# BEFORE THE LAW

## An Introduction to the Legal Process

SEVENTH EDITION

John J. Bonsignore
Ethan Katsh
Peter d'Errico
Ronald M. Pipkin
Stephen Arons
Janet Rifkin

*Department of Legal Studies*
*The University of Massachusetts at Amherst*

Houghton Mifflin Company    BOSTON    NEW YORK

*Sponsoring Editor*   Mary Dougherty
*Editorial Assistant*   Tonya  Lobato
*Senior Project Editor*   Rosemary R. Jaffe
*Senior Production/Design Coordinator*   Jodi O'Rourke
*Senior Manufacturing Coordinator*   Priscilla Bailey
*Marketing Manager*   Nicola Poser

Cover image: Peter Samuels, Stone

*Printed in the U.S.A.*

Library of Congress Control Number: 2001089047

ISBN: 0-618-15558-9

456789-QF-07 06 05 04 03

# Contents

# Preface

*Before the Law: An Introduction to the Legal Process,* Seventh Edition, provides a foundation in the liberal arts study of law. Its aim is to develop critical, intellectual capacities in the reader. The book contains material taken from many and varied sources, including court opinions; sociological, psychological, and anthropological analyses of legal phenomena; and historical and philosophical approaches to law. The book also includes literary views of law, in selections from fiction and poetry.

As the contents of the book are varied, so are its applications. Although the table of contents displays an arrangement oriented toward institutional structures and functions, the materials lend themselves to many other arrangements. The kindest compliment ever paid about previous editions of *Before the Law* was that it was difficult to tell from which disciplines the editors come. We are in fact all law-trained, but since we have worked with many teachers of law-related subjects over many years, our legal training has no doubt been influenced by other understandings.

Teachers who have used earlier versions of the book have come from various disciplines themselves; thus they determine the best sequence of materials to suit their perspective and the needs of their students. An historical or political approach, for example, might result in an arrangement of the readings that takes advantage of current events. A systems approach might organize selections to focus on legal processes, and a sociological approach on legal actors—and under either approach, the readings can be sequenced in different ways. The editors encourage teachers to experiment with the book's contents, taking advantage of individual interests and expertise, using the index to facilitate such experimentation. Over the years the Department of Legal Studies at the University of Massachusetts—Amherst has received many inquiries as to how various selections in the book might be used and also syllabi that show the myriad ways in which the book has

been approached. We continue to invite inquiries as to how *Before the Law* might be suitable in different contexts, and we also welcome syllabi of courses in which the book has been a principal text.

This seventh edition of *Before the Law* contains substantial editorial comment at the start of each part and chapter. Some concluding and interstitial comments are also provided. These comments encourage the reader to analyze materials, to compare divergent perspectives, and to reflect on issues spanning different sections of the book. Our intention is to maintain a broad, non-legalistic and open-textured approach, while nonetheless guiding and orienting the reader. In this way, the themes of the text as a whole are developed without an overly didactic method.

## CHANGES IN THE SEVENTH EDITION

All chapters have been revised, updated, and reorganized to reflect developments in legal theory and practice, emerging issues in legal culture, and the experience of teachers using previous editions.

Part I, "Law in Theory and Practice," surveys explanations of the functions and disfunctions of the law. It includes essays, cases and other materials for testing the sometimes-rival explanations of law in theory and practice. This part includes new readings on the death penalty, feminist issues, and more extensive coverage of race and gay rights. The breadth and depth of Part I are shown by the range of authors represented: They include Franz Kafka (noted Czech lawyer and writer); Karl Llewellyn, Jerome Frank, Marc Galanter, Roscoe Pound (American jurists); E. Adamson Hoebel, Laura Nader, Claude Levi-Strauss (anthropologists); and Karl Marx, V. I. Lenin and Peter Kropotkin (socialist and anarchist writers).

Part II, "Law Enforcement," explores two conflicting images of law in American society: revolutionary freedom and established order.

Chapter 8, focused on law's use of violence, includes new material about federal mandatory sentences. Chapter 9 has been expanded to present an array of specific historical and contemporary legal issues, including racial segregation, slavery, pornography (within a feminist perspective), and intellectual property (especially software patents and bio-technology). Chapter 10 focuses on issues of surveillance, privacy, and search and seizure, and includes new material on investigation technologies.

Part III, Lawyers," was revised to introduce potential changes to the legal profession as it moves deeper into the "information age." Race and gender diversity are probably no longer the dominant forces for change in the profession, as they have been in recent years. Chapter 11 alerts the reader to ways in which the profession is beginning to be transformed by globalism and information technologies, perhaps—as Herbert Kritzer argues in a new reading—to the point of "post-professionalism." Chapter 12 retains familiar themes on legal education and reintroduces the powerful piece by Patricia Williams on race in the imaginary legal landscape of law school. Chapter 13, on lawyers in the adversary process, introduces new material and reprises the reflections of Harry Subin on defending a known-guilty client.

Part IV, "The Jury," has been shortened and revised. Chapters 14 and 15 still deal with the jury in cultural and political contexts. Chapter 16, on jury selection, is now focused on two current issues: keeping racism out of the jury room and determining whether people with scruples against the death penalty should or should not be excluded from juries in capital cases. The discussion of tort reform as an attack on trial by jury (in Chapter 17 on the decline of the jury) has been updated with material about the $145 billion jury award in the Florida tobacco case.

Part V, "Conflict Resolution," includes new materials on the history of "community mediation," a practice that was founded on a critique of formal legal processes, but is now an integral part of, and even indistinguishable from, the court system itself. There are new readings on models of mediation used around the United States and raising questions about the legitamacy of mediation as a diversion from formal prosecution. In addition, new material on Navajo mediation processes illustrates the significance of cultural beliefs and social values on mediation practices.

Part VI, "Cyberspace and the Future of Law," first appeared in the sixth edition of this book. Since then, cyberspace has become clearly a "place" that touches important commercial, political, and educational processes. It is also a "place" that touches law. It does this in two ways. First, legal standards and processes of dispute resolution are needed to regulate behavior in cyberspace and resolve disputes that arise out of online activities. Second, cyberspace challenges many traditional legal doctrines and opens up opportunities for law to be applied in new ways. For the seventh edition, new materials have been added to this Part, discussing marketing, privacy, and managing Internet access in libraries.

## DISTINCTIVE FEATURES

A key pedagogical feature of *Before the Law* is the arrangement of readings to provoke questioning and discussion, and to preclude simplistic conclusions to various difficult issues. Our intention is to juxtapose selections to demonstrate the open-ended quality of law and legal knowledge, despite the definitive nature of legal authority. There is never an attempt to reduce an area of law to "black letter" answers. Law is presented as a field of argument: continually changing; multifaceted; responding to social, political, and economic forces; evolving in different ways in different cultures and historical eras.

The thought-provoking quality of the book's editorial structure is reinforced throughout by questions, suggestions for contemplation and discussion, and notes to elaborate specific issues. References for additional reading are provided at the conclusion of each part.

In short, *Before the Law* supports a problem-solving, inquiry-based approach to teaching legal issues. Whether enhanced by films, presentations, or other readings, or as the sole component to the syllabus, *Before the Law* provides the basis for exploring law as a facet of liberal arts education.

## ACKNOWLEDGMENTS

We thank students and teachers who have used prior editions of the book for their comments and suggestions, which helped us shape the present edition. In particular, we thank the following reviewers for their intensive reviews of this edition: Richard Chesteen, University of Tennessee at Martin; Susan J. Siggelakis, University of New Hampshire; Mark Silverstein, Boston University; and Robert C. Wigton; Eckerd College.

We also gratefully acknowledge the continuing strong support of the Department of Legal Studies and the College of Social and behavioral Sciences at the University of Massachusetts at Amherst, and we thank our editors at Houghton Mifflin for their thorough attention to our manuscript.

# Introduction

*Before the Law: An Introduction to the Legal Process* is an unusual textbook. It does not pretend to be the "last word" on the subject. Instead, it raises questions and leaves many topics open-ended. *Before the Law* is not written in linear fashion from beginning to end. Instead, it presents an array of perspectives, any of which may be the start of a discussion leading to other readings.

This book is intended to inspire its readers to think. To this end, the materials and their arrangement are provocative. They criticize accepted ideas, raise questions about values, and provide glimpses into the difficult choices underlying the everyday operation and historical development of the legal system. What one writer or one case may assert is set next to a different assertion by another author or case. The result is that the book reads like a dialogue rather than a monologue. Each selection is presented as part of a discussion, even if its author has written it as though its facts are unquestionable.

The editors of this book regard law as an ongoing process in society. Law itself may speak with the authority of the state, but its meaning and content are as changeable as the political, social, and economic forces of the society. Any reader who comes to this book with expectations of finding legal answers to legal questions—such as "When can the police arrest?" or "What is the liability of the manufacturer for injury to the consumer?"—will probably be disappointed, although there are selections that deal with such specific questions and answers. But the reader who comes to this book hoping to understand the nature and functions of law in society will probably be satisfied. For this is a book in *legal studies,* designed to reach those who are interested in law, with or without a pressing legal problem or the intention to make a career in law.

This book is therefore not simply a legal text. More than being a book *in* law, it is a book *about* law. It is designed to encourage a variety of approaches to the study of law: political, sociological, anthropological, historical, literary, and philosophical. All of these facets are represented in readings throughout the chapters. Some selections are written by famous authors, and many readings come from works by scholars who are recognized as experts in their fields. A few selections are excerpted from popular magazines. The legal materials include court decisions and law review articles. But whatever their sources, the readings are always arranged to present aspects of law in the broad context of culture and history. No legal issue is presented only as a technical rule to be memorized. Rather, each issue is shown as part of a process of law operating in society.

To help you reach for these broad perspectives, we have provided comments before and sometimes after each part and chapter. These editors' comments describe the major themes in the readings, and help orient and guide you. In addition, we have included many notes and questions specifically relating to the selections. These notes include suggestions to prompt discussion and contemplation, and may also provide short excerpts about particular points. We encourage you to use the Notes and Questions in working with the ideas presented in the main selections.

The comments, notes, and questions provide a basis for you to criticize, understand, and discuss each reading by itself and in conjunction with other readings. It is important to remember, however, that the readings may contain issues other than those pointed out by the editors. Our approach is to provide many starting points and connecting themes, and to prompt your own curiosity and intelligence to be a guide to further inquiry.

A list of Suggested Additional Readings is appended to each part. These are meant to be useful to readers who wish to pursue further the major ideas raised in the part. Since bibliographical information is provided for each reading in the book, including excerpts in the notes and questions, readers interested in a fuller review of the original sources can look them up at their library. You are encouraged to use the Contents and the Index to seek additional information on a topic, and to find further correlations among selections.

This is the beginning of the book. From here you may go to any other part of it. But first, you may wish to read the Foreword, which follows this Introduction. In the Foreword you will find the source of the book's title in a parable told by a character in a novel by Franz Kafka. The parable itself is written as a teaching about law, about the confusion and contradiction that seems to exist within and around it. We do not know what specific legal questions were troubling the man in the story, but we are forced to see the trouble he has in finding a solution to his questions.

The Foreword explores the meaning of the parable in a way that demonstrates how this book works: raising questions, suggesting answers, exploring alternatives, and ultimately leaving the final answer open. Like Kafka's protagonist, you may be left with a melancholy feeling after reading this. Perhaps you too would rather have simple answers to the questions you ask about law. On the other hand, you may react to this story as you would to a dream: its logical meaning eludes you, but the power of its imagery inspires much thinking and prods you to further inquiry.

# Foreword

## F.1    Before the Law    *Franz Kafka*

"BEFORE THE LAW STANDS a doorkeeper on guard. To this doorkeeper there comes a man from the country who begs for admittance to the Law. But the doorkeeper says that he cannot admit the man at the moment. The man, on reflection, asks if he will be allowed, then, to enter later. 'It is possible,' answers the doorkeeper, 'but not at this moment.' Since the door leading into the Law stands open as usual and the doorkeeper steps to one side, the man bends down to peer through the entrance. When the doorkeeper sees that, he laughs and says: 'If you are so strongly tempted, try to get in without my permission. But note that I am powerful. And I am only the lowest doorkeeper. From hall to hall keepers stand at every door, one more powerful than the other. Even the third of these has an aspect that even I cannot bear to look at.' These are difficulties which the man from the country has not expected to meet; the Law, he thinks, should be accessible to every man and at all times, but when he looks more closely at the doorkeeper in his furred robe, with his huge pointed nose and long, thin, Tartar beard, he decides that he had better wait until he gets permission to enter. The doorkeeper gives him a stool and lets him sit down at the side of the door. There he sits waiting for days and years.

He makes many attempts to be allowed in and wearies the doorkeeper with his importunity. The doorkeeper often engages him in brief conversation, asking him about his home and about other matters, but the questions are put quite impersonally, as great men put questions, and always conclude with the statement that the man cannot be allowed to enter yet. The man, who has equipped himself with many things for his journey, parts with all he has, however valuable, in the hope of bribing the doorkeeper. The doorkeeper accepts it all, saying, however, as he takes each gift: 'I take this only to keep you from feeling that you have left something undone.' During all these long years the man watches the doorkeeper almost incessantly. He forgets about the other doorkeepers, and this one seems to him the only barrier between himself and the Law. In the first years he curses his evil fate aloud; later, as he grows old, he only mutters to himself. He grows childish, and since in his prolonged watch he has learned to know even the fleas in the doorkeeper's fur collar, he begs the very fleas to help him and to persuade the doorkeeper to change his mind. Finally, his eyes grow dim and he does not know whether the world is really darkening around him or whether his eyes are only deceiving him. But in the darkness he can now perceive a radiance that streams immortally from the door of the Law. Now his life is drawing to a close. Before he dies, all that he has experienced during the whole time of his sojourn condenses in his mind into one question, which he has never yet put to the doorkeeper. He beckons the doorkeeper, since he can no longer raise his stiffening body. The doorkeeper has to bend far down to hear him, for the difference in size between them has increased very much to the man's disadvantage. 'What do you want to know now?' asks the doorkeeper, 'you are insatiable.' 'Everyone strives to attain the Law,' answers the man, 'how does it come about,

From *The Trial: Definitive Edition* by Franz Kafka, translated by Willa & Edwin Muir. Copyright 1937, 1956 and renewed 1965, 1984 by Alfred A. Knopf, a Division of Random House, Inc. Used by permission of Alfred A. Knopf, a Division of Random House, Inc.

Franz Kafka (1883–1924) was born in Prague, Czechoslovakia, where he lived and practiced law until his death of tuberculosis. As his diaries reflect, he sometimes found his work as a lawyer incompatible with his art, but there is no doubt that law, from its imposing architecture down to its sometimes overwhelming effects on the average person, permeated all his writings. The parable "Before the Law" was not published during his lifetime; it was part of his unfinished novel, *The Trial*. —ED.

then, that in all these years no one has come seeking admittance but me?' The doorkeeper perceives that the man is at the end of his strength and that his hearing is failing, so he bellows in his ear: 'No one but you could gain admittance through this door, since this door was intended only for you. I am now going to shut it.'"

## Notes and Questions

1. The parable is both an old and an odd form of education. Parables are extensively used for instructional purposes in both the Old and New Testaments, not to mention in Middle and Far Eastern religions. What makes the parable so rich as a teaching-learning device is our inability to reduce a parable to a single point, message, or slogan. Both teachers and students are left in doubt, even after having studied the parable for some time.

   The parable has other unique features as well. It cannot be dismissed as mere abstraction or as consummate vagueness that leads nowhere. By the time we might be inclined to dismiss the parable, we have become hooked. Our minds struggle to find the meaning that is at once at hand and escaping us. Each line of the parable considered separately is intelligible, but the totality slips away. One more reading might suffice, we think. Well, not quite. Perhaps a third, and so on. We can allow ourselves multiple readings, because the parable is so short and each time through we seem to gain something. What is Kafka telling you about law? Has he drawn a pleasant or an unpleasant picture? In what settings, legal or otherwise, might his lessons be applicable?

2. Richard Delgado, a principal scholar in a group called the Critical Race Theorists, argues that story telling and other forms of narrative can have a revolutionary potential:

   > Stories, parables, chronicles and narratives are powerful means for destroying mindset—the bundle of presuppositions, received wisdoms and shared understandings against a background of which legal and political discourse takes place. They are like eyeglasses we have worn a long time. They are nearly invisible; we use them to scan and interpret the world and only rarely examine them for themselves. Ideology—the received wisdom—makes current social

arrangements seem fair and natural. Those in power sleep well at night—their conduct does not seem to them like oppression.*

So much for the accepted form of discourse—the discourse in straight academic materials, of insiders and would-be insiders. What magic can narrative work to reduce the power of insiders and give outsiders a better place to stand in their resistance and gain a say? Delgado contends that stories told by underdogs are

> frequently ironic and satiric . . . bringing low, down to earth . . . Storytelling [has] community building functions: Stories build consensus, a common culture of shared understandings, and a deeper, more vital ethics. But stories and counterstories can serve an equally important destructive function. They can show that what we believe is ridiculous, self-serving, or cruel. They can show us the way out of the trap of unjustified exclusion. They can help us understand when it is time to reallocate power. They are the other half—the destructive half—of the creative dialectic.†

Before going further, consider what Delgado has said about narrative, the powerful, underdog's satire, irony, and the constructive/destructive aspects of storytelling as they might apply to Kafka's *Before the Law*. For example, does Kafka's parable have revolutionary potential?

3. What effects does Kafka's parable have on you? Are you frustrated, angry or otherwise disturbed by it? If so what lies behind these unwanted feelings?

4. You might want to try the narrative form yourself by writing a short report on an occasion in your life when your sense of injustice was aroused. It is always easier to think of an episode of injustice than one of justice. Of course, the episode need not concern police, courts, or other encounters with legal officialdom, since most of us run into formal law only occasionally, but participate in many other institutions such as the family, schools, athletic teams, social clubs, and workplaces where decisions can be unjust.

---

*R. Delgado, "Storytelling for Oppositionists and Others: A Plea for Narrative," in *Critical Race Theory*, 2nd ed., 61.
†Ibid., 61.

&#x267a; Kafka follows the parable of the man from the country and the door-keeper with a discussion of the parable between a priest and a character named simply K. In doing so, Kafka gives us as much to think about as he resolves. Impishly, but like a great teacher, he both helps us and opens new questions at the same time.

## F.2 | Dialogue Between a Priest and K.    *Franz Kafka*

"SO THE DOORKEEPER DELUDED the man," said K. immediately, strongly attracted by the story.

"Don't be too hasty," said the priest, "don't take over an opinion without testing it. I have told you the story in the very words of the scriptures. There's no mention of delusion in it."

"But it's clear enough," said K., "and your first interpretation of it was quite right. The doorkeeper gave the message of salvation to the man only when it could no longer help him."

"He was not asked the question any earlier," said the priest, "and you must consider, too, that he was only a doorkeeper, and as such he fulfilled his duty."

"What makes you think he fulfilled his duty?" asked K. "He didn't fulfill it. His duty might have been to keep all strangers away, but this man, for whom the door was intended, should have been let in."

"You have not enough respect for the written word and you are altering the story," said the priest. "The story contains two important statements made by the doorkeeper about admission to the Law, one at the beginning, the other at the end. The first statement is: that he cannot admit the man at the moment, and the other is: that this door was intended only for the man. But there is no contradiction. The first statement, on the contrary, even implies the second. One could almost say that in suggesting to the man the possibility of future admittance the doorkeeper is exceeding his duty. At that moment his apparent duty is only to refuse admit-

tance, and indeed many commentators are surprised that the suggestion should be made at all, since the doorkeeper appears to be a precisian with a stern regard for duty. He does not once leave his post during these many years, and he does not shut the door until the very last minute; he is conscious of the importance of his office, for he says: 'I am powerful'; he is respectful to his superiors, for he says: 'I am only the lowest doorkeeper'; he is not garrulous, for during all these years he puts only what are called 'impersonal questions'; he is not to be bribed, for he says in accepting a gift: 'I take this only to keep you from feeling that you have left something undone'; where his duty is concerned he is to be moved neither by pity nor rage, for we are told that the man 'wearied the doorkeeper with his importunity'; and finally even his external appearance hints at a pedantic character, the large, pointed nose and the long, thin, black Tartar beard. Could one imagine a more faithful doorkeeper? Yet the doorkeeper has other elements in his character which are likely to advantage anyone seeking admittance and which make it comprehensible enough that he should somewhat exceed his duty in suggesting the possibility of future admittance. For it cannot be denied that he is a little simple-minded and consequently a little conceited. Take the statements he makes about his power and the power of the other doorkeepers and their dreadful aspect which even he cannot bear to see—I hold that these statements may be true enough, but that the way in which he brings them out shows that his perceptions are confused by simpleness of mind and conceit. The commentators note in this connection: 'The right perception of any matter and a misunderstanding of the same matter do not wholly exclude each other.' One must at any rate assume that such simpleness and conceit, however, sparingly indicated, are likely to weaken his defense of the door; they are breaches in the character of the doorkeeper. To this must be added the fact that the doorkeeper seems to be a friendly creature by nature, he is by no means always on his official dignity. In the very first moments he allows himself the jest of inviting the man to enter in spite of the strictly maintained veto against entry; then he does not, for instance, send the man away, but gives him, as we are told, a stool and lets him sit down beside the door. The patience with which he endures the man's appeals during so many years, the brief conversations, the acceptance of the gifts, the politeness with which he allows the man to curse loudly in his presence the fate for which he himself is responsible—all this lets us deduce certain motions of sympathy. Not every doorkeeper would have acted thus. And finally, in answer to a gesture of the man's he stoops low down to give him the chance of putting a last question. Nothing but mild impatience—the doorkeeper knows that his is the end of it all—is discernible in the words: 'You are insatiable.' Some push this mode of interpretation even further and hold that these words express a kind of friendly admiration, though not without a hint of condescension. At any rate the figure of the doorkeeper can be said to come out very differently from what you fancied."

"You have studied the story more exactly and for a longer time than I have," said K. They were both silent for a while. Then K. said: "So you think the man was not deluded?"

"Don't misunderstand me," said the priest, "I am only showing you the various opinions concerning that point. You must not pay too much attention to them. The scriptures are unalterable and the comments often enough merely express the commentator's bewilderment. In this case there even exists an interpretation which claims that the deluded person is really the doorkeeper."

"That's a far-fetched interpretation," said K. "On what is it based?"

"It is based," answered the priest, "on the simple-mindedness of the doorkeeper. The argument is that he does not know the Law from inside, but he knows only the way that leads to it, where he patrols up and down. His ideas of the interior are assumed to be childish, and it is supposed that he himself is afraid of the other guardians whom he holds up as bogies before the man. Indeed, he fears them more than the man does, since the man is determined to enter after hearing about the dreadful guardians of the interior, while the doorkeeper has no desire to enter, at least not so far as we are told. Others again say that he must have been in the interior already, since he is after all engaged in the service of the Law and can only have been appointed from inside. This is countered by arguing that he may have been appointed by a voice calling from the interior, and that anyhow he cannot have been far inside, since the aspect of the third doorkeeper is more than he can endure. Moreover, no indication is given that all these years he ever made any remarks showing a knowledge of the interior except for the one remark about the doorkeepers. He may have been forbidden to do so, but there is no mention of that either. On these grounds the conclusion is reached that he knows nothing about the aspect and significance of the interior so that he is in a state of delusion. But he is deceived also about his relation to the man from the country, for he is subject to the man and does not know it. He treats the man instead as his own subordinate, as can be recognized from many details that must still be fresh in your mind. But, according to this view of their story, it is just as clearly indicated that he is really subordinated to the man. In the first place, a bondman is always subject to a free man. Now the man from the country is really free, he can go where he likes, it is only the Law that is closed to him, and access to the Law is forbidden him only by one individual, the doorkeeper. When he sits down on the stool by the side of the door and stays there for the rest of his life, he does it of his own free will; in the story there is no mention of any compulsion. But the doorkeeper is bound to his post by his very office, he does not dare strike out into the country, nor apparently may he go into the interior of the Law, even should he wish to. Besides, although he is in the service of the Law, his service is confined to this one entrance; that is to say, he serves only this man for whom alone the entrance is intended. On that ground too he is subject to the man. One must assume that for many years, for as long as it takes a man to grow up to the prime of life, his service was in a sense empty formality, since he had to wait for a man to come, that is to say, someone in the prime of life, and so had to wait a long time before the purpose of his service could be fulfilled, and, moreover, had to wait on the man's pleasure, for the man came of his own free will. But the termination of his service also depends on the man's term of life, so that to the very end he is subject to the man. And it is emphasized throughout that the doorkeeper apparently realizes nothing of all this. That is not in itself remarkable, since according to this interpretation the doorkeeper is deceived in a much more important issue, affecting his very office. At the end, for example, he says regarding the entrance to the Law: 'I am now going to shut it,' but at the beginning of the story we are told that the door leading into the Law stands always open, and if it stands open always, that is to say, at all times, without reference to the life or death of the man, then the doorkeeper is incapable of closing it. There is some difference of opinions about the motive behind the doorkeeper's statement, whether he said he was going to close the door merely for the sake of giving an answer, or to emphasize his devotion to duty, or to bring the man into a state of grief and regret in his last moments. But there is no lack of agreement that the doorkeeper will not be able to shut the door. Many indeed profess to find that he is subordinate to the man even in wisdom, towards the end, at least, for the man sees the radiance that issues from the door of the Law while the doorkeeper in his official position must stand with his back to the door, nor does he say anything to show that he has perceived the change."

"That is well argued," said K., after repeating to himself in a low voice several passages from the priest's exposition. "It is well argued, and I am inclined to agree that the doorkeeper is deluded. But that has not made me abandon my former opinion, since both conclusions are to some extent compatible. Whether the doorkeeper is clear-sighted or deluded does not dispose of the matter. I said the man is deluded. If the doorkeeper is clear-sighted, one might have doubts about that, but if the doorkeeper himself is deluded, then his delusion must of necessity be communicated to the man. That makes the doorkeeper not, indeed, a swindler, but a creature so simple-minded that he ought to be dismissed at once from his office. You mustn't forget that the doorkeeper's delusions do himself no harm but do infinite harm to the man."

"There are objections to that," said the priest. "Many aver that the story confers no right on anyone to pass judgment on the doorkeeper. Whatever he may seem to us, he is yet a servant of the Law; that is, he belongs to the Law and as such is set beyond human judgment. In that case one dare not believe that the doorkeeper is subordinate to the man. Bound as he is by his service, even at the door of the Law, he is incomparably freer than anyone at large in the world. The man is only seeking the Law, the doorkeeper is already attached to it. It is the Law that has placed him at his post; to doubt his integrity is to doubt the Law itself."

"I don't agree with that point of view," said K. shaking his head. "for if one accepts it, one must accept as true everything the doorkeeper says. But you yourself have sufficiently proved how impossible it is to do that."

"No," said the priest, "it is not necessary to accept everything as true, one must only accept it as necessary,"

"A melancholy conclusion," said K. "It turns lying into a universal principle."

## Notes and Questions

1. Compare your earlier reflections about the parable with the commentaries of the priest and K. Which of them comes closer to your own?

2. What are the priest and K. arguing about? Who won the argument? Is there a difference between winning an argument and being right?

3. K.'s argument seems to come down to the idea that justice was denied the man from the country. Was justice done, in your judgment?

4. In the dialogue, the priest does most of the talking and K. does very little. (Follow the comments of K. all the way through to see this.) What does this imbalance in the

conversation tell you? Does Kafka, the author, speak through the priest or through K.?

5. The priest seems expert and confident, whereas K. appears amateurish and tentative. What effect do these characteristics have on the ability of either to win the argument or to convince readers of the worth of K.'s contentions?

6. In the parable, the doorkeeper is portrayed as a low-level insider to the law and the man from the country as an outsider. In the discussion, the priest looks more like an insider and K. like an outsider. Would either the man from the country or K. have been helped by hiring a lawyer? By having studied law themselves?

7. The position of the priest seems to shift as each new question is raised by K. Do the priest's arguments get stronger or weaker as he goes along? What about K.'s arguments?

8. The final argument of the priest is that "it is not necessary to accept everything as true, one must only accept it as necessary." What are the implications of this contention? How does K. respond to it? Which position would you endorse?

9. It is sometimes said that bad order may be better than no order at all. What makes bad order compelling? Which would you prefer? Which would the man from the country prefer?

10. In the encounter between the doorkeeper and the man from the country, the rules seem to change as they are made: at first the door is denied the man from the country, presumably because he has no right to enter; but later he is told that the door was intended only for him—that it was always his right to enter and, in fact, that it was his exclusively. Is it possible to have "order" where there are shifting rules?

   However, it could also be said that despite surface inconsistencies there is a deeper consistency across the entire story. The rules may be different, but the result stays constant— the man from the country can never enter into the domain of law. If the law never serves him, then for whom is it intended?

11. With what characters—the man from the country, the doorkeeper, the priest, or K.— should most readers identify? With whom do they want to identify? What social roles and positions are represented by these characters?

    ☙ In the next reading, Kafka raises problems for the well-intentioned lawyer who chooses the calling as a means to serve people or render the world more just. Kafka's thumbnail rendition of the legal order leaves us with a deep contradiction: law is for the few and those associated with the few, but the many do not rebel.

## F.3    The Problem of Our Laws    *Franz Kafka*

OUR LAWS ARE NOT generally known; they are kept secret by the small group of nobles who rule us. We are convinced that these ancient laws are scrupulously administered; neverthe-

From *The Trial: Definitive Edition* by Franz Kafka, translated by Willa & Edwin Muir. Copyright 1937, 1956 and renewed 1965, 1984 by Alfred A. Knopf, a Division of Random House, Inc. Used by permission of Alfred A. Knopf, a Division of Random House, Inc.

less, it is an extremely painful thing to be ruled by laws that one does not know. I am not thinking of possible discrepancies that may arise in the interpretation of the laws, or of the disadvantages involved when only a few and not the whole people are allowed to have a say in their interpretation. These disadvantages are perhaps of no great importance. For the laws are very ancient; their interpretation has been the work of centuries, and has itself doubtless acquired the status of law; and though there is still a possible freedom of interpretation left, it has now become very restricted. Moreover the nobles have obviously no cause to be influenced in their interpretation by personal interests inimical to us, for the laws were made to the advantage of the nobles from the very beginning, they themselves stand above the laws, and that seems to be why the laws were entrusted exclusively into their hands. Of course, there is wisdom in that—who doubts the wisdom of the ancient laws?—but also hardship for us; probably that is unavoidable.

The very existence of these laws, however, is at most a matter of presumption. There is a tradition that they exist and that they are a mystery confided to the nobility, but it is not and cannot be more than a mere tradition sanctioned by age, for the essence of a secret code is that it should remain a mystery. Some of us among the people have attentively scrutinized the doings of the nobility since the earliest times and possess records made by our forefathers—records which we have conscientiously continued—and claim to recognize amid the countless number of facts certain main tendencies which permit of this or that historical formulation; but when in accordance with these scrupulously tested and logically ordered conclusions we seek to orient ourselves somewhat towards the present or the future, everything becomes uncertain, and our work seems only an intellectual game, for perhaps these laws that we are trying to unravel do not exist at all. There is a small party who are actually of this opinion and who try to show that, if any law exists, it can only be this: The Law is whatever the nobles do. This party see everywhere only the arbitrary acts of the nobility, and reject the popular tradition, which according to them possesses only certain trifling and incidental advantages that do not offset its heavy drawbacks, for it gives the people a false, deceptive and over-confident security in confronting coming events. This cannot be gainsaid, but the overwhelming majority of our people account for it by the fact that the tradition is far from complete and must be more fully enquired into, that the material available, prodigious as it looks, is still too meager, and that several centuries will have to pass before it

becomes really adequate. This view, so comfortless as far as the present is concerned, is lightened only by the belief that a time will eventually come when the tradition and our research into it will jointly reach their conclusion, and as it were gain a breathing space, when everything will have become clear, the law will belong to the people, and the nobility will vanish. This is not maintained in any spirit of hatred against the nobility; not at all, and by no one. We are more inclined to hate ourselves, because we have not yet shown ourselves worthy of being entrusted with the laws. And that is the real reason why the party which believes that there is no law has remained so small—although its doctrine is in certain ways so attractive, for it unequivocally recognizes the nobility and its right to go on existing.

Actually one can express the problem only in a sort of paradox: Any party which would repudiate, not only all belief in the laws, but the nobility as well, would have the whole people behind it; yet no such party can come into existence, for nobody would dare to repudiate the nobility. We live on this razor edge. A writer once summed the matter up in this way: The sole visible and indubitable law that is imposed upon us is the nobility, and must we ourselves deprive ourselves of that one law?

## Notes and Questions

1. According to Kafka, what is the central problem of law and what are the obstacles to its resolution?
2. Where do doorkeepers and lawyers fit into the legal structure as outlined by Kafka?
3. If people were to come to know that law is *of*, *by*, and *for* the nobility, would they necessarily rebel?
4. Kafka says, "We are more inclined to hate ourselves, because we have not yet shown ourselves worthy of being entrusted with the laws." Does this suggest that the problem of law lie within people and their excessive humility or in the institutions they encounter that inhibit their assertion of autonomy? Put another way, is the problem in the man from the country or in the system symbolized by the doorkeeper? In both?

5. What helps officials of law, like doorkeepers, priests, judges, and lawyers, feel worthy enough to be entrusted with the law? If they felt more like ordinary people, would the problem of law be resolved?

6. Kafka seems to talk in circles. Try to present his central ideas "in a straight line." Imagine, if it helps, explaining Kafka's argument to a roommate who has not read him.

❧ A final selection from Kafka has the virtue of being short, but compact.

## $\boxed{F.4}$ Couriers  *Franz Kafka*

THEY WERE OFFERED THE choice between becoming kings or the couriers of kings. The way children would, they all wanted to be couriers. Therefore there are only couriers who hurry about the world, shouting to each other—since there are no kings—messages that have become meaningless. They would like to put an end to this miserable life of theirs but they dare not because of their oaths of service.

### Notes and Questions

1. It might be said that this parable calls for strong leadership, since leadership might give meaning to the couriers' messages, which are now meaningless. But how would strong leadership be distinguished from an embryonic nobility (today's leaders, tomorrow's aristocrats), which is said to be the integral part of "The Problem of Our Laws"? Are there alternatives to the recommendation of strong leadership?

2. It is also sometimes said that people are "happy" in courier roles and would not abandon them, even if given the opportunity; but Kafka says that couriers lead miserable lives. What are the sources of misery in the courier's life? Are there alternatives to resentful acceptance?

   Other street wisdom finds its expression in the need to "go with the flow," "adapt to situations," or, especially when trying to get a job, "sell yourself." These strategies may at first seem expedient—that is why they are considered street wisdom—but what if the cost of accommodation becomes too destructive, so that advice designed to assure survival guarantees death?

   Richard Wright in *Black Boy* defines a non-negotiable core that he dared not violate:

   > What was it that made the hate of whites for blacks so steady, seemingly so woven into the texture of things? What kind of life was possible under that hate? How had this hate come to be? Nothing about the problems of Negroes was ever taught in the classrooms at school; and whenever I would raise these questions with the boys, they would either remain silent or turn the subject into a joke. They were vocal about the petty individual wrongs they suffered, but they possessed no desire for a knowledge of the picture as a whole. Then why was I worried about it? . . .
   >
   > Why was it considered wrong to ask questions? . . . It was inconceivable that one should surrender to what seemed wrong, and most of the people I had met seemed wrong. Ought one to surrender to authority even if one believed that that authority was wrong? If the answer was yes, then I knew that I would always be wrong because I could never do it. Then how could one live in a world in which one's mind and perceptions meant nothing and authority and tradition meant everything?*

*Richard Wright, *Black Boy* (New York: Harper, 1966 ed., first published 1937), pp. 181, 182.

3. In what sense are doorkeepers and lawyers couriers? In what sense are they kings? To whom or to what do they owe their "oaths of service"? Could they revoke their oaths? Should they?

4. You have considered several writings from Kafka on law. What is Kafka's position on law, legal order and its effects?

❧ The philosopher Alfred North Whitehead once said that all of Western philosophy was nothing more than footnotes to Plato. It might similarly be said that all discourses on Western law may be nothing more than footnotes to Franz Kafka. If this is true, Kafka's guidance and careful observation might give students all that they will ever need for an understanding of modern legal order.

A *Scholar in His Study Watching a Magic Disk.* Rembrandt van
Rijn: *Faust,* c. 1652. (National Gallery of Art, Washington.
Gift of R. Horace Gallatin.)

# Law in Theory and Practice

They tell you out at the Law School that the law is a wonderful science—the perfection of reason. 'Tis in fact a hodge-podge of Roman law, Bible texts, canon law, superstitions, scraps of feudalism, crazy fictions, and long dead statutes. Your professors try to bring order out of chaos and make sense where the devil himself couldn't find any.

> Ephraim Tutt, *Yankee Lawyer* (1944)

Political philosophies are intellectual and moral creations; they contain high ideals, easy slogans, dubious facts, crude propaganda, sophisticated theories. Their adherents select some facts and ignore others, urge the acceptance of ideals, the inevitability of events, argue with this theory and debunk that one.

> C. Wright Mills, *The Marxists* (1962)

All logical systems, East-West, scientific-religious, cyclic or linear, originate in an analysis of the way reality is structured.

> Joseph Pearce, *Crack in the Cosmic Egg* (1982)

᳁ Definitions of law are statements of belief akin to political philosophies, articles of faith in religion, or intuition in science. The person who defines has a flash of genius, and the whole legal universe falls momentarily into place. Once a definition is reached, events are shaped to fit the definition, and what is at first only a psychic reality becomes a reality "out there" as well. It is this phenomenon that makes definitions so important and yet so dangerous; they provide concentrated explanations of the legal world but also foreclose possibilities that would disrupt the definition.

Law as a system of thought is only one of many possible structures of reality. As with other systems of thought, model precedes rather than follows data—map often both precedes and supersedes the territory itself. For example, an African river trader looking at a map his son brought back from school objected to the way the map made differences look alike. On the map everything was homogenized, so many inches to the theoretical mile. His son recalled:

> Distances measured in miles had no meaning to him. "Maps are liars," he told me briefly. From his tone of voice I could tell I had offended him. . . . The truth of a place is in the joy and the hurt that come from it. I had better not put my trust in anything as inadequate as a map, he counseled. . . .

*1*

> I understand now, although I did not at the time, that my airy sweep of . . .
> staggering distances belittled the journeys he had measured on tired feet.
> With my big map-talk I had effaced the magnitude of his cargo-laden, heat-
> weighted treks.*

The map is comparable to conventional wisdom that tells us what to see.
The trader-father puts the price tag on conventional wisdom. What is said
to be wise may be simple-minded and rules out—puts beyond its boundaries—what could turn out to be very important. The father knows what the
person faithful to the map does not know: the traveler who takes the map
more seriously than the actual terrain stands a greater chance of dying.

Unconventional wisdom says that we see only what we are taught to
see, or only what we instruct ourselves to see. The foregoing may fly in the
face of ideas generally held about learning. We might think of ourselves
as wanting to learn and being open to new ideas no matter how startling
they might be. Why else would students enroll in a university? Why else
would people teach in universities? But what if the opposite is true, that
although we may want to give ourselves credit for an abiding desire to
learn, we really want to get by on what we already know? We all may be engaging in more and more schooling with less and less real impact, hoping
and praying that the map we already have will get us across the territory.
Since it has gotten us this far, it may—but what if it doesn't?

Beginning law students often feel they know little about law, and that
their lack of knowledge of law is the very reason why they are taking an introductory law course. In fact, everyone has models of law and expectations that can be traced to television, newspapers, personal experiences,
family history, and other sources. This incoming knowledge map can
both interfere with and facilitate new learning. Parts of this map can be
revealed by the first few words that come to mind on hearing the word
*law.* Write down a few sentences describing what law involves, where legal
activity most commonly takes place, and the desirable and undesirable aspects of law. You may be surprised at how much this inventory reveals; it is
your incoming map of law (which may or may not fit the territory).

The study of law should be complex enough to require humility-
bravery, the kind of humility that Kafka's parables force on us, and
enough bravery to let us abandon views of the world that do not explain
enough of what we need to understand. One purpose of an introductory
law text is to provide new guides for perception about law, so that the
strengths and weaknesses of the existing legal order can be adequately
evaluated. The act of teaching and learning should break down stereotypical thinking and also offer new possibilities.

By looking across a range of definitions about law, you can gain more
critical insight. Each definition includes the flash of genius of its propo-

---

*Marshall McLuhan, *Understanding Media* (New York: Signet, 1964), pp. 145–146.

nent; each is the element of limited vision caused by exclusion of the un-explainable. For example, law can be defined as a system of rules and regulations, a cover for the whimsy of officials, a forum for value inquiry, a regime for the resolution of conflict, a power play of elites, a reflection or repression of popular will, or a regime to preserve inequality and denial of freedom. These thumbnail explanations offer promising leads for study. Thinking across a field of explanations promotes clearer insight, because competing ideas create tensions and provide a dynamic in law. These tensions create similar conflicts within students of law, who may be inclined to seek the one best way to explain law. Yet these tensions also make law study a unique educational experience.

The following chapters explore some of the major explanations of law both in theory and in practice. Because no conversation about law can proceed for very long without a discussion of rules, Chapter 1 describes what lawyers and judges do with legal precedents. Chapter 2 discusses official discretion in finding facts, selecting rules, and making decisions. Chapters 3 and 4 concern the articulation of values through law and the role of the legal order in "balancing conflicting interests." All of these chapters can be squared nicely with conventional legal training: learning rules, understanding the options and limits of legal officials, engaging in value inquiry via contested cases, and identifying the countervailing pressures found in all legal systems.

As one would expect, not everyone has been satisfied with the way law has been made and enforced. Nor have all groups been satisfied with the overall effects of legal order on the allocation of political power or economic returns. Marxists (see Chapter 5) have always argued that law enacts and preserves privilege and undercuts broad political participation and economic equality. Anarchists (see Chapter 6) historically have made an even more fundamental challenge to law than Marxists, contending that the institutionalization of values, through law or other state agencies, will *inevitably* pervert values. According to them, the state destroys the very purposes for which it was said to be needed.

A third and more recent critique of law has come from feminist jurists and critical race theorists who have questioned the premises and style of professional legal education, reexamined virtually all areas of law as written and applied, or challenged the entire worth of the legal order, either in undoing inequalities or limitations on freedom (see Chapter 7).

Another form of lawmaking—what anthropologists have designated lawmaking in "non-state settings"—the informal community, the family, the school, and the workplace, to name a few of the principal ones—will be integrated into these chapters and others via questions and comments. There is no doubt that most applications of rules occur informally, with low visibility, and in these settings. Where we spend most of our time, rule-making makes up in intensity and volume what it may lack in publicity.

# 1 LAWMAKING AND PRECEDENT: HOW JUDGES AND LAWYERS REASON FROM PRIOR CASES

> What great king, is the Jewel of the Analytical Powers proclaimed by the Exalted one? Four in number, great king, are the Analytical Powers: Understanding of the Meaning of Words, Understanding of the Doctrine, Grammar and Exegesis, and Readiness in Speaking. Adorned, great king with these Four Analytical Powers, a monk, no matter what manner of assemblage he approaches, whether it be an assemblage of Warriors or an assemblage of Brahmans or an assemblage of householders or an assemblage of religious, approaches confidently, approaches that assemblage untroubled, unafraid, unalarmed, untrembling with no bristling of the hair of the body.
>
> A Buddhist parable

  How does a lawyer decide whether a client has a "good" or a "bad" case? Typically, lawyers begin with facts told them by clients and, after other investigation, "apply" the law to the facts and predict a result. Lawyers assume that judges will decide like cases in like manner; that is, when cases involve comparable facts, prior results will be repeated. Two sources of ambiguity arise in conventional legal work: factual ambiguity ("What happened?") and legal ambiguity ("What law might apply to what happened?").

How do lawyers know what the law is? Oliver Wendell Holmes, Jr. (1841–1935), the famous American jurist, observed:

> Take the fundamental question, what constitutes the law? You will find some text writers telling you that it is something different from what is decided by the courts of Massachusetts or England, that it is a system of reason, that it is a deduction from principles or ethics or admitted axioms . . . which may or may not coincide with decisions. But if we take the view of our friend the bad man we shall find that he does not care two straws for the axioms or deductions, but that he does want to know what the Massachusetts or English courts are likely to do in fact. I am much of his mind. The prophecies of what the courts will do in fact, and nothing more pretentious, are what I mean by the law.*

---

*Oliver Wendell Holmes, "The Path of the Law," *Harvard Law Review,* 10(1897), 457.

Prophecies about law rest in part on a comparison between cases in question and prior cases that have been decided. Skill in finding similarities and differences among cases—the case method—is thus a fundamental part of professional law study. In this section the writing of Karl Llewellyn (1893–1962) and a line of cases from North Carolina show what judges and lawyers do with cases.

## 1.1   The Bramble Bush   *Karl N. Llewellyn*

FIRST, WHAT IS PRECEDENT? In the large, disregarding for the moment peculiarities of our law and of legal doctrine—in the large, precedent consists in an official doing over again under similar circumstances substantially what has been done by him or his predecessor before. The foundation, then, of precedent is the official analogue of what, in society at large, we know as folkways, or as institutions, and of what, in the individual, we know as habit. And the things which make for precedent in this broad sense are the same which make for habit and for institutions. It takes time and effort to solve problems. Once you have solved one it seems foolish to reopen it. Indeed, you are likely to be quite impatient with the notion of reopening it. Both inertia and convenience speak for building further on what you have already built; for incorporating the decision once made, *the solution once worked out,* into your operating technique *without reexamination* of what *earlier went into* reaching your solution. From this side you will observe that the urge to precedent will be present in the action of any official, irrespective of whether he wants it, or not; irrespective likewise of whether he thinks it is there, or not. From this angle precedent is but a somewhat dignified name for the *practice* of the officer or of the office. And it should be clear that unless there were such practices it would be hard to know there was an office or an officer. It is further clear that with the institution of written

records the background range of the practice of officers is likely to be considerably extended; and even more so is the possible outward range, the possibility of outside imitation. Finally, it is clear that if the written records both exist and are somewhat carefully and continuously consulted, the possibility of change creeping into the practices unannounced is greatly lessened. At this place on the law side the institution of the bar rises into significance. For whereas the courts might make records and keep them, but yet pay small attention to them; or might pay desultory attention; or might even deliberately neglect an inconvenient record if they should later change their minds about that type of case, the lawyer searches the records for convenient cases to support his point, presses upon the court what it has already done before, capitalizes the human drive toward repetition by finding, by making explicit, by urging, the prior cases. . . .

To continue past practices is to provide a new official in his inexperience with the accumulated experience of his predecessors. If he is ignorant, he can learn from them and profit by the knowledge of those who have gone before him. If he is idle he can have their action brought to his attention and profit by their industry. If he is foolish he can profit by their wisdom. If he is biased or corrupt the existence of past practices to compare his action with gives a public check upon his biases and his corruption, limits the frame in which he can indulge them unchallenged. Finally, even though his predecessors may themselves, as they set up the practice, have been idle, ignorant, foolish and biased, yet the knowledge that he will continue what they have done gives a basis from which men may predict the action of the courts; a basis to which they can adjust their expectations and their affairs in advance. To know the law is helpful, even when the law is bad. Hence it is readily understandable that in our system there has grown up first the habit of following precedent, and then the legal norm that precedent is to be followed. The main form that this principle takes we have seen. It is essentially the canon that each case must be decided as one instance under a general rule. This much is common to almost all systems of law. The other canons are to be regarded rather as subsidiary canons that have been built to facilitate working with and reasoning from our past decisions.

### Notes and Questions

1. The doctrine of *stare decisis* means that courts will decide like cases in like manner, or that past decisions will be followed. Is there a theory of justice implicit in this doctrine? What are the sources of injustice in such a system?

2. Compare with Llewellyn the following excerpt from the late Aldous Huxley:

   > To make biological survival possible, Mind at Large has to be funneled through the reducing valve of the brain and nervous system. . . . To formulate and express the contents of this reduced awareness man has invented and endlessly elaborated those symbol-systems and implicit philosophies that we call languages.

   Every individual is at once the beneficiary and the victim of the linguistic tradition into which he has been born—the beneficiary inasmuch as language gives access to the accumulated records of other people's experience, the victim insofar as it confirms . . . the belief that reduced awareness is the only awareness, and as it bedevils [the] sense of reality, so that [s]he is all too apt to take . . . concepts for data, . . . words for actual things. That which, in the language of religion, is called "this world" is the universe of reduced awareness expressed and, as it were, petrified by language.*

3. Llewellyn says that it is helpful to know the law even when the law is bad. How is it helpful?

4. Precedent in law becomes more possible by having written records, and so when we think of a precedent system as a general reference to "the past" we should remember that we most often refer to a written record of the past. Is there a difference? What is the written record of your life? Does the record adequately encompass your past?

5. Do you use a precedent system in making personal decisions? Does a precedent system operate in your home, in the various classes you attend, at work, in social groups, and so on?

6. Does each of us carry around a precedent system into which we cram all of our experiences, whether they fit perfectly or not, or are we open to the new experiences we encounter?

---

*Aldous Huxley, *The Doors of Perception* (New York: Harper & Row, 1954), pp. 22–23.

 

🖜 All the following cases in this section are drawn from reports of the North Carolina Supreme Court. These cases illustrate the doctrine of *stare decisis.*

## 1.2  State v. Pendergrass   *2 Dev. & B., N.C. 365 (1837)**

INDICTMENT FOR ASSAULT AND battery. The offense consisted of a whipping with a switch, inflicted

by defendant, a schoolmistress, upon one of her younger pupils. The switching left marks upon the body of the child, upon which were also found marks apparently made by some blunter instrument than a switch. All of these marks,

---

*Case citations are to volume and page numbers of court reports, in this instance North Carolina reports.—ED.

however, disappeared in a few days. The nature of the charge to the jury appears from the opinion. Verdict was against defendant, who thereupon appealed. . . .

GASTON, J.

It is not easy to state with precision, the power which the law grants to schoolmasters and teachers, with respect to the correction of their pupils. It is analogous to that which belongs to parents, and the authority of the teacher is regarded as a delegation of parental authority. One of the most sacred duties of parents, is to train up and qualify their children, for becoming useful and virtuous members of society; this duty can not be effectually performed without the ability to command obedience, to control stubbornness, to quicken diligence, and to reform bad habits; and to enable him to exercise this salutary sway, he is armed with the power to administer moderate correction, when he shall believe it to be just and necessary. The teacher is the substitute of the parent; is charged in part with the performance of his duties, and in the exercise of these delegated duties, is invested with his power.

The law has not undertaken to prescribe stated punishments for particular offenses, but has contented itself with the general grant of the power of moderate correction, and has confided the graduation of punishments, within the limits of this grant, to the discretion of the teacher. The line which separates moderate correction from immoderate punishment, can only be ascertained by reference to general principles. The welfare of the child is the main purpose for which pain is permitted to be inflicted. Any punishment, therefore, which may seriously endanger life, limbs, or health, or shall disfigure the child, or cause any other permanent injury, may be pronounced in itself immoderate, as not only being unnecessary for, but inconsistent with, the purpose for which correction is authorized. But any correction, however severe, which produces temporary pain only, and no permanent ill, can not be so pronounced, since it may have been necessary for the reformation of the child, and does not injuriously affect its future welfare. We hold, therefore, that it may be laid down as a general rule, that teachers exceed the limits of their authority when they cause lasting mischief; but act within the limits of it, when they inflict temporary pain.

When the correction administered, is not in itself immoderate, and therefore beyond the authority of the teacher, its legality or illegality must depend entirely, we think, on the qui animo [the intention—ED.] with which it was administered. Within the sphere of his authority, the master is the judge when correction is required, and of the degree of correction necessary; and like all others intrusted with a discretion, he can not be made penally responsible for error of judgment, but only for wickedness of purpose. The best and the wisest of mortals are weak and erring creatures, and in the exercise of functions in which their judgment is to be the guide, can not be rightfully required to engage for more than honesty of purpose, and diligence of exertion. His judgment must be presumed correct, because he is the judge, and also because of the difficulty of proving the offense, or accumulation of offenses, that called for correction; of showing the peculiar temperament, disposition, and habits, of the individual corrected; and of exhibiting the various milder means, that may have been ineffectually used, before correction was resorted to.

But the master may be punishable when he does not transcend the powers granted, if he grossly abuse them. If he use his authority as a cover for malice, and under pretense of administering correction, gratify his own bad passions, the mask of the judge shall be taken off, and he will stand amenable to justice, as an individual not invested with judicial power.

We believe that these are the rules applicable to the decision of the case before us. If they be, there was error in the instruction given to the jury, that if the child was whipped by the defendant so as to occasion the marks described by the prosecutor, the defendant had exceeded her authority, and was guilty as charged. The marks were all temporary, and in a short time all disappeared. No permanent injury was done to the child. The only appearances that could warrant the belief or suspicion that the correction threatened permanent injury, were the bruises on the neck and the arms; and these, to say the least, were too equivocal to justify the court in assuming that they did threaten such mischief. We think that the instruction on this point should have been, that unless the jury could clearly infer from the evidence, that the correction inflicted had produced, or was in its nature calculated to produce, lasting injury to the child, it did not exceed the limits of the power which had been granted to the defendant. We think also, that the jury should have been further instructed, that however severe the pain inflicted, and however in their judgment it might seem disproportionate to the alleged negligence or offense of so young and tender a child, yet if it did not produce nor threaten lasting mischief, it was their duty to acquit the defendant; unless the facts testified induced a conviction in their minds, that the defendant did not act honestly in the performance of duty, according to her sense of right, but under the pretext of duty, was gratifying malice.

We think that rules less liberal towards teachers, can not be laid down without breaking in upon the authority necessary for preserving discipline, and commanding respect; and that although these rules leave it in their power to commit acts of indiscreet severity, with legal impunity, these indiscretions will probably find their check and correction, in parental affection, and in public opinion; and if they should not, that they must be tolerated as a part of those imperfections and inconveniences, which no human laws can wholly remove or redress.

By Court.

Judgment reversed.

## Notes and Questions

1. The *Pendergrass* case follows the pattern of all judicial opinions: Facts are discussed, legal questions are raised, and a rule or rules are applied. Usually courts give some explanation justifying the application of rules to convince readers that the result reached in the case is appropriate. The analysis of cases for facts, issues, rules, and reasons is a central feature in lawyer training. With modest practice, anyone can master this technique and see the strengths and weaknesses of the case method.

2. Several decades after the *Pendergrass* case, a woman sued for divorce in North Carolina on the grounds that her husband had "rendered her life insupportable." The husband had struck her with a horsewhip on one occasion and with a switch on another, leaving bruises. The lawyer who represented the husband wanted to use the *Pendergrass* case as authority in his efforts to oppose the divorce. Is the *Pendergrass* case applicable?

3. The court acknowledges that no human law can "wholly remove or redress" certain "imperfections and inconveniences." This is said in support of the court's refusal to take on school discipline cases and instead to delegate power to teachers, parents, and others who have day-to-day control over the lives of children. Do you agree with the court's reluctance to intervene?

4. The court observes that "the best and wisest of mortals may be weak and erring creatures" and that therefore people in authority need room to make mistakes. Would this idea be even more pertinent to the behavior of children than to adults?

5. How effective as a limitation on teacher power is parental influence or public opinion? If the court had chosen to intervene here, would it have dulled parental activism or community outrage?

6. If you were a teacher or a student interested in the law of corporal punishment at the time of the *Pendergrass* case, what would the case tell you? If you were a lawyer giving advice based on the case, would you find the case useful in predicting the outcome of a similar case?

7. The principal reason for the court's decision seems to be the protection of established authority or the maintenance of hierarchical relationships. Is nonhierarchical education thinkable? A powerless teacher? Can law require nonhierarchy? Is law itself inherently hierarchical? If school and the legal order are hierarchical, what are the institutions for training in democratic governance?

8. Many years have passed between the time of the case and contemporary times in which we are continually confronted with cases of mental, physical, and sexual abuse of children which arise in almost every conceivable context. Whatever the wisdom of courts' deferring to other authority systems at the time

the case was decided, that position is no longer held, and courts, social agencies, police, and others are expected to intervene in such cases.

A critical aspect of the problem has not been resolved, however. Some of the settings in which children are likely to be abused are also the settings that are regarded as most private and sacrosanct. Even if all acknowledge that privacy must yield in the interests of the child, there will, nevertheless, be continual tension over who should intervene, in what circumstances, and with what remedies.

## 1.3 Joyner v. Joyner  *59 N.C. 322 (1862)*

PETITION FOR DIVORCE. Appeal from an interlocutory order allowing alimony *pendente lite* [during the lawsuit—ED.]. The petitioner alleged her marriage with the defendant; that she herself was well-bred and of respectable family, and that her husband was not less than a fair match for her; that her husband had struck her with a horse-whip on one occasion, and with a switch on another, leaving several bruises on her person; and that on several occasions, he had used abusive and insulting language towards her. The petition concluded as set forth in the opinion of the court.

*By Court,* PEARSON, C. J.

The legislature has deemed it expedient to enlarge the grounds upon which divorces may be obtained; but as a check or restraint on applications for divorces, and to guard against abuses, it is provided that the cause or ground on which the divorce is asked for shall be set forth in the petition "particularly and specially. . . ."

By the rules of pleading in actions at the common law, every allegation of fact must be accompanied by an allegation of "time and place." This rule was adopted in order to insure proper certainty in pleading, but a variance in the *allegata* and *probata* [allegations and proof—ED.], that is, a failure to prove the precise time and place, as alleged in the pleading, was held not to be fatal, unless time or place entered into the essence, and made a material part of the fact relied on, in the pleading.

There is nothing on the face of this petition to show us that time was material, or a part of the essence of the alleged cause of divorce, that is, that the blows were inflicted at a time when the wife was in a state of pregnancy, with an intent to cause a miscarriage, and put her life in danger; and there is nothing to show us that the place was a part of the essence of the cause of divorce, that is, that the blows were inflicted in a public place, with an intent to disgrace her, and make her life insupportable—so we are inclined to the opinion that it was not absolutely necessary to state the time and place, or if stated, that a variance in the proof, in respect to time and place, would not be held fatal.

But we are of opinion that it was necessary to state the circumstances under which the blow with the horse-whip, and the blows with the switch, were given; for instance, what was the conduct of the petitioner; what had she done, or said, to induce such violence on the part of the husband? We are informed by the petitioner that she was a woman, "well-bred, and of respectable family, and that her husband was not less than a fair match for her." There is no allegation that he was drunk, nor was there any imputation of unfaithfulness on either side (which is the most common ingredient of applications for divorce), so there was an obvious necessity for some explanation, and the cause of divorce could not be set forth, "particularly and specially," without stating the circumstances which gave rise to the alleged grievances.

It was said on the argument that the fact that a husband on one occasion "struck his wife with a horse-whip, and on another occasion with a switch, leaving several bruises on her person," is of itself a sufficient cause of divorce, and consequently the circumstances which attended the infliction of these injuries are immaterial, and need not be set forth. This presents the question in the case.

The wife must be subject to the husband. Every man must govern his household, and if by reason of an unruly temper, or an unbridled tongue, the wife persistently treats her husband with disrespect, and he submits to it, he not only loses all sense of self-respect, but loses the respect of the other members of his family, without which he cannot expect to govern them, and forfeits the respect of his neighbors. Such have been the incidents of the marriage relation from the beginning of the human race. Unto the woman it is said: "Thy desire shall be to thy husband, and he shall rule over thee": Gen. iii. 16. It follows that the law gives the husband power to use such a degree of force as is necessary to make the wife behave herself and know her place. Why is it, that by the principles of the common law, if a wife slanders or assaults and beats a neighbor, the husband is made to pay for it? Or if the wife commits a criminal offense, less than felony, in the presence of her husband, she is not held responsible? Why is it that the wife cannot make a will disposing of her land, and cannot sell her land without a privy examination, "separate and apart from her husband," in order to see that she did so voluntarily, and without compulsion on the part of her husband? It is for the reason that the law gives this power to the husband over the person of the wife, and has adopted proper safeguards to prevent an abuse of it.

We will not pursue the discussion further. It is not an agreeable subject, and we are not inclined unnecessarily to draw upon ourselves the charge of a want of proper respect for the weaker sex. It is sufficient for our purpose to state that there may be circumstances which will mitigate, excuse, and so far justify the husband in striking the wife "with a horse-whip on one occasion and with a switch on another, leaving several bruises on the person," so as not to give her a right to abandon him, and claim to be divorced. For instance, suppose a husband comes home, and his wife abuses him in the strongest terms—calls him a scoundrel, and repeatedly expresses a wish that he was dead and in torment; and being thus provoked in the *furor brevis* [sudden anger—ED.], he strikes her with the horse-whip, which he happens to have in his hands, but is afterwards willing to apologize, and expresses regret for having struck her; or suppose a man

and his wife get into a discussion and have a difference of opinion as to a matter of fact, she becomes furious and gives way to her temper, so far as to tell him he lies, and upon being admonished not to repeat the word, nevertheless does so, and the husband taking up a switch, tells her if she repeats it again he will strike her, and after this notice she again repeats the insulting words, and he thereupon strikes her several blows,—these are cases in which, in our opinion, the circumstances attending the act, and giving rise to it, so far justify the conduct of the husband as to take from the wife any ground of divorce for that cause, and authorize the court to dismiss her petition, with the admonition, "If you will amend your manners, you may expect better treatment": See Shelford on Divorce. So that there are circumstances under which a husband may strike his wife with a horse-whip, or may strike her several times with a switch, so hard as to leave marks on her person, and these acts do not furnish sufficient ground for a divorce. It follows that when such acts are alleged as the causes for a divorce, it is necessary in order to comply with the provisions of the statute to state the circumstances attending the acts, and which gave rise to them. . . .

## Notes and Questions

1. The matter-of-factness with which Judge Pearson speaks of relationships between husbands and wives may shock contemporary readers. Besides the Bible, Pearson could have cited some venerable authorities in support of the idea that certain relationships are "traditional" and "natural." From *The Politics* of Aristotle:

   It was out of the association formed by men of these two, women and slaves, that the first household was formed; and the poet Hesiod was right when he wrote, "Get first a house and a wife and an ox to draw the plow." (The ox is the poor man's slave.) This association of persons, established according to the law of nature, and continuing day after day, is the household.*

---

*Aristotle, *The Politics*, tr. T. Sinclair (Harmondsworth: Penguin, 1962), p. 27.

# 1.4 State v. Black   *60 N.C. 262 (1864)*

*By Court,* PEARSON, C. J.

A HUSBAND IS RESPONSIBLE for the acts of his wife, and he is required to govern his household, and for that purpose the law permits him to use towards his wife such a degree of force as is necessary to control an unruly temper and make her behave herself; and unless some permanent injury be inflicted, or there be an excess of violence, or such a degree of cruelty as shows that it is inflicted to gratify his own bad passions, the law will not invade the domestic forum or go behind the curtain. It prefers to leave the parties to themselves, as the best mode of inducing them to make the matter up and live together as man and wife should.

Certainly the exposure of a scene like that set out in this case can do no good. In respect to the parties, a public exhibition in the courthouse of such quarrels and fights between man and wife widens the breach, makes a reconciliation almost impossible, and encourages insubordination; and in respect to the public, it has a pernicious tendency; so, *pro bono publico* [for the public good—ED.], such matters are excluded from the courts, unless there is a permanent injury or excessive violence or cruelty indicating malignity and vindictiveness.

In this case, the wife commenced the quarrel. The husband, in a passion provoked by excessive abuse, pulled her upon the floor by the hair, but restrained himself, did not strike a blow, and she admits he did not choke her, and she continued to abuse him after she got up. Upon this state of facts the jury ought to have been charged in favor of the defendant: *State v. Pendergrass, . . . Joyner v. Joyner . . .*

It was insisted by Mr. Winston that, admitting such to be the law when the husband and wife lived together, it did not apply when, as in this case, they were living apart. That may be so when there is a divorce from bed and board, because the law then recognizes and allows the separation, but it can take no notice of a private agreement to live separate. The husband is still responsible for her acts, and the marriage relation and its incidents remain unaffected.

## Notes and Questions

1. The court cites the *Pendergrass* and *Joyner* cases as precedent. What are the similarities between those cases and the facts of the *Black* case? The differences?

2. How clear were the prior cases as a guide in the *Black* case? Was the result in *Black* preordained by the earlier cases?

3. In the *Joyner* case, no evidence was given as to who started the fight, whereas in the *Black* case, there was evidence that the wife started it. Is this case, therefore, easier for the court to decide than the *Joyner* case? Which case is the stronger precedent regarding a husband's "right" to chastise his wife?

4. In the *Pendergrass* case, the court said that intervention in the school situation would depend on the *qui animo,* or intentions, of the teacher in punishing. Only for wickedness of purpose would the court find an assault. In the *Black* case, the court spoke of cruelty or the use of force "to gratify his own bad passions." How can these interior states of teachers or husbands be proved?

5. The court indicates in the *Black* case that if the parties make a private agreement to live apart it need not be recognized. Why is the preservation of this agreement less compelling as a public good than the preservation of the privacy of the "domestic forum"?

6. In reading these cases, do you have difficulty in dealing with anything other than whether it is a good idea for teachers to beat students or for husbands to beat their wives? With contemporary eyes you can see that the power mismatch in families has been dodged.

   The court does not stay on larger questions, but instead moves to questions of how, when, and where a beating may take place. The latter questions are seen as more manageable than the ones that first come to mind, and can be handled with "less emotion."

   What does this approach say about legal analysis? About rules of law? Can a profession, such as law, be based on emotion? What would emotional rules of law look like? Are "Stop it now" or "Cut it out" possibilities as rules of law?

## 1.5 State v. Rhodes   *61 N.C. 453 (1868)*

ASSAULT AND BATTERY, IN which it appeared that the husband struck the wife three blows with a switch about the size of one of his fingers. The other facts are stated in the opinion.

*By Court*, READE, J.

The violence complained of would, without question, have constituted a battery, if the subject of it had not been the defendant's wife. The question is, how far that fact affects the case.

The courts have been loth to take cognizance of trivial complaints arising out of the domestic relations—such as master and apprentice, teacher and pupil, parent and child, husband and wife. Not because those relations are not subject to the law, but because the evil of publicity would be greater than the evil involved in the trifles complained of, and because they ought to be left to family government. On the civil side of this court, under our divorce laws, such cases have been unavoidable and not infrequent. On the criminal side, there are but two cases reported. In one, the question was whether the wife was a competent witness to prove a battery by the husband upon her, which inflicted no great or permanent injury. It was decided that she was not. In discussing the subject, the court said that the abstract question of the husband's right to whip his wife did not arise: *State* v. *Hussy*. . . . The other case was one of a slight battery by the husband upon the wife after gross provocation. He was held not to be punishable. In that case, the court said that unless some permanent injury be inflicted, or there be an excess of violence, or such a degree of cruelty as shows that it is inflicted to gratify his own bad passions, the law will not invade the domestic forum, or go behind the curtain: *State* v. *Black*. . . . Neither of those cases is like the one before us. The first case turned upon the competency of the wife as a witness, and in the second there was a slight battery upon a strong provocation.

In this case no provocation worth the name was proved. The fact found was, that it was "without any provocation except some words which were not recollected by the witness." The words must have been of the slightest import to have

made no impression on the memory. We must therefore consider the violence as unprovoked. The question is therefore plainly presented whether the court will allow a conviction of the husband for moderate correction of the wife without provocation.

Our divorce laws do not compel a separation of husband and wife, unless the conduct of the husband be so cruel as to render the wife's condition intolerable or her life burdensome. What sort of conduct on the part of the husband would be allowed to have that effect has been repeatedly considered. And it has not been found easy to lay down any iron rule upon the subject. In some cases it has been held that actual and repeated violence to the person was not sufficient; in others, that insults, indignities, and neglect, without any actual violence, were quite sufficient;—so much does each case depend upon its peculiar surroundings.

We have sought the aid of the experience and wisdom of other times and of other countries.

Blackstone says: "That the husband, by the old law, might give the wife moderate correction; for as he was to answer for her misbehavior, he ought to have the power to control her; but that in the polite reign of Charles the Second this power of correction began to be doubted": 1 Bla. Com. 444. Wharton says that by the ancient common law, the husband possessed the power to chastise his wife; but that the tendency of criminal courts in the present day is to regard the marital relation as no defense to a battery: Crim. Law, secs. 1259, 1260. Chancellor Walworth says of such correction that it is not authorized by the law of any civilized country; not, indeed, meaning that England is not civilized, but referring to the anomalous relics of barbarism which cleave to her jurisprudence: Bishop on Marriage and Divorce, 446, note. The old law of moderate correction has been questioned even in England, and has been repudiated in Ireland and Scotland. The old rule is approved in Mississippi, but it has met with but little favor elsewhere in the United States. . . . In looking into the discussions of the other states, we find but little uniformity.

From what has been said, it will be seen how much the subject is at sea. And probably it will ever be so; for it will always be influenced by the habits, manners, and condition of every community. Yet it is necessary that we should lay down something as precise and practical as the nature of the subject will admit of for the guidance of our courts.

Our conclusion is, that family government is recognized by law as being as complete in itself as the state government is in itself, and yet subordinate to it; and that we will not interfere with or attempt to control it in favor of either husband or wife, unless in cases where permanent or malicious injury is inflicted or threatened, or the condition of the party is intolerable. For however great are the evils of ill temper, quarrels, and even personal conflicts inflicting only temporary pain, they are not comparable with the evils which would result from raising the curtain and exposing to public curiosity and criticism the nursery and the bed-chamber. Every household has and must have a government of its own, modeled to suit the temper, disposition, and condition of its inmates. Mere ebullitions of passion, impulsive violence, and temporary pain, affection will soon forget and forgive; and each member will find excuse for the other in his own frailties. But when trifles are taken hold of by the public, and the parties are exposed and disgraced, and each endeavors to justify himself or herself by criminating the other, that which ought to be forgotten in a day will be remembered for life.

It is urged in this case that as there was no provocation the violence was of course excessive and malicious; that every one, in whatever relation of life, should be able to purchase immunity from pain by obedience to authority and faithfulness in duty. And it is insisted that in *State* v. *Pendergrass* . . . , which was the case of a schoolmistress whipping a child, that doctrine is laid down. It is true that it is there said that the master may be punishable even when he does not transcend the powers granted; i.e., when he does not inflict permanent injury, if he grossly abuse his powers, and use them as a cover for his malice. But observe, the language is if he grossly abuse his powers. So that every one would say at once there was no cause for it, and it was purely malicious and cruel. If this be not the rule, then every violence which would amount to an assault upon a stranger would have to be investigated to see whether there was any provocation. And that would contravene what we have said, that we will punish no case of trifling importance. If in every such case we are to hunt for the provocation, how will the proof be supplied? Take the case before us. The witness said there was no provocation except some slight words. But then, who can tell what significance the trifling words may have had to the husband? Who can tell what had happened an hour before, and every hour for a week? To him they may have been sharper than a sword. And so in every case it might be impossible for the court to appreciate what might be offered as an excuse, or no excuse might appear at all, when a complete justification exists. Or suppose the provocation could in every case be known, and the court should undertake to weigh the provocation in every trifling family broil, what would be the standard? Suppose a case coming up to us from a hovel, where neither delicacy of sentiment nor refinement of manners is appreciated or known. The parties themselves would be amazed if they were to be held responsible for rudeness or trifling violence. What do they care for insults and indignities? In such cases, what end would be gained by investigation or punishment? Take a case from the middle class, where modesty and purity have their abode, but nevertheless have not immunity from the frailties of nature, and are sometimes moved by the mysteries of passion. What could be more harassing to them or injurious to society than to draw a crowd around their seclusion? Or take a case from the higher ranks, where education and culture have so refined nature that a look cuts like a knife, and a word strikes like a hammer; where the most delicate attention gives pleasure, and the slightest neglect pain; where an indignity is disgrace, and exposure is ruin. Bring all these cases into court side by side, with the same offense charged and the same proof made, and what conceivable charge of the court to the jury would be alike appropriate to all the cases, except that they all have domestic government, which they have formed for themselves, suited to their own peculiar conditions, and that those governments are supreme, and from them there is no appeal, except in cases of great importance requiring the strong arm of the law, and that to those governments they must submit themselves?

It will be observed that the ground upon which we have put this decision is not that the husband has the right to whip his wife much or little, but that we will not interfere with family government in trifling cases. We will no more interfere where the husband whips the wife than where the wife whips the husband, and yet we would hardly be supposed to hold that a wife has a right to whip her husband. We will not inflict upon society the greater evil of raising the curtain upon domestic privacy to punish the lesser evil of trifling violence. Two boys under fourteen years of age fight upon the playground, and yet the courts will take no notice of it, not for the reason that boys have the right to fight, but because the interests of society require that they should be left to the more appropriate discipline of the schoolroom and of home. It is not true that boys have a right to fight; nor is it true that a husband has a right to whip his wife. And if he had, it is not easily seen how the thumb is the standard of size for the instrument which he may use, as some of the old authorities have said, and in deference to which was his honor's charge. A light blow, or many light blows, with a stick larger than the thumb might produce no injury; but a switch half the size might be so used as to produce death. The standard is the effect produced, and not the manner of producing it, or the instrument used.

Because our opinion is not in unison with the decisions of some of the sister states, or with the philosophy of some very respectable law-writers, and could not be in unison with all because of their contrariety, a decent respect for the opinions of others has induced us to be very full in stating the reasons for our conclusion. There is no error. [The husband won.—ED.]

*Notes and Questions*

1. In light of the prior cases in North Carolina, is it fair for the court to say that the subject at issue is "at sea," meaning that it has not been resolved?

2. If the courts will not involve themselves in family quarrels below a certain threshold and it is likely that husbands will be the aggressors in family assaults, has not the court, through a promise of inaction, acknowledged the right of the husband to chastise up to the threshold?

3. If the family is a government, what kind of government is it? What is the relationship between the government of the family and the government of the state? Does the analogy of the family to a government help the court to reach a resolution of the questions before it? Is the court's use of the analogy persuasive to you?

4. What is the status of the "rule of thumb" (that the circumference of the instrument used could be no larger than the circumference of the thumb) after this case?

5. Why does the court cite examples from other countries and other states that seem to differ from its decision? Do these references strengthen or weaken the case as precedent for the rule that a husband may chastise his wife?

## 1.6 | State v. Mabrey    *64 N.C. 592 (1870)*

*Assault, tried before* WALLS, J., *at Spring Term, 1870, of Halifax.*

THE JURY FOUND, BY a special verdict, that on 7 June, 1869, at the house of the defendant, etc., the latter and his wife had some words and he threatened to leave her; after some very improper language by him, she started off, when he caught her by the left arm and said he would kill her, and drew his knife and struck at her with it, but did not strike her; that he drew back as if to strike again, and his arm was caught by a bystander, whereupon the wife got away and ran about fifteen steps; that the defendant did not pursue her, but told her not to return, if she did he would kill her; that he did not strike her or inflict any personal injury, and that he was a man of violent character, etc., etc.

His Honor thereupon being of opinion that the defendant was not guilty, there was a verdict and judgment accordingly; and the Solicitor for the State appealed.

READE, J.

The facts present a case of savage and dangerous outrage, not to be tolerated in a country of laws and Christianity. We rigidly adhere to the doctrine, in *State* v. *Rhodes, . . .* and precedent cases . . . , that the courts will not invade the domestic forum, to take cognizance of trifling cases of violence in family government; but there is no relation which can shield a party who is guilty of malicious outrage or dangerous violence committed or threatened. In *State* v. *Rhodes* the jury had been charged that "the husband had the right to whip his wife with a switch no larger than his thumb." In combating that error the Court said: "A light blow, or many light blows with a stick larger than the thumb, might produce no injury; but a switch half the size might be so used as to produce death. The standard is the *effect produced,* and not the manner of producing it, or the instrument used." Those words were used as ap-

plicable to the facts in that case. But on the argument at the bar in this case they were perverted to mean that in any case, no matter what weapon was used or from what motive or intent, unless permanent injury were inflicted, the Court would not interfere; therefore, *here,* although death was threatened and a deadly knife used, yet as it was averted by a bystander, the Court will not interfere. We repudiate any such construction of *State* v. *Rhodes.* Upon the special verdict there ought to have been judgment against the defendant.

Per Curiam.

Error.

### Notes and Questions

1. Judge Reade wrote the opinions in both the *Rhodes* and *Mabrey* cases. Are there any words that he wished he had not written in the earlier opinion? Are there any he might have wished he had included?

2. What is the combined effect of the *Rhodes* and *Mabrey* cases?

⨭ Keep the foregoing cases in mind as you read additional material on precedent from Llewellyn.

## 1.7   The Bramble Bush (continued)   *Karl N. Llewellyn*

WE TURN FIRST TO what I may call the orthodox doctrine of precedent, with which, in its essence, you are already familiar. Every case lays down a rule, the rule of the case. The express ratio decidendi is prima facie the rule of the case, since it is the ground upon which the court chose to rest its decision. But a later court can reexamine the case and can invoke the canon that no judge has power to decide what is not before him, can, through examination of the facts or of the procedural issue, narrow the picture of what was actually before the court and can hold that the rul-

ing made requires to be understood as thus restricted. In the extreme form this results in what is known as expressly "confining the case to its particular facts." This rule holds only of red-headed Walpoles in pale magenta Buick cars. And when you find this said of a past case you know that in effect it has been overruled. Only a convention, a somewhat absurd convention, prevents flat overruling in such instances. It seems to be felt as definitely improper to state that the court in a prior case was wrong, peculiarly so if that case was in the same court which is speaking now. It seems to be felt that this would undermine the dogma of the infallibility of courts. So lip service is done to that dogma, while the rule which the prior court laid down is disembowelled. The execution proceeds with due respect, with mandarin courtesy.

Now this orthodox view of the authority of precedent—which I shall call the *strict* view—is but *one of two views* which seem to me wholly contradictory to each other. It is in practice the dogma which is applied to *unwelcome* precedents. It is the recognized, legitimate, honorable technique for whittling precedents away, for making the lawyer, in his argument, and the court, in its decision, free of them. It is a surgeon's knife. . . .

. . . when you turn to the actual operations of the courts, or, indeed, to the arguments of lawyers, you will find a totally different view of precedent at work beside this first one. That I shall call, to give it a name, the *loose view* of precedent. That is the view that a court has decided, and decided authoritatively, *any* point or all points on which it chose to rest a case, or on which it chose, after due argument, to pass. No matter how broad the statement, no matter how unnecessary on the facts or the procedural issues, if that was the rule the court laid down, then that the court has held. . . . In its extreme form this results in thinking and arguing exclusively from language that is found in past opinions, and in citing and working with that *language* wholly without reference to the facts of the case which called the language forth.

Now it is obvious that this is a device not for cutting past opinions away from judges' feet, but for using them as a springboard when they are found convenient. This is a device for *capitalizing welcome precedents*. And both the lawyers and the judges use it so. And judged by the *practice* of the most respected courts, as of the courts of ordinary stature, this doctrine of precedent is like the other, recognized, legitimate, honorable.

What I wish to sink deep into your minds about the doctrine of precedent, therefore, is that it is two-headed. It is Janus-faced.* That it is not one doctrine, nor one line of doctrine, but two, and two which, *applied at the same time to the same precedent, are contradictory of each other*. That there is one doctrine for getting rid of precedents deemed troublesome and one doctrine for

making use of precedents that seem helpful. That these two doctrines exist side by side. That the same lawyer in the same brief, the same judge in the same opinion, may be using the one doctrine, the technically strict one, to cut down half the older cases that he deals with, and using the other doctrine, the loose one, for building with the other half. Until you realize this you do not see how it is possible for law to change and to develop, and yet to stand on the past. . . .

. . . The strict view—that view that cuts the past away—is *hard* to use. An ignorant, an unskillful judge will find it hard to use: the past will bind him. But the skillful judge—he whom we would make free—is thus made free. He has the knife in hand; and he can free himself. Nor, until you see this double aspect of the doctrine-inaction, do you appreciate how little, in detail, you can predict *out of the rules alone;* how much you must turn, for purposes of prediction, to the reactions of the judges to the facts and to the life around them. . . .

. . . The first question is, how much can this case fairly be made to stand for by a later court to whom the precedent is welcome? . . . The second question is, how much is there in this case that cannot be got around, even by a later court that wishes to avoid it?

You have now the tools for arguing from that case as counsel on *either* side of a new case. You turn then to the problem of prediction. Which view will this same court, on a later case on slightly different facts, take: will it choose the narrow or the loose? Which use will be made of this case by one of the other courts whose opinions are before you? Here you will call to your aid the matter of attitude that I have been discussing. Here you will use all that you know of individual judges, or of the trends in specific courts, or, indeed, of the trend in the line of business, or in the situation, or in the times at large—in anything which you may expect to become apparent and important to the court in later cases. But always and always, you will bear in mind that each precedent has not one value, but two, and that the two are wide apart, and that whichever value a later court assigns to it, such assignment will be respectable, traditionally sound, dogmatically correct. Above all, as you turn this information to your own training you

---

*Janus was a Roman god with two faces, and so capable of looking in opposite directions simultaneously.

will, I hope, come to see that in most doubtful cases the precedents *must* speak ambiguously until the court has made up its mind whether each one of them is welcome or unwelcome. And that the job of persuasion which falls upon you will call, therefore, not only for providing a technical ladder to reach on authority the result that you contend for, but even more, if you are to have your use of the precedents made as *you* propose it, the job calls for you, on the facts, to persuade the court your case is sound.

People—and they are curiously many—who think that precedent produces or ever did produce a certainty that did not involve matters of judgment and of persuasion, or who think that what I have described involves improper equivocation by the courts or departure from the courtways of some golden age—such people simply do not know our system of precedent in which they live.

## Notes and Questions

1. Llewellyn gives two views of precedent, strict and loose. One point of confusion about his explanation can come from his using the word *strict* in a different way than is customary in constitutional law. In constitutional law, strict construction involves the finding of the intention of the framers of the Constitution and *following* that intention in a contemporary case. As Llewellyn uses the term, a strict view of precedent is used by a judge or lawyer who wishes to *reject* a past case in whole or in part. The strict view thus sometimes contradicts the intentions of the judges in the prior case.

2. Using Llewellyn's explanation, would the lawyer representing the husband in the *Mabrey* case have found the prior cases of *Pendergrass, Joyner, Black,* and *Rhodes* welcome or unwelcome? In part welcome, in part unwelcome? How would the lawyer have presented the facts and rules of the prior cases so as to capitalize on the welcome features and minimize the impact of the unwelcome features?

   How would the opposition read and interpret the prior cases?

3. Could the judge in *Mabrey* have decided in favor of Mabrey using the precedents available? The judge in fact decided against Mabrey. Does the opinion make a fair application of precedent?

4. Does any of the foregoing material on what judges and lawyers do with cases smack of dishonesty?

5. Assume that the following occurred in North Carolina in 1873: A man came home intoxicated one morning. After complaining to his wife about the food that was around for him to eat, he went out in the yard, cut some thin switches, and struck her several times with them until he was told to stop by some people who were there. The beating left bruises that lasted two weeks, but did not disable her from her work. She went to the prosecutor and asked what could be done about it. What could he have advised her in light of the prior cases?

---

## 1.8   State v. Oliver     *70 N.C. 60 (1874)*

*Indictment for an assault and battery, tried before,* MITCHELL, JUDGE, *at Fall Term, 1873, Alexander Superior Court.*

ON THE TRIAL THE jury found the following facts:

Defendant came home intoxicated one morning after breakfast was over; got some raw bacon, said it had skippers on it, and told his wife she [*sic*] would not clean it. He sat down and ate a little, when he threw the coffee cup and pot into the corner of the room and went out; while out he cut two switches, brought them in, and, throwing them on the floor, told his wife that if he whipped her she would leave; that he was going to whip her, for she and her d—d mother had aggravated him near to death. He then struck her five licks with the two switches, which were about four feet long, with the branches on them about half way and some leaves. One of the switches was about half as large as a man's little finger; the other not so large. He had them in both hands, and inflicted bruises on her arm which remained for two weeks, but did not disable her from work.

One of the witnesses swore he struck as hard as he could. Others were present, and after defendant had struck four licks told him to desist. Defendant stopped, saying if they had not been there he would have worn her out.

Upon these facts the Court found defendant guilty and fined him $10. Defendant appealed.

*Armfield,* for defendant.

*Attorney General Hargrove,* for the State, called the attention of the Court to the cases of *State* v. *Black* . . . ; *State* v. *Mabrey* . . . ; *State* v. *Rhodes* . . . ; *State* v. *Hussey* . . . ; and *State* v. *Pendergrass.* . . .

SETTLE, J.

We may assume that the old doctrine that a husband had a right to whip his wife, provided he used a switch no larger than his thumb, is not law in North Carolina. Indeed, the Courts have advanced from that barbarism until they have reached the position that the husband has no right to chastise his wife under any circumstances.

But from motives of public policy, and in order to preserve the sanctity of the domestic circle, the Courts will not listen to trivial complaints.

If no permanent injury has been inflicted, nor malice, cruelty nor dangerous violence shown by the husband, it is better to draw the curtain, shut out the public gaze, and leave the parties to forget and forgive.

No general rule can be applied, but each case must depend upon the circumstances surrounding it.

Without adverting in detail to the facts established by the special verdict in this case, we think that they show both malice and cruelty.

In fact it is difficult to conceive how a man who has promised upon the altar to love, comfort, honor and keep a woman can lay rude and violent hands upon her without having malice and cruelty in his heart.

Let it be certified that the judgment of the Supreme Court is affirmed.

*Per curiam.*

Judgment affirmed.

### Notes and Questions

1. The court had several cases called to its attention, but cited none of them in the opinion. How can this be explained? Could the outcome reached here have been predicted in light of the earlier cases?

2. If Oliver had seen his lawyer shortly before his trial and asked bluntly, "What are my chances?" how might the lawyer have responded?

3. Is an injustice done to Oliver here? Could he say that he had planned his affairs in reliance upon the state of the prior law?

4. Has the court at last solved the problem of family quarreling? Are future cases predictable?

5. Consider the following presentation of time perspectives of a decision maker:

    *Past* (historical or precedent [general sense] oriented): What are the past decisions where the same or equivalent facts, issues, and so forth, have been involved?

    *Present* (existential): To what extent does this case (transaction, event) present dimensions that are unanswerable by reference to the past? To what extent is "the answer" of the past inadequate to meet the "felt needs" of the present?

    *Future* (impact orientation): Will a result contribute to or detract from purposes that the law is designed to serve? Will a result lead to improvement? To a better society?

    One or another of these orientations emerges in each of the various North Carolina cases. Reread the cases with this in mind.

    What is particularly noteworthy about these cases is that the court appears to be making a turnabout, without even acknowledging it. In thinking about this odd way in which change occurs with all pretenses of stability, one is reminded of the story of the ax that had been in the family for hundreds of years— with two new heads and six new handles!

6. After having studied these cases from North Carolina, how is your understanding of precedent and legal reasoning different from that of someone who has not studied them?

    There might be an easy way to test your powers of legal reasoning. Imagine yourself to be a lawyer practicing in North Carolina in 1875 one year after the decision in the *Oliver* case. Assume that either the husband or the wife involved in the following case has consulted you for a professional opinion:

    The husband and his wife had an argument in their home. Two children, both eight years old, were playing where they could see and hear what was going on. One was the child of the couple, the other of a neighbor. The discussion was over finances, the husband's sporadic work, and his drinking, which according to his wife made all their problems worse. The husband insisted that he had not been drinking and that if his wife didn't shut up he would hit her. She continued to shout at him, and he went over to a stack of wood that was piled by the fireplace and picked up a piece of kindling two inches in diameter. He approached his wife with the piece of wood raised up, but when she screamed, he dropped the wood and slapped her with his hand. Her nose started to bleed and her eye later blackened, but there was no sign of injury after five days.

7. How is a lawyer's exploration of the foregoing hypothetical case different from a layperson's? What is the role of legal rules in rendering advice?

8. What do you now see as the essential strengths and weaknesses in legal reasoning? When is legal reasoning preferable to nonlegal reasoning? If thinking like a lawyer involves careful reading of cases and legal reasoning, do you want to think like one?

9. How applicable is the idea of precedent in out-of-court settings, such as the home, among family members, or at school? Are precedents used in those situations? Do strict and loose interpretations of precedents operate? Who gets to "set" precedents in such groups?

ﷺ Despite the North Carolina cases having been used in this text to illustrate the doctrine of stare decisis and how judges and lawyers argue from cases, the issue of violence against women cries out for a discussion of recent developments. In 1994 the U.S. Congress passed a law entitled the Violence Against Women Act which attempted to protect women from "crimes of violence based on gender," and provide a damage remedy to the victims of violence. The plaintiff in *Brzonkala* v. *Morrison et al.* alleged that while a student at Virginia Polytechnic Institute she was raped by the two defendants, members of the varsity football team. Her case was dismissed and the United States Supreme Court upheld the dismissal. According to Chief Justice Rehnquist the Congress had no power to pass the law either under the Commerce Clause or the XIV Amendment.

Justice Souter, writing in dissent[†], observed that Congress had found extensive violence toward women and concluded that there was ample power under the Commerce Clause[*] for Congress to enact the law. According to Souter:

. . . Congress through hearings had received evidence for the following findings:

Three out of four women will be victims of violent crimes sometime during their life . . . (cit.)[‡]

---

[*]Article I of the U.S. Constitution.

[†]68 U.S.L.W. 4360,4361 (2000).

[‡]The citations to congressional reports and other studies are omitted but can be found in the text of the opinion.

Violence is the leading cause of injuries to women ages 15–44 . . .

[A]s many as 50 percent of homeless women and children are fleeing domestic violence . . .

Since 1974, the assault rate against women has outstripped the rate for men by at least twice for some age groups and far more for others . . .

[B]attering is the largest single cause of injury to women in the United States . . .

An estimated 4 million women are battered each year by their husbands or partners . . .

Over 1 million women in the United States seek medical assistance each year for injuries sustained [from] their husbands or other partners . . .

Between 2,000 and 4,000 women die every year from [domestic] abuse . . .

[A]rrest rates may be as low as 1 for every 100 domestic assaults . . .

Partial estimates show that violent crime against women costs this country at least 3 billion—not million, but billion—dollars a year . . .

[E]stimates suggest that we spend $5 to $10 billion a year on health care, criminal justice, and other costs of domestic violence . . .

Souter then went on to consider the incidence and impact of rape and fear of rape:

The evidence as to rape was similarly extensive . . .

[The incidence of rape] rose four times as fast as the national crime rate over the past 10 years . . .

According to one study, close to half a million girls now in high school will be raped before they graduate . . .

[One hundred twenty-five thousand] college women can expect to be raped during this—or any—year . . .

[T]hree quarters of women never go to the movies alone after dark because of the fear of rape, and nearly 50 percent do not use public transit alone after dark for the same reason . . .

[Forty-one] percent of judges surveyed believed that juries give sexual assault victims less credibility than other crime victims . . .

Less than 1 percent of all [rape] victims have collected damages . . .

[A]n individual who commits rape has only about 4 chances in 100 of being arrested, prosecuted, and found guilty of any offense. . .

Almost one-quarter of convicted rapists never go to prison and another one-quarter received sentences in local jails where the average sentence is 11 months . . .

[A]lmost 50 percent of rape victims lose their jobs or are forced to quit because of the crime's severity . . .

Based on the data . . . Congress found:

Crimes of violence motivated by gender have a substantial adverse effect on interstate commerce, by deterring potential victims from travelling interstate, from engaging in employment in interstate business, and from transacting with business, and in places involved in interstate commerce . . . by diminishing national productivity, increasing medical and other costs, and decreasing the supply of and the demand for interstate products . . .

Justice Souter then concluded:

Congress thereby explicitly stated the predicate for the exercise of the commerce power. Is its conclusion irrational in view of the data amassed? True, the methodology of particular studies may be challenged, and some of the figures arrived at may be disputed. But the sufficiency of the evidence before Congress to provide a rational basis for the finding cannot be seriously questioned.

# 2 | LAW AND OFFICIAL DISCRETION

A crow can pass for a peacock or a nightingale when there is no rivalry and nobody knows the difference.

　　B. Traven, *Government* (1971)

Law is what is read, not what is written.

　　Donald Kingsbury, *Courtship Rite* (1981)

❧ When a Hollywood studio was casting for the role of judge in a movie or television series, what would it traditionally have looked for? Probably a white man, fiftyish, flowing gray hair—or at least hair graying at the temples—horn-rimmed glasses, mildly imperious but not devoid of compassion, sober, thoughtful, remote, and so on. There is now more diversity among judges but many of the earlier stereotypes as to how judges should look and act persist. These images have been perpetuated for so long in popular culture that they take on a life of their own that may mask the realities of the judging process. Ordinary mortals feel one-down in a courtroom and when appearing before a judge. Popular myths can also be highly useful to professionals in law: For example, rather than make a frontal assault on judicial wisdom and authority or their own ineptitude in handling a case, lawyers can explain to disaffected clients that a judge was "forced" to rule in a certain way.

　　Your study of the mixed doctrines of precedent has already suggested that legal professionals have a range of action and are not necessarily constrained by prior law. Judges likewise can and must choose courses of action, and are not simply automatons who slavishly follow the pronouncements laid down by their predecessors on the bench. What are some of the factors that lie below the surface of judicial opinions?

　　Jerome Frank (1889–1957), a teacher, a lawyer, and later a judge, began to expose the realities of judicial process in *Law and the Modern Mind,* which stands as perhaps one of the finest books ever written about American law. There he uncovered dominant popular and professional myths about law and process, probed them psychoanalytically, and recommended changes that he thought would be helpful. Since judges, police, prosecutors, and other decision makers exercise discretion and therefore filter the competing notions of law, justice, and process, and control day-to-day outcomes in law, Frank's writing adds a vital link between law in theory and law in practice.

## 2.1 The Judging Process and the Judge's Personality    *Jerome Frank*

AS THE WORD INDICATES, the judge in reaching a decision is making a judgment. And if we would understand what goes into the creating of that judgment, we must observe how ordinary men dealing with ordinary affairs arrive at their judgments.*

The process of judging, so the psychologists tell us, seldom begins with a premise from which a conclusion is subsequently worked out. Judging begins rather the other way around—with a conclusion more or less vaguely formed; a man ordinarily starts with such a conclusion and afterwards tries to find premises which will substantiate it.[1] If he cannot, to his satisfaction, find proper arguments to link up his conclusion with premises which he finds acceptable, he will, unless he is arbitrary or mad, reject the conclusion and seek another.

In the case of the lawyer who is to present a case to a court, the dominance in his thinking of the conclusion over the premises is moderately obvious. He is a partisan working on behalf of his client. The conclusion is, therefore, not a matter of choice except within narrow limits. He must,

that is if he is to be successful, begin with a conclusion which will insure his client's winning the lawsuit. He then assembles the facts in such a fashion that he can work back from this result he desires to some major premise which he thinks the court will be willing to accept. The precedents, rules, principles and standards to which he will call the court's attention constitute this premise.

While "the dominance of the conclusion" in the case of the lawyer is clear, it is less so in the case of the judge. For the respectable and traditional descriptions of the judicial judging process admit no such backward-working explanation. In theory, the judge begins with some rule or principle of law as his premise, applies this premise to the facts, and thus arrives at his decision.

Now, since the judge is a human being and since no human being in his normal thinking processes arrives at decisions (except in dealing with a limited number of simple situations) by the route of any such syllogistic reasoning, it is fair to assume that the judge, merely by putting on the judicial ermine, will not acquire so artificial a method of reasoning. Judicial judgments, like other judgments, doubtless, in most cases, are worked out backward from conclusions tentatively formulated.

As Jastrow says, "In spite of the fact that the answer in the book happens to be wrong, a considerable portion of the class succeeds in reaching it. . . . The young mathematician will manage to obtain the answer which the book requires, even at the cost of a resort to very unmathematical processes." Courts, in their reasoning, are often singularly like Jastrow's young mathematician. Professor Tulin has made a study which

Selections from *Law and the Modern Mind* by Jerome Frank, copyright 1930, 1933, 1949 by Coward McCann, Inc., copyright 1930 by Brentano's, Inc., are from the Anchor Books edition, 1963. Copyright renewed in 1958 by Florence K. Frank. Reprinted by arrangement with the estate of Barbara Frank Kirstein.

*Frank wrote in 1931 before the language was purged of sexist forms as a way of describing "everyone." He uses "he" throughout, but this usage was not completely inapt since at the time he wrote the overwhelming percentage of lawyers and judges were men.—ED.

[1]A convenient analogy is the technique of the author of a detective story.

prettily illustrates that fact. While driving at a reckless rate of speed, a man runs over another, causing severe injuries. The driver of the car is drunk at the time. He is indicted for the statutory crime of "assault with intent to kill." The question arises whether his act constitutes that crime or merely the lesser statutory crime of "reckless driving." The courts of several states have held one way, and the courts of several other states have held the other.

The first group maintain that a conviction for assault with intent to kill cannot be sustained in the absence of proof of an actual purpose to inflict death. In the second group of states the courts have said that it was sufficient to constitute such a crime if there was a reckless disregard of the lives of others, such recklessness being said to be the equivalent of actual intent.

With what, then, appears to be the same facts before them, these two groups of courts seem to have sharply divided in their reasoning and in the conclusions at which they have arrived. But upon closer examination it has been revealed by Tulin that, in actual effect, the results arrived at in all these states have been more or less the same. In Georgia, which may be taken as representative of the second group of states, the penalty provided by the statute for reckless driving is far less than that provided, for instance, in Iowa, which is in the first group of states. If, then, a man is indicted in Georgia for reckless driving while drunk, the courts can impose on him only a mild penalty; whereas in Iowa the judge, under an identically worded indictment, can give a stiff sentence. In order to make it possible for the Georgia courts to give a reckless driver virtually the same punishment for the same offense as can be given by an Iowa judge, it is necessary in Georgia to construe the statutory crime of assault with intent to kill so that it will include reckless driving while drunk. If, and only if, the Georgia court so construes the statute can it impose the same penalty under the same facts as could the Iowa courts under the reckless driving statute. On the other hand, if the Iowa court were to construe the Iowa statute as the Georgia court construes the Georgia statute, the punishment of the reckless driver in Iowa would be too severe.

In other words, the courts in these cases began with the results they desired to accomplish: they wanted to give what they considered to be adequate punishment to drunken drivers: their conclusions determined their reasoning.

But the conception that judges work back from conclusions to principles is so heretical that it seldom finds expression.[2] Daily, judges, in connection with their decisions, deliver so-called opinions in which they purport to set forth the bases of their conclusions. Yet you will study these opinions in vain to discover anything remotely resembling a statement of the actual judging process. They are written in conformity with the time-honored theory. They picture the judge applying rules and principles to the facts, that is, taking some rule or principle (usually derived from opinions in earlier cases) as his major premise, employing the facts of the case as the minor premise, and then coming to his judgment by processes of pure reasoning.

Now and again some judge, more clear-witted and outspoken than his fellows, describes (when off the bench) his methods in more homely terms. Recently Judge Hutcheson essayed such an honest report of the judicial process. He tells us that after canvassing all the available material at his command and duly cogitating on it, he gives his imagination play,

> and brooding over the cause, waits for the feeling, the hunch—that intuitive flash of understanding that makes the jumpspark connection between question and decision and at the point where the path is darkest for the judicial feet, sets its light along the way. . . . In feeling or "hunching" out his decisions, the judge acts not differently from but precisely as the lawyers do in working on their cases, with only this exception, that the lawyer, in having a predetermined destination in view,—to win the lawsuit for his client—looks for and regards

[2]Years ago the writer, just after being admitted to the bar, was shocked when advised by S. S. Gregory, an ex-president of the American Bar Association—a man more than ordinarily aware of legal realities—that "the way to win a case is to make the judge want to decide in your favor and then, and then only, to cite precedents which will justify such a determination. You will almost always find plenty of cases to cite in your favor." All successful lawyers are more or less consciously aware of this technique. But they seldom avow it—even to themselves.

only those hunches which keep him in the path that he has chosen, while the judge, being merely on his way with a roving commission to find the just solution, will follow his hunch wherever it leads him. . . .

And Judge Hutcheson adds:

> I must premise that I speak now of the judgment or decision, the solution itself, as opposed to the apologia for that decision; the decree, as opposed to the logomachy, the effusion of the judge by which the decree is explained or excused. . . . The judge really decides by feeling and not by judgment, by hunching and not by ratiocination, such ratiocination appearing only in the opinion. The vital motivating impulse for the decision is an intuitive sense of what is right or wrong in the particular case; and the astute judge, having so decided, enlists his every faculty and belabors his laggard mind, not only to justify that intuition to himself, but to make it pass muster with his critics. Accordingly, he passes in review all of the rules, principles, legal categories, and concepts which he may find useful, directly or by an analogy so as to select from them those which in his opinion will justify his desired result.

We may accept this as an approximately correct description[3] of how all judges do their thinking. But see the consequences. If the law consists of the decisions of the judges and if those decisions are based on the judge's hunches, then the way in which the judge gets his hunches is the key to the judicial process. Whatever produces the judge's hunches makes the law.

What, then, are the hunch-producers? What are the stimuli which make a judge feel that he should try to justify one conclusion rather than another?

The rules and principles of law are one class of such stimuli.[4] But there are many others, concealed or unrevealed, not frequently considered in discussions of the character or nature of law. To the infrequent extent that these other stimuli have been considered at all, they have been usually referred to as "the political, economic and moral prejudices" of the judge.[5] A moment's reflection would, indeed, induce any open-minded person to admit that factors of such character must be operating in the mind of the judge.

But are not those categories—political, economic and moral biases—too gross, too crude, too wide? . . . What are the hidden factors in the inferences and opinions of ordinary men? The answer surely is that those factors are multitudinous and complicated, depending often on peculiarly individual traits of the persons whose inferences and opinions are to be explained. These uniquely indi-

---

[3]. . . A century ago a great American judge, Chancellor Kent, in a personal letter explained his method of arriving at a decision. He first made himself "master of the facts." Then (he wrote) "I saw where justice lay, and the moral sense decided the court half the time; I then sat down to search the authorities. . . . I might once in a while be embarrassed by a technical rule, *but I almost always found principles suited to my view of the case.*". . .

[4]If Hutcheson were to be taken with complete literalness, it would seem that such legal rules, principles and the like are merely for show, materials for window dressing, implements to aid in rationalization. They are that indeed. But although impatience with the orthodox excessive emphasis on the importance of such devices might incline one at times to deny such formulations any real value, it is necessary—and this even Hutcheson would surely admit—to concede them more importance. In part, they help the judge to check up on the propriety of the hunches. They also suggest hunches. . . .

[5]Most of the suggestions that law is a function of the undisclosed attitudes of judges stress the judges' "education," "race," "class," "economic, political and social influences" which "make up a complex environment" of which the judges are not wholly aware but which affect their decisions by influencing their views of "public policy," or "social advantage" or their "economic and social philosophies" or "their notions of fair play or what is right and just."

It is to the economic determinists and to the members of the school of "sociological jurisprudence" that we owe much of the recognition of the influence of the economic and political background of judges upon decisions. For this much thanks. But their work has perhaps been done too well. . . . [T]hey over-stressed a few of the multitude of unconscious factors and oversimplified the problem.

Much the same is to be said of the views of the "historical school" with respect to the effect of custom on judicial decisions. "Whether a custom will or will not be ratified by the courts depends after all on the courts themselves," says Dickinson. . . . "Whatever forces can be said to influence the growth of the law, they exert that influence only by influencing the judges. . . ."

vidual factors often are more important causes of judgments than anything which could be described as political, economic, or moral biases.

. . . A man's political or economic prejudices are frequently cut across by his affection for or animosity to some particular individual or group, due to some unique experience he has had; or a racial antagonism which he entertains may be deflected in a particular case by a desire to be admired by someone who is devoid of such antagonism.

Second (and in the case of the judge more important), is the consideration that in learning the facts . . . the judge's sympathies and antipathies are likely to be active with respect to the persons of the witness, the attorneys and the parties to the suit. His own past may have created plus or minus reactions to women, or blonde women, or men with beards, or Southerners, or Italians, or Englishmen, or plumbers, or ministers, or college graduates, or Democrats. A certain twang or cough or gesture may start up memories painful or pleasant in the main. Those memories of the judge, while he is listening to a witness with such a twang or cough or gesture, may affect the judge's initial hearing of, or subsequent recollection of, what the witness said, or the weight or credibility which the judge will attach to the witness's testimony.

That the testimony of witnesses is affected by their experiences and temperaments has been often observed. . . .

Men are prone to see what they want to see. . . .

Even where witnesses are upright or honest, their belief is apt to be more or less warped by their partiality or prejudice for or against the parties. It is easy to reason ourselves into a belief in the existence of that which we desire to be true, whereas the facts testified to, and from which the witness deduces his conclusions, might produce a very different impression on the minds of others.

It frequently happens that a person, by long dwelling on a subject, thinks that a thing may have happened, and he at last comes to believe that it actually did occur.

The courts have been alive to these grave possibilities of error and have therefore repeat-edly declared that it is one of the most important functions of the trial judge, in determining the value and weight of the evidence, to consider the demeanor of the witness.

They have called attention, as of the gravest importance, to such facts as the tone of voice in which a witness's statement is made, the hesitation or readiness with which his answers are given, the look of the witness, his carriage, his evidences of surprise, his gesture, his zeal, his bearing, his expression, his yawns, the use of his eyes, his furtive or meaning glances, or his shrugs, the pitch of his voice, his self-possession or embarrassment, his air of candor or of seeming levity. It is because these circumstances can be manifest only to one who actually hears and sees the witnesses that upper courts have frequently stated that they are hesitant to overturn the decision of the trial judge in a case where the evidence has been based upon oral testimony; for the upper courts have recognized that they have before them only a stenographic or printed report of the testimony, and that such a black and white report cannot reproduce anything but the cold words of the witness. . . .

Strangely enough, it has been little observed that, while the witness is in this sense a judge, the judge, in a like sense, is a witness. He is a witness of what is occurring in his courtroom. He must determine what are the facts of the case from what he sees and hears; that is, from the words and gestures and other conduct of the witnesses. And like those who are testifying before him, the judge's determination of the facts is no mechanical art. If the witnesses are subject to lapses of memory or imaginative reconstruction of events, in the same manner the judge is subject to defects in his apprehension of the testimony, so that long before he has come to the point in the case where he must decide what is right or wrong, just or unjust, with reference to the facts of the case as a whole, the trial judge has been engaged in making numerous judgments or inferences as the testimony dribbles in. His beliefs as to what was said by the witnesses and with what truthfulness the witnesses said it, will determine what he believes to be the "facts of the case." If his final decision is based upon a hunch and that hunch is a function of the "facts," then of course what, as a fallible witness of what went on in his courtroom, he believes to be the "facts," will often be of controlling importance. So that the judge's innumerable unique traits, dispositions and habits often get in their work in shaping his decisions not only in his determination of what he thinks fair or just with reference to a given set of facts, but in the very processes by which he becomes convinced what those facts are. . . .

. . . The following is from the reminiscences of a man who has served both as prosecuting attorney and as judge:

> The jockeying for a judge is sometimes almost humorous. Lawyers recognize the peculiarities, previous opinions, leanings, strength and weakness, and likes or dislikes of a particular judge in a particular case. Some years ago one of the bright lawyers of Chicago conferred with me as an assistant state's attorney, to agree on a judge for the trial of a series of cases. We proceeded to go over the list. For the state's attorney, I objected to but one judge of all the twenty-eight Cook County judges, and as I went through the list I would ask him about one or another, "How about this one?" As to the first one I named he said, "No, he decided a case a couple of weeks ago in a way that I didn't like. . . ." As to another, he said, "No, he is not very clear-headed; he is likely to read an editorial by the man who put him on the ticket, and get confused on the law." Of another he said, "No, he might sneer at my witnesses, and I can't get the sneer in the record." To another he objected that "If my clients were found guilty this judge would give them the limit.". . .

One bit of statistical evidence as to the differences between judges is available: A survey was made of the disposition of thousands of minor criminal cases by the several judges of the City Magistrate's Court in New York City during the years 1914 to 1916 with the express purpose of finding to what extent the "personal equation" entered into the administration of justice. It was disclosed that "the magistrates did differ to an amazing degree in their treatment of similar classes of cases." Thus of 546 persons charged with intoxication brought before one judge, he discharged only one and found the others (about 97%) guilty, whereas of the 673 arraigned before another judge, he found 531 (or 79%) not guilty. In dis-

orderly conduct cases, one judge discharged only 18% and another discharged 54%. "In other words, one coming before Magistrate Simons had only 2 chances in 10 of getting off. If he had come before Judge Walsh he would have had more than 5 chances in 10 of getting off.". . . When it came to sentences, the same variations existed. One judge imposed fines on 84% of the persons he found guilty and gave suspended sentences to 7%, while one of his fellows fined 34% and gave suspended sentences to 59%. . . .

But if we determine that the personality of the judge has much to do with law-making, have we done enough? Can we rest content with this mere recognition? Can we stop with the blanket statement that our judicial process at its best will be based upon "the trained intuition of the judges," on the hunches of experienced men? . . .

. . . What we may hope some day to get from our judges are detailed autobiographies containing the sort of material that is recounted in the autobiographical novel; or opinions annotated, by the judge who writes them, with elaborate explorations of the background factors in his personal experience which swayed him in reaching his conclusions. For in the last push, a judge's decisions are the outcome of his entire life-history. Judges can take to heart the counsel Anatole France gave to the judges of literature:

> All those who deceive themselves into the belief that they put anything but their own personalities into their work are dupes of the most fallacious of illusions. The truth is that we can never get outside ourselves. . . . We are shut up in our own personality as if in a perpetual prison. The best thing for us, it seems to me, is to admit this frightful condition with a good grace, and to confess that we speak of ourselves every time we have not strength enough to remain silent. . . .

. . . The judge's decision is determined by a hunch arrived at long after the event on the basis of his reaction to fallible testimony. It is, in every sense of the word, *ex post facto* [after the fact]. It is fantastic, then, to say that usually men can warrantably act in reliance upon "established law." Their inability to do so may be deplorable. But mature persons must face the truth, however unpleasant.

Why such resistance to the truth? . . .

It is a marked characteristic of the young child, writes Piaget, that he does very little thinking about his thinking. He encounters extreme difficulty if asked to give an account of the "how" of his mental processes. He cannot reflect on his own reasoning. If you ask him to state how he reached a conclusion, he is unable to recover his own reasoning processes, but instead invents an artificial account which will somehow seem to lead to the result. He cannot correctly explain what he did to find this result. "Instead of giving a retrospect he starts from the result he has obtained as though he had known it in advance and then gives a more or less elaborate method for finding it again. . . . He starts from his conclusion and argues towards the premises as though he had known from the first whither those premises would lead him."

Once more these difficulties find their explanation in the child's relative unawareness of his self, of his incapacity for dealing with his own thoughts as subjective. For this obtuseness produces in the child an overconfidence in his own ideas, a lack of skepticism as to the subjectivity of his own beliefs. As a consequence, the child is singularly nonintrospective. He has, according to Piaget, no curiosity about the motives that guide his thinking. His whole attitude towards his own thinking is the antithesis of any introspective habit of watching himself think, of alertness in detecting the motives which push him in the direction of any given conclusion. The child, that is, does not take his own motives into account. They are ignored and never considered as a constituent of thinking.

. . . One recalls a dictum of Piaget in talking of the child:

The less a mind is given to introspection the more it is the victim of the illusion that it knows itself thoroughly.

## Notes and Questions

1. Llewellyn, whose work on precedent appears in the preceding chapter, thought that Jerome Frank had overstated the psychological and uncertain in law and had understated the legal and predictable:

Law . . . is in fact more predictable, and hence more certain than his treatment would indicate. In his very proper enthusiasm for illusion smashing, he paints the illusion as somewhat more illusive than it is. . . . (W)e . . . must recognize that ways of deciding, ways of thinking, ways of sizing up facts "in terms of legal relevance" are distinctly enough marked in our courts so that we know a lawman, by his judging reactions, from a layman.*

How might Jerome Frank have answered Llewellyn?

2. Does the fact that decisions are made publicly, with lawyers and litigants present, with records and published results that are subject to appeal, present additional limitations on the free flow of psychological forces and intuition? (Students can test these ideas through court visitations.)

3. Frank himself notes that in addition to psychological determinants there are other forces affecting judgment—political, economic and moral biases. He thought these "environmental forces" less important. Do you agree?

4. Using Frank's leads, reevaluate the cases on child and spousal abuse. Can factors of decision other than legal rules be identified?

5. To some, judges would do well to avoid intuition and hunching in decision making and "stick to the law and the facts." Judge Hutcheson, quoted by Frank, found intuition and hunching indispensable to good decision making. What role should intuition play?

Can intuition be cultivated and improved, or is intuition "just there"? Can intuition peacefully coexist with professionalism and "objectivity," or are they irreversibly opposed? If any of these elements can be controlled, i.e., rules or intuition, objectivity or subjectivity, which one ought to be?

6. Unlike Llewellyn, Frank believed that for all their professional training and case study, judges make decisions just as ordinary people do, although they have much fancier ways of dressing their decisions up. What do you see to be the political implications of regarding

---

*Karl N. Llewellyn, *Jurisprudence* (Chicago: University of Chicago Press, 1962), p. 107. See also Karl N. Llewellyn, *The Common Law Tradition* (Boston: Little, Brown, 1960), pp. 17, 18.

judges as ordinary mortals? For example, could "folk judges" or rotating judges be used instead of legally trained ones?

7. How deeply does Frank's illusion-busting go? Does he undercut the legitimacy of professionalism completely, or is he simply advocating more introspection by professionals to improve their performance without putting them out of work?

8. How do you reach decisions? Do you get a flash of intuition or a hunch and rationalize it later, or do you assemble all the pros and cons and only then reach a conclusion? Which sources or methods of decision making do you regard as legitimate and which indefensible?

By what criteria do the people whom you routinely encounter make decisions? Does actual decision making match the officially prescribed ways of making decisions? Would the decision process be different if all people who made decisions were called judges and put on robes?

How does your teacher determine your grades? How are decisions made in your family? Where you work? In your social club? On your athletic team? Can Frank's insights help you understand these settings better and find ways to improve the decision processes used in them?

&. During the late 1960s, judges became embarrassed by the evident disparities in criminal sentences. A person sentenced in one court might receive dramatically different treatment from a person convicted in another court for the same offense.

The criminal law context is especially sensitive because contradictory claims are made on decision makers. They are to provide "equality before the law," which seems to require comparable dispositions in comparable cases. And yet there is an element of discretion expected so that each person will get justice based in part on the uniqueness of his or her own life and the peculiarities of the case.

In an unprecedented development, not currently done, judges in California and elsewhere convened annually to more openly discuss their sentencing practices. The following case was prepared for discussion at the 1968 California Sentencing Institute.

## 2.2 | A Forgery Case   *1968 California Sentencing Institute, 77 Cal. Rptr. (Appendix)*

### OFFENSE: FORGERY

DEFENDANT CASHED A FORGED check amounting to $145 at a department store. The blank check was taken from the company by which he was formerly employed. There were other checks involved but they were uncharged. Defendant pleaded guilty.

Case History Information   This is a 24-year-old man, the third of five children of a Mexican-American working-class family. The father died when defendant was six years of age and there-

after the family was supported by public assistance. He claims he got along well with his mother and the members of his family. However, he asserts they regard him as a "black sheep" because of his difficulties as a youth and as an adult.

Probation officer in Arizona indicates that defendant suffered from rheumatic fever as a child and was overindulged by his mother. He has withdrawn from his family.

Defendant claims high school graduation but verification shows he only completed the ninth grade. His employment record has also been quite spotty. He worked for one year as a warehouse

**TABLE 2.2-A\***  *Prior Criminal History*

|  | Auto theft and burlary second | Committed to boys' school |
|---|---|---|
| [Five years later] | Drunk driving | One year probation |
| [Six years later] | Burglary | Six months county jail, one year probation |
| [Six and one-half years later] | Present offense |  |

*Table has been numbered.

helper and quit because creditors attached his wages. He also has worked as a bus boy.

For the past year and a half subject has been married and one child was born of that union. Wife indicates that marriage has been satisfactory although defendant has difficulty managing finances and friction developed. They have also been plagued by large bills as a result of time payments for furniture and other household goods. Wife had been employed until the time baby was born three months ago.

Subject has a drinking problem which has caused him some difficulty and it has gotten progressively worse in recent years.

Case Evaluation   This is a 24-year-old immature man of average intelligence. He gives the appearance of being friendly and likeable but obviously has been unable to accept responsibility. There are a total of eight checks outstanding, amounting to approximately $1,000 worth of purchases in various types of business establishments. He said he would like to have probation so that he could make restitution. His adjustment on probation for the burglary has been marginal and he was placed in a special caseload where the probation officer could furnish intensive supervision. His wife says this simply worried the defendant and may have contributed to his present offense. He appears to have support from his wife, who assumes major responsibility for family stability. The recent birth of his child has created more anxiety for the defendant and he says that this has affected his relationship with his wife.

*Notes and Questions*

1. The foregoing information is comparable to that which a sentencing judge would receive. On the basis of this report, would you grant probation? Probation with conditions? County jail time? A state prison sentence? Prepare one page giving your decision and your reasons for making it.

2. Now proceed with the opinions of California judges who also considered the case, and compare them with your opinion.

JUDGE SCHOENIG: I would place this man on three years' probation on the condition that he take treatment at DeWitt State Hospital for both alcoholism and emotional problems. Upon his release from the hospital he would be placed under the intensive supervision unit of the probation department and the family would be outpatients at the mental health clinic or Family Service Agency. Work could be secured for him in the food processing plants and deductions would be made from his checks for restitution.

There are other alternatives, of course, which embody the thoughts behind this sentence and that would be first a work furlough program if one was available in the county of sentencing. The same supervision and payroll deduction could be made through the Sheriff's office, but added to the work furlough program would be a continuing period of time under the probation department for proper supervision and outpatient care.

Also to be considered would be the right of the defendant to refuse probation. Since probation has bothered this defendant in the past, he might indicate to the court that the terms of probation are too onerous and refuse same. If such is the case, I would then impose a state prison sentence.

My reasons for the sentence are as follows: In reviewing the case of this 24-year-old Mexican-American, it appears that he does not have a lengthy arrest record and there is no history of violence. His first offense for burglary 2nd degree occurred when he was 16 years of age and he was committed to a boys' school. I assume this was not a State Correctional Institution. Six years later, he was again arrested for burglary and given 6 months in county jail and 1 year probation. His present offense occurred when he was not under probation.

As of this time, this young man is not a confirmed "paper hanger," but merely used this offense as a means to make certain purchases which were evidently for his family. These checks were given as payment in full for various articles that he bought. Inasmuch as we know he has a drinking problem, this undoubtedly is a factor in lowering his will power so that he breaches the rules and regulations set up by society.

His case history indicates that he is an inadequate individual, which has affected his employment and ability to manage his finances. It is also noted that his wife has a certain amount of awareness of his problems. However, I am not in agreement with her statement relative to probation. Her husband's present arrest occurred after he completed his probationary period. The wife is the dominant figure in this family because it appears the husband has refused to face or accept responsibility. I would consider this a further reason for psychiatric help and further, from all indications, this defendant is amenable to such counsel. It would appear that this defendant again needs the intensive supervision of the probation department for the purpose of obtaining professional help for his drinking problem and counselling for him and his wife.

If he were given a straight county jail sentence or committed to state prison, that would defer the treatment that must be implemented to help this man adjust to society and with his family.

I am aware that his previous adjustment on probation was marginal but I am not averse to taking this risk with the defendant when there is some definite goal in mind. If this defendant resided in my jurisdiction, employment could be obtained for him in food processing for the year round with one of the corporate farms in that area. This type of employment would prevent the defendant from handling any money other than his paycheck. Also, the defendant, through the probation department, would be helped in managing his financial obligations, inasmuch as I would order restitution payments on his outstanding checks.

I would recommend outpatient treatment at the mental health facility because of the history of rejection of this defendant by his family and his inability to face problems.

JUDGE COAKLEY: I've had several bad check cases and this is always the type of person you find. What do you do with a fellow who is repeatedly this kind of a customer and yet doesn't have too bad a record otherwise? . . .

JUDGE ROSS A. CARKEET . . .: I voted for prison . . . This guy needs a real good scare. It might do him good to send him to prison and put a recall on him, and see if you want to take him back.

JUDGE D. STERRY FAGAN . . .: I gave this man a straight jail sentence. My feeling was that he had a shot at probation and didn't do well. The only reason I would think of probation is that he could make some restitution. His background as presented here is marginal so I feel that it's touch and go between a prison sentence or a county jail sentence. I choose the county jail because of the nonviolence of his criminal activity . . .

JUDGE LEONARD M. GINSBURG . . .: I would have sentenced the man to prison on the basis that he's been around the track. He's been in everything from boys' school to apparently ordinary probation on the drunk driving charge, county jail and intensive probation on the burglary. To me, he's reached the point where there's nothing left to do with him. . . .

JUDGE COAKLEY: Dr. Olivier, have you any comments?

DR. OLIVIER: . . . I feel this is a man who hasn't been violent and for whom psychiatry hasn't been tried. I also feel that he's a rather inadequate, dependent guy and . . . I think this fellow would develop a relationship rather easily with a psychotherapist. I don't think prison would do anything at all for him. I think it would increase his dependency and his inadequacy and I think this man would be easily led and if he were to stay in prison very long he would form more identification with the antisocial element. I think he has a lot of problems around his sexual identification and his being a man and if he could stay employed and make restitution, this would be the most ego-enhancing thing that he could do. I think it would well be worth probation on the condition that he obtain psychiatric treatment.

JUDGE HAYDEN: How much treatment do you think would be likely to be developed? Assume he had a service such as yours, how often and how long would you be seeing this man?

DR. OLIVIER: Well, we don't have any kind of standard for length of treatment. If we feel that someone needs a lot of treatment initially to get into a treatment contract then we often recommend our day treatment program where the person can come in eight hours a day, five days a week, for somewhere between two to six weeks. Then, we follow them up with a once a week basis in the out-patient clinic. For a man like this who has been nonviolent and whose latest offense has to do with check forgery, I would think it would be reasonable to start on a once a week basis and I would predict reasonably good results within a matter of six months to a year.

JUDGE GARDINER: I recognize the different kinds of treatment that are available, but I don't see how you come to the conclusion that this fellow hasn't had any treatment . . .

DR. OLIVIER: Well, I'm making a distinction between probation where he sees a probation officer periodically and seeing a psychotherapist for a half hour to an hour each and every week with great regularity.

JUDGE GARDINER: There is obviously a tremendous quality difference between the different kinds of people, but must we not recognize the fact that probation officers are giving something which is not unlike psychiatric treatment? Isn't this their objective?

DR. OLIVIER: Well, most of them are not professionally trained. Certainly they can do a great deal of good in a warm human relationship with an individual. That's the vehicle for any professional treatment, but . . . I think that we can do more to help him alter his maladapted patterns of life than a probation officer can. . . .

JUDGE J. KELLY STEELE . . .: You mentioned several times that this party is nonviolent. . . . My question is what difference does it make whether he's violent or nonviolent? . . .

DR. OLIVIER: . . . I mean the kind of a guy that isn't very aggressive at all and tends to be passive and, I feel, unlikely to commit violent, aggressive acts. . . .

JUDGE SCHAUER: . . . I'm not quite ready to give up on this man. He needs one more chance anyway, although I think I'd give him a long term in custody as a condition of probation, such as county jail. I probably would impose a felony on him by suspending an execution of a state prison sentence, but I think I would try probationary supervision with a condition of probation, possibly that he attend Alcoholics Anonymous. I smell in his background here the odor of alcohol. . . .

DR. OLIVIER: Well, I think that could be a very useful adjunct to the program. . . . I think it's interesting that when I recently participated in a Municipal & Justice Court Judges Institute in San Diego one of the judges pointed out that when there were crimes against property, judges tended to be more punitive than in cases of aggression against individuals. Someone who had stolen 50¢ worth of meat from a super market would get a more severe sentence than someone who had threatened his girl friend with a knife, or even injured her and had been assaultive before. I think it's kind of an interesting sidelight of the way society views crimes against property.

JUDGE HAYDEN: You may have gotten a distorted sample . . . I would much rather have a guy hang a thousand dollar bad check on me than take $10 out of my pocket with a gun. I have a different hierarchy of values there.

MR. SHAIN: . . . The reference that Dr. Olivier had involved discussion of a case in which there was a husband and wife conflict. I think all of us would agree that the violence that emerges from a husband and wife conflict is a far different cry from violence in the more commonly accepted term of assaulting somebody that you don't know. That's the mitigating circumstance in those cases.

DR. OLIVIER: Yes, that is an important point that I had forgotten.

JUDGE DELL: I just don't think it's our function to lock up everybody who is a hazard to property. Now in this case, I would have imposed a felony sentence and as a condition of probation have given the man a maximum period in the county jail with work furlough which we have in Los Angeles County. There are certain crimes that you just have a price tag for. I'd be very reluctant to send a person who is a "paper hanger" to the state prison. I don't think it accomplishes a great deal except to fill up the state prison with people who don't belong there . . . [T]his is a burglary and an embezzlement besides. . . . But generally speaking, I don't think a property crime . . . should carry a state prison sentence. On the other hand I think that a violent crime is another matter and there we are talking about protecting life and person. . . .

JUDGE EDWARD P. FOGG . . .: This man's employment record had been quite spotty. . . . Wouldn't state prison and his commitment to the Department of Corrections give the Department an opportunity to offer this man vocational training of some type that would eventually assist in his rehabilitation?

JUDGE SHOENIG: . . . What bothered me with that is you're giving him a felony rap and saying you're rehabilitating him so that he can get a job. When he comes out he's got a felony rap sheet and who's going to hire him, a Mexican-American with a felony rap? . . .

JUDGE HAYDEN: If you have an adequate probation office in your county, which we do not, you should be able to get in much more satisfactory vocational training on probation than he would ever get in a state prison. . . .

MR. SHAIN: Here is the vote for this case: 2/3 would have committed him to jail with probation; a little more than 1/4 would have sent him to prison, about 1 out of 14 would have just given him jail without probation and about 3 percent would have granted him probation using the time that he had already served in jail as fulfilling his incarceration term.

*Notes and Questions*

1. Using Jerome Frank as a source for criteria, compare the commentaries of the various judges. What are some of the differences among the judges? How would you rank the judges for leniency or severity?

2. As a member of the general public, which judge would you want to decide the case? What does your preference tell you about yourself? About professional perspectives as compared to public perspectives?

3. If you or a member of your family were convicted of a forgery-type offense, which judge would you prefer?

4. Included in the deliberations are the remarks of a psychotherapist, Dr. Olivier. Compare the approaches of the judges with that of the psychotherapist. Would you recommend using one or more psychotherapists, rather than judges, for sentencing decisions?
   Would psychotherapists follow the same decisional sequence that Frank noted about judges, i.e., would they draw their conclusions first and only later provide psychiatric explanations?

5. One of the judges distinguishes between domestic cases and cases between strangers. Does this comment suggest that the older thinking found in the North Carolina cases is still prevalent?

&ampersand; The following case was considered by the California judges at the 1969 Sentencing Institute.

## 2.3 | A Case of Attempted Murder   *1969 California Sentencing Institute*
*85 Cal. Rptr. (Appendix)*

### OFFENSE: ATTEMPTED MURDER

ABOUT 1:30 IN THE afternoon defendant entered the place of employment of his common-law wife, with whom he had been living for approximately seven years and asked her to leave the room to sign some legal forms. She refused his request and attempted to phone a boyfriend but couldn't reach him. Defendant drew out a .38 revolver and shot her twice in the right chest and also shot another employee who attempted to intervene. Both victims have recovered after varying lengths of time in the hospital.

Prior Criminal History None.

Case History Information Defendant is the oldest of nine children of an intact midwestern farm family. Mother was very religious and a strict disciplinarian although the father was the dominant figure in the home. Four siblings who live in the area have visited him since his incarceration and other relatives have aided him financially in his legal defense. He is a high school graduate who was an average student in school. Subsequent to graduating high school he served four years in the U.S. Air Force and received a bad conduct discharge because he went AWOL. The Army psychiatrist diagnosed him as having an "acute situational maladjustment."

For the past several years he has maintained a common-law relationship with the victim whom he had known since childhood. She had been married and had a six-year-old son but had been separated from her husband. She never formally got a divorce. She assumed defendant's name as did her son and defendant is still concerned about the boy's future education. He claims they were happy during their first years together but the relationship began to deteriorate as their financial situation improved. The specific problem was that his common-law wife was having an affair with a co-worker. Defendant hoped that the affair would terminate. Following a trip out of town defendant found his common-law wife in liaison with her boyfriend which produced a severe argument.

Defendant has been regularly employed in a semi-skilled job with an aircraft factory for the past seven years.

Case Evaluation   Defendant had no prior criminal record and also has an exemplary employment record. His supervisor submitted a very favorable written report regarding his work and his character. He is basically a serious responsible man. Defendant says he came to frighten his common-law wife rather than to shoot her or her fellow employee. The immediate cause of the present offense was jealousy. In interviews he revealed that she had acted contemptuously of him and the offense represented an explosion of accumulated feelings of anger. Psychiatric report indicates that he was comfortable in the interview and is evaluated as an obsessive-compulsive individual. He did not seem emotionally involved while reciting the history of the relationship although he described a series of incidents as very traumatic to him. He claimed he would have married her if she had been legally divorced from her husband. He feels guilty about the present offense and says that he could not face the prospect of losing her.

### Notes and Questions

1. Prepare a written opinion about what should be done. As in this and other cases, usually there are a range of choices open to a judge: straight prison, county jail (usually regarded as less severe even if the sentence is for the same time as prison), probation, or probation with conditions such as psychiatric counseling.

2. Form a small group of people who have also prepared individual opinions. Discuss each person's decision and the reasons for it.
   A. Compare the individual results with group deliberations. Are minds changed or do they stay pretty much constant?

*B.* If there had to be a group decision rather than an individual one, what results? (This compares to a panel of judges who sometimes join in a single opinion.)

*C.* Does the individual decision look more reasonable and responsible than the group one or less reasonable and responsible?

&. The next case, commonly studied by first-year law students, raises every problem in criminal law, from determining responsibility to assessing appropriate penalties once guilt has been found. The case also can be studied as a decision at the intersection of precedent, judicial discretion, and the value dilemmas of choosing one rule over another.

## 2.4  The Queen v. Dudley and Stephens   *L.R. 14 Q.B.D. 273 (1884)*

INDICTMENT FOR THE MURDER of Richard Parker on the high seas within the jurisdiction of the Admiralty.

At the trial before Huddleston, B., . . . the jury, at the suggestion of the learned judge, found the facts of the case in a special verdict, which stated "that on July 5, 1884, the prisoners, Thomas Dudley and Edward Stephens, with one Brooks, all able-bodied English seamen, and the deceased also an English boy, between seventeen and eighteen years of age, the crew of an English yacht, a registered English vessel, were cast away in a storm on the high seas 1600 miles from the Cape of Good Hope, and were compelled to put into an open boat belonging to the said yacht. That in this boat they had no supply of water and no supply of food, except two 1 lb. tins of turnips, and for three days they had nothing else to subsist upon. That on the fourth day they caught a small turtle, upon which they subsisted for a few days, and this was the only food they had up to the twentieth day when the act now in question was committed. That on the twelfth day the remains of the turtle were entirely consumed, and for the next eight days they had nothing to eat. That they had no fresh water, except such rain as they from time to time caught in their oilskin capes. That the boat was drifting on the ocean, and was probably more than 1000 miles away from land. That on the eighteenth day, when they had been seven days without food and five without water,

the prisoners spoke to Brooks as to what should be done if no succour came, and suggested that some one should be sacrificed to save the rest, but Brooks dissented, and the boy, to whom they were understood to refer, was not consulted. That on the 24th of July, the day before the act now in question, the prisoner Dudley proposed to Stephens and Brooks that lots should be cast who should be put to death to save the rest, but Brooks refused to consent, and it was not put to the boy, and in point of fact there was no drawing of lots. That on that day the prisoners spoke of their having families, and suggested it would be better to kill the boy that their lives should be saved, and Dudley proposed that if there was no vessel in sight by the morrow morning the boy should be killed. That next day, the 25th of July, no vessel appearing, Dudley told Brooks that he had better go and have a sleep, and made signs to Stephens and Brooks that the boy had better be killed. The prisoner Stephens agreed to the act, but Brooks dissented from it. That the boy was then lying at the bottom of the boat quite helpless, and extremely weakened by famine and by drinking sea water, and unable to make any resistance, nor did he ever assent to his being killed. The prisoner Dudley offered a prayer asking forgiveness for them all if either of them should be tempted to commit a rash act, and that their souls might be saved. That Dudley, with the assent of Stephens, went to the boy and telling him that his time was come, put a knife into his throat and killed him then and there; that the three men fed upon the body and blood of the boy for four days; that on the fourth day after the act had been committed the boat was picked up by a passing vessel, and the prisoners were rescued, still alive, but in the lowest state of prostration. That they were carried to the port of Falmouth, and committed for trial at Exeter. That if the men had not fed upon the body of the boy they would probably not have survived to be picked up and rescued, but would within the four days have died of famine. That the boy, being in a much weaker condition, was likely to have died before them. That at the time of the act in question there was no sail in sight, nor any reasonable prospect of relief. That under these circumstances there appeared to the prisoners every probability that unless they then fed or very soon fed upon the boy or one of themselves they would die of starvation. That there was no appreciable chance of saving life except by killing some one for the others to eat. That assuming any necessity to kill anybody, there was no greater necessity for killing the boy than any of the other three men." But whether upon the whole matter . . . the killing of Richard Parker by Dudley and Stephens be felony and murder the jurors are ignorant, and pray the advice of the Court thereupon, and if upon the whole matter the Court shall be of opinion that the killing of Richard Parker be felony and murder, then the jurors say that Dudley and Stephens were each guilty of felony and murder as alleged in the indictment. . . .

LORD COLERIDGE, C. J.

. . . It was further objected that, according to the decision of the majority of the judges in the *Franconia Case,* there was no jurisdiction in the Court at Exeter to try these prisoners. But in that case the prisoner was a German, who had committed the alleged offence as captain of a German ship; these prisoners were English seamen, the crew of an English yacht, cast away in a storm on the high seas, and escaping from her in an open boat; the opinion of the minority in the *Franconia Case* has been since not only enacted but declared by Parliament to have been always

the law; . . . "All offences against property or person committed in or at any place either ashore or afloat, out of her Majesty's dominions by any master seaman or apprentice who at the time when the offence is committed is or within three months previously has been employed in any British ship, shall be deemed to be offences of the same nature respectively, and be inquired of, heard, tried, determined, and adjudged in the same manner and by the same courts and in the same places as if such offences had been committed within the jurisdiction of the Admiralty of England." We are all therefore of opinion that this objection . . . must be overruled.

There remains to be considered the real question in the case—whether killing under the circumstances set forth in the verdict be or be not murder. The contention that it could be anything else was, to the minds of us all, both new and strange, and we stopped the Attorney General in his negative argument in order that we might hear what could be said in support of a proposition which appeared to us to be at once dangerous, immoral, and opposed to all legal principle and analogy. . . . First it is said that it follows from various definitions of murder in books of authority, which definitions imply, if they do not state, the doctrine, that in order to save your own life you may lawfully take away the life of another, when that other is neither attempting nor threatening yours, nor is guilty of any illegal act whatever towards you or any one else. But if these definitions be looked at they will not be found to sustain this contention. The earliest in point of date is the passage cited to us from Bracton, who lived in the reign of Henry III. It was at one time the fashion to discredit Bracton . . . There is now no such feeling . . . Sin and crime are spoken of as apparently equally illegal . . . [I]n the very passage as to necessity, one which reliance has been placed, it is clear that Bracton is speaking of necessity in the ordinary sense—the repelling by violence, violence justified so far as it was necessary for the object, any illegal violence used towards oneself. If, says Bracton, the necessity be "evitabilis, et evadere posset absque occisione, tunc erit reus homicidii" [avoidable and he can escape without harm, then it will be homicide]—words which shew clearly that he is thinking of physical danger from which *escape* may be possible, and that the "inevitabilis necessitas" [unavoidable necessity] of which he speaks as justifying homicide is a necessity of the same nature.

It is, if possible, yet clearer that the doctrine contended for receives no support from the great authority of Lord Hale. It is plain that in his view the necessity which justified homicide is that only which has always been and is now considered a justification. "In all these cases of homicide by necessity," says he, "as in pursuit of a felon, in killing him that assaults to rob, or comes to burn or break a house, or the like, which are in themselves no felony." . . . Again, he says that "the necessity which justifies homicide is of two kinds: (1) the necessity which is of a private nature; (2) the necessity which relates to the public justice and safety. The former is that necessity which obligeth a man to his own defence and safeguard, and this takes in these inquiries:—What may be done for the safeguard of a man's own life;" and then follow three other heads not necessary to pursue. Then Lord Hale proceeds:—"As touching the first of these—viz., homicide in defence of a man's own life, which is usually styled se defendendo." It is not possible to use words more clear to shew that Lord Hale regarded the private necessity which justified, and alone justified, the taking the life of another for the safeguard of one's own to be what is commonly called "self-defence.". . .

But if this could be even doubtful upon Lord Hale's words, Lord Hale himself has made it clear. For in the chapter in which he deals with the exemption created by compulsion or necessity he thus expresses himself:—"If a man be desperately assaulted and in peril of death, and cannot otherwise escape unless, to satisfy his assailant's fury, he will kill an innocent person then present, the fear and actual force will not acquit him of the crime and punishment of murder, if he commit the fact, for he ought rather to die himself than kill an innocent; but if he cannot otherwise save his own life the law permits him in his own defence to kill the assailant, for by the violence of the assault, and the offence committed upon him by the assailant himself, the law of nature, and necessity, hath made him his own protector. . . ."

But, further still, Lord Hale in the following chapter deals with the position . . . , that in a case of extreme necessity, either of hunger or clothing; "theft is no theft, or at least not punishable as theft, as some even of our own lawyers have asserted the same." "But," says Lord Hale, "I take it that here in England, that rule, at least by the laws of England, is false; and therefore, if a person, being under necessity for want of victuals or clothes, shall upon that account clandestinely and animo furandi steal [with intent to steal] another man's goods, it is felony, and a crime by the laws of England punishable with death." . . . If, therefore, Lord Hale is clear—as he is—that extreme necessity of hunger does not justify larceny, what would he have said to the doctrine that it justified murder?

It is satisfactory to find that another great authority, second, probably, only to Lord Hale, speaks with the same unhesitating clearness on this matter. Sir Michael Foster, in the 3rd chapter of his Discourse on Homicide, deals with the subject of "homicide founded in necessity"; and the whole chapter implies, and is insensible unless it does imply, that in the view of Sir Michael Foster "necessity and self-defence" (which he defines as "opposing force to force even to the death") are convertible terms. There is no hint, no trace, of the doctrine now contended for; the whole reasoning of the chapter is entirely inconsistent with it.

In East's Pleas of the Crown (i. 271) the whole chapter on homicide by necessity is taken up with an elaborate discussion of the limits within which necessity in Sir Michael Foster's sense (given above) of self-defence is a justification of or excuse for homicide. There is a short section at the end very generally and very doubtfully expressed, in which the only instance discussed is the well-known one of two shipwrecked men on a plank able to sustain only one of them, and the conclusion is left by Sir Edward East entirely undetermined.

What is true of Sir Edward East is true also of Mr. Sarjeant Hawkins. The whole of his chapter on justifiable homicide assumes that the only justifiable homicide of a private nature is the defence against force of a man's person, house, or goods. In the 26th section we find again the case of the two shipwrecked men and the single plank, with the significant expression from a careful writer, "*It is said* to be justifiable." So, too, Dalton c. 150, clearly considers necessity and self-defence in Sir Michael Foster's sense of that expression, to be convertible terms, though he prints without comment Lord Bacon's instance of the two men on one plank as a quotation from Lord Bacon, adding nothing whatever to it of his own. And there is a remarkable passage at page 339, in which he says that even in the case of a murderous assault upon a man, yet before he may take the life of the man who assaults him even in self-defence, "cuncta prius tentanda" [delay must be attempted—ED.]. . . .

Is there, then, any authority for the proposition which has been presented to us? Decided cases there are none. The case of the seven English sailors referred to by the commentator on Grotius and by Puffendorf has been discovered by a gentleman of the Bar, who communicated with my Brother Huddleston, to convey the authority (if it conveys so much) of a single judge of the island of St. Kitts, when that island was possessed partly by France and partly by this country, somewhere about the year 1641. It is mentioned in a medical treatise published at Amsterdam, and is altogether, as authority in an English court, as unsatisfactory as possible. The American case cited by my Brother Stephen in his Digest, from Wharton on Homicide, in which it was decided, correctly indeed, that sailors had no right to throw passengers overboard to save themselves, but on the somewhat strange ground that the proper mode of determining who was to be sacrificed was to vote upon the subject by ballot, can hardly, as my Brother Stephen says, be an authority satisfactory to a court in this country. The observations of Lord Mansfield in the case of *Rex. v. Stratton and Others,* striking and excellent as they are, were delivered in a political trial, where the question was whether a political necessity had arisen for deposing a Governor of Madras. But they have little application to the case before us, which must be decided on very different considerations.

The one real authority of former time is Lord Bacon, who, . . . lays down the law as follows:—"Necessity carrieth a privilege in itself. Necessity is of three sorts—necessity of conservation of life, necessity of obedience, and necessity of the act of God or of a stranger. First of conservation of life; if a man steal viands to satisfy his present hunger, this is no felony nor larceny. So if divers be in danger of drowning by the casting away of some boat or barge, and one of them get to some plank, or on the boat's side to keep himself above water, and another to save his life thrust him from it, whereby he is drowned, this is neither se defendendo nor by misadventure, but justifiable." On this it is to be observed that Lord Bacon's proposition that stealing to satisfy hunger is no larceny is hardly supported by Staundforde, whom he cites for it, and is expressly contradicted by Lord Hale in the passage already cited. And for the proposition as to the plank or boat, it is said to be derived from the canonists. At any rate he cites no authority for it, and it must stand upon his own. Lord Bacon was great even as a lawyer; but it is permissible to much smaller men, relying upon principle and on the authority of others, the equals and even the superiors of Lord Bacon as lawyers, to question the soundness of his dictum. There are many conceivable states of things in which it might possibly be true, but if Lord Bacon meant to lay down the broad proposition that a man may save his life by killing, if necessary, an innocent and unoffending neighbour, it certainly is not law at the present day.

. . . Neither are we in conflict with any opinion expressed upon the subject by the learned persons who formed the commission for preparing the Criminal Code. They say on this subject:—

"We are certainly not prepared to suggest that necessity should in every case be a justification. We are equally unprepared to suggest that necessity should in no case be a defence; we judge it better to leave such questions to be dealt with when, if ever, they arise in practice by applying the principles of law to the circumstances of the particular case."

It would have been satisfactory to us if these eminent persons could have told us whether the received definitions of legal necessity were in their judgment correct and exhaustive, and if not, in what way they should be amended, but as it is we have, as they say, "to apply the principles of law to the circumstances of this particular case."

Now, except for the purpose of testing how far the conservation of a man's own life is in all cases and under all circumstances, an absolute, unqualified, and paramount duty, we exclude from our consideration all the incidents of war. We are dealing with a case of private homicide, not one imposed upon men in the service of their Sovereign and in the defence of their country. Now it is admitted that the deliberate killing of this unoffending and unresisting boy was clearly murder, unless the killing can be justified by some well-recognized excuse admitted by the law. It is further admitted that there was in this case no such excuse, unless the killing was justified by what has been called "necessity." But the temptation to the act which existed here was not what the law has ever called necessity. Nor is this to be regretted. Though law and morality are not the same, and many things may be immoral which are not necessarily illegal, yet the absolute divorce of law from morality would be of fatal consequence; and such divorce would follow if the temptation to murder in this case were to be held by law an absolute defence of it. It is not so. To preserve one's life is generally speaking a duty, but it may be the plainest and the highest duty to sacrifice it. War is full of instances in which it is a man's duty not to live, but to die. The duty, in case of shipwreck, of a captain to his crew, of the crew to the passengers, of soldiers to women and children, as in the noble case of the *Birkenhead*; these duties impose on men the moral necessity, not of the preservation, but of the sacrifice of their lives for others, from which in no country, least of all, it is to be hoped, in England, will men ever shrink, as indeed, they have not shrunk. It is not correct, therefore, to say that there is any absolute or unqualified necessity to preserve one's life. . . . It would be a very easy and cheap display of commonplace learning to quote from Greek and Latin authors, from Horace, from Juvenal, from Cicero, from Euripides, passage after passage, in which the duty of dying for others has been laid down in glowing and emphatic language as resulting from the principles of heathen ethics; it is enough in a Christian country to remind ourselves of the Great Example whom we profess to follow. It is not needful to point out the awful danger of admitting the principle which has been contended for. Who is to be the judge of this sort of necessity? By what measure is the comparative value of lives to be measured? Is it to be strength, or intellect, or what? It is plain that the principle

leaves to him who is to profit by it to determine the necessity which will justify him in deliberately taking another's life to save his own. In this case the weakest, the youngest, the most unresisting, was chosen. Was it more necessary to kill him than one of the grown men? The answer must be "No"—

> So spake the Fiend, and with necessity,
> The tyrant's plea, excused his devilish deeds.

It is not suggested that in this particular case the deeds were "devilish," but it is quite plain that such a principle once admitted might be made the legal cloak for unbridled passion and astrocious crime. There is no safe path for judges to tread but to ascertain the law to the best of their ability and to declare it according to their judgment; and if in any case the law appears to be too severe on individuals, to leave it to the Sovereign to exercise that prerogative of mercy which the Constitution has intrusted to the hands fittest to dispense it.

It must not be supposed that in refusing to admit temptation to be an excuse for crime it is forgotten how terrible the temptation was; how awful the suffering; how hard in such trials to keep the judgment straight and the conduct pure. We are often compelled to set up standards we cannot reach ourselves, and to lay down rules which we could not ourselves satisfy. But a man has no right to declare temptation to be an excuse, though he might himself have yielded to it, nor allow compassion for the criminal to change or weaken in any manner the legal definition of the crime. It is therefore our duty to declare that the prisoners' act in this case was wilful murder, that the facts as stated in the verdict are no legal justification of the homicide; and to say that in our unanimous opinion the prisoners are upon this special verdict guilty of murder.

The court then proceeded to pass sentence of death upon the prisoners.[1]

### Notes and Questions

1. Did Coleridge do justice here? How does one judge the quality of judgments? What values are at stake in this case? What good is accomplished by the decision? What harm?

---

[1]This sentence was afterwards commuted by the Crown to six months' imprisonment.

2. Many students, on reading the case, agree with the decision of Coleridge *and* the decision of the queen to commute the sentence to six months. Can one consistently agree with both?

3. What impels Coleridge to rule against the men while at the same time almost inviting the queen to commute the sentence?

4. Coleridge seems afraid—"It is not needful to point out the awful danger of admitting the principle which has been contended for." Is justice done if the basis for a decision is not so much the case at hand but some future case that might come up?

    Return to Note 5 on page 18. Can the classification of time perspectives presented there be applied to the *Dudley and Stephens* case?

5. How does Coleridge's sense of values affect his treatment of prior cases or other authority? What prior materials were available to him? Could he have written a persuasive contrary opinion based on available authority? Prepare an opinion of acquittal on the ground of necessity, using *only* the material to which Coleridge refers in his opinion.

6. Judge Coleridge states, "We are often compelled to set standards we cannot reach ourselves and to lay down rules which we could not ourselves satisfy." Compare this with the following statement of Oliver Wendell Holmes:

It may be the destiny of man that the social instincts shall grow to control his actions absolutely, even in antisocial situations. But they have not done so, and as the rules of law are or should be based on a morality that is generally accepted, no rule of law founded on a theory of absolute unselfishness can be laid down without a breach between law and working beliefs.*

Which contention should be the predominant value in law?

7. Earlier in this chapter, Jerome Frank described the importance of psychological factors in decision making. Can Coleridge's personal preferences be found in his opinion?

8. Should the attorneys representing either Dudley and Stephens or the Crown be expected to believe in their cases, or is it enough for them to do a craftsmanlike job?

9. Some jurists have said that procedure is the heart of the law—the *way* a decision is made is more important than *what* decision is made. Evaluate. If Coleridge makes his decision in a judicious way, should we be satisfied?

---

*Oliver Wendell Holmes, *The Common Law* (Boston: Little, Brown, 1886), p. 44.

---

 # 3 | LAW AND VALUES

My intention was to write it in a cool and detached manner but it came to naught; indignation and pity kept seeping in. This is perhaps just as well, for capital punishment is not merely a problem of statistics and expediency, but also of morality and feeling.

Arthur Koestler, *Reflections on Hanging* (1956)

Even a fairy story—a single fairy story—can call up a normative generalization about the right behavior of mice and pumpkins, and of fairy godmothers and princes. . . .

Karl N. Llewellyn, "The Normative, the Legal and the Law Jobs" (1941)

    ❧ Studying the relationship of values to any subject matter, including law, is generally out of favor. Scholars in fledgling disciplines are reluctant to delve into such matters lest their colleagues in the hard sciences consider them "prescientific" or just plain soft-headed. This drive for respectability leads to the selection of "manageable" questions for teaching and research.

    Part of the reluctance to consider values is traceable to relativism, which takes both crude and sophisticated forms. Relativism—crude form—is captured in such conversation stoppers as "Well, that depends upon your point of view." At times, the refusal to discuss competing points of view takes on similarities to the small-town diplomat who piously proclaims, "There are two topics I never discuss—politics and religion." Underlying such contentions may be a deep fear of exposing oneself to the psychic risks accompanying the exploration of values.

Sophisticated relativism is typified by the academician's contention that all values are situational, that is, depend on time and place. Having concluded thus, instead of relentlessly pursuing a detailed inquiry into the various situations, times, and places and the moralities pertinent to them, some academicians drop inquiry altogether, thereby eliminating wide areas of necessary thought. In addition, it is commonly asserted by academicians that research (good research) is (ought to be) value-free. Apart from the nonrecognition that this assertion is itself value-laden—as the parenthetical material indicates—the tenet leads "scholars" to put little psychic investment into their work and aggravates the already excessive anti-ethical and apolitical bias that characterizes most schoolwork.

Lawyers are not immune from the pressures of relativism and value freedom. Law students are schooled in the mixed doctrines of precedent, taught that any side of a case has merit and can be argued with vigor. If they forget that *technical* arguments are not necessarily *good* arguments, they do not prepare themselves to meet the public demand for improvement of law. As practitioners, their readiness to argue any cause anywhere for any client will at times be of great social benefit, but at its worst can produce a neglect of the value dimensions of law practice. By default, lawyers as a group often simply adopt the values of their clients.

A gross breach between personal views and the causes that one is expected to advocate can have a corrosive effect on a lawyer's own sense of self-worth and contribute to a nagging disillusionment that many practitioners feel once they have been out of law school for a while and settled into law practice. It is difficult to defend environmental polluters during the day and read Sierra Club magazines at night.

In judicial process, when technique and mere craft predominate, legalism results—to the misery of all those who encounter the results. Jacques Ellul, a French jurist, observes,

> The judicial element (which becomes principally organization) is no longer charged with pursuing justice or creating law in any way whatsoever. It is charged with applying the laws. This role can be perfectly mechanical. It does not call for a philosopher or a man with a sense of justice. What is needed is a good technician, who understands the principles of the technique, the rules of interpretation, the legal terminology, and the ways of deducing consequences and finding solutions.*

---

*Jacques Ellul, *The Technological Society* (New York: Random House, 1964), p. 294.

Ellul further explains the hesitancy of professionals to get too philosopical:

> Justice is not a thing to be grasped or fixed. If one pursues genuine justice . . . one never knows where one will end. A law created as a function of justice has something unpredictable in it which embarrasses the jurist.[†] And yet, as he later adds, "Men of law have certain scruples and are unable to eliminate justice from the law completely without the twinges of conscience."[‡]

Because most contested cases are situational and brim over with questions of value, statements about relativism or value freedom are misplaced maxims with respect to them. Values must be explained, demonstrated where possible or otherwise fully debated if law and legal process are to transcend mere technique. As the dialectic over values unfolds, a socially desirable tension arises between rules and values, pressuring decision makers to integrate the present with the past in anticipation of the future. Perhaps no case demonstrates this tension better than *Queen* v. *Dudley and Stephens,* found in the previous chapter. Llewellyn poignantly describes the potency of some contested cases:

> The case of trouble . . . is the case of doubt, or is that in which discipline has failed, or is that in which unruly personality is breaking through into new paths of action or of leadership, or is that which an ancient institution is being tried against emergent forces. It is the case of trouble which makes, breaks, twists, or flatly establishes a rule, an institution, an authority. Not all such cases do so. There are also petty rows, the routine of law-stuff which exists among primitives as well as among moderns. For all that, if there be a portion of a society's life in which tensions of the culture come to expression, in which the play of variant urges can be felt and seen, in which emergent power-patterns, ancient security-drives, religion, politics, personality, cross-purposes, and views of justice tangle in the open, that portion of the life will concentrate in the case of trouble or disturbance. Not only the making of new law and the effect of old, but the hold and the thrust of all other vital aspects of the culture, shine clear in the crucible of conflict.[§]

Llewellyn's guide for the social study of law applies in both informal and formal settings, the home as well as the courtroom, the schoolroom as well as the boardroom. If you wish to study how any group hammers out its values—making the abstract concrete—then it is the occasions of conflict where the group is forced to dwell that will inform the best.

Being mindful of the difficulties that have always plagued value inquiry and its connection to any field including law, how can a brief opening to the subject be made without being totally superficial or settling for

---

[†]Ibid., p. 292.

[‡]Ibid., p. 295.

[§]Excerpt from *The Cheyenne Way: Conflict and Case Law in Primitive Jurisprudence,* by Karl N. Llewellyn and E. Adamson Hoebel. Copyright University of Oklahoma Press. Reprinted by permission.

the biblical mandate: "Do unto others as you would have them do unto you" and "Love thy neighbor as thyself"?

Two approaches are taken here. The first looks at how professionalism and values are interconnected—is some critical dimension of life lost as a person moves from being an outsider to being an insider to a calling? The second approach looks at how the legal system deals with cases that raise profound value questions.

When people decide to pursue a profession, they usually want to do two things that turn out to be incompatible. First they want to be changed and take on the attributes of the profession—law, medicine, or even sorcery. Second, they want to keep their previous selves intact, with the expectation that their profession will be an addition to their lives and not a replacement of who they are and the principles they stand for. In short, they want to be able to pick and choose the ways that the profession will change their lives. The next selections, from a variety of specialties, show how becoming a professional can have both intended and unintended consequences.

---

## 3.1 | The Sorcerer and His Magic   *C. Levi-Strauss*

QUESALID (FOR THIS WAS the name when he became a sorcerer) did not believe in the power of the sorcerers—or, more accurately shamans, since this is the better term for their specific type of activity in certain regions of the world. Driven by curiosity about their tricks and by the desire to expose them, he began to associate with the shamans until one of them offered to make him a member of their group. Quesalid did not wait to be asked twice, and his narrative recounts the details of his first lessons, a curious mixture of pantomime, prestidigitation, and empirical knowledge, including the art of simulating fainting and nervous fits, the learning of sacred songs, the technique for inducing vomiting, rather precise notions of auscultation and obstetrics, and the use of "dreamers," that is, spies who listen to private conversations and secretly convey to the shaman bits of information concerning the origins and symptoms of the ills suffered by differ-

Excerpt from "The Sorcerer and His Magic" from *Structural Anthropology*, Volume I by Claude Levi-Strauss. English translation copyright © 1963 by Basic Books, Inc. Reprinted by permission of Basic Books, a member of Perseus Books, LLC.

ent people. Above all, he learned the *ars magna* of one of the shamanistic schools of the Northwest Coast: The shaman hides a little tuft of down in a corner of his mouth, and he throws it up, covered with blood, at the proper moment—after having bitten his tongue or made his gums bleed—and solemnly presents it to his patient and the onlookers as the pathological foreign body extracted as a result of his sucking and manipulations.

His worst suspicions confirmed, Quesalid wanted to continue his inquiry. But he was no longer free. His apprenticeship among the shaman began to be noised about, and one day he was summoned by the family of a sick person who had dreamed of Quesalid as his healer. The first treatment (for which he received no payment, any more than he did for those which followed, since he had not completed the required four years of apprenticeship) was an outstanding success. Although Quesalid came to be known from that moment as a "great shaman," he did not lose his critical faculties. He interpreted his success in psychological terms—it was successful "because he [the sick person] believed strongly in his dream about me." A more complex adventure made him, in his own words "hesitant and thinking about many things." Here he encountered several varieties of a "false supernatural," and was led to conclude that some forms were less false than others—those of course, in which he had a personal stake and whose system he was, at the same time surreptitiously building up in his mind. A summary of the adventure follows.

While visiting the neighboring Koskimo Indians, Quesalid attends a curing ceremony of his illustrious colleagues of the other tribe. To his great astonishment he observes a difference in their technique. Instead of spitting out the illness in the form of a "bloody worm" (the concealed down), the Koskimo shamans merely spit a little saliva into their hands, and they dare to claim that this is "the sickness." What is the value of this method? What is the theory behind it? In order to find out "the strength of the shamans, whether it was real or whether they only pretended to be shamans" like his fellow tribesmen, Quesalid requests and obtains permission to try his method in an instance where the Koskimo method has failed. The sick woman then declares herself cured.

And here our hero vacillates for the first time. Though he had few illusions about his own technique, he has now found one that is more false, more mystifying, and more dishonest than his own. For he at least gives his clients something: he presents them with their sickness in a visible and tangible form, while his foreign colleagues show nothing at all and only claim to have captured the sickness. Moreover, Quesalid's method gets results while the other is futile. Thus our hero grapples with a problem which perhaps has its parallel in the development of modern science. Two systems which we know to be inadequate present (with respect to each other) a differential validity, from both a logical and an empirical perspective. From which frame of reference shall we judge them? On the level of fact, where they merge, or on their own level, where they take on different values, both theoretically and empirically?

Meanwhile the Koskimo shamans, "ashamed" and discredited before their tribesmen are also plunged into doubt. Their colleague has produced, in the form of a material object, the illness which they had always considered to be spiritual in nature and had never dreamed of rendering visible. They send Quesalid an emissary to invite him to a secret meeting in a cave. Quesalid goes and his foreign colleagues expound their system to him: "Every sickness is a man: boils and swellings, and itch and scabs, and pimples and coughs and consumption and scrofula; and also this, stricture of the bladder and stomach aches. . . . As soon as we get the soul out of the sickness which is a man, then dies the sickness which is a man. Its body just disappears in our insides." If this theory is correct, what is there to show? And why, when Quesalid operates, does "the sickness stick to his hand"? But Quesalid takes refuge behind professional rules which forbid him to teach before completing four years of apprenticeship, and refuses to speak. He maintains his silence even when the Koskimo shamans send him their allegedly virgin daughters to try to seduce him and discover his secret.

Thereupon Quesalid returns to his village at Fort Rupert. He learns that the most reputed shaman of a neighboring clan, worried about Quesalid's growing renown, has challenged all his colleagues, inviting them to compete with him in curing several patients. Quesalid comes to the contest and observes the cures of his elder. Like the Koskimo, this shaman does not show the illness. He simply incorporates an invisible object, "what he called the sickness," into his head-ring, made of bark, or into his bird-shaped ritual rattle. These objects can hang suspended in mid-air, owing to the power of the illness which "bites" the house-posts of the shaman's hand. The usual drama unfolds. Quesalid is asked to intervene in cases judged hopeless by his predecessor, and he triumphs with his technique of the bloody worm.

Here we come to the truly pathetic part of the story. The old shaman, ashamed and despairing because of the ill-repute into which he has fallen and by the collapse of his therapeutic technique, sends his daughter to Quesalid to beg him for an interview. The latter finds his colleague sitting under a tree and the old shaman begins thus: "It won't be bad what we say to each other, friend, but only I wish you to try and save my life for me, so that I may not die in shame, for I am a plaything of my people on account of what you did last night. I pray you to have mercy and tell me what stuck on the palm of your hand last night. Was it the true sickness or was it only made up? For I beg you to have mercy and tell me about the way you did it so I can imitate you. Pity me friend."

Silent at first, Quesalid begins by calling for explanations about feats of the head-ring and the rattle. His colleague shows him the nail hidden in the head-ring which he can press at right angles into the post, and the way in which he tucks the head of his rattle between his finger joints to make it look as if the bird were hanging by its beak from his hand. He himself probably does nothing but lie and fake, simulating shamanism for material gain, for he admits to being "covetous for the property of the sick men." He knows the shamans cannot catch souls, "for . . . we all own a soul"; so he resorts to using tallow and pretends that it is a soul . . . that white thing . . . sitting on my hand." The daughter then adds her entreaties to those of her father: "Do have mercy that he may live." But Quesalid remains silent. That very night, following this tragic conversation, the shaman disappears with his entire family, heartsick and feared by the community, who think that he may be tempted to take revenge. Needless fears: He returned a year later, but both he and his daughter had gone mad. Three years later, he died.

And Quesalid, rich in secrets, pursued his career, exposing the impostors and full of contempt for the profession. "Only one shaman was seen by me, who sucked at a sick man and I never found out whether he was a real shaman or only made up. Only for this reason I believe that he is a shaman; he did not allow those who are made well to pay him. I truly never once saw him laugh." Thus his original attitude has changed considerably. The radical negativism of the free thinker has given way to more moderate feelings. Real shamans do exist. And what about him? At the end of the narrative we cannot tell, but it is evident that he carries on his craft conscientiously, takes pride in his achievements, and warmly defends the technique of the bloody down against all rival schools. He seems to have completely lost sight of the fallaciousness of the technique which he had so disparaged at the beginning.

### Notes and Questions

1. What are the steps in Quesalid's becoming a sorcerer and what becomes of his incoming values in the process? Is he better or worse off with his newfound sense of professional realism?

   Are he and the community where he lives better off with his newfound values or would they be better off if he had stuck with his initial plan to expose shamanism?

2. If Quesalid decided that he could no longer continue "with the charade," then what would he do?

3. What do Quesalid and his fellow tribespeople need? How can these needs be met?

4. Is becoming a lawyer like becoming a sorcerer? Are incoming values kept intact with the professional expertise accompanying law simply added to what a person was before the study of law or is there more of a top-to-bottom shift that accompanies becoming a lawyer?

🐦 Movies like *The Paper Chase* or books like Scott Turow's *One L* suggest that people studying law get caught up in a process of transformation that is not entirely within their control. Consider the following written by one of the authors of this text based on his post-law school reflections:

> Most lawyers have at some point felt themselves to be at the edge of law. In my own case, since my entry into law school was more a matter of chance than design and my post law school career somewhat deviant, I sometimes wonder whether I ever entered the realm of law more than provisionally. As a neophyte in law school I was reluctant to subject myself to legal ways of thought—although the full implications of this reluctance were admittedly

only dimly perceived. I can recall my first impressions of the early cases: most seemed to be unjustly decided; law seemed overly technical and neglectful of matters of substance. Most importantly, the ways of thought and the content of thought in law seemed destructive of what I had developed prior to law school, and I often wondered about the value of the "law school experience."

But the tug of law school, as reinforced by family, friends, and classmates, is very strong, and what I now look upon as a healthy distrust of law ways withered in the boot-camp atmosphere that is law school. I continued with study, explaining my doubts as a kind of personal lunacy, and carried by this momentum went on to sample private and governmental practice. . . .*

Compare the following by the same author:

[W]hat a discipline says should be seen, and nothing else, can be understood as a highly painful and unnatural process of closing down perception, intuition, emotions, and other aspects of being that are not relevant to the calling. While it is sometimes said that law students have too much inclination toward certainty, the deeper need may be in quite the opposite direction; rather students intuitively feel the gross neglect of fundamental questions of justice, good policy and fairness in the theory and practice of law. But it is through the closing down of vision that the paradigm of the calling is developed and shared vision through community become the abiding reality."†

Some of the main critiques of law school, and of law generally, have come from women since the number of women attending law school has increased. Patricia Williams writes about her law school experiences:

My abiding recollection of being a student at Harvard Law School is the sense of being invisible. I spent three years wandering in a murk of unreality. I observed large, mostly male bodies assert themselves against one another like football players caught in the gauzy mist of intellectual slow motion. I stood my ground amid them, watching them deflect from me, unconsciously, politely, as if I were a pillar in a crowded corridor. Law school was for me like being on another planet, full of alienated creatures with whom I could make little connection. The school created a dense atmosphere that muted my voice to inaudibility. All I could do to communicate my existence was to posit carefully worded messages into hermetically sealed, vacuum-packed blue books, place them on the waves of that foreign sea, and pray that they would be plucked up by some curious seeker and understood.

Perhaps there were others who felt what I felt. Perhaps we were all aliens, all silenced. . . .‡

---

*John Bonsignore, "At the Edge of Law," © 1973 by The American Business Law Journal.

†John Bonsignore, "Law as a Hard Science," 2 *ALSA Forum* (1977).

‡Reprinted by permission of the publisher from *The Alchemy of Race and Rights* by Patricia J. Williams, Cambridge, Mass.: Harvard University Press, Copyright © 1991 by the President and Fellows of Harvard College.

ᴥ The next selection is a story of a physician who has worked among the rural poor of Kentucky. As a professional she had been taught to practice medicine. As a person, she found that the borders of "her field" gave way at every turn, and had to yield to a need to live life consciously.

## 3.2    Simple Living and Hard Choices    *Maureen A. Flannery*

AS A FAMILY PHYSICIAN in rural Appalachia, I do not confront many of the issues that pervade the literature of contemporary medical ethics. In my county, we do not debate which facilities should have CAT scanners; we are just trying to replace an outmoded x-ray machine so that we can obtain clearer chest films while exposing our patients to less scatter radiation.

Amniocentesis is not much of an issue in my practice. My patients are astonished at the suggestion that they drive three hours to the university medical center to have a risky procedure simply because they are pregnant past the age of thirty-five or forty, because childbearing into these years remains common in Appalachia. Within large families, it is not unexpected that one or two of the children will be "slow" or "strange"; most women reject an invasive test to predict whether a subsequent child might turn out similarly.

For most Appalachian women, abortion is not an option, even in the case of an unplanned and desperately unwanted pregnancy. This is partly because of strong family ties and the value placed on children within the extended mountain family; and perhaps because Appalachian women are resigned to the fact that motherhood is one of the few potentially fulfilling roles available to them in their home communities. The unavailability of abortions, physically and economically, within the region is less of a factor; the unusual woman who elects abortion as a solution to an unwanted pregnancy prefers that the procedure be done far from the gossip of her home community and without the knowledge of the local "welfare office."

I do not see the daughters or sons of women who took DES during pregnancy and are therefore at risk for a rare cancer. The mothers of most of my patients received little, if any, prenatal care, thereby avoiding that particular pharmacologic tragedy. Decisions around "exotic medical lifesaving therapy" and "scarce lifesaving medical resources," to use the jargon of bioethics, are issues only in their general unavailability, sparing me from difficult decisions about the individual allocation of these technologies. . . . When a city friend asked me whether the medical community had criticized my midwife-attended home birth, I responded, "What medical community?"

The ethical issues I face daily are less dramatic than those involved in decisions around critically ill neonates, organ transplants, and brain death; but they are no less difficult to resolve. Some of them are peculiar to practice in a rural and impoverished area; some are shared by practitioners in other poor areas, such as urban slums; many are faced by all primary-care providers. And with the current health budget cuts, ethical issues around allocation of resources are concerns for all health workers.

My definition of medical ethics is simple: it is ordinary ethics applied to the practice of medicine. Medical ethics is what I do when I stop short in the middle of a busy day in the clinic or have difficulty returning to sleep after an early-morning telephone call from the emergency room because I am asking myself, "What ought I to do in this case?" or "What is the right solution to this problem?"—where the answer to my question cannot be found by checking *Medical Letter* or dialing the neonatologist on the medical center hotline.

Sometimes the situation is a new one, like having a member of one of my families with *osteo-*

From *Simple Living and Hard Choices* by Maureen A. Flannery from *Hastings Center Report* (1982). Reproduced by permission. © The Hastings Center.

*genesis imperfecta* (a genetic disease in which the bones are abnormally brittle) become pregnant, despite contraceptive and genetic counseling. More often the problem the patient presents is familiar, but something about the patient or the family situation confounds me, calls my assumptions into question, makes me stop and think.

The nature of the situations that present ethical dilemmas are quite different for the family physician than for the specialist. They tend to be personal and unpredictable. As one family doctor described her practice in North Carolina, "I never did specialize in anything except just people and what came along next." I. R. McWhinney's description of the family medicine perspective is useful:

> Family physicians have in common the fact
> that they obtain fulfillment from personal
> relations more than from the technical
> aspects of medicine. Their commitment is
> to a group of people more than to a body of
> knowledge. . . . It is difficult for a doctor to
> commit himself [or herself, throughout] to a
> person and at the same time to limit his com-
> mitment to certain diseases or certain types of
> problem. . . . the kind of commitment I am
> speaking of implies that the physician will "stay
> with" a person whatever his problem may be,
> and he will do so because his commitment is
> to people more than to a body of knowledge
> or a branch of technology. To such a physi-
> cian, problems become interesting and impor-
> tant not only for their own sake but because
> they are Mr. Smith's or Mrs. Jones's problem.
> Very often in such relations there is not even a
> very clear distinction between a medical prob-
> lem and a nonmedical one. The patient de-
> fines the problem.

For a family physician in a rural area, often the only limit to practice is geographic; everyone within a one- or two-hour driving distance may be the doctor's responsibility. Depending upon the other resources of the area, the physician's commitment may even extend beyond human patients. . . .

Given the general commitment a rural family physician has to the surrounding community, the realities of life for the people nearby largely determine the issues that arise in practice. Survival in rural America involves a unique set of struggles, many of which influence health.

One major factor is *low income.* A disproportionate number of the nation's poor live in rural America. About 25 percent of the U.S. population lives in nonmetropolitan areas, yet the rural population accounts for 40 percent of those people living below the poverty level. Furthermore, of this 40 percent, ethnic minority groups and the elderly make up a significant proportion. Fifty percent of rural Native Americans, 27 percent of rural Hispanics, and 41 percent of rural blacks have incomes below the poverty level, as compared to 11 percent of rural whites. Poverty increases health problems because of its association with poor nutrition, inadequate housing, unsafe living conditions, and inability to purchase health services.

Low income becomes a greater liability when wages are earned in a *hazardous occupation.* According to 1976 Department of Labor statistics, rural Americans represented the majority of workers in those industries that rank first and second in job-related fatalities: mining and agriculture. Despite the well-known health and safety risks of these occupations, they often represent the only available or the only well-paying jobs for rural Americans.

Not only are rural occupations more likely to be low paying and hazardous, these industries generally provide *fewer health benefits* for their employees. Many rural workers cannot get workers' compensation and they are rarely provided with health insurance. In Texas, for instance, workers' compensation is mandatory for all workers except the farmworkers, who constitute the majority of the rural population of the state. Farm workers are rarely provided with health insurance. Employed rural residents in low-benefit industries are often unable to make payments for their health care, generating insufficient revenue for the facilities that provide them services.

A related disadvantage for rural dwellers is a *lower-than-average* educational level, a characteristic that correlates closely with poor usage of health services. Less-educated persons tend not to have had the opportunity to learn about health, hygiene, and preventive measures. Often they are not informed about governmental programs for which they are eligible, programs that might help with some of the costs or remove some of the obstacles to needed health care services.

Rural dwellers tend to have *closer family ties* than city dwellers because of the preservation of traditional values and also because other societal structures upon which a family can depend are limited in rural areas. Divorce is less common than in urban areas; traditional nuclear and/or extended families are the rule. Since 70 percent of rural families have two parents in the home, compared to 39 percent in the inner cities, the rural poor often fail to meet eligibility criteria for governmental insurance programs that were designed to deal with urban poverty, such as Medicaid and Aid to Dependent Children.

The *particular age structure* of rural America affects the health care of its inhabitants. The number of elderly persons and of children under ten is proportionately higher in rural areas. Since women not only constitute the largest number of health care consumers in general, but also live longer than men and bear children, they are disproportionately represented among rural persons in need of health care. Institutions that care for dependent members of society, such as nursing homes and day care centers, are not prevalent in rural areas; nor are they well accepted, since traditional rural families "care for their own."

In addition to these epidemiological characteristics that militate against good health care, many rural areas have a history of *substandard health care providers*. In Appalachia, the most dramatic example is the coal company doctor. In many communities, the first "professional" health provider was a physician brought in by the local coal company to treat all its employees and their families. There was no alternative to the company doc; he was part of the paternalistic monopoly, just like the company store. Rather than health insurance benefits, workers received free care or else scrip for the company doc's services. Since miners were poorly paid and other health providers were scarce, there was essentially no consumer choice for health care. For a variety of reasons, the coal companies did not attract particularly qualified physicians. And patients saw quite clearly that their doctor's allegiance was to the company management, not to their health. (It was not until the United Mine Workers developed its visionary system of hospitals and clinics in the late 1950s that qualified physicians came in any number to the mountains.) . . .

I became particularly aware of the influence of all these characteristics on the health of rural dwellers this fall when my partner and I taught a self-care course for the patients in our clinic, modifying a curriculum taught in several Kentucky cities. In dealing with our class of twenty layfolk, we came up against the many conditions that hinder outpatients in taking care of themselves—poverty, environmental hazards, dangerous occupations, lack of education, unemployment, socialization into dependence upon "experts," and lack of support for healthy behavior within a society that condones and often encourages self-destructive habits. Trying to modify a curriculum developed for urban middle-class folk to our rural participants made me realize that much of the self-care and holistic health movements does not apply to people who lack control over many of the basic conditions of their lives.

For instance, self-responsibility is a basic concept of the holistic health movement. The notion that individuals are responsible for their health is sometimes extended to assume that people are also responsible for their diseases. Although this idea can be useful for individuals seeking to understand the meaning of their illnesses—particularly illnesses with significant psychological components—much of the popular self-care literature fails to acknowledge that there are some factors over which we have control in our lives and other factors (known and unknown) over which we have little or no control. For the people in our class, the latter often clearly dominated. Black lung victims, for instance, do not create their health problems (unless they also smoke heavily); unhealthy working conditions do. It is wrong to suggest that the victims must change themselves in order to survive; it is the workplace that must be changed. The problem and its treatment are not individual but societal.

Many specifics of the curriculum were as inappropriate to our class as the underlying philosophy. For example, how do you start a jogging regimen when you live up a creek bed, when the nearby public roads have no shoulders and are dominated by overfull and uncovered coal trucks? When "just getting by" occupies most of your time, leaving little for leisure activities, however healthful? And when jogging itself is a foreign concept: in the mountains, anyone who would run for any reason other than to get somewhere—or else to get away from something—is a fool. . . .

Many of the female patients I see tell me that they have come to my office because of "bad nerves"; or else they may use it as a tag-on at the visit's end ("By the way, doc, I've got these bad nerves. . . ."). A doctor who practiced nearby several years ago recorded a number of interviews with "bad nerve" patients in which she explored the origin of the diagnosis and the patient's concept of the nature of the malady. Her discovery was that "bad nerves" was largely an iatrogenic complaint [doctor-created illness—ED.]. Asked when they became aware of their bad nerves, patients generally said that they had visited a physician with a somatic complaint, say a headache or a stomach ache, and had been told, "No, you don't have a brain tumor," or "There's no ulcer causing your stomach to hurt," but rather, "What you have is *bad nerves*." And the treatment in most cases was a prescription for "nerve pills." Patients took this medical diagnosis and its pharmacological treatment very seriously, seeing "bad nerves" as an illness as physical and concrete as a tumor or an ulcer. One woman vividly described her concept of the nerves coursing through her body as "frayed and tarnished" rather than "silvery smooth" as in a fifth-grade health book picture. Another understood the doctor who performed her hysterectomy to say that he saw her nerves "all aquiver" on the operating table, clearly the worst case of "bad nerves" he had witnessed. . . .

A common dilemma I face in my practice is what to do when a woman comes in requesting (and requests unmet soon escalate to demands) drug treatment for her "bad nerves." A thorough history usually confirms the iatrogenic labeling of the "bad nerves" and in addition uncovers a difficult and complex social situation that perpetuates the symptoms. Given a busy practice, a bare-bones staff, and poor human service re-

sources in the area; given that patients who discontinue benzodiazepine tranquilizers after more than four months of regular use have a physiological as well as psychological addiction to overcome; and given that there are no transcendental meditation sessions, yoga or exercise classes, or even competent individual or group therapists within a reasonable driving distance, is it right for me to refuse to refill the patient's Valium, cutting off her way of dulling her responses to the problems of her life? Is it right for me to support her habit? Must a good family physician in a rural area play the roles of counselor, social worker, recreation therapist, and scout leader as well as doctor? Is it possible for one person, however committed, to handle such multiple and demanding roles?

Another frequent complaint, one so common that it is difficult to get patients to clarify it, is "smothering." In the mountains, "smothering" describes everything from the sudden shortness-of-breath of an acute asthmatic attack to the labored breathing of poor physical condition to the short-windedness of chronic obstructive lung disease. I imagine that the frequency of this description is related to the prevalence of black lung, an occupational disease of enormous significance in our single-industry region. Almost everyone knows a neighbor or relative, retired from years in the coal mines, spending his days bound to his home "breathing machine," coughing into a cut-off milk carton in front of the television set. The image is so familiar that even children pick it up: the other day an asthmatic five-year-old described his problem to me as "smothering." I can't help but think that the image is metaphorical for a group of people as oppressed and accustomed to outside control of their lives, their money, and their land as Appalachians. Is it right for a physician simply to treat "smothering" with epinephrine or aminophylline without attempting to deal with the root causes of the oppression? Must a good rural family physician also be a political activist?

And what do patients' rights mean when dealing with people so oppressed and unassertive that they are reluctant to take any responsibility for the care that they receive? It takes hard work and time to bring such folk to demand any of the rights that they have traditionally signed away, just as their foreparents signed away the mineral rights to the land on which they live. In the midst of a busy practice, it is far easier to lapse into the paternalistic pattern to which patients are accustomed. Must a conscientious rural doc also be a part-time community organizer?

A patient came to me the other day to see whether I could "do something" about the dust accumulation in her parents' home. They live up an isolated holler near the clinic, and the dirt road that once ended at their cabin now provides access to a newly developed strip mine. Huge coal trucks now rumble past day and night—their daughter counted five in the space of an hour. Since her parents are the only inhabitants along the road, the coal company ignores the requirement that it "water" the road several times a day to reduce dust accumulation. My patient was concerned that the particles in the air were exacerbating her father's severe chronic obstructive pulmonary disease, a result of thirty-five years of coal dust exposure in underground mines. And it was certainly affecting the couple's quality of life: her elderly mother, a fastidious housekeeper with an early organic brain syndrome, was wearing herself out in a hopeless situation.

Certainly this is an appropriate problem for a family physician. But how far do I go? Write a letter to the owner of the coal company? Report the violation to the Office of Surface Mining when the owner does not respond? Pursue the matter to the state or federal level when lower officials do not act because they are in league with one of the biggest coal operators in the region? How much time and energy can I consume hassling a nonresponsive bureaucracy to benefit one family? Would it be right for me to do nothing?

. . . [T]he rural physician must constantly ask, how much can one individual do? Can one be a good and ethical physician just by treating symptoms, or must a doctor become deeply involved in addressing the sources of disease in the people she or he cares for? And if a doctor neglects continuing medical education because of political involvements, or "burns out" from the stress of trying to do too much, do the patients and community ultimately benefit or not?

## THE WISE OLD WOMAN OF THE VILLAGE

In struggling with the issue of setting limits to commitment, a rural health care provider must deal with a related question: personal survival in a rural community. For a physician in a rural area, there is no boundary between professional and private life. Living among the people whom I serve in a close-knit community, I do not have the luxury of retreating to a suburban lifestyle surrounded by other "young professionals" when I end my day at an inner-city clinic. I am one of a few professionals in my county, and everyone knows where I live, how I spend my days off, and whether I dug up my potatoes before the first frost. . . .

Physicians have traditionally considered their private lives immune to this sort of public scrutiny. Although they have almost unlimited access to patients' minds and bodies, an unwritten ethic of the relationship generally prevents patients from intruding into their doctors' private lives. But is it unreasonable for patients to demand that I connect my public and private lives? To challenge me to be consistent in the values I profess in the clinic and at home? How I spend my time and money, what political convictions I hold—do these not affect my doctoring?

Many urban physicians make a sharp distinction between the people with whom they spend social or after-hours time and those they see as patients. The director of my residency program felt very strongly that a doctor should not accept friends as patients. He believed that confusing friend-friend and doctor-patient relationships created problems for both physician and patient: the blurring made medical judgments more difficult for the physician and detracted from the role of "authority figure" that the physician plays. He also believed in the value of friends who relate to the physician as a person, and who can help him or her escape from medicine after hours. Whatever the merits of that position, a rural physician has little choice in the matter. I would have to drive a long way for friends or my friends would have to travel a long way for their medical care if I followed his advice. Instead, I trust my patient/friends to understand that I need "time off" in order to be there for them as physician/friend.

Given the high visibility of a physician in a small community, anonymity is impossible. From an income disproportionately higher than that of hard-working neighbors to preferential treatment in scheduling a haircut, the "myriad and often subtle privileges of physician status" are striking in a rural community. Should I accept these favors as compensation for the pressing and demanding work I do? Or should I refuse them as elitist and unnecessary? The absence of boundaries between personal and public lives makes it difficult for the rural physician to lead a "well-rounded" life in the sense of an urban or suburban colleague. Yet those of us who are content with our lives as country docs discover ways of dealing with our situations. Mary Howell describes a model that works for me:

> My vision of how I like to work and relate to the people I serve does not correspond to the usual understanding of the professional role. I have found a different "role model" altogether—that of the wise old woman of the village, the witch healer, who has been privileged to learn from her predecessors and to share with many generations of village folk their experiences as family members, and who can convey what she has distilled (what she "knows") to others so that they too can use that wisdom.

For rural primary health care providers, finding the wisdom to cope with work that specializes only in "people and what comes along next" is often an overwhelming task. How well we seek that wisdom and resolve the everyday ethical issues that arise in our work ultimately determines our effectiveness in helping the people with whom we live and whom we serve.

## Notes and Questions

1. The cases in Chapter 1 on spousal abuse showed that lawyers and judges use rules of law to convert large questions into small, manageable, and answerable ones. Those cases turned on the permanence of injury, the presence or absence of lethal weapons, or drunkenness rather than on the imponderables of marriage, or how a man who at one point pledges his eternal love can later become an abuser.

Dr. Flannery seems to violate the main tenet of all professions—that no question will be asked unless it can readily be answered by even the most unenlightened practitioner. For her, problems grow more complex rather than less. Could she behave ethically were she to narrow questions to medical symptoms and the answers found in her black bag? (Is the "black bag" male?)

Did the lawyers and judges in the spousal abuse cases behave ethically when they stuck to the law and the facts relevant to the law? Were they duty bound to change the law itself rather than to do fancy legal footwork within unjust rules? Should lawyers of the time have gone beyond the law to help eliminate the root causes of spousal abuse? This activism would be analogous to Dr. Flannery's going beyond treating patients to the causes of illnesses.

2. What problems do professionals encounter when they go wherever problems take them? For example:
   A. Should Dr. Flannery simply treat black lung or other occupationally related diseases, or must she become active in preventive medicine—mine safety, and environmental health?
   B. In the case of patients with "bad nerves," should she rewrite prescriptions for addictive tranquilizers (as her medical colleagues might do), or should she take a longer and more burdensome approach, e.g., address the problem of addiction, or the real causes of "bad nerves"?
   C. Should Dr. Flannery ally herself with activist lawyers, family counselors, or schoolteachers who see that the problems of Appalachia do not fall conveniently within professional specialties?
   D. If many problems of Appalachia are subsets of poverty—technically outside everyone's field—what is the appropriate stance for the concerned professional on economic issues?
   E. Must the doctor be more than doctor, the lawyer more than lawyer, or the teacher more than teacher to reach the problems that their patients, clients, and students have?

*3.* What can the "wise old woman" model do for Dr. Flannery that her professional model cannot? Can her "prescription" for ethical activism be transferred to other settings?

*4.* Dr. Flannery does not seem like a member of the country club set. Must she accept less income than her professional peers if she is to work with the poor?

🔊 The previous reading shows that professionals often answer ethical questions on their own. In the following case involving sterilization, a court of law must integrate law, medicine, and psychiatry.

## 3.3  Cook v. State  *495 P. 2d 768 Or. (1972)*

FOLEY, J.

THIS IS AN APPEAL from an order of the circuit court which affirmed an order of the State Board of Social Protection after trial . . . in the circuit court.

On May 21, 1971, the State Board of Social Protection entered an order for plaintiff's sterilization based on findings:

(2) . . . That in the judgment of a majority of the Board the condition of the examinee is such that procreation by the examinee would produce a child or children: . . . (b) who would become neglected or dependent children as a result of the parent's inability by reason of mental illness or mental retardation to provide adequate care.

(3) That in the judgment of the majority of the Board there is no probability that the condition of the examinee investigated and examined will improve to such an extent as to avoid the indicated consequences as set forth in paragraph (2) hereof. . . .

Plaintiff contends that the trial court erred in denying her motion that the state elect between mental retardation and mental illness as the basis for sterilization and that the trial court erred in affirming the Board's order. The remaining assignment of error alleges that ORS 436.070(1) (b) is unconstitutional because it discriminates against indigents in violation of the

equal protection provisions of the state and federal constitutions. ORS 436.070 provides:

(1) The investigation, findings and orders of the board . . . shall be made with the purpose in view of avoiding the procreation of children:

. . . (b) Who would become neglected or dependent children as a result of the parent's inability by reason of mental illness or mental retardation to provide adequate care. . . .

Plaintiff is a 17-year-old girl with a history of severe emotional disturbance. At age 13 she was declared a ward of the court and was taken out of her home under circumstances which indicate that she had been physically and sexually abused by her family for some period of time. During the last four years she has been placed in two foster homes, juvenile detention home, F. W. Dammasch State Hospital and Hillcrest School of Oregon. The longest period in any one place was one and one-half years at Dammasch. Her behavior has vacillated between periods of stability that lasted up to three months and aggressive hostility expressed in verbal or physical threats towards others, self-inflicted injury and running away. A petition was filed with the Board of Social Protection[1] after appellant engaged in a se-

---

Footnotes have been renumbered.—ED.

[1] ORS 436.025 provides:

"Any two persons or any person licensed to practice medicine and surgery by the State Board of Medical Examiners may file a petition with the State Board of Social Protection alleging that any other person within the state is within the jurisdiction of the board as provided in subsection (1) of ORS 436.070."

ries of indiscriminate and impulsive sexual involvements while she was in the hospital.

A psychiatrist who specializes in child guidance has followed plaintiff's care since she became a ward of the court. His uncontradicted testimony was that she would never be able to provide the parental guidance and judgment which a child requires even though she might be able to master the skills necessary to take physical care of herself and a child. He based this conclusion on the girl's lack of emotional control, her consistent low scores in areas of judgment on psychological tests, and the likelihood that she would abuse a child. He said the prognosis is poor because the presence of brain damage makes her condition inherently unstable despite continuous medication. He testified further that both mental illness and mental retardation are contributing factors and are interrelated.

Because of their interrelated nature, plaintiff's condition could not be intelligently considered without reference to both mental illness and mental retardation. The statute provides for, and the plaintiff was accorded, counsel at public expense, adequate notice and opportunity to be heard. The statute thus satisfies the due process clause. The trial court's denial of the motion to elect was proper. . . .

It is now necessary to determine whether the statute denies plaintiff equal protection of the laws.

In *Buck* v. *Bell* . . . (1927), the United States Supreme Court upheld a Virginia sterilization law. Sterilization was considered beneficial to the patient and to society because it allowed people to be discharged from state institutions, to return to the community, and to become self-supporting.

The only other case involving sterilization laws to come before the United States Supreme Court was *Skinner* v. *Oklahoma* . . . (1942). The purpose of the Oklahoma law was to prevent criminal traits from being inherited by ordering the sterilization of those who had been thrice-convicted of various specified felonies. The law was held unconstitutional as a violation of equal protection because there was no rational basis for distinguishing those felonies which would result in sterilization (one of petitioner's convictions was for chicken stealing) from other felonies which were exempt (embezzlement, for example). The

premise that state sterilization laws are constitutional when validly drawn was not disturbed.

The statute with which we are concerned does not discriminate on its face between rich and poor. Plaintiff contends that the statute actually applies only to the poor because a mentally ill or mentally retarded person with money would be able to hire others to care for his child and would never allow the child to become neglected or dependent.[2]

The words "neglected or dependent" are not defined in ORS ch. 436. Plaintiff urges us to interpret both as dependent on state support and to adopt the reasoning in *Smith* v. *Wayne Probate Judge,* . . . (1925). The purpose of the statute in that case was to protect the state from public charges:

> That he would not be able to support and care for his children, if any, and such children would probably become public charges by reason of his own mental defectiveness. . . .

The Oregon law specifies that the potential offspring would become dependent or neglected as a result of the parent's inability to provide adequate care and is not concerned with the parent's financial status.[3]

The state's concern for the welfare of its citizenry extends to future generations and when there is overwhelming evidence, as there is here,

---

[2]The statute denies the fundamental right of procreation to those who come within its terms. The usual deference given to the judgment of state legislatures does not apply to laws affecting fundamental human rights. . . .

". . . [S]trict scrutiny of the classification which a State makes in a sterilization law is essential, lest unwittingly or otherwise invidious discriminations are made against groups or types of individuals in violation of the constitutional guaranty of just and equal laws. . . ." *Skinner* v. *Oklahoma,* . . . 1113.

[3]Plaintiff has referred us to the minutes of the House Judiciary Committee, May 17, 1967, and the testimony of one of the principal witnesses who replied, when asked if the legislation was for the welfare of child or parent:

> ". . . Many of these girls can be trained for ordinary housework or simple skills in a community, but if they had the added stress and strain of the responsibility of infants are then unable to function properly. Furthermore, the children become public charges. . . ."

The same witness stated that the children become neglected and "have all sorts of problems." Hearing, Senate Judiciary Committee, May 2, 1967.

that a potential parent will be unable to provide a proper environment for a child because of his own mental illness or mental retardation, the state has sufficient interest to order sterilization.

Affirmed.

*Notes and Questions*

1. The court states that due process has been provided under the statute allowing sterilization. Due process generally means that the state must go about what it does in a prescribed manner. For example, in the famous case of *in re Gault,* a case involving juvenile proceedings, the U.S. Supreme Court said that due process includes the right to be informed about the nature of charges, the right to counsel, the right to confront and cross-examine witnesses, the privilege against self-incrimination, the right to a transcript of proceedings, and the right to appellate review.

    Given these protections, does the woman in the *Cook* case have anything to fear?

2. In reading the case, one is struck by at least two areas of vagueness. A first is the language of the statute itself—"the condition of the examinee," "adequate care," "no probability of improvement," and so on. A second concerns the group that stands to benefit from the sterilization. The board bears the name Board for Social Protection. Elsewhere the court says that the sterilization will be beneficial to society, or that the state has a concern that children be raised in a "proper environment." Is it clear enough who is to benefit and what evil is being eradicated? In cases of doubt, should ambiguity be resolved in favor of the individual or the interests of "the state" or "society"?

3. The court says that the statute *on its face* does not discriminate between rich and poor, which probably means that the statute as written is potentially applicable to all people within the state of Oregon.

    Compare the foregoing idea of equality with the following observation by Justice Douglas in the case of *Furman* v. *Georgia,* a death penalty case to be considered next:

    > A law that stated that anyone making more than $50,000 would be exempt from the death penalty would plainly fall, as would a law that in terms said that blacks, those who never went beyond the fifth grade in school, those who made less than $3,000 a year, or those who were unpopular or unstable should be the only people executed. A law which in the overall view reaches that result in practice has no more sanctity than a law which in terms provides the same.*

*Furman* v. *Georgia* 92 S.Ct. 2726 (1972) 2735.

To put it crudely, the *Cook* case might be considered the elimination of welfare at retail—one undesirable candidate for reproduction at a time. In the thirty years since the case, the antipathy to welfare has assumed wholesale proportions. The direction has been unmistakable: less and less welfare, to fewer and fewer people, for shorter and shorter periods of time. The shift in attitude from helping the poor to blaming the poor can be found in the commonplace comments that it is one thing to help the "truly needy" and another to subsidize fancy cars, allow people to breed themselves into higher payments, and condone fraud. The belief that people would rather be on welfare than work pitted welfare recipients against the working poor. Despite the fact that many receiving welfare are white, disabled, aged, and living in rural areas, recipients were seen in racial terms—young black deadbeats in city tenements.

Elimination of welfare—wholesale—reached a high point when Congress enacted the Personal Responsibility and Work Opportunity Act of 1996, which was designed to limit welfare to "temporary assistance for needy families." The words headlining the law give the reasons why the president claimed to be eliminating "welfare as we know it." First, if help would continue to be forthcoming it would be "temporary." Second, the problem with the welfare system was that people were not taking responsibility for their own actions and lives and instead were relying on a social safety net that was destroying initiative; initiative that might have to be restored by something analogous to "tough love." Third, people would have to go to work after two years and, with certain exceptions, this included women with children who would have to find work and use day care for their children. The amount of time on welfare, over a lifetime, could not exceed five years; welfare to legal immigrants was at the discretion of states, and in general the states had discretion on how to allocate the block grants they would receive from the federal government.*

The legislation included an interesting amalgam of policies:

1. [providing] assistance to needy families so that the children may be cared for in their homes or in the homes of relatives;
2. [ending] the dependency of needy parents on government benefits by promoting job preparation, work and marriage;
3. [preventing] and [reducing] the incidence of out of wedlock pregnancies and establishing annual numerical goals for preventing and reducing the incidence of these pregnancies;
4. [encouraging] the formation and maintenance of two-parent families.†

In the years following the enactment of the welfare law politicians proclaimed its success in "getting people off welfare." But it is not clear what those who went off welfare did. Some did get jobs at the low end of the labor force in a tight labor market. Some did not. Apolitical appraisals of the impact of the new law might be found by consulting food banks, homeless shelters, and religious and secular community assistance groups who often found resources stretched to the limits.

Homelessness is a large and growing subset of poverty.‡ It is difficult to access just how many people are homeless since many are homeless for limited periods of time. Being homeless can involve living with relatives, in a shelter, or on the street; this makes some forms of homelessness as invisible as the homeless themselves. In its own studies, which included children, the government estimated that between 4.5 and 9 million people experienced homelessness from 1985 to 1990, and the National Law Center on Homelessness estimated that 600,000 to 2 million people will be homeless at some point during a year.§ The usual stereotypes of who are homeless no longer apply. There are still mental patients, alcoholics, and drug dependent people among the homeless, but they are now joined by spouses and children escaping abuse, unattached children, and the working poor who cannot afford housing.* Meanwhile, the commitment to provide adequate housing

---

*M. Greenberg and S. Savner, A Brief Summary of Key Provisions of the Temporary Assistance of Needy Families . . . H.R.3734, Center for Law and Social Policy, 1997.

†Ibid, p. 6.

‡National Coalition on Homelessness, Homelessness in America: Unabated and Increasing—A Ten Year Perspective (1997).

§National Coalition on Homelessness, How Many People Experience Homelessness? (1993), p. 3.

*National Coalition, . . . Homelessness Unabated, pp. 3, 4.

to all people has been fitful and largely pious. In the 1949 Housing Act Congress established the goal of a "decent home and living environment for every American family," a goal that was never met. In 1993 President Clinton announced "Priority home!", a plan to break "the cycle of homelessness and [prevent] future homelessness." Nothing appreciable happened; confronting homelessness was overwhelmed by welfare law changes that made a decent life, including adequate shelter, even less attainable for the poor. The National Coalition on Homelessness summarized the Clinton years as follows:

> The shift away from addressing the systemic causes of homelessness to focusing on individual "responsibility" for homelessness and poverty only serves to legitimatize and perpetuate homelessness. . . . This shift, as well as the abdication of responsibility for social welfare programs to state and local government, ignores the ample research and data collection on homelessness . . . President Clinton may well succeed President Reagan as the president under whose tenure homelessness increased most dramatically and broadly—particularly among children and the employed.[†]

The presidential campaign of 2000 added fresh ironies to the homelessness crisis. Al Gore, who promised to be a champion for working families, said virtually nothing about the working poor except that he advocated increasing the minimum wage and making incremental increases in the budget for HUD, the federal agency concerned with housing. George Bush would turn to the private market to increase housing supply with $1.7 billion through investor tax credits and a $1 billion American Dream Downpayment Fund whereby the government would contribute $1,500 to help low income families buy homes.

---

❧ The use of the death penalty is a related issue to the crisis in the handling of poverty-related issues. Justice Douglas in the famous case of *Furman* v. *Georgia* made the following observation:

> [W]e know that the discretion of judges in imposing the death penalty enables the penalty to be selectively applied, feeding prejudices against the accused if he is poor and despised, and lacking political clout, or if he is a member of a suspect or unpopular minority, and saving those who by social position may be in a more protected position. In ancient Hindu law a Brahmin was exempt from capital punishment, and under that law . . . punishment increased as social status diminished. We have, I fear, taken in practice the same position, partially as a result of making the death penalty discretionary and partially as a result of the ability of the rich to purchase the services of the most respected and most resourceful legal talent in the nation.[‡]

A majority of the American people sit astride two positions that are difficult to reconcile: endorsing the death penalty, while knowing that Justice Douglas' observations about its selective use are true.

---

[†]Ibid, p. 4.

[‡]*Furman* v. *Georgia* 92 Sup.Ct. 2726, 2735 (1972).

# 3.4 | Furman v. Georgia    *408 U.S. 238 (1972)*

MR. JUSTICE MARSHALL . . .

THESE THREE CASES PRESENT the question whether the death penalty is a cruel and unusual punishment prohibited by the Eighth Amendment to the United States Constitution. . . . Furman was convicted of murder for shooting the father of five children when he discovered that Furman had broken into his home. . . . [The two other cases being appealed] involve state convictions for forcible rape. Jackson was found guilty of rape during the course of a robbery in the victim's home. The rape was accomplished as he held the pointed ends of scissors at the victim's throat. Branch was also convicted of a rape committed in the victim's home. No weapon was utilized, but physical force and threats of physical force were employed.

The criminal acts with which we are confronted are ugly, vicious, reprehensible acts. Their sheer brutality cannot and should not be minimized. But we are not called upon to condone the penalized conduct; we are asked only to examine the penalty imposed on each of the petitioners and to determine whether or not it violates the Eighth Amendment. The question then is not whether we condone rape or murder, for surely we do not; it is whether capital punishment is a "punishment no longer consistent with our own self-respect" and therefore violative of the Eighth Amendment. . . .

[W]e must proceed with caution. . . . By first examining the historical derivation of the Eighth Amendment and the construction given it in the past, and then exploring the history and attributes of capital punishment in this country, we can answer the question presented with objectivity and a proper measure of self-restraint.

Candor is critical to such inquiry. All relevant material must be marshaled and sorted and forthrightly examined. . . .

Candor compels me to confess that I am not oblivious to the fact that this is truly a matter of life and death. Not only does it involve the lives of these three petitioners, but those of the almost 600 other condemned men and women in the country currently awaiting execution. While this fact cannot affect our ultimate decisions it necessitates that the decision be free from any possibility of error.

[Justice Marshall reviews the origins of the constitutional provision against cruel and unusual punishment in the history of the Bill of Rights. He then turned to an appraisal of prior court decision where the word "cruel" had been interpreted. After discussing two cases upholding execution by shooting and execution by electrocution, Marshall considers the *Weems* case, decided in 1910—ED.]

Weems . . . was convicted of falsifying a "public and official document." He was sentenced to 15 years incarceration at hard labor with chains on his ankles, to an unusual loss of his civil rights, and to perpetual surveillance. Called upon to determine whether this was cruel and unusual punishment, the Court found that it was. . . . In striking down the penalty . . . the Court examined the punishment in relation to the offense, compared the punishment to those inflicted for other crimes and to those imposed in other jurisdictions and concluded that the punishment was excessive. Justices . . . dissented . . . that the cruel and unusual prohibition was meant to prohibit only those things that were objectionable at the time the constitution was adopted.

*Weems* is a landmark case because it represents the first time the Court invalidated a penalty prescribed by a legislature for a particular offense. . . .

Then came another landmark case, . . . *Francis* v. *Resweber* . . . (1947). . . . Francis had been convicted of murder and sentenced to be executed. The first time the current passed through him, there was a mechanical failure and he did not die. Thereafter Francis sought to prevent a second execution. . . . Five members of the court . . . held that the legislature adopted electrocution for a humane purpose, and that its will should not be thwarted because . . . it may have inadvertently increased suffering in one particular case. . . .

*Trop* v. *Dulles* (1958) . . . marked the next major . . . case. . . . Trop, a native-born American, was declared to have lost his citizenship by reason of conviction by court-martial for wartime desertion. . . . Emphasizing the flexibility inherent in the words "cruel and unusual" the Chief Justice wrote that [t]he amendment must draw its meaning from the evolving standards of decency that mark the progress of a maturing society. . . . He scrutinized the penalty in relation to the offense . . . and concluded that involuntary statelessness was excessive. . . .

[F]our years later a majority . . . in *Robinson* v. *California* [ruled] that a sentence of 90 days imprisonment for violation of a California statute making it a crime to "be addicted to the use of narcotics" was cruel and unusual. . . . Mr. Justice Stewart . . . reiterated . . . that the cruel and unusual clause was not a static concept but one that must be continually examined "in light of contemporary human knowledge." . . . We distinguished *Robinson* in *Powell* v. *Texas* (1968) where we sustained a conviction for drunkenness in a public place.* Four justices dissented. . . .

Perhaps the most important principle in analyzing "cruel and unusual punishment questions is . . . the "cruel and unusual" language "must draw its meaning from the evolving standards of decency that mark the progress of a maturing society." Thus a penalty permissible at one time in our nation's history is not necessarily permissible today.

The fact therefore that the Court, or individual justices may have in the past expressed an opinion that the death penalty is constitutional is not now binding on us. . . . [Marshall then surveys the standards for decision of the case: (1) cases that involve so much physical pain and suffering as to be intolerable—the rack, the thumbscrew; (2) cases that involve an innovative punishment "more cruel than that punishment which it superseded"; (3) cases where the penalty serves no valid legislative purpose; (4) cases in which popular sentiment abhors the penalty even though it serves a valid legislative purpose. This survey brings Marshall to the discussion of whether capital punishment is unconstitutional because abhorrent to "currently existing moral values." But before beginning, he surveys the history of capital punishment, noting a reduction

of the use of capital punishment. However, at the time the *Furman* case arose Marshall noted that "41 States, the District of Columbia, and other federal jurisdictions still authorized the death penalty for at least one crime."—ED.]

The foregoing history demonstrates that capital punishment was carried from Europe to America, but once here, was tempered considerably. At times in our history strong abolitionist movements have existed. But they have never been completely successful, as no more than a quarter of the States of the Union have, at any time, abolished the death penalty. They have had partial success, however, especially in reducing the number of capital crimes, replacing mandatory death sentences with jury discretion, and developing more humane forms of executions.

This is where our historical foray leads. The question now faced is whether American society has reached a point where abolition is not dependent on a grass roots movement in particular jurisdictions, but is demanded by the Eighth Amendment. . . .

In order to assess whether or not death is an excessive or unnecessary penalty, it is necessary to consider the reasons why a legislature might select it as a punishment . . . and examine whether a less severe penalty would satisfy the legitimate legislative wants. . . .

There are six purposes conceivably served by capital punishment: retribution, deterrence, prevention of repetitive criminal acts, encouragement of guilty pleas and confessions, eugenics, and economy. . . .

A   The concept of retribution is one of the most misunderstood in all of our criminal jurisprudence. The principal cause of confusion derives from the fact that . . . most people confuse the question "why do men in fact punish?" with the question "what justifies men in punishing?" Men may in fact punish for any number of reasons, but the one reason that punishment is morally good or morally justifiable is that someone has broken the law. . . .

The fact that the state may seek retribution against those who have broken its laws does not mean that retribution may then become the state's sole end in punishing. . . . Our jurisprudence has always accepted deterrence in gen-

---

*It had been alleged in that case that the defendant as an alcoholic could not be punished for his illness.—ED.

eral, deterrence of individual recidivism, isolation of dangerous persons, and rehabilitation as proper goals of punishment. . . . Retaliation, vengeance, and retribution have been roundly condemned as intolerable aspirations for a government in a free society.

Punishment as retribution has been condemned by scholars for centuries, and the Eighth Amendment itself was adopted to prevent punishment from becoming synonymous with vengeance. . . .

Retribution surely underlies the imposition of some punishment on one who commits a criminal act. But the fact that *some* punishment may be imposed does not mean that *any* punishment is permissible. . . .

At times a cry is heard that morality requires vengeance to evidence society's abhorrence of the act. But the Eighth Amendment is our insulation from our baser selves. The "cruel and unusual" language limits the avenues through which vengeance may be channeled.

B   The most hotly contested issue regarding capital punishment is whether it is better than life imprisonment as a deterrent to crime. Admittedly there are some persons who would rather die than languish in prison for a lifetime. But whether or not they should be able to choose death as an alternative is a far different question from that presented here—*i.e.,* whether the state can impose death as a punishment. Death is irrevocable; life imprisonment is not. Death of course makes rehabilitation impossible; life imprisonment does not. . . .

It must be kept in mind, then, that the question to be considered is not simply whether capital punishment is a deterrent, but whether it is a better deterrent than life imprisonment.

There is no more complex problem than determining the deterrent efficacy of the death penalty. Capital punishment has obviously failed as a deterrent when a murder is committed. We can number its failures. But we cannot number its successes. No one can ever know how many people have refrained from murder because of the fear of being hanged. . . .

The two strongest arguments in favor of capital punishment as a deterrent are both logical hypotheses devoid of evidentiary support.

The first proposition was best stated by Sir James Stephen in 1864:

> No other punishment deters men so effectively. . . . No one goes to certain inevitable death except by compulsion. . . . Why is this? It can only be because "all that a man has he will give for his life." In any secondary punishment, however terrible, there is hope, but death is death; its terrors cannot be described more forcibly."

. . . The second proposition is that "if life imprisonment is the maximum penalty for a crime such as murder, an offender who is serving a life sentence cannot be deterred from murdering a fellow inmate or a prison officer.". . .

Abolitionists attempt to disprove these hypotheses by amassing statistical evidence to demonstrate that there is no correlation between criminal activity and the existence or nonexistence of a capital sanction. . . .

Thorstein Sellin, one of the leading theorists on capital punishment, has urged that if the death penalty deters prospective murderers, the following hypotheses should be true:

- Murders should be less frequent in states that have the death penalty than those that have abolished it. . . .
- Murders should increase when the death penalty is abolished and should decline when it is restored.
- The deterrent effect should be greatest . . . in those communities where the crime occurred and its consequences are most strongly brought home to the population.
- Law enforcement officers should be safer from murderous attacks in states that have the death penalty.

Sellin's research indicates that not one of these propositions are true. . . . Sellin's statistics demonstrate that there is no correlation between the murder rate and the presence or absence of the capital sanction. . . .

Statistics also show that the deterrent effect of capital punishment is no greater in those communities where executions take place than in other communities. In fact there is some evidence that imposition of capital punishment may actually encourage crime rather than deter it. And while police and law enforcement are the strongest advocates of capital punishment, the evidence is overwhelming that police are no safer in communities that retain the sanction than in those that have abolished it.

There is also a substantial body of evidence that the existence of the death penalty has virtually no effect on the homicide rate in prisons. . . .

The United Nations Committee that studied capital punishment found . . . that the data which now exist show no correlation between the existence of capital punishment and lower rates of capital crimes. . . .

C   Much of what must be said about the death penalty as a device to prevent recidivism is obvious—if a murderer is executed, he cannot possibly commit another offense. The fact is, however, that murderers are extremely unlikely to commit other crimes either in prison or upon their release. For the most part they are first offenders, and when released from prison they are known to become model citizens. . . .

D   The three remaining purposes . . . encouraging guilty pleas and confessions, eugenics, and reducing state expenditures may be dealt with quickly. If the death penalty is used to encourage guilty pleas and thus to deter suspects from exercising their rights under the Sixth Amendment to jury trials, it is unconstitutional. . . . Its elimination would do little to impair the State's bargaining position in criminal cases, since life imprisonment remains a severe sanction. . . .

[A]ny suggestions concerning the eugenic benefits of capital punishment are obviously meritless. . . . No test or procedure presently exists by which incurables can be screened from those who would benefit from treatment. . . . More importantly, this nation has never formally professed eugenic goals, and the history of the world does not look kindly upon them. . . .

As for the argument that it is cheaper to execute a capital offender than to imprison him for life, even assuming that such an argument if true would support a criminal sanction, it is simply incorrect. A disproportionate amount of money spent on prisons is attributable to death row. Condemned men are not productive members of the prison community, although they could be, and executions are expensive. Appeals are often automatic and courts admittedly spend more time with death cases. . . .

At trial the selection of jurors is likely to become a costly, time-consuming problem in a capital case, and defense lawyers will reasonably exhaust every possible means to save his client from execution no matter how long the trial takes.

During the period between conviction and execution, there are an inordinate number of collateral attacks on the conviction and attempts to obtain executive clemency, all of which exhaust time, money and effort of the state. . . . When all is said and done . . . it costs more to execute a man than to keep him in prison for life.

There is but one conclusion that can be drawn from all of this—i.e., the death penalty is an excessive and unnecessary punishment. . . . The point has now been reached at which the deference to the legislatures is tantamount to abdication of our judicial roles as factfinders, judges, and ultimate arbiters of the Constitution. . . . There is no rational basis for concluding that capital punishment is not excessive. . . .

In addition, even if capital punishment is not excessive, it nonetheless violates the Eighth Amendment because it is merely unacceptable to the people of the United States at this time in their history.

In judging whether or not a given penalty is morally acceptable, most courts have said that the punishment is valid unless it shocks the conscience and sense of justice of the people.

Judge Frank[†] once noted . . .

"[I]n any context, such a standard—the community's attitude is usually unknowable. It resembles a slithery shadow, since one can seldom learn, at all accurately, what the community, or a majority, actually feels. Even a carefully taken "public opinion poll" would be inconclusive in a case like this." [*Rosenberg*]

While a public opinion poll obviously is of some assistance in indicating public acceptance

---

[†]Judge Frank wrote the material on discretion in Chapter 2; see Reading 2.1.—Ed.

or rejection of a specific penalty, its utility cannot be very great. This is because whether or not a punishment is cruel and unusual depends, not on whether its mere mention "shocks the conscience and sense of justice of the people," but on whether people who were fully informed as to the purposes of the penalty and its liabilities would find the penalty shocking, unjust and unacceptable.

In other words, the question with which we must deal is not whether a substantial number of American citizens would today, if polled, opine that capital punishment is barbarously cruel, but whether they would find it to be so in light of all information presently available. . . .

It has often been noted that American citizens know almost nothing about capital punishment. Some of the conclusions arrived at in the preceding section and the supporting evidence would be critical to an informed judgment . . . : e.g., that the death penalty is no more effective deterrent than life imprisonment . . . ; that convicted murderers are rarely executed but are usually sentenced to a term in prison; that convicted murderers are usually model prisoners; and that they almost always become law abiding citizens on their release . . . ; that the costs of executing . . . exceed the costs of imprisoning for life; that while in prison a convict under sentence of death performs none of the useful functions that life prisoners perform; that no attempt is made in the sentencing process to ferret out recidivists for execution; and that the death penalty may actually stimulate criminal activity.

This information would almost surely convince the average citizen. . . . [The] problem arises from the . . . public's desire for retribution, even though this is a goal that the legislature cannot constitutionally pursue as its sole justification for capital punishment. . . . I cannot believe that at this point in our history, the American people would ever knowingly support purposeless vengeance. . . .

But if this information needs supplementing, I believe that the following facts would serve to convince even the most hesitant of citizens to condemn death as a sanction: capital punishment is imposed discriminatorily against identifiable classes of people; there is evidence that innocent people have been executed . . . and the death penalty wreaks havoc with our entire criminal justice system. . . .

Regarding discrimination it has been said that "[i]t is usually the poor, the illiterate, the underprivileged, the members of the minority group—the man who because he is without means, and is defended by a court-appointed attorney—who becomes society's sacrificial lamb. . . . Indeed a look at the bare statistics regarding executions is enough to betray much of the discrimination. A total of 3,859 persons have been executed since 1930, of whom 1,751 were white and 2,066 were Negro. Of the executions, 3,334 were for murder; 1,664 of the executed murderers were white and 1,630 were Negro. 455 persons including 48 whites and 405 Negroes were executed for rape. It is immediately apparent that Negroes were executed far more often than whites in proportion to their percentage of the population. Studies indicate that while the higher rate of executions among Negroes is partially due to a higher rate of crime, there is evidence of racial discrimination. . . .

There is also overwhelming evidence that the death penalty is employed against men and not women. Only 32 women have been executed since 1930. . . .

It is also evident that the burden of capital punishment falls upon the poor, the ignorant, and the underprivileged members of society. It is the poor and the members of minority groups who are least able to voice their complaints against capital punishment. Their impotence leaves them victims of a sanction that the wealthier, better represented just-as-guilty person can escape. So long as the capital sanction is used against the forlorn, easily forgotten members of society, legislators are content to maintain the status quo, because change would draw attention to the problem and concern might develop. . . .

Just as Americans know little about who is executed and why, they are unaware of the potential dangers of executing an innocent man. . . .

Proving one's innocence after a jury finding of guilt is almost impossible. . . . [R]eviewing courts . . . rarely dispute the jury's interpretation of the evidence. [The innocent man] . . . must then depend on the good faith of the prosecutor's office to help him establish his innocence. There is evidence, however, that prosecutors do not welcome the idea of having convictions . . . overturned. . . .

While it is difficult to ascertain with certainty the degree to which the death penalty is discriminatorily imposed or the number of innocent persons sentenced to die, there is one conclusion about the penalty that is universally accepted . . . it tends to distort the course of criminal law. . . .

For example its very existence "inevitably sabotages a social and institutional program of reformation." . . . [The] presence of the death penalty as a keystone of our penal system bedevils the administration of criminal justice all the way down the line and is the stumbling block in the path of general reform. . . .

To arrive at the conclusion that the death penalty violates the Eighth Amendment we have had to engage in a long and tedious journey. The amount of information that we have assembled and sorted is enormous. Yet I do not believe that we have deviated in the slightest from the principles with which we began.

At a time in our history when the streets of the Nation's cities inspire fear and despair, rather than pride and hope, it is difficult to maintain objectivity and concern for our fellow citizens. But the measure of a country's greatness is its ability to retain compassion in time of crisis. No nation in recorded history of men has a greater tradition of revering justice and fair treatment for all its citizens in time of turmoil, confusion and tension than ours.

In striking down capital punishment, the court does not malign our system of government. On the contrary it pays homage to it. . . . In recognizing the humanity of our fellow beings, we pay ourselves the highest tribute. We achieve "a major milestone in the long road up from barbarism and join approximately 70 other jurisdictions in the world which celebrate their regard for civilization and humanity by shunning capital punishment. . . ."

## Notes and Questions

1. Jerome Frank in his essay on judging discounts any allusions to objectivity or *self-restraint* as a mask for subjectivity. Is this true of Justice Marshall's opinion too?

Compare the beginning of Justice Marshall's opinion to Justice Blackmun's opinion in the case of *Roe* v. *Wade* on abortion:

> We forthwith acknowledge our awareness of the sensitive and emotional nature of the abortion controversy, of the vigorous opposing views even among physicians, and of the deep and seemingly absolute convictions that the subject inspires. One's philosophy, one's experiences, one's exposure to the raw edges of human existence, one's religious training, one's attitude toward life and family and their values, and the moral standards one establishes and seeks to observe, are all likely to influence and to color one's thinking and conclusions about abortion.
>
> In addition, population growth, pollution, poverty and racial overtones tend to complicate and not to simplify the problem.
>
> Our task, of course, is to resolve the issue by constitutional measurement, free of emotion and predilection.[‡]

Is this "detachment" the commendable temperament of an able jurist or merely a smoke screen?

Compare the following statement of Justice Brennan in the *Furman* case in agreement with Justice Marshall's decision that the death penalty *in itself* is cruel and unusual punishment:

> The basic concept underlying the Amendment is nothing less than the dignity of man. While the state has the power to punish, the Clause stands to assure that the power be exercised within civilized standards.
>
> Death is truly an awesome punishment. The calculated killing of a human being by the State involves, by its very nature, a denial of the executed person's humanity. . . . When a man is hung, there is an end of our relationship with him. His execution is a way of saying, you are not fit for this world. Take your chances elsewhere.[§]

2. It might be instructive to briefly excerpt the opening paragraphs of two other opinions in the *Furman* case in view of our sensitivity to the relationship of objectivity to subjectivity, and the overall direction of judicial discretion.

---

[‡]*Roe* v. *Wade*, 93 S. Ct. 756.

[§]*Furman* v. *Georgia*, 92 S. Ct. 272 (1972).

MR. JUSTICE BURGER, *dissenting.*

At the outset it is important to note that only two members of the Court, Mr. Justice Brennan and Mr. Justice Marshall have concluded that the Eighth Amendment prohibits capital punishment for all crimes and under all circumstances. . . .

If we were possessed of legislative power, I would either join with Mr. Justice Brennan and Mr. Justice Marshall or, at the very least, restrict the use of capital punishment to a small category of the most heinous crimes. Our constitutional inquiry however must be divorced from personal feelings as to the morality and efficacy of the death penalty, and be confined to the meaning and applicability of the uncertain language of the Eighth Amendment. . . .

Yet it is essential to our role as a court that we not seize upon the enigmatic character of the guarantee as an invitation to enact our personal predilections into law. . . . (Opinion pp. 375, 376)

MR. JUSTICE BLACKMUN, *dissenting.*

I join [the dissenters] and add only the following, somewhat personal, comments.

1. Cases such as these provide for me an excruciating agony of the spirit. I yield to no one in the depth of my distaste, and, indeed, abhorrence, for the death penalty with all its aspects of physical distress and fear and of moral judgment exercised by finite minds. The distaste is buttressed by a belief that capital punishment serves no useful purpose that can be demonstrated. For me, it violates childhood training and life experiences, and is not compatible with the philosophical convictions I have been able to develop. It is antagonistic to any sense of "reverence for life." Were I a legislator, I would vote against the death penalty for the policy reasons argued by counsel for the respective petitioners . . . and adopted . . . by the Justices who vote to reverse. . . .

[U]ntil today capital punishment was accepted and assumed as not unconstitutional *per se* under the Eighth Amendment. . . .

Suddenly, however the course of decision is now the other way, with the Court evidently persuaded that somehow the passage of time has taken us to a place of greater maturity and outlook. The argument, plausible and high sounding as it might be is not persuasive. . . .

My problem . . . is the suddenness of the Court's perception of progress of the human attitude since decisions of only a short while ago.

To reverse the judgments . . . is, of course the easy choice. It is easier to strike the balance in favor of life and against death. It is comforting to relax in the thoughts—perhaps the rationalizations—that this is the compassionate decision for a maturing society; that this is the moral and the "right" thing to do; that thereby we convince ourselves that we are moving down the road toward human decency; that we value life even though that life has taken another or others or has grievously scarred another or others and their families and that we are less barbaric than we were in 1789 . . .

This for me is a good argument, and it makes some sense. But it is good argument, and it makes sense only in a legislative and executive way and not as a judicial expedient. . . . (Opinion pp. 405–410)

3. The dissenting opinions in the *Furman* case picked up on a number of other themes that readers can deduce from tensions in the Marshall opinion itself: that the death penalty was in place at the time of the ratification of the Constitution and has been on the books of most of the states ever since; that the Supreme Court in prior cases has never questioned the ability of a state to impose the death penalty; that in cases of estimating policy alternatives the Supreme Court as a judicial body ought to defer to legislators and not arrogate power to itself; that where narrower grounds for a decision can be found—e.g., the way the statutes in question were worded or the procedure by which capital penalties were decided—those narrower grounds for reversal of convictions ought to be used instead of making a wholesale denunciation of the death penalty as Justice Marshall seemed willing to do.

How does Marshall answer these contentions? Can Marshall's opinion be analyzed along the lines suggested by Llewellyn (Chapter 1), when he contended that material available to a judge will rarely be uniformly helpful in reaching a particular result and that in preparing opinions judges have certain techniques for accentuating what is helpful and deemphasizing what is unhelpful? Can we see in Marshall's opinion what he found helpful and what he found unhelpful and needed to explain away?

4. Marshall cites the universal condemnation of vengeance as a justification for capital punishment. Compare "Revenge is a kind of wild justice." What is wild about revenge? What is

corrupting about vengeance such that a state dare not condone it as a policy? Is vengeance inevitably cruel? Who is the victim of the vengeance?

5. Marshall discusses the expense of convicting and keeping capital offenders. The thrust of his position is that capital punishment is expensive. But is not part of the argument of the current enthusiasts for the death penalty that conviction should be sure and swift and executions immediate? How might Marshall answer these newer "economic" arguments in favor of a revised, extended, and expedited death penalty, or the opinion polls that seem to give overwhelming support to the death penalty "without all the appeals"?

   Was Marshall talking to a less hardened population at the time he wrote his opinion than the current populace?

 ❧ The post-*Furman* world can be described as one that has been more and more hospitable to the death penalty, expeditiously administered. After *Furman,* state criminal statutes were revised to bring them into greater compliance with those Supreme Court justices who did not regard the death penalty as an outright violation of the Constitution. The following article updates developments over the almost quarter century since the case was decided.

## 3.5 | The Hanging Judges   *Bryan Stevenson**

TWENTY YEARS AGO, THE Supreme Court reauthorized the death penalty after it had been briefly banned by the Court's landmark 1972 decision in *Furman* v. *Georgia.* Warren Burger's Court sanctioned the reintroduction of capital punishment into American society on the premise that states would recognize that "death is different." The new legal framework of "guided discretion" in death penalty cases imposed on states an obligation to exercise a higher degree of care, review and scrutiny than had existed prior to *Furman.* The "death is different" doctrine, the Court proclaimed, would shield the modern death penalty from the historic problems of unfairness, arbitrariness, racism and discrimination against the poor that had long accompanied its application.

From the very beginning the courts have struggled with the demands of the new doctrine. Between 1976 and 1982, 70 percent of death sentences were reversed by federal courts due to fundamental constitutional violations. During this period there were only six executions, four carried out on suicidal death-row prisoners who forfeited appeals and demanded death. It became increasingly clear that states were unable to meet basic constitutional requirements in death cases.

By the mid-eighties, the inability of most states to avoid constitutional error in capital cases prompted the Supreme Court to erect procedural barriers to postconviction review, relieving federal courts of the growing burden of insuring fairness in every case. By restricting the scope of habeas corpus—the federal remedy for challenging most death sentences—the Court began limiting the power of federal courts to address even gross violations of the Constitution. Racially biased jury selection, prosecutorial misconduct, even evidence of innocence could all be ignored by federal courts if somewhere along the line an

"The Hanging Judges" by Bryan Stevenson from the October 14, 1996 issue of *The Nation.* Copyright © 1996. Reprinted with permission.

*Bryan Stevenson, director of the Equal Justice Initiative of Alabama, has represented dozens of death-row prisoners.

unwary defense lawyer had failed to object at precisely the right moment, cited the wrong amendment or legal authority or otherwise failed to comply with proper procedure. Twenty-one executions took place in 1984, a 400 percent increase over the previous year.

Despite the procedural restrictions on capital litigation, challenges to the death penalty continued to be brought before the Court on such grounds as inadequate legal representation, disproportionate imposition on black or Hispanic defendants, police or prosecutorial misconduct, and unreliable evidence. In response, the Court retracted even substantive constitutional rights to accommodate more executions.

In the past ten years the Rehnquist Court has clearly tired of the idealistic expectations raised in the seventies. The decade has seen a strengthening of the inverted notion that due process, equal protection of the law and reliability in criminal case adjudications are not nearly as important as finality when a state wants to execute someone. It is only this bizarre reformulation of "death is different" that could explain the Court's 1987 decision in *McCleskey* v. *Kemp*. Warren McCleskey argued to the Court that Georgia's use of the death penalty was racially biased. A study conducted by University of Iowa Professor David Baldus, hailed by many as the most sophisticated examination of race and the criminal justice system ever undertaken, supported McCleskey's claim and established that defendants accused of killing white people were 4.3 times more likely to receive the death penalty than defendants accused of killing African-Americans. Black defendants accused of killing whites faced an even greater likelihood of execution.

In a 5-to-4 opinion written by Justice Lewis Powell, the Court accepted the compelling data documenting racial bias in Georgia's death penalty but nonetheless upheld McCleskey's death sentence. Justice Powell concluded that certain disparities based on race in the administration of capital punishment were "inevitable" and more properly an issue for the legislature to address. Powell later stated after retiring from the Court that if he could change one vote during his tenure it would be *McCleskey*. However, in the grim world of capital litigation there are no sec-ond chances. Warren McCleskey was executed and the doctrine of race bias inevitability lives on.

The Rehnquist Court's perverse interpretation of the "death is different" formulation has led to some strange outcomes. In 1991 the Court held in *Payne* v. *Tennessee* that a murder victim's family members may testify at the penalty phase of a capital case even though the Court had rejected this same practice four years earlier. Victim-impact evidence simply gives more constitutional space for jurors to consider arbitrarily the social status, race and character of victims and consequently gives legal force to the idea that we punish offenders based on how much we identify with the victim.

More amazing, the Court has even abandoned the commitment to insuring review for innocent men and women facing imminent execution. In *Herrera* v. *Collins* (1993), the Court held that the Constitution does not protect condemned state prisoners from execution *even if there is new evidence of innocence.* Chief Justice Rehnquist wrote the opinion, which rejected federal protections for such prisoners because of "the very disruptive effect that entertaining claims of actual innocence would have on the need for finality in capital cases."

The consequence of the Court's continuing retreat in capital jurisprudence has been a modern death penalty that is no more predictable, fairly applied or nondiscriminatory than the death penalty the Court struck down in *Furman* almost twenty-five years ago. There are more than 3,100 people now awaiting execution in the United States. Supreme Court rulings that states may execute the mentally retarded and teenagers as young as 16 have triggered an increased number of such death sentences. In Alabama, Georgia and Mississippi, two-thirds of those executed have been black.

Perhaps even more worrisome is the enthusiasm for executions that has emerged in American political and legal culture. Despite a record number of fifty-six executions in 1995, Congress passed a crime bill this year that further limits capital appeals and seeks to increase dramatically the number of executions. From presidential debates to gubernatorial campaigns the death penalty is exploited as an issue. At a time when drunken crowds gather at executions to cheer on the executioner and when governors and politicians brag about the number of people they have killed, the Court has rejected the heightened review called for by the Burger Court; instead, it has adopted the philosophy of "Let's get on with it," as Chief Justice Rehnquist put it in his campaign to limit appeals by death-row prisoners.

Sadly, for the nearly 300 prisoners who have been lethally injected, electrocuted, gassed, hanged or shot in the past ten years, the fairness of the process leading to death has not been so different from the inglorious years prior to *Furman*. Nor has any meaningful difference been made for the thousands of people who die each year from violent crime in America. Instead,

politicians avoid the more vexing and complex causes of violence by posturing on the death penalty, and the Supreme Court continues to retreat from the debilitating problems caused by an unequal and discriminatory system of criminal justice.

It is hard to imagine how in the next ten years the Court will revive a vision of justice that insists on fairness and reliability in capital cases. Perhaps at some point the excess and extremism frequently authorized by judicial decisions and constantly solicited in political discussions will force the Court to reconsider its current course. As the death penalty moves toward the twenty-first century, it is likely that no other area of constitutional law will reveal as honestly the Court's commitment to equal justice under the law. One can only hope that there are better days ahead.

 

&#10087; As this book goes to press it is difficult to predict the future of the death penalty in the United States. Several things are clear. From the international perspective the United States is increasingly alone, not only in the number of executions carried out in recent years, but also in having so many people in prison. But a plurality in opinion polls still favors the death penalty, and in the 2000 presidential debates both candidates said they favored the death penalty as a deterrent to murder. Meanwhile, the doubts about the death penalty are gathering at least some support, as the next article suggests.

## 3.6   The End of Executions? The Anti-Death Penalty Movement Is Gathering Force   *Linda Lutton*

WHEN BILL RYAN STARTED visiting Death Row prisoners in Illinois some five years ago, he got a lot of unsympathetic reactions from friends. "It used to be that I would talk about being opposed to the death penalty and people would look at me like I was crazy," says Ryan, a retired social worker who helped form the Illinois Death Penalty Moratorium Project in 1996. "I live in

suburbia, and there are a lot of very conservative people out here. They'd look at me like I was nuts."

No longer, he says.

For death penalty activists, the landscape has undergone a sea change in a very short time. Not long ago, people like Bill Ryan were toiling in an environment where politicians embraced executions as evidence they were tough on crime, and where the death penalty had such overwhelming support that it barely registered as a debatable issue.

"The End of Executions?" Linda Lutton, *In These Times,* October 30, 2000. Copyright © 2000 In These Times. Reprinted by permission. www.inthesetimes.com

Now, particularly after Illinois' pro-death penalty Gov. George Ryan declared a moratorium on executions in that state, the movement to end the death penalty has been catapulted forward. Six states are currently conducting reviews of their capital punishment systems, as is the federal government. Both chambers of the New Hampshire state legislature voted to abolish the death penalty in that state (though the measure was vetoed by the Democratic governor). Moratorium legislation is pending in Pennsylvania, Ohio, New Jersey and Missouri, and similar bills have been introduced in 10 other states over the past two years. A spate of city governments have passed resolutions supporting moratoriums. In Congress, several bills are pending that would impose moratoriums or institute safeguards against wrongful convictions.

For the first time in decades, it's arguable that abolitionists have the upper hand. How things arrived at this point is a combination of hard work—on the part of activists, lawyers, journalists and the civil rights and religious communities—and, as in any movement, an element of timing and luck. A look at how the movement to abolish the death penalty has changed gives insights into how strong the movement is—and where it might be headed.

Last year 98 people were executed in the United States—more than in any year since death penalty laws were put back on the books in 1976. By comparison, 63 people were put to death in the entire decade after the death penalty was reinstated. Executions have seen their sharpest increases in the '90s, as have the rolls of Death Row inmates (currently at more than 3,600). According to Amnesty International, only China and the Democratic Republic of Congo executed more people than the United States in 1998, and this country is the world leader in executions of prisoners who were under 18 at the time of their capital crime.

The increase in executions and death sentences can be traced to a politically motivated get-tough-on-crime spree embraced by politicians from both major parties that dates back to Nixon and went through a revival in the early '90s. "The death penalty was the poster issue of the whole tough-on-crime movement," says actor and activist Mike Farrell, president of Death Penalty Focus in California.

In 1988, the federal death penalty was revived for murder committed in the course of large-scale drug trafficking. Under President Clinton, the Violent Crime Control and Law Enforcement Act of 1994 expanded the federal death penalty to some 60 additional crimes, including several that didn't involve murder: treason, espionage and large-scale drug trafficking. Two years later, following the Oklahoma City bombing, Clinton signed the Anti-Terrorism and Effective Death Penalty Act. In an effort to shorten the amount of time between conviction and execution, the law established tighter filing deadlines, limited the opportunity for evidentiary hearings, and allowed only a single *habeas corpus* filing in federal court. It was passed a year after Congress eliminated all federal funding for post-conviction capital defense organizations, which had assisted Death Row inmates in *habeas* proceedings.

The outlook even a few years ago was bleak. "You'd go to executions—I even went to double executions—and nothing was happening," Bill Ryan says. "It was frustrating."

What has happened since is all about critical mass. "A confluence of events came to a head," Farrell says. "There was the conference on the wrongly convicted at Northwestern University in Chicago, the whole explosion of the issue of innocents on Death Row, Governor Ryan's decision to declare a moratorium, the *Chicago Tribune*'s articles, the movie of Sister Helen Prejean's book *Dead Man Walking*—there were so many things that were happening. All of these things kind of collided at a time and . . . people suddenly began to wake up. And I think it has established a momentum that in my view is irreversible."

This has left activists somewhere between dumbstruck and giddy. "It was like they finally heard us," says JoAnn Patterson, mother of Illinois Death Row prisoner Aaron Patterson, who has worked with the Illinois Death Penalty Moratorium Project.

Bill Ryan adds that for the first time in his five years working on the issue, it feels like he's part of a movement. "I didn't think it was a movement until the last six or eight months," he says. "But it's fast becoming a movement."

For the past three decades, the foot soldiers in the movement against the death penalty have worked out of churches and makeshift home offices. They've maintained a consistent presence at executions, drawn attention to the wrongfully convicted, and undoubtedly saved dozens of lives. At times they've put enough people in the streets—particularly in the case of Pennsylvania Death Row prisoner Mumia Abu-Jamal—to attract media attention. But despite being able to mobilize thousands and attract international support, abolitionists were unable to get mainstream Americans to buy into their cause.

Abolitionists haven't suddenly won the ear of Americans because they're presenting new arguments. "Eighteen years ago when I started investigating these cases, nobody would pay any attention," says Rob Warden, executive director of Northwestern University's Center for Wrongful Convictions and former editor of *Chicago Lawyer,* where seven of the first 10 wrongfully convicted Death Row prisoners in Illinois were first exposed. The Death Penalty Information Center has a library of studies—some of them nearly 10 years old—that bring up issues only recently catapulted into the public consciousness and being seriously reviewed: innocents on Death Row, prosecutorial misconduct, ineffective counsel. So why now?

More than anything else it has been the recent parade of exonerated men marching off of Death Row—13 of them in the past two years—that has triggered movement on this issue. "The issue of innocence, the presence of a number of innocent people who have been freed from Death Row and stories people have now heard—that convinced people outside of the usual opponents that there was something wrong," says Richard Dieter, executive director of the Death Penalty Information Center.

The debate over the death penalty, which in the past has focused on ethics and morality, now centers on the justice system as a whole. "I don't think that people are being morally convinced that the death penalty is wrong," Dieter says. "That's not what's changing. What's changing is a practical, fact-based concern about how the death penalty is applied. That's where the numbers are shifting." . . .

Changes in public opinion may allow politicians an opportunity to reconsider their stand. A Gallup poll taken in February registered support for the death penalty at a 19-year low; but that just means support is overwhelming, rather than nearly unanimous: 66 percent surveyed said they favored the death penalty for people convicted of murder. But recent polls are showing that similar majorities support a moratorium on executions. In a nationwide, bipartisan poll released by the Justice Project in September, 64 percent of those surveyed said that they favored suspending the death penalty until its fairness could be studied—in light of Death Row prisoners who have been released based on new evidence or DNA testing. The *San Francisco Chronicle* reported in June that 73 percent of voters surveyed in California—which has the largest Death Row in the country—are in favor of suspending executions to study the fairness of the state's capital punishment system. And even in Texas, which accounts for 33 executions so far this year (about half of the national total), a *Houston Chronicle* survey showed that 3 out of 4 respondents said the state should declare a moratorium on death sentences in cases that might be affected by DNA testing.

In a year when the Democratic Party might have anticipated a shift in public opinion on this issue, it went in the other direction and inserted a pro-death penalty plank in the formerly neutral platform. . . .

## WHAT PUSHED THE MOVEMENT FORWARD

• Dead Man Walking (May 1994). The book by Sister Helen Prejean, which was turned into a movie by director Tim Robbins in 1995, told the story of Prejean's friendship with a convicted killer on Death Row, and propelled the death penalty debate into mainstream popular culture. "We never had a way of bringing [the issue of the death penalty] close to the American public," Prejean said shortly after the release of the film. "Mostly it's been caught up in rhetoric."

• DNA and the Ford Heights Four (July 1996). The story of Death Row inmates being acquitted by science has been given big play in the media and registered strongly with the public. In one high-profile case, DNA testing exonerated four prisoners (two on Death Row) in a 1978 rape and murder case on Chicago's

Southside, and corroborated the confession of another prisoner.

By law just two states (Illinois and New York) allow post-conviction access to DNA, but that's likely to change. In a March 2000 Gallup poll, 92 percent of those surveyed said prisoners convicted before DNA tests were developed should be allowed access to them now if they might prove their innocence.

• American Bar Association calls for a moratorium on executions (February 1997). The traditionally middle-of-the-road body gives credibility to the notion that there is something wrong with the capital punishment system. The high-profile introduction of the idea of a "moratorium" (rather than abolition) offered a third option in a debate that had been deadlocked.

• Karla Faye Tucker is executed (February 1998). "Anytime a human face is put on the death penalty it changes things," says Richard Dieter, executive director of the Death Penalty Information Center. "People support the death penalty abstractly. Karla Faye Tucker was a face, a woman who really was no threat to anybody. It was a pivotal case: If the image that people have of the death penalty is Karla Faye Tucker, they're not going to be as vehement about executions as they are if the image is some faceless horror." Tucker's case was also pivotal because staunch death penalty supporters on the Christian right voiced support for clemency. Pat Robertson said the Born-Again Christian should be spared so she could continue to preach God's word to other prisoners.

• National Conference on Wrongful Convictions and the Death Penalty (November 1998). This conference at Northwestern University in Chicago brought together 30 former Death Row inmates who had been exonerated on a single stage and threw an international spotlight on wrongful convictions. The conference helped shift the debate over the death penalty away from moral rhetoric, focused media attention on systemic problems and highlighted the issue of innocence.

• Anthony Porter exonerated (February 1999). Forty-eight hours from execution, Porter was saved by the work of journalism students who had investigated his case. Porter, whose case made international headlines, was the 10th

Death Row prisoner to be exonerated since the death penalty was reinstated in Illinois.

• *Chicago Tribune* articles (November 1999). The five-part series "Failure of the Death Penalty in Illinois" charged that capital punishment in Illinois is "a system so riddled with faulty evidence, unscrupulous trial tactics and legal incompetence that justice has been forsaken." Illinois Governor George Ryan has cited the *Tribune* investigation as pivotal in deciding to impose a moratorium on executions in Illinois.

• Illinois declares moratorium on executions (January 2000). "I have grave concerns about our state's shameful record of convicting innocent people and putting them on Death Row," said Illinois Governor George Ryan, in a speech declaring a moratorium on executions. "I cannot support a system, which, in its administration, has proven to be so fraught with error and has come so close to the ultimate nightmare, the state's taking of innocent life."

• Gary Graham executed (June 2000). Most executions garner no more than a small note in the newspaper, but Gary Graham's got front-page headlines nationwide. Radio and TV stations counted down the hours to Graham's execution, drama building as the nation waited to see if George W. Bush would intervene in the 135th execution carried out in Texas under his administration. Graham (aka Shaka Sankofa) was convicted largely on the testimony of a single eyewitness, and attention to his case centered around his possible innocence. Graham had to be forcibly strapped and handcuffed to a gurney. His final words: "They are killing me tonight. They're murdering me tonight."

*Notes and Questions*

1. What have been the developments on capital punishment in your state? Have executions taken place? Has the criminal law been revised?
   What is the general approval rating by the public in your state? Does the public know enough about criminal law, or its administration for the opinions to be informed, or is the absymal state of public knowledge about the death penalty that Marshall noted still the abiding condition?

2. One teacher of criminology stopped teaching about capital punishment around the time of

the *Furman* case on the ground that it looked like all the trends were away from the use of capital punishment. He believed that talking about capital punishment was like talking about plantation slavery—a chapter of history, a past barbarity, with no contemporary importance.

Then the electric chair (or more accurately the firing squad in Utah) was reactivated, and what had become a vestigial topic took on new life, if that is the proper word. The same teacher now finds such overwhelming consensus in his classes in favor of the death penalty that capital punishment seems beyond debate. In fact, he was wondering what students can learn about a subject when "their minds are made up."

He also mentioned that it is the serial killer stories that come up immediately in class discussions as the best justification for the death penalty. Even though serial killings, however chilling, are not the main problem criminal law systems must deal with—most assaults occur in the home between people who are related or know each other— nevertheless these episodes are fueling a retributive impulse which makes the worth of the death penalty unassailable in the imagination of some.

3. On June 11, 2001, Timothy McVeigh was executed by lethal injection for his bombing of a federal building in Oklahoma City that killed 168 people. It is impossible to say what long-term impacts this highly-publicized case will have on the capital punishment debate.

᠔ For most people, professional training, the practice of law, sorcery or medicine, or the sterilization of a person determined by the state to be unfit for procreation remain abstractions. And when someone has received the death sentence we may read in a newspaper that the person "has paid his (or her) debt to society." Someone we do not know has been executed, by people we do not know and are unlikely to meet, in places we will never see. George Orwell, the famous British writer, enjoyed no such "luxury."

## 3.7 | A Hanging   *George Orwell*

IT WAS IN BURMA, a sodden morning of the rains. A sickly light, like yellow tinfoil, was slanting over the high walls into the jail yard. We were waiting outside the condemned cells, a row of sheds fronted with double bars, like small animal cages. Each cell measured about ten feet by ten and was quite bare within except for a plank bed and a pot of drinking water. In some of them brown silent men were squatting at the inner bars, with their blankets draped round them. These were the condemned men, due to be hanged within the next week or two.

One prisoner had been brought out of his cell. He was a Hindu, a puny wisp of a man, with a shaven head and vague liquid eyes. He had a thick, sprouting moustache, absurdly too big for his body, rather like the moustache of a comic man on the films. Six tall Indian warders were guarding him and getting him ready for the gallows. Two of them stood by with rifles and fixed bayonets, while the others handcuffed him, passed a chain through his handcuffs and fixed it to their belts, and lashed his arms tight to his sides. They crowded very close about him, with their hands always on him in a careful, caressing grip, as though all the while feeling him to make sure he was there. It was like men handling a fish which is still alive and may jump back into the water. But he stood quite unresisting, yielding his arms limply to the ropes, as though he hardly noticed what was happening.

Eight o'clock struck and a bugle call, desolately thin in the wet air, floated from the distant barracks. The superintendent of the jail, who was standing apart from the rest of us, moodily prodding the gravel with his stick, raised his head at the sound. He was an army doctor, with a grey toothbrush moustache and a gruff voice. "For God's sake hurry up, Francis," he said irritably. "The man ought to have been dead by this time. Aren't you ready yet?"

Francis, the head jailer, a fat Dravidian in a white drill suit and gold spectacles, waved his black hand. "Yes sir, yes sir," he bubbled. "All iss satisfactorily prepared. The hangman iss waiting. We shall proceed."

"Well, quick march, then. The prisoners can't get their breakfast till this job's over."

We set out for the gallows. Two warders marched on either side of the prisoner, with their rifles at the slope; two others marched close against him, gripping him by arm and shoulder, as though at once pushing and supporting him. The rest of us, magistrates and the like, followed behind. Suddenly, when we had gone ten yards, the procession stopped short without any order or warning. A dreadful thing had happened—a dog, come goodness knows whence, had appeared in the yard. It came bounding among us with a loud volley of barks, and leapt round us wagging its whole body, wild with glee at finding so many human beings together. It was a large woolly dog, half Airedale, half pariah. For a moment it pranced round us, and then, before anyone could stop it, it had made a dash for the prisoner, and jumping up tried to lick his face. Everyone stood aghast, too taken aback even to grab at the dog.

"Who let that bloody brute in here?" said the superintendent angrily. "Catch it, someone!"

A warder, detached from the escort, charged clumsily after the dog, but it danced and gambolled just out of his reach, taking everything as part of the game. A young Eurasian jailer picked up a handful of gravel and tried to stone the dog away, but it dodged the stones and came after us again. Its yaps echoed from the jail walls. The prisoner, in the grasp of the two warders, looked on incuriously, as though this was another formality of the hanging. It was several minutes before someone managed to catch the dog. Then we put my handkerchief through its collar and moved off once more, with the dog still straining and whimpering.

It was about forty yards to the gallows. I watched the bare brown back of the prisoner marching in front of me. He walked clumsily with his bound arms, but quite steadily, with that bobbing gait of the Indian who never straightens his knees. At each step his muscles slid neatly into place, the lock of hair on his scalp danced up and down, his feet printed themselves on the wet gravel. And once, in spite of the men who gripped him by each shoulder, he stepped slightly aside to avoid a puddle on the path.

It is curious, but till that moment I had never realized what it means to destroy a healthy, conscious man. When I saw the prisoner step aside to avoid the puddle, I saw the mystery, the unspeakable wrongness, of cutting a life short when it is in full tide. This man was not dying, he was alive just as we were alive. All the organs of his body were working—bowels digesting food, skin renewing itself, nails growing, tissues forming—all toiling away in solemn foolery. His nails would still be growing when he stood on the drop, when he was falling through the air with a tenth of a second to live. His eyes saw the yellow gravel and the grey walls, and his brain still remembered, foresaw, reasoned—reasoned even about puddles. He and we were a party of men walking together, seeing, hearing, feeling, understanding the same world; and in two minutes, with a sudden snap, one of us would be gone—one mind less, one world less.

The gallows stood in a small yard, separate from the main grounds of the prison, and overgrown with tall prickly weeds. It was a brick erection like three sides of a shed, with planking on top, and above that two beams and a crossbar with the rope dangling. The hangman, a grey-haired convict in the white uniform of the prison, was waiting beside his machine. He greeted us with a servile crouch as we entered. At a word from Francis the two warders, gripping the prisoner more closely than ever, half led, half pushed him to the gallows and helped him clumsily up the ladder. Then the hangman climbed up and fixed the rope round the prisoner's neck.

We stood waiting, five yards away. The warders had formed in a rough circle round the gallows. And then, when the noose was fixed, the prisoner began crying out to his god. It was a high, reiterated cry of "Ram! Ram! Ram! Ram!", not urgent and fearful like a prayer or a cry for help, but steady, rhythmical, almost like the tolling of a bell. The dog answered the sound with a whine. The hangman, still standing on the gallows, produced a small cotton bag like a flour bag and drew it down over the prisoner's face. But the sound, muffled by the cloth, still persisted, over and over again: "Ram! Ram! Ram! Ram! Ram!"

The hangman climbed down and stood ready, holding the lever. Minutes seemed to pass. The steady, muffled cry from the prisoner went on and on, "Ram! Ram! Ram!" never faltering for an instant. The superintendent, his head on his chest, was slowly poking the ground with his stick; perhaps he was counting the cries, allowing the prisoner a fixed number—fifty, perhaps, or a hundred. Everyone had changed colour. The Indians had gone grey like bad coffee, and one or two of the bayonets were wavering. We looked at the lashed, hooded man on the drop, and listened to his cries—each cry another second of life; the same thought was in all our minds: oh, kill him quickly, get it over, stop that abominable noise!

Suddenly the superintendent made up his mind. Throwing up his head he made a swift motion with his stick. "Chalo!" he shouted almost fiercely.

There was a clanking noise, and then dead silence. The prisoner had vanished, and the rope was twisting on itself. I let go of the dog, and it galloped immediately to the back of the gallows; but when it got there it stopped short, barked, and then retreated into a corner of the yard, where it stood among the weeds, looking timorously out at us. We went round the gallows to inspect the prisoner's body. He was dangling with his toes pointed straight downwards, very slowly revolving, as dead as a stone.

The superintendent reached out with his stick and poked the bare body; it oscillated, slightly. "*He's* all right," said the superintendent. He backed out from under the gallows, and blew out a deep breath. The moody look had gone out of his face quite suddenly. He glanced at his wrist-watch. "Eight minutes past eight. Well, that's all for this morning, thank God."

The warders unfixed bayonets and marched away. The dog, sobered and conscious of having misbehaved itself, slipped after them. We walked out of the gallows yard, past the condemned cells with their waiting prisoners, into the big central yard of the prison. The convicts, under the command of warders armed with lathis, were already receiving their breakfast. They squatted in long rows, each man holding a tin pannikin, while two warders with buckets marched round ladling out rice; it seemed quite a homely, jolly scene, after the hanging. An enormous relief had come upon us now that the job was done. One felt an impulse to sing, to break into a run, to snigger. All at once everyone began chattering gaily.

The Eurasian boy walking beside me nodded towards the way we had come, with a knowing smile: "Do you know, sir, our friend (he meant the dead man), when he heard his appeal had been dismissed, he pissed on the floor of his cell. From fright.—Kindly take one of my cigarettes, sir. Do you not admire my new silver case, sir? From the boxwallah, two rupees eight annas. Classy European style."

Several people laughed—at what, nobody seemed certain.

Francis was walking by the superintendent, talking garrulously: "Well, sir, all hass passed off with the utmost satisfactoriness. It wass all finished—flick! like that. It iss not always so—oah, no! I have known cases where the doctor wass obliged to go beneath the gallows and pull the prisoner's legs to ensure decease. Most disagreeable!"

"Wriggling about, eh? That's bad," said the superintendent.

"Ach, sir, it iss worse when they become refractory! One man, I recall, clung to the bars of hiss cage when we went to take him out. You will scarcely credit, sir, that it took six warders to dislodge him, three pulling at each leg. We reasoned with him. 'My dear fellow,' we said, 'think of all the pain and trouble you are causing to us!' But no, he would not listen! Ach, he wass very troublesome!"

I found that I was laughing quite loudly. Everyone was laughing. Even the superintendent grinned in a tolerant way. "You'd better all come out and have a drink," he said quite genially. "I've got a bottle of whisky in the car. We could do with it."

We went through the big double gates of the prison, into the road. "Pulling at his legs!" exclaimed a Burmese magistrate suddenly, and burst into a loud chuckling. We all began laughing again. At that moment Francis's anecdote seemed extraordinarily funny. We all had a drink together, native and European alike, quite amicably. The dead man was a hundred yards away.

*Notes and Questions*

1. In Chapter 2, on judging and discretion, there was some discussion of the role of intuition in decisions. Does the vivid description of an execution give rise to certain intuitions or evaluations that require no special philosophizing or gathering of pros and cons? What reactions does Orwell want to excite in his readers? Which of his images are most effective in bringing us closer to the events he wants us to understand?

2. Orwell's sense of injustice was aroused by the execution. Interview a friend regarding an episode in which your friend felt that injustice occurred. (Since injustices occur in settings other than formal legal ones or where officials of law are not involved, the episodes need not be "law related.") Compare the episode you gathered with those gathered by other students. Do common themes appear?

3. Orwell does not tell us the offense for which the prisoner was executed. He seems to reach his adverse reaction to the death penalty without needing to know more. Must the execution by the state stand on its own or should he, as a good reporter, have told us the offense, so that we might evaluate whether the killing of the man by the state was an unconscious and needless act or a necessary one?

   Compare these considerations with the claim that people who reject the death penalty fail to consider the victims of an offense.

4. How is a story unlike a legal opinion? How like it?

 Orwell was a minor official of the state, a person at the end of the line between the decision to execute a person and the execution itself. Many moral dilemmas are far from officialdom, where each person must make the connection between evaluation and action. Each person has an array of experiences that might be loosely termed precedents or moral habits. Each has a sphere of action and at least some discretion, to be exercised for better or worse. Each operates in a time, place, and circumstance and draws no consolation from the contention that nothing in general can be said about values, that they depend upon the situation.

# 4 | LAW AND CONFLICTING INTERESTS

> It is the best expedient that can be devised in any government, to secure a steady, upright, and impartial administration of the laws.
>
> *The Federalist,* No. 78

In Greek mythology, Themis is the blindfolded, impartial goddess of justice who carries scales to weigh competing contentions and a sword to enforce her decrees. This powerful metaphor was most extensively developed in the jurisprudence of Roscoe Pound (1870–1964), who observed:

> [W]e all want the earth. We all have a multiplicity of desires and demands which we seek to satisfy. There are very many of us but there is only one

earth. The desires of each continually conflict with or overlap those of his neighbors. So there is, as one might say, a great task of social engineering. There is a task of making the goods of existence, the means of satisfying the demands and desires of men living together in a politically organized society, if they cannot satisfy all the claims that men make upon them, at least go round as far as possible. This is what we mean when we say that the end of law is justice. We do not mean justice as an individual virtue. We do not mean justice as the ideal relation among men. We mean a regime. We mean such an adjustment of relations and ordering of conduct as will make the goods of existence the means of satisfying human claims to have things and do things, go round as far as possible with the least friction and waste.*

According to Pound, legal systems are designed to determine which of the competing claims to material wealth and life space are to be recognized and secured, and which are to be denied.

How does a legal system provide for the evaluation of claims? Pound suggested that the first way is pragmatic: results that have worked or are likely to work are used. He stated, "In the whole development of modern law, courts and lawmakers and law teachers, very likely with no clear theory of what they were doing but guided by a clear instinct of practical purpose, have been at work finding practical adjustments and reconcilings and, if nothing more was possible, practical compromises of conflicting and overlapping interests."† Prior dispositions of trouble provide a start, but fresh conflict may indicate inadequacies in prior solutions.

A second method of evaluation is by reference to what Pound termed jural postulates, the goals that all legal orders strive to achieve:

1. In civilized society men must be able to assume that others will commit no intentional aggressions upon them.

2. In civilized society men must be able to assume that they may control for beneficial purposes what they have discovered and appropriated to their own use, what they have created by their own labor, and what they have acquired under the existing social and economic order.

3. In civilized society men must be able to assume that those with whom they deal in the general intercourse of society will act in good faith and hence

(a) will make good reasonable expectations which their promises or other conduct reasonably create;

(b) will carry out their undertakings according to the expectations which the moral sentiments of the community attaches thereto;

(c) will restore specifically or by equivalent what comes to them by mistake or unanticipated or not fully intended situation whereby they receive at another's expense what they could not reasonably have expected to receive under the circumstances.

---

*From Roscoe Pound, *Social Control Through Law,* pp. 64–65. Copyright © 1942 by Yale University Press. Reprinted by permission of the publisher.

†Ibid., p. 111.

**FIGURE 4-A**  *Pound's Model of Conflict and the Role of Legal Systems*

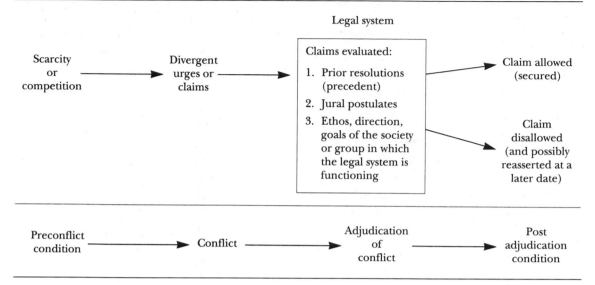

4. In civilized society men must be able to assume that those who are engaged in some course of conduct will act with due care not to cast an unreasonable risk of injury upon others.

5. In civilized society men must be able to assume that those who maintain things likely to get out of hand or to escape and do damage will restrain them or keep them within their proper bounds.[‡]

A third way that he considered is more diffuse; he suggested that a legal system reflects the overall ethos, directions, and goals of the society in which it functions. In Pound's time, American society was shifting from individualistic-agrarian values to collective, urban-industrial values, and this trend could be noted in legal outcomes. If Pound were alive today, he might be interested in the way that social pressures such as the drive for racial equality, equitable distribution of wealth, ecology, suburbanization, ruralization, and decentralization intrude on legal consciousness and determine legal results. Pound's assumptions about society and the resulting legal order are presented diagrammatically in Figure 4-A.

Pound thus provided a theory of justice (the reduction of waste); a theory of the source of conflict (scarcity); an explanation of the function of legal systems (the adjudication of competing claims and interests); a theory of change (the reassertion of previously unrecognized claims); and a theory as to the way claims are evaluated (through experience, the jural postulates, and what officials in the legal system perceive as the overall value orientations of the society in which they function).

[‡]Ibid., pp. 113–115.

❧ Roscoe Pound, who over a long career was a judge, scholar, and dean at the Harvard Law School, had an enormous influence. His understanding of how legal systems worked and the role of lawyers in them went virtually unchallenged. However, Marc Galanter's essay posed a challenge to his theories.

## 4.1 | Why the "Haves" Come Out Ahead: Speculations on the Limits of Legal Change    *Marc Galanter*

### I. A TYPOLOGY OF PARTIES

. . . Most analyses of the legal system start at the rules end and work down through institutional facilities to see what effect the rules have on the parties. I would like to reverse that procedure and look through the other end of the telescope. Let's think about the different kinds of parties and the effect these differences might have on the way the system works.

Because of differences in their size, differences in the state of the law, and differences in their resources, some of the actors in the society have many occasions to utilize the courts (in the broad sense) to make (or defend) claims; others do so only rarely. We might divide our actors into those claimants who have only occasional recourse to the courts (one-shotters or OS) and repeat players (RP) who are engaged in many similar litigations over time. The spouse in a divorce case, the auto-injury claimant, the criminal accused are OSs; the insurance company, the prosecutor, the finance company are RPs. Obviously this is an oversimplification; there are intermediate cases such as the professional criminal. So we ought to think of OS-RP as a continuum. . . . Typically, the RP is a larger unit and the stakes in any given case are smaller (relative to total worth). OSs are usually smaller units and the stakes represented by the tangible outcome of

the case may be high relative to total worth, as in the case of injury victim or the criminal accused. Or, the OS may suffer from the opposite problem: his claims may be so small and unmanageable (the shortweighted consumer or the holder of performing rights) that the cost of enforcing them outruns any promise of benefit. . . .

Let us refine our notion of the RP . . . —a unit which has had and anticipates repeated litigation, which has low stakes in the outcome of any one case, and which has the resources to pursue its long-run interests. . . .

An OS, on the other hand, is a unit whose claims are too large (relative to his size) or too small (relative to the cost of remedies) to be managed routinely and rationally.

We would expect an RP to play the litigation game differently from an OS. Let us consider some of his advantages:

1. RPs, having done it before, have advance intelligence; they are able to structure the next transaction and build a record. It is the RP who writes the form contract, requires the security deposit, and the like.

2. RPs develop expertise and have ready access to specialists. They enjoy economies of scale and have low start-up costs for any case.

3. RPs have opportunities to develop facilitative informal relations with institutional incumbents.

4. The RP must establish and maintain credibility as a combatant. His interest in his "bargaining reputation" serves as a resource to establish "commitment" to his bargaining positions. With no bargaining reputation to maintain, the OS has more difficulty in convincingly committing himself in bargaining.

"Why the 'Haves' Come Out Ahead" by Marc Galanter in *Law & Society Review,* Vol. 9, No. 1, pp. 95–151. Copyright © 1974. Reprinted by permission of the Law and Society Association.

Footnotes have been deleted and figures renumbered—Ed.

5. RPs can play the odds. The larger the matter at issue looms for OS, the more likely he is to adopt a minimax strategy (minimize the probability of maximum loss). Assuming that the stakes are relatively smaller for RPs, they can adopt strategies calculated to maximize gain over a long series of cases, even where this involves the risk of maximum loss in some cases.

6. RPs can play for rules as well as immediate gains. First, it pays an RP to expend resources in influencing the making of the relevant rules by such methods as lobbying. . . .

7. . . . Because his stakes in the immediate outcome are high and because by definition OS is unconcerned with the outcome of similar litigation in the future, OS will have little interest in that element of the outcome which might influence the disposition of the decision-maker next time around. For the RP, on the other hand, anything that will favorably influence the outcomes of future cases is a worthwhile result. The larger the stake for any player and the lower the probability of repeat play, the less likely that he will be concerned with the rules which govern future cases of the same kind. Consider two parents contesting the custody of their only child, the prizefighter vs. the IRS for tax arrears, the convict facing the death penalty. On the other hand, the player with small stakes in the present case and the prospect of a series of similar cases (the IRS, the adoption agency, the prosecutor) may be more interested in the state of the law.

Thus, if we analyze the outcomes of a case into a tangible component and a rule component, we may expect that in case 1, OS will attempt to maximize tangible gain. But if RP is interested in maximizing his tangible gain in a series of cases 1 . . . *n,* he may be willing to trade off tangible gain in any one case for rule gain (or to minimize rule loss). . . . We would then expect RPs to "settle" cases where they expected unfavorable rule outcomes. Since they expect to litigate again, RPs can select to adjudicate (or appeal) those cases which they regard as most likely to produce favorable rules. On the other hand, OSs should be willing to trade off the possibility of making "good law" for tangible gain. Thus, we would expect the body of "precedent" cases—that is, cases capable of influencing the outcome of future cases—to be relatively skewed

toward those favorable to RP. . . . The point here is merely to note the superior opportunities of the RP to trigger promising cases and prevent the triggering of unpromising ones.

8. RPs, by virtue of experience and expertise, are more likely to be able to discern which rules are likely to "penetrate" and which are likely to remain merely symbolic commitments. RPs may be able to concentrate their resources on rule-changes that are likely to make a tangible difference. They can trade off symbolic defeats for tangible gains.

9. Since penetration depends in part on the resources of the parties (knowledge, attentiveness, expert services, money), RPs are more likely to be able to invest the matching resources necessary to secure the penetration of rules favorable to them.

It is not suggested that RPs are to be equated with "haves" (in terms of power, wealth and status) or OSs with "have-nots." In the American setting most RPs are larger, richer and more powerful than are most OSs, so these categories overlap, but there are obvious exceptions. . . . OSs such as criminal defendants may be wealthy. What this analysis does is to define a position of advantage in the configuration of contending parties and indicate how those with other advantages tend to occupy this position of advantage and to have their other advantages reinforced and augmented thereby. This position of advantage is one of the ways in which a legal system formally neutral as between "haves" and "have-nots" may perpetuate and augment the advantages of the former.

We may think of litigation as typically involving various combinations of OSs and RPs. We can then construct a matrix such as Figure 1 and fill in the boxes with some well-known if only approximate American examples.

On the basis of our incomplete and unsystematic examples, let us conjecture a bit about the content of these boxes:

**Box I: OS vs. OS**   The most numerous occupants of this box are divorces and insanity hearings. Most (over 90 per cent of divorces, for example) are uncontested. A large portion of these are really pseudo-litigation, that is, a settle-

**FIGURE 1** ***A Taxonomy of Litigation by Strategic Configuration of Parties***

| *Defendant* \ *Initiator, Claimant* | ONE-SHOTTER | REPEAT PLAYER |
|---|---|---|
| ONE-SHOTTER | Parent v. Parent (Custody)<br>Spouse v. Spouse (Divorce)<br>Family v. Family Member (Insanity Commitment)<br>Family v. Family (Inheritance)<br>Neighbor v. Neighbor<br>Partner v. Partner<br>OS vs OS<br>I | Prosecutor v. Accused<br>Finance Co. v. Debtor<br>Landlord v. Tenant<br>I.R.S. v. Taxpayer<br>Condemnor v. Property Owner<br>RP vs OS<br>II |
| REPEAT PLAYER | Welfare Client v. Agency<br>Auto Dealer v. Manufacturer<br>Injury Victim v. Insurance Company<br>Tenant v. Landlord<br>Bankrupt Consumer v. Creditors<br>Defamed v. Publisher<br>OS vs RP<br>III | Union v. Company<br>Movie Distributor v. Censorship Board<br>Developer v. Suburban Municipality<br>Purchaser v. Supplier<br>Regulatory Agency v. Firms of Regulated Industry<br>RP vs RP<br>IV |

ment is worked out between the parties and ratified in the guise of adjudication. When we get real litigation in Box I, it is often between parties who have some intimate tie with one another, fighting over some unsharable good, often with overtones of "spite" and "irrationality." Courts are resorted to where an ongoing relationship is ruptured; they have little to do with the routine patterning of activity. The law is invoked *ad hoc* and instrumentally by the parties. There may be a strong interest in vindication, but neither party is likely to have much interest in the long-term state of the law (of, for instance, custody or nuisance). There are few appeals, few test cases, little expenditure of resources on rule-development. Legal doctrine is likely to remain remote from everyday practice and from popular attitudes.

**Box II: RP vs. OS** The great bulk of litigation is found in this box—indeed every really numerous kind except personal injury cases, insanity hearings, and divorces. The law is used for routine processing of claims by parties for whom the making of such claims is a regular business activity. Often the cases here take the form of stereotyped mass processing with little of the individuated attention of full-dress adjudication. Even greater numbers of cases are settled "informally" with settlement keyed to possible litigation outcome (discounted by risk, cost, delay).

The state of the law is of interest to the RP, though not to the OS defendants. . . .

**Box III: OS vs. RP** All of these are rather infrequent types except for personal injury cases which are distinctive in that free entry to the arena is provided by the contingent fee. In auto injury claims, litigation is routinized and settlement is closely geared to possible litigation outcome. Outside the personal injury area, litigation in Box III is not routine. It usually represents the attempt of some OS to invoke outside help to create leverage on an organization with which he has been having dealings but is now at the point of divorce (for example, the discharged employee or the cancelled franchisee). The OS claimant generally has little interest in the state of the law; the RP defendant, however, is greatly interested.

**Box IV: RP vs. RP**  Let us consider the general case first and then several special cases. We might expect that there would be little litigation in Box IV, because to the extent that two RPs play with each other repeatedly, the expectation of continued mutually beneficial interaction would give rise to informal bilateral controls. This seems borne out by studies of dealings among businessmen and in labor relations. Official agencies are invoked by unions trying to get established and by management trying to prevent them from getting established, more rarely in dealings between bargaining partners. Units with mutually beneficial relations do not adjust their differences in courts. Where they rely on third parties in dispute-resolution, it is likely to take a form (such as arbitration or a domestic tribunal) detached from official sanctions and applying domestic rather than official rules.

However, there are several special cases. First, there are those RPs who seek not furtherance of tangible interests, but vindication of fundamental cultural commitments. An example would be the organizations which sponsor much church-state litigation. Where RPs are contending about value differences (who is right) rather than interest conflicts (who gets what) there is less tendency to settle and less basis for developing a private system of dispute settlement.

Second, government is a special kind of RP. . . .

. . . [W]e would expect litigation by and against government to be more frequent than in other RP vs. RP situations. There is a second reason for expecting more litigation when government is a party. That is, that the notion of "gain" (policy was well as monetary) is often more contingent and problematic for governmental units than for other parties, such as businesses or organized interest groups. In some cases courts may, by proffering authoritative interpretations of public policy, redefine an agency's notion of gain. Hence government parties may be more willing to externalize decisions to the courts. And opponents may have more incentive to litigate against government in the hope of securing a shift in its goals.

A somewhat different kind of special case is present where plaintiff and defendant are both RPs but do not deal with each other repeatedly (two insurance companies, for example.) In the government/monopoly case, the parties were so inextricably bound together that the force of informal controls was limited; here they are not sufficiently bound to each other to give informal controls their bite; there is nothing to withdraw from! The large one-time deal that falls through, the marginal enterprise—these are staple sources of litigation.

Where there is litigation in the RP vs. RP situation, we might expect that there would be heavy expenditure on rule-development, many appeals, and rapid and elaborate development of the doctrinal law. . . .

On the basis of these preliminary guesses, we can sketch a general profile of litigation and the factors associated with it. The great bulk of litigation is found in Box II; much less in Box III. Most of the litigation in these Boxes is mass routine processing of disputes between parties who are strangers (not in mutually beneficial continuing relations) or divorced—and between whom there is a disparity in size. One party is a bureaucratically organized "professional" (in the sense of doing it for a living) who enjoys strategic advantages. Informal controls between the parties are tenuous or ineffective; their relationship is likely to be established and defined by official rules; in litigation, these rules are discounted by transaction costs and manipulated selectively to the advantage of the parties. On the other hand, in Boxes I and IV, we have more infrequent but more individualized litigation between parties of the same general magnitude, among whom there are or were continuing multi-stranded relationships with attendant informal controls. Litigation appears when the relationship loses its future value; when its "monopolistic" character deprives informal controls of sufficient leverage and the parties invoke outside allies to modify it; and when the parties seek to vindicate conflicting values.

## II. LAWYERS

What happens when we introduce lawyers? Parties who have lawyers do better. Lawyers are themselves RPs. Does their presence equalize the parties, dispelling the advantage of the RP client? Or does the existence of lawyers amplify the advantage of the RP client? We might assume that RPs (tending to be larger units) who can buy legal services more steadily, in larger quantities, in bulk (by retainer) and at higher rates, would get services of better quality. They would have better information (especially where restrictions on information about legal services are present). Not only would the RP get more talent to begin with, but he would on the whole get greater continuity, better record-keeping, more anticipatory or preventive work, more experience and specialized skill in pertinent areas, and more control over counsel. . . .

The more close and enduring the lawyer-client relationship, the more the primary loyalty of lawyers is to clients rather than to courts or guild, the more telling the advantages of accumulated expertise and guidance in overall strategy. . . .

What about the specialization of the bar?

Most specializations cater to the needs of particular kinds of RPs. Those specialists who service OSs have some distinctive features:

First, they tend to make up the "lower echelons" of the legal profession. Compared to the lawyers who provide services to RPs, lawyers in these specialties tend to be drawn from lower socio-economic origins, to have attended local, proprietary or part-time law schools, to practice alone rather than in large firms, and to possess low prestige within the profession. . . .

Second, specialists who service OSs tend to have problems of mobilizing a clientele. . . .

Third, the episodic and isolated nature of the relationship with particular OS clients tends to elicit a stereotyped and uncreative brand of legal services. . . . [O]bserve that:

> The quality of service rendered poorer clients is . . . affected by the non-repeating character of the matters they typically bring to lawyers (such as divorce, criminal, personal injury): this combined with the small fees encourages a mass processing of cases. As a result, only a limited amount of time and interest is usually expended on any one case—there is little or no incentive to treat it except as an isolated piece of legal business. . . .

Fourth, while they are themselves RPs, these specialists have problems in developing optimizing strategies. . . .

## III. INSTITUTIONAL FACILITIES

We see then that the strategic advantages of the RP may be augmented by advantages in the distribution of legal services. Both are related to the advantages conferred by the basic features of the institutional facilities for the handling of claims: passivity and overload.

These institutions are passive, first, in the sense that Black refers to as "reactive"—they must be mobilized by the claimant—giving advantage to the claimant with information, ability to surmount cost barriers, and skill to navigate restrictive procedural requirements. They are passive in a further sense that once in the door the burden is on each party to proceed with his case. The presiding official acts as umpire, while the development of the case, collection of evidence and presentation of proof are left to the initiative and resources of the parties. Parties are treated as if they were equally endowed with economic resources, investigative opportunities and legal skills. . . . Where, as is usually the case, they are not, the broader the delegation to the parties, the greater the advantage conferred on the wealthier, more experienced and better organized party.

The advantages conferred by institutional passivity are accentuated by the chronic overload which typically characterizes these institutions. Typically there are far more claims than there are institutional resources for full-dress adjudication of each. In several ways overload creates pressures on claimants to settle rather than to adjudicate:

(a) by causing delay (thereby discounting the value of recovery);

(b) by raising costs (of keeping the case alive);

(c) by inducing institutional incumbents to place a high value on clearing dockets, discouraging full-dress adjudication in favor of bargaining, stereotyping and routine processing;

(d) by inducing the forum to adopt restrictive rules to discourage litigation.

Thus, overload increases the cost and risk of adjudicating and shields existing rules from challenge, diminishing opportunities for rule-change. This tends to favor the beneficiaries of existing rules.

Second, by increasing the difficulty of challenging going practice, overload also benefits those who reap advantage from the neglect (or systematic violation) of rules which favor their adversaries.

Third, overload tends to protect the possessor—the party who has the money or goods—against the claimant. For the most part, this amounts to favoring RPs over OSs, since RPs typically can structure transactions to put themselves in the possessor position.

Finally, the overload situation means that there are more commitments in the formal system than there are resources to honor them—more rights and rules "on the books" than can be vindicated or enforced. There are, then, questions of priorities in the allocation of resources. We would expect judges, police, administrators and other managers of limited institutional facilities to be responsive to the more organized, attentive and influential of their constituents. Again, these tend to be RPs.

Thus, overloaded and passive institutional facilities provide the setting in which the RP advantages in strategic position and legal services can have full play.

## IV. RULES

We assume here that rules tend to favor older, culturally dominant interests. This is not meant to imply that the rules are explicitly designed to favor these interests, but rather that those groups which have become dominant have successfully articulated their operations to pre-existing rules. To the extent that rules are evenhanded or favor the "have-nots," the limited resources for their implementation will be allocated, I have argued, so as to give greater effect to those rules which protect and promote the tangible interests of organized and influential groups. Furthermore, the requirements of due process, with their barriers or protections against precipitate action, naturally tend to protect the possessor or holder against the claimant. Finally, the rules are sufficiently complex and problematic (or capable of being problematic if sufficient resources are expended to make them so) that differences in the quantity and quality of legal services will affect capacity to derive advantages from the rules.

Thus, we arrive at Figure 2 which summarizes why the "haves" tend to come out ahead. It points to layers of advantages enjoyed by different (but largely overlapping) classes of "haves"—advantages which interlock, reinforcing and shielding one another.

. . . . . . . . . . . . . . . . . . . .

## VI. STRATEGIES FOR REFORM

Our categorization of four layers of advantage (Figure 2) suggests a typology of strategies for "reform" (taken here to mean equalization—conferring relative advantage on those who did not enjoy it before). We then come to four types of equalizing reform:

(1) rule-change
(2) improvement in institutional facilities
(3) improvement of legal services in quantity and quality
(4) improvement of strategic position of have-not parties

. . . . . . . . . . . . . . . . . . . .

**A. Rule-change** Obtaining favorable rule changes is an expensive process. The various kinds of "have-nots" have fewer resources to accomplish changes through legislation or administrative policy-making. The advantages of the organized, professional, wealthy and attentive in these forums are well-known. Litigation, on the other hand, has a flavor of equality. . . .

Litigation may not, however, be a ready source of rule-change for "have-nots." Complexity, the need for high inputs of legal services and cost barriers (heightened by overloaded

---

**FIGURE 2***   *Why the "Haves" Tend to Come Out Ahead*

| Element | Advantages | Enjoyed by |
|---|---|---|
| PARTIES | —ability to structure transaction<br>—specialized expertise, economies of scale<br>—long-term strategy<br>—ability to play for rules<br>—bargaining credibility<br>—ability to invest in penetration | —repeat players large, professional |
| LEGAL SERVICES | —skill, specialization, continuity | —organized, professional, wealthy |
| INSTITUTIONAL FACILITIES | —passivity<br>—cost and delay barriers<br><br><br>—favorable priorities | —wealthy, experienced, organized<br>—holders, possessors<br><br>—beneficiaries of existing rules<br><br>—organized, attentive |
| RULES | —favorable rules<br>—due process barriers | —older, culturally dominant<br>—holders, possessors |

---

*Figure has been renumbered. —ED.

institutional facilities) make challenge of rules expensive. OS claimants, with high stakes in the tangible outcome, are unlikely to try to obtain rule changes.

**B.  Increase in Institutional Facilities**  Imagine an increase in institutional facilities for processing claims such that there is timely full-dress adjudication of every claim put forward—no queue, no delay, no stereotyping. Decrease in delay would lower costs for claimants, taking away this advantage of possessor-defendants. . . . Greater institutional "activism" might be expected to reduce advantages of party expertise and of differences in the quality and quantity of legal services. Enhanced capacity for securing compliance might be expected to reduce advantages flowing from differences in ability to invest in enforcement. It is hardly necessary to point out that such reforms could be expected to en-

counter not only resistance from the beneficiaries of the present passive institutional style, but also massive ideological opposition from legal professionals whose fundamental sense of legal propriety would be violated.

. . . . . . . . . . . . . . . . . . . . . . .

**D.  Reorganization of Parties**  The reform envisaged here is the organization of "have-not" parties (whose position approximates OS) into coherent groups that have the ability to act in a coordinated fashion, play long-run strategies, benefit from high-grade legal services, and so forth.

One can imagine various ways in which OSs might be aggregated into RPs. They include (1) the membership association-bargaining agent (trade unions, tenant unions); (2) the assignee-manager of fragmentary rights (performing rights associations like ASCAP); (3) the interest group-sponsor (NAACP, ACLU, environmental action groups). All of these forms involve upgrading capacities for managing claims by gathering and utilizing information, achieving continuity and persistence, employing expertise, exercising bargaining skill and so forth. These advantages are combined with enhancement of the OS party's strategic position either by aggregating claims that are too small relative to the cost of remedies (consumers, breathers of polluted air, owners of performing rights); or by reducing claims to manageable size by collective action to dispel or share unacceptable risks (tenants, migrant workers). . . .

An organized group is not only better able to secure favorable rule changes, in courts and elsewhere, but is better able to see that good rules are implemented. It can expend resources on surveillance, monitoring, threats, or litigation that would be uneconomic for an OS. Such new units would in effect be RPs. . . .

Our analysis suggests that breaking the interlocked advantages of the "haves" requires attention not only to the level of rules, but also to institutional facilities, legal services and organization of parties. It suggests that litigating and lobbying have to be complemented by interest organizing, provisions of services and invention of new forms of institutional facilities.

The thrust of our analysis is that changes at the level of parties are most likely to generate changes at other levels. If rules are the most abundant resource for reformers, parties capable of pursuing long-range strategies are the rarest. The presence of such parties can generate effective demand for high grade legal services—continuous, expert, and oriented to the long run—and pressure for institutional reforms and favorable rules. This suggests that we can roughly surmise the relative strategic priority of various rule-changes. Rule changes which relate directly to the strategic position of the parties by facilitating organization, increasing the supply of legal services (where these in turn provide a focus for articulating and organizing common interests) and increasing the costs of opponents—for instance authorization of class action suits, award of attorneys fees and costs, award of provisional remedies—these are the most powerful fulcrum for change. . . .

**[Lawyers]**   The contribution of the lawyer to redistributive social change, . . . depends upon the organization and culture of the legal profession. We have surmised that court-produced substantive rule-change is unlikely in itself to be a determinative element in producing tangible redistribution of benefits. The leverage provided by litigation depends on its strategic combination with inputs at other levels. The question then is whether the organization of the profession permits lawyers to develop and employ skills at these other levels. The more that lawyers view themselves exclusively as courtroom advocates, the less their willingness to undertake new tasks and form enduring alliances with clients and operate in forms other than courts, the less likely they are to serve as agents of redistributive change. Paradoxically, those legal professionals most open to accentuating the advantages of the "haves" (by allowing themselves to be "captured" by recurrent clients) may be most able to become (or have room for, more likely) agents of change, precisely because they provide more license for identification with clients and their "causes" and have a less strict definition of what are properly professional activities.

## Notes and Questions

1. Before going further, note the principal differences between Pound's and Galanter's explanations of how litigation works and its social effects.

   If you were contemplating a career in law with which explanation would you feel most comfortable?

2. In Pound's schema, courts, judges, and other legal professionals are not part of the problem, but are part of the solution to problems. Does this theory make law, the legal order, and functionaries within it look better than they really are? (Use Kafka's parables, the North Carolina cases, and the materials in Chapter 2 on judging to develop your answer.)

    ❧ The following case, drawn from the work of Laura Nader, shows the way a court in Mexico attempts to "make a balance" between contending parties.

## 4.2 The Case of the Spoiled Chiles    *Laura Nader*

ON FEBRUARY 24, 1964, in the town of Ralu'a, District of Villa Alta, State of Oaxaca [Mexico], there arrived at nine thirty before this municipal authority a Mr. Ignacio Andres Zoalage, merchant, fifty-five years of age. He explained the following: "I am coming to make a complaint about the chauffeur of the cream-colored truck that is on the platform, in the middle of which is a bruised basket of chiles weighing forty-seven and a half kilograms." The chauffeur of the cream-colored truck was called; he arrived fifteen minutes later and said that his name was Mario Valdex Herrero, chauffeur of the truck. The Court President asked him whether it was true that he had bruised the basket of chiles, and he answered: "Actually, I bruised it, but this happened because I don't have anyone to advise me. It is also the truck owner's fault because he ought to let me have a helper. Also, I could not see because the driver's compartment is high. Besides, it is the senor's fault—they put the things they have for sale on the ground, knowing that there is truck traffic."

    The Municipal Court President asked Mr. Ignacio Andres: "Why did you put your merchandise down, knowing that the truck would go by?" Mr. Andres answered that there was room for the truck to pass. The chauffeur then said that this was not true, as the space there was at an angle. Mr. Andres said: "Look, Mr. President, the truck came this way, then this way and that way." The Municipal Court President said that it would be most convenient in this case if the chauffeur paid for the damage he had caused, and that the basket of chiles should be brought in, so that an estimate could be made of how much of it had been spoiled.

    The plaintiff left and the Municipal Court President ordered the magistrate to have the

merchandise brought in. The magistrate returned with the owner, carrying a basket of chiles. They emptied it on the floor. The court magistrate observed the chiles on the floor and put aside the damaged chiles; he then told the President that the quantity ruined was about one and a half kilograms. The Municipal Court President asked the owner of the basket how much he wanted to be paid for the damage. Mr. Andres answered that it was not much—three pesos. The President told the chauffeur that he had to pay three pesos for the damage. Upon this the chauffeur said: "All right, I will go right now for the three pesos." Meanwhile the Municipal Court President reminded the plaintiff to be more careful on the next occasion and to watch where he put his booth—not to put it just anywhere and especially not in front of a truck. Thus this case was closed and the owner walked out with his load of chiles, leaving the damaged merchandise with the municipal authority.

### Notes and Questions

1. What is the function of the court in this case?

2. How can the ideas of Pound be applied here? Galanter?

3. It appears that the court has no interest in the matter beyond getting the dispute settled to the satisfaction of both of the parties. Is this always the case, or are there some cases of clear winners and clear losers? Must courts take into account interests that transcend the particular case or can they simply focus on matters at hand? Does even this case, as straightforward and simple as it sounds, become part of the borderland between truckers and merchants?

4. Do courts sometimes have interests of their own to foster; e.g., rendering consistent results, preserving respect for law, the court, and so forth? In case of a conflict between the interests of the parties, and personal or systemic interest, which should yield?

"The Case of the Spoiled Chiles" from *Law in Culture and Society,* Chicago, Aldine, 1969, p. 74. Reprinted by permission of the author.

&#10086; The *Spoiled Chiles* case suggests the involvement of a court in rudimentary balancing. In the cases that follow on the early judicial response to air pollution, richer dimensions emerge.

## 4.3 | Susquehanna Fertilizer Co. v. Malone   *20 A.900 73 Md. 268 (1890)*

ROBINSON, J.

THIS IS AN ACTION for a nuisance, and the questions to be considered are questions of more than ordinary interest and importance. At the same time, it does not seem to us that there can be any great difficulty as to the principles by which they are governed. The plaintiff is the owner of five dwelling-houses on Eighth avenue, in Canton, one of the suburbs of Baltimore city. The corner house is occupied and kept by the plaintiff as a kind of hotel or public house, and the other houses are occupied by tenants. On the adjoining lot is a large fertilizer factory, owned and operated by the defendant, from which the plaintiff alleges noxious gases escape, which not only cause great physical discomfort to himself and his tenants, but also cause material injury to the property itself. The evidence on the part of the plaintiff shows that this factory is used by the defendant for the manufacture of sulphuric acid and commercial fertilizers; that noxious gases escape therefrom, and are driven by the wind upon the premises of the plaintiff, and of his tenants; that they are so offensive and noxious as to affect the health of the plaintiff's family, and at times to oblige them to leave the table, and even to abandon the house. It further shows that these gases injure, materially, his property, discolor and injure clothing hung out to dry, slime the glass in the windows, and even corrode the tin spouting on the houses. The evidence on the part of the defendant is in direct conflict with the evidence offered by the plaintiff; but still, assuming the facts testified to by plaintiff's witnesses to be true,—and this was a question for the jury,—an actionable injury was done to the plaintiff, for which he was entitled to recover. No principle is better settled than that where a trade or business is carried on in such a manner as to interfere with the reasonable and comfortable enjoyment by another of his property, or which occasion material injury to the property itself, a wrong is done to the neighboring owner for which an action will lie; and this, too, without regard to the locality where such business is carried on; and this, too, although the business may be a lawful business, and one useful to the public, and although the best and most approved appliances and methods may be used in the conduct and management of the business. . . .

. . . As far back as *Poynton* v. *Gill*, . . . an action, it was held, would lie for melting lead so near the plaintiff's house as to cause actual injury to his property, even though the business was a lawful one, and one needful to the public, "for the defendant," say the court, "ought to carry on his business in waste places and great commons remote from enclosures so that no damage may happen to the owner of adjoining property." And the doctrine thus laid down has been, to this day, the doctrine of every case in which a similar question has arisen.

We cannot agree with the appellant that the court ought to have directed the jury to find whether the place where this factory was located was a convenient and proper place for the carrying on of the appellant's business, and whether such a use of his property was a reasonable use, and if they should so find the verdict must be for the defendant. It may be convenient to the defendant, and it may be convenient to the public, but, in the eye of the law, no place can be convenient for the carrying on of a business which is a nuisance, and which causes substantial injury to the property of another. Nor can any use of one's own land be said to be a reasonable use, which deprives an adjoining owner of the lawful use and enjoyment of his property.

. . . So we take the law to be well settled that, in actions of this kind, the question whether the place where the trade or business is carried on is a proper and convenient place for the purpose, or whether the use by the defendant of his own land is, under the circumstances, a reasonable use, are questions which ought not to be submitted to the finding of the jury. We fully agree that, in actions of this kind, the law does not regard trifling inconveniences; that everything must be looked at from a reasonable point of view; that, in determining the question of nuisance in such cases, the locality and all the surrounding circumstances should be taken into consideration; and that, where expensive works have been erected and carried on, which are useful and needful to the public, persons must not stand on extreme rights, and bring actions in respect of every trifling annoyance, otherwise, business could not be carried out in such places. But still, if the result of the trade or business thus carried on is such as to interfere with the physical comfort, by another, of his property, or such as to occasion substantial injury to the property itself, there is wrong to the neighboring owner for which an action will lie. . . .

But then it is said there was a fertilizer factory on the lot on which the appellant's works are now erected, and that this factory was used for the manufacture of sulphuric acid and fertilizers several years before the plaintiff built his house, and that the plaintiff has no right to complain, because he "came to the nuisance." But this constitutes no defense in this action. If the appellant had acquired a prescriptive right, that is to say, a user of the place for 20 years, that would present a different question. But no such right is claimed in this case; and, that being so, the appellant had no right to erect works which would be a nuisance to the adjoining land owned by the plaintiff, and thus measurably control the uses to which the plaintiff's land may in the future be subject. It could not, by the use of its own land, deprive the plaintiff of the lawful use of his property. The question of coming to a nuisance was fully considered in *Bliss* v. *Hall,* . . . where, in an action for a nuisance arising from carrying on the business of making candles, the defendant pleaded that he had carried on his business at the same place, in the same manner, and to the same extent, three years before the plaintiff became possessed of his messuage. In sustaining the demurrer to this plea, TINDAL, C. J., says: "That is no answer to the complaint in the declaration, for the plaintiff came to the house he now occupies with all the rights which the com-

mon law affords, and one of them is a right to wholesome air. Unless the defendant shows a prescriptive right to carry on his business, the plaintiff is entitled to judgment." . . .

It does not seem to us, therefore, that the defendant has any reason to complain of the several instructions granted by the court. . . . Now, as to the evidence offered in the first exception, it does not seem to us that the fact that $500,000 had been invested in other fertilizer factories in the neighborhood could have any bearing upon the issues before the jury. The defendant had already proved that there was a number of fertilizer factories in the neighborhood, and had offered evidence tending to prove that the nuisance complained of was caused by these factories. Such evidence as this was admissible and proper evidence. But the fact that $500,000 had been invested in other works in the neighborhood could not in any manner affect the plaintiff's right to recover. The only effect of such evidence, it seems to us, would be to show what loss or injury the owners of these factories might sustain if the business carried on by them should be found to be a nuisance. But that was not a question for the consideration of the jury. The law, in cases of this kind, will not undertake to balance the conveniences, or estimate the difference between the injury sustained by the plaintiff and the loss that may result to the defendant from having its trade and business, as now carried on, found to be a nuisance. No one has a right to erect works which are a nuisance to a neighboring owner, and then say he has expended large sums of money in the erection of his works, while the neighboring property is comparatively of little value. The neighboring owner is entitled to the reasonable and comfortable enjoyment of his property, and, if his rights in this respect are invaded, he is entitled to the protection of the law, let the consequences be what they may. [Plaintiff got money.—ED.]

Judgment affirmed.

## Notes and Questions

*1.* Compare this opinion with Pound's theory, pages 73–75 and with Galanter's opinion, pages 76–83. Would Pound commend the court for its decision?

# 4.4 Madison v. Ducktown Sulphur, Copper & Iron Co.

*83 S.W. 658, 13 Tenn. 331 (1904)*

NEIL, J.

THESE THREE CASES WERE instituted separately in the court below, but tried together here. They embrace, in the main, the same facts and the same questions of law, and will be disposed of in a single opinion.

The bills are all based on the ground of nuisance, in that the two companies, in the operation of their plants at and near Ducktown, in Polk county, in the course of reducing copper ore, cause large volumes of smoke to issue from their roast piles, which smoke descends upon the surrounding lands, and injures trees and crops, and renders the homes of complainants less comfortable and their lands less profitable than before. The purpose of all the bills is to enjoin the further operation of these plants; the first bill having been filed against the first-named company, the last bill against the second company, and the intermediate bill against both companies.

The following general facts are applicable to all of the cases:

Prior to 1870 one Rhat began the operation of a copper mine at Ducktown, and worked it for several years. Subsequently it was owned by the Union Consolidated Mining Company, Mr. Rhat's successor. These operations were continued until the year 1879, and were then suspended until 1891. During the latter year the Ducktown Sulphur, Copper & Iron Company commenced operating the properties formerly owned and operated by the Union Consolidated Mining Company, and has continued to operate them ever since. The Pittsburgh & Tennessee Copper Company began operations at Ducktown about the year 1881, and continued until about 1899, when it sold out to the defendant Tennessee Copper Company. The latter began its operations in 1900, and commenced roasting ores in May, 1901. It has continued its works ever since.

Ducktown is in a basin of the mountains of Polk county, in this state, not far from the state line of the states of Georgia and North Carolina. This basin is six or eight miles wide. The complainants are the owners of small farms situated in the mountains around Ducktown.

The method used by the defendants in reducing their copper ores is to place the green ore, broken up, on layers of wood, making large open-air piles, called "roast piles," and these roast piles are ignited for the purpose of expelling from the ore certain foreign matters called "sulphurets." In burning, these roast piles emit large volumes of smoke. This smoke, rising in the air, is carried off by air currents around and over adjoining land.

The lands of the complainants in the first bill, Carter, W. M. Madison and Margaret A. Madison, Verner, and Ballew, lie from two to four miles from the works. The land of Farner, complainant in the last bill, lies six or eight miles away. The distance of McGhee's land is not shown. . . .

These lands are all thin mountain lands, of little agricultural value. Carter's land consists of 80 acres, assessed at $80; Verner's, 89 acres, at $110; Ballew's, 40 acres, at $66; Madison and wife, 43 acres, at $83; W. M. Madison, about 100 acres, at $180; Isaac Farner, 100 acres, at $180. Avery McGee has 75 acres. W. M. Madison has a tract across the Georgia line, and Mrs. Madison also one of 100 acres there. The assessed value of these last three tracts does not appear. All of these lands, however, lie in the same general section of country, and we assume their value to average about the same in proportion to acreage.

All of the complainants have owned their several tracts since time anterior to the resumption of the copper industry at Ducktown in 1891. . . .

The general effect produced by the smoke upon the possessions and families of the complainants is as follows, viz.:

Their timber and crop interests have been badly injured, and they have been annoyed and discommoded by the smoke so that the complainants are prevented from using and enjoying their farms and homes as they did prior to the inauguration of these enterprises. The smoke makes it impossible for the owners of farms within the area of the smoke zone to subsist their families thereon with the degree of comfort they enjoyed before. They cannot raise and harvest their customary crops, and their timber is largely destroyed. . . .

There is no finding in either of the cases that the output of smoke by the Ducktown Sulphur, Copper & Iron Company has increased to any extent since 1891, when the business of mining and reducing copper ore was resumed at Ducktown. There is likewise no finding as to this matter in respect of the Tennessee Copper Company since it began roasting ores in May, 1901.

There is a finding that the Ducktown Sulphur, Copper & Iron Company acquired its plant in 1891, and that it has spent several hundred thousand dollars since that time in improving and enlarging the plant.

The Court of Chancery Appeals find that the defendants are conducting and have been conducting their business in a lawful way, without any purpose or desire to injure any of the complainants; that they have been and are pursuing the only known method by which these plants can be operated and their business successfully carried on; that the open-air roast heap is the only method known to the business or to science by means of which copper ore of the character mined by the defendants can be reduced; that the defendants have made every effort to get rid of the smoke and noxious vapors, one of the defendants having spent $200,000 in experiments to this end, but without result.

It is to be inferred from the description of the locality that there is no place more remote to which the operations referred to could be transferred.

It is found, in substance, that, if the injunctive relief sought be granted, the defendants will be compelled to stop operations, and their property will become practically worthless, the immense business conducted by them will cease, and they will be compelled to withdraw from the state. It is a necessary deduction from the foregoing that a great and increasing industry in the state will be destroyed, and all of the valuable copper properties of the state become worthless.

The following facts were also found, viz.:

That the total tax aggregate of Polk County for the year 1903 was $2,585,931.43, of which total the assessments of the defendants amounted to $1,279,533. It is also found that prior to the operations of these companies there lived in the district where these works are located only 200 people, whereas there are now living in this district, almost wholly dependent upon these copper industries, about 12,000 people.

It is also found that one of the defendants, the Tennessee Copper Company, employs upon its pay roll 1,300 men, and that the average pay roll is about $40,000 per month, nearly all of which employees have been drawn from the population of Polk and neighboring counties.

It is further found that one of the defendants, the Tennessee Copper Company, consumes approximately 3,000 tons of coke, 2,800 tons of coal, and 1,000 cords of wood per month, and that it purchases and uses 2,110 car loads of coal, coke, wood, etc., per annum. In the year 1901 it purchased and used approximately 1,100 car loads of cord wood, cross-ties, lumber, and quartz. It was also found that 80 percent of these supplies were purchased from, and delivered by, the citizens of Polk county. The aggregate paid out for supplies is not stated in the findings of the Court of Chancery Appeals, and cannot be here stated accurately, but certainly the amount is very large; and it seems from the figures stated that one of the defendants alone, the Tennessee Copper Company, pays out annually in wages in Polk county nearly a half million of dollars. The Court of Chancery Appeals finds that the other company employs between 1,100 and 1,200 people, and from this it may be inferred that the company pays out in wages and for supplies annually nearly as much as the Tennessee Copper Company.

It is quite apparent that the two companies pay out annually vast sums of money, which are necessarily of great benefit to the people of the county, and that they are conducting and maintaining an industry upon which a laboring population of from ten to twelve thousand people are practically dependent; and it is found, in substance, by the Court of Chancery Appeals, that, if these industries be suppressed, these thousands of people will have to wander forth to other localities to find shelter and work. . . .

We shall now state the principles which, as we conceive, should control the merits of the controversy involved in the several cases before the court:

While there can be no doubt that the facts stated make out a case of nuisance, for which the complainants in actions at law would be entitled to recover damages [money—ED.], yet the remedy in equity is not a matter of course. Not only must the bill state a proper case, but the right must be clear and the injury must be clearly established, as in doubtful cases the party will be turned over to his legal remedy; and, if there is a reasonable doubt as to the cause of the injury, the benefit of the doubt will be given to the defendant, if his trade is a lawful one, and the injury is not the necessary and natural consequence of the act; and, if the injury can be adequately compensated at law by a judgment for damages, equity will not interfere.

And the equitable remedy by injunction must be applied for with reasonable promptness. . . .

In addition to the principles already announced, the following general propositions seem to be established by the authorities: If the case made out by the pleadings and evidence show with sufficient clearness and certainty grounds for equitable relief it will not be denied because the persons proceeded against are engaged in a lawful business, *Susquehanna Fertilizer Co.* v. *Malone,* . . . or because the works complained of are located in a convenient place, if that place be one wherein an actionable injury is done to another (*Susquehanna Fertilizer Co.* v. *Malone . . .*); nor will the existence of another nuisance of a similar character at the same place furnish a ground for denying relief if it appears that the defendant has . . . contributed to the injury complained of. . . . Nor is it a question of care and skill, but purely one of results.

But there is one other principle which is of controlling influence in this department of the law, and in the light of which the foregoing principle must be weighed and applied. This is that the granting of an injunction is not a matter of absolute right, but rests in the sound discretion of the court, to be determined on a consideration of all of the special circumstances of each case, and the situation and surroundings of the parties, with a view to effect the ends of justice.

A judgment for damages in this class of case is a matter of absolute right, where injury is shown. A decree for an injunction is a matter of sound legal discretion, to be granted or withheld as that discretion shall dictate, after a full and careful consideration of every element appertaining to the injury.

These propositions will be found to be substantially confirmed and enforced in the following authorities:

In *Powell* v. *Bentley & Gerwig Furniture Co.* (W. Va.) it is said:

"Although a court of equity in such cases follows precedent and goes by rule, as far as it can, yet it follows its own rules, and among them is the one that to abate or restrain in case of nuisance is not a matter of strict right, but of orderly and reasonable discretion, according to the right of the particular case, and hence will refuse relief, and send the party to a court of law, when damages would be a fairer approximation to common justice, because to silence a useful and costly factory is often a matter of serious moment to the state and town as well as to the owner."

In *Clifton Iron Co.* v. *Dye* it is said:

"Counsel have pressed the proposition that mere convenience in the use of its property by the company does not entitle it to pour down upon the appellee's land and into the stream on his land, the debris from the washers erected by it, and we think the contention is reasonable. But it is not every case of nuisance or continuing trespass which a court of equity will restrain by injunction. In determining this question the court should weigh the injury that may accrue to the one or the other party, and also to the public, by granting or refusing the injunction.

"The court will take notice of the fact that in the development of the mineral interests of this state, recently made, very large sums of money have been invested. The utilization of these ores, which must be washed before using, necessitates in some measure the placing of sediment where it may flow into streams which constitute the natural drainage of the section where the ore banks are situated. This must cause a deposit of sediment on the lands below, and, while this invasion of the rights of the lower riparian owner may produce injury, entitling him to redress, the great public interests and benefits to flow from the conversion of these ores into pig metal should not be lost sight of. As said by the vice chancellor in *Wood* v. *Sutcliffe,* supra: "Whenever a court of equity is asked for an injunction . . . it must have regard not only to the dry, strict rights of the plaintiff and defendant, but also to the surrounding circumstances." . . .

A recent statute passed in this state (Acts 1901 . . .) gives legislative expression to the same considerations of duty and public policy. . . .

The Act referred to reads as follows:

> An Act . . . to authorize courts to determine in assessing damages for injuries to real estate, whether the nuisance complained of is a work of public utility and to give to said courts discretionary powers. . . . In all suits brought for the recovery of damages resulting from any nuisance and the finding that the matter complained of is a nuisance, the court exercising a sound discretion may immediately upon petition of plaintiff, order or decline to order the nuisance to be abated.
>
> Sec. 2. Be it further enacted, that on the trial of any action for the recovery of damages . . . either party may show by proof the extent if any of the injury or injuries complained of, and how the alleged nuisance is caused or originates. . . .

It cannot be doubted, therefore, that although the amending acts above copied purport, in terms, to apply to suits brought for the recovery of damages resulting from nuisances, the purpose was to declare the legislative will in respect of the use of the injunctive power in nuisance cases . . . the court should exercise a sound discretion, and either "order or decline to order the nuisance to be abated." . . . This act must be regarded as declaring the policy of the state upon the subject referred to. . . .

. . . [W]hat is the proper exercise of discretion, under the facts appearing in the present case? Shall the complainants be granted, in the way of damages, the full measure of relief to which their injuries entitle them, or shall we go further, and grant their request to blot out two great mining and manufacturing enterprises, destroy half of the taxable values of a county, and drive more than 10,000 people from their homes?

We think there can be no doubt as to what the true answer to this question should be.

In order to protect by injunction several small tracts of land, aggregating in the value less than $1,000, we are asked to destroy other property worth nearly $2,000,000, and wreck two great mining and manufacturing enterprises, that are engaged in work of very great importance, not only to their owners, but to the state, and to the whole country as well, to depopulate a large town, and deprive thousands of working people of their homes and livelihood, and scatter them broadcast. The result would be practically a confiscation of the property of the defendants for the benefit of the complainants—an appropriation without compensation. The defendants cannot reduce their ores in a manner different from that they are now employing, and there is no more remote place to which they can remove. The decree asked for would deprive them of all of their rights. We appreciate the argument based on the fact that the homes of the complainants who live on the small tracts of land referred to are not so comfortable and useful to their owners as they were before they were affected by the smoke complained of, and we are deeply sensible of the truth of the proposition that no man is entitled to any more rights than another on the ground that he has or owns more property than that other. But in a case of conflicting rights, where neither party can enjoy his own without in some measure restricting the liberty of the other in the use of property, the law must make the best arrangement it can between the contending parties, with a view to preserving to each one the largest measure of liberty possible under the circumstances. We see no escape from the conclusion in the present case that the only proper decree is to allow the complainants a reference for the ascertainment of damages, and that the injunction must be denied to them. . . .

### Notes and Questions

1. Compare the decision reached here with the decision in *Susquehanna.* Looking back to Llewellyn's theory of welcome and unwelcome precedent in Chapter 1, would the court in the *Ducktown* case have found the *Susquehanna* case helpful or unhelpful in reaching a pro-company result? The court

cites the *Susquehanna* case as precedent for its decision; is this a distortion of the earlier decision?

2. If the court could have used prior law to rule either for the farmers or for the smelter, what appeared to be the basis for ruling for the smelter?

3. Make an appraisal of the *Ducktown* case first using Pound, then using Galanter and then comparing the two.
   Using Galanter, what aspects of the case enabled the smelter to come out ahead?

4. How does the *Ducktown* case look from a contemporary perspective? If it looks like a long-term ecological problem could have been nipped in the bud with a decision against the company, where did the court in *Ducktown* go wrong? Is there something wrong with the way that the competing claims were evaluated?

5. In a later case, *Georgia* v. *Tennessee Copper*,* the Supreme Court ruled against the Ducktown Sulphur companies in an action brought by the state of Georgia to enjoin the pollution. Even though the damage to Georgia lands was not as consequential as the damage to the lands immediately adjacent to the factories in the Ducktown basin, Justice Oliver Wendell Holmes ruled for the state:

   > The case has been argued largely as if it were one between two private parties; but it is not. . . . This is a suit by a State for an injury to it in its capacity of "quasi-sovereign." In that capacity the State has an interest independent of and behind the titles of its citizens, in all the earth and air within its domain. It has the last word as to whether its mountains shall be stripped of their forests and its inhabitants shall breathe pure air. It might have to pay individuals before it could utter that word, but with it remains the final power. . . .
   >
   > [W]e cannot give . . . weight . . . to a comparison between the damage threatened to the plaintiff and the calamity of a possible stop to the defendants' business, the question of health, the character of the forests as a first or second growth, the commercial possibility or impossibility of reducing the fumes to sulphuric acid, the special adaptation of the business to the place.
   >
   > It is a fair and reasonable demand on the part of a sovereign that the air over its territory should not be polluted on a great scale by sulphurous acid gas, that the forests on its mountains, be they better or worse, and whatever domestic destruction they have suffered, should not be further destroyed or threatened by the act of persons beyond its control, that the crops and orchards on its hills should not be endangered from the same source. . . .
   >
   > The proof requires but a few words. It is not denied that the defendants generate in their works near the Georgia line large quantities of sulphur dioxide which becomes sulphurous acid by its mixture with the air. It hardly is denied and cannot be denied with success that this gas often is carried by the wind great distances and over great tracts of Georgia land. . . . [I]t is proper to add that we are satisfied by a preponderance of evidence that the sulphurous fumes cause and threaten damage on so considerable a scale to the forests and vegetable life, if not to health, within the plaintiff State as to make out a case. . . . Whether Georgia by insisting upon this claim is doing more harm than good to her own citizens is for her to determine.
   >
   > [T]here is no alternative to issuing an injunction, after allowing a reasonable time to the defendants to complete the structures that they now are building, and the efforts that they are making, to stop the fumes . . .

   Should Justice Holmes have done more careful balancing and regarded the state of Georgia just like any other party and not eligible for an injunction solely on the basis of its being a state? Should the state as sovereign have the last word on what is good for its citizens and not be limited by the acts of private companies?

6. In *Diamond* v. *General Motors* (20 Cal. App. 3d 374, 97 Cal. Rptr. 639, 1971), a class action was brought on behalf of all the residents of Los Angeles County against 293 corporations engaged in automobile manufacture, refining and distributing oil products, generating energy, transportation for damages, and injunctive relief for air pollution. Their suit was dismissed, and they appealed. In their brief on appeal, the plaintiffs argued,

   > This lawsuit was prompted by the steady deterioration of the air supply of Los Angeles County, and the lack of any significant response by the executive and legislative

---

*\**Georgia* v. *Tennessee Copper*, 206 U.S. 236 (1906).

branches of various levels of government. Legislative tinkering with ineffective laws, illusory, periodic bureaucratic reorganizations, and industry controlled administrators have led to drastic increases in discomfort, disease, and death. More and more, legal scholars have concluded that judicial intervention is necessary and proper.

Later they contended,

The defendants who ask this Court to defer to the legislative and executive branches of the government are the same persons who continue to corrupt the system with their lobbying, influence peddling, and campaign contributions. Defendants do not come into court with clean hands. This honorable Court is the only institution which they cannot contaminate. If there is to be a solution to this environmental tragedy, it will have to come from the judiciary.

The court upheld the dismissal, stating,

Once it is acknowledged that a superior court cannot, by decree, abolish air pollution, it is appropriate to face some demonstrable realities of the problem which plaintiff is asking the court to solve. We do not deal with a simple dispute between those who breathe the air and those who contaminate it. The need for controls is not in question. The issue is not "shall we," but "what kind, how much, how soon."

Both the United States Congress and the California Legislature have decided that the discharge of air contaminants must be controlled. Legislative enactments have provided for administrative machinery at the federal, state and local levels. These agencies conduct research, hold public hearings, and, upon the knowledge thereby acquired, set and revise the allowable limits for the discharge of the various kinds of contaminants. The statutory systems provide means for enforcement of the standards through license revocation, civil injunctions and criminal prosecution.

Plaintiff's brief makes it clear that his case is not based upon violation of any existing air

pollution control law or regulation. His position is that the present system of statutes and administrative rules is inadequate, and that the enforcement machinery is ineffective. Plaintiff is simply asking the court to do what the elected representatives of the people have not done: adopt stricter standards over the discharge of air contaminants in this country, and enforce them with the contempt power of the court.

It is indisputable that there exists, within the community, a substantial difference of opinion as to what changes in industrial processes should be required and how soon, what new technology is feasible, what reduction in the volume of goods and services should result and what increase in production costs for the sake of cleaner air will be acceptable. These issues are debated in the political arena and are being resolved by the action of those elected to serve in the legislative and executive branches of government.

We assume, for the purposes of this decision, that notwithstanding the existing administrative machinery, anyone claiming to have sustained personal injury or property damage caused by an unreasonable discharge of contaminants into the atmosphere by one or more of the defendants could state a cause of action for his damages and for injunctive relief. But the class action attempted by plaintiff, as the purported representative of every resident of the county, is a wholly different kind of suit. The objective, which plaintiff envisions to justify his class action, is judicial regulation of the processes, products and volume of business of the major industries of the county.

It was entirely reasonable for the trial court to conclude from the face of the pleading that such an undertaking was beyond its effective capability.

How does the court anticipate that the varying interests in environmental questions will be accommodated? Is this expectation reasonable? Desirable? What should the people of Los Angeles do next to eliminate pollution?

🍃 In the *Diamond* case, the action was brought in the courts of California. In the following case, the state of Ohio took the question of the pollution of Lake Erie to the top of the legal order, the United States Supreme Court, against alleged polluters. This special procedure open to states is the same as the one used in *Georgia* v. *Tennessee Copper*, discussed above.

# 4.5 | Ohio v. Wyandotte Chemicals Corp.   *401 U.S. 494 (1971)*

MR. JUSTICE HARLAN . . .

THE ACTION, FOR ABATEMENT of a nuisance, is brought on behalf of the State and its citizens, and names as defendants Wyandotte Chemicals Corp. (Wyandotte), Dow Chemical Co. (Dow America), and Dow Chemical Company of Canada, Ltd. (Dow Canada). Wyandotte is incorporated in Michigan and maintains its principal office and place of business there. Dow America is incorporated in Delaware, has its principal office and place of business in Michigan, and owns all the stock of Dow Canada. Dow Canada is incorporated, and does business, in Ontario. A majority of Dow Canada's directors are residents of the United States.

The complaint alleges that Dow Canada and Wyandotte have each dumped mercury into streams whose courses ultimately reach Lake Erie, thus contaminating and polluting that lake's waters, vegetation, fish, and wildlife, and that Dow America is jointly responsible for the acts of its foreign subsidiary. Assuming the State's ability to prove these assertions, Ohio seeks a decree: (1) declaring the introduction of mercury into Lake Erie's tributaries a public nuisance; (2) perpetually enjoining these defendants from introducing mercury into Lake Erie or its tributaries; (3) requiring defendants either to remove the mercury from Lake Erie or to pay the costs of its removal into a fund to be administered by Ohio and used only for that purpose; (4) directing defendants to pay Ohio monetary damages for the harm done to Lake Erie, its fish, wildlife, and vegetation, and the citizens and inhabitants of Ohio. . . .

## I

That we have jurisdiction seems clear enough. Beyond doubt, the complaint on its face reveals the existence of a genuine "case or controversy" between one State and citizens of another, as well as a foreign subject. . . .

. . . [M]uch would be sacrificed, and little gained, by our exercising original jurisdiction over issues bottomed on local law. This Court's paramount responsibilities to the national system lie almost without exception in the domain of federal law. As the impact on the social structure of federal common, statutory, and constitutional law has expanded, our attention has necessarily been drawn more and more to such matters. We have no claim to special competence in dealing with the numerous conflicts between States and nonresident individuals that raise no serious issues of federal law. . . .

Thus, we think it apparent that we must recognize "the need [for] the exercise of a sound discretion in order to protect this Court from an abuse of the opportunity to resort to its original jurisdiction in the enforcement by States of claims against citizens of other States." . . .

## II

[W]e believe that the wiser course is to deny Ohio's motion for leave to file its complaint. . . .

In essence, the State has charged Dow Canada and Wyandotte with the commission of acts, albeit beyond Ohio's territorial boundaries, that have produced and, it is said, continue to produce disastrous effects within Ohio's own domain. . . .

. . . History reveals that the course of this Court's prior efforts to settle disputes regarding interstate air and water pollution has been anything but smooth. The difficulties that ordinarily beset such cases are severely compounded by the particular setting in which this controversy has reached us. . . . [A] number of official bodies are already actively involved in regulating the conduct complained of here. A Michigan circuit court has enjoined Wyandotte from operating its mercury cell process without judicial authorization. The company is, moreover, currently utilizing a recycling process specifically approved by the Michigan Water Resources Commission and remains subject to the continued scrutiny of that agency. Dow Canada reports monthly to the Ontario Water Resources Commission on its compliance with the commission's order prohibiting the company from passing any mercury into the environment.

Additionally, Ohio and Michigan are both participants in the Lake Erie Enforcement Conference, convened a year ago by the Secretary of the Interior pursuant to the Federal Water Pollution Control Act. . . . The Conference is studying all forms and sources of pollution, including mercury, infecting Lake Erie. The purpose of this Conference is to provide a basis for concerted remedial action by the States or, if progress in that regard is not rapidly made, for corrective proceedings initiated by the Federal Government . . . and the International Joint Commission, . . . between the United States and Canada, . . . issued . . . a comprehensive report, the culmination of a six-year study . . . concerning the contamination of Lake Erie. That document makes specific recommendations for joint programs to abate these environmental hazards and recommends that the IJC be given authority to supervise and coordinate this effort.

In view of all this, granting Ohio's motion for leave to file would, in effect, commit this Court's resources to the task of trying to settle a small piece of a much larger problem that many competent adjudicatory and conciliatory bodies are actively grappling with on a more practical basis.

The nature of the case Ohio brings here is equally disconcerting. It can fairly be said that what is in dispute is not so much the law as the facts. And the fact finding process we are asked to undertake is, to say the least, formidable. We already know . . . that Lake Erie suffers from several sources of pollution other than mercury; that the scientific conclusion that mercury is a serious water pollutant is a novel one; that whether and to what extent the existence of mercury in natural waters can safely or reasonably be tolerated is a question for which there is presently no firm answer: and that virtually no published research is available describing how one might extract mercury that is in fact contaminating water. Indeed, Ohio is raising factual questions that are essentially ones of first impression to the scientists. The notion that appellate judges . . . might appropriately undertake at this time to unravel these complexities is, to say the least, unrealistic. . . . Other factual complexities abound. For example, the Department of the Interior has stated that eight American companies are discharging, or have discharged, mercury into Lake Erie or its tributaries. We would, then, need to assess the business practices and relative culpability of each to frame appropriate relief as to the one now before us.

. . . Thus, entertaining this complaint not only would fail to serve those responsibilities we are principally charged with, but could well pave the way for putting this Court into a quandary whereby we must opt either to pick and choose arbitrarily among similarly situated litigants or to devote truly enormous portions of our energies to such matters. . . .

## III

What has been said here cannot, of course, be taken as denigrating in the slightest the public importance of the underlying problem Ohio would have us tackle. Reversing the increasing contamination of our environment is manifestly a matter of fundamental import and utmost urgency. What is dealt with above are only considerations respecting the appropriate role this Court can assume in efforts to eradicate such environmental blights. We mean only to suggest that our competence is necessarily limited. . . .

Motion denied.

MR. JUSTICE DOUGLAS, *dissenting.*

The complaint in this case presents basically a classic type of case congenial to our original jurisdiction. It is to abate a public nuisance. Such was the claim of Georgia against a Tennessee company which was discharging noxious gas across the border into Georgia. *Georgia* v. *Tennessee Copper Co.* . . . [t]he Court said:

> It is a fair and reasonable demand on the part of a sovereign that the air over its territory should not be polluted on a great scale by sulphurous acid gas, that the forests on its mountains, be they better or worse, and whatever domestic destruction they have suffered, should not be further destroyed or threatened by the act of persons beyond its control, that the crops and orchards on its hills should not be endangered from the same source. . . .

Dumping of sewage in an interstate stream, *Missouri* v. *Illinois,* . . . or towing garbage to sea only to have the tides carry it to a State's beaches, *New Jersey* v. *New York City,* . . . have presented analogous situations which the Court has entertained in suits invoking our original jurisdiction. The pollution of Lake Erie or its tributaries by the discharge of mercury or compounds thereof, if proved, certainly creates a public nuisance of a seriousness and magnitude which a State by our historic standards may prosecute. . . .

The suit is not precluded by the Boundary Waters Treaty of 1909. . . . [It] does not evince a purpose on the part of the national governments of the United States and Canada to exclude their States and Provinces from seeking other remedies for water pollution. Indeed, Congress in later addressing itself to water pollution in the Federal Water Pollution Control Act, . . . said in 1(c):

> Nothing in this chapter shall be construed as impairing or in any manner affecting any right or jurisdiction of the States with respect to the waters (*including boundary waters*) of such States. (Emphasis added.)

This litigation, as it unfolds, will, of course, implicate much federal law. The case will deal with an important portion of the federal domain—the navigable streams and the navigable inland waters which are under the sovereignty of the Federal Government. It has been clear since Pollard's *Lessee* v. *Hagan,* . . . decided in 1845, that navigable waters were subject to federal control. . . .

Congress has enacted numerous laws reaching that domain. One of the most pervasive is the Rivers and Harbors Act of 1899, . . . which forbids discharge of "any refuse matter of any kind or description whatever other than that flowing from streets and sewers and passing therefrom in a liquid state" as including particles in suspension. . . .

In the 1930's fish and wildlife legislation was enacted granting the Secretary of the Interior various heads of jurisdiction over the effects on fish and wildlife of "domestic sewage, mine, petroleum, and industrial wastes, erosion silt, and other polluting substances." . . .

The Federal Water Pollution Control Act, . . . gives broad powers to the Secretary to take action respecting water pollution on complaints of States, and other procedures to secure federal abatement of the pollution. . . . The National Environmental Policy Act of 1969, . . . gives elaborate ecological directions to federal agencies and supplies procedures for their enforcement.

On December 23, 1970, the President issued an Executive Order which correlates the duties of the Corps of Engineers and the Administrator of the new Environmental Protection Agency under the foregoing statutes. . . .

Yet the federal scheme is not preemptive of state action. Section 1(b) of the Water Pollution Control Act declares that the policy of Congress is "to recognize, preserve, and protect the primary responsibilities and rights of the States in preventing and controlling water pollution." . . .

The new Environmental Quality Improvement Act of 1970, . . . while stating the general policy of Congress in protecting the environment, also states: "The primary responsibility for implementing this policy rests with State and local governments." . . .

There is much complaint that in spite of the arsenal of federal power little is being done. That, of course, is not our problem. But it is our concern that state action is not pre-empted by federal law. Under existing federal law, the States do indeed have primary responsibility for setting water quality standards; the federal agency only sets water quality standards for a State if the State defaults. . . .

There is not a word in federal law that bars state action. . . .

Much is made of the burdens and perplexities of these original actions. Some are complex, notably those involving water rights. The drainage of Lake Michigan with the attendant lowering of water levels, affecting Canadian as well as United States interests, came to us in an original suit. . . .

The apportionment of the waters of the Colorado between Arizona and California was a massive undertaking entailing a searching analysis. . . .

The apportionment of the waters of the North Platte River among Colorado, Wyoming, and Nebraska came to us in an original action. . . .

But the practice has been to appoint a Special Master which we certainly would do in this case. We could also appoint—or authorize the Special Master to retain—a panel of scientific advisers. The problems in this case are simple compared with those in the water cases discussed above. It is now known that metallic mercury deposited in water is often transformed into a dangerous chemical. This lawsuit would determine primarily the extent, if any, to which the defendants are contributing to that contamination at the present time. . . .

The problem, though clothed in chemical secrecies, can be exposed by the experts. It would indeed be one of the simplest problems yet posed in the category of cases under the head of our original jurisdiction.

The Department of Justice in a detailed brief tells us there are no barriers in federal law to our assumption of jurisdiction. I can think of no case of more transcending public importance than this one.

## Notes and Questions

1. The U.S. Supreme Court said a number of things to the state of Ohio: that the Court has other and more important business to attend to, and cannot undertake fact finding and the determination of remedies; that the companies have already come under the scrutiny of the states of Michigan and Ohio and the province of Ontario, and that the Court's taking the case would deal with only one dimension of a larger problem; and finally, that whatever relief Ohio needs can be secured through its own court system rather than by a special proceeding in the United States Supreme Court.

    Compare these contentions with those of the dissent. Also compare the reasoning of the Court in the *Wyandotte* case with the reasoning of the *Diamond* case that appears in the notes preceding the *Wyandotte* case.

    Has the Supreme Court adequately weighed the competing interests and minimized friction and waste, which Pound observed to be the central functions of law in adjudicating controversies?

2. The *Diamond* and *Wyandotte* cases demonstrate that as a pollution problem becomes more intense and affects wider geographical areas the elimination of the problem through court, legislative, or administrative action becomes *more,* and not less, difficult. If solutions are sought locally through court action, as was the case in *Diamond,* the inclination may be to buck the problem to political or administrative agencies. If relief is sought at the top of the judicial system, as was the case in *Wyandotte,* the question may be referred to either lower courts or political authorities, sometimes international in their scope.

If there are to be independent "efforts" at all levels and in all branches of government or through international consortia of nations, might it mean that *everyone*'s being able to act will mean that *no one* will act in fact, that the pollution question will be confounded and left unresolved because of competing power structures and policies?

If that happens, could it be that the only constants across all the activity are the passage of time and the persistence of pollution?

3. Walter Rosenbaum* counted several hundred environmental statutes administered by the EPA and a number of other agencies, such as the Occupational Safety and Health Administration (OSHA) and the Department of the Interior. These agencies have different personnel, budgets, and philosophies of enforcement. In Congress there were the same divided and subdivided responsibilities; in the House and Senate, committees and subcommittees with at least a piece of the environmental agenda numbered over one hundred.

4. Environmental litigation has continued to be a fertile ground for complexities and delays, both of which contribute to the persistence and growth of pollution. Asked over and over again are questions such as these: What parties can bring suit? Against whom? In what courts? According to what law? With what remedies?

    For example, in a 1987 case arising over the pollution of Lake Champlain, suit was brought against the International Paper Company by Vermont landowners in the Vermont state courts under the common law of nuisance of Vermont.† The remedies sought were compensatory damages of $20,000,000, punitive damages of $100,000,000, and injunctive relief. The company operated on the New York side of the lake with its diffusion pipe emptying just before the boundary on the lake between New York and Vermont.

    The company first moved that the case be transferred to the federal district court that sits for Vermont. Once in the federal court, the company moved to dismiss on the ground that common-law remedies such as damages and injunctions had been preempted (displaced)

---

*W. Rosenbaum, "Environmental Politics and Policy" (Washington: Cong. Qtly Pr., 1991) 17, 18; pp. 82–96.

†*International Paper Co.* v. *Ouelette,* 479 U.S. 481 (1987).

by national law (The Clean Water Act) and were no longer available.

It was over these procedural questions and not the merits of the claims that the case moved up through the federal court system to the U.S. Supreme Court. The Supreme Court had to decide whether there was any state law left after the passage of the federal Clean Water Act, and if so, was the law that was left intact the law of Vermont (affected state), or the law of New York (source state), or both. The Supreme Court ruled that the federal law did not totally preempt the state law remedies on pollution, but that the law of the *source* state rather than the law of the *affected* state should be applied (to eliminate confusion).

When the case was sent back it was settled for $5,000,000 and an elaborate formula for sharing the judgment was worked out by the plaintiff's attorney, Peter Langrock of Middlebury, Vermont. Langrock, by telephone conversation, said that he "must have done 40 drafts" of the settlement agreement, finely tuning the amounts to which each person was entitled (for example, some of the claimants were closer to the pollution than others; some had purchased their property with knowledge of the pollution and had presumably paid less than they would have, had the property been pristine; the property owners affected by the pollution received an average of about 25 percent of the value of their property).

Langrock's work on the case had spanned two decades and involved two trips to the U.S. Supreme Court. (He also said that his clients turned out to be better off under New York law than they would have been under Vermont law, an ironic twist of fate, since he had argued for the application of Vermont law in the Supreme Court!)

5. In this chapter we have sampled some of the ways by which pollution cases have reached the court system: suits by one landowner against polluters for damage to property (*Susquehanna, Ducktown, International Paper*); suits brought by states against polluters for injunctions and the expenses of cleanup (*Tennessee Copper, Wyandotte Chemical*); and suits by citizens against hundreds of corporations, in which the cumulative effect of the corporate behavior was manifest, but the particular source of the pollution was not (*Diamond* v. *General Motors*).

Lawsuits can also be brought against polluters for deaths and injuries caused by pollution. One such case, *Anderson* v. *W. R. Grace and Company,* has been made famous by a book, *A Civil Action,*[‡] which chronicles many of the twists and turns of the case during the period of almost a decade over which it was fought. This best-selling book, written from the standpoint of Jan Schlichtmann, the attorney who represented the Woburn, Massachusetts claimants, is both an indispensable guide to the difficulties in establishing the causal connection between polluting acts and their consequences, and a compendium of the procedural intricacies that can be fully exploited by corporate defendants with virtually unlimited war chests to fight a case. The use and abuse of legal technicalities in such cases dwarfs their use in the criminal context, where they are commonly thought to thrive.

The story line of the Woburn cases was straightforward, but not without imponderables. There had been a high incidence of leukemia and other serious diseases in certain sections of the town. The affected families had all drunk water from town wells that drew on an aquifer near the defendant companies. The defendant companies had both used toxic chemicals in their businesses, one in tanning leather, the other as a cleaning agent. If the chemicals got into the water supply they could have dangerous health effects, but the precise effects and the amount of chemicals necessary to produce them was not fully understood when the cases began.

In the *Wyandotte* case on the pollution of Lake Erie, the causation of pollution and the effects of pollution were contested. In the *Woburn* case, the causal relationships were even more difficult to establish. The plaintiffs had to prove that chemicals from the companies had polluted the aquifer, entered the wells, entered the households, and affected the health of the families bringing the action. Every one of the elements called for the careful development of proof, a very expensive process involving experts in the areas of toxicology, hydrology, and medicine. On every point there were rival experts. The connection between the chemicals from the companies and the etiology of leukemia and a number of neurological, genetic, and respiratory diseases was at the edge of medical understanding.

---

[‡]Jonathan Harr, *A Civil Action* (New York: Random House, 1995).

Here were the makings for a very long case, with numerous delays and enormous expense.

Jan Schlichtmann, caught in the quagmire of the case, realized that he could be driven crazy if he continued the fight, but that he could also be driven crazy if he stopped fighting; Schlichtmann might pick the form of insanity, but he could not avoid insanity altogether. His resolution of the dilemma would be spoiled if it were told here. (See *A Civil Action,* which should be required reading for any student who wishes to understand the legal system and the use of wrongful death and injury actions to remedy environmental pollution.)

 Cases like *Ohio* v. *Wyandotte, International Paper Company* v. *Ouelette,* and *Anderson* v. *W. R. Grace and Company* give rise to a troubling conclusion: it may not be so important what the law of pollution says, based on either federal or state sources, but more important to consider the strategic position of the defendants and their ability relative to that of their opponents to sustain the burden of litigation: that is, to secure expensive lawyers for long periods of time, move cases around among the possible courts, argue about what law applies, create delays and complexities, impose costs, and otherwise tie courts and opponents into knots.

Where opponents have not been dismayed by preliminaries and are still on their legal feet, there remains the trial or successive trials of the cases and the expenses of gathering evidence, scientific and otherwise, all within a limited litigation budget. Then there are the rounds of appeal which, if allowed, can start a case all over again, with fresh burdens of litigation. If, as in the *Ouelette* case, it takes two decades of litigation and expense to get $5,000,000 from a polluting corporation, who has won? Has the polluter lost? In the case of *Anderson,* how much tenacity and resources are required to get justice?

# 5    LAW, STATUS, WEALTH, AND POWER

When leaving his surgery on the morning of April 16 Dr. Bernard Rieux felt something soft under his foot. It was a dead rat lying in the middle of the landing. On the spur of the moment he kicked it to one side and without giving it further thought, continued on his way downstairs. Only when he stepped forth into the street did it occur to him that a dead rat had no business to be on his landing.

Albert Camus, *The Plague*

The preservation of power is a vital necessity for the powerful, since it is their power which provides their sustenance; but they have to preserve it both against their rivals and against their inferiors, and these latter cannot do otherwise than try to rid themselves of dangerous masters; for, through a vicious circle, the master produces fear in the slave by the very fact that he is afraid of him, and vice versa; and the same is true as between rival powers.

Simone Weil, *Oppression and Liberty* (1973)

If you're strong, you don't have to say thank you.

Fenna Lee Bonsignore, at age 4

ॐ Max Weber, German lawyer and sociologist, defined law as coercive order, an order that has the potential backing of the full force of the state. He thus distinguished law from other norms such as custom, ethics, and religion, which have different sanctions like the cold shoulder, internal guilt, or the threat of eternal damnation. Elsewhere, he observed that a society has two basic ways of providing rewards to its membership—honor (status) and economic return (wealth, class). A troublesome question arises when law and social rewards are considered together: Is the legal system used to perpetuate prevailing patterns in the allocation of status and wealth? And of power?

These are unpleasant questions in U.S. law, since our society is said to be classless and each citizen is deemed equal before the law. Notable jurists like Holmes, Llewellyn, Frank, and Pound rarely developed the power dimension in law, perhaps because it is almost unthinkable that law and legal process may do no more than reinforce social and economic positionings; it is more comfortable to think of law as impartial, administered with just the right amount of discretionary flexibility, or as a balancing process, than as a power play to accomplish the wishes of a few well-placed elites.

And yet a number of concrete instances can be explained in no other way. Certain rules of law inhibit the raising of large questions that cut to the quick of the social, political, and economic order. Disputes involving housing, welfare, employment, and other areas that have wide impact are channeled into discrete confines so that contesting parties do not see themselves as representatives of a large group of persons who have a similar interest in redressing parallel grievances concerning control of property or the allocation of power.

Beyond the dampening of threats to the status quo by rules that inhibit legal action, the powerful spend large sums of money and energy to keep the law favorable through legislation. Most notable is the growth of PACs [political action committees] and other forms of influence peddling at the state and national levels either to head off unwanted laws or to get favorable legislation passed, but also significant are the resources devoted to win contested cases that threaten the status quo. (See the cases in Chapter 4). Most of the law of contract and property has been shaped to perpetuate existing power and property relationships. Not surprisingly, fine print, which is almost always inimical to the interests of the poor and low-income wage earners—to say nothing of people in small businesses or the general public—becomes the currency of the powerful. It is the powerful who furnish the documentation for most transactions, and it is they who benefit from the documents. Insurance policies, promissory notes, mortgages, conditional sales contracts, leases, and other papers that people are expected to sign are as often instruments of domination as they are evidence of an evenly bargained deal. Courts typically do not look behind the documentation to discover the economic realities of a transaction.

Legislation can have highly stratified effects, that is, the benefits and burdens of the legislation may not be distributed across the entire population, but instead pile up in one stratum or group. The ability of corporations to move revenues and costs around in worldwide production and marketing networks benefits those few who are at or near the control centers of major multinational corporations, while producing gigantic leaks in tax collection that must be made up by ordinary taxpayers. Case law and legislation that allows corporations to freely move capital from place to place benefit those who do the moving but not workers who are displaced by those decisions or the communities where production once took place.

Other examples of the differential impacts of law can readily be found. For decades, it has been known that laws "regulating" corporations have been shaped to meet managerial and financial interests rather than the needs of the ordinary shareholder or the public generally. Taxation, which is theoretically progressive in nature and should over time be a force for greater equality in income and wealth, has tended in exactly the opposite direction, leading one writer to characterize the preferential treatment of the rich as a "great Treasury raid" (perhaps the wrong metaphor, since the money never made it to the U.S. Treasury). Inequalities in the sharing of income and wealth have grown since the mid 1970s rather than narrowed.

Administrative agencies covering activities like public utilities, communication, transportation, and other vital services are often as much directed by the businesses to be controlled as by public officials acting independently. A single group of people may circulate between businesses and the government agencies charged with the regulation of the very same businesses from which the "public" officials are recruited.

Criminal law and enforcement has always been a highly visible demonstration of the importance of wealth, status, and power in affecting legal outcomes. Gentlemanly offenses like business tax evasion, insider trading of corporate securities, defense contract fraud, robbing banks from the inside without guns (as in the savings and loan cases), antitrust violations, and embezzlement have often been treated differently from poor people's offenses such as theft, burglary, and purse snatching. It is expected that discretion will be exercised by police and prosecutors so that people who are not "real criminals" will be saved from the opprobrium that accompanies arrest, the criminal process, and jail or prison. Watergate, which led to criminal convictions of many high officials of the Nixon administration, was an unusual and distinctly small exception to the rule of preferential treatment. And even after Watergate, President Nixon was given a handsome pension and a personal staff at government expense. Like other Watergate "ex-cons" who returned to the public eye after serving token sentences, Nixon published his memoirs, engaged in television interviews, was consulted, and in the end received a heroic funeral as if he had never needed a presidential pardon to be saved from criminal prosecution.

After a relatively scandal-free Carter administration, the Reagan administration added numerous cases of corruption and illegality in high places. These included perjury to congressional committees investigating the Environmental Protection Agency; conflicts of interest and influence peddling by former White House assistants; and violations of congressional prohibitions on aid to the Contras in Honduras and Nicaragua (via arms sales to Iran, numbered Swiss bank accounts, and even allowing the Contras to fund their army with drug trafficking proceeds).* Some were asked to resign from office and others were convicted. President Bill Clinton barely escaped impeachment.

The net effect of these cases looked to some observers like differential treatment according to the social class and political connections of the offenders. In the almost thirty years since Watergate, scandals in Washington have become so common that the line between legality and illegality, propriety and impropriety has been obliterated. Many people, upon hearing news of what in former times might have produced outrage, simply shrug their shoulders as if to say, "What do you expect?"

---

&◆ It was Karl Marx who sensitized the world to the intimate connection between economic power and political and legal power. He concluded that once it was discovered who controlled property and the means of production, the controllers of political and legal order could readily be found as well. New means of production, later termed the Industrial Revolution, obliterated craft methods, and moved populations from farm to factory. If to many contemporaries Marxism is a series of general slogans, the readers of *Das Capital* will find a detailed investigation into the day-to-day workings of the British factory system and its impact on workforces. Hours and wages were Marx's principal focus, but he also documented the impact of overworking and of poor working environments on the health of workers. In fact, he might have been among the first to introduce the idea of occupational diseases. Workers were being asked to contribute their lungs and part of their life expectancies to their employers.

A 1981 Supreme Court case on "brown lung," a disease caused by the inhalation of dust in cotton mills, suggests the contemporary relevance of Marx's finding that manufacturing processes can destroy workforces.

---

*Peter D. Scott and Jonathan Marshall, *Cocaine Politics: Drugs, Armies, and the CIA in Central America* (Berkeley: University of California Press, 1991).

## 5.1 | Das Capital, "The Working Day"    *Karl Marx*

The potteries of Staffordshire have, during the last 22 years, been the subject of three parliamentary inquiries. The result is embodied in Mr. Scriven's report of 1841 to the Children's Employment Commissioners, in the report of Dr. Greenhow of 1860, published by order of the medical officer of the Privy Council . . . ; lastly, in the report of Mr. Longe of 1862 . . . For my purpose it is enough to take from the reports of 1860 and 1863 some depositions of the exploited children themselves. From the children we may form an opinion as to the adults, especially the girls and women, and that in a branch of industry by the side of which cotton spinning appears an agreeable and healthful occupation.

William Wood, 9 years old, was 7 years and 10 months when he began to work. He "ran moulds" (carried ready-moulded articles into the drying room, afterwards bringing back the empty mould) from the beginning. He came to work every day in the week at 6 A.M., and left off about 9 P.M. "I work till 9 o'clock at night six days in the week. I have done so seven or eight weeks." Fifteen hours of labor for a child 7 years old! J. Murray, 12 years of age, says: "I turn jigger, and run moulds. I come at 6. Sometimes I come at 4. I worked all night last night, till 6 o'clock this morning. I have not been in bed since the night before last. There were eight or nine other boys working last night. All but one have come this morning. I get 3 shillings and sixpence. I do not get any more for working at night. I worked two nights last week." Fernyhough, a boy of ten: "I have not always an hour (for dinner). I have only half an hour sometimes; on Thursday, Friday, and Saturday."

Dr. Greenhow states that the average duration of life in the pottery districts of Stoke-on-Trent and Wolstanton is extraordinarily short. Although in the district of Stoke, only 36.6%, and in Wolstanton only 30.4%, of the adult male population above 20 are employed in the potteries, among the men of that age in the first district more than half, in the second, nearly two-fifths of the deaths are the result of pulmonary diseases among the potters. . . .

From the report of the Commissioners in 1863, the following: Dr. J. T. Arledge, senior physician of the North Staffordshire Infirmary, says: "The potters as a class, both men and women, represent a degenerated population, both physically and morally. They are, as a rule, stunted in growth, ill-shaped, and frequently ill-formed in the chest; they become prematurely old, and are certainly short-lived; they are phlegmatic and bloodless, and exhibit their debility of constitution by obstinate attacks of dyspepsia, and disorders of the liver and kidneys, and by rheumatism. But of all diseases they are especially prone to chest disease, to pneumonia, phthisis, bronchitis, and asthma. One form would appear peculiar to them, and is known as potter's asthma, or potter's consumption. Scrofula attacking the glands, or bones, or other parts of the body, is a disease of two-thirds or more of the potters. . . . That the "degenerescence" of the population of this district is not even greater than it is, is due to the constant recruiting from the adjacent country, and intermarriages with more healthy races."

From *Das Capital*, "The Working Day," Chicago: Great Books, Vol. 50, p. 118.

Footnotes have been omitted.—ED.

# 5.2 | American Textile Mfrs. Inst. v. Donovan   *452 U.S. 490 (1981)*

JUSTICE BRENNAN . . .

Congress enacted the Occupational Safety and Health Act of 1970 (Act) "to assure so far as possible every working man and woman in the Nation safe and healthful working conditions. . . ." The Act authorizes the Secretary of Labor to establish, after notice and opportunity to comment, mandatory nationwide standards governing health and safety in the workplace. . . . In 1978, the Secretary, acting through the Occupational Safety and Health Administration (OSHA), promulgated a standard limiting occupational exposure to cotton dust, an airborne particle byproduct of the preparation and manufacture of cotton products, exposure to which induces a "constellation of respiratory effects" known as "byssinosis." . . .

Petitioners[1] . . . contend in this Court, as they did below, that the Act requires OSHA to demonstrate that its Standard reflects a reasonable relationship between the costs and benefits associated with the Standard. Respondents, the Secretary of Labor and two labor organizations,[2] counter that Congress balanced the costs and benefits in the Act itself, and that the Act should therefore be construed not to require OSHA to do so. They interpret the Act as mandating that OSHA enact the most protective standard possible to eliminate a significant risk of material health impairment, subject to the constraints of economic and technological feasibility. The Court of Appeals held that the Act did not require OSHA to compare costs and benefits. . . .

## I

Byssinosis, known in its more severe manifestations as "brown lung" disease, is a serious and potentially disabling respiratory disease primarily caused by the inhalation of cotton dust.[3] . . . Byssinosis is a "continuum . . . disease," . . . that has been categorized into four grades.[4] In its least serious form, byssinosis produces both subjective symptoms, such as chest tightness, shortness of breath, coughing, and wheezing, and objective indications of loss of pulmonary functions. . . . In its most serious form, byssinosis is a chronic and irreversible obstructive pulmonary disease, clinically similar to chronic bronchitis or emphysema, and can be severely disabling. . . . At worst, as is true of other respiratory diseases including bronchitis, emphysema, and asthma, byssinosis can create an additional strain on cardiovascular functions and can contribute to death from heart failure. . . . ("there is an association between mortality and the extent of dust exposure"). One authority has described the increasing seriousness of byssinosis as follows:

---

Some footnotes have been omitted; others have been renumbered.—ED.

[1]Petitioners in No. 79–1429 include 12 individual cotton textile manufacturers and the American Textile Manufacturers Institute, Inc. (ATMI), a trade association representing approximately 175 companies. . . . In No. 79–1583, petitioner is the National Cotton Council of America, a nonprofit corporation chartered for the purpose of increasing the consumption of cotton and cotton products. . . .

[2]The two labor organizations are the American Federation of Labor and Congress of Industrial Organizations, Industrial Union Department, AFL–CIO, and the Amalgamated Clothing & Textile Workers Union, AFL–CIO. In the Court of Appeals, the labor organizations challenged the Cotton Dust Standard as not sufficiently stringent.

[3]Cotton dust is defined as "dust present in the air during the handling or processing of cotton, which may contain a mixture of many substances including ground up plant matter, fiber, bacteria, fungi, soil, pesticides, non-cotton plant matter and other contaminants which may have accumulated with the cotton during the growing, harvesting and subsequent processing or storage periods. Any dust present during the handling and processing of cotton through the weaving or knitting of fabrics, and dust present in other operations or manufacturing processes using new or waste cotton fibers or cotton fiber by-products from textile mills are considered cotton dust." . . .

[4]Known generally as the Schilling classification grades, they include: "[Grade] ½: slight acute effect of dust on ventilatory capacity; no evidence of chronic ventilatory impairment." "[Grade] 1: definite acute effect of dust on ventilatory capacity; no evidence of chronic ventilatory impairment." "[Grade] 2: evidence of slight to moderate irreversible impairment of ventilatory capacity." "[Grade] 3: evidence of moderate to severe irreversible impairment of ventilatory capacity." . . .

"In the first few years of exposure [to cotton dust], symptoms occur on Monday, or other days after absence from the work environment; later, symptoms occur on other days of the week; and eventually, symptoms are continuous, even in the absence of dust exposure." . . .[5]

While there is some uncertainty over the manner in which the disease progresses from its least serious to its disabling grades, it is likely that prolonged exposure contributes to the progression. . . . It also appears that a worker may suddenly contract a severe grade without experiencing milder grades of the disease. . . .

Estimates indicate that at least 35,000 employed and retired cotton mill workers, or 1 in

---

[5]Descriptions of the disease by individual mill workers, presented in hearings on the Cotton Dust Standard before an Administrative Law Judge, are more vivid:

"When they started speeding the looms up the dust got finer and more and more people started leaving the mill with breathing problems. My mother had to leave the mill in the early fifties. Before she left, her breathing got so short she just couldn't hold out to work. My stepfather left the mill on account of breaching [*sic*] problems. He had coughing spells til he couldn't breath [*sic*], like a child's whooping cough. Both my sisters who work in the mill have breathing problems. My husband had to give up his job when he was only fifty-four years old because of the breathing problem." . . .

"I suppose I had a breathing problem since 1973. I just kept on getting sick and began losing time at the mill. Every time that I go into the mill I get deathly sick, choking and vomiting losing my breath. It would blow down all that lint and cotton and I have clothes right here where I have wore and they have been washed several times and I would like for you all to see them. That will not come out in washing.

"I am only fifty-seven years old and I am retired and I can't even get to go to church because of my breathing. I get short of breath just walking around the house or dressing [or] sometimes just watching T.V. I cough all the time." . . .

". . . I had to quit because I couldn't lay down and rest without oxygen in the night and my doctor told me I would have to get out of there. . . . I couln't [*sic*] even breathe, I had to get out of the door so I could breathe and he told me not to go back in [the mill] under any circumstances." . . .

Byssinosis is not a newly discovered disease, having been described as early as in the 1820's in England, App. 404–405, and observed in Belgium in a study of 2,000 cotton workers in 1845, . . .

12 such workers, suffer from the most disabling form of byssinosis. . . . The Senate Report accompanying the Act cited estimates that 100,000 active and retired workers suffer from some grade of the disease. . . . One study found that over 25% of a sample of active cotton-preparation and yarn-manufacturing workers suffer at least some form of the disease at a dust exposure level common prior to adoption of the current Standard. . . . Other studies confirm those general findings . . .

Not until the early 1960's was byssinosis recognized in the United States as a distinct occupational hazard associated with cotton mills. . . . In 1966, the American Conference of Governmental Industrial Hygienists (ACGIH), a private organization, recommended that exposure to total cotton dust be limited to a "threshold limit value" of 1,000 micrograms per cubic meter of air (1,000 µg/m$^3$) averaged over an 8-hour workday. See 43 Fed. Reg. 27351, col. 1 (1978). The United States Government first regulated exposure to cotton dust in 1968, when the Secretary of Labor, pursuant to the Walsh-Healey Act, 41 U. S. C. § 35 (e), promulgated airborne contaminant threshold limit values, applicable to public contractors, that included the 1,000 µg/m$^3$ limit for total cotton dust. 34 Fed. Reg. 7953 (1969). Following passage of the Act in 1970, the 1,000 µg/m$^3$ standard was adopted as an "established Federal standard" under § 6 (a) of the Act, 84 Stat. 1593, 29 U. S. C. § 655 (a), a provision designed to guarantee immediate protection of workers for the period between enactment of the statute and promulgation of permanent standards.

In 1974, ACGIH, adopting a new measurement unit of respirable rather than total dust, lowered its previous exposure limit recommendation to 200 µg/m$^3$ measured by a vertical elutriator, a device that measures cotton dust particles 15 microns or less in diameter. . . . That same year, the Director of the National Institute for Occupational Safety and Health (NIOSH), . . . submitted to the Secretary of Labor a recommendation for a cotton dust standard with a permissible exposure limit (PEL) that "should be set at the lowest level feasible, but in no case at an environmental concentration as high as 0.2 mg lint-free cotton dust/cu m," or 200 µg/m$^3$ of lint-free respirable dust.[6] . . . Several months later, OSHA published an Advance Notice of Proposed Rulemaking, 39 Fed. Reg. 44769 (1974), requesting comments from interested parties on the NIOSH recommendation and other related matters. Soon thereafter, the Textile Worker's Union of America, joined by the North Carolina Public Interest Research Group, petitioned the Secretary, urging a more stringent PEL of 100 µg/m³.

On December 28, 1976, OSHA published a proposal to replace the existing federal standard on cotton dust with a new permanent standard . . . The proposed standard contained a PEL of 200 µg/m³ of vertical elutriated lint-free respirable cotton dust for all segments of the cotton industry. . . . It also suggested an implementation strategy for achieving the PEL that relied on respirators for the short term and engineering controls for the long term. . . . OSHA invited interested parties to submit written comments . . .

Following the comment period, OSHA conducted three hearings in Washington, D. C., Greenville, Miss., and Lubbock, Tex., that lasted over 14 days. Public participation was widespread, involving representatives from industry and the work force, scientists, economists, industrial hygienists, and many others. . . .

The Cotton Dust Standard promulgated by OSHA establishes mandatory PEL's over an 8-hour period of 200 µg/m³ for yarn manufacturing, 750 µg/m³ for slashing and weaving operations, and 500 µg/m³ for all other processes in the cotton industry.[7] . . . These levels represent a relaxation of the proposed PEL of 200 µg/m³ for all segments of the cotton industry.

OSHA chose an implementation strategy for the Standard that depended primarily on a mix of engineering controls, such as installation of ventilation systems,[8] and work practice controls, such as special floor-sweeping procedures. Full compliance with the PEL's is required within four years, except to the extent that employers can establish that the engineering and work practice controls are infeasible. . . . During this compliance period, and at certain other times, the Standard requires employers to provide respirators to employees. . . . Other requirements include monitoring of cotton dust exposure, medical surveillance of all employees, annual medical examinations, employee education and training programs, and the posting of warning signs. A specific provision also under challenge in the instant case requires employers to transfer employees unable to wear respirators to another position, if available, having a dust level at or below the Standard's PEL's, with "no loss of earnings or other employment rights or benefits as a result of the transfer." . . .

On the basis of the evidence in the record as a whole, the Secretary determined that exposure to cotton dust represents a "significant health hazard to employees," . . . and that "the prevalence of byssinosis should be significantly reduced" by the adoption of the Standard's PEL's, . . . In assessing the health risks from cotton dust and the risk reduction obtained from lowered exposure, OSHA relied particularly on data showing a strong linear relationship between the prevalence of byssinosis and the concentration of lint-free respirable cotton dust. . . . Even at the 200 µg/m³ PEL, OSHA found that the prevalence of at least Grade ½ byssinosis would be 13% of all employees in the yarn manufacturing sector. . . .

In promulgating the Cotton Dust Standard, OSHA interpreted the Act to require adoption of the most stringent standard to protect against material health impairment, bounded only by

---

[6]NIOSH presented its recommendation in a lengthy and detailed document entitled "Criteria for a Recommended Standard: Occupational Exposure to Cotton Dust." . . . The report examined the effects of cotton dust exposure and suggested implementation of work practices, engineering controls, medical surveillance, and monitoring to decrease exposure to the recommended level.

[7]The manufacturing of cotton textile products is divided into several different stages. (1) In the operations of *opening, picking, carding, drawing,* and *roving,* raw cotton is cleaned and prepared for spinning into yarn. . . . (2) In the operations of *spinning, twisting, winding, spooling,* and *warping,* the prepared cotton is made into yarn and readied for weaving and other processing. . . . (3) In *slashing* and *weaving,* the yarn is manufactured into a woven fabric. . . . The Cotton Dust Standard defines "yarn manufacturing" to mean "all textile mill operations from opening to, but not including, slashing and weaving." . . .

[8]Ventilation systems include general controls, such as central air-conditioning, and local exhaust controls, which capture emissions of cotton dust as close to the point of generation as possible.

technological and economic feasibility. . . . OSHA therefore rejected the industry's alternative proposal for a PEL of 500 µg/m³ in yarn manufacturing, a proposal which would produce a 25% prevalence of at least Grade ½ byssinosis. The agency expressly found the Standard to be both technologically and economically feasible based on the evidence in the record as a whole. Although recognizing that permitted levels of exposure to cotton dust would still cause some byssinosis, OSHA nevertheless rejected the union proposal for a 100 µg/m³ PEL because it was not within the "technological capabilities of the industry." . . . Similarly, OSHA set PEL's for some segments of the cotton industry at 500 µg/m³ in part because of limitations of technological feasibility. . . . Finally, the Secretary found that "engineering dust controls in weaving may not be feasible even with massive expenditures by the industry," . . . and for that and other reasons adopted a less stringent PEL of 750 µg/m³ for weaving and slashing.

The Court of Appeals upheld the Standard in all major respects. . . .

## II

The principal question presented in these cases is whether the Occupational Safety and Health Act requires the Secretary, in promulgating a standard pursuant to . . . to determine that the costs of the standard bear a reasonable relationship to its benefits. . . . [P]etitioners urge not only that OSHA must show that a standard addresses a significant risk of material health impairment . . . but also that OSHA must demonstrate that the reduction in risk of material health impairment is significant in light of the costs of attaining that reduction.[9] . . . Respondents on the other hand contend that the Act re-

quires OSHA to promulgate standards that eliminate or reduce such risks "to the extent such protection is technologically and economically feasible."[10] . . . To resolve this debate, we must turn to the language, structure, and legislative history of the Act.

### A

The starting point of our analysis is the language of the statute itself. . . .

> "The Secretary, in promulgating standards dealing with toxic materials or harmful physical agents under this subsection, shall set the standard which most adequately assures, *to the extent feasible,* on the basis of the best available evidence, that no employee will suffer material impairment of health or functional capacity even if such employee has regular exposure to the hazard dealt with by such standard for the period of his working life."[11] (Emphasis added.)

. . . The plain meaning of the word "feasible" supports respondents' interpretation of the statute. . . . "[F]easible" means "capable of being done, executed, or effected." . . . In effect then, as the Court of Appeals held, Congress itself defined the basic relationship between costs and benefits, by placing the "benefit" of worker health above all

---

[9]Respondent Secretary disputes petitioners' description of the exercise, claiming that any meaningful balancing must involve "placing a [dollar] value on human life and freedom from suffering," . . . and that there is no other way but through formal cost-benefit analysis to accomplish petitioners' desired balancing, . . . Cost-benefit analysis contemplates "systematic enumeration of all benefits and all costs, tangible and intangible, whether readily quantifiable or difficult to measure, that will accrue to all members of society if a particular project is adopted."

[10]As described by the union respondents, the test for determining whether a standard promulgaged to regulate a "toxic material or harmful physical agent" satisfies the Act has three parts:

"First, whether the 'place of employment is unsafe—in the sense that significant risks are present and can be eliminated or lessened by a change in practices.' . . . Second, whether of the possible available correctives the Secretary has selected '*the* standard . . . that is most protective.' *Ibid.* Third, whether that standard is 'feasible.'" . . .

[11][T]he Act . . . also provides "Development of standards under this subsection shall be based upon research, demonstrations, experiments, and such other information as may be appropriate. In addition to the attainment of the highest degree of health and safety protection for the employee, other considerations shall be the latest available scientific data in the field, the feasibility of the standards, and experience gained under this and other health and safety laws. Whenever practicable, the standard promulgated shall be expressed in terms of objective criteria, and of the performance desired."

other considerations save those making attainment of this "benefit" unachievable. Any standard based on a balancing of costs and benefits by the Secretary that strikes a different balance than that struck by Congress would be inconsistent with the command set forth . . . Thus, cost-benefit analysis by OSHA is not required by the statute because feasibility analysis is. . . .

When Congress has intended that an agency engage in cost-benefit analysis, it has clearly indicated such intent on the face of the statute. One early example is the Flood Control Act of 1936, 33 U. S. C. § 701:

> "[T]he Federal Government should improve or participate in the improvement of navigable waters or their tributaries, including watersheds thereof, for flood-control purposes if the *benefits to whomsoever they may accrue are in excess of the estimated costs,* and if the lives and social security of people are otherwise adversely affected." (Emphasis added.)

A more recent example is the Outer Continental Shelf Lands Act Amendments of 1978, 43 U. S. C. § 1347 (b) (1976 ed., Supp. III), providing that offshore drilling operations shall use

> "the best available and safest technologies which the Secretary determines to be economically *feasible,* wherever failure of equipment would have a significant effect on safety, health, or the environment, except where the Secretary determines that the *incremental benefits are clearly insufficient to justify the incremental costs of using such technologies.*"

These and other statutes demonstrate that Congress uses specific language when intending that an agency engage in cost-benefit analysis. . . . We therefore reject the argument that Congress required cost-benefit analysis in §6(b)(5).

.   .   .   .   .   .   .   .   .   .   .   .   .   .   .   .   .   .   .   .   .

**C**

The legislative history of the Act, while concededly not crystal clear, provides general support for respondents' interpretation of the Act. The congressional Reports and debates certainly confirm that Congress meant "feasible" and nothing else in using that term. Congress was concerned that the Act might be thought to require achievement of absolute safety, an impossible standard, and therefore insisted that health and safety goals be capable of economic and technological accomplishment. Perhaps most telling is the absence of any indication whatsoever that Congress intended OSHA to conduct its own cost-benefit analysis before promulgating a toxic material or harmful physical agent standard. The legislative history demonstrates conclusively that Congress was fully aware that the Act would impose real and substantial costs of compliance on industry, and believed that such costs were part of the cost of doing business. . . .

*Notes and Questions*

1. The companies argued that there ought to be a cost-benefit analysis as part of the establishment of the permissible level of cotton dust. Justice Rehnquist argued that without setting out more explicit guidelines for agency action, Congress had unconstitutionally delegated its responsibilities to work out policy conflicts. Had a cost-benefit analysis been undertaken, how would the incidence of "brown lung" and its impacts on health and longevity be monetized? In setting the standard, the agency estimated the feasibility of putting remedial measures in place, but not every financial impact on the textile industry, impacts that might be included in a full cost-benefit analysis. They also set the permitted level of dust at twice as high some evidence might have justified. Do you consider these enough to justify the standard set?

   What would you estimate to be the effect if the establishment of permitted levels of cotton dust were to be retained as a legislative matter in Congress and not delegated to the Occupational Safety and Health Administration (OSHA)?

2. How should the following impinge on the setting of health and safety standards: perfect competition in textiles; the risk that foreign competition will gain an edge over domestic producers by virtue of the increased cost of compliance; or the possibility that the U.S.-based companies might move their enterprises abroad where health and safety standards are nonexistent or unenforced?

## 5.3 | The State   *V. I. Lenin*

IN PRIMITIVE SOCIETY, WHEN people lived in small family groups and were still at the lower stages of development, in a condition approximating to savagery . . . there were yet no signs of the existence of a state. We find the predominance of custom, authority, respect, the power enjoyed by the elders of the clan; we find this power sometimes accorded to women—the position of women then was not like the downtrodden and oppressed condition of women today—but nowhere do we find a special *category* of people who are set apart to rule others and, for the sake and purpose of rule, systematically and permanently to wield a certain apparatus of coercion, an apparatus of violence, such as is represented at the present time, as you all realize, by the armed detachments of troops, the prisons and the other means of subjugating the will of others by force—all that which constitutes the essence of the state.

If we abstract ourselves from the so-called religious teachings, subtleties, philosophical arguments and the various opinions advanced by bourgeois scholars, . . . and try to get at the real essence of the matter, we shall find that the state really does amount to such an apparatus of rule separated out from human society. When there appears such a special group of men who are occupied with ruling and nothing else, and who in order to rule need a special apparatus of coercion and of subjugating the will of others by force—prisons, special detachments of men, armies, etc.—then there appears the state.

. . . History shows that the state as a special apparatus for coercing people arose only wherever and whenever there appeared a division of society into classes, that is, a division into groups of people some of whom are permanently in a position to appropriate the labour of others, where some people exploit others.

And this division of society into classes must always be clearly borne in mind as a fundamental fact of history. The development of all human so-

cieties for thousands of years, in all countries without exception, reveals a general conformity to law, a regularity and consistency in this development; so that at first we had a society without classes—the original patriarchal, primitive society, in which there were no aristocrats; then we had a society based on slavery—a slaveowning society. The whole of modern civilized Europe has passed through this stage—slavery ruled supreme two thousand years ago. . . . Among the less developed peoples traces of slavery survive to this day; you will find the institution of slavery in Africa, for example, at the present time. Slaveowners and slaves were the first important class divisions. The former group not only owned all the means of production—the land and the implements, however primitive they may have been in those times—but also owned people. . . .

This form was followed . . . by . . . feudalism. In the great majority of countries slavery in the course of its development evolved into serfdom. The fundamental division of society was now into feudal landlords and peasant serfs. The form of relations between people changed. The slaveowners had regarded the slaves as their property; the law had confirmed this view and regarded the slave as a chattel completely owned by the slaveowner. As far as the peasant serf was concerned, class oppression and dependence remained, but it was not considered that the feudal landlord owned the peasants as chattels, but that he was only entitled to their labour and to compel them to perform certain services. In practice . . . serfdom, especially in Russia, where it survived longest of all and assumed the grossest forms, in no way differed from slavery.

Further, with the development of trade, the appearance of the world market and the development of money circulation, a new class arose within feudal society—the capitalist class. From the commodity, the exchange of commodities and the rise of the power of money, there arose the power of capital. During the eighteenth century—or rather, from the end of the eighteenth century and during the nineteenth century—revolutions took place all over the world. Feudalism was eliminated in all the countries of

Western Europe. This took place latest of all in Russia. In 1861 a radical change took place in Russia as well, as a consequence of which one form of society was replaced by another—feudalism was replaced by capitalism, under which division into classes remained, as well as various traces and relics of serfdom, but in which the division into classes fundamentally assumed a new form.

The owners of capital, the owners of the land, the owners of the mills and factories in all capitalist countries constituted and still constitute an insignificant minority of the population who have complete command of the labour of the whole people, and, consequently, command, oppress and exploit the whole mass of labourers, the majority of whom are proletarians, wage workers, that procure their livelihood in the process of production only by the sale of their own workers' hands, their labour power. With the transition to capitalism, the peasants, who were already disunited and downtrodden in feudal times, were converted partly (the majority) into proletarians, and partly (the minority) into wealthy peasants who themselves hired workers and who constituted a rural bourgeoisie.

This fundamental fact—the transition of society from primitive forms of slavery to serfdom and finally to capitalism—you must always bear in mind, for only by remembering this fundamental fact, only by inserting all political doctrines into this fundamental framework will you be able properly to appraise these doctrines . . . ; for each of these great periods in the history of mankind—slaveowning, feudal and capitalist—embraces scores and hundreds of centuries and presents such a mass of political forms, such a variety of political doctrines, opinions and revolutions, that this extreme diversity and immense variety can be understood . . . only by firmly holding, as to a guiding thread, to this division of society into classes, this change in the forms of class rule, and from this standpoint examining all social questions—economic, political, spiritual, religious, etc.

. . . People are divided into ruled, and into specialists in ruling, those who rise above society and are called rulers, representatives of the state. This apparatus, this group of people who rule others, always takes possession of a certain apparatus of coercion, of physical force, irrespective of whether this violence over people is expressed in the primitive club, or, in the epoch of slavery, in more perfected types of weapons, or in the firearms which appeared in the Middle Ages, or, finally, in modern weapons, which in the twentieth century are marvels of technique and are entirely based on the latest achievements of modern technology. The methods of violence changed, but whenever there was a state there existed in every society a group of persons who ruled, who commanded, who dominated and who in order to maintain their power possessed an apparatus of physical coercion. . . . And by examining these general phenomena, by asking ourselves why no state existed when there were no classes, when there were no exploiters and exploited, and why it arose when classes arose . . . shall we find a definite answer to the question of the essence of the state and its significance.

## Notes and Questions

1. E. B. Pashukanis, a Soviet legal philosopher, argued that it is in the area of criminal law where class antagonisms reach their highest intensity. People accused of crime are transformed by the system into "juridic objects," enabling lawmakers to intrude more roughly upon their personalities and, through the accused people so transformed, impose class domination. According to him, the standard of justification of criminal law as being vital to the protection of the safety of the community conceals reality, since the true role of criminal law, from feudalism through industrialism, has been nothing more than the preservation of hierarchy, privilege, and property.*

   Return to the case of the check forger in Chapter 2. Using Lenin and Pashukanis, reexamine the case and the judges' deliberations.

2. When sentencing convicted offenders, judges apply sentencing criteria to determine whether a person should get probation, local jail time, or a prison term. Sentencing factors include prior criminal record, age, intelligence, educational

---

*Hugh W. Babb, tr. *Soviet Legal Philosophy* (1951), pp. 206–207, 211–213.

background, family and marital status, church record, military experience, work history, and neighborhood environment.[†] These factors are used by judges to predict probation success.

Do sentencing criteria discriminate against lower-class offenders? Are the factors relevant

---

†See, for example, 1965 California Sentencing Institute 45 Cal. Rptr. (Appendix).

in determining sentences the same as those denoting "success" in society? To what extent does the achievement of success in society result from the prior achievement of status, wealth, and power by one's family or by happening to be born into the "right environment"?

3. Return to the case of *Cook* v. *State* in Chapter 3, and review the questions following that case.

## 5.4 | Streich v. General Motors Corp.

### *126 N.E. 2d 389 5. Ill. App. 2d 485 (1955)*

MCCORMICK, J. . . .

. . . THE COMPLAINT WAS FILED in an action for damages occasioned by the defendant's alleged wrongful cancellation of a contract. . . .

A motion to dismiss the complaint was filed by the defendant, in which, among other things, it was alleged that purchase order No. 11925 shows on its face that the plaintiff need not make or deliver, and that the defendant need not buy, any air magnet valves as therein identified, except when and as specified in written releases issued by the defendant. . . .

The trial court . . . dismissed the suit. . . .

There were three exhibits attached to the complaint. Purchase Order No. 11925 provided that it was a purchase order for air magnet valves, drawing 8024271 Rev. A, at a price of $13.50 net each. On the face of the purchase order it was provided:

> This Purchase Order is issued to cover shipments of this part, to be received by us from September 1, 1948, to August 31, 1949, as released and scheduled on our series 48 "Purchase Order release and Shipping Schedule" No. 478412 attached and all subsequent Purchase Order releases.
>
> The total quantity covered by this Purchase Order will always be included in the amount shown under "Total Released" on the latest "Purchase Order Release and Shipping Schedule."

This order was dated April 19, 1948. It provided that the order, including the terms and conditions on the face and reverse side, constitute "the complete and final agreement between Buyer and Seller and no other agreement in any way modifying any of said terms and conditions will be binding upon Buyer unless made in writing and signed by Buyer's authorized representative."

On the reverse side are twenty-three provisions, among which are the following:

> The contract resulting from the acceptance of this order is to be construed according to the laws of the state. . . . This contract is nonassignable by Seller.
>
> Deliveries are to be made both in quantities and at times specified in schedules furnished by Buyer. Buyer will have no liability for payment for material or items delivered to Buyer which are in excess of quantities specified in the delivery schedules. Buyer may from time to time change delivery schedules or direct temporary suspension of scheduled shipments.
>
> Buyer reserves the right to cancel all or any of the undelivered portion of this order if Seller does not make deliveries as specified in the schedules, or if Seller breaches any of the terms hereof including the warranties of Seller.
>
> Unless otherwise herein agreed, Seller at its own expense shall furnish, keep in good

condition and replace when necessary all dies, tools, gauges, fixtures and patterns necessary for the production of the material ordered. . . . Buyer has the option, however, to take possession of and title to any dies, tools, gauges, fixtures and patterns that are special for the production of the material covered by this order and shall pay to Seller the unamortized cost thereof; provided, however, that this option shall not apply if the material hereby ordered is the standard product of Seller or if a substantial quantity of like material is being sold by Seller to others. . . .

It is the contention of the plaintiff, Frank Streich, . . . that the defendant, General Motors Corporation . . . had entered into a binding contract to purchase all the requirements of the buyer from September 1, 1948, through August 31, 1949, from the seller, and that, while the amount of the requirements was not specified, parol evidence [oral agreements] might be properly introduced to show what the requirements were. . . .

. . . The promise of the seller to furnish identified items at a stated price is merely an offer and cannot become a contract until the buyer issues a release or order for a designated number of items. Until this action is taken the buyer has made no promise to do anything, and either party may withdraw. The promise is illusory, and the chimerical contract vanishes. "An agreement to sell to another such of the seller's goods, wares, and merchandise as the other might from time to time desire to purchase is lacking in mutuality because it does not bind the buyer to purchase any of the goods of the seller, as such matter is left wholly at the option or pleasure of the buyer." . . .

. . . The agreement in question is an adaptation of what was termed an "open end contract," which was used extensively by the federal government during the late war. However, it was used only in cases where the commodities dealt with were staples and either in the possession of or easily accessible to the seller. In this case the use of the contract is shifted and extended to cover commodities which must be manufactured before they are available for sale. According to the admitted statements in the complaint, special tools had to

be manufactured in order to produce the item herein involved. The seller here, misled by the many and detailed provisions contained in purchase order No. 11925 and ordinarily applicable to an enforceable bilateral contract, undoubtedly, as he alleged in his complaint, did go to considerable expense in providing tools and machines, only to find that by the accepted agreement the buyer had promised to do absolutely nothing. A statement of expectation creates no duty. Courts are not clothed with the power to make contracts for parties, nor can they, under the guise of interpretation, supply provisions actually lacking or impose obligations not actually assumed.

. . . The seller also argues the fact that he has alleged in his complaint he was advised by the defendant it would release approximately 1,600 units for shipment under the said purchase order. The written purchase order 11925 contains a provision that the terms and conditions thereof are the complete and final agreement between the buyer and the seller. . . .

> In *Sterling-Midland Coal Co.* v. *Great Lakes Coal [& Coke] Co.,* . . . at page 797, . . . the Supreme Court . . . said: "If a written contract purports on its face to be a complete expression of the whole agreement, it is to be presumed that the parties introduced into it every material item and term, and parol evidence is not admissible to add another term to the agreement about which the contract is silent. . . . The clause of the contract . . . expressly negatives the fact that there are any understandings, whether arising by implication of law or otherwise, between the parties, as to the subject-matter of the contract. . . . This clause of the contract is just as binding upon the parties as any other clause, and the . . . Courts had no right to disregard it."

. . . [T]he seller argues that . . . he should be permitted to introduce parol evidence for the purpose of showing an agreement on the part of the buyer to purchase approximately 1,600 valves. The formal agreement contained in purchase order 11925 purports to be a final and complete agreement. A provision therein contained so recites. Parol evidence of this character would vary and contradict the terms of the agreement, and such evidence is inadmissible.

Professor Fuller, discussing insurance and correspondence school contracts, says:

> One often has the impression of a kind of running battle between draftsmen and the courts, with much shifting of ground on the part of both.
>
> Back of this development lies a problem that touches the basic philosophy of contract law. The law of contracts is founded generally on the principle that it is the business of the courts to interpret and enforce the agreements that the parties have negotiated. This theory confronts the social reality that in many cases no real negotiations take place, and the terms of the contract are in fact set by the will of one party alone. This situation may arise where one party is indifferent or ignorant, or it may result from a superiority of bargaining power on one side. In such situations, there seems to be emerging a principle of law not yet frankly acknowledged which might be phrased something as follows: where one party to a contract has the power to dictate its terms, the terms of the contract are subject to judicial review, and may be modified by the court if they are unduly harsh.

The courts have many times passed on cases involving insurance contracts, which in many respects are similar to the agreement in this case. Concerning such cases it has been said:

> The history of the cases is, very largely, the history of a struggle between the insurance companies and the courts. . . . The courts, endeavoring to compel fair play, but trammelled and often thwarted by the stringent terms of the contracts, have devised doctrines and asserted principles which are sometimes more creditable to the ingenuity and subtlety of the judges than easily harmonized with decisions rendered, under less violent bias, in other departments of the law.

The agreement contained in purchase order No. 11925 was artfully prepared. It contains, in print so fine as to be scarcely legible, more than twenty-three clauses, most of which are applicable to bilateral contracts. It has all the indicia of a binding and enforceable contract, but it was not a binding and enforceable contract because the promise was defective. Behind the glittering facade is a void. This agreement was made in the higher echelons of business, overshadowed by the aura of business ethics. To say the least, the agreement was deceptive. In a more subterranean atmosphere and between persons of lower ethical standards it might, without any strain on the language, be denominated by a less deterged appellation.

Nevertheless, as the law is today . . . the trial court could do nothing but sustain the motion to dismiss the complaint. . . .

## Notes and Questions

1. The judge seems to be saying at the end of his opinion that the result is legally correct, but ethically wrong. What rules of law kept him from reaching the opposite conclusion? What interests stand to benefit most from such rules of law?

2. Some of the provisions of the purchase order are set out in the opinion. Who drew them up? Who stands to benefit from them? Why would a person disadvantaged under a proposed agreement sign it? What does that person's signature indicate?

3. The court states that the parties here had an agreement, but no contract. What is the difference? Would most people think that there is a difference?

4. Sometimes agreements are compared to private governments set up to accomplish a result. What kind of government was established by the parties here?

5. In the 1972 issue of Martindale-Hubbell (a directory of lawyers), Robert J. Gorman, counsel to Streich, is shown to be a solo practitioner. Pope and Ballard, attorneys for General Motors, is a firm with forty-eight lawyers in Chicago and eleven in Washington, D.C. While it must be conceded that a legal David can slay a Goliath with a well-placed stone, the figures demonstrate that there can be gross differences in the availability of legal resources in contested cases. Under U.S. practice, parties must pay for their own lawyers

whether they win or lose (unless a contrary provision is written into the agreement!).

6. At the most General Motors stood to pay $23,600 to Streich. So why all the commotion and high-priced legal talent?

7. Streich is regarded as having his own personal lawsuit against General Motors. Suppose that he could find other suppliers to General Motors who were in situations similar to his. Would it be appropriate for them to gather their claims and other grievances in one lawsuit? Should Streich be able to introduce proof of General Motors' contracting and cancellation practices across a number of contracts?

8. The contract made between General Motors and Streich has been called a "contract of adhesion," that is, a contract where one party has greater bargaining power and can impose terms on the less powerful party. Streich had the choice of doing business with General Motors on the latter's terms or not doing it at all. As for setting some of the terms of the supply contract, Streich's input was unthinkable.

Can courts safely assume that contracts have been entered freely and that the terms of the contract, by definition, must be considered of mutual benefit?

  ❧ The power of big buyers over suppliers in the automotive network has become more extensive rather than less in the years since the *Streich* case was decided. One congressional committee, while investigating the effect of NAFTA (the free trade agreement with Canada and Mexico) on small business in the United States, heard testimony from the president of AES, a small automotive supply company.

## 5.5 | Testimony of John Higbie*

. . . AES IS A SUPPLIER of wiring harnesses to the automotive industry. At peak levels, AES employs 200 people, has sales of $8 million a year, and 65 percent of our business ships to a supplier of the General Motors Corp. based in Kokomo, Indiana. This supplier operates two maquiladora [Mexican industrial processing zones—ED.] facilities in Mexico, and 50 percent of our product ships to these factories in Mexico. The remainder of our product supplies the truck and bus industry in the United States and Canada, the U.S. Navy, as well as two Japanese transplant automotive radio manufacturers.

AES is known as a contract manufacturer. AES manufactures product to blueprint. Our expertise is in our assembly skills and product knowledge. We sell no product on the consumer market. Our bank considers us a strong company and we consider ourselves a conservative company. . . .

The story of AES, I suppose, would have to be one of adapting to the comings and goings of the large industrial concerns of the Midwest in the 1970's and 1980's. There are two major events which have influenced our actions in the last decade.

The first event was an upward wage spiral in the late 1970's. By nature, our product requires labor-intensive hand assembly. By 1986, it became apparent that AES was pricing itself out of its hand assembly operations at our Avon location. Company and union-negotiated labor costs

U.S. House of Representatives, Committee on Small Business, "United States-Mexico Free Trade Agreement: The Small Business Perspective," 100th Congress, 1st Session, May, 1991.

*President AES Interconnects, Avon, Indiana.

were averaging nearly $7 an hour in relation to our competitor's minimum wage levels.

In order to maintain our . . . sales, AES opened a second facility in Kirklin, Indiana, 30 miles north of Indianapolis, at 25 cents above minimum wage. An IUE[†] local was organized in mid-1988, to which half of the Kirklin employees now belong. The opening of our Kirklin factory allowed us, and still allows us, to ship product at prices acceptable to our Midwestern customers.

By 1988, Kirklin was shipping product to Kokomo, Indiana and to the maquiladora facilities located across the Texas border from Brownsville and McAllan. The employees at our original Avon, Indiana location were retrained for high-technology work such as mil-spec soldering for the Navy, and building higher-priced cable assemblies for the truck and bus industry.

. . . Our customer's Reynosa, Mexico facility decided to fill excess capacity by producing internally one particular product line that had been assembled at Kirklin. This business equaled $1 million a year in sales and 14 full-time employees. . . .

However our customer has since backfilled the Kirklin facility with additional business, in order to maintain competitive pricing for the harness business remaining in Indiana. . . . It is fortunate for AES and its employees that our customer had additional product to award that was deliverable within Indiana. Whether that business remains in Indiana and, therefore, whether our business remains in Indiana, is a source of friction between our customer and the UAW[‡], AES will remain adaptable to our larger business needs in order to maintain satisfactory business levels and also by obtaining new lines of business.

The second event was, and continues to be, a requirement of the transportation industry, brought on by foreign competition, for continuous improvement of our product . . . and closer

---

[†]International Union of Electrical Workers—ED.

[‡]United Auto Workers—ED.

contact between customer and supplier. . . .

By mid-1988, our customer's Matamoras, Mexico facility expressed a desire to be supplied from a location closer than Kirklin, Indiana in order to allow their personnel in Mexico to assist AES in maintaining higher quality and process control.

Again we were faced with a decision of losing 50 percent of our business or moving south. Accordingly, AES decided to open a facility in Harlingen, Texas, 20 miles from the border.

Why did we not move to Mexico at that time? Being from the Midwest, and not familiar with the Hispanic culture, I felt that learning the customs and legal requirements for doing business in Mexico too great a burden, considering the short time allotted to begin production. . . .

*Notes and Questions*

1. What is happening here? What is your prediction as to future events?

2. How would the events described by Higbie be fitted to a larger theory of the relationship between economy and law?

   It is assumed that companies in a free-market economy can buy and sell wherever they choose. The law generally supports this assumption. Given this, AES has no standing to complain when others in the production hierarchy make decisions that render AES's business less secure. If this is so, is the economy freer for some businesses than it is for others?

3. Are the unions (IUE and UAW) causing the problems for AES and its principal customer?

   Average wages in northern Mexico are less than $1 per hour with minimum fringe benefits. What should American workers and their unions do in face of these figures?

4. The strategy of Higbie and AES is adaptation to the decisions of companies more powerful than they are. Is the handwriting on the wall for Higbie, AES, and other small U.S. manufacturers? Compare AES to Streich, the supplier to G.M. in the previous case.

&❧ The organization of plantation slavery in the antebellum South is the subject of the next excerpt.

# 5.6  From Day Clean to First Dark   *Kenneth Stampp*

ONE SUMMER AFTERNOON IN 1854, a traveler in Mississippi caught a vivid picture of a gang of field-hands returning to their toil after a thundershower. "First came, led by an old driver carrying a whip, forty of the largest and strongest women I ever saw together; they were all in a simple uniform dress of a bluish check stuff, the skirts reaching little below the knee; their legs and feet were bare; they carried themselves loftily, each having a hoe over the shoulder, and walking with a free, powerful swing, like chasseurs on the march." Then came the plow-hands with their mules, "the cavalry, thirty strong, mostly men, but a few of them women. . . . A lean and vigilant white overseer, on a brisk pony, brought up the rear." In this procession were the chief components of the plantation's production machinery—the regimented laborers whom slavery was expected to provide.

Slavery was above all a labor system. Wherever in the South the master lived, however many slaves he owned, it was his bondsmen's productive capacity that he generally valued most. And to the problem of organizing and exploiting their labor with maximum efficiency he devoted much of his attention.

On small agricultural units—and the great majority of them were small—the organization was simple: the masters usually gave close personal supervision to the unspecialized labor of a few slaves. Most of these masters could not afford merely to act as managers; and many of them were obliged to enter the fields with their bondsmen and drive a plow or wield a hoe. Farmers who worked alongside their slaves could be found throughout the South. The son of a small slaveholder in the South Carolina Low Country remembered that his mother ran a spinning wheel, wove cloth, did her own cooking, and milked the cows, while his father plowed, drove the wagon, and made shoes. In the Upper South, as a contemporary student of southern

society observed, it was not unusual to see "the sturdy yeoman and his sons working in company of their negroes." One could hear "the axe of master and man falling with alternate strokes" and watch "the negroes and their masters ploughing side by side."

Masters who had at their command as few as a half dozen field-hands, however, were tempted to improve their social status by withdrawing from the fields and devoting most of their time to managerial functions. Lacking skilled craftsmen in their small slave forces, they still found it necessary to perform certain specialized tasks such as carpentering and repairing tools; and in an emergency (a crop rarely went from spring planting to fall harvesting without a crisis of some kind) they temporarily forgot their pride. If some of the land needed to be replanted, if a crop was "in the grass"—i.e., overgrown with weeds—after a long spell of wet weather, or if illness created a shortage of plowhands, a master often had to choose between losing his crop and pitching in with his slaves. Cotton farmers who did not do ordinary field work helped with the picking in the fall, for that was a time when the labor force was seldom adequate.

But most slaves never saw their masters toiling in the fields, because most did not live on farms of the size where such intimate relationships and unspecialized economic functions existed. The great majority of bondsmen belonged to those whose holdings were large enough to enable them to escape routine farm labor. Even the slaves in the more modest holdings did not always work with their masters on small farms. Some of them worked in the cities. Others belonged to overseers and hence labored on the plantations. Still others belonged to the children or grandchildren of large planters and were used on the family estates. Hence the normal relationship between field-hands and their masters was not that of fellow workers but of labor and management. . . .

The substantial farmers and small planters who owned from ten to thirty slaves had at their disposal enough field-hands to make the problems of organization and supervision more complex. Members of this class usually handled these problems themselves without the aid of an overseer—unless they operated more than one farm or combined farming with some other business or profession. In such cases the owner often required his overseer to work in the field as well as to manage the slaves. . . .

The planters who owned more than thirty slaves were the ones who achieved maximum efficiency, the most complex economic organization, and the highest degree of specialization within their labor forces. Slightly less than half of the slaves belonged to the approximately twenty-five thousand masters operating plantations of these dimensions. Planters in this group who did not use overseers were as rare as the smaller slaveholders who did. In 1860 the number of Southerners who were employed as overseers about equalled the number of plantations with more than thirty slaves.

The planter who hired a full-time overseer limited his direction of routine crop cultivation to periodic inspections of the fields and concentrated upon problems of marketing, finance, and general plantation administration. Being free from the need to give constant attention to his labor force, he enjoyed greater leisure and was able to absent himself from the plantation more or less at his discretion. He employed his overseer on a year-to-year basis, usually by a written contract which could be terminated at the will of either party. The planter paid his overseer an annual salary ranging all the way from $100 to $1200, in addition to furnishing a house, an allowance of corn and pork, and a slave servant.

A prudent planter defined the overseer's duties in a detailed set of written instructions. Each planter had his own peculiar notions about the proper way to manage an estate, but his instructions tended to follow a somewhat standardized pattern. A Mississippian generalized about the overseer's responsibilities in a way that almost any planter would have endorsed: "The Overseer will never be expected to work in the field, but he must always be with the hands when not otherwise engaged in the Employers business and must do every thing that is required of him, provided it is directly or indirectly connected with the planting or other pecuniary interest of the Employer." Specific instructions related to the care and control of the slaves, the amount and kinds of labor to be performed, the care of plantation tools and livestock, and the behavior and activities of the overseer himself. The owner often required his overseer to keep a daily record of general plantation activities and to make regular oral or written reports. In short, he expected the overseer to be an efficient general manager and a careful guardian of his employer's property. . . .

In working the slave force the overseer generally made use of one or more slave drivers. If there were several of them one was designated head driver and acted almost as a sub-overseer. Sometimes the drivers were required to work and thus to set the pace for the rest of the slaves; sometimes they were exempted from labor and urged the gangs on by word or whip. A South Carolina rice planter defined their duties in his plantation rules: "Drivers are, under the Overseer, to maintain discipline and order on the place. They are to be responsible for the quiet of the negro-houses, for the proper performance of tasks, for bringing out the people early in the morning, and generally for the immediate inspection of such things as the Overseer only generally superintends." Planters thus called upon trusted slaves to become part of the plantation's command hierarchy. A Georgia planter described the efficient managerial system that existed on his estate:

> Every evening the drivers . . . make a report to the overseer in my presence of the employment of their respective hands. The drivers report . . . the quantity and kind of work they have done, and the field in which it is done. . . . These reports . . . are copied into the "Journal of Plantation Work," which forms a minute and daily record of the occupation and quantity of work done by the different gangs. After the reports are received, the work for the following day is arranged, and the head driver is directed what is to be done, and the manner in which it is to be executed. He distributes the orders to the sub-drivers and others:—the sub-drivers to the hands composing the gangs.

As the quantity of land in each field is accurately known, a constant check is had on the fidelity of the reports as to the quantity of work done. It only remains, by a daily inspection, to see that all operations have been well performed.

On a plantation containing more than thirty slaves there was always considerable labor specialization, the amount depending upon its size. The minimum was a clear distinction between household servants and field-hands, the latter in turn being divided into plow and hoe gangs. On the larger plantations some slaves devoted their full time to such occupations as ditching, tending livestock, driving wagons, and cultivating vegetable gardens. Here, too, there were substantial numbers of skilled slave artisans, and a high degree of specialization among household servants. In addition, each of the southern staples demanded its own kinds of specialists. These agricultural enterprises, with their business directors, production managers, labor foremen, and skilled and unskilled workers, approached the organizational complexity of modern factories. Though agriculture was not yet mechanized, the large plantations were to a considerable extent "factories in the fields."

## Notes and Questions

1. Lenin contended that the modern organization replicates the formal arrangements of slavery and feudalism. Therefore, it is more than an exercise in antiquarianism or the study of the roots of modern racism that impels the investigation of slavery. In order to appraise current conditions, modern students need to know the extent to which form persists while surfaces change.

    Non-Marxists have also sometimes endorsed the idea that there are constants across organizational history. Max Weber, a German sociologist and lawyer, traced the evolution of organizations from charismatic types (led by dynamic and visionary leaders who had compelling personal qualities) to routine forms where systems are established and goals are pursued by elaborate divisions of labor and specialization. The routine form does not completely displace the charismatic form, but actually builds upon it—the antique army with provisional leadership, willingly followed, influences the arrangement of peacetime affairs. Later, the expectation that leaders be dazzling or earn respect of their followers gets lost, but the leader-follower notion is retained. Over time, hierarchies become permanent and not dependent upon the consent of underlings.*

2. What contemporary questions are suggested by the investigation of slavery? Can modern-day roles be placed in the paradigm of masters, overseers, drivers, and slaves?

    What is the connection between role and rule, the relationship between position in organization and determination of the direction and activities of organizations, and what is done to noncooperative participants? Over centuries, has there been progress, or no change, or decline in the distribution of power and wealth?

    And finally, how does the form of organizations affect the achievement of the central democratic values of liberty and equality?

3. The position of the driver under slavery was especially difficult. He was vital to the success of the plantation, for he was responsible for the maintenance of production and discipline, and yet as a black slave, he was disqualified from full status; thus, he must have suffered serious crises of conscience. To do well in the master's eyes and gain material success and a measure of status would help the master prosper, thereby contributing to the perpetuation of slavery and the profound indignities experienced by both him and his brethren. As a person of influence, the driver could beneficially affect the day-to-day lives of his fellow slaves, but winning battles could mean the loss of the war.

    The unenviable position of the driver typifies those in the middle ranks of many organizations. They are neither in positions of appreciable wealth and power nor at the lower levels where their kin loyalties and origins lie. To make gains, they inevitably suffer losses.

    What modern-day parallels do you see to the driver-slave relationship? What difficulties would there be for slavery or for the modern

---

*See, generally, Hans Gerth and C. Wright Mills, *From Max Weber* (New York: Oxford University Press, 1946); Frederick Thayer, *An End to Hierarchy and Competition* (New York: Watts, 1981).

organization were there no such relationships?

Compare the position of the driver with the position of the doorkeeper in Kafka's parable "Before the Law."

4. A. Were you to find yourself in a culture and economy with only four organizational positions—master, overseer, driver, or slave—which position would you prefer? Before jumping to the conclusion that the answer is obvious, consider the nature of each role and how you would be able to act and be expected to act in each.

   B. If you were not able to exercise your preference, but instead were assigned a position by lot or by birth, how would this affect your thinking?

   C. In the modern organization with top, middle, and bottom levels, where would you prefer to be? How would your thinking about organizations be affected if roles were assigned rather than being subject to your preference?

   How does the relative scarcity of upper-level positions affect your thinking about the way organizations should be designed?

5. What did law have to do with slavery? Students might think that since slavery was and is inherently unjust, there could have been no relationship between law and slavery—the system would keep quiet about it, so to speak. The contrary was the case. Summaries of cases dealing with slavery fill five volumes, and every slave state had numerous statutes dealing with the subject.[†] This substantial body of law demonstrates conclusively that the legal order was indispensable to the maintenance and nurturance of slavery.

   But what made law so vital to the system? Preeminently important was the definition of slaves as personal property to be used, traded, put up as collateral for loans, and inherited at death. A second critical aspect of law involved the delegation of power over the slave to the masters and their appointees, meaning that the day-to-day governance and discipline on plantations were of no concern to the courts.

   In addition to being property, slaves were considered persons for purposes of criminal law so that the police power of the state could be invoked at critical times in aid of masters whose slaves got out of control. Under law,

slavery was a system of property and delegated power, with state power available in times of emergency.

6. Slaves naturally did not willingly subject themselves to bondage. At the plantation level where the law decreed that slavery relationships be fought out on a daily basis, slaves used a variety of tactics to undo master-overseer power. Since the slave was simultaneously a valuable property, a source of labor, and an "object" requiring constant discipline, there were limits on the physical abuse that could be inflicted on a slave. A dead slave was valueless for sale or labor.

   Beginning with this outside limit, slaves engaged in a full range of tactics that led one master to characterize them as a "troublesome property." Common tactics were work slow-downs, feigning of illness or ineptitude, shoddy workmanship, the playing off of masters against overseers, thefts from masters, arson on crops and buildings, assaults and murders of masters and overseers, and running away.

   These tactics limited the otherwise complete control by masters and were vital ingredients in daily working arrangements.

   There are still countless situations when as a matter of formal rule "all the power" is held by one or a few persons over others who have "no power." What do people who are in powerless situations do to preserve a measure of their autonomy and dignity? Compare these actions with the tactics of the slaves on plantations. Are these challenges to power a form of lawmaking?

7. Some slavemasters, seeing the futility of controlling people by force alone, injected reward structures such as holiday treats, small payments, letting slaves hire themselves out for pay, or allotting them small plots of land for personal use. One antebellum North Carolina case involved the practice of allowing slaves to grow small amounts of cotton for themselves; their harvests were added to the plantation's and the cash proceeds were distributed to the slaves. The case arose because the slaveowner died. Did the slaves have the right to the proceeds from their crop, as had been customary, or should the proceeds have been lumped together with the rest of the slaveowner's estate?

   The court, in deciding the issue, reveals just where everyone stood with respect to power and property—master, slave, and, in passing, married women:

---

[†]Helen Catterall, ed., *Judicial Cases* (Westport, Conn.: Greenwood, 1926).

[I]t has never been considered that the negro's little crops . . . were assets, any more than the little sums of money which they might have received for the crop of a preceding year, if any remnant were left in their chests, or their poultry, or their dog, or their extra clothing. Those petty gains and property have been allowed our servants by usage, and may be justified by policy and law, upon the same principle, that the savings of a wife in housekeeping, by the sale of milk, butter, cheese, vegetables, and so forth, are declared to be, by the husband's consent, the property of the wife. It is true a slave cannot have property . . . But it is equally true that a married woman can have no property in money or personal chattels in possession; but they belong in strict law to the husband . . . Nevertheless, the wife may claim them . . . [A]n executor is not bound to strip a poor negro of the things his master gave him . . . which promote his health, cheerfulness and contentment and increase his value. In many instances, what the slave, with a pride that makes him happy, buys for himself, would, if not thus procured, be of necessity supplied directly by the master; so that . . . leaving to the negro the spending of his money at his own pleasure, is then a pecuniary saving . . . and these slight indulgences are repaid by the attachment of the slave to the master . . . In fine, experience has proved so fully the advantages of these minor benefactions to a dependent race, which humanity at first prompted, there is scarcely an owner who does not act as the testator did . . .[‡]

---

[‡]*Waddill* v. *Martin*, 38 N.C. 487 (1845).

 

&#10086; We follow the cotton northward to Lowell, Massachusetts, which in the 1850s was the center of the New England textile industry. Most of the factory "hands" were women, who were recruited first from the farms of the area and later from successive groups of immigrants—Irish, French-Canadians, and southern Europeans. The following case arose in the same period as the preceding excerpt on slavery and shows the early organization of the textile industry.

## 5.7  Thornton and Wife v. The Suffolk Manufacturing Company

*64 Mass. 376 (1852)*

ACTION OF CONTRACT FOR the breach of an agreement under which the female plaintiff, Catherine Cassidy, before her marriage, worked in the manufactory of the defendants, at Lowell.

. . . [T]he female plaintiff went to work for the defendants under the agreement that if she faithfully performed her duties in their employ for the term of at least twelve months, at the expiration of such period, upon giving a fortnight's notice, she would be entitled to leave, and to receive from them "a line," or honorable discharge, by means of which she might obtain employment in the other mills in Lowell. It was also alleged that there was an agreement among the several manufacturing companies in Lowell, that if an operative did not receive such "line" or honorable discharge, he could not afterwards obtain employment in any other of the mills in Lowell. It was also alleged that the female plaintiff faithfully performed services for the defendants for more than twelve months, and became thereby entitled to such discharge, or "line," upon giving a fortnight's notice of her intention to leave, and working for that period; but that the defendants, regardless of their contract, wrongfully discharged her without such "line," and thereby deprived her of work in any other mill in Lowell.

At the trial . . . the plaintiffs called Alexander P. Wright. He testified: "I am agent of the Lowell (carpet) company; have been so for about twenty-three years; am generally acquainted with the rules and customs of the Lowell companies. I know of no certain agreement between companies to require a 'line'; I believe the custom is to require a 'line' wherever an operative has been previously employed in other mills in Lowell, or not to hire them. Our company requires it; . . . the invariable custom is to give a line if there is no objection to the conduct of the help from the overseer; never have known any difference for twenty-three years that I have been here; if the help work properly it is usual to give a line; there may be cases of opposition on the part of the overseers, but this is usually for cause. I never have known an overseer to refuse arbitrarily, but always for cause shown; if help work a year, and give a fortnight's notice, they are entitled to a 'line'; this is a general custom, and . . . the help hire with knowledge of this custom; if a line is refused by the overseers they apply to me. I should say improper conduct is the only cause of refusal. . . . [B]ad temper, producing disturbance in [the] room, would be sufficient cause of discharge; any such conduct as would render the hand unserviceable elsewhere, such as insulting the overseer, trying to get other hands discontented. I know of no right in operatives to demand a line; this line is like a recommendation to a servant in a family. . . ."

John B. McAlvin testified: "I have been paymaster on the Suffolk for eighteen years; have the books of the company in my hands; it appears from this book that the plaintiff came to work for the company, May 29, 1848, and was discharged, July 19, 1849; the entry is, 'discharged for improper conduct. . . . Suffolk Dressing Room, No. 3. Catherine Cassidy, has worked since pay-day, thirteen days; pay her for warping nineteen beams, at 22c. per beam, $6.08. John C. Clark, overseer. Discharged for improper conduct, July 18, 1849. She has worked in this room ——— months. She leaves with notice.' If the blank is filled up, namely, has worked here twelve months, and leaves with notice, I should give a line, but should generally ask the overseer; giving her a line would be a compliance with the rules of the Suffolk company . . . ;

if she leaves with notice, it would be a compliance with rules to give her a line, but of late years I have usually asked the overseer, if there is any objection to her having a line. . . .

". . . Soon after she left, she came to me with another woman; brought me this bill, (the one signed by Clark,) and demanded a line; I told her I could not give her a line. If the bill comes from the overseer in this form, by the rules, I cannot give a line or honorable discharge. I told her to go to the overseer, and she went out as if to go to see him. . . . My business is paymaster, I have nothing to do with hiring or discharging hands, this is done by the overseers. The help go to the overseer and make their engagements with him as to what price they are to have, and how they are to be employed, and then come to the counting-room. . . ."

James Montague testified: "I have lived in Lowell twelve years; have known the female plaintiff four years; she has worked in the mill since I knew her; she lived next door to me with her mother; her father was dead; she has worked with the Suffolk Company; after she was discharged she requested me to go to the company and get an honorable discharge for her. I called on Mr. Clark, her overseer, to give her a discharge or a line so she could get work in the other factories in Lowell, as she had a crippled mother dependent on her. He said he would not give her an honorable discharge, or a line, though she might come back and work there. I told him I thought it a rather hard discharge. . . . [H]e said he would go and see Mr. Wright, the agent, and it might be arranged. We went to see Mr. Wright; I told him the same I had told Mr. Clark. Wright said that he would not give her a line, but that she might come back; assured her that she was a very good girl, there was nothing against her. This was in October, 1849. I then told Mr. Wright I thought there would be some trouble about it, that she would prosecute; he said he would spend $5,000 rather than change the line he had given her, and I left."

William Markland testified: "I am overseer in Lowell Company; have been so five years, but have been employed there ten years. The female plaintiff applied to me for work in our company, August 2, 1849; got work, and worked six and three-fourth days at that time; she left because she could not get a line from the Suffolk Company. . . . [S]he appeared to do well so far as I could see, and I was satisfied with her. She began to learn to weave; this was new business to her, and could at first earn at it only fifty cents per day; a good weaver can earn from seventy-five to eighty cents per day. I don't know as there is any specified rule, but it is necessary, as I understand it, to have a line before a hand can get work who has worked in Lowell before. If they work twelve months, and give a fortnight's notice, they are entitled to a line, as I consider it; this has always been my practice. . . . I hired myself with this understanding when I came to work for the company. I hire my own help with this understanding. I have twenty-two men, four boys, and one hundred and thirty-five girls under me; they are frequently changing. . . . After she left, because she could not get a line, she came back December 31, 1849, and brought a line from the Merrimack Company; I then employed her for thirteen months; she was an average good weaver, and did an average quantity of work; she made about eighty cents per day; I can't tell exactly how much. I . . . had no difficulty with her. I suppose it is a matter of discretion with the overseer whether he will give a line; it is so with me; but I never refused one without a cause; disobedience is sufficient." . . .

Bridget Gaiten testified: "After the female plaintiff was discharged from the Suffolk, I went with her to the Boott Mills to get work; she engaged work with the overseer, and went to the counting-room to get her regulation paper, and they asked her for her line; she showed them the one she had; they said that would not do, she must go to the Suffolk and get a line. I went with her to the paymaster, and she asked him for a line; he said he could not give one, she must get one from her overseer. We went to the overseer, and he said that he would not do any thing about it; it was left at the counting-room; she did not get a line, and came away." . . .

SHAW, C. J.

In this action, brought by Catherine Cassidy, whilst sole, we see no ground on which the plaintiffs can recover, as upon a contract. The ground relied on is, that in consideration of services, the employer engages that if the operative remains in the service a certain time, he will give her an honorable discharge; or in other words, that her service and conduct have been good and satisfactory. Were such a contract made in express terms, intended to be absolute, it seems to us that it would be bad in law, as plainly contrary to good morals and public policy. Such a discharge is a certificate of a fact; but if the fact is otherwise, if the conduct of the operative has not been satisfactory, it would be the certificate of a falsehood, tending to mislead and not to inform other employers. Besides; if such a custom were general, such a discharge would be utterly useless to other employers and utterly worthless to the receiver. It could give other employers no information, upon which they could rely. To avoid such illegality, it must be taken with some limitation and qualification, to wit, that the conduct of the operative has been such in all respects, including not only skill and industry in the employment, but conduct in point of morals, temper, language, and deportment, and the like, so that a certificate of good character would be true. Then it stands upon the same footing with the custom which governs most respectable persons in society, upon the termination of the employment of a servant, to give him a certificate of good character, if entitled to it. In such case, it is for the employer to give or withhold such certificate, according to his own conviction of the truth, arising from his own personal knowledge, or from other sources. It is the state of the employer's mind, his belief of the good character of the servant, or the contrary, which other employers desire to know, and have a right to know. It must therefore necessarily depend upon the employer's own determination, when so applied to for a certificate, whether with a just regard to truth and honesty, he can certify to the good character or not. If an assurance of an employer on engaging a servant, that at the end of the time he will give him a certificate of good character, if he should then think him entitled to it, could in any respect be deemed a contract, and not the promise of an ordinary act of courtesy, it would be no breach of such contract, to aver and prove that the servant, after the termination of the service, demanded such certificate, and was refused it. . . .

[The corporation] could only know the truth of the facts, of such good conduct and behavior, by the report of the superintendent under whom such operative may have been employed. He alone may know the facts and be able to state them. Should they certify to good character without, or against such report, they might certify to a falsehood, and only mislead those who should rely upon such certificate. This certainly they cannot be legally obliged to do. When therefore the overseer certifies that the operative is discharged for impropriety, as in the present case, this evidence must be conclusive with the corporation, because they can have no other to justify them in giving a certificate.

It is said by way of objection to this, that an overseer may arbitrarily refuse to certify a good character, or falsely certify a bad one. This is possible, and if he does it capriciously, or without cause, it is extremely dishonorable and wrong, and would tend soon to impair his own reputation and standing for honesty and uprightness. Still, when an appeal is necessarily made to a man's own personal knowledge, judgment, and conscience, his decision must be presumed to be according to the truth, and conclusive. . . .

The fact, that on account of the peculiar situation of the various companies in Lowell, in relation to each other, the common interest they have in maintaining their discipline, the certificate of good character is of so much more importance to the servant, than elsewhere, can make no difference to the servant, in regard to his rights. In the same proportion in which it is important to the servant out of employ, to hold a certificate of good character and honorable discharge, it is important to corporations, their agents and servants, and all interested in them, to be cautious and conscientious, in giving such discharges and recommendations, when they are honestly deserved, and in withholding them when they are not. . . .

## Notes and Questions

1. In the textile industry, the owners appointed agents who in turn named overseers to direct the factory workers. Compare the organization of large southern plantations with the organization of cotton textile factories.

Southern planters who went North for visits said they found little difference between life on their slave plantations and life in the cotton mills of New England as to working conditions and the food, clothing, and shelter available to workers and slaves.

Karl Marx in *Das Capital* noted that employers in England had less compunction about wearing out workforces than a slaveholder who had a vested interest in the slave as property. These statements are extreme, given the lifetime servitude of black slaves, but they are worth thinking about.

2. If a person wanted to leave a factory in Lowell, what inhibitions would she or he have had? Can quitting a job in a factory in Lowell be compared to a slave's running away?

3. Compare the judge's reasoning in the *Thornton* case with the commentary in an 1823 case from North Carolina:

> With the services and labours of a slave the law has nothing to do; they are the master's by the law; the government and control of them being exclusively to him. Nor will the law interfere upon the ground that the state's rights and not the master's have been violated.
>
> In establishing slavery then, the law vested in the master the absolute and uncontrolled right to the services of the slave, and the means of enforcing those services follow as necessary consequences; nor will the law weigh with the most scrupulous niceties his acts in relation thereto.*

Both slavery and early industrial organization involved delegations of power to those in charge. The legal system would not be concerned with the internal affairs of plantations or the early factory (these delegations of power are analogous to those found in the very first cases studied in this text on discipline in the school or in the household). An important topic for "law" study becomes the consequences of legal neglect, or systemic disregard: those occasions when there is no recourse to the legal system can be far

---

*State v. Read 9, N.C. 365 (1823). Quoted in Mark Tushnet, *The American Law of Slavery* (Princeton, N.J.: Princeton University Press, 1981).

more important than those occasions when recourse to the legal system is available.

4. The court leaves fairness in the terms of a worker's departure to the discretion of the overseer "who alone may know the facts and be able to state them." The limitation on arbitrariness comes from the overseer's desire to protect his own reputation for honesty. Compare this limitation with those placed on schoolteachers in punishing children and on husbands in chastising wives as reported in the early North Carolina cases in Chapter 1.

5. What large questions seemed to be riding on the outcome of the case? What would impel the agent of the company to say that he was willing to spend $5,000—an enormous sum in 1850—on the defense of a case involving a weaver who earned $3 to $5 a week?

6. Catherine Cassidy, as a married woman, could not bring the action for breach of contract in her own name. Compare the commentary of the judges in the North Carolina spousal abuse cases on the limited legal capacity of women.

૨▲ Until the emergence of organized labor and collective bargaining, workers like Catherine Cassidy were expected to bargain individually with employers to set the terms and conditions of their employment. From the mid-nineteenth century until the 1930s, there was ongoing resistance to unions and collective action. Samuel Gompers (the first president of the AFL) prayed, "God save labor from the courts." Decades of discriminatory uses of the antitrust laws and the labor injunction, to say nothing of the use of police, state militias, and the U.S. army, had led him to conclude that no law at all would be preferable to the anti-labor law that had inhibited the development of organized labor from the outset.

During the Great Depression, Congress softened the law affecting organized labor and collective bargaining. Whether the resulting National Labor Relations Act of 1935 (the Wagner Act) was passed out of a desire to head off more radical activism by labor, or out of a genuine interest in bringing about greater mutuality in the dealings between owner-managers and labor has long been debated by labor historians. But most agree that the Wagner Act marked a significant shift in national labor policy.

At the center of the act were provisions to secure the free choice of workers regarding unions and union representatives, to mandate collective bargaining, and to protect collective action in the form of strikes, boycotts, and picketing. The National Labor Relations Board (NLRB) was created to be the first point of adjudication of disputes between labor and management.

One of the main areas of conflict under the Wagner Act and subsequent labor legislation concerned the scope of collective bargaining. About what subjects did the law require labor and management to bargain? The law stated that bargaining was to take place over "wages, hours, and other terms and conditions of employment." If the phrase were given a broad interpretation, literally anything might find its way into a collective bargaining agreement, for example, the purposes and scope of the business, what products or services would be made or furnished, the manner of making or furnishing them, to whom they would go and at what prices, and the formula for sharing the proceeds from their sale.

If given a narrow interpretation—how much money and for how long, and matters close to money and time—owner-manager discretion would remain virtually unaffected by congressionally mandated bargaining. Labor would be reduced to a commodity like any other factor of production such as land or capital. Definite limits would have been imposed upon the gains that workers could make through the formation of unions and collective bargaining.

In 1964, the U.S. Supreme Court rendered a decision that has had a profound impact on the scope of collective bargaining and on whether the congressional intention of bringing about labor peace through the rule of law can be realized. On the surface the case of *Fibreboard Paper Products Corp* v. *NLRB* would not have looked momentous enough to shape labor law to the present day. A union workforce had done the maintenance at a manufacturing plant in California, but when the time for renewal of the contract came up, the employer refused to bargain with the employees saying that because of its plans to use an outside contractor to perform maintenance services, bargaining would be "pointless."

After all the rounds of administrative and lower court decisions, the U.S. Supreme Court had before it the question of whether the Wagner Act required an employer to bargain with a union before "contracting out" to an outside firm the work that had been done previously by its own employees. The Court ruled for the union, out of an impulse to promote collective bargaining and reduce "industrial strife," noting that the work still had to be performed and that the employer was in effect substituting an outside workforce for the one previously under union contract.

Justice Stewart agreed with the decision, but saw far-reaching implications of a broad interpretation of Wagner Act language—"wages, hours and other terms and conditions of employment."

## 5.8 | Fibreboard Paper Products Corp. v. NLRB    *379 U.S. 204 (1964)*

MR. JUSTICE STEWART,. . . *concurring:*

VIEWED BROADLY, THE QUESTION before us stirs large issues. [T]he Court's opinion radiates implications of such disturbing breadth that I am persuaded to file this separate statement of my own views.

Section 8(a) (5) of the National Labor Relations Act . . . makes it an unfair labor practice for an employer to "refuse to bargain collectively with the representatives of his employees." Collective bargaining is defined in §8(d) as:

the performance of the mutual obligation of the employer and the representative of the employees to meet at reasonable times and confer in good faith with respect to wages, hours, and other terms and conditions of employment.

. . . Fibreboard had performed its maintenance work at its Emeryville manufacturing plant through its own employees, who were represented by a local of the United Steelworkers.

Estimating that some $225,000 could be saved annually by dispensing with internal maintenance, the company contracted out this work, informing the union that there would be no point in negotiating a new contract since the employees in the bargaining unit had been replaced by employees of the independent contractor, Fluor. Maintenance work continued to be performed within the plant, with the work ultimately supervised by the company's officials and "functioning as an integral part" of the company. Fluor was paid the cost of operations plus $2,250 monthly. The savings in costs anticipated from the arrangement derived largely from the elimination of fringe benefits, adjustments in work scheduling, enforcement of stricter work quotas, and close supervision of the new personnel. Under the cost-plus arrangement, Fibreboard remained responsible for whatever maintenance costs were actually incurred. On these facts, I would agree that the employer had a duty to bargain collectively concerning the replacement of his internal maintenance staff by employees of the independent contractor.

The basic question is whether the employer failed to "confer in good faith with respect to . . . terms and conditions of employment" in unilaterally deciding to subcontract this work. . . . The phrase "conditions of employment" is no doubt susceptible of diverse interpretations. At the extreme, the phrase could be construed to apply to any subject which is insisted upon as a prerequisite for continued employment. Such an interpretation, which would in effect place the compulsion of the Board behind any and all bargaining demands, would be contrary to the intent of Congress, as reflected in this legislative history. Yet there are passages in the Court's opinion today which suggest just such an expansive interpretation, for the Court's opinion seems to imply that any issue which may reasonably divide an employer and his employees must be the subject of compulsory collective bargaining.

Only a narrower concept of "conditions of employment" will serve the statutory purpose of delineating a limited category of issues which are subject to the duty to bargain collectively. . . . In common parlance, the conditions of a person's employment are most obviously the various physical dimensions of his working environment.

What one's hours are to be, what amount of work is expected during those hours, what periods of relief are available, what safety practices are observed, would all seem conditions of one's employment. There are other less tangible but no less important characteristics of a person's employment which might also be deemed "conditions". . . . Thus, freedom from discriminatory discharge, seniority rights, the imposition of a compulsory retirement age, have been recognized as subjects upon which an employer must bargain, although all of these concern the very existence of the employment itself.

While employment security has thus properly been recognized in various circumstances as a condition of employment, it surely does not follow that every decision which may affect job security is a subject of compulsory collective bargaining. Many decisions made by management affect the job security of employees. Decisions concerning the volume and kind of advertising expenditures, product design, the manner of financing, and sales, all may bear upon the security of the workers' jobs. Yet it is hardly conceivable that such decisions so involve "conditions of employment" that they must be negotiated with the employees' bargaining representative. In many of these areas the impact of a particular management decision upon job security may be extremely indirect and uncertain, and this alone may be sufficient reason to conclude that such decisions are not "with respect to . . . conditions of employment." Yet there are other areas where decisions by management may quite clearly imperil job security, or indeed terminate employment entirely. An enterprise may decide to invest in labor-saving machinery. Another may resolve to liquidate its assets and go out of business. Nothing the Court holds today should be understood as imposing a duty to bargain collectively regarding such managerial decisions, which lie at the core of entrepreneurial control. Decisions concerning the commitment of investment capital and the basic scope of the enterprise are not in themselves primarily about conditions of employment, though the effect of the decision may be necessarily to terminate employment. If, as I think clear, the purpose of §8(d) is to describe a limited area subject to the duty of collective bargaining, those management decisions which are fundamental to the basic direction of a corporate enterprise or which impinge only indirectly upon employment security should be excluded from that area. . . .

This kind of subcontracting falls short of such larger entrepreneurial questions as what shall be produced, how capital shall be invested in fixed assets, or what the basic scope of the enterprise shall be. In my view, the Court's decision in this case has nothing to do with whether any aspects of those larger issues could under any circumstances be considered subjects of compulsory collective bargaining under the present law.

I am fully aware that in this era of automation and onrushing technological change, no problems in the domestic economy are of greater concern than those involving job security and employment stability. Because of the potentially cruel impact upon the lives and fortunes of the working men and women of the Nation, these problems have understandably engaged the solicitous attention of government, of responsible private business, and particularly of organized labor. It is possible that in meeting these problems Congress may eventually decide to give organized labor or government a far heavier hand in controlling what until now have been considered the prerogatives of private business management. That path would mark a sharp departure from the traditional principles of a free enterprise economy. Whether we should follow it is, within constitutional limitations, for Congress to choose. But it is a path which Congress certainly did not choose when it enacted the Taft-Hartley Act.

&❧ The union won the battle in *Fibreboard* over subcontracting but lost the war over the scope of mandatory bargaining. Justice Stewart's granting to owner-managers prerogatives on "larger entrepreneurial questions" has remained to this day the center of bargaining law.

Plant closings and partial terminations of businesses have become increasingly visible areas of conflict between workers and corporations, as corporations moved more operations overseas, or sharply curtailed activity in the severe recession (depression) that began in the early 1980s. Can workers do anything about the security of their employment through the collective bargaining process? Returning to the testimony of the president of AES before Congress on the movement of the company to another site in Indiana and later to Texas, could unionized workers have blocked the decision to move and demanded collective bargaining to determine the direction of the company?

The U.S. Supreme Court in 1981 had before it a case where a union contended that an employer had a duty to collectively bargain regarding the termination of a major contract with a customer, which would have led to large layoffs.

# 5.9  First National Maintenance Corp. v. NLRB

*452 U.S. 666, 101 S.Ct. 2573 (1981)*

JUSTICE BLACKMUN *delivered the opinion of the Court.*

MUST AN EMPLOYER, UNDER its duty to bargain in good faith "with respect to wages, hours, and other terms and conditions of employment," . . . negotiate with the certified representative of its employees over its decision to close a part of its business? In this case, the National Labor Relations Board (Board) imposed such a duty on petitioner with respect to its decision to terminate a contract with a customer. . . .

## I

Petitioner, First National Maintenance Corporation (FNM), is a New York corporation engaged in the business of providing housekeeping, cleaning, maintenance, and related services for commercial customers in the New York City area. It supplies each of its customers, at the customer's premises, contracted-for labor force and supervision in return for reimbursement of its labor costs . . . and payment of a set fee. It contracts for and hires personnel separately for each customer, and it does not transfer employees between locations.

During the spring of 1977, petitioner was performing maintenance work for the Greenpark Care Center, a nursing home in Brooklyn. Its written agreement dated April 28, 1976, with Greenpark specified that Greenpark "shall furnish all tools, equipment, materials, and supplies," and would pay petitioner weekly "the sum of five hundred dollars plus the gross weekly payroll and fringe benefits." . . . Its weekly fee, however, had been reduced to $250 effective November 1, 1976. . . . Petitioner employed approximately 35 workers in its Greenpark operation.

Petitioner's business relationship with Greenpark, seemingly, was not very remunerative or smooth. . . . On June 30, by telephone, it asked

that its weekly fee be restored at the $500 figure and, on July 6, it informed Greenpark in writing that it would discontinue its operations there on August 1 unless the increase were granted. . . . By telegram on July 25, petitioner gave final notice of termination. . . .

While FNM was experiencing these difficulties, District 1199, National Union of Hospital and Health Care Employees, Retail, Wholesale and Department Store Union, AFL-CIO (union), was conducting an organization campaign among petitioner's Greenpark employees. On March 31, 1977, at a Board-conducted election, a majority of the employees selected the union as their bargaining agent. On July 12, the union's vice president, Edward Wecker, wrote petitioner, notifying it of the certification and of the union's right to bargain, and stating: "We look forward to meeting with you or your representative for that purpose. Please advise when it will be convenient." . . . Petitioner neither responded nor sought to consult with the union.

On July 28, petitioner notified its Greenpark employees that they would be discharged three days later. . . .

## II

. . . Congress deliberately left the words "wages, hours, and other terms and conditions of employment" without further definition, for it did not intend to deprive the Board of the power further to define those terms in light of specific industrial practices. . . .

Some management decisions, such as choice of advertising and promotion, product type and design, and financing arrangements, have only an indirect and attenuated impact on the employment relationship. See *Fibreboard*, . . . (Stewart, J., concurring). Other management decisions, such as the order of succession of layoffs and recalls, production quotas, and work rules, are almost exclusively "an aspect of the relationship" between employer and employee. . . . The present case concerns a third type of management deci-

---

Footnotes deleted—ED.

sion, one that had a direct impact on employment, since jobs were inexorably eliminated by the termination, but had as its focus only the economic profitability of the contract with Greenpark, a concern under these facts wholly apart from the employment relationship. This decision, involving a change in the scope and direction of the enterprise, is akin to the decision whether to be in business at all, "not in [itself] primarily about conditions of employment, though the effect of the decision may be necessarily to terminate employment." *Fibreboard, . . .* At the same time, this decision touches on a matter of central and pressing concern to the union and its member employees: the possibility of continued employment and the retention of the employees' very jobs. . . .

. . . The concept of mandatory bargaining is premised on the belief that collective discussions backed by the parties' economic weapons will result in decisions that are better for both management and labor and for society as a whole. . . . This will be true, however, only if the subject proposed for discussion is amenable to resolution through the bargaining process. Management must be free from the constraints of the bargaining process to the extent essential for the running of a profitable business. It also must have some degree of certainty beforehand as to when it may proceed to reach decisions without fear of later evaluations labeling its conduct an unfair labor practice. . . . [I]n view of an employer's need for unencumbered decision-making, bargaining over management decisions that have a substantial impact on the continued availability of employment should be required only if the benefit, for labor-management relations and the collective-bargaining process, outweighs the burden placed on the conduct of the business. . . .

### III

. . . We conclude that the harm likely to be done to an employer's need to operate freely in deciding whether to shut down part of its business purely for economic reasons outweighs the incremental benefit that might be gained through the union's participation in making the decision. . . .

JUSTICE BRENNAN, *with whom* JUSTICE MARSHALL *joins, dissenting.* . . .

The Court bases its decision on a balancing test. It states that "bargaining over management decisions that have a substantial impact on the continued availability of employment should be required only if the benefit, for labor-management relations and the collective-bargaining process, outweighs the burden placed on the conduct of the business." . . . I cannot agree with this test, because it takes into account only the interests of management; it fails to consider the legitimate employment interests of the workers and their union. . . . This one-sided approach hardly serves "to foster in a neutral manner" a system for resolution of these serious, two-sided controversies. . . .

. . . Apparently, the Court concludes that the benefit to labor-management relations and the collective-bargaining process from negotiation over partial closings is minimal, but it provides no evidence to that effect. The Court acknowledges that the union might be able to offer concessions, information, and alternatives that might obviate or forestall the closing, but it then asserts that "[i]t is unlikely, however, that requiring bargaining over the decision . . . will augment this flow of information and suggestions." . . . Recent experience, however, suggests the contrary. Most conspicuous, perhaps, were the negotiations between Chrysler Corporation and the United Auto Workers, which led to significant adjustments in compensation and benefits, contributing to Chrysler's ability to remain afloat. . . .

. . . I therefore agree with the Court of Appeals that employers presumptively have a duty to bargain over a decision to close an operation, and that this presumption can be rebutted by a showing that bargaining would be futile, that the closing was due to emergency financial circumstances, or that, for some other reason, bargaining would not further the purposes of the National Labor Relations Act. . . .

### Notes and Questions

1. In general companies need not bargain about the *decision* to totally or partially close a portion of its business when there is economic

justification for it, but it must bargain over the *effects* of the decision. How does this distinction between the decision and effects of the decision make a difference to workers?

2. Should the phrase "wages, hours and other terms and conditions of employment" be broad enough to include bargaining about total or partial plant closings?

3. If there is to be no "equal partnership" between unions and managers, what is the relationship to be? Without equality, what are the prospects of bringing about labor peace through collective bargaining?

4. After the *Fibreboard* and *First National Maintenance* decisions, is it fair to say that the more important a question is to worker welfare, the less likely it is to be considered by the courts as a mandatory subject for collective bargaining?

5. Given the limits of collective bargaining, what is the future role of unions? Since only about 15 percent of the workforce of the United States is unionized (one of the lowest percentages in the industrialized world), what is the role of nonunion workers in setting the terms and conditions of their employment?

How is their position different from that of Catherine Cassidy described in *Thornton* v. *Suffolk Manufacturing?*

6. Return to the contention that early hierarchical organization appears under different guises at a later time. What perennial themes do you see being replayed through the conflict over the scope of collective bargaining?

7. In a slightly earlier case, *Yeshiva* v. *NLRB,* the U.S. Supreme Court had before it the question of whether teachers in a private university could unionize. The Court ruled that they could not, because *supervisory personnel* are excluded from statutes permitting unionization and collective bargaining. The Court contrasted faculty with workers in industry, stating that collective bargaining "was intended to accommodate the type of management-employee relations that prevail in the *pyramidal hierarchies of private industries.*" In short, university professors are too unlike industrial workers at the bottom of manufacturing companies.

Although the decision was about teachers, what does the case say about the Court's estimation of "ordinary workers"?

⁂ The labor law following the *Fibreboard* case was bleak from the standpoint of organized labor; no challenge could be made to owner-manager decisions to discontinue production, regardless of how long the company had been at a place or how much workforces and communities had come to depend on the continued presence of companies. That Flint, Michigan, was virtually synonymous with General Motors, Peoria, Illinois, with Caterpillar, and Youngstown, Ohio, with U.S. Steel and other steel companies seemed to make little difference to owner-managers. Looking to the bottom line, they made decisions utterly incompatible with the longstanding dependence of workforces or communities where the companies were located.

One group of creative lawyers tried to raise questions that were otherwise unreachable in *Local 1330, United Steelworkers* v. *U.S. Steel,* 631 F.2d 1264 (1980). The case concerned the closing of very old steel mills in Youngstown which affected 3500 workers. The claim in the case was that the company had assured workforces that if they cooperated in making the mills profitable, the company would not close; that because the city of Youngstown had become so synonymous with steel, the company could not pick up and leave without compensating the community for the damages its departure would inevitably cause; and finally—if the company were unstoppable in its decision to close plants—then the company should be required to sell the facilities to the workers and the city.

The union and the city eventually lost on all issues. The court was not without sympathy for the large workforce to be left unemployed and the plight of Youngstown, Ohio, and other places in the Mahoning Valley where steelmaking and community had been virtually synonymous:

> For all of the years United States Steel has been operating in Youngstown, it has been a dominant factor in the lives of its thousands of employees and their families, and in the life of the city itself. The contemplated abrupt departure of United States Steel from Youngstown will, of course, have direct impact on 3,500 workers and their families. It will doubtless mean a devastating blow to them, to the business community and to the City of Youngstown itself. While we cannot read the future of Youngstown from this record, what the record does indicate clearly is that we deal with an economic tragedy of major proportion to Youngstown and Ohio's Mahoning Valley.

Quoting the trial court, the judge continued:

> Everything that has happened in the Mahoning Valley has been happening for many years because of steel. Schools have been built, roads have been built. Expansion that has taken place is because of steel. And to accommodate that industry, lives and destinies of the inhabitants of that community were based and planned on the basis of that institution: Steel.

The gravity of the situation acknowledged, the court had to determine whether the company had incurred obligations beyond the collective bargaining agreement which gave management prerogatives over operations and severance pay in the event of shutdown.* The court found that even though the company over the last years of operation had exhorted the workforce to bring the plants to profitability to avert closing them, either the company made no enforceable promises to its employees, or profits, as computed by the company, were never forthcoming.

Nor could the court find that the company owed any compensation to the city for its long accommodation to the companies, or that by long employment workers had acquired a property right to a job. The trial court had asked a crucial question:

> We are talking about an institution, a large corporate institution that is virtually the reason for the existence of that segment of this nation [Youngstown]. Without it, that segment of this nation perhaps suffers, instantly and severely. Whether it becomes a ghost town or not, I don't know. I am not aware of its capability for adapting.

---

*Workers with ten years or more would receive eight weeks pay in a lump sum on termination—ED.

But what has happened over the years between U.S. Steel, Youngstown and the inhabitants? Hasn't something come out of that relationship . . . not reaching for a case on property law or a series of cases, but looking at the law as a whole . . . that [a court] is to adjust human relationships in keeping with the whole spirit and foundation of the American system of law, to preserve property rights. . . .

In the end, the court could find no legal answer to match its apparent concern:

Neither in brief nor oral argument have plaintiffs pointed to any constitutional provision contained in either the Constitution of the United States or the Constitution of the State of Ohio, nor any law enacted by the United States Congress or the Legislature of Ohio, nor any case decided by the courts . . . which would convey authority to this court to require the United States Steel Corporation to continue operations in Youngstown which its officers and Board of Directors had decided to discontinue on the basis of unprofitability.

Whether to reassert its historical awareness, or to pour salt in the wounds, the court then added:

The problem of plant closing and plant removal from one section of the country to another is by no means new in American history. The former mill towns of New England, with their empty textile factory buildings, are monuments to the migration of textile manufacturers to the South, without hindrance from the Congress of the United States, from the legislatures of the states concerned, or, for that matter, from the courts of the land.

The last claim—that the company be required to sell the plants being closed to the workforces being terminated—added a further irony to the case. The company, after having successfully argued that the plants could no longer be profitably operated, refused to sell them to the workers and their community on the ground that they did not have to help *a potential competitor:*

U.S. Steel has now four times refused to deal with Steelworkers: first, when Chairman of the Board Roderick stated on January 31, 1980, in response to a question about Steelworkers' hope of buying the Youngstown Works, that the company would not sell to a subsidized competitor; second, when a representative of U.S. Steel's Realty Division told Steelworkers on February 14, 1980, that the property was not for sale to them; third, when Mr. Roderick testified to the same effect, and fourth, when Mr. Roderick formally communicated this position to Steelworkers by letter of April 18, 1980.

Time eventually ran out on the workforce and Youngstown; the case was closed and the steelmaking properties demolished. . . .

For decades, the U.S. Congress had a number of proposals on plant closings and the flight of capital to the Third World. Legislation provided federal assistance to workers whose jobs are lost through international competition, and in 1988, after a veto by President Reagan, Congress finally passed a law containing a requirement that employers give sixty days' *notice* of a plant closing. The *decision* to operate or close a plant has not been affected by this legislation and, to this day, remains an exclusive managerial prerogative.

In the *Youngstown* case, the obligation of U.S. Steel to the community was stated in general terms: the city had come to be synonymous with steel, and the company could not close down and leave the community flat. In a later case, the town of Ypsilanti, Michigan, firmed up the community position by arguing that the town's granting property tax abatements to General Motors (50 percent of $175 million worth of property devoted to Caprice production) created a promise that the company would remain in Ypsilanti for so long as the Caprice was made. General Motors announced a move of Caprice production to Texas.[†]

The lower court found a promise:

> There would be a gross inequity and patent unfairness if General Motors, having lulled the people of the Ypsilanti area into giving up millions of tax dollars which they so desperately need to educate their children and provide basic governmental services, is allowed to simply decide it will desert 4500 workers and their families because it thinks it can make these same cars cheaper somewhere else.[‡]

On appeal, the decision was reversed, first, the granting of tax abatements created no promise to continue production. Second, as for employment, General Motors was certifying only that *at the time of the issuance* of the certificate for tax abatement, would there be a likelihood "to create employment, retain employment, prevent a loss of employment . . ." Third, the fact that a manufacturer uses hyperbole and puffery (the court used as examples "We're partners" and "We look forward to growing together") does not necessarily create a promise. In short, Ypsilanti's brief victory in the lower court was turned into a defeat. General Motors was free to move production despite having applied for tax abatements.

The late 1980s and early 1990s brought into the foreground a problem even more ominous than the creation of a "rust belt" in the industrial heartland of the United States, or companies running away from relatively strong union states in the North to lower-paid nonunion labor in the Sunbelt. By the end of the 1980s, the South was losing the industrial base it had painfully been building. This time the loss was to production outside the United States. Workforces everywhere in the United States were being told to adapt to a "world economy," but most did not have the vaguest idea about how to adapt, and intuitively knew that the political leadership did not really know either. What workers everywhere could see, with their own eyes, was the disappearance of the better paying jobs from the United States.

---

[†]*Ypsilanti TP* v. *GMC*, 506 N.W.2d 556 (1993).
[‡]Ibid., 558.

# 5.10   Testimony of William H. Bywater

I AM WILLIAM H. Bywater, President of the . . . IUE. . . . I appreciate this opportunity to submit this statement on . . . a free trade agreement . . . with Mexico. It is our view that this agreement would be devastating for millions of American workers. . . .

The IUE represents production and maintenance workers in a wide spectrum of industries, including electrical-electronics, transportation, fabricated metal, power-generation equipment, furniture and automotive parts. At one time, our union had 360,000 members. Today we have 165,000. This dramatic decline . . . has been due, in large part, to our members having been displaced, as their employers have cut back or completely closed their U.S. operations in favor of offshore lower wage labor markets. While millions of American homes now contain color televisions, compact disc players, major appliances and other electronic goods with American brand names, the majority of these products are no longer made in this country. *The United States has already lost entire industries—radio and black and white television manufacturing are but two examples—and many others are sure to follow if exploitation of cheap foreign labor continues to be a cornerstone of U.S. trade policy.*

Cheap labor, however is precisely the foundation of the proposed agreement with Mexico. "Free trade" . . . means that all workers are put into competition with the most impoverished workers of the world. It does not mean decent wages and full employment. Indeed, for the FTA proponents, Mexico's most outstanding attraction is the poverty of its citizens and their corresponding willingness to work for subsistence wages. The skill and productivity of American workers becomes irrelevant in this context. Under no circumstances can U.S. workers compete with Mexican workers who earn, on average, 59 cents per hour. A free trade pact between countries of such unequal economic status is, in fact, unprecedented.

IUE members know first-hand from our experience with the Mexican maquiladora program what happens when companies go abroad for cheap labor. The "maquiladoras" are assembly plants that have been established in Mexico by foreign corporations. Ninety percent of them are U.S. owned. Maquila workers are paid the abysmal wage of 60 to 70 cents an hour.

. . . During the past decade many of our employers, including Bendix, Chrysler, General Electric, General Motors, Litton Industries, North American Philips, RCA, Sylvania, United Technologies, Westinghouse, and Zenith have abandoned assembly operations in this country and relocated them . . . across the Rio Grande. . . .

Our experience with the maquiladora program offers a preview of what American workers may expect from a free trade agreement. . . . The proposed pact would vastly expand the territory from which the companies could recruit low-wage workers. It would increase opportunities for multinational corporations to circumvent U.S. laws intended to protect workers and the environment.

It is a widespread practice of American-based companies to make components here, ship them to their maquila plants . . . for assembly, and then return the finished product to this country for sale. Currently about 95% of the components used in the maquilas are produced in the U.S. . . . [T]he proposed pact would allow Mexico to produce *more* of the *component parts.* . . . Such a shift would mean the exportation of even more jobs from this country.

Five years ago U.S. firms had invested nearly $2 billion in the maquilas and we lost nearly 300,000 manufacturing jobs. Since 1986, many American-based companies have expanded their existing operations in Mexico. . . . There are now some 2000 maquilas along the border employing nearly a half million workers. . . .

Such investment abroad has not been without domestic repercussions. The number of workers officially counted as unemployed is now 8.6 million. When the millions of others who have been forced to accept part-time employ-

U.S. House of Representatives, Committee on Small Business, April 24, 1991.

ment are counted, along with those who are too discouraged to continue their search for work, the number of Americans suffering from partial or total income loss is a staggering 15.8 million. . . .

Our members are enraged that the Bush Administration is forging ahead to negotiate a FTA . . . against this backdrop of recession, job loss, and increasing demands that U.S. workers take wage and benefit cuts. . . .

The following are but a few examples of the disastrous impact that our economic relationship with Mexico has already had on IUE members:

1. *IUE . . . Jefferson City, Tennessee* in 1978 with 2000 production workers. . . . IUE members made electronic components for televisions and video games, and television cabinets for Magnavox, Philco and Sylvania.

In 1982, the Company (North American Philips) shifted production . . . and laid off 950. . . . Eight hundred jobs were relocated to Mexico. . . . With wages at only $5.40 an hour NAP was hard pressed to argue that its labor costs were making it unprofitable. Indeed the company did not even try to seek wage concessions from the local union because it realized that even at minimum wage, the Tennessee workers could not possibly compete with Mexican workers . . . [at] *65 cents an hour—$5.20 a day.* . . .

2. *IUE . . . Evansville, Indiana:* . . . 850 Zenith workers. . . . Today we no longer represent any Zenith workers there. Both plants have been closed. The work was moved to Mexico. . . .

3. *IUE . . . Louisville, Kentucky:* Roper range is now being built in Mexico.

4. *IUE . . . Warwick, Rhode Island:* In 1987, 550 wiring assembly jobs at this GE plant were lost to Mexico. . . .

5. *IUE . . . Warren, Ohio:* In 1973, IUE represented some 13,000 production workers. . . . By 1986 GM's Packard Division had seven plants along the Mexican border, with more than 15,000 workers. . . . [O]nly 8,200 jobs remain in Warren.

6. *IUE . . . Brooklyn, New York:* . . . 600 jobs . . . Matamoras, Mexico. . . .

7. *IUE . . . Pittsfield, Mass.* Fifteen years ago GE employed 15,000. . . . Today, only 1000 hourly jobs remain. . . .

8. *IUE . . . Memphis, Tennessee:* In 1989 . . . 400 workers . . . GE announced that . . . jobs would be moved to Mexico. . . .

9. *IUE . . . Troy, Illinois:* Since 1982 employment at Basler Electric has declined . . . relocated to Reynosa and Matamoras, Mexico.

10. *IUE . . . Kirkland, Indiana:* . . . Many IUE members work for small companies which rely on larger corporations for their business. . . . Delco Products, a General Motors subsidiary, subcontracts to AES. . . . IUE members at this plant . . . make $5.00 an hour. The business there has been threatened and the jobs of members lost because Delco turned to another supplier across the border. . . .

## Notes and Questions

1. When businesses from the United States operate in Mexico, what do they encounter? First, they find massive *un*regulation in the fields of labor and the environment. The word *deregulation* is not appropriate since it conveys the idea that regulations may have once been in place and are now being rolled back; in Mexico no regulations of consequence have existed. There may be laws on the books concerning child labor, unions, workers' rights, hours of employment, paid holidays, housing taxes, and retirement plans, but one cannot know the extent to which a law on the books finds its way into day-to-day practice.

Simple assembly in textiles, electronics, and automobile subcomponents, once the whole of maquiladora enterprises, now exists alongside manufacturing with more basic inputs and more complex outputs. Factory output is still for export or is subsidiary to other manufacturing for export, with Mexican production and labor conditions more a function of external decisions than of internal choice. Peso devaluation reflects the sometimes precarious connection between Mexican production and external factors. The following chart* shows daily minimum wage

*"The Mexican Option," *Twin Plant News,* 1997, p. 18.

rates, the rate of exchange between the peso and the U.S. dollar, and the wages per hour in U.S. dollars.

|      | Daily Minimum (pesos) | Rate of Exchange (pesos per dollar) | U.S. Dollars per hour |
|------|-----------------------|-------------------------------------|-----------------------|
| 1980 | 160.00                | 26.26                               | 0.8886                |
| 1985 | 1060–1250             | 195–364.8                           | 0.81–0.49             |
| 1990 | 11,900                | 2929.8                              | 0.59                  |
| 1995 | 16.4*–18.30           | 4.94–6.78                           | 0.48–0.396            |
| 1-4-96 | 22.60               | 7.55                                | 0.44                  |

*In 1992 the Mexican peso was set at 1 new peso for 3,000 old pesos.

The chart tells us that the fluctuations in the value of the peso have had dramatic effects on the wage bills of the U.S. manufacturers located in Mexico. The fate of the Mexican workforce has turned on the domestic rate of inflation. For them, the short answer is that wages have not kept up with increases in prices: it takes more pesos to get less.[†]

On the ground, the workweek is 48 hours, which has been "gringoized" to run over a five-day week (about 9.5 working hours per day). Workers receive breakfast and lunch at the employer's expense but take meal breaks on their own time. The following chart based on the Mexican minimum wage gives some idea of the *on-paper* costs per worker, based on an eight-hour day. The on-paper costs are (those required by law—it is not known whether legally required payments are monitored or actually paid). At the time the chart was made, the peso was 7 to the dollar. It was lower in early 1997.[‡]

---

[†]See generally K. Kopinak, *Desert Capitalism: Maquiladoras in North America's Western Industrial Corridor* (Tucson: University of Arizona Press, 1996), pp. 146–150.

[‡]Nogales–Santa Cruz County Economic Development Foundation, Inc., undated, p. 20.

---

**Mexican Minimum Wage Fully Fringed, as of April 1, 1996**

| Rate of Exchange 7.0 Pesos to 1 U.S. Dollar | U.S./Mexico Border* | |
|---|---|---|
| | Minimum Wage | |
| | PESOS | DOLLARS |
| 1.  Regional Minimum Salary (D.R. = Daily Rate) | 22.60 | $3.23 |
| 2.  Annual Salary (365 Days × D.R.) | 8,249.00 | $1,178.43 |
| 3.  Christmas Bonus (15 Days × D.R.) | 339.00 | 48.43 |
| 4.  Vacations 6 Days included in the 365 days plus 25% of 6 days × D.R. | 33.90 | 4.84 |
| 5.  Payroll Taxes—Employer | | |
|     A)  Social Security (Computed on Annual Salary) | 2,139.67 | 305.67 |
|     B)  1% Children's Nursery Tax (Computed on Annual Salary) | 82.49 | 11.78 |
|     C)  5% Housing Tax (Computed on 2 + 3 + 4) | 431.10 | 61.59 |
|     D)  2.50% State Tax (Computed on 2 + 3 + 4) | 215.55 | 30.79 |
|     E)  2.00% Retirement Savings Fund (Computed on 2 + 3 + 4) | 172.44 | 24.63 |
| TOTAL ANNUAL COST | 11,663.12 | $1,666.16 |

*(table continues on next page)*

---

**Mexican Minimum Wage Fully Fringed, as of April 1, 1996**   *(Continued)*

| | | U.S./Mexico Border* | |
| :--- | :---: | :---: | ---: |
| *Rate of Exchange* | | *Minimum Wage* | |
| *7.0 Pesos to 1 U.S. Dollar* | | PESOS | DOLLARS |
| 6.  Yearly Worked Hours | | | |
|     A)  Days in a Year | 365 | | |
|         Less: Sundays | 52 | | |
|             Legal Holidays | 8 | | |
|             Vacations | 6 | | |
|         Total Working Days | 299 | | |
|         8 Hours per Day | × 8 | | |
|     B)  Total Annual Worked Hours | 2,392 | | |
| 7.  Fully Fringed Hourly Minimum Wage | | 4.88 | $0.70 |
|     (Annual Cost Divided by Annual Worked Hours) | | | |

---

$$\frac{\text{Minimum Wage in Pesos}}{\text{Rate of Exchange}} = \begin{array}{c}\text{Minimum wage}\\ \text{fully fringed}\\ \text{in dollars}\end{array} \quad \text{For example:} \quad \frac{4.88}{7.00} = 0.70 \text{ U.S. dollars}$$

---

*The daily minimum wage for cities in the interior of the state of Sonora, Mexico is 7.5 percent less than the daily minimum wage for cities along the Arizona-Mexico border.

 &#42690; The following excerpt shows how international production is organized in Indonesia for the assembly of Nike footwear by a Korean subcontractor of Nike.

## 5.11 | The New Free-Trade Heel   *Jeffrey Ballinger*

HER ONLY NAME IS Sadisah [1 in Figure 5.11-A], and it's safe to say that she's never heard of Michael Jordan. Nor is she spending her evenings watching him and his Olympic teammates gliding and dunking in prime time from Barcelona. But she *has* heard of the shoe company he endorses—Nike, whose logo can be seen on the shoes and uniforms of many American Olympic athletes this summer. Like Jordan, Sadisah works on behalf of Nike. You won't see her, however, in the flashy TV images of freedom and individuality that smugly command us to JUST DO IT!—just spend upward of $130 for a pair of basketball shoes. Yet Sadisah is, in fact, one of the people who *is* doing it—making the actual shoes, that is, and earning paychecks such as this one in a factory in Indonesia. . . .

In the 1980s, Oregon-based Nike closed its last U.S. footwear factory, in Saco, Maine, while establishing most of its new factories in South Korea, where Sung Hwa Corp. [2] is based. Sung Hwa is among many independent producers Nike has contracted with. Nike's actions were part of the broader "globalization" trend that saw the United States lose 65,300 footwear jobs between 1982 and 1989 as shoe companies sought non-unionized Third World workers who didn't require the U.S. rubber-shoe industry average of $6.94 an hour. But in the late 1980s, South Ko-

**FIGURE 5.11-A**

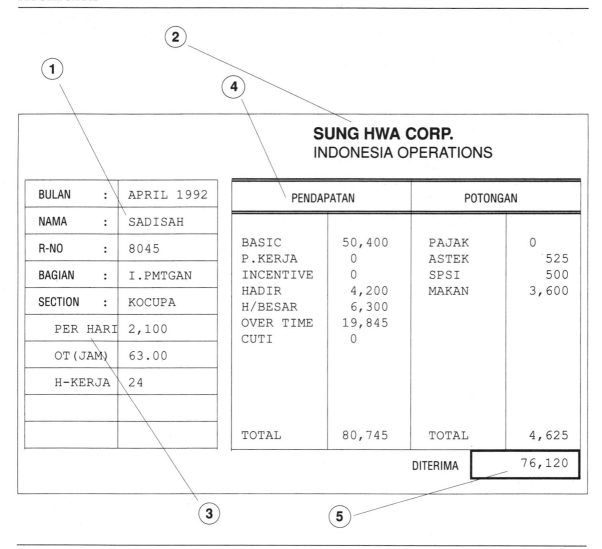

## SUNG HWA CORP.
### INDONESIA OPERATIONS

| BULAN | : | APRIL 1992 |
|---|---|---|
| NAMA | : | SADISAH |
| R-NO | : | 8045 |
| BAGIAN | : | I.PMTGAN |
| SECTION | : | KOCUPA |
| PER HARI | | 2,100 |
| OT (JAM) | | 63.00 |
| H-KERJA | | 24 |
| | | |
| | | |

| PENDAPATAN | | POTONGAN | |
|---|---|---|---|
| BASIC | 50,400 | PAJAK | 0 |
| P.KERJA | 0 | ASTEK | 525 |
| INCENTIVE | 0 | SPSI | 500 |
| HADIR | 4,200 | MAKAN | 3,600 |
| H/BESAR | 6,300 | | |
| OVER TIME | 19,845 | | |
| CUTI | 0 | | |
| TOTAL | 80,745 | TOTAL | 4,625 |
| | | DITERIMA | 76,120 |

rean laborers gained the right to form independent unions and to strike. Higher wages cut into Nike's profits. The company shifted new factories to poorer countries such as Indonesia, where labor rights are generally ignored and wages are but one seventh of South Korea's. (The Sung Hwa factory and others like it are located in Tangerang, a squalid industrial boomtown just outside Jakarta.) Today, to make 80 million pairs of shoes annually, Nike contracts with several dozen factories globally, including six in Indonesia. Others are in China, Malaysia, Thailand, and Taiwan. By shifting factories to cheaper labor pools, Nike has posted year after year of growth; in 1991 the company grossed more than $3 billion in sales—$200 million of which Nike attributes to Jordan's endorsement—and reported a net profit of $287 million, its highest ever. . . .

The words [3] printed on the pay stub are in Bahasa Indonesia, a language created by fusing Roman characters with a dominant Malay dialect. The message, however, is bottom-line capitalism. "Per hari" is the daily wage for seven and a half hours of work, which in Sadisah's case is 2,100 Indonesia rupiah—at the current rate of exchange, $1.03 *per day*. That amount, which works out to just under 14 cents per hour, is less than the Indonesian government's figure for "minimum physical need." A recent International Labor Organization survey found that 88 percent of Indonesian women working at Sadisah's wage rates are malnourished. And most workers in this factory—over 80 percent—are women. With seldom more than elementary-school educations, they are generally in their teens or early twenties, and have come from outlying agricultural areas in search of city jobs and a better life. Sadisah's wages allow her to rent a shanty without electricity or running water. . . .

"Pendapatan" [4] is the earnings column, and five lines below the base pay figure for the month (50,400 rupiah) is one for overtime. Sadisah and the other workers in this factory are compelled to put in extra hours, both by economic necessity and by employer fiat. Each production line of 115 workers is expected to produce about 1,600 pairs of Nikes a day. According to the column at left, next to "OT (JAM)," Sadisah worked 63 hours of overtime during this pay period, for which she received an extra 2 cents per hour. At this factory, which makes mid-priced Nikes, each pair of shoes requires .84 man-hours to produce; working on an assembly line, Sadisah assembled the equivalent of 13.9 pairs every day. The profit margin on each pair is enormous. The labor costs to manufacture a pair of Nikes that sells for $80 in the United States is approximately 12 cents. . . .

Here [5] are Sadisah's net earnings for a month of labor. She put in six days a week, ten and a half hours per day, for a paycheck equivalent to $37.46—about half the retail price of one pair of the sneakers she makes. Boosters of the global economy and "free markets" claim that creating employment around the world promotes free trade between industrializing and developing countries. But how many West-ern products can people in Indonesia buy when they can't earn enough to eat? The answer can't be found in Nike's TV ads showing Michael Jordan sailing above the earth for his reported multiyear endorsement fee of $20 million—an amount, incidentally, that at the pay rate shown here would take Sadisah 44,492 years to earn. . . .

## Notes and Questions

1. A. In some ways Nike is "well known" in the United States, but in other ways it is not. Tell a friend about Nike in Indonesia, Sadisah, and "offshore assembly." Record your friend's reaction to the story and your discussion.

   B. Nike is only one example of the many companies that choose to manufacture overseas. Nike's response to criticism of employment practices may be narrow— Nike does not own or control the companies doing the assembly—or broad— Nike operates in an internationally competitive market that is not of its own making.

   If you are upset over the exploitation of workers in Indonesia, how would you refute Nike's responses?

2. Did the author pick the right comparison to demonstrate the dismal fate of Sadisah? Michael Jordan's earnings from endorsements are impressive, and it is stunning to think that Sadisah would have to work over 44,000 years to match his contract with Nike. Closer study, based on Nike company reports, reveals that Michael Jordan, big fish that he is, is not the biggest fish that might be found in the story of Nike production.

   Michael Jordan makes no production decisions for Nike; he is simply part of their sales force. On the other hand, Philip Knight, the Nike president and CEO, does. [At the time the article was written,—Ed.] he owned enough stock (about 25 million shares) to control the board of directors. If he converted his shares and sold them over the stock exchange they would bring almost $2 billion (Oct. 9, 1992 closing price was $79 per share). In addition to his stock, Knight makes almost $1 million a year plus perks. If you have a talent for high numbers, you can calculate how long Sadisah would have to work at $37 per month to amass the fortune that Knight already has.

Nike has no labor problems of its own because it has very little labor in the usual sense of the word. Footwear and apparel are manufactured by subcontractors and Nike is essentially a marketing company. All Nike footwear and half of Nike apparel are made overseas. (The other half is made by subcontractors in the southern United States. Nike now operates in Vietnam as well as Indonesia.)

        ❧ Is Indonesia exceptional as a place of low wage, export-oriented assembly? Next is a description of industrial processing zones as they have been established all over the world.

## 5.12 | Industrial Processing Zones   *John J. Bonsignore*

IN THE STORY FROM Indonesia, the factory where Sadisah works is said to be located in "a squalid industrial boomtown just outside Jakarta." In other countries there have been more clearly identified zones set aside for the establishment of factories most commonly called "export processing zones" (EPZs). Virtually every underdeveloped country has them, and after the Los Angeles riot, industrial zones for depressed urban and rural areas of the United States were proposed as a way to reduce unemployment, while providing incentives for businesses to locate in areas where they might not otherwise choose to do so.

The idea behind zones is easy to grasp even though the many effects of zones are not. A country offers international companies a place or zone where they can set up factories, import factory machinery and other inputs duty-free, employ locals, and export the product from the zone. On the other end of the line—the final destination of the products—there is either no import duty imposed, or the duty imposed is reduced.

Decisions about production are controlled by the international company. The "home" country, where the multinational company is "based," sometimes gets the benefit of employment from making inputs for export to the zone for further processing—parts to an electronic game, components for electrical equipment for a car, or dyed leather for a handbag. In addition, there may be some import duties collected by the home country, and "cheap products" are available to home country consumers. But the government of the home country may also furnish financial and nonfinancial subsidies—sometimes low visibility subsidies—to the companies going abroad. For example, the home country may make grants or extend loans to the "host country" to pay for the infrastructure necessary to make the processing zone feasible. And perhaps some food aid might be allocated to the cooperating country that opens itself to processing zones.

The home country loses "labor intensive" work, hence the contradictory impulse at the present time in the United States to subsidize labor intensive assembly work in urban and rural areas where there has been chronic unemployment, while at the same time promoting the movement of assembly and other work "offshore" through free trade agreements which can intensify the movement of production overseas.

The "host" country, where the enterprise zones are located, gets employment, and contributes what it must to attract industry to the zone. In addition, contributions of the host country to EPZ's can include assistance in finance, free factory space, roads, harbor and trans-

From *Law and Multinationals: A Study in Law and Political Economy.*

portation improvement, water and sewage systems, job training, policing and security, public transportation, housing, health facilities, and so on. The host country also usually abdicates most of its rights to impose legal regulations in the zone either by express grant, that is, "on the law books," or by the nonenforcement of law that would, strictly speaking, be applicable in the zone. Despite the general endorsement in business of good organization and precise control, when it comes to some aspects of law, businesses prefer lawlessness, usually termed "deregulation." This latter preference becomes the working understanding in most zones.

Those in favor of zones defend them as a great way for underdeveloped countries to promote growth, create employment, and generate needed foreign exchange. Those more skeptical of zones look on them as publicly-subsidized enclaves for gain that accrues primarily to the multinational corporate participants, and leaves zone workforces as a permanent underclass. Whatever growth is counted is usually accompanied by uncounted losses: the employment is marginal and often below subsistence, the infrastructure is pushed beyond environmentally sound limits, and countries are caught in endless rounds of debt from which improvement in the levels of foreign exchange never seem to extricate them.

## Questions and Comments

1. The identification of benefits and detriments, and beneficiaries and victims, is difficult to make in that the gains and losses from the zones are *stratified* in both the "home" and the "host" countries. Return briefly to the Nike case: Can it be said that the United States *as a whole* gained, or that Indonesia *as a whole* gained, or must there be a more careful assessment of just what groups or social strata we are talking about?

Did the owners of Nike gain? The workers in Saco, Maine? Do consumers of Nike footwear in the United States and Europe gain? The principals of the South Korean subcontractor?

Do the workers in Indonesia gain? Are there other people in Indonesia who gain through their allegiances with international companies or their willingness to deliver a tractable workforce?

2. The primary focus during the 1980s was on the exploitation of women in Third World production. In the 1990s concern for children came into greater visibility. For example, in the last days of the Clinton administration, Alexis Herman, secretary of labor, appeared with the secretaries of state and treasury to discuss child labor across the world. Two-hundred and fifty thousand children between the ages of nine and fourteen were working. Half of the children were working full time. Secretary of State Albright commented on "initiatives" to curtail child labor, but one wondered just what was being undertaken and what was designed to gloss over prior inaction. Lawrence Summers of the Treasury Department spoke of using customs to head off products produced with child labor. With respect to child labor there is understatement and overstatement: understatement of the use of child labor in products commonly sold in the United States and overstatement of actions taken to curtail the exploitation of children.

3. When we see a "cheap shirt" at a shopping mall should we add all of the costs that are not necessarily reflected in the ticket price? Compare the production in industrial processing zones where workforces are unprotected to the conditions in the U.S. textile industry, described in the *American Textile Manufacturers* case (page 103).

4. According to the Marxian explanation of legal systems, a legal system will reflect relationships of status, power, and stratification extrinsic to the system rather than imposing limits or counterweights to those relationships. Marxists also argue that although surface appearances and labels change—slavery, feudalism, national industrialization, and now worldwide industrialization—the deep structure of legal systems remains the same.

Using the various readings found in this chapter, evaluate the Marxian thesis.

# 6  LAW AND POPULAR WILL

The Chief Magistrate derives all of his authority from the people.

>    Abraham Lincoln, First Inaugural Address (1861)

When the great lord passes, the wise peasant bows deeply and silently farts.*

>    Ethiopian proverb

. . . that this nation, under God, shall have a new birth of freedom—and that government of the people, by the people and for the people shall not perish from the earth.

>    Abraham Lincoln, Gettysburg Address (1863)

Whoever puts his hand on me to govern me is a usurper and a tyrant. I declare him my enemy.

>    Joseph Proudhon

    ❧ In a period when alienation from virtually all institutions is proceeding swiftly, one may begin to wonder when people might wake up and shake government and law off their backs. Those voters who have faith enough to cast periodic ballots labor under no illusion that their voting makes a grand difference. There might have been less alienation in the nineteenth century when scholars took an interest in tracing the origin of law and the evolution of legal institutions. They believed that law evolved out of the customary practices of people. At first, practices occurred and unarticulated sentiments were felt in a group of people. There was no consciousness that certain activities were the *right* ones, or the *only* ones that would be tolerated. After a time, and particularly on occasions of deviance from prior practice, *a* way of acting or behaving became *the* way of acting and behaving; what previously was customary had become law.

    Readers of this early literature are left with the idea that there is an organic connection between law and custom. Law grows out of custom, or in other words, custom contains embryonic law, practice on its way to becoming perfect—as soon as the appropriate level of consciousness has been reached. The *Spoiled Chiles* case which appeared in Chapter 4 suggests that there is not always a breach between people and their dispute resolution system. The cases from the Cheyenne that appear in this section also suggest that there can be an organic connection between the exercise of authority and custom.

    As society grows larger and more specialized, people feel less correspondence between their understandings and the institutions around them. Whereas a Cheyenne might know intimately much of "the law" of the tribe, it is highly unlikely that in modern America citizens will know, let alone agree with, much of the law that could touch their lives. Under-

---

*Quoted by James Scott, *Domination and the Arts of Resistance* (New Haven, Conn.: Yale University Press, 1990).

standably, the expression "Can *they* do that?" displaces "This is how *we* handle situations like that"; hierarchy, bewilderment, resentment, and fear replace mutuality, understanding, voluntary compliance, and love.

Stanley Diamond, a contemporary anthropologist rejected the earlier theory of the congenial relationship between custom and law, describes the relationship between custom and law as follows:

> Efforts to legislate conscience by external political power are the antithesis of custom; customary behavior comprises precisely those aspects of social behavior which are traditional, moral and religious, which are in short, conventional and nonlegal. Put another way, custom is social morality. The relationship between custom and law is basically one of contradiction, not continuity.[†]

For Diamond, then, the advent of law is a sign of social breakdown rather than a mark of heightened consciousness and civility. Life under law becomes less liveable and not more liveable for the average person.

There are numerous difficulties in charting the relationship between law and popular will. Who are *the* people whose will is expressed or frustrated by the creation and operation of law? We have already seen in the previous chapters that it is an ill wind that blows no good; that is, to get at the effects of law, one must look across all strata of society and all groups whose life may be touched by the law in question.

*The* people may mean a numerical majority, an influential elite, the poor, the middle class once referred to as the "silent majority," blacks and minorities, women, white Anglo-Saxon Protestant males, the young, the aged, and so on. Although popular sentiments may be shared among these groups on many questions, there can also be large differences.

How does popular will get expressed? By voting? Street protest? Boycotts? "Public interest" groups? PACs? Lobbyists in the halls of Congress, at the Executive Branch or in the state legislatures? What is the link between tactics and legal action and outcomes?

Is activism designed to get law made or unmade? Do people want better law, more law, less bad law, or no law at all? The difficulties in making a coherent statement on the relationship between people and law might make it tempting to scrap the inquiry altogether, or at least limit the explanation to "simple" societies. However, there are too many occasions for tension between people and their institutions for the question to be abandoned. In the North Carolina cases on spousal abuse, the courts—unless mindless and diabolical—must have had some feel for the probable reception of their decisions, however chauvinistic their decisions look from today's perspectives. Similarly in the *Ducktown Sulphur* case in Chapter 4,

---

[†]Stanley Diamond, "The Rule of Law versus the Order of Custom," in *In Search of the Primitive* (New Brunswick, N.J.: Transaction Books, 1974).

the court might have been afraid that closing the plant would cause a local furor among the nonelite as well as the elite.

Although the influence of ordinary people on law has been sporadic and diffuse, there have been notable instances of popular pressure. In the nineteenth century, Populism took the form of advocating soft money for the repayment of debt, opposing the power of railroads, pressing for the recognition of labor unions and collective bargaining, and demanding equal legal and political status for women. Not surprisingly, people who have sought changes in the status quo—from farmers to trade unionists to blacks to feminists—have found themselves on the wrong side of law. As one example, during the first seven years of the Sherman Antitrust Act—an act supposedly designed to curb the power of large business—the federal courts found twelve violations of the act by labor and only one by business! The familiar cordon of police around street protesters conveys the not so subtle message that the protesters are on the edge of criminality.

The last thirty years have been marked by black activism, resistance to the Vietnam War, farmers' strikes for parity, the women's movement, gay rights initiatives, antinuclear protests, and, more recently, a fundamentalist Christian revolt against artistic expression, abortion, and the prohibition of school prayer.

In the late 1980s, economic questions crowded out earlier causes of popular unrest. Many workers were permanently laid off by a changing economy and the flight of capital and industry abroad for higher profits. Small businesses, especially in home building, experienced the highest rate of bankruptcies since the Great Depression. Farmers on prime land, with the best cash crops in a hungry world, found themselves caught in a cost-price squeeze that took many of them out of farming. In the 1990s corporate mergers and downsizing added middle managers to the ranks of those hanging onto their jobs for dear life.

In addition, women, minorities, and aliens, who had never really received systemic advantages in terms of job opportunities, adequate health care, housing, and schooling were declared to have been excessively advantaged and found themselves caught in a backlash of antagonisms, fueled in part by the fear that power and property might have to be shared and not monopolized.

When people assert themselves, they are usually regarded as criminals, people out of control, crazies, or revolutionaries. To the extent that challenges to authority disrupt the prevailing order, activists are at least provisional anarchists, that is, willing to openly declare that all is not well with "the system." The deeper the distrust of institutions and their alleged salutary effects, the more anarchical the sentiment, a theme that will be developed in the second part of this chapter. But first, how did custom-law-government work in so-called simple societies?

## 6.1 | The Cheyenne Way    *Karl N. Llewellyn and E. Adamson Hoebel*

### WHEN WALKING RABBIT RAISED A PROBLEM THE TRIBAL OSTRACISM AND REINSTATEMENT OF STICKS EVERYTHING UNDER HIS BELT

ONCE, AT A TIME when all the Cheyenne tribe was gathered together, Sticks Everything Under His Belt went out hunting buffalo alone. "I am hunting for myself," he told the people. He was implying that the rules against individual hunting did not apply to him because he was declaring himself out of the tribe—a man on his own.

All the soldier chiefs and all the tribal chiefs met in a big lodge to decide what to do in this case, since such a thing had never happened before. This was the ruling they made: no one could help Sticks Everything Under His Belt in any way, no one could give him smoke, no one could talk to him. They were cutting him off from the tribe. The chiefs declared that if anyone helped him in any way that person would have to give a Sun Dance.

When the camp moved, Sticks Everything Under His Belt moved with it, but the people would not recognize him. He was left alone and it went to his heart, so he took one of his horses (he had many) and rode out to the hilltops to mourn.

His sister's husband was a chief in the camp. This brother-in-law felt sorry for him out there mourning, with no more friends. At last he took pity on his poor brother-in-law; at last he spoke to his wife, "I feel sorry for your poor brother out there and now I am going to do something for him. Cook up all those tongues we have! Prepare a good feast!"

Then he invited the chiefs to his lodge and sent for his brother-in-law to come in. This was after several years had passed, not months.

When the chiefs had assembled, the brother-in-law spoke. "Several years ago you passed a ruling that no one could help this man. Whoever

should do so you said would have to give a Sun Dance. Now is the time to take pity on him. I am going to give a Sun Dance to bring him back in. I beg you to let him come back to the tribe, for he has suffered long enough. This Sun Dance will be a great one. I declare that every chief and all the soldiers must join in. Now I put it up to you. Shall we let my brother-in-law smoke before we eat, or after?"

The chiefs all answered in accord, "Ha-ho, ha-ho [thank you, thank you]. We are very glad you are going to bring back this man. However, let him remember that he will be bound by whatever rules the soldiers lay down for the tribe. He may not say he is outside of them. He has been out of the tribe for a long time. If he remembers these things, he may come back."

Then they asked Sticks Everything Under His Belt whether he wanted to smoke before or after they had eaten. Without hesitation he replied, "Before," because he had craved tobacco so badly that he had split his pipe stem to suck the brown gum inside of it.

The lodge was not big enough to hold all the chiefs who had come to decide this thing, so they threw open the door, and those who could not get in sat in a circle outside. Then they filled a big pipe and when it was lighted they gave it to Sticks Everything Under His Belt. It was so long since he had tobacco that he gulped in the smoke and fell over in a faint. As he lay there the smoke came out of his anus, he was so empty. The chiefs waited silently for him to come to again and then the pipe was passed around the circle.

When all had smoked, Sticks Everything Under His Belt talked. "From now on I am going to run with the tribe. Everything the people say, I shall stay right by it. My brother-in-law has done a great thing. He is going to punish himself in the Sun Dance to bring me back. He won't do it alone, for I am going in, too."

After a while the people were getting ready for the Sun Dance. One of the soldiers began to get worried because he had an ugly growth on his body which he did not want to reveal to the people. He was a good-looking young man named Black Horse. Black Horse went to the head chiefs asking them to let him sacrifice himself alone on the hilltops as long as the Sun Dance was in progress.

"We have nothing to say to that," they told him. "Go to the pledger. This is his Sun Dance."

Black Horse went to the brother-in-law of Sticks Everything Under His Belt, who was a brother-in-law to him as well. "Brother-in-law," he begged, "I want to be excused from going into the lodge. Can't you let me go into the hills to sacrifice myself as long as you are in there, to make my own bed?"

"No," he was rebuffed, "you know my rule is that all must be there."

"Well, brother-in-law, won't it be all right if I set up a pole on the hill and hang myself to it through my breasts? I shall hang there for the duration of the dance."

This brother-in-law of his answered him in these words. "Why didn't you take that up when all the chiefs were in the lodge? I have agreed with them that everyone must be in the lodge. I don't want to change the rule. I won't give you permission to go outside."

Then Black Horse replied, "You will not make the rules my way. Now I am going to put in a rule for everybody. Everyone in there has to swing from the pole as I do."

"No," countered the brother-in-law. "That was not mentioned in the meeting. If you want to swing from the pole, that is all right, but no one else has to unless he wishes to."

When they had the Sun Dance everyone had a good time. Black Horse was the only one on the pole, and there were so many in the lodge that there was not room enough for all to dance. Some just had to sit around inside the lodge. Though they did not dance, they starved themselves for four days. This dance took place near Sheridan, Wyoming, seven years before Custer. I was only a year old at that time, but what I have said here was told by Elk River and others. We call this place "Where the Chiefs Starved Themselves."

## CRIES YIA EYA BANISHED FOR THE MURDER OF CHIEF EAGLE

Cries Yia Eya had been gone from the camp for three years because he had killed Chief Eagle in a whiskey brawl. The chiefs had ordered him away for his murder, so we did not see anything of him for that time. Then one day he came back, leading a horse packed with bundles of old-time tobacco. He stopped outside the camp and sent a messenger in with the horse and tobacco who was to say to the chiefs for him, "I am begging to come home."

The chiefs all got together for a meeting, and the soldier societies were told to convene, for there was an important matter to be considered. The tobacco was divided up and chiefs' messengers were sent out to invite the soldier chiefs to come to the lodge of the tribal council, for the big chiefs wanted to talk to them. "Here is the tobacco that man sent in," they told the soldier chiefs. "Now we want you soldiers to decide if you think we should accept his request. If you decide that we should let him return, then it is up to you to convince his family that it is all right." (The relatives of Chief Eagle had told everybody that they would kill Cries Yia Eya on sight if they ever found him. "If we set eyes on him, he'll never make another track," they had vowed.) The soldier chiefs took the tobacco and went out to gather their troops. Each society met in its own separate lodge to talk among themselves, but the society servants kept passing back and forth between their different lodges to report on the trend of the discussion in the different companies.

At last one man said, "I think it is all right. I believe the stink has blown from him. Let him return!" This view was passed around, and this is the view that won out among the soldiers. Then the father of Chief Eagle was sent for and asked whether he would accept the decision. "Soldiers," he replied, "I shall listen to you. Let him return! But if that man comes back, I want never to hear his voice raised against another person. If he does, we come together. As far as that stuff of his is concerned, I want nothing that belonged to him. Take this share you have set aside for me and give it to someone else."

Cries Yia Eya had always been a mean man, disliked by everyone, but he had been a fierce fighter against the enemies. After he came back to the camp, however, he was always good to the people.

## WHEN WALKING RABBIT RAISED A PROBLEM

A war party was organizing. Walking Rabbit approached the leader with a question. "Is it true that you have declared we must all go afoot? If so, I would like to be able to lead a horse to pack my moccasins and possibles." The leader gave him an answer. "There is a reason for my ruling. I want no horses, that it may be easier for us to conceal our movements. However, you may bring one horse." Then Walking Rabbit asked for instructions concerning the location of the first and second nights' camps, for he would start late and overtake the party.

Walking Rabbit's sweetheart had been married only recently to another. "My husband is not the man I thought he was," she told her former suitor. So Walking Rabbit took her to join the war party. [The Cheyennes have a phrase for the single man who marries a one-time married woman—"putting on the old moccasin."] In this way, it turned out that the "moccasin" he was packing was a big woman.

When they saw this woman there, the warriors got excited. The party turned into the hills and stopped. The leader opened his pipe. The leader's pipe was always filled before they left the camp, but it was not smoked until the enemy was seen or their tracks reported. Now the leader spoke. "When we take a woman with us it is usually known in the camp. Here is a man who has sneaked off with another's wife. Now what is going to happen?" That is what they were talking about.

The leader declared, "The only thing this man can do is return and make a settlement with the husband. Then he may follow us up."

One warrior was for aiding Walking Rabbit. "Why can't we let him stay?" was his proposal. "If we take any horses, we can give them to her husband." That was rejected.

The decision was that he had to go back. "If you had told us you wanted her so badly, we might have waited for you to settle for her. Then we could have taken her the right way. If you really want to go to war with us, you will be able to overtake us. We are afoot."

Then three or four warriors spoke up, each promising Walking Rabbit a horse to send to the husband. Everyone gave one or two arrows to be sent as well.

In the meantime Walking Rabbit's father had fixed it up with the aggrieved husband. Since he and his wife were incompatible, he was willing to release her. When Walking Rabbit came in and told his father the story of the soldiers' action, the father said, "Just let that stand. The thing is fixed. When those fighters come back they may want to give to the girl's parents. You go back after your party." But Walking Rabbit preferred to stay at home.

When Walking Rabbit did not go out, his closest relatives raised a big tipi. When they heard of the approach of the returning war party, everything was in readiness.

The warriors came charging in, shooting; they had taken many horses. The first coup-counters were in the van. Walking Rabbit's father had a right to harangue; he was a crier. "Don't go to your homes! Don't go to your own lodges! Come here to the lodge of Walking Rabbit, your friend!"

When they were all in this lodge the old man entered and told them his story. "I had this thing all settled before my son returned. You have sent arrows and promised horses. Now I have kept this girl here pending your return. I shall send her back to her parents with presents. I have waited to see what you are going to do."

The leader replied for his followers. "Yes, we will help you. We promised to help your son. When you send her back, we'll send presents with her. The men who had promised horses went out to get them. Others gave captured horses.

Sending her back with these presents was giving wedding gifts. Her relatives got them all. They gathered up their goods to send back. The war party was called together once more; to them this stuff was given. It was a great thing for the people to talk about. It was the first and last time a woman was sent home on enemy horses the day they came in.

*Notes and Questions*

1. What was the law in these cases, and who made it?

2. What was the relationship between the exercise of tribal authority and the popular sentiments of the Cheyenne?

3. Was a precedent system operating here?

4. What values were at stake in the cases?

5. How were the varying positions or interests delineated, recognized, and secured?

6. Did the Cheyenne equivalent of the person on the street have anything to complain about regarding the way trouble was handled or the outcomes reached?

Llewellyn concluded that the Cheyenne found a correspondence between their personal beliefs and the exercise of tribal authority, but many modern Americans may frequently feel that there is no accord between themselves and the institutions they come "under." Today the "system" and "law" are "out there"—potentially menacing, remote creations. Whereas Lincoln could speak comfortably of government "*of, by,* and *for* the people," today Americans might think—sometimes for excellent reasons—of government as *of, by,* and *for* someone else. Yet, like Kafka's commoners, they might be inclined to blame troubles on "personal problems" rather than structural failures. To think and act otherwise might take them to political stances which they do not want to take. One such stance is *anarchism,* which not one person in a thousand would publicly endorse.

But just what is anarchism? For most it stands simply for chaos, or finding a special relish in disrupting order, preferably by violence. Those who dismiss anarchism with a wave of the hand are not aware of the substantial literature that exists on anarchism reaching back to ancient times, or that anarchists respect order—if it is created and maintained in the right way, that is, if the order is *of, by,* and *for* the people. Moreover, anarchists count many pacifists in their midst.

Another misunderstanding arises when anarchism is lumped in with Marxism, a lumping that neglects the antipathy between anarchists and Marxists that has persisted for over one hundred years; one of the first tasks of the Bolsheviks after the 1917 Russian Revolution was to purge the revolution of anarchists!

Michael Bakunin, a famous anarchist, had this to say about Karl Marx, whom he may have wanted to like, but couldn't:

> Marx and I were friendly enough in those days (the 1840's). We saw one another often, for I respected him a great deal for his science and his passionate and serious devotion—mingled as it was with a certain personal vanity—to the cause of the proletariat, and I sought avidly his ever instructive and intelligent conversation. Yet there was no intimacy between us. Our temperaments did not suit each other. He called me a sentimental idealist—and he was right. I called him vain, perfidious and sly—and I was right too.*

---

*George Woodcock, *The Anarchist Reader* (London: Fontana, 1977), p. 37.

Joseph Proudhon in a letter to Marx in 1846 spelled out some of the differences that led ultimately to a total breach between Marxists and anarchists which has lasted to this day. If anarchists and Marxists concurred on the maldistribution of power and wealth, they differed dramatically on what to do if they succeeded in upsetting it:

> [F]or God's sake, after having demolished all the a priori dogmatisms, do not let us in turn dream of indoctrinating the people; do not let us in our turn fall into the contradiction of your compatriot Martin Luther . . . let us carry on a good and loyal polemic; let us give the world an example of learned and far-sighted tolerance, but let us not pose as apostles of a new religion, even if it be the religion of logic, the religion of reason. Let us gather together and encourage all protests, let us brand all exclusiveness, all mysticism; let us never regard a question as exhausted, and when we have used our last argument, let us begin again, if need be, with eloquence and irony. On that condition I will enter your association. Otherwise no.[†]

The dogmatism of Marx was anathema to the anarchists, who believed that there could be no "blueprint" for the future. To try to impose one, no matter how clear-sighted the planners thought themselves to be, would resurrect the very tyranny which impelled the revolution in the first place. If the Marxists advocated a proletarian-run state, the anarchist advocated no state at all: the Marxist prophecy of the disappearance of the state, once economic relationships were made equitable, is a partial borrowing from the anarchists, who were not inclined toward the state at all.

It is the disagreement over the role of the state that has created chasms between the two predominant left philosophies. Power to the people is perhaps more anarchist than Marxist, although both groups endorse a power shift from the powerful to the powerless. Marxists anticipate a transfer of power back to the state to hold fast revolutionary gains; anarchists want to maximize the opportunities for direct action by the people themselves. If this sounds reminiscent of current political rhetoric, it is because politicians in both major parties frequently tap the American antipathy to government. The invocation of anarchist-like slogans is often rhetorical, however, since defense spending, national debt, and other centrist practices inevitably lead to more government rather than less.

Under neither left philosophy does legal order, as generally constituted, get much respect. Under both it is seen as a regime of domination rather than a source of protection for average people. To give a better idea of the unique features of anarchistic thought, here follows a reading from the most famous modern anarchist, Peter Kropotkin (1841–1921).

---

[†]Ibid., pp. 72,73.

# 6.2 | Law and Authority   *Peter Kropotkin*

## I

WE ARE SO PERVERTED by an education which from infancy seeks to kill in us the spirit of revolt, and to develop that of submission to authority; we are so perverted by this existence under the ferrule of a law, which regulates every event in life—our birth, our education, our development, our love, our friendship—that, if this state of things continues, we shall lose all initiative, all habit of thinking for ourselves. Our society seems no longer able to understand that it is possible to exist otherwise than under the reign of law, elaborated by a representative government and administered by a handful of rulers. And even when it has gone so far as to emancipate itself from the thralldom, its first care has been to reconstitute it immediately. "The Year I of Liberty" has never lasted more than a day, for after proclaiming it men put themselves the very next morning under the yoke of law and authority.

Indeed, for some thousands of years, those who govern us have done nothing but ring the changes upon "Respect for law, obedience to authority." This is the moral atmosphere in which parents bring up their children, and school only serves to confirm the impression. Cleverly assorted scraps of spurious science arc inculcated upon the children to prove necessity of law; obedience to the law is made a religion; moral goodness and the law of the masters are fused into one and the same divinity. The historical hero of the schoolroom is the man who obeys the law, and defends it against rebels.

Later when we enter upon public life, society and literature, impressing us day by day and hour by hour as the water-drop hollows the stone, continue to inculcate the same prejudice. Books of history, of political science, of social economy, are stuffed with this respect for law. Even the physical sciences have been pressed into the service by introducing artificial modes of expression, borrowed from theology and arbitrary power, into knowledge which is purely the result of observation. Thus our intelligence is successfully befogged, and always to maintain our respect for law. The same work is done by newspapers. They have not an article which does not preach respect for law, even where the third page proves every day the imbecility of that law, and shows how it is dragged through every variety of mud and filth by those charged with its administration. Servility before the law has become a virtue, and I doubt if there was ever even a revolutionist who did not begin in his youth as the defender of law against what are generally called "abuses," although these last are inevitable consequences of the law itself. . . .

The confused mass of rules of conduct called law, which has been bequeathed to us by slavery, serfdom, feudalism, and royalty, has taken the place of those stone monsters, before whom human victims used to be immolated, and whom slavish savages dared not even touch lest they should be slain by the thunderbolts of heaven.

This new worship has been established with especial success since the rise to supreme power of the middle class—since the great French Revolution. Under the ancient regime, men spoke little of laws; . . . Obedience to the good pleasure of the king and his lackeys was compulsory on pain of hanging or imprisonment. But during and after the revolutions, when the lawyers rose to power, they did their best to strengthen the principle upon which their ascendancy depended. The middle class at once accepted it as a dyke to dam up the popular torrent. The priestly crew hastened to sanctify it, to save their bark from foundering amid the breakers. Finally the people received it as an improvement upon the arbitrary authority and violence of the past.

To understand this, we must transport ourselves in imagination into the eighteenth century. Our hearts must have ached at the story of the atrocities committed by the all-powerful nobles of that time upon the men and women of the people before we can understand what must have been the magic influence upon the peasant's mind of the words, "Equality before the law, obedience to the law without distinction of birth or fortune." He who until then had been treated more cruelly than a beast, he who had never had any rights, he who had never obtained justice

From *Kropotkin's Revolutionary Pamphlets,* ed. by Roger N. Baldwin (Vanguard Press, 1927).

against the most revolting actions on the part of a noble, unless in revenge he killed him and was hanged—he saw himself recognized by this maxim, at least in theory, at least with regard to his personal rights, as the equal of his lord. Whatever this law might be, it promised to affect lord and peasant alike; it proclaimed the equality of rich and poor before the judge. The promise was a lie, and to-day we know it; but at that period it was an advance, a homage to justice, as hypocrisy is a homage rendered to truth. This is the reason that when the saviors of the menaced middle class . . . proclaimed "respect for law, the same for every man," the people accepted the compromise; for their revolutionary impetus had already spent its force in the contest with a foe whose ranks drew closer day by day; they bowed their neck beneath the yoke of law to save themselves from the arbitrary power of their lords.

The middle class has ever since continued to make the most of this maxim, which with another principle, that of representative government, sums up the whole philosophy of the bourgeois age, the nineteenth century. It has preached this doctrine in its schools, it has propagated it in its writings, it has molded its art and science to the same purpose, it has thrust its beliefs into every hole and corner . . . and it has done all this so successfully that . . . men who long for freedom begin the attempt to obtain it by entreating their masters to be kind enough to protect them by modifying the laws which these masters themselves have created!

But times and tempers are changed. Rebels are everywhere to be found who no longer wish to obey the law without knowing whence it comes, what are its uses, and whither arises the obligation to submit to it, and the reverence with which it is encompassed. The rebels of our day are criticizing the very foundations of society which have hitherto been held sacred, and first and foremost amongst them that fetish, law.

The critics analyze the sources of law, and find there either a god, product of the terrors of the savage, and stupid, paltry and malicious as the priests who vouch for its supernatural origin, or else, bloodshed, conquest by fire and sword. They study the characteristics of law, and instead of perpetual growth corresponding to that of the human race, they find its distinctive trait to be immobility, a tendency to crystallize what should be modified and developed day by day. They ask how law has been maintained, and in its service they see the atrocities of Byzantinism, the cruelties of the Inquisition, the tortures of the middle ages, living flesh torn by the lash of the executioner, chains, clubs, axes, and gloomy dungeons of prisons, agony, curses and tears. In our own days they see, as before, the axe, the cord, the rifle, the prison; on the one hand, the brutalized prisoner, reduced to the condition of a caged beast by the debasement of his whole moral being, and on the other, the judge, stripped of every feeling which does honor to human nature, living like a visionary in a world of legal fictions, revelling in the infliction of imprisonment and death, without even suspecting, in the cold malignity of his madness, the abyss of degradation into which he has himself fallen before the eyes of those whom he condemns.

They see a race of law-makers legislating without knowing what their laws are about; to-day voting a law on the sanitation of towns, without the faintest notion of hygiene, tomorrow making regulations for the armament of troops, without so much as understanding a gun; making laws about teaching and education without ever having given a lesson of any sort, or even an honest education to their own children; legislating at random in all directions, but never forgetting the penalties to be meted out to ragamuffins, the prison and the galleys, which are to be the portion of men a thousand times less immoral than these legislators themselves.

Finally, they see the jailer on the way to lose all human feeling, the detective trained as a blood-hound, the police spy despising himself; "informing," metamorphosed into a virtue; corruption, erected into a system; all the vices, all the evil qualities of mankind countenanced and cultivated to insure the triumph of law.

All this we see, and, therefore, instead of inanely repeating the old formula, "Respect the law," we say, "Despise law and all its attributes!" In place of the cowardly phrase, "Obey the law," our cry is "Revolt against all laws!"

Only compare the misdeeds accomplished in the name of each law with the good it has been able to effect, and weigh carefully both good and evil, and you will see if we are right.

## II

Relatively speaking, law is a product of modern times. For ages and ages mankind lived without any written law, even that graved in symbols upon the entrance stones of a temple. During that period, human relations were simply regulated by customs, habits and usages, made sacred by constant repetition, and acquired by each person in childhood, exactly as he learned how to obtain his food by hunting, cattle rearing, or agriculture. . . .

Every tribe has its own manners and customs; customary law, as the jurists say. It has social habits, and that suffices to maintain cordial relations between the inhabitants of the village, the members of the tribe or community. Even amongst ourselves—the "civilized" nations—when we leave large towns, and go into the country, we see that there the mutual relations of the inhabitants are still regulated according to ancient and generally accepted customs, and not according to the written law of the legislators. The peasants of Russia, Italy and Spain, and even of a large part of France and England, have no conception of written law, it only meddles with their lives to regulate their relations with the State. As to relations between themselves, though these are sometimes very complex, they are simply regulated according to ancient custom. Formerly, this was the case with mankind in general.

Two distinctly marked currents of custom are revealed by analysis of the usages of primitive people.

As man does not live in a solitary state, habits and feelings develop within him which are useful for the preservation of society and the propagation of the race. Without social feelings and usages, life in common would have been absolutely impossible. It is not law which has established them; they are anterior to all law. Neither is it religion which has ordained them; they are anterior to all religions. They are found amongst all animals living in society. They are spontaneously developed by the very nature of things, like those habits in animals which men call instinct. They spring from a process of evolution, which is useful,

and, indeed, necessary, to keep society together in the struggle it is forced to maintain for existence. . . . The hospitality of primitive peoples, respect for human life, the sense of reciprocal obligation, compassion for the weak, courage, extending even to the sacrifice of self for others which is first learnt for the sake of children and friends, and later for that of members of the same community—all these qualities are developed in man anterior to all law, independently of all religion, as in the case of the social animals. Such feelings and practices are the inevitable results of social life. Without being, as say priests and metaphysicians, inherent in man, such qualities are the consequence of life in common.

But side by side with these customs, necessary to the life of societies and the preservation of the race, other desires, other passions, and therefore other habits and customs, are evolved in human association. The desire to dominate others and impose one's own will upon them; the desire to seize upon the products of the labor of a neighboring tribe; the desire to surround oneself with comforts without producing anything, while slaves provide their master with the means of procuring every sort of pleasure and luxury—these selfish, personal desires give rise to another current of habits and customs. The priest and the warrior, the charlatan who makes a profit out of superstition, and after freeing himself from the fear of the devil cultivates it in others; and the bully, who procures the invasion and pillage of his neighbors that he may return laden with booty and followed by slaves. These two, hand in hand, have succeeded in imposing upon primitive society customs advantageous to both of them, but tending to perpetuate their domination of the masses. Profiting by the indolence, the fears, the inertia of the crowd, and thanks to the continual repetition of the same acts, they have permanently established customs which have become a solid basis for their own domination. . . .

The spirit of routine, originating in superstition, indolence, and cowardice, has in all times been the mainstay of oppression. In primitive human societies it was cleverly turned to account by priests and military chiefs. They perpetuated customs useful only to themselves, and succeeded in imposing them on the whole tribe.

So long as this conservative spirit could be exploited so as to assure the chief in his encroachments upon individual liberty, so long as the only inequalities between men were the work of nature, and these were not increased a hundredfold by the concentration of power and wealth, there was no need for law and the formidable paraphernalia of tribunals and ever augmenting penalties to enforce it.

But as society became more and more divided into two hostile classes, one seeking to establish its domination, the other struggling to escape, the strife began. Now the conqueror was in a hurry to secure the results of his actions in a permanent form, he tried to place them beyond question, to make them holy and venerable by every means in his power. Law made its appearance under the sanction of the priest, and the warrior's club was placed at its service. Its office was to render immutable such customs as were to the advantage of the dominant minority. Military authority undertook to ensure obedience. This new function was a fresh guarantee to the power of the warrior; now he had not only mere brute force at his service; he was the defender of law.

If law, however, presented nothing but a collection of prescriptions serviceable to rulers, it would find some difficulty in insuring acceptance and obedience. Well, the legislators confounded in one code the two currents of custom of which we have just been speaking, the maxims which represent principles of morality and social union wrought out as a result of life in common, and the mandates which are meant to ensure external existence to inequality. Customs, absolutely essential to the very being of society, are, in the code, cleverly intermingled with usages imposed by the ruling caste, and both claim equal respect from the crowd. "Do not kill," says the code, and hastens to add, "And pay tithes to the priest." "Do not steal," says the code, and immediately after, "He who refuses to pay taxes, shall have his hand struck off."

Such was law; and it has maintained its twofold character to this day. Its origin is the desire of the ruling class to give permanence to customs imposed by themselves for their own advantage. Its character is the skilful commingling of customs useful to society, customs which have no need of law to insure respect, with other customs useful only to rulers, injurious to the mass of the people, and maintained only by the fear of punishment.

Like individual capital, which was born of fraud and violence, and developed under the auspices of authority, law has no title to the respect of men. Born of violence and superstition, and established in the interests of consumer, priest and rich exploiter, it must be utterly destroyed on the day when the people desire to break their chains. . . .

## Notes and Questions

1. The promise of equality after the French Revolution must have looked especially appealing to those who had suffered under the old regime of royalty and nobility. Should people have rejected the promise of more equality through the rule of law, on the grounds that other tyrannies would creep in with the institutions that were said to be necessary to preserve equality?

   If they did, how would the gains of the revolution have been consolidated, or is the idea of consolidation itself an illusion?

2. Kropotkin argues that law has a mixed character, that is, something to hold the interest of average people and preserve the legitimacy of law-as-a-whole, while providing substantial gains to a minority. Could the desirable elements of law be retained while preferential elements are purged, or is the whole institution of law *inherently* flawed?

3. Could there be a society where there are no leaders? Or where every person is a leader with no followers? Would it be possible to have a society in which all people agreed with Kropotkin? While skeptical about the prospects of peace through law, Kropotkin did have great faith in mutual aid and wrote a book to counter Darwin's theory of relentless competition.

   How would the people involved in strictly voluntary relationships settle their differences?

4. In the society ordered through custom, Kropotkin states that upon occasions of dispute people "prefer appealing to a third party to settle their differences." Would such reference of disputes to third parties give rise to law? To a hierarchy with people who settle differences between disputants being in a

preferred place? Should good anarchists like Kropotkin reject third-party intervention in disputes because they are suspicious of the beneficial effects of the state?

5. According to Kropotkin, the usual relationship between law and custom is the incorporation into law of prior practices *both* of equality and of inequality and domination. Compare this view of Kropotkin with the observations by Stanley Diamond found in the introduction to this chapter. Is Diamond more enamored of custom than Kropotkin?

6. Kropotkin argues that people who make laws about health know nothing of hygiene, those who legislate about education know nothing of teaching, and so on. Would he advocate the transferring of questions from law to scientists and other experts? Would experts come to rule the inexpert?

  Should experts be in authority, or are they just as unfit to rule as are bourgeois lawyers?

7. What is the relationship between anarchy and democracy?

8. In previous sections of the text, questions of school discipline, marital conflict, criminal law violations, pollution, and labor have come to the courts. Did the operation of law have beneficial effects in those instances, or would people have been just as well off, and possibly better off, if there were no law?

9. Select a rule of law of the state where you live. Try to find the origins of the rule, determine who benefits and loses from it, and then estimate the effect of its repeal.

  As an alternative, select a rule that is enforced where you work or go to school and follow the same steps.

10. Make an inventory of newspaper articles relating to state law or institutional rules and policies. Assess whether the writers are calling for more law, less law, or different law. How anarchical does your inventory suggest people to be?

How can one make an assessment of the contemporary relationship between people and the legal system? The popular expression "money talks" captures at least four sentiments: that money creates outcomes, legal and otherwise; that the outcomes produced by money are not necessarily what a majority of people who do not have much money would prefer; that people without money do not have a voice; and that this lack of voice does them harm. A fifth sentiment might be that a person without money can make no difference—activism would be an exercise in futility.

Although the expression about money talking rolls easily off the tongue, most people do not know how money is translated into concrete results, since the pathway through which money enters law-government systems may be subtle, hidden, and serpentine. Consider the complex elements of Galanter's analysis of litigation. Recall Kafka's statement in "The Problem of Our Laws": "Our laws are not generally known; they are kept secret by the small group of nobles who rule us." The obvious example, bribery, is only one way, a crude one, that money operates in this system.

In the same way, some aspects of power (and its partner, powerlessness) are well understood, some partially understood, and some not understood at all. When the order "Do it, or else," is accompanied by a threat of physical force most of us can see that the person or group of persons against whom the threat is directed must comply or risk bad consequences. But just as out-and-out bribery is only one way in which money talks, the threat of naked force is only one way that power talks to powerlessness.

More subtle exercises of power take place when one party has the ability to set an agenda for discussion that forecloses other agendas. In the early North Carolina cases on spousal abuse (Chapter 1), some courts viewed the damage by degrees, talking about the size of sticks or the permanence of injury instead of dealing squarely with household terror. Power also enters into issues like national health care. Is the debate to be about getting health care to the over forty million of the working poor who do not have any health care at all, or about cutting down on paperwork for doctors treating those who already have health care coverage? The first is a far more radical agenda than the second, and whether the first or the second becomes the agenda for debate determine who gets health care and how the system is administered, since once an agenda has been set, alternative approaches become invisible.

The least understood dimension of power and powerlessness occurs when power relationships are fully internalized, so that when faced with injustice, the powerless quit before they start. Powerlessness becomes a fact of life. In the parable "Before the Law," Kafka describes a countryman who has so thoroughly internalized the requirement that laws be unswervingly obeyed that he can think of no alternative to begging for admission. Turning to the parable "The Problem of Our Laws," we learn that Kafka traces the inability to confront noble rule to the psyches of commoners; people are more inclined to hate themselves than to hate their oppressors. But how are unresourceful psyches created? Could the ineffectiveness attributed to the psyche be the result of prior conditioning? Surrender to unjust rule may be the *effect* of prior exercises of power—a spontaneous *cause* of paralysis. A complete social psychology of power would include the experiences of people in power systems. Each of us has accumulated a personal record that makes certain courses of actions practical and thinkable and others impractical and unthinkable. It could be that, in systems, nothing succeeds like a history of success and nothing fails like a history of failure.

When a power relationship is fully internalized in the psyche of the powerless, the power of the powerful will be complete. Fortunately, this end point may never be reached, since most powerless people resent their lack of choices, even as they are saying, "How can I change things?— They're going to do what they want to do anyway."

Plantation slavery presents a vivid model of power and the lack of it. Masters, who lived off the labor of others and destroyed most human prerogatives, used force where necessary, but also attempted to imbue habits of obedience (powerlessness) in their slaves. Most masters were not experts in human relations; they sought to establish control through repetitive practices. Kenneth Stampp, whose historical accounts were included in Chapter 5, outlines the steps masters took to control slaves.

1. Establish and maintain strict discipline.
2. Implant in the bondsmen a consciousness of personal inferiority.
3. Awe slaves with a sense of the master's enormous power.
4. Persuade slaves to take an interest in the master's enterprise.

5. Create a habit of perfect dependence (helplessness without the master's benevolence).

As Stampp indicates, force, agenda setting, and the inculcation of certain thought patterns all assist the master in gaining power. The full force of the state and the legal system supported the master's use of force on a plantation. The agenda was the master's. If the master was successful, physical force was used only sparingly and the slave willingly obeyed rather than rebelled. The system never fully succeeded, as it was full of limits, counterpressures, and contradictions—for example, slave discipline could not permanently damage black flesh, which had property value; and slaves pushed too far toward passivity could not take an interest in a master's enterprise. Nonetheless, it is instructive to see the dynamics of power in a diabolical system that persisted for centuries.

John Gaventa, in his text *Power and Powerlessness,** presents an example from modern industrial development. As a young VISTA volunteer, he arrived in a coal mining region of Appalachia and found glaring injustices: the area was rich in coal, but the people who lived there were among the most impoverished and destitute in the United States. Although their ancestors had been in the area for several hundred years, they owned nothing, and they had a right to nothing other than what they were accorded by absentee landowners. To Gaventa's amazement, the people were also silent. He could not uncritically accept the assumption that the people's silence meant approval of the existing economic and power relationships: their lives were so miserable that any idea of contentment made no sense to him. Yet he found neither political activism, which political scientists predict in a democracy when there are grievances, nor class warfare or revolution, as Marxists would

**Power, Coal Valley***

| *1st Dimension* | *2nd Dimension* | *3rd Dimension* |
|---|---|---|
| Control of material resources—land, transportation, and related businesses | Control of institutions—lawyers, politicians, education, religion | Control of images—"progress," "prosperity," "hillbilly"; ideology—"Hard work rewards all," and myths—"Everyone gains, unless personally deficient" |
| Coercion—law, court orders, sheriff | Barriers against effective protest | Internalized restraints—surrender without fight, or even being conscious of surrender |
| Protest | Protest deflected or put in harmless channels | Silence |
| Visible power | Secondary actors visible, primary power holders not visible | Hegemonic power—generally invisible |

*John Gaventa, *Power and Powerlessness* (Urbana: University of Illinois Press, 1982), pp. 3–83.

anticipate. Gaventa found plenty of reasons for political activism and rebellion, but no activism and no rebellion.

To find an answer to the puzzle, he studied the historical and contemporary uses of power:

The table on page 155 records the sequence of power consolidation by the absentee landlords in three stages. First, landlords took control of material resources and the force of the local legal system. At the earliest stages the deprivation is visible to those on the losing ends of land deals or coercive systems, who at that point voice their opposition since a different past is still within memory. After further consolidation, secondary institutions are used to establish barriers that impede resistance by those who see their life chances worsening. Meanwhile lawyers, business people, and "civic leaders" see their own material futures tied to those who control the wealth in coal and related enterprises. These smaller players form a perimeter of defense around the more powerful, who might otherwise have to use brute force to maintain their position. Eventually, not only do economic and legal relationships come under the control of the powerful, but also local government, churches, schools, and all other potentially rival sources of organizing principles are fully colonized.

Gaventa concluded that political surrender, apathy, silence, and even taking stands contrary to one's own best interest were *caused* by power; long experience with powerlessness implanted an abiding expectation of powerlessness, which was in turn caused by the history of power use in the valley. What surprised him more was that, once consolidated, power relationships remained largely unchanged over the one hundred years he studied.

If power is consolidated in stages, it might also be inferred that power relationships can be confronted in stages, by force, challenges to agenda setting, and the rejection of destructive images. It is not accidental that the first step in any social movement is to restudy history and to reconstitute alternative images of reality that have been purged in the interest of preserving power relationships.

James Scott, in a more recent book,[†] argues that Gaventa is far too pessimistic about the success of powerful people in taking over the thinking of the powerless. He says that one has to go to places where the powerless feel free to speak their minds if one is to find their true sentiments—to the slave quarters to find what slaves think, and to the households of the people of Appalachia to find the people's thoughts about absentee property holders. Taking Scott as a lead, one would get a more faithful picture of what students think about college by going into dormitories, snack bars, and other places where students feel free to express their views. Their comments in places where they confront teachers or administrative power would be of dubious reliability.

---

[†]James Scott, *Domination and the Arts of Resistance* (New Haven, Conn.: Yale University Press, 1990).

❧ Next is another short parable by Kafka that offers, as one should expect, an odd angle on power relationships.

## 6.3 | The Watchman    *Franz Kafka*

I ran past the first watchman. Then I was horrified, ran back again and said to the watchman: "I ran through here while you were looking the other way." The watchman gazed ahead of him and said nothing. "I suppose I really oughtn't to have done it," I said. The watchman still said nothing. "Does your silence indicate permission to pass?" . . .

### Notes and Questions

1. Here there are just two characters. What does the description of each tell us, and how might we use Kafka's insights to better understand power and the lack of it?

2. Return to the epigram at the start of this chapter that describes a peasant who bows deeply and then silently farts. What does this epigram tell us about power relationships? What might be the king's reaction to learning that the peasant's bow was followed by a fart?

❧ The following case introduces the subject of the influence of money in lawmaking. The state of Massachusetts tried to limit corporate contributions to groups supporting or opposing ballot referenda where the referendum is not "one materially affecting . . . the property, business, or assets of the corporation." If money talks, does it also have a constitutionally protected right of free speech?

## 6.4 | First National Bank of Boston v. Bellotti    *435 U.S. 765 (1978)*

MR. JUSTICE POWELL

In sustaining a state criminal statute that forbids certain expenditures by banks and business corporations for the purpose of influencing referendum proposals, the Massachusetts Supreme Judicial Court held that the First Amendment rights of a corporation are limited to issues that materially affect its business, property or assets . . . We now reverse.

The statute . . . prohibits appellants, two national banks and three business corporations, from making contributions or expenditures "for the purposes of . . . influencing or affecting the vote on any question submitted to the voters, other than one materially affecting . . . the property, business, or assets of the corporation." The statute further specifies that "[n]o question submitted to the voters solely concerning the taxation of the income, property, or transactions of individuals shall be deemed materially to affect the property, business or assets of the corporation." A corporation that violates [the statute] may receive a maximum fine of $50,000; a corporate officer, director or agent who violates this section may receive a maximum fine of $10,000 or be imprisoned for up to one year, or both.

Appellants wanted to spend money to publicize their views on a proposed constitutional amendment . . . [which] would have permitted the legislature to impose a graduated income tax on the income of individuals . . . [T]hey brought this action [originally in Massachusetts courts.—ED.] to have the statute declared unconstitutional . . . Appellants argued that [the statute] violates the First Amendment, the Due Process and Equal Protection Clauses of the Fourteenth Amendment, and similar clauses of the Massachusetts Constitution . . . [T]he court . . . viewed the principal question as "whether business corporations . . . have First Amendment rights coextensive with natural persons or associations of natural persons" . . . [T]he court held that "only when a general political issue materially affects a corporation's business property or assets may that corporation claim First Amendment protection. . . .

If the speakers here were not corporations, no one would suggest that the state could silence the proposed speech. It is the type of speech indispensable to decision making in a democracy, and this is no less true because the speech comes from a corporation rather than an individual . . . Freedom of speech and the other freedoms encompassed by the First Amendment always have been viewed as fundamental components of liberty safeguarded by the Due Process Clause . . . and the Court has not identified a separate source for the right when it has been asserted by corporations . . . Nor do our recent commercial speech cases lend support to appellees' business interest theory. They illustrate that the First Amendment goes beyond protection of the press and the self-expression of individuals to prohibit government from limiting the stock of information from which members of the public may draw. A commercial advertisement is constitutionally protected not so much because it pertains to the seller's business as because it furthers the societal interest in the "free flow of commercial information" . . .

Appellee nevertheless advances two principal justifications for the prohibition of corporate speech. The first is the State's interest in sustaining the active role of the individual citizen in the electoral process and thereby preventing elimination of the citizen's confidence in government. The second is the interest of protecting the rights of shareholders whose views differ from those expressed by management on behalf of the corporation. However weighty these inter-

ests may be in the context of partisan candidates elections they are not [implicated . . . or . . . served by this prohibition].

Preserving the integrity of the electoral process, preventing corruption and "sustain[ing] the active, alert, responsibility of the individual citizen . . . are interests of the highest importance . . . Preservation of the individual citizen's confidence in government is equally important.

Appellee . . . arguments . . . hinge upon the assumption that [corporate] participation would exert an undue influence on the outcome of the referendum vote . . . and destroy the confidence of the people in the democratic process and the integrity of government. According to the appellee, corporations are wealthy and powerful and their views may drown out other points of view . . . [T]here has been no showing that the relative voice of corporations has been overwhelming or even significant in influencing referenda in Massachusetts or that there has been any threat to the confidence of the citizenry in government . . .

Finally, appellee argues that [the statute] protects corporate shareholders . . . Ultimately shareholders may decide through the procedures of corporate democracy whether their corporation should engage in debate on public issues. Acting through their power to elect the board of directors or to insist upon protective provisions in the corporate charter, shareholders are presumed competent to protect their own interests . . .

MR. JUSTICE BURGER, *concurring* . . .

[T]he First Amendment does not "belong" to any definable category of persons or entities; it belongs to all who exercise its freedoms.

MR. JUSTICE WHITE . . . *dissenting*

[T]he issue is whether a State may prevent a corporate management from using the corporate treasury to propagate views having no connection with the corporate business . . . The Court invalidates the Massachusetts statute and holds that the First Amendment guarantees corporate managers the right to use not only their personal funds, but also those of the corporation to circulate fact and opinion irrelevant to the business placed in their charge and necessarily representing their own personal or collective views about political and social questions . . .

By holding that Massachusetts may not prohibit corporate expenditures or contributions . . . the Court not only invalidates a statute which has been on the books in one form or another for many years, but also casts considerable doubt on the constitutionality of legislation passed by some 31 States restricting corporate political activity, as well as upon the Federal Corrupt Practices Act . . . The Court's fundamental error is its failure to realize that the state regulatory interests . . . are themselves derived from the First Amendment. The question posed by this case, as approached by the Court, is whether the State has struck the best possible balance . . . What is inexplicable, is for the Court to substitute its judgment as to the proper balance for that of Massachusetts where the State has passed legislation reasonably designed to further First Amendment interests in the context of the political arena where the expertise of the legislators is at its peak and that of judges is at its very lowest . . .

There is now little doubt that corporate communications come within the scope of the First Amendment. This, however, is merely the starting point of analysis, because corporate expression . . . is not fungible with communications coming from individuals and is subject to restrictions which individual expression is not. Indeed what some have considered to be the principal function of the First Amendment, the use of communication as a means of self-expression, self-realization, and self-fulfillment, is not at all furthered by corporate speech. It is clear that the communications of profit making corporations are not "an integral part of the development of ideas, of mental exploration and of the affirmation of self. They do not represent a manifestation of individual freedom of choice . . ."

Of course it may be assumed that corporate investors are united by a desire to make money, for the value of their investment to increase. Since even communications which have no purpose other than that of enriching the communicator have some First Amendment protection, activities such as advertising . . . may be viewed as furthering the desires of individual shareholders. The unanimity of purpose breaks down, however, when corporations make expenditures or undertake activities designed to influence the opinion or general public on political and social issues that have no material connection with or effect upon their business, property or assets . . .

Ideas which are not a product of individual choice are entitled to less First Amendment protection. Secondly, the restriction of corporate speech . . . impinges much less upon the availability of ideas to the general public than do restrictions on individual speech. Even the complete curtailment of corporate speech concerning political or ideological questions not integral to the day-to-day business functions would leave individuals, including corporate shareholders, employees and customers, free to communicate their thoughts. . . . These individuals would remain perfectly free to communicate any ideas which could be conveyed by the corporate form. Indeed such individuals could even form associations for the very purpose of promoting personal or ideological causes . . .

Corporations are artificial entities created by law for the purpose of furthering certain economic goals. In order to facilitate the achievement of such ends, special rules relating to . . . limited liability, perpetual life, and the accumulation, distribution and taxation of assets are normally applied to them . . . It has long been recognized, however, that the special status of corporations has placed them in a position to control vast amounts of economic power which may, if not regulated, dominate not only the economy but also the very heart of our democracy, the electoral process. The interest of Massachusetts and . . . many other states . . . is . . . preventing institutions which have been permitted to amass wealth as a result of special advantages extended by the State for certain economic purposes from using that wealth to acquire an unfair advantage in the political process . . . The State need not permit its own creation to consume it . . .

The Court's opinion appears to recognize at least the possibility that the fear of corporate domination . . . would justify restrictions . . . but brushes this interest aside by asserting that "there has been no showing that the relative voice of corporations have been overwhelming or even significant in influencing referenda in Massachusetts . . . It fails to even allude to the fact, however, that Massachusetts' most recent experience with unrestrained corporate expenditures in connection with ballot questions establishes precisely the contrary. In 1972, a proposed amendment to the Massachusetts Constitution which would have authorized . . . a graduated income tax on both individuals and corporations was put to the voters. The Committee for Jobs and Government Economy, an organized political committee, raised and expended $120,000 to oppose the proposed amendment, the bulk of it raised through large corporate contributions . . . In contrast the Coalition for Tax Reform, the only political committee organized to support the 1972 amendment, was able to raise and expend only $7,000.

The necessity of prohibiting corporate political expenditures in order to prevent the use of corporate funds for purposes with which shareholders may disagree is not a unique perception of Massachusetts . . . [O]ne of the purposes of the Corrupt Practices Act [passed by the U.S. Congress.—ED.] was to prevent the use of corporate or union funds for political purposes without the consent of the shareholders or union members and to protect minority interests from domination by corporate or union leadership . . .

MR. JUSTICE REHNQUIST, *dissenting.*

The question presented today . . . has never been squarely addressed by any previous decision of this Court. However, Massachusetts, The Congress . . . and the legislatures of 30 other States . . . have considered the matter, and have concluded that restrictions upon the political activity of business corporations are both politically desirable and constitutionally permissible. The judgment of such a broad consensus . . . is entitled to considerable deference . . .

Early in our history, Mr. Justice Marshall described the status of the corporation in the eyes of the federal law:

> A corporation is an artificial being, invisible, intangible, and existing only in contemplation of law. Being the mere creature of law, it possesses only those properties which the charter of creation confers upon it, either expressly, or as incidental to its very existence. These are such

as are supposed best calculated to effect the object for which it was created.

Dartmouth College v. Woodward (1819)

. . . There can be little doubt that when a State creates a corporation with the power to acquire and utilize property, it necessarily and implicitly guarantees that the corporation will not be deprived of that property absent due process . . . Likewise when a State charters a corporation for purpose of publishing a newspaper, it necessarily assumes that the corporation is entitled to the liberty of the press . . . Until recently it was not thought that any persons, natural or artificial, had any protected right to engage in commercial speech . . . Although the Court has never explicitly recognized a corporation's right of commercial speech, such a right might be considered necessarily incidental to the business of a commercial corporation.

It cannot be so readily concluded that the right of political expression is equally necessary to carry out the functions of a corporation organized for commercial purposes. A State grants to a business corporation the blessings of potentially perpetual life and limited liability to enhance its efficiency as an economic entity. It might reasonably be concluded that those properties, so beneficial in the economic sphere, pose special dangers in the political sphere. Furthermore, it might be argued that liberties of political expression are not at all necessary to effectuate the purposes for which States permit commercial corporations to exist . . . Indeed the States might reasonably fear that the corporation would use its economic power to obtain further benefits beyond those already bestowed. I would think that any particular form of organization upon which the state confers special privileges or immunities different from those of natural persons would be subject to like regulation, whether the organization is a labor union, a partnership, a trade association, or a corporation.

The free flow of information is in no way diminished by the Commonwealth's decision to permit the operation of business corporations with limited rights of political expression. All natural persons who owe their existence to a higher sovereign than the Commonwealth, remain as free as before to engage in political activity . . .

*Notes and Questions*

1. The U.S. Supreme Court has ruled that corporations are persons for purposes of the Constitution, as amended. It is from this starting place that the debate in the *Bellotti* case arose. What is the appropriate role of corporations in the political process? Would the political activism of shareholders acting on their own rather than via the corporation establish enough corporate presence?

2. The graduated income tax proposed in Massachusetts was a *personal* tax and not a *corporate* tax. Would the approval or disapproval of the referendum have a material effect on the welfare of the corporation?

   If the state of Massachusetts failed to limit corporate contributions in this case, is it likely that the contributions of corporations concerning *any* referendum question can be challenged?

3. Justice White compared the contributions of corporations to those of noncorporate contributors and was disturbed by the imbalance in favor of the corporations.

   If there have been ballot referenda in your state, find out who contributed what to secure or to defeat passage. Then make a comparison between your findings and the commentaries of the Supreme Court in the *Bellotti* case.

4. The committee whose contributions were challenged was called the Committee on Jobs and Government Economy. Does one get the idea from the name that the principal supporters of the committee were corporations? Should there be disclosure requirements so that onlookers will not be fooled by names that can confuse the public about what an association stands for and who contributes to it?

5. In the health care reform debate during the first Clinton administration, the stakes were very high. Haynes Johnson and David Broder, who wrote *The System*,* a record of the debate,

estimated that $100 to $300 million was spent either to defeat reform or to secure its passage. Some of the money took the form of campaign contributions to members of Congress, and some was spent to influence the public directly, so that they could in turn pressure their representatives. The following advertisement, featuring a typical American couple at home, was very effective:

> *Announcer:*  The government may force us to pick from a few health care plans designed by the government.
>
> *Louise:*  Having choices we don't like is no choice at all.
>
> *Harry:*  They choose.
>
> *Louise:*  We lose.[†]

It may seem absurd that something as complicated as a health care system that would cover all Americans could be reduced to a few lines, but the ad was regarded as highly influential in defeating health care reform.

The advertisement was paid for by the Health Insurance Association of America, the lobbying group for health insurance companies, that stood to lose if health reform were enacted as proposed. Insurers have power in the existing health system. They would prefer an agenda that discusses general antipathies toward government to one that discusses the nuts and bolts of health care. (For example, health insurers can make far more money by "cherry picking"—insuring those who are least likely to be sick—than they can if they are forced to broaden coverage and take more risks.) They also understand the strength of image creation; hence the advertisements that reduced the health care questions to a few slogans that persuaded people that changes in health care were not in their interest.

---

*David Broder, *The System* (Boston: Little, Brown, 1996).
[†]Ibid., p. 205.

❧  The ballot referendum has become a common vehicle through which citizens can more actively participate in lawmaking, a means by which voters can "take the law into their own hands." Over the last twenty years, ballot initiatives have come from people of all political persuasions and interests: to put ceilings on local property taxes, to go from a flat tax to a graduated income tax, to require term limits, to make seat belts optional, to require deposits on cans and bottles, to enact gun control, to control automobile insurance, to secure victims' rights, to require nonpolluting cars, to legalize gambling, to prohibit leg traps to capture wild animals, to prohibit illegal aliens from getting access to schooling or health care, to allow the use of marijuana by people suffering from certain illnesses, to prevent affirmative action, and so on.

If the sources and the underlying political preferences of the advocates and opponents of referenda differ, there is a common underlying principle that makes ballot questions germane to our study of the relationship between popular will and law. People must be seeing a need to act directly in lawmaking rather than through their elected representatives or other established channels. If proponents would not acknowledge a tinge of anarchical preference, the referenda attest to a measure of distrust of government left on its own. Californians, who are out front on the number and range of ballot questions, seem to spend as much time debating ballot initiatives as deciding which candidates should be elected. And the rest of the country seems to be following California's lead.

In the remainder of this chapter, two ballot initiatives will be considered: the California referendum on the medical uses of marijuana, and an earlier Colorado referendum designed to invalidate local ordinances prohibiting discrimination based on "homosexual, lesbian or bisexual orientation, conduct, practices or relationships." As the variety of ballot questions in the above list shows, these samples in no sense exhaust the possibilities for study. Yet they do show some of the mood of the times, and the complications that arise in going from mood to law.

## 6.5 | Proposition 215: The Compassionate Use Act of 1996

To The Honorable Secretary Of State Of California;

We, the undersigned, registered, qualified voters of California, residents of _____ County (or City and Country), hereby propose an addition to the Health and Safety Code, relating to the compassionate use of marijuana, and petition the Secretary of State to submit the same to the voters of California for their adoption or rejection at the next succeeding general election or at any special statewide election held prior to that general election or otherwise provided by law. The proposed addition to the Health and Safety Code shall read as follows:

Section 1. Section 11362.5 is added to the Health and Safety Code, to read:

11362.5 (a) This section shall be known and may be cited as the Compassionate Use Act of 1996.

(b) (1) The people of the State of California hereby find and declare that the purposes of the Compassionate Use Act of 1996 are as follows:

(A) To ensure that seriously ill Californians have the right to obtain and use marijuana for medical purposes where that medical use is deemed appropriate and has been recommended by a physician who has determined that the person's health would benefit from the use of marijuana in the treatment of cancer, anorexia, AIDS, chronic pain, spasticity, glaucoma, arthritis, migraine, or any other illness for which marijuana provides relief.

(B) To ensure that patients and their primary caregivers who obtain and use marijuana for medical purposes upon the recommendation of a physician are not subject to criminal prosecution or sanction.

(C) To encourage the federal and state governments to implement a plan to provide for the safe and affordable distribution of marijuana to all patients in medical need of marijuana.

(2) Nothing in this act shall be construed to supersede legislation prohibiting persons from engaging in conduct that endangers others, nor to condone the diversion of marijuana for nonmedical purposes.

(c) Notwithstanding any other provision of law, no physician in this state shall be punished, or denied any right or privilege, for having recommended marijuana to a patient for medical purposes.

(d) Section 11357, relating to the possession of marijuana, and Section 11358, relating to the cultivation of marijuana, shall not apply to a patient, or to a patient's primary caregiver, who possesses or cultivates marijuana for the personal medical purposes of the patient upon the written or oral recommendation or approval of a physician.

(e) For the purposes of this section "primary caregiver" means the individual designated by the person exempted under this act who has consistently assumed responsibility for the housing, health, or safety of that person.

Sec. 2. If any provision of this measure or the application thereof to any person or circumstance is held invalid, that invalidity shall not affect other provisions or applications of the measure which can be given effect without the invalid provision or application, and to this end the provisions of this measure are severable.

## Notes and Questions

1. After the passage of the referendum, U.S. Attorney General Janet Reno stated that the California law ran contrary to the federal drug laws and that federal authorities would continue to prosecute cases arising in California, using federal law. Under the law of preemption, where a state's law runs contrary to national law on the same subject, the national law precludes or "preempts" the enforcement of the contradictory state law. In May 2001, the United States Supreme Court in an 8–0 decision (*U.S. v. Oakland Cannabis Cooperative*), ruled that medical necessity could not justify an exception to the federal law on marijuana.

2. There is also tension between the medical community and drug law enforcers. Does marijuana have proven therapeutic uses, or is the California referendum just a way to begin to legalize marijuana?

    Related to this question is the argument that the California initiative was so vaguely worded that not only would patients who are severely ill have legal access to marijuana, but also just about anyone who wanted to use marijuana could find a pretext for doing so. Read the initiative in its entirety, and evaluate the claim that it is so vague that its long-term effect will be to legalize marijuana.

3. As of a few weeks before the 1996 election, a total of $1,754,445 had been contributed in support of the referendum, with $311,545 coming from within California and $1,442,900 from out of state. Among the California contributors, the largest was the Life Aids Lobby of Sacramento ($194,750), and among the out-of-state contributors, the largest were George Soros of New York ($550,000), Peter Lewis of Ohio ($500,000), John Sperling of Arizona ($200,000), The Dennis Trading Group of Illinois ($100,000), and Laurance Rockefeller ($50,000). Individual contributions of less than $100 totaled $12,962.*

    Statistics like the foregoing can now be retrieved using the Web, but it is not clear what is to be made of them. For some additional biographical material on the large contributors, see E. Bailey, "Six Wealthy Donors Aid Measure on Marijuana," *Los Angeles Times,* November 2, 1996.

---

*Campaign Contributors, www.emory.edu/NFIA/NEW/MARIJUANA/MONEY.html.

&clubs; The following case arose in Colorado. Some Colorado communities had passed ordinances prohibiting discrimination in a number of settings based on sexual orientation. A ballot initiative was then passed that would amend the Colorado Constitution to prohibit such ordinances. The referendum was challenged in the Colorado courts, and the Supreme Court of Colorado affirmed a decision that held that the referendum was unconstitutional as a denial of equal protection of laws. The case then was brought before the U.S. Supreme Court.

## 6.6 | Romer v. Evans    *116 S.Ct. 1620 (1996)*

JUSTICE KENNEDY...

### I

The enactment challenged in this case is an amendment to the Constitution of the State of Colorado, adopted in a 1992 statewide referendum. The parties and the state courts refer to it as "Amendment 2," its designation was submitted to the voters. The impetus for the amendment and the contentious campaign that preceded its adoption came in large part from ordinances that had been passed in various Colorado municipalities. For example, the cities of Aspen and Boulder and the City and County of Denver each had enacted ordinances which banned discrimination in many transactions and activities, including housing, employment, education, public accommodations, and health and welfare services. . . . What gave rise to the statewide controversy was the protection the ordinances afforded to persons discriminated against by reason of their sexual orientation. See Boulder Rev. Code . . . (defining "sexual orientation" as "the choice of sexual partners, i.e., bisexual, homosexual or heterosexual"); Denver Rev. Municipal Code, . . . (defining "sexual orientation" as "[t]he status of an individual as to his or her heterosexuality, homosexuality or bisexuality"). Amendment 2 repeals these ordinances to the extent they prohibit discrimination on the basis of "homosexual, lesbian or bisexual orientation, conduct, practices or relationships." . . .

Yet Amendment 2, in explicit terms, does more than repeal or rescind these provisions. It prohibits all legislative, executive or judicial action at any level of state or local government designed to protect the named class, a class we shall refer to as homosexual persons or gays and lesbians. The amendment reads:

> No Protected Status Based on Homosexual, Lesbian, or Bisexual Orientation. Neither the State of Colorado, through any of its branches or departments, nor any of its agencies, political subdivisions, municipalities or school districts, shall enact, adopt or enforce any statute, regulation, ordinance or policy whereby homosexual, lesbian or bisexual orientation, conduct, practices or relationships shall constitute or otherwise be the basis of or entitle any person or class of persons to have or claim any minority status, quota preferences, protected status or claim of discrimination. This Section of the Constitution shall be in all respects self-executing. . . .

### II

The State's principal argument in defense of Amendment 2 is that it puts gays and lesbians in the same position as all other persons. So, the State says, the measure does no more than deny homosexuals special rights. This reading of the amendment's language is implausible. We rely not upon our own interpretation of the amendment but upon the authoritative construction of Colorado's Supreme Court. The state court, deeming it unnecessary to determine the full extent of the amendment's reach, found it invalid even on a modest reading of its implications. . . .

The immediate objective of Amendment 2 is, at a minimum, to repeal existing statutes, regulations, ordinances, and policies of state and local entities that barred discrimination based on sexual orientation. . . . *See* Aspen, Colo., Mun. Code . . . (prohibiting discrimination in employment, housing and public accommodations on the basis of sexual orientation); Boulder, Colo., . . . (same); Denver, Colo., . . . (same); Executive Order No. D0035 . . . (prohibiting employment discrimination for "all state employees, classified and exempt" on the basis of sexual orientation); Colorado Insurance Code, . . . (forbidding health insurance providers from determining insurability and premiums based on an applicant's, a beneficiary's, or an insured's sexual orientation); and various provisions prohibiting discrimination based on sexual orientation at state colleges.

The "ultimate effect" of Amendment 2 is to prohibit any governmental entity from adopting similar, or more protective statutes, regulations, ordinances, or policies in the future unless the state constitution is first amended to permit such measures. . . .

Sweeping and comprehensive is the change in legal status effected by this law. So much is evident from the ordinances that the Colorado Supreme Court declared would be void by operation of Amendment 2. Homosexuals, by state decree, are put in a solitary class with respect to transactions and relations in both the private and governmental spheres. The amendment withdraws from homosexuals, but no others, specific legal protection from the injuries caused by discrimination, and it forbids reinstatement of these laws and policies.

The change that Amendment 2 works in the legal status of gays and lesbians in the private sphere is far-reaching, both on its own terms and when considered in light of the structure and operation of modern anti-discrimination laws. That structure is well illustrated by contemporary statutes and ordinances prohibiting discrimination by providers of public accommodations. "At common law, innkeepers, smiths, and others who 'made profession of a public employment,' were prohibited from refusing, without good reason, to serve a customer." . . . The duty was a general one and did not specify protection for particular groups. The common law rules, however, proved insufficient in many instances . . . In consequence, most States have chosen to counter discrimination by enacting detailed statutory schemes.

Colorado's state and municipal laws typify this emerging tradition of statutory protection and follow a consistent pattern. The laws first enumerate the persons or entities subject to a duty not to discriminate. The list goes well beyond the entities covered by the common law. The Boulder ordinance, for example, has a comprehensive definition of entities deemed places of "public accommodation." They include "any place of business engaged in any sales to the general public and any place that offers services, facilities, privileges, or advantages to the general public or that receives financial support through solicitation of the general public or through governmental subsidy of any kind." . . . The Denver ordinance is of similar breadth, applying, for example, to hotels, restaurants, hospitals, dental clinics, theaters, banks, common carriers, travel and insurance agencies, and "shops and stores dealing with goods or services of any kind," . . .

These statutes and ordinances also depart from the common law by enumerating the groups or persons within their ambit of protection. Enumeration is the essential device used to make the duty not to discriminate concrete and to provide guidance for those who must comply. In following this approach, Colorado's state and local governments have not limited anti-discrimination laws to groups that have so far been given the protection of heightened equal protection scrutiny under our cases. . . . Rather, they set forth an extensive catalogue of traits which cannot be the basis for discrimination, including age, military status, marital status, pregnancy, parenthood, custody of a minor child, political affiliation, physical or mental disability of an individual or of his or her associates—and, in recent times, sexual orientation. . . .

Amendment 2 bars homosexuals from securing protection against the injuries that these public-accommodations laws address. That in itself is a severe consequence, but there is more. Amendment 2, in addition, nullifies specific legal protections for this targeted class in all trans-actions in housing, sale of real estate, insurance, health and welfare services, private education, and employment.

Not confined to the private sphere, Amend-ment 2 also operates to repeal and forbid all laws or policies providing specific protection for gays or lesbians from discrimination by every level of Colorado government.

. . . The State Supreme Court cited two ex-amples . . . The first is Colorado Executive Order D0035 (1990), which forbids employment discrim-ination against " 'all state employees, classified and exempt' on the basis of sexual orientation." . . . Also repealed, and now forbidden, are "vari-ous provisions prohibiting discrimination based on sexual orientation at state colleges." . . .

Amendment 2's reach may not be limited to specific laws passed for the benefit of gays and lesbians. It is a fair, if not necessary, inference from the broad language of the amendment that it deprives gays and lesbians even of the protec-tion of general laws and policies that prohibit arbitrary discrimination in government and pri-vate settings. . . . At some point in the systematic administration of these laws, an official must de-termine whether homosexuality is an arbitrary and thus forbidden basis for decision. Yet a deci-sion to that effect would itself amount to a policy prohibiting discrimination on the basis of homo-sexuality, and so would appear to be no more valid under Amendment 2 than the specific pro-hibitions against discrimination the state court held invalid.

If this consequence follows from Amend-ment 2, as its broad language suggests, it would compound the constitutional difficulties the law creates. The state court did not decide whether the amendment has this effect, however, and nei-ther need we. In the course of rejecting the argu-ment that Amendment 2 is intended to conserve resources to fight discrimination against suspect classes, the Colorado Supreme Court made the limited observation that the amendment is not intended to affect many anti-discrimination laws protecting non-suspect classes . . . In our view, that does not resolve the issue. In any event, even if, as we doubt, homosexuals could find some safe harbor in laws of general application, we cannot accept the view that Amendment 2's

prohibition on specific legal protections does no more than deprive homosexuals of special rights. To the contrary, the amendment imposes a special disability upon those persons alone. Homosexuals are forbidden the safeguards that others enjoy or may seek without constraint. They can obtain specific protection against dis-crimination only by enlisting the citizenry of Colorado to amend the state constitution or per-haps, on the State's view, by trying to pass helpful laws of general applicability. This is so no matter how local or discrete the harm, no matter how public and widespread the injury. We find noth-ing special in the protections Amendment 2 withholds. These are protections taken for granted by most people either because they al-ready have them or do not need them; these are protections against exclusion from an almost limitless number of transactions and endeavors that constitute ordinary civic life in a free society.

## III

The Fourteenth Amendment's promise that no person shall be denied the equal protection of the laws must co-exist with the practical necessity that most legislation classifies for one purpose or another, with resulting disadvantage to various groups or persons. . . . [T]he amendment has the peculiar property of imposing a broad and undifferentiated disability on a single named group, an exceptional and, as we shall explain, invalid form of legislation. Second, its sheer breadth is so discontinuous with the reasons of-fered for it that the amendment seems inexplica-ble by anything but animus toward the class that it affects; it lacks a rational relationship to legiti-mate state interests. . . .

Taking the first point, even in the ordinary equal protection case calling for the most defer-ential of standards, we insist on knowing the re-lation between the classification adopted and the object to be attained. The search for the link between classification and objective gives sub-stance to the Equal Protection Clause; it pro-vides guidance and discipline for the legislature, which is entitled to know what sorts of laws it can pass; and it marks the limits of our own author-ity. In the ordinary case, a law will be sustained if it can be said to advance a legitimate govern-ment interest, even if the law seems unwise or works to the disadvantage of a particular group, or if the rationale for it seems tenuous. . . . By requiring that the classification bear a rational relationship to an independent and legitimate legislative end, we ensure that classifications are not drawn for the purpose of disadvantaging the group burdened by the law. (If the adverse impact on the disfavored class is an apparent aim of the legislature, its impartiality would be suspect.)

Amendment 2 confounds this normal process of judicial review. It is at once too narrow and too broad. It identifies persons by a single trait and then denies them protection across the board. The resulting disqualification of a class of persons from the right to seek specific protection from the law is unprecedented in our jurisprudence. . . .

It is not within our constitutional tradition to enact laws of this sort. Central both to the idea of the rule of law and to our own Constitution's guarantee of equal protection is the principle that government and each of its parts remain open on impartial terms to all who seek its assistance. . . . Respect for this principle explains why laws singling out a certain class of citizens for disfavored legal status or general hardships are rare. A law declaring that in general it shall be more difficult for one group of citizens than for all others to seek aid from the government is itself a denial of equal protection of the laws in the most literal sense . . . A second and related point is that laws of the kind now before us raise the inevitable inference that the disadvantage imposed is born of animosity toward the class of persons affected. "[I]f the constitutional conception of 'equal protection of the laws' means anything, it must at the very least mean that a bare . . . desire to harm a politically unpopular group cannot constitute a *legitimate* governmental interest." . . . Even laws enacted for broad and ambitious purposes often can be explained by reference to legitimate public policies which justify the incidental disadvantages they impose on certain persons. Amendment 2, however, in making a general announcement that gays and lesbians shall not have any particular protections from the law, inflicts on them immediate, continuing, and real injuries that outrun and belie any legitimate justifications that may be claimed for it. We conclude that, in addition to the far-reaching deficiencies of Amendment 2 that we have noted, the principles it offends, in another sense, are conventional and venerable; a law must bear a rational relationship to a legitimate governmental purpose. . . . The primary rationale the State offers for Amendment 2 is respect for other citizens' freedom of association, and in particular the liberties of landlords or employers who have personal or religious objections to homosexuality. Colorado also cites its interest in conserving resources to fight discrimination against other groups. The breadth of the Amendment is so far removed from these particular justifications that we find it impossible to credit them. . . . It is a status-based enactment divorced from any factual context from which we could discern a relationship to legitimate state interests; it is a classification of persons undertaken for its own sake, something the Equal Protection Clause does not permit.

We must conclude that Amendment 2 classifies homosexuals not to further a proper legislative end but to make them unequal to everyone else. This Colorado cannot do. A State cannot so deem a class of persons a stranger to its laws. . . .

JUSTICE SCALIA, *with whom* THE CHIEF JUSTICE *and* JUSTICE THOMAS *join, dissenting.*

The Court has mistaken a Kulturkampf [cultural battle—ED.] for a fit of spite. The constitutional amendment before us here is not the manifestation of a " 'bare . . . desire to harm' " homosexuals, but is rather a modest attempt by seemingly tolerant Coloradans to preserve traditional sexual mores against the efforts of a politically powerful minority to revise those mores through use of the laws. That objective, and the means chosen to achieve it, are not only unimpeachable under any constitutional doctrine hitherto pronounced (hence the opinion's heavy reliance upon principles of righteousness rather than judicial holdings); they have been specifically approved by the Congress of the United States and by this Court.

In holding that homosexuality cannot be singled out for disfavorable treatment, the Court contradicts a decision, unchallenged here, pronounced only 10 years ago, see *Bowers v. Hardwick* . . . (1986), and places the prestige of this institution behind the proposition that opposition to homosexuality is as reprehensible as racial or religious bias. Whether it is or not is *precisely* the cultural debate that gave rise to the Colorado constitutional amendment (and to the preferential laws against which the amendment was directed). Since the Constitution of the United States says nothing about this subject, it is left to be resolved by normal democratic means, including the democratic adoption of provisions in state constitutions. This Court has no business imposing upon all Americans the resolution favored by the elite class from which the Members of this institution are selected, pronouncing that "animosity" toward homosexuality . . . is evil. I vigorously dissent.

The amendment prohibits *special treatment* of homosexuals, and nothing more. It would not affect, for example, a requirement of state law that pensions be paid to all retiring state employees with a certain length of service; homosexual employees, as well as others, would be entitled to that benefit. But it would prevent the State or any municipality from making death-benefit payments to the "life partner" of a homosexual when it does not make such payments to the long-time roommate of a nonhomosexual employee. Or again, it does not affect the requirement of the State's general insurance laws that customers be afforded coverage without discrimination unrelated to anticipated risk. Thus, homosexuals could not be denied coverage, or charged a greater premium, with respect to auto collision insurance; but neither the State nor any municipality could require that distinctive health insurance risks associated with homosexuality (if there are any) be ignored. . . .

## II

I turn next to whether there was a legitimate rational basis for the substance of the constitutional amendment—for the prohibition of special protection for homosexuals. It is unsurprising that the Court avoids discussion of this question, since the answer is so obviously yes. . . . In *Bowers v. Hardwick* . . . (1986), we held that the Constitution does not prohibit what virtually all States had done from the founding of the Republic until very recent years—making homosexual con-

duct a crime. That holding is unassailable, except by those who think that the Constitution changes to suit current fashions. But in any event it is a given in the present case: Respondents' briefs did not urge overruling *Bowers,* and at oral argument respondents' counsel expressly disavowed any intent to seek such overruling . . . If it is constitutionally permissible for a State to make homosexual conduct criminal, surely it is constitutionally permissible for a State to enact other laws merely *disfavoring* homosexual conduct. . . . "After all, there can hardly be more palpable discrimination against a class than making the conduct that defines the class criminal." . . . And *a fortiori* [even stronger—ED.] it is constitutionally permissible for a State to adopt a provision *not even* disfavoring homosexual conduct, but merely prohibiting all levels of state government from bestowing *special protections* upon homosexual conduct. . . . As Justice KENNEDY wrote, when he was on the Court of Appeals, in a case involving discharge of homosexuals from the Navy: "Nearly any statute which classifies people may be irrational as applied in particular cases. Discharge of the particular plaintiffs before us would be rational, under minimal scrutiny, not because their particular cases present the dangers which justify Navy policy, but instead because the general policy of discharging all homosexuals is rational." . . .

## III

The foregoing suffices to establish what the Court's failure to cite any case remotely in point would lead one to suspect: No principle set forth in the Constitution, nor even any imagined by this Court in the past 200 years, prohibits what Colorado has done here. But the case for Colorado is much stronger than that. What it has done is not only unprohibited, but eminently reasonable, with close, congressionally approved precedent in earlier constitutional practice.

First, as to its eminent reasonableness. The Court's opinion contains grim, disapproving hints that Coloradans have been guilty of "animus" or "animosity" toward homosexuality, as though that has been established as Unamerican. Of course it is our moral heritage that one should not hate any human being or class of human beings. But I had thought that one could consider certain conduct reprehensible—murder, for example, or polygamy, or cruelty to animals—and could exhibit even "animus" toward such conduct. Surely that is the only sort of "animus" at issue here: moral disapproval of homosexual conduct, the same sort of moral disapproval that produced the centuries-old criminal laws that we held constitutional in *Bowers*. The Colorado amendment does not, to speak entirely precisely, prohibit giving favored status to people who are *homosexuals;* they can be favored for many reasons—for example, because they are senior citizens or members of racial minorities. But it prohibits giving them favored status *because of their homosexual conduct*—that is, it prohibits favored status *for homosexuality. . . .*

But though Coloradans are, as I say, *entitled* to be hostile toward homosexual conduct, the fact is that the degree of hostility reflected by Amendment 2 is the smallest conceivable. The Court's portrayal of Coloradans as a society fallen victim to pointless, hate-filled "gay-bashing" is so false as to be comical. Colorado not only is one of the 25 States that have repealed their antisodomy laws, but was among the first to do so. . . . But the society that eliminates criminal punishment for homosexual acts does not necessarily abandon the view that homosexuality is morally wrong and socially harmful; often, abolition simply reflects the view that enforcement of such criminal laws involves unseemly intrusion into the intimate lives of citizens. . . .

There is a problem, however, which arises when criminal sanction of homosexuality is eliminated but moral and social disapprobation of homosexuality is meant to be retained. The Court cannot be unaware of that problem; it is evident in many cities of the country, and occasionally bubbles to the surface of the news, in heated political disputes over such matters as the introduction into local schools of books teaching that homosexuality is an optional and fully acceptable "alternate life style." The problem (a problem, that is, for those who wish to retain social disapprobation of homosexuality) is that, because those who engage in homosex-

ual conduct tend to reside in disproportionate numbers in certain communities, . . . and of course care about homosexual-rights issues much more ardently than the public at large, they possess political power much greater than their numbers, both locally and statewide. Quite understandably, they devote this political power to achieving not merely a grudging social toleration, but full social acceptance, of homosexuality. . . . ("[T]he task of gay rights proponents is to move the center of public discourse along a continuum from the rhetoric of disapprobation, to rhetoric of tolerance, and finally to affirmation").

By this time Coloradans were asked to vote on Amendment 2, their exposure to homosexuals' quest for social endorsement was not limited to newspaper accounts of happenings in places such as New York, Los Angeles, San Francisco, and Key West. Three Colorado cities—Aspen, Boulder, and Denver—had enacted ordinances that listed "sexual orientation" as an impermissible ground for discrimination, equating the moral disapproval of homosexual conduct with racial and religious bigotry. . . . The phenomenon had even appeared statewide: the Governor of Colorado had signed an executive order pronouncing that "in the State of Colorado we recognize the diversity in our pluralistic society and strive to bring an end to discrimination in any form," and directing state agency-heads to "ensure non-discrimination" in hiring and promotion based on, among other things, "sexual orientation." . . . I do not mean to be critical of these legislative successes; homosexuals are as entitled to use the legal system for reinforcement of their moral sentiments as are the rest of society. But they are subject to being countered by lawful, democratic countermeasures as well.

That is where Amendment 2 came in. It sought to counter both the geographic concentration and the disproportionate political power of homosexuals by (1) resolving the controversy at the statewide level, and (2) making the election a single-issue contest for both sides. It put directly, to all the citizens of the State, the question: Should homosexuality be given special protection? They answered no. The Court today asserts that this most democratic of procedures is unconstitutional. . . .

But there is a much closer analogy, one that involves precisely the effort by the majority of citizens to preserve its view of sexual morality statewide, against the efforts of a geographically concentrated and politically powerful minority to undermine it. The constitutions of the States of Arizona, Idaho, New Mexico, Oklahoma, and Utah *to this day* contain provisions stating that polygamy is "forever prohibited." . . . Polygamists, and those who have a polygamous "orientation," have been "singled out" by these provisions for much more severe treatment than merely denial of favored status; and that treatment can only be changed by achieving amendment of the state constitutions. The Court's disposition today suggests that these provisions are unconstitutional, and that polygamy must be permitted in these States on a state-legislated, or perhaps even local-option, basis—unless, of course, polygamists for some reason have fewer constitutional rights than homosexuals.

The United States Congress, by the way, *required* the inclusion of these antipolygamy provisions in the constitutions of Arizona, New Mexico, Oklahoma, and Utah, as a condition of their admission to statehood. . . .—so that not only were "each of [the] parts" of these States not "open on impartial terms" to polygamists, but even the States as a whole were not; polygamists would have to persuade the whole country to their way of thinking. Idaho adopted the constitutional provision on its own, but the 51st Congress, which admitted Idaho into the Union, found its constitution to be "republican in form *and . . . in conformity with the Constitution of the United States.*" Act of Admission of Idaho, . . . Thus, this "singling out" of the sexual practices of a single group for statewide, democratic vote—so utterly alien to our constitutional system, the Court would have us believe—has not only happened, but has received the explicit approval of the United States Congress. . . . In *Davis v. Beason,* . . . (1890), Justice Field wrote for a unanimous Court:

In our judgment, §501 of the Revised Statutes of Idaho Territory, which provides that "no person . . . who is a bigamist or polygamist or who teaches, advises, counsels, or encourages any person or persons to become bigamists or polygamists, or to commit any other crime defined by law, or to enter into what is known as plural or celestial marriage, or who is a member of any order, organization or association which teaches, advises, counsels, or encourages its members or devotees or any other persons to commit the crime of bigamy or polygamy, or any other crime defined by law . . . is permitted to vote at any election, or to hold any position or office of honor, trust, or profit within this Territory," *is not open to any constitutional or legal objection.*

. . . It remains to be explained how §501 of the Idaho Revised Statutes was not an "impermissible targeting" of polygamists, but (the much more mild) Amendment 2 is an "impermissible targeting" of homosexuals. Has the Court concluded that the perceived social harm of polygamy is a "legitimate concern of government," and the perceived social harm of homosexuality is not?

## IV

I strongly suspect that the answer to the last question is yes, which leads me to the last point I wish to make: The Court today, announcing that Amendment 2 "defies . . . conventional [constitutional] inquiry" . . . and "confounds [the] normal process of judicial review" . . . employs a constitutional theory heretofore unknown to frustrate Colorado's reasonable effort to preserve traditional American moral values. . . . The Court's stern disapproval of "animosity" towards homosexuality might be compared with what an earlier Court said [in a polygamy case—ED.]:

[C]ertainly no legislation can be supposed more wholesome and necessary in the founding of a free, self-governing commonwealth, fit to take rank as one of the co-ordinate States of the Union, than that which seeks to establish it on the basis of the idea of the family, as consisting in and springing from the union for life of one man and one woman in the holy estate of matrimony; the sure foundation of all that is stable and noble in our civilization; the best guaranty of that reverent morality which is the source of all beneficent progress in social and political improvement. . . .

I would not myself indulge in such official praise for heterosexual monogamy, because I think it no business of the courts (as opposed to the political branches) to take sides in this culture war. . . .

When the Court takes sides in the culture wars, it tends to . . . reflect . . . the views and values of the lawyer class from which the Court's Members are drawn. How that class feels about homosexuality will be evident to anyone who wishes to interview job applicants at virtually any of the Nation's law schools. The interviewer may refuse to offer a job because the applicant is a Republican; because he is an adulterer; because he went to the wrong prep school or belongs to the wrong country club; because he eats snails; because he is a womanizer; because she wears real-animal fur; or even because he hates the Chicago Cubs. But if the interviewer should wish not to be an associate or partner of an applicant because he disapproves of the applicant's homosexuality, *then* he will have violated the pledge which the Association of American Law Schools requires all its member-schools to exact from job interviewers: "assurance of the employer's willingness" to hire homosexuals. . . .

Today's opinion has no foundation in American constitutional law, and barely pretends to. The people of Colorado have adopted an entirely reasonable provision which does not even disfavor homosexuals in any substantive sense, but merely denies them preferential treatment. Amendment 2 is designed to prevent piecemeal deterioration of the sexual morality favored by a majority of Coloradans, . . .

## Notes and Comments

1. After the approval of the marijuana referendum, a conflict arose over the applicability of national and state drug laws.

As noted earlier, under the usual rule, the national law would apply, regardless of the vote of Californians. In *Romer*, the conflict involved an approved initiative and the U.S. Constitution. Under the doctrine of judicial review, the U.S. Supreme Court is the final arbiter of the constitutional limits upon state and local power. These two limitations upon lawmaking by referendum need to be kept in mind.

Also to be kept in mind is the power of popular will in the face of unwanted law. At a minimum, one can expect widespread violations when the rule of law strays too far from working beliefs. For example, school prayers have long been ruled unconstitutional as a violation of the First Amendment, but this has not prevented defiance of the rule in some schools, since rules of law are not self-enforcing.

2. The majority of the Court has ruled that the Colorado amendment would result in singling out a group and denying them equal protection of law. The dissent argues that the amendment does no more than deny *special* privileges over and above those available to every citizen. Evaluate the arguments.

3. The main thrust of the Scalia dissent is that Coloradans ought to have a right to select, by majority vote, among competing "cultures," in this case heterosexuality and other sexual preferences. But an essential principle in constitutional law is that some areas are not open to majority rule. If the contrary were the case, all minorities would be at the mercy of hostile majorities and could by the exercise of rules like those envisioned in Amendment 2 of the Colorado Constitution be held in permanent subordination. This point would apply with equal vigor to all those groups who have historically been (1) disfavored for a variety of reasons and (2) in the minority—immigrants, aliens, blacks, Asians, and many others who at various times have been on the wrong side of popular will.

4. The dissent seems to favor some results of majority vote and to disfavor others. Justice Scalia favors the Colorado amendment as a legitimate exercise of majority rule but disfavors the rules of the communities where anti-discrimination ordinances were passed, presumably by majority rule. He looks beneath the surface of the

anti-discrimination ordinances to see whether they were the product of an ardent minority or a real majority of the communities. Evaluate.

He also criticizes law schools for having special rules prohibiting discrimination in hiring based on sexual orientation, arguing that these rules are the result of elite bias and not majority rule. Should a law school make explicit its policy against discrimination in hiring based on sexual orientation?

5. There is a battle over sexual preferences taking place in churches, in schools, and in the courts. What should be the place of legal institutions in cultural battles? Before concluding that the courts should stay out of them, remember from our earliest case study that nonintervention is never neutral.

Gay rights received a setback in the Supreme Court case that considered the right to exclude homosexuals from the Boy Scouts.* By all admissions James Dale had been an exemplary scout up to the time of his exclusion from scouting on the grounds of his homosexuality. He entered scouting at age eight and continued as a scout until age eighteen, by which time he had attained the rank of eagle scout. He then became an adult scout and an assistant troop leader. All went well until he attended Rutgers and joined a gay/lesbian alliance. A newspaper interviewed him and he stated the need for teenagers to have gay role models. He received a letter dismissing him from the scouts and he challenged the decision based on the New Jersey statute for public accommodation which prohibited discrimination on the grounds of sexual preference. Chief Justice Rehnquist ruled for the scouts, stating their First Amendment rights of association and expression would be violated if an avowed

homosexual were to be made a member against their wishes:

> The forced inclusion of an unwanted person in a group infringes the group's freedom of expressive association if the presence of that person affects in a significant way the group's ability to advocate public or private viewpoints[†]

Rehnquist also concluded that Dale's very presence would run counter to the scouts' policy against homosexuality:

> Dale's presence in the Boy Scouts would, at the very least, send a message, both to the youth members and the world, that the Boy Scouts accepts homosexual conduct as a legitimate form of behavior[‡]

Nor could he find the Boy Scouts a "place" to which Dale had been refused accommodation.

Justice Souter dissented, concluding that the Boy Scouts really had no policy, other than the one the Scouts cobbled together to exclude Dale. The idea of "place" for purposes of accommodations law had been interpreted to cover more than physical locations and included organizations. But his most passionate criticism of the majority opinion is found in the following:

> The only apparent explanation for the majority's holding then, is that homosexuals are simply so different from the rest of society that their presence alone—unlike any other individuals—should be singled out for special First Amendment treatment. Under the majority's reasoning, an openly gay male is irreversibly affixed with the label "homosexual." That label even though unseen, communicates a message that permits his exclusion wherever he goes. His openness is the sole and sufficient justification for his ostracism.[§]

---

*Boy Scouts of America . . . v. Dale* 68 U.S. Law Week 4625 (2000) 4627.

[†]Ibid., 4627.

[‡]Ibid., at 4629.

[§]Ibid., 4641.

# 7 FEMINIST PERSPECTIVES ON LAW AND LEGAL ORDER

I myself have never been able to find out precisely what feminism is: I only know that people call me a feminist whenever I express sentiments that distinguish me from a doormat.

Rebecca West, *The Clarion* (1913)

The desire to please must not master the desire for truth.

Judith Baer (1999)

Antifeminism is a direct expression of misogyny: it is a political defense of woman hating.

Andrea Dworkin (1983)

True, true happiness will follow
If you only follow me.
*True True Happiness,* popular song (1959)

[W]hatever new obstacles are mounted against the future march toward equality, whatever new myths are invented, penalties levied, opportunities rescinded, or degradations imposed, no one can ever take from the American woman the justness of her cause.

Susan Faludi, *Backlash* (1991)

&larr; It is not always clear just what a feminist critique of law is—as one should expect about a field that is relatively new, there has been no fully unified theory. And it is not clear how deep the critique goes; whether, like anarchistic orientations studied in the last chapter, feminists find law fundamentally, inherently, and irretrievably flawed—a gigantic wrong turn in human history—or instead believe there is something left for progressive change through the rule of law, after the critique has run its course. What is clear is that feminism is alive and well in legal circles as elsewhere, and there is an abundance of high-quality literature questioning every aspect of law in theory and practice.

We already sensed gender bias in the legal order from the readings in the preceding chapters of this text. In the jurisprudential readings, including left-leaning ones, the masculine form abounds—he did this, men do that, and so on. These forms indicate that women were not simply considered of a lower economic class, or in lower places in status and power hierarchies, but, until comparatively recent times, women were nowhere in the thinking at all. Women of color have been less than nowhere across jurisprudential history; indeed, until the Civil War they were most probably slaves.

The cases in Chapter 1 on spousal abuse get contemporary readers thinking about man-made law, and male lawyers practicing conservatively—that is, within rule structures designed to reduce women to property—rather than radically, by delegitimatizing the rule system wholesale, along with its administration. One need only think of the case of *State* v. *Black*, where instead of challenging the right of a husband to abuse his wife in *all* cases, the lawyer for the state argued that since the husband and wife were living apart they were the legal equivalent of strangers.

(Thus the propriety of the rule giving the husband the "right" to chastise his wife did not have to be squarely faced.) Moreover, the standards for criminality were always based on the abuser's standard—what state of mind *he* was in—and not on the recipient's standard, a distortion still prevalent in cases of rape where the state of mind of the rapist displaces the state of mind of the victim.

Under common law there were some special rules that applied to women; it was presumed that a woman was incapable of forming criminal intent if an alleged crime were done in the presence of her husband. But this "extenuating circumstance" carried debilitating premises: she was presumed to be under the domination and control of her husband and therefore incapable of intending anything. A wife could not be a criminal in such circumstances because she was a nonperson—no penalty, but no humanity either.

Regarding the related common law understanding that after marriage there was a unity and no longer two independent individuals with separate legal standing, a number of commentators have observed that the marriage merged the wife into her husband. (In the 1858 case of *Thornton and Wife* v. *Suffolk Manufacturing* in Chapter 5 we saw a situation in which, after her marriage, Catherine Cassidy had no independent standing to sue, and her husband used his standing to bring an action based on *her* employment contract!)

What makes contemporary readers especially uncomfortable about spousal abuse cases and related doctrines, apart from the realization that gender permeates legal concepts, is the knowledge that while official criteria may appear to provide greater protection for battered women, in fact the police and courts may not protect them. Even without formal authorization to do so, police sometimes still ask, "Is the husband or mate drunk? Has he inflicted or is he likely to inflict serious injury? Is the victim of abuse to be believed when she says everything is all right now?" Based on ad hoc evaluations, the police may decide that a dispute will "blow over" and conclude that noninvolvement by the state is the best course of action. Thus the working criteria for police or court intervention may be more similar to those of a hundred years ago than one would suppose.

The domestic circle as an inviolable sanctum, which for purposes of spousal abuse means a male-dominated sanctum, may still be the abiding assumption today. For example, when one hears that the courts of Massachusetts issued 45,000 restraining orders against husbands or mates in the first nine months of 1992, several thoughts flash through the mind (besides the general approval of greater judicial activism): (1) there is a huge amount of violence against women, and (2) whatever the claims of criminal law or family law as "systems of social control," the number of cases show that law has had precious little deterrent effect in controlling or reducing domestic violence. The prevalence of violent behavior and the number of serious assaults preceded by a history of abuse dwarf the fact that courts are more willing to issue the orders.

In Chapter 3 on values, there appeared an observation by Patricia Williams about her experiences as a black woman at the Harvard Law School. She felt herself to be an inanimate obstruction to be politely avoided. She had lost both her presence and her voice. Men around her seemed to be full-fledged students with presence, movement, and voice. How widespread are the sentiments she felt about legal training and being a woman, a black woman, in a law school?

Her experience is common. Women writing about Yale Law School in the mid-1980s found four levels of "alienation": "from [them]selves, from the law school community, from the classroom, and from the content of legal education."* Their answer was to develop tactics by which to insinuate their way into the imagination of the school. Whether gazing into the legal abyss would let the legal abyss gaze further into them cannot be determined from their account. They could not empower themselves without entering, but entering could transform them in ways that they might not have preferred at the outset. Recall the story of Quesalid (Chapter 3), who after study and membership in a group of sorcerors discarded his early skepticism about the efficacy of sorcery.

The choices of the women at Yale Law School parallels the choices faced by practicing professionals as discussed by Catharine MacKinnon in her book on the relationship between feminism and the state, *Toward a Feminist Theory of the State*. By an ironic twist, contemporary feminist advocates may find themselves confronting the same dilemma as advocates opposed to spousal abuse in North Carolina. Those lawyers might have been torn between making radical challenges that would be difficult to achieve and putting aside fundamental claims in order to *win a case* on whatever grounds the unjust system recognized.

Should feminist lawyers radically attack a legal system dominated by male perceptions—of reality, of what equality means and when it has been achieved, of a "woman's place," etc.—or should advocates argue for gains *within the system* when by their own analysis the system is more deeply flawed than most "legal" victories will remedy? Or is there a third way that uses available legal principles like equality in ways that do not turn small-scale victories into large-scale defeats?

MacKinnon recognizes the problem and makes a choice:

> Is the state to some degree autonomous of the interest of men or an integral expression of them? Does the state embody and serve male interests in its form, dynamics, relation to society, and specific policies? Is the state constructed upon the subordination of women? If so, how does male power become state power? Can such a state be made to serve the interests of those upon whose powerlessness its power is erected? Would a different relation between state and society, such as may exist under socialism, make a difference? If not, is masculinity inherent in the state form *as such,* or is

---

*C. Weiss and L. Melling, "Legal Education of Twenty Women," *Stanford Law Review* 40, (1988), 1299.

some other form of state, or some other form of governing, distinguishable or imaginable? In the absence of answers to these questions, feminism has been caught between *giving more power to the state in each attempt to claim it for women and leaving unchecked power in the society of men. Undisturbed, meanwhile, like the assumption that women consent to sex is the assumption that women consent to this government.*[†] [Emphasis added]

MacKinnon answers that the symbolic implications of law are too powerful to be neglected by feminists:

> [L]aw is a particularly potent source and badge of legitimacy, and site and cloak of force. The force underpins the legitimacy as the legitimacy conceals the force. When life becomes law in such a system, the transformation is both formal and substantive. It reenters life marked by power."[‡]

With heightened consciousness, feminist lawyers can practice and not simply wait for a revolution, but their work will always be on the edge of problematic for the reasons MacKinnon herself states: to argue within a system legitimates the system and, for the critical present, the system is male.

The kinds of cases that must be pressed most strongly in the system are those in which gender issues cannot be trivialized or defined in male terms—for example, "unequal pay, allocation to disrespected work, demeaned physical characteristics, . . . rape, domestic battery, sexual abuse . . . and systemic sexual harassment."[§] These areas raise problems which by historical-precedential [male] terms the system cannot answer; the cases, while "conventional" on the surface—they can be talked about via legal categories—simultaneously have a radically transforming potential. Over time such cases become comparable to successive laboratory experiments that disprove the scientific model pursuant to which the experiments are done.

The foregoing questions mirror the perennial conflict between Marxists and anarchists, who debated whether the powerless should seek more powerful roles in the state and law, or whether activism ought to be directed toward other ends, for example, building nonstate networks open to direct action and control. Are the state and law *inherently flawed,* as Kropotkin contended, so that it will not do to transfer power from malevolent hands to benevolent hands? The anarchist contention has been that malevolence comes from power, regardless of good intentions, that the state will "deprive" as it "gives," and inevitably will pervert the values for which capture of the state was deemed necessary.

MacKinnon comes close to the anarchist position through her continual denunciation of hierarchy regardless of incumbents and wherever

---

[†]Catharine A. MacKinnon, *Toward a Feminist Theory of the State* (Cambridge, Massachusetts: Harvard University Press, 1989), p. 161.

[‡]Ibid., p. 237.

[§]Ibid., p. 244.

it is found. But even if increased access for women to flawed structures may not warrant complete optimism, it appears to be an indispensable first step toward bigger transformations.

These differences on the appropriate role of the state, if any, have not been resolved either within the feminist literature or outside it. Potential conflicts can be raised by assuming that the state is eventually made female instead of remaining male. If power tells all, the remarks of the anarchist Proudhon to Marx come to mind: fresh dogma could destroy the very purposes for which the state was taken over—that is, the elimination of tyranny. On the other hand, liberal theory of reform does not go far enough, and may simply fine-tune oppressive rule structures and their administration.

For the present, we are stuck with Albert Camus' observation that in the modern world, "Power settles everything." Women, who might be reluctant to assume power because of its corrosive effects on the soul, nevertheless rightly see the need for more empowerment of women. To simply withdraw from the contest tacitly legitimatizes male power, the male state, the male legal order, and the male-based hierarchy. Liberal reform or greater power in the state, as inadequate as they might turn out to be over a longer run, may be the only practical alternatives to submission.

This chapter introduces some feminist perspectives on law and legal order. It cannot pretend to encompass the experience of women in America, although that experience has helped to fuel the abundance of high-quality feminist literature in all fields of study including law. The experiences of women have not been of a single piece and, as noted above, the study of feminist perspectives on law will not yield a unified theory that all women and men everywhere will unqualifiedly embrace.

Having acknowledged that there are differences, we also recognize there is a shared commonality that motivates the study and application of gender theory in legal life. Women are women, and as women their experiences with legal training and with the law as enacted and applied presents an organizing principle for inquiry. The jurisprudence that explains the interconnections between women and legal order—past and contemplated—is feminist jurisprudence, and that jurisprudence pushes toward a more just world, both within and outside the formal legal realm.

The jurisprudential debate has been open and intense. Sometimes people antagonistic to women's claims for more justice will use this or that thread of the debate as ammunition *against* women, as was the case in *EEOC v. Sears, Roebuck.* An explanation of the uses and misuses of feminist scholarship by and about women can be found in the best-selling book by Susan Faludi, *Backlash.* In the *Sears* case, aspects of the open exploration of the nature and nurture of women provided the lawyers representing Sears with the argument that women were not "interested" in higher-paying jobs selling big-ticket items on commission. According to the court, the gross underrepresentation of women in certain jobs had not been due to discriminatory behavior of Sears but rather originated in the personal preferences of women.

Faludi found that the debate between feminist and nonfeminist women can feed a general backlash against women as this or that aspect of the ongoing dialogue is selectively invoked to support the repression of women. That such a misuse of scholarship goes against the whole purpose of feminist study should go without saying, but this selective invocation is a fact of political-legal life. It is not unlike the selective uses of precedent which were dissected in Chapter 1.

The efforts of women to improve their employment opportunities can be undercut by new meanings given to "protection." On the surface the requirement of a safe work environment for men and women and for fetal protection from workplace hazards seems commendable. But it was found in the *Johnson Controls* case that occupational restrictions for fetal protection actually resulted in discrimination against women. As the U.S. Supreme Court held, employers cannot use fetal protection to rationalize the discriminatory exclusion of women from certain employment.

That women of various ethnicities, races, and religions may have unique experiences and political-legal agendas cannot be brushed casually to one side. Included in the chapter readings are cases in which black women challenged race and sex discrimination in court and an appraisal of the cases and feminist jurisprudence from a black woman's perspective. Just as there can be no clean fit between Marxist and anarchist analysis of law and feminism, so too race and class can complicate feminist scholars' speaking with one voice and for all.

The impulse in the face of the stresses and strains of scholarship that "feed the opposition" might be for feminists to attempt self-censorship or to engage in consensus scholarship designed to present a "unified front" to groups antagonistic to the betterment of the lives of women of all backgrounds and persuasions. Fortunately, this temptation to act like a political party rather than a group of scholars and thoughtful people either has been resisted or cannot be put into practice. The result has been the most creative branch of modern legal scholarship, which, for all its disparate viewpoints, has a deep momentum that can only transform, for the better, law as made, studied, practiced, and applied.

No case in recent history has enraged feminists more than *EEOC* v. *Sears, Roebuck.* A first feminist critique of the case concerned the overall failure of enthusiasm in the Reagan administration for zealously pursuing any cases impinging on employer prerogatives, including those contesting gender discrimination under the Civil Rights Act. The second critique concerned the bypassing of impressive statistics compiled by the Equal Employment Opportunities Commission on discrimination in hiring and promotion at Sears. Both the trial and appellate courts concluded that the statistical material, consistent with discrimination in hiring and promotion by Sears, was simply irrelevant *"given"* a lack of interest of women in commission sales; Sears did not have anything to do with the underrepresentation of women in high-commission jobs. Also, by giving greater value to anecdotal evidence from Sears' managers than to the EEOC's statistical material, the courts freed themselves to rule that despite the company's hope that women would be attracted to straight commission positions, women were simply not forthcoming to take the jobs.

In the following excerpt we focus on the court's definition of women's interests, by nature or nurture, and, given those interests, the type of work women select and don't select. Sears would have been legally accountable if discrimination in hiring or promotion to commission sales were pinned on their behavior. They would be innocent—as the courts eventually found—if by nature or nurture women were choosing to avoid commission sales work.

---

## 7.1  EEOC v. Sears, Roebuck & Co.    *628 F. Supp. 1264 (1986)*

NORDBERG, JUDGE.

THE MOST CREDIBLE AND convincing evidence offered at trial regarding women's interest in commission sales at Sears was the detailed, uncontradicted testimony of numerous men and women who were Sears store managers, personnel managers and other officials, regarding their efforts to recruit women into commission sales. As discussed above, attracting women to commission sales has been an important priority in Sears' affirmative action programs since the first affirmative action questionnaire was circulated in 1968. Sears managers and other witnesses with extensive store experience over the entire relevant time period testified that far more men than women were interested in commission selling at Sears. Numerous managers described the difficulties they encountered in convincing women to sell on commission.

> Sears' witnesses with extensive experience testified that the ratio of men interested in commission sales to women was at least 8 or 10 to 1.
>
> The court finds the testimony of the Sears officials and employees in this case to be very credible and persuasive. Their testimony in the case was supported by a substantial number of other employees whose uncontradicted written testimony was also persuasive.

Sears managers continually attempted to persuade women to accept commission selling or other non-traditional jobs. Women who expressed an interest in commission selling were given priority over men when an opening occurred. Managers attempted to persuade even marginally qualified women to accept commission selling positions. They would sometimes guarantee a woman her former position if she would try commission selling for a certain period. Store managers reported that they had interviewed every woman in the store and none were willing to sell on commission. Managers often had to "sell" the job to reluctant women, even though enthusiasm and interest in the positions were qualities management valued highly in commission salespeople. Despite these unusual efforts, managers had only limited success in attracting women to commission sales.

Female applicants who indicated an interest in sales most often were interested in selling soft lines of merchandise, such as clothing, jewelry, and cosmetics, items generally not sold on commission at Sears. Male applicants were more likely to be interested in hard lines, such as hardware, automotive, sporting goods and the more technical goods, which are more likely to be sold on commission at Sears. These interests generally paralleled the interest of customers in these product lines. Men, for example, were usually not interested in fashions, cosmetics, linens, women's or children's clothing, and other household small

---

Footnotes and exhibits have been deleted.—ED.

ticket items. Women usually lacked interest in selling automotives and building supplies, men's clothing, furnaces, fencing and roofing. Women also were not as interested as men in outside sales in general, and did not wish to invest the time and effort necessary to learn to sell in the home improvements divisions. Women often disliked Division 45 (men's clothing) because it sometimes involved taking personal measurements of men.

Custom draperies, however, was one division in which women were willing to sell on a commission basis, even though it could require some outside selling. More women were willing to sell custom draperies on commission because they enjoyed the fashion and creative aspect of the job, most had past experience in the field, and it was a relatively low pressure commission division. Applicants expressing an interest in the division were almost all women. Very few men were willing to sell draperies.

The percentage of women hired in the various categories generally paralleled their interests and background in the product line involved. This illustrates how much an applicant's interest in the product sold can influence his willingness to accept a particular commission sales position. As is evident from the above discussion, interests of men and women often diverged along patterns of traditional male and female interest.

This lack of interest of women in commission sales was confirmed by the number of women who rejected commission sales positions. Although evidence was presented only for the Eastern territory, this evidence showed that many women turned down commission sales job offers or otherwise expressly indicated that they were not interested in commission selling at Sears. . . .

Women at Sears who were not interested in commission sales expressed a variety of reasons for their lack of interest. Some feared or disliked the perceived "dog-eat-dog" competition. Others were uncomfortable or unfamiliar with the products sold on commission. There was fear of being unable to compete, being unsuccessful, and of losing their jobs. Many expressed a preference for noncommission selling because it was more enjoyable and friendly. They believed that the increased earnings potential of commission sales was not worth the increased pressure, tension, and risk.

These reasons for women not taking commission sales jobs were confirmed in a study performed by Juliet Brudney on behalf of Sears. Ms. Brudney conducted structured interviews of women in nontraditional jobs at Sears, including women in automotive and service technician jobs, and their supervisors. She also interviewed women who were seeking jobs or changing jobs, and found that they perceived commission sales as requiring cut-throat competitiveness that prevents friendships at work. They were also reluctant to sell products with which they were unfamiliar and preferred the security of a steady salary to the risks of making less in commission sales.

The results of Ms. Brudney's study were supported by the testimony of Sears' expert, Dr. Rosalind Rosenberg, who testified that women generally prefer to sell soft-line products, such as apparel, housewares or accessories sold on a noncommission basis, and are less interested in selling products such as fencing, refrigeration equipment and tires. Women tend to be more interested than men in the social and cooperative aspects of the workplace. Women tend to see themselves as less competitive. They often view noncommission sales as more attractive than commission sales, because they can enter and leave the job more easily, and because there is more social contact and friendship, and less stress in noncommission selling. This testimony is consistent with the uncontradicted testimony of Sears' witnesses regarding the relative lack of interest of women in commission selling at Sears, and with the testimony of Ms. Brudney, and is further evidence that men and women were not equally interested in commission sales at Sears.

## SURVEY EVIDENCE

Sears also introduced a number of surveys taken of Sears employees and applicants which also demonstrate that women were much less interested than men in commission selling at Sears. This evidence also showed that women were particularly less interested than men in selling products in divisions where EEOC found the greatest disparities between the expected and actual proportions of women.

First, Sears presented extensive evidence of differences in the general interests and attitudes of men and women in American society over the past 50 years. This evidence was developed by Dr. Irving Crespi. . . . Dr. Crespi found that: (1) men were more likely than women to be interested in working at night or on weekends, (2) women were more likely than men to be interested in regular daytime work; (3) men were more likely than women to be interested in sales jobs involving a high degree of competition among salespersons; (4) men were more likely to be interested in jobs where there was a chance of making more money, even though it involved a risk of losing the job if they did not sell enough; and (5) men more likely than women to be motivated by the pay of a job than by the nature of the job and whether they like it. . . .

Sears' evidence also demonstrated that women's attitudes toward work changed measurably between 1970 and 1980. During this time, significant changes occurred in the sexual compositions of the workforce. The number of females in many traditionally male-dominated fields doubled or tripled (e.g., securities and financial services salespeople, lawyers, hardware and building supplies). The female proportion of college students majoring in business subjects rose from 10 percent to nearly one-third in each category. Sears evidence also showed that, by the late 1970's, women were more open to commission sales positions than in the early 1970's, but it was still necessary to "sell" the job to them in many cases. Some reasons for the increased willingness of women to accept commission sales jobs were: (1) commission sales jobs changed from being almost exclusively full time to largely part time, and many more women preferred to work part time; (2) the change in compensation for commission sales from draw versus commission to salary plus commission, which reduced the risk perceived by some women in commission selling; (3) a group of successful commission saleswomen that over time provided role models for other women; and (4) the increased availability of day care, which increased the hours many women were available to work. Thus, female interest in and availability for commission sales increased during the period from 1973 through 1980.

In addition, specific surveys of the interests of Sears employees reveal that far more men than women are interested in commission sales. Sears has taken regular morale surveys of its employees in every retail store approximately once every three years since 1939. Sears has also conducted a number of special surveys to ascertain employee opinions on particular subjects.

The morale surveys demonstrated that most noncommission salespeople were happy with their work, and that more noncommission saleswomen preferred to stay in their present jobs than noncommission salesmen. In 1974–1976, noncommission saleswomen were much less interested than noncommission salesmen in promotion to division management or a higher level. They were far more likely than noncommission salesmen to want to remain in the job they had or one like it. In 1978–1980, only 14% of full time noncommission salesmen and 8.4% of noncommission saleswomen were interested in a different position. Thus, although only a small percentage were interested in other jobs, almost twice as many men as women were interested in new jobs. In addition, almost twice the percentage of female (56.4%) as male (30.3%) full time noncommission salespeople expressed a preference to remain in their present jobs.

The morale of noncommission salespersons was higher than that of all other time-card nonsupervisory employees. Noncommission salespersons were satisfied with their work, and noncommission saleswomen were more satisfied than noncommission salesmen. Most noncommission salespersons, and especially females, enjoyed their work and took pride in their jobs.

Noncommission saleswomen were more likely than noncommission salesmen to believe that their pay levels favorably influenced their attitudes toward their jobs, and were less likely to feel underpaid and to report that their pay at Sears was inadequate to meet their needs. Noncommission saleswomen were also more likely than noncommission salesmen to feel good about their futures at Sears.

This survey evidence, which has not been challenged by EEOC, demonstrates that noncommission saleswomen were generally happier with their present jobs at Sears, and were much less likely than their male counterparts to be interested in other positions, such as commission sales. These results confirm the reports of Sears' witnesses that women were less interested in commission sales than men.

Sears also presented the results of a special Job Interest Survey taken in 1976. . . .

. . . Twice as many male as female noncommission salespersons reported that they were interested in another job at Sears (80.6% of the males, 36.6% of the females). . . . After stating whether they were interested in any other job at Sears, respondents were asked to list what other jobs they would be interested in at Sears. Almost three times as many males (33.7%) as females (12.3%) stated that they were interested in commission sales. . . .

The survey next provided a definition of big ticket commission selling . . . The survey then asked if the respondent would be interested in such a job. After reading the definition, 32% of the men, but only 3.5% of the women, expressed a definite interest in a big ticket commission sales job at Sears. . . . The clear majority of females (69.4%) responded that they were definitely not interested in such a job, while only 37.9% of the males responded "definitely no." . . .

. . . The survey provides a sufficiently fair and useful estimate of the interest of noncommission salesmen and saleswomen in big ticket commission sales to corroborate the highly credible testimony of Sears' store witnesses regarding the lack of female interest in commission sales positions.

. . . Sears' National Timecard Nonsupervisory Special Survey taken in 1982 . . . asked questions about the attitudes, interests, and the personal beliefs and lifestyles of the employee. . . .

Question 42 of the survey asked respondents which three positions they wanted to be considered for next at Sears. Commission sales was one of the many alternative responses provided to the question. More than three times as many full time noncommission salesmen as noncommission saleswomen responded that they wanted to be considered for commission sales (20% of the males, 6% of the females), and more than twice as many part time noncommission salesmen as saleswomen (23% of the males, 9% of the females) were interested in commission sales.

. . . EEOC contends that Question 13C, not Question 42, is the most appropriate predictor of whether a noncommission salesperson is interested in commission sales. Question 13C asks whether the respondent would accept a commission sales job if offered one. However, as Dr. Crespi testified, Question 42 is a better indicator of real interest in the position, since the respondent must affirmatively choose commission sales. A "yes" answer to Question 13C requires less affirmative interest in the position. As discussed above, a strong interest in commission sales is an important factor which Sears managers look for in hiring commission sales applicants. The court therefore finds that Question 42 is the better indicator of the interest in commission sales. In any event, responses to Question 13C also indicate that noncommission salesmen are considerably more interested than noncommission saleswomen in commission selling. . . .

As Sears' witness Dr. Roper testified, perhaps the best indication of interest in commission sales can be derived from a combined analysis of the two questions. His combined analysis produced results similar to the responses to Question 42. Of the full time respondents, 20% of the men but only 6% of the women were actively interested in commission sales. For part time, 22% of the men and 9% of the women were actively interested. A slightly higher percentage of women would prefer another position but would accept commission sales (9% of full time women, 16% of part time women). Equally revealing is that 64% of the full time women were not interested in and would not accept a commission sales job, contrasted with 34% of the men giving the same responses. . . .

. . . [T]he NTNSS provided other useful information about the interests of men and women in noncommission sales. Noncommission salesmen, both full time and part time, were more interested in advancement at Sears in general than noncommission saleswomen. . . . Noncommission salesmen were more willing to make sacrifices for advancement, including working overtime, working more off-hours and weekends, and being assigned to bigger divisions. . . . In addition, among those with prior commission or big ticket sales experience, noncommission salesmen were much more likely than noncommission saleswomen to want to return to commission sales job. . . .

The court finds that, again, although there are some flaws in the design and administration of the NTNSS, they are not significant enough to undermine the essential validity of the results. The responses described above corroborate the uncontradicted testimony of Sears' store witnesses, the results of the morale surveys, and the 1976 Job Interest Survey discussed above. Together, this evidence provides clear and essentially uncontroverted proof that the interests of men and women in commission sales is far from equal. To the contrary, men have consistently indicated far more interest than women in commission selling, leaving EEOC's foundational assumption of the equal interest of men and women in commission sales without any credible factual support in the record.

## COMPARING SEARS TO NATIONAL DATA

In addition to Sears' evidence of actual interest of its employees in commission sales, Sears analyzed national labor force data as another measure of both interest in and availability for commission sales positions. . . . Sears expert Dr. Joan Haworth analyzed publicly available labor force data to obtain a reasonable benchmark for comparison with Sears. She examined data from the Panel Study of Income Dynamics, collected by the University of Michigan Institute for Social Research, and data from the Income Survey Development Program, based on surveys conducted by the Department of Commerce. She also relied on census data. This data demonstrated that the percentage of women selling on commission in the national workforce was far lower than the percentage of women EEOC estimated were available based on its overinclusive "sales" applicant pool during the years 1976–1980. . . . This data also revealed that the percentage of women interested in selling a product depended to a great extent on the nature of the product. For example, as late as 1980, females were 83.5 percent of the sales cashiers and 81.8 percent of the persons selling apparel, but only 7.8 percent of the persons selling motor vehicles and boats and 25 percent of the sales workers in hardware and building supplies. . . .

Dr. Haworth analyzed the number of male-owned and female-owned businesses by the type of product sold as a measure of interest in the product, since owning a business is the ultimate form of commission sales. She found wide differences in the percent of female-owned business depending on the product involved. For example, women owned 42.3 percent of the apparel and accessory stores, but only 3.9 percent of automobile dealerships and service stations. . . . Dr. Haworth also found a wide divergence of male and female interests within product lines. For example, within the apparel and accessories businesses, in 1980, women owned 68.5 percent of women's ready-to-wear stores, but only 13.1 percent of shoe stores, and none of the men's apparel stores. . . .

. . . National data revealed that women owned 60.5 percent of the drapery, curtain and upholstery stores in 1980, but they owned only 14.2 percent of the furniture stores and 1.2 percent of the floor coverings stores. . . .

This difference in male and female interests by product line is important in this case, because most of the disparities produced by EEOC's analysis are concentrated in five product lines: automotive, home building materials, electronics, appliances, and home improvements. All of these are product lines in which women have been substantially less interested than men.

This national data corroborates Sears' strong evidence of female lack of interest in commission sales and in the particular product lines discussed above. It is further proof that EEOC's assumption of equal male and female interest in commission sales and in all product lines has absolutely no basis in fact.

## OTHER EVIDENCE OF INTEREST

The only evidence introduced by EEOC regarding the interest of women in commission sales is the testimony of several witnesses regarding women's interests and aspirations in the workforce in general. These witnesses described the general history of women in the workforce, and contend essentially that there are no significant differences between the interests and career aspirations of men and women. They assert that women are influenced only by the opportunities presented to them, not by their preferences. . . .

However, these experts provided little persuasive authority to support their theories. The particular examples of unknown numbers and proportions of women in history to which they refer generally focus on small groups of unusual women and their demonstrated abilities in various historical contexts, not on the majority of women or their interests at the time of this case. The sweeping generalizations these witnesses sought to make are not supported by credible evidence. None of these witnesses had any specific knowledge of Sears, or provided any specific evidence to contradict the strong evidence presented by Sears of the actual differences between the interests of men and women in commission sales positions at Sears.

More convincing testimony in this area was offered by Sears expert Dr. Rosalind Rosenberg. Dr. Rosenberg testified that, although differences between men and women have diminished in the past two decades, these differences still exist and may account for different proportions of men and women in various jobs. She offered the more reasonable conclusion that differences in the number of men and women in a job could exist without discrimination by an employer.

In conclusion, EEOC's statistical analyses are dependent upon the crucial arbitrary assumption that men and women are equally interested in commission sales jobs at Sears. As is evident from the above discussion, EEOC has provided nothing more than unsupported generalizations by expert witnesses with no knowledge of Sears to support that assumption. Sears has offered a wide variety of credible evidence that, during 1973 to 1980, women in fact were far less interested in commission selling at Sears than men. All the evidence presented by Sears indicates that men are at least two times more interested in commission selling than women. Thus, EEOC's assumption of equal interest is unfounded and fatally undermines its entire statistical analysis.

## Notes and Questions

1. The lawyers for Sears countered the EEOC statistics that showed the gross underrepresentation of women in certain jobs by saying that those statistics did not show *cause,* i.e. that underrepresentation was attributable to discriminatory behavior by Sears.

Can this defense be constructed in every case, making it difficult for women to oppose well-funded employer-defendants who assemble rival statistics or anecdotal material showing employer benevolence?

Is the use of statistical material an indispensable shortcut to determine the probable presence of discrimination?

After the *Sears* case, women who claim discrimination may be confronted by a dilemma: if statistics are presented, courts may dispute the causal connection between the statistics and the employer's behavior; if individual accounts of discrimination are told, the stories may be considered "isolated instances" and not representative of the whole picture.

2. Susan Faludi, in her book *Backlash,* writes about the peculiar role of Professor Rosalind Rosenberg as a witness for Sears. A feminist and teacher at Barnard College, Professor Rosenberg had written a book, *Beyond Separate Spheres: Intellectual Roots of Modern Feminism,* in which she discussed feminist social scientists who broke into academic fields that had been exclusively male. Faludi then described how such an unlikely witness came to support the validity of what can best be termed gender roles and stereotypes, the opposite of what Rosenberg had written about pioneering feminist social scientists:

Rosenberg was originally drawn into the Sears case for personal reasons; she was friendly with Sears' chief defense lawyer, Charles Morgan, Jr., employer of her former husband. But when Morgan first asked her to testify she was reluctant. "My gut personal feeling was EEOC were the good guys and private employers weren't . . . I suggested some other names." Besides, as she told Morgan at the time, labor history wasn't even her field. But when the labor historians that Sears approached refused to testify, Morgan asked her again, and this time she consented . . . [T]he scholar also says she was influenced by the new relational feminist scholarship that had emerged on women's "difference." These academic ideas, she says, inspired her to rethink her attitudes about feminism and to regard the demand for simple gender equality in a new light— as "old '70s feminism" and "simpleminded androgyny."*

3. Vicki Schultz, one of the legal commentators on the *Sears* and other employment cases, outlines three "stories" of women and work. The first is the conservative story—the one which is adopted by the court in the *Sears* case:

> [W]omen are "feminine," nontraditional work is "masculine," and therefore women do not want to do it. The story rests on the appeal to masculinity and femininity as oppositional categories. Women are "feminine" because that is the definition of what makes them women. Work itself is endowed with the imagined human characteristics of masculinity or femininity based on the sex of the workers who do it. "Femininity" refers to a complex of womanly traits and aspirations that by definition precludes any interest in the work of men. Even though the story follows this same logic, the story changes across class lines in the way it is told. Cases involving blue-collar work emphasize the "masculinity" of the work drawing on images of physical strength and dirtiness. Cases involving white-collar work focus on the "femininity" of women, appealing to traits and values associated with domesticity.†

Compare the conservative story with the language of the court in the *Sears* case.

Schultz also outlines the liberal story of women as follows:

> Like their conservative counterparts, liberal courts assume that women form their job preferences before they begin working. This shared assumption, however, drives liberal courts to a rhetoric that is the opposite of conservative rhetoric. Whereas the conservative story has a strong account of gender that implies a preference for "feminine" work, the liberal account has no coherent account of gender. To the contrary, liberal courts suppress gender difference, because the assumption of stable preexisting preferences means that they can hold employers responsible for sex segregation only by portraying women as ungendered subjects who emerge from early life realms with the

same experiences and values, and therefore the same work aspirations, as men.

The liberal story centers around the prohibition against stereotyping. Courts reject the lack of interest argument by reasoning that "Title VII was intended to override stereotypical views" of women. . . . This anti-stereotyping reasoning is the classic rhetoric of gender neutrality; it invokes the familiar principle that likes are to be treated as likes. The problem lies in determining the extent to which women are "like" men. On its face the anti-stereotyping reasoning seems to deny the existence of group-based gender differences and asserts that, contrary to the employer's contention, the women in the proposed labor pool are no less interested than the men in nontraditional work. Below the surface, however, this reasoning reflects a basic ambiguity (and ambivalence) about the extent of gender differences. For the anti-stereotyping rule may be interpreted to admit that women are *as a group* less interested than men in nontraditional work and to assert only that some *individual* women may nonetheless be exceptions who do not share the preferences of most women. Under such an individualized approach, the employer is forbidden merely from assuming that *all* women are so "different" from men that they do not aspire to nontraditional work.‡

Schultz sees some perils in casually adopting the liberal approach in discrimination cases. What are they?

Schultz then proceeds to a "new story" to escape the confines of both the conservative and liberal approaches:

> This new account traces gendered work attitudes and behaviors to organizational structures and cultures in the workplace. Like all workers, women adapt their work aspirations and orientations rationally and purposefully, but always within and in response to the constraints of organizational arrangements not of their own making. Providing women with the formal opportunity to enter nontraditional jobs is a necessary but insufficient condition to empower them to claim those jobs, because deeper aspects of work systems pose powerful disincentives for women to enter and remain in nontraditional employment. The new account of work and gender thus reverses the causation

---

*Susan Faludi, *Backlash* (New York: Crown, 1991), pp. 381–382.

†Vicki Schultz, "Telling Stories about Work," *Harvard Law Review,* 103 (1990), p. 1801. Copyright © 1990 by the Harvard Law Review Association.

‡Ibid., p. 1806.

implicit in the current judicial framework. Sex segregation persists not because most women bring to the workworld fixed preferences for traditionally female jobs, but rather because employers structure opportunities and incentives and maintain work cultures and relations so as to disempower most women from aspiring to and succeeding in traditionally male jobs.

The new account suggests a more transformative role for the law in dismantling sex segregation at work. Once we realize that women's work aspirations are shaped not solely by amorphous "social" forces operating in pre-work realms . . . it becomes clear that title VII can play a major role in producing the needed changes. Title VII cases challenging segregation seek to alter . . . the very structural conditions that prevent women from developing and realizing aspirations for higher-paid, more challenging nontraditional jobs. By attributing women's aspirations to forces external and prior to the workworld, courts deny their own ability to (re)construct workplace arrangements and the work aspirations that arise out of these arrangements. In a very real sense, the legal system has perpetuated the status quo of sex segregation by refusing its own power to dismantle it.§

Identify the critical differences between the first two approaches and this one.

In the *Sears* case, what would have been the implications of shifting the burden from the women and their alleged "pre-work" preferences to the employer and the employers' duty to structure a nondiscriminatory work environment?

4. While some of the discussion of the differences between men and women can fill women with a rosy glow, they also can provide rationalizations for legal results that are not in women's interest, as the *Sears* case attests. Judith Baer in her provocative new text puts it this way:

> . . . [C]haracter is based on sexist role expectations [that] militate against any acceptance of gender-specific laws based on women's physical or social functions. Whatever good these laws may do they also reinforce unjust social arrangements. The need for policies that recognize the contributions of mothers, caregivers, and nurturers can be met by gender-neutral laws. The need for policies that compensate women for the disadvantages they incur from performing socially assigned functions can be met by sex-specific ameliorative legislation. The need for policies that authorize the female view of the world can be met at least in part by a radical rewriting of equal protection doctrine. . . . Character theory starts with people and fails to understand power.*

---

§Ibid., p. 1816.

*J. Baer, *Our Lives Before the Law*, Princeton, N.J.: Princeton University Press, 1999, p. 55.

---

## 7.2 | International Union, UAW v. Johnson Controls

*111 S.Ct. 1196 (1991)*

JUSTICE BLACKMUN

IN THIS CASE WE are concerned with an employer's gender-based fetal-protection policy. May an employer exclude a fertile female employee from certain jobs because of its concern for the health of the fetus the woman might conceive?

### I

Respondent Johnson Controls, Inc., manufactures batteries. In the manufacturing process, the element lead is a primary ingredient. Occupational exposure to lead entails health risks, in-

cluding the risk of harm to any fetus carried by a female employee.

Before the Civil Rights Act of 1964 . . . Johnson Controls did not employ any woman in a battery-manufacturing job. In June 1977, however, it announced its first official policy concerning its employment of women in lead-exposure work:

"[P]rotection of the health of the unborn child is the immediate and direct responsibility of the prospective parents. While the medical profession and the company support them in the exercise of this responsibility, it cannot assume it for them without simultaneously infringing their rights as persons.

. . . . Since not all women who can become mothers wish to become mothers (or will become mothers) it would appear to be illegal discrimination to treat all who are capable of pregnancy as though they will become pregnant. . . ."

Consistent with that view, Johnson Controls "stopped short of excluding women capable of bearing children from lead exposure" . . . but emphasized that a woman who expected to have a child should not choose a job in which she would have such exposure. The company also required that a woman who wished to be considered for employment to sign a statement that she had been advised of the risk of having a child while she was exposed to lead. The statement informed the woman that although there was evidence "that women exposed to lead have a higher rate of abortion," this evidence was "not as clear . . . as the relationship between cigarette smoking and cancer," but that it was, "medically speaking, just good sense not to run that risk if you want children and you do not want to expose the unborn child to risk, however small. . . ."

Five years later, in 1982, Johnson Controls shifted from a policy of warning to a policy of exclusion. Between 1979 and 1983, eight employees became pregnant while maintaining blood levels in excess of 30 micrograms per deciliter. . . . This appeared to be the critical level noted by . . . OSHA for a worker who was planning to have a family. . . . The company responded by announcing a broad exclusion of women from jobs that exposed them to lead: "[I]t is [Johnson Controls'] policy that women who are pregnant or who are capable of bearing children will not be placed into jobs involving lead exposure. . . ."

The policy defined "women . . . capable of bearing children" as "[a]ll women except those whose inability to have children is medically documented. . . ."

## II

In 1984, petitioners filed . . . a class action challenging Johnson Control's fetal protection policy as sex discrimination that violated Title VII. . . . Among the individual plaintiffs were Mary Craig who had chosen to be sterilized in order to avoid losing her job, Elsie Nason, a 50-year-old divorcee who had suffered a loss of compensation when she was transferred out of a job where she was exposed to lead, and Donald Penney, who had been denied a request for a leave of absence for purpose of lowering his lead level because he intended to become a father. . . .

The district court granted summary judgment for . . . Johnson. . . . The Court of Appeals . . . affirmed. The majority held that the proper standard for evaluating the fetal protection policy was the defense of business necessity . . . and that even if the proper standard was a BFOQ* Johnson Controls was still entitled to a summary judgment. . . .

[Appeal court] opinions established a three-step business necessity inquiry: whether there is a substantial health risk to the fetus; whether transmission of the hazard to the fetus occurs only through women; and whether there is a less discriminatory alternative equally capable of preventing the health hazard to the fetus. . . . Applying the business necessity defense, the Court . . . ruled that Johnson Controls should prevail. . . . The Court . . . also concluded that unlike the evidence of risk to the fetus from the mother's exposure, the evidence of risk from the father's exposure . . . "is, at best, speculative and unconvincing." . . .

[T]he court proceeded to discuss the BFOQ defense and concluded that Johnson Controls met that test too. . . . [I]ndustrial safety is part of the essence of respondent's business and that the fetal protection policy is reasonably necessary to further that concern. . . .

## III

The bias in Johnson Controls' policy is obvious. Fertile men, but not fertile women, are given a choice as to whether they wish to risk their reproductive health for a particular job. Section 703(a) of the Civil Rights act of 1964 . . . prohibits sex-based classifications. . . . Respondent's fetal-protection policy explicitly discriminates against women on the basis of their sex. The policy excludes women with childbearing capacity from lead-exposed jobs and so creates a facial classification based on gender. . . .

Nevertheless, the Court of Appeals assumed, as did . . . two appellate courts . . . that sex-specific fetal protection policies do not involve

---

*Bona fide occupational qualification—ED.

facial discrimination. . . . These courts analyzed the policies as though they were facially neutral, and had only a discriminatory effect on the employment opportunities of women. Consequently, the courts looked to see if each employer in question had established that its policy was justified as a business necessity. The business necessity standard is more lenient . . . than the statutory BFOQ defense. . . . The court assumed that because the asserted reason for the sex-based exclusion (protecting women's unconceived offspring) was ostensibly benign, the policy was not sex-based discrimination. That assumption, however, was incorrect.

First, Johnson Controls' policy classifies on the basis of gender and childbearing capacity, rather than fertility alone. Respondent does not seek to protect the unconceived children of all its employees. Despite evidence in the record about the debilitating effect of lead exposure on the male reproductive system, Johnson Controls is concerned only with . . . the unborn offspring of its female employees. . . .

This Court faced a conceptually similar situation in *Phillips* . . . and found sex discrimination because the policy established "one hiring policy for women and another for men—each having pre-school age children." . . .

Our conclusion is bolstered by the Pregnancy Discrimination Act of 1978, (PDA) . . . in which Congress . . . provided . . . discrimination "on the basis of sex" includes discrimination "because of or on the basis of pregnancy, childbirth, or related medical conditions." . . . In its use of the words "capable of bearing children" in the 1982 policy . . . Johnson Controls explicitly classifies on the basis of potential for pregnancy. . . . Respondent has chosen to treat all its female employees as potentially pregnant. . . .

The absence of malevolent motive does not convert a facially discriminatory policy into a neutral policy with a discriminatory effect. . . . In sum, Johnson Control's policy does not pass the simple test of . . . "treatment in a manner which but for the person's sex would be different."

## IV

Under 703(e)(1) of Title VII, an employer may discriminate . . . where religion, sex, or national origin is a bona fide occupational qualification reasonably necessary to the normal operation of that particular business or enterprise.

[T]he exception reaches only special situations. . . . Johnson Controls argues that its fetal protection policy falls within the so-called safety exception. . . . In *Dothard* . . . this court indicated that danger to a woman herself does not justify discrimination. . . . We there allowed the employer to hire only male guards in contact areas of maximum-security male penitentiaries only because more was at stake than the "individual woman's decision to weigh and accept the risks of employment." . . . Sex discrimination was tolerated because sex was related to the guard's ability to do the job—maintaining prison security. . . . We also required . . . a high correlation between sex and ability to perform job functions and refused to allow employers to use sex as a proxy for strength. . . .

Similarly, some courts have approved airlines' layoffs of pregnant flight attendants at different points during the first five months of pregnancy on the ground that the employer's policy was necessary to ensure the safety of passengers. . . .

Our case law, therefore, makes clear that the safety exception is limited to instances in which sex or pregnancy actually interferes with the employee's ability to perform the job. . . .

The PDA's amendment . . . contains a BFOQ standard of its own: unless pregnant employees differ from others "in their ability or inability to do the work" they must be "treated the same" as other employees. . . . Women who are either pregnant or potentially pregnant must be treated like others. . . .

## V

. . . Decisions about the welfare of future children must be left to the parents who conceive, bear, support, and raise them rather than the employers who hire those parents. . . . Title VII and the PDA simply do not allow a woman's dismissal because of her failure to submit to sterilization. . . .

## Notes and Questions

1. There is a growing awareness of the danger of working with lead and other toxic chemicals.

How can legal regulations or company policies be drawn in order to both take into account manifest industrial hazards *and* avoid discrimination based on gender or the possibility of pregnancy?

2. The Johnson case did not end all measures that would inhibit choices of women in the interest of fetal protection. Judith Baer finds fetal protection a threat to "all women— pregnant or not, prospectively pregnant or not, vulnerable to pregnancy or not"[†]

> Between 1985 and 1992, at least 167 women had been prosecuted for delivering drugs to a minor—(through the umbilical chord) child abuse, or (where the infant died) homicide. Most of these prosecutions ended with courts' dismissing charges or overturning convictions, usually on the grounds that existing statutes do not apply to these situations. In April, 1997 the Wisconsin Supreme Court ruled that the state had acted wrongfully in detaining Angela M. W., a pregnant woman who tested positively for cocaine. But in October the South Carolina Supreme Court upheld Cornelia Whitner's conviction and eight-year sentence for child neglect after she gave birth to a baby boy who tested positive for cocaine. Nothing prevents a legislature from enacting criminal laws which explicitly punish pregnant women, but only Florida had done so by 1995. The legality of forced treatment has been problematic since the ruling in *Mater of A.C.* that a cancer patient should not have been subjected to a cesarean section that neither she nor the baby survived. . . .[‡]

[†]Baer, op. cit., p. 151.

[‡]Ibid., pp. 152, 153.

❧ The term sexual harassment, in a wide variety of contexts has been appearing in the news more and more frequently. Former Senator Packwood of Oregon was accused of decades of "improprieties," documented in his own diary. A Supreme Court appointee, Clarence Thomas, was accused of sexually harassing one of his staff members during the time he was head of EEOC (by an ironic twist, the federal agency charged with enforcement of equal employment opportunity). Naval aviators "at play" at the 1991 Tailhook Association Convention were accused of sexual harassment, including assault. The Mitsubishi Corporation in 1995 was accused of being a place where sexual harassment was rampant and affected hundreds of women. In 1996, throughout the military there were charges of sexual harassment of female recruits by their superiors. These examples suggest the intensity of the problem and some of the contexts in which allegations of sexual harassment arise: the offices of elected officials, regulatory agencies, the military, and in the workplace.

Closer to home for students, faculty, and administration of colleges and universities, sexual harassment claims have been made under policies now in place in most colleges and universities. The University of Massachusetts, for example, has a policy whereby a person alleging sexual harassment can bring either an informal or a formal complaint against the harasser. There is a Sexual Harassment Board of twenty-five made up of faculty, professional staff, classified employees, graduate students, and four members appointed at large. These policies and their implementation are undergoing continual revision, just as newly created courts would hammer out policies, rules, and procedures as their experience builds and the problems of the institution become more visible.

One way to provide a modest introduction to this complicated subject is through a Supreme Court case involving workplace harassment. The case can be extended to raise some of the principal issues in the field. Legally, workplace sexual harassment cases fall into two overall categories: cases where there is a *quid pro quo*—sexual favors are demanded in exchange for work-related benefits and consequences—and cases alleging a "hostile employment environment" where "unwanted actions of a sexual nature have the purpose of unreasonably interfering with an individual's work performance, or creating an intimidating, hostile, or offensive working environment."* The *Harris* case which follows is in the second category.

---

*M. Stockdale, "What We Know and What We Need to Learn About Sexual Harassment," in M. Stockdale (ed.), *Sexual Harassment in the Workplace* (Thousand Oaks, Calif.: Sage, 1996) p. 6.

## 7.3 | Harris v. Forklift Systems, Inc.     *114 S.Ct. 367 (1993)*

JUSTICE O'CONNOR . . .

In this case we consider the definition of a discriminatorily "abusive work environment" (also known as a "hostile work environment") under Title VII of the Civil Rights Act of 1964 . . .

Teresa Harris worked as a manager at Forklift Systems, Inc., an equipment rental company, from April 1985 until October 1987. Charles Hardy was Forklift's president.

The Magistrate found that, throughout Harris' time at Forklift, Hardy often insulted her because of her gender and often made her the target of unwanted sexual innuendos. Hardy told Harris on several occasions, in the presence of other employees, "You're a woman, what do you know" and "We need a man as the rental manager"; at least once, he told her she was "a dumb ass woman." . . . Again in front of others, he suggested that the two of them "go to the Holiday Inn to negotiate [Harris'], raise." . . . Hardy occasionally asked Harris and other female employees to get coins from his front pants pocket. . . . He threw objects on the ground in front of Harris and other women, and asked them to pick the objects up. . . . He made sexual innuendos about Harris' and other women's clothing. . . .

In mid-August 1987, Harris complained to Hardy about his conduct. Hardy said he was surprised that Harris was offended, claimed he was only joking, and apologized. . . . He also promised he would stop, and based on this assurance Harris stayed on the job. . . . But in early September, Hardy began anew: While Harris was arranging a deal with one of Forklift's customers, he asked her, again in front of other employees, "What did you do, promise the guy . . . some [sex] Saturday night?" . . . On October 1, Harris collected her paycheck and quit.

Harris then sued Forklift, claiming that Hardy's conduct had created an abusive work environment for her because of her gender. The United States District Court . . . found this to be "a close case," . . . but held that Hardy's conduct did not create an abusive environment. The court found that some of Hardy's comments "offended [Harris], and would offend the reasonable woman," . . . but that they were not[:]

> so severe as to be expected to seriously affect [Harris'] psychological well-being. A reasonable woman manager under like circumstances would have been offended by Hardy, but his conduct would not have risen to the level of interfering with that person's work performance.
>
> Neither do I believe that [Harris] was subjectively so offended that she suffered injury. . . . Although Hardy may at times have genuinely offended [Harris], I do not believe that he created a working environment so

poisoned as to be intimidating or abusive to "Harris." . . .

We granted certiorari . . . to resolve a conflict among the Circuits on whether conduct, to be actionable as "abusive work environment" harassment (no *quid pro quo* harassment issue is present here), must "seriously affect [an employee's] psychological well-being" or lead the plaintiff to "suffe[r] injury." Compare *Rabidue* (requiring serious effect on psychological well-being) . . . with *Ellison v. Brady* . . . (rejecting such a requirement).

## II

Title VII of the Civil Rights Act of 1964 makes it "an unlawful employment practice for an employer . . . to discriminate against any individual with respect to his compensation, terms, conditions, or privileges of employment, because of such individual's race, color, religion, sex, or national origin." . . . [T]his language "is not limited to 'economic' or 'tangible' discrimination. The phrase 'terms, conditions, or privileges of employment' evinces a congressional intent 'to strike at the entire spectrum of disparate treatment of men and women' in employment," which includes requiring people to work in a discriminatorily hostile or abusive environment. . . . When the workplace is permeated with "discriminatory intimidation, ridicule, and insult," . . . that is "sufficiently severe or pervasive to alter the conditions of the victim's employment and create an abusive working environment," . . . Title VII is violated.

This standard, which we reaffirm today, takes a middle path between making actionable any conduct that is merely offensive and requiring the conduct to cause a tangible psychological injury. As we pointed out in *Meritor,* "mere utterance of an . . . epithet which engenders offensive feelings in a employee," . . . does not sufficiently affect the conditions of employment to implicate Title VII. Conduct that is not severe or pervasive enough to create an objectively hostile or abusive work environment—an environment that a reasonable person would find hostile or abusive—is beyond Title VII's purview. Likewise, if the victim does not subjectively perceive the environment to be abusive, the conduct has not actually altered the conditions of the victim's employment, and there is no Title VII violation.

But Title VII comes into play before the harassing conduct leads to a nervous breakdown. A discriminatorily abusive work environment, even one that does not seriously affect employees' psychological well-being, can and often will detract from employees' job performance, discourage employees from remaining on the job, or keep them from advancing in their careers. Moreover, even without regard to these tangible effects, the very fact that the discriminatory conduct was so severe or pervasive that it created a work environment abusive to employees because of their race, gender, religion, or national origin offends Title VII's broad rule of workplace equality. The appalling conduct alleged in *Meritor,* and the reference in that case to environments "'so heavily polluted with discrimination as to destroy completely the emotional and psychological stability of minority group workers,'" . . . merely present some especially egregious examples of harassment. They do not mark the boundary of what is actionable. . . .

We therefore believe the District Court erred in relying on whether the conduct "seriously affect[ed] plaintiff's psychological well-being" or led her to "suffe[r] injury." Such an inquiry may needlessly focus the factfinder's attention on concrete psychological harm, an element Title VII does not require. Certainly Title VII bars conduct that would seriously affect a reasonable person's psychological well-being, but the statute is not limited to such conduct. So long as the environment would reasonably be perceived, and is perceived, as hostile or abusive, . . . there is no need for it also to be psychologically injurious.

This is not, and by its nature cannot be, a mathematically precise test. We need not answer today all the potential questions it raises, nor specifically address the EEOC's new regulations on this subject . . . But we can say that whether an environment is "hostile" or "abusive" can be determined only by looking at all the circumstances. These may include the frequency of the discriminatory conduct; its severity; whether it is physically threatening or humiliating, or a mere offensive utterance; and whether it unreasonably interferes with an employee's work performance.

The effect on the employee's psychological well-being is, of course, relevant to determining whether the plaintiff actually found the environment abusive. But while psychological harm, like any other relevant factor, may be taken into account, no single factor is required.

## III

Forklift, while conceding that a requirement that the conduct seriously affect psychological well-being is unfounded, argues that the District Court nonetheless correctly applied the *Meritor* standard. We disagree. Though the District Court did conclude that the work environment was not "intimidating or abusive to [Harris]," . . . it did so only after finding that the conduct was not "so severe as to be expected to seriously affect plaintiff's psychological well-being," . . . and that Harris was not "subjectively so offended that she suffered injury," . . . The District Court's application of these incorrect standards may well have influenced its ultimate conclusion, especially given that the court found this to be a "close case," . . .

We therefore reverse the judgment of the Court of Appeals, and remand the case for further proceedings consistent with this opinion.

JUSTICE SCALIA, *concurring.*

*Meritor Savings Bank v. Vinson* . . . (1986), held that Title VII prohibits sexual harassment that takes the form of a hostile work environment. The Court stated that sexual harassment is actionable if it is "sufficiently severe or pervasive 'to alter the conditions of [the victim's] employment and create an abusive work environment.'" . . . Today's opinion elaborates that the challenged conduct must be severe or pervasive enough "to create an objectively hostile or abusive work environment—an environment that a reasonable person would find hostile or abusive." . . .

"Abusive" (or "hostile," which in this context I take to mean the same thing) does not seem to me a very clear standard—and I do not think clarity is at all increased by adding the adverb "objectively" or by appealing to a "reasonable person's" notion of what the vague word

means. Today's opinion does list a number of factors that contribute to abusiveness, . . . but since it neither says how much of each is necessary (an impossible task) nor identifies any single factor as determinative, it thereby adds little certitude. As a practical matter, today's holding lets virtually unguided juries decide whether sex-related conduct engaged in (or permitted by) an employer is egregious enough to warrant an award of damages. One might say that what constitutes "negligence" (a traditional jury question) is not much more clear and certain than what constitutes "abusiveness." Perhaps so. But the class of plaintiffs seeking to recover for negligence is limited to those who have suffered harm, whereas under this statute "abusiveness" is to be the test of whether legal harm has been suffered, opening more expansive vistas of litigation.

Be that as it may, I know of no alternative to the course the Court today has taken. One of the factors mentioned in the Court's nonexhaustive list—whether the conduct unreasonably interferes with an employee's work performance—would, if it were made an absolute test, provide greater guidance to juries and employers. . . . the term "conditions of employment" as the law, the test is not whether work has been impaired, but whether working conditions have been discriminatorily altered. I know of no test more faithful to the inherently vague statutory language than the one the Court today adopts. For these reasons, I join the opinion of the Court.

JUSTICE GINSBURG, *concurring.*

. . . The critical issue, Title VII's text indicates, is whether members of one sex are exposed to disadvantageous terms or conditions of employment to which members of the other sex are not exposed. . . . As the Equal Employment Opportunity Commission emphasized, . . . the adjudicator's inquiry should center, dominantly, on whether the discriminatory conduct has unreasonably interfered with the plaintiff's work performance. To show such interference, "the plaintiff need not prove that his or her tangible productivity has declined as a result of the harassment." . . . It suffices to prove that a reasonable person subjected to the discriminatory conduct would find, as the plaintiff did, that the harassment so altered working conditions as to "ma[k]e it more difficult to do the job." . . .

## Notes and Questions

1. Based upon their survey of court cases, Ramona Paetzold and Anne O'Leary Kelly* compiled a chart of conduct alleged in harassment cases and the frequency of cases where the conduct appears. See Table 7.3-A below.

   As to whether the court cases accurately reflect the whole universe of sexual harassment behavior, the researchers compared behavior alleged in court cases with behavior elicited in surveys based on self-reporting. There was overlap, but the court cases involved more serious behavior than that mentioned in surveys based on self-reports.

They also found what could be termed a class stratification of sexual harassment. As one goes down the power-status hierarchy of an enterprise, it is more likely that allegations of more serious forms of sexual harassment will be found.

The most common types of sexually harassing conduct reported by both professional and nonprofessional women were plaintiff-specific offensive language and nonphysical contact. On the other hand, plaintiffs holding clerical positions most frequently complained of nonviolent physical contact and sexual assault.[†]

The Supreme court in the *Harris* case said that the conduct in the 1985 *Meritor Savings Bank* case was appalling. In the *Meritor* opinion, the court summarized the plaintiff's testimony as follows:

. . . [D]uring her probationary period as teller-trainee, Taylor [Vice President of the bank] treated her in a fatherly way and made no sexual advances. Shortly thereafter, however,

**Table 7.3-A.**  *Types of Conduct Alleged in Court Cases*

| Conduct | Overall[a] (N = 55) | Supervisor Is Harasser (N = 40) | Coworker Is Harasser (N = 23) |
|---|---|---|---|
| Date request | 13% (7)[b] | 15% (6) | 9% (2) |
| Offensive language | | | |
| plaintiff specific | 56% (31) | 48% (19) | 70% (16) |
| nonspecific | 29% (16) | 23% (9) | 22% (5) |
| Graffiti/pornography | | | |
| plaintiff specific | 18% (10) | 10% (4) | 13% (3) |
| nonspecific | 11% (6) | 3% (1) | 13% (3) |
| Sexual propositions | 44% (24) | 50% (20) | 17% (4) |
| Physical contact | | | |
| nonviolent | 58% (32) | 53% (21) | 26% (6) |
| violent | 18% (10) | 10% (4) | 22% (5) |
| Sexual assault | 22% (12) | 25% (10) | 9% (2) |

a. Percentages do not sum to 100% because of allegations of multiple types of behavior within cases.
b. Number in parentheses indicates the number of cases in the category.

*R. Paetzold and A. O'Leary-Kelly, "The Implications of U.S. Supreme Court and Circuit Court Decisions for Hostile Environmental Sexual Harassment Cases," in M. Stockdale (ed.), *Sexual Harassment in the Workplace* (Thousand Oaks, Calif.: Sage, 1996), p. 91.

[†]Ibid., pp. 89–92.

he invited her out to dinner and during the course of the meal, suggested that they go to a motel to have sexual relations. At first she refused, but out of what she called fear of losing her job she eventually agreed. According to respondent, Taylor therefore made repeated demands upon her for sexual favors, usually at the branch, both during and after business hours; she estimated that over the next several years she had intercourse with him some 40 of 50 times. In addition, respondent testified that Taylor fondled her in front of other employees, followed her into the restroom when she went there alone, exposed himself to her, and even forcibly raped her on several occasions. These activities ceased . . . when she started going with a steady boyfriend."[‡]

2. The court has advanced two standards by which behavior alleged to be harassment is to be judged: (1) the person has herself (it is not inaccurate to use the feminine gender here, since the overwhelming majority of cases involve women) considered the behavior abusive or harassing, *and* (2) a reasonable person would also conclude that the behavior is abusive or harassing. One depends upon the testimony of the claimant and is *subjective,* while the other is one step removed from her characterization of events and is *objective.*

The "reasonable man" standard found in older tort cases would seem absurd in sexual harassment cases given the gender of most claimants. In 1991, the federal court discussed the differing standards, before recommending a *reasonable woman* standard:

> [W]e believe that in evaluating the severity and pervasiveness of sexual harassment, we should focus on the perspective of the victim . . . (courts "should consider the victim's perspective and not stereotyped notions of acceptable behavior"). If we only examined whether a reasonable person would have engaged in allegedly harassing conduct, we would run the risk of reinforcing the prevailing level of discrimination. Harassers could continue to harass merely because a discriminatory practice was common, and victims of harassment would have no remedy.

We therefore prefer to analyze harassment from the victim's perspective. A complete understanding of the victim's view requires, among other things, an analysis of the different perspectives of men and women. Conduct that many men consider unobjectionable may offend many women . . . (a male superior might believe, for example, that it is legitimate for him to tell a female subordinate that she has a "great figure" or "nice legs"); . . . ("men and women are vulnerable in different ways and offended by different behavior") . . . (men tend to view some forms of sexual harassment as a "harmless social interaction to which only overly-sensitive women would object") . . . (the characteristically male view that depicts sexual harassment as comparatively harmless amusement).

We realize that there is a broad range of viewpoints among women as a group, but we believe that many women share common concerns which men do not necessarily share. For example, because women are disproportionately victims of rape and sexual assault, women have a stronger incentive to be concerned with sexual behavior. Women who are the victims of mild forms of sexual harassment may understandably worry whether a harasser's conduct is merely a prelude to violent sexual assault . . .

In order to shield employers from having to accommodate the idiosyncratic concerns of the rare hyper-sensitive employee, we hold that a female plaintiff states a prima facie case of hostile environment sexual harassment when she alleges conduct which a reasonable woman would consider sufficiently severe or pervasive to alter the conditions of employment and create an abusive working environment . . .[§]

Discuss the differing standards by which sexual harassment can be judged and compare the results of your discussion with the opinion rendered in the *Harris* case.

3. There has also been debate as to the type and extent of injuries actionable in harassment cases. In some cases there are economic losses—the job, pay, raises, promotion, or other economic benefits. There can also be psychological injury, which can range from

---

[‡]*Meritor Savings Bank v. Vinson,* 477 U.S. 57 (1985), 60.

[§]*Ellison v. Brady,* 924 F.2d 872 (1991), 878–879.

dreading to go to work or feeling ill at ease at work, to suffering a nervous breakdown. Review the discussion of psychic injury in the *Harris* case. Is it true, as Justice Scalia states in his separate opinion, that after this case courts will be left with little guidance?

4.  A.  When does the behavior of *particular employees* lead to a conclusion that the *work environment* is hostile? Can a firm charged with harassment say that it does not want women to be harassed and therefore cannot be held accountable for harassment by employees who are "acting on their own"? Some courts have applied strict agency principles to harassment—the employer is held accountable for the behavior of those acting in its place. Other courts seem to favor *notice* to the enterprise as a precondition for liability. Which rule ought to be applied?

   B.  It is common in sexual harassment cases for witnesses to say: "She didn't mind it";

"she seemed to like the attention"; "she at times joked in return"; "everyone was surprised when there was an accusation of harassment." These remarks are made to support either the argument that there was no harassment or the argument that the claimant "welcomed" behavior that was later alleged to be "unwelcome." Most sexual harassment cases are open to a wide range of proof covering both on-the-job and off-the-job evidence. The bringing of a harassment case can become as painful to a claimant as bringing a criminal complaint for rape can be for a victim of rape.

Where there is a possibility of substantial compensatory and punitive damage claims against a company, as there was in the case against Sears in the earlier part of this chapter, the full resources of a large law firm may be mobilized, and cases can be made long and very expensive to carry to a conclusion.

᛭ We have sampled only a few corners of the contemporary inquiry into feminism and the law. The world of work has been one of the main topics of feminist research, but there are many others of equal importance, as the perusal of a daily newspaper will disclose: spousal and mate abuse, rape, and reproductive rights. Had any of these topics been chosen as the focus of this section, an equally large array of cases and jurisprudential analyses could have been assembled.

What was once a gloss on professional legal education that found its way into law school curricula through single courses called Women and the Law has now become an indispensable means for appraising law and legal order as a whole. The field can no longer be trivialized by pretending that it can be encompassed in a three-credit course. To study law and gender is to study the legal order and the interconnection between law and society. To study the way in which the legal order affects women takes the professional beyond the field of mere law to the field of social relationships at large, and, for good reasons, feminist jurists do as much reading outside the usual parameters of legal study as within.

Every jurisprudential insight that has been developed in the Western world can be tested in the crucible of gender. Whether law in theory and practice is defined as rules, discretion, evaluation, balancing, class stratification, or plain hierarchy, new insights can be found at the intersection of law and gender.

Whether the system can be reformed by changing rules and their application or whether consequential change cannot come via law remains an open question. Despite the history of the relationship between legal order and gender being bleak, law has too much impact to be written off as a waste of energy. Moreover, it is simply too early to tell what the impact will be of the dramatic increase in the number of women teaching and practicing law, or using their legal training in political careers.

What about cases where women *of color* claim discrimination? In these cases, issues of race and gender intersect. It is clear that people can simultaneously find themselves at the bottom of a series of hierarchies of preference: for example, white over black, white women over black men and black women, and black men over black women. Cases with different factual elements can arise where this or that aspect of the foregoing hierarchies intersect.

How have the courts handled cases where multiple forms of discrimination are claimed in the same case? And how are such cases especially instructive not only about the place of black women in the law of discrimination, but also about the place of black women in thinking about gender? We turn to an essay by Kimberle Crenshaw, discussing the intersection of gender and race.

## 7.4 | Demarginalizing the Intersection of Race and Sex

*Kimberle Crenshaw*

I WILL CENTER BLACK women in this analysis in order to contrast the multidimensionality of Black women's experience with the single-axis analysis that distorts these experiences. Not only will this juxtaposition reveal how Black women are theoretically erased, it will also illustrate how this framework imports its own theoretical limitations that undermine efforts to broaden feminist and antiracist analyses. . . . I want to suggest further that this single-axis framework erases Black women in the conceptualization, identification, and remediation of race and sex discrimination by limiting inquiry to the experience of other-

wise-privileged members of the group. In other words, in race discrimination cases, discrimination tends to be viewed in terms of sex- or class-privileged Blacks; in sex discrimination cases, the focus is on race- and class-privileged women.

This focus on the most privileged group members marginalizes those who are multiply-burdened and obscures claims that cannot be understood as resulting from discrete sources of discrimination. . . . [T]he operative conceptions of race and sex become grounded in experiences that actually represent only a subset of a much more complex phenomenon.

After examining the doctrinal manifestations of this single-axis framework, I will discuss how it contributes to the marginalization of Black women in feminist theory and in antiracist politics. I argue that Black women are sometimes excluded from feminist theory and antiracist policy discourse because both are predicated on a discrete set of experiences that often does not accurately reflect the interaction of race and gender. These problems of exclusion cannot be solved simply by including Black women within an already established analytical structure. Because the intersectional experience is greater than the sum of racism and sexism, any analysis that does not take intersectionality into account cannot sufficiently address the particular manner in which Black women are subordinated. . . .

## THE ANTIDISCRIMINATION FRAMEWORK

**The Experience of the Intersectionality and the Doctrinal Response** One way to approach the problem of intersectionality is to examine how courts frame and interpret the stories of Black women plaintiffs. . . . To illustrate the difficulties inherent in judicial treatment of intersectionality, I will consider three Title VII cases, *DeGraffenreid* v. *General Motors, Moore* v. *Hughes Helicopters* and *Payne* v. *Travenol.*

[In] *DeGraffenreid* . . . the court stated:

> [P]laintiffs have failed to cite any decisions which have stated that Black women are a special class to be protected from discrimination. The Court's own research has failed to disclose such a decision. The plaintiffs are clearly entitled to a remedy if they have been discriminated against. However, they should not be allowed to combine statutory remedies to create a new "super-remedy" which would give them relief beyond what the drafters of the relevant statutes intended. Thus, this lawsuit must be examined to see if it states a cause of action for race discrimination, sex discrimination, or alternatively either, but not a combination of both. . . .

After refusing to consider plaintiffs' sex discrimination claim, the court dismissed the race discrimination complaint . . . and recommended its consolidation with another case alleging race discrimination against the same employer. The plaintiffs responded that such consolidation would defeat the purpose of their suit since theirs was not purely a race claim, but an action brought specifically on behalf of Black women alleging race *and* sex discrimination. The court, however, reasoned:

> The legislative history surrounding Title VII does not indicate that the goal of the statute was to create a new classification of "black women" who would have greater standing than, for example, a black male. . . .

Thus the court apparently concluded that Congress either did not contemplate that Black women could be discriminated against as "Black women" or did not intend to protect them when such discrimination occurred. The court's refusal in *DeGraffenreid* to acknowledge that Black women encounter combined race and sex discrimination implies that the boundaries of sex and race discrimination are defined respectively by white women's and Black men's experiences. Under this view, Black women are protected only to the extent that their experiences coincide with those of either of the two groups. Where their experiences are distinct, Black women can expect little protection as long as approaches . . . completely obscure problems of intersectionality. . . .

*Moore* . . . presents a different way in which courts fail to understand or recognize Black women's claims. . . .

> Moore had never claimed before the EEOC that she was discriminated against as a female, *but only* as a Black female. . . . [T]his raised serious doubts as to Moore's ability to adequately represent white female employees.

The curious logic in *Moore* reveals not only the narrow scope of antidiscrimination doctrine and its failure to embrace intersectionality, but also the centrality of white female experiences in the conceptualization of gender discrimination. One inference that could be drawn from the court's statement that Moore's complaint did not entail a claim of discrimination "against females" is that discrimination against Black females is something less than discrimination against females. More than likely, however, the court meant to imply that Moore did not claim that *all* females were discriminated against *but only* Black females. But even thus recast, the court's rationale is problematic for Black women. . . .

A white woman claiming discrimination against females may be in no better position to represent all women than a Black woman who claims discrimination as a Black female and wants to represent all females. The court's preferred articulation of "against females" is not necessarily more inclusive—it just appears to be so because the racial contours of the claim are not specified.

The court's preference for "against females" rather than "against Black females" reveals the implicit grounding of white female experiences in the doctrinal conceptualization of sex discrimination. For white women, claiming sex discrimination is simply a statement that but for gender, they would not have been disadvantaged. For them there is no need to specify discrimination as *white* females because their race does not contribute to the disadvantage for which they seek redress. The view of discrimination that is derived from this grounding takes race privilege as a given.

Discrimination against a white female is thus the standard sex discrimination claim. . . . The effect of this approach is that even though a challenged policy or practice may clearly discriminate against all females, the fact that it has particularly harsh consequences for Black females places Black female plaintiffs at odds with white females.

*Moore* illustrates one of the limitations of antidiscrimination law's remedial scope and normative vision. The refusal to allow a multiply-disadvantaged class to represent others who may be singularly-disadvantaged defeats efforts to restructure the distribution of opportunity and limits remedial relief to minor adjustments within an established hierarchy. Consequently, "bottom up" approaches, those which combine all discriminatees in order to challenge an entire employment system, are foreclosed by the limited view of the wrong and the narrow scope of the available remedy. If such "bottom up" intersectional representation were routinely permit-

ted, employees might accept the possibility that there is more to be gained by challenging the hierarchy rather than by each discriminatee individually seeking to protect her source of privilege within the hierarchy. But as long as antidiscrimination doctrine proceeds from the premise that employment systems need only minor adjustments, opportunities for advancement by disadvantaged employees will be limited. Relatively privileged employees probably are better off guarding their advantage while jockeying against others to gain more. As a result Black women—the class of employees which because of its intersectionality, is best able to challenge all forms of discrimination—are essentially isolated and forced to fend for themselves. . . .

Black female plaintiffs have also encountered difficulty in their efforts to win certification as class representatives in some race discrimination actions. This problem typically arises in cases where statistics suggest significant disparities between Black and white workers and further disparities between Black men and Black women. . . .

[T]he plaintiffs in [*Payne* v.] *Travenol* fared better than the similarly situated plaintiff in *Moore:* they were not denied use of meaningful statistics showing an overall pattern of race discrimination simply because there were no men in their class. The plaintiffs' bid to represent all Black employees, however, like Moore's attempt to represent all women employees, failed as a consequence of the court's narrow view of class interest.

Even though *Travenol* was a partial victory for Black women, the case specifically illustrates how antidiscrimination doctrine creates a dilemma for Black women. It forces them to choose between specifically articulating the intersectional aspects of their subordination, thereby risking their ability to represent Black men, or ignoring intersectionality in order to state a claim that would not lead to the exclusion of Black men. When one considers the political consequences of this dilemma, there is little wonder that many people within the Black community view the articulation of Black women's interests as dangerously divisive. . . .

Perhaps it appears to some that I have offered inconsistent criticisms of how Black women are treated in antidiscrimination law: I seem to be saying that in one case, Black women's claims were rejected and their experiences obscured because the court refused to acknowledge that the employment experience can be distinct from that of white women, while in other cases, the interests of Black women are harmed because Black women's claims were viewed as so distinct from the claims of either white women or Black men that the court denied to Black females representation of the larger class. It seems that I have to say that Black women are the same and harmed by being treated differently, or that they are different and harmed by being treated the same. But I cannot say both. . . .

The point is that Black women can experience discrimination in any number of ways and that the contradiction arises from our assumptions that their claims of exclusion must be unidirectional. . . . I am suggesting that Black women can experience discrimination in ways that are both similar to and different from those experienced by white women and Black men. Black women sometimes experience discrimination in ways similar to white women's experiences; sometimes they share very similar experiences with Black men. Yet often they experience double-discrimination—the combined effects of practices which discriminate on the basis of race, and on the basis of sex. And sometimes they experience discrimination as Black women—not the sum of race and sex discrimination, but as Black women.

**The Significance of Doctrinal Treatment of Intersectionality** . . . [N]ot only courts but feminist and civil rights thinkers as well have treated Black women in ways that deny both the unique compoundedness of their situation and the centrality of their experiences to the larger classes of women and Blacks. Black women are regarded either as too much like women or Blacks and the compounded nature of their experience is absorbed into the collective experiences of either group or as too different, in which case Black women's Blackness or femaleness sometimes has placed their needs and perspectives at the margins of the feminist and Black liberationist agendas.

. . . [T]he following analogy can be useful in describing how Black women are marginalized in the interface between antidiscrimination law and race and gender hierarchies: Imagine a basement which contains all people who are disadvantaged on the basis of race, sex, class, sexual preference, age, and/or physical ability. These people are stacked—feet standing on shoulders—with those on the bottom being disadvantaged by the full array of factors, up to the very top, where the heads of all those disadvantaged by a singular factor brush up against the ceiling. Their ceiling is actually the floor above which only those who are *not* disadvantaged in any way reside. In efforts to correct some aspects of domination, those above the ceiling admit from the basement only those who can say that "but for" the ceiling, they too could be in the upper room. A hatch is developed through which those placed immediately below can crawl. Yet this hatch is generally available only to those who—due to the singularity of their burden and their otherwise privileged position relative to those below—are in a position to crawl through. Those who are multiply-burdened are generally left below unless they can somehow pull themselves into the groups that are permitted to squeeze through the hatch. . . .

## FEMINISM AND BLACK WOMEN; AIN'T WE WOMEN?

. . . In 1851 Sojourner Truth declared "Ain't I a woman?" and challenged the sexist imagery used by male critics to justify the disenfranchisement of women. . . . [W]hite male hecklers, invoking the stereotypical images of "woman-hood" argued that women were too frail and delicate to take on the responsibilities of political activity. When Sojourner Truth rose to speak, many white women urged that she be silenced, fearing that she would divert attention from women's suffrage to emancipation. Truth, once permitted to speak recounted . . .

Look at my arms! I have ploughed and
planted and gathered into barns, and no man

could head me—and ain't I a woman? I would work as much and eat as much as a man—when I could get it—and bear the lash as well! And ain't I a woman? I have born thirteen children, and seen most of 'em sold into slavery, and when I cried out with my mother's grief, none but Jesus heard me—and ain't I a woman?

. . . [T]his 19th Century Black feminist challenged not only patriarchy, but she also challenged white feminists to embrace Black women's history to relinquish their vestedness in whiteness. . . . Even today, the difficulty that white women have traditionally experienced in sacrificing racial privilege to strengthen feminism renders them susceptible to Truth's critical question. When feminist theory and politics that claim to reflect *women's* experience and *women's* aspirations do not include or speak to Black women, Black women must ask: Ain't We Women? . . .

The value of feminist theory to Black women is diminished because it evolves from a white racial context that is seldom acknowledged. Not only are women of color in fact overlooked, but their exclusion is reinforced when *white*

women speak for and as *women*. The authoritative universal voice—usually white male subjectivity masquerading as non-racial, non-gendered objectivity—is merely transferred to those who, but for gender, share many of the same cultural, economic, and social characteristics. When feminist theory attempts to describe women's experience through analyzing patriarchy, sexuality, or separate spheres ideology, it often overlooks the role of race. Feminists thus ignore how their own race functions to mitigate some aspects of sexism, and moreover, how it often privileges them over and contributes to the domination of other women. Consequently, feminist theory remains *white* and its potential to broaden and deepen its analysis by addressing non-privileged women remains unrealized. . . .

## Notes and Questions

1. What transformation in the judicial approach to cases at the intersection of race and gender would be required for Crenshaw's criticism of the cases to be met?

2. What transformation in feminist analysis of gender would be required?

---

## 7.5 | A Critique of "Our Constitution Is Color-Blind"
### *Neil Gotanda*

WE ACCEPT AS UNREMARKABLE an employer who asserts, "Yes, I noticed that she was Black, but I did not consider her race in making my hiring or promotion decision." This technique of "noticing but not considering race" implicitly involves recognition of the employee's racial category

and a transformation or sublimation of that recognition so that the racial label is not "considered" in the employer's decisionmaking process. Advocates of the color-blind model argue that nonrecognition by government is clearly superior to any race-conscious process. Indeed, nonrecognition advocates apparently find the political and moral superiority of this technique so self-evident that they think little or no justification is necessary.

But just how adequate is color-blind constitutionalism as a technique for combating racial subordination? I argue that nonrecognition is self-contradictory. Not only that—nonrecogni-

---

tion fosters the systematic denial of racial subordination and the psychological repression of an individual's recognition of that subordination, thereby allowing it to continue.

Nonrecognition has three elements. First, there must be something which is cognizable as a racial characteristic or classification. Second, the characteristic must be recognized. Third, the characteristic must not be considered in a decision. For nonrecognition to make sense, it must be possible to recognize something while not including it in making a decision.

Nonrecognition is a technique, not a principle of traditional substantive common law or constitutional interpretation. It addresses the question of race, not by examining the social realities or legal categories of race, but by setting forth an analytical methodology. This technical approach permits a court to describe, to accommodate, and then to ignore issues of subordination. This deflection from the substantive to the methodological is significant. Because the technique appears purely procedural, its normative, substantive impact is hidden. Color-blind application of the technique is important because it suggests a seemingly neutral and objective method of decisionmaking that avoids any consideration of race.

## SELF-CONTRADICTION AND REPRESSION

Decisions that use color-blind nonrecognition are often regarded as superior to race-conscious ones. Proponents of nonrecognition argue that it facilitates meritocratic decisionmaking by preventing the corrupting consideration of race. They regard race as a "political" or "special interest" consideration, detrimental to fair decisionmaking.

To use color-blind nonrecognition effectively in the private sphere, we would have to fail to recognize race in our everyday lives. This is impossible. One cannot literally follow a color-blind standard of conduct in ordinary social life. Moreover, the technique of nonrecognition ultimately supports the supremacy of white interests.

In everyday American life, nonrecognition is self-contradictory because it is impossible

not to think about a subject without having first thought about it at least a little. Nonrecognition differs from nonperception. Compare color-blind nonrecognition with medical color-blindness. A medically color-blind person is someone who cannot see what others can. It is a partial nonperception of what is "really" there. To be racially color-blind, on the other hand, is to ignore what one has already noticed. The medically color-blind individual never perceives color in the first place; the racially color-blind individual perceives race and then ignores it. This is not just a semantic distinction. The characteristics of race that are noticed (before being ignored) are situated within an already existing understanding of race. That is, race carries with it a complex social meaning. This pre-existing race consciousness makes it impossible for an individual to be truly nonconscious of race. To argue that one did not really consider the race of an African American is to concede that there was an identification of Blackness. Suppressing the recognition of a racial classification in order to act as if a person were not of some cognizable racial class is inherently racially premised.

[One author] offers a bizarre example of this enforced nonrecognition when she recounts Professor Patricia Williams's struggle with the editors of the University of Miami Law Review. In an article published with them, Williams describes her exclusion from a New York store as follows:

> Two Saturdays before Christmas, I saw a sweater that I wanted to purchase for my mother. I pressed my brown face to the store window and my finger to the buzzer, seeking admittance. A narrow-eyed white youth who looked barely seventeen, wearing tennis sneakers and feasting on bubble gum, glared at me, evaluating me for signs that would pit me against the limits of his social understanding. After about five seconds, he mouthed, "We're closed," and blew pink rubber at me. It was one o'clock in the afternoon. There were several white people in the store who appeared to be shopping for things for their mothers.

I was enraged. At that moment I literally wanted to break all of the windows in the store and take lots of sweaters for my mother.

[When editing her account,] "the editors initially deleted all references to [Williams's] racial identity informing her that references to physiogomy [*sic*] were irrelevant. . . . [But] if the racial identity of the speaker is not included, the point of the story is unintelligible." Had the editors prevailed, Williams would have appeared irrational for being so angry at a store clerk over a minor incident. The editors sought to suppress the existence of race from a narrative in which race was the center of the incident. Their attempted use of nonrecognition would have produced a misleading "nonracial" narrative.

While the actions of the University of Miami Law Review editors appear nonsensical, similar efforts in most other contexts would be regarded as perfectly legitimate. For example, in a recent empirical study, Professor Ian Ayres examined whether race and gender substantively affected automobile showroom sales transactions. Ayres found that white men purchasing automobiles in the Chicago area were offered substantially lower prices than were women or Blacks and concluded that car salespersons were unwilling to negotiate better prices with Black and female buyers. If a salesperson were to say that he "did not consider race," in his sales transactions, it would not be regarded as a complex assertion. Yet Professor Ayres's study reveals a wide range of socioeconomic considerations involved in such a seemingly simple statement.

From a psychological or psychoanalytic perspective, nonrecognition may be considered a mode of repression. The claim that race is not recognized is an attempt to deny the reality of internally recognized social conflicts of race. This internal psychological conflict between recognition and repression of racial identity is reflected in legal discourse. More concretely, an individual's assertion that he "saw but did not consider race," can be interpreted as a recognition of race and its attendant social implications, followed by suppression of that recognition. The legal mode of racial nonrecognition is, then, the external extension of this psychological mode of denial of race. As explained by Charles Lawrence, "[w]hen an individual experiences conflict between racist ideas and the societal ethic that condemns those ideas, the mind excludes his racism from consciousness." The impetus for that conflict may be moral, legal, or both. But the suppression does take place, and the external world accommodates it by accepting and institutionalizing the repression rather than attempting to expose and alter the conditions of racial exploitation.

The inherent self-contradictions of nonrecognition can be summarized in terms of dialectical logic: A subject is defined by its negation, hence, an assertion of nonconsideration necessarily implies consideration. The stronger and more defined the character of racial recognition, the clearer and more sharply drawn its dialectical opposite, racial nonrecognition. The assertion "I noticed but did not consider race" divides the dialectic into two components, consideration and nonconsideration. It then focuses exclusively on the nonconsideration by denying the existence of the consideration component. While this is a complex maneuver surrounded by assertions of moral superiority, the attempt to deny racial consideration is, at its root, an attempt to hide the underlying racial oppression, a reality no amount of hand-waving and obfuscation can eliminate.

# CONCLUSION

&. Part I has introduced some of the major explanations of law and tested them in a variety of legal settings. Most of the themes recur in later chapters, and there will be numerous opportunities to see their worth in a number of contexts. Each explanation—law as rules, discretion, value conflict, a balance of competing interests, a power play, the voice of the people, or an extension of patriarchy or racism—tends to drive competing contenders from attention. But law resembles a field of forces rather than one force operating for all time, and more is gained through surveying an array of perspectives than through preoccupation with a single vision.

The strengths and weaknesses of alternative explanations can be put succinctly. Rule lovers drive toward certainty only to be brought up short by difficulties of interpretation and vagaries of fact. Students of discretion find choice everywhere but neglect constraint, not only from rules but also from the pressures of context. Those inclined toward the study of values that are advanced or retarded by law often become royal philosophers without territory who must settle for a running dialogue with the less thoughtful who nevertheless have power. Legal professionals who see themselves as balancing conflict and minimizing waste fail to see that involvement is never neutral and that they may be creating as much waste as, or even more than, they hoped to arrest. Power theorists can raise the current contradictions, but they rarely tell what should be done next, leaving their adherents waiting patiently for a spontaneous revolution. Neo-populists, seeking a demise of hierarchy and endemic alienation, sometimes overlook the less desirable aspects of popular will and the reasons earlier institutions failed. And feminists and critical race theorists stand between reforming law that has been a source of oppression and more radical answers that sweep them beyond mere law.

The contradictory elements emerging from the study of different perspectives about law can leave people so confused that they assume the role of Kafka's commoners—aware that life can be miserable but in need of a more definitive clincher before attempting to work their way out of their misery. Nothing could be a more undesirable outcome from a broad-based study of law. After study, one must choose a best course of action rather than flounder among the pros and cons. To do otherwise simply perpetuates the status quo. The confusion we experience differs from unalloyed relativism where anything goes and power settles everything.

Clearly some understandings about law are more conducive to maintaining the status quo, whereas others support the need for profound change if not revolution. Judges and lawyers can be proud and the citizenry thankful if legal officials with prudent discretion apply legitimate rules to advance agreed-upon values and alleviate conflict. But what if the

Marxists, the anarchists, the feminists, and critical race theorists are right in their finding that law enacts power and privilege while leaving many people on the outside looking in? If the more radical jurists are reading the contemporary system correctly, then law study becomes part of the documentation of the decline of the American dream of equality and freedom and a painful prelude to transforming activism in courts, in legislatures, or in the nonstate settings in which we inevitably find ourselves.

# Suggested Additional Readings

Baer, Judith. *Our Lives Before the Law*. Princeton, N.J.: Princeton University Press, 1999.

Barnet, Richard, et al. *Global Reach*. New York: Simon and Schuster, 1974.

———. *Global Dreams*. New York: Simon and Schuster, 1994.

Bartlett, Katherine, and Rosanne Kennedy. *Feminist Legal Theory*. Boulder: Westview, 1991.

Benjamin, Medea, ed. *Don't Be Afraid, Gringo*. New York: HarperCollins, 1987.

Berry, Wendell. *The Unsettling of America*. New York: Avon Books, 1978.

Bok, Sissela. *Lying*. New York: Pantheon, 1978.

Bonsignore, John. *Law and Multinationals*. Englewood Cliffs, N.J.: Prentice-Hall, 1994.

Bottomly, Anne. *Feminist Perspectives on Foundational Subjects of Law*. London: Cavendish Press, 1996.

Delgado Richard, ed. *Critical Race Theory*, 2d ed. Philadelphia: Temple University Press, 2000.

Edelman, Peter. *Searching for America's Heart*. Boston: Houghton Mifflin, 2001.

Ehrlich, Eugen. *Fundamental Principles of the Sociology of Law*. Translated by W. Moll. New York: Russell & Russell, 1962.

Faludi, Susan. *Backlash*. New York: Crown, 1991.

Fernandez-Kelly, Maria. *For We Are Sold*. Albany: SUNY Press, 1983.

Frank, Jerome. *Courts on Trial*. Princeton, N.J.: Princeton University Press, 1949.

Gaventa, John. *Power and Powerlessness*. Urbana: University of Illinois Press, 1982.

Genovese, Eugene. *Roll Jordan Roll*. New York: Pantheon, 1974.

Greider, William. *Who Will Tell the People?* New York: Simon and Schuster, 1994.

———. *One World, Ready or Not*. New York: Simon and Schuster, 1977.

Guerin, Daniel. *Anarchism from Theory to Practice*. New York: Monthly Review Press, 1970.

Herman, Edward, and Noam Chomsky. *Manufacturing Consent*. New York: Pantheon, 1988.

Lall, Sanjaya. *The Multinational Corporation*. New York: Holmes and Meier, 1980.

Levi, Edward. *An Introduction to Legal Reasoning*. Chicago: University of Chicago Press, 1949.

Llewellyn, Karl. *The Bramble Bush*. New York: Oceana Publications, 1930.

Llewellyn, Karl, and E. Adamson Hoebel. *The Cheyenne Way*. Norman: University of Oklahoma Press, 1941.

MacKinnon, Catherine. *Toward a Feminist Theory of the State*. Cambridge, Mass.: Harvard University Press, 1989.

Mills, C. Wright. *The Power Elite*. New York: Oxford University Press, 1957.

Noonan, John. *Persons and Masks of the Law*. New York: Farrar, Straus & Giroux, 1976.

Olsen, Frances, ed. *Feminist Legal Theory.* New York: New York University Press, 1995.

Ong, Aihwa. *Spirits of Resistance and Capitalist Discipline.* Albany: SUNY Press, 1987.

Rawls, John. *A Theory of Justice.* Cambridge, Mass.: Harvard University Press, 1971.

Rosenbaum, Walter. *Environmental Politics and Policy.* Washington: Congressional Quarterly Press, 1991.

Scott, James. *Domination and the Arts of Resistance.* New Haven: Yale University Press, 1992.

Stockdale, Margaret, ed. *Sexual Harassment in the Workplace.* Thousand Oaks, Calif.: Sage, 1996.

Weber, Max. *On Law in Economy and Society.* Translated with introduction by Max Rheinstein et al. Cambridge, Mass.: Harvard University Press, 1954.

Williams, Patricia. *The Alchemy of Race and Rights.* Cambridge, Mass.: Harvard University Press, 1991.

Woodcock, George. *Anarchism.* New York: New American Library, 1962.

Zelermyer, William. *The Process of Legal Reasoning.* Englewood Cliffs, N.J.: Prentice-Hall, 1963.

*Police Court.* (The Bettmann Archive, Inc.)

# Law Enforcement

An injunction duly issuing out of a court of general jurisdiction with equity powers, upon pleadings properly invoking its action, and served upon persons made parties therein and within the jurisdiction, must be obeyed by them, however erroneous the action of the court may be. . . . [A]nd until its decision is reversed for error by orderly review, either by itself or by a higher court, its orders based on its decision are to be respected, and disobedience of them is contempt of its lawful authority, to be punished.

*Howat* v. *Kansas* (42 S.Ct. 277, 280–281, 1921)

[W]henever any Form of Government becomes destructive of these ends, it is the Right of the People to alter or to abolish it. . . . [E]xperience hath shown, that mankind are more disposed to suffer, while evils are sufferable, than to right themselves by abolishing the forms to which they are accustomed. But when a long train of abuses and usurpations, pursuing invariably the same Object evinces a design to reduce them under absolute Despotism, it is their right, it is their duty, to throw off such Government.

The Declaration of Independence (1776)

❧ American society presents two conflicting images of law. One is expressed by the revolutionary message in the Declaration of Independence: law is subordinate to society and may be overthrown if it fails to meet social needs. In this image, the legitimacy of government is dependent on its ability to support human freedom. Law enforcement is to be judged by whether it serves "Life, Liberty, and the pursuit of Happiness."

The other image of law is of established order, of constituted government with rules and procedures, as in the *Howat* case quoted above. In that case, the state of Kansas enjoined 150 members of the United Mine Workers of America from striking against a coal company. When the miners struck anyway, they were sentenced to one-year jail terms for violating the injunction. In their appeal they argued that the Kansas statute on which the injunction was based violated the federal Constitution. The U.S. Supreme Court refused to consider this argument, on the grounds that the miners should have appealed the injunction itself instead of violating it and then appealing their convictions. The message of this decision is that human freedom is subordinate to law, a relationship often explicitly stated on courthouse buildings—for example, "Obedience to the law is liberty." In this view, life, liberty, and perhaps even happiness are presumed to be based on law enforcement.

Perhaps every legal system that begins with revolution is characterized by this conflict of images. On one hand, the revolution is justified as an overthrow of oppressive law. On the other hand, when the revolution succeeds, the new government must justify its authority to enforce new law. Yet the revolutionary image cannot be completely forgotten, and so the contradictory images coexist in the culture.

The materials in this part focus on issues of "freedom" and "order" in a wide range of situations. The readings present a variety of perspectives on the enforcement of and resistance to law, including political, economic, philosophical, anthropological, and historical considerations. Chapter 8 explores how law depends on violence as a method to secure its rules. Chapter 9 presents conflicts about enforcement of specific laws, including racial segregation, slavery, pornography, and patent law. Chapter 10 focuses on surveillance, with discussions of privacy, search and seizure, and investigative technologies.

# 8 | THE FORCE OF LAW

> State is the name of the coldest of all cold monsters. Coldly it tells lies too; and this lie crawls out of its mouth: "I, the state, am the people." That is a lie! It was creators who created peoples and hung a faith and a love over them: thus they served life.
>
> Friedrich Nietzsche, "On the New Idol,"
> in *Thus Spoke Zarathustra* (1891)

By the beginning of the nineteenth century, the practice of public punishment (pillory, stocks, and so on) and the use of prisoners for public work (the chain gang) were dying out. Similarly, public executions were increasingly seen as problematic, as repeating or exceeding the savagery of the crime against which they were directed. But this does not mean that the law was no longer involved with punishment. On the contrary, as French philosopher Michel Foucault has pointed out, punishment became "the most hidden part of the penal process. . . . As a result, justice no longer takes public responsibility for the violence that is bound up with its practice. If it too strikes, if it too kills, it is not as a glorification of its strength, but as an element of itself that it is obliged to tolerate, that it finds difficult to account for."*

By the end of the nineteenth century, the institutions of incarceration, which had been developed as alternatives to public punishment, had

---

*Michel Foucault, *Discipline and Punish: The Birth of the Prison* (New York, Vintage, 1979), p. 9.

themselves become the targets of criticism. Investigators saw filth, corruption, and brutality behind the prison walls, and noted no reduction of crime outside. The result of these findings, however, was neither a return to public punishment nor an abandonment of incarceration. Instead, they became the basis for recommending more prisons and more guards.

The problem of punishment is the problem of law enforcement generally: the use of force to sustain law. Law presents itself as the embodiment of reason, but it depends on violence for its efficacy. In other words, law does not banish force and violence, but organizes it as a state monopoly. Attempts to regulate or ban the sale of firearms to the public are an example of this; if such attempts succeed, only officials and those they authorize will have weapons. Looking at law as a system of rules tends to obscure this view of law as the social organization of violence. Both aspects are present.

---

## 8.1 | The Violence of Legal Acts    *Robert M. Cover*

LEGAL INTERPRETATION TAKES PLACE in a field of pain and death. This is true in several senses. Legal interpretive acts signal and occasion the imposition of violence upon others: A judge articulates her understanding of a text, and as a result, somebody loses his freedom, his property, his children, even his life. Interpretations in law also constitute justifications for violence which has already occurred or which is about to occur. When interpreters have finished their work, they frequently leave behind victims whose lives have been torn apart by these organized, social practices of violence. Neither legal interpretation nor the violence it occasions may be properly understood apart from one another. . . .

The deliberate infliction of pain . . . we call torture. The interrogation that is part of torture, [Elaine] Scarry* points out, is rarely designed to elicit information. More commonly, the torturer's interrogation is designed to demonstrate the end of the normative world of the victim— the end of what the victim values, the end of the bonds that constitute the community in which

the values are grounded. Scarry thus concludes that "in compelling confession, the torturers compel the prisoner to record and objectify the fact that intense pain is world-destroying." That is why torturers almost always require betrayal— a demonstration that the victim's intangible normative world has been crushed by the material reality of pain and its extension, fear. . . .

. . . But the relationship between legal interpretation and the infliction of pain remains operative even in the most routine of legal acts. The act of sentencing a convicted defendant is among these most routine of acts performed by judges.[1] Yet it is immensely revealing of the way

---

[1] I have used the criminal law for examples throughout this essay for a simple reason. The violence of the criminal law is relatively direct. If my argument is not persuasive in this context, it will be less persuasive in most other contexts. I would be prepared to argue that all law which concerns property, its use and its protection, has a similarly violent base. But in many, perhaps most, highly visible legal transactions concerning property rights, that violent foundation is not immediately at issue. My argument does not, I believe require that every interpretive event in law have the kind of direct violent impact on participants that a criminal trial has. It is enough that it is the case that where people care passionately about outcomes and are prepared to act on their concern, the law officials of the nation state are usually willing and able to use either criminal or violent sanctions to control behavior.

---

Reprinted by permission of The Yale Law Journal Company and Fred B. Rothman and Company from *The Yale Law Journal,* Vol. 95, p. 1601. Some footnotes have been omitted and the rest are renumbered.

*Author of *The Body in Pain* (1985), an analysis of pain.— ED.

in which interpretation is distinctively shaped by violence. First, examine the event from the perspective of the defendant. The defendant's world is threatened. But he sits, usually quietly, as if engaged in a civil discourse. If convicted, the defendant customarily walks—escorted—to prolonged confinement, usually without significant disturbance to the civil appearance of the event. It is, of course, grotesque to assume that the civil facade is "voluntary" except in the sense that it represents the defendant's autonomous recognition of the overwhelming array of violence ranged against him, and of the hopelessness of resistance or outcry. . . .

If I have exhibited some sense of sympathy for the victims of this violence it is misleading. Very often the balance of terror in this regard is just as I would want it. But I do not wish us to pretend that we talk our prisoners into jail. The "interpretations" or "conversations" that are the preconditions for violent incarceration are themselves implements of violence. To obscure this fact is precisely analogous to ignoring the background screams or visible instruments of torture in an inquisitor's interrogation. The experience of the prisoner is, from the outset, an experience of being violently dominated, and it is colored from the beginning by the fear of being violently treated.

The violence of the act of sentencing is most obvious when observed from the defendant's perspective. Therefore, any account which seeks to downplay the violence or elevate the interpretive character or meaning of the event within a community of shared values will tend to ignore the prisoner or defendant and focus upon the judge and the judicial interpretive act. Beginning with broad interpretive categories such as "blame" or "punishment" meaning is created for the event which justifies the judge to herself and to others with respect to her role in the acts of violence. I do not wish to downplay the significance of such ideological functions of law. But the function of ideology is much more significant in justifying an order to those who principally benefit from it and who must defend it than it is in hiding the nature of the order from those who are its victims. . . .

. . . The best known study and theory of social codes and their role in overcoming normal inhibitions against inflicting pain through violence is Milgram's *Obedience to Authority*. In the Milgram experiments, subjects administered what they thought were actually painful electric shocks to persons who they thought were the experimental subjects. This was done under the direction or orders of supposed experimenters. The true experimental subjects—those who administered the shocks—showed a disturbingly high level of compliance with authority figures despite the apparent pain evinced by the false experimental subjects. From the results of his experiment, Milgram has formulated a theory that . . . relies heavily on the distinction he draws between acting in an "autonomous" state and acting in an "agentic" state. Milgram posits the evolution of a human disposition to act "agentically" within hierarchies. . . .

The judge in imposing a sentence normally takes for granted the role structure which might be analogized to the "transmission" of the engine of justice. The judge's interpretive authorization of the "proper" sentence can be carried out as a deed only because of these others; a bond between word and deed obtains only because a system of social cooperation exists. That system guarantees the judge massive amounts of force—the conditions of effective domination—if necessary. It guarantees—or is supposed to—a relatively faithful adherence to the word of the judge in the deeds carried out against the prisoner. . . .

We have done something strange in our system. We have rigidly separated the act of interpretation—of understanding what ought to be done—from the carrying out of this "ought to be done" through violence. At the same time we have, at least in the criminal law, rigidly linked the carrying out of judicial orders to the act of judicial interpretation by relatively inflexible hierarchies of judicial utterances and firm obligations on the part of penal officials to heed them. Judges are both separated from, and inextricably linked to, the acts they authorize. . . .

. . . Judges, officials, resisters, martyrs, wardens, convicts, may or may not share common texts; they may or may not share a common vocabulary, a common cultural store of gestures and rituals; they may or may not share a common philosophical framework. There will be in the immense human panorama a continuum of degrees of commonality in all of the above. But as long as legal interpretation is constitutive of violent behavior as well as meaning, as long as people are committed to using or resisting the social organizations of violence in making their interpretations real, there will always be a tragic limit to the common meaning that can be achieved.

The perpetrator and victim of organized violence will undergo achingly disparate significant experiences. For the perpetrator, the pain and fear are remote, unreal, and largely unshared. They are, therefore, almost never made a part of the interpretive artifact, such as the judicial opinion. On the other hand, for those who impose the violence the justification is important, real and carefully cultivated. Conversely, for the victim, the justification for the violence recedes in reality and significance in proportion to the overwhelming reality of the pain and fear that is suffered.

Between the idea and the reality of common meaning falls the shadow of the violence of law, itself.

## Notes and Questions

1. In thinking about Cover's analysis of the violence of legal acts, consider the following comment on the link between punishment and social values:

   . . . The social values which are given the protection of the law, the rules which are enforced by the political power of the state because they are embodied in the criminal code, are those which are deemed desirable by those social groups within the state who have the power to make law. This fact is not so easy to discern when we confine our observations to democratic states, but in other forms of political organization it is obvious. The class distinctions in the criminal law—different penalties for masters and slaves, for nobles and commoners, for instance—furnish good illustrations. Fundamentally, then, the aim of all punishment is the protection of those social values which the dominant social group of a state regard as good for "society."

   The multiplicity of theories of punishment and the confusion of thinking they have produced seems to be due to a confusion of ends with means. The means to secure the protection of "society" have varied greatly because the law-enforcing powers of different societies have chosen those means which they believed to be at a given time most likely to secure obedience to their law. These beliefs are in turn dependent on tradition, the level of knowledge, and the nature of social and economic institutions and conditions. The sanguinary punishments and tortures of old are no evidence of blood-thirstiness or sadism on the part of those who used them. They rather testify to the fact that those who designed them could conceive of no better, that is more efficient, way of securing protection for the social values which they treasured. The character of punishments, then, is inextricably associated with and dependent on the cultural values of the state that employs them.[†]

2. Consider as well the following:

   The ideas of the ruling class are in every epoch the ruling ideas: i.e., the class, which is the ruling material force of society, is at the same time its ruling intellectual force. The class which has the means of material production at its disposal has control at the same time over the means of mental production, so that thereby, generally speaking, the ideas of those who lack the means of mental production are subject to it. The ruling ideas are nothing more than the ideal expression of the dominant material relationships, the dominant material relationships grasped as ideas; hence of the relationships which make the one class the ruling one, therefore, the ideas of its dominance. The individuals composing the ruling class possess among other things consciousness, and therefore think. In so far, therefore, as they rule as a class and determine the extent and compass of an epoch, it is self-evident that they do this in their whole range, hence among other things rule also as thinkers, as producers of ideas, and regulate the production and distribution of the ideas of their age: thus their ideas are the ruling ideas of the epoch.[‡]

3. In thinking further about how violence may be justified in law enforcement, consider the following account of how Mengele, the Nazi doctor, once explained why he killed Jewish

---

[†]George Rusche and Otto Kirchheimer, *Punishment and Social Structure* (New York: Columbia University Press, 1939), pp. v–vi.

[‡]Karl Marx, "German Ideology," trans. by T. B. Bottomore (1845), in Erich Fromm, ed., *Marx's Concept of Man* (New York: Ungar, 1966), pp. 212–213.

women together with their children at Auschwitz:

> Orli had told me once how Mengele explained to her why he killed Jewish women together with their children. "When a Jewish child is born, or when a woman comes to the camp with a child already," he had explained, "I don't know what to do with the child. I can't set the child free because there are no longer any Jews who live in freedom. I can't let the child stay in the camp because there are no facilities in the camp that would enable the child to develop normally. It would not be humanitarian to send a child to the ovens without permitting the mother to be there to witness the child's death. That is why I send the mother and the child to the gas ovens together." Imagine that cynical criminal justifying his hideous crimes in the name of humanitarianism, making a mockery of the tenderest of all feelings, a mother's love for her children.§

§Sara Nomberg-Przytyk, *Auschwitz,* trans. by Roslyn Hirsch (Chapel Hill: University of North Carolina Press, 1985), p. 69.

---

## 8.2 | Address to the Prisoners in the Cook County Jail

*Clarence Darrow*

IF I LOOKED AT jails and crimes and prisoners in the way the ordinary person does, I should not speak on this subject to you. The reason I talk to you on the question of crime, its cause and cure, is that I really do not in the least believe in crime. There is no such thing as a crime as the word is generally understood. I do not believe there is any sort of distinction between the real moral conditions of the people in and out of jail. One is just as good as the other. The people here can no more help being here than the people outside can avoid being outside. I do not believe that people are in jail because they deserve to be. They are in jail simply because they cannot avoid it on account of circumstances which are entirely beyond their control and for which they are in no way responsible.

From *Address to the Prisoners in the Cook County Jail* by Clarence Darrow. From the 1975 edition of the 1902 speech to the prisoners. Copyright Charles H. Kerr Publishing Company. Reprinted by permission (abridged).

Clarence Seward Darrow (1857–1938), a social reformer as well as a criminal lawyer, is remembered today for his defense in the landmark Scopes trial in 1925. He defended John Scopes, who was being tried for teaching evolution theory in a Tennessee public school, which was against state law; Scopes was convicted, but released on a technicality. The well-known opposing counsel was the statesman William Jennings Bryan.

I suppose a great many people on the outside would say I was doing you harm if they should hear what I say to you this afternoon, but you cannot be hurt a great deal anyway, so it will not matter. Good people outside would say that I was really teaching you things that were calculated to injure society, but it's worth while now and then to hear something different from what you ordinarily get from preachers and the like. These will tell you that you should be good and then you will get rich and be happy. Of course we know that people do not get rich by being good, and that is the reason why so many of you people try to get rich some other way, only you do not understand how to do it quite as well as the fellow outside.

There are people who think that everything in this world is an accident. But really there is no such thing as an accident. A great many folks admit that many of the people in jail ought not to be there, and many who are outside ought to be in. I think none of them ought to be here. There ought to be no jails; and if it were not for the fact that the people on the outside are so grasping and heartless in their dealings with the people on the inside, there would be no such institutions as jails.

I do not want you to believe that I think all you people here are angels. I do not think that. You are people of all kinds, all of you doing the best you can—and that is evidently not very well. You are people of all kinds and conditions and under all circumstances. In one sense everybody is equally bad. We all do the best we can under the circumstances. But as to the exact things for which you are sent here, some of you are guilty and did the particular act because you needed the money. Some of you did it because you are in the habit of doing it, and some of you because you are born to it, and it comes to be as natural as it does, for instance, for me to be good.

Most of you probably have nothing against me, and most of you would treat me the same way as any other person would, probably better than some of the people on the outside would treat me, because you think I believe in you and they know I do not believe in them. While you would not have the least thing against me in the world, you might pick my pockets. I do not think all of you would, but I think some of you would. You would not have anything against me, but that's your profession, a few of you. Some of the rest of you, if my doors were unlocked, might come in if you saw anything you wanted—not out of any malice to me, but because that is your trade. There is no doubt there are quite a number of people in this jail who would pick my pockets. And still I know this—that when I get outside pretty nearly everybody picks my pockets. There may be some of you who would hold up a man on the street, if you did not happen to have something else to do, and needed the money; but when I want to light my house or my office the gas company holds me up. They charge me one dollar for something that is worth twenty-five cents. Still all these people are good people; they are pillars of society and support the churches, and they are respectable.

When I ride on the streetcars I am held up—I pay five cents for a ride that is worth two and a half cents, simply because a body of men have bribed the city council and the legislature, so that all the rest of us have to pay tribute to them.

If I do not want to fall into the clutches of the gas trust and choose to burn oil instead of gas, then good Mr. Rockefeller holds me up, and he uses a certain portion of his money to build universities and support churches which are engaged in telling us how to be good.

Some of you are here for obtaining property under false pretenses—yet I pick up a great Sunday paper and read the advertisements of a merchant prince—"Shirtwaists for 39 cents, marked down from $3.00."

When I read the advertisements in the paper I see they are all lies. When I want to get out and find a place to stand anywhere on the face of the earth, I find that it has all been taken up long ago before I came here, and before you came here, and somebody says, "Get off, swim into the lake, fly into the air; go anywhere, but get off." That is because these people have the police and they have the jails and the judges and the lawyers and the soldiers and all the rest of them to take care of the earth and drive everybody off that comes in their way.

A great many people will tell you that all this is true, but that it does not excuse you. These facts do not excuse some fellow who reaches into my pocket and takes out a five-dollar bill. The fact that the gas company bribes the members of the legislature from year to year, and fixes the law, so that all you people are compelled to be "fleeced" whenever you deal with them; the fact that the streetcar companies and the gas companies have control of the streets; and the fact that the landlords own all the earth—this, they say, has nothing to do with you.

Let us see whether there is any connection between the crimes of the respectable classes and your presence in the jail. . . .

The reformers who tell you to be good and you will be happy, and the people on the outside who have property to protect—they think that the only way to do it is by building jails and locking you up in cells on weekdays and praying for you Sundays.

I think that all of this has nothing whatever to do with right conduct. I think it is very easily seen what has to do with right conduct. Some so-called criminals—and I will use this word because it is handy, it means nothing to me—I speak of the criminals who get caught as distinguished from the criminals who catch them—some of these so-called criminals are in jail for their first offenses, but nine tenths of you are in jail because you did not have a good lawyer and, of course, you did not have a good lawyer because you did not have enough money to pay a good lawyer. There is no very great danger of a rich man going to jail.

Some of you may be here for the first time. If we would open the doors and let you out, and leave the laws as they are today, some of you would be back tomorrow. This is about as good a place as you can get anyway. There are many people here who are so in the habit of coming that they would not know where else to go. There are people who are born with the tendency to break into jail every chance they get, and they cannot avoid it. You cannot figure out your life and see why it was, but still there is a reason for it; and if we were all wise and knew all the facts, we could figure it out.

In the first place, there are a good many more people who go to jail in the wintertime than in summer. Why is this? Is it because people are more wicked in winter? No, it is because the coal trust begins to get in its grip in the winter. A few gentlemen take possession of the coal, and unless the people will pay seven or eight dollars a ton for something that is worth three dollars, they will have to freeze. Then there is nothing to do but to break into jail, and so there are many more in jail in the winter than in summer. It costs more for gas in the winter because the nights are longer, and people go to jail to save gas bills. The jails are electric-lighted. You may not know it, but these economic laws are working all the time, whether we know it or do not know it.

There are more people who go to jail in hard times than in good times—few people, comparatively, go to jail except when they are hard up. They go to jail because they have no other place to go. They may not know why, but it is true all the same. People are not more wicked in hard times. That is not the reason. The fact is true all over the world that in hard times more people go to jail than in good times, and in winter more people go to jail than in summer. Of course it is pretty hard times for people who go to jail at any time. The people who go to jail are almost always poor people—people who have no other place to live, first and last. When times are hard, then you find large numbers of people who go to jail who would not otherwise be in jail.

Long ago, Mr. Buckle, who was a great philosopher and historian, collected facts, and he showed that the number of people who are arrested increased just as the price of food increased. When they put up the price of gas ten cents a thousand, I do not know who will go to jail, but I do know that a certain number of people will go. When the meat combine raises the price of beef, I do not know who is going to jail, but I know that a large number of people are bound to go. Whenever the Standard Oil Company raises the price of oil I know that a certain number of girls who are seamstresses, and who work night after night long hours for somebody else, will be compelled to go out on the streets and ply another trade, and I know that Mr. Rockefeller and his associates are responsible and not the poor girls in the jails.

First and last, people are sent to jail because they are poor. Sometimes, as I say, you may not need money at the particular time, but you wish to have thrifty forehanded habits, and do not always wait until you are in absolute want. Some of you people are perhaps plying the trade, the profession, which is called burglary. No man in his right senses will go into a strange house in the dead of night and prowl around with a dark lantern through unfamiliar rooms and take chances of his life, if he has plenty of the good things of the world in his own home. You would not take any such chances as that. If a man had clothes in his clothes-press and beefsteak in his pantry and money in the bank, he would not navigate around nights in houses where he knows nothing about the premises whatever. It always requires experience and education for this profession, and people who fit themselves for it are no more to blame than I am for being a lawyer. A man would not hold up another man on the street if he had plenty of money in his own pocket. He might do it if he had one dollar or two dollars, but he wouldn't if he had as much money as Mr. Rockefeller has. Mr. Rockefeller has a great deal better hold-up game than that.

The more that is taken from the poor by the rich, who have the chance to take it, the more poor people there are who are compelled to resort to these means for a livelihood. They may not understand it, they may not think so at once, but after all they are driven into that line of employment.

There is a bill before the legislature of this state to punish kidnaping children with death.

We have wise members of the legislature. They know the gas trust when they see it and they always see it—they can furnish light enough to be seen; and this legislature thinks it is going to stop kidnaping children by making a law punishing kidnapers of children with death. I don't believe in kidnaping children, but the legislature is all wrong. Kidnaping children is not a crime, it is a profession. It has been developed with the times. It has been developed with our modern industrial conditions. There are many ways of making money—many new ways that our ancestors knew nothing about. Our ancestors knew nothing about a billion-dollar trust, and here comes some poor fellow who has no other trade and he discovers the profession of kidnaping children.

This crime is born, not because people are bad; people don't kidnap other people's children because they want the children or because they are devilish, but because they see a chance to get some money out of it. You cannot cure this crime by passing a law punishing by death kidnapers of children. There is one way to cure it. There is one way to cure all these offenses, and that is to give the people a chance to live. There is no other way, and there never was any other way since the world began; and the world is so blind and stupid that it will not see. If every man and woman and child in the world had a chance to make a decent, fair, honest living, there would be no jails and no lawyers and no courts. There might be some persons here or there with some peculiar formation of their brain, like Rockefeller, who would do these things simply to be doing them; but they would be very, very few, and those should be sent to a hospital and treated, and not sent to jail; and they would entirely disappear in the second generation, or at least in the third generation.

I am not talking pure theory. I will just give you two or three illustrations.

The English people once punished criminals by sending them away. They would load them on a ship and export them to Australia. England was owned by lords and nobles and rich people. They owned the whole earth over there, and the other people had to stay in the streets. They could not get a decent living. They used to take their criminals and send them to Australia—

I mean the class of criminals who got caught. When these criminals got over there, and nobody else had come, they had the whole continent to run over, and so they could raise sheep and furnish their own meat, which is easier than stealing it. These criminals then became decent, respectable people because they had a chance to live. They did not commit any crimes. They were just like the English people who sent them there, only better. And in the second generation the descendants of those criminals were as good and respectable a class of people as there were on the face of the earth, and then they began building churches and jails themselves.

A portion of this country was settled in the same way, landing prisoners down on the southern coast; but when they got here and had a whole continent to run over and plenty of chances to make a living, they became respectable citizens, making their own living just like any other citizen in the world. But finally the descendants of the English aristocracy who sent the people over to Australia found out they were getting rich, and so they went over to get possession of the earth as they always do, and they organized land syndicates and got control of the land and ores, and then they had just as many criminals in Australia as they did in England. It was not because the world had grown bad; it was because the earth had been taken away from the people.

Some of you people have lived in the country. It's prettier than it is here. And if you have ever lived on a farm you understand that if you put a lot of cattle in a field, when the pasture is short they will jump over the fence; but put them in a good field where there is plenty of pasture, and they will be law-abiding cattle to the end of time. The human animal is just like the rest of the animals, only a little more so. The same thing that governs in the one governs in the other.

Everybody makes his living along the lines of least resistance. A wise man who comes into a country early sees a great undeveloped land. For instance, our rich men twenty-five years ago saw that Chicago was small and knew a lot of people would come here and settle, and they readily saw that if they had all the land around here it would be worth a good deal, so they grabbed the land. You cannot be a landlord because somebody has got it all. You must find some other calling. In

England and Ireland and Scotland less than five per cent own all the land there is, and the people are bound to stay there on any kind of terms the landlords give. They must live the best they can, so they develop all these various professions—burglary, picking pockets, and the like.

Again, people find all sorts of ways of getting rich. These are diseases like everything else. You look at people getting rich, organizing trusts and making a million dollars, and somebody gets the disease and he starts out. He catches it just as a man catches the mumps or the measles; he is not to blame, it is in the air. You will find men speculating beyond their means, because the mania of money-getting is taking possession of them. It is simply a disease—nothing more, nothing less. You cannot avoid catching it; but the fellows who have control of the earth have the advantage of you. See what the law is: when these men get control of things, they make the laws. They do not make the laws to protect anybody; courts are not instruments of justice. When your case gets into court it will make little difference whether you are guilty or innocent, but it's better if you have a smart lawyer. And you cannot have a smart lawyer unless you have money. First and last it's a question of money. Those men who own the earth make the laws to protect what they have. They fix up a sort of fence or pen around what they have, and they fix the law so the fellow on the outside cannot get in. The laws are really organized for the protection of the men who rule the world. They were never organized or enforced to do justice. We have no system for doing justice, not the slightest in the world. . . .

The people who are on the outside, who are running banks and building churches and making jails, they have no time to examine 600 or 700 prisoners each year to see whether they are guilty or innocent. If the courts were organized to promote justice the people would elect somebody to defend all these criminals, somebody as smart as the prosecutor—and give him as many detectives and as many assistants to help, and pay as much money to defend you as to prosecute you. We have a very able man for state's attorney, and he has many assistants, detectives, and policemen without end, and judges to hear the cases—everything handy.

Most all of our criminal code consists in offenses against property. People are sent to jail because they have committed a crime against property. It is of very little consequence whether one hundred people more or less go to jail who ought not to go—you must protect property, because in this world property is of more importance than anything else.

How is it done? These people who have property fix it so they can protect what they have. When somebody commits a crime it does not follow that he has done something that is morally wrong. The man on the outside who has committed no crime may have done something. For instance: to take all the coal in the United States and raise the price two dollars or three dollars when there is no need of it, and thus kill thousands of babies and send thousands of people to the poorhouse and tens of thousands to jail, as is done every year in the United States—this is a greater crime than all the people in our jails ever committed; but the law does not punish it. Why? Because the fellows who control the earth make the laws. If you and I had the making of the laws, the first thing we would do would be to punish the fellow who gets control of the earth. Nature put this coal in the ground for me as well as for them and nature made the prairies up here to raise wheat for me as well as for them, and then the great railroad companies came along and fenced it up.

Most all of the crimes for which we are punished are property crimes. There are a few personal crimes, like murder—but they are very few. The crimes committed are mostly those against property. If this punishment is right the criminals must have a lot of property. How much money is there in this crowd? And yet you are all here for crimes against property. The people up and down the Lake Shore have not committed crime: still they have so much property they don't know what to do with it. It is perfectly plain why these people have not committed crimes against property: they make the laws and therefore do not need to break them. And in order for you to get some property you are obliged to break the rules of the game. I don't know but what some of you may have had a very nice chance to get rich by carrying a hod for one dollar a day, twelve hours. Instead of taking that nice, easy profession, you are a burglar. If you had been given a chance to be a banker you would rather follow that. Some of you may have had a chance to work as a switchman on a railroad where you know, according to statistics, that you cannot live and keep all your limbs more than seven years, and you can get fifty dollars or seventy-five dollars a month for taking your lives in your hands; and instead of taking that lucrative position you chose to be a sneak thief, or something like that. Some of you made that sort of choice. I don't know which I would take if I was reduced to this choice. I have an easier choice.

I will guarantee to take from this jail, or any jail in the world, five hundred men who have been the worst criminals and lawbreakers who ever got into jail, and I will go down to our lowest streets and take five hundred of the most abandoned prostitutes, and go out somewhere where there is plenty of land, and will give them a chance to make a living, and they will be as good people as the average in the community.

There is a remedy for the sort of condition we see here. The world never finds it out, or when it does find it out it does not enforce it. . . .

And this has been the history of the world. It's easy to see how to do away with what we call crime. It is not so easy to do it. I will tell you how to do it. It can be done by giving the people a chance to live—by destroying special privileges. So long as big criminals can get the coal fields, so long as the big criminals have control of the city council and get the public streets for streetcars and gas rights—this is bound to send thousands of poor people to jail. So long as men are allowed to monopolize all the earth, and compel others to live on such terms as these men see fit to make, then you are bound to get into jail.

The only way in the world to abolish crime and criminals is to abolish the big ones and the little ones together. Make fair conditions of life. Give men a chance to live. Abolish the right of private ownership of land, abolish monopoly, make the world partners in production, partners in the good things of life. Nobody would steal if he could get something of his own some easier way. Nobody will commit burglary when he has a house full. No girl will go out on the streets when she has a comfortable place at home. The man who owns a sweatshop or a department store may not be to blame himself for the conditions of his girls, but when he pays them five dollars, three dollars, and two dollars a week, I wonder where he thinks they will get the rest of their money to live. The only way to cure these conditions is by equality. There should be no jails. They do not accomplish what they pretend to accomplish. If you would wipe them out there would be no more criminals than now. They terrorize nobody. They are a blot upon any civilization, and a jail is an evidence of the lack of charity of the people on the outside who make the jails and fill them with the victims of their greed.

*Notes and Questions*

1. Do you think these images of law should have been given to prisoners? In the introduction to the lecture, which he had printed in pamphlet form and sold for 5 cents, Darrow wrote:

   Realizing the force of the suggestion that the truth should not be spoken to all people, I have caused these remarks to be printed on rather good paper and in a somewhat expensive form. In this way the truth does not become cheap and vulgar, and is only placed before those whose intelligence and affluence will prevent their being influenced by it.

   It was said that one of the prisoners in the audience commented that the speech was "too radical." What might Darrow have said that this remark showed about that prisoner?

2. If Darrow thinks that jails are the invention of the ruling class, how can he say that some people are "born with the tendency to break into jail"?

3. Does Darrow assume that the basic motivation of all people is to get rich? Why does he view the drive for wealth as a basic social problem? What are the implications of the fact that the law may protect and even encourage the accumulation of wealth? In considering this question, note the following analysis of the relation between law and wealth in the U.S. Constitution:

   The nation's Founding Fathers were acutely aware of the latent contradiction in the democratic form of government, as indeed were most political thinkers in the late eighteenth and early nineteenth centuries. They recognized the possibility that the propertyless majority might, once it had the vote, attempt to turn its nominal sovereignty into real power and thereby jeopardize the security of property, which they regarded as the very foundation of civilized society. They therefore devised the famous system of checks and balances, the purpose of which was to make it as difficult as possible for the existing system of property relations to be subverted. American capitalism later developed in a context of numerous and often bitter struggles among various groups and segments of the moneyed classes—which had never been united, as in Europe, by a common struggle against feudal power. For these and other reasons, the governmental institutions which have taken shape in the United States have been heavily weighted on the side of protecting the rights and privileges of minorities: the property-owning minority as a whole against the people, and various groups of property-owners against each other.*

4. Clarence Darrow abandoned a lucrative career in corporate law to represent Eugene Debs and other workers in the 1894 Pullman strike. He was a strong opponent of the death penalty. Why do you suppose that Darrow's images of law are not more widely known in America, especially since his reputation as a criminal defense lawyer is almost legendary? (How do you suppose Darrow would answer this question?)

5. Does it seem reasonable to you to think of kidnapping and theft as ways of surviving in a capitalist economy?

6. What do you think people's main aim in life would be if "every man and woman and child in the world had a chance to make a decent, fair, honest living"?

7. Emma Goldman, 1869–1940, became famous as an anarchist and feminist in America, and was imprisoned several times on such charges as inciting to riot, advocating birth control, and obstructing the draft. As you think further about what Darrow said to the prisoners, consider Goldman's remarks on law, order, and crime:

Order derived through submission and maintained by terror is not much of a safe guaranty; yet that is the only "order" that governments have ever maintained. True social harmony grows naturally out of solidarity of interests. In a society where those who always work never have anything, while those who never work enjoy everything, solidarity of interests is non-existent; hence social harmony is but a myth. The only way organized authority meets this grave situation is by extending still greater privileges to those who have already monopolized the earth, and by still further enslaving the disinherited masses. Thus the entire arsenal of government—laws, police, soldiers, the courts, legislatures, prisons—is strenuously engaged in "harmonizing" the most antagonistic elements in society. . . .

Crime is naught but misdirected energy. So long as every institution of today, economic, political, social, and moral, conspires to misdirect human energy into wrong channels; so long as most people are out of place doing the things they hate to do, living a life they loathe to live, crime will be inevitable, and all the laws on the statutes can only increase, but never do away with, crime.[†]

8. In thinking about the relationship between democratic government and wealth, consider the following comments by Henry Carter Adams, historian and political economist:

When a . . . government desires to borrow money it must divest itself for the time being of all sovereign powers, and come before its subjects as a private corporation. It must bargain with those who have money to lend, and satisfy them as to questions of payment and security. . . . The broad theory of constitutional liberty is that the people have the right to govern themselves; but the historical fact is that, in the attempt to realize this theory, the actual control of public affairs has fallen into the hands of those who possess property. It follows from this that when property-owners lend to the government, they lend to a corporation controlled by themselves.[‡]

---

*Paul A. Baran and Paul M. Sweezy, *Monopoly Capital* (New York: Modern Reader, 1966), pp. 157–158.

[†]Alix Schulman, ed., *Red Emma Speaks* (New York: Vintage, 1972), p. 57.

[‡]Henry Carter Adams, *Public Debts: An Essay in the Science of Finance* (New York: D. Appleton, 1887), pp. 7, 9.

9. Consider also the following comments by Adam Smith about the relationship between property and law:

> . . . Wherever there is great property, there is great inequality. For one very rich man, there must be at least five hundred poor, and the affluence of the few supposes the indigence of the many. The affluence of the rich excites the indignation of the poor, who are often both driven by want, and prompted by envy, to invade his possessions. It is only under the shelter of the civil magistrate that the owner of that valuable property, which is acquired by the labor of many years, or perhaps of many successive generations, can sleep a single night in security. He is at all times surrounded by unknown enemies, whom, though he never provoked, he can never appease, and from whose injustice he can be protected only by the powerful arm of the civil magistrate continually held up to chastise it. The acquisition of valuable and extensive property, therefore, necessarily requires the establishment of civil government. Where there is no property, or at least none that exceeds the value of two or three days labor, civil government is not so necessary. . . .
>
> . . . The rich, in particular, are necessarily interested to support that order of things, which can alone secure them in the possession of their own advantages. Men of inferior wealth combine to defend those of superior wealth in the possession of their property, in order that men of superior wealth may combine to defend them in the possession of theirs. All the inferior shepherds and herdsmen feel that the security of their own herds and flocks depends upon the security of those of the great shepherd or herdsmen; that the maintenance of their lesser authority depends upon that of his greater authority, and that upon their subordination to him depends his power of keeping their inferiors in subordination to them. They constitute a sort of little nobility, who feel themselves interested to defend the property and to support the authority of their own little sovereign, in order that he may be able to defend their property and to support their authority. Civil government, so far as it is instituted for the security of property, is in reality instituted for the defense of the rich against the poor, or of those who have some property against those who have none at all.[§]

---

[§]Adam Smith, *An Inquiry into the Nature and Causes of the Wealth of Nations*, 4th ed., vol. 2 (Dublin: Colles, Moncrieffe, et al., 1785), pp. 224–225, 229.

---

## 8.3   America's Crude Approach to Crime and Punishment

*James Carroll*

WHAT WILL IT MEAN for America if Bill Clinton is charged as a criminal? The question emerges from reports that independent counsel Robert W. Ray is reiterating the perjury and misconduct case against the president before a new grand jury, issues tied to the Paula Jones and Monica Lewinsky matters. To some, an indictment of the president, before or after he leaves office, would be a welcome reassertion of the principle that no one is above the law. To others, such an event would be a sordid exercise in partisan politics, a sign more of the pathology of Clinton's enemies than of the virtue of justice. I fall into this latter group.

But the question has larger implications than the old debates between Democrats and Republicans, liberals and conservatives, or between libertarians and puritans, for that matter. In the unfolding presidential campaign, much attention is being paid to the rhetoric of values and religion, but the test of a society's spiritual health is a matter not of the gods invoked but of the way it responds to certain fundamental human problems. Most obviously, how a nation deals with war and peace provides a far more reliable measure of its moral character than how it worships.

For example, religious life in Germany remained vital throughout the Nazi period, and the overt spiritual commitments of the population proved to be remarkably irrelevant to its capacity for moral discernment. According to the scholar William Sheridan Allen, by 1940, seven years after Hitler came to power and after he had launched his brutal war, 95 percent of the German population was still affiliated with a church. From all reports, instead of that affiliation prompting dissent from the quite evident Nazi program, it reinforced broad German cooperation with evil.

As revealing as attitudes toward war and peace are, so are social responses to crime and punishment. That the two phrases are enshrined in the titles of great Russian novels is a clue to their significance as signals of communal character. In fact the question of judicial retribution goes even deeper than that of military ethics, since even before confronting enemies abroad, society must organize itself around norms and their observance. Are those who violate such norms automatically dealt with as enemies within? Or can we distinguish among kinds of violation, and can we construct a judicial system on the basic fact of life that no member of society perfectly realizes its ideal? How do we respond to one another when we make mistakes, or when we fail to keep promises, or when we abuse the trust we've been given? When offenses are committed, how do we balance the human need for revenge against the social benefit of rehabilitation? And how do we know when an offender has been punished enough?

These questions seem so fundamental that it is hard to believe an advanced democracy like ours regularly shows itself incapable of answering them. The solid American commitment to capital punishment, which subliminally manifests a quasi-religious faith in human sacrifice, is one indicator that something is askew in our moral reasoning about crime and punishment. Another is the burgeoning prison industry: A few days ago the Justice Department reported that last year, 1,284,894 people were incarcerated in this country.

The figure, presumably, is higher today. An even greater number of children under 18 has a parent in prison. No country in the world approaches such rates of social breakdown. And as is well known, many of the incarcerated have been consigned to the hyper-violent culture of prison for crimes that involved no violence. Indeed, many violations of social norms are simplistically defined as crimes when in fact they could be more humanely and practically dealt with as problems of mental health, consequences of addiction, or even failures to learn.

In most aspects of American culture, we have developed tremendously nuanced responses to economic, organizational, and political challenges, but when it comes to crime and punishment, we are content to respond with the crude, often discredited methods of the past. Our prisons are the social and moral equivalents of the poor houses and debtors' jails to which the destitute were once routinely condemned. Someday the hyper-prisons that salt the American landscape will offend moral sensibility the way the grotesque insane asylums and cruel orphanages of the past do today.

The unsubtle American way of dealing with crime and punishment is to say, If you cross us, we will smash you. And that is where Bill Clinton's fate comes in. If the legal system deems that this most profoundly disgraced man has not been punished enough; if his fully admitted and acknowledged abuse of the public trust is now criminalized, with an indictment and trial; if the media rituals of humiliation are now to be performed over his head again—it will, alas, only be business as usual in this country.

Thousands upon thousands of men and women whose names we do not know have already been shown as little mercy for their mistakes. Their cases have been adjudicated with as little concern for the broader social welfare. The presidential campaign reveals an America profoundly self-satisfied with its religion, values, morality, virtue—but this same America blithely maintains an approach to human fallibility and, yes, criminal behavior that knows nothing of mercy, wisdom, forgiveness or the time to say, Enough!

## Notes and Questions

1. Carroll asks, " . . . Can we distinguish among kinds of violation. . . . ?" In thinking about this question, consider the following:

The federal Anti-Drug Abuse Act of 1986 created minimum sentences for drug crimes, based solely on the weight of the drug—or in the case of LSD, the "mixture or substance" containing the drug. One gram gets five years, ten grams gets ten years; double it for a second offense. Other than the standard 15 percent reduction for good behavior, the law forbids parole. There is no consideration of character or circumstances. The judge may not even consider the defendant's role in the crime—mastermind or messenger, if a gram was involved, everybody gets five years. The only way around the minimum is to give "substantial assistance," i.e. to snitch. Since the passage of mandatory minimums the number of drug convicts in the U.S. has more than tripled.

A breathtaking list of organizations have come out in opposition to mandatory minimums, including the U.S. Sentencing Commission, the Federal Courts Study Committee, the American Bar Association, the National Association of Veteran Police Officers, and the American Civil Liberties Union.

"There is no single issue affecting the work of the federal courts with respect to which there is such unanimity," according to Judge Vincent Broderick, chair of the Criminal Law Committee of the Judicial Conference of the U.S. "Most federal judges . . . believe . . . that mandatory minimums are the major obstacle to the development of a fair, rational, honest and proportional federal criminal justice sentencing system."

At least one federal judge has resigned in protest. Reagan appointee J. Lawrence Irving left the bench in 1991 because he felt that the drug sentences he was forced to impose were often "Draconian." "The sentences are too long; there is no logic to them," . . . "I just hope that sometime Congress comes to their senses and changes the laws."

Supreme Court Justice John Paul Stevens has written that the law's consequences for LSD defendants are "so bizarre that I cannot believe they were intended by Congress."

Eric Sterling, former counsel to the House Judiciary Committee, helped write the law. He now calls it "frighteningly unjust" and says Congress's primary aim when it rushed to pass the legislation was "to vaccinate the Democrats against soft-on-crime charges after Reagan had pounded them on the issue in 1984." Today he is president of the Criminal Justice Policy Foundation in Washington, DC.*

*Thea Kelley and Dennis Bernstein, "LSD, Deadheads, and the Law," *Z Magazine*, April, 1996, p. 43.

## 8.4 | The Rule of Law Versus the Order of Custom  *Stanley Diamond*

The lowest police employee of the civilized state has more "authority" than all the organs of gentilism combined. But the mightiest prince and the greatest statesman or general of civilization may look with envy on the spontaneous and undisputed esteem that was the privilege of the least gentile sachem. The one stands in the middle of society, the other is forced to assume a position outside and above it.

[Friedrich] Engels

. . . WE LIVE IN A law-ridden society; law has cannibalized the institutions which it presumably rein-

Stanley Diamond, "The Rule of Law Versus the Order of Custom" in *In Search of the Primitive* (New Brunswick, NJ: Transaction Books, 1974).

forces or with which it interacts. . . . [W]e are encouraged to assume that legal behavior is the measure of moral behavior. . . . Efforts to legislate conscience by an external political power are the antithesis of custom: customary behavior comprises precisely those aspects of social behavior which are traditional, moral and religious—in short, conventional and nonlegal. Put another way, custom is social morality. The relation between custom and law is basically one of contradiction, not continuity.

. . . William Seagle writes:

> The dispute whether primitive societies
> have law or custom, is not merely a dispute
> over words. Only confusion can result
> from treating them as interchangeable
> phenomena. If custom is spontaneous and
> automatic, law is the product of organized
> force. . . .

Thus, law is symptomatic of the emergence of the state. . . . Custom—spontaneous, traditional, personal, commonly known, corporate, relatively unchanging—is the modality of primitive society; law is the instrument of civilization, of political society sanctioned by organized force, presumably above society at large and buttressing a new set of social interests. Law and custom both involve the regulation of behavior but their characters are entirely distinct. . . .

## ARCHAIC LAW AND LOCAL CUSTOM

The simple dichotomy between primitive society and civilization does not illustrate the passage from the customary to the legal order. The most critical and revealing period in the evolution of law is that of archaic societies, the local segments of which are the cultures most often studied by anthropologists. More precisely, the earlier phases of these societies, which I call proto-states, represent a transition from the primitive kinship-based communities to the class-structured polity. In such polities, law and custom exist side by side; this gives us the opportunity to examine their connections, distinctions and differential relationship to the society at large. The customary behavior typical of the local groups—joint families, clans, villages—maintains most of its force; the Vietnamese, for example, still say: "The customs of the village are stronger than the law of the emperor." Simultaneously, the civil power, comprising bureaucracy and sovereign, the dominant emerging class, issues a series of edicts that

have the double purpose of confiscating "surplus" goods and labor for the support of those not directly engaged in production, while attempting to deflect the loyalties of the local groups to the center. These archaic societies are the great historical watershed; it is here that Sir Henry Maine and Paul Vinogradoff [legal historians] located the passage from status to contract, from the kinship to the territorial principle, from extended familial controls to public law. For our understanding of the law, we need not be concerned with the important distinctions among archaic societies, or with the precise language or emphases of those scholars who have recognized their centrality. The significant point is that they are transitional. Particularly in their early phase, they are the agencies that transmute customary forms of order into legal sanction. . . . The following example from the archaic proto-state of Dahomey, prior to the French conquest in 1892, will make this process clear.

Traditionally in Dahomey, each person was said to have three "best" friends, in descending order of intimacy and importance. This transitional institution, . . . of the same species as blood brotherhood, reinforced the extended family structure, which continued to exist in the early state, but was being thrown into question as a result of the political and economic demands made by the emerging civil power. So for example, the best friend . . . of a man charged with a civil crime could be seized by the king's police in his stead. However, these traditional friendships were so socially critical, so deeply held, so symbolically significant that the person charged, whether or not he had actually committed a civil breach, would be expected to turn himself in rather than implicate a friend in his punishment. Whether or not he did so, the custom of friendship was given a legal edge and converted by the civil power into a means of enforcing its will. This example . . . has the virtue of explicitly revealing the contradiction between law and custom. But there are other examples in which the law appears as a reinforcement of customary procedure.

In eleventh-century Russia, for instance, Article 1 of the codified law states:

> If a man kills a man . . . the brother is to
> avenge his brother; the son, his father; or the

father, his son; and the son of the brother (of the murdered man) or the son of his sister, their respective uncle. If there is no avenger (the murderer) pays 40 grivna wergeld. . . .

Similarly, circa A.D. 700, the law of the Visigoths states: "Whoever shall have killed a man, whether he committed a homicide intending to or not intending to . . . let him be handed over into the potestas of the parents or next of kin of the deceased. . . ." In these instances, a custom has been codified by an external agency, thus assuming legal force, with its punitive character sharpened. Such confirmation is both the intimation of legal control and the antecedent of institutional change beyond the wish or conception of the family. . . .

[Sydney P.] Simpson and [Julius] Stone [law and society scholars] explain this apparent reinforcement of custom by the civil power as follows:

> Turning then to the role of law in the emergent political society . . . it is true that political institutions, independent of the kin and the supernatural, had risen to power; yet these institutions were young, weak and untried. Their encroachment on the old allegiance was perforce wary and hesitating. Social cohesion still seemed based on nonpolitical elements, and these elements were therefore protected. . . .

Ultimately, local groups have maintained their autonomy when their traditional economies were indispensable to the functioning of the entire society. They could be hedged around by restrictions, harassed by law or as we have seen, they could be "legally" confirmed in their customary usage. But so long as the central power depended on them for support, in the absence of any alternative mode or source of production, their integrity could be substantially preserved. . . .

As the state develops, according to Maine, "the individual is steadily substituted for the family as the unit of which civil laws take account." And in R. von Jhering's [scholar of Roman law] words, "The progress of law consists in the destruction of every natural tie, in a continued process of separation and isolation." . . . The legal stipulation that spouses may not testify against each other appears as one of the last formal acknowledgements of familial integrity and the exception that proves the historical case. Clearly, the nuclear family in contemporary, urban civilization, although bound by legal obligations, has minimal autonomy; obviously, the means of education, subsistence and self-defense are outside the family's competence. It is in this sense that, given the absence of mediating institutions having a clearly defined independent authority, the historical tendency of all state structures vis-à-vis the individual may be designated as totalitarian. Indeed, the state creates the disaffiliated individual whose bearings thus become bureaucratic or collective; the juridical "person," who may even be a corporation doing business, is merely the legal reflection of a social process. If "totalization" is the state process, totalitarianism cannot be confined to a particular political ideology but is, so to speak, the ideology, explicit or not, of political society.

This étatist tendency has its origins in archaic society. We can observe it with unusual clarity in the proto-states of sub-Saharan Africa. In East Africa, pastoralists, competing for land, and in West Africa, militaristic clans, catalyzed by the Arab, and later, the European trade, notably in slaves, conquered horticulturalists, thereby providing the major occasions for the growth of civil power. . . . [W]e can reconstruct through chronicles extending back for centuries and by means of contemporary field work, the structure of early state controls. . . .

In such societies, [anthropologist R. S.] Rattray tells us, referring to Ashanti:

> the small state was ever confronted with the kindred organization which was always insidiously undermining its authority by placing certain persons outside its jurisdiction. It could only hold its own, therefore, by throwing out an ever-widening circle to embrace those loyalties which were lost to it owing to the workings of the old tribal organization which has survived everywhere. . . .

Concerning the Islamized Nupe of the Nigerian Middle Belt, [anthropologist S. F.] Nadel saw "a much more subtle development and a deeper kind of antagonism [than interstate warfare], namely, the almost eternal antagonism of developed State versus that raw material of the Community which, always and everywhere, must form the nourishing soil from which alone the state can grow." And Engels refers to the "irreconcilable opposition of gentile society to the state."

I have documented this conflict in detail in a study of the Dahomean proto-state. There, as elsewhere, it is apparent that the contradictory transition from customs to specified laws . . . is by no means the major source of law. Whether the law arises latently in confirmation of previous usage or through the transformation of some aspect of custom which the law itself may have provoked, as in the ambiguous example of the "best friend," neither circumstance brings us to the heart of the matter. For we learn, by studying intermediate societies, that the laws so typical of them are unprecedented. . . . They arise in opposition to the customary order of the antecedent kin or kin-equivalent groups; they represent a new set of social goals pursued by a new and unanticipated power in society. These goals can be reduced to a single complex imperative: the imposition of the census-tax-conscription system. The territorial thrust of the early state, along with its vertical social entrenchment, demanded conscription of labor, the mustering of an army, the levying of taxes and tribute, the maintenance of a bureaucracy and the assessment of the extent, location and numbers of the population being subjected. These were the major direct or indirect occasions for the development of civil law.

The primary purpose of a census is indicative. Census figures provide the basis on which taxes are apportioned among conquered districts and on which tribute in labor is exacted from kin units. The census is also essential for conscripting men into the army. . . .

The census figures represented the potential power of the state and were carefully guarded; perhaps they were the first state secret. The act and intent of the census turned persons into ciphers and abstractions; people did all they could to avoid being counted. Suspicion persists; even in the United States the authorities during the period of census taking find it necessary to assert that census information will not be used to tax or

otherwise penalize the individual and in fact, to do so is said to be against the law.

The double meanings of certain critical terms in common English use—"custom," "duty" and "court," reveal this conflict between local usage and the census-tax-conscription system of the early state. We have been speaking of custom as traditional or conventional nonlegal behavior, but custom also refers to a tax routinely payable to the state for the transportation of goods across territorial borders. . . .

Fiscal or legal coercion and political imposition were not the purpose of . . . ancestral ceremonies which ritually reenacted reciprocal bonds. The customs of the sovereign were laws, the ceremonies of the kin groups were customs.

Similarly, the term duty implies a moral obligation on the one hand and a tax on the other. . . . [T]he paradox inherent in the term becomes more obvious as we examine archaic civilizations.

The term *court* is analogously ambivalent. On the one hand, it refers to the residence or entourage of the sovereign; on the other, to a place where civil justice is dispensed, but at their root the functions fuse. The prototypical juridical institution was, in fact, the court of the sovereign where legislation was instituted, for which no precedent or formal analogue existed on the local level. . . .

Clearly, the function of the court was not primarily the establishment of order. In primitive societies, as in the traditional sectors of proto-states, there already existed built-in mechanisms for the resolution of conflict. Generally speaking (as Max Gluckman, among others, has shown), in such societies conflicts generated by the ordinary functioning of social institutions were resolved as part of the customary ritual cycle integral to the institutions themselves. With regard to more specific breaches, we recall Rattray's observation on the Ashanti: "Corporate responsibility for every act was an established principle which survived even the advent of . . . the administration of public justice." That is to say the kin unit was the juridical unit, just as it was the economic and social unit. Furthermore,

Causes which give rise to the greater part of present "civil" actions were practically nonexistent. Inheritance, ownership of moveable and nonmoveable property, status of individuals, rules of behavior and morality were matters inevitably settled by the customary law, with which everyone was familiar from childhood, and litigation regarding such matters was . . . almost inconceivable. Individual contract, moreover, from the very nature of the community with which we are concerned, was also unknown, thus removing another possible, fruitful source of litigation.

. . . In the census-tax-conscription system, every conceivable occasion was utilized for the creation of law in support of bureaucracy and sovereign. We observe no abstract principle, no impartial justice, no precedent, only the spontaneous opportunism of a new class designing the edifice of its power. It should be re-emphasized, however, that in certain instances . . . analogues . . . existed on the local level, but no formal or functional precedents. Civil taxation, for example, can be rationalized in the context of reciprocal gift-giving in the localities . . . , similarly, corvee labor is a political analogue of local cooperative work groups. But such evolutionary and dialectical relationships are most important for their distinctions.

[Legal historian William] Stubbs writes about the Norman kings that "it was mainly for the sake of the profits that early justice was administered at all." [Captain Sir Richard] Burton relates that at Whydah in Dahomey in the event of a financial dispute, the Yevogan, the leading bureaucrat in the district, sat in judgment. For his services, he appropriated half the merchandise involved, in the name of the king and another quarter for various lesser officials. The remainder presumably went to the winning contestant in the judicial duel. Among the Ashanti, the central authority relied on the proceeds of litigation as a fruitful means for replenishing a depleted treasury. Litigation, Rattray notes, came actually to be encouraged.

Tolls were an important source of revenue. In Ashanti, the king had all the roads guarded; all traders were detained until inquiries were made about them, whereupon they were allowed to pass on payment of gold dust. [Explorer]

W. Bosman writes that in early eighteenth century Whydah, "in proportion to his country, the king's revenue is very large, of which I believe, he hath above one thousand collectors who dispose themselves throughout the whole land in all market roads and passages, in order to gather the king's toll which amounts to an incredible sum, for there is nothing so mean sold in the whole kingdom that the king hath no toll for it. . . ."

The punishment for the theft of property designated as the king's was summary execution by kangaroo courts organized on the spot by the king's agents. . . .

In [legal historian Frederic William] Maitland's words, "the king has a peace that devours all others." If in these proto-states, the sovereign power is not yet fully effective, it nonetheless strives to that monopoly of force which characterizes the mature state.

The purpose and abundance of laws inevitably provoked breaches. The civil authority, in fact, continually probed for breaches and frequently manufactured them. . . .

Thus, rape was invented as a civil crime. If rape had occurred in the traditional joint-family villages . . . , the wrong could have been dealt with by composition (the ritualized giving of goods to the injured party), ritual purification, ridicule and, perhaps for repeated transgressions, banishment; the customary machinery would have gone into effect automatically, probably on the initiative of the family of the aggressor. Such examples as this only sharpen the point that in early states crimes seem to have been invented to suit the laws. The latent purpose of the law was punishment in the service and profit of the state, not prevention or the protection of persons, not the healing of the breach. . . .

. . . For [another] example, civil protection of the market place or highway was certainly not necessary to the degree implied in the archaic edicts at the time they were issued. Joint-family markets and village trails were not ordinarily dangerous places, if we are to believe the reports of the earliest chroniclers as well as those of more contemporary observers. More significantly if trouble had developed, the family, clan or village was capable of dealing with it. But, in an evolving state, the presence of the king's men would itself be a primary cause of disruption. Indeed, as

[M.] Quenum, a descendant of Dahomean commoners, informs us the soldiers were referred to as bandits and predators who victimized many people. Sometimes their forays were confined to a compound, where someone, whether man, woman, or child, resided who had spoken badly of the sovereign or whom the king suspected. . . .

As the integrity of the local groups declined, a process which . . . must have taken generations or even centuries, conditions doubtless developed which served as an ex post facto rationalization for edicts already in effect. In this sense, laws became self-fulfilling prophecies. Crime and the laws which served it were, then, covariants of the evolving state. . . .

The intention of the civil power is epitomized in the sanctions against homicide and suicide; indeed, they were among the very first civil laws. Just as the sovereign is said to own the land, intimating the mature right of eminent domain, so the individual is ultimately conceived as the chattel of the state. In Dahomey, persons were conceived as *les choses du monarque* [property of the monarch]. Eminent domain in persons and property, even where projected as a fiction, is the cardinal prerequisite of the census-tax-conscription system. We recall that Maine designated the individual the unit of which the civil law steadily takes account. [Legal historian William] Seagle stated the matter as follows: "By undermining the kinship bond, they [the early civil authorities] made it easier to deal with individuals, and the isolation of the individual is a basic precondition for the growth of law."

Homicide, then, was regarded as an offense against the state. In Rattray's words, "The blow which struck down the dead man would thus appear to have been regarded as aimed also at the . . . central authority." In Ashanti, homicide was punishable by death in its most horrible form as customarily defined, in Dahomey, by death or conscription into the army. . . .

Traditionally, murder in a joint-family village was a tort—a private, remediable wrong—which could stimulate a blood feud, not to be confused with the *lex talionis* [law of revenge], until redress, though not necessarily injury in kind, was achieved. But a breach was most often settled by composition. As [anthropologist] Paul Radin put it: "The theory of an eye for an eye . . . never really held for primitive people. . . . Rather it was replacement for loss with damages." And this is echoed by [anthropologist J. G.] Peristiany: "they claim restitution or private damages and not social retribution." In any case, the family was fully involved. "The family was a corporation," said Rattray, and "it is not easy to grasp what must have been the effect . . . of untold generations of thinking and acting . . . in relation to one's group. The Ashanti's idea of what we term moral responsibility for his actions must surely have been more developed than in peoples where individualism is the order of the day." This more or less typical anthropological observation makes it clear that the law against homicide was not a "progressive" step. . . . "Anti-social conduct [is] exceptional in small kinship groups," writes [anthropologist] Margery Perham of the Igbo. Crimes of violence were rare, Richard Burton reported of Dahomey, and "murder virtually unknown."

Acts of violence, of course, must be distinguished from crimes of violence. The incidence, occasion for, and character of violence in primitive societies is a subject of the utmost importance. But the question here has to do with crimes in which violence is used as a means to an end, such as the theft of property. In contemporary societies, unpremeditated acts of personal violence that have no ulterior motive, so-called crimes of passion, may not be penalized or carry minor degrees of guilt, that is, their status as legally defined crimes is ambiguous. This would certainly seem to reflect a historically profound distinction between crime and certain types of violence; in primitive societies violence tends to be personally structured, nondissociative and thereby self-limiting. As with other crimes defined by civil law, crimes of violence may have increased as the social autonomy, economic communalism and reciprocity of the kin units weakened. . . .

The law against suicide, a capital offense, was the apotheosis of political absurdity. The individual, it was assumed, had no right to take his own life; that was the sole prerogative of the state, whose property he was conceived to be. The fanatical nature of the civil legislature in claiming sole prerogative to the lives of its subjects is conclusively revealed among the Ashanti, where, if the suicide was a murderer, "the central authority refused to be cheated thus and the long arm of the law followed the suicide to the grave from which, if his kinsmen should have dared to bury him, he was dragged to stand trial." This contrasts remarkably, if logically, with the behavior of the more primitively structured Igbo, as reported by Victor Uchendu, an anthropologist who is himself an Igbo:

> Homicide is an offense against ala—the earth deity. If a villager is involved, the murderer is expected to hang himself, after which . . . daughters of the village perform the rite of . . . sweeping away the ashes of murder. If the murderer has fled, his extended family must also flee, and the property of all is subject to raids. When the murderer is eventually caught, he is required to hang himself to enable the [daughters of the village] to perform their rites. It is important to realize that the village has no power to impose capital punishment. In fact, no social group or institution has this power. Everything affecting the life of the villager is regulated by custom. The life of the individual is highly respected; it is protected by the earth-goddess. The villagers can bring social pressure, but the murderer must hang himself.

It can hardly be argued that the purpose of the civil sanction against suicide was to diminish its incidence or to propagate a superior moral consciousness. Dare we say, as with other crimes, that attempts at suicide increased as society became more thoroughly politicized? The law against suicide reveals, in the extreme, the whole meaning and intent of civil law at its origins. In the proto-state, the quintessential struggle was over the lives and labor of the people, who, still moving in a joint family context, were nonetheless conceived to be *les choses du monarque.*

## LAW AND DISORDER

If revolutions are the acute, episodic signs of civilizational discontent, the rule of law, from Sumer or Akkad to New York or Moscow, has been the chronic symptom of the disorder of institutions. [Anthropologist] E. B. Tylor stated: "A constitutional government, whether called republic or kingdom, is an arrangement by which the nation governs itself by means of the machinery of a military despotism."

The generalization lacks nuance, but we can accept it if we bear in mind what seems to be Tylor's point of reference: "Among the lessons to be learnt from the life of rude tribes is how society can go without the policeman to keep order." When he alludes to constitutional government, Tylor was not distinguishing its ultimate sanction from that of any other form of the state: all political society is based on repressive organized force. In this he was accurate. For pharaohs and presidents alike have always made a public claim to represent the common interest, indeed to incarnate the common good. Only a Plato or a Machiavelli in search of political harmony, or a Marx in search of political truth, has been able to penetrate this myth of the identity between ruler and ruled, of equality under the law. The tradition of Plato and Machiavelli commends the use of the "royal" or "noble lie," while that of Marx exposes and rejects the power structure (ultimately the state) that propagates so false a political consciousness. On this issue I follow Marx. . . .

The legal order, which Plato idealized, is as Tylor maintained and Marx understood, synonymous with the power of the state. "The state," writes Paul Vinogradoff, "has assumed the monopoly of political co-ordination. It is the state which rules, makes laws and eventually enforces them by coercion. Such a state did not exist in ancient times. The commonwealth was not centered in one sovereign body towering immeasurably above single individuals and meting out to everyone his portion of right." And Engels, on reflecting on the origins of the state, asserts: "The right of the state to existence was founded on the preservation of order in the interior and the protection against the barbarians outside, but this order was worse than the most disgusting disorder, and the barbarians against whom the state pretended to protect its citizens were hailed by them as saviors." Moreover, "The state created a public power of coercion that did no longer coincide with the old self-organized and (self) armed population." Finally, in a passage that epitomizes the West's awareness of itself, Engels writes:

> The state, then, is by no means a power forced on society at a certain stage of evolution. It is the confession that this society has become hopelessly divided against itself, has estranged itself in irreconcilable contradictions which it is powerless to banish. In order that these contradictions, these classes with conflicting economic interests may not annihilate themselves and society in a useless struggle, a power becomes necessary that stands apparently above society and has the function of keeping down the conflicts and maintaining "order." And this power, the outgrowth of society, but assuming supremacy over it and becoming more and more divorced from it, is the state. . . .

In a word, the state is the alienated form of society. . . .

## THE RESPONSE TO CIVIL LAW

. . . Finally, we are led to ask, as did Nadel about the Nupe:

> What did the tax-paying law-abiding citizen receive in return for allegiance to king and nobility? Was extortion, bribery, brutal force, the only aspect under which the state revealed itself to the populace? The people were to receive, theoretically, on the whole, one thing: security—protection against external and internal enemies, and general security for carrying out the daily work, holding markets, using the roads. We have seen what protection and security meant in reality. At their best, they represented something very unequal and very unstable. This situation must have led to much tension and change within the system and to frequent attempts to procure better safeguards for civil rights.

The struggle for civil rights, then, is a response to the imposition of civil law. . . .

Procedure is the individual's last line of defense in contemporary civilization, wherein all other associations to which he may belong have become subordinate to the state. The elaboration of procedure is a unique if fragile feature of more fully evolved states, in compensation, so to speak, for the radical isolation of the individual; procedure permits the individual to hold the line, while working toward associations designed to replace the state. In the proto-states, the harshness of rudimentary procedure was countered by the role of the kinship units which, as we recall, retained a significant measure of functional socio-economic autonomy and, therefore, of local political cohesion. But "law has its origin in the pathology of social relations and functions only when there are frequent disturbances of the social equilibrium." Law arises in the breach of a prior customary order and increases in force with the conflicts that divide political societies internally and among themselves. Law and order is the historical illusion; law versus order is the historical reality. . . .

## *Notes and Questions*

1. Diamond says that custom is definite and known, whereas law is vague and uncertain. What does he mean? Consider the following court opinion:

   > [The Naturalization Law provides] that the court must "be satisfied that" the applicant . . . "has behaved as a man of a good moral character, attached to the principles of the constitution of the United States, and well disposed to the good order and happiness of the same." It is of course true that repeated and deliberate violation of any ordinance indicates the absence, *pro tanto,* of that obedience to the will of the community that is the duty of all citizens. That would be true, for example, of those regulations now common that provide waste baskets for litter which one must use so as not to clog the pavement or the roadway. A purist may indeed argue that, if clean streets are a part of the "good order" of a city, when anyone deliberately and persistently refuses to use such baskets, it proves that he is not "well disposed to the good order" of the city. However, such a rigid interpretation of the words seems to us unduly to enlarge their proper scope. Like any other statute, this one is to be read with its purposes in mind, which

are to admit as citizens only those who are in general accord with the basic principles of the community. Disregard of parking regulations, even when repeated as often as this was, is not inimical to its "good order," so construed. . . .

We should of course yield to the text, when the text is plain, but "good order" is a word of vague content: particularly when used as an alternate to "good moral character." If it be answered that this bases our construction on our personal judgment of the public importance of the conduct involved, we agree. Not infrequently a legislature means to leave to the judges the appraisal of some of the values at stake. For example, those rights, criminal and civil, that are measured by what is "reasonable," really grant to courts such a "legislative" power, although we call the issues questions of fact. They require of the judges the compromise that they think in accord with the general purposes of the measure as the community would understand it. We are of course aware of the resulting uncertainties involved in such an interpretation; but the alternative would be specifically to provide for each situation that can arise, a substitute utterly impractical in operation. We can say no more than that we think it plain that this statute did not mean to make naturalization depend upon obedience to such a regulation as that before us. . . . In the case at bar we hold that disobedience to the parking regulations of a great city, even though repeated and deliberate, does not show a disposition contrary to the "good order" of the United States; and was a permissible delegation of power.*

2. Vine Deloria, Jr., has contrasted the "two concepts of community" that differentiate Native American Indian tribal culture from Anglo-European civilization. Compare his description of contemporary American society with Diamond's analysis of the economic basis of law:

Today the land is dotted with towns, cities, suburbs, and the like. Yet very few of these political subdivisions are in fact communities. They are rather transitory locations for the temporary existence of wage earners. People come and go as the economics of the situation demand. They join churches and change churches as their business and economic successes dictate. . . . People may live side by side for years having in common only their property boundaries and their status as property taxpayers. . . . Today many of the Indian tribes are undergoing profound changes with respect to their traditional solidarity. . . . Massive economic development programs on the reservations have caused population shifts that have tended to break down traditional living groups and to cause severe strain in the old clan structure.†

3. Diamond discusses how the administration of justice served as a source of revenue for the early nation-state. Compare his analysis with the following remarks by Adam Smith on "the expense of justice":

. . . In the Tartar governments of Asia, in the governments of Europe which were founded by the German and Scythian nations who overturned the Roman empire, the administration of justice was a considerable source of revenue, both to the sovereign and to all the lesser chiefs or lords who exercised under him any particular jurisdiction, either over some particular tribe or clan, or over some particular territory or district. Originally both the sovereign and the inferior chiefs used to exercise this jurisdiction in their own persons. Afterwards they universally found it convenient to delegate it to some substitute, bailiff, or judge. This substitute, however, was still obliged to account to his principal or constituent for the profits of the jurisdiction. Whoever reads the instructions which were given to the judges of the circuit in the time of Henry II will see clearly that those judges were a sort of itinerant factors, sent round the country for the purpose of levying certain branches of the king's revenue. In those days the administration of justice not only afforded a certain revenue to the sovereign, but to procure this revenue seems to have been one of the principal advantages which he proposed to obtain by the administration of justice.

---

*Yin-Shing Woo v. United States,* 288 F2d 434, 435 (1961).

†Vine Deloria, Jr., *God Is Red* (New York: Delta, 1973), pp. 221–22.

This scheme of making the administration of justice subservient to the purposes of revenue could scarce fail to be productive of several very gross abuses. The person who applied for justice with a large present in his hand was likely to get something more than justice; while he who applied for it with a small one was likely to get something less. Justice too might frequently be delayed, in order that this present might be repeated. The amercement, besides, of the person complained of, might frequently suggest a very strong reason for finding him in the wrong, even when he had not really been so. That such abuses were far from being uncommon, the ancient history of every country in Europe bears witness.‡

4. Consider the relations today between "developed" nations and "underdeveloped" nations and between "multinational" corporations and their "host" countries. Do you think these relations involve a rearrangement of customary social structures by powerful groups competing for legal control? What different images of law and society are involved in these situations? The following report by a German duke visiting Africa before World War I may help you respond to these questions:

Ruanda is certainly the most interesting country in the German East African Protectorate—in fact, in all Central Africa—chiefly on account of its ethnographical and geographical position. Its interest is further increased by the fact that it is one of the last negro kingdoms governed autocratically by a sovereign sultan, for German supremacy is only recognized to a very limited extent.

Added to this, it is a land flowing with milk and honey, . . . a land which offers the brightest of prospects to the white settler. . . .

To anyone with an intimate knowledge of African affairs it seemed a sheer impossibility that so powerful a sovereign, the ruler over some one and a half million people, would voluntarily submit to the new regime and agree to enter upon no undertakings within his vast, thickly populated, and unexplored realms except by permission of the European Resident.

To compel him to do so would have meant bloody wars and an enormous sacrifice of human life as the inevitable consequence. The sudden change of existing conditions, too, would have involved a heavy pecuniary sacrifice, as the government would have found it necessary, with such a large population, to appoint a relatively large number of European officials. As such measures would have proved impracticable, complete anarchy would have followed.

So the country was therefore allowed to retain its traditional organization, and the sultan was given full jurisdiction over his fellow-people, under control of the Resident, who was to suppress cruelty as far as possible. In one word, the government does not acknowledge the Sultan as a sovereign lord, but fully recognizes his authority as chief of his clan. Kindred tribes, non-resident in Ruanda, are therefore not subject to the Sultan's jurisdiction, but are under the administration of the Resident.

The fundamental principle is the same with all Residents. It is desired to strengthen and enrich the Sultan and persons in authority, and to increase thereby their interest in the continuance of German rule, so that the desire for revolt shall die away, as the consequence of a rebellion would be a dwindling of their revenues. At the same time, by steadily controlling and directing the Sultan and using his powers, civilizing influences would be introduced. Thus by degrees, and almost imperceptibly to the people and to the Sultan himself, he eventually becomes nothing less than the executive instrument of the Resident. . . .

Similarly to their sovereign ruler, the chiefs are descended from various distinguished families or clans. These clans hold land, pay taxes to the Sultan, are keen to avenge the bloodshed of kinsmen, and possess a totem—some object of adoration, which usually takes the shape of an animal or plant. . . .

From what I have written it will easily be seen that the greater part of Ruanda is eminently adapted for colonization by white men, . . . and that there is a splendid opening here for the establishment of business on a vast scale. . . .

When we took our leave of the Sultan, at early dawn on the 12th of August, it was with a certain amount of satisfaction. We had been afforded an insight into the court life of a

‡Adam Smith, *An Inquiry into the Nature and Causes of the Wealth of Nations,* 4th ed., vol. 2 (Dublin: Colles, Moncrieffe, et al., 1785), pp. 230–231.

negro prince and favored with a display of his power such as no one had ever experienced previously or would probably ever experience again. When the illimitable power of this Sultan has receded before European influence, and when busy throngs of traders encroach upon the haughty aloofness of this most aristocratic of all negro tribes and the white man's herds graze in its pastures, then we shall be able to appreciate to the full the value of our remarkable experience.§

5. Farley Mowat, naturalist and historian, has written about life among some of the Inuit people in Canada. Their social order, he asserts, is based on principles that diverge widely from the legal order of the Canadian state. In a sense, one might say that the Inuit law is not based on "principles" at all, but rather on concrete, existential experience stretching over many generations. Compare Mowat's description of Inuit society with Diamond's contrast between "customary law" and "civilized law":

> [T]here are deviations from law, and there are crimes in the land; for no race of men can be free of these things. But there are also certain forces which the People control and which in turn direct the actions of men, and these forces keep the law-breaking within narrow bounds. To understand these forces is to realize why the Ihalmiut have no need of our laws to maintain the security of their way of life.
>
> There is absolutely no internal organization to hold authority over the People. No one man, or body of men, holds power in any other sense than the magical. There is no council of elders, no policeman. There are no assemblies of government and, in the strictest sense, the Ihalmiut may be said to live in an anarchistic state, for they do not even have an inflexible code of laws.
>
> Yet the People exist in amity together, and the secret of this is the secret of cooperative endeavor, limited only by the powers of human will and endurance. It is not blind obedience or obedience dictated by fear. Rather it is intelligent obedience to a simple

code that makes sense to those who must live by its rules. . . .

> . . . Should a man continuously disregard the Law of Life, then little by little he finds himself isolated and shut off from the community. There can be no more powerful punishment . . . in a world where man must work closely with man in order to live. . . . The law does not call for an eye for an eye. If possible the breaker of law is brought back to become an asset to the camps. His defection is tacitly forgotten, and to all intents and purposes it never happened at all.*

6. In thinking further about the contemporary significance of the difference between custom and law, consider the following remarks of Jane Jacobs:

> The first thing to understand is that the public peace—the sidewalk and street peace—of cities is not kept primarily by the police, necessary as police are. It is kept primarily by an intricate, almost unconscious, network of voluntary controls and standards among the people themselves, and enforced by the people themselves. In some city areas—older public housing projects and streets with very high population turnover are often conspicuous examples—the keeping of public sidewalk law and order is left almost entirely to the police and special guards. Such places are jungles. No amount of police can enforce civilization where the normal, casual enforcement of it has broken down. . . .
>
> An incident at . . . , a public housing project in New York illustrates this point. A tenants' group . . . put up three Christmas trees. The chief tree, so cumbersome it was a problem to transport, erect, and trim, went into the project's . . . landscaped central mall and promenade. The other two trees, each less than six feet tall and easy to carry, went on two small fringe plots at the outer corners of the project where it abuts a busy avenue and lively cross streets of the old city. The first night, the large tree and all its trimmings were stolen. The two smaller trees remained intact, lights, ornaments and all, until they were taken down at New Year's. "The place where the tree was stolen, which is *theoretically* the most safe and sheltered place in the project, is the same

§Duke Adolphus Frederick of Mecklenburg, "A Land of Giants and Pygmies," in *In the Heart of Africa* (London: Cassell, 1912).

*From Farley Mowat, *People of the Deer* (Boston: Little, Brown, 1951), pp. 176–178.

place that is unsafe for people too, especially children," says a social worker. . . ." People are no safer in that mall than the Christmas tree. On the other hand, the place where the other trees were safe, where the project is just one corner out of four, happened to be safe for people."[†]

Jacobs says that city planners, architects, politicians, real estate developers, bankers, and others who make decisions about the building and rebuilding of cities often act from false ideas about how communities work. These false ideas center on making things look good rather than on creating good places for people to live. Jacobs believes that community life consists of people watching out for each other, and that people do this unless the environment they live in prevents or obstructs them. The basic problem, she maintains, is to understand and provide for the complexity of healthy social relations. She says, for example, that no amount of law enforcement can take the place of a living network of relations among people. What qualities do living relations have that law does not? Can you see how law enforcement might actually damage a living network of people's lives? What other forces might damage a network of human relations?

7. The "cyber-society" of the Internet has been analyzed from a perspective similar to Diamond's:

> Legal institutions must back up the social ethic by punishing those who transgress the social bounds, but reliance on legal mechanisms alone is inadequate to create a society of trust. A strong "civil society" with its network of non-governmental institutions and relations invariably exists in a high-trust society. Once government superimposes itself on that society and begins to intervene in interpersonal relationships, relationships of trust are replaced with relationships in which the intervention of the state becomes necessary to mediate disputes. . . .

> Cyberspace may also be on the cusp of a decision point as to whether it will be a high-trust or low-trust environment. This decision is gradually being made by a series of technical working groups developing Internet standards. This will have a profound effect on society in decades to come, as cyberspace becomes the medium in which many, if not most, major transactions will be developed. The U.S. Government and many large institutions favor the "X.509" certification system (a means of guaranteeing the authenticity of a transaction in cyberspace), a hierarchical chain of encryption-guarded certificates, resting in the final analysis on a "root certificate" issued by an institution considered reliable (for example, a large bank). Of course, the dependence on root certificates issued by large institutions permits the government to insert a control point. . . .

> "Cypherpunks"—anarchistic hackers battling the concept of governmental control of cyberspace—have proposed an alternate model, sometimes called "circles of trust," in which networks of people pass along public keys, essentially creating a web of personal endorsements validating the trustworthiness of identities represented by public keys. This inserts a larger element of human judgment into the system, with both the advantages and drawbacks of that quality. An error in judgment by an acquaintance of an acquaintance can leave "downstream" users of the system in trouble, just as with the corruption of the root authority in the hierarchical model. However, damage is likely to be discovered sooner and mitigated more easily in this model.[‡]

---

[†]From Jane Jacobs, *The Death and Life of Great American Cities* (New York: Random House, 1961), pp. 31–32, 34.

[‡]James Bennett, "Cyberspace and the Return of Trust," *Strategic Investment Newsletter,* October 16, 1996, pp. 11, 12.

# *9* RULES OF LAW

> Law reflects but in no sense determines the moral
> worth of a society. . . . The better the society, the
> less law there will be. In Heaven, there will be no
> law, and the lion will lie down with the lamb. . . .
> The worse the society, the more law there will be.
> In Hell, there will be nothing but law, and due
> process will be meticulously observed.
>
> Grant Gilmore, "The Age of Anxiety," *Yale
> Law Journal* (1975)

⁂ The principal of law enforcement is to make people obey rules. This is called "the rule of law." The idea is that without enforced rules society would become disorderly. The problem is that rules do not exist apart from society. People create rules to accomplish political, economic, moral, and other social organization purposes. Therefore, law enforcement becomes entangled with disagreements about these purposes, especially when different ideas of "social order" are in conflict. For example, some rules may serve the interests of a segment of society, at the expense of others. Some rules may be based on purposes that are regarded as outmoded or oppressive. There is a special tension in law enforcement when moral issues are involved. The readings in this section explore historical and contemporary examples of social conflict about which rules should be enforced. Law enforcement is shown to involve not only the application of force to coerce obedience to rules, but the determination of the shape and content of the rules themselves.

## *9.1*   The Law Is Terror Put into Words   *Peter d'Errico*

We are living in a time of changing consciousness about the meaning and function of authority. Law, which is often taken to be the backbone of authority structures in society, has come increasingly under scrutiny, both for its role in maintaining oppressive social conditions and for the exceeding narrowness of legalism as a world-view.

In a sense, we no longer believe in our system of legal rules the way we used to. We are

A selection from "The Law Is Terror Put into Words," by Peter d'Errico, *Learning and the Law* 1975 issue. Copyright © 1975 by the American Bar Association. Reprinted by permission.

beginning to see through the facade of a "government of laws" to the people who animate that system. And further, we are coming to understand that legalism is as much an obscuring veil as a clarifying lens for approaching social problems. Law and legal thinking are as frequently the cause of social trouble as the means of resolving it. Thus, as Addison Mueller has noted, in our "free-enterprise" economy, "freedom of contract" is the consumer's losing card.

This growing skepticism and criticism about law is part of the decline of legalism in our culture. The decline, however, is not a simple matter. It is beset with resistance and contradiction.

For example, even as the evidence becomes more and more clear that prison is a dysfunctional, self-defeating, self-perpetuating social institution, the force of the state is called again and again into action against the victims of that institution. Likewise, even though crime is increasingly understood to be a product of social stratification, rather than a phenomenon of human nature against which society structures itself, the state spends ever more money to preserve the existing social structure and to thwart the forces of social change.

In an overall way, these contradictions are forcing us to realize that our justice system is only another social institution, subject to all the ills that befall any other institution: bureaucracy, preoccupation with its own maintenance and expansion, depersonalization of those whom it is supposed to serve, etc. Disenchantment with law as the basis for authority in social and personal life is now so pervasive that we are at a crisis in the history of law itself.

. . . . . . . . . . . . . . . . . .

## WE ARE AUTHORITY ADDICTS

Daily life under legalism is permeated in all its aspects by a belief in authority, and an accompanying tension between authoritative descriptions of the world and our own individual perceptions of life. We are authority addicts, hooked on rules. As Judith Shklar has noted, the institutional and personal levels of commitment to legalism form a social continuum: "At one end of the scale of legalistic values and institutions stand its most highly articulate and refined expressions, the courts of law and the rules they follow; at the other end is the personal morality of all those men and women who think of goodness as obedience to the rules that properly define their duties and rights."

At every moment, even to the level of how and when to eat, smile, sleep, talk, touch and move, and beyond this to the level of how and what we are supposed to think, fantasy and dream, there are rules. Life for most people seems to be a project of obedience, of duty and responsibility to authority. Constantly there is the struggle to fit ourselves into someone else's dream, someone else's definition of reality. And with this struggle,

as part of it and in turn perpetuating it, goes a fear of letting go of authority as well as attempts to impose our authority on others, preoccupation with what others think, feelings of isolation from others and the world, and fear that we will not exist if we do not define ourselves, label our relationships and categorize ourselves and each other.

David Cooper, studying such phenomena in *The Death of the Family* (1971), writes:

> If, then, we wish to find the most basic level of understanding of repression in society, we have to see it as a collectively reinforced and institutionally formalized panic about going mad, about the invasion of the outer by the inner and of the inner by the outer, about the loss of the illusion of "self." The Law is terror put into words.

Under legalism, we are constantly trying to control ourselves and each other within limits laid down by authority, all the time not seeing any alternative to this positivistic world, accepting it as necessary and inevitable. . . .

. . . . . . . . . . . . . . . . . .

The concept of a person's "rights," for example, is basic to legalism. It is one of the most powerful formulations in gaining and sustaining popular support for the operation of the legal system.

The common understanding of this concept is that law takes the side of the people against governmental or other systematic injustice. This uncritical view is elaborated upon in law school and throughout the legal system. Actually, however, once one understands that the central concern of legalism is with the maintenance of its own power system, one sees that the law only *appears* to take the side of the people. In fact, the real concern of legalism in its recognition of popular claims of right (civil rights, etc.) is *to preserve the basic governmental framework in which the claims arise.*

The concept of civil rights has meaning only in the context of an over-arching system of legal power against which the civil rights are supposed to protect. Ending the system of power would also end the need for civil rights. But it is precisely here that one sees the impossibility of ending the oppression by means of civil rights law. In the end, this analysis points to the concept of personal "rights" as being a technique for depersonalizing people. We are taught to respect the rights of others, and in doing so we focus on the abstract bundle of rules and regulations which have been set up by judges and other officials to govern the behavior of people. In this focus, we miss the actual reality of the others as whole, real individuals. We end up, in short, respecting the law rather than people; and this, for legalism, is the essential aim.

Due process is another sacred cow become fair game. Legalism would have us regard this notion as the key to freedom under law, the means by which fairness and regularity are incorporated into legal decision-making. In reality, due process is the attempt of the system to insure that claim and counterclaim, freedom and grievance, both occur and only within the existing legal universe and in its terms.

Every due process decision is thus only a further elaboration of the pre-existing legalist mazeway. People confront the claim of law to control social life, and the law responds; whatever the legal response to the confrontation, the law is concerned with itself first and foremost. The basic due process problem, as far as legalism is concerned, is only to preserve the apparatus of official legal control, even when the framework of that control must bend to meet the demands and needs of the people whose lives the officials govern. In a critical view, due process is essentially a technique for co-opting social change forces that threaten, or appear to threaten, official control of society.

In my own experience in practice—in an urban ghetto, on an Indian reservation, and in a middle class college community—I found again and again the people were able to see through law and legal processes in ways that I had been taught to close my eyes to. When their vision was rebuffed by law, it became the basis for a deep cynicism about legal process. I saw, moreover, that even when lawyers succeeded in legalism's own game—the creation of a new rule, or the vindication of an old one—that we didn't really win anything, because legalism wasn't dealing with the roots of problems, but only with their surface appearances.

And it is not only "radical" law or legal services practice which generates such insight and skepticism. I found many traditional lawyers in conventional practices who were well aware that the law was not reaching their clients' real problems: economic, familial, psychological, and so on. These lawyers were sometimes deeply troubled by this awareness, and yet they remained unable even to articulate their experience. Locked into the mazeway of legalism in their education, and bereft of any critical viewpoint, they seemed resigned to a life of legal routine.

. . . I have come to regard legalism as a defunct social ideology. Capable at one time of unleashing tremendous productive social forces, legalism is now only a source of confusion and contradiction. Far from uniting America into a coherent and just society, traditional ideas of law foster division and give the stamp of approval to inequality.

## ONE LEGACY OF LEGAL REALISM

If "authority" is needed for this iconoclastic view of legalism, one need only look back to the last major jurisprudential shakeup in American history, legal realism. Karl Llewellyn, one of the most profound thinkers and observers in the realist movement, commenting on "the place and treatment of concepts," wrote: ". . . categories and concepts, once formulated and once they have entered into thought processes, tend to take on an appearance of solidity, reality and inherent value which has no foundation in experience." In a time like the present, when belief in the central myths, or explanations of reality, around which our social life has been organized is increasingly breaking down, it becomes especially important to go beyond superficial exploration of social phenomena to an examination of concepts. The legal realist movement opened the door to new ways of thinking about the law, ways colored by non- or even anti-legalist perspectives.

The cry to go beyond legalism has come from other quarters, too. Brainerd Currie, writing about the materials of law study in the early and middle 1950's put forth an unmistakable critique:

Solutions to the problems of a changing social order are not implicit in the rules and principles which are formally elaborated on the basis of past decision, to be evoked by merely logical processes; and effective legal education cannot proceed in disregard of this fact. If men are to be trained for intelligent and effective participation in legal processes, and if law schools are to perform their function of contributing through research to the improvement of law administration, the formalism which confines the understanding and criticism of law within limits fixed by history and authority must be abandoned, and every available resource of knowledge and judgment must be brought to the task.

A humanistic legal studies accepts this challenge in a context that is wider than Currie's concern for legal process and law administration. Dealing with the central themes of human social life in a problem-oriented, question-posing way, this mode of study is free to pick up on even the most radical and far-reaching changes which are occurring in human consciousness. Legalism's continuous attempt to preserve old values by giving them new meaning can be replaced by an attempt to follow new meanings into a transvaluation of the central features of law and social life.

## Notes and Questions

1. Do you agree that there is widespread disenchantment with law? What current examples of this can you find? What examples of belief in law can you find?

2. What are the sources of disenchantment or belief? Do the mass media tend in either direction in presenting legal issues?

3. David Cooper is quoted on "the loss of the illusion of 'self.'" What relationship do you see between self-control and legal control? How might images of law be seen as illusions?

4. In thinking further about the relationship of law to new social forms, consider the following discussion:

> **As an LA native, I've witnessed the ups and downs of the city's rave scene firsthand: A lot has happened since the summer of 1990.** Back then, map points set up on downtown LA street corners would indicate an abandoned warehouse less than a mile away where $20 could get you inside and cover all the fruit, water and kegs you could consume. Yeah, these parties were illegal, but my high school friends and I felt like we were flying by the seat of our pants until the cops caught on and broke up the festivities before midnight and $20 came and went just as quickly. In 1990, candy ravers were still in elementary school, whistles came before glow sticks, Fatboy Slim was in an indie pop band, and *URB* was a seed waiting to be planted. Now, most people have to drive for hours to find a safe, licensed massive that is ever more under the watchful eye of the media and law enforcement. However, there are smaller local happenings that still reaffirm why "the party" is still the nucleus of our scene—it's where the music is heard and experienced. Raving in America at the end of the century is in a precarious position due to an emerging generation gap and severe growing pains. But we all can remember what brought us here in the first place and why we will always return. Surveyed here are a sampling of DJs, promoters and ravers from across the country sharing their experiences and projections on raving's future.

> **Participants:**
> **AK1200,** 28, Orlando, FL, drum & bass DJ
> **Sandra Collins,** 20-something, New York, NY, trance DJ/producer
> **Donnie,** 29, New Orleans, LA, promoter, Freebass Society
> **Wade Randolph Hampton aka WishFM aka W,** 31, San Francisco, CA, drum & bass DJ/producer
> **John Kelley,** 29, Los Angeles, CA, funky breaks DJ
> **Brian Alper,** 25, Huntington Beach, CA, marketing manager at Raveworld.net and co-owner of B3Cande Productions
> **Chris Esparza,** 20, Fond du lac, WI
> **Kellie Allen,** 19, Bloomington, IN, student
> **Sarah Krug,** 19, Fond du Lac, WI, mother of 21-month-old daughter Chloe Amara, student/office assistant
> **DJ Brian,** 23, Victoria, B.C., trance DJ

> *Do you think law enforcement in the U.S. will ever become more friendly to people organizing raves? How?*

> **AK:** No, I don't think it will ever be easy to organize a "rave" now that law enforcement have their minds made up on what they think

a rave is all about. They may decide to compromise and allow raves to go on, but in a severely controlled surrounding.

**SC:** The only way law enforcement will be more friendly is if promoters are stricter and people are more responsible for their actions.

**Donnie:** Yes, we have already infiltrated the rave scene and are working closely with many promoters. Oops, what I meant to say was that I think raves and law enforcement go hand in hand, it's a perfect marriage.

**WH:** Yes, as soon as enough money lands in the right hands. Check the entire rock & roll story for further details. Let's hope we survive the inevitable degradation of the art form. In order for the law to lighten up, the city will need to benefit, not just the promoters. Simple civil politics.

**JK:** Yes, as raves become more legalized, I think law enforcement will become correspondingly more "friendly." There will be less illegal things for them to get all in a huff about.

**CE:** I think as the older law enforcement group retires, a new form will emerge. Younger cops who are familiar with experimental activities. A lot of the raves I've been to have had cops inside not knowing what to expect, and just find kids dancing and having a good time. The only time most raves have been shut down is because of fire codes, etc., like when they find 1000 people inside a 400-person max recreation center, and they were "just looking out for us." It's the promoters' fault. The rave is becoming more of a concert these days, which means bigger legal venues. With security guards who are ravers themselves, they will come in, check it out and leave, and if they hang, they feel the vibe and enjoy it. The more organized the scene gets, the less enforcement. If you want to be old-school and break into churches and warehouses, it's not gonna happen. We're not criminals now, are we?

**BA:** I see law enforcement becoming more tolerant, but not more friendly. At some point, when the promoters and the rave community are strong enough to raise legal questions and get legal counsel to support the claims of discrimination against rave organizers and the community, will this change occur. Being a promoter, I know how difficult it is dealing with city officials and local law enforcement and the only way their attitudes will change is if they are forced to change.

**KA:** Because of the way raves operate, I'd say law enforcement won't become friendly to organizers any time in the near future. Regardless of how promoters may feel, drug culture is far too embedded in raves. Obviously there is the stereotype: ravers = drug users. Cops are never friendly to that sort of atmosphere. Again, another stereotype. People tend to think that anything that happens at night must be associated with some evil. Unfortunately, I've seen far too many examples of pure irresponsibility with drugs. People fucked up on whatever will go up to cops and ask them for acid, E, K, etc. It's this kind of irresponsibility that causes the parties to be shut down. Moderate, responsible drug use could probably continue (as it does at many concerts) but not with incidents like that.

**SK:** No, I think promoters have given local law enforcement a bunch of bullshit and usually it ends up being illegal/out of control anyway. I've been to parties where the building capacity is over the limit, people/music is too loud or there is public drinking/drug use. The promoters need to be honest with themselves, ravers and law enforcement or everyone just gets ripped off in the end anyway.

**Brian:** I think all that will happen is that it will become more accepted. Somewhat like rock shows, therefore as easy to pull off as rock shows (not really that easy to begin with).*

---

*Excerpt from "Rave 2k: A Survey on Raving at the Millennium and Beyond," moderated by Stacy Osbaum, *URB*, Vol. 9, No. 70, December 1999, p. 64. Reprinted by permission.

    ❧ The 1963 Easter civil rights demonstration in Birmingham, Alabama, is a famous example of challenge to law enforcement. Rev. Martin Luther King, Jr., and others planned to protest racial discrimination by demonstrating against segregation laws. The city obtained a state court injunction to block the demonstrations, but the ministers went ahead with their plans and carried out the civil rights protests. The city responded by arresting the demonstrators. The case eventually reached the United States Supreme Court. The Court agreed with the ministers that the city's action "unquestionably raised substantial constitutional issues" (*Walker* v. *Birmingham,* 87 S.Ct. 1824 (1967)) but ruled against the demonstrators on the ground that an unconstitutional injunction must be obeyed, until a court has overturned it.

## 9.2   Excerpt from "Letter from Birmingham Jail"

*Martin Luther King, Jr.*

YOU EXPRESS A GREAT deal of anxiety over our willingness to break laws. This is certainly a legitimate concern. Since we so diligently urge people to obey the Supreme Court's decision of 1954 outlawing segregation in the public schools, at first glance it may seem rather paradoxical for us consciously to break laws. One may well ask: "How can you advocate breaking some laws and obeying others?" The answer lies in the fact that there are two types of laws: just and unjust. I would be the first to advocate obeying just laws. One has not only a legal but a moral responsibility to obey just laws. Conversely, one has a moral responsibility to disobey unjust laws. I would agree with St. Augustine that "an unjust law is no law at all."

    Now, what is the difference between the two? How does one determine whether a law is just or unjust? A just law is man-made code that squares with the moral law or the law of God. An unjust law is a code that is out of harmony with the moral law. To put it in the terms of St. Thomas Aquinas: An unjust law is a human law that is not rooted in eternal law and natural law. Any law that uplifts human personality is just. Any law that de-

grades human personality is unjust. All segregation statutes are unjust because segregation distorts the soul and damages the personality. It gives the segregator a false sense of superiority and the segregated a false sense of inferiority. Segregation, to use the terminology of the Jewish philosopher Martin Buber, substitutes an "I-it" relationship for an "I-thou" relationship and ends up relegating persons to the status of things. Hence segregation is not only politically, economically and sociologically unsound, it is morally wrong and sinful. Paul Tillich has said that sin is separation. Is not segregation an existential expression of man's tragic separation, his awful estrangement, his terrible sinfulness? Thus it is that I can urge men to obey the 1954 decision of the Supreme Court, for it is morally right; and I can urge them to disobey segregation ordinances, for they are morally wrong.

    Let us consider a more concrete example of just and unjust laws. An unjust law is a code that a numerical or power majority group compels a minority group to obey but does not make binding on itself. This is difference made legal. By the same token, a just law is a code that a majority compels a minority to follow and that it is willing to follow itself. This is sameness made legal.

    Let me give another explanation. A law is unjust if it is inflicted on a minority that, as a result of being denied the right to vote, had

From *Why We Can't Wait* by Martin Luther King, Jr. Reprinted by arrangement with the Estate of Martin Luther King, Jr., c/o Writers House as agents for the Proprietor. Copyright Martin Luther King 1963, copyright renewed 1991 by Coretta Scott King.

no part in enacting or devising the law. Who can say that the legislature of Alabama which set up that state's segregation laws was democratically elected? Throughout Alabama all sorts of devious methods are used to prevent Negroes from becoming registered voters, and there are some counties in which, even though Negroes constitute a majority of the population, not a single Negro is registered. Can any law enacted under such circumstances be considered democratically structured?

Sometimes a law is just on its face and unjust in its application. For instance, I have been arrested on a charge of parading without a permit. Now, there is nothing wrong in having an ordinance which requires a permit for a parade. But such an ordinance becomes unjust when it is used to maintain segregation and to deny citizens the First-Amendment privilege of peaceful assembly and protest.

I hope you are able to see the distinction I am trying to point out. In no sense do I advocate evading or defying the law, as would the rabid segregationist. That would lead to anarchy. One who breaks an unjust law must do so openly, lovingly, and with a willingness to accept the penalty. I submit that an individual who breaks a law that conscience tells him is unjust and who willingly accepts the penalty of imprisonment in order to arouse the conscience of the community over its injustice, is in reality expressing the highest respect for law.

Of course, there is nothing new about this kind of civil disobedience. It was evidenced sublimely in the refusal of Shadrach, Meshach and Abednego to obey the laws of Nebuchadnezzar, on the ground that a higher moral law was at stake. It was practiced superbly by the early Christians, who were willing to face hungry lions and the excruciating pain of chopping blocks rather than submit to certain unjust laws of the Roman Empire. To a degree, academic freedom is a reality today because Socrates practiced civil disobedience. In our own nation, the Boston Tea Party represented a massive act of civil disobedience.

We should never forget that everything Adolf Hitler did in Germany was "legal" and everything the Hungarian freedom fighters did in Hungary was "illegal." It was "illegal" to aid and comfort a Jew in Hitler's Germany. Even so, I am sure that,

had I lived in Germany at the time, I would have aided and comforted my Jewish brothers. If today I lived in a Communist country where certain principles dear to the Christian faith are suppressed, I would openly advocate disobeying that country's antireligious laws.

I must make two honest confessions to you, my Christian and Jewish brothers. First, I must confess that over the past few years I have been gravely disappointed with the white moderate. I have almost reached the regrettable conclusion that the Negro's great stumbling block in his stride toward freedom is not the White Citizen's Counciler or the Ku Klux Klanner, but the white moderate, who is more devoted to "order" than to justice; who prefers a negative peace which is the absence of justice; who constantly says: "I agree with you in the goal you seek, but I cannot agree with your methods of direct action"; who paternalistically believes he can set the timetable for another man's freedom; who lives by a mythical concept of time and who constantly advises the Negro to wait for a "more convenient season." Shallow understanding from people of good will is more frustrating than absolute misunderstanding from people of ill will. Lukewarm acceptance is much more bewildering than outright rejection.

I had hoped that the white moderate would understand that law and order exist for the purpose of establishing justice and that when they fail in this purpose they become the dangerously structured dams that block the flow of social progress. I had hoped that the white moderate would understand that the present tension in the South is a necessary phase of the transition from an obnoxious negative peace, in which the Negro passively accepted his unjust plight, to a substantive and positive peace, in which all men will respect the dignity and worth of human personality. Actually, we who engage in nonviolent direct action are not the creators of tension. We merely bring to the surface the hidden tension that is already alive. We bring it out in the open, where it can be seen and dealt with. Like a boil that can never be cured so long as it is covered up but must be opened with all its ugliness to the natural medicines of air and light, injustice must be exposed, with all the tension its exposure creates, to the light of human conscience and the air of national opinion before it can be cured.

In your statement you assert that our actions, even though peaceful, must be condemned because they precipitate violence. But is this a logical assertion? Isn't this like condemning a robbed man because his possession of money precipitated the evil act of robbery? Isn't this like condemning Socrates because his unswerving commitment to truth and his philosophical inquiries precipitated the act by the misguided populace in which they made him drink hemlock? Isn't this like condemning Jesus because his unique God-consciousness and never-ceasing devotion to God's will precipitated the evil act of crucifixion? We must come to see that, as the federal courts have consistently affirmed, it is wrong to urge an individual to cease his efforts to gain his basic constitutional rights because the quest may precipitate violence. Society must protect the robbed and punish the robber.

I had also hoped that the white moderate would reject the myth concerning time in relation to the struggle for freedom. I have just received a letter from a white brother in Texas. He writes: "All Christians know that the colored people will receive equal rights eventually, but it is possible that you are in too great a religious hurry. It has taken Christianity almost two thousand years to accomplish what it has. The teachings of Christ take time to come to earth." Such an attitude stems from a tragic misconception of time, from the strangely irrational notion that there is something in the very flow of time that will inevitably cure all ills. Actually, time itself is neutral; it can be used either destructively or constructively. More and more I feel that the people of ill will have used time much more effectively than have the people of good will. We will have to repent in this generation not merely for the hateful words and actions of the bad people but for the appalling silence of the good people. Human progress never rolls in on wheels of inevitability; it comes through the tireless efforts of

men willing to be co-workers with God, and without this hard work, time itself becomes an ally of the forces of social stagnation. We must use time creatively, in the knowledge that the time is always ripe to do right. Now is the time to make real the promise of democracy and transform our pending national elegy into a creative psalm of brotherhood. Now is the time to lift our national policy from the quicksand of racial injustice to the solid rock of human dignity.

## Notes and Questions

1. As you reflect on King's letter, consider what the Supreme Court stated in its ruling that the civil rights marchers had to go to jail for violating an injunction:

    [P]recedents clearly put the petitioners on notice that they could not bypass orderly review of the injunction before disobeying it. . . . This Court cannot hold that the petitioners were constitutionaly free to ignore all the procedures of the law and carry their battle to the streets. One may sympathize with the petitioners' impatient commitment to their cause. But respect for judicial process is a small price to pay for the civilizing hand of law, which alone can give abiding meaning to constitutional freedom.*

2. In thinking further about the Supreme Court's statement above, compare it with a statement from an earlier case:

    [S]overeign power in our government belongs to the people, and the government of the United States and the government of the several states are but the machinery for expounding or expressing the will of the sovereign power.†

    Do you think these statements are contradictory? Explain why or why not.

---

* 87 S.Ct. at 1832.

† *Cherokee Nation* v. *So. Kans. Ry. Co.*, D.C. 33 F 900, 906 (1888).

🐦 Notwithstanding that law enforcement involves the use of official force and violence to secure obedience to rules, law also involves the establishment of ideas and concepts that are the basis for the rules. One of the key ideas in U.S. racial segregation laws was that black people were subordinate to white. In slave laws, this resulted in a paradoxical situation: black persons were legally categorized as property; at the same time, black persons were subject to criminal laws premised on the idea that a black person could intentionally commit a crime. The laws of slavery were thus in conflict with themselves: how could a piece of property have the capacity to commit a crime?

## 9.3   Virginian Liberators   *John T. Noonan, Jr.*

### THE LEGAL STRUCTURE OF PRE-REVOLUTIONARY SLAVERY

ON THE EVE OF the Revolution, slavery in Virginia did not exist as a relationship of brute power. A social institution, it was given its shape by a hundred assumptions and omissions, intentions and neglects, customs and conventions. Law formed a part of these multiple pressures and, although far from the whole institution, was essential to it. The statutes on the control of slaves provided not a set of detailed instructions which the slaves meticulously obeyed but a message primarily directed at the white community. The statutes defining the legal status of slaves determined the dispositions to be made at a slave's birth and at a master's death. Slavery was not a transient condition: the law gave it immortality. Control statutes and status statutes together were indispensable to the creation and maintenance of the institution.

The statutes on control were designed on the model of a criminal code regulating public behavior. No slave was to leave his or her owner's plantation without a pass. No slave was to carry a club, staff, or other weapon. No slave was to own a horse, hog, or cow. No slave was to run away and lie out, hiding and lurking in swamps, woods, or other obscure places. No slave was to resist his

A selection adapted from "Virginian Liberators" from *Persons and Masks of the Law* by John T. Noonan, Jr. Copyright © 1976 by John T. Noonan, Jr. Reprinted with the permission of the author.

or her owner administering correction. No slave was to lift his or her hand in opposition to a Christian, provided the Christian was not a Negro, mulatto, or Indian. No slave was to attempt to rape (the possibility of successful rape was not contemplated) a white woman. No slave was to prepare or administer medicine. No slave was to meet with four or more other slaves. No slave was to attend a religious service except with his or her "white family." The statutes were accompanied by provisions, specifying punishments for their violation, ranging from whipping to castration to death. . . .

The statutes, the legislature prescribed, were to be read aloud at the door of each parish church twice a year, on the first sermon Sundays in March and September, so that the slaves could make no pretense of ignorance if they disobeyed. . . .

The pedagogy of the statutes pointed to the slaves as creatures who must be coerced, upon whom it was right to exercise force. The statutes measured the amount of violence that masters might employ. The owner's boisterous passions were to be modeled to the community's norm. Violence on the slaves was authorized and rationalized by being put in the form of a rule. Punishments were set as though each penalty had been measured to the act prohibited. The model of this approach was an act of 1723 whose ostensible purpose was to put slave witnesses "under greater obligation to tell the truth." If their testimony was shown to be false, not by "due proof," but merely by "pregnant circumstances," then every such offender shall, without further trial, be ordered by said court to have one ear nailed to the pillory, and there to stand for the space of one hour, and then the said ear to be cut off; and thereafter, the other ear nailed in like manner, and cut off, at the expiration of one other hour; and moreover to order every such offender thirty-nine lashes, well laid on, on his or her bare back, at the common whipping-post.

Sadistic in its precision of detail, this statute appeared to focus on the witnesses. It was to be read to them before they gave testimony, in the only case in which they could give testimony—the trial of another black. . . . Directed to read it to black witnesses, the judge was reminded of their unreliability, their subjection, their amenability to physical threats. Compelled to bring these brutal threats into the actual conduct of his court, he was instructed in the act of administering justice.

The communication made by the statute to the judge in the paradigm case of a trial was the communication transmitted by other control laws to sheriffs, deputy sheriffs, constables, prosecutors, county courts, and owners. More powerful in intensity than the standards mumblingly communicated to the slaves was the clear word brought to the masters: the community is with you in your exercise of domination.

"Without force, the alienability of the title to the human capital of blacks would have been worthless," write [Robert Williams] Fogel and [Stanley L.] Engerman, stressing in their fundamental reevaluation of Southern slavery that the plantation system required a judicious blending of economic incentive with coercion. But what made it possible for slavery to continue for more than a generation? Without acceptance of the rule that the slaves could be transferred by their owners and by the testaments of their owners, neither force nor economic incentive could have maintained the system. To regulate birth and overcome death, and incidentally to determine the transmission and distribution of slaves, a special world had to be created in which rules had a force, a magic, of their own. This second function of the law of slavery depended on a mass of concepts, decisions, and statutes, whose exact application to human beings required the industry and imagination of lawyers.

"Slaves," said the index to the first laws of Virginia, "See Negroes." From the beginning of the colony, "slave" and "Negro" were terms of art indicating a special legal status. The content of these terms was largely given by the popular understanding of what a slave or Negro was. From the beginning, Africans were distinguished from Europeans by complexion, physiognomy, customs, language, and treatment. Lawyers did not single-handedly determine their definition. Yet when it came to the key questions posed by death and birth, answers could not be given by popular perception. What happened to an African when the one for whom he worked died? What happened to a child born of an African? Answers to these questions issued from the use of concepts and rules which, even before they were written up as a code, had the character of law. Africans in Virginia, having arrived by means of purchase, were viewed as *property*.

"For the better settling and preservation of estates within this dominion"—so their desire for immortality was confessed—the Burgesses in 1705 decreed that plantation slaves "shall be held, taken, and adjudged to be real estate (and not chattels)." The object of the statute was to secure the perpetuity of ownership in plantations, insuring that slaves would descend with the land they worked. Designation of plantation slaves as real estate dramatized the triumph of landed proprietorship over death. The dead owner's slave was not cast into a state of nature. The slave was to pass "to the heirs and widows of persons departing this life, according to the manner and custom of land of inheritance held in fee simple." Slaves in the possession of merchants and factors were exempted from the operation of the statute and were to be held "as personal estate in the same condition as they should have been, if this act had never been made." Whether real estate or personal estate, slaves were property, subject to all the rules by which the rights of the dead were imparted to their spouses or to their descendants.

Overcoming the death of the master, determining the status of the offspring, the legislators and courts of Virginia presented a doctrine on the morality of slavery. They taught that it was good. In the pedagogy of the law, slaves were identified with the soil—the literal foundation of prosperity in the colony—or, generically, with property. As long as the teaching of the lawgivers was accepted, slavery could not be criticized without aspersion on the goodness of wealth itself. . . .

Locke's notion that a purpose of government was to protect property could justify all measures taken to secure the stability of the slaveholder's domain. The masters' ties of commerce, marriage, and kindred, so often intertwined with the masters' property arrangements, and dependent upon them, confirmed the position of the slaves. Property was the most comprehensive and most necessary of social categories. Catalogued within it, slaves fell within a classification which announced that it was right and good to maintain their enslavement.

The concept of property performed a further function. It put the slaves at a distance from the world of men and women. "Slave" and "Negro" functioned in the same way, but neither term by itself carried a primary meaning suggesting the non-human. "Property" obliterated every anthropoid feature of the slave. Consistently inculcating this description, the statutes assured the owning class that they did not need to attend to the person of the slave in any conveyance, lease, mortgage, or devise [transfer by will] they cared to make of their human possessions.

Addresses of the property statutes were only in an incidental way the slaves themselves. In theory, as real estate or personal estate, they could not be addressed at all. Definition as property determined their physical location, their employment, their sexual opportunities, and their familial relationships whenever they were made the object of sale, lease, mortgage, foreclosure, gift, bequest, intestacy, or entailment. They could not, however, apply this law to themselves. If they grasped the general idea that they and their children were always at the direction of another, they had deciphered the message of the law for themselves.

The law treating slaves as property conflicted with the control statutes which treated the slaves as responsible, triable, teachable human beings. . . .

Inconsistency was not fatal to the dominant message communicated to the trustees and executors, lawyers and judges, auctioneers and sheriffs who had to manage the transfer of particular persons when ownership in them passed, and to the testators and heirs, donors and donees, buyers and sellers, mortgagors and creditors, who wanted to know the terms upon which ownership in particular persons could be conveyed. To all those interested in the disposition and distribution of slaves, the message communicated was single: individuals do not have to be looked at when a conveyance is made. . . .

Between 1705, when the definition of plantation slaves as real estate was enacted, and the Revolution, legislators and lawyers argued how far the metaphor of real estate should be pressed. Lenders wanting the largest tangible assets of the plantations as collateral wished that the slaves be as freely transmissible as other forms of personal property. Owners seeking credit had a corresponding need for slaves to be readily disposable. Against these interests ran the dynastic desire of the planters to have the slaves descend with the land to their families in perpetuity. . . .

Virginian lawyers of the eighteenth century, even when they were revolutionaries, it might be supposed, were so imprisoned by traditional legal assumptions about slavery that they had no choice but to ratify the legal institution. However universalist their proclamations of liberty, they lacked, it might be imagined, a concept which would correspond in law to what they announced as ideology. Suppositions of this sort would be mistaken. Only a dozen years old, new but already popular and prestigious, the *Commentaries on the Laws of England,* by the Professor of the Laws of England at Oxford [Sir William Blackstone], provided both a legal critique of slavery and a concept on which to base a law of universal liberty.

In retrospect, [Thomas] Jefferson recalled two reasons for refusing to make the laws afresh with Blackstone as a basis. First, new laws would have to be "systematical." . . . Second, the result would be to "render property uncertain." The first reason could not have been controlling. The old law was not systematized. Why should the new have been? . . .

The key difficulty is focused on in Jefferson's "render property uncertain." The property which would have been made most fundamentally uncertain was property in slaves. John Quincy Adams accurately described the committee's dilemma: If they had started afresh, "they must have restored slavery after having abolished it; they must have assumed to themselves all the odium of establishing it as a positive institution, directly in face of all the principles they had proclaimed."

Slavery, nonetheless, had to be dealt with. . . . Jefferson did the text on the control laws. The bill was reported to the legislature in 1779. Managed by James Madison, it was adopted without substantial alteration in 1785. . . .

Jefferson discarded the detail which had made the old control laws exact and hideous and substituted a simple scheme of elegant generality. Instead of specifically proscribing meetings of groups of slaves, the practice of medicine by slaves, hiding out by runaway slaves, and the lifting of a slave's hand in opposition to a white Christian, he prohibited "riots, routs, and unlawful assemblies, and seditious speeches." Instead of specifically designating thirty-nine lashes, castration, or death as sanction, he made each crime punishable by whipping at the discretion of a justice of the peace. The statute on false testimony of slaves disappeared. The new provision on seditious speeches was a far broader control of the use of language. Milder but more comprehensive, functionally the new statute did not differ from the colonial grotesquerie it replaced. Its message to the white community—the message of the legislature, the message drafted by Jefferson and approved by Jefferson, [Edmund] Pendleton, and [George] Wythe*—was: We are with you in the use of measured force.

The opening clause of the new legislation parodied the revolutionaries' statement on the inalienable liberty of human beings. "Be it enacted by the General Assembly," the committee bill said, "that no persons shall henceforth be slaves within this commonwealth, except such as were so on the first day of this present session of the Assembly, and the descendants of the females of them." This was not unlike saying, "Be it enacted that no persons shall henceforth be convicts within this commonwealth except such as are already convicted and those subsequently found guilty by process of law." No one was born a hereditary slave in Virginia unless he was the descendant of a female slave. Still, the provision was not wholly innocuous or tautological: it banned the importation of slaves. But the ban on imports, increasing the value of slaves already within the commonwealth and to be born within it, did not touch the institution. The new statute proclaimed the lawfulness of slavery in Virginia, provided for its perpetuation, and left the slaves the option of "locking up their faculties" or providing the slaves of the next generation. . . .

The [work of] Wythe and Jefferson . . . may be measured not only against the principles of Blackstone but against the work of Edmund Burke, who in 1780 drafted and in 1792 proposed a code for the amelioration of the conditions of slavery in the British colonies. . . .

The difference between Burke's draft and the Virginians' statutes is this: accepting the slaves as human beings, Burke worked toward their enjoyment of human liberties; Jefferson and Wythe treated the slaves as human beings for the purposes of the control laws; they proposed no law by which their enjoyment of human liberties was recognized. . . .

For that decision they were responsible— that is, it must be recognized that they as human beings performed the acts by which slavery was continued as a legal institution. They chose to participate in the system. With their own hands they put on the masks of the law and imposed them on others.

## THE VIRGINIA PARADOX

. . . In 1768, in *Blackwell* v. *Wilkinson*, Wythe had argued that the real nature of a slave was "personality." In 1770 he had won *Howell* v. *Netherland* by standing on the power of the legislature to cancel freedom. In 1792, in *Turpin* v. *Turpin*, he had ruled that slaves passed by will "as if they were chattels." In 1798, in *Fowler* v. *Saunders*, he had declared that a transfer of slaves was like a transfer of a quadruped or kitchen utensil. As a

---

*Both Pendleton and Wythe were lawyers. Pendleton was First Judge, the Virginia Court of Appeals, and Wythe was Chancellor of the Commonwealth of Virginia—ED.

lawyer and as a judge, he had not challenged the power of legislatures and judges to suppress a birthright. . . . The split between the ideals of the American Revolution and the maintenance of slavery was evident to contemporaries like [St. George] Tucker [a professor and judge]; it has now been comprehensively explored by David Brion Davis, who has probed with particular sensitivity Jefferson's "uncertain commitment" to universal liberty. The liberators were divided, knew they were divided, and were able to function because they entered a universe with distinctive rules.

Jefferson did not apply his reproach to Wythe. Wythe did not apply it to himself. . . . He took the legal universe to be self-contained. When he entered that special world, he accepted the masks of the law—they were the law's creations, not his. He did not see it as his fault that these fictions effected the distribution of slaves and the perpetuation of slavery. . . .

The Virginia paradox was this: Wythe believed that human beings are by nature free. He believed that the legislature is not omnipotent over nature. He believed that the legislature can enslave human beings. Rule-centered, he perceived with sharpness the injustice of an unjust rule; he did not perceive the injustice of removing human beings from consideration as persons. The Virginia paradox is the legal paradox, generally.

At least half of the property cases before the Chancellor involved the disposition of slaves. He could not have compassion for each of them as a person and still be a judge. His role in a slave system necessitated the use of masks. If he acted at all in his judicial office, those he disposed of had to fall within an appropriate subdivision of property. He needed to suppress humanity in the objects he transferred. He had to impress upon them the mask of property. The operation was not wholly external. . . . He could not pay attention to his torment. He had to act with apathy. He had to suppress humanity in himself. He had to put on himself the mask of the court.

When one reads of the earnest efforts of young eighteenth-century lawyers to master Roman law, one could weep at their futility—what possible relevance had the learning of fifth-century Byzantium to the affairs of America?

Tears would be misplaced. Learning the Roman law was far from ineffective indoctrination in the fiction-making power of a legal system. Citation of Roman law, as Wythe cited it in *Turpin* v. *Turpin,* was not mere harmless display of erudition; it was active evocation of the magic of the law. Roman law could make a horse a consul and did make a horse a priest; it could and did extinguish a person's past; and if it did these "impossible" things, it could and did unmake persons. Legal education has often been education in the making and unmaking of persons. Wythe was a superb teacher.

The essential was that no exceptions be permitted to break the spell. The control statutes, modeled on criminal law, had judges' options, sheriffs' options, prosecutors' options, owners' options. No one had options under the property concept, save the owner who had the option, following a prescribed ritual, to end the spell altogether and make his slave free. If emancipation was not granted, the property concept was absolute and all-enveloping for purposes of distribution and perpetuation. . . .

George Wythe is the first of all the lawyers of the United States who from 1775 to 1865, North and South, kept slavery in existence. He is first not in that he caused the others to follow him, but in that, as professor of law, as legislator, as Chancellor of the Commonwealth of Virginia, he taught the others. His pupils followed in his path. Jefferson wanted to end the evil of slavery. So did Henry Clay, James Monroe, and John Marshall. Deploring the evil, they overcame their objections to it as Speaker, President, and Chief Justice, respectively, and sustained the system, accepting the power of the law to convert persons into personality. They could believe in the natural law of freedom, and champion emancipation, and enforce slavery, so long as the legal universe was a special world with its own rules.

Like Wythe himself, they personally owned slaves. Their acceptance of the masks of the law did not blind them to the personalities of those they knew domestically. Sally Hemings, for example, his wife's half-sister and his slave, was a person Thomas Jefferson responded to when on an April day in Paris he spent two hundred francs on "clothes for Sally." Yet when he died her ownership moved under the property clauses of his will and her eventual fate had to depend on the claims of Jefferson's creditors not consuming the estate. The masks he had accepted, constructed, sustained, permitted him to distribute Sally Hemings in a fashion that would have been impossible if in the act of transmission he had to confront another living person. At the critical moments the masks of the law covered the faces of the slaves. Only an act of violence could shatter the concealing forms.

Slavery survived in Virginia after the Revolution not as an act of brute power and not as a discredited social habit, a colonial vestige repudiated by an enlightened ideology. It survived as a full-blown social institution with the control mechanisms and metaphors for transfer and distribution of the colonial regime intact. As an institution its survival was assured by the cataloguing power, the rule-making capacity, the indifference to persons of—the law? That is to depersonalize those responsible; better say—the lawyers. Without their professional craftsmanship, without their management of metaphor, without their loyalty to the system, the enslavement by words more comprehensive than any shackles could not have been forged.

### Notes and Questions

1. What image of law enforcement do you think the Virginia legislature saw when it required the slave laws to be read in churches? What image did it want the people to see?

2. Noonan says that the message of the slave laws to the masters was, "[T]he community is with you." Why would the masters need to hear this message?

3. What social institutions besides slavery can you think of in which personal domination is supported by law? Does managerial control of employees fall into this category? teachers' control of students? parents' control of children? husbands' of wives? In each of these situations, what image of the relationship between the dominant person(s) and the society does the law enforce?

4. What significance do you find in the following facts? George Wythe had emancipated his mulatto slave, Michael Brown, and his housekeeper, Lydia Brodnax, and had prepared a will leaving property and stock in trust to support them. The rest of his estate was to go to his grandnephew, George Wythe Swinney. Apparently unhappy with this arrangement, Swinney poisoned both Wythe and Brown. Wythe lived long enough to disinherit Swinney, but Swinney could not be successfully prosecuted for murder. The reason: the chief witness, Lydia Brodnax, was prevented from testifying by the application of a Virginia law that permitted blacks to testify only against blacks.

Women have often been subjected to special legal rules based on a presumption of female subordination to males. Enforcement of these rules is sometimes said to be for the "protection" of women and sometimes to "control" them. The rules have included marriage, birth control, abortion, and gender inequality. Feminist perspectives have called all this into question. But within feminism there are also disagreements about the need for certain kinds of legal rules. The following article argues that "protection" laws and "control" laws are inextricably linked and that their enforcement undercuts women's freedom.

## 9.4 | Feminism and Porn: Fellow Travelers    *Wendy McElroy*

Comstockery is the world's standing joke at the expense of the United States. Europe likes to hear of such things. It confirms the deep-seated conviction of the Old World that America is a provincial place, a second-rate country-town civilization after all.

George Bernard Shaw

SEXUALLY CORRECT HISTORY CONSIDERS the graphic depiction of sex to be the traditional and immutable enemy of women's freedom. Exactly the opposite is true.

Historically, feminism and pornography have been fellow travelers on the rocky road of unorthodoxy. This partnership was natural, perhaps inevitable. After all, both feminism and pornography flout the conventional notion that sex is necessarily connected to marriage or procreation. Both view women as sexual beings who should pursue their sexuality for pleasure and self-fulfillment. Indeed, most of feminism's demands have been phrased in terms of women's sexuality: equal marriage, lesbianism, birth control, abortion, gender justice. . . .

In the nineteenth century, critics of feminism yelled from pulpits and soapboxes that feminists were corrupting the sanctity of the family and motherhood. Similar charges were also hurled at pornography, then called "obscenity." A century later, right-wing critics of feminism and pornography sound strangely similar to their early counterparts. Perhaps this sort of criticism endures because it contains truth. Both feminism and pornography *do* call the traditional institutions and assumptions of sexuality into question.

The similarity does not end here. Both feminism and pornography flourish in an atmosphere of tolerance, where questions are encouraged and differing attitudes are respected. Not surprisingly, both feminism and pornography are suppressed whenever sexual expression is regulated.

The current backlash of censorship is an alliance between the Moral Majority (the Right) and the politically correct (the Left). This alliance is threatening the freedom of both women and sexual expression. The Right defines the explicit depiction of sex as evil; the Left defines it as violence against women. The result is the same.

The censorship net has been cast so widely that feminist classics, such as Susan Brownmiller's *Against Our Will,* are in the same peril as such porn icons as *Debbie Does Dallas.* This is inevitable. Both works address the same theme: sexual freedom in a sexually repressive world. They merely arrive at antagonistic conclusions.

Why are feminists linking hands with the Right? Perhaps they believe themselves to be in a position of power, at last. Perhaps they dream of having their view of sex become the status quo.

It is a realistic hope. Radical feminists have been successful in establishing sexual correctness as a form of orthodoxy in the university system, where no one currently dares to question concepts like sexual harassment. The media now censors itself to avoid sexually incorrect references. The workplace has turned into halls of paranoia. Anti-pornography feminists have good reason to believe they have a shot at becoming the new power structure.

Meanwhile, pornography is left as a lonely voice to depict the less popular sexual choices that women have available to them.

Feminists desperately need to reacquaint themselves with their own history. What passes for feminist scholarship these days has too often been filtered through ideology. Feminists must come to terms with two of the important lessons that history has taught over and over again:

1. Censorship—or any sexual repression—inevitably rebounds against women, especially against those women who wish to question their traditional roles. Freedom of sexual expression, including pornography, inevitably creates an atmosphere of inquiry and exploration. This promotes women's sexuality and their freedom.

2. Censorship strengthens the position of those in power. This has never been good news for women, who are economically, politically, and socially among the weakest members of society.

Freedom of speech is the freedom to demand change. It will always benefit those who seek to reform society far more than those who wish to maintain the status quo.

. . . . . . . . . . . . . . . . . .

## A CASE OF SEXUALLY INCORRECT HISTORY

... In the social turbulence following the Civil War, thousands of men and women enlisted in a purity campaign. They sought to establish a single standard of sexual morality for both sexes. This was not a drive for greater freedom; it was a puritanical campaign to narrow the choices of individuals down to socially acceptable ones.

These crusaders considered a free and open sexuality to be a reflection of the selfish appetites of men, who disrespected women. After all, women were naturally chaste. They were the mothers and the wives and the cornerstone of the church. Purity—the curbing of men's appetites—required social control. Thus, the purity crusaders rallied for laws against prostitution, alcohol, and pornography—then called obscenity.

Many female and male reformers climbed on the purity band wagon. In doing so, they destroyed a small but growing feminist movement. That movement was virtually the only voice of its time crying out for women's sexual rights. It focused on the twin goals of marriage reform and the distribution of birth control.

The story of how this movement was coldly killed is one of the most tragic episodes in feminist history. Yet it has been virtually ignored by modern feminist scholars. The tale is as follows:

By 1865—the year the Civil War ended—the U.S. Congress had adopted its first law barring obscenity from the U.S. mails. The mailing of obscenity was officially declared to be a criminal offense. But there was an enforcement problem: The post office had no legal right to refuse to deliver anything. Penalties could be imposed only after the obscene material had gone through the mail. This was awkward, both legally and tactically.

In 1868, the New York branch of the Young Men's Christian Association (YMCA) began to urge the state legislature to outlaw "the traffic in obscenity" in order to keep corrupting material out of the hands of impressionable young men. In this cause, the YMCA found a zealous champion named Anthony Comstock.

Born in 1844, Comstock was one of ten children—three of whom died before reaching majority. One might think this background would make Comstock pro-birth control. But Comstock was deeply religious and seemed to blame man's animal nature, rather than poor medical techniques, for his family's tragedies.

A passionate rejection of sexuality led Comstock to attack the dime novels, popular in his day, as "devil-traps for the young." Indeed, one of his early slogans was "Books Are Feeders for Brothels."

Affluent members of the YMCA provided their crusader with an annual salary of $3,000 plus expenses. This allowed him to quit his employment as a dry-goods clerk and devote full time to anti-obscenity work.

Comstock spent his days tracking down those who dealt in books that offended him. Then, he arranged for their arrest. But his jurisdiction extended only to the borders of New York State. To get at the publishers of obscenity—the source of the vileness!—Comstock needed a federal law that let him cross state lines. In 1872, the Committee for the Suppression of Vice was founded in New York, with Comstock as its agent. (The "Committee" later became the "Society.") Together with the YMCA, the Committee pushed for a sweeping federal law.

Comstock went to Washington, D.C., where he vigorously lobbied in the halls of Congress. Like some current anti-pornography crusaders, Comstock carried pornographic displays with him, with which he shocked and manipulated people's sensibilities. He must have put on a good show, because what came to be known as the Comstock Act passed at two a.m. Sunday March 2, 1873. The Act was pushed through in a rowdy closing session of Congress, with less than one hour of debate.

Through this legislation, Congress amended the United States criminal code to prohibit the transport by public mail of material that included the following:

> . . . [A]ny obscene book, pamphlet, paper, writing, advertisement, circular, print, picture, drawing or other representation, figure, or image on or of paper or other material, or any cast, instrument or other article of an immoral nature, or any drug or medicine, or any article whatever, for the prevention of conception, or for unlawful abortion, or . . . advertise same for sale. . . .

Birth control information was now obscene. The Act provided for up to ten years' imprisonment for anyone who knowingly mailed or received such "obscene, lewd, or lascivious" printed and graphic material.

A series of state laws modeled on the federal one quickly ensued. Every state but New Mexico took some form of action. Twenty-four states passed legislation that banned contraceptive information and devices from the public mails, *and* from being circulated through private publication. Fourteen states banned speech on the subject. Connecticut prohibited people from using birth control. Collectively, these became known as the Comstock laws.

Meanwhile, the post office assumed independent powers of censorship and confiscation. *And* Congress appointed Comstock as a special agent of the post office to inspect mail and to hunt down those who violated federal standards of what was mailable. The Society for the Suppression of Vice—which Comstock headed until his death in 1915—received a large chunk of every fine collected from these prosecutions.

Using blatant entrapment, the purity crusader racked up a large list of "victories." With no due process, postal officials confiscated, refused to accept, or simply destroyed any mail they didn't like. Postmaster General Wanamaker

interpreted "obscenity" in very broad terms indeed: For example, he declared a book by the Christian pacifist Leo Tolstoy to be obscene. Comstock's major target, however, was contraception, which he associated with prostitution.

Comstock zealously pursued birth control advocates. Using false signatures, he wrote decoy letters which asked for information. These letters appealed to the sympathy of doctors and reformers in order to entrap them. At one point, he arrested a woman doctor for selling him a syringe to be used for birth control—a syringe that was legally available in any drugstore. By January 1874, Comstock had traveled 23,500 miles by rail, seized 194,000 obscene pictures and photos, 134,000 pounds of books, 14,200 stereo plates, 5,500 decks of playing cards, had made 55 arrests, secured 20 convictions, and seized 60,300 "obscene rubber items."

Soon, he started to run out of birth control advocates to persecute. Reformers fell silent rather than become targets. Books that discussed birth control before 1873 simply removed these sections from later editions. Even periodicals which were sympathetic to women's sexual rights refused to back birth control in print.

Those brave enough to protest Comstock's methods were ignored. For example, in February 1878, the influential Liberal League presented Congress with a petition 2,100 feet long bearing 70,000 names. It protested the Comstock Act. The petition was tabled.

Many of the Comstock laws are still in force today. Contraception was not removed from the postal prohibition list until 1971, after four years of effort by Representative James H. Scheuer of New York. He became involved in this cause when a U.S. customs officer made one of Scheuer's constituents throw her diaphragm into the harbor before allowing her to re-enter the country.

The real tragedy of the Comstock laws is best appreciated by looking at how it devastated the lives of the brave reformers—both male and female—who tried to better the lot of women.

## THE BACKGROUND OF SEXUAL REPRESSION

For most of the nineteenth century, women were the chattel of their husbands. Men had legal title to their wives' property and wages, to children, and even to their wives' bodies. Women could be locked away in insane asylums at the discretion of their husbands or other male relatives. They had no voice in government. They could not enter into contracts without their husband's consent. Even labor unions shut out the most needy of workers: women. Those seats of enlightenment—the universities—locked their doors against women who dared to ask for knowledge.

To be a woman was to be powerless.

Before the Civil War, a vibrant feminist movement arose to address the abysmal condition of women.

Feminism in America, as an organized self-conscious force, grew out of the abolitionist movement of the 1830s. Here women played prominent roles as lecturers, writers, and political organizers. Abolitionism was the radical anti-slavery movement that demanded an immediate cessation to slavery on the grounds that every human being is a self-owner. In other words, every human being has moral jurisdiction over his or her own body.

Abolitionist women began to ask themselves how much better off they were than slaves. The anti-slavery feminist Abbie Kelly observed: "We have good cause to be grateful to the slave, for the benefit we have received to ourselves, in working for him. In striving to strike his irons off, we found most surely that we were manacled ourselves."

And, in case anyone missed the parallel being drawn between slavery and the condition of women, the Grimke sisters—Sarah and Angelina—explicitly compared the two. Sarah began by quoting the foremost legal authority of the day, Judge Blackstone, who declared: "If the wife be injured in her person or property, she can bring no action for redress without her husband's concurrence, and in his name as well as her own.' "

Sarah went on to observe: "[T]his law is similar to the law respecting slaves: 'A slave cannot bring suit against his master or any other person for an injury—his master must bring it.' "

Sarah also compared a Louisiana law that said everything possessed by a slave belonged to his master with a law that said, "A woman's personal property by marriage becomes absolutely her husband's which, at his death, he may leave entirely from her."

The issue that united the anti-slavery and feminist movements was a demand for the right of every human being to control *his or her* own body and property. This same principle is the core of individualist feminism today.

The Civil War derailed the drive for women's rights. Women were explicitly asked to put aside their own complaints and fight for a larger cause: freedom for the slaves through victory for the North. After the War, when the Fourteenth and Fifteenth Amendments to the Constitution passed Congress, women were left out in the political cold. The Fourteenth Amendment ensured the right to vote to every law-abiding *male* American (excluding Native Americans). The Fifteenth Amendment assured that the right to vote could not be abridged because of "race, color, or previous condition of servitude." Not sex. Women were omitted from both Amendments.

From this point onward, feminists tended to take one of three paths toward women's rights. The mainstream reformers worked for woman's suffrage. Some radical women worked for social change as expressed through "social-purity crusades"—e.g., raising the age of consent, the reformation of prostitutes, and the censorship of obscenity. In *Woman's Body, Woman's Right*, Linda Gordon commented on this period: "The closer we look, the harder it is to distinguish social-purity groups from feminist ones. Feminists from very disparate groups were advocates of most major social purity issues. . . ."

Abolitionist feminists had also believed in purity, but for them it had to emerge from the purity of an individual's conscience; social-purity feminists seemed quite willing to enforce morality by law.

Other radicals fought for sexual rights, for freedom rather than for purity. This movement offered an ideological home for those who believed in self-ownership: a woman's body, a woman's right. It was called free love.

The free-love movement is best remembered by a witticism from the twentieth-century radical Emma Goldman. When asked if she believed in free love, Emma retorted, "I certainly don't believe in paying for it." The theory of free love, however, is a bit more complicated than this response implies.

The philosophy of free love has no connection with promiscuity. For example, the banner flying over a nineteenth-century free-love community in Ohio proclaimed, "Freedom, Fraternity, Chastity." Why was such a chaste community considered a haven for free-lovers? Because it lived by the principle that no coercion should exist in sexual relations between adults. Free-lovers vehemently denied the state had any right to intervene in the sexual arrangements of consenting adults. They focused on empowering the weakest and most abused partner in sex: the woman.

There were two keys to securing sexual rights for women. The first was to reform the marriage laws, which gave husbands almost absolute authority over their wives. Marriage—free-lovers insisted—should be a voluntary and equal association between two people who shared a spiritual affinity.

The second key was access to birth control information and devices.

As Comstock tried to push the door closed on women's sexuality, the free-love movement tried to take that door off its hinges. Although it is not politically correct to acknowledge the fact, two of the most courageous figures in the fight for women's freedom were white males: Ezra Heywood and Moses Harman. Both men were destroyed because they tried to help women.

**The Heywoods and *The Word***   Ezra H. Heywood was an abolitionist and an outspoken advocate for women's rights. In 1865, he married Angela Fiducia Tilton. Although they were a devoted couple with four children, Ezra and Angela became convinced that marriage was the single greatest obstacle to true love. Indeed, the Heywoods considered traditional marriage to be prostitution. They reasoned: Men had reduced women to such socioeconomic dependence that, in order to live, the women were forced to choose between selling their labor for next to nothing or selling their bodies into unwanted unions.

In 1872, Ezra launched his periodical, *The Word,* from Princeton, Massachusetts, as a vehicle for labor reform. The Prospectus of *The Word* declared, "*THE WORD* favors the abolition of speculative income, of women's slavery, and war government. . . ." Almost from the beginning, *The Word* had a wide circulation with subscribers in every state of the union, as well as internationally. The Heywoods began with the declared intention of rescuing women from economic subordination; but, slowly, *The Word* was drawn deeper and deeper into the free-love issue. Soon, it began to focus on sexual freedom in a direct and candid manner that can be directly attributed to Angela.

. . . . . . . . . . . . . . . . . . . . . . .

The Heywoods established The Co-operative Publishing Company, from which they launched a full frontal attack on marriage. In 1873, they founded the New England Free Love League and began to date their correspondence and writings with the chronological designation Y.L., "Year of Love."

In 1873, The Co-operative Publishing Company put out a pamphlet entitled *Uncivil Liberty,* which had been written by Ezra, with Angela's active assistance. It called for women's suffrage and argued that the political enfranchisement of women would lead to the social emancipation of both sexes. Eighty thousand copies of the pamphlet were distributed.

Then, in 1876, the Company put out another pamphlet entitled *Cupid's Yokes,* subtitled *The Binding Forces of Conjugal Life: An Essay to Consider Some Moral and Physiological Phases of Love and Marriage, Wherein Is Asserted the Natural Right and Necessity of Sexual Self-Government.* The distribution of this twenty-three-page essay has been estimated variously at from fifty thousand to two hundred thousand. The term "Cupid's Yokes" referred to the healthy ties of love that should replace a legal certificate as the true evidence of marriage. Ezra also argued for birth control and called for the immediate repeal of the Comstock laws. He even ridiculed the august Anthony Comstock as "a religious monomaniac."

Indeed, Ezra seemed to delight in ridiculing Comstock. At one point, *The Word* offered a contraceptive device for sale—a vaginal-douche syringe—which was called the Comstock syringe.

. . . . . . . . . . . . . . . . . .

Ezra was charged with circulating obscene material through the mail. At the commencement of the trial, the prosecution held that *Cupid's Yokes* was too obscene to be placed upon the records of the court. Thus, the obscenity of the pamphlet was assumed when the trial started. The court also forbade any investigation into the purpose or merits of the work, as well as any medical or scientific testimony.

On June 25, 1878, Ezra Heywood was sentenced to pay a $100 fine and to be confined for two years at hard labor. On August 1, six thousand people demonstrated in Faneuil Hall in Boston. They demanded the editor's release and the repeal of the Comstock laws. After serving six months, Ezra was released under a special pardon from President Hayes. Comstock was outraged; he renewed his determination to stop *Cupid's Yokes* from circulating.

. . . . . . . . . . . . . . . . . .

Persecutions only made Ezra harden his stand. In 1882, he was again arrested for distributing *Cupid's Yokes* along with other "obscene" materials, including two of Walt Whitman's poems. He was acquitted on April 12, 1883, then quickly arrested again for distributing an essay written by Angela, which argued for birth control.

This obscenity charge, along with one in 1887, was never prosecuted, largely due to public protest. Then, in 1890, *The Word* reprinted a letter from the free-love periodical *Lucifer, the Light Bearer*—a letter which had occasioned the trial of *Lucifer*'s editor, Moses Harman, on charges of mailing obscenity.

Heywood was arrested and indicted on three counts of obscenity. He was sentenced to two years at hard labor, which he served in its entirety. Released in poor health, Ezra Heywood died a year later, on May 22, 1893, after catching a cold.

*The Word* ceased publication. It had been killed by those who sought to control sexual expression.

It was left to Moses Harman, publisher of *Lucifer, the Light Bearer,* and the circle of courageous reformers who gathered about him, to continue the fight for women's sexual rights.

**The Lucifer Circle**   On a hot June Sunday in 1879, the widower Moses Harman and his two children, George and Lillian, arrived in the sleepy midwestern town of Valley Falls, Kansas. The small town would become a center of sexual reform in America. Although his neighbors must have initially approved of Harman's respectable appearance and well-mannered ways, they soon saw a more controversial side of the man. For Moses Harman was an uncompromising crusader for free love and against what he labeled the Twin Despots: the paternalistic state and the church.

In his private life, Harman was something of a prude, but he insisted that everyone be free to make decisions concerning sex without requiring permission from a church or the state. In particular, he demanded uncontrolled access to birth control, and marriage by contract.

In 1883, Harman began publishing a periodical entitled *Lucifer, the Light Bearer* (1883–1907). The paper was so named because it was Lucifer, not God, who offered man the knowledge of good and evil. Like Prometheus, Lucifer brought light to man; like Prometheus, he became an outcast for doing so. Lucifer was the first political rebel; he questioned the status quo of authority called God.

*Lucifer* quickly became the outstanding journal of sexual liberty of its day. It almost defined the limits of sexual freedom in late nineteenth-century America.

*Lucifer* also became a prime target of Anthony Comstock, who bristled at the periodical's open discussion of birth control, and of forced marital sex as rape. Although Harman knew the risk involved in addressing such issues, he maintained: "Words are not deeds, and it is not the province of civil law to take preventative measures against remote or possible consequences of words, no matter how violent or incendiary."

On February 23, 1887, a federal marshal arrived in Valley Falls to arrest the staff of *Lucifer* on 270 counts of obscenity, which resulted from its publication of four letters to the editor. The number of counts was somewhat arbitrary, since *Lucifer* was considered too obscene to be read before a judge or jury.

Moses Harman was sentenced to serve five years in prison and to pay a $300 fine. After serving seventeen weeks, he was released on a technicality, retried without a jury on a slightly different charge, and sentenced to one year. After eight months, he was again released on a technicality.

The renowned British playwright George Bernard Shaw lamented Harman's plight in a front-page interview in *The New York Times*:

"... A journal has just been confiscated and its editor imprisoned in America for urging that a married woman should be protected from domestic molestation when childbearing. Had that man filled his paper with aphrodisiac pictures and aphrodisiac stories of duly engaged couples, he would be a prosperous, respected citizen."

Harman's last imprisonment for obscenity was in 1906, when he was seventy-five years old. Moses was sentenced to a year at hard labor in Joliet. When breaking rocks for eight-and-a-half hours a day in the bitter winter cold threatened his health, his friends pressured the authorities and managed to get him transferred.

At about this time, Shaw was asked why he did not visit America. He answered bluntly:

The reason I do not go to America is that I am afraid of being arrested by Mr. Anthony Comstock and imprisoned like Mr. Moses Harman.... If the brigands can, without any remonstrance from public opinion, seize a man of Mr. Harman's advanced age, and imprison him for a year under conditions which amount to an indirect attempt to kill him, simply because he shares the opinion expressed in my *Man and Superman* that "marriage is the most licentious of human institutions," what chance should I have of escaping?

No thank you; no trips to America for me.

If these ignored radicals were the only people persecuted by social purity laws, then anti-porn feminists could argue they were unaware of an historical connection between sexual freedom and women's rights. But there is at least one woman persecuted by Anthony Comstock of whom no educated feminist can be ignorant: Margaret Sanger.

Sanger first came into conflict with the Comstock laws as a result of her column entitled "What Every Girl Should Know," which ran in the socialist periodical *The Call*. The offending column graphically described venereal disease. In early 1913, Comstock banned it. In place of the column, *The Call* ran an empty box, with the headline "What Every Girl Should Know—Nothing; by order of the U.S. Post Office."

On October 16, 1916, Margaret Sanger opened America's first birth control clinic in a storefront tenement in Brooklyn. Handbills advertising the clinic were printed in English, Yiddish, and Italian. They urged women not to have abortions, but to prevent conception in the first place. On October 26, Sanger was arrested by the vice squad for distributing contraceptive information. Released that afternoon, she re-opened the clinic. This time the police strong-armed the landlord into evicting her and closed the place down.

As Sanger was driven away in a police vehicle, she looked out the back at the crowds of poor women still standing at the door of her clinic. They had come to her for help. Sanger wrote:

"I heard ... a scream. It came from a woman wheeling a baby carriage, who had just come around the corner, preparing to visit the clinic. She saw the patrol wagon ... left the baby carriage, rushed through the crowd to the wagon and cried to me: 'Come back and save me!'"

Sanger was sentenced to thirty days in the workhouse. Because the authorities feared she would go on a hunger strike, she served the term in a less harsh and more obscure prison.

In a provocative move, the first issue of her periodical, *Woman Rebel,* announced an intention to disperse contraceptive information. When the postal authorities declared this issue "obscene," Sanger avoided having it confiscated by mailing it in small batches all over the city. As subscriptions poured in, the post office declared five other issues unmailable.

Meanwhile, Sanger prepared a pamphlet entitled *Family Limitation,* which provided contraceptive information. Before it could be published, the federal government indicted her for the August issue of *Woman Rebel.* Facing a possible forty-five years in prison, Sanger fled to England.

Before doing so, she arranged to have copies of *Family Limitation* printed by a radical publisher, who virtually guaranteed himself a jail term. In early 1915, Comstock personally arrested her husband, William Sanger. He was sentenced to thirty days. Ironically, his trial created a backlash of public support for birth control advocates. Fake subpoenas were sold to those who wished to sit in the extremely crowded courtroom. By the time Margaret Sanger returned to the U.S. in 1916, the political climate had changed. She was a cause célèbre and the government prudently refrained from prosecuting her.

## CONCLUSION

Sexual freedom—especially pornography, which is sexual free speech—is an integral part of the battle for *women's* freedom. The censoring of sexual words and images does not simply lead to the suppression of women's sexual rights. It is an attempt to control women themselves. For women's rights have traditionally been phrased in terms of their sexuality: marriage, abortion, birth control. To surrender one iota of women's control over their own sexual expression is to deny that it is *their* sexuality in the first place.

Today, both pornography and women's sexuality are victims of sexual correctness.

Anti-porn feminists need look no further back than to the February 1992 Supreme Court of Canada decision in *Butler* v. *Regina.* The *Butler* decision mandated the seizure of pornography by customs on the grounds that such material threatened the safety of women. In praising the decision, which she considers a victory for women, Catharine MacKinnon speculated: "Maybe in Canada, people talk to each other, rather than buy and sell each other as ideas." Customs has used the decision almost exclusively against lesbian, gay, and feminist material.

*Notes and Questions*

1. McElroy argues that attacks on pornography are linked to legal regulation of feminism's demands related to women's sexuality. As you think about this, consider the following:

> Law reaches every silent space. It invades the secrecy of women's wombs. It breaks every silence, uttering itself. Law-language, jurisdiction. It defines. It commands. It forces.
>
> Law as the seamless web we believe and die in. I cannot think of a single case involving legal regulation of motherhood without thinking of all. They constitute an interconnected network of variegated threads. Abortion. "Surrogacy." Supervision of women's pregnancies. Exclusion of pregnant women from the workplace. Termination of the parental rights of indigent or battered women. Enforcement of the "relinquishments" for adoption executed by confused and vulnerable women. Forced Caesarean sections. Policings of home births. Following the thread which is any one, I find it intertwined with each of the others. When I loosen a single thread, it tightens the others. Each knotted and entangled in fabrications of legal doctrine; each attached to notions of neutrality and generality.*

2. Do you think that McElroy would agree with Marie Ashe that:

> The self-accounts of mothers and of all women—pregnant, birthing, aborting, suffering violations or growing in power—constitute utterances closer to the reality of women's experiences than does any formulation of law or of medicine. While our generalizations and extrapolations from those experiences may be in conflict, when we attend to one another we discover truths that, rising out of our natural and acculturated bodies, do not conflict. . . .
>
> I want a law that will let us be—women. That, recognizing the violence inherent in every regulation of female "reproduction," defines an area of non-regulation, within which we will make, each of us, our own "mortal decisions."†

3. Do you think that the law could recognize "an area of nonregulation"? Explain why or why not.

*Excerpted from Marie Ashe, "Zig-Zag Stitching and the Seamless Web: Thoughts on 'Reproduction' and the Law," *Nova Law Review,* Vol. 13, 1989. Reprinted by permission of the author. Some footnotes have been omitted, others renumbered.

†Excerpted from Marie Ashe, "Zig-Zag Stitching and the Seamless Web: Thoughts on 'Reproduction' and the Law," *Nova Law Review,* Vol. 13, 1989. Reprinted by permission of the author. Some footnotes have been omitted, others renumbered.

 

    🐌 Business relations are among the oldest and most controversial areas of law enforcement. From the earliest phases of contract law to the most recent developments in intellectual property law, issues of "freedom" and "obligation" have provoked debte and challenge about the relationship between law and economics. The following article explores these issues in the controversy about legal "ownership" of ideas produced in the development of computer software.

## 9.5   Softwars   *Seth Shulman*

NOVEMBER 1993, LAS VEGAS, NEVADA. Technophiles flock to Comdex, the computer industry's biggest trade show, for the thrill of the new. In a field renowned for a breakneck pace of technological innovation, the enormous, bustling event has showcased a cavalcade of cutting-edge products from laptop computers to virtual-reality software. Vendors here do everything they can to ensure that their newly minted high-tech products delight, dazzle, and even shock. In 1993, though, one of the biggest shocks of the event came from neither hardware nor software but from one small company's announcement at a carefully staged press conference.

    Stanley Frank, then president of a California-based firm called Compton's New Media, used the Comdex show to focus industry attention on the broad intellectual property rights his company had recently secured. Compton's had already made a name for itself by publishing one of the earliest and most successful CD-ROMs—*Compton's Interactive Encyclopedia*—a so-called multimedia reference disk that combined sound, graphics, and text. People in the industry had closely tracked the growing popularity of the CD-ROM encyclopedia. What they didn't know, however, is that in 1989, when Compton's first launched the product, the company had also filed for a patent covering all multimedia software. And just months before the Comdex show, the U.S. Patent Office had granted the company the sweeping ownership rights it had sought.

    To Stanley Frank, Comdex offered the perfect venue at which to gloat about the monopoly the government had handed his company. "We in-

vented multimedia," he told a packed crowd at the Comdex press conference. His company's patent substantiated the claim.

    In this case the sanctioned title of "inventor" had powerful implications indeed. Compton's patent did not cover specific programming language. Rather, in some forty-one separate claims, it gave the company exclusive ownership rights over any multimedia database software that allowed users to search simultaneously for text, graphics, and sounds. According to the patent's broad language, Compton's was the exclusive owner of the "process and concept" of so-called retrieval technology in multimedia databases.

    Frank couched his initial announcement of the patent in magnanimous terms. "We simply want the public to recognize Compton's New Media as the pioneer in this industry," he said, adding that the company hoped to "promote a standard that can be used by every developer." But as the press conference wore on, it quickly became clear that recognition was only part of what Frank sought. As the sole owner of a patented technology, the company could legally exact royalties from anyone else who wanted to use it. As Frank put it, Compton's was determined to be "compensated for the investments we have made to make multimedia a reality for developers and end users." In the terms the company laid out, all other multimedia CD-ROM manufacturers would have to either pay between 1 and 3 percent of their revenues to Compton's or negotiate a joint venture with the company if they wanted to sell multimedia products over the course of the seventeen-year lifetime of the patent.

    While there was no overt mention of it at Comdex, Compton's message also carried an implicit threat. Any multimedia publisher that didn't comply with the company's terms could face a costly patent infringement lawsuit. And if this unlucky firm lost the case, it would have to pay even more dearly: patent infringers can be subject to treble damages—a punitive payment three times greater than any economic harm Compton's might allege in the case.

To competitors of Compton's New Media, the prospect of a broad patent in their promising new field posed a serious and inescapable problem. The search tools Compton's now claimed to own were a basic feature of virtually every multimedia product. With scores of multimedia CD-ROM titles already on the market—many of them on display at Comdex—the patent not surprisingly fostered a good deal of outrage. The larger implications were particularly troubling. If other companies secured similarly broad patents, the proliferating royalty demands would seriously erode the potential for profits in the multimedia field.

. . . . . . . . . . . . . . . . . . . .

At Compton's press conference, Norm Bastin, the company's executive vice president and general manager, contended that the company had earned exclusive ownership rights because "this sort of search system was unique" at the time it filed for the patent. The company's patent lawyers had evidently convinced the U.S. government of Bastin's contention. But now Compton's faced a tougher audience. Assembled experts asserted that the techniques the patent described were widely used before the 1989 filing date. Some noted, for instance, that the technique for indexing and searching multimedia databases had been explored originally at the Xerox Corporation's Palo Alto Research Center—Xerox PARC—almost two decades before Compton's made its claims.

But whether or not Compton's originated the concept, most competitors objected to the breadth of the claim. "Patenting multimedia is like patenting the English language," said Robert Carberry, president of Fireworks Partners, a New York-based IBM affiliate, when he heard the news. As one former Microsoft executive put it, the absurdity of one company owning exclusive rights to something as broad as multimedia technology made most competitors want to jump on Compton's "like a herd of elephants on a mambo snake."

. . . . . . . . . . . . . . . . . . . .

Eventually, as the aftershocks of Compton's earthquake subsided, industry representatives began to shift their attention away from the firm at the epicenter, directing their ire instead at the U.S. Patent Office. How could the examiners have overlooked the fact that the concept of multimedia had been in circulation long before Compton's claimed to have invented it? The Compton's announcement focused the attention of the entire software field on the proliferation of software patents that threatened to wreak havoc on the industry.

To most programmers, Compton's patent represented much more than a mistake by an inexperienced patent examiner, and it concerned more than an assessment of what the Patent Office terms "prior art." Even if Compton's could unequivocally establish that it was the first to develop a multimedia database, the patent's breadth opened the door for a crippling tangle of similar claims, with royalty demands that could choke off the field's prized pace of innovation. At the heart of the Compton's debacle was a multibillion-dollar question: What exclusive ownership claims, if any, were viable over concepts that the entire software field needed to use to develop new products? Could the industry, or the patent system, ever hope to reliably distinguish between specific innovations that might merit individual recompense and broad chokeholds over shared concepts?

## SILICON VALLEY'S LAMENT

The Compton's saga posed the classic and increasingly familiar dilemma of broad conceptual ownership claims threatening to distort and stifle development in high-tech fields. It also presented precisely the kind of nightmare that some in the software industry had predicted for years. The fact is, software has proven exceptionally troublesome to the U.S. legal system since it first appeared in the 1960s.

On the one hand, software code can alter a computer's functioning so significantly that it can be seen as creating an entirely new machine. And, following this line of reasoning, the invention of new machines in the United States has always been allowed the protection of patents. On the other hand, though, software code itself is not a machine. It is made up of strings of instructions, something like the recipes in a cookbook. Historically, the U.S.

legal system has tended to treat instruction sets—even useful and lucrative ones—as forms of expression protected solely by copyright law.

The distinction is far from trivial. The different kinds of ownership systems imply widely different rights. Most notably copyright allows practitioners more latitude. A composer's symphony may be protected by copyright but the constituent parts—the musical notes, chords, and conventions of time and meter—cannot normally be privately owned. Under the copyright regime these constituent parts are held by all of us in common, reused from one piece of music to the next.

Despite its utilitarian nature, software shares many of the features of a piece of music or a written work. It is made up of a progression of subroutines that are roughly equivalent to the specific steps or directions outlined in a musical score or a recipe. And, as programmers are keenly aware, these subroutines are widely repeated from one program to another. Programmers need to have unfettered access to the language of software in order to write new programs.

Recognizing the need to maintain widespread access to these shared features, the Patent Office simply refused to grant patents on software programs in the early days of the computer age. The Supreme Court ruled in 1972 that software fell into the category of "mental processes" and held that its logical steps had to be preserved in the public domain "as they are basic tools of scientific and technological work." Copyright therefore remained the only legal method available to programmers seeking to protect their developments, and the industry thrived and blossomed with that protection.

But in a global economy increasingly fixated on the value of knowledge assets, some companies sought tighter private control over their particular advances in software design. A key shift occurred in a 1981 Supreme Court case involving a company whose application for a patent on a system for manufacturing rubber included a software program to control the temperature throughout the process. In *Diamond v. Diehr,* the Court ruled by a narrow margin that the inclusion of a software program in a patent application should not automatically disqualify it from consideration by the Patent Office.

*Diamond v. Diehr* pushed the door to software patents slightly ajar. But the Patent Office's liberal interpretation of the ruling soon flung it wide open. Before long the agency was awash in a flood of applications for patents on software programs. By the early 1990s software patents were one of the fastest-growing sectors of the U.S. patent system, being issued at nearly three times the rate of other kinds of patents.

Many in the software field began to complain that the agency's patent examiners were ill prepared to rule on the profusion of patents in this fast-paced field. They charged that the Patent Office's decisions often seemed capricious and that many of the patents it issued seemed unreasonably broad. Patents were beginning to divide the emerging software field into arbitrary monopolies that squelched newcomers and new developments alike.

Mounting tensions came to a head in the aftermath of the multimedia patent issued to Compton's New Media. With the Compton's patent and a growing number of high-profile intellectual property lawsuits in the software field, many contended that urgent action was required to address the situation. Bruce Lehman, commissioner of the Patent and Trademark Office, stepped into the breach early in 1994. He took the highly unusual step of second-guessing his own examiners, personally calling for the agency to reexamine Compton's patent application. In addition, he scheduled an unprecedented hearing in Silicon Valley to hear the industry's views on what to do about proliferating software patents to defuse the sense of imminent crisis.

By the standards of Washington, D.C., the hearing was anything but typical. First of all, the packed hall in the San Jose Convention Center, normally home to annual meetings of chiropractors and Rotarians, lacked the staid authority of Capitol Hill. More notable, though, was the distinctive character of the crowd. The youthful software programmers and entrepreneurial executives tended to mistrust the federal government. In their views and demeanor, they would prove to be far different from the lawyers and lobbyists Lehman and his fellow Patent Officer officials normally dealt with.

Opening the meeting, Lehman laid out his agenda. The best kind of patent system, he said to the hushed crowd, is clear, understood by everyone, and requires little litigation. "Our concern is that we're not quite seeing that kind of patent system, particularly in the software-related inventions area." Over the next two days, Lehman and his team would be pummeled with criticism and complaints. Only the patent lawyers who testified were uniformly sanguine about the direction of development in the field; the overwhelming majority of programmers and executives had little good to say about the way the rules of intellectual property were affecting their industry.

Douglas Brotz, principal scientist at Adobe Systems, was one of the first to testify. Adobe, based in Mountain View, California, was well respected in the field for its widely used PostScript programming language and desktop publishing tools. Brotz got right to the point. "The emergence of patents on software has hurt Adobe and the industry," he contended, relaying a tale of woe that would be repeated many times before the two-day hearing was over. "Resources that could have been used to further innovation have been diverted to the patent problem," he complained. "Engineers and scientists such as myself, who could have been creating new software, instead are focusing on analyzing patents, applying for patents, and preparing defenses. Revenues are being sunk into legal costs instead of into research and development."

As Brotz recounted, Adobe had already been sued for patent infringement by a competitor in a lengthy and costly lawsuit. Although Adobe had won the initial case and the appeal, it had cost the company more than $4.5 million in legal fees and expenses. Employees had spent thousands of work hours on the case, with the chairman of the board devoting a month just to appear at the trial. "I myself have spent over 3,500 hours of my time—that's equivalent to almost two years of working time," Brotz said.

Consequently, Brotz called for the Patent Office to return to its policy of refusing to patent software. "I take this position as the creator of software and as the beneficiary of the rewards that innovative software can bring in the marketplace," he said. A world without software patents hadn't stopped his company from creating new programs, nor had it deterred the venture capitalists who helped Adobe with early investment. Perhaps software patents might be justified if they brought some other kind of benefit to the field, Brotz said, "but I see none." He concluded that conferring monopoly positions "will promote stagnation rather than increased innovation. When companies turn from competing by offering the best products to earning money by the threat of patent litigation, we will see our best hope for job creation in this country disappear."

Jim Warren, a director of the California-based computer firm Autodesk, had a similar message for Lehman and the panelists from the Patent Office, but he was more direct in his exasperation and anger. Warren's credentials and wealth of experience gave his testimony added authority: he was the founding president of the Microcomputer Industry Trade Association, the founder of the field's first subscription newspaper, *InfoWorld,* and had helped start a number of successful software firms. He also held graduate degrees in medical information science, mathematics, and statistics, as well as computer engineering. Warren did not mince words. "There is absolutely no evidence whatsoever—not a single iota—that software patents have promoted or will promote progress," he said.

Facing the panel directly and referring only occasionally to the prepared remarks before him, Warren testified that of the thousands of programmers he had known over the past quarter century, not a single one ever said they developed a program because they wanted a monopoly on it. But in the current climate, Warren said, Autodesk, like most other firms, felt forced to try to secure patents on its software techniques to defend itself against others who might try to monopolize them. All the effort to secure patents, he said, represented "an infuriating waste of our technical talent and financial resources made necessary only by the lawyers' invention of software patents."

According to Warren's testimony, Autodesk had faced no fewer than seventeen patent infringement claims over the past several years. The company had spent well over a million dollars defending itself. And, Warren lamented, "millions more are certain to pour down the bottomless patent pit." Warren said his company was fortunate: it had the financial and technical resources to rebuff baseless ownership claims made against it. But he was not happy about having to devote such significant resources to the cause. "Your office has issued at least sixteen patents that we have successfully rebutted," Warren charged, the frustration evident in his voice. "We never paid a penny in these attempted extortions that your office assisted. But they have caused an enormous waste of resources that could better be invested in useful innovation."

Warren's complaints were also voiced by larger firms. Jerry Baker, senior vice president of Oracle Corporation, recommended that patent protection be eliminated for computer software. On behalf of Oracle, a fast-growing company boasting $1.5 billion in revenues and employing more than 11,000 people worldwide, Baker asserted that "software patents are failing to achieve the Constitutional mandate of promoting innovation and indeed are having a chilling effect on innovative activity in our industry."

Baker said the rapid pace of development in the software field put the patent system's seventeen-year monopoly "completely out of context with industry reality." More importantly, though, he stressed the difference between software and other types of inventions. "Software seldom includes substantial leaps in technology," he said, "but rather consists of adept combinations of several ideas." As Baker put it, "Whether a software program is a good one does not generally depend as much on the newness of each specific technique, but instead depends on how well these are incorporated into the unique combination of known algorithms and methods. Patents simply should not protect such a technology."

Like Warren, Baker said that his company felt coerced into participating in a patent system it believed to be fundamentally flawed. "Our engineers and patent counsel have advised me that it may be virtually impossible to develop a complicated software product today without infringing numerous broad existing patents." As a result, "Oracle has selectively been applying for patents which will present the best opportunities for cross-licensing between Oracle and other companies who may allege patent infringement."

Nearly all of the programmers who testified over the course of the hearing voiced similar complaints. Each seemed to have a favorite analogy for what was happening. One likened the situation to individual schools suing one another, claiming exclusive ownership of techniques like long division. Another compared it to carpenters having to pay a royalty every time they picked up a tool.

Tim Boyle, head of a consortium of software companies that included Compton's New Media, had his own analogy. Undaunted by the prospect of alienating one of his prominent constituent firms, Boyle urged the Patent Office officials to allow fundamental concepts like "multimedia" to remain in the public domain. As he quipped, "How would theater have developed if the concept of 'plot' were owned by someone? William Shakespeare never could have afforded a license."

Late in the proceedings, someone challenged Lehman with the fact that the only people testifying in favor of the patent system were lawyers. The point was not lost on Lehman. "There is no question that the lawyers seem to be very much in favor of patent protection," he reflected. When a programmer griped that the panel was made up exclusively of lawyers, Lehman deflected the evident hostility in the audience with humor. "Sorry, we run the world," he retorted. "Julius Caesar was a lawyer, you know. The pharoah was a lawyer. You can't get away from that."

The clash of cultures represented at the Silicon Valley hearings was perhaps most clearly highlighted in the testimony of Richard Stallman. Stallman, a respected programmer and recipient of a MacArthur Foundation "genius" award, was well known in the field as a champion of shareware—software programs disseminated freely by their creators, who receive voluntary nominal payments from users. And he had come prepared with a few crowd-pleasing missives.

"The Supreme Court has ruled that no one can patent an algorithm or other law of nature," Stallman said, "but skilled patent lawyers have been tricking the Patent Office into regularly doing precisely this in the software field." Stallman testified that a colleague of his, curious to test the limits of the system, had applied for and won a patent on Kirchoff's Law—an 1845 scientific theory holding that the electric current flowing into a junction equals the current flowing out. Stallman said his colleague sought the patent not to reap any financial benefit but to confirm his suspicion of serious deficiencies in the system. "If the Patent Office couldn't understand electricity after a century," Stallman ventured amid murmurs of approval from the audience, "how can we expect it to understand software in another decade or two?"

Like many of the other speakers, Stallman emphasized the difference between software and other types of patented inventions. "In some fields, like pharmaceuticals, one patent goes with one product," Stallman said. "Software is the extreme opposite. A typical patent covers many dissimilar programs, and even an innovative program is likely to infringe many patents. That's because a substantial program must combine a large number of different techniques and implement many features."

To illustrate his point, Stallman produced a voluminous, unwieldy printout of a computer program he had written with several colleagues, explaining that the program is in use on more than a million computers, including those of the U.S. Air Force and major companies like Intel and Motorola. "Just a few lines of code can be enough to infringe a patent, and this compiler has ten thousand pages," Stallman said, gesturing to the document. "How many patents does it infringe? I don't know. Nobody does. Perhaps you can read the code and tell me?" he challenged Lehman. His guerrilla theater made his point effectively, drawing hoots of laughter from the crowd.

"An invalid patent is a dangerous weapon," Stallman explained forcefully. "Defending a patent suit typically costs a million dollars and the outcome depends mostly on legal technicalities." But he also underscored the fact that the problem went beyond the question of technical validity. Suppose the Patent Office stopped making mistakes and issued no more invalid patents, he said. "Suppose that it is the year 2010 and you're a software developer. You want to write a program combining 200 patentable techniques. Suppose 15 of them are new; you might patent those. Suppose 120 of them were known before 1990; those would not be patented any longer. That leaves 65 techniques probably patented by others, more than enough to make the project infeasible. This is the gridlock we are headed for.

"A decade ago, the field of software functioned without patents, and it produced innovations such as Windows, virtual reality, spreadsheets, and networks. And because of the absence of patents, programmers could develop software using these innovations," Stallman said. "We did not ask for the change that was imposed on us. There is no doubt that software patents tie us in knots. If there's no clear and vital public need to tie us up in bureaucracy, untie us and let us get back to work."

As the hearing wore on, it appeared that Silicon Valley's lament was making an impression on Lehman. When twenty-nine-year-old Ted Lemon, a software engineer at Network Computer Devices, reviewed a series of broad, harassing patent infringement claims leveled against his company, the tale seemed to particularly catch Lehman's attention.

"The essence of the problem, then," Lehman summarized, is "that there was a patent issued that didn't meet the test of patentability."

"Right," said Lemon.

"And now, in effect it's being used to extort money out of people, and they just buy into the extortion scheme and then they pay up rather than solve it.

"You know," Lehman reflected, "it reminds me a little bit of the old thrillers that you used to see on television when I was a kid about the Mafia holding up the candy store, and people would let that happen, you know, getting protection money out of them." He paused for an awkward moment. "Maybe that makes me the vigorous prosecutor; maybe that's my role to do that," he mused in an odd moment of self-reflection that the audience greeted with a sustained round of applause.

## SIGNS OF TROUBLE

Within a year of the Silicon Valley hearing, the U.S. Patent Office reexamined Compton's patent and rejected every one of its forty-one claims, citing "new evidence" of prior art that had come to light. To the relief of many, the Compton's debacle had been successfully defused. Despite Lehman's intervention, however, the overarching question about the viability of software patents has grown ever more confounding and ominous since Compton's patent first surfaced in 1993.

. . . . . . . . . . . . . . . .

From this byzantine maze of intellectual property claims, two distinctly problematic types of patents emerge: those monopolizing the algorithms present in many different software packages and those claiming exclusive rights to overly broad concepts.

Computer programmers particularly disdain the annoyance of patents on the small chunks of computer code called algorithms, the discrete mathematical strings of rules that allow a computer to perform such basic tasks as moving a cursor around the screen or alphabetically sorting a list—both of which have been patented. Technically, algorithms are not patentable, but patent lawyers continue to cleverly disguise them as computer-implemented processes.

. . . . . . . . . . . . . . . .

Why do so many questionable patents continue to slip through the system? Some answers can be found in ten bland office buildings in the sterile, concrete landscape of Crystal City, across the Potomac River from the nation's capital. A visit to the U.S. Patent and Trademark headquarters here finds an agency that, despite its age and pedigree, must surely rank as one of the oddest and least-known branches of the federal government. In these buildings some 1,800 well-paid federal examiners (aided by thousands of support staff) process and pass judgment on roughly 175,000 patent applications annually.

The first thing to impress a visitor is the scale of the enterprise. The patent library holds some 23 million documents pertaining to the nearly 6 million patents issued to date. Leafing through these stacks, the extent to which patents pervade our lives becomes clear. No mundane gadget has been forgotten. Before reaching the breakfast table, almost all Americans make use of household items covered by scores of U.S. patents—from toothbrushes and shampoos to showerheads, not to mention alarm clocks, light fixtures, door hinges, and sneakers.

The team responsible for issuing patents on "computer software-related inventions" is called Group 2300, a section of examiners that exudes a feeling of fast-paced change. Having grown tremendously over the past five years, Group 2300 is now one of the Patent Office's largest departments, employing some 200 examiners. The group's document handling room, where software patent applications are processed, looks like a good-sized post office. Alan MacDonald, a supervisor and senior examiner in Group 2300, leads a brisk tour of the area. As he explains, the department used to be divided by subject matter into two separate units. Now it has fifteen. Some 15,000 patents are currently pending here. And the cases are often notoriously complex. MacDonald points out shelves upon shelves of pending applications, many in folders that are more than a foot thick.

. . . . . . . . . . . . . . . . . . . .

What is to come? . . .

Currently, though, an eerie standoff has developed. With major software firms building sizable arsenals of intellectual property as a deterrent, needless barriers to innovation are rising, as are fear and confusion on the part of even the larger players. The situation is especially poignant because so few of those involved respect the validity of the legal protections most companies have garnered.

. . . . . . . . . . . . . . . . . . . .

The kind of problem exemplified by the Compton's case has not gone away. To the contrary, it has become institutionalized. For a sense of the kind of regular eruptions we can expect in the future, consider the shock wave a virtually unknown company called E-data sent through the industry in the spring of 1996.

## THREE MEN AND A PATENT

E-data made its public debut in the spring of 1996. The tiny, three-person firm sent a letter to 75,000 separate companies warning that if these firms were conducting business over the Internet, they were likely infringing E-data's broad patent on Internet commerce.

E-data outlined its stance in a series of advertisements that supplemented the company's mail campaign. The message was simple. The ads, featuring a picture of a carrot and a stick, read, "Your choice." The "carrot" E-data offered companies was amnesty: companies that signed up immediately for a licensing arrangement—involving a relatively modest annual fee of $5,000 to $50,000, depending on the company's revenues—would be exempted from royalties on past infringement of E-data's alleged intellectual property. The "stick," of course, was the threat of a patent infringement lawsuit.

How did E-data ever obtain a patent on something as broad as financial transactions on the Internet? The story begins in 1985, when computer programmer Charles Freeny won a patent by outlining a system in which products are purchased on line and delivered electronically. It was a simple but prescient idea. Anticipating a world of networked computers, Freeny sought to patent on-line transactions such as downloading music or magazine articles on demand. With little prior art to be found, the U.S. patent examiners granted Freeny Patent No. 4,528,643, entitled a "System for Reproducing Information in Material Objects at a Point of Sale Location."

Despite Freeny's farsightedness, though, he could not have envisioned the patent's universal applicability to the mushrooming on-line commerce of the World Wide Web. In 1989, unsure what his patent might ever be worth, Freeny sold it to an entrepreneur for $200,000. (Less than ten years later, E-data publicly estimated that it expected to collect licensing fees on some $20 billion of digital transactions by the year 2000.)

Freeny's patent resurfaced with a vengeance in 1994 when it was bought by an enterprising businessman named Arnold Freilich. Seeing the patent's lucrative potential, Freilich moved fast. With two partners, he built the corporate shell for E-data on the back of a tiny company called Interactive Gift Express, Inc., which, something like an FTD florist, distributed gift packages of stuffed animals, bathroom soaps, and specialty foods.

Establishing himself as president and CEO of E-data, Freilich hired patent lawyer David Fink, whom he fondly describes as "the pit bull of patent infringement." Early on, Freilich and his partners at E-data were lampooned in the trade press as "three men and a patent," but the joking quickly dissipated as a number of financial analysts recognized that E-data's strategy, if its patent held up in court, might well succeed in exacting royalties from every company that wanted to buy and sell in cyberspace.

In response to E-data's "carrot and stick" campaign, a number of firms, including IBM, Adobe, Intermind Corporation, and Kidsoft, Inc., agreed to license the patent rather than risk fighting it. In royalty negotiations with IBM in 1996, one of the less discreet negotiators on the IBM team speculated publicly that E-data's patent, if valid, could be worth billions. In a heady three weeks that year, E-data's stock price soared from $1.63 to $11 per share.

Meanwhile, though, the vast majority of the 75,000 firms E-data had contacted by mail failed to sign up for licenses, opting instead to see whether E-data's patent would hold up in court. As a result, in the summer of 1996, E-data began to make good on its threat to sue infringers. So far the company has filed lawsuits against forty-one companies, including the Internet provider CompuServe, the financial firm Dun and Bradstreet, various software makers, including Broderbund and Intuit, and publishers McGraw-Hill and Ziff-Davis. These firms have been forced to sink millions of dollars into fighting the case in court.

"Part of our marketing strategy was to sue everybody and get noticed," Freilich said. "Well, we went ahead and sued, and everyone now knows that we're very serious about defending our claims."

"We don't want to affect anyone's ability to do business," he says, adding that he is only trying to provide his company's shareholders with "a fair return on their investment." As he puts it, "I hate being called a leech, but such is life."

Needless to say, few of the 75,000 companies targeted by E-data have much nice to say about the company. Its tactics have been derided as "patently offensive," a "nuisance," and even an "abomination." It doesn't help matters that the firm exists merely to exploit a patent.

Nonetheless, compared to the stir caused just a few years earlier by Compton's multimedia patent, most players seem surprisingly resigned to a sanctioned system in which companies extort money from each other by claiming to own absurdly broad and seemingly obvious conceptions. As Stewart Baker, a Washington, D.C., attorney who's fighting E-data's patent on behalf of several businesses, says, "We have clients who have said that at my level of business right now it is cheaper just to pay the license than to even ask my lawyers to examine what the defenses might be."

Much of the cynicism comes from the myopic limitations of the court system in dealing with the underlying problem presented by patents like E-data's. The legal battle against its claims, for example, hinges on an interpretation of Freeny's initial conception. The lawyers for CompuServe and many other defendants seek to declaw the claim by arguing that the "point of sale" described in the broad language of Freeny's patent actually envisioned a kind of on-line cash register for dispensing information at retail outlets. Whether this line of argument will win in court remains to be seen. The patent language is so vague that even if the court rules for a narrowed interpretation, the hair-splitting, semantic legal battle will fall far short of addressing the problem in future cases.

Regardless of Freeny's precise vision, if he even was the first person to ever think of on-line commerce (a highly dubious proposition by the early 1980s), the broader question is whether anyone should be able to own exclusive rights to such a sweeping concept—precisely the same question that caused the uproar in 1994 over Compton's multimedia patent. The question will undoubtedly cause numerous battles in the years to come, yet it is one that is outside the jurisdiction of the courts. It must be dealt with on a broader level of policy or legislation.

As Stallman puts it, for instance, "Two kinds of patents hurt programmers: valid patents and invalid patents. Even a valid patent can and will obstruct software development."

The E-data case is currently still pending. Recent developments in the trial indicate that the judge might be receptive to the defendants' arguments for a narrow interpretation of the Freeny patent, but the outcome remains unclear. A definitive verdict, including the appeals process, is likely to be several years and many millions of dollars away.

.   .   .   .   .   .   .   .   .   .   .   .   .   .   .   .

Certainly, the prospect of many more companies . . . seeking to exact royalties from everyone in the industry is enough to give pause to almost any player in the software field. There is little clear justification for a state of affairs in which patent holders—especially those who have made no contribution to the field—can hold the entire industry hostage to dubious conceptual claims. It is simply another example of our inability so far to set limits on the scope of ownership claims in the emerging knowledge-based economy.

## Notes and Questions

1.  Shulman asserts an "inability . . . to set limits on the scope of ownership claims." As you think about this, consider the following:

    In 1988, the U.S. Patent and Trademark Office (PTO) granted the first patent on a "nonnaturally occurring non-human multicellular living organism": a mouse genetically engineered to be particularly susceptible to cancer. Although Congress had earlier provided limited protection for certain cultivated plants, bioengineered animals— ranging from single-celled bacteria to mammals and amphibians—were barred from patent protection on ethical and moral grounds. In 1980, the U.S. Supreme Court drew upon a growing trend in the law to allow patents for "anything under the sun that is made by man," thereby opening the universe of patentable subject matter to living organisms. The Court, however, failed to define the boundaries of this new area of patent doctrine, choosing instead to induce the fledgling biotechnology industry to draw policymakers into the issue. But Congress and the PTO tacitly refused to address the growing concerns and let the question of animal patentability go unresolved. As a result, over 6000 biotechnology patent applications were filed, which were then held in limbo until the PTO's 1988 action.

    The PTO's decision to grant the mouse patent was its second attempt to force Congress or the courts to end the tumultuous and confusing decade-long struggle over animal patentability. In response to the PTO's new policy, a flood of legal and political challenges flowed from numerous special interest groups that feared the detrimental moral and economic effects such patents could have on nature and society. In 1991, the PTO obtained partial closure on the issue when the U.S. Court of Appeals for the Federal Circuit consolidated and disposed of the legal challenges, dismissing the claims for lack of standing. Although the Federal Circuit failed to address any questions of morality or law effectively, its conclusion cleared the way for the PTO's declaration that bioengineered animals and plants were appropriate subject matter for patent protection, provided that they met the traditional standards set forth in 35 U.S.C. 101. Both the Federal Circuit and the PTO relied heavily on the Supreme Court's earlier opinion and did little to clarify the guidelines or definitions for patentability. They merely established a case-by-case review process that gave the PTO arbitrary discretion over the factors it would consider in determining acceptable subject matter. This system, akin to the ill-constructed "I know it when I see it" analysis that Justice Potter Stewart employed for pornography, remains the regime under which patent review for bioengineered organisms operates today.*

---

*"From Chakrabarty to Chimeras: The Growing Need for Evolutionary Biology in Patent Law," by Ryan M.T. Iwasaka. Reprinted by permission of The Yale Law Journal Company and William S. Hein Company from *The Yale Law Journal*, Vol. 109, pages 1505–1534, April 2000.

2. The U.S. Supreme Court decision that opened the way to patent living organisms is the basis for broad claims to ownership of genetic materials:

> Today, most biotechnology inventions are filed as utility patents and not as plant patents. Instead of only protecting the plant, utility patents make protection of plant genes possible, as well as allow the breeder to protect the use of the genetic material of a number of plants, and to protect for multiple uses such as pharmaceutical, pest protection, and herbicide resistance. Prior to 1980, the U.S. Patent and Trademark Office (PTO) and the federal courts were reluctant to allow utility patents to extend to living matter. This practice ended when, in *Diamond v. Chakrabarty,* the U.S. Supreme Court recognized the patentability of living inventions. Chakrabarty, a microbiologist, challenged a denial of his patent application for a bacterium he invented that broke down crude oil. The Court held that Chakrabarty's bacterium was a product of human labor, contained characteristics "markedly different" from any found in nature, and showed the potential for "significant utility," thus making Chakrabarty's bacterium eligible for a patent.[†]

3. Controversies over "ownership of knowledge" have global, international implications:

> The uncompensated "harvesting" of biological resources from developing states can be seen as an insidious new form of colonialism, since multinational companies reap huge benefits while none of the profits flow back to the states providing the resources. In this sense, some observers refer to the Western innovators as "pirates": they engage in an illegal and immoral operation of stealing indigenous knowledge and genes with the ultimate aim of making themselves richer while keeping the poorer nations poor. According to Vandana Shiva, one of the world's most prominent activists on this issue, this practice of plundering the developing world's natural resources has a long history. For her, biological "strip-mining" is simply a continuation of the British Empire's efforts to

take India's riches while oppressing her subjects. She points out that the West also used the promise of a "better life" to dupe developing nations into consenting to increased dependence on the industrial world in the Green Revolution—a revolution which, she asserts, ultimately resulted in more crop failure, poverty, and disease.[‡]

4. The existence of international legal instruments may not resolve the problems caused by ownership of knowledge and may actually exacerbate the problem:

> . . . [I]ndigenous communities have long used their knowledge and creativity to utilize plants native to their surroundings for a variety of needs, including food, shelter, clothing, and medicine. Even early colonists who set out to conquer and subjugate what are now lesser developed countries transported discovered plant species from the South back to their own countries as new foods and raw materials for plant breeding. Northern explorers traditionally considered the knowledge and biological resources of local and indigenous communities to be public domain. This view continues to survive today as Northern transnational corporations use it, along with international treaties, to support their ability to make a large profit off of indigenous knowledge without having to compensate indigenous communities.

> . . . . . . . . . . . . . . . . . . . .

> As the usurpation of indigenous knowledge continues, a pressing need arises to protect the legal interests of indigenous and local communities, especially those in lesser developed countries. Public international law gives countries jurisdiction over all persons and things found within their borders, so lesser developed countries could take legal steps to protect indigenous and local knowledge within their borders. However, these countries face economic pressure from developed countries to sign international treaties such as TRIPs [Trade-Related Intellectual Property Rights], which try to take such sovereign rights away from the lesser developed countries. Even those treaties that vest sovereign rights to indigenous knowledge, like the Convention

---

[†]Lara E. Ewens, "Note: Seed Wars: Biotechnology, Intellectual Property, and the Quest for High Yield Seeds," 23 B.C. *Int'l & Comp. L. Rev.* 285, 293–294 (Spring, 2000).

[‡]Emily Marden, "The Neem Tree Patent: International Conflict over the Commodification of Life," 22 B.C. *Int'l & Comp. L. Rev.* 279, 280 (Spring, 1999).

on Biological Diversity (Biodiversity Convention), force lesser developed countries to choose between the potential to profit on sales of indigenous innovation and the ability to protect the indigenous knowledge system from exploitation. This conflict arises because the underdevelopment of many Southern countries, due to remnants of colonialism, causes the governments of these countries to continually seek ways to equalize their economies with those of developed countries. If governments of lesser developed countries resist pressure from developed countries, lesser developed countries could take legal steps to protect indigenous and local knowledge within their bor-

ders. Unfortunately most governments would rather use this knowledge as a profitable economic resource, enabling them to gain more power in the global marketplace. Furthermore, pressure from developed countries to force lesser developed countries to comply with TRIPs could create a legal system that not only weakens the economic situation in lesser developed countries, but also speeds the destruction of Southern indigenous knowledge systems.[§]

---

[§]From "Note & Comment: Biopiracy: Twentieth Century Imperialism in the Form of International Agreements," Lakshmi Sarma, *Temple International and Comparative Law Journal,* Vol. 13, Spring 1999, pp. 107, 108, 109.

# *10*  SURVEILLANCE

Most of the time, when one analyzes the role of the state in our society, either one focuses attention on institutions—armies, civil service, bureaucracy, and so on—and on the kind of people who rule them, or one analyzes the theories or the ideologies which were developed in order to justify the existence of the state.

What I am looking for, on the contrary, are the techniques, the practices, which give a concrete form to [the] . . . relationship between the social entity and the individual.

Michel Foucault, "The Political Technology of Individuals" (1981).

à A precondition of law enforcement is the ability to detect disobedience and discover law-breakers. Investigation and surveillance are necessary ingredients of the "rule of law." But, like the methods and content of law enforcement, these preconditions of information-gathering activities give rise to debates about "freedom." The debates include arguments about the limits of police authority to search for evidence of illegality, the importance of privacy in human relations, the nature of "data," and the propriety of new technologies.

The readings in this chapter begin with an exploration of the notion that the law's ability to acquire knowledge is a measure of its power. This is followed by a series of cases and a discussion about rules for police searches under the U.S. Constitution, as interpreted by the Supreme Court.

## 10.1  The New Outlawry and Foucault's Panoptic Nightmare

*Steve Russell*

BOTH CIVIL LAW AND COMMON LAW provided for a diminution of citizenship rights based upon misconduct. Under Roman law, in which the civil law is rooted, citizenship might be wholly lost or simply diminished. In common law countries, a citizen might, because of misconduct, become completely estranged from the community, a status called outlawry.

Such *outlawry* is putting a person outside the protection of the law so that he is incapable of bringing any action for redress of injuries; it is also attended with a forfeiture of all one's goods and chattels to the king.

Outlawry was a powerful punishment to those few citizens who had a stake in feudal society. To a person who owned nothing and had no access to law in the best of times, a more salient feature of the King's justice was its power to torture and to kill, a power commonly exercised before the rise of imprisonment as an alternative.

In its earliest form, as a criminal sanction rather than as a method of coercing submission to legal process, outlawry did implicate the full force of royal power:

> He who breaks the law has gone to war with the community; the community goes to war with him. It is the right and duty of every man to pursue him, to ravage his land, to burn his house, to hunt him down like a wild beast and slay him; for a wild beast he is; not merely is he a 'friendless man,' he is a wolf. . . .

The power of life and death contained within it the power to imprison. And if "the body of the condemned" could be dismembered, it could also be set to labor to benefit the sovereign. Since the dungeon was an impractical way to house workers, the penitentiary has become an exercise in architecture as well as in social policy.

As the penitentiary caught on in the United States, ". . . prison architecture and arrangements became the central concern of reformers of the period." A great policy debate between backers of the Auburn (New York) and Pennsylvania models for prison construction raged for many years in the United States, a debate that largely ignored an English design thought by its author to embody the final solution to most problems in prison architecture.

The Panopticon was Jeremy Bentham's architectural innovation, a central tower within a circle of pie-slice cells where a small number of guards could observe, "inspect" a much larger number of prisoners. This design is not just an efficiency, Michel Foucault perceived, but an intensification of the power relationship by ". . . dissociating the see/being seen dyad: in the peripheral ring, one is totally seen, without ever seeing; in the central tower, one sees everything without ever being seen." To see in this sense is to discipline; to watch is to order, to keep track of, to put in place, to keep in place. For Foucault, this panoptic discipline is a metaphor for much of what really controls behavior in any post-industrial society.

"The Panopticon," said Foucault, "is a marvellous machine which, whatever use one may wish to put it to, produces homogeneous effects of power." But Foucault's primary interest was in "(t)he minute disciplines, the panopticisms of every day. . . ."

> Take, for example, the ubiquitous case file, wherein . . . the child, the patient, the madman, the prisoner, were to become, with increasing ease from the eighteenth century and according to a curve is that of the mechanisms of discipline, the object of individual descriptions and biographical accounts. This turning of real lives into writing is no longer a procedure of heroization; it functions as a procedure of objectification and subjection.

. . . . . . . . . . . . . . . . . . . .

A reported felony creates a file with the police. If a suspect is arrested, a file is created with the sheriff, who runs the jail, and the magistrate who accepts the accusation, as well as with the District Attorney. If an indictment is returned, the District Clerk creates a file. A conviction means the probation office must open a file to do a presentence investigation and potentially the department of corrections will create a file that will eventually spawn a parole file. If children are involved, if official corruption is involved—any number of ifs—can result in another file in another agency documenting one incident in one citizen's life and intersecting with other files on other criminals, victims, investigations, crimes, and incidents in ways that can be collated and cross-referenced to formulate governmental policies of control.

Control is only for the outlaws, of course, and we must watch the outlaws to control them, but the cybernetic webs we are now capable of weaving trap the innocent with the guilty or, more precisely, render guilt irrelevant. Solzhenitsyn visualized data as power even before computers became a common repository for dossiers:

Every person fills out quite a few forms in his life, and each form contains an uncounted number of questions. The answer of just one person to just one question in one form is already a thread linking that person forever with the local center of the dossier department. Each person thus radiates hundreds of such threads, which, all together, run into the millions. If these threads were visible, the heavens would be webbed with them, and if they had substance and resilience, the buses, streetcars, and the people themselves would no longer be able to move; and no wind would ever again sweep the autumn leaves or scraps of newspaper down the streets. They were neither visible, nor material, but they were constantly felt by man. The point was that a so-called crystal dossier—the absolute and ideal truth—was almost unachievable. One could always find something negative and suspicious about every human being alive, for everyone was guilty of something, if one got down to it.

Constant awareness of these invisible threads naturally bred respect for the people in charge of that most intricate dossier department. It bolstered their authority.

Each exertion of State power creates another datum, another bit of knowledge and, of necessity, a Kafkaesque breach between the known and the knower. Computers never forget unless so instructed, and seldom are they so instructed. This has led to the surreal experience I have had many times of opening a file in the presence of a citizen and "remembering" *more of his history than he remembers.*

. . . . . . . . . . . . . . . . . . . .

Studs Terkel, interviewing a telephone operator, elicited this example of panopticism at its most efficient:

This company is the kind who watches you all the time. The supervisor does listen to you a lot. She can push a button on this special console. Just to see if I'm pleasant enough, if I talk too much to the customers, if I'm charging the right amount, if I make a personal call. Ma Bell is listening. And you don't know. That's why its's smart to do the right thing most of the time. Keep your nose clean.

Ma Bell's execution of the panoptic principle here exceeds Bentham's technological reach. In his first version of the *Panopticon,* Bentham imagined an acoustic surveillance, operated by means of pipes leading from the cells to the central tower. In the *Postscript* he abandoned the idea, perhaps because he could not introduce into it the priciple of dissymmetry and prevent the prisoners from hearing the inspector as well as the inspector hearing them.

Kafka understood panopticism. Joseph K., awaiting trial before an invisible court on unknowable charges, is always the object rather than the subject. His every attempt to take charge of the process, to become the doer rather than the recipient sinks him more deeply into irrationality. His lack of knowledge makes his lack of power a forgone conclusion. Something is happening, and everyone seems to know what it is except the person to whom it is happening.

Kafka's name is eponymous for that feeling of falling through some existential void, of feeling there is some pattern behind apparent absurdity but knowing that trying to discover it would be a futile enterprise. Futility in the face of the absurd is what the powerful find salutary for the powerless, and accepting absurdity as normal is the ultimate submission to authority.

. . . . . . . . . . . . . . . . . .

If arguments against any particular form of surveillance are directed at flaws in the technology, the argument can quickly become one about how much less than perfection is acceptable. We do, after all, accept capital punishment, and very few workers within the criminal justice system believe that it finds facts perfectly—or that they could really trust *their own* lives to it.

It is for most of us not a question of what is being done, but to whom. Like Joseph K., we do not expect to ring for our breakfast and be confronted by the authorities. For criminals, such happenings are an occupational harzard. As we do not expect to be treated like criminals, they should not expect to be treated like us. Outlawry is not an outmoded concept in the area of privacy. A criminal is properly subject to surveillance by a probation officer (*Griffin v. Wisconsin*, 483 U.S. 868, 1987) as is a welfare client by her case worker (*Wyman v. James*, 400 U.S. 309, 1971) or a student by his teachers. An alien—the quintessentially anonymous other—may lawfully be held incommunicado until she defecates into a waste basket while under surveillance! (*United States v. De Hernandez*, 473 U.S. 531, 1985).

Surveillance is the common element in most of our cutting edge alternatives to incarceration—electronic monitoring being the most obviously intrusive. Surveillance, especially when used to deinstitutionalize mental patients, is functioning here in the service of humane impulses, just as prisons and mental hospitals originally did. Giving rein to these impulses may be the proper thing to do, but if so we should do it with open eyes, realizing that we are creating a constitutional underclass, further obscuring lines of privacy that exist only imperfectly for persons who have been found guilty of no misconduct. Accepting panoptic discipline for any-one starts us down a slippery slope from criminal to mental patient to soldier to employee to student to ordinary citizen. "Is it surprising," Foucault asked, "that prisons resemble factories, schools, barracks, hospitals, which all resemble prisons?"

One answer to slippery slope reasoning might be called spikes-on-our-boots: the feared result will not happen if we stoutly resolve not to let it happen. Unfortunately, the United States Supreme Court in *Laird v. Tatum* (408 U.S. 1, 1972) has clipped the best spike from our boots by refusing to recognize in the constitutional right of privacy the right of innocent citizens to be free of governmental surveillance.

More precisely, the Court created an insurmountable barrier for any citizen ever asserting such a right, if it exists. The plaintiffs—victims of surveillance by the U.S. Army—argued that the mere existence of governmental surveillance had a chilling effect on their rights to freedom of association, speech, and the press, all guaranteed by the First Amendment. The Court found that the mere existence of the lawsuit rebutted the plaintiffs' claims of a chilling effect on their constitutional rights; since the plaintiffs were not harmed, they had no standing to sue.

In *Laird v. Tatum,* the Supreme Court has created one of the great jurisprudential Catch-22s of all time: chilled citizens will not sue and citizens who are not chilled have no standing to sue. By demanding a more tangible harm than chilling effect, the Court has legalized governmental surveillance by taking away the means for declaring it to be illegal. Justice William O. Douglas observed correctly in dissent that such a standing requirement ". . . would in practical effect immunize from judicial scrutiny all surveillance activities, regardless of their misuses and their deterrent effect" (408 U.S. at 26).

The possibilities of "misuse" or even "deterrent effect" are not really the point. These possibilities link the question of governmental surveillance to what an honest citizen would want to hide. Our need for privacy, if it must be justified to the government, has no sanctity as a fundamental principle and little chance of recognition by executives, legislatures or courts. Foucault reminded us that the question of surveillance (knowledge) is a question of power, distribution of power between the government and the governed. Justice Douglas, dissenting in *Laird v. Tatum,* articulated one view of the appropriate distribution:

> This case involves a cancer in our body politic. It is a measure of the disease which afflicts us. Army surveillance, like Army regimentation, is at war with the principles of the First Amendment. Those who already walk submissively will say there is no cause for alarm. But submissiveness is not our heritage. The First Amendment was designed to allow rebellion to remain as our heritage. The Constitution was designed to keep the government off the backs of the people. The Bill of Rights was added to keep the precinct of belief and expression, of the press, of political and social activities free from surveillance. The Bill of Rights was designed to keep agents of government and official eavesdroppers away from assemblies of people. The aim was to allow men to be free and independent and to assert their rights against government.

Other respectable views of the appropriate distribution of power between government and the people are common, which is why Justice Douglas expressed his in dissent. But the debate about surveillance is a debate about power, and one word for a society in which governmental surveillance may not be challenged in court is "panoptic." Bentham's efforts to gain governmental imprimatur for the Panopticon stirred up the issue of power even in the heyday of the utilitarians.

There was no question of the "rights" of prisoners and paupers, for there was no such thing as rights at all. There were only interests, and the interests of the majority had to prevail. The greatest happiness of the greatest number might thus require the greatest misery of the few.

The principle of the greatest happiness of the greatest number was as inimical to the idea of liberty as to the idea of rights. Just as Bentham attacked those parents whose scruples about liberty made them apprehensive of a Panopticon-school, so he attacked those who expressed the same scruples and apprehensions in matters of government.

With federal and state prison populations rising 115 percent between 1980 and 1990, it is fair to question how many scruples and apprehensions about surveillance we can afford. The cost of incarcerating even a fraction of the 3.2 million Americans on probation or parole would be staggering. Numbers of persons under court-ordered surveillance, therefore, rise as quickly as surveillance becomes available. Use of electronic monitoring—a technology only available since 1984—climbed about 300 percent between 1988 and 1989.

Persons under court-ordered surveillance are, in terms of most rights to privacy, the new outlaws—their homes, financial affairs, sex habits and bodily fluids subject to inspection by the government. We have outlawed, in this sense, shocking percentages of some subgroups—33.2% of young black males in California, for example. This disparate impact on some communities may or may not be the result of differing patterns of criminality, but the sheer numbers of all people under surveillance-as-punishment combined with the Supreme Court's position in *Laird v. Tatum* that governmental surveillance is constitutionally benign are ample cause to apprehend panopticism as not just a design for a prison, but a design for a society.

Panoptic architecture might be dismissed as an overblown metaphor, but the digital computer—the simple ability to count great numbers of like occurrences—has given eyes to power beyond Bentham's wildest dreams. Geographical distribution of crime is plotted by computer and used to assign police patrols. Neighborhoods with more reported deviancy get more surveillance and therefore more reported deviancy. Computers find stolen property by tracking pawnshop transactions, while incidentally inspecting thousands of innocent loans. In a country where the freedom of interstate travel is taken for granted, individual movements of most citizens who do travel are easily traced by credit card transactions. While the Panopticon made short range and small scale surveillance more efficient, computers and electronic communications could potentially make nationwide surveillance of whole communities and troublesome individuals nearly perfect.

This potential is far from realization because civil libertarians have opposed it and because civil libertarians might dominate the political discourse if the government were to move into information technology on a grand and obviously intrusive scale. Foucault warned, however, that ". . . although the universal juridicism of modern society seems to fix limits on the exercise of power, its universally widespread panopticism enables it to operate, on the underside of the law, a machinery that is both immense and minute, which supports, reinforces, multiplies the asymmetry of power and undermines the limits that are traced around the law."

Our new conception of outlawry is this: there are people, outlaws, for whom privacy is not important as a matter of policy or as a matter of law. This conception contains what Corbett and Marx call "(t)he fallacy of the sure shot," the idea that privacy can exist for *anyone* in a society they call "maximum security" and I call panoptic.

Such a society is transparent and porous. Information leakage is rampant. Barriers and boundaries—distance, darkness, time, walls, windows, and even skin, which have been fundamental to our conceptions of privacy, liberty, and individuality—give way.

It is probably a good thing that power may assert itself in ways that are more economical and less barbaric, but the "panopticisms of every day" are no less intrusive for their subtlety. We should be thankful for Foucault's forceful reminder that *surveiller* is to assert power. A decision about surveillance is a decision about apportionment of power, and once a citizen has to justify privacy, to say what might be hidden from the government, *power has already been apportioned.*

If the power to maim and to kill contains the power to incarcerate, it is equally clear that the power to incarcerate contains the power to place under surveillance. That this new form of outlawry may lawfully take place is beyond question. But, unlike the old form of outlawry, it may not always be based on misconduct. As more citizens are placed under closer surveillance for misconduct, incidental surveillance of innocent others is inevitable. The technological tools to use the resulting data exist; the legal tools to prevent data gathering against innocent persons do not.

Surveillance is now omnipresent but not omniscient. Bentham failed to achieve perfect panoptic discipline for lack of technology; we fail only because of a lack of political will. Foucault does not condemn this state of affairs; he merely describes it, and only our political principles can determine whether Foucault's description is a nightmare or a dream or just an invitation to wake up.

## Notes and Questions

1. Russell asserts that the system of "files," especially computerized databases, allows a bureaucrat to "remember" more of a person's history than the person remembers. Do you think there are people who know more about you than you know of yourself? Who might they be? How and when might the information have been collected?

2. Russell refers to "arguments . . . about how much less than perfection is acceptable" in the technology of law enforcement. Do you think that police surveillance should be allowed greater leeway if and when a "silver bullet" search technology (that can only discover illegal acts or objects) is developed? If your answer is yes, consider that the U.S. Supreme Court has held that a police search cannot be justified by the fact that it discovers something: *Sibron* v. *New York*, 392 U.S. 40 (1968); *Byars* v. *United States*, 273 U.S. 28 (1927).

3. What does Russell mean by his argument that increased surveillance will create "a constitutional underclass"?

4. Russell discusses Foucault's view that the Panopticon is a metaphor for a power arrangement. As you think about this, consider the following:

> I would say that in this kind of analysis of the relationships between the individual and the state, the individual becomes pertinent for the state insofar as he can do something for the strength of the state. But there is in this perspective something which we could call a kind of political marginalism, since what is in question here is only political utility. From the state's point of view, the individual exists insofar as what he does is able to introduce even a minimal change in the strength of the state, either in a positive or in a negative direction. It is only insofar as an individual is

able to introduce this change that the state has to do with him. And sometimes what he has to do for the state is to live, to work, to produce, to consume; and sometimes what he has to do is to die.

. . . . . . . . . . . . . . . . . .

The police govern [therefore] not by the law but by a specific, a permanent, and a positive intervention in the behavior of individuals.*

5. The United States does not have an official identity card for citizens. Although the social security card states that it is not to be used for identification, it appears to be used this way. In thinking about the implications of identity cards, consider the following:

Delta, like other airlines, is using a directive from the Federal Aviation Administration to require passengers to provide a Government-issued identification to board an airplane. If it could be shown that this in fact enhances airline safety, then we would all readily accept this invasion of privacy. The Government and the airlines, however, have never shown a connection between the ID card and the prevention of explosives or weapons in luggage.

I object to the requirement on the grounds that it forces me to satisfy the Government that I am a real person before I may exercise the constitutional right to travel within the United States. I object also that it is part of an accelerating trend toward requiring every citizen to carry a Government-issued ID card—in essence, a national identity document.

Attention seems to be focused on asking passengers for more identification rather than on subjecting all carry-on and checked luggage to complete screening for weapons or bombs. The ID requirement, in fact, serves only to lead the public to believe that somehow we are more secure on an airplane if our "papers are in order" before boarding. Probably the only effective consequence of such requirements is to get us used to the idea

of presenting identification in all aspects of our lives.

I'm shocked that more Americans are not shocked by the idea. Don't we remember the Nazi experience in Europe, where identity documents listing religion and ethnic background facilitated the roundup of Jews? Don't we remember how we condemned South Africa in the 1970's and 80's for using a domestic passport to limit the movements of certain citizens but not others? Don't we realize the dangers of allowing the Government to establish identity and legitimacy? Isn't it, in fact, the responsibility of the citizenry to establish the legitimacy of the Government?

Faced with rising crime, illegal immigration, welfare fraud and absentee parents, many bureaucrats and members of Congress insist that the nation would run more smoothly if we all had counterfeit-proof plastic identity cards. In considering immigration legislation this spring, the House came within a few votes of requiring a national identification card for all working Americans. Congress is about to authorize pilot programs with employers in several states verifying the legal identity of new employees by using central data bases. And it has already established a National Directory of New Hires containing the name, Social Security number and birth date of every person newly hired in the private and public sector.

These are precursors of a national ID card. The machinery, in fact, is now in place. All that is missing is the piece of plastic—and apparently most Americans are ready for it. Senator Dianne Feinstein, Democrat of California, has increased the stakes; she wants to create an identity card with a fingerprint, digitized photo, eye retina scan or some other biometric identity device.

Would an ID card work? It would make it easy to track illicit cash transactions, to discover after the fact all persons at the scene of a crime, to know immediately whether an adult accompanying a child is a parent or legal guardian, to keep a list of suspicious persons in a neighborhood each night, to know who purchased a gun or knife or fertilizer or Satanic books, or to know who carries the H.I.V. virus.

A suspicious police officer could demand to see your identity document and then query an on-line data base that would display identifying information about you. An

---

*Michel Foucault, "The Political Technology of Individuals." In *Technologies of the Self: A Seminar with Michel Foucault,* edited by Luther H. Martin, Huck Gutman, Patrick H. Hutton (Amherst: The University of Massachusetts Press, 1988).

employer could check the card to see whether you are a citizen or legal alien, have a criminal record or have filed previous workers' compensation claims.

But listing possible uses of a national ID card makes evident how it could be a nightmare to each of us. And that's not even considering the errors inevitable in such a data base. Even a remarkably low error rate of 1 percent would impose hardship on 650,000 innocent Americans who would be excluded from work, travel, commerce or schooling if their identity were somehow confused with a criminal's.

And that doesn't take into account the lucrative market in counterfeit ID cards. The advocates of an identity document want us to believe that it would be counterfeit-proof. But experts know there is no such thing.

Many people, charmed by the convenience of credit-card shopping by number over the phone or the Internet, think we already have a national identity system anyway. But that practice is wholly voluntary and doesn't involve centralized Government depositories of information. It is true that Social Security numbers are used in all kinds of ways. But the number is not issued to every person in the country as a national ID number would be.

Nor is a driver's license a true national identity document. While it is issued by a governmental agency, people are not required to have it when they do not drive, a photograph is not always required and a person who moves may apply for a new and different license.

A true national identity document would be mandatory; everyone would have to carry it and present it upon demand. It would be issued to everyone, probably at birth. And the identity of the bearer of each card would be recorded in a national data bank, usually along with other personal history. It would be the universally accepted proof of identity everywhere in the society. Without the card, you would have no acceptable proof of your citizenship.

Let's be clear that this is a one-way street. Once having established a requirement to carry photo ID, it will be difficult if not impossible to reverse. It's hard to imagine that the Government can begin issuing an identifying number at birth, then later tell all the agencies that have come to rely on it that they must disregard it.

What would a national ID card mean to American life? By accepting it, we will have removed the spontaneity in our lives. Every time we leave home, it will be necessary for each of us to gather up "our documents"— and those of our children, of course—before we venture out, to jog in a park, stroll in the neighborhood, lounge at the beach, buy a six-pack of beer or cross a state line. We will have empowered police officers to stop citizens engaged in law-abiding activities and demand that they produce proof of identity and "give a good account of themselves." There would be no excuse for not carrying the card—only criminals would not be carrying the card. By acting strangely at any time or by simply passing someone who doesn't like our looks, we can trigger a demand to produce the ID card. This, in turn, will trigger a search of an electronic data base to confirm our identity and perhaps provide other bits of personal data. . . .

After we have come to accept this, politicians will point out that technology allows for other means of establishing identity. Many parents would welcome computer-readable implants to identify their children in the event of kidnapping. Relatives of Alzheimer's disease patients would want these microchip implants too, so that wandering patients could be located.

Laurence N. Gold, a former vice president of Nielsen Marketing Research, has written futuristically about voluntary "devices that can be carried, worn—or even implanted under the skin. These sensors will store and transmit data . . . identifying not only who is in the room but also his or her physiological state in response to both TV programs and advertising messages." Would people stand for it? Gold speculated that, despite "20th century sensibilities, future children may have much different attitudes about this." Well, not my children, I hope. We must draw the line now. Identifying people by a number is dehumanizing, and in the end destructive of a free society.[†]

---

[†]"The True Terror Is in the Card," Robert Ellis Smith, *New York Times Magazine*, September 8, 1996. Copyright © 1996 New York Times, Inc. Reprinted by permission of New York Times, Inc.

# 10.2  Terry v. State of Ohio    *392 U.S. 1 (1968)*

MR. CHIEF JUSTICE WARREN *delivered the opinion of the Court.*

THIS CASE PRESENTS SERIOUS questions concerning the role of the Fourth Amendment in the confrontation on the street between the citizen and the policeman investigating suspicious circumstances.

Petitioner Terry was convicted of carrying a concealed weapon and sentenced to the statutorily prescribed term of one to three years in the penitentiary. Following the denial of a pretrial motion to suppress, the prosecution introduced in evidence two revolvers and a number of bullets seized from Terry and a codefendant, Richard Chilton,[1] by Cleveland Police Detective Martin McFadden. At the hearing on the motion to suppress this evidence, Officer McFadden testified that while he was patrolling in plain clothes in downtown Cleveland at approximately 2:30 in the afternoon of October 31, 1963, his attention was attracted by two men, Chilton and Terry, standing on the corner of Huron Road and Euclid Avenue. He had never seen the two men before, and he was unable to say precisely what first drew his eye to them. However, he testified that he had been a policeman for 39 years and a detective for 35 and that he had been assigned to patrol this vicinity of downtown Cleveland for shoplifters and pickpockets for 30 years. He explained that he had developed routine habits of observation over the years and that he would "stand and watch people or walk and watch people at many intervals of the day." He added: "Now, in this case when I looked over they didn't look right to me at the time."

His interest aroused, Officer McFadden took up a post of observation in the entrance to a store 300 to 400 feet away from the two men. "I get more purpose to watch them when I seen their movements," he testified. He saw one of the men leave the other one and walk southwest on Huron Road, past some stores. The man paused for a moment and looked in a store window, then walked on a short distance, turned around and walked back toward the corner, pausing once again to look in the same store window. He rejoined his companion at the corner, and the two conferred briefly. Then the second man went through the same series of motions, strolling down Huron Road, looking in the same window, walking on a short distance, turning back, peering in the store window again, and returning to confer with the first man at the corner. The two men repeated this ritual alternately between five and six times apiece—in all, roughly a dozen trips. At one point, while the two were standing together on the corner, a third man approached them and engaged them briefly in conversation. This man then left the two others and walked west on Euclid Avenue. Chilton and Terry resumed their measured pacing, peering and conferring. After this had gone on for 10 to 12 minutes, the two men walked off together, heading west on Euclid Avenue, following the path taken earlier by the third man.

By this time Officer McFadden had become thoroughly suspicious. He testified that after observing their elaborately casual and oft-repeated reconnaissance of the store window on Huron Road, he suspected the two men of "casing a job, a stick-up," and that he considered it his duty as a police officer to investigate further. He added that he feared "they may have a gun." Thus, Officer McFadden followed Chilton and Terry and saw them stop in front of Zucker's store to talk to the same man who had conferred with them earlier on the street corner. Deciding that the situation was ripe for direct action, Officer McFadden approached the three men, identified himself as a police officer and asked for their names. At this point his knowledge was confined to what he had observed. He was not acquainted with any of the three men by name or by sight, and he had received no information concerning them from any other source. When the men "mumbled something" in response to his inquiries, Officer

---

Some footnotes and case citations omitted, and footnotes have been renumbered.—ED.

[1]They prosecuted their state court appeals together through the same attorney, and they petitioned this Court for certiorari together. Following the grant of the writ upon this joint petition, Chilton died. Thus, only Terry's conviction is here for review.

McFadden grabbed petitioner Terry, spun him around so that they were facing the other two, with Terry between McFadden and the others, and patted down the outside of his clothing. In the left breast pocket of Terry's overcoat Officer McFadden felt a pistol. He reached inside the overcoat pocket, but was unable to remove the gun. At this point, keeping Terry between himself and the others, the officer ordered all three men to enter Zucker's store. As they went in, he removed Terry's overcoat completely, removed a .38-caliber revolver from the pocket and ordered all three men to face the wall with their hands raised. Officer McFadden proceeded to pat down the outer clothing of Chilton and the third man, Katz. He discovered another revolver in the outer pocket of Chilton's overcoat, but no weapons were found on Katz. The officer testified that he only patted the men down to see whether they had weapons, and that he did not put his hands beneath the outer garments of either Terry or Chilton until he felt their guns. So far as appears from the record, he never placed his hands beneath Katz' outer garments. Officer McFadden seized Chilton's gun, asked the proprietor of the store to call a police wagon, and took all three men to the station, where Chilton and Terry were formally charged with carrying concealed weapons.

On the motion to suppress the guns the prosecution took the position that they had been seized following a search incident to a lawful arrest. The trial court rejected this theory, stating that it "would be stretching the facts beyond reasonable comprehension" to find that Officer McFadden had had probable cause to arrest the men before he patted them down for weapons. However, the court denied the defendants' motion on the ground that Officer McFadden, on the basis of his experience, "had reasonable cause to believe . . . that the defendants were conducting themselves suspiciously, and some interrogation should be made of their action." Purely for his own protection, the court held, the officer had the right to pat down the outer clothing of these men, who he had reasonable cause to believe might be armed. The court distinguished between an investigatory "stop" and an arrest, and between a "frisk" of the outer clothing for weapons and a full-blown search for evidence of crime. The frisk, it held, was essential to the proper performance of the officer's investigatory duties, for without it "the answer to the police officer may be a bullet, and a loaded pistol discovered during the frisk is admissible."

After the court denied their motion to suppress, Chilton and Terry waived jury trial and pleaded not guilty. The court adjudged them guilty, and the Court of Appeals for the Eighth Judicial District, Cuyahoga County, affirmed. *State* v. *Terry,* 5 Ohio App.2d 122, 214 N.E.2d 114 (1966). The Supreme Court of Ohio dismissed their appeal on the ground that no "substantial constitutional question" was involved. We granted certiorari, 387 U.S. 929, 87 S.Ct. 2050, 18 L.Ed.2d 989 (1967), to determine whether the admission of the revolvers in evidence violated petitioner's rights under the Fourth Amendment, made applicable to the States by the Fourteenth. *Mapp* v. *Ohio,* 376 U.S. 643, 81 S.Ct. 1684, 6 L.Ed.2d 1081 (1961). We affirm the conviction.

The Fourth Amendment provides that "the right of the people to be secure in their persons, houses, papers, and effects, against unreasonable searches and seizures, shall not be violated. . . ." We have recently held that "the Fourth Amendment protects people, not places," *Katz* v. *United States,* 389 U.S. 347, 351, 88 S.Ct. 507, 511, 19 L.Ed.2d 576 (1967), and wherever an individual may harbor a reasonable "expectation of privacy," id., at 361, 88 S.Ct. at 507 (Mr. Justice Harlan, concurring), he is entitled to be free from unreasonable governmental intrusion. . . . Unquestionably petitioner was entitled to the protection of the Fourth Amendment as he walked down the street in Cleveland. The question is whether in all the circumstances of this on-the-street encounter, his right to personal security was violated by an unreasonable search and seizure. . . .

On the one hand, it is frequently argued that in dealing with the rapidly unfolding and often dangerous situations on city streets the police are in need of an escalating set of flexible responses, graduated in relation to the amount of information they possess. For this purpose it is urged that distinctions should be made between a "stop" and an "arrest" (or a "seizure" of a person), and between a "frisk" and a "search." Thus, it is argued, the police should be allowed to "stop" a person and detain him briefly for questioning upon suspicion that he may be connected with criminal activity. Upon suspicion that the person may be armed, the police should have the power to "frisk" him for weapons. If the "stop" and the "frisk" give rise to probable cause to believe that the suspect has committed a crime, then the police should be empowered to make a formal "arrest," and a full incident "search" of the person. This scheme is justified in part upon the notion that a "stop" and a "frisk" amount to a mere "minor inconvenience and petty indignity," which can properly be imposed upon the citizen in the interest of effective law enforcement on the basis of a police officer's suspicion.

On the other side the argument is made that the authority of the police must be strictly circumscribed by the law of arrest and search as it has developed to date in the traditional jurisprudence of the Fourth Amendment.... The heart of the Fourth Amendment, the argument runs, is a severe requirement of specific justification for any intrusion upon protected personal security, coupled with a highly developed system of judicial controls to enforce upon the agents of the State the commands of the Constitution. Acquiescence by the courts in the compulsion inherent in the field interrogation practices at issue here, it is urged, would constitute an abdication of judicial control over, and indeed an encouragement of, substantial interference with liberty and personal security by police officers whose judgment is necessarily colored by their primary involvement in "the often competitive enterprise of ferreting out crime." *Johnson* v. *United States,* 33 U.S. 10, 14, 68 S.Ct. 367, 369, 92 L.Ed. 436 (1948). This, it is argued, can only serve to exacerbate police-community tensions in the crowded centers of our Nation's cities.

... The State has characterized the issue here as "the right of a police officer ... to make an on-the-street stop, interrogate and pat down for weapons (known in street vernacular as 'stop and frisk')." But this is only partly accurate. For the issue is not the abstract propriety of the police conduct, but the admissibility against petitioner of the evidence uncovered by the search and seizure. Ever since its inception, the rule excluding evidence seized in violation of the Fourth Amendment has been recognized as a principal mode of discouraging lawless police conduct. Thus its major thrust is a deterrent one, and experience has taught that it is the only effective deterrent to police misconduct in the criminal context, and that without it the constitutional guarantee against unreasonable searches and seizures would be a mere "form of words." The rule also serves another vital function—"the imperative of judicial integrity...."

The exclusionary rule has its limitations, however, as a tool of judicial control.... In some contexts the rule is ineffective as a deterrent. Street encounters between citizens and police officers are incredibly rich in diversity. They range from wholly friendly exchanges of pleasantries or mutually useful information to hostile confrontations of armed men involving arrests, or injuries, or loss of life. Moreover, hostile confrontations are not all of a piece. Some of them begin in a friendly enough manner, only to take a different turn upon the injection of some unexpected element into the conversation. Encounters are initiated by the police for a wide variety of purposes, some of which are wholly unrelated to a desire to prosecute for crime.[2] Doubtless some police "field interrogation" conduct violates the Fourth Amendment. But a stern refusal by this Court to condone such activity does not necessarily render it responsive to the exclusionary rule. Regardless of how effective the rule may be where obtaining convictions is an important objective of the police, it is powerless to deter invasions of constitutionally guaranteed rights where the police either have no interest in prosecuting or are willing to forgo successful prosecution in the interest of serving some other goal.

---

[2]This sort of police conduct may, for example, be designed simply to help an intoxicated person find his way home, with no intention of arresting him unless he becomes obstreperous. Or the police may be seeking to mediate a domestic quarrel which threatens to erupt into violence. They may accost a woman in an area known for prostitution as part of a harassment campaign designed to drive prostitutes away without the considerable difficulty involved in prosecuting them. Or they may be conducting a dragnet search of all teenagers in a particular section of the city for weapons because they have heard rumors of an impending gang fight.

Proper adjudication of cases in which the exclusionary rule is invoked demands a constant awareness of these limitations. The wholesale harassment by certain elements of the police community, of which minority groups, particularly Negroes, frequently complain, will not be stopped by the exclusion of any evidence from any criminal trial. Yet a rigid and unthinking application of the exclusionary rule, in futile protest against practices which it can never be used effectively to control, may exact a high toll in human injury and frustration of efforts to prevent crime. No judicial opinion can comprehend the protean variety of the street encounter, and we can only judge the facts of the case before us. Nothing we say today is to be taken as indicating approval of police conduct outside the legitimate investigative sphere. Under our decision, courts still retain their traditional responsibility to guard against police conduct which is overbearing or harassing, or which trenches upon personal security without the objective evidentiary justification which the Constitution requires. When such conduct is identified, it must be condemned by the judiciary and its fruits must be excluded from evidence in criminal trials. . . .

> . . . The scheme of the Fourth Amendment becomes meaningful only when it is assured that at some point the conduct of those charged with enforcing the laws can be subjected to the more detached, neutral scrutiny of a judge who must evaluate the reasonableness of a particular search or seizure in light of the particular circumstances. And in making that assessment it is imperative that the facts be judged against an objective standard: would the facts available to the officer at the moment of the seizure or the search "warrant a man of reasonable caution in the belief" that the action taken was appropriate?

. . . [W]e cannot blind ourselves to the need for law enforcement officers to protect themselves and other prospective victims of violence in situations where they may lack probable cause for an arrest. When an officer is justified in believing that the individual whose suspicious behavior he is investigating at close range is armed and presently dangerous to the officer or to others, it would appear to be clearly unreasonable to deny the officer the power to take necessary measures to determine whether the person is in fact carrying a weapon and to neutralize the threat of physical harm. . . .

Our evaluation of the proper balance that has to be struck in this type of case leads us to conclude that there must be a narrowly drawn authority to permit a reasonable search for weapons for the protection of the police officer, where he has reason to believe that he is dealing with an armed and dangerous individual, regardless of whether he has probable cause to arrest the individual for a crime. The officer need not be absolutely certain that the individual is armed; the issue is whether a reasonably prudent man in the circumstances would be warranted in the belief that his safety or that of others was in danger. And in determining whether the officer acted reasonably in such circumstances, due weight must be given, not to his inchoate and unparticularized suspicion or "hunch," but to the specific reasonable inferences which he is entitled to draw from the facts in light of his experience.

We must now examine the conduct of Officer McFadden in this case to determine whether his search and seizure of petitioner were reasonable, both at their inception and as conducted. He had observed Terry, together with Chilton and another man, acting in a manner he took to be preface to a "stick-up." We think on the facts and circumstances Officer McFadden detailed before the trial judge a reasonably prudent man would have been warranted in believing petitioner was armed and thus presented a threat to the officer's safety while he was investigating his suspicious behavior. The actions of Terry and Chilton were consistent with McFadden's hypothesis that these men were contemplating a daylight robbery—which, it is reasonable to assume, would be likely to involve the use of weapons—and nothing in their conduct from the time he first noticed them until the time he confronted them and identified himself as a police officer gave him sufficient reason to negate that hypothesis. Although the trio had departed the original scene, there was nothing to indicate abandonment of an intent to commit a robbery at some point. Thus, when Officer McFadden approached the three men gathered before the display window at Zucker's store he had observed enough to make it quite reasonable to fear that they were armed; and nothing in their response to his hailing them, identifying himself as a police officer, and asking their names served to dispel that reasonable belief. We cannot say his decision at that point to seize Terry and pat his clothing for weapons was the product of a volatile or inventive imagination, or was undertaken simply as an act of harassment; the record evidences the tempered act of a policeman who in the course of an investigation had to make a quick decision as to how to protect himself and others from possible danger, and took limited steps to do so. . . .

. . . The sole justification of the search in the present situation is the protection of the police officer and others nearby, and it must therefore be confined in scope to an intrusion reasonably designed to discover guns, knives, clubs, or other hidden instruments for the assault of the police officer. The scope of the search in this case presents no serious problem in light of these standards. Officer McFadden patted down the outer clothing of petitioner and his two companions. He did not place his hands in their pockets or under the outer surface of their garments until he had felt weapons, and then he merely reached for and removed the guns. He never did invade Katz' person beyond the outer surfaces of his clothes, since he discovered nothing in his pat-down which might have been a weapon. Officer McFadden confined his search strictly to what was minimally necessary to learn whether the men were armed and to disarm them once he discovered the weapons. He did not conduct a general exploratory search for whatever evidence of criminal activity he might find.

We conclude that the revolver seized from Terry was properly admitted in evidence against him. At the time he seized petitioner and searched him for weapons, Officer McFadden had reasonable grounds to believe that petitioner was armed and dangerous, and it was necessary for the protection of himself and others to take swift measures to discover the true facts and neutralize the threat of harm if it materialized. The policeman carefully restricted his search to what was appropriate to the discovery of the particular items which he sought. Each case of this sort will, of course, have to be decided on its own facts. We merely hold today that where a police officer observes unusual conduct which leads him reason-

ably to conclude in light of his experience that criminal activity may be afoot and that the persons with whom he is dealing may be armed and presently dangerous, where in the course of investigating this behavior he identifies himself as a policeman and makes reasonable inquiries, and where nothing in the initial stages of the encounter serves to dispel his reasonable fear for his own or others' safety, he is entitled for the protection of himself and others in the area to conduct a carefully limited search of the outer clothing of such persons in an attempt to discover weapons which might be used to assault him. Such a search is a reasonable search under the Fourth Amendment and any weapons seized may properly be introduced in evidence against the person from whom they were taken.

Affirmed.

[Concurring opinion of MR. JUSTICE HARLAN has been omitted.—ED.]

MR. JUSTICE DOUGLAS *dissenting*.

I agree that petitioner was "seized" within the meaning of the Fourth Amendment. I also agree that frisking petitioner and his companions for guns was a "search." But it is a mystery how that "search" and that "seizure" can be constitutional by Fourth Amendment standards, unless there was "probable cause" to believe that (1) a crime had been committed or (2) a crime was in the process of being committed or (3) a crime was about to be committed.

The opinion of the Court disclaims the existence of "probable cause." If loitering were in issue and that was the offense charged, there would be "probable cause" shown. But the crime here is carrying concealed weapons; and there is no basis for concluding that the officer had "probable cause" for believing that that crime was being committed. Had a warrant been sought, a magistrate would, therefore, have been unauthorized to issue one, for he can act only if there is a showing of "probable cause." We hold today that the police have greater authority to make a "seizure" and conduct a "search" than a judge has to authorize such action. We have said precisely the opposite over and over again.

In other words, police officers up to today have been permitted to effect arrests or searches without warrants only when the facts within their personal knowledge would satisfy the constitutional standard of *probable cause.* At the time of their "seizure" without a warrant they must possess facts concerning the person arrested that would have satisfied a magistrate that "probable cause" was indeed present. The term "probable cause" rings a bell of certainty that is not sounded by phrases such as "reasonable suspicion." Moreover, the meaning of "probable cause" is deeply imbedded in our constitutional history. As we stated in *Henry* v. *United States,* 361 U.S. 98, 100–102, 80 S.Ct. 168, 170:

> The requirement of probable cause has roots that are deep in our history. The general warrant, in which the name of the person to be arrested was left blank, and the writs of assistance, against which James Otis inveighed, both perpetuated the oppressive practice of allowing the police to arrest and search on suspicion. Police control took the place of judicial control, since no showing of "probable cause" before a magistrate was required. . . .
>
> That philosophy [rebelling against these practices] later was reflected in the Fourth Amendment. And as the early American decisions both before and immediately after its adoption show, common rumor or report, suspicion, or even "strong reason to suspect" was not adequate to support a warrant for arrest. And that principle has survived to this day. . . .

. . . To give the police greater power than a magistrate is to take a long step down the totalitarian path. Perhaps such a step is desirable to cope with modern forms of lawlessness. But if it is taken, it should be the deliberate choice of the people through a constitutional amendment. . . .

There have been powerful hydraulic pressures throughout our history that bear heavily on the Court to water down constitutional guarantees and give the police the upper hand. That hydraulic pressure has probably never been greater than it is today.

Yet if the individual is no longer to be sovereign, if the police can pick him up whenever they do not like the cut of his jib, if they can "seize" and "search" him in their discretion, we enter a new regime. The decision to enter it should be made only after a full debate by the people of this country.

## Notes and Questions

1. Why did Chief Justice Warren say that the exclusionary rule is not very effective in regulating police actions in which arrest is not the police officer's aim?

2. The famous decisions of the Warren court concerning police officers [e.g., *Miranda* v. *Arizona,* 384 U.S. 436 (1966), *Escobedo* v. *Illinois,* 378 U.S. 478 (1964), and *Mapp* v. *Ohio,* 367 U.S. 643 (1961)] all involved cases in which the defendant had been convicted after trial. What role can the U.S. Supreme Court play in the vast majority of cases, in which defendants plead guilty and do not have a trial?

3. If police officers are more afraid of attack than are other citizens, how can the judge, when determining the reasonableness of the officer's perception, evaluate the "specific reasonable inferences which he is entitled to draw from the facts in light of his experience"? Under this test, would it be permissible for police officers to stop and frisk blacks more often than whites? Youths more often than the elderly? Men more often than women?

4. Why does Douglas believe that "probable cause" is a more meaningful concept than "reasonable suspicion"? Is either standard more or less "objective" than the other? Why or why not?

5. The Court says, "Encounters are initiated by the police for a wide variety of purposes, some of which are wholly unrelated to a desire to prosecute for crime." In what ways are such purposes within the scope of the police work? How do the examples given by the Court fit within the framework of surveillance described by Steve Russell in "The New Outlawry and Foucault's Panoptic Nightmare"?

6. The Court rationalizes its ruling in part by saying, "we cannot blind ourselves to the need for law enforcement officers to protect themselves . . ." How reasonable is this rationale in light of the statistics cited by Kris Hundley in "The High Costs of Cop Stress" (in notes after *Florida* v. *Bostick*), which show that the rate of police suicide is more than double the rate of police murder? Is the Court blinding itself to the real dangers involved in law enforcement? What purposes are served by focusing on one cause of death and not the other?

# 10.3 | Brown v. Texas    *99 S.Ct. 2637 (1979)*

MR. CHIEF JUSTICE BURGER *delivered the opinion of the Court.* . . .

## I

AT 12:45 IN THE afternoon of December 9, 1977, Officers Venegas and Sotelo of the El Paso Police Department were cruising in a patrol car. They observed appellant [Brown] and another man walking in opposite directions away from one another in an alley. Although the two men were a few feet apart when they were first seen, Officer Venegas later testified that both officers believed the two had been together or were about to meet until the patrol car appeared.

The car entered the alley, and Officer Venegas got out and asked appellant to identify himself and explain what he was doing there. The other man was not questioned or detained. The officer testified that he stopped appellant because the situation "looked suspicious and we had never seen that subject in the area before." The area of El Paso where appellant was stopped has a high incidence of drug traffic. However, the officers did not claim to suspect appellant of any specific misconduct, nor did they have any reason to believe that he was armed.

Appellant refused to identify himself and angrily asserted that the officers had no right to stop him. Officer Venegas replied that he was in a "high drug problem area"; Officer Sotelo then "frisked" appellant, but found nothing.

When appellant continued to refuse to identify himself, he was arrested for violation of Texas Penal Code Ann. §38.02(a) (1974), which makes it a criminal act for a person to refuse to give his name and address to an officer "who has lawfully stopped him and requested the information."[1] Following the arrest the officers searched appellant; nothing untoward was found.

While being taken to the El Paso County Jail appellant identified himself. Nonetheless, he was held in custody and charged with violating §38.02(a). When he was booked he was routinely searched a third time. Appellant was convicted in the El Paso Municipal Court and fined $20 plus court costs for violation of §38.02. He then exercised his right under Texas law to a trial *de novo* [anew—ED.] in the El Paso County Court. There, he moved to set aside the information on the ground that §38.02(a) of the Texas Penal Code violated the First, Fourth, and Fifth Amendments and was unconstitutionally vague in violation of the Fourteenth Amendment. The motion was denied. Appellant waived a jury, and the court convicted him and imposed a fine of $45 plus court costs. . . .

## II

When the officers detained appellant for the purpose of requiring him to identify himself, they performed a seizure of his person subject to the requirements of the Fourth Amendment. In convicting appellant, the County Court necessarily found as a matter of fact that the officers "lawfully stopped" appellant. The Fourth Amendment, of course, "applies to all seizures of the person, including seizures that involve only a brief detention short of traditional arrest." *Davis* v. *Mississippi,* 394 U.S. 721, 89 S.Ct. 1394, 22 L.Ed.2d 676 (1969); *Terry* v. *Ohio,* 392 U.S. 1, 16–19, 88 S.Ct. 1868, 1877, 20 L.Ed.2d 889 (1968) "'[W]henever a police officer accosts an individual and restrains his freedom to walk away, he has "seized" that person,' *id.,* at 16, 88 S.Ct., at 1877, and the Fourth Amendment requires that the seizure be 'reasonable.'" *United States* v. *Brignoni-Ponce,* 422 U.S. 873, 878, 95 S.Ct. 2574, 2578, 45 L.Ed.2d 607 (1975).

The reasonableness of seizures that are less intrusive than a traditional arrest, depends "'on a balance between the public interest and the individual's right to personal security free from arbitrary interference by law officers.'" *Pennsylvania* v. *Mimms,* 434 U.S. 106, 109, 98 S.Ct. 330, 332, 54 L.Ed.2d 331 (1977); *United States* v. *Brignoni-Ponce, supra,* 422 U.S., at 878, 95 S.Ct., at 2578. Consideration of the constitutionality of

---

Some case citations have been omitted. One footnote has also been omitted.—ED.

[1]The entire section reads as follows:
   "§38.02 Failure to Identify as Witness
   "(a) A person commits an offense if he intentionally refuses to report or gives a false report of his name and residence address to a peace officer who has lawfully stopped him and requested the information."

such seizures involves a weighing of the gravity of the public concerns served by the seizure, the degree to which the seizure advances the public interest, and the severity of the interference with individual liberty.

A central concern in balancing these competing considerations in a variety of settings has been to assure that an individual's reasonable expectation of privacy is not subject to arbitrary invasions solely at the unfettered discretion of officers in the field. To this end, the Fourth Amendment requires that a seizure must be based on specific, objective facts indicating that society's legitimate interests require the seizure of the particular individual, or that the seizure must be carried out pursuant to a plan embodying explicit, neutral limitations on the conduct of individual officers.

The State does not contend that appellant was stopped pursuant to a practice embodying neutral criteria, but rather maintains that the officers were justified in stopping appellant because they had a "reasonable, articulable suspicion that a crime had just been, was being, or was about to be committed." We have recognized that in some circumstances an officer may detain a suspect briefly for questioning although he does not have "probable cause" to believe that the suspect is involved in criminal activity, as is required for a traditional arrest. . . . However, we have required the officers to have a reasonable suspicion, based on objective facts, that the individual is involved in criminal activity. . . .

The flaw in the State's case is that none of the circumstances preceding the officers' detention of appellant justified a reasonable suspicion that he was involved in criminal conduct. Officer Venegas testified at appellant's trial that the situation in the alley "looked suspicious," but he was unable to point to any facts supporting that conclusion.[2]

There is no indication in the record that it was unusual for people to be in the alley. The fact that appellant was in a neighborhood frequented by drug users, standing alone, is not a basis for concluding that appellant himself was engaged in criminal conduct. In short, the appellant's activity was no different from the activity of other pedestrians in that neighborhood. When pressed, Officer Venegas acknowledged that the only reason he stopped appellant was to ascertain his identity. The record suggests an understandable desire to assert a police presence; however, that purpose does not negate Fourth Amendment guarantees.

In the absence of any basis for suspecting appellant of misconduct, the balance between public interest and appellant's right to personal security and privacy tilts in favor of freedom from police interference. The Texas statute under which appellant was stopped and required to identify himself is designed to advance a weighty social objective in large metropolitan centers: prevention of crime. But even assuming that purpose is served to some degree by stopping and demanding identification from an individual without any specific basis for believing he is involved in criminal activity, the guarantees of the Fourth Amendment do not allow it. When such a stop is not based on objective criteria, the risk of arbitrary and abusive police practices exceeds tolerable limits.

The application of Tex. Penal Code Ann., Tit. 8, §38.02 (1974), to detain appellant and require him to identify himself violated the Fourth Amendment because the officers lacked any reasonable suspicion to believe appellant was engaged or had engaged in criminal conduct. Accordingly, appellant may not be punished for refusing to identify himself, and the conviction is
*Reversed.*

## APPENDIX TO OPINION OF THE COURT

THE COURT: . . . What do you think about if you stop a person lawfully, and then if he doesn't want to talk to you, you put him in jail for committing a crime.

MR. PATTON [Prosecutor]: Well first of all, I would question the Defendant's statement in his mo-

---

[2]This situation is to be distinguished from the observations of a trained, experienced police officer who is able to perceive and articulate meaning in given conduct which would be wholly innocent to the untrained observer. See United States v. Brignoni-Ponce, 422 U.S. 873, 884–885, 95 S.Ct. 2574, 2582, 45 L.Ed.2d 607 (1975); Christensen v. United States, 104 U.S. App.D.C. 35, 36, 259 F.2d 192, 193 (1958).

tion that the First Amendment gives an individual the right to silence.

THE COURT: . . . I'm asking you why should the State put you in jail because you don't want to say anything.

MR. PATTON: Well, I think there's certain interests that have to be viewed.

THE COURT: Okay, I'd like you to tell me what those are.

MR. PATTON: Well, the Governmental interest to maintain the safety and security of the society and the citizens to live in the society, and there are certainly strong Governmental interests in that direction and because of that, these interests outweigh the interests of an individual for a certain amount of intrusion upon his personal liberty. I think these Governmental interests outweigh the individual's interests in this respect, as far as simply asking an individual for his name and address under the proper circumstances.

THE COURT: But why should it be a crime to not answer?

MR. PATTON: Again, I can only contend that if an answer is not given, it tends to disrupt.

THE COURT: What does it disrupt?

MR. PATTON: I think it tends to disrupt the goal of this society to maintain security over its citizens to make sure they are secure in their . . . homes.

THE COURT: How does that secure anybody by forcing them, under penalty of being prosecuted, to giving their name and address, even though they are lawfully stopped?

MR. PATTON: Well I, you know under the circumstances in which some individuals would be lawfully stopped, it's presumed that perhaps this individual is up to something, and the officer is doing his duty simply to find out the individual's name and address, and to determine what exactly is going on.

THE COURT: I'm not questioning, I'm not asking whether the officer shouldn't ask questions. I'm sure they should ask everything they possibly could find out. *What I'm asking is what's the State's interest in putting a man in jail because he doesn't want to answer something.* I realize lots of times an officer will give a defendant a *Miranda* warning which means a defendant doesn't have to make a statement. Lots of defendants go ahead and confess, which is fine if they want to do that. But if they don't confess, you can't put them in jail, can you, for refusing to confess to a crime? [Emphasis added.]

### Notes and Questions

1. The appellant in this case argued that the Texas statute violated the federal Constitution. The Court decided that "the application" of the statute violated the Constitution. What is the difference? Is the statute still valid after this decision?

2. The Court says that the situation in this case, where the officer testified that the appellant "looked suspicious," is to be distinguished from a situation in which an officer "is able to perceive and articulate meaning." Does this mean that the validity of police conduct is dependent on how articulate the officer is? Does this case provide a "script" for officers to use in describing their actions?

---

## 10.4 | Florida v. Bostick    *111 S. Ct. 2382 (1991)*

JUSTICE O'CONNOR *delivered the opinion of the Court.*
WE HAVE HELD THAT the Fourth Amendment permits police officers to approach individuals at random in airport lobbies and other public places to ask them questions and to request consent to search their luggage, so long as a reasonable person would understand that he or she could refuse to cooperate. This case requires us to determine whether the same rule applies to police encounters that take place on a bus.

---

Some footnotes and case citations omitted.—ED.

## I

Drug interdiction efforts have led to the use of police surveillance at airports, train stations, and bus depots. Law enforcement officers stationed at such locations routinely approach individuals, either randomly or because they suspect in some vague way that the individuals may be engaged in criminal activity, and ask them potentially incriminating questions. Broward County has adopted such a program. County Sheriff's Department officers routinely board buses at scheduled stops and ask passengers for permission to search their luggage.

In this case, two officers discovered cocaine when they searched a suitcase belonging to Terrance Bostick. The underlying facts of the search are in dispute, but the Florida Supreme Court, whose decision we review here, stated explicitly the factual premise for its decision:

> "Two officers, complete with badges, insignia and one of them holding a recognizable zipper pouch, containing a pistol, boarded a bus bound from Miami to Atlanta during a stopover in Fort Lauderdale. Eyeing the passengers, the officers admittedly without articulable suspicion, picked out the defendant passenger and asked to inspect his ticket and identification. The ticket, from Miami to Atlanta, matched the defendant's identification and both were immediately returned to him as unremarkable. However, the two police officers persisted and explained their presence as narcotics agents on the lookout for illegal drugs. In pursuit of that aim, they then requested the defendant's consent to search his luggage. Needless to say, there is a conflict in the evidence about whether the defendant consented to the search of the second bag in which the contraband was found and as to whether he was informed of his right to refuse consent. However, any conflict must be resolved in favor of the state, it being a question of fact decided by the trial judge," 554 So. 2d 1153, 1154–1155 (1989), quoting 510 So. 2d 321, 322 (Fla. App. 1987) (Letts, J., *dissenting in part*). . . .

Bostick was arrested and charged with trafficking in cocaine. He moved to suppress the co-caine on the grounds that it had been seized in violation of his Fourth Amendment rights. The trial court denied the motion but made no factual findings. Bostick subsequently entered a plea of guilty, but reserved the right to appeal the denial of the motion to suppress. . . .

. . . The [Florida] Supreme Court reasoned that Bostick had been seized because a reasonable passenger in his situation would not have felt free to leave the bus to avoid questioning by the police. . . .

## II

The sole issue presented for our review is whether a police encounter on a bus of the type described above necessarily constitutes a "seizure" within the meaning of the Fourth Amendment. The State concedes, and we accept for purposes of this decision, that the officers lacked the reasonable suspicion required to justify a seizure and that, if a seizure took place, the drugs found in Bostick's suitcase must be suppressed as tainted fruit.

Our cases make it clear that a seizure does not occur simply because a police officer approaches an individual and asks a few questions. So long as a reasonable person would feel free "to disregard the police and go about his business," . . . the encounter is consensual and no reasonable suspicion is required. The encounter will not trigger Fourth Amendment scrutiny unless it loses its consensual nature. The Court made precisely this point in *Terry* v. *Ohio*, 392 U.S. 1, 19, n. 16 (1968): "Obviously, not all personal intercourse between policemen and citizens involves 'seizures' of persons. Only when the officer, by means of physical force or show of authority, has in some way restrained the liberty of a citizen may we conclude that a 'seizure' has occurred."

Since Terry, we have held repeatedly that mere police questioning does not constitute a seizure. In *Florida* v. *Royer*, 460 U.S. 491 (1983) (plurality opinion), for example, we explained that "law enforcement officers do not violate the Fourth Amendment by merely approaching an individual on the street or in another public place, by asking him if he is willing to answer some questions, by putting questions to him if the person is willing to listen, or by offering in evidence in a criminal prosecution his voluntary answers to such questions." *Id.,* at 497; see *id.,* at 523, n. 3 (REHNQUIST, J., *dissenting*).

There is no doubt that if this same encounter had taken place before Bostick boarded the bus or in the lobby of the bus terminal, it would not rise to the level of a seizure. The Court has dealt with similar encounters in airports and has found them to be "the sort of consensual encounters that implicate no Fourth Amendment interest," *Florida* v. *Rodriguez,* 469 U.S. 1, 5–6 (1984). We have stated that even when officers have no basis for suspecting a particular individual, they may generally ask questions of that individual, see *INS* v. *Delgado,* 466 U.S. 210, 216 (1984); *Rodriguez, supra,* at 5–6; ask to examine the individual's identification, see *Delgado, supra,* at 216; *Royer, supra,* at 501 (plurality opinion); *United States* v. *Mendenhall,* 446 U.S. 544, 557–558 (1980); and request consent to search his or her luggage, see *Royer, supra,* at 501 (plurality opinion)—as long as the police do not convey a message that compliance with their requests is required.

Bostick insists that this case is different because it took place in the cramped confines of a bus. A police encounter is much more intimidating in this setting, he argues, because police tower over a seated passenger and there is little room to move around. Bostick claims to find support in language from *Michigan* v. *Chesternut,* 486 U.S. 567, 573 (1988), and other cases, indicating that a seizure occurs when a reasonable person would believe that he or she is not "free to leave." Bostick maintains that a reasonable bus passenger would not have felt free to leave under the circumstances of this case because there is nowhere to go on a bus. Also, the bus was about to depart. Had Bostick disembarked, he would have risked being stranded and losing whatever baggage he had locked away in the luggage compartment.

The Florida Supreme Court found this argument persuasive, so much so that it adopted a *per se* rule prohibiting the police from randomly boarding buses as a means of drug interdiction. The state court erred, however, in focusing on whether Bostick was "free to leave" rather than on the principle that those words were intended

to capture. When police attempt to question a person who is walking down the street or through an airport lobby, it makes sense to inquire whether a reasonable person would feel free to continue walking. But when the person is seated on a bus and has no desire to leave, the degree to which a reasonable person would feel that he or she would leave is not an accurate measure of the coercive effect of the encounter. . . .

. . . In such a situation, the appropriate inquiry is whether a reasonable person would feel free to decline the officers' requests or otherwise terminate the encounter. This formulation follows logically from prior cases and breaks no new ground. We have said before that the crucial test is whether, taking into account all of the circumstances surrounding the encounter, the police conduct would "have communicated to a reasonable person that he was not at liberty to ignore the police presence and go about his business." . . .

The facts of this case, as described by the Florida Supreme Court, leave some doubt whether a seizure occurred. Two officers walked up to Bostick on the bus, asked him a few questions, and asked if they could search his bags. As we have explained, no seizure occurs when police ask questions of an individual, ask to examine the individual's identification, and request consent to search his or her luggage—so long as the officers do not convey a message that compliance with their requests is required. Here, the facts recited by the Florida Supreme Court indicate that the officers did not point guns at Bostick or otherwise threaten him and that they specifically advised Bostick that he could refuse consent.

Nevertheless, we refrain from deciding whether or not a seizure occurred in this case. The trial court made no express findings of fact, and the Florida Supreme Court rested its decision on a single fact—that the encounter took place on a bus—rather than on the totality of the circumstances. We remand so that the Florida courts may evaluate the seizure question under the correct legal standard. . . .

The dissent characterizes our decision as holding that police may board buses and by an "*intimidating* show of authority," *post,* at 8 (emphasis added), demand of passengers their "voluntary" cooperation. That characterization is incorrect. Clearly, a bus passenger's decision to cooperate with law enforcement officers authorizes the police to conduct a search without first obtaining a warrant *only* if the cooperation is voluntary. "Consent" that is the product of official intimidation or harassment is not consent at all. Citizens do not forfeit their constitutional rights when they are coerced to comply with a request that they would prefer to refuse. The question to be decided by the Florida courts on remand is whether Bostick chose to permit the search of his luggage. . . .

The dissent reserves its strongest criticism for the proposition that police officers can approach individuals as to whom they have no reasonable suspicion and ask them potentially incriminating questions. But this proposition is by no means novel; it has been endorsed by the Court any number of times. *Terry, Royer, Rodriguez,* and *Delgado* are just a few examples. As we have explained, today's decision follows logically from those decisions and breaks no new ground. . . .

This Court, as the dissent correctly observes, is not empowered to suspend constitutional guarantees so that the Government may more effectively wage a "war on drugs." See *post,* at 1, 11–12. If that war is to be fought, those who fight it must respect the rights of individuals, whether or not those individuals are suspected of having committed a crime. By the same token, this Court is not empowered to forbid law enforcement practices simply because it considers them distasteful. The Fourth Amendment proscribes unreasonable searches and seizures; it does not proscribe voluntary cooperation. The cramped confines of a bus are one relevant factor that should be considered in evaluating whether a passenger's consent is voluntary. We cannot agree, however, with the Florida Supreme Court that this single factor will be dispositive in every case.

We adhere to the rule that, in order to determine whether a particular encounter constitutes a seizure, a court must consider all the circumstances surrounding the encounter to determine whether the police conduct would have

communicated to a reasonable person that the person was not free to decline the officers' requests or otherwise terminate the encounter. That rule applies to encounters that take place on a city street or in an airport lobby, and it applies equally to encounters on a bus. The Florida Supreme Court erred in adopting a *per se* rule.

The judgment of the Florida Supreme Court is reversed, and the case remanded for further proceedings not inconsistent with this opinion.

*It is so ordered.*

JUSTICE MARSHALL, *with whom* JUSTICE BLACKMUN *and* JUSTICE STEVENS *join, dissenting.*

Our Nation, we are told, is engaged in a "war on drugs." No one disputes that it is the job of law-enforcement officials to devise effective weapons for fighting this war. But the effectiveness of a law-enforcement technique is not proof of its constitutionality. The general warrant, for example, was certainly an effective means of law enforcement. Yet it was one of the primary aims of the Fourth Amendment to protect citizens from the tyranny of being singled out for search and seizure without particularized suspicion *notwithstanding* the effectiveness of this method. In my view, the law-enforcement technique with which we are confronted in this case—the suspicionless police sweep of buses in intrastate or interstate travel—bears all of the indicia of coercion and unjustified intrusion associated with the general warrant. Because I believe that the bus sweep at issue in this case violates the core values of the Fourth Amendment, I dissent.

## I

At issue in this case is a "new and increasingly common tactic in the war on drugs": the suspicionless police sweep of buses in interstate or intrastate travel. . . . Typically under this technique, a group of state or federal officers will board a bus while it is stopped at an intermediate point on its route. Often displaying badges, weapons or other indicia of authority, the officers identify themselves and announce their purpose to intercept drug traffickers. They proceed to approach individual passengers, requesting them to show identification, produce their tickets, and explain the purpose of their travels. Never do the officers advise the passengers that they are free not to speak with the officers. An "interview" of this type ordinarily culminates in a request for consent to search the passenger's luggage. . . .

These sweeps are conducted in "dragnet" style. The police admittedly act without an "articulable suspicion" in deciding which buses to board and which passengers to approach for interviewing.[1] By proceeding systematically in this fashion, the police are able to engage in a tremendously high volume of searches. See, e.g., *Florida* v. *Kerwick,* 512 So. 2d 347, 348–349 (Fla. App. 1987) (single officer employing sweep technique able to search over 3,000 bags in nine-month period). The percentage of successful drug interdictions is low. See *United States* v. *Flowers, supra,* at 710 (sweep of 100 buses resulted in seven arrests).

To put it mildly, these sweeps "are inconvenient, intrusive, and intimidating." *United States* v. *Chandler,* 744 F. Supp. at, 335. They occur within cramped confines, with officers typically placing themselves in between the passenger selected for an interview and the exit of the bus. See, e.g., *id.,* at 336. Because the bus is only temporarily stationed at a point short of its destination, the passengers are in no position to leave as a means of evading the officers' questioning. Undoubtedly, such a sweep holds up the progress of the bus. See *United States* v. *Fields,* 909 F. 2d 470, 474 n. 2 (CA11 1990); cf. *United States* v. *Rembert,* 694 F. Supp. 163, 175 (WDNC 1988) (reporting testimony of officer that he makes "'every effort in the world not to delay the bus'" but that the driver does not leave terminal until sweep is complete). Thus, this "new and increasingly common tactic," *United States* v. *Lewis,* . . . burdens the experience of traveling by bus with a degree of governmental interference to which, until now, our society has been proudly unaccustomed. See, e.g., *State ex rel. Ekstrom* v. *Justice Court,* 136 Ariz. 1, 6, 663 P. 2d 992, 997 (1983) (Feldman, J., *concurring*) ("The thought that an American can be compelled to 'show his papers' before exercising his right to walk the streets, drive the highways or board the trains is repugnant to American institutions and ideals.")

This aspect of the suspicionless sweep has not been lost on many of the lower courts called upon to review the constitutionality of this practice. Remarkably, the courts located at the heart of the "drug war" have been the most adamant in condemning this technique. As one Florida court put it:

> "'[T]he evidence in this cause has evoked images of other days, under other flags, when no man traveled his nation's roads or railways without fear of unwarranted interruption, by individuals who held temporary power in the Government. The spectre of American citizens being asked, by badge-wielding police, for identification, travel papers— in short a *raison d'etre*—is foreign to *any* fair reading of the Constitution, and its guarantee of human liberties. This is not Hitler's Berlin, nor Stalin's Moscow, nor is it white supremacist South Africa. Yet in Broward County, Florida, these police officers approach every person on board buses and trains ("that time permits") and check identification [and] tickets, [and] ask to search luggage—all in the name of "voluntary cooperation" with law enforcement. . . .'" 554 So. 2d, at 1158, quoting *State* v. *Kerwick, supra,* at 348–349 (quoting trial court order).

The District Court for the District of Columbia spoke in equally pointed words:

---

[1]That is to say, the police who conduct these sweeps decline to offer a reasonable, articulable suspicion of criminal wrongdoing sufficient to justify a warrantless "stop" or "seizure" of the confronted passenger. See *Terry* v. *Ohio,* 392 U. S. 1, 20–22, 30–31 (1968); *Florida* v. *Royer,* 460 U. S. 491, 498–499 (1983) (plurality opinion). It does not follow, however, that the approach of passengers during a sweep is completely random. Indeed, at least one officer who routinely confronts interstate travelers candidly admitted that *race* is a factor influencing his decision whom to approach. See *United States* v. *Williams,* No. 1:89CR0135 (ND Ohio, June 13, 1989), p. 3 ("Detective Zaller testified that the factors initiating the focus upon the three young black males in this case included: (1) that they were young and black. . . ."), aff'd, No. 89–4083 (CA6, Oct. 19, 1990), p. 7 (the officers "knew that the couriers, more often than not, were young black males"), vacated and remanded, 500 U. S. 901 (1991). Thus, the basis of the decision to single out particular passengers during a suspicionless sweep is less likely to be *inarticulable* than *unspeakable.*

"It seems rather incongruous at this point in the world's history that we find totalitarian states becoming more like our free society while we in this nation are taking on their former trappings of suppressed liberties and freedoms."

"The random indiscriminate stopping and questioning of individuals on interstate busses seems to have gone too far. If this Court approves such 'bus stops' and allows prosecutions to be based on evidence seized as a result of such 'stops,' then we will have stripped our citizens of basic Constitutional protections. Such action would be inconsistent with what this nation has stood for during its 200 years of existence. If passengers on a bus passing through the Capital of this great nation cannot be free from police interference where there is absolutely no basis for the police officers to stop and question them, then the police will be free to accost people on our streets without any reason or cause. In this 'anything goes' war on drugs, random knocks on the doors of our citizens' homes seeking 'consent' to search for drugs cannot be far away. This is not America." *United States* v. *Lewis,* 728 F. Supp. 784, 788–789, rev'd, 287 U.S. App. D.C. 306, 921 F. 2d 1294 (1990). . . .

The question for this Court, then, is whether the suspicionless, dragnet-style sweep of buses in intrastate and interstate travel is consistent with the Fourth Amendment. The majority suggests that this latest tactic in the drug war is perfectly compatible with the Constitution. I disagree.

## II

I have no objection to the manner in which the majority frames the test for determining whether a suspicionless bus sweep amounts to a Fourth Amendment "seizure." I agree that the appropriate question is whether a passenger who is approached during such a sweep "would feel free to decline the officers' requests or otherwise terminate the encounter." . . . What I cannot understand is how the majority can possibly suggest an affirmative answer to this question. . . .

As far as is revealed by facts on which the Florida Supreme Court premised its decision, the officers did not advise respondent that he was free to break off this "interview." Inexplicably, the majority repeatedly stresses the trial court's implicit finding that the police officers advised respondent that he was free to refuse permission to search his travel bag. This aspect of the exchange between respondent and the police is completely irrelevant to the issue before us. For as the State concedes, and as the majority purports to "accept," if respondent was unlawfully seized when the officers approached him and initiated questioning, the resulting search was likewise unlawful no matter how well advised respondent was of his right to refuse it. . . . Consequently, the issue is not whether a passenger in respondent's position would have felt free to deny consent to the search of his bag, but whether such a passenger—without being apprised of his rights—would have felt free to terminate the antecedent encounter with the police.

Unlike the majority, I have no doubt that the answer to this question is no. Apart from trying to accommodate the officers, respondent had only two options. First, he could have remained seated while obstinately refusing to respond to the officers' questioning. But in light of the intimidating show of authority that the officers made upon boarding the bus, respondent reasonably could have believed that such behavior would only arouse the officers' suspicions and intensify their interrogation. Indeed, officers who carry out bus sweeps like the one at issue here frequently admit that this is the effect of a passenger's refusal to cooperate. The majority's observation that a mere refusal to answer questions, "without more," does not give rise to a reasonable basis for seizing a passenger, is utterly beside the point, because a passenger unadvised of his rights and otherwise unversed in constitutional law has no reason to know that the police cannot hold his refusal to cooperate against him.

Second, respondent could have tried to escape the officers' presence by leaving the bus altogether. But because doing so would have required respondent to squeeze past the gun-wielding inquisitor who was blocking the aisle of the bus, this hardly seems like a course that respondent reasonably would have viewed as available to him. The majority lamely protests that nothing in the stipulated facts shows that the questioning officer "pointed gun at [respondent] or otherwise threatened him" with the weapon. Our decisions recognize the obvious point, however, that the choice of the police to "display" their weapons during an encounter exerts significant coercive pressure on the confronted citizen. We have never suggested that the police must go so far as to put a citizen in immediate apprehension of being shot before a court can take account of the intimidating effect of being questioned by an officer with weapon in hand.

Even if respondent had perceived that the officers would let him leave the bus, moreover, he could not reasonably have been expected to resort to this means of evading their intrusive questioning. For so far as respondent knew, the bus' departure from the terminal was imminent. Unlike a person approached by the police on the street, see *Michigan* v. *Chesternut, supra,* or at a bus or airport terminal after reaching his destination, see *United States* v. *Mendenhall, supra,* a passenger approached by the police at an intermediate point in a long bus journey cannot simply leave the scene and repair to a safe haven to avoid unwanted probing by law-enforcement officials. The vulnerability that an intrastate or interstate traveler experiences when confronted by the police outside of his "own familiar territory" surely aggravates the coercive quality of such an encounter. See *Schneckloth* v. *Bustamonte,* 412 U.S. 218, 247 (1973). . . .

Rather than requiring the police to justify the coercive tactics employed here, the majority blames respondent for his own sensation of constraint. The majority concedes that respondent "did not feel free to leave the bus" as a means of breaking off the interrogation by the Broward County officers. *Ante,* at 436. But this experience of confinement, the majority explains, "was the natural result of *his* decision to take the bus." *Ibid.* (emphasis added). Thus, in the majority's view, because respondent's "freedom of movement was restricted by a factor independent of police conduct—*i.e.,* by his being a passenger on a bus," *ante,* at 436—respondent was not seized for purposes of the Fourth Amendment.

This reasoning borders on sophism and trivializes the values that underlie the Fourth Amendment. Obviously, a person's "voluntary decision" to place himself in a room with only one exit does not authorize the police to force an encounter upon him by placing themselves in front of the exit. It is no more acceptable for the police to force an encounter on a person by exploiting his "voluntary decision" to expose himself to perfectly legitimate personal or social constraints. By consciously deciding to single out persons who have undertaken interstate or intrastate travel, officers who conduct suspicionless, dragnet-style sweeps put passengers to the choice of cooperating or of exiting their buses and possibly being stranded in unfamiliar locations. It is exactly because this "choice" is no "choice" at all that police engage this technique.

In my view, the Fourth Amendment clearly condemns the suspicionless, dragnet-style sweep of intrastate or interstate buses. Withdrawing this particular weapon from the government's drug-war arsenal would hardly leave the police without any means of combatting the use of buses as instrumentalities of the drug trade. The police would remain free, for example, to approach passengers whom they have a reasonable, articulable basis to suspect of criminal wrongdoing. Alternatively, they could continue to confront passengers without suspicion so long as they took simple steps, like advising the passengers confronted of their right to decline to be questioned, to dispel the aura of coercion and intimidation that pervades such encounters. There is no reason to expect that such requirements would render the Nation's buses law-enforcement-free zones.

## III

The majority attempts to gloss over the violence that today's decision does to the Fourth Amendment with empty admonitions. "If the [war on drugs] is to be fought," the majority intones, "those who fight it must respect the rights of individuals, whether or not those individuals are suspected of having committed a crime." The majority's actions, however, speak louder than its words.

I dissent.

*Notes and Questions*

1. The dissenting opinion refers to "dragnet" style searches and says that the basis of police conduct in these situations is "less likely to be *inarticulable* than *unspeakable*." What does this mean? Is this a reference to the kind of "script" that would be an unacceptable explanation for an officer's conduct? In what ways is the concept of surveillance discussed by Steve Russell applicable here?

2. Here is a story about "the high costs of cop stress" in America. What similarities and differences do you find between the situations described here and those in the preceding cases? What are some implications of police stress for systems of law enforcement?

> Gary Berte is one frustrated man. A former Springfield policeman who watched colleagues turn to drink, drugs or the barrel of a gun under pressure of the job, Berte has a simple plan. He wants a police support services program implemented in criminal justice training centers throughout the state to offer peer counseling, stress management seminars and support groups for cops, their wives and their kids. . . .
>
> While state agencies play politics with the funding, Berte has no doubt that a comprehensive, non-departmentalized approach to police stress, run by cops themselves, is desperately needed. Life expectancy for a cop who works to age 55 is just 59. On a national level, suicides among police are estimated to be 100 to 200 per 100,000 (depending on the study) as opposed to 12 per 100,000 for the general population. Police are murdered, on the other hand, at a rate of just 54 per 100,000. "In other words, cops are killing themselves twice as fast as the bad guys [are killing us]," Berte says. Yet of more than 16,000 police departments across the country, only 75 have stress units.
>
> In the last 18 months in Massachusetts, three police recruits committed suicide either during or soon after training. And just last week in one area police department, an officer had to be physically restrained by his colleagues from attacking a suspect. Earlier that day at roll call, that officer had asked for time off the streets, telling his superiors to take his gun away from him or they would be sorry. "But the department had no place to turn," Berte says. "They were just trying to get the guy through the next eight hours."

> Though he cites such stories, Berte says the "crisis stuff" is good hype and good type but puts the wrong focus on police stress. "What research is showing is that the violence is not the most stressful part of police work. It's the organizational stuff and the hours that are the killers. And who's going to help you out when you're bored to death?"
>
> Citing his own work, as well as recent studies by the National Institute of Justice, Berte says policemen tend to handle the "cop and robber" aspect of their work quite well. "What creates the most difficulty is the inflexibility of departmental policies, fears of liability, bad equipment and inadequate opportunities for advancement. Then there are the mixed messages given to a cop every day. One year it's OK to do something, the next year it's not. Internal policies can be really absurd—you can't leave town without getting permission. And you can't leave the job at the office. If a crime is being committed, you're sworn to take appropriate action, whether you're on duty or off."
>
> Though Berte agrees that cops aren't the only ones facing stress at work, he believes that their isolation and willingness to cover up for their colleagues combine to make cop stress extremely costly and dangerous for both the individual and society at large. Sworn to protect the public at all times, cops begin viewing everything through "blue eyes." "They become very lonely, cynical people, who entrench themselves in their minority status and divide the world into two parts: assholes and cops," says Berte. "Once you become a police officer, you change. It's a whole social status. There's definitely isolation and I think we fail to take responsibility for how much we cause damage to ourselves."
>
> There are also misconceptions about what cops do, with all the focus on the Dirty Harry deeds and little fanfare for the mundane routine. "Only about 10 percent of our time is spent on the criminal work and the other 90 percent of the time we're doing social service-type stuff. Now, social workers average 18 months on the job before they burn-out and that's understood. Cops do that kind of work day in and day out, but our way of coping with it, our maladaptive behaviors, are more acceptable. If you become drunk and violent, we'll cover up for you."
>
> Policemen attending Berte's seminars have expressed what being part of this insulated blue universe means. "I want to shoot myself and shoot my chief," wrote one participant. Another,

echoing a desire to escape the pressure with a disability pension, said, "I was blessed by having the accident I had." "The longer I'm on the job, the more negative my attitude," wrote a third. "Consequently the public has to pay."[†]

---

[†]Kris Hundley, "The High Costs of Cop Stress," *Valley Advocate,* October 12, 1987. Copyright © 1987 by The Valley Advocate.

3. In the preceding note, Gary Berte is quoted as saying, ". . . cops are killing themselves twice as fast as the bad guys [are killing us]." What implications can be drawn from this fact? Compare these statistics with the rationale used by the Supreme Court in the *Terry* case: "we cannot blind ourselves to the need for law enforcement officers to protect themselves. . . ." How might police officers protect themselves from suicide?

---

| 10.5 | This Is Not America   *Stephen Arons*

*Florida* v. *Bostick* is disturbing not only because it approves such a draconian attack upon the privacy and liberty of ordinary citizens, but because it is merely one of many Supreme Court opinions in which significant elements of the Fourth Amendment have fallen victim to state power. The War on Drugs has substantially increased the rate of these constitutional casualties.

The War on Drugs is supported by many Americans and tolerated by others because drug abuse is viewed as an indicator of despair and hopelessness at the economic bottom of society and hedonistic, there-is-no-future living at the top. To most Americans, some kind of government drug policy seems essential as drug abuse erodes individual integrity and personal security and dissolves the basis of a sane society, but the War on Drugs is also fueled by irrational fears and politically profitable hysteria whipped up by cynical politicians and exploited by rigid ideologues and power-hungry government agencies.

Like the anti-communist witch hunts of the 1950s and the literal witch hunts of late seventeenth-century Massachusetts, the War on Drugs includes a number of people whose self-interests are served by extending police power at the expense of individual privacy and personal liberty. Of the ten billion dollars the U.S. federal government proposed to spend in fiscal year 1992 on the War on Drugs, over eighty percent would go not to drug treatment for the thousands who

seek it, nor to education for the millions who need it, but to prisons, drug interdiction, and other forms of law enforcement.

The militaristic logic of emphasizing criminalization and enforcement now extends beyond police, politicians, and prosecutors to the Supreme Court itself. Since 1982, the Supreme Court has heard thirty Fourth Amendment cases involving drugs. In twenty-seven of those, police power prevailed in spite of the fact that in twenty-nine of the thirty the government had lost in a lower court. The end result of the legal substance of these decisions has been the virtual repeal of Fourth Amendment protections against unreasonable searches and seizures by a Court almost totally dominated by right-wing ideologues.

In the demise of the Fourth Amendment, the War on Drugs has claimed its most significant and tragic casualty, for the primary victims of the steady erosion of the right to privacy at the hands of police-state tactics have not been criminals and drug traffickers, but ordinary citizens. The impact of this casualty is magnified by the fact that the right to privacy protected by the Fourth Amendment is integral to virtually all the liberties that Americans hold dear—freedom to travel, security in one's home, freedom of belief and expression, the right not to be required to incriminate oneself, even the political franchise.

As adopted in 1791, the Fourth Amendment reads: The right of the people to be secure in their persons, houses, papers, and effects, against unreasonable searches and seizures,

---

Stephen Arons, "This Is Not America," excerpted from *The Threefold Review,* Issue 6, Winter 91–92, p. 15. Used by permission of the author.

shall not be violated, and no Warrants shall issue, but upon probable cause, supported by oath or affirmation, and particularly describing the place to be searched, and the persons or things to be seized.

The new, operative form of the Fourth Amendment as rewritten by the Rehnquist Court has a long and a short form. The long form would probably read as follows:

The right of the police to engage, without probable cause, in warrantless searches and seizures of persons, houses, papers, and effects shall not be challenged in a court of law except upon a showing of probable cause to believe that such search or seizure was known by police to be totally without merit and upon showing that no contraband or incriminating evidence whatsoever was thereby uncovered.

The short-form rewrite of the Constitution's great statement of privacy makes clearer the brave new world order the government seems to envision arising at the end of the War on Drugs: *A police search is justified by what it finds.*

*Florida* v. *Bostick* is a sad testament to the fact that a majority of Americans increasingly find themselves without intellectual, moral, or legal defenses against an overbearing governmental power to invade and manipulate private lives. . . .

The exercise of oppressive police power to search and seize persons and property on interstate buses and trains in 1991 is merely a modern expression of the violations of privacy practiced by the British prior to the American Revolution. Indeed, it was the historical experience of just this kind of violation of persons and forcible government intrusion into homes, papers, and personal effects without probable cause that prompted the Founding Fathers to draft the Fourth Amendment as a protection of individual liberty in 1791.

Unfortunately, few Americans seem to have learned about eighteenth-century police-state tactics such as public intimidation, forcible entry without reason, and the general warrant; and not having learned our history, we are of course condemned to repeat it. Worse still, those charged with upholding a Constitution and Bill of Rights written precisely to prevent this repeat of oppres-

sion have not only failed in their duty, they have become part of the problem. . . .

In virtually all of the Court's Fourth Amendment drug war cases the message is the same: No human liberty, least of all privacy, is important enough to slow the police juggernaut or to temper the national mania for punitive enforcement as the preferred means of reducing drug abuse. Those who wrote and adopted the Fourth Amendment were aware that liberty is forever at risk of being eroded by an overzealous and unduly powerful state. They did not anticipate, however, that an independent judiciary would become the agent of such a state.

In inflicting a grievous wound upon the right to privacy, the Court has, in effect, rewritten the Fourth Amendment. As the Founding Fathers would undoubtedly exclaim if they were able to return to the United States on the bicentennial of its Bill of Rights, "This is not America."

*Notes and Questions*

1. How does the "war on drugs" involve issues of surveillance discussed by Steve Russell?

2. Arons points out that in nearly all drug cases decided by the Supreme Court in favor of police power, the lower courts had ruled against this power. Compare this to the lower court opinions quoted in the dissent in *Bostick*. What is the significance of the fact that the higher court is more favorable to police power than those courts closer to actual law enforcement?

3. Consider the following in thinking about the "political rationality" of the "war on drugs":

    After declaring a stepped up "war on drugs" a few months ago, for example, the federal government last October launched simultaneous raids in 46 states on *garden supply stores,* seeking customer lists so they could apprehend people who might be growing marijuana indoors! In the 1950s, it was dangerous to join a political organization for fear the FBI would get your name and harass you. Today, tomato growers are in danger."*

---

*Ira Glasser, "Taboo No More?" *Civil Liberties,* Fall/Winter, 1989, p. 12.

# CONCLUSION

> . . . in so far as we believe in law, we condemn
> existence. . . .
>
> Peter Goodrich, *Reading the Law* (1986)

The philosophy of the rule of law is that humans are rational beings (capable of conforming to rules) motivated by self-interest (susceptible to reward and punishment). This philosophy says that wrongful behavior is the result either of an intentional violation of the rules in pursuit of self-interest, or of an incapacity to be rational. It asserts that the function of law enforcement is to provide a stable context for working out competing individual intentions. The function of law enforcement in the case of intentional violation is to increase self-interest in obedience by penalizing misbehavior. Its function in the case of inability to obey the rules is to remove the actor from the general population.

This philosophy of the rule of law requires a certain kind of utopian faith. First, there must be faith in reason as a foundation of behavior, despite evidence that chance and fate play a part in life and that emotion motivates much behavior. Second, there must be faith in the ability of lawmakers to design a set of rules broad enough to cover the full range of human interactions, yet narrow enough to be applied in particular conflicts; flexible enough to permit change, yet rigid enough to permit predictability. The rule of law is thus a belief system, rather than an unquestionable aspect of human existence.

The issues that arise when we examine the theory and practice of law enforcement under the rule of law are ultimately metaphysical issues—questions about human nature, the nature of society, the meaning of life. Politics, insofar as it deals with these same issues, has an impact on law and presents alternative conceptions of the rules that ought to be enforced and the methods of enforcement. Economics, insofar as it involves systems of behavior motivation and control, is likewise implicated in any discussion of law enforcement. History and anthropology may also be brought to bear in a study of the rule of law. History presents the possibility of seeing the development of rules and rule systems in a society, and anthropology allows cross-cultural comparison and contrast. Analyses from these and other perspectives have been presented in the materials in this part of the book.

Probably every field of inquiry has some relevance to an understanding of law enforcement, once one sees what the deepest issues are. Law enforcement is especially involved with issues of self and other, life and death. It is not surprising, therefore, that the meaning of life and death and the nature of human relations are at the center of an interdisciplinary study of law. When questions challenge fundamental faiths that support the rule of law, some people may become afraid of anarchy, of lawlessness.

This fear reflects a will to believe in the rule of law even, as Llewellyn says, "when the law is bad." We must face this fear if our commitment is to human freedom based on self-knowledge and self-respect and on knowledge of and respect for others. Our questioning can be a powerful force to create modes of social organization adequate to the multicultural, global society of Earth.

# Suggested Additional Readings

Acosta, Oscar Zeta. *The Autobiography of a Brown Buffalo.* San Francisco: Straight Arrow Books, 1972.

Ballard, J. G. *Running Wild.* New York: Farrar, Straus, Giroux, 1988.

Bankowski, Zenon, and Geoff Mungham. *Images of Law.* London: Routledge & Kegan Paul, 1976.

Berman, Harold J. *Law and Revolution.* Cambridge, Mass.: Harvard University Press, 1983.

Berry, Wendell. *Sex, Economy, Freedom & Community.* New York: Pantheon, 1992.

Bloch, Marc. *Feudal Society.* Trans. by L. Manyon. Chicago: University of Chicago Press, 1961.

Boyer, Richard O., and Herbert M. Morais. *Labor's Untold Story.* New York: United Electrical, Radio, and Machine Workers, 1955.

Braverman, Harry. *Labor and Monopoly Capital.* New York: Monthly Review Press, 1974.

Brinton, Maurice. *The Irrational in Politics.* Montreal: Black Rose Books, 1974.

Deloria, Vine, Jr. *God Is Red.* New York: Dell, 1973.

Douglass, James W. *Resistance and Contemplation.* New York: Dell, 1972.

Edwards, David. *Burning All Illusions: A Guide to Personal and Political Freedom.* Boston: South End Press, 1996.

Ellison, Ralph. *The Invisible Man.* New York: New American Library, 1952.

Engels, Frederick. *The Origin of the Family, Private Property, and the State.* Trans. by Alec West. Ed., with an introduction by Eleanor Burke Leacock. New York: International Publishers, 1973.

F. C., *The Unabomber Manifesto: Industrial Society and Its Future.* Berkeley, Calif.: Jolly Roger Press, 1995.

Foucault, Michel. *Discipline and Punish.* New York: Vintage, 1979.

Freire, Paulo. *Pedagogy of the Oppressed.* Trans. by Myra Bergman Ramos. New York: Seabury Press, 1973.

Fudge, Judy, and Harry Glasbeek. "The Politics of Rights: A Politics with Little Class." *Social and Legal Studies* (1992), p. 45.

Gierke, Otto. *Political Theories of the Middle Age.* Trans., with an introduction by Frederic William Maitland. Boston: Beacon Press, 1958.

Goldman, Emma. *Living My Life.* 2 vols. New York: Dover Publications, 1970.

Goodrich, Peter. *Reading the Law.* Oxford, England: Blackwell, 1986.

Hamilton, Jane. *A Map of the World.* New York: Anchor Books, 1995.

Harr, Jonathan. *A Civil Action.* New York: Random House, 1995.

Haudenosaunee. *Basic Call to Consciousness.* Mohawk Nation: Akwesasne Notes, 1978.

Hermer, Joe, and Alan Hunt. "Official Graffiti of the Everyday." *Law & Society Review* 30 (1996), p. 455.

Horwitz, Morton J. *The Transformation of American Law, 1780–1860.* Cambridge, Mass.: Harvard University Press, 1977.

Howard, Philip K. *The Death of Common Sense.* New York: Warner Books, 1994.

Hughes, Richard. *A High Wind in Jamaica.* New York: Harper & Row, 1929.

Keeble, John. *Broken Ground.* New York: Harper & Row, 1987.

Kingsolver, Barbara. *High Tide in Tucson.* New York: HarperCollins Publishers, 1995.

Kinoy, Arthur. *Rights on Trial*. Cambridge, Mass.: Harvard University Press, 1983.

Koestler, Arthur. *Darkness at Noon*. Trans. by Daphne Hardy. New York: Bantam, 1966.

Lame Deer, John (Fire), and Richard Erdoes. *Lame Deer, Seeker of Visions*. New York: Simon & Schuster, 1972.

Lao Tzu. *The Way of Life According to Lao Tzu*. Trans. by Witter Bynner. New York: Capricorn Books, 1962.

Larner, Christina. *Witchcraft and Religion*. Oxford, England: Blackwell, 1985.

LeGuin, Ursula. *The Dispossessed*. New York: Avon Books, 1974.

——. *Always Coming Home*. New York: Harper & Row, 1985.

Lessing, Doris. *The Wind Blows Away Our Words*. New York: Vintage Books, 1987.

Lester, John, and Pierre Spoerri. *Rediscovering Freedom*. London: Grosvenor Books, 1992.

Logsdon, Gene. *At Nature's Pace: Farming and the American Dream*. New York: Pantheon Books, 1994.

Lumumba, Patrice. *Lumumba Speaks*. Ed. by Jean van Lierde, ed. Trans. by Helen R. Lane. Introduction by Jean-Paul Sartre. Boston: Little, Brown, 1972.

MacPherson, C. B. *The Political Theory of Possessive Individualism*. Oxford, England: Oxford University Press, 1962.

Malcolm X and Alex Haley. *The Autobiography of Malcolm X*. New York: Grove Press, 1965.

Manitonquat (Medicine Story). *Ending Violent Crime*. Greenville, N.H.: Story Stone Publishing, 1996.

Nietzsche, Friedrich. *The Portable Nietzsche*. Trans., with an introduction by Walter Kaufman. New York: Viking Press, 1954.

Nomberg-Przytyk, Sara. *Auschwitz*. Trans. by Roslyn Hirsch. Chapel Hill: University of North Carolina Press, 1985.

Orwell, George. *1984*. New York: New American Library, 1961.

Polanyi, Karl. *The Great Transformation*. Boston: Beacon Press, 1957.

Prejean, Helen. *Dead Man Walking: An Eyewitness Account of the Death Penalty in the United States*. New York: Random House, 1993.

Quinney, Richard. *Critique of Legal Order*. Boston: Little, Brown, 1974.

Reich, Wilhelm. *The Mass Psychology of Fascism*. Trans. by Vincent Carfagno. New York: Farrar, Straus & Giroux, 1970.

Rowbotham, Sheila. *Woman's Consciousness, Man's World*. New York: Penguin, 1973.

Settle, Mary Lee. *Prisons*. New York: Charles Scribner's Sons, 1987.

Sharp, Paula. *Crows Over a Wheatfield*. New York: Hyperion, 1996.

Shklar, Judith. *Legalism*. Cambridge, Mass.: Harvard University Press, 1964.

Silko, Leslie. *Almanac of the Dead*. New York: Simon & Schuster, 1991.

Skillen, Anthony. *Ruling Illusions: Philosophy and the Social Order*. Hassocks, England: Harvester Press, 1977.

Sloterdijk, Peter. *Critique of Cynical Reason*. Trans. by Michael Eldred. Minneapolis: University of Minnesota Press, 1987.

Smart, Carol. "The Woman of Legal Discourse." *Social and Legal Studies* 1 (1992), p. 29.

Smedley, Agnes. *Daughter of Earth*. Old Westbury, N.Y.: Feminist Press, 1973.

Spence, Gerry. *From Freedom to Slavery: The Rebirth of Tyranny in America*. New York: St. Martin's Press, 1996.

Strauss, Gerald. *Law, Resistance, and the State*. Princeton, N.J.: Princeton University Press, 1986.

Thompson, E. P. *Whigs and Hunters*. New York: Pantheon Books, 1975.

Traven, B. *Government*. New York: Hill and Wang, 1971.

Unger, Roberto. *Knowledge and Politics*. New York: Free Press, 1975.

Waters, Frank. *The Man Who Killed the Deer*. Chicago: Swallow, 1942.

Weinstein, James. *The Corporate Ideal in the Liberal State*. Boston: Beacon Press, 1968.

Woodward, Bob, and Scott Armstrong. *The Brethren*. New York: Simon & Schuster, 1979.

Zamiatin, Evgenii Ivanovich. *We*. Trans., with a foreword by Gregory Zilboorg. New York: Dutton, 1952.

Zaretsky, Eli. *Capitalism, the Family, and Personal Life*. New York: Harper & Row, 1976.

Zola, Emile. *Germinal*. Trans. by Havelock Ellis. New York: Nonesuch Press, 1942.

*"Arming for the Fray," Nineteenth-Century British Barrister.* (Courtesy of Art & Visual Materials, Special Collections Department, Harvard Law School Library)

# PART III

# Lawyers

Woe unto you also, ye lawyers! for ye lade men with burdens grievous to be borne, and ye yourselves touch not the burdens with one of your fingers.

New Testament (Luke 11:46)

Could the ambivalence toward law . . . be related to the possibility that the lawyer must do things the community regards as necessary—but still disapproves of? Hence is the lawyer something of a scapegoat? Now to be sure this does not distinguish lawyers from prostitutes, politicians, prison wardens, some debtors and many other occupational groups. What does distinguish lawyers in the role is that they are feared and disliked—but needed—because of their matter-of-factness, their sense of relevance, their refusal to be impressed by magical solutions to people's problems.

David Riesman, *Individualism Reconsidered* (1954)

᛭᛭ Law regulates the relationships in society concerning property, wealth, and commerce, which are central to the general welfare of society. It also orders the particular concerns of self-aggrandizement, personal mishap, violence, and domestic felicity, which are important to individuals. The legal system is backed by the repressive power of the state. It is tempered by popular demand to do justice. In matters of power, justice, property, personal fortune, and crime, people's sentiments differ and conflict. No wonder the profession associated with articularing partisan interests in the legal system should itself elicit strong and ambivalent reactions. Probably no other legitimate occupation has simultaneously been the subject of honor and vilification to the extent that lawyers have. They are seen as champions or as despicable villains.

This part focuses closely on the legal profession: its role in society; the education of its novices; the lawyers' relationship to clients and the meaning of advocacy; and the role of lawyers in the processes of social control and social change.

The readings in Chapter 11 introduce several themes that run through the part: the relationship of lawyers to sources of power; popular conceptions of lawyers; the role lawyers play in maintaining democratic institutions, social stability, transfer of wealth and, most importantly, society's claims of doing justice. But as society moves from the industrial era to the information age, the legal profession and its traditional roles are being transformed. The last reading in the chapter asks us to contemplate the death of the legal profession, as we have known it.

Chapter 12 focuses on law school—the site for initiation of students into legal culture and professional reproduction. Themes from the previous chapter are developed further, showing how people of ordinary origins take on the lawyer's habits of mind and social posture that Tocqueville called aristocratic, and how novice lawyers are channeled into the hierarchies in this stratified profession. Also, considered here is the interplay of pedagogy, race and gender stereotypes, and student powerlessness in the teaching of "thinking like a lawyer."

Chapter 13 concerns lawyers in court and the adversary process. The central question here involves the nature and meaning of client representation. What are the limits of advocacy? How much loyalty does a lawyer owe a client? What about truth? What kind of justice can there be without truth? And, the perennial question asked of lawyers by those outside the profession: "How can you, in good conscience, represent a person you know to be guilty?" Also considered is the question, most relevant as increasing numbers of women are becoming lawyers, is whether the primary lawyer's role, that of litigator, is gender neutral.

For the past three decades, law as a profession has enjoyed unprecedented popularity among college students. Many readers of this book are probably themselves seriously considering whether they want to become lawyers or have already committed themselves to the profession. This part aims to provide an understanding of the place of lawyers in society and the legal system, to provoke conversations about some issues in the practice of law that are important for all citizens to consider, and to ask oneself to contemplate the implications for the legal profession of the emerging information age. Readers may also wish to use these conversations to envision themselves in situations of legal practice in order to answer questions about their own values, aspirations, and whether law is likely to be the career they hope it will be.

# 11 THE PROFESSION OF LAW

[The lawyer's] profession enables him to serve the State. As well as any other, better than any other profession or business or sphere, more directly, more palpably, it enables and commands him to perform certain grand and difficult and indispensable duties of patriotism,—certain grand, difficult and indispensable duties to our endeared and common native land. . . . [Service to the state raises the profession] from a mere calling by which bread, fame, and social place may be earned, to a function by which the republic may be served. It raises it from a dexterous art and a subtle and flexible science,—from a cunning logic, a gilded rhetoric, and an ambitious learning, wearing the purple robe of the sophists, and letting itself to hire,— to the dignity of almost a department of government,—an instrumentality of the State for the well-being and conservation of the State.

> Rufus Choate, "The Position and Functions of the American Bar, as an Element of Conservatism in the State," Address delivered before the Harvard Law School (1845)

[T]he function of law is not so much to guide society, as to comfort it. . . . Though the notion of a "rule of law" may be the moral background of revolt, it ordinarily operates to induce acceptance of things as they are. It does this by creating a realm somewhere within the mystical haze beyond the courts, where all our dreams of justice in an unjust world come true. . . . From a practical point of view it is the greatest instrument of social stability because it recognizes every one of the yearnings of the underprivileged, and gives them a forum in which those yearnings can achieve official approval without involving any particular action which might joggle the existing pyramid of power.

> Thurman Arnold, *The Symbols of Government* (1935)

After all, let's ask ourselves: Does America really need 70 percent of the world's lawyers?

> Daniel Quayle, "The Most Litigious Society in the World" (1992)

[T]he law is a hustle, . . .

> Florynce Kennedy, "The Whorehouse Theory of Law," in Robert Lefcourt, ed., *Law Against the People* (1971)

❧ The tension in American society between lawyers and other social elements is as old as the country itself. In 1640, when the Massachusetts Bay Colony founded its short-lived utopia in the New World, it, like Plato's Republic, had no room for lawyers. That men trained in the law should defend with equal tenacity the cause of the righteous and that of the sinner, the aggrieved and those who injure, the interests of society and the evils of its most pernicious elements, was completely unacceptable to the Puritan moral community.

Nor were lawyers welcomed elsewhere in the colonies. In Virginia, the landed aristocracy jealously guarded its governing powers from the intrusion of lawyers by restricting the practice of law to the most petty circumstances. In New York, under first the Dutch and later the English occupation, the practice of law was permitted, but with licensing and limits on fees imposed by the dominant merchant and land-holding class.

For the first seventy years after the settlement of Pennsylvania, no lawyers practiced in that colony. The hostility of Quakers to the tyranny of English law and their religious antipathy to the lawyer's preoccupation with conflict and social strife was carried over to their frontier society.

The absence of lawyers did not mean that the colonies were lawless, nor did the hostility toward lawyers prevent "law-jobs" from being done. Acting for others as legal advocates, counselors, and advisors were a plethora of clergymen, court clerks and justices, traders and merchants, sheriffs, and people called pettifoggers, who had the gift of clever penmanship or sharp oratory. In addition, frontier self-sufficiency often included knowing enough law to get by. For the greater part of the seventeenth century, the American colonies had a legal system without lawyers.

The demand for a trained bar came at the close of the seventeenth century, with the first stages of urban growth and increasing commercialism. Earlier reluctance to encourage a professional lawyer class succumbed to the immediate legal needs of a growing country.

In the fifty years before the Revolutionary War, the bar flourished in the colonies. Many prosperous Southern families sent sons to England to be trained in law at the Inns of Court. In the North, the more typical path was apprenticeship to a successful attorney after having attended Harvard, Yale, Dartmouth, or one of the other colleges for gentlemen. By the time of the Revolution, the majority of the lawyers in the colonies were college-educated, the practice of law by laymen was at a minimum, and entrance to the profession was tightly controlled by the legal elite.

Twenty-five of the fifty-two signers of the Declaration of Independence were lawyers. But the Revolutionary War decimated the bar. Consistent with their conservative views, many lawyers, including some of the most prominent, aligned themselves with the interests of the state and king and had to flee when the legal government toppled. Massachusetts lost nearly a third of its lawyers to the Tory cause.

After the Revolution, the popular antilawyer sentiment, submerged during most of the century, resurfaced when the chief law business became cleaning up the war's legal debris: collecting debts, imprisoning intractable debtors, foreclosing mortgages, assisting the collection of ruinous taxes, and litigating the cases of returning Tories and English creditors. In 1787, Daniel Shays led an army of farmers out of the hills of Massachusetts in the country's first antilawyer riot.

In the early nineteenth century, under the influence of Jeffersonian—later Jacksonian—persuasions, state legislatures began dismantling the restrictive license requirements for practice of law that had garrisoned the bar from "the common man." Individual omnicompetence was the prevailing view. Anyone could be a lawyer—an idea supported by the newly established national principles of equality and democracy, by American repudiation of the class privileges associated with European societies, and by the demonstrated self-sufficiency of life on the frontier. In nearly all states, admission to legal practice became a right granted with citizenship, with no restricting requirements of advanced education or high social position (although, like most other rights at the time, this right was limited to white males). The era of easy access to a lawyer's license for socially mobile aspirants began. The bar lost, for a century, its traditional power of self-regulation and its position as gatekeeper to the profession.

Americans of this period were ambivalent as to what the place of law and lawyers in society should be. On the one hand, the U.S. Supreme Court, constitutionally an equal branch in the governmental triumvirate, was considered too insignificant to merit special space in the Capitol Building in Washington. From 1801 to 1860, the highest court in the land "was driven, like a poor-paying tenant, from one abode to another: from the marshal's office to the clerks' office, to the Law Library in the basement, to the clerk's home on Pennsylvania Avenue, thence to the North Wing of the Capitol Building, then back to the Law Library, then to the old Senate Chamber, then to the District of Columbia Committee Room, then to the Judiciary Committee Room, and finally back to the Senate Chamber."* The justices were made to ride judicial circuits, spending as much as six months of the year traveling the muddy back roads of the country.

The legislative loosening of license requirements was meant to lower the status of the legal profession. However, at the same time, it recognized the importance of law and lawyers for society. With the opening of the legal profession to those who were not well-born, people assumed that the ranks of lawyers would include representatives from many more segments of society. Thus, the bar would be democratic, and law would be democratic.

Into this milieu, in 1831, arrived a young French lawyer, Alexis de Tocqueville—one of history's most extraordinarily perceptive tourists. His official mission was to study U.S. prison reform. His personal mission was to satisfy himself—and report to his countrymen—as to whether this new experiment in democracy could succeed. He saw the antagonism between populism and lawyers' elitism, between a fundamental faith in the common man and a claim for the legitimacy of authority, and between a "tyranny of the masses" and the restraint required for the maintenance of democratic institutions. He concluded that lawyers have a special role in this democracy. Not only is his analysis historically relevant, but it frames the issues surrounding the legal profession today.

---

*Drew Pearson and Robert S. Allen, *The Nine Old Men* (New York: Doubleday, Doren, 1937), p. 7.

## 11.1 The Temper of the Legal Profession in the United States

*Alexis de Tocqueville*

IN VISITING THE AMERICANS and studying their laws, we perceive that the authority they have entrusted to members of the legal profession, and the influence that these individuals exercise in the government, are the most powerful existing security against the excesses of democracy. This effect seems to me to result from a general cause, which it is useful to investigate, as it may be reproduced elsewhere. . . .

Men who have made a special study of the laws derive from this occupation certain habits of order, a taste for formalities, and a kind of instinctive regard for the regular connection of ideas, which naturally render them very hostile to the revolutionary spirit and the unreflecting passions of the multitude.

The special information that lawyers derive from their studies ensures them a separate rank in society, and they constitute a sort of privileged body in the scale of intellect. This notion of their superiority perpetually recurs to them in the practice of their profession: they are the masters of a science which is necessary, but which is not very generally known; they serve as arbiters between the citizens; and the habit of directing to their purpose the blind passions of parties in litigation inspires them with a certain contempt for the judgment of the multitude. Add to this that they naturally constitute a body; not by any previous understanding, or by an agreement that directs them to a common end; but the analogy of their studies and the uniformity of their methods connect their minds as a common interest might unite their endeavors.

Some of the tastes and the habits of the aristocracy may consequently be discovered in the characters of lawyers. They participate in the same instinctive love of order and formalities; and they entertain the same repugnance to the actions of the multitude, and the same secret contempt of the government of the people. I do not mean to say that the natural propensities of lawyers are sufficiently strong to sway them irresistibly; for they, like most other men, are governed by their private interests, and especially by the interests of the moment.

In a state of society in which the members of the legal profession cannot hold that rank in the political world which they enjoy in private life, we may rest assured that they will be the foremost agents of revolution. . . .

I am in like manner inclined to believe that a monarch will always be able to convert legal practitioners into the most serviceable instruments of his authority. There is a far greater affinity between this class of persons and the executive power than there is between them and the people, though they have often aided to overturn the former; just as there is a greater natural affinity between the nobles and the monarch than between the nobles and the people, although the higher orders of society have often, in concert with the lower classes, resisted the prerogative of the crown.

Lawyers are attached to public order beyond every other consideration, and the best security of public order is authority. It must not be forgotten, also, that if they prize freedom much, they generally value legality still more: they are less afraid of tyranny than of arbitrary power; and, provided the legislature undertakes of itself to deprive men of their independence, they are not dissatisfied.

I am therefore convinced that the prince who, in presence of an encroaching democracy, should endeavor to impair the judicial authority in his dominions, and to diminish the political influence of lawyers, would commit a great mistake: he would let slip the substance of authority to grasp the shadow. He would act more wisely in introducing lawyers into the government; and if he entrusted despotism to them under the form of violence, perhaps he would find it again in their hands under the external features of justice and law.

The government of democracy is favorable to the political power of lawyers; for when the wealthy, the noble, and the prince are excluded from the government, the lawyers take possession of it, in their own right, as it were, since they are the only men of information and sagacity, beyond the sphere of the people, who can be the object of the popular choice. If, then, they are led by their tastes towards the aristocracy and the prince, they are brought in contact with the people by their interests. They like the government of democracy without participating in its propensities and without imitating its weaknesses; whence they derive a two-fold authority from it and over it. The people in democratic states do not mistrust the members of the legal profession, because it is known that they are interested to serve the popular cause; and the people listen to them without irritation, because they do not attribute to them any sinister designs. The lawyers do not, indeed, wish to overthrow the institutions of democracy, but they constantly endeavor to turn it away from its real direction by means that are foreign to its nature. Lawyers belong to the people by birth and interest, and to the aristocracy by habit and taste; they may be looked upon as the connecting link between the two great classes of society.

The profession of the law is the only aristocratic element that can be amalgamated without violence with the natural elements of democracy and be advantageously and permanently combined with them. I am not ignorant of the defects inherent in the character of this body of men; but without this admixture of lawyer-like sobriety with the democratic principle, I question whether democratic institutions could long be maintained; and I cannot believe that a republic could hope to exist at the present time if the influence of lawyers in public business did not increase in proportion to the power of the people.

This aristocratic character, which I hold to be common to the legal profession, is much more distinctly marked in the United States and in England than in any other country. This proceeds not only from the legal studies of the English and American lawyers, but from the nature of the law and the position which these interpreters of it occupy in the two countries. The English and the Americans have retained the law of precedents; that is to say, they continue to found their legal opinions and the decisions of their courts upon the opinions and decisions of their predecessors. In the mind of an English or American lawyer a taste and a reverence for what is old is almost always united with a love of regular and lawful proceedings.

This predisposition has another effect upon the character of the legal profession and upon the general course of society. The English and American lawyers investigate what has been done; the French advocate inquires what should have been done; the former produce precedents, the latter reasons. A French observer is surprised to hear how often an English or an American lawyer quotes the opinions of others and how little he alludes to his own, while the reverse occurs in France. There the most trifling litigation is never conducted without the introduction of an entire system of ideas peculiar to the counsel employed; and the fundamental principles of law are discussed in order to obtain a rod of land by the decision of the court. This abnegation of his own opinion and this implicit deference to the opinion of his forefathers, which are common to the English and American lawyer, this servitude of thought which he is obliged to profess, necessarily gives him more timid habits and more conservative inclinations in England and America than in France.

The French codes are often difficult to comprehend, but they can be read by everyone; nothing, on the other hand, can be more obscure and strange to the uninitiated than a legislation founded upon precedents. The absolute need of legal aid that is felt in England and the United States, and the high opinion that is entertained of the ability of the legal profession, tend to separate it more and more from the people and to erect it into a distinct class. The French lawyer is simply a man extensively acquainted with the statutes of his country; but the English or American lawyer resembles the hierophants of Egypt, for like them he is the sole interpreter of an occult science. . . .

In America there are no nobles or literary men, and the people are apt to mistrust the wealthy; lawyers consequently form the highest political class and the most cultivated portion of society. They have therefore nothing to gain by innovation, which adds a conservative interest to their natural taste for public order. If I were asked where I place the American aristocracy, I should reply without hesitation that it is not among the rich, who are united by no common tie, but that it occupies the judicial bench and the bar.

The more we reflect upon all that occurs in the United States, the more we shall be persuaded that the lawyers, as a body, form the most powerful, if not the only, counterpoise to the democratic element. In that country we easily perceive how the legal profession is qualified by its attributes, and even by its faults, to neutralize the vices inherent in popular government. When the American people are intoxicated by passion or carried away by the impetuosity of their ideas, they are checked and stopped by the almost invisible influence of their legal counselors. These secretly oppose their aristocratic propensities to the nation's democratic instincts, their superstitious attachment to what is old to its love of novelty, their narrow views to its immense designs, and their habitual procrastination to its ardent impatience. . . .

The influence of legal habits extends beyond the precise limits I have pointed out. Scarcely any political question arises in the United States that is not resolved, sooner or later, into a judicial question. Hence all parties are obliged to borrow, in their daily controversies, the ideas, and even the language, peculiar to judicial proceedings. As most public men are or have been legal practitioners, they introduce the customs and technicalities of their profession into the management of public affairs. The jury extends this habit to all classes. The language of the law thus becomes, in some measure, a vulgar tongue; the spirit of law, which is produced in the schools and courts of justice, gradually penetrates beyond their walls into the bosom of society, where it descends to the lowest classes, so that at last the whole people contract the habits and the tastes of the judicial magistrate. The lawyers of the United States form a party which is but little feared and scarcely perceived, which has no badge peculiar to itself, which adapts itself with great flexibility to the exigencies of the time and accommodates itself without resistance to all the movements of the social body. But this party extends over the whole community and penetrates into all the classes which compose it; it acts upon the country imperceptibly, but finally fashions it to suit its own purposes.

## Notes and Questions

1. Tocqueville described lawyers as all having the following characteristics: a taste for formalism, dislike of arbitrary power, conservatism, a contempt for the judgment of the masses, and a natural affinity with sources of power. How do lawyers acquire these attributes? Some argue that such changes occur during education for the law. In what ways do these qualities contribute to the profession's function in maintaining democratic institutions?

2. Tocqueville wants us to understand the legal profession in the role of power broker. Contrast the following views:

   > It should need no emphasis that the lawyer is today, even when not himself a "maker" of policy, the one indispensable advisor of every responsible policy-maker of our society—whether we speak of the head of a government department or agency, of the executive of a corporation or labor union, of the secretary of a trade or other private association, or even of

the humble independent enterprise or professional man. As such an advisor the lawyer, when informing the policy-maker of what he can or cannot *legally* do, is, as policy-makers often complain, in an unassailably strategic position to influence, if not create, policy.*

> A profession attains and maintains its position by virtue of the protection and patronage of some elite segment of society which has been persuaded that there is some special value in its work. Its position is thus secured by the political and economic influence of the elite which sponsors it. . . .
>
> If the source of the special position of the profession is granted, then it follows that professions are occupations unique to high civilizations, for there it is common to find not only full-time specialists but also elites with organized control over large populations. Further, the work of the chosen occupation is unlikely to have been singled out if it did not represent or express some of the important beliefs or values of that elite. . . .†

Can lawyers be both brokers and servitors of power? What does Tocqueville suggest?

3. Tocqueville states that lawyers "are less afraid of tyranny than of arbitrary power" and that they can turn despotism into "the external features of justice and law." What do these ideas imply in the context of a democratic society?

4. One of Tocqueville's themes, that the legal profession serves the state as an agent of social control, has many contemporary advocates. Much of the evidence for this view comes from the analysis of poverty law practice, where clients are powerless and controlled by their lawyers, and usually have their grievances given short shrift by the legal system. Maureen Cain, however, has argued that the idea of lawyers as controllers misses the fact that most clients are not working-class people.‡ Rather, except for the restricted case of criminal law practice,

---

*Harold Lasswell and Myres McDougal, "Legal Education and Public Policy," *Yale Law Journal* 52 (1943): 208–209.

†Eliot Freidson, *Profession of Medicine* (New York: Dodd, Mead, 1970), pp. 72–73.

‡Maureen Cain, "The General Practice Lawyer and the Client: Towards a Radical Reconception," in Robert Dingwall and Philip Lewis, eds., *The Sociology of the Professions: Lawyers, Doctors and Others* (London: Macmillan, 1983), pp. 106–131.

lawyers' clients are primarily middle- or upper-class individuals (or their organizations), who are themselves the primary beneficiaries of state power in capitalist society. By her interpretation, lawyers do—as Tocqueville and many contemporary theorists have noted—translate the grievances of clients into other terms. But it is not a translation intended to repress the desires and interests of clients; rather, it merely converts these claims into the universalistic discourse of law where middle- and upper-class values and interests are sustained. Thus for most clients in law, the interests of state, class, and client coincide.

If this view is accepted, does it answer Questions 2 and 3?

5. Tocqueville predicted that in the United States law would become a "vulgar tongue" of the people—the language and concepts of law would pervade all institutions and daily interactions in the society. Has the prediction been borne out?

6. What do you think Tocqueville might have thought of *Bush* v. *Gore* (121 S. Ct. 525, 2000)—the case where the U.S. Supreme Court essentially determined the outcome of the 2000 U.S. presidential election?

❧ At the end of the twentieth century, it is rather difficult to see lawyers as Tocqueville did—as America's aristocracy with a grand role to play in our democracy. Still, our view is complex. We have become a highly litigious society. Lawsuits and the threat of lawsuits order almost all aspects of our daily lives. Many simple acts have legal consequences. Fear of legal liability has become a standard reason for limiting fun. While we may personally know few, if any, lawyers, there is a sense that they are everywhere. Almost every night on the evening TV news, mixed in with stories of weather disasters, wars, famines, health scares, and political events, there are stories of lawsuits and criminal cases, and lawyers speaking for their clients. We see lawyers as champions of "good" and "bad" causes; defenders of the virtuous and of the nefarious; wielders of great power and the butt of crude jokes. They entertain us as players in engaging dramas, both real and fictional; we know that they have firsthand access to the "inside story." They are, themselves, actors and storytellers. They are wise, cynical, naive, obfuscating, truth-telling, altruistic, greedy, self-sacrificing, money-loving, generous, arrogant, empathetic, colorful, bland, warm-hearted, cold-hearted, tough-fighting, caring . . . human beings. It is nearly impossible not to have opinions about lawyers.

The following excerpt introduces us to some lawyers, the clients who employ them, and what they both want from law. It was written by a flamboyant contemporary legal practitioner, Roy Grutman, who represented the Reverend Jerry Falwell in his suit against Larry Flynt (dramatized in the Oliver Stone film *The People vs. Larry Flynt*). As you read, think about what Tocqueville might have made of these lawyers and the author's conception of what the practice of law is about.

## 11.2 | The Big Casino    *Roy Grutman and Bill Thomas*

TO CERTAIN PEOPLE . . . LAWYERS are an everyday necessity. For others, needing a lawyer is the equivalent of needing major surgery—the ultimate horror. By the time they hire an attorney, clients usually feel they have been through enough, but . . . a lawyer not only has to prepare their case, he also has to toughen them up for the long fight that lies ahead.

To find out what I have to work with, I give all my new clients a simple stress test. First I ask them to tell me everything they can about themselves and their case; then, using that information, I hit them with a barrage of insults and sarcasm. Some break down, go home and never come back; the serious contenders stick around.

A trial is a contest between two attorneys to see who has more nerve and whose client is more determined to win. People sue one another to inflict suffering. That's natural. To some extent trials are meant for revenge. Yet, for a growing number of litigants, lawsuits are not just a form of vengeance; they have become a way to strike it rich. . . .

Centuries ago, justice was largely do-it-yourself. If someone harmed you, you harmed him back. There were no lawyers, no judges or juries, and the outcome was generally fast and final. The urge to get even still motivates people to fight it out in court, only today it takes longer to see the results.

One cause for the delay is the nature of the legal process itself; in America anybody can sue you for any valid reason. Another is the financial reward at stake. A principal function of the courts is to separate right from wrong through the redistribution of wealth. If a person injures someone and is found liable, he has to pay. If a company's product hurts someone and the company is at fault, it has to pay. Almost everybody who goes to court . . . expects to come out with money.

That's because a lawsuit is an investment in the legal economy. Taking someone to court is not simply an act of hostility, it's a complicated capital venture for attorneys as well as their clients. All it takes is a quick glance through the newspapers to see how profitable cases can be. Without them, lawyers would have nothing to do but write wills and close real estate deals. Suing and the threat of being sued are what scare people, and wherever there is fear, there are attorneys looking for bigger and better ways to make it pay off.

Looking the hardest are negligence lawyers, who literally comb the streets in search of clients. . . .

The image of an ambulance-chasing lawyer waiting for customers outside a hospital emergency room is part of legal folklore. Obviously, no self-respecting ambulance chaser would be caught dead working that way today. Some pay police and paramedics to deliver their cards at the scene of an accident; others hire what are known in the trade as "steerers" to patrol hospitals looking for patients whose cases seem promising. Using newspaper stories about six- and seven-figure damage awards as enticements, steerers are paid a commission for signing up clients. This practice is against the law in most states; still it accounts for millions of dollars' worth of business every year.

Despite some of their methods, negligence and personal-injury lawyers offer their clients a way to change misfortune into money. Like medieval alchemists who claimed to make gold out of ordinary metals, they sell the promise of a fast fortune. And in that sense the service they provide defines the main economic ingredient in every lawyer-client relationship.

In addition, there is also a psychological bond that connects an attorney to the person he represents. Every day people are injured, hurt and abused. The rest of the world may be indifferent to their broken bones and broken hearts; lawyers not only listen to their woes, they make them the center of attention. . . .

Most people hire lawyers for the same reason they hire doctors, to repair some damaged part of their lives. But in court, damage is in the

From *Lawyers and Thieves: Experiences of a Trial Lawyer,* by Norman Grutman and Bill Thomas (Simon & Schuster, 1990). Copyright © 1990 by Norman Grutman and Bill Thomas. Reprinted by permission of the Estate of Norman P. Grutman.

eyes of the jury, and winning always depends on how well an attorney tells his client's story, no matter how unbelievable it seems.

Manny Katz, a New York personal-injury lawyer I know, likes to say he believes in "the reality of pain." The problem is conveying that belief to a jury. Pain, except to the person experiencing it, is an abstraction. In order to convince the court that his client deserves to be rewarded for his anguish, an attorney has to make it real, paint a picture of torment and sadness so vivid that no jury could deny his request for damages. . . .

There are some lawyers who weep and wail to get their message across in court. Others bring in a cast of expert witnesses. Manny Katz does it with cinéma-vérité videos he calls "A Day in the Life of ———." One particularly lucrative production showed his client, a welfare mother, during a typical day, caring for a severely retarded infant while her normal children romped in the background. She was suing the hospital where the baby was born, claiming that doctors had botched the delivery. It was a complex case, asking for damages in the millions. Six physicians testified, but the only piece of evidence the jurors needed to see was the film, which had most of them crying their eyes out by the time it was over.

Juries are particularly susceptible to misery in movie form, and there is no doubt that the medium conveys the message with maximum impact. Yet there are still a few purists left in the legal profession who rely on the spoken word to do the job.

While it is hard for a fair-minded jury to turn its back on a person who sincerely needs help, there is a big difference between feeling sorry for someone and handing him a half-million dollars. For that the lawyer has to tell a sob story so powerful that the only sympathetic response is cash. One of the masters of the technique was Manhattan attorney "Mo" Levine, who never met a victim he didn't like.

Levine's voice choked with emotion when he described lost income. He could make a fender bender sound like the end of the world. In one particular case, he represented a man who had both hands amputated in an accident. The defense summed up its argument in the morning, and in the afternoon, Levine, a firm believer in high-impact imagery, got his turn.

"Ladies and gentlemen," he told the jurors, "I just had lunch with my client." Then, pausing between each word, he said, "He . . . eats . . . like . . . a . . . dog."

Period. That was his entire summation. The jury sat there in stunned silence, picturing the meal, and after deliberating for less than half an hour, gave Levine's client everything he asked for.

Levine was so good that he made money on the side by selling tape recordings of his final arguments. There are weepers for every occasion. Some lawyers bought the tapes and memorized every word he said. None, however, could copy Mo Levine's all-purpose sense of tragedy. . . .

Airplane crashes, fires and construction cave-ins are made for attorneys who know how to build up a case. Paying doctors to exaggerate injuries is a common method for inflating damage claims. Some attorneys even defy medical science to make money. After a resort hotel in Puerto Rico burned down in 1986, disaster master Melvin Belli was fined $5,000 for filing a lawsuit on behalf of a dead man. The suit claimed that the plaintiff's wife, who was injured in the fire, was unable "to perform her duties as a spouse" and cited the loss of family income from the woman's missed earnings. An astute judge determined that the man could not have authorized Belli to file the suit, since he had been dead for twelve years at the time the litigation was started.

Lamentably, these kinds of shenanigans occur everywhere law is practiced. They especially thrive when an attorney's fee is based on how much he earns for his client. That is not to say the contingency-fee system lacks necessary and important benefits. Without it, how could poor people ever have their day in court? . . .

Wealthy clients, regardless of how unpopular they are, can always find good lawyers. Oil spills, chemical pollution and plane crashes may mean bad press for big business, but they are easy money for elite law firms, most of which have no moral qualms about representing anyone who can pay their fees.

"Hail me, I'm a cab," said Simon Rifkind, a partner with the respected New York firm of Paul, Weiss and one of the top American litigators. Still, no cabbie gives away free rides, and good attorneys rarely work for nothing. The choice of clients, even in charity cases, can be a business decision. Lawyers like to pay lip service to the idea that no individual, corporation or foreign country should be denied legal representation; however, from Bhopal to Bedford-Stuyvesant, the cases they fight the hardest for are the ones they can take to the bank.

A negligence lawyer, working on contingency, is like a boxer who only gets paid when he wins. "You don't need an Ivy League education in our profession," said a New Jersey attorney in the field understandably proud of his ring record. "A Phi Beta Kappa key never won over a jury," he added. "For that, you have to be street smart." . . .

All lawyers are essentially confidence men, some in the best sense, many in the worst. What they market is the belief that for a price they can solve their client's problems and put cash in his pockets. In most cases the problems are not solved comfortably, and the money usually travels in the opposite direction. But knowing that does not stop some people from calling a lawyer every time something goes wrong.

We live in an imperfect world, and attorneys are part of it. However, an imperfect world is full of economic opportunities, and given the right legal advice a person can pick up a nice piece of change.

Joe Flom of the New York firm of Skadden, Arps may be the highest-paid attorney in America. The Harvard-educated mergers-and-acquisitions expert would never be confused with a leg-off man. Yet every year Flom earns between $3 million and $5 million cleaning up after corporate collisions.

A generation ago, the American business world was a far more peaceful environment than it is today. Bankers, CEOs and their lawyers closed as many deals at the country club as they did at company headquarters. Competition followed a sportsmanlike set of rules, and hostile takeovers—buying businesses not wanting to be sold—were strictly out of bounds.

Skadden, Arps changed all that. Under Flom's guidance, the takeover has become a commonplace corporate strategy—and his firm's device for charging whatever it wants.

Using the grandfatherly Flom and a bloody proxy fight as an implied threat, Skadden, Arps has converted fear of unfriendly buyouts into a private cash machine. If a lawyer works for you, he's not available to help someone else take away your business. That would be a conflict of interest. So just to be safe, corporations reportedly pay Skadden, Arps over $20 million a year in retainer fees to avoid facing Flom and company in court. Keep in mind, this is money Skadden, Arps collects for being on call. In the event that actual legal work is required the cost goes up.

Normally, law firms charge 1 percent of the total dollar value of a deal to handle a takeover. Skadden, Arps is generally more expensive, yet that has not hurt business. It's easy to see why. The fact that clients include such notorious corporate raiders as Sir James Goldsmith and Carl Icahn (whose Flom-assisted takeover of Trans World Airlines inspired the movie *Wall Street*) is encouragement enough for most companies to sign on.

Corporations live in terror of Flom, and even those that hire him do not like to talk about it. In today's corporate world, Flom is the modern equivalent of a Wild West gunfighter. When he rides into town, every businessman wants to be his friend, since to be anything else is suicidal.

"Takeover insurance" is just one of Skadden, Arps's protective services. If a corporate war goes to trial, the firm calls in its corps of cutthroat litigators. A kinder, gentler world would not have lawyers from Skadden, Arps in it. Their instinct for the bottom line is legendary, and so are their bills, structured to reflect both the time they spent working on a case and how well they performed. The more lucrative the outcome is for clients, the more Skadden, Arps takes off the top.

Like negligence lawyers, mergers-and-acquisitions specialists can be a mean and reckless breed. "Watching these deals get done," said an investment banker who helps do them, "is like watching a herd of drunk drivers take to the highway on New Year's Eve." One of their favorite maneuvers is the scorched-earth discovery process. Takeover lawyers are experts at depleting the other side's resources with endless motions for documents and data. There are attorneys in takeover firms who are assigned to do nothing but create correspondence and bury the opposition with paperwork. The issues in a case become secondary to bombarding the targeted company with demands for more and more information until it finally gives up.

Defensive strategies, known as "shark repellent," require even more ingenuity. One is the so-called Nancy Reagan defense, where companies "just say no" to buyout offers. Another more elaborate maneuver known as the "onion shield" was devised for Unocal, the Southern California oil company, when it became a target of takeover king T. Boone Pickens. Designed by the New York firm of Sullivan & Cromwell, the onion defense called for the creation of a series of holding companies between Unocal and its present Union Oil of California. Under the plan, if Pickens succeeded in buying Unocal, he would acquire a business in name only. Every time he took aim at one of the holding companies, another would be created. Like peeling the skin off an onion, Pickens would have to spend years looking for the real Unocal.

When the company settled with Pickens by going deeply into debt to buy back its stock, Unocal chairman Fred Hartley triumphantly described the long struggle and its outcome this way: "Mad dog bites man, man bites back; man, with superior intellect, defeats mad dog." But the mad dog in this instance claimed to have taken millions of dollars with him.

Other takeover-avoidance techniques are more ruthless than clever. In one case, Joe Flom acted on behalf of a corporation that eliminated 27,000 jobs to avoid an unfriendly buyout. The decision, he explained later, was in the "best interest of the company."

A philanthropist in his spare time, Flom justifies what he does as a way to increase earnings for his firm and the raiders he works for. "This is capitalism," he declared after a recent victory. "I thought profit was what it was all about."

But lawyers do not add value to the economy, they add cost, and in the mergers-and-acquisitions business the amounts of money involved can be staggering. When a law firm can earn $15 million for a month's work, not an unusual payoff for handling a big takeover, realities like cost and labor tend to lose all their normal meaning.

"I remember spending months on a billion-dollar buyout," said one acquisitions specialist.

"We were talking about seven figures for this and that as if it was chump change. One night my wife was complaining about how expensive everything was, and when she said tuna fish just went up a nickel a can, I told her to let me know when it hits a million. How jaded can you get?"

According to Carl Icahn, one of Joe Flom's big clients, "The takeover boom is a treatment for the disease . . . destroying American productivity: gross and . . . incompetent mismanagement." Viewed another way, takeover mania, like the glut of negligence suits, is the symptom of a different sickness. Under the guise of improving corporate efficiency, buyouts are a way of rearranging assets for the benefit of the investment bankers and lawyers who make the deals. In 1988, the $24 billion takeover of RJR Nabisco produced "professional fees" totaling over $1 billion. Roughly two-thirds went to bankers and the rest to lawyers. Whatever happened to productivity?

This is the Age of the Middleman, and never before have so many earned more for doing less. Arbitrageurs and acquisition attorneys have become entrepreneurs in reverse, buying companies in order to break them up and sell the pieces. If productivity is suffering from mismanagement, as Icahn claims, it's because making deals and money has become more important than making products.

Lawyers thrive in a hostile environment where doing business means doing unto others before they do unto you. As a rule, the more unfriendly the opposing parties, the longer they fight, and since, for attorneys, time is money, drawn-out conflicts can be a valuable source of revenue. Quick-strike takeovers and mega-payoffs may get headlines in *The Wall Street Journal*, but sustained legal warfare is what lawyers love.

The predatory psychology that attracts clients like Icahn to firms like Skadden, Arps is the same thing most attorneys rely on to generate business. Just as the only protection against Joe Flom is to hire him, the only way to be safe from someone else's lawyer is to hire one of your own.

Whether the case involves personal injury or a multimillion-dollar merger, a lawyer is always the weapon, an instrument for threatening harm and inflicting damage. The strongest incentive to retain an attorney is the thought of what might happen to you without one, and it's that fear that lawyers use to intimidate their opponents and profit from their clients.

The first step in the litigation process, and frequently the last, is putting the other side on notice that legal action is about to begin. This is usually done by a letter, whose main purpose is to scare the recipient into immediate surrender.

Recently I took the case of a love-torn lady in Seattle who was suing her gynecologist. The doctor had just ended their affair and, in addition, left her with a nasty case of herpes. Under ordinary circumstances the woman's claim for damages might have been difficult to prove in court, but before their breakup she had tape-recorded a conversation with the doctor in which he not only confessed to infecting her but also admitted having affairs with other female patients as well.

The gynecologist was cornered. He had to be convinced that it would be in his best interest to resolve the matter quickly and quietly, and here (with appropriate name changes) was the letter I sent him:

[*First the bad news*]
Dear Dr. Jones:

We write to you in our capacity as counsel to Jane Smith, on whose behalf we have been instructed to promptly initiate an action at law against you, if necessary, to recover for the severe damages she has suffered at your hands.

[*Then a dilemma*]

To place before you in the clearest way possible the nature of Ms. Smith's grievances, the bearer of this letter is delivering the accompanying copy of a proposed draft of a complaint which will be served upon you within two weeks in the event that you do not give this matter the immediate attention it requires.

[*Then the solution*]

We invite you and your counsel to meet with us next week at the earliest mutually convenient time to discuss the possibilities of an out-of-court resolution of this matter.

[*Then another dilemma*]

We have fully investigated the allegations contained in the complaint. We are also perfectly aware that they involve highly sensitive material that could result in severe damages to you with attendant unwelcome publicity.

[*Then a warning*]

This matter should not be sloughed off. We have in our possession incontrovertible evidence, proving beyond a doubt that the allegations contained in the complaint are the facts and are true.

The evidence to which I refer consists in part of your own confession and admission. We also have evidence that what my client suffered on account of you is no isolated episode.

[*And finally, the handshake and the ultimatum*]

On behalf of Ms. Smith, we are prepared in the spirit of cooperation to explore the possibility of settling this matter with you. If you are amenable to meeting and conferring for that purpose, we will be reasonable, but if you are otherwise disposed, then you will have only yourself to blame for the consequences, distasteful as they may be, which appear to us to be inescapable.

Trusting that you yourself or your counsel will respond to us within the next week, we remain,

Very truly yours

To protect himself and his reputation, the doctor had no choice but to settle with my client. Sometimes, though, the tables are turned and it is the attorney who needs protection. The agreement between a lawyer and his client is like a military alliance. The objective is to defeat the enemy or at least push him back into his own territory. For some clients winning is never enough. They want to demolish the opposition and frequently end up venting their anger by turning on their lawyers.

Once I represented a Florida real estate executive who was so determined to get revenge on his ex-partner that he hired five different law firms to go after him. His plan was to drive the man crazy. With so many lawyers second-guessing each other, that idea soon backfired. Several years—and several law firms—later the irate executive is still obsessed with destroying his former partner, but the only people going crazy are the attorneys who have yet to be paid.

People who need lawyers are either angry or afraid. The ones who are afraid can overcome their fear by getting angry; those who show up angry only get worse.

Clients who seek attorneys as a necessary evil when they have a legal problem often see no reason to pay them when the problem is solved. Indeed, they can be very ungrateful. The assumption is that lawyers get paid for winning arguments and vanquishing their foes. Actually, they get paid when, and if, their clients feel like it, and in certain cases that can mean never. . . .

There are two things at stake in every legal case: profit and principle. The system works best when all parties get what they deserve, but that does not happen by accident. Before attorneys sit down to cut deals, they always separate "the issues" from the bottom line. Lawyers and clients should do the same by agreeing on who gets what before either side gets anything. That way there is less chance of a misunderstanding when principles are compromised for money—and the money (as it usually does) turns out to be less than everyone expected.

Liking each other is not a requirement for a successful lawyer-client relationship, but trusting each other is. I have had clients who lied to me about everything: women who claimed they were being sexually harassed by men they were sleeping with; businessmen who were stealing from people they accused of stealing from them; and, in one case I'll never forget, an acquitted murderer who wanted me to bring a libel suit against the district attorney who tried him for homicide and the unfriendly newspaper that had written about the case. It made no difference to the man that he had committed the crime, as he freely confessed. The trial had inconvenienced him, and he was determined to make everyone who had anything to do with it pay, although I declined the offer to help.

No attorney can ever do enough for his client. If he loses a case, it's always his fault; if he wins, he should have gotten more money from the other side. The only predictable thing about people in legal distress is that they always take out their worst dissatisfactions and frustrations on their lawyers.

Clients come to attorneys with complaints, some justified, some exaggerated and some totally imagined. There are those who truly need help and those who chronically require it. People in this latter group are not just shopping for legal advice, they need psychotherapy.

Several years ago, a client of mine thought he was being followed by spies from Mars. His predicament was laughable, although to him it was very real. Substitute a hated boss, an ex-spouse or a corporate raider for the Martian spies and you have just the sort of paranoia that attorneys depend on for their livelihood. Spies from Mars are exactly what lawyers are to most people—mysterious creatures from another planet who invade their lives. The only way to beat them is to join them. The man had come to the right place for help.

With him sitting there in my office, I picked up the phone and pretended to call the FBI.

"J. Edgar? Roy Grutman . . . Fine, and you? . . . Great. Listen, J. Edgar, I've got someone here who's being followed by spies from Mars. That's right. From Mars, and I was wondering . . . You can? . . . A dozen agents? . . . I'm sure they will. Thanks a million. I'll tell him. . . . You too, J. Edgar, and keep up the good work."

The long-deceased FBI chief, I assured the man, had promised to take care of everything right away.

A few weeks later he stopped by to thank me, obviously happy with the results of his first visit. "The spies from Mars are still following me," he said. "But I'm happy to see the FBI agents are right behind them."

The service was free, and I have never had a case with a happier ending.

*Notes and Questions*

1. What do you think of the metaphor of law as a big casino? Who are the gamblers—the clients, the lawyers, or both? What kind of games are being played—blackjack, poker, slot machines? In slot machine or lottery gambling, a little is taken from many, accumulated into a large amount, and returned to a few—minus, of course, a house cut. In blackjack, dice, and roulette, the gambler bets against the house, with the long-run odds favoring the house. In poker, gamblers wager against each other, with the house claiming an administration fee from each pot. What kinds of legal cases might have characteristics similar to those of casino games? For example, what form of gambling may describe a personal injury suit against an insurance company, a divorce case, a criminal case, an antitrust case to break up a large corporation?

2. Without a doubt, one of the best books written on a single case is *A Civil Action* by Jonathan Harr (New York: Random House, 1995). The author tells the story of an environmental lawsuit against two large corporations by several families in Woburn, Massachusetts, who had lost several children and other family members to cancer, apparently caused by the pollution of the town's groundwater. Jan Schlichtmann, the principal lawyer in a small law firm, was strongly moved by the plight of the families and agreed to take the case on a contingency fee basis (agreeing to accept a portion of the final judgment as his fee should he win, and receiving no fee should he lose). The case began in 1966 and concluded in 1990. Ultimately, Schlichtmann and his two partners had to spend over $2 million to cover costs and develop the scientific and medical evidence needed for the plaintiff's case. The defendants spent nearly an equal amount in legal fees and settlement costs. Each of the plaintiff families recovered less than $500,000, and Schlichtmann ended up in bankruptcy. The cost of the environmental cleanup was estimated to be $69 million. What kind of casino game is this?

3. Those interested in learning more about the story of Joseph Flom and the Skadden, Arps law firm should read *Skadden: Power, Money, and the Rise of a Legal Empire* by Lincoln Caplan (New York: Farrar, Straus, Giroux, 1993). For a story of the collapse of a giant law firm (in which Grutman also had a part), see *Conduct Unbecoming: The Rise and Ruin of Finley, Kumble* by Steven J. Kumble and Kevin J. Lahart (New York: Carroll & Graf, 1990).

## 11.3 | Legal Practice in a Postprofessional World   *Herbert M. Kritzer*

THE AMERICAN LEGAL PROFESSION is facing challenges that are sending tremors through its institutional foundations. On the one hand, U.S. lawyers appear to be wielding ever increasing power. . . . At the same time, the profession finds its traditional prerogatives under increasing challenge with the push for multidisciplinary professional practices, direct encroachment by a variety of service providers (accountants, consultants, paralegals, etc), and mounting political attacks on the profession for its apparent greed (e.g., huge fees from the tobacco litigation) and apparent arrogance. . . .

We are moving into a period in which the role of professions . . . is radically changing and may be in sharp decline. Although I hesitate to add another "post-xxx" to a lexicon now overflowing with "posts" (postmodernism, poststructuralism, postmaterialism, postindustrialism, post-Soviet, post-this, and post-that), a concept that begins to capture the full dimensions of these developments is *postprofessionalism*. . . .

### PROFESSIONALISM AND POSTPROFESSIONALISM

What specifically do I mean by postprofessionalism? The starting point to answer this is a definition of "profession."

**Professions: Multiple Conceptions** One problem with thinking about professions is that the term *profession* can be defined and conceptualized in many different ways, three of which I label the common parlance definition, the "historical" definition, and the sociological definition, with the first as the most inclusive and the last as the least. . . .

Profession, according to the "lay definition," is almost synonymous with "occupation" and is distinguished primarily by means of its antonym, "amateur." As commonly used in lay parlance, a "professional" can refer to a firefighter, a plumber, an auto mechanic, a secretary, a teacher, a salesperson, a social worker, a lawyer, a doctor, or a member of the military as well as many other occupations. Members of all of these occupations often choose to pride them-

Excerpts from "The Professions are Dead, Long Live the Professions: Legal Practice in a Post-Professional World" Herbert M. Kritzer in *Law and Society Review,* Vol. 33, No. 3, pp. 713–759. Copyright © 1999. Reprinted by permission of the Law and Society Association.

Footnotes have been omitted.—ED.

selves on their "professionalism," and by referring to themselves as a "professional" (e.g., a "professional secretary" or a "professional firefighter"), they mean that they perform a particular line of work as a means of livelihood and are committed to what they view as a set of standards of performance. . . .

Professions, according to the "historical" definition, include a broad class of occupations that are characterized by "trained expertise and selection by merit, a selection made not by the open market but by the judgment of similarly educated experts." These professions are built on human capital, and typically involve some recognition of qualifications and some sort of career hierarchy. Some occupations are able to restrict entry by enforceable licensing rules based on recognized expertise. . . . Others may be able to achieve a recognition of a strong credentialing process outside a state-based enforcement structure (e.g., librarians, engineers, college professors). Still other occupations have no licensing process and at best a weak credentialing process, but nonetheless are associated with an expertise that has led to the appellation "professional" (e.g., managers, computer programmers). The key elements to professionalism in this broad sense are the creation of and recognition of trained expertise and the structuring of occupations around this expertise. Within developed economies, professionalism of this type is endemic and is one of today's key features. I refer to professions defined in this sense as "general professions."

The sociological definition uses "professional" in a still more restrictive sense. . . . Professions are specific occupational groups that are at a minimum defined as "exclusive occupational groups applying somewhat abstract knowledge to particular cases." Two key elements to this definition go beyond the historical definition: *exclusive* occupational groups and the application of *abstract* knowledge. As noted above, many occupational groups enjoy exclusivity (through licensing or union structures), and abstract knowledge is today applied by many technical occupations (e.g., computer programmers, electronic repair technicians). It is the combination of recognized exclusivity with the application of abstract knowledge that defines what sociologists label as professions. Professions in the sociological sense have further distinguished

themselves by adding notions of altruism, regulatory autonomy through peer review processes, and autonomy vis-à-vis the service recipient (i.e., the professional tends to control the relationship with and the service provided to the client/patient/customer). By combining these characteristics with their abstract knowledge-based expertise, these professions have regularly asserted claims of independence that other occupational groups have never successfully advanced. . . .

For purposes of clarity, I will refer to these as "formal professions." As should be obvious, formal professions are a subset of general professions.

.   .   .   .   .   .   .   .   .   .   .   .   .   .   .

**Postprofessionalism**   Postprofessionalism refers to the combination of three elements:

1. the formal professions' loss of exclusivity
2. the increased segmentation in the application of abstract knowledge through increased specialization
3. the growth of technology to access information resources

The end result is that services previously provided only by members of formal professions can now be delivered by specialized general professionals or nonprofessionals. The type of political and economic power that members of the formal professions and their organizations were able to wield to secure their control through much of the twentieth century cannot withstand the pressures created by the combination of segmentation of tasks and improved access to information. Equally important is that although at one time professions might have been able to control what information was available through the control of journals—sponsorship, editorial control, peer review processes, and the like—the Internet and the World Wide Web have reduced much of that control. . . .

## MOVING INTO THE POSTPROFESSIONAL WORLD

. . . [I]deas of practitioner independence and autonomy lie at the core of the standard image of the formal professional. Over a 15-year period

(1980 to 1995), the percentage of private practice lawyers working in firms of six or more went from 29% to 38%. Increasingly, we are coming to see formal professionals, not just lawyers, as working in institutional or bureaucratic settings that are designed to control workers rather than to foster autonomy. . . .

The traditional image of the formal professional as having substantial control over the substance and conditions of his or her work has increasingly come to be questioned. . . . [T]he lament that the practice of law has become "just a business" has become common, and the struggle to recapture the supposed spirit of professionalism is a theme that has regularly recurred. . . . Abel has characterized the loss of control experienced by the legal profession as the "decline of professionalism." . . . Abel argues that professions are largely economic entities designed to limit entry ("control the production of producers") and limit competition from within and without ("control the production by producers"). In the late twentieth century, . . . the legal profession in particular lost these kinds of controls.

. . . . . . . . . . . . . . . . . .

## WHY THE PROFESSIONS ARE LOSING CONTROL . . .

### Changing Nature of Work . . .

*Rationalization*

Rationalization of the professional workplace involves three elements: the formalization and systematization of the distribution of knowledge, the development of standardized procedures, and the segmentation of professional practice. The impact of rationalization is evident both with regard to the production of producers of professional services and the production of those services by producers.

The rationalization of entry processes for the professions has radically altered the production of producers of professional services. Historically, professions such as medicine and law (at least in the common-law world) controlled entry through a process akin to apprenticeship. The apprenticeship model was highly personalistic and particularistic, with decisionmaking resting largely in the hands of individuals who had incentives to limit entry, both in terms of who was

permitted entry and how many were permitted entry. Over the course of the twentieth century, however, entry moved to a system of formal education and at the same time access to educational opportunities was no longer limited to members of the social and economic elite. Control over entry has shifted from the professionals themselves to educational authorities whose incentives are to increase, not control, enrollments. . . . The overall effects of these developments is to rationalize the process around "objective" criteria (grades, examinations, etc.) as opposed to the more personalized criteria of the apprentice system and to increase the opportunities to enter the profession radically.

Rationalization is also evident in the production of services. Traditional controls such as limits on advertising, mandatory fee schedules, and the like have either disappeared or have been greatly relaxed. Professional practice is increasingly marked by a combination of specialization and delegation. . . . Where we once thought of doctors or lawyers, we now have doctors who describe themselves as allergists, cardiologists, dermatologists, endocrinologists, nephrologists, neurologists, pediatricians, obstetricians, oncologists, ophthalmologists, orthopedists, radiologists, rheumatologists, urologists, and a whole host of surgeons and legal specialists in the fields of criminal defense, divorce and family, elder law, insurance defense, labor law, litigation, patents and trademarks, personal injury, real estate, environmental law, mergers and acquisitions, workers compensation, and wills and estates. Although the American legal profession (unlike the medical profession) has resisted formalizing specializations, the reality is that all but the small town lawyer and the most marginal of urban practitioners have come to specialize in the services that they offer. . . .

As professionals have recognized the quality and efficiency gains of specialization, they have built on the identification of tasks within their specialized areas of work to delegate to nonprofessionals or general professionals. Many of these tasks are extremely routine, but not always. In some areas of practice, professionals are able to design their practices so that relatively little of the client . . . contact is directly with the professional. As clients . . . increase in sophistication (through education, access to information, etc.), they begin to demand direct access to lower-cost, nonprofessional providers of specific services previously the domain of professions. Some of these nonprofessional specialties were effectively created by professionals as means of increasing efficiency. The result is that professionals have themselves created many of the conditions for postprofessionalism to take hold.

*Information Technology*

The second major force is information technology and the resulting changes in how knowledge is accumulated and then distributed in society. . . . Given the very close linkage between information and knowledge, the rapidly improving tools for accessing information reduce the need to rely on highly trained individuals who have acquired extensive information as part of their training. . . .

Among providers of legal services, the traditional tools for accessing legal information (i.e., case law) was a sophisticated set of categories closely tied to a variety of legal concepts. . . . To access case law effectively, one needed training in the central concepts that lie at the core of the category system. Modern information technology has led to an alternative system for accessing case law: free text searches using massive electronic databases (most prominently Westlaw and LEXIS). The result is to make it possible for persons with a much less sophisticated understanding of legal categories and principles to perform at least rudimentary legal research. . . .

**Challenges to Professional Autonomy and Control**   Modern formal professions in the English-speaking world have often enjoyed the protection of the state. These protections (e.g., licensing laws, unauthorized practice laws) have been the primary device used to exclude potential competitors from domains considered to belong to members of a profession. . . . As evidence mounts that nonprofessionals can deliver quality services at lower cost, it is becoming more difficult to maintain those protections.

As tasks become specialized and it becomes possible for persons to acquire the limited set of knowledge necessary to deliver highly specific services traditionally the domain of a member of a formal profession, it becomes increasingly difficult for the profession to maintain any exclusivity over those tasks. A common claim by formal professionals seeking to protect their domain is that someone without the level of training required to be a full member of the profession will not be able to recognize the complex interrelationships and subtle issues raised in a specific case. . . . Yet whenever previously restricted tasks have been opened to new providers, the problems predicted by the profession opposing relaxation of restrictions have failed to materialize in significant numbers (if at all). . . .

**Globalization of the Professional Services Sector**   The last development has been the globalization of the professional services sector. . . . At one time, professional services were delivered almost exclusively on a local basis: doctors, lawyers, and accountants practiced locally, drew clients locally, and relied on local institutions (courts, hospitals, etc.). Accountants were the first of the professions to develop nationally (and then internationally), primarily because they serviced large corporations with operations in many locales and many countries. The corporate sector of the legal profession was next, as it too devised new ways to meet the needs of large corporate clients; developments such as the European Union have spurred these developments along. In recent years, elements of the personal services sector of the bar have also begun to reach out beyond their local communities (e.g., statewide law firms advertising for personal injury clients, securities specialists seeking clients around the country, and mass tort specialists flying off to sign up clients at the most recent international disaster). . . .

The geographic widening of the market for professional services reflects the combination of improvement in transportation, communication technology, and information technology. Today, . . . information technology allows lawyers in New York, London, and Singapore to work simultaneously on documents needed for a complex financial transaction in Hong Kong. A personal injury lawyer in Charleston, South Carolina, can obtain copies of previous depositions by an opposing expert witness via overnight courier (or even within the hour using facsimile transmission) from an attorney in Portland, Oregon. Or, a solicitor in England working on tobacco-related cases can access key documents obtained from American tobacco companies via the Internet.

Once it becomes difficult to control competition from players beyond a professional group's area of political influence, the ability to maintain the group's professional monopoly is doomed. It is only a matter of time before competition from within the local community (i.e., nonprofessionals) will join the competition from without.

## LAWYERS CONFRONT POSTPROFESSIONALISM

For the lawyers, postprofessionalism is real and immediate:

• Although corporate lawyers have for many years been very attentive to the demands of their fee-paying clients, corporations have become increasingly sophisticated in their use of legal services. In the 1970s, corporations might have automatically turned to "their" outside law firm, but today corporations put work out for bid, inviting interested firms to participate in a "beauty contest." Furthermore, corporations regularly demand that their outside firms consider alternatives to hourly billing in pricing their services. More generally, lawyers are having to recognize and deal with growing consumer consciousness. . . .

• Until recently, a lawyer who achieved partner status in a large corporate law firm could look forward to a secure position and many years of a substantial income, but today corporate legal practice has become a world of change and turmoil. Employment structures have radically changed to include a variety of types of positions, and firms regularly shed partners, dissolve and merge. Life in a large corporate law firm increasingly resembles life in the management sector of any large business.

• In the 1980s and 1990s, a number of bar-related groups and commissions have been appointed to examine the issue of whether it is time for the legal profession to come to grips with the reality of nonlawyers providing a wide range of legal services; typically, the resulting report has recommended finding a way to accommodate (and regulate) the competing providers.

• We are beginning to see the development of computer-based "expert systems" that can be employed to handle routine cases such as valuing personal injury claims or uncontested divorces.

The response by the legal profession to these and other developments has been to try to hold onto an outmoded image of professionalism. Compared with other professions, the legal profession may have had a stronger ally in the state because of its close connection to state functions. Nonetheless, although lawyers have avoided coming to grips with the "brave new world" of postprofessionalism, that avoidance has not prevented that new world from emerging.

### Resisting Competitors . . .

Whereas previously the legal profession lost control over the production of producers to the legal academy, the near future is likely to see substantial erosion in the profession's control over the production by producers. This erosion will come from challenges by potential competitors (other professions such as accounting and paraprofessionals), from economic pressures to reduce the cost of legal services, and from politicians seeking to capitalize on the apparent public disaffection with lawyers. What specific changes might we see in the legal profession? Let us now turn to that question.

## THE NEXT ROUND OF CHANGES IN LEGAL PRACTICE

**Specialization**  The issue of specialization, which is by no means new, continues to be extremely controversial. Anglo-American legal professions cling to the image of the general practitioner, and there are many such practitioners at work across the country, particularly in smaller cities and towns, but they are increasingly the exception. In addition to the general structure of corporate legal firms, some substantive areas (e.g., tax and intellectual property) have long been the province of specialists. . . .

Only a minority of states have actually adopted systems for certifying specialists, and proposals for such systems have often been controversial.

Would recognizing specialties give some lawyers an advantage over others in getting clients?

Would uncertified lawyers who actually practice in an area be more at risk for claims of malpractice in the event of a negative outcome?

Would specialization drive up fees?

Added to the controversy over the impact of recognizing specialization is the dilemma of which *dimensions* of specialization to recognize. . . .

Generally, the developments with regard to specialization have been experience related rather than training related. Unlike the medical profession, where one enters a formal training program (a residency) to become a specialist, a lawyer works in the field to become certified as a specialist. Only after a number of years of experience can the lawyer seek such certification. One can argue that training for a specialization today is where legal training was at the beginning of the twentieth century: it is essentially an apprentice system (but often without the guidance of an experienced mentor). Just as legal training moved from the law office to the law school, it may be time that specialized training made a similar move. . . .

**Dissolving Disciplinary Boundaries: The Coming Rise of Multidisciplinary Practices**  Although specialization will increasingly define the nature of legal practice, pressures also work in the opposite direction. One is the development of multidisciplinary practices and partnerships. Until very recently, the American (and English) legal professions staunchly maintained the position that lawyers must not work in private practice situations where they are under the supervision or control of nonlawyers. Among other things, this position means that all partners in a private practice that provides legal services must be lawyers. The stated rationale for these restrictions turns on the types of ethical obligations lawyers have that do not apply to nonlawyers: the attorney-client privilege, conflict of interest rules, the lawyer's role as an officer of the court, and so on. . . .

In the years to come, the lines among professions, both formal and general, as they were known throughout the twentieth century will become much less distinct and will perhaps begin to disappear. The groupings of services will probably be less along the lines of professions as defined today and much more along substantive or client lines. Thus, for a corporation, rather than turning to (1) a law firm to handle labor negotiations, (2) a specialized service firm to handle unemployment compensation issues, and (3) an insurance company to handle workers' compensation, one might see a generalized employee services firm that serviced all those areas with a combination of lawyers, mediators, accountants, risk managers, and so on. Similarly, where today a residential property purchase might involve a real estate broker, an attorney, a title insurer, an engineering firm to inspect a property, an insurance broker to provide casualty insurance and a home buyer's warranty, and a mortgage company to provide a mortgage, in the future all these services might be grouped into a single "home buyers' service corporation." . . . How far these kinds of combinations will extend is the unanswered question.

**Changing Structures of Firms**  For those law firms that remain focused solely on law, the structure of the firms will almost certainly change. . . . Two changes are already obvious.

The first is the changing status of lawyers within firms. The modern American law firm developed along the distinction between lawyers who were partners (owners) and those who were associates (employees). The corporate firm today has myriad categories: equity partner, nonequity partner, of counsel, associate (partner track and nonpartner track), contract lawyer, and so on. These categories have developed in significant part to allow firms to be more responsive to client needs. The traditional partner/associate model effectively locked firms into particular patterns of staff and services. The much more diverse set of categories allows firms to be much more responsive to the needs of clients and the flow of work.

Outside the coporate firm, it is increasingly common for lawyers to speak about positions in terms of "owners" and "employees." Most often, these terms reflect the reality that in small firms, the expectation is often that a lawyer-employee (a non-owner) will work in the firm for a period of time to gain experience and then move on;

the labels avoid any suggestion of an expectation of partnership. In other situations, a law practice may be built around the reputation of the "owner," which is probably most common in more entrepreneurial areas of practice such as plaintiffs' personal injury. Often, these practices stay relatively small, in part because of the owner's dominance and in part because the work does not itself require large groupings of lawyers. In either case, the "owner"/"employee" distinction sees the law practice in a more clearly business-oriented mode. Despite the frequent cries of members of the legal profession that the practice of law is becoming "too much like a business," this trend will in fact only increase in the future.

One way the "business" pressures will be evident will be in increasing pressure to find cost-efficient ways to deliver legal services. For both corporate and personal services firms, one route will be in the increasing use of nonlawyer staff, whether called paralegals, legal assistants, legal secretaries, or something else. These staff members will handle relatively routinized aspects of the legal work, including basic computerized legal research, review of documents, drafting of relatively standard documents, interaction with outside parties (experts, service firms, etc.), and anything else the lawyers believe that a particular paralegal is capable of handling. The pressures for efficiencies will break down many of the traditional barriers. . . .

A second way that business, or "commercial," pressures on corporate law firms is already evident is in the shift from departmental structures based largely on substantive areas of law (e.g., property, finance, contracts, tax, trusts and estates, litigation) to structures based on the industries of the targeted clients. Today large law firms commonly have groups organized around major client groups such as the computer industry, healthcare, pharmaceuticals, transportation. . . .

### Changing Demands on (Corporate) Firms

Increasingly, the concern of legal practitioners is one of efficiently delivering their product in a way that ensures quality. Previously, large firms viewed the partner/associate system as a vehicle for achieving these ends, but firms today are confronting corporate clients who demand efficiences and accountability that are the anathema of the . . . system. These clients no longer rely on strong ongoing relations with a single (or primary) outside law firm; rather corporations today look to outside lawyers for "specialized services on a case-by-case, transaction-by-transaction basis." Thus, the corporate client might once have seen a value to subsidizing "their" outside law firm's development of new legal talent, but that is no longer the case.

One impact of this change is that the organizational language of a large firm practice today looks very much like the language of other large organizational providers of services: teams, accountability, total quality management, information technology, and so on. Another impact is that where previously firms recruited at only the entry level and promoted from within, firms today seek legal talent across the experience spectrum; this type of staff recruitment is also an important means of securing clients (experienced lawyers bring their existing clients with them to their new firm). The emphasis within the firms is no longer on professional development and professional autonomy, but on marketing and delivering the kind of service for which wealthy clients are prepared to pay. . . .

### Subcontracting Elements of Legal Services

One way that industrial production has been rationalized is through subcontracting. Rather than producing every element of a product, manufacturers turn to subcontractors to produce major elements that can be incorporated into their products. This case is particularly true when the product has highly specialized elements that must be produced in a manner that is tangential to the primary manufacturer's production process. . . .

Although it is common today for lawyers to refer cases and clients to other lawyers, either because a case is outside a lawyer's areas of expertise or because of the resources needed to handle a case, it is unusual for lawyers to subcontract elements of a case to other law firms (although tasks such as litigation management are already being subcontracted). As the demands for efficiencies increase, one might expect to see specialized service providers develop that concentrated on very specific aspects of a case. Legal research or legal writing are possible examples. If a lawyer needed a brief on a particular issue, a specialized legal research firm employing skilled paralegals, legal writers, and editors might be employed to produce the brief.

**Connecting Lawyers and Clients**   One side effect of the technology that is pushing change in legal practice will affect the "marketing" of legal services. Large corporations have long had the ability to seek legal counsel in a national market. Clients on the "personal services" side, however, have relied almost exclusively on the local market. In turn, although some lawyers have used modern advertising techniques to attract clients, most have continued to rely on traditional word-of-mouth referrals from prior clients, repeat clients, and referrals from other local lawyers. The Internet provides a vehicle for potential clients to locate lawyers in a wholly new way, particularly if the potential client has some sort of fairly esoteric legal problem (e.g., an injury arising from the use of a particular machine or tool). By using a site that searches lawyer directories or an online lawyer referral service, potential users of lawyers' services can find lawyers purporting to work in the area of the person's needs. More general searches of the Internet allow the potential client to find others outside his or her own community with similar problems and to get information on and recommendations regarding lawyers. Lawyers, in turn, are provided with a new advertising medium. Carefully designed Web sites can provide "hits" on searches made by potential clients. Legal referral services increasingly have a presence on the Internet, and they may be another new vehicle for connecting lawyers and clients.

Although there are still major issues concerning who may practice law where (and what constitutes the location where law is being practiced), information technology is radically changing markets from local to national and even international. Particularly where practice does not require a physical presence (or where "appearance" may be made over an electronic hookup, which is increasingly practical with improvements in interactive television), lawyers will no longer be bound to a relatively small geographic area and potential clients will have a wider range of lawyers from which to choose.

**Increased Role of Electronic Tools in Legal Research and Practice**   Information tools such as Westlaw and LEXIS have radically altered how lawyers can carry out legal research. Until recently, however, the cost of using these tools was quite high and was often prohibitive for the provider of services to clients without the resources of a large corporation. The cost of accessing electronic research resources has been plummeting in recent years. . . .

These types of research tools are familiar to all practitioners and researchers. What will lead to more change are the new types of services that are becoming available. Take CyberSettle.com, for example. This service was initially marketed as a tool to assist in settlement processes by allowing parties to make a series of settlement offers confidentially and then letting the service provider determine whether there is a settlement based on a set of matching rules. More important, however, is that over time, the provider of the service will develop a large database of cases with the kind of information that will allow the valuing of claims; this information could then be marketed both to lawyers and to claimants themselves. Another example of an online service that is breaking new ground is VirtualJury.com; this site is designed to provide an online focus group type of review of cases similar to what jury consultants do on a face-to-face basis.

· · · · · · · · · · · · · · · · · · · ·

**Increased Reliance on Self-Help**   As discussed previously, one important implication of information technologies is the relatively easy access to information that was previously the exclusive domain of the professional. The amount of information readily available from a computer keyboard is staggering. In years past, it took significant training to learn how to access technical (including legal) information, but today, any junior high school student with access to the Internet can find much of that information. . . .

Finding information and knowing how to use it are two different things. . . . As people recognize this capability, there will be an increase in the availability of simple training regimes that give nonlawyers (or laypersons vis-à-vis other professions) the basic knowledge to assimilate the information they can access. Already one can find such courses in areas such as family law, auto insurance, consumer rights, and workers' compensation. In addition, people who find information on the Internet may also turn to the Internet to seek out individualized legal advice, either through lawyer referral services or through some sort of online legal consultation. . . .

Self-help will not eliminate the need for legal professionals or other legal practitioners, except perhaps in the simplest, most routinized of legal tasks. . . . The impact of self-help activities is going to be less in terms of eliminating the service provider and more in changing the types of services provided and modifying the relationship between the service providers and the recipients of the providers' services. With better information available, someone who previously sought professional-level services might feel more comfortable using a non-professional (in the formal sense) service provider. The user of that provider's services would be in a better position to make some judgments about the quality of the services being provided.

## CONCLUSION

I am sure that the types of developments described only scrape the surface of what postprofessionalism will mean for the legal profession, the practice of law, and the provision of legal services. To the degree that current changes result from the combination of increased rationalization in knowledge and the growing power of information technology, the shape of the world with which today's formal professionals will have to cope will depend on yet unseen developments in that rationalization process and the information technologies that have exploded recently.

In this new world, "professionals" will continue to be central, but the special place of the traditional professions will wither. Although I have called this development postprofessionalism, others might choose to label it professionalism, referring not to the withering of the formal professions but to the growth in what I referred to as general professions. Whatever the label, professionalism as Anglo-American societies have known it is fading. The new professionalism will be much more dynamic, reflecting the rapidity of change in the workplace and the accompanying demands of the market.

The professions are dead. Long live the professions. . . .

## Notes and Questions

1. Kritzer discusses the increasingly common reorganization of law firms to make partnership (ownership) of the firm less available to associates (lawyer-employees). Until now the history of large law firms has been that partnership was the prize held out to all young attorneys to induce them to devote all their time and most of their lives to the firm. (For a good description, albeit fictionalized, see Louis Auchincloss, *Diary of a Yuppie*, Houghton-Mifflin, 1986).

Robert Nelson, a researcher at the American Bar Foundation, reported from a study of Chicago lawyers in 1975 and repeated in 1995, that "[i]n 1975 lawyers in firm settings had about a 37% chance of making partner, but by 1995 the figure had dropped to 22%. . . . For the youngest cohort, however, there was a striking difference, with only an 11% chance of making partner in 1995 compared to a 30% chance in 1975." Further, exit rates during that period jumped from 40% to 61% in mid-size firms and 22% to 43% in large firms.* Clearly, career employment in a single professional setting has become a thing of the past.

Given that the chance of making partner in a large firm is now only about 1 in 10, the incentive appears to be approaching gamblers' odds. What does it cost to become a lawyer—that is, to make this bet?

Lawrence Dieker, Jr., added it up for his law degree:

Using Tulane's projected costs for 1999–2000 as a model, the cost of a private law school education today looks something like this:

| | |
|---|---|
| Tuition and fees for three years | $72,984 |
| Room and board, health, miscellaneous | $35,160 |
| Lost opportunity costs for three years | $105,000 |
| Total | $213.144† |

Certainly, this is a daunting price for an entry ticket. And, of course, that does not include the

---

*From "Structural Transformations in the Legal Profession and Legal Practice," *Researching Law,* Chicago: American Bar Foundation Newsletter (Volume 12, Number 1, Winter 2001), pp. 2–3.

†See, *Letters From Law School: The Life of a Second-Year Law Student* by Lawrence Dieker, Jr. (Lincoln, NE: Writers Club, 2000), p. 67.

cost of the prior undergraduate education. What is the payoff? In the largest law firms in the United States annual compensation can easily be more than a million dollars in some years. But this accounts for only a few thousand of the nearly 900,000 lawyers in the United States. In 1998, according to Career Infonet (www.acinet.org) the median (half above and below) salary for lawyers in the United States was $78,200, or $37.58 per hour. Perhaps the big casino metaphor applies here as well. If you are law school bound, how do you calculate the costs-benefits?

2. The possibility of multidisciplinary practices—firms with a mix of lawyers, accountants, and other business specialists (called MDPs)—is a particularly "hot" topic at this time. At present they are proscribed by the lawyer's Code of Professional Responsibility. The ethically problematic assumption is that lawyers might not be permitted to be zealous and devoted advocates for their clients, as demanded by law and society, if they were subordinate to the economically-driven motives and policies of nonlawyer superiors. During the debates at the 1999 Annual Meeting of the American Bar Association to amend the legal profession's ethical code to allow MDPs, one opponent reported his great fear that by 2050 law firms would no longer exist. In their place, would be law practiced under the names of Pricewaterhouse Coopers, KPMG, and Ernst & Young. "It was a world in which those who were once known as lawyers now kowtowed to accountants in the servile role as clerks. The accountant principals, moreover, were without principles . . . [who] treated clients like commodities, traded client secrets like Pokeman trading cards, and embraced the ideal of legal services for the public good with a variation: What's good for Ernst & Young, is good for the public."‡

On the other side, is the reality-based argument that MDPs are exactly what large corporate clients want and need.

Serving client needs is professionally accepted as doing public good. The corporate market for legal services is changing and a responsive legal profession must adapt to survive.

At this time, the issue is still unresolved. Opponents of MDPs, although granting that this form of organization could be very lucrative for lawyers, perhaps even more than in current large firm practice, still believe MDPs are the legal profession's doomsday machine. Kritzer seems to agree.

3. It is trite to say that the Internet and new information technologies are revolutionary developments. But, in fact, their implications are vast and still not clearly understood. Kritzer considers this one of the social forces undermining lawyers' authority and expertise. The Internet permits public access to legal materials that were previously accessible only to the specially trained. Do-it-yourself legal software is taking routine legal practice out of the lawyer's office and moving it to a personal computer. Some lawyers from all around the country give legal advice online, free or sometimes for a fee, to anyone who asks. Clients share their law stories, give advice based on personal experience, and form interest groups through chat groups and websites. Software engineers are working on developing legal expert systems that use large databases to respond to legal queries—robolawyers?

Most likely you are also an extensive user of the Internet. Do you see in this experience the possibility of the death of the legal profession?

To read about some of these developments see "Technology Time Capsule: What Does the Future Hold?" by Patricia Hassett in 50 *Syracuse Law Review,* 1223 (2000); "Attorney-Client Relationships in Cyberspace: The Peril and the Promise" by Catherine J. Lancetot in 49, 147 (1999); and "Gandy Dancers on the Web: How the Internet Has Raised the Bar on Lawyers' Professional Responsibility to Research and Know the Law," by Lawrence Duncan MacLachlan in 13 *Georgetown Journal of Legal Ethics* (Summer, 2000).

---

‡From "The Future of the Profession: A Symposium on Multidisciplinary Practice: Flight from the Center: Is It Just About Money?" by Burnele V. Powell in *Minnesota Law Review* (Vol. 84: 1439 at p. 1457, June, 2000).

# *12*  THE EDUCATION OF LAWYERS

You are sitting, let us say, in a class in Contracts, or Personal Property, or Domestic Relations. John Smith in the third row is reciting on a case, and has got the facts confused, or he has misread the Restatement section in the footnote. A dozen hands are up, and a dozen eager faces reflect the desire to close in for the kill. The professor delays the moment of slaughter and deliberately passes over the volunteer matadors in order to call on Dick Jones in the tenth row. The professor knows from previous experience that he can count on Jones not only to set Smith right, but to introduce a new misconception that will transfer the error to a still deeper level of confusion. Jones performs according to expectation. More hands go up as more of the class come to share the illumination, taking it either from an inner flame or from the whispered coachings of neighbors. The whole discussion is lively and stimulating; everyone is put on his mettle and seeks to show his best capacities.

> Lon L. Fuller, "On Teaching Law," *Stanford Law Review* (1950)*

Students learn from the emotional content of the law curriculum that they ought to distrust their own deepest moral sensibilities; that they ought to avoid global moral and political inquiry (because it is dangerous, simplistic, and unlawyerlike); that they ought to revere hierarchy; and that manipulating vulnerable people is an acceptable form of professional behavior.

> Karl E. Klare, "The Law-School Curriculum in the 1980s: What's Left?" *Journal of Legal Education* (1982)

❧ Law schools are the gatekeepers for the legal profession. For those who aspire to be lawyers but lack financial resources or are academically uncompetitive, law schools, like Kafka's guard, are the barrier to law. For those allowed to enter, law schools are the profession's initiation—a rite of passage all lawyers share, a basis of community.

The purpose of law school is to change people, to make them different by the experience—to transform them from laypeople into novice lawyers. Law school provides them with some competence in legal rules and legal problem solving. It develops in them a nascent concept of themselves as professionals, a commitment to the values of the calling, and a claim to that elusive and esoteric style of reasoning called "thinking like a lawyer."

Many issues have been raised about the quality, substance, and effects of legal education. People have asked whether this education actually teaches students how to practice law (would you allow a doctor to operate on you if you knew his or her only training was reading books on surgery?), whether it is morally numbing (Watergate and all that) or unnecessarily harsh (a world of Professor Kingsfields from Jay Osborne's *Paper Chase*). Although recently increasing in number and proportion of law students, women and minorities can find it difficult to adjust to this domain, where sitting in classrooms or the library (or just walking down the hall) subjects them to the fixed, oily stares from the omnipresent portraits of eminent white men who came before.

The readings here are directed toward some of these issues. But the major themes are the transmission of the profession's values through legal education, the role of legal education in reproducing the profession's hierarchies, and the subtle consequences of socialization into the adversarial role.

---

## 12.1  Law School: Caught in the Paradigmatic Squeeze

*John J. Bonsignore*

There was a man in our town
and he was wondrous wise;
he jumped into a BRAMBLE BUSH
and scratched out both his eyes—
and when he saw that he was blind,
with all his might and main
he jumped into another one
and scratched them in again.

With this nursery rhyme, Karl Llewellyn opened a book of first lectures to beginning Columbia law students, *The Bramble Bush.* Law students, likewise men, could expect to become blinded in the thicket of law and only upon bold reentry would they regain their vision. One wonders why the most apt metaphor for law is a bramble, why a wise man would jump into it to be blinded, why once blinded he would come back for more, and why more of what takes vision away will yield it again. . . .

Entering law students, unlike graduate students in other disciplines, who have already sampled their fields at the undergraduate level, come to law school with very little knowledge of what it will mean to study law and become lawyers. Admission is difficult (hence, law school *must* be good for you), law offers "more options" than does a Ph.D. in English, and parents and friends think that law is a good career. Beyond

this, there floats what Llewellyn earlier termed "a pleasant haze."

Erving Goffman's classic work *Asylum* offers the best model on the remaking of visions in institutional settings. Although law students are voluntary entrants, they will find the psychic-social process of change a sharp intrusion into their lives and may wonder, after the first few days, what happened to the pleasant haze.

A key concept for Goffman is that all social institutions, such as the home, schools, work places, prisons, asylums, or monasteries have "*encompassing tendencies,*" that is, the ability to capture the time and interest of participants. Although most people carry on several activities in several institutions at different times and places with different participants and different authorities, there are some people who are encompassed by more *total institutions* which crowd out competing value sets and alternative identities that people in them would otherwise experience. The more encompassing or total an institution, the more influence it can exert over its participants.

Upon entry into an institution of whatever type; a person carries a *home world* or *presenting culture,* which Goffman impressionistically defines as "a record of experience that confirmed a tolerable conception of self and allowed a set of defense maneuvers, exercised at his own discretion, for coping with conflicts, discreditings and failures." The more the "home world" can be kept intact in an institution, the less influence that institution can have in altering values or identities of participants.

"Law as a Hard Science" by John Bonsignore, *ALSA Forum* (December, 1977), Vol. 2, No. 3, pp. 65–74, published by the American Legal Studies Association. Reprinted by permission of the author.

One additional preliminary idea is necessary before beginning to make application of Goffman to the law school setting. The idea of novices to an institution presupposes veterans or other regulars in the institution, who establish the institutional values and the permitted personal identities. Thus, home world or presenting culture meets *institutional* world and its culture. A clash of competing cultures may occur upon entry into an institution, even when the entry is voluntary; and the institution must develop *strategies* to eliminate the "home world" and replace it with the "institutional world." The more total an institution, the more effective it will be in prevailing in this contest of values and identities.

Some questions immediately arise as these abstractions are brought closer to the question of law schools and their impact. How total is the law school as an institution? How antithetical are its values and prescribed identities to the values and presenting identities of incoming participants? When there is conflict, what strategies are employed by regulars of the law school, particularly its faculty and veteran students, in overcoming "presenting cultures" and in replacing presenting cultures with the institutional culture? Some tentative answers to these questions can be put forth before going into the details of the "contest of wills" in law schools.

1. Law schools appear to be quite total, exerting strong encompassing tendencies that sharply curtail the regular rhythm among competing institutions of work, play, family, friendships, etc.

2. Even though entry is voluntary, there is a substantial conflict between the values and expected identities of entrants and the values and prescribed identities available in the institution.

3. Given that law schools are relatively total, the school has the edge in reshaping values and identities, but given the clash between "home world" and "institutional world," the law school must employ distinctive strategies to prevail.

4. At stake, behind this contest of wills is nothing other than the paradigm of law, from world view through technique. Learning to see the world as a lawyer and to use legal techniques to the exclusion of other organizing principles appears at most to be only a semivoluntary process. . . .

Judging from the types of strategies used in law school teaching, it seems safe to assume that a law school has more than ordinary leverage over its student body. (Of course, it must be acknowledged that some do leave the school entirely and to this extent the institution is more open than a prison.) That entrants are in conflict with the institutional culture can also be assumed from the intensity with which strategies are employed in the early months of law school. (There is either overkill on willing subjects or necessary intensity of strategies on at least semi-unwilling subjects; the latter appears to be the better explanation.) These heroic assumptions made, this essay can focus on the strategies employed in eliminating the presenting culture and replacing it with the institutional culture.

The pleasant haze in the first days of law school is traceable to the fact the "home world" of most entrants has been good: having graduated from college, usually with at least a modicum of academic honor; having satisfactorily performed tests, particularly the LSAT which is supposedly predictive of law school success; having passed through the "careful screening" of the law school admission committee; and so on. In addition to these acceptable images possessed by all entrants, each entrant has additional sources of contentment and is assured of his or her capacity for self-determination, autonomy, freedom of action, and self-expression. It must be that the pleasant haze and its underlying causes are deemed undesirable in a good law school, because in the next few months there will be a vigorous institutional effort to cut the individual loose from all of these psycho-social anchoring points.

How can individuals who are relatively well satisfied with past experiences, identities, and values be made to want to get rid of them? According to Goffman, institutions (at least the more encompassing ones) provide a unique kind of "welcome" which entails the mortification of entrants through a series of abasements, degradations, humiliations, and profanations of self. If the institution is to prevail, the ways that entrants have defined their identity and role must never find outlet in behavioral opportunities within the institution.

Goffman focused in part on the physical side of "identity stripping such as the admission practices of photographing, head shaving, removal of personal possessions and property, issuance of drab institutional clothing, forcing intimacy with batches of other people, and curtailing privacy in such institutions as mental hospitals, prisons, and the army. But he also considered psychological forms of mortification which are more pertinent in the law school setting. The classroom is the primary situs, the teacher the mortifier and the students the mortified. When the process is over, former selves will be largely abandoned and new selves will be born to think and act in ways not anticipated upon entry.

The pedagogy of a law school is said to be Socratic, but it has nothing to do with Socrates except that two people are talking to each other. The manifest aim in all early law school communication is to avoid common understandings through dialogue and to make the student into a fool whose past academic life and ways of thought are not only unhelpful in doing law, but are positively in the way. This is done primarily in two ways: (1) by a process called *looping,* in which the students' verbal responses and defenses are *themselves* made the objects of attack and rejected as improper and worthless, and (2) a disruption in the students' sense of economy of action. Looping makes for the evershifting ground in law school dialogue, the only constant being that whatever students say exceeds the wildest image of incomprehensibility. Every expression down to the face-saving aside thus becomes a fit subject matter for this process. And given the useful hangup of law students of seeking teacher praise, the student struggles desperately to determine what has gone wrong with the academic success formula that worked in undergraduate settings. Students who observe the looping process on other students are happy not to have been the subject of ridicule before the entire class, but at the same time they identify with the victim and try to find out what earns rewards in this peculiar institution. When students *en masse* begin to feel inferior, weak, blameworthy, and guilty and are constantly looking over their shoulders to see if criticism or other sanctions are once again coming, the process of mortification (literally, the killing off of a self) has reached full effectiveness.

The second major strategy in bringing entrants into institutions involves a disruption of the students' sense of *economy of action,* that is, the way each individual balances needs and objectives in a personally efficient way in the ordering of events, scheduling of time, determining the relative importance of things, and so on. For the law student, personal economies, derived from prior academic experience, also become the subject of criticism. In preparing for class, the usual student technique of reading for point or mood rather than trifling detail becomes—it is learned from class—an improper technique. The very thing left out of preparation is said to be the thing needed, and *vitally* needed. Once again, the need for recognition of academic competence surfaces and students grow compulsive, scrapping their old economies of action, studying longer, reading more slowly, underlining everything, taking more notes or even copying whole sections of casebooks, or memorizing material, so as to be "thoroughly prepared" and not a target of academic ridicule. . . .

Of interest here is the transformation in attitudes that law students have about themselves and the worth of their past. In the foregoing ways, the pleasant haze is burned off, people become dissatisfied with their home worlds or presenting cultures and become amenable to the institution's culture and its privilege system. As Goffman states:

> Total institutions do not really look for total cultural victory. They create and sustain a particular kind of tension between the home world and the institutional world and use the persistent tension as strategic leverage in the management of men.

The tension explains why students do not rebel *en masse* at institutional demands. First, as noted above, each student has a need for teacher praise in academic matters and each believes that the odd pedagogy of law school must somehow be necessary to becoming a lawyer. Secondly, the usual student competition for an edge over fellow students militates against solidarity and collective political action at the formative period when such action is desperately needed. Thirdly, students are in such a state of personal stress and chaos that they seek personal solutions and have literally no energy left for resistance. (It also may be that those who would be so inclined simply leave the law school.)

As the mortification process runs its course, the privilege system of the law school is slowly introduced and some students are restored to a state of partial grace. Law school questions and ways of answering them, though alien at first, become slowly intelligible. (Repetitive practice in legal technique begins to take hold.) Students starved for favorable recognition begin to build whole worlds around a favorable nod or facial expression, or in lasting a few seconds longer in "dialogue" before being put down. Beginners also get solace from the fact that most of the class will pass and ultimately some people do get out of law school. But the fewness of examinations and the postponing of those that are given until late in the first year prolongs and intensifies anxieties and facilitates the changing process. By the start of the second year, students have adjusted and anxiety yields to quiet boredom.

How does the stripping and conversion process of the first year of law school relate to the main question of paradigms and their practice in community? The shortest answer to this question is that much of the first year struggles may be traceable to the unwillingness of law students to accept the legal world view, the kinds of questions asked in law, and the way lawyers answer questions. If cases are presented in the raw—that is, factually—there may be a wide variety of organizational principles that can be invoked in their resolution. It is only after discipline that students will "know" what questions arise from facts. (That is what the phrase "spotting the issues" so commonly heard in law school means.) For example, it is not a legal question to ask about the happiness of marriage. Rather, one must learn to ask about the presence or absence of statutory grounds for divorce. Similarly, one does not ask about the fairness of bargains after learning the rule that adequacy of consideration is not significant in contract law. Becoming case-hardened thus means the ability to read the legal world and to share understandings of it with other professionals. (If law students wonder why they have difficulty in talking with former college acquaintances, it is because of the deep transformation that has taken place in law school; the intensity of the law school has so displaced the home culture of students that they are literally different people when visiting old friends.)

In summary, seeing what a discipline says should be seen, and nothing else, can be understood as a highly painful and unnatural process of closing down perception, intuition, emotions, and other aspects of being that are not relevant to the calling. While it is sometimes said that law students have too much inclination toward certainty, the deeper need may be quite in the opposite direction; rather students intuitively feel the gross neglect of fundamental questions of justice, good policy, and fairness, in the theory and practice of law. But it is through the closing down of vision that the paradigm of the calling is developed and shared vision through community becomes the abiding reality. It is this process that lies behind the blindness-seeing metaphor of Llewellyn.

*Notes and Questions*

1. Of course, law schools do not call themselves "total institutions," or draw parallels between what they do and what happens in a mental hospital. They describe the teaching and learning experiences in law school as a preparation for legal practice. If so, what does Bonsignore's analysis imply about conceptions of the lawyer's role in legal education?

2. Law school teaching in the student's first year primarily uses two techniques, the Socratic dialogue and the case method. In this pedagogic combination, a teacher intensively interrogates individual students concerning the facts and principles presumed to be operative in an appellate opinion. The method is rationalized through two goals. The first is information: instruction in the substantive rules of discrete bodies of law. The second is to develop in the student a cognitive restructuring for the style of analysis generally called "thinking like a lawyer." In that analysis, a student is trained to account for the factual minutiae as well as for the legal issues determined by the court to be at the core of the dispute, so as to allow an intelligent prediction of what another court would do with a similar set of facts. The technique is learner-centered: students are closely questioned, and the teacher often takes their responses to further direct the dialogue. One student described the dialogue from the student's perspective as follows:

Even knowing all the answers affords scant protection against the awful moment when you are plucked from the sea of faces and forced to perform. As you sit drowning in adrenaline, rational thought becomes impossible. Facts are forgotten or jumbled together. Basic principles of coherent sentence structure and logical argument are irretrievably lost. Answers that would be brilliant in any other context fall flat. Creativity is strictly taboo. Each response must be carefully tailored to the demands of the question. Too complete an answer can be as damaging as none at all. Law professors jump at each opportunity for sarcasm or outright cruelty. It's not that they are sadistic. They're simply indifferent. It doesn't matter that some students cry or vomit or pass out in class. How else will they learn?*

This teaching method has been at the center of much criticism of law education. Paul Savoy, in a frequently cited article, compared the pedagogy to game playing:

The Socratic method . . . consists largely of a set of "games," the most popular of which is "Corner." . . . The objective in each case is to drive the student into a corner by refuting any position he takes. In being presented with . . . a Socratic question, the student is cast on the horns of a dilemma: he is made to feel that there is some answer he must find, but in seeking it out, he begins to despair of finding it because everything he says is rejected as wrong. . . .

A variation of the game of "Corner" is "One Up":

*Student:* Do you think that custodial interrogation in the absence of counsel is a violation of the dignity of the individual?

*Teacher:* "What do you mean by "dignity"? . . .

Then there is the familiar "chamber of horrors" gambit—the logical paradigm of which is the *reductio ad absurdum* argument or what I prefer to call the game of "Now I've Got You, You Son-of-a-Bitch." By the time a law student reaches his second year, he knows the game and either stops playing it, plays along cynically, or initiates the counter-game of "Wooden Leg" ("What can you expect of a 'dumb' student like me"). . . . Another

popular pastime of professors that often passes for Socratic dialogue is the game of "Guess What I'm Thinking"; the student counter-game is "Mindreading I, II or III," depending on the number of previous courses the student has had with the professor.[†]

Andrew Watson, a psychiatrist and law professor, sees the pedagogy of law education as causing students to lose their willingness to care about other people:

It is my contention that law school education explicitly shapes the character development of law students in certain ways which are detrimental to efficient professional performance. The character adaptation is necessary in order to resolve and escape the tensions of the classroom. The principle [sic] characterological development change is to become "unemotional." In addition to being told that this is a desirable attribute to develop, it is also a reaction to classroom anxiety. . . . Marked stoicism and emotional unresponsiveness may be regarded as characterological defenses against underlying emotions. Intellectual means in the form of cynicism about the human aspect of the lawyer's role may also be used to accomplish this purpose. This cynicism is a kind of characterological defense which enables a person to avoid the necessity of caring about people with its intrinsic capacity to stir up anxiety.[‡]

Robert Nagel provides the common justification of the Socratic method:

Many students see their teachers as a self selected group of the meanest of the legal profession, a group that seems to get a personal thrill out of brow beating students. Every reasonable answer begets just another question, and it is frustrating and embarrassing to be put on the spot. But to conclude, because of such feelings, that the teacher is trying to hurt is for the student to confuse his personal reactions with the motive of the professor. It is to ignore the teacher as a person in his own right, with his own

---

*Victoria Steinberg, "Why I Quit Law School," *College Digest* (Spring 1982): 7A.

†"Toward a New Politics of Legal Education," by Paul Savoy. Reprinted by permission of The Yale Law Journal Company and William S. Hein Company from *The Yale Law Journal*, Vol. 79, pages 444–504, 1970.

‡Andrew Watson, "The Quest for Professional Competence: Psychological Aspects of Legal Education," *University of Cincinnati Law Review* 37 (1968): 131.

objectives. The teacher's aim is to enable the student to respond under pressure, even in situations where at first the student thinks he has no response. The objective is to encourage the student to think and communicate even more precisely and effectively than he thought he could. Law students are in training to be professional advocates and counselors. For a professional, arguments cannot be merely adequate or normal or bright. Lawyers are paid to be always clear and sometimes moving and brilliant in their communications: they must meet this professional obligation even when they feel embarrassed, even when they are distracted, even when at first they think they have no response.§

Alan Stone, a psychiatrist and law teacher, responded to law education's critics as follows:

> Despite its admitted potential for destructive interaction, Socratic dialogue also has enormous value in channeling group emotions into structural academic inquiry. As individuals vie for status during the period when a group evolves into a coherent entity the entire gamut of intense feelings and personal motivations, including a certain amount of free floating hostility, is inevitably generated. . . . What the Socratic technique can do at its best is to channel the inevitable hostility into the academic inquiry. Most professors do not allow one student to become the constant target, nor do they accept the role of target themselves; rather, the ritual has evolved such that hopefully a student's ideas rather than the student are the impersonal target; at worst, a number of students in turn will be the focus. . . . Its functional value is, however, that group hostility is controlled, and the class knows that the teacher's authority—in this context his capacity to control group hostility and other emotional excesses—is unquestioned.*

Lastly, in Scott Turow's book *One L,* a student remarks:

> At moments during the year, it sometimes appeared to me that my female classmates

were not themselves entirely comfortable with the open aggression that law and law school demanded. In class, they tended to be retiring. . . . Moreover, if I could believe Gina, many of the women were sometimes even more uncomfortable than the men when they were called on.

> "I know how this sounds," she told me once, "but a lot of the women say the same thing. When I get called on, I really think about rape. It's sudden. You're exposed. You can't move. You can't say no. And there's this man who's in control, telling you exactly what to do. Maybe that's melodramatic," she said, "but for me, a lot of the stuff in class shows up all kinds of male/female power relations that I've sort of been training myself to resent."[†]

That the Socratic dialogue provokes anxiety, hostility, and aggression seems to be generally agreed on. Savoy's analogy to game playing and Watson's observation that students are encouraged to become unemotional suggest that an important part of law training is to develop in novice lawyers a sense of detachment from the emotion-laden fray. Stone and the student focused on the domination by the law teacher as authority figure, suggesting that another aspect of the training is to enforce a respect for authoritative power. What are the implications of such training for the roles these new lawyers are ultimately to fill? Should the nonprofessional population—both lawyers' clients and members of society generally—be concerned about the psychological aspects of law education?

3. The process of taking on professional attitudes and identity, called professional socialization by sociologists, can be traumatic. The following is a quote from a first-year law student:

> In my two and a half months here I have felt myself deteriorate mentally, emotionally and spiritually. My high level of self-confidence and self-pride that I carried with me is gone. For the first time in any academic or intellectual phases of my life I feel completely inadequate and find myself losing sleep. I am unable to communicate with former friends of mine from college who are not in law school. Law school has made me a miserable person and the worst thing about it is that I can sense

---

§Robert F. Nagel, "Invisible Teachers: A Comment on Perceptions in the Classroom," *Journal of Legal Education,* Vol. 32, p. 359, 1982. Reprinted by permission of Journal of Legal Education.

*From "Legal Education on the Couch," by Alan Stone, *Harvard Law Review,* Vol. 85, pp. 412–413. Copyright © 1971 by the Harvard Law Review Association.

†Scott Turow, *One L* (New York: Farrar, Straus and Giroux, Inc.).

it happening. I had quite a creative talent when I came here; I feel I have lost it. I had quite a flair with the subject matter of my undergraduate major. I find it inapplicable now. Is it necessary that I am doing this to myself? How much longer will I last? Does anybody in this law school care?[‡]

This experience is largely a phenomenon of the first year in law school. The intensity of the experience diminishes as students adopt the accepted style of thinking, develop coping devices (academic ploys as suggested by Savoy, or the psychological defenses that Watson noted), and class rank becomes established through the first battery of examinations.

In a study of Harvard law students, Robert Granfield observes that it is in the passive resistance to the Socratic method and classroom pedagogy that a sense of collectivity emerges.

> Students begin regaining self-esteem and building solidarity through their symbolic rejection of the distinctive characteristics and authority relations of the law school . . . and . . . feeling that they have personally triumphed over a stressful, demeaning and pretentious environment. Such experiences in common help foster the collective identity students soon develop.[§]

Wilbert Moore, the late famous sociologist of professions, developed a theory of professional training called "punishment-centered socialization." He noted that suffering is a prominent component in the training of all developed professions. The training includes hazing, demands that are "unpleasant and even hazardous to . . . good standing," and "challenging and painful experiences." These experiences are shared with other initiates "who thus have a sort of fellowship of suffering." He concluded that occupational identity and commitment are proportional to the degree that initiates are compelled to suffer, have a realistic fear of failure, have acceptable role models available, and develop collective bonds based on hardships. The greater the amount of suffering and mortification in professional preparation, the more likely students are to take on the proffered professional identities and values.[*]

Even if this analysis correctly describes a common experience of students in law school, the reader should not be left with the impression that all students suffer in law school, do not find excitement, or have traumatic anxieties. For many students it is, on balance, a positive experience. The degree of personal turmoil for any individual is likely tied to the resistance of that person's "home culture" and its distance from the institutionally imposed culture of legal education.

4. Many legal educators object to the characterizations of law school such as those in notes 2 and 3. They say these practices are no longer common in legal education or, at least, have been substantially softened in the past decade or so. Teachers more often use lectures, question students lightly, and accept unpreparedness. They attribute this to the increasing presence of women in law school, a new focus on "customer satisfaction" coming with high law school tuition, and/or competition between schools for students and ratings of law schools in popular media (e.g., annual rankings in *U.S. News and World Report*). But of course, this is the teacher's point of view. Student literature still appears to see games. For example, Lawrence Dieker, Jr., writes:

> There's a joke in law school that if you can't learn the course material in three days it's not worth knowing. And if exams can be justified in no other way, they do at least test one's ability to convey a sense of expertise. After all, being a lawyer means continually becoming an expert on different subjects in a short period of time. Your client's business is your business. Law school exams test one's ability to put on an impromptu show.
>
> I don't know why I should have been surprised. Our vegetables are artificially colored, our food flavor-enhanced. On the evening news, the anchorman asks prepared questions to correspondents who give prepared answers. They read their lines from cue cards like actors. Everything is a play, a production put on for the American public. Why should the education of lawyers be any different? Once students learn not to beat themselves, they get

[‡]Ronald M. Pipkin, "Legal Education: The Consumers' Perspective," American Bar Foundation Research Journal 1976, no. 4 (1976): 1191.

[§]Robert Granfield, Making Elite Lawyers: Visions of Law at Harvard and Beyond (New York: Routledge, 1992), p. 131.

[*]Wilbert E. Moore, *The Professions: Roles and Rules* (New York: Russell Sage Foundation, 1970), pp. 76–79.

through, sometimes even do quite well. It may take a few semesters to learn the tricks, but once they learn, they can really be said to be lawyers. They have the confidence of lawyers, They can take on the world.[†]

---

[†]Lawrence Dieker, Jr., *Letters from Law School: The Life of a Second-Year Law Student* (Lincoln, NE: Writers Club, 2000), pp. 239–240.

5. For a comprehensive review of the literature and report of an extensive empirical study on the question of whether law school classroom dynamics have been changed by the greater inclusion of women and minorities in law schools, see Elizabeth Mertz, with Wamucii Njogu and Susan Gooding, "What Difference Does Difference Make? The Challenge for Legal Education," in *Journal of Legal Education* (Vol. 48, No. 1, 1998, pp. 1–87).

---

# 12.2 | Legal Education and the Reproduction of Hierarchy

*Duncan Kennedy*

ONE CAN DISTINGUISH IN a rough way between two aspects of legal education as a reproducer of hierarchy. A lot of what happens is the inculcation through the formal curriculum and the classroom experience of a set of political attitudes toward the economy and society in general, toward law, and toward the possibilities of life in the profession. These have a general ideological significance, and they have an impact on the lives even of law students who never practice law. Then there is a complicated set of institutional practices that orient students to willing participation in the specialized hierarchical roles of lawyers. In order to understand these, one must have at least a rough conception of what the world of practice is like.

Students begin to absorb the more general ideological message before they have much in the way of a conception of life after law school, so I will describe this formal aspect of the educational process first. I will then try to sketch in the realities of professional life that students gradually learn about in the second and third year, before describing the way in which the institutional practices of law schools bear on those realities. . . .

## THE FORMAL CURRICULUM: LEGAL RULES AND LEGAL REASONING

The intellectual core of the ideology is the distinction between law and policy. Teachers convince

---

Abridged from *Legal Education and the Reproduction of Hierarchy: A Polemic Against the System* (Cambridge, Mass.: Afar, 1983). Reprinted with permission of the author.

students that legal reasoning exists, and is different from policy analysis, by bullying them into accepting as valid in particular cases arguments about legal correctness that are circular, question begging, incoherent, or so vague as to be meaningless. Sometimes these are just arguments from authority, with the validity of the authoritative premise put outside discussion by professorial fiat. Sometimes they are policy arguments (security of transaction, business certainty) that are treated in a particular situation as though they were rules that everyone accepts, but that will be ignored in the next case when they would suggest that the decision was wrong. Sometimes they are exercises in formal logic that wouldn't stand up for a minute in a discussion between equals. . . .

Within a given subfield, the teacher is likely to treat cases in three different ways. There are the cases that present and justify the basic rules and basic ideas of the field. These are treated as cursory exercises in legal logic. Then there are cases that are anomalous—sometimes they are "outdated," sometimes "wrongly decided" because they don't follow the supposed inner logic of the area. There won't be many of these, but they are important because their treatment persuades students that the technique of legal reasoning is at least minimally independent of the results reached by particular judges, is capable of criticizing as well as legitimating.

Finally, there will be an equally small number of peripheral or "cutting edge" cases the teacher sees as raising policy issues about growth or change in the law. Whereas in discussing the first two kinds of cases the teacher behaves in an authoritarian way supposedly based on his objective knowledge of the technique of legal reasoning, here everything is different. Because we are dealing with "value judgments" that have "political" overtones, the discussion will be much more free-wheeling. Rather than every student comment being right or wrong, all student comments get pluralist acceptance, and the teacher will reveal himself to be either a liberal or a conservative, rather than merely a legal technician.

The curriculum as a whole has a rather similar structure. It is not really a random assortment of tubs on their own bottoms, a forest of tubs. First, there are contracts, torts, property, criminal law and civil procedure. The rules in these courses are the ground-rules of late nineteenth century laissez-faire capitalism. Teachers teach them as though they had an inner logic, as an exercise in legal reasoning with policy (e.g., promissory estoppel in the contracts course) playing a relatively minor role.

Then there are second and third year courses that expound the moderate reformist program of the New Deal and the administrative structure of the modern regulatory state (with passing reference to the racial egalitarianism of the Warren Court). These courses are more policy oriented than first year courses, and also much more ad hoc. Teachers teach students that limited interference with the market makes sense, and is as authoritatively grounded in statutes as the ground rules of laissez faire are grounded in natural law. But each problem is discrete, enormously complicated, and understood in a way that guarantees the practical impotence of the reform program.

Finally, there are peripheral subjects, like legal philosophy or legal history, legal process, clinical legal education. These are presented as not truly relevant to the "hard" objective, serious, rigorous analytic core of law. They are a kind of playground or a finishing school for learning the social art of self-presentation as a lawyer.

This whole body of implicit messages is nonsense. Legal reasoning is not distinct, *as a method for reaching correct results,* from ethical and political discourse in general (i.e., from policy analysis). It is true that there is a distinctive lawyers' body of knowledge of the rules in force. It is true that there are distinctive lawyers' argumentative techniques for spotting gaps, conflicts and ambiguities in the rules, for arguing broad and narrow holdings of cases, and for generating pro and con policy arguments. But these are only argumentative techniques. There is never a "correct legal solution" that is other than the correct ethical and political solution to that legal problem.

Put another way, everything taught, except the formal rules themselves and the argumentative techniques for manipulating them, is policy and nothing more. It follows that the classroom distinction between the unproblematic legal case and the policy oriented case is a mere artifact: each could as well be taught in the opposite way. And the curricular distinction between the "nature" of contract law as highly legal and technical by contrast, say, with environmental law, is equally a mystification.

These errors have a bias in favor of the center-liberal program of limited reform of the market economy and pro forma gestures toward racial and sexual equality. The bias arises because law school teaching makes the choice of hierarchy and domination, which is implicit in the adoption of the rules of property, contract and tort, look as though it flows from legal reasoning, rather than from politics and economics. The bias is reenforced when the center-liberal reformist program of regulation is presented as equally authoritative, but somehow more policy oriented, and therefore less fundamental. . . .

## INCAPACITATION FOR ALTERNATIVE PRACTICE

Law schools channel their students into jobs in the hierarchy of the bar according to their own standing in the hierarchy of schools. Students confronted with the choice of what to do after they graduate experience themselves as largely helpless: they have no "real" alternative to taking a job in one of the conventional firms that hires from their school. Partly, faculties generate this sense of student helplessness by propagating myths about the character of the different kinds of practice. They extol the forms that are accessible to their students; they subtly denigrate or express envy about the jobs that will be beyond their students' reach; they dismiss as ethically and socially suspect the jobs their students won't have to take.

As for any form of work outside the established system—for example, legal services for the poor, and neighborhood law practice—they convey to students that, although morally exalted, the work is hopelessly dull and unchallenging, and that the possibilities of reaching a standard of living appropriate to a lawyer are slim or nonexistent. These messages are just nonsense—the rationalizations of law teachers who long [to move] upward, fear status degradation, and above all hate the idea of risk. Legal services practice, for example, is far more intellectually stimulating and demanding, even with a high case load, than most of what corporate lawyers do. It is also more fun.

Beyond this dimension of professional mythology, law schools act in more concrete ways to guarantee that their students will fit themselves into their appropriate niches in the existing system of practice. First, the actual content of what is taught in a given school will incapacitate students from any other form of practice than that allotted graduates of that institution. This looks superficially like a rational adaptation to the needs of the market, but it is in fact almost entirely unnecessary. Law schools teach so little, and that so incompetently, that they cannot, as now constituted, prepare students for more than one career at the bar. But the reason for this is that they embed skills training in mystificatory nonsense, and devote most of their teaching time to transmitting masses of ill-digested rules. A more rational system would emphasize the way to learn law, rather than rules, and skills rather than answers. Student capacities would be more equal as a result, but students would also be much more flexible in what they could do in practice.

A second incapacitating device is the teaching of doctrine in isolation from practice skills. Students who have no practice skills tend to exaggerate how difficult it is to acquire them. There is a distinct lawyers' mystique of the irrelevance of the "theoretical" material learned in school, and of the crucial importance of abilities that cannot be known or developed until one is out in the "real world," "on the firing line" and "in the trenches." Students have little alternative to getting training in this dimension of things after law school. If you have any choice in the matter, it will seem impractical to think about setting up your own law firm, and only a little less impractical to go to a small or political or unconventional firm rather than to one of those that offers the standard package of post-graduate education. Law schools are wholly responsible for this situation. They could quite easily revamp their curricula so that any student who wanted it would have a meaningful choice between independence and servility.

A third form of incapacitation is more subtle. Law school, as an extension of the educational system as a whole, teaches students that they are weak, lazy, incompetent and insecure. And it also teaches them that if they are fortunate, and willing to accept dependency, large institutions will take care of them almost no matter what. The terms of the bargain are relatively clear. The institution will set limited, cognizable tasks, and specify minimum requirements in their performance. The student/associate has no other responsibilities than performance of those tasks. The institution takes care of all the contingencies of life, both within the law (supervision and back up from other firm members; firm resources and prestige to bail you out if you make a mistake) and in private life (firms offer money, but also long term job security and delicious benefits packages aimed to reduce risks of disaster). In exchange, you renounce any claim to control your work setting or the actual content of what you do, and agree to show the appropriate form of deference to those above you and condescension to those below.

By comparison, the alternatives are risky. Law school does not train you to run a small law business, to realistically assess the outcome of a complex process involving many different actors, or to enjoy the feeling of independence and moral integrity that comes of creating your own job to serve your own goals. It tries to persuade you that you are barely competent to perform the much more limited roles it allows you, and strongly suggests that it is more prudent to kiss the lash than to strike out on your own.

## HIERARCHIES OF THE LEGAL PROFESSION

Throughout their legal education, students are engaged in reconceiving themselves and the legal profession. Partly this is an affair of knowledge. Students find out things about the bar and about themselves that they didn't know before, and the process has a direction—it is a process of loss, of possibilities foreclosed. Knowledge of professional life renders irrelevant capacities you have but will not be allowed to use. Newly discovered incapacities of the self make it impossible to play roles it was easy to fantasize as a college student.

To begin with, there is the fact that most law jobs, and almost all the jobs at the top of the hierarchy, consist of providing marginally important services to businesses in their dealings among themselves and with consumers and stray victims. Of the remaining jobs, the great majority involve trying to get money out of the business community in the form of compensation for injuries to individuals, or of arranging the private affairs of middle class or upper class people. The total number of jobs that directly serve the public interest is small, and the number of jobs that integrate law and left political action is tiny. The notion that lawyers as a group work at a profession which is intrinsically involved with justice, or that lawyers are at least on the front lines of class struggle, is one of the things that allows left students to resolve their ambivalence enough to go to law school. But in fact the profession is mainly engaged in greasing the wheels of the economy.

A second crucial piece of information is that this is partly drudge work, partly puzzle solving (with the narcotically fascinating and morally vacuous quality of, say, bridge), and partly a macho battle of wills in which all that counts is winning. Most of this work has no discernible moral spin to it, let alone a political spin. It is not that it is "evil," it is that it is socially inconsequential, even when you look at it in terms of the profession as a whole rather than in terms of individual lawyers. It is fulfilling to help people achieve their objectives (theirs, not yours), to exercise one's skills, to make money and be respected. That's it.

As dreams of pursuing careers that would be unambiguously good begin to fade, it becomes important that lawyers submit to hierarchy in concrete ways, as well as in the more abstract way of abandoning their hope of integrating their jobs and their politics. One will drudge, solve puzzles and fight the battle of wills in a law firm.

Many students have a clear sense of the hierarchical role of lawyers in society, but little sense of just how stratified is the bar itself. Getting into law school, or getting into an elite law school seems to parachute them beyond the land of struggle into a realm of assured superiority. They discover some of how wrong this is through the admissions process, which firmly establishes that law schools exist on a scale of rank which has its ambiguities but is unequivocal in its rejections. But it is still a shock that what your background is, where you went to law school, and how well you did seem to make an enormous difference to where you can get a job, what the actual content of your job will be, and what you can reasonably look forward to in the way of professional advancement over your whole career.

Law firms are ranked just as law schools are (with the same ambiguity and the same near finality). The lawyers in the "top" firms make more money, exercise more power and have more prestige than lawyers in the next rank, these lawyers lord it over those below them, and so forth to the bottom. The top firms have top clients, work in the top courts, have top office conditions, do more "challenging" work, and are less subject to all kinds of minor pains and humiliations than those lower down. . . .

The hierarchy of firms is based in part on the general class, sexual and racial structure of American society. There are lower middle class, middle class and upper middle class lawyers, and because they congregate in groups mainly according to class criteria, there are lower middle, middle and upper middle class law firms. In some, lawyers wear leisure suits, in others, three piece worsted suits. In some there are photographs of lawyers' sailboats on the office walls along with the diplomas; in others there are reproductions of seascapes bought by wives to brighten things up. There are regional accents, but also class accents; fancy colleges and unfancy colleges. There are few blacks anywhere to be seen. Women are underrepresented in the top firms; within those firms, they tend to do legal jobs with relatively low prestige (trusts and estates rather than litigation). In general, the legal universe just reproduces the society around it: most people live in homogeneous enclaves within which they rigidly observe the rituals and guard the prerogatives of their station, while vigorously denying that the concept of station has any relevance to their lives.

The hierarchy of firms is also in part a professional hierarchy. Lawyers in top firms went to higher ranked law schools and got better grades than lawyers in the next-to-top, and so through gradations to the bottom. Within the bar, it is possible to distinguish oneself as a technically terrific lawyer and move up a notch or two, or to be *such* a bad lawyer one is disgraced and tumbled a rung or two down.

At first glance, it might appear that there would be a constant tension between the demands of the two hierarchies, since there is no reason to believe that professional merit is distributed other than randomly with regard to class, sex or race. But there are practices within the system that work to minimize or altogether eliminate any such tension. The first is that the class/sex/race system gets hold of people long before the professional one, and *creates* them in such a way that they will, with some legitimating exceptions, appear to deserve on professional grounds the position that is in fact based on other things. Your chances of ending up at a "top" law school are directly proportional to your status at birth.

Second, people who are able to succeed according to existing professional criteria learn that they must also put themselves through a process of assimilation that has nothing to do with professionalism. Law schools are finishing schools as well as trade schools, where everyone learns to act more or less according to the behavioral criteria of the rung of the profession they hope to enter. There are children of lower middle class parents at Yale, but the student culture is relentlessly upper middle class. There are children of working class parents at Boston College, but the student culture mixes only lower middle and middle class styles. The result of the initial stacking of the system combined with the norm of upward assimilation is that the class/sex/race

hierarchy controls the professional hierarchy rather than being disrupted by it.

Law firms offer security and training only in exchange for complicity in various further forms of hierarchy. The first of these is internal to the firm. There is the generational hierarchy of lawyers, and the sharp occupational hierarchy that separates the lawyers from the secretaries and the secretaries from messengers and maintenance people. The pecking order conditions all of working life. Young lawyers are no more free to disown their hierarchical superiority to the staff than to cast off deference and dependence on partners. It is almost as bad to treat your secretary like a partner as to do the reverse, and no one smiles on a perverse rejection of the rewards and reassurances (flexible hours and expense accounts, for example) that go along with your particular place in the scheme of things.

A second hierarchy is that of the judicial system, in which judges play the role of tin gods, exacting an extraordinary servility from their court personnel and the lawyers and litigants who appear before them. Judges are free to treat, and often do treat those who come before them with a degree of personal arrogance, a sense of entitlement to arbitrariness, and an insistence on deference that provide an extreme model of everything that is wrong with legal hierarchy.

Lawyers are complicit in this behavior: they expect it, and even enjoy the purity of the experience—the absolute character of the submission demanded, with its suggestion of playing a game which is really and truly for keeps. Beyond that, the judicial system is based on the same extreme specialization of function and differentiation of capacities as the hierarchy of the bar and the internal hierarchy of particular firms. All of this deforms the very idea of justice, rendering it at once impersonal, inaccessible to ordinary human understanding and ordinary human practice, and intensely personal, since everything depends, most of the time, on the crotchets and whims of petty dictators.

The third hierarchy relates lawyers to their clients. It works differently for different firms, according to their rank in the hierarchy of the bar. Top firms deal with the managers of large corporations. They engage with them on the basis of an implicit deal: the lawyers accept, even participate enthusiastically in the self-interested, or immoral, or downright criminal behavior of the client, in return for client acquiescence in the charging of ludicrous fees for work that is mainly elementary or mindless, and vastly swollen by conventions of over-research and over-writing. Within their assigned province, the lawyers behave as though they possessed the knowledge of the Delphic oracle.

At the lower levels of the hierarchy, there are different patterns of domination, mainly involving lawyers making decisions for clients, where the client was perfectly capable of deciding on his own or her own, in ways that make things easy for the lawyer, or profitable, or correspond to the lawyer's own morality or preferences. As in corporate law, the whole thing is based on excluding clients from knowledge they would need to decide on their own, while at the same time mystifying that knowledge. But in many lawyer/client encounters below the top level, that is also social inequality between the parties, with the lawyer of higher social class than the client, and this hierarchy reenforces and is reenforced by the professional one.

The final hierarchy that concerns us is the general social arrangement in which lawyers are treated—even in a country with a long tradition of anti-lawyer polemicizing—as among the elite of the nation. Partly this is simply a reflection of the fact that many lawyers come from the upper middle class to start with. But it has some small basis in the usefulness of lawyers' skills and lawyers' knowledge in the actual operation of legislative and executive politics, and some small basis in the real importance and value of the legal profession as an expression both of commitment to truth and to helping people. On this foundation, lawyers have managed to erect a massive edifice of social prestige and material over-reward. At each level of the class system, lawyers are granted a measure of deference and a measure of power altogether disproportionate to their objective merit. In their group activities, but also in their individual social lives, they tend to exploit this deference and to accentuate it by emphasizing the arcane character of what they know and do.

The legal hierarchies I have been describing have three features in common. First, the people involved in each of them have roles, and the roles require different activities and draw on different capacities. There are partners, associates, secretaries and janitors. There are corporate lawyers, business litigation lawyers, real estate lawyers, small time personal injury lawyers. There are lawyers and mere lay people. Second, if we look at each hierarchy as a joint enterprise within which people are producing things, participants playing different roles receive unequal rewards, and exercise unequal degrees of power, both over production decisions and over the organization and style of the workplace. This is most obviously true in the highly organized, oligarchical world of the individual firm, but also true of the bar taken as a unit, and of the hierarchical relations of the profession to its clients and to society at large.

Third, each hierarchy operates within a cultural framework that gives a meaning to the differences in activities and capacities, and to the inequality of power and reward. The meaning is that the whole arrangement is based on the natural differences between people, with respect to talent and energy, that it serves the social function of maximizing the quantity and quality of legal services to society, and that it is therefore just. Hierarchy reflects desert. The parties signify their participation in this universe of shared meanings (whether or not they really believe in it) through deferential or imperious behavior towards others, and by "explaining" what is going on in its terms. "Why do some firms make so much more than others, year after year?" "Well, the best firms can charge higher prices than the less good firms. Since they can charge more, they can hire the best law students, so they make even more money. And so on."

Besides having common features (differentiation of activities and capacities, inequality of power and reward, meritocratic legitimating ideology), the hierarchies are related to one another in a functional way. Internally hierarchical firms are the building blocks of the hierarchy of firms, and it is the bar as a whole that is in a hierarchical relation to society at large. The structure of the parts reproduces the structure of the whole, or vice versa, depending on how you look at it. Individuals are to firms as firms are to the bar as the bar is to society. . . .

## THE CONTRIBUTION OF LEGAL EDUCATION TO THE HIERARCHIES OF THE BAR

The relationship between legal education and legal hierarchy is complex, and I think it's worth going into in some detail because it offers insight into the issue of how hierarchy works in general. I want to distinguish three different ways in which one can see legal education as a causal factor in the persistence of hierarchy within the bar.

**The Analogy Effect**    The first of these is the simplest and the weakest—it might be called the analogy effect. Legal education has an internal structure very much like that of the bar. Each law school has its arrangement of professors, assistant professors, students and staff, roughly analogous to the internal arrangement of a law firm. Law schools themselves are ranked, with differences in what they teach, how they teach it, how much power they have in the field of legal education, and what rewards their faculties receive. Within the world of legal education, there is a legitimating ideology which explains and justifies these rankings in terms of natural differences in capacities, social utility and fairness. . . .

**Legal Ideology as an "Input"**    A second way in which legal education relates to legal hierarchy after law school arises from its specialized character as education. Law teachers are constantly involved in explaining how the world works, and also in formulating notions of how it should work. As it presently operates, legal education is like education in general in that it propagates the message that things are the way they are because it is best, or close to best that they should be that way. In others words, the legal education system produces ideology. Ideology is one of its "inputs" into the rest of the social system. Since the bar is part of the social system, it benefits from this legitimating contribution.

I am not here speaking of anything law schools teach about law practice, but about their general message about the legal rules in force. Law schools, as we saw above, do more than teach these rules. They also teach why they are a good thing, and that they are there because they are a good thing. These rules provide the framework within which social actors create all the hierar-

chies of our society, including the hierarchies of the bar. If the rules were different—for example, if all bosses were legally obligated to spend part of every day on their own typing, or if secretaries had a legal right to education for upward job mobility—the hierarchies would be different too. In so much as legal education legitimates the rules in force, it legitimates the consequences, in terms of the division of labor and inequality of power and reward, that flow from the rules. By teaching law students that the rules are groovy, law teachers also teach them that they are entitled to the six figure salaries they will earn in corporate law practice, just as doctors and business managers are entitled to theirs.

Within its general ideological message, legal education has some particular things to say to lawyers—namely, that what they do is more than just a craft, like, say carpentry. What they do is "legal reasoning." Law schools are largely (though not exclusively) responsible for persuading lawyers and the lay public that lawyers do more than exercise the skills I described in the section on the curriculum. So they are also at least partly responsible for the hierarchical relations that lawyers manage to erect on that shadowy foundation. The mystique of legal reasoning reenforces all these hierarchies because it makes it seem that people who have gone to law school are privy to secrets that are loaded with social value.

The actual capacities of lawyers—knowledge of rule systems, of issue spotting, case analysis and pro/con policy argument—have real social value; they are difficult to acquire; and one can't practice law effectively without them. But they are nowhere near as inaccessible as they are made to seem by the mystique of legal education. By mystifying them, law schools make it seem necessary to restrict them to a small group, presumed to be super-talented. That, in turn, makes it seem necessary to divide the labor in the joint enterprise of providing legal services so that most of the participants (secretaries, paralegals, office assistants, court clerks, janitors, marshalls, and so on) are firmly and permanently excluded from doing the things that are most challenging and rewarding within the overall activity. Once they have devalued everyone else on "professional" grounds, it also seems natural for those who have gone to law school to specialize in the most desirable tasks, while controlling the whole show and reaping the lion's share of the rewards.

**The Hierarchical Structuring of the Group of Prospective Lawyers**   The third way in which legal education contributes causally to the hierarchies of the bar is by structuring the population of potential lawyers so that it will seem natural, efficient and fair that they should incorporate themselves into the existing hierarchy of law firms without much changing it. To grasp this, imagine that by some bizarre chance all the lawyers in the country decided to create a bar of roughly equal firms, in place of the existing hierarchy. Such a program would have many things in its way, even supposing the decision to pursue it was unanimous, including the influence by analogy of all the other hierarchies of our society, and the ideological messages about existing legal arrangements, and about the nature of legal reasoning, that the schools now propagate.

But the program of equalization would also have to contend with the fact that law school graduates enter practice as a group already structured hierarchically. They already have different capacities, different values and expectations, and different visions of what law practice should be. There is more to it than difference: they are unequal, in many though by no means all respects, before they have even begun.

The internal structure of the group corresponds roughly to the structure of the bar: some prospective lawyers are prepared for elite practice, others for small time solo practice. The whole group tends most of the time to believe that these differences among themselves, these inequalities, flow from individual characteristics, from their personal virtues and vices, talents and energies.

*Notes and Questions*

1. Kennedy makes the point that political values are often fused with the learning of legal dogma. Ralph Nader wrote of this process,

   Students are conditioned to react to questions and issues which they have no rule in forming or stimulating. Such teaching forms have been crucial in perpetuating the status quo in teaching content. For decades, the law school curriculum reflected with remarkable fidelity the commercial demands of law firm practice.*

   Another critic of law education suggests that the reliance of the case method on appellate opinions, which are elicited primarily by those who are sufficiently affluent to pursue costly appeals, biases the instruction:

   The emphasis placed on the study of appellate decisions omits consideration of the actual problem of trial work, such as the prejudices of judges and juries, the deals which are made in criminal courts, or the political focus affecting various classes of interested parties, such as tenants. This coincides with the insistence of many law schools that emphasis be placed on a supposedly value-free theoretical approach to law. In practice this means that law students draw only from theory heavily tinged with corporate values. They will thus be able to offer solutions for corporate problems, but not for the problems posed by injustices in the judicial system or other injustices caused by corporate interests."[†]

   If this criticism is taken seriously, what kind of measures should be considered to control or balance such political messages in law training? What interests should society have in this matter?

2. Reinforcing for students the experiences ascribing elite status noted by Kennedy is the ritual of the summer internship—a time when law firms take on students to look them over for potential hiring. Richard D. Kahlenberg describes his internship as follows:

   As the summer at Ropes & Gray progressed, there were more lunches and outings. There was the Labor Law Lunch, where the firm's lawyers discussed the ways to counter various worker claims, including how to combat an age discrimination case. . . . There was the Corporate Lunch . . . where I learned that women at Ropes do trusts and estates and health care but not corporate law. . . . There was the summer associates night at Fenway, where an R&G attorney sat with a stack of twenty-dollar bills to cover whatever food or drink people desired. . . .

---

*Ralph Nader, "Law Schools and Law Firms," *New Republic* (October 11, 1969): p. 21.

[†]David N. Rockwell, "The Education of the Capitalist Lawyer: The Law School," in Robert Lefcourt, ed., *Law Against the People* (New York: Vintage Books, 1971), p. 97.

Amid it all, I did end up doing a little bit of work. . . . I spent time trying to help the New England Patriots avoid paying John Hannah damages for allegedly making him play when they knew it would cripple him. I helped a number of wealthy individuals make sure that their money would stay in their families. . . . And I worked on one "*pro bono*" project to revise the Massachusetts Corporate Law to make it more favorable to corporations.[‡]

3. Kennedy says that people generally accept the idea that hierarchies express the net value of each individual's worth, and thus they also accept not only other people's unequal relationship to themselves, but also their own location in unequal systems. Do you agree?

4. The role of law schools in the reproduction of profession hierarchies, access to law school, and therefore ultimately the legal profession, has been mediated for many years by the Law School Admission Test (LSAT), required of all applicants to accredited law schools. This "objectified" assessment of aptitude for law study has been believed to filter out social distinctions so that entry into the profession becomes largely meritocratic—i.e., restricted to the best and the brightest. Some research suggests, however, that the process has not been totally freed of social bias:

A study by Franklin Evans and Donald Rock . . . analyzed the scores and backgrounds of incoming students at eight law schools. The LSAT distinguished not only rich and poor, but also rich and middle class. Students of "high" socioeconomic status had a mean LSAT score about forty points higher than those of "average" background who in turn ranked higher than the "low" status students by about thirty points.

Evans and Rock also found scores to be related to an aspect of the candidate's personality, their test anxiety. . . . When the effects of social class and anxiety were combined, the impact was considerable: low-income people with high test anxiety received an average LSAT of 505 [on an earlier LSAT scale of 200–800]; high income people with low anxiety averaged 622.[§]

Cappell and Pipkin reported that even when students' LSAT scores, college grade-point averages, and quality of undergraduate college attended were comparable, social factors influenced the allocation of students to law schools of differing status. With seven law schools classified in three categories of prestige—elite, regional, and local—they found, within the same levels of academic background, women were about forty percent less likely than men to attend an elite versus a regional or local law school. Catholics were 48 percent less likely than Protestants and 64 percent less likely than Jews to attend an elite rather than regional law school. And, those of the highest socioeconomic class were 40 to 60 percent more likely than students from the other three social groups to attend an elite rather than a regional or local law school. In other words, the "inside tracks" to elite law schools were largely awarded to those with the highest academic qualifications from high-status colleges. However, once the field was thereby narrowed, the advantages went to males from the highest social class backgrounds who were Jewish or Protestant.[*]

On the point that the status of the law school attended has a strong effect on the status of law practice, Frances Kahn Zemans and Victor G. Rosenblum found in their study of the practicing bar in Chicago that 73 percent of all lawyers in Chicago's largest law firms (over fifty members) were graduates of only twelve national law schools—Harvard, Yale, Columbia, Chicago, Michigan, Northwestern, Georgetown, New York University, Pennsylvania, Stanford, Virginia, and Wisconsin—only two of which were located in Chicago. In contrast, solo practitioners came primarily from four local law schools—Loyola, IIT-Kent, DePaul, and John Marshall.[†]

---

[‡]Richard D. Kahlenberg, *Broken Contract: A Memoir of Harvard Law School* (New York: Hill and Wang, 1992), 153–154.

[§]Allan Nairn and Associates, *The Reign of ETS* (Washington, D.C.: The Ralph Nader Report on the Educational Testing Service, 1980), pp. 222–223.

[*]Charles L. Cappell and Ronald M. Pipkin, "The Inside Tracks: Status Distinctions in Allocations to Elite Law Schools," in Paul William Kingston and Lionel S. Lewis, *The High-Status Track: Studies of Elite Schools and Stratification* (Albany: State University of New York Press, 1990), pp. 211–230.

[†]Frances Kahn Zemans and Victor G. Rosenblum, *The Making of a Public Profession* (Chicago: American Bar Foundation, 1981).

❧ Professional legal education, as the previous readings have shown, is not just simply a technical or skills education—becoming a lawyer is not simply just becoming an expert. Rather, law school is the place to learn a new way of thinking and to begin absorption into the role of lawyer. On one hand, it is a familiar environment for students taking the overt form of previous academic experiences—books, classrooms, lectures, grade competitions, and so forth. But, as Bonsignore and the legal education critics tell us, law school is about much more than this. Lawyer thinking is primarily taught in the ideational realm—a fantasy domain of constructed hypotheticals and abstracted fact patterns—a realm of images and imagination. Kennedy describes this as teachers explaining to students "how the world works."

The following reading extends the understanding of this ideational realm to include racial and gender characterizations that reinforce derogatory images, and which by being attached to evaluations of legal thinking skills compel students from those groups to sacrifice their sense of self for academic success. This argument would be powerful at any time, but in a period of increasing openness of law to women and minorities, it provokes a particular need for consideration of legal socialization in law school.

## 12.3   Diary of a Law Professor   *Patricia J. Williams*

IT IS EARLY ON a Tuesday morning. I am feeling most like a law professor—prolific, published, powerful. There is a knock on my office door. It is K., a first-year student, in tears.

"What's wrong?" I ask. A school administrator has called her an activist. My first instinct is to ask again, so what's wrong? But we're in the middle of a presidential election in which the word "liberal" has become a synonym for "better dead," so I try to put myself in tune with this upside-down new world in which "activist" might mean something like "troublemaker." "Why?" I ask instead.

K. had gone to an administrator to complain about an exam she and her classmates were given by their criminal-law professor. The problem was an updated version of Shakespeare's *Othello,* in which Othello is described as a "black

militaristic African leader" who marries the "young white Desdemona" whom he then kills in a fit of sexual rage. Othello is put on trial. The students were to identify the elements of murder. The model answer gives points for ability to "individualize the test" of provocation by recognizing that "a rough untutored Moor might understandably be deceived by the wiles of a more sophisticated European." K. had gone first to the professor and told him she thought the exam racist; the professor denied it, saying it was not he who had dreamed up the facts but Shakespeare. Then K. went to the administrator, who called her an "activist" but not before he said that she should be more concerned about learning the law and less about the package in which it comes.

As I read the exam, I think about this assertion that the exercise is not racist because, after all, it was Shakespeare who made race part of the problem. But the exam used race in a peculiarly gratuitous fashion; it seems to me that its offensiveness does not depend on whether race and cultural "unsophistication" play any part in the play *Othello;* the issue is what role they played in the fact pattern (Othello-as-legal-problem) that students had to resolve. In fact, the play is irrelevant to the resolution of Othello-as-defendant, and the opening paragraph of the exam says as much (that students don't need to have read the play to understand the dynamic contained in the problem). So the complex dramatic motivations, ironies, subtleties, and complications of character development in the original play are, again, rendered unimportant—gratuitous in this context. . . .

I grow angry as I continue to read. Even though the problem follows the facts of the original play, the analogy stops there. To say that this is "the same as" is to accept blindly the authority of "Shakespeare" as some universalized canon. Moreover, it does not acknowledge the fact that, while Shakespeare may have produced great literature, he was also a historical being, a product of an Elizabethan world that was in some ways quite as racist as our own. This is not to say that we should therefore suppress *Othello,* for it allows us to view ourselves and to evaluate a range of still valid human dilemmas.

Unfortunately, those human dilemmas do not seem to be the subject of this problem; instead there is a flattening of universal emotions and events to mere stereotype because all the artful, evocative context of the original is missing. The problem presents a defendant who is black, militaristic, unsophisticated, insecure, jealous, and sexually enraged. It reduces the facts to the very same racist generalizations and stereotypes this nation has used to subjugate black people since the first wave was brought from Africa. Moreover, it places an enormous burden on black students in particular who must assume, for the sake of answering these questions, these things about themselves that is the trauma of gratuitous generalization. The frame places blacks in the position of speaking against ourselves. It forces us to accept as "truth" constructions that go to the heart of who we are.

In the Othello problem, the exam is put in a frame where to contest those subtly generalized "truths" (blacks are sexually dangerous, blacks are militaristic) (would the Capulets or the Montagues ever be characterized as "militaristic"?) is not only irrelevant but costs the student points:

it is, according to the model answer, *necessary* to argue that "a rough untutored Moor might understandably be deceived by the wiles of a more sophisticated European." In other words, a student who refuses to or cannot think like a racist—most people of color, I would guess—will receive a lower grade. My further guess is that everyone, including perhaps the students of color, will rationalize this result away as an inability to "think like a lawyer."

I agree to speak to the professor on behalf of K. "Just make sure he understands I'm not an activist," implores K. "This could ruin my career."

I visit Professor L. the next day and present our concerns. L.'s explanation is that this was merely his attempt to respect the minority and feminist quest to bring issues of race, class, and gender more directly into the curriculum. I say I'm concerned that he shares a deep misunderstanding of the struggle, a misunderstanding that threatens to turn the quest for empowering experiential narrative into permission for the most blatant expressions of cynical stereotypification. I cite the example of an exam given by another professor at another school, who handed out to his class a detailed and luridly violent wife-battering hypothetical in which a man knocks out his wife's teeth, urinates on the floor and throws their baby down into it, rips her blouse off, calls her a "castrating bitch," and arranges for a friend to come in and rape her. At the top of the question there is a disclaiming explanation that it only reflects "the world" where "there is a lot of violence directed at women" and that "the legal system has (often in response to organized feminist concerns) at least partly shifted its responses to situations involving that violence." I use this example to question the potential, no doubt unintended, voyeuristic repercussions of well-meaning attempts to include race and gender without also attempting to examine the *way* in which such material is included. I don't do a good job of making this point, and L. sees no comparison.

L. asks me: "Are you suggesting that race and gender issues be censored from the law-school classroom?"

I answer: The catch-22 of using terms like "black" and "white" has to do with fathoming when and why race or gender or violence or any-thing else is important. On the one hand, race isn't important because it isn't important; most of us devoutly wish this to be a colorblind society, in which removing the words "black" and "white" from our vocabulary would render the world, in a miraculous flash, free of all division. On the other hand, real life isn't that simple. Often we have to use the words in order to acknowledge the unde-niable psychological and cultural power of racial constructions upon all our lives; we have to be able to call out against the things that trouble us, whether racism or other forms of suffering.

This is not the same, I say, as retreating to a completely race-neutral point of view for any and all circumstances. That would be like saying we should never study Shakespeare, particularly *Othello* and *The Merchant of Venice*—or, to take it to an extreme, that we should never discuss why racism is racist. (And we desperately need to get past the point of angst about whether we're guilty of guilt-tripping each other.) But it is something quite again if I were to use the au-thority of what this culture considers "classical" to justify every instance of violent gratuity: It sim-ply would not be valid for me to say, "Well, these are Shakespeare's facts, not mine"—as if "Shake-speare" were some fixed object, some physically determinate piece of marble, as if I could dis-count all my own interpretive power and respon-sibility over what I render from it.

"What you are proposing," says L., "sounds like the very antithesis of academic freedom."

Over the next few weeks, I think about ways in which to clarify what I am trying to say. Word has gotten out among my students and friends that I am interested in this sort of thing, and they bring me sheaves of exams; in addition I do my own research. I end up with a stack of exams written on a variety of subjects, and given at schools around the country. I find:

• a tax exam that asks students to calculate the tax implications for Kunta Kinte's master when the slavecatchers cut off his foot.

• a securities-regulation exam in which the professor muses about whether white-collar defendants should go to jail, since "unlike ghetto kids" they are not equipped to fare in that environment.

• a constitutional-law exam in which students are given the lengthy text of a hate-filled polemic entitled "How To Be a Jew-Nigger" and then told to use the first amendment to defend it.

• a description of the "typical criminal" as "a young black male with an I.Q. of 87 who is one of eight children and has always lived on welfare and who spends his time hanging out in pool halls with his best friend Slick."

• numerous criminal-law exams whose questions feature exclusively black or Hispanic or Asian criminals and exclusively white victims.

• many questions depicting gay men as the exclusive spreaders of AIDS, asking students to find the elements of murder.

• many, many questions in which women are beaten, raped, and killed in descriptions pornographically detailed (in contrast to streamlined questions, by the same professors, that do not involve female victims).

I review all these exams and ponder what to do with them, how to raise the issues in a way that can best be heard, and heard in a way that will not be taken as "censorship." Finally I decide to write a memorandum to the faculty, worded generally, without names of professors or schools, but using real exams to illustrate real is-sues of propriety. I write:

I have been looking at law-school exams and studying them as a genre of legal writing involving complex relations of power and influence. I am interested in opening discussion about the extent to which what we write into exams, as much as what we teach, conveys stereotypes, delimits the acceptable, and formulates ideals. I have been reviewing a collection of exams that exploit race and gender and violence in ways that I think are highly inappropriate. By "inappropriate" I mean that they use race, gender, and violence in ways that have no educational purpose, that are gratuitous and voyeuristic, and that simultaneously perpetuate inaccurate and harmful stereotypes as "truthful." This is accomplished by a variety of devices:

1. Compartmentalizing the relevant from the irrelevant is one of the primary skills law students are expected to master during their

education. Frequently, professors employ red-herring facts from which the legally dispositive kernel facts must be clearly identified. But in the exams about which I am concerned, race, ethnicity, class, and gender are irrelevant even to the process of winnowing the relevant from the irrelevant. They function as sheer gratuity. Their mention has absolutely nothing to do with the manipulation of rules necessary to resolve the fact patterns as constructed.

Furthermore, in the one or two questions in which a specified characteristic (e.g., a "gay male prostitute" being tried for murder in the spread of AIDS) is arguably important to the disposition, or reflective of some current controversy in the law, students are specifically instructed not to consider it, or to consider it only to a limited extent (e.g., that same exam contained the following instruction: "while we're all concerned about homophobia, don't consider it in answering this problem"). I found exams whose basic message was: M. is black, N. is a white racist, but you, you're color blind. O. is [a] battered wife, P. is her vicious spouse-battering husband, but you, you must not consider provocation if O. hits P.

It is thus that information that is quite important in real life and real courtrooms becomes unimportant for purposes of answering a law school exam. Students are left to deal with raised issues of race and gender as unframed information, as mere backdrop in a society where large numbers of people hold powerful, if not always spoken, impressions that "most blacks are criminals" or "women can't be raped by their husbands" or "all Chicanos belong to gangs."

The message that is reinforced by such exams is that while racist, sexist stereotypes may be part of life, it's not important or important *not* to deal with them in the law. (And yet of course we know it is.) Or that it's not so important that it can't be severed, caged, and neatly suppressed. Actual importance is thus not legitimated.

Nevertheless, although devalued expressly or implicitly, race, gender, sexual preference are part of these problems. They're written in

them by virtue of some inscrutable design. And they do have a power and a function in such questions, if beyond the answer to that question; yet that function is rendered invisible—not less powerful, just not acknowledged. They become powerful as external markers of what must be suppressed or ignored, of what must be rendered unconscious as "unsightly." These interrogatories, in so directly turning students' attention away from precisely what is most provocative and significant in these problems, reiterates exactly what is so difficult about raising these issues in any kind of social setting: the feeling of impropriety, the sheer discourtesy of talking about what has been, by our teachers at every stage of life, explicitly tabooed: it's o.k. to purvey these unchallenged images as gratuity, but not to talk about them in a way that matters, that changes outcomes.

2. These problems draw for their justification upon one of the law's best-loved inculcations: the preference for the impersonal above the personal, the "objective" above the "subjective." Most of these problems require blacks, women who have been raped, gays and lesbians, to not just re-experience their oppression, but to write *against* their personal knowledge. They actually require the assumption of an "impersonal" (but racist/sexist/homophobic) mentality in order to do well in the grading process. Consider, for example, the exam in which a white woman premeditatedly lures a 13-year-old black would-be thief to her balcony and then kills him, her actions motivated by racial hatred. In one interrogatory, students are asked to "make the best argument you can that [the white woman] ought to be exculpated entirely, ignoring arguments (say that she might be diplomatically immune or insane) grounded in general incapacity to be convicted." This requires students either to indulge the imaginative flowering of their most insidious rationalizations for racial hatred; or it requires them to suppress any sense of social conscience. It requires them to devalue their own and others' humanity for the sake of a

grade. (This is also how, over time, perfectly rational and humanitarian insights and concerns are devalued, as a matter of habit rather than wisdom, as "merely experiential" and "irrelevant to the law." Law professors can thus set up irresponsibly authoritarian constructs that give permission to, and legitimize, some really warped world views. The result will be students who are cultured to hate; yet who still think of themselves as very very good people; who will be deeply offended, and *personally* hurt if anyone tries to tell them otherwise. I think this sort of teaching, rampant throughout the educational system, is why racism and sexism remain so routine, so habitually dismissed, as to be largely invisible.)

3.  While styled as hypotheticals, these collected exams set themselves up as instructional mirrors of real life. In talking to some of the professors whose exams concerned me, I was always given some version of the following explanation: "Well, (people of color) (women) (gays) do commit crimes after all. It's naive to assume this doesn't happen in the real world." The problem with this reasoning, however, is that everything under the sun could be rationalized by the open-ended authority of "what happens," no matter how depraved, singular, or despicable.

We, as law teachers, create miniworlds of reality, by the faith that students put in our tutelage of the rules of reality. We define the boundaries of the legitimate and the illegitimate, in a more ultimately powerful way than almost anyone else in the world. It is enormously important therefore to consider the process by which we include as well as the process by which we exclude. It is thus that an exam, which includes only three problems, two of which feature black criminality and the third of which deals with gay criminality, constructs a miniworld that reinforces the widely held misperceptions that blacks commit most of the crimes, that only gays carry AIDS, or that all gays are promiscuous.

It is not that there aren't racially or sexually motivated crimes of all sorts in the world; what is problematic about casting problems (directed to a hypothetically diverse student body) repeatedly and persistently in racially or sexually stereotypical terms is that it not only perpetuates the idea, for example, that most blacks commit most crimes, but that it makes invisible white criminality. In any event, race has nothing to do with the resolution of these problems, which for the most part are problems going beyond race and class; yet students are set up to believe that this is "what happens."

Furthermore, there is a relativistic, cynical majoritarianism in the idea that "it happens in the real world," akin to the childish excuse the "everybody does it." I am struck, for example, by the general absence of reference to white people in exams written by people who do specify race when they are referring to nonwhites. Yet we all know that there are white gangs (e.g. skinheads, the White Aryan Resistance) as well as black, Asian, and Chicano gangs. None of these exams, or any I could find, present gratuitous "white-people" problems. "White" is used only to distinguish from blacks and other nonwhites. The absence of "white" thus signals that "everyone" is white. "Blacks" therefore become distanced, different, "othered." In order to deal with such a problem on an exam, moreover, students are required to take the perspective of "everybody"; for black students this requires their taking a stance in which they objectify themselves with reference to the interrogatories. (I use the word "objectify" in the literal, grammatical sense of subject-verb-object: the removing of oneself from the subject position of power, control, and direction over the verb-action. "We," blacks, become "them.") The law becomes less than universally accessible or participatory: The point of view assumes a community of "everybody's" that is in fact exclusionary.

When my sister was in the fourth grade, she was the only black child in the class. One Valentine's Day, when the teacher went out of the room, all her white classmates ripped up the valentines she had sent them and dumped them on her desk. It was so traumatic that my sister couldn't speak again in that class, she refused to participate: so completely had they made her feel not part of that group. For a while she stopped performing altogether. Ultimately my mother convinced her that she could "show them" by outperforming them, but I think the joy of education for its own sake was seriously impaired, in both her and me (for I felt it almost as much as she did; we had made the valentines together).

Our roles repeatedly defined as "outsiders" in both cruel and unintentional ways, we were faced with a curious dilemma: we could continually try to be insiders, which would have been quite frustrating, because "insider" is not an act of will but a cooperative relation, defeated as easily as the turn of a head; or we could resign ourselves to being outsiders. A few exceptionally strong people, usually reinforced by an alternative sense of communty, can just ignore it and carry on, despite the lack of that part of education which flows from full participation, perhaps thus resulting in a brand of knowledge that is more abstract than relational. But most others become driven to transform the outsider status into its own excuse, either by obsessional and abstracted overachievement, or by underachievement occasioned by the loss of relation and loss of interest. Either way the outsider status is a kind of unresolved wound, driven by pain, for after all that is the seeded prophecy contained in the word and the concept of those who are designated "outsider."

The students who have seen coming to my office have been describing occurrences, in class as well as on exams, that if true are just as powerfully and complexly traumatizing. Perhaps if all we value is toughness of spirit in our interactions, then what happened to my sister was a good lesson. It's certainly not just-as-easy to inflict the same lesson on women and students of color, or white men for that matter, if the project is only to toughen them up. We will, in the forge of exam pressure and general humiliation, be able to produce a tough human being totally split inside. But I trust that is not the exclusive project of institutions engaged in the training of ethical servants of either private or public interest.

This brings me back to my original issue how to distinguish the appropriate introduction of race, gender, class, social policy, into law-school classrooms. I don't think there's an easy answer or a formula that can be applied. That's why I think such discussion should be ongoing, constant, among faculties willing to hear diverse points of view—as difficult as such conversations are, and as long-term and noisier as they may have to be.

Nor do I think that handling these exams should be limited to discussions of wording in specific instances, or to specific professors who may have suffered momentary lapses of consciousness or whose motives may have been misunderstood. I think that the ultimate resolution has to do with understanding relations of power. It is significant that in my sister's class everyone ripped up her valentines; it might not have been more than a few hours of hurt feelings if only one person had done it. Similarly, it is significant when not just one but many law professors feel free to propagate (if unintentionally) racism in fanciful classroom hypotheticals and in publicly disseminated exams, bound for posterity in volumes in the library. It is significant that professors feel that they *can't talk* about exams like these without interfering with the first-amendment rights or the academic freedom of their colleagues. It is significant that we are teachers and have power over our students. It is significant that significant numbers of students are desperately unhappy about what they consider the abusive exercise of that power, and yet are too afraid to speak openly of their unhappiness. It is significant because people are hired and fired and graded and held to accountability under the law, based on factors about which we cannot or will not speak.

The response to my memo is not good. I am accused of being didactic, condescending, "too teacherly." I am told that I have humiliated a number of professors because, although no names were used, identities were easily divined. I have, I am told, "reduced the conversation to one of personalities and pot shots."

These accusations frighten me. I share the lawyerly resistance to the windy, risky plain of exposure that the "personal" represents. I am just as fearful of my own personality having been put into public debate as my critics are of theirs. My instinct is to retreat—the responses to my memo render the debate too subjective, complicated, messy, detailed. Somewhere inside, I know that my fear of being called didactic, condescending, and teacherly is related to K.'s fear of being called an activist. . . .

In the meantime, I avoid K. whenever I see her on the other side of the student union.

## Notes and Questions

1. Others have also explored the phantasm of the law school exam. Here is an example from British legal education:

> It all takes place in a region variously referred to as Ruritania, Urbania, Imperia and Proletania. With weird consistency a mad dystopia is created, whose citizens are exclusively involved in horrible crimes and complex litigation. The names . . . narrow character to some quintessentially lawless quality. We have Messrs Shady, Lustful, Lusty and Playboy. Mr. Lightfingers cashes bad cheques under the assumed name of Goldbags. The ladies are Miss Flighty or Miss Tattle. . . . They are often worse for drink. They are usually armed, but often with such objects as bicycle pumps, which might or might not be construed as dangerous weapons. People invited to dinner are shown sketch maps of how to get to the rendezvous which lead them to drive over ravines. "Dr Jekyll" has sexual intercourse with a woman patient with her consent under the pretense that he is performing a surgical operation which will cure her of whooping cough.*

*Timothy Hilton, "Lawyers at Play," (*New Statesman,* Jan. 26, 1968, 117) in James Boyd White, *The Legal Imagination* (1973).

The law school exam pretends to be about the real world—of course its purpose is to test legal knowledge and skills. And, given that testing is stressful, some professors may consider the use of ridiculous characterizations as simply a way to introduce some humor or lightness into exams. Even if they are an attempt at humor (or race/gender relevance), what do they imply about the law teachers who construct these fantasies and what should students make of these images of the population they are being trained to serve?

2. Professor Williams, by taking up the student's cause, comes to suffer the same fate as the student—ostracism and blaming the victim. What does this imply about law school culture, pedagogy and hierarchies, and about advocacy?

3. Before we leave the topic of legal education, it is worth while to think about the readings in this chapter and speculate on the possible consequences for legal education of the trends Kritzer described in his reading in the previous chapter. Could Bonsignore's "paradigmatic squeeze" still happen if law classes were primarily taught through distance learning and the Internet? Could the Socratic method endure in a move to cyberspace? What about Kennedy's idea about law schools training for legal hierarchies if the practice of law is fragmented into hundreds of highly-specialized areas of expertise subsumed into the large-scale organizations of multidisciplinary practices? Will race and gender have any particular significance in legal education in the postprofessional world? If, as Kritzer envisons, the legal profession is drastically changed in the information age, what shape will law schools take? Will they survive as distinct places with buildings, mock courts, libraries, and students coming together, or perhaps simply as brands and logos attached to electronically distributed courses and degrees? If the latter happens, what would be lost and what gained?

# 13 LAWYERS AND THE ADVERSARY PROCESS

From the moment I left on the trip until I returned, every penny I spent, even for the newspaper, was charged to the client's account. Every quarter I handed a shoeshine man or dollar I put down for a drink was not my own money. And if anyone thinks this was great, I would like to point out one fact. Every motion I made, every word I uttered, every thought I had was also not my own. It belonged to somebody else.

Charles Reich, *The Sorcerer of Bolinas Reef* (1976)

Lawyers are not savages. They are basically decent, concerned, well-educated citizens. Their sense of moral outrage can be extracted if the subject is man's capacity for cruelty and brutality. They would be first in line to suggest corrections aimed at curbing our more base instincts. . . . Yet change the focus, ask them about litigation or trial practice, and their sense of moral outrage goes only as far as the villainy of their current adversary. They often greet the subject with a cynicism worthy of Machiavelli.

Abraham P. Ordover, "The Lawyer as Liar," *American Journal of Trial Advocacy* (1979)

A lawyer is a utensil, like a knife or fork. It makes no difference who ate with it last, only that it was sufficiently sanitized between meals.

Roy Grutman, *Lawyers and Thieves* (1990)

[T]he adversary ethic is an inadequate aspiration for a community, and it is a pernicious moral principle. As an idea about power in the community, it depends not on goodness but on force and therefore reaches only the small, desperate residues of the community's life. As a moral principle it depends on the idea that one person should be able to buy the loyalty of another and often poisons the hope that people can grow together.

Thomas L. Shaffer, *On Being a Christian and a Lawyer* (1982)

The feature of the U.S. legal system that is most fundamental to its definition, operation, and character is its central tenet: that conflict resolution is best achieved through an adversary process. The adversary process assumes: (1) that the primary responsibility for articulating the sides in a dispute is best left to those most closely affected by the dispute; (2) that the biases of self-interest necessarily produced by forcing partisan dialogue between disputants can best be offset by having this dialogue take place in a neutral forum before impartial arbiters; and (3) that the conflict and dialogue can be constrained by a system of universalistic procedural and substantive rules (that is, law) that sets forth the interests of the state in the outcome of disputes. The ultimate objective in the adversary process—winning a case—is realized when the state is enticed into joining the side of one disputant against the other.

Thus, in the adversary process, disputants are expected to marshall and present the best (that is, most effectively self-serving) arguments and evidence they can. Lawyers act as advocates for their clients in this process. In court, they stand in the place of their clients. Their credentials, their skills, their special knowledge, their influence, and even their personalities are for rent. As noted earlier, lawyers are sometimes said to be modern-day "hired guns." Each of the readings in this chapter calls into question the meaning of advocacy, the relationship between lawyer and client, the neutrality of the law, and gender assumptions in the adversary system.

# 13.1 | The Ethics of Advocacy   *Charles P. Curtis*

## I

I WANT FIRST OF all to put advocacy in its proper setting. It is a special case of vicarious conduct. A lawyer devotes his life and career to acting for other people. So too does the priest, and in another way the banker. The banker handles other people's money. The priest handles other people's spiritual aspirations. A lawyer handles other people's troubles.

But there is a difference. The loyalty of a priest or clergyman runs, not to the particular parishioner whose joys or troubles he is busy with, but to his church; and the banker looks to his bank. It is the church or the bank, not he, but he on its behalf, who serves the communicant or the borrower. Their loyalties run in a different direction than a lawyer's.

So too when a lawyer works for the government. His loyalties hang on a superior peg, like the priest's or the clergyman's. For it is fiction to say that he only has the government for his client. The government is too big. It absorbs him. He is part of it.

Likewise with the general counsel for a corporation. His identification with his client is all but complete. Taft in some lectures at the Albany Law School,[1] referring to work in the legal department of a corporation, said, "Such employment leads to a lawyer's becoming nothing more than an officer of the corporation as closely identified with it as if he was the president, the secretary or the treasurer."[2] Indeed, he usually is a director or a vice-president.

Not so the lawyer in private practice. His loyalty runs to his client. He has no other master. Not the court? you ask. Does not the court take the same position as the church or the bank? Is not the lawyer an officer of the court? Doesn't the court have first claim on his loyalty? No, in a paradoxical way. The lawyer's official duty, required of him indeed by the court, is to devote himself to the client. The court comes second by the court's, that is the law's, own command. . . .

. . . How far must a lawyer accompany his client and turn his back on the court? . . .

The person for whom you are acting very reasonably expects you to treat him better than you do other people, which is just another way of saying that you owe him a higher standard of conduct than you owe to others. This goes back a long way. It is the pre-platonic ethics which Socrates had disposed of at the very outset of the *Republic;* that is that justice consists of doing good to your friends and harm to your enemies. A lawyer, therefore, insensibly finds himself treating his client better than others; and therefore others worse than his client. A lawyer, or a trustee, or anyone acting for another, has lower standards of conduct toward outsiders than he has toward his client or his beneficiaries or his patrons against the outsiders. He is required to treat outsiders as if they were barbarians and enemies. The more good faith and devotion the lawyer owes to his client, the less he owes to others when he is acting for his client. It is as if a man had only so much virtue, and the more he gives to one, the less he has available for anyone else. The upshot is that a man whose business it is to act for others finds himself, in his dealings on his client's behalf with outsiders, acting on a lower standard than he would if he were acting for himself, and lower, too, than any standard his client himself would be willing to act on, lower, in fact, than anyone on his own.

You devote yourself to the interests of another at the peril of yourself. Vicarious action tempts a man too far from himself. Men will do for others what they are not willing to do for themselves—noble as well as ignoble things. What I want to do now is to illustrate this in the practice of law by a number of perplexing situations. They raise ethical problems, but none of them, I think, has a simple right or wrong answer, and I know of no canons of ethics or morals which lead to any answer. How could there be

From "The Ethics of Advocacy," by Charles P. Curtis from *4 Stanford Law Review* 3 (1931). Copyright 1951, 1952 by the Board of Trustees of the Leland Stanford Junior University. Reprinted by permission.

[1] The Hubbard Lectures in May 1914.

[2] Cheatham, *Cases and Materials on the Legal Profession* 60 (1938).

when the cause of the perplexity is the difference between acting for another and acting for yourself? . . .

## II

A lawyer is called on the telephone by a former client who is unfortunately at the time a fugitive from justice. The police want him and he wants advice. The lawyer goes to where his client is, hears the whole story, and advises him to surrender. Finally he succeeds in persuading him that this is the best thing to do and they make an appointment to go to police headquarters. Meanwhile the client is to have two days to wind up his affairs and make his farewells. When the lawyer gets back to his office, a police inspector is waiting for him, and asks him whether his client is in town and where he is. Here are questions which the police have every right to ask of anybody, and even a little hesitation in this unfortunate lawyer's denials will reveal enough to betray his client. Of course he lies.

And why not? The relation between a lawyer and his client is one of the intimate relations. You would lie for your wife. You would lie for your child. There are others with whom you are intimate enough, close enough, to lie for them when you would not lie for yourself. At what point do you stop lying for them? I don't know and you are not sure.

To every one of us come occasions when we don't want to tell the truth, not all of it, certainly not all of it at once, when we want to be something less than candid, a little disingenuous. Indeed, to be candid with ourselves, there are times when we deliberately and more or less justifiably undertake to tell something else or something different. Complete candor to anyone but ourselves is a virtue that belongs to the saints, to the secure, and to the very courageous. Even when we do want to tell the truth, all of it, ultimately, we see no reason why we should not take our own time, tell it as skillfully and as gracefully as we can, and most of us doubt our own ability to do this as well by ourselves and for ourselves as another could do it for us. So we go to a lawyer. He will make a better fist of it than we can.

I don't see why we should not come out roundly and say that one of the functions of a lawyer is to lie for his client; and on rare occasions, as I think I have shown, I believe it is. Happily they are few and far between, only when his duty gets him into a corner or puts him on the spot. Day in, day out, a lawyer can be as truthful as anyone. But not ingenuous.

A lawyer is required to be disingenuous. He is required to make statements as well as arguments which he does not believe in. But the further his statements descend toward the particular, the more truthful he may be, indeed must be, because no one appreciates the significance of the particular better than a lawyer. In the higher brackets of generality, he has to be freed from his own beliefs and prejudices, for they are irrelevant, unless they are pressed into service for the client. But his insincerity does not extend to the particular, except, of course, particulars which do not belong to him, but are his client's secrets. Barring these, when he is talking for his client, a lawyer is absolved from veracity down to a certain point of particularity. And he must never lose the reputation of lacking veracity, because his freedom from the strict bonds of veracity and of the law are the two chief assets of the profession.

I have said that a lawyer may not lie to the court. But it may be a lawyer's duty not to speak. Let me give you a case from the autobiography of one of the most distinguished and most conscientious lawyers I or any other man has ever known, Samuel Williston. In his autobiography, *Life and Law,* he tells of one of his early cases. His client was sued in some financial matter. The details of the claim are not important. Williston, of course, at once got his client's letter file and went through it painstakingly, sorting, arranging, and collating it. The letters, we may well believe, told the whole story, as they usually do in such a case. Trial approached, but the plaintiff's lawyers did not either demand to see the correspondence, nor ask for their production. "They did not demand their production and we did not feel bound to disclose them."[3] At the close of the trial, "In the course of his remarks the Chief Justice stated as one reason for his decision a supposed fact which I knew to be unfounded. I had in front of me a letter that showed his error. Though I have no doubt of the propriety of my behavior in keep-

---

[3] Williston, *Life and Law* 271 (1940).

ing silent, I was somewhat uncomfortable at the time."

This was a letter, a piece of evidence, a fact. Suppose it had been a rule of law. Suppose the Chief Justice had equally mistakenly given as a reason for his decision some statute or regulation which Williston knew had been repealed or amended, and it was not a letter but a copy of the new statute which he had in front of him. Williston would have interrupted the Chief Justice and drawn his attention to it. This is sometimes debated, but it is beyond dispute that this would have been Williston's duty, and there is no doubt at all that he would have performed it as scrupulously as he respected his duty to his client. . . .

## III

"I must be cruel only to be kind," said Hamlet, on his way to his mother. And so likewise a lawyer has to tell himself strange things on his way to court. But they are strange only to those who do not distinguish between truth and justice. Justice is something larger and more intimate than truth. Truth is only one of the ingredients of justice. Its whole is the satisfaction of those concerned. It is to that end that each attorney must say the best, and only the best, of his own case.

This is not the method we have used in other endeavors, with not only more, but with conspicuous success. But the law has other things than success to think about. It must give the losing party, and his friends and his sympathizers, as much satisfaction as any loser can expect. At least the most has been said for him. The whole has been shaken out into the sun, and everyone concerned is given a feeling akin to the feeling of security which you get when you have told yourself the worst before you make a decision. The administration of justice is no more designed to elicit the truth than the scientific approach is designed to extract justice from the atom.

Advocacy requires a lawyer to start with something to be proved, and this is as true of facts as it is of propositions of law. When he goes to interview a witness as well as when he goes to the law library, he goes to get something. He will waste a lot of time if he goes with an open mind. He must, of course, first formulate the issue in his mind, but he does this only to make it the easier to find what lies on his side of the issue. He fixes on the conclusion which will best serve his client's interests, and then he sets out to persuade others to agree.

The problem presented to a lawyer when he is asked to defend a man he knows is guilty or to take a case he knows is bad is perplexing only to the laymen. Brandeis said, "As a practical matter, I think the lawyer is not often harassed by this problem, partly because he is apt to believe at the time in most of the cases that he actually tries, and partly because he either abandons or settles a large number of those he does not believe in."[4]

It is profoundly true that the first person a lawyer persuades is himself. A practicing lawyer will soon detect in himself a perfectly astonishing amount of sincerity. By the time he has even sketched out his brief, however skeptically he started, he finds himself believing more and more in what it says, until he has to hark back to his original opinion in order to orient himself. And later, when he starts arguing the case before the court, his belief is total, and he is quite sincere about it. You cannot very well keep your tongue in your cheek while you are talking. He believes what he is saying in a way that will later astonish himself as much as now it does others.

Not that he cares how much we are astonished. What he does care is whether we are persuaded, and he is aware that an unsound argument can do much worse than fall flat. For it may carry the implication that he has no better one. He will not want to make it unless he really has no better.

## IV

The classical solution to a lawyer taking a case he knows is bad is Dr. Johnson's. It is perfectly simple and quite specious. Boswell asked Johnson whether as a moralist Johnson did not think that the practice of the law, in some degree, hurt the nice feeling of honesty.

"What do you think," said Boswell, "of supporting a cause which you know to be bad?"

Johnson answered, "Sir, you do not know it to be good or bad till the Judge determines it. I

---

[4]Brandeis, The Opportunity in the Law, 39 *Am. L. Rev.* 561 (1905).

have said that you are to state facts fairly; so that your thinking, or what you call knowing, a cause to be bad, must be from reasoning, must be from your supposing your arguments to be weak and inconclusive. But, Sir, that is not enough. An argument which does not convince yourself, may convince the Judge to whom you urge it: and if it does convince him, why, then, Sir, you are wrong, and he is right."

Dr. Johnson ignored the fact that it is the lawyer's job to know how good or how bad his case is. It is his peculiar function to find out. Dr. Johnson's answer is sound only in cases where the problem does not arise.

A lawyer knows very well whether his client is guilty. It is not the lawyer, but the law, that does not know whether his case is good or bad. The law does not know, because it is trying to find out, and so the law wanted everyone defended and every debatable case tried. Therefore the law makes it easy for a lawyer to take a case, whether or not he thinks other people think it bad. It is particularly important that it be made as easy as possible for a lawyer to take a case that other people regard as bad.

We want to make it as easy as we can for a lawyer to take a bad case, and one of the ways the bar helps go about it is the canon of ethics which says, "It is improper for a lawyer to assert in argument his personal belief in his client's innocence or in the justice of his cause." It is called improper just so that the lawyer may feel that he does not have to. This, I think, must be its only purpose, for it is honored in no other way. . . .

No, there is nothing unethical in taking a bad case or defending the guilty or advocating what you don't believe in. It is ethically neutral. It's a free choice. There is a Daumier drawing of a lawyer arguing, a very demure young woman sitting near him, and a small boy beside her sucking a lollypop. The caption says, "He defends the widow and the orphan, unless he is attacking the orphan and the widow." And for every lawyer whose conscience may be pricked, there is another whose virtue is tickled. Every case has two sides, and for every lawyer on the wrong side, there's another on the right side.

I am not being cynical. We are not dealing with the morals which govern a man acting for himself, but with the ethics of advocacy. We are talking about the special moral code which governs a man who is acting for another. Lawyers in their practice—how they behave elsewhere does not concern us—put off more and more of our common morals the farther they go in a profession which treats right and wrong, vice and virtue, on such equal terms. Some lawyers find nothing to take its place. There are others who put on new and shining raiment. . . .

I have talked perhaps too lovingly about the practice of the law. I have spoke unsparingly, as I would to another lawyer. In a way the practice of the law is like free speech. It defends what we hate as well as what we most love. I don't know any other career that offers ampler opportunity for both the enjoyment of virtue and the exercise of vice, or, if you please, the exercise of virtue and the enjoyment of vice, except possibly the ancient rituals which were performed in some temples by vestal virgins, in others by sacred prostitutes.

## V

Let us now go back and reconsider, and perhaps reconstruct, in the light of my examples and our discussion, this "entire devotion" which a lawyer owes to his client.

The fact is, the "entire devotion" is not entire. The full discharge of a lawyer's duty to his client requires him to withhold something. If a lawyer is entirely devoted to his client, his client receives something less than he has a right to expect. For, if a man devotes the whole of himself to another, he mutilates or diminishes himself, and the other receives the devotion of so much the less. This is no paradox, but a simple calculus of the spirit.

There is authority for such detachment. It is not Christian. Nor is the practice of law a characteristically Christian pursuit. The practice of law is vicarious, not altruistic, and the lawyer must go back of Christianity to Stoicism for the vicarious detachment which will permit him to serve his client.

E. R. Bevan, in his *Stoics and Sceptics,*[5] summarized the Stoic faith as follows: "The Wise Man was not to concern himself with his brethren . . . he was only to serve them. Benevolence he was to have, as much of it as you can conceive; but there was one thing he must not have, and

---

[5]As quoted in 6 Toynbee, *A Study of History,* 146–47 (1939).

that was love. . . . He must do everything which it is possible for him to do, shrink from no extreme of physical pain, in order to help, to comfort, to guide his fellow men, but whether he succeeds or not must be a matter of pure indifference to him. If he has done his best to help you and failed, he will be perfectly satisfied with having done his best. The fact that you are no better off for his exertions will not matter to him at all. Pity, in the sense of a painful emotion caused by the sight of other men's suffering, is actually a vice. . . . In the service of his fellow men he must be prepared to sacrifice his life; but there is one thing he must never sacrifice: his own eternal calm.". . .

The Stoics gave us a counsel of perfection, but it is none the less valid. If a lawyer is to be the best lawyer he is capable of being, and discharge his "entire duty" to his clients, here in the Stoic sage is his exemplar. Here in Stoicism is his philosophy. Let him be a Christian if he choose outside the practice of the law, but in his relations with his clients, let him be a Stoic, for the better Stoic, the better lawyer.

A lawyer should treat his cases like a vivid novel, and identify himself with his client as he does with the hero or the heroine in the plot. Then he will work with "the zest that most people feel under their concern when they assist at existing emergencies, not actually their own; or join in facing crises that are grave, but for somebody else. . . ."[6]

How is a lawyer to secure this detachment? There are two ways of doing it, two devices, and all lawyers, almost all, are familiar with one or the other of them.

One way is to treat the whole thing as a game. I am not talking about the sporting theory of justice. I am talking about a lawyer's personal relations with his client and the necessity of detaching himself from his client. Never blame a lawyer for treating litigation as a game, however much you may blame the judge. The lawyer is detaching himself. A man who has devoted his life to taking on other people's troubles, would be swamped by them if he were to adopt them as his own. He must stay on the upland of his own personality, not only to protect himself, but to give his client the very thing that his client came for. . . .

The other way is a sense of craftsmanship. Perhaps it comes to the same thing, but I think not quite. There is a satisfaction in playing a game the best you can, as there is in doing anything else as well as you can, which is quite distinct from making a good score. . . .

A Lawyer may have to treat the practice of law as if it were a game, but if he can rely on craftsmanship, it may become an art. . . .

. . . I wonder if there is anything more exalted than the intense pleasure of doing a job as well as you can irrespective of its usefulness or even of its purpose. At least it's a comfort.

I have compared the lawyer to the banker who handles other people's money and to the priest who handles other people's spiritual aspirations. Let me go further. Compare the lawyer with the poet whose speech goes to the heart of things. "Yet he is that one especially who speaks civilly to Nature as a second person and in some sense is the patron of the world. Though more than any he stands in the midst of Nature, yet more than any he can stand aloof from her."[7]

### Notes and Questions

1. Curtis asserts that lawyers who work for government or corporations are absorbed by their clients. Should such lawyers have no obligations to the public beyond those of their employers? Consider the following from the ethical code for lawyers in federal government employment:

   The situation of the federal lawyer which may give rise to special considerations, not applicable to lawyers generally, includes certain limitations on complete freedom of action in matters relating to Canon 8. [Canon 8 of the *American Bar Association Code of Professional Responsibility* states, "a lawyer should assist in improving the legal system."] For example, a lawyer in the Office of the Chief Counsel of the Internal Revenue Service may reasonably be expected to abide, without public criticism, with certain policies or rulings closely allied to his sphere of responsibility even if he disagrees with the position taken by the agency. But even if involved personally in the process of formulating policy or ruling there may be rare

---

[6]Cozzens, *Guard of Honor* 479 (1948).

[7]*VII Writings of Henry David Thoreau*, 289 (1906).

occasions when his conscience compels him publicly to attack a decision which is contrary to his professional, ethical or moral judgment. In that event, however, he should be prepared to resign before doing so, and he is not free to abuse professional confidence reposed in him in the process leading to the decision.*

What about lawyers who serve the government as prosecutors? Should they resign rather than prosecute someone whose behavior may be illegal but not "wrong" in the prosecutor's own moral or ethical judgment?

2. What about lawyers in firm practices? Recall the readings in the last chapter about preparing young lawyers for practice by dulling their moral sensitivity in this excerpt:

> Before I ever became a lawyer, I both respected and was intrigued by lawyers' ability to put their personal beliefs aside and zealously advocate positions they themselves didn't support. Rather than perceiving lawyers as prostitutes of their legal skills, I saw their ability to defend seemingly indefensible positions as the purest form of advocacy. . . . But now I recognize that separating yourself from your work comes at a high price. The lawyer in the office for 12 or more hours a day is the same person who has to go home each night, and live with the consequences of their actions.
>
> The nature of large firm practice often masks the harsh reality of selling out. As a general rule, as an associate you are expected to work on cases assigned to you, unless you have—and can articulate—very strong moral or ethical objections. This pressure means that associates must take a stand to get off cases they don't want to work on, and that's a potentially career-jeopardizing move. It leaves people looking down on you for not being a "team-player." . . . Surrounded by other professionals who routinely put their personal beliefs aside, and surrounded by plush offices, expensive artwork, and state-of-the-art technology, I found it depressingly easy to overlook any distaste I harbored for certain clients and cases.[†]

3. In a case in Lake Pleasant, New York, two lawyers appointed to defend a man charged with murder were told by their client of two other murders that, unknown to police, he had committed. The lawyers, following the client's directions, discovered the bodies in an abandoned mine shaft and photographed them. They did not, however, inform the police until several months later, after their client confessed to those killings. In addition, the parents of one victim had approached one of the lawyers seeking information about their missing daughter. The attorney denied having any information.

Monroe Freedman, a law school dean and prominent writer on legal ethics, wrote of this case,

> The adversary system, within which the lawyer functions, contemplates that the lawyer frequently will learn from the client information that is highly incriminating and may even learn, as in the Lake Pleasant case, that the client has in fact committed serious crimes. In such a case, if the attorney were required to divulge that information, the obligation of confidentiality would be destroyed, and with it, the adversary system itself.[‡]

Should there be any limits to a lawyer's advocacy? Should society have any interest in the lawyer-client relationship so long as the lawyer is ethical?

4. Curtis claims that lawyers must be understood as playing a game. Lawyers commonly refer to legal practice as a game. Why is that? Other professionals—doctors, ministers, engineers, social workers, scientists, academics—don't do it. Lawyer and novelist Louis Auchincloss also uses this metaphor when his character in *Diary of a Yuppie,* Attorney Robert Service explains how things work to junior lawyers in the firm:

> The trouble with you and Blakelock is that neither of you has the remotest understanding of the moral climate in which we live today. It's all a game, but a game with very strict rules. You have to stay meticulously within the law; the least misstep, if caught, involves an instant

---

*Federal Bar Association, *Federal Ethical Considerations* (Washington, D.C.: FBA, adopted November 17, 1973).

†William R. Keates, *Proceed with Caution: A Diary of the First Year at One of America's Largest, Most Prestigious Law Firms.* (Chicago: Harcourt Brace Legal and Professional Publications, 1997), 132–133.

‡Monroe H. Freedman, *Lawyers' Ethics in an Adversary System* (Indianapolis, Inc.: Bobbs-Merrill, 1975), p. 5.

penalty. But there is no particular moral opprobrium in incurring a penalty, any more than there is being offside in football. A man who is found to have bought or sold stock on inside information, or misrepresented his assets in a loan application, or put his girl friend on the company payroll, is not "looked down on," except by sentimentalists. He's simply been caught, that's all. Even the public

understands that. . . . You break the rules, pay the penalty and go back to the game.§

Does Curtis's perspective necessarily lead a lawyer to the kind of cynical understanding of moral action described by Service?

---

§Louis Auchincloss, *Diary of a Yuppie* (New York: St. Martin's Press, 1986), pp. 26–27.

 

❧ The courtroom is not merely a field upon which personal grievances are settled by rhetorical combat. It is not a closed scene in which only the parties to the dispute have an interest. Adjudication is a process of state governance. The court represents the government and, less directly, the society. Judgments of the court are backed by state power. Adjudication is imbued with the public interest.

## 13.2 | The "Fight" Theory Versus the "Truth" Theory

*Jerome Frank*

### I

WHEN WE SAY THAT present-day trial methods are "rational," presumably we mean this: The men who compose our trial courts, judges and juries, in each law-suit conduct an intelligent inquiry into all the practically available evidence, in order to ascertain, as near as may be, the truth about the facts of that suit. That might be called the "investigatory" or "truth" method of trying cases. Such a method can yield no more than a guess, nevertheless an educated guess.

The success of such a method is conditioned by at least these two factors: (1) The judicial inquirers, trial judges or juries, may not obtain all the important evidence. (2) The judicial inquirers may not be competent to conduct such an inquiry. Let us, for the time being, assume that the second condition is met—i.e., that we have competent inquirers—and ask whether we so conduct trials as to satisfy the first condi-

tion, i.e., the procuring of all the practically available important evidence.

The answer to that question casts doubt on whether our trial courts do use the "investigatory" or "truth" method. Our mode of trials is commonly known as "contentious" or "adversary." It is based on what I would call the "fight" theory, a theory which derives from the origin of trials as substitutes for private out-of-court brawls.

Many lawyers maintain that the "fight" theory and the "truth" theory coincide. They think that the best way for a court to discover the facts in a suit is to have each side strive as hard as it can, in a keenly partisan spirit, to bring to the court's attention the evidence favorable to that side. Macaulay said that we obtain the fairest decision "when two men argue, as unfairly as possible, on opposite sides," for then "it is certain that no important consideration will altogether escape notice."

Unquestionably that view contains a core of good sense. The zealously partisan lawyers sometimes do bring into court evidence which, in a dispassionate inquiry, might be overlooked. Apart from the fact element of the case, the opposed lawyers also illuminate for the court niceties of

From Jerome Frank, *Courts on Trial: Myth and Reality in American Justice.* Copyright 1949 by Jerome Frank, ©1976 renewed by Princeton University Press. Reprinted with permission of Princeton University Press.

the legal rules which the judge might otherwise not perceive. The "fight" theory, therefore, has invaluable qualities with which we cannot afford to dispense.

But frequently the partisanship of the opposing lawyers blocks the uncovering of vital evidence or leads to a presentation of vital testimony in a way that distorts it. I shall attempt to show you that we have allowed the fighting spirit to become dangerously excessive.

## II

This is perhaps most obvious in the handling of witnesses. Suppose a trial were fundamentally a truth-inquiry. Then, recognizing the inherent fallibilities of witnesses, we would do all we could to remove the causes of their errors when testifying. Recognizing also the importance of witnesses' demeanor as clues to their reliability, we would do our best to make sure that they testify in circumstances most conducive to a revealing observation of that demeanor by the trial judge or jury. In our contentious trial practice, we do almost the exact opposite.

No businessman, before deciding to build a new plant, no general before launching an attack, would think of obtaining information on which to base his judgment by putting his informants through the bewildering experience of witnesses at a trial. "The novelty of the situation," wrote a judge, "the agitation and hurry which accompanies it, the cajolery or intimidation to which the witness may be subjected, the want of questions calculated to excite those recollections which might clear up every difficulty, and the confusion of cross-examination . . . may give rise to important errors and omissions." "In the court they stand as strangers," wrote another judge of witnesses, "surrounded with unfamiliar circumstances giving rise to an embarrassment known only to themselves."

In a book by Henry Taft (brother of Chief Justice Taft, and himself a distinguished lawyer) we are told: "Counsel and court find it necessary through examination and instruction to induce a witness to abandon for an hour or two his habitual method of thought and expression, and conform to the rigid ceremonialism of court procedure. It is not strange that frequently truthful witnesses are . . . misunderstood, that they nervously react in such a way as to create the impression that they are either evading or intentionally falsifying. It is interesting to account for some of the things that witnesses do under such circumstances. An honest witness testifies on direct examination. He answers questions promptly and candidly and makes a good impression. On cross-examination, his attitude changes. He suspects that traps are being laid for him. He hesitates; he ponders the answer to a simple question; he seems to 'spar' for time by asking that questions be repeated; perhaps he protests that counsel is not fair; he may even appeal to the court for protection. Altogether the contrast with his attitude on direct examination is obvious; and he creates the impression that he is evading or withholding," Yet on testimony thus elicited courts every day reach decisions affecting the lives and fortunes of citizens.

What is the role of the lawyers in bringing the evidence before the trial court? As you may learn by reading any one of a dozen or more handbooks on how to try a law-suit, an experienced lawyer uses all sorts of stratagems to minimize the effect on the judge or jury of testimony disadvantageous to his client, even when the lawyer has no doubt of the accuracy and honesty of that testimony. The lawyer considers it his duty to create a false impression, if he can, of any witness who gives such testimony. If such a witness happens to be timid, frightened by the unfamiliarity of court-room ways, the lawyer, in his cross-examination, plays on that weakness, in order to confuse the witness and make it appear that he is concealing significant facts. Longenecker, in his book *Hints on The Trial of a Law Suit* (a book endorsed by the great Wigmore), in writing of the "truthful, honest, over-cautious" witness, tells how "a skilful advocate by a rapid cross-examination may ruin the testimony of such a witness." The author does not even hint any disapproval of that accomplishment. Longenecker's and other similar books recommend that a lawyer try to prod an irritable but honest "adverse" witness into displaying his undesirable characteristics in their most unpleasant form, in order to discredit him with the judge or jury. "You may," writes Harris, "sometimes destroy the effect of an adverse witness by making him appear more hostile than he really is. You may make him exaggerate or unsay something and say it again." Taft says that a clever cross-examiner, dealing with an honest but egotistic witness, will "deftly tempt the witness to indulge in his propensity for exaggeration, so as to make him 'hang himself.' And thus," adds Taft, "it may happen that not only is the value of his testimony lost, but the side which produces him suffers for seeking aid from such a source"—although, I would add, that may be the only source of evidence of a fact on which the decision will turn. . . .

The lawyer not only seeks to discredit adverse witnesses but also to hide the defects of witnesses who testify favorably to his client. If, when interviewing such a witness before trial, the lawyer notes that the witness has mannerisms, demeanor-traits, which might discredit him, the lawyer teaches him how to cover up those traits when testifying: He educates the irritable witness to conceal his irritability, the cocksure witness to subdue his cocksureness. In that way, the trial court is denied the benefit of observing the witness's actual normal demeanor, and thus prevented from sizing up the witness accurately.

Lawyers freely boast of their success with these tactics. They boast also of such devices as these: If an "adverse," honest witness, on cross-examination, makes seemingly inconsistent statements, the cross-examiner tries to keep the witness from explaining away the apparent inconsistencies. "When," writes Tracy, counseling trial lawyers, in a much-praised book, "by your cross-examination, you have caught the witness in an inconsistency, the next question that will immediately come to your lips is, 'Now, let's hear you explain.' Don't ask it, for he may explain and, if he does, your point will have been lost. If you have conducted your cross-examination properly (which includes interestingly), the jury will have seen the inconsistency and it will have made the proper impression on their minds. If, on re-direct examination the witness does explain, the explanation will have come later in the case and at the request of the counsel who originally called the witness and the jury will be much more likely to look askance at the explanation than if it were made during your cross-examination." Tracy adds, "Be careful in your questions on cross-examination not to open the door that you have every reason to wish kept closed." That

is, don't let in any reliable evidence, hurtful to your side, which would help the trial court to arrive at the truth. . . .

Nor, usually, will a lawyer concede the existence of any facts if they are inimical to his client and he thinks they cannot be proved by his adversary. If, to the lawyer's knowledge, a witness has testified inaccurately but favorably to the lawyer's client, the lawyer will attempt to hinder cross-examination that would expose the inaccuracy. He puts in testimony which surprises his adversary who, caught unawares, has not time to seek out, interview, and summon witnesses who would rebut the surprise testimony. "Of course," said a trial lawyer in a bar association lecture in 1946, "surprise elements should be hoarded. Your opponent should not be educated as to matters concerning which you believe he is still in the dark. Obviously, the traps should not be uncovered. Indeed, you may cast a few more leaves over them so that your adversary will step more boldly on the low ground believing it is solid."

These, and other like techniques, you will find unashamedly described in the many manuals on trial tactics written by and for eminently reputable trial lawyers. The purpose of these tactics—often effective—is to prevent the trial judge or jury from correctly evaluating the truthworthiness of witnesses and to shut out evidence the trial court ought to receive in order to approximate the truth.

In short, the lawyer aims at victory, at winning in the fight, not at aiding the court to discover the facts. He does not want the trial court to reach a sound educated guess, if it is likely to be contrary to his client's interest. Our present trial method is thus the equivalent of throwing pepper in the eyes of a surgeon when he is performing an operation. . . .

## III

That brings me to a point which the fighting theory obscures. A court's decision is not a mere private affair. It culminates in a court order which is one of the most solemn of governmental acts. Not only is a court an agency of government, but remember that its order, if not voluntarily obeyed, will bring into action the police, the sheriff, even the army. What a court orders, then, is no light matter. The court represents the government, organized society, in action.

Such an order a court is not supposed to make unless there exist some facts which bring into operation a legal rule. Now any government officer, other than a judge, if authorized to do an act for the government only if certain facts exist, will be considered irresponsible if he so acts without a governmental investigation. For instance, if an official is empowered to pay money to a veteran suffering from some specified ailment, the official, if he does his duty, will not rely solely on the applicant's statement that he has such an ailment. The government officer insists on a governmental check-up of the evidence. Do courts so conduct themselves?

In criminal cases they seem to, after a fashion. In such cases, there is some recognition that so important a governmental act as a court decision against a defendant should not occur without someone, on behalf of the government itself, seeing to it that the decision is justified by the actual facts so far as they can be discovered with reasonable diligence. For, in theory at least, usually before a criminal action is begun, an official investigation has been conducted which reveals data sufficient to warrant bringing the defendant to trial. In some jurisdictions, indigent defendants charged with crime are represented by a publicly-paid official, a Public Defender. . . . And the responsibility of government for mistakes of fact in criminal cases, resulting in erroneous court judgments, is recognized in those jurisdictions in which the government compensates an innocent convicted person if it is subsequently shown that he was convicted through such a mistake.

In civil cases (non-criminal cases), on the whole a strikingly different attitude prevails. Although, no less than a criminal suit, a court's order is a grave governmental act, yet, in civil cases, the government usually accepts no similar responsibilities, even in theory. Such a suit is still in the ancient tradition of "self help." The court usually relies almost entirely on such evidence as one or the other of the private parties to the suit is (a) able to, and (b) chooses to, offer. Lack of skill or diligence of the lawyer for one of those parties, or that party's want of enough funds to finance a pre-trial investigation necessary to obtain evidence, may have the result, as I explained,

that crucial available evidence is not offered in court. No government official has the duty to discover, and bring to court, evidence, no matter how important, not offered by the parties.

In short, the theory is that, in most civil suits, the government, through its courts, should make orders which the government will enforce, although those court-orders may not be justified by the actual facts, and although, by reasonable diligence, the government, had it investigated, might have discovered evidence—at variance with the evidence presented—coming closer to the actual facts.

Yet the consequence of a court decision in a civil suit, based upon the court's mistaken view of the actual facts, may be as grave as a criminal judgment which convicts an innocent person. If, because of such an erroneous decision, a man loses his job or his savings and becomes utterly impoverished, he may be in almost as serious a plight as if he had been jailed. His poverty may make him a public charge. It may lead to the delinquency of his children, who may thus become criminals and go to jail. Yet in no jurisdiction is a man compensated by the government for serious injury to him caused by a judgment against him in a non-criminal case, even if later it is shown that the judgment was founded upon perjured or mistaken testimony.

I suggest that there is something fundamentally wrong in our legal system in this respect. If a man's pocket is picked, the government brings a criminal suit, and accepts responsibility for its prosecution. If a man loses his life's savings through a breach of contract, the government accepts no such responsibility. Shouldn't the government perhaps assume some of the burden of enforcing what we call "private rights"? . . .

## IV

Suppose, that, in a crude "primitive" society, A claims that B took A's pig. If that is true, B violated a well-settled tribal rule. But B denies that he took the pig. A attacks B and kills him. Does A's killing of B prove that B was wrong about the facts? Does that killing constitute the enforcement of the tribal rule? Now suppose somewhat the same sort of dispute in the U.S.A. A sues B, claiming that by fraud and deceit, B got A's pig. A legal rule says that if B did those acts, then A has a legal right to get back the pig or its money value. If A wins that suit, does the decision in his favor constitute the enforcement of that legal rule, even if A won through perjured testimony or because the trial court erroneously believed an honest but mistaken witness?

A lawyer friend of mine, to whom I put this question, replied, "Yes, in theory. In theory, the facts as found must be assumed to be true." His answer does not satisfy me. That we must accept the facts found by a trial court does not mean that a rule against fraud is really enforced when a court holds a man liable for a fraud he did not commit. My friend is saying, in effect, that, even were it true that the courts misfound the facts in 90% of all cases, still the courts would be enforcing the rules.

The conclusion does not bother the hardened cynic. "In the long run," one may imagine him saying, "what is the difference whether courts make many mistakes in fact-finding, and, as a result, render erroneous decisions—as long as the public generally doesn't learn of those mistakes? . . . [I]f a noncriminal legal rule is of a desirable kind—for instance, a rule concerning the duty of a trustee to the beneficiaries of a trust—why bother whether, in particular lawsuits, the courts, through failure to discover the actual facts, apply it to persons who haven't violated it? Public respect for that rule, and its infiltration into community habits, will come just as well from its misapplications as from its correction applications—if only the public doesn't learn of its misapplications. If you call it injustice to punish the innocent or mistakenly to enter money judgments against men who have done no legal wrongs, then I answer that effectively concealed instances of injustice are not only harmless but socially beneficial. They serve as useful examples. Don't get squeamish about such mistakes." I doubt whether any reader will agree with the cynic.

## V

No one can doubt that the invention of courts, which preserve the peace by settling disputes, marked a great step forward in human progress. But are we to be so satisfied with this forward step that we will rest content with it? Should not a modern civilized society ask more of its courts than that they stop peace-disrupting brawls? The basic aim of the courts in our society should, I think, be the just settlement of particular disputes, the just decision of specific law-suits.

The just settlement of disputes demands a legal system in which the courts can and do strive tirelessly to get as close as is humanly possible to the actual facts of specific court-room controversies. Court-house justice is, I repeat, done at retail, not at wholesale. The trial court's job of fact-finding in each particular case therefore looms up as one of the most important jobs in modern court-house government. With no lack of deep admiration and respect for our many able trial judges, I must say that that job is not as well done as it could and should be.

## Notes and Questions

1. Curtis commented that "the administration of justice is no more designed to elicit the truth than the scientific approach is designed to extract justice from the atom." Would Judge Frank agree? How can there be justice without truth?

   Can there be truth without knowledge? Does Socrates' dialogue with Theaetetus help or make the problem even more complicated?

   *Socrates:* [There is] a whole profession to prove that true belief is not knowledge.

   *Theaetetus:* How so? What profession?

   *Socrates:* The profession of those paragons of intellect known as orators and lawyers. There you have men who use their skill to produce conviction, not by instruction, but by making people believe whatever they want them to believe. You can hardly imagine teachers so clever as to be able, in the short time allowed by the clock, to instruct their hearers thoroughly in the true facts of a case of robbery or other violence which those hearers had not witnessed.

   *Theaetetus:* No, I cannot imagine that; but they can convince them.

   *Socrates:* And by convincing you mean making them believe something.

   *Theaetetus:* Of course.

   *Socrates:* And when a jury is rightly convinced of facts which can be known only by an eye-witness, then, judging by hearsay and accepting a true belief, they are judging without knowledge, although, if they find the right verdict, their conviction is correct?

*Theaetetus:* Certainly.

*Socrates:* But if true belief and knowledge were the same thing, the best of jurymen could never have a correct belief without knowledge. It now appears that they must be different things.*

2. How would Frank be likely to view the following quote?

> Justice as a professional aspiration is corrupting the extent that the culture of justice finds it hard to say that a lawyer's life is ministry and that that ministry aims beyond justice to compassion and hope. Compassion is the heart of counseling, and counseling is what lawyers do most of the time. Lawyers do not, most of the time, "dispense" or "administer" or serve justice; they serve people who know and who want to know how to live together. The professional culture's proclaimed concern with justice, became justice is often irrelevant to this enterprise, makes compassion more rather than less difficult, and, therefore, the professional

culture makes things worse. The practice of hope in a lawyer's professional life involves the use of knowledge and intellectual skill as an expression of truth; but exclusive concern with justice in the professional culture often comes out expressing itself in terms of coercion, rather than truth, and in that way, too, professional culture makes things worse. Justice is an important professional virtue, no doubt, but it is not an adequate aspiration for the life the average lawyer leads.†

3. In criminal cases, the state is a party to the legal dispute. Does this fact explain why the government may be more diligent in searching for truth in such cases than in civil cases between private parties? If the court were to conduct its own truth-seeking inquiries to settle private disputes, would it jeopardize its own status as impartial arbiter? If so, how could that outcome be avoided?

4. What is Frank's view of the interests of the state and society in private litigation? Does he suggest a role for lawyers different from that put forth by Curtis?

---

*From Plato, *Theaetetus* in *Plato's Theory of Knowledge,* translated by Francis M. Cornford. Copyright © 1957 Liberal Arts Press. Reprinted by permission of Pearson Education, Inc., Upper Saddle River, NJ 07458.

†Thomas L. Shaffer, *On Being a Christian and a Lawyer* (Provo, Utah: Brigham Young University Press, 1982), p. 162.

---

## 13.3  The Criminal Lawyer's "Different Mission": Reflections on the "Right" to Present a False Case  *Harry I. Subin*

ABOUT FIFTEEN YEARS AGO I represented a man charged with rape and robbery. The victim's account was as follows: Returning from work in the early morning hours, she was accosted by a man who pointed a gun at her and took a watch from her wrist. He told her to go with him to a nearby lot, where he ordered her to lie down on the ground and disrobe. When she complained that the ground was hurting her, he took her to his apartment, located across the street. During the next hour there, he had intercourse with her. Ultimately, he said that they had to leave to avoid

being discovered by the woman with whom he lived. The complainant responded that since he had gotten what he wanted, he should give her back her watch. He said that he would.

As the two left the apartment, he said he was going to get a car. Before leaving the building, however, he went to the apartment next door, leaving her to wait in the hallway. When asked why she waited, she said that she was still hoping for the return of her watch, which was a valued gift, apparently from her boyfriend.

She never did get the watch. When they left the building, the man told her to wait on the street while he got the car. At that point she went to a nearby police precinct and reported the incident. She gave a full description of the assailant that matched my client. She also accu-

Harry I. Subin, "The Criminal Lawyer's Different Mission," *Georgetown Journal of Legal Ethics,* Vol. 1, 1987, pp. 125–136. Copyright 1987 The Georgetown Journal of Legal Ethics. Reprinted by permission.

rately described the inside of his apartment. Later, in response to a note left at his apartment by the police, my client came to the precinct, and the complainant identified him. My client was released at that time but was arrested soon thereafter at his apartment, where a gun was found.[1] No watch was recovered.

My client was formally charged, at which point I entered the case. At our initial interview and those that followed it, he insisted that he had nothing whatever to do with the crime and had never even seen the woman before.[2] He stated that he had been in several places during the night in question: visiting his aunt earlier in the evening, then traveling to a bar in New Jersey, where he was during the critical hours. He gave the name of a man there who would corroborate this. He said that he arrived home early the next morning and met a friend. He stated that he had no idea how this woman had come to know things about him such as what the apartment looked like, that he lived with a woman, and that he was a musician, or how she could identify him. He said that he had no reason to rape anyone, since he already had a woman, and that in any event he was recovering from surgery for an old gunshot wound and could not engage in intercourse. He said he would not be so stupid as to bring a woman he had robbed and was going to rape into his own apartment.

I felt there was some strength to these arguments, and that there were questionable aspects to the complainant's story. In particular, it seemed strange that a man intending rape would be as solicitous of the victim's comfort as the woman said her assailant was at the playground. It also seemed that a person who had just been raped would flee when she had the chance to, and in any case would not be primarily concerned with the return of her watch. On balance, however, I suspected that my client was not telling me the truth. I thought the complaining witness could not possibly have known what she knew about him and his apartment, if she had not had any contact with him. True, someone else could have posed as him, and used his apartment. My client, however, could suggest no one who could have done so.[3] Moreover, that hypothesis did not explain the complainant's accurate description of him to the police. Although the identification procedure used by the police, a one person "show up," was suggestive, the woman had ample opportunity to observe her assailant during the extended incident. I could not believe that the complainant had selected my client randomly to accuse falsely of rape. By both her and my client's admission, the two had not had any previous association.

That my client was probably lying to me had two possible explanations. First, he might have been lying because he was guilty and did not see any particular advantage to himself in admitting it to me. It is embarrassing to admit that one has committed a crime, particularly one of this nature. Moreover, my client might well have feared to tell me the truth. He might have believed that I would tell others what he said, or, at the very least, that I might not be enthusiastic about representing him.

He also might have lied not because he was guilty of the offense, but because he thought the concocted story was the best one under the circumstances. The sexual encounter may have taken place voluntarily, but the woman complained to the police because she was very angry at my client for refusing to return the valued wrist watch, perhaps not stolen, but left, in my client's apartment. My client may not have been able to admit this, because he had other needs that took precedence over the particular legal one that brought him to me. For example, the client might have felt compelled to deny any involvement in the incident because to admit to having had a sexual encounter might have jeopardized his relationship with the woman with whom he lived. Likewise, he might have decided to "play lawyer," and put forward what he believed to be his best defense. Not understanding the heavy burden of proof on the state in criminal cases, he might have thought that any version

---

[1] The woman was not able to make a positive identification of the gun as the weapon used in the incident.

[2] A student working on the case with me photographed the complainant on the street. My client stated that he could not identify her.

---

[3] The woman had indicated that her assailant opened the door with a key. There was no evidence of a forced entry.

of the facts that showed that he had contact with the woman would be fatal because it would simply be a case of her word against his.

I discussed all of these matters with the client on several occasions. Judging him a man of intelligence, with no signs of mental abnormality, I became convinced that he understood both the seriousness of his situation, and that his exculpation did not depend upon maintaining his initial story. In ensuring that he did understand that, in fact, I came close enough to suggesting the "right" answers to make me a little nervous about the line between subornation of perjury and careful witness preparation, known in the trade as "horseshedding." In the end, however, he held to his original account.

At this point the case was in equipoise for me. I had my suspicions about both the complainant's and the client's version of what had occurred, and I supposed a jury would as well. That problem was theirs, however, not mine. All I had to do was present my client's version of what occurred in the best way that I could.

Or was that all that was required? Committed to the adversarial spirit . . . , I decided that it was not. The "different mission" took me beyond the task of presenting my client's position in a legally correct and persuasive manner, to trying to untrack the state's case in any lawful way that occurred to me, regardless of the facts.

With that mission in mind, I concluded that it would be too risky to have the defendant simply take the stand and tell his story, even if it were true. Unless we could create an iron-clad alibi, which seemed unlikely given the strength of the complainant's identification, I thought it was much safer to attack the complainant's story, even if it were true. I felt, however, that since my client had persisted in his original story I was obligated to investigate the alibi defense, although I was fairly certain that I would not use it. My students and I therefore interviewed everyone he mentioned, traveled and timed the route he said he had followed, and attempted to find witnesses who may have seen someone else at the apartment. We discovered nothing helpful. The witness my client identified as being at the bar in New Jersey could not corroborate the client's presence there. The times the client gave were consistent with his presence at the place of the crime when the victim claimed it took place. The

client's aunt verified that he had been with her, but much earlier in the evening.

Because the alibi defense was apparently hopeless, I returned to the original strategy of attempting to undermine the complainant's version of the facts. I demanded a preliminary hearing, in which the complainant would have to testify under oath to the events in question. Her version was precisely as I have described it, and she told it in an objective manner that, far from seeming contrived, convinced me that she was telling the truth. She seemed a person who, if not at home with the meanness of the streets, was resigned to it. To me that explained why she was able to react in what I perceived to be a nonstereotypical manner to the ugly events in which she had been involved.

I explained to my client that we had failed to corroborate his alibi, and that the complainant appeared to be a credible witness. I said that in my view the jury would not believe the alibi, and that if we could not obtain any other information, it might be appropriate to think about a guilty plea, which would at least limit his exposure to punishment. The case, then in the middle of the aimless drift towards resolution that typifies New York's criminal justice system, was left at that.

Some time later, however, my client called me and told me that he had new evidence; his aunt, he said, would testify that he had been with her at the time in question. I was incredulous. I reminded him that at no time during our earlier conversations had he indicated what was plainly a crucial piece of information, despite my not too subtle explanation of the elements of an alibi defense. I told him that when the aunt was initially interviewed with great care on this point, she stated that he was not with her at the time of the crime. Ultimately, I told him that I thought he was lying, and that in my view even if the jury heard the aunt's testimony, they would not believe it.

Whether it was during that session or later that the client admitted his guilt I do not recall. I do recall wondering whether, now that I knew the truth, that should make a difference in the way in which the case was handled. I certainly wished that I did not know it and began to understand, psychologically if not ethically, lawyers who do not want to know their clients' stories.

I did not pause very long to ponder the problem, however, because I concluded that knowing the truth in fact did not make a difference to my defense strategy, other than to put me on notice as to when I might be suborning perjury. Because the mission of the defense attorney was to defeat the prosecution's case, what I knew actually happened was not important otherwise. What did matter was whether a version of the "facts" could be presented that would make a jury doubt the client's guilt.

Viewed in this way, my problem was not that my client's story was false, but that it was not credible, and could not be made to appear so by legal means. To win, we would therefore have to come up with a better theory than the alibi, avoiding perjury in the process. Thus, the defense would have to be made out without the client testifying, since it would be a crime for him to assert a fabricated exculpatory theory under oath. This was not a serious problem, however, because it would not only be possible to prevail without the defendant's testimony, but it would probably be easier to do so. Not everyone is capable of lying successfully on the witness stand, and I did not have the sense that my client would be very good at it.

There were two possible defenses that could be fabricated. The first was mistaken identity. We could argue that the opportunity of the victim to observe the defendant at the time of the original encounter was limited, since it had occurred on a dark street. The woman could be made out to have been in great emotional distress during the incident.[4] Expert testimony would have to be adduced to show the hazards of eyewitness identification. We could demonstrate that an unreliable identification procedure had been used at the precinct. On the other hand, given that the complainant had spent considerable time with the assailant and had led the police back to the defendant's apartment, it seemed doubtful that the mistaken identification ploy would be successful.

The second alternative, consent, was clearly preferable. It would negate the charge of rape

and undermine the robbery case.[5] To prevail, all we would have to do would be to raise a reasonable doubt as to whether he had compelled the woman to have sex with him. The doubt would be based on the scenario that the woman and the defendant met, and she voluntarily returned to his apartment. Her watch, the object of the alleged robbery, was either left there by mistake or, perhaps better, was never there at all.

The consent defense could be made out entirely through cross-examination of the complainant, coupled with argument to the jury about her lack of credibility on the issue of force. I could emphasize the parts of her story that sounded the most curious, such as the defendant's solicitude in taking his victim back to his apartment, and her waiting for her watch when she could have gone immediately to the nearby precinct that she went to later. I could point to her inability to identify the gun she claimed was used (although it was the one actually used), that the allegedly stolen watch was never found, there was no sign of physical violence, and no one heard screaming or any other signs of a struggle. I could also argue as my client had that even if he were reckless enough to rob and rape a woman across the street from his apartment, he would not be so foolish as to bring the victim there. I considered investigating the complainant's background, to take advantage of the right, unencumbered at the time, to impeach her on the basis of her prior unchastity.[6] I did not pursue this, however, because to me this device, although lawful, was fundamentally wrong. No doubt in that respect I lacked zeal, perhaps punishably so.

Even without assassinating this woman's character, however, I could argue that this was

---

[4]This would be one of those safe areas in cross-examination, where the witness was damned no matter what she answered. If she testified that she was distressed, it would make my point that she was making an unreliable identification; if she testified that she was calm, no one would believe her. . . .

[5]Consent is a defense to a charge of rape. E.g., N.Y. Penal Law § 130.05 (McKinney 1975 & Supp. 1987). While consent is not a defense to a robbery charge, N.Y. Penal Law § 160.00–15 (McKinney 1975 & Supp. 1987), if the complainant could be made out to be a liar about the rape, there was a good chance that the jury would not believe her about the stolen watch either.

[6]When this case arose it was common practice to impeach the complainant in rape cases by eliciting details of her prior sexual activities. Subsequently the rules of evidence were amended to require a specific showing of relevance to the facts of the case. *N.Y. Crim. Proc. Law* § 60.42 (McKinney 1981 & Supp. 1987).

simply a case of a casual tryst that went awry. The defendant would not have to prove whether the complainant made the false charge to account for her whereabouts that evening, or to explain what happened to her missing watch. If the jury had reason to doubt the complainant's charges it would be bound to acquit the defendant.

How all of this would have played out at trial cannot be known. Predictably, the case dragged on so long that the prosecutor was forced to offer the unrefusable plea of possession of a gun. As I look back, however, I wonder how I could justify doing what I was planning to do had the case been tried. I was prepared to stand before the jury posing as an officer of the court in search of the truth, while trying to fool the jurors into believing a wholly fabricated story, i.e., that the woman had consented, when in fact she had been forced at gunpoint to have sex with the defendant. I was also prepared to demand an acquittal because the state had not met its burden of proof when, if it had not, it would have been because I made the truth look like a lie. If there is any redeeming social value in permitting an attorney to do such things, I frankly cannot discern it.

Others have discerned it, however, and while they have been criticized, they seem clearly to represent the majority view. They rely on either of two theories. The first is that the lawyer cannot possibly be sufficiently certain of the truth to impose his or her view of it on the client's case. The second is that the defense attorney need not be concerned with the truth even if he or she does know it. Both are misguided.

## Notes and Questions

1. When legal authorities debate the "truth" theory versus the "fight" theory, most take the side of the latter. In *United States* v. *Wade* (388 *U.S.* 218, 1967) Justice Byron White wrote,

> Law enforcement officers have the obligation to convict the guilty and to make sure they do not convict the innocent. They must be dedicated to making the criminal trial a procedure for the ascertainment of the true facts surrounding the commission of the crime. To this extent, our so-called adversary system is not adversary at all; nor should it be. But defense counsel has no comparable obligation to ascertain or present the truth. . . . He must be and is interested in preventing the conviction of the innocent, but . . . we also insist that he defend his client whether he is innocent or guilty. . . . Our interest in not convicting the innocent permits counsel to put the State to its proof, to put the State's case in the worst possible light, regardless of what he thinks or knows to be the truth. . . . [A]s part of the duty imposed on the most honorable defense counsel, we countenance or require conduct which in many instances has little if any, relation to the search for truth.

2. Criminal law examples are typically used to support the "fight" theory. These examples usually invoke rights given to citizens by the U.S. Constitution to inhibit the ready use of state force. What happens to the "fight" theory in civil dispute cases—for example, in divorce, contract disputes, and negligence cases? What about cases of administrative regulation, such as pollution controls, product safety and labeling, workplace safety, antimonopoly regulations, consumer protection, insider stock trading, and campaign contribution regulations? Is zealous legal advocacy as appropriate here as when a defendant's life or liberty is at stake? What might adoption of the "truth" theory in these areas do to the adversary process? What would be the lawyer's role?

⁊ With the advent of *Court TV* and the increasing acceptance of news cameras in courtrooms, the public no longer has only fictionalized images of lawyers in movies and on TV to provide an understanding of legal advocacy-in-action. But what almost no TV program, news or fictional, covers is the day-to-day routine, low-profile, large-scale processing of cases in a big city criminal court. Here lawyers on opposing sides grind through their days handling overwhelming caseloads of largely poor defendants by negotiating guilt and punishment through plea bargaining. The following reading tells that story and highlights more questions about advocacy, justice, truth, and society's interests in the processes and outcomes of law through combat advocacy.

## 13.4   "I Have Nothing to Do with Justice"   *James Mills*

MARTIN ERDMANN THINKS HE might be antisocial. When he was 6 he liked to sneak across his family's red-carpeted, spiral-staircased entrance hall to the potted palm, and spit in it. At Yankee Stadium, he rooted for the Red Sox. When he went to Dartmouth, he cheered for Yale. He didn't make a lot of friends. He says he doesn't need them. Today he's 57 years old, an unmarried millionaire lawyer, and he has defended more criminals than anyone else in the world. Because he is one of the five or 10 best defense lawyers in New York, he gets those criminals turned back into the streets months or years earlier than they had any right to hope for. His clients are not Mafia bosses or bank embezzlers or suburban executives who've shot their wives. He defends killers, burglars, rapists, robbers—the men people mean when they talk about crime in the streets. Martin Erdmann's clients *are* crime in the streets.

In 25 years, Martin Erdmann has defended more than 100,000 criminals. He has saved them tens of thousands of years in prison and in those years they have robbed, raped, burglarized and murdered tens upon tens of thousands of people. The idea of having had a very personal and direct hand in all that mayhem strikes him as boring and irrelevant. "I have nothing to do with justice," he says. "Justice is not even part of the equation. If you say I have no moral reaction to what I do, you are right."

And *he* is right. As right as our adversary judicial system, as right as jury trials, as right as the presumption of innocence and the Fifth Amendment. If there is a fault in Erdmann's eagerness to free defendants, it is not with Erdmann himself, but with the system. Criminal law to the defense lawyer does not mean equity or fairness or proper punishment or vengeance. It means getting everything he can for his client. And in perhaps 98% of his cases, the clients *are* guilty. Justice is a luxury enjoyed by the district attorney. He alone is sworn "to see that justice is done." The defense lawyer does not bask in the grandeur of any such noble oath. He finds himself most often working for the guilty and for a judicial system based upon the sound but paradoxical principle that the guilty must be freed to protect the innocent.

And Erdmann does free them, as many as he possibly can. He works for the Legal Aid Society, a private organization with a city contract to represent the 179,000 indigent defendants who flood each year into New York City courtrooms. He heads the society's supreme court branch, has 55 lawyers working under him, makes $23,500 a year. Next to the millions left him by his father, a Wall Street bond broker, the money means nothing. Twenty-five years ago, until the accounting office told him he was messing up their books, he kept his paychecks stuffed in a desk drawer. In private practice he could have a six-figure income and, probably, the fame of Edward Bennett Williams, or F. Lee Bailey, or Percy Foreman. He is disgusted when people accuse him of dedication. "That's just plain nonsense. The one word that does *not* describe me is dedicated. I reserve that word for people who do something that requires sacrifice. I don't sacrifice anything. The only reason I'm any good is because I have an ego. I like to win."

Martin Erdmann does not look like a winner. He is slight, unimposing, with balding hair cut short every Monday on his way to work, custom-made suits that come out baggy anyway and a slightly stooped, forward-leaning walk that makes him look in motion like Groucho Marx.

His face is lean, bony, taut-skinned, with thin lips and bulging eyes. He lives in a one-bedroom co-op on Manhattan's East Side, has no television and rarely answers his phone ("I learned that from my father—he could sit in a room for hours with a ringing phone"). He plays chess by post-card, buys Christmas presents from catalogues and seldom goes out except to work and eat. Defendants who ask him for loans, get them. He finances black student scholarships and is listed as a patron of New York's City Center. His only self-indulgences are a 75-acre weekend Connecticut retreat and a one-month-a-year fishing trip, alone, to the Adirondacks. "I discovered a long time ago," he says, "that I am a very self-contained person."

Like most men who are alone without lone-liness, Martin Erdmann is emotionally compact: self-centered, stubborn, at times perverse. He is also a failed idealist. "I had an English professor in college," he says, "who read an essay I wrote and told me, 'Martin, you are looking for better bread than is made of wheat.' I've never forgotten that."

Martin Erdmann gets up at 4:45, reads till 6:30, then subways three miles downtown to the Criminal Court Building. He moves through the dark, empty hallway to his office and unlocks the door. He is there at 7:30, two and a half hours before the courts open, and he is alone. In another 10 or 15 minutes Milton Adler will arrive, his boss, chief attorney in the criminal branch. Then, one or two at a time, come the phone operator and clerks, the other lawyers, the defendants on bail, mothers of men in jail, sick-looking junkies with vomit-stained shirts, frightened people who sit quietly on the seven wooden chairs along the wall, angry people mumbling viciously, insane people dressed in costumes with feathers in their hair.

Before the rush begins, Martin Erdmann sits at his desk in a side office and goes over the folders of the day's cases. Anthony Howard, a 21-year-old Negro, is accused of using a stick and knife to rob a man of his wallet. Howard's mother visits him in jail, brings clean clothes and takes out his laundry. She doesn't know that the greatest danger to her son is not the robbery charge, but the man who sleeps above him in the eight-by-six-foot cell. Robert Phillips, Howard's cellmate, escaped from a state mental hospital seven years ago, was recaptured, released, then arrested for the murder of a 22-year-old girl and an infant boy. After three more years in a mental hospital, he has been declared legally sane and is now awaiting trial for the murders. Erdmann looks over the file. "Prisoners who've been in mental hospitals," he says, "tell me they keep them there until they admit the charges against them. Then they mark them sane and send them down for pleading." He decides to give the Anthony Howard case to Alice Schlesinger, a young lawyer who can still believe her clients are innocent. She's good at what Erdmann calls "hand-holding," giving a defendant and his family more time than the case might need.

Milton Adler walks in and says something about a meeting he went to yesterday with DAs and judges to discuss ways of getting more prisoners out on bail. Erdmann listens and says nothing. What's left of his idealism, the wreckage, he defends against the day's events by affecting an air of playful cynicism. He smiles and laughs and pricks the pretty little bubbles of naïveté that rise around him from other lawyers. Listening to Adler, his face flashes now with the playful-cynic smile. "If they do reduce bail," he says, "it'll be the last they see of the defendants."

Alice Schlesinger appears in the doorway, a small young woman, about 30, with long black hair. She wants to know what she can do to pressure the DA to start the trial of a bailed defendant charged with robbery. "Can't we put the screws to them a little? My client is very nervous and upset. He wants to get the trial over with."

"Well," says Erdmann, "of course you can always make a motion to dismiss for lack of prosecution. Say your client is suffering great emotional stress at having this dreadfully unjust accusation hanging over his head."

"Don't *smile* like that," she says. "He *is* innocent, this time."

Erdmann gets rid of the smile. "Well, you know," he says, "maybe the DA is having a little trouble locating the complainant, and your defendant's on bail anyway, so why urge them to go right out and track him down? Because if they find the complainant and go to trial and if from some extremely unfortunate occurrence your client should be convicted, then he's going to jail and he'll be a lot worse off than just nervous."

She agrees reluctantly and leaves. Erdmann sits silently at his desk, staring into the piles of papers. Then he says, "She has a lot to learn. She'll learn. With some tears, but she'll learn."

Erdmann gathers up the folders and takes the elevator to a courtroom on the 13th floor. He sits in one of the soft upholstered chairs in the jury box and takes another look at the 30 folders of the day's cases: a forgery, robberies (mostly muggings), burglaries, drug sales, assault with a gun, arson, sodomy, an attempted murder. He arranges them on the shelf in front of the jury box and then sits back to await the DAs and the judge. He is alone in the courtroom, a dimly lighted, solemn place—meant to be imposing, it is only oppressive. Brown walls, brown tables, brown church-pew seats soak up what little light the low-watt overhead bulbs surrender.

A DA comes in and Erdmann asks him about a kidnapping case that's approaching trial. "The DA on that one's on trial on another case, Marty. He won't be finished for a month at least."

"Wonderful," Erdmann laughs. "I hope he stays on trial until the complainant's 30. Then it won't look so bad. She was 8 when it happened and she's already 11." The DA shakes his head and walks away. Two more DAs arrive and Erdmann talks to them, joking with them, making gentle fun of them, establishing his presence: twice their age, more experienced, more knowledgeable, more cunning. "There's no question that my reputation is much too high," he says. "It's been carefully cultivated. Myths are very important in this business."

The judge enters: Mitchell Schweitzer, tall, thin, gray-haired, on the bench 26 years, 16 of them working closely with Erdmann. He flashes a look around the room, greeting private lawyers, Erdmann and the two assistant DAs.

The clerk calls a name: "José Santiago!"

Erdmann fumbles through his folders and pulls one out. "He's mine," he says. An assistant DA looks at the rows of folders on his table and picks one up. Erdmann and the DA walk slowly toward the judge's bench, pulling out papers as they go. Erdmann has, among other things, a copy of the complaint and a hand-written interview that another Legal Aid lawyer had earlier with the defendant. The DA has a synopsis of the grand jury testimony and a copy of the defendant's record. With these documents, in the next

three or four minutes, while the defendant himself sits unaware in a detention pen beneath the courtroom, the judge, DA and Erdmann will determine the likelihood of guilt and the amount of time the man will serve.

Trials are obsolete. In New York City only one arrest in thousands ends in trial. The government no longer has time and money to afford the luxury of presuming innocence, nor the belief that the truest way of determining guilt is by jury trial. Today, in effect, the government says to each defendant, "If you will abandon your unsupportable claim of innocence, we will compensate you with a light sentence." The defendant says, "How light?"—and the DA, defense lawyer and judge are drawn together at the bench. The conference there is called "plea bargaining," and it proceeds as the playing of a game, with moves and countermoves, protocol, rules and ritual. Power is in the hands of the prisoners. For as increasing crime has pushed our judicial system to the crumbling edge of chaos and collapse, the defendant himself has emerged as the only man with a helping hand. The government needs guilty pleas to move the cases out of court, and the defendants are selling their guilty pleas for the only currency the government can offer—time. But no matter what sentence is finally agreed upon, the real outcome of this bargaining contest is never truly in doubt. The guilty always win. The innocent always lose.

To play the game well, a lawyer must be ruthless. He is working within, but *against* a system that has been battered to its knees. He must not hesitate to kick it when it's down, and to take every advantage of its weakness. No one is better at the game than Martin Erdmann.

Judge Schweitzer glances through the grand jury extract handed him by the DA, a young bespectacled man named Jack Litman. Then the judge looks up over his glasses. "What are you looking for, Marty?"

Erdmann isn't sure yet. His client is accused of robbing a man on the street after stabbing him in the face, neck, chest, stomach and back. The victim was held from behind by an accomplice. "They have a big identification problem," Erdmann says. He is looking at a copy of a police report. "The DD-5 says the complaining witness refused to look at pictures in the hospital the next day because he said he wouldn't be able to identify the assailants from photographs."

"Your honor," Litman says, "they put 65 stitches in him."

"Just a minute," says the judge, and proceeds to read quickly to Erdmann from the grand jury extract: "They fled into an apartment house, the cop asked the super if he'd seen them, the super said they went into apartment 3-A, the cop went in, placed them under arrest and took them to the hospital where they were identified by the victim." He looks up. Erdmann has never heard the grand jury testimony before, and it hasn't exactly made his day. "So, you see, Marty, it's not such a bad case." He leans back. "I'll tell you what. A year with credit for time served." Santiago already has been in jail for 10 months. With time off for good behavior, that sentence will let him out today. Erdmann agrees. The DA nods and starts stuffing papers back into the folder. "Bring him up," he says.

Santiago's accomplice is brought in with him. Both men are 21, short and defiant-looking. The accomplice, Jesus Rodriguez, has his own lawyer, who now joins Erdmann in agreeing to the sentence. The lawyers explain the offer to the defendants. They tell them that the offer can be made only if they are in fact guilty. Neither the judge nor the DA nor the lawyers themselves would permit an innocent man to plead guilty. Santiago and Rodriguez look bewildered. They say they are innocent, they did nothing. Much mumbling and consternation at the counsel table. Then Schweitzer says, "Would you like a second call?"

"Yes, your honor," says Erdmann. "A second call." The defendants are led out and downstairs to a detention pen. Erdmann looks at Santiago's interview sheet, a mimeographed form with blanks for name, age, address, education, employer, and then at the bottom, space for his version of what happened. Santiago's statement begins, "I am not guilty. I did nothing wrong." He has never been arrested before. He says he and Rodriguez were asleep in their apartment when the police charged in and grabbed them. At his arraignment some weeks ago, he pleaded not guilty.

"Talk to them," Judge Schweitzer suggests. Erdmann and his co-counsel walk over to the door of the pen. A court officer opens it and they step from the court's dark, quiet brownness into a

bright, noisy, butt-littered hallway. The door slams shut behind them. From somewhere below come voices shouting, and the clang of cell doors closing. A guard yells, "On the gate!" and precedes them down a dark stairway to a barred steel door. An inside guard unlocks the door and they walk into a yellow, men's-room-tiled corridor with windows on the left and a large bench-lined cell on the right. Twenty men are in the cell, almost all of them dirty and bearded, some young and frightened sitting alone on the benches, others older, talking, standing, as at home here as on a Harlem street corner. Suddenly the voices stop and the prisoners, like animals expecting to be fed, turn their heads toward Erdmann and his co-counsel. Three other lawyers walk in, too, and in a moment the voices begin again—prisoners and lawyers arguing with each other, explaining, pleading, conning in the jailhouse jargon of pleas and sentences: "I can get you one and one running wild [two years consecutive].... I know a guy got an E and a flat [a Class E felony with a year].... So you want a bullet [a year]? You'll take a bullet? ..."

Erdmann walks to the far end of the cell and Santiago meets him at the bars. Erdmann puts his toe on a cross strip between the bars and balances Santiago's folder and papers on his knee. He takes out a Lucky Strike, lights it and inhales. Santiago watches, and then a sudden rush of words starts violently from his mouth. Erdmann silences him. "First let me find out what I have to know," he says calmly, "and then you can talk as much as you want." Santiago is standing next to a chest-high, steel-plate partition. On the other side of it, a toilet flushes. A few steps away, Rodriguez is talking through the bars to his lawyer.

"If you didn't do anything wrong," Erdmann says to Santiago, "then there's no point even discussing this. You'll go to trial."

Santiago nods desperately. "I ain't done nothing! I was asleep! I *never* been in trouble before." This is the first time since his initial interview seven months ago that he has had a chance to tell his story to a lawyer, and he is frantic to get it all out. Erdmann cannot stop the torrent, and now he does not try. "I never been arrested." Santiago shouts, "never been to jail, never been in *no* trouble, no trouble, *nothing*. We just asleep in the apartment and the police break in and grab us out of bed and take us, we ain't done nothing. I *never* been in trouble, I never saw this man before, and he says we did it. I don't even know what we did, and I been here 10 months, I don't see no lawyer or nothing, I ain't had a shower in two months, we locked up 24 hours a day, I got no shave, no hot food, I ain't *never* been like this before, I can't stand it, I'm going to kill himself, I got to get out, I ain't—"

Now Erdmann interrupts, icily calm, speaking very slowly, foot on the cross strip, drawing on his cigarette. "Well, it's very simple. Either you're guilty or you're not. If you're guilty of anything you can take the plea and they'll give you a year, and under the circumstances that's a very good plea and you ought to take it. If you're *not* guilty, you have to go to trial."

"I'm not guilty." He says it fast, nodding, sure of that.

"Then you should go to trial. But the jury is going to hear that the cop followed you into the building, the super sent him to apartment 3-A, he arrested you there, and the man identified you in the hospital. If they find you guilty, you might get 15 years."

Santiago is unimpressed with all of that. "I'm innocent. I didn't do nothing. But I got to get out of here. I got to—"

"Well, if you *did* do anything and you are a little guilty, they'll give you time served and you'll walk."

That's more like it. "Today? I walk today?"

"If you are guilty of something and you take the plea."

"I'll take the plea. But I didn't do nothing."

"You can't take the plea unless you're guilty of something."

"I want the year. I'm innocent, but I'll take the year. I walk today if I take the year?"

The papers start to fall from Erdmann's knee and he grabs them and settles them back. "You walk if you take the plea, but no one's going to let you take the plea if you aren't guilty."

"But I didn't *do* nothing."

"Then you'll have to stay in and go to trial."

"When will that be?"

"In a couple of months. Maybe longer."

Santiago has a grip on the bars. "You mean if I'm guilty I get out today?"

"Yes." Someone is urinating on the other side of the partition.

"But if I'm innocent, I got to stay in?"

"That's right." The toilet flushes.

It's too much for Santiago. He lets go of the bars, takes a step back, shakes his head, turns around and comes quickly back to the bars. "But, *man*—"

Back upstairs at the bench, Erdmann says to Schweitzer, "He's got no record, your honor, and I've had no admission of guilt. You know I'm very careful with people who have no records—"

"And I am too, Marty, you know that."

"He says he hasn't had a shower in two months, he's in a 24-hour-a-day lockup, and he wants to get out, and I don't blame him."

"Marty, I'm not taking a guilty plea just because he wants a shower."

"Of course not."

"Do you want me to talk to them?"

"I think it might be a good idea, your honor."

Santiago and Rodriguez are brought up again and led into a small jury room adjoining the courtroom. Schweitzer reads the grand jury extract to the defendants, making sure they know the case against them.

Now Rodriguez says he'll take the plea. Schweitzer asks him to tell what happened the night of the robbery. Rodriguez says he and Santiago were on the street and they ran into the complainant and spoke with him and the complainant had a knife in his pocket and ended up getting cut, "but I didn't do nothing."

This departure from the original story, the admission that they had been with the victim and that there was indeed a knife, is enough for Erdmann. He looks at Schweitzer. "Now I'm convinced he's guilty." Schweitzer and Litman go back to court. Erdmann says to Santiago, "Do you want the plea?"

"Yes, man, I *told* you that, I got to get out—"

"Then the judge will ask you certain questions and you have to give the appropriate answers." He nods toward Rodriguez. "He held him and you stabbed him. Let's go."

They return to the courtroom and stand before the bench. Three times Schweitzer asks Santiago if he wants to change his plea, and three times Santiago refuses to answer. What if this is just a ruse to trick him into confessing? In exasperation Schweitzer gives up and moves on to Rodriguez. Rodriguez pleads guilty and is sentenced. Erdmann leans against the clerk's desk, his arms crossed over his chest, his eyes burning into Santiago. This ignorant, stupid, vicious kid has been offered a huge, heaping helping of the Erdmann talent, the experience, the knowledge, the *myth*—and has shoved it away. Erdmann's face is covered with disgust. Through his eyes, way beyond them, is fury—and unclouded, clear contempt.

The defendants are led from the courtroom. The clerk calls a case for a private lawyer, and Erdmann takes advantage of the break to get a cigarette. He goes into a small side room the court officers use for a lounge. The room has lockers, a desk, a refrigerator, toaster and hotplate—all of them old and beaten and scarred. Cops' jackets hang from the chair backs. Erdmann has forgotten Santiago. He stands by the window with his foot up on a radiator and looks across at the Tombs, home of many of his clients, a desperate place of rats and rapes, beatings, murders and, so far this year, six suicides. Eighty percent of the 1,800 men in the Tombs are clients of the Legal Aid Society. A few weeks ago, some of the prisoners, angry at the overcrowding, vermin and lack of official attention, decided to find out what could be accomplished by rioting. The riots were followed by avalanches of studies, committees, investigations and reports—some helpful, some hysterical.

Erdmann is looking at workmen on a Tombs setback clearing away shattered glass and broken furniture from beneath burned-out windows. "It will never be the same," he says. "Once they've found out they can riot and take hostages, it will never be the same. Today defendants are telling the judges what sentences they'll take. I had a guy the other day who told me he knew the system was congested and that they needed guilty pleas, and he was willing to help by pleading guilty for eight months. The guilty are getting great breaks, but the innocent are put under tremendous pressure to take a plea and get out. The innocent suffer and the community suffers.

"If the defendants *really* get together, they've got the system by the balls. If they all decide to plead not guilty, and keep on pleading not guilty, then what will happen? The offered pleas will get lower and lower—six months, three months. If that doesn't work, and they still plead

not guilty, maybe the court will take 15 or 20 and try them and give them the maximum sentences. And if *that* doesn't work—I don't know. I don't know. They have the power, and when they find out, you're in trouble."

Two workmen standing on a plank are lowering themselves on ropes down the side of the Tombs. "Fixing the windows," Erdmann says. "Or escaping."

Forty minutes have been wasted with the stubborn Santiago, and now comes another problem. An Erdmann client named Richard Henderson says he was asleep in a Welfare Department flophouse when another man "pounced" on him with a stick. The other man says he was trying to wake Henderson when Henderson "jumped up like a jack rabbit" and stabbed him in the chest. Henderson is charged with attempted murder.

Erdmann talks to him in the pen hallway just outside the courtroom door. It has started to rain. A casement window, opaque, with chicken wire between the plates, has been cranked open and cold air and rain are blowing in and making things miserable for Henderson. He's a 21-year-old junkie—wire-thin, with deep, lost, wandering eyes, and a face sad and dead, as if all the muscles that could make it laugh or frown or show fear or anger had been cut. He stands there shivering in a dirty white shirt, no socks, no shoelaces, the backs of his shoes pushed in like slippers, hands stiff-armed down into the pockets of beltless khaki pants. Quietly, he tells Erdmann he wants to go to trial.

"Well you certainly have that right. But if you're guilty, I've spoken to the judge, and he'll give you a year with credit for time served. How long have you been in?" Erdmann turns the folder and looks at a date. "Six months. So with good behavior you'll have four left. It simply depends on whether you're guilty of anything or not."

Henderson nods. "Yes, that's why I want a jury trial."

"Why?"

"To find out if I'm innocent or not."

"Don't you know?" Erdmann takes another look in the folder. Henderson was psychiatrically examined at Bellevue Hospital and returned as legally sane.

"No. I don't know. But I have an opinion." His eyes leave Erdmann and begin to examine the hallway. He has withdrawn from the conversation. Erdmann watches him a moment, then brings him back.

"What is your opinion?"

"That I am."

"Well, if you go to trial, it may be four months anyway before you *get* a trial, and then you'll be gambling zero against five or 10 years. And even if you're acquitted, you'll still have done the four months."

Henderson moves his feet and shivers. "I understand," he says meekly. "So I think I'd better do that."

"What?"

"Go to trial."

Erdmann just looks at him, not angry as he was with Santiago, but questioningly, trying to figure him out.

"I think I'd better have a trial," Henderson says.

Erdmann leaves him and walks back into court. "Ready for trial," he announces. "Don't even bother bringing him out." Litman makes a note on his file and they move on to another case.

Erdmann sits down in the jury box. The next few defendants have private lawyers, so he just waits there: watching, smiling, his bulging eyes gently ridiculing those around him who have failed to see as clearly as he into the depths of this charade, and to have found the joke there.

The judge is asking a defendant where he got the loaded gun. "He found it," Erdmann whispers before the man answers.

"I found it," the man says.

"Where?" asks the judge.

"Someone just gave it to him," Erdmann says.

"Someone walked by and handed it to me," says the defendant.

Erdmann smiles. "It's amazing," he says, "how often people rush by defendants and thrust things into their hands—guns, watches, wallets, things like that."

One of the two DAs is Richie Lowe, a black man—young, tall, slender, double-breasted, mod, Afro-haircut. Black defendants coming into court glance quickly around, and they see a white judge, white defense lawyers, white clerk, white stenographer, white guards, and then, over there, at that table over there, a *black,* the *only* black in the room, and he's—the enemy. Lowe, the black kid with a law degree from St. John's, sits next to mil-

lionaire Erdmann with the Wall Street father and Dartmouth and Yale Law.

But the irony is superficial—inside, Erdmann's character belies his background. He says he was "far to the left" of his parents, and he spent much of his youth trying to radicalize them. After law school he went to work in "a stuffy Wall Street law firm" where his first assignment was discovering whether or not a Florida gambling casino had acted legally in denying admittance to a female client's poodle. He quit, spent World War II in the Army and then joined the Legal Aid Society. "When I run into someone I can't place, I just say, 'Good to see you again, when did you get out?' That covers college, the Army and prison."

Guards bring in an old, toothless black man with wild white hair and an endless record of rapes, assaults, sodomy and armed robbery. He's accused of trying to rape a 4-year-old Puerto Rican girl. Some people driving in a car saw the man sitting on a wall with the girl struggling in his lap, and rescued her. Erdmann, Lowe and Judge Schweitzer talk it over. Schweitzer suggests a year. Lowe runs his eyes again over the grand jury extract. He usually goes along with Schweitzer, but this time he balks. "I can't see it, your honor. I just can't see it."

Erdmann speaks a few urging words, but Lowe won't budge. "No," he says, "I just can't see it, your honor. If these people hadn't come by in the car and seen the girl, this could have been—it could have been anything."

Schweitzer, himself under great Appellate Division pressure to dispose of cases, now pressures Lowe, politely, gently. He points out that the girl was not injured.

"I just can't, your honor," Lowe says. "I just can't. This is abhorrent, this—"

Schweitzer breaks in. "It's abhorrent to *me,* too, and it's being discussed *only* in the light of the calendar."

"Your honor, we've been giving away the courthouse for the sake of the calendar. I can't do it. I won't do it." He stuffs his papers back in the folder. "Ready for trial, your honor."

He moves back to the prosecution table and announces for the record, "The people are ready for trial."

Erdmann has been saying nothing. As he passes Lowe's table on his way to the jury box, Lowe says, "Am I being unreasonable, Marty?"

Erdmann stops for a moment, very serious, and then shakes his head. "No, I don't think you are."

Lowe is upset. The next case has not yet been called. He moves around the table, fumbling folders. Then loudly he says, "Your honor, if he takes it *right now* I'll give him a year."

The judge fires Lowe a look. "You'll *recommend* a year. *I'll* give him a year."

Erdmann talks to the defendant at the counsel table. Lowe keeps shaking his head. He is suffering. He takes a step toward the bench. "Your honor," he says desperately, "he should get zip to three, at *least*."

"I *know* he should," Schweitzer says.

Erdmann now stands and for the record makes the customary speech. "Your honor, the defendant at this time wishes to withdraw his plea of not guilty, previously entered, and plead guilty to the second count of the indictment, attempted assault in the second degree, a Class E felony, that plea to cover the entire indictment."

Now it's Lowe's turn to make the speech of acceptance for the people, to accept the Class E felony, the least serious type of felony in the penal code. He stands. "Your honor, the people respectfully recommend acceptance of this plea, feeling that it will provide the court with adequate scope for punishment—" He stops. The next words should be, "in the interest of justice." He sits down and pretends to write something on a folder. Then softly, as if hoping he might not be heard, he speaks down into the table: ". . . in the interest of justice."

He walks over to a visitor. "What do you think about *that*?" he demands. "That took a little *piece* out of me. He got a *year* for trying to *rape* a *4-year-old* girl."

Schweitzer recesses for lunch, and Lowe and Erdmann ride down in the elevator. Lowe is still upset. "What do I tell that girl's mother when she calls me and wants to know what happened to the man who tried to rape her daughter?"

Erdmann smiles, the playful cynic. *Better bread than is made of wheat.* "Tell her, 'No speaka English, no speaka English, no speaka English.'"

Because Manhattan's Criminal Court Building is on the Lower East Side, in the midst of the ethnic no-man's-land where Little Italy collides with Chinatown, it is surrounded by some of the city's best Italian and Chinese restaurants. But every lunch-time Erdmann ignores these and walks two blocks north to Canal Street, a truck-choked crosstown conduit littered with derelicts overflowing from the Bowery, and eats in the sprawling, Formica-filled, tray-crashing chaos of the foulest cafeteria east of Newark. No number of threats, insults or arguments can persuade him into any other eating place. He has, every day, one scoop of cottage cheese, a slice of melon, and one slice of rye bread, buttered. (They give you two slices, want them or not, but he never succumbs.) Today he is at a table with a friend, not a lawyer, who asks how he feels when he goes to trial with a man he knows is guilty, and gets the man freed.

"Lovely! Perfectly beautiful! You're dancing on air and you say to yourself, 'How could that have happened? I must have done a wonderful job!' It's a euphoric feeling. Just to see the look of shock on the judge's face when the jury foreman says 'Not guilty' is worth something. It's the same sense of greed you get if a horse you bet on comes in at 15 to 1. You've beaten the odds, the knowledgeable opinion, the wise people." He laughs. "The exultation of winning dampens any moral feelings you have."

"But what," he is asked, "if you defended a man who had raped and murdered a 5-year-old girl, and he was acquitted and went free, and a year later was arrested for raping and murdering another 5-year-old girl. Would you defend him again with the same vigor?"

"I'm afraid so."

"Why afraid?"

"Because I think most people would disapprove of that."

"Do you care?"

"No."

"It doesn't concern you?"

"I'm not concerned with the crime committed or the consequences of his going free. If I were, I couldn't practice. I'm concerned with seeing that every client gets as good representation as he could if he had $200,000. I don't want him to get screwed just because there wasn't anyone around to see that he not get screwed. If you're a doctor and Hitler comes to you and says you're the one man in the world who can cure him, you do it."

"How much of that is ego?"

"Ninety-nine percent."

Erdmann eats his cottage cheese. An old derelict—bearded, toothless, with swollen lips—puts his tray down next to Erdmann and sits slurping soup and eyeing the untouched slice of rye.

In the courthouse lobby after lunch, Erdmann stops to buy a candy bar. Someone says he saw a story in the *Times* that 5,000 of that brand had been recalled after rodent hair was found in some of them. Erdmann smiles and buys two more.

A court officer sees Erdmann coming down the hall. "Hey, Marty," he yells, "he's on the bench, he's starting to call your cases."

"So what do you want me to do," Erdmann says, "break into a run?"

Guards bring in a 20-year-old girl charged with robbery with a knife. Erdmann is talking to her at the counsel table when Lowe strolls over and says, "Marty, an E and a flat?"

The girl looks at Lowe. "What's he saying, who's he?"

Lowe starts away. "Don't listen to me, I'm the enemy."

She wants to know why she has to go to jail. "Well, rightly or wrongly," Erdmann tells her, "people think they shouldn't be robbed. So when they get robbed, they give a little time." She asks if the year can run concurrent with another sentence pending against her. Erdmann asks Lowe and he agrees. She still hesitates, and finally refuses the offer.

"What's wrong?" Lowe says. "She wanted a year, I gave her a year. She wanted it concurrent, I made it concurrent. It's unreal. They tell us what they want and we're supposed to genuflect."

"José Sanchez!" the clerk calls. A drug-sale case.

"Your honor, he hasn't been seen yet," Erdmann says.

"Let me see the file," Schweitzer says to Lowe.

"Your honor," Erdmann says, "he hasn't even been interviewed. I haven't seen him."

"Well, just let's look at it, Marty," the judge says. He goes over Lowe's file. "It's one sale, Marty. He doesn't have any robberies. Burglaries, petty larceny. Mostly drugs, I'll tell you what, Marty, I'll give him an E and a flat." Lowe agrees.

Erdmann walks into the pen hallway, and they bring up a defendant. "They're offering an E and a flat," Erdmann says to him. "For a single sale, that's about the—"

The defendant looks mystified. He says nothing. The guard interrupts. "This isn't Sanchez, Marty. It's Fernandez."

Erdmann drops his arms in disgust, and without a word he turns and goes back into court and sits down in the jury box. A defendant has in effect been tried, convicted and sentenced before his lawyer even knew what he looked like.

After court, Alice Schlesinger comes into Erdmann's office to brief him on a client of hers, a woman, who will be in Schweitzer's court tomorrow. "She's absolutely not guilty," Alice says. When she leaves, Erdmann's smile turns wistful and nostalgic. "It must be wonderful," he says, "to have an *absolute* sense of who's guilty and who isn't. I wish I had it."

Adler walks into the office. "What can I tell them?" he asks Erdmann. "Jack says he's leaving because the job's making a cynic of him. He says he thought he was going to defend the down-trodden and he finds out they're hostile and they lie to him. So he's leaving. Alice comes to me and says, 'The system's wonderful for the guilty, but for the innocent it's awful. Some of them *must* be innocent.' What do you *say* to that?"

"You say nothing," Erdmann answers, "because it's true."

"No. You say that in a good system of government the vast majority get fair treatment, but there are bound to be a few who don't." He looks at Erdmann. "You think that's sentimental."

"I think you're a Pollyanna."

Adler turns to another man in the office. "He's called me sentimental, and he's called me a Pollyanna. And you know what? It's *true.*"

Erdmann laughs. "What difference does *that* make?"

That night Erdmann goes home, has three Scotches on the rocks, meets a former judge for dinner, has a double Scotch, and thus fortified appears before the judge's evening seminar at the New York University Law School. Ten students are sitting in upholstered, stainless-steel swivel chairs in a red-carpeted conference room—all very new and rich and modern. Erdmann is supposed to tell them about jury selection and trial tactics, subjects on which he is a recognized master.

He unwraps a pack of cigarettes, lights up, and leans close over the table. Two of the students are girls. Most of the men are in jeans and long hair. Erdmann knows the look in their eyes. They think they will have innocent clients, they think they'll be serving their fellow man, the community, justice. They don't know that what they'll be serving is the system. He wants to give them some of the facts of life. "You are salesmen," he begins, "and you are selling a product that no one particularly wants to buy. You are selling a defendant who in all likelihood is guilty." They give him looks. "So you're going to disguise the product, wrap it in the folds of justice, and make it a symbol of justice. You have to convince the jurors that you're sincere, and that the product you are selling is not really this defendant, but justice. You must convince them that your defendant is not on trial. Justice is on trial."

The students are cautious. No one has taken any notes. "Your job is at the beginning and the end of the trial—the jury-picking and the summation. In between comes that ugly mess of evidence. In examining prospective jurors you have to sell your product before they get a look at him, before they hear the evidence. You want also to plant the seeds of your defense, and soften the blow of the prosecution's case. If you know that a cop is going to testify that the defendant stabbed the old lady 89 times, you can't hide from it. You might just as well bring it out yourself, tell them that they're going to hear a police officer testify that the defendant stabbed the old lady 89 times, and then when the testimony comes you will be spared the sudden indrawing of breath. And maybe you can even leave the impression that the cop is lying."

A girl mentions the Tombs riots and asks Erdmann what could be done to give the prisoners speedy trials. During the riots, inmates' demands for less crowding, better food, extermination of rats and vermin were supported even by the hostage guards. But their demands for speedy trials, though they found strong support in the press, were less sincere. Virtually every prisoner in the Tombs is guilty, either of the crime charged or of some lesser but connected crime. He knows that he will either plead guilty or be convicted in a trial, and that he will serve time. He knows, too, that delays will help his case. Witnesses disappear, cops' memories fade, complainants lose their desire for vengeance. As prosecutors see their cases decaying, they lower and lower the pleas. Meanwhile, time served in the Tombs before sentencing counts as part of the sentence. Erdmann wants to explain that to the students, but he knows he will not find many believers.

"Let me disabuse you," he says, "of the idea that the prisoners in the Tombs want speedy trials. Most of them are guilty of something, and the *last* thing they want is a trial. They know that if every case could be tried within 60 days, the pleas of one-to-three for armed robbery would be back up to 15-to-25."

"What about the defendants out on bail?" a student asks.

"People out on bail almost *never* have to go to trial. If you can get your client out on bail, he won't be tried for at least three years, if at all. The case will go from one DA's back drawer to another's until it either dissolves into dust or the DA agrees to a plea of time served."

A student asks about the defense lawyer's responsibility to be honest. That triggers Erdmann's smile. "My *only* responsibility," he says, "is to my client. And not to suborn perjury, and not to lie personally. My client may lie as much as he wants."

So mired have the courts become that there now arises the nightmare possibility of a prisoner sinking forever out of sight in the quicksand of judicial chaos. In the post-riot panic to relieve overcrowding in the Tombs, a special court was set up to facilitate the return to state prisons of inmates who had been brought to the Tombs to await hearings on various motions of appeal. One defendant entered the court in a rage. He was doing 20-to-life at Sing Sing for stabbing someone to death with an umbrella. A year ago he was brought to New York for an appeal hearing. He never got the hearing, and went 11 months without seeing a lawyer. Finally in court—unsure as to when, if ever, he would reappear—he shouted furiously at the judge. Guards moved in around him.

The judge got things sorted out, scheduled the hearing for the following week, and the prisoner was removed. After a year in limbo in the Tombs, he had finally been found. The judge waited until the door closed behind the prisoner, then looked at Erdmann, at the DA and back at Erdmann. He said, "Now there's a man who's got a *beef*."

Since the case of Richard Henderson, the junkie who didn't know if he was guilty, was marked ready for trial, he has been returned each day to the detention pen beneath Schweitzer's courtroom—on the almost nonexistent chance that his lawyer, and the DA assigned to the case, and a judge and courtroom might all become simultaneously available for trial. Each day he sits there in the pen while upstairs in court his case is called and passed, with no more certain consequence than that he will be back again the next day, so that it can be called and passed once more. After several days of this, Erdmann speaks to him again to see if he has changed his mind. He is the same—same clothes, same dead expression, same mad insistence on trial. Erdmann tries to encourage him to take the plea, "if you are guilty of anything."

Henderson still wants a trial.

"What will happen today?" he asks.

"Nothing. They'll set another date for trial, and that date will mean about as much as any date they set, which is nothing. You'll just have to wait in line."

Henderson picks at some mosquito-bite-size scars on his arm. "The other prisoners intimidate me," he says. "They keep asking me about my case, what I did, what I'm in for."

"What do you say?"

"I don't answer them. I don't want to talk about it."

Henderson is adamant. Erdmann leaves him and goes back to court.

Erdmann's disrespect for judges (Schweitzer is a rare exception) is so strong and all-inclusive that it amounts at times to class hatred. When one of his young lawyers was held in contempt and fined $200, Erdmann left Schweitzer's court and rushed to the rescue. He argued with the judge and conned him into withdrawing the penalty. Then, outside the courtroom in the corridor, Erdmann's composure cracked. "He's a bully," he said angrily. "I'll put Tucker [one of his senior lawyers]in there a couple of days and tell him, 'No pleas.' That'll fix *that* wagon." He makes a note, then crumples it up. "No. I'll take it myself—and it'll be on the record this time." Erdmann remembers that two days earlier the judge's car was stolen in front of the courthouse. "I should have told him not to let the theft of his Cadillac upset him so much."

"There are so few trial judges who just judge," Erdmann says, "who rule on questions of law, and leave guilt or innocence to the jury. And Appellate Division judges aren't any better. They're the whores who became madams."

Would he like to be a judge?

"I would like to—just to see if I could be the kind of judge I think a judge should be. But the only way you can get it is to be in politics or buy it—and I don't even know the going price."

Erdmann is still in the hallway fuming over the contempt citation when a lawyer rushes up and says a defendant who has been in the Tombs five months for homicide has been offered time served and probation—and won't take it. Erdmann hurries to the courtroom. The defendant and his girl friend had been playing "hit and run," a ghetto game in which contestants take turns hitting each other with lead pipes. He said he was drunk when he played it and didn't know how hard he was hitting the girl. They both passed out and when he awoke the next morning she was dead. He had no previous record, and the judge is considering the extraordinarily light sentence agreed upon by the lawyer and DA. Neither the judge nor the DA is in a mood for any further haggling from the defendant. Erdmann talks with the defendant and gets the plea quickly accepted. Five months for homicide. As he leaves the courtroom, a DA says, "Marty, you got away with murder."

Erdmann is gleeful. "I always get away with murder."

He goes down to his office. Alice Schlesinger walks by his desk and Erdmann remembers something he saw in the *Times* that morning about Anthony Howard, the man with an insane cellmate whose case he assigned to her three weeks ago.

"Hey, Alice," he calls to her, "congratulations on winning your first case."

She shrugs. A lawyer named James Vinci walks in and Erdmann says to him, "Don't forget to congratulate Alice. She just won her first case."

"Really?" says Vinci. "That's great."

"Yeah," Erdmann laughs. "Anthony Howard. His cellmate strangled him to death last night."

Every evening Martin Erdmann walks crosstown to a small French restaurant in the theater district. He sits always at the same table in a rear

corner, with his back to whatever other customers there are, and he is happiest when there
are none. The owner and his wife are always
pleased to see him, and when he does not come
they call his apartment to see if everything is all
right.

Not long ago he reluctantly agreed to allow
a reporter to join him for dinner. The reporter
asked him if he could be positive after 25 years
that he had ever defended an innocent man.

"No. That you never know. It is much easier
to know guilt than innocence. And anyway, it's
much easier to defend a man if you know he's
guilty. You don't have the responsibility of saving
him from unjust punishment."

"What do you think about the courts today,
the judicial system?"

"I think it's time people were told what's
really going on. Everyone's so cowardly. Nobody
wants to tell the public that the minimeasures
proposed to clear up the mess *won't* do it. If you
only had two roads going in and out of New York
and someone said, 'What can we do about the
traffic problem?' the answer would be, 'Nothing—until we get more roads.' You couldn't help
it by tinkering around with the lights. Well, tinkering with the courts isn't going to help. We
need more courts, more DAs, more Legal Aids,
more judges—and it's going to cost a massive
amount of money. I wonder how much money
you could raise if you could guarantee safety
from mugging and burglary and rape for $50 per
person. Eight million people in New York?
Could you get $20 million? And if you asked for
$20 million to provide a workable system of crim-
inal justice, how much would you get? People are
more interested in their safety than in justice.
They can pay for law and order, or they can be
mugged."

"So what's the solution?"

"I've never really felt it was my problem.
Everything up to now has benefited the defendant, and he's a member of the community, too.
When you say, 'The people versus John Smith'—
well, John Smith is part of the people, too. As a
Legal Aid lawyer, I don't think it's my problem to
make things run smoothly so my clients will get
longer sentences. That's the court's problem."

He stops talking and thinks for a minute.
Something is burning inside. "That's the wrong

attitude, I suppose, but then the Appellate Division has never approached me and asked me
what can be done to improve justice for the *accused*. They *never* ask *that* question. It's just how
can we clear the calendars. It's how can we get
these bastards in jail faster for longer. Not in
those words—*certainly* not. They *never* in all these
years asked, how can we have more justice for
the defendants. That's why I'm not too concerned about the system." He has become angry
and impassioned and now draws back. He con-
centrates on a lamb chop.

"I'm loquacious when I'm tired," he says.

After several minutes, he begins again. "You
know, I really don't think there *is* any solution
to the problem, any more than there is to the
traffic problem. You do what you can within the
problem."

"Is the day coming when the traffic won't
move at all?"

"Yes. If every defendant refused to plead
and demanded a trial, within a year the system
would collapse. There would be three-year delays in reaching trial, prison riots, defendants
would be paroled into the streets."

"What's Martin Erdmann going to do when
that happens?"

"That's an interesting question. It would be
too late by then to do anything. It's going to be
too late very soon."

Every Friday, Erdmann assigns himself to a
courtroom with a half-day calendar and catches
the 1:35 bus for Danbury, Conn. From there he
drives to his estate in Roxbury and spends the
weekend walking, gardening "and talking to myself." He has a three-story house with a junk-
jammed attic, a cellar filled with jarred fruit he
preserved years ago and never ate, and a library
cluttered with unread books and magazines. A
brook runs down from the acres of Scotch pine,
past his garden and under a small bridge to the
country below. He walks along the brook, and
stops on the bridge to stare down at the trout.
He never fishes here. "These are my friends," he
says, "and you don't catch your friends."

Most of the weekend he spends trying to
coax cooperation from the flowers and vegetables. "I worry most about the tomatoes because I
like to eat them. The most difficult is what I
don't grow anymore, roses. They demand con-

stant care and that's why I don't have them." Tulips he likes. He spent a recent four-day weekend putting in 400 bulbs sent by a friend from Holland. "They're not difficult. You just dig 400 holes and put them in and they come up in the spring. The only problem is moles. The moles make runs to eat insects and then the mice use the mole runs to eat the tulip bulbs. Years ago I used to be out with spray guns. And then I figured, what the hell, this is nature, the mice don't know they're not supposed to eat tulip bulbs. So I gave up the spraying. I can't be hostile to something that's just doing what comes naturally."

The tulips are all in, it's 9 A.M., and Erdmann is back in his office going through the *Times*. He is stopped by an item about a former Legal Aid client, a 25-year-old homosexual named Raymond Lavon Moore. Charged with shooting a policeman in a bar, Moore had been in the Tombs 10 months, made 24 appearances in court, and steadfastly refused to plead guilty to anything more serious than a misdemeanor. He went into the Tombs weighing 205 pounds, and wasted slowly down to 155. He had never been in jail before. Five times Moore was removed to hospitals for mental observation, and each time he was returned to the Tombs. He twice tried unsuccessfully to kill himself. For fighting with a guard, Moore was sentenced to 20 days' solitary confinement in a small iron box whose only openings were a barred window and a four-inch-wide glass slit in the door. Last weekend, while Erdmann was on his hands and knees in T-shirt and dungarees digging the 400 tulip holes, Moore stripped the white ticking from his mattress, knotted it into a noose and hanged himself from the barred window.

Erdmann slowly folds the paper around the clipping and without expression hands it across his desk to another lawyer. He says nothing.

That noon, Erdmann is back talking through the bars of the detention pen beneath Schweitzer's courtroom. He's asking a drug pusher if there's someone who will make bail for him.

"I can't get in touch with no one from in here, man."

"Can I?"

"Yeah. My mama in Cincinnati." He is about to give Erdmann the phone number when Erd-

mann moves aside to allow a guard to open the door and insert more prisoners. One of the prisoners is Richard Henderson, the junkie who wants to go to trial. He walks in, foggy and listless, and his momentum carries him to the center of the cell. He stops there, staring straight ahead. He does not move or look around for three minutes. Then he takes two steps to the bench, sits down and puts his hands between his knees. He sits there, rubbing his palms together.

Five hours later, Judge Schweitzer is almost at the end of the day's calendar. The spectators have all left, and no one remains but court personnel. Everyone is tired. To speed things up, Schweitzer has told the guards to bring up everyone left in the pen and keep them in the hall by the door till their names are called. Five come up. Their cases already have been adjourned and what's happening now is more or less a body count to make sure no one is missed.

The last is Henderson. A guard walks him in, holding his arm, and someone says, "That's Henderson. He's been adjourned."

The guard, just four steps into the courtroom when he hears this news, quickly wheels Henderson around and heads him back out the door. Something in the wide, crack-the-whip arc of Henderson's swift passage through the court, something in his dead, unaware, zombie-eyed stare as he banks around the pivoting guard, strikes everyone who sees it as enormously funny. It's strange and it's pathetic, and no one can keep from laughing.

## Notes and Questions

1. Erdmann says at one point, "We need more courts, more DAs, more Legal Aids, more judges . . ." and at another point, "It's just how can we clear the calendars. It's how can we get these bastards in jail faster for longer. . . . They *never* in all these years asked, how can we have more justice for the defendants." How will the provision of more courts and the like result in more justice if justice is *not* just a matter of "clearing the calendars"?

2. Do you feel that Erdmann is justified in obstructing the DA and the judge even to the point of the system's collapse if he believes that the defendant is not getting justice?

3. Why are the judge and the lawyers careful to get the defendant to state a guilty plea openly in court?

4. What are the underlying goals of the state in plea bargaining: rehabilitation, deterrence, retribution, or something else?

5. Is it proper for a judge or lawyer who has lost faith in the prison system to allow defendants to bargain out of going to prison? Should the conditions in prison influence the sentencing process?

🐦 For most of its history, the legal profession has been a male domain. While there have been some women lawyers in America since colonial days, until recently they were few in number and confined to office practice—certainly not litigators. Now that has changed. We return to Curtis's metaphor of litigation as a game to consider, is it a boy's game? The following reading is from a sociologist's study of the interaction between gender and expectations for practice in the adversarial system.

## 13.5 | Rambo Litigators: Emotional Labor in a Male-Dominated Job

*Jennifer L. Pierce*

Late in the afternoon, I was sitting with Ben and Stan. . . . They were complaining about being litigators, or as they put it, how "litigation turns people into bastards—you don't have any real choices." Stan said that if you don't fit in, you have to get out because you won't be successful. And Ben added, "To be a really good litigator, you have to be a jerk. Sure you can get by being a nice guy, but you'll never be really good or really successful."

Field notes

THE COMMENTS MADE BY these two young lawyers suggest that the legal profession often requires behavior that is offensive not only to other people, but to oneself: "To be a really good litigator, you have to be a jerk." In popular culture and everyday life, jokes and stories abound that characterize lawyers as aggressive, manipulative, unreliable, and unethical. . . . Our popular wisdom is that lawyers are ruthless con artists who are more concerned with making money than they are with fairness. Few consider, as these two

young men do, that the requirements of the profession itself support and reinforce this behavior.

How does the legal profession support such behavior? Legal scholar Carrie Menkel-Meadow suggests that the adversarial model, with its emphasis on "zealous advocacy" and "winning," encourages a "macho ethic" in the courtroom. Lawyers and teachers of trial lawyers argue that the success of litigators depends on their ability to manipulate people's emotions. Trial lawyers must persuade judges and juries and must intimidate witnesses and opposing counsel in the courtroom, in deposition, and in negotiations. The National Institute of Trial Advocacy, for example, devotes a three-week training seminar to teaching lawyers to hone such emotional skills. Furthermore, attorneys recognize that to attract and retain clients they must not only provide a competent professional service, but spend considerable energy wooing potential business as well as listening to current clients, reassuring them and impressing them with their professional competence and expertise. . . .

. . . Litigators make use of their emotions to persuade juries, judges, and witnesses in the courtroom, in depositions, and in communications with opposing counsel and with clients. However, in contrast to the popular image, intimidation and aggression constitute only one component of the emotional labor of lawyering. Lawyers also make use of strategic friendliness, that is, charm or flattery to manipulate others. Despite apparent differences in these two types of emotional labor, both involve the manipulation of others for a specific end—winning a case. While other jobs require the use of manipulation to achieve specific ends, such labor may serve different purposes and be embedded in a different set of relationships. Flight attendants, for example, are trained to be friendly and reassuring to passengers to alleviate their anxiety about flying. However, flight attendants' friendliness takes the form of deference: their relationship to passengers is supportive and subordinate. In litigation the goal of strategic friendliness is to "win over" or dominate another. As professionals who have a monopoly over specialized knowledge, attorneys hold a superordinate position with respect to clients, witnesses, and jurors, and they take a competitive position with other lawyers. To win their cases, trial lawyers must manipulate and ultimately dominate others for their professional ends.

By doing whatever it takes, within the letter of the law, to win a case, lawyers fulfill the goal of zealous advocacy: persuading a third party that the client's interests should prevail. In this way, intimidation and strategic friendliness serve to reproduce and maintain the adversarial model. By exercising dominance and control over others, trial lawyers also reproduce gender relations. The majority of litigators who "do dominance" are men, and those who defer are either women— such as secretaries and paralegals—or men who become feminized in the process of losing. In addition to creating and maintaining a gendered hierarchy, the form such emotional labor takes is itself gendered. It is a masculinized form of emotional labor not only because men do it but because dominance is associated with masculinity in our culture. . . . In the case of trial lawyers, the requirements of the profession deem it appropriate to dominate women as well as other men. Such "conquests" or achievements at once serve the goals of effective advocacy and become means for the trial lawyer to demonstrate his masculinity.

Of course, not all litigators are men. My usage of the masculine pronoun in this chapter is meant to reflect not only that this area of law is male-dominated but also that the norms and idioms of appropriate emotional labor are masculinized. Furthermore, use of *he* highlights the contradictions women trial attorneys face as women in this profession: how can a woman be a woman and a lawyer who strives to prove his masculinity? . . .

## GAMESMANSHIP AND THE ADVERSARIAL MODEL

Popular wisdom and lawyer folklore portray lawyering as a game, and the ability to play as gamesmanship. As one of the trial attorneys I interviewed said,

> The logic of gamesmanship is very interesting to me. I like how you make someone appear to be a liar. You know, you take them down the merry path and before they know it, they've said something pretty stupid. The challenge is getting them to say it without violating the letter of the law.

Lawyering is based on gamesmanship—legal strategy, skill, and expertise. But trial lawyers are much more than chess players; their strategies are not simply cerebral, rational, and calculating moves, but highly emotional, dramatic, flamboyant, shocking presentations that evoke sympathy, distrust, or outrage. In litigation practice, gamesmanship involves the utilization of legal strategy through a presentation of an emotional self that is designed specifically to influence the feelings and judgment of a particular legal audience—the judge, the jury, the witness, or opposing counsel. Furthermore, in my definition, the choices litigators make about selecting a particular strategy are not simply individual; they are institutionally constrained by the structure of the legal profession, by formal and informal professional norms, such as the American Bar Association's Model Code of Professional Responsibility (1982), and by training in trial advocacy, through programs such as those sponsored by the National Institute of Trial Advocacy.

The rules governing gamesmanship derive from the adversarial model that underlies the basic structure of our legal system. This is a method of adjudication in which two advocates (the attorneys) present their sides of the case to an impartial third party (the judge and the jury), who listens to evidence and argument and declares one party the winner. As Menkel-Meadow (1985) observes, the basic assumptions that underlie this set of arrangements are "advocacy, persuasion, hierarchy, competition and binary results (win/lose)." She writes: "The conduct of litigation is relatively similar . . . to a sporting event—there are rules, a referee, an object to the game, and a winner is declared after play is over."

Within this system, the attorney's main objective is to persuade the impartial third party that his client's interests should prevail. However, clients do not always have airtight, defensible cases. How then does the "zealous advocate" protect his client's interests and achieve the desired result? When persuasion by appeal to reason breaks down, an appeal to emotions becomes paramount. . . .

By appealing to emotions, the lawyer becomes a con man. He acts as if he has a defensible case; he puffs himself up; he bolsters his case. Thus, the successful advocate must not only be smart, but . . . he must also be a good actor. . . .

This emphasis on acting is also evident in the courses taught by the National Institute for Trial Advocacy, where neophyte litigators learn the basics of presenting a case for trial. NITA's emphasis is on "learning by doing." Attorneys do not simply read about cases but practice presenting them in a simulated courtroom with a judge, a jury, and witnesses. In this case, doing means acting. As one of the teachers/lawyers said on the first day of class, "Being a good trial lawyer means being a good actor. . . . Trial attorneys love to perform." Acting, in sociological terms, constitutes emotional labor, that is, inducing or suppressing feelings in order to produce an outward countenance that influences the emotions of others. The instructors discuss style, delivery, presentation of self, attitude, and professionalism. Participants, in turn, compare notes about the best way to "handle" judges, jurors, witnesses, clients, and opposing counsel. The efforts of these two groups constitute the teaching and observance of "feeling rules," or professional norms that govern appropriate lawyerly conduct in the courtroom.

The tone of the three-week course I attended in Boulder, Colorado, was set by one of the introductory speakers, a communications expert and actor. He began his lecture by describing his personal "presentation of self":

> Let's see, tall, blond, Scandinavian looking. Can't change that. But let's think about what I can change." He stands erect, imperious, and exclaims, "A Nordic Viking!" The class laughs. He doubles over, limps along the dais, and says in a shaky voice, "A bent, old man." There is more laughter. He stands erect again and begins making exaggerated faces—he smiles, grimaces, frowns; he looks sad, stern, angry. There is more laughter. "So you see, I do have something to work with! Now let's start with you. Everyone stand up." People stand. "Are you a sloucher, do you walk with a ramrod up your. . . . Let's practice by standing for awhile and try thinking confidence. You want to convey confidence in the courtroom! How do you do that?" He addresses one of the students: "No, you do not slouch!" There is more laughter. "Stand tall. . . . Stand tall." He looks around the room. "Have any of you ever heard of animation? Standing tall is great, but—" he pauses and looks significantly at a woman student—"standing tall and looking bored does not convey confidence! How do you convey confidence? It helps to look confident—but you also have to feel confident.

In his lecture, he provided a list of acting techniques that attorneys could use in the courtroom. He encouraged the litigators to practice facial expressions in front of a mirror for at least fifteen minutes a day. However, his lecture was not just a lesson in "surface acting," that is, the display of facial expressions, but in "deep acting," as well. Deep acting is similar to the Stanislavski method, in which the actor induces the actual feeling called upon by the role. NITA's communications expert, for example, encouraged students to visualize themselves in situations where they had felt confident, to "hold on to that feeling" and "project it" into the current situation.

The remainder of the three-week course took students through various phases of a hypothetical trial—jury selection, opening and closing statements, direct and cross-examination. In each stage of the trial the lawyer has a slightly different purpose. For example, the objective in jury selection is to uncover the biases and prejudices of the jurors and to develop rapport with them. The opening statement sets the theme for the case, whereas direct examination lays the foundation of evidence for the case. Cross-examination is intended to undermine the credibility of the opposition's witness, and closing represents the final argument. Despite the differing goals of each phase, the means to achieve the lawyer's goals is similar in each case, that is, to attempt to persuade a legal audience to be favorably disposed to one's client through a particular emotional presentation of self.

In their sessions on direct and cross-examination, students were given primarily stylistic rather than substantive responses to their presentations. They were given finer criticisms on the technicalities of their objections and the strength or weakness of their arguments. But in the content analysis of my field notes of each session I found that 50 to 80 percent of comments were directed toward the attorney's particular style. These comments fell into five categories: (1) personal appearance; (2) presentation of self (nice, aggressive, or sincere manner); (3) tone and level of voice; (4) eye contact and (5) rapport with others in the courtroom.

For example, in one of the sessions, Tom, a young student in the class, did a direct examination of a witness to a liquor-store robbery. He solemnly questioned the witness about his work, his special training in enforcing liquor laws, and his approach to determining whether someone was intoxicated. At one point, the witness provided a detail that Tom had not expected, but rather than expressing surprise, Tom appeared nonchalant and continued with his line of questions. At the end of his direct, the teacher provided the following feedback:

> Good background development of witness. Your voice level was appropriate but try modulating it a bit more for emphasis. You also use too many thank you's to the judge. You should ingratiate yourself with the judge, but not overly so. You also made a good recovery when the witness said something unexpected.

When Patricia, a young woman attorney, proceeded nervously through the same direct exam-ination, opposing counsel objected repeatedly to some of her questions, which flustered her. The teacher told her:

> You talk too fast. And, you didn't make enough eye contact with the judge. Plus, you got bogged down in the objections and harassment from opposing counsel. Your recovery was too slow. You've got to be more forceful.

In both these examples, as in most of the sessions I observed, the focus of the comments is not on the questions asked but on how the questions are asked. Tom is told to modulate his voice; Patricia is told not to talk so fast. In addition, the teacher directs attention to rapport with others in the courtroom, particularly the judge. Moreover, the teacher commends Tom for his "recovery," that is, regaining self-composure and control of the witness. He criticizes Patricia, on the other hand, for not recovering well from an aggressive objection made by opposing counsel.

In my fieldwork at NITA and in the two law offices, I found two main types of emotional labor: intimidation and strategic friendliness. Intimidation entails the use of anger and aggression, whereas strategic friendliness utilizes politeness, friendliness, and/or playing dumb. Both types of emotional labor are related to gamesmanship. . . .

Intimidation and strategic friendliness not only serve the goals of the adversarial model but also exemplify a masculine style of emotional labor. They become construed as masculine for several reasons. First, emotional labor in the male-dominated professional strata of the gendered law firm is interpreted as masculine simply because men do it. . . . Male trial attorneys participate in shaping this idiom by describing their battles in the courtroom and with opposing counsel as "macho," "something men get into" and "a male thing." In addition, by treating women lawyers as outsiders and excluding them from professional networks, they further define their job as exclusively male.

The underlying purpose of gamesmanship itself, that is, the control and domination of others through manipulation, reflects a particular cultural conception of masculinity. Connell (1987), for example, describes a hegemonic form of masculinity which emphasizes the domination of a certain class of men—middle- to upper-middle-class—over other men and over women. Connell's cultural conception of masculinity dovetails neatly with feminist psychoanalytic accounts that interpret domination as a means of asserting one's masculinity. The lawyers I studied also employed a ritual of degradation and humiliation against other men and women who were witnesses, opposing counsel, and, in some cases, clients. . . .

## INTIMIDATION

> Litigation is war. The lawyer is a gladiator and the object is to wipe out the other side.
>
> Cleveland lawyer quoted in the *New York Times,* August 5, 1988

The most common form of emotional labor associated with lawyers is intimidation. In popular culture, the tough, hard-hitting, and aggressive trial lawyer is portrayed in television shows such as *L.A. Law* and *Perry Mason* and in movies such as *The Firm, A Few Good Men,* and *Presumed Innocent.* The news media's focus on famous trial attorneys such as Arthur Liman, the prosecutor of Oliver North in the Iran-Contra trial, also reinforces this image. Law professor Wayne Brazil (1978) refers to this style of lawyering as the "professional combatant." Others have termed it the "Rambo litigator" (a reference to the highly stylized, super-masculine role Sylvester Stallone plays in his action movies), "legal terrorists," and "barbarians of the bar." Trial attorneys themselves call litigators from large law firms "hired guns." . . .

The recurring figure in these images is not only intimidating but strongly masculine. In the old West, hired guns were sharpshooters; men who were hired to kill other men. The strong, silent movie character Rambo is emblematic of a highly stylized, supermasculinity. . . . Finally, most of the actors who play tough, hard-hitting lawyers in the television shows and movies mentioned above are men. Thus, intimidation is not simply a form of emotional labor associated with trial lawyers, it is a masculinized form of labor. . . .

This stance is tied to the adversarial model's conception of the "zealous advocate." The purpose of this strategy is to intimidate the witness or opposing counsel into submission. A destructive cross-examination is the best example. The trial attorney is taught to intimidate the witness in cross-examination, "to control the witness by never asking a question to which he does not already know the answer and to regard the impeachment of the witness as a highly confrontational act."

In the sections on cross-examination at NITA, teachers trained lawyers to "act mean." The demonstration by the teachers on cross-examination best exemplified this point. Two male instructors reenacted an aggressive cross-examination in a burglary case. The prosecutor relentlessly hammered away until the witness couldn't remember any specific details about the burglar's appearance. At the end of his demonstration, the audience clapped vigorously. Three male students who had been asked to comment responded unanimously and enthusiastically that the prosecutor's approach had been excellent. One student commentator said, "He kept complete control of the witness." Another remarked, "He blasted the witness's testimony." And the third added, "He destroyed the witness's credibility." The fact that a destructive cross-examination served as the demonstration for the entire class underscores the desirability of aggressive behavior as a model for appropriate lawyer-like conduct in this situation. Furthermore, the students' praise for the attorney's tactics collectively reinforce the norm for such behavior.

Teachers emphasized the importance of using aggression to motivate oneself as well. Before a presentation on cross-examination, Tom, one of the students, stood in the hallway with one of the instructors trying to "psyche himself up to get mad." He repeated over and over to himself, "I hate it when witnesses lie to me. It makes me so mad!" The teacher coached him to concentrate on that thought until Tom could actually evoke the feeling of anger. He said later in an interview, "I really felt mad at the witness when I walked into the courtroom." In the actual cross-examination, each time the witness made an inconsistent statement, Tom became more and more angry: "First, you told us you could see the burglar, now you say your vision was obstructed! So, which is it, Mr. Jones?" The more irate he became, the more he intimidated and confused the witness, who at last completely backed down and said, "I don't know" in response to every question. The teacher characterized Tom's performance as "the best in the class" because it was "the most forceful" and "the most intimidating." Students remarked that he deserved to "win the case."

NITA's teachers also utilized mistakes to train students in the rigors of cross-examination. For example, when Laura cross-examined the same witness in the liquor store case, a teacher commented on her performance:

> Too many words. You're asking the witness for information. Don't do that in cross-examination. You tell them what the information is. You want to be destructive in cross-examination. When the other side objects to an answer, you were too nice. Don't be so nice! Next time, ask to talk to the judge, tell him, "This is crucial to my case." You also asked for information when you didn't know the answer. Bad news. You lost control of the witness.

By being nice and losing control of the witness, Laura violated two norms underlying the classic confrontational cross-examination. A destructive cross-examination is meant to impeach the witness's credibility, thereby demonstrating to the jury the weakness in opposing counsel's case. In situations that call for such an aggressive cross-examination, being nice implies that the lawyer likes the witness and agrees with her testimony. By not being aggressive, Laura created the wrong impression for the jury. Second, Laura lost control of the witness. Rather than guiding the witness through the cross with leading questions that were damaging to opposing counsel's case, she allowed the witness to make his own points. As we will see in the next section of the chapter, being nice can also be used as a strategy for controlling a witness; however, such a strategy is not effective in a destructive cross-examination.

Laura's violation of these norms also serves to highlight the implicitly masculine practices utilized in cross-examination. The repeated phrase, "keeping complete control of the witness," clearly signals the importance of dominating other women and men. Further, the language used to describe obtaining submission— "blasting the witness," "destroying his credibility," pushing him to "back down"—is quite violent. In addition, the successful control of the witness often takes on the character of a sexual conquest. One brutal phrase used repeatedly in this way is "raping the witness." Within this discursive field, men who "control," "destroy," or "rape" the witness are seen as "manly," while those who lose control are feminized as "sissies" and "wimps," or in Laura's case as "too nice." . . .

Masculine images of violence and warfare—destroying, blasting, shredding, slaying, burying—are used repeatedly to characterize the attorney's relationship to legal audiences. They are also used to describe discovery tactics and filing briefs. Discovery tactics such as enormous document requests are referred to as "dropping bombs" or "sending missiles" to the other side. And at the private firm, when a lawyer filed fourteen pretrial motions the week before trial, over three hundred pages of written material, he referred to it as "dumping an avalanche" on the other side.

## STRATEGIC FRIENDLINESS

> Mr. Choate's appeal to the jury began long before final argument. . . . His manner to the jury was that of a friend, a friend solicitous to help them through their tedious investigation; never an expert combatant, intent on victory, and looking upon them as only instruments for its attainment.
>
> (Wellman, 1986 [1903]: 16–17)

The lesson implicit in Wellman's anecdote about famous nineteenth century lawyer Rufus Choate's trial tactics is that friendliness is another important strategy the litigator must learn and use to be successful in the courtroom. Like aggression, the strategic use of friendliness is a feature of gamesmanship, and hence, a component of emotional labor. As Richard, one of the attorney/teachers, at NITA stated, "Lawyers have to be able to vary their styles; they have to be able to have multiple speeds, personalities, and style." In his view, intimidation did not always work, and he proposed an alternative strategy, what he called "the toe-in-the-sand, aw-shucks routine." Rather than adopting an intimidating stance toward the witness, he advocated "playing dumb and innocent": "Say to the witness, 'Gee, I don't know what you mean. Can you explain it again?' until you catch the witness in a mistake or an inconsistent statement." . . .

Being nice, polite, welcoming, playing dumb, or behaving courteously are all ways that a trial lawyer can manipulate the witness in order to create a particular impression for the jury. I term this form of gamesmanship strategic friendliness. Rather than bully or scare the witness into submission, this tactic employs friendliness, politeness and tact. Yet it is simply another form of emotional manipulation of another person for a strategic end—winning one's case. . . .

This emphasis on winning is tied to traditional conceptions of masculinity and competition. Sociologist Mike Messner (1989) argues that achievement in sporting competitions such as football, baseball, and basketball serve as a measure of men's self-worth and their masculinity. This can also be carried over into the workplace. . . .

For litigators, keeping score of wins in the courtroom and the dollar amount of damages or settlement awards allows them to interpret their work as manly. . . . [T]he first question lawyers often asked others after a trial or settlement conference was "Who won the case?" or "How big were the damages?" . . . Trial attorneys who did not "win big" were described as "having no balls," or as being "geeks" or "wimps." The fact that losing is associated with being less than a man suggests that the constant focus on competition and winning is an arena for proving one's masculinity. . . .

Strategic friendliness is also utilized in the cross-examination of sympathetic witnesses. In one of NITA's hypothetical cases, a woman dies of an illness related to her employment. Her husband sues his deceased wife's employer for her medical bills, lost wages, and "lost companionship." One of the damaging facts in the case, which could hurt his claim for "lost companionship," was the fact that he had a girlfriend long before his wife died. In typical combative, adversarial style, some of the student lawyers tried to bring this fact out in cross-examination to discredit his claims about his relationship with his wife. The teacher told one lawyer who presented such an aggressive cross-examination:

> It's too risky to go after him. Don't be so confrontational. And don't ask the judge to reprimand him for not answering the question. This witness is too sensitive. Go easy on him.

The same teacher gave the following comments to another student who had "come on too strong":

> Too stern. Hasn't this guy been through enough already! Handle him with kid gloves. And, don't cut him off. It generates sympathy for him from the jury when you do that. It's difficult to control a sympathetic witness. It's best to use another witness's testimony to impeach him.

And to yet another student:

> Slow down! This is a dramatic witness. Don't lead so much. He's a sympathetic witness— the widower—let him do the talking. Otherwise you look like an insensitive jerk to the jury.

In the cross-examination of a sympathetic witness, teachers advised students to be gentle. Their concern, however, is not for the witness's feelings but for how their treatment of the witness appears to the jury. The jury is already sympathetic to the witness because he is a widower. As a result, the lawyers were advised not to do anything which would make the witness appear more sympathetic and them less so. The one student who did well on this presentation demonstrated great concern for the witness. She gently asked him about his job, his marriage, his wife's job and her illness. Continuing with this gentle approach, she softly asked him whether anyone had been able to provide him comfort during this difficult time, and thus was able to elicit the testimony about the girlfriend in a sensitive manner. By extracting the testimony about the girlfriend, she decreased the jury's sympathy for the bereaved widower. How much companionship did he lose, if he was having an affair? At the same time, because she treated the witness gently, she increased the jury's regard for herself. Her approach is similar to Laura's in utilizing "niceness" as a strategy. However, in Laura's case, being nice was not appropriate to a destructive cross-examination. In the case of cross-examining a sympathetic witness, such an approach is effective.

### Notes and Questions

1. At the time Curtis and Frank wrote their essays, women lawyers were a very small portion of the bar and almost always confined to office practice—never litigators. How do

you think women litigators might react to Pierce's observations? Do you find language in their essays that suggests litigation is a distinctly masculine activity? Would Frank be inclined to view women litigators, as described by Pierce, as more likely to want truth than a fight?

2. Why should anyone care if the role of litigator is better suited to those with masculine characteristics? Is court something more than a modern "gladiatorial ring"?

3. Carrie Menkel-Meadow, in the article cited in the reading, sees a future in which women lawyers may change the adversarial process entirely. She writes:

. . . [T]he growing strength of women's voice in the legal profession may change the adversarial system into a more cooperative, less war-like system of communication between disputants in which solutions are mutually agreed upon rather than dictated by an outsider, won by the victor, and imposed upon the loser. Some seeds of change may already be found in existing alternatives to the litigation model, such as mediation.*

Does this seem plausible to you?

---

*Carrie Menkel-Meadow, "Portia in a Different Voice: Speculations on a Women's Lawyering Process." *Berkeley Women's Law Review* 1, No. 1 (Fall 1985): 39–63.

# Suggested Additional Readings

Abel, Richard L. *American Lawyers*. New York: Oxford University Press, 1989.

Auerbach, Jerome. *Unequal Justice*. New York: Oxford University Press, 1976.

Caplan, Lincoln. *Skadden: Power, Money and the Rise of a Legal Empire*. New York: Farrar, Straus, Giroux, 1993.

Carlin, Jerome E. *Lawyers on Their Own*. New Brunswick, N.J.: Rutgers University Press, 1962.

Galanter, Marc, and Thomas Paley. *Tournament of Lawyers: The Transformation of the Big Law Firm*. Chicago: University of Chicago Press, 1991.

Granfield, Robert. *Making Elite Lawyers: Visions of Law at Harvard and Beyond*. New York: Routledge & Kegan, Paul, 1992.

Harr, Jonathan. *A Civil Action*. New York: Random House, 1995.

Heinz, John P., and Edward O. Laumann. *Chicago Lawyers: The Social Structure of the Bar*. New York: Basic Books, 1983.

Jack, Rand, and Dana Crowley Jack. *Moral Vision and Professional Decisions: The Changing Values of Women and Men Lawyers*. New York: Cambridge University Press, 1989.

Morello, Karen Berger. *The Invisible Bar: The Woman Lawyer in America: 1638 to the Present*. New York: Random House, 1986.

Nelson, Robert L. *Partners with Power: Social Transformation of the Large Law Firm*. Berkeley: University of California Press, 1988.

Pierce, Jennifer. *Gender Trials: Emotional Lives in Contemporary Law Firms*. Berkeley: University of California Press, 1995.

Sarat, Austin, and Stuart Scheingold, eds. *Cause Lawyering: Political Commitments and Professional Responsibilities*. New York: Oxford University Press, 1998.

Spangler, Eve. *Lawyers for Hire: Salaried Professionals at Work*. New Haven, Conn.: Yale University Press, 1986.

Stevens, Robert. *Law School: Legal Education in America from the 1850s to the 1980s*. Chapel Hill: University of North Carolina Press, 1983.

Turow, Scott. *One L*. New York: Putnam's, 1977.

Wilkins, David A. "Everyday Practice Is the Troubling Case: Confronting Context in Legal Ethics" in Austin Sarat, Marianne Constable, David Engel, Valerie Hans, and Susan Lawrence, eds. *Everyday Practice and Trouble Cases*. Chicago: Northwestern University Press, 1998. pp. 68–108.

*A Jury of Whites and Blacks, 1867.* (The Bettmann
Archive, Inc.)

# The Jury

Were I called upon to decide, whether the people had best be omitted in the legislative or in the judiciary department, I would say it is better to leave them out of the legislative. The execution of the laws is more important than the making of them.

Thomas Jefferson

❧ Every culture answers, by its structure as well as by its stated beliefs, the question of how much and in what way the community shall participate in the legal process. The handling of conflict may be separated from the daily round of human existence and entrusted to professionals, or these functions may be widely dispersed among citizens and become a means of expressing current community beliefs and standards of behavior. What is at stake in the answer to this question of participation is the relationship of law to group life and individual autonomy.

From one point of view, of course, it is always "the people" who create conflict by their behavior and define it through their beliefs. But the fragmentation of society, the specialization of labor, and the rise of the state have contributed to such a thorough separation of the legal institution from the rest of society that law cannot be studied without asking questions about community participation. What function does law serve in establishing or reinforcing community cohesion? What role do group values play in determining the scope of individual liberty? Do the standards of judgment imposed by law reflect the values of the population as a whole? Of some special interest group? Of a deity or other source of transcendent morality? How are standards that derive from past wisdom balanced against changes in current values?

The adjudication of conflict—like the making of legislative policy—is a form of governance about which one may ask, "Who is politically sovereign?" But the depth, ambiguity, and complexity of human conflict raise still broader issues, for disputing inevitably involves challenges to a group's beliefs and values, and law authoritatively defines the relationship of the challengers to culture.

Studying the form of community participation in law thus becomes a means to examine an important aspect of culture. In the following chapters, we present materials about the jury. The goal is to learn what we can, not only about how this legal institution functions, but about the society that fashioned and continues to use the jury. What, for example, does a comparison of the ordeal, the jury, and trial by "truth serum" tell us about the origins and ultimate fate of participation? What does the definition of a jury of one's peers tells us about the meaning of America for its multiple subgroups? Here, as with other materials, the reader is invited, in legal philosopher Karl Llewellyn's words, to use the study of conflict and of legal institutions as "a candle to illumine the nature of society."

The Anglo-American legal system is nearly unique in its use of the jury as a forum for the determination of truth and the exploration and expression of community ethics. It is the most visible and, perhaps, the most effective engine in the formal legal system for the deprofessionalization of law.

We begin the examination of jury trials in Chapter 14 with materials intended to place the jury in its historical and cultural context and to provoke speculation about whether changes in the basic values of American culture may eventually render trial by jury vestigial. The materials form a kind of time line, with the historical development of legal institutions paralleling historical changes in culture, and with the "trial of the future" suggesting a culture of the future with which we may be less than comfortable.

Chapter 15 considers the political importance of the jury in our own society and confronts the issue of popular sovereignty directly. Alexis de Tocqueville, a French lawyer and author, observed 170 years ago that in the United States, the jury is essentially a political institution. He pointed out that jury trials also instill legal culture in the minds of ordinary citizens, thus reversing, perhaps, the direction of the flow of political influence so that it moves from legal institutions to people as well as from the people to their legal institutions. How much of Tocqueville's seemingly contradictory description of the jury is accurate today? Does the answer to this question depend on the status of jury nullification, by which jurors can determine both law and fact in a criminal case regardless of the judge's instructions? Readings in Chapter 15 ask us to estimate how much power the jury should have as an instrument of popular participation in law, and what are the political consequences of the jury's power or lack of it. The issue is one that continues to occupy not only legal scholars but populist political organizations, the courts, and students of American society.

New materials on jury selection in Chapter 16 take on added importance in view of the political role of the jury as the voice of community values. The selection of a jury of peers secures fair trials and contributes, if properly done, to the legitimacy of the legal system in the public mind. But defining what constitutes a jury of peers also requires answering the question, "Who belongs to America?" Chapter 16 focuses on problems of jury selection in two areas—race-based challenges to jury participation and the creation of "death-qualified" juries in capital cases. These issues permeate American culture. But the question of who belongs is always thorny in a multicultural society. In the U.S. context, upon its answer may depend not only the adequacy of the jury trial as legal process, but the continuing fairness and vitality of a society in which all are entitled to participate in the ongoing process of defining America.

Finally, materials in Chapter 17 presume that the conclusion has already been reached, based on Chapters 14 to 16, that the jury is an institution of vital importance to the survival of the democratic experiment in the United States. This chapter asks whether jury trial still exists in the United States. The materials in the chapter should help in evaluating whether historical and current changes in the U.S. jury system have contributed to the decline of the jury as a legal and democratic institution. In the overall operation of the legal system, the jury is not very much used. Most civil cases result in out-of-court settlements or trial by judge, and more than 85 percent of criminal cases end in plea bargains rather than jury trials. Still, the jury retains a symbolic significance, and it is used in many of what seem to be the most notable and publicly significant trials. Since we seem to want the jury to be important as a form of public participation in law, it is essential that we examine changes in the jury system to determine whether they enhance or undercut the jury's importance and effectiveness.

Since this introduction begins with a quotation from Thomas Jefferson about the importance of trial by jury in a democracy, it will end by reiterating Alexis de Toqueville's warning about the possible decline of jury trial and its consequences for democracy in America:

> All the sovereigns who have chosen to govern by their own authority, and to direct society instead of obeying its directions, have destroyed or enfeebled the institution of the jury.

Part IV asks how and whether the jury is in decline, what such a decline might mean about the changing nature of American culture, whether the weakening of the trial by jury puts democracy at risk, and finally, who or what stands to benefit from enfeebling the institution of the jury?

# 14   THE JURY IN A CULTURAL CONTEXT

&#10086; At the simplest level, the petit or trial jury is charged with determining the facts and applying the law in a particular case. The grand jury, a somewhat larger group of citizens, has the responsibility of deciding whether the prosecutor has sufficient evidence to warrant making a formal criminal accusation (an indictment) against a person, or, in some cases, whether an indictment should be issued even though a prosecutor has been unwilling to bring charges. To understand the petit jury's function and its relationship to the culture that created and developed it, we begin by examining the jury's predecessors in medieval England to discover what legitimized such an apparently irrational process as the ordeal. What changes would be required in the values of those who used the ordeal, so as to allow them to consider jury trial as anything but heresy? Can we place the Lateran Council of 1215 (which forbade priests to officiate at ordeals) and the *Collins* case of 1968 (in which an appeals judge overturned the use of statistical evidence in a jury trial) on a time line with ordeals, jury trials, and trial by injection in order to trace the development of our cultural beliefs and assumptions? What might such a historical and cultural view of trial by jury teach us about the legal policy issues of today and the nature of law in the future?

In what way do the cultural beliefs that lead us to accept jury trials condition us against accepting other forms of legal decision making? Does the proliferation of what might be called "show trials"—in which the media saturate the public with facts, emotional appeals, and speculations about a crime before, during, and after a trial—undermine trial by jury? Under what conditions might we be willing to abandon the commitment to community participation, through jury service, in formal law? What effects might our shifting cultural values and experiences have on the strengths and weaknesses of the system of trial by jury?

---

## 14.1  The Ordeal As a Vehicle for Divine Intervention in Medieval Europe   *William J. Tewksbury*

THE ORDEAL IS A primitive form of trial used to determine the guilt or innocence of the accused, the result being regarded as a divine or preterhuman judgment. The fundamental idea upon which the ordeal rests is that it is a device for regulating, under conditions of comparative fairness, the primitive law of force. The concept that victory would inure to the right—that divine intervention would prevail on behalf of the innocent—was a belief that was subsequently engrafted upon the concept of the ordeal. The earliest occurrences, which can be referred to as pseudo-ordeals, seem to turn on the idea of brute strength. Such was the wager of battle and other "*bilateral* ordeals" to which both sides had to submit. Only later do we see man,

alleging his innocence and facing his Creator, on trial by himself.

To understand the ordeal and the use for which it was designed, one must recognize the tremendous impact that religion has on the daily lives of the people who rely on it. The usual conception of divine intervention to vindicate innocence and to punish guilt is illustrated through an occurrence which happened in 1626 in France. A master had two servants, one stupid, and the other cunning. The latter stole from the master and so framed the stupid servant that he could not justify himself. The doltish servant, allegedly guilty, was tied to a flagstaff and guarded by the accuser. In the night, the flagstaff broke, the upper part falling upon and killing the guilty cunning servant, leaving the innocent servant unhurt. Beliefs such as this lead to irregular judicial proceedings. One might refer to them as ordeals of chance. The innocence of a man often turned on pure luck.

From William J. Tewksbury, "The Ordeal as a Vehicle for Divine Intervention," in Paul Bohanon, ed., *Law and Warfare* (Garden City, N.Y.: Natural History Press, 1967), pp. 267–70. Reprinted by permission.

## I. ORDEALS BY FIRE AND HEAT

The ordeal of boiling water is important in medieval Europe and elsewhere because it combines the elements of fire and water. Water represents the deluge which was the judgment inflicted upon the wicked of old. Fire represented the fiery doom of the future—the day of judgment. This ordeal compelled the accused with his naked hand to find a small pebble within a caldron of boiling water. After the hand had been plunged into the seething caldron, it was carefully enveloped in a cloth, sealed with the signet of a judge, and three days later was unwrapped. It was at this subsequent unwrapping that the accused's guilt or innocence was announced, determined by the condition of the hand.

A related ordeal was that of the red-hot iron. Two forms of this ordeal were found in medieval Europe. The first, which can best be categorized as one of chance, is the ordeal of the red-hot ploughshares. Ploughshares are heated until they glow and are then placed at certain intervals. The accused walks blindfolded and barefooted through the prescribed course. If he escapes injury, he is acquitted. The second form of the ordeal is more widely discussed. The accused is compelled to carry a piece of hot iron for a given distance. The weight of the iron varies with the magnitude of the crime alleged. If the accused can carry the piece of iron without sustaining any burn, he is regarded as innocent.

## II. ORDEALS BY WATER AND MEANS OTHER THAN A DIRECT APPEAL TO GOD

The basis of the ordeal of cold water was that water, being a pure element, will not receive into her bosom anyone stained with the crime of a false oath. Water was recognized as capable of ascertaining those things which had been injected with untruths. The result seems, today, somewhat anomalous: the guilty floated and the innocent sank.

The success of this ordeal was less than perfect. Throughout the sources on the mode of ordeal were examples of malfunctions. Witches would sink like rocks, while leading members of the community, offering themselves to the rigors of the ordeal to test their validity, would float, often not sinking at all, even with the efforts of the officiating executioner.

Some ordeals were designed for people with some type of infirmity, such as blindness, lameness, or old age. Such people had to endure less trying ordeals to determine their guilt or innocence. A person burdened by such an incapacity is placed in one scale of the balance with an equivalent weight to counterbalance him in the other scale. The accused then went before the administering official, who then addressed a customary adjuration to the ordeal of the balance. The accused ascended the balance again, and if he was lighter than before, he was acquitted. This association of lightness with innocence would seem to be contrary to the European belief that lightness is associated with the Devil, as the Devil was regarded as nothing but a spirit of air.

## III. ORDEAL BY DIRECT APPEAL TO GOD

The ordeal of the cross is characterized by placing two parties, the accused and the accuser, in front of a cross with their arms uplifted. Divine service was performed, and victory was adjudged to the one who was able to maintain his arms in the upraised position for the longest period of time. If this procedure led to a stalemate, the accused was given a piece of bread or cheese over which prayers had been said. If the accused could swallow the consecrated morsel, he was acquitted. We must remember that at the time these ordeals were the vogue, the people had great faith in Christ. The criminal, conscious of his guilt, standing before God and pledging his salvation, was expected to "break" under the weight of his own conscience. The truth of the matter lies in the fact that bread or cheese is difficult to swallow when the saliva secretion in one's mouth is not functioning properly. The exorcisms which were said beforehand were subject only to the imagination of the presiding priest. The more ingenious and devising he was, the more constricted became the throat of the most hardened criminal (as well as God-fearing innocents), and, therefore, the more difficult became the function of swallowing.

It was only a slight modification of the above which resulted in the Eucharist as an ordeal. "He that eateth and drinketh unworthily eateth and drinketh damnation to himself" (I Corinthians XI). When the consecrated wafer was offered under appropriate adjuration, the guilty would not receive it; or if it were taken, immediate convulsions and speedy death would ensue.

The basis for all ordeals is that men are asking for divine help to relieve themselves of the responsibility of decision. The ordeal has as its greatest characteristics the element of certainty. Such dependence on ordeals could be had whenever man waived his own judgment and undertook to test the inscrutable ways of his Creator—i.e., the laws of Nature are to be set aside whenever man chooses to tempt his God with the promise of right and the threat of injustice to be committed in His name. This passing the buck to God was particularly prevalent when there was no evidence as to the crime or where the crime was very difficult to prove judicially. The ordeal offered a ready and satisfactory solution to the doubts of a timid judge. Man believed that God would reverse the laws of Nature to accomplish a specified object.

The ordeal was thoroughly and completely a judicial process. It seems to have been used mostly to supplement deficient evidence and amounts to nothing more than an appeal to God.

⁊ Trial by jury and trial by ordeal could hardly seem less alike; yet like the opposite faces of a coin, they share the same center. The almost mystical reverence in which we hold the jury today is probably neither greater nor less than the public reverence toward the ordeal in its day. Each produces, for a different society, that degree of certainty of truth and acceptability of decision necessary for the settling of disputes and the imposition of authority.

The differences between jury and ordeal are not in their function, but in the underlying cultural values of the societies that these seemingly antithetical institutions served. Medieval England looked to the judgment of God and the power of the Church. Twenty-first century America looks to rationalism, the mystique of technology, and the state. Since trial by jury is the successor to trial by ordeal, we may learn something by examining briefly a historical point of contact between them—thirteenth-century England.

The earliest juries in England were not concerned with determining guilt or innocence or civil liability, but rather with making accusations on behalf of the Crown and thereby extending its authority. At a time when the monarchy was still struggling to bring the private resolution of conflict under its own control through the extension of "law," Henry II, in the Assize of Clarendon, 1166, made the jury of presentment a nationwide phenomenon, and twelve local knights or "free lawful men" of each village were charged with producing accusations of murder, theft, or arson. Having been thus accused, the defendant had to proceed to "the judgment of the water" (ordeal or trial by water).

By the first part of the thirteenth century, something a little more like jury trial as we know it began to appear in murder cases in England. Those who felt that they had been accused of murder "out of spite and hate" could purchase from the king a "writ" entitling them to a trial by twelve "recognitors" on the issue of whether the accusation was malicious. If the recognitors found that it was, no ordeal was required. If the accusation was not found to be malicious, trial by ordeal was prescribed. This preliminary determination, not of guilt but of the good faith of the accusation, began to bring considerable revenue to the royal coffers, as it was claimed more and more as a matter of course by accused murderers seeking to avoid the ordeal.

As this procedure was developing, the Church dealt a heavy blow to the ordeal and gave the jury more room to develop. In 1215, the Fourth Lateran Council forbade the clergy to perform any religious ceremonies in connection with the ordeal. The reason for this decision is unclear, but without this religious seal of approval, this system of determining guilt began to lose its legitimacy, and substantial confusion was created among the king's justices as to how such determinations were to be reached. In the confusion and experimentation that ensued, the jury trial began to emerge as one way of deciding issues of fact. But it was not a jury trial we would recognize today.

The central problem with using what were then called jury trials seems to have been the reluctance of the populace to accept them as a legitimate means of determining guilt. Despite the increased use of juries to determine whether accusations of murder were malicious, the general attitude of most people still seemed to be confidence in the ordeal as the judgment of God and uncertainty about juries' verdicts as the judgment of men. In fact, not until 1275 did the king feel it was reasonable to impose the jury trial even on notorious felons. Up to that point people had to voluntarily accept a jury trial ("throw themselves on the country"), and some endured death by torture (being sandwiched between two boards, which were then slowly loaded with stones) rather than accept trial by jury when conviction meant forfeiture of land and chattels. What was at issue during the formative period of trial by jury was whether this institution could confer legitimacy on decisions or whether it was too inscrutable, heretical, and unfamiliar to be trusted with such an important task.

While this transformation of the mind was beginning, the early jury was at best a makeshift procedure from our point of view. It had not yet been rationalized or even settled in its procedure. In fact, it was very much like the inquisition that preceded it, which made accusations (jury of presentment) or determined the existence of taxable property (the Domesday Book of 1066). Instead of hearing evidence and making an allegedly impartial decision based on the evidence, the jury relied solely on its own knowledge of local affairs. As the king's justices traveled on circuit, they convened a jury in each village; these men were then charged with the duty of determining the guilt or innocence of the accused on the basis of whatever they knew personally or were able to find out on their own. In fact, there were often members of the accusing jury on the trial jury, and what was on trial was probably primarily the person's general reputation in the village. It was not until the 1500s that witnesses were even *allowed* to present information to the jury, and it was almost 1700 before the accused gained the right to compel the attendance of witnesses to help in presenting his or her case. The later history of trial by jury, especially in the United States, can be traced from the *Duncan* case and from Tocqueville's analysis which appear on pages  400-402 .

Whatever its shortcomings from the viewpoint of modern U.S. legal process, the jury did serve the purpose even then of relieving the king's justices of the responsibility of deciding issues of guilt or innocence and civil liability. In so doing, it shifted the focus, though perhaps not the reality, of authority from king to subjects, from rule of man to rule of men and ultimately rule of law. And it began to shift the justification for decisions resolving disputes from God to rational man, an equally inscrutable entity. By the 1700s, the transformation began to be layered over with the Enlightenment philosophy of individualism, rationalism, and what we now call due process of law. The value of privacy and the sanctity of the individual as a decision-maker in private life and political democracy were added early in the United States' experience with juries. Likewise, individual conscience and an awareness of the community's sense of justice became important to the jury's role in law. By 1954 the values that underlay jury trial had become so sacred, yet so little understood, that a scholarly attempt to probe its workings was met with an investigation by the Internal Security Subcommittee of the Senate Judiciary Committee and by legislation forbidding the recording of jury deliberations. Today jury deliberations are as jealously protected as they were in the 1950s, but calls for reducing the cost and time taken by jury trials indicate that perhaps the jury's importance in the American psyche is declining.

Perhaps something about the function of the jury in the legal process requires this protectiveness and even mystery, lest we lose our legitimized decision-making process at the hands of objective consciousness—just as Henry II lost the ordeal in the thirteenth century at the hands of progressive religion. In any case, its symbolic role can be no less important than its practical utility.

## $\boxed{14.2}$ Constitution of the United States, Amendments

### ARTICLE III

SECTION 2. (3) THE trial of all Crimes, except in Cases of Impeachment, shall be by Jury; and such Trial shall be held in the State where the said Crimes shall have been committed; but when not committed within any State, the Trial shall be at such Place or Places as the Congress may by Law have directed.

### AMENDMENT VI (1791)

In all criminal prosecutions, the accused shall enjoy the right to a speedy and public trial, by an impartial jury of the State and district wherein the crime shall have been committed, which district shall have been previously ascertained by law, and to be informed of the nature and cause of the accusation; to be confronted with the witnesses against him; to have compulsory process for obtaining witnesses in his favor, and to have the Assistance of Counsel for his defence.

### AMENDMENT VII (1791)

In Suits at common law, where the value in controversy shall exceed twenty dollars, the right of trial by jury shall be preserved, and no fact tried by jury, shall be otherwise re-examined in any Court of the United States, than according to the rules of the common law.

## $\boxed{14.3}$   People v. Collins   *66 Cal. Rptr. 497, 438 P.2d 33 (S.Ct., 1968)*

SULLIVAN, JUSTICE

WE DEAL HERE WITH the novel question whether evidence of mathematical probability has been properly introduced and used by the prosecution in a criminal case. While we discern no inherent incompatibility between the disciplines of law and mathematics and intend no general disapproval or disparagement of the latter as an auxiliary in the fact-finding processes of the former, we cannot uphold the technique employed in the instant case. As we explain in detail *infra,* the testimony as to mathematical probability infected the case with fatal error and distorted the jury's traditional role of determining guilt or innocence according to long-settled rules. Mathematics, a veritable sorcerer in our computerized society, while assisting the trier of fact in the search for truth, must not cast a spell over him. We conclude that on the record before us defendant should not have had his guilt determined by the odds and that he is entitled to a new trial. We reverse the judgment. . . .

A jury found defendant Malcolm Ricardo Collins and his wife defendant Janet Louise Collins guilty of second degree robbery (Pen. Code, §211, 211a, 1157). Malcolm appeals from the judgment of conviction. Janet has not appealed.

On June 18, 1964, about 11:30 A.M. Mrs. Juanita Brooks, who had been shopping, was walking home along an alley in the San Pedro area of the City of Los Angeles. She was pulling behind her a wicker basket carryall containing groceries and had her purse on top of the packages. She was using a cane. As she stooped down to pick up an empty carton, she was suddenly pushed to the ground by a person whom she neither saw nor heard approach. She was stunned by the fall and felt some pain. She managed to look up and saw a young woman running from the scene. According to Mrs. Brooks the latter appeared to weigh about 145 pounds, was wearing "something dark," and had hair "between dark blonde and a light blonde," but lighter than the color of defendant Janet Collins' hair as it appeared at trial. Immediately after the incident, Mrs. Brooks discovered that her purse, containing between $35 and $40, was missing.

About the same time as the robbery, John Bass, who lived on the street at the end of the alley, was in front of his house watering his lawn. His attention was attracted by "a lot of crying and screaming" coming from the alley. As he looked in that direction, he saw a woman run out of the alley and enter a yellow automobile parked across the street from him. He was unable to give the make of the car. The car started off immediately and pulled wide around another parked vehicle so that in the narrow street it passed within six feet of Bass. The latter then saw that it was being driven by a male Negro, wearing a mustache and beard. At the trial Bass identified defendant as the driver of the yellow automobile. However, an attempt was made to impeach his identification by his admission that at the preliminary hearing he testified to an uncertain identification at the police lineup shortly after the attack on Mrs. Brooks, when defendant was beardless.

In his testimony Bass described the woman who ran from the alley as a Caucasian, slightly over five feet tall, of ordinary build, with her hair in a dark blond ponytail, and wearing dark clothing. He further testified that her ponytail was "just like" one which Janet had in a police photograph taken on June 22, 1964.

In an apparent attempt to bolster the identifications, the prosecutor called an instructor of mathematics at a state college. Through this witness he sought to establish that, assuming the robbery was committed by a Caucasian woman with a blond ponytail who left the scene accompanied by a Negro with a beard and mustache, there was an overwhelming probability that the crime was committed by any couple answering such distinctive characteristics. The witness testified, in substance, to the "product rule," which states that the probability of the joint occurrence of a number of *mutually independent* events is equal to the product of the individual probabilities that each of the events will occur. *Without presenting any statistical evidence whatsoever in support of the probabilities for the factors selected,* the prosecutor then proceeded to have the witness assume probability factors for the various characteristics which he deemed to be shared by the guilty couple and all other couples answering to such distinctive characteristics.[1]

Applying the product rule to his own factors the prosecutor arrived at a probability that there was but one chance in 12 million that any couple possessed the distinctive characteristics of the defendants. Accordingly, under this theory, it was to be inferred that there could be but one chance in 12 million that defendants were innocent and that another equally distinctive couple actually committed the robbery. Expanding on what he had thus purported to suggest as a hypothesis, the prosecutor offered the completely unfounded and improper testimonial assertion that, in his opinion, the factors he had assigned were "conservative estimates" and that, in reality, "the chances of anyone else besides these defendants being there, . . . having every similarity, . . . is somewhat like one in a billion." . . .

Defendant makes two basic contentions before us: First, . . . ; and second, that the introduc-

tion of evidence pertaining to the mathematical theory of probability and the use of the same by the prosecution during the trial was error prejudicial to defendant. We consider the latter claim first.

As we shall explain, the prosecution's introduction and use of mathematical probability statistics injected two fundamental prejudicial errors into the case: (1) The testimony itself lacked an adequate foundation both in evidence and in statistical theory; and (2) the testimony and the manner in which the prosecution used it distracted the jury from its proper and requisite function of weighing the evidence on the issue of guilt, encouraged the jurors to rely upon an engaging but logically irrelevant expert demonstration, foreclosed the possibility of an effective defense by an attorney apparently unschooled in mathematical refinements, and placed the jurors and defense counsel at a disadvantage in sifting relevant fact from inapplicable theory.

We initially consider the defects in the testimony itself. As we have indicated, the specific technique presented through the mathematician's testimony and advanced by the prosecutor to measure the probabilities in question suffered from two basic and pervasive defects—an inadequate evidentiary foundation and an inadequate proof of statistical independence. First, as to the foundation requirement, we find the record devoid of any evidence relating to any of the six individual probability factors used by the prosecutor and ascribed by him to the six characteristics as we have set them out in footnote [1], ante. . . .

We now turn to the second fundamental error caused by the probability testimony. Quite apart from our foregoing objections to the specific technique employed by the prosecution to estimate the probability in question, we think that the entire enterprise upon which the prosecution embarked, and which was directed to the objective of measuring the likelihood of a random couple possessing the characteristics allegedly distinguishing the robbers, was gravely misguided. At best, it might yield an estimate as to how infrequently bearded Negroes drive yellow cars in the company of blonde females with ponytails.

---

[1]Although the prosecutor insisted that the factors he used were only for illustrative purposes—to demonstrate how the probability of the occurrence of mutually independent factors affected the probability that they would occur together—he nevertheless attempted to use factors which he personally related to the distinctive characteristics of defendants. In his argument to the jury he invited the jurors to apply their own factors, and asked defense counsel to suggest what the latter would deem as reasonable. The prosecutor himself proposed the individual probabilities set out in the table below. Although the transcript of the examination of the mathematics instructor and the information volunteered by the prosecutor at that time create some uncertainty as to precisely which of the characteristics the prosecutor assigned to the individual probabilities, he restated in his argument to the jury that they should be as follows:

| Characteristic | Individual probability |
|---|---|
| A.  Partly yellow automobile | 1/10 |
| B.  Man with mustache | 1/4 |
| C.  Girl with ponytail | 1/10 |
| D.  Girl with blonde hair | 1/3 |
| E.  Negro man with beard | 1/10 |
| F.  Interracial couple in car | 1/1000 |

In his brief on appeal defendant agrees that the foregoing appeared on a table presented in the trial court.

Two footnotes have been omitted and the third is renumbered.—ED.

The prosecution's approach, however, could furnish the jury with absolutely no guidance on the crucial issue: *Of the admittedly few such couples, which one, if any, was guilty of committing this robbery?* Probability theory necessarily remains silent on that question, since no mathematical equation can prove beyond a reasonable doubt (1) that the guilty couple in fact possessed the characteristics described by the People's witnesses, or even (2) that only *one* couple possessing those distinctive characteristics could be found in the entire Los Angeles area.

As to the first inherent failing we observe that the prosecution's theory of probability rested on the assumption that the witnesses called by the People had conclusively established that the guilty couple possessed the precise characteristics relied upon by the prosecution. But no mathematical formula could ever establish beyond a reasonable doubt that the prosecution's witnesses correctly observed and accurately described the distinctive features which were employed to link defendants to the crime. . . .

The foregoing risks of error permeate the prosecution's circumstantial case. Traditionally, the jury weighs such risks in evaluating the credibility and probative value of trial testimony, but the likelihood of human error or of falsification obviously cannot be quantified; that likelihood must therefore be excluded from any effort to assign a number to the probability of guilt or innocence. Confronted with an equation which purports to yield a numerical index of probable guilt, few juries could resist the temptation to accord disproportionate weight to that index; only an exceptional juror, and indeed only a defense attorney schooled in mathematics, could successfully keep in mind the fact that the probability computed by the prosecution can represent, at best, the likelihood that a random couple would share the characteristics testified to by the People's witnesses—*not necessarily the characteristics of the actually guilty couple.* . . .

In essence this argument of the prosecutor was calculated to persuade the jury to convict defendants whether or not they were convinced of their guilt to a mortal certainty and beyond a reasonable doubt. (Pen. Code, §1096.) Undoubtedly the jurors were unduly impressed by the mystique of the mathematical demonstration but were unable to assess its relevancy or value. Although we make no appraisal of the proper applications of mathematical techniques in the proof of facts, . . . we have strong feelings that such applications, particularly in a criminal case, must be critically examined in view of the substantial unfairness to a defendant which may result from ill conceived techniques with which the trier of fact is not technically equipped to cope. (See *State v. Sneed, supra,* 414 P.2d 858; Note, *supra,* Duke L.J. 665.) We feel that the technique employed in the case before us falls into the latter category.

We conclude that the court erred in admitting over defendant's objection the evidence pertaining to the mathematical theory of probability and in denying defendant's motion to strike such evidence. . . . [W]e think that under the circumstances the "trial by mathematics" so distorted the role of the jury and so disadvantaged counsel for the defense, as to constitute in itself a miscarriage of justice. After an examination of the entire case, including the evidence, we are of the opinion that it is reasonably probable that a result more favorable to defendant would have been reached in the absence of the above error. . . . The judgment against defendant must therefore be reversed.

The judgment is reversed.

TRAYNOR, C.J., *and* PETERS, TOBRINER, MOSK *and* BURKE, JJ., *concur.* . . .

## 14.4 | The Trial of the Future    *Bernard Botein and Murray A. Gordon*

FOR A LONG TIME science has been deflating our notions about the infallibility of the trial process. More recently, the technicians have gone even further. There have been developed startling, effective techniques for "eavesdropping on man's unconscious," as it has been termed. If these techniques fulfill the expectations of many sober-minded men of science, the laboratory will be equipped to reveal truth much more efficiently and inexorably than the courtroom. We may reach the point where our present methods of resolving legal disputes may seem as archaic and barbaric as trial by ordeal seems to us today, and courtroom procedures as we know them may have to be scrapped.

Because we stand at the threshold of such a possibility, it should be profitable to review briefly the progress of science in the ascertainment of truth and to consider its implications for the administration of law in this country. If science can reproduce truth more reliably and effectively than our present system, we shall not be able long to defer our rendezvous with progress. The judicial test for admitting the fruits of scientific research is whether they have won general acceptance in the appropriate discipline. Because of this stringent test various newer truth-revealing techniques have not yet won admittance to the courthouse, but they are storming its steps. . . .

Fact-finding for trial purposes today depends in large measure upon articulate, communicable testimony reflecting the recollection of witnesses. As indicated, limitations of conscious memory, even aside from the distorting factors of self-interest and partisanship, made this process painfully fallible; and its deficiencies often cannot be cured by cross-examination, that revered rectifier of purposeful fabrication or unwitting error. And many times, even when recollection is accurate, tense and frightened witnesses fail to communicate accurately to judge or jury.

Recent experience with drugs such as scopolamine and the barbiturates (sodium pentothal and sodium amytal), techniques such as hypnosis and devices such as the lie detector should be, accordingly, of profound significance in our current trial procedures. These devices suggest the eventual emergence of scientifically accepted procedures for inducing the full and truthful recollection and the relaxed narration of events. . . .

Narcoanalysis, a term loosely blanketing procedures for interrogating subjects while they are in a state of partial unconsciousness induced by drugs, is the most dramatic of the techniques mentioned. The drugs employed in narcoanalysis serve as central nervous system depressants and thereby lessen inhibitions and other blocks to disclosures. . . .

The slow and limited judicial acceptance of drug-induced revelations must be viewed in the light of similar judicial skepticism which existed and was ultimately dispelled by scientific progress leading eventually to court acceptance of fingerprint evidence, blood tests, and handwriting, X-ray and psychiatric testimony. . . .

. . . The likely timetable of judicial acceptance of drug-induced disclosures will, no doubt, reflect the observation of our outstanding authority on the law of evidence, the late Professor Wigmore: "If there is ever devised a psychological test for the evaluation of witnesses, the law will run to meet it. . . . Whenever the psychologist is ready for the courts, the courts are ready for him."

In short, recent and probable future advances in the technique of inducing revelations by narcoanalysis and the general judicial receptivity to scientifically validated evidence remove this subject from the realm of science-fiction fantasy and dictate a sober consideration of the consequences to the judicial process. . . .

As the novel methods of proof we have discussed assume greater scientific validity, serious questions must also arise as to whether findings of fact, of intention or of motive can be left, as now, to the nonscientific community of judges or juries, or whether that function will be for those whose special skills and training more particularly qualify them to appraise the materials resulting from such methods. Indeed, there would no doubt be agitation for the elimination of judge, jury and courtroom, as we know them, in favor of the more clinical precincts of the technician. . . .

More subtle than the scuttling of the traditional trial process, but probably more critical in its societal implications, would be the effect of truth-revealing techniques on rights of the individual which have long been cherished and associated with protection of his person and dignity. We shall be unable to avoid re-examining the present practice of imposing upon the claimant in a civil action the burden of proving his version by a fair preponderance of the evidence, or requiring the prosecution in a criminal case to prove the defendant guilty beyond a reasonable doubt. The trial process is usually weighted on the side of the defending party. The law places a heavy burden on the complaining party who would enlist its resources to obtain relief. This is particularly true in criminal cases, where society seeks to balance the uneven resources of government and the accused individual so as to protect him from tyrants and powerful masters who possess the means to employ the courts as instruments of oppression.

But what need will remain to such weighting and protective rules, it will be argued, if the management of litigation by the parties themselves become minimal? Constitutional and common law safeguards, such as the provisions against self-incrimination, the presumption of innocence, the right to due process, are all commonly believed to be for the protection of the innocent. Again, what need in law or logic for invoking these protections when science can reliably establish such innocence without them? . . .

It will be contended that since the end to be attained by the provisions of constitutional and common law is protection of the innocent, and since science will accomplish this so much more effectively than all of the legal doctrines laid end to end, *ergo*, this is one end that justifies the means. In such a view the presumption of innocence would be dissolved because it would become unnecessary. Likewise, a major justification

for asserting the right against self-incrimination— that the innocent might become entangled in the toils of the law through his own lip—falls away. The innocent person would no longer have to hack his way through the jungle of uncertainties and technicalities which made all these legal safeguards necessary. He would be able to establish his innocence more easily and directly through science. Indeed, if the reliability of narcoanalysis is demonstrated, but it is not received as evidence, an innocent man ready to submit to the testing may be deemed to be deprived unfairly of the right to clear himself. . . .

. . . [T]he public intuitively looks to those administering justice not only to elicit truth and enforce law, but to satisfy other social and community values. Such protective rules as the privilege against self-incrimination, the presumption of innocence, and the exclusion from evidence of confidential communications between husband and wife, doctor and patient, lawyer and client, all have evolved to maintain the high value the community has set on the grandeur of the individual. Each of these principles subordinates full disclosure of the facts to some other higher social value. . . .

. . . It is . . . frequently the case that where investigatory or trial procedures for the disclosure of facts impinge upon deeply held values sustaining the integrity and the dignity of the individual, those values prevail at the expense of the facts. . .

Each of the techniques associated with narcoanalysis involves dredging facts from the unconscious that the person interrogated might be unwilling consciously to reveal. To that extent, each of these techniques entails an invasion of his privacy, as well as his freedom of will. Each abrades the dignity of man; and such indignities can become contagious, if not epidemic. Our traditional and adversary system of litigation, though it may not prove to be the most exact medium for ascertaining truth, embodies the democratic emphasis upon respect for human dignity at every step of the way. If we do not act to anticipate, it remains for us to await—and not without anxiety—the balance finally to be struck between the service of dignity and of truth in the trial process as truth comes more surely within reach as a result of scientific validation of fact-finding through unconscious disclosures. The issue posed is, in the end, no less than an uneasy search for the character of our society of the future. For the balance finally struck between dignity and truth in our courts will be cast in the image of a society which has opted either for efficiency or for freedom.

## Notes and Questions

1. Tewksbury's analysis of the ordeal as a medieval legal institution reveals something about the epistemology and beliefs of medieval society. The society and its legal process are both based on a belief in Divine intervention. What does trial by jury imply about the epistemology and basic beliefs of the society that spawned it? Is it significant that belief in trial by jury reached its pinnacle in Anglo-American history at the time of the Enlightenment?

2. The cultural values that underlay ordeals (like the different values underlying jury trials) provided the legitimacy that legal decisions need if society is to function. Why did the court in the *Collins* case resist the legitimizing power of statistics, technology, and "hard" science? Was the resistance to statistics based only on their unreliability in the particular case? Or would the judge in *Collins* have rejected even reliable statistics in a situation like this? Does this resistance reflect at all on the values and training of lawyers and judges?

3. If courts today are accepting statistical evidence when it is more properly presented and carefully calculated than it was in *Collins,* does that imply that American society is in the process of rejecting the Enlightenment values of the jury's heyday?

4. Trial by jury is said to involve the use of rational techniques by ordinary citizens in determining facts and applying the law to them. Can the resulting judgments be anything more than probabilistic? If certainty is unattainable, why might the court in *Collins* be opposed to the use of even *reliable* statistical evidence of guilt? What do you think is the judge's opinion of juror values and intelligence?

5. The mysticism involved in ordeals conducted under religious auspices concerned revelation of the Divine will. What mysticism is evoked by statistics? What does the court in *Collins* protect by excluding such mysticism from the trial? Where between Divine revelation and technological proof does the jury's function lie?

6. Consider the Botein and Gordon reading as a portent of things to come in trials and other legal processes aimed at certifying the "truth." What kind of society will we be when these new methods are accepted by law and the public? What values underlie your own resistance to or approval of these new methods?

7. Among the values that underlie the U.S. commitment to trial by jury (including faith in reason and in the judgment of the common person), do privacy, individual dignity, and restriction of police power to reasonable searches have a place? Would a reduction of individual privacy undercut the commitment to trial by jury?

## 15 | THE JURY AS A POLITICAL INSTITUTION

☙ As the previous materials imply, the function of the jury extends beyond determining the facts and applying the law in a particular case. One difficulty inherent in determining the adequacy of technological methods of finding the "truth" is that the jury is really asked to do much more than determine the facts in a particular case and apply to them the law as stated by the judge. The jury injects the community's sense of justice into the judicial process. In the jury room, reaching a verdict requires making judgments about the significance of the facts and the fairness of applying written law in a particular case. Relying on polygraphs, truth serums, and other methods of probing the unconscious of witnesses or defendants implies that no judgment about the significance of these facts is required—that there is no necessary political content to jury decisions. Even the use of technological evidence such as fingerprinting, ballistics, and DNA testing—which do not deal with the consciousness of witnesses or the parties in a trial—may imply to some jurors that there are no normative judgments to be made by a jury in reaching its verdict. The existence of such methods, moreover, might deflect us from considering how the very existence of jury trials is a political phenomenon.

The first reading in this chapter, the *Duncan* case, gives a conservative Supreme Court Justice's view of the historical importance of the jury as a political institution. Seeing the jury described as a protection against government oppression in a democracy is a wake-up call to all those who imagine or hope that democratic self-government can survive without active citizen involvement in law.

In the next reading, written in 1830, Alexis de Tocqueville gives a view of the complexities of the U.S. jury system as a political institution. It is a view that still resonates in the twenty-first century. Tocqueville's perspective may seem contradictory, because it suggests that the jury is both an agent for extending the power and legitimacy of formal law, and an important part of popular political sovereignty in a democracy. But such ambiguity is at the heart of the political functions of jury trial in a democracy. All of this suggests that any discussion of the political function of juries inevitably involves questions of the jury's power and of the jurors' attitude toward their involvement in the jury.

In connection with Tocqueville, you may wish to look at some historical and modern examples of the political significance of the jury system. If so, examine the excerpt from Horwitz's *Transformation of American Law* (pages 461–463), which describes how the politics of the early nineteenth century shaped the jury system to suit the commercial interests of the time. Look also at the piece on modern tort reform legislation by Philip Corboy, which suggests how such reforms may alter the role of the jury for similar antidemocratic reasons. This article appears on pages 465–467.

Following the Tocqueville excerpt, Scheflin's 1972 article discusses the issue of jury nullification, beginning with the unquestioned and unquestionable right of the jury to reach its verdict in a criminal case as a matter of conscience even when that conscience is at odds with the law. In Scheflin and Van Dyke's 1991 article, "Merciful Juries," a populist movement to educate jurors about the power of nullification and to bring the democratic role of the jury out in the open is discussed and evaluated.

Following these materials, we present examples of widely differing jury instructions from two states, one acknowledging the existence of jury nullification and the other implicitly denying it. The 1972 case of *United States* v.

*Dougherty* then discusses the question of how the right of nullification ought to be treated by the trial judge. So that the difficulty and significance of the nullification issue in the *Dougherty* case can be fully appreciated, the case is preceded by "A Call to Resist Illegitimate Authority," which appeared in 1967 as an expression of the anguish and determination of those who, like the defendants in *Dougherty,* sought to end the war in Vietnam.

---

## 15.1 | Duncan v. Louisiana    *391 U.S. 145 (1968)*

MR. JUSTICE WHITE *delivered the opinion of the Court.* APPELLANT, GARY DUNCAN, WAS convicted of simple battery in the Twenty-fifth Judicial District Court of Louisiana. Under Louisiana law simple battery is a misdemeanor, punishable by a maximum of two years' imprisonment and a $300 fine. Appellant sought trial by jury, but because the Louisiana Constitution grants jury trials only in cases in which capital punishment or imprisonment at hard labor may be imposed, the trial judge denied the request. Appellant was convicted and sentenced to serve 60 days in the parish prison and pay a fine of $150. Appellant sought review in the Supreme Court of Louisiana, asserting that the denial of jury trial violated rights guaranteed to him by the United States Constitution. The Supreme Court, finding "[n]o error of law in the ruling complained of," denied appellant a writ of certiorari. . . .

[A]ppellant sought review in this Court, alleging that the Sixth and Fourteenth Amendments to the United States Constitution secure the right to jury trial in state criminal prosecutions where a sentence as long as two years may be imposed. . . .

The test for determining whether a right extended by the Fifth and Sixth Amendments with respect to federal criminal proceedings is also protected against state action by the Fourteenth Amendment has been phrased in a variety of ways in the opinions of this Court. The question has been asked whether a right is among those "fundamental principles of liberty and justice which lie at the base of all our civil and political institutions,'" . . . whether it is "basic to our system of jurisprudence," and whether it is "a fundamental right, essential to a fair trial." The claim before us is that the right to trial by jury guaranteed by the Sixth Amendment meets these tests. The position of Louisiana, on the other hand, is that the Constitution imposes upon the States no duty to give a jury trial in any criminal case, regardless of the seriousness of the crime or the size of the punishment which may be imposed. Because we believe that trial by jury in criminal cases is fundamental to the American scheme of justice, we hold that the Fourteenth Amendment guarantees a right of jury trial in all criminal cases which—were they to be tried in a federal court—would come within the Sixth Amendment's guarantee. Since we consider the appeal before us to be such a case, we hold that the Constitution was violated when appellant's demand for jury trial was refused.

The history of trial by jury in criminal cases has been frequently told.[1] It is sufficient for present purposes to say that by the time our Constitution was written, jury trial in criminal cases had been in existence in England for several centuries and carried impressive credentials traced by many to Magna Carta.[2] Its preservation and proper operation as a protection against ar-

---

[1] E.g., W. Forsyth, History of Trial by Jury (1852); J. Thayer, A Preliminary Treatise on Evidence at the Common Law (1898); W. Holdsworth, History of English Law.

[2] E.g., 4 W. Blackstone, Commentaries on the Laws of England 349 (Cooley ed. 1899). Historians no longer accept this pedigree. See, e.g., 1 F. Pollock & F. Maitland, The History of English Law Before the Time of Edward I, at 173, n. 3 (2d ed. 1909).

bitrary rule were among the major objectives of the revolutionary settlement which was expressed in the Declaration and Bill of Rights of 1689. . . .

Jury trial came to America with English colonists, and received strong support from them. Royal interference with the jury trial was deeply resented. Among the resolutions adopted by the First Congress of the American Colonies (the Stamp Act Congress) on October 19, 1765—resolutions deemed by their authors to state "the most essential rights and liberties of the colonists"—was the declaration:

> That trial by jury is the inherent and invaluable right of every British subject in these colonies.

The First Continental Congress, in the resolve of October 14, 1774, objected to trials before judges dependent upon the Crown alone for their salaries and to trials in England for alleged crimes committed in the colonies; the Congress therefore declared:

> That the respective colonies are entitled to the common law of England, and more especially to the great and inestimable privilege of being tried by their peers of the vicinage, according to the course of that law.

The Declaration of Independence stated solemn objections to the King's making "judges dependent on his will alone, for the tenure of their offices, and the amount and payment of their salaries," to his "depriving us in many cases, of the benefits of Trial by Jury," and to his "transporting us beyond Seas to be tried for pretended offenses." The Constitution itself, in Art. III, §2, commanded:

> The Trial of all Crimes, except in Cases of Impeachment, shall be by Jury; and such Trial shall be held in the State where the said Crimes shall have been committed.

Objections to the Constitution because of the absence of a bill of rights were met by the immediate submission and adoption of the Bill of Rights. Included was the Sixth Amendment which, among other things, provided:

> In all criminal prosecutions, the accused shall enjoy the right to a speedy and public trial, by an impartial jury of the State and district wherein the crime shall have been committed.

The constitutions adopted by the original States guaranteed jury trial. Also, the constitution of every State entering the Union thereafter in one form or another protected the right to jury trial in criminal cases.

Even such skeletal history is impressive support for considering the right to jury trial in criminal cases to be fundamental to our system of justice, an importance frequently recognized in the opinions of this Court. . . .

The guarantees of jury trial in the Federal and State Constitutions reflect a profound judgment about the way in which law should be enforced and justice administered. A right to jury trial is granted to criminal defendants in order to prevent oppression by the Government.

Those who wrote our constitutions knew from history and experience that it was necessary to protect against unfounded criminal charges brought to eliminate enemies and against judges too responsive to the voice of higher authority. The framers of the constitutions strove to create an independent judiciary but insisted upon further protection against arbitrary action. Providing an accused with the right to be tried by a jury of his peers gave him an inestimable safeguard against the corrupt or overzealous prosecutor and against the compliant, biased, or eccentric judge. If the defendant preferred the common-sense judgment of a jury to the more tutored but perhaps less sympathetic reaction of the single judge, he was to have it. Beyond this, the jury trial provisions in the Federal and State Constitutions reflect a fundamental decision about the exercise of official power—a reluctance to entrust plenary powers over the life and liberty of the citizen to one judge or to a group of judges. Fear of unchecked power, so typical of our State and Federal Governments in other respects, found expression in the criminal law in this insistence upon community participation in the determination of guilt or innocence. The deep commitment of the nation to the right of jury trial in serious criminal cases as a defense against arbitrary law enforcement qualifies for protection under the Due Process Clause of the Fourteenth Amendment, and must therefore be respected by the States.

Of course jury trial has "its weaknesses and the potential for misuse." We are aware of the long debate, especially in this century, among those who write about the administration of justice, as to the wisdom of permitting untrained laymen to determine the facts in civil and criminal proceedings. . . .[3] At the heart of the dispute have been express or implicit assertions that juries are incapable of adequately understanding evidence or determining issues of fact, and that they are unpredictable, quixotic, and little better than a roll of dice. Yet, the most recent and exhaustive study of the jury in criminal cases concluded that juries do understand the evidence and come to sound conclusions in most of the cases presented to them and that when juries differ with the result at which the judge would have arrived, it is usually

---

[3]A thorough summary of the arguments that have been made for and against jury trial and an extensive bibliography of the relevant literature is available at Hearings on Recording of Jury Deliberations before the Subcommittee to Investigate the Administration of the Internal Security Act of the Senate Committee on the Judiciary, 84th Cong., 1st Sess., 63-81 (1955). A more selective bibliography appears at H. Kalven, Jr. & H. Zeisel, The American Jury 4, n. 2 (1966).

because they are serving some of the very purposes for which they were created and for which they are now employed.

. . . In determining whether the length of the authorized prison term or the seriousness of other punishment is enough in itself to require a jury trial, we . . . refer to objective criteria, chiefly the existing laws and practices in the nation. In the federal system, petty offenses are defined as those punishable by no more than six months in prison and a $500 fine. In 49 of the 50 States crimes subject to trial without a jury, which occasionally include simple battery, are punishable by no more than one year in jail. Moreover, in the late 18th century in America crimes triable without a jury were for the most part punishable by no more than a six-month prison term, although there appear to have been exceptions to this rule. We need not, however, settle in this case the exact location of the line between petty offenses and serious crimes. It is sufficient for our purposes to hold that a crime punishable by two years in prison is, based on past and contemporary standards in this country, a serious crime and not a petty offense. Consequently, appellant was entitled to a jury trial and it was error to deny it.

The judgment below is reversed and the case is remanded for proceedings not inconsistent with this opinion.

Reversed and remanded.

## 15.2 | Trial by Jury in the United States   *Alexis de Tocqueville*

. . . SINCE MY SUBJECT HAS led me to speak of the administration of justice in the United States, I will not pass over it without referring to the institution of the jury. Trial by jury may be considered in two separate points of view: as a judicial, and as a political institution. . . .

---

From *Democracy in America* by Alexis de Tocqueville, translated by Henry Reeve. Copyright 1945 and renewed 1973 by Alfred A. Knopf, a division of Random House, Inc. Used by permission of Alfred A. Knopf, a division of Random House, Inc. (Some footnotes omitted.)

My present purpose is to consider the jury as a political institution; any other course would divert me from my subject. . . .

. . . The jury is, above all, a political institution, and it must be regarded in this light in order to be duly appreciated.

By the jury I mean a certain number of citizens chosen by lot and invested with a temporary right of judging. Trial by jury, as applied to the repression of crime, appears to me an eminently republican element in the government, for the following reasons.

The institution of the jury may be aristocratic or democratic, according to the class from which the jurors are taken; but it always preserves its republican character, in that it places the real direction of society in the hands of the governed, or of a portion of the governed, and not in that of the government. Force is never more than a transient element of success, and after force comes the notion of right. A government able to reach its enemies only upon a field of battle would soon be destroyed. The true sanction of political laws is to be found in penal legislation; and if that sanction is wanting, the law will sooner or later lose its cogency. He who punishes the criminal is therefore the real master of society. Now, the institution of the jury raises the people itself, or at least a class of citizens, to the bench of judges. The institution of the jury consequently invests the people, or that class of citizens, with the direction of society.

. . . Every American citizen is both an eligible and a legally qualified voter. The jury system as it is understood in America appears to me to be as direct and as extreme a consequence of the sovereignty of the people as universal suffrage. They are two instruments of equal power, which contribute to the supremacy of the majority. All the sovereigns who have chosen to govern by their own authority, and to direct society instead of obeying its directions, have destroyed or enfeebled the institution of the jury. The Tudor monarchs sent to prison jurors who refused to convict, and Napoleon caused them to be selected by his agents.

. . . The jury is preeminently a political institution; it should be regarded as one form of the sovereignty of the people: when that sovereignty is repudiated, it must be rejected, or it must be adapted to the laws by which that sovereignty is established. The jury is that portion of the nation to which the execution of the laws is entrusted, as the legislature is that part of the nation which makes the laws; and in order that society may be governed in a fixed and uniform manner, the list of citizens qualified to serve on juries must increase and diminish with the list of electors. This I hold to be the point of view most worthy of the attention of the legislator; all that remains is merely accessory.

I am so entirely convinced that the jury is preeminently a political institution that I still consider it in this light when it is applied in civil causes. Laws are always unstable unless they are founded upon the customs of a nation: customs are the only durable and resisting power in a people. When the jury is reserved for criminal offenses, the people witness only its occasional action in particular cases; they become accustomed to do without it in the ordinary course of life, and it is considered as an instrument, but not as the only instrument, of obtaining justice.

When, on the contrary, the jury acts also on civil causes, its application is constantly visible; it affects all the interests of the community; everyone co-operates in its work: it thus penetrates into all the usages of life, it fashions the human mind to its peculiar forms, and is gradually associated with the idea of justice itself.

. . . In whatever manner the jury be applied, it cannot fail to exercise a powerful influence upon the national character; but this influence is prodigiously increased when it is introduced into civil causes. The jury, and more especially the civil jury, serves to communicate the spirit of the judges to the minds of all the citizens; and this spirit, with the habits which attend it, is the soundest preparation for free institutions. It imbues all classes with a respect for the thing judged and with the notion of right. If these two elements be removed, the love of independence becomes a mere destructive passion. It teaches men to practice equity; every man learns to judge his neighbor as he would himself be judged. And this is especially true of the jury in civil causes; for while the number of persons who have reason to apprehend a criminal prosecution is small, everyone is liable to have a lawsuit. The jury teaches every man not to recoil before the responsibility of his own actions and impresses him with that manly confidence without which no political virtue can exist. It invests each citizen with a kind of magistracy, it makes them all feel the duties which they are bound to discharge toward society and the part which they take in its government. By obliging men to turn their attention to other affairs than their own, it rubs off that private selfishness which is the rust of society.

The jury contributes powerfully to form the judgment and to increase the natural intelligence of a people; and this, in my opinion, is its greatest advantage. It may be regarded as a gratuitous public school, ever open, in which every juror learns his rights, enters into daily communication with the most learned and enlightened members of the upper classes, and becomes practically acquainted with the laws, which are brought within the reach of his capacity by the efforts of the bar, the advice of the judge, and even the passions of the parties. I think that the practical intelligence and political good sense of the Americans are mainly attributable to the long use that they have made of the jury in civil causes.

I do not know whether the jury is useful to those who have lawsuits, but I am certain it is highly beneficial to those who judge them; and I look upon it as one of the most efficacious means for the education of the people which society can employ.

. . . [I]n civil causes . . . the judge appears as a disinterested arbiter between the conflicting passions of the parties. The jurors look up to him with confidence and listen to him with respect, for in this instance, his intellect entirely governs theirs. It is the judge who sums up the various arguments which have wearied their memory, and who guides them through the devious course of the proceedings; he points their attention to the exact question of fact that they are called upon to decide and tells them how to answer the question of law. His influence over them is almost unlimited. . . .

The jury, then, which seems to restrict the rights of the judiciary, does in reality consolidate its power; and in no country are the judges so powerful as where the people share their privileges. It is especially by means of the jury in civil causes that the American magistrates imbue even the lower classes of society with the spirit of their profession. Thus the jury, which is the most energetic means of making the people rule, is also the most efficacious means of teaching it how to rule well.

## 15.3 | Jury Nullification: The Right to Say No   *Alan Scheflin*

ACCORDING TO THE DOCTRINE of jury nullification, the jurors have the inherent right to set aside the instructions of the judge and to reach a verdict of acquittal based upon their own consciences, and the defendant has the right to have the jury so instructed. There was a time when "conscience" played a legally recognized and significant role in jury deliberations. . . .

In the British colonies, the role of the jury in criminal trials is exemplified by the *Zenger* case. A New York jury in 1735, at the urging of Andrew Hamilton, generally considered to be the foremost lawyer in the Colonies, gave John Peter Zenger his freedom by saying "no" to government repression of dissent. Zenger was the only printer in New York who would print material not authorized by the British mayor. He

Alan Scheflin, "Jury Nullification: The Right to Say No," *Southern California Law Review*, Vol. 45, No. 167, 1972. Reprinted with the permission of the *Southern California Law Review*. (Footnotes omitted.)

published the *New York Weekly Journal*, a newspaper designed to expose some of the corruption among government officials. All of the articles in the papers were unsigned; the only name on the paper was that of its printer, Zenger. Although a grand jury convened by the government refused to indict Zenger, he was arrested and charged by information with seditious libel. Although Zenger did not write any of the articles and it was not clear that he even agreed with their content, had the jury followed the instructions of the court they would have had to find him guilty.

Against this obstacle, Hamilton insisted that the jurors:

> . . . have the right beyond all dispute to determine both the law and the facts, and where they do not doubt of the law, they ought to do so.

He urged the jury "to see with their own eyes, to hear with their own ears, and to make use of their consciences and understanding in judging of the lives, liberties or estate of their fellow subjects." The closing words of his summation to the jury are as vital today as they were when they were uttered over 200 years ago:

> [T]he question before the Court and you gentlemen of the jury, is not of small or private concern, it is not the cause of a poor printer, nor of New York alone, which you are now trying: No! It may in its consequence, affect every freeman that lives under a British government on the main of America. It is the best cause, it is the cause of liberty; and I make no doubt but your upright conduct this day will not only entitle you to the love and esteem of your fellow citizens; but every man who prefers freedom to a life of slavery will bless and honor you as men who have baffled the attempt of tyranny; and, by an impartial and uncorrupt verdict, have laid a noble foundation for securing to ourselves, our posterity, and our neighbors that to which nature and the laws of our country have given us a right—the liberty—both of exposing and opposing arbitrary power (in these parts of the world) at least, by speaking and writing truth.

[In behavior similar to the *Zenger* case] colonial juries regularly refused to enforce the navigation acts designed by the British Parliament to channel all colonial trade through the mother country. Ships impounded by the British for violating the acts were released by colonial juries, often in open disregard of law and fact. In response to this process of jury nullification, the British established courts of vice-admiralty to handle maritime cases, including those arising from violations of the navigation acts. The leading characteristic of these courts was the absence of the jury; this resulted in great bitterness among the colonists and was one of the major grievances which ultimately culminated in the American Revolution.

In the period immediately before the Revolution, jury nullification in the broad sense had become an integral part of the American judicial system. The principle that juries could evaluate and decide questions of both fact and law was accepted by leading jurists of the period.

John Adams, writing in his Diary for February 12, 1771, noted that the jury power to nullify the judge's instructions derives from the general verdict itself, but if a judge's instructions run counter to fundamental constitutional principles

> is a juror obliged to give his verdict generally, according to his direction or even to the fact specially, and submit the law to the court? Every man, of any feeling or conscience, will answer, no. It is not only his right, but his duty, in that case to find the verdict according to his own best understanding, judgment, and conscience, though in direct opposition to the direction of the court.

Adams based this reasoning in part on the democratic principle that "the common people . . . should have as complete a control, as decisive a negative, in every judgment of a court judicature" as they have in other decisions of government. At the time of the adoption of the Constitution, this view of jury nullification prevailed. Without jury nullification, as the Founding Fathers well knew, government by judge (or through the judge by the rulers in power) became a distinct possibility and had in fact been a reality. In the *Zenger* case, two lawyers were held in contempt and ordered disbarred by the judge when they argued that he should not sit because he held his office during the King's "will and pleasure." The Court of Star Chamber was not too distant in memory for the colonists to have forgotten the many perversions perpetrated there in the name of justice and law. It was likely, therefore, that the once unchecked, unresponsive power of the judge would have been limited by the Founding Fathers through some method of public control. One method chosen was the jury function most closely guarded by the colonists: the power to say no to oppressive authority. . . .

Proper understanding of the concept of jury nullification requires it to be viewed as an exercise of discretion in the administration of law and justice. Jury discretion in this context may be a useful check on prosecutorial indiscretion. No system of law can withstand the full application of its principles untempered by considerations of justice, fairness and mercy. Every technical violation of law cannot be punished by a court structure that attempts to be just. As prosecutorial discretion weeds out many of these marginal cases, jury discretion hopefully weeds out the rest.

"Jury lawlessness," according to Dean Roscoe Pound, "is the great corrective" in the administration of law. Thus, the jury stands between the will of the state and the will of the people as the last bastion in law to avoid the barricades in the streets. To a large extent, the jury gives to the judicial system a legitimacy it would otherwise not possess. Judge control of jury verdicts would destroy that legitimacy.

A juror who is forced by the judge's instructions to convict a defendant whose conduct he applauds, or at least feels is justifiable, will lose respect for the legal system which forces him to reach such a result against the dictates of his conscience. The concept of trial by a jury of one's peers is emasculated by denying to the juror his right to act on the basis of his personal morality. For if the jury is the "conscience of the community," how can it be denied the right to function accordingly? A juror compelled to decide against his own judgment will rebel at the system which made him a traitor to himself. No system can be worthy of respect if it is based upon the necessity of forcing the compromise of a man's principles. . . .

If jury discretion leads to a lawless society, as some critics of nullification have argued, what does no discretion lead to? Several years ago the New York police went on "strike" on the Long Island Expressway and ticketed every motorist failing to observe any traffic regulation presently on the books. Though the police did not ticket non-violators, there was still a great outcry against their conduct. While much of the wrath was vented on the devious tactic used to get the raises, much of it was also against the lack of discretion in the enforcement of the laws. Without such discretion, the legal system becomes a mockery. But unlimited discretion in the hands of persons in power can become despotic. Accountability of such discretion to the people is the fundamental principle of democracy. It is also the underlying rationale for jury nullification.

One of the most significant principles of democracy calls for the involvement or participation of the "man in the street" in the formation of public policy. Within the framework of the judicial process, the jury has evolved as an institutional reflection of such a commitment. The "man in the street" becomes the "man in the jury box," and as such sits as the representative of the community in question. As the embodiment of the "conscience of the community" he functionally legitimizes and effectuates the authoritativeness of decisions made by and through the judicial process.

The chief distinguishing characteristic of any democratic system is effective popular control over policymakers. With reference to the judicial process this can mean only one thing: If the "man in the jury box" is to fulfill his role as the representative of the "conscience of the community," participating effectively in the making of public policy, then he must possess the power and the right to check the "misapplication" of any particular value distribution. Beyond this, he must be informed that he has such a power and the constitutional right to exercise it.

Thus, jury service is a two-way street. Community values are injected into the legal system making the application of the law responsive to the needs of the people, and participation on the jury gives the people a feeling of greater involvement in their government which further legitimizes that government. This dual aspect of the concept of the jury, flowing from its role as a political institution in a constitutional democracy, serves to keep both the government and the people in touch with each other. But should there be a divergence of sufficient magnitude, as the Founding Fathers were aware there often is, the jury can serve as a corrective with a final veto power over judicial rigidity, servility or tyranny.

In the words of Thomas Jefferson, "Were I called upon to decide, whether the people had best be omitted in the legislative or in the judiciary department, I would say it is better to leave them out of the legislative. The execution of the laws is more important than the making of them." The power of the people as a community conscience check on governmental despotism is manifested in their ability to sit on juries and limit the thrust of governmental abuse of discretion.

The jury provides an institutional mechanism for working out matters of conscience within the legal system. Jury nullification allows the community to say of a particular law that it is too oppressive or of a particular prosecution that it is too punitive or of a particular defendant that his conduct is too justified for the criminal sanction to be imposed. As William Kunstler put it,

> Unless the jury can exercise its community conscience role, our judicial system will have become so inflexible that the effect may well be a progressive radicalization of protest into channels that will threaten the very continuance of the system itself. To put it another way, the jury is . . . the safety valve that must exist if this society is to be able to accommodate itself to its own internal stresses and strains.

. . . In any politically-charged case where there is a jury acquittal, it is not always clear whether the verdict was a product of the inability of the prosecutor to prove his case beyond a reasonable doubt or rather was a demonstration that the case was so well proven that the real motive for prosecution became all too clear; stifling political dissent. Or the verdict could quite easily be a combination of deficient proof and juror outrage over governmental repression. Because of this ambiguity, and because questions of intent are vague enough to give jurors room to nullify subconsciously by honestly believing that criminal intent is not consistent with good faith resistance to seemingly unjust laws or applications of laws, any description of an acquittal as an instance of jury nullification may not be entirely accurate. . . .

# 15.4 | Merciful Juries: The Resilience of Jury Nullification

*Alan W. Scheflin\* and Jon M. Van Dyke†*

THE POWER OF A jury to soften the harsh commands of the law and return a verdict that corresponds to the community's sense of moral justice has long been recognized.[1] Widely disputed, however, is whether jurors should be told they have this authority. Proponents have seen a right to a jury nullification instruction as an inalienable part of the heritage of democracy, whereas opponents have argued that it is tantamount to anarchy. Although in the past judges did instruct jurors about their role, and judges in Maryland and Indiana still do, most courts now refuse to explain honestly to jurors that they have the ultimate power to decide whether it is appropriate to apply the law to the facts presented to them.

This judicial lack of candor has been periodically challenged; during the past few years a persistent grass roots movement has developed to promote the notion that our juries should be fully informed of their powers. Information about jury nullification has been spreading to an increasingly larger group of citizens and potential jurors. This movement serves to illustrate the resilience of the "jury nullification" concept and its link to fundamental notions of democracy.

This article discusses this new populist movement, analyzes some recent court decisions, reports some of the significant developments related to jury nullification during the past decade, and concludes that our judicial system would be better served if judges instructed jurors of their true powers. . . .

## FROM THE JUDICIAL TO THE POLITICAL ARENA

The controversy over the propriety of a jury nullification instruction lay dormant for most of this century until resurrected in the 1960s as

"Merciful Juries: The Resilience of Jury Nullification" by Scheflin and Van Dyke, *Washington and Lee Law Review,* No. 48, Winter 1991, pp. 165–184. Copyright © 1991. Reprinted by permission. (Some footnotes omitted and the rest renumbered.)

\*Professor of Law, Santa Clara University. B.A. 1963, University of Virginia; J.D. 1966, George Washington University; LL.M. 1967, Harvard University; M.A. in Counseling Psychology 1987, Santa Clara University.

†Professor of Law, William S. Richardson School of Law, University of Hawaii. B.A. 1964, Yale; J.D. 1967, Harvard University. The authors would like to thank Gerald W. Berkley, William S. Richardson School of Law, University of Hawaii, class of 1991, for assistance with research on this article.

[1]*See, e.g.,* Lessard v. State, 719 P.2d 227, 231 (Wyo. 1986) (citing numerous other cases).

part of the defense strategy in anti-Vietnam War demonstration trials.[2] As mentioned above, it did not meet with a warm judicial reception, and most judges still refuse to instruct juries honestly about their nullification power. Such refusal in the 1960s did not significantly undermine the legitimacy of the judiciary because few people knew about nullification. This is no longer true in the 1990s. The jury nullification movement is more active now than at any previous period. Journalists have noted that juries have appeared to invoke their nullification power in many prominent recent cases.[3] More significantly,

frustration with the judicial system, and in particular the perception that judges are dishonest with juries, has caused proponents of jury nullification to seek satisfaction from two more hospitable forums—voters and legislators.

**Voters and Legislators** Debate about jury nullification raises fundamental, and unanswered, questions about sovereignty in a constitutional democracy. It was therefore natural that nullification proponents would seek out the two major forums for lawmaking, the popular vote and legislation.

In the summer of 1989, Larry Dodge, a Montana businessman, joined with his friend Don Doig to found the Fully Informed Jury Association (FIJA). This "national nonprofit nonpartisan group [is] dedicated to jurors being fully informed of their rights."[4] Within eighteen months, the organization had jury rights lobbyists in thirty-five states.[5]

FIJA sponsored the first Bill of Jury Rights Conference in November 1990. The purpose of the gathering was to plan strategy to lobby legislators to enact "fully informed jury" statutes, and to urge voters to pass initiatives, referenda, or constitutional amendments to protect the heritage of the jury's right of nullification. The Conference concluded with a ceremony at the federal courthouse to kick off a national Jury Rights Campaign.

Because public sentiment supports jury nullification, FIJA's appeal spans the political and social spectrum:

> Conservatives and constitutionalists, liberals and progressives, libertarians, populists, greens, gun owners, peace groups, taxpayer rights groups, home schoolers, alternative medicine practitioners, drug decriminalization groups, criminal trial lawyers, seat belt and helmet law activists, environmentalists, women's groups, anti-nuclear groups, ethnic minorities, . . . and judges (yes, some judges are sympathetic).[6] . . .

---

[2]Credit goes to Professor Sax for rekindling the flame of jury nullification. *See* Sax, *supra* note 2.

[3]Among the recent highly publicized trials where jury nullification appears to have played a role are those of Mayor Marion Barry of Washington, D.C., for drug use, Oliver L. North for his role in the Iran-Contra Affair, and Bernhard Goetz for his assault in a New York City subway.

After Mayor Barry's jury returned a conviction for a relatively minor charge and acquittals on the other counts, the trial judge Thomas Penfield Jackson spoke at Harvard Law School and expressed his dismay that the jurors had failed to return more convictions even though the evidence was "overwhelming" on at least a dozen counts. Bruce Fein then wrote a column chastising Judge Jackson for his "acid carping at jurors for nullifying the law." Fein, *Judge, Jury . . . and the Sixth*, Wash. Times, Nov. 8, 1990, at G3. Judge Jackson had said:

> The jury is not a minidemocracy or a minilegislature. They are not to go back and do right as they see fit. That's anarchy. They are supposed to follow the law.

Commentator Fein responded by saying:

> Jury nullification in a particular case is no more a legislative repeal of a criminal law, or anarchy, than are the commonplace decisions of presecutors to resist prosecutions where the crime is deemed inconsequential or mitigated by special circumstances.

*Id.; see also* Thompson, *Sifting the Pool; Juror Questionnaires Explore Drug Addiction, Prejudice,* Wash. Post, June 5, 1990, at A1.

The jury in Oliver North's trial similarly returned a verdict that indicated sympathy with the accused, convicting him on only three of the twelve charges against him. Georgetown University Law Professor Paul F. Rothstein analyzed the trial by saying: "It's jury nullification. . . . The instructions on aiding and abetting left [the jurors] little choice, but I think they sort of vaguely felt in their minds that his superiors ordered it and he was in a bind. . . ." Strasser, *Jury in North's Trial Settled on the Concrete; Abstractions Rejected,* Nat'l. L.J., May 15, 1989, at 9; *see also* Schultz, *supra* note 2.

Regarding the Goetz case and jury nullification, *see* G. Fletcher, *supra* note 9; Pinsley, *Goetz Appeal Explores Jury Nullification Issue,* Manhattan Lawyer, Nov. 1, 1988, at 11; April 5, 1987, sec. 4, at 6, col. 1.

---

[4]Fully Informed Jury Association, Media Handout 2 (Oct. 30, 1990).

[5]Adler, *Courtroom Putsch?,* Wall St. J., Jan. 4, 1991, at A1, col. 1.

[6]The FIJActivist 1 (Special Outreach Issue, 1990).

## JURIDICAL DISHONESTY

Essential to the success of the grass roots jury nullification movement is publicity. People need to be informed about the right to fully informed juries. Jury nullification makes news in most major criminal trials where a clash of values attracts public attention. Articles about jury nullification now appear in newspapers and magazines with great frequency. When the Public Broadcast System (PBS) aired *Inside the Jury Room,* an estimated twenty-five million viewers saw the program. Jury nullification is getting more press coverage than ever before. Millions of people are learning what the judges refuse to tell them.

**Contacting Potential Jurors**   Press coverage has the advantage of reaching many people, but it does so at a time in their lives when the jury nullification issue is not very pressing. For potential jurors, however, information about jury nullification may have a more direct impact on the juror's deliberations.

On January 25, 1990, the *San Diego Reader* published a three-quarter page advertisement[7] with the following headline:

ATTENTION JURORS & FUTURE JURORS
You Can Legally Acquit Anti-Abortion
"Trespassers" Even If They're "Guilty"

The advertisement began by saying "[s]uppose you're on the jury in the trial of pro-life 'rescuers' who blocked the entrances to an abortion facility. The judge will probably tell you it makes no difference whether you agree with their actions. . . . He's Not Telling the Truth." The text went on to praise a Philadelphia jury that had used its "common-law right to 'nullify'" a trespass law.

The timing of the appearance of the advertisement was well planned. Trials were beginning for Operation Rescue defendants accused of trespass and other offenses at the site of a medical clinic. That the advertisement was designed to influence jury verdicts cannot be in doubt. Indeed, the publisher of *The Reader* was one of the defendants and his lawyer told the press that he was aware the advertisement would be run.[8]

Three weeks before the San Diego advertisement appeared, leaflets were distributed outside the courthouse in El Cajon, California. The demonstrators stopped when warned by the marshal that they could be arrested for felony jury-tampering. To combat the information being handed out, judges gave jurors special instructions to disregard the leaflets.

California was not the first location where such leaflets appeared. Operation Rescue adherents in Jackson, Mississippi distributed leaflets urging jurors to "nullify every rule or 'law' that is not in accordance with the principles of Natural, God-given, Common, or Constitutional Law."[9]

Many of these leaflets present a distorted and incorrect discussion of nullification. Potential jurors who read them may taint the deliberations of actual juries with misinformation. Only an accurate jury nullification instruction from the judge can eliminate this problem.

In fact, many of the pamphlets and leaflets go further than presenting misinformation. They suggest or hint that potential jurors should deceive judges.

**Should Jurors Be Honest with Judges?**   Sir Walter Scott wrote the much quoted phrase, "Oh! what a tangled web we weave [w]hen first we practice to deceive!"[10] Proponents of jury nullification have written about the lack of candor involved when the judge fails to tell the jury about nullification. This dishonesty now has spawned a more virulent deception in the reverse direction: jurors lying to judges.

---

[7]At the bottom right of the advertisement there is a small box, labelled "ATTENTION LAWYERS," which contains a reference to our article in 43:4 Law & Contemp. Prob. 52 (1980). Neither of us was contacted before this reference was used. Statements in the advertisement are in direct contradiction to our position. We categorically and emphatically do not endorse jurors lying to judges nor do we endorse telling jurors to disbelieve everything they hear from judges.

[8]*See* Jackson, *DA's Office Decries 'Jury Nullification' Ad,* San Diego Union, Jan. 26, 1990, at B1.

[9]The authors thank Jerry Mitchell, reporter for the Jackson, Mississippi *Clarion-Ledger,* for sending us the leaflet. This particular leaflet was sponsored by the Christian Action Group of Jackson, Mississippi.

[10]Sir Walter Scott, *Marmion,* Canto VI, Stanza 17, in *Complete Poetical Works* 145 (1900).

In 1988, the authors received a four-page pamphlet entitled "The Informed Juror." Written by Paul deParrie and sponsored by an Oregon group called Advocates for Life, the pamphlet gives a very brief description of nullification before calling on conservatives, "especially Christians," to refrain from showing during voir dire that they have strong feelings about abortion. The pamphlet's author advises:

> During jury selection it may be wise to refrain from elaborating on answers to questions asked by attorneys. Any appearance of being educated, involved or opinionated may be sufficient cause to be rejected, thus being removed from the opportunity to be a watchman for abuses by the executive and judicial departments of government. This does not mean that you would be untruthful in answering questions. Simply keep your answers brief if you would like to improve your chances of serving on a jury.

Not all anti-abortion activists have been content with silence or brevity. For some, outright deception appears justified. One such illustration surfaced in San Diego where a published advertisement stopped just short of advocating lying. Noting that "before you even *get on* the jury, they may ask you whether you know about your right to 'nullify,'" the advertisement then offered a suggested response:

> *Don't believe a word they say. . . .*
> *Here's How to Do It*
> It's easy. The most important rule is, *don't let the judge and prosecutor know that you know about this right.*
> It is unjust and illegal for them to deny you this right. So, if you have to, it's perfectly all right for you to make a "mental reservation."
> Give them the same answer you would have given if you were hiding fugitive slaves in 1850 and the 'slave catchers' asked if you had runaways in your attic. Or if you were hiding Jews from the Nazis in Germany.

This recommendation for "pious dishonesty" was then followed by two other suggestions:

The second rule is, *educate the other jurors* about jury nullification and, if possible, persuade them to vote "not guilty."
The third rule is *stick to your guns.* Don't let other jurors make you change your position.

Millions of potential jurors may be exposed to similar advertisements, leaflets, or pamphlets. That means that countless juries may contain members who have concealed their awareness of nullification, who hold seriously incorrect views about it, and who intend to "educate" the other jurors to rebuff laws they do not like.

When jury nullification was a judicial secret, it was easier to refuse to give jury nullification instructions.[11] Such refusal today, however, may seriously compromise the justice of our jury verdicts.

**Should Judges Be Honest with Jurors?** What should the judge do about the fact that jurors may know something about nullification, accurate or not? Suppose, for example, we have a panel of potential jurors in a criminal case that has attracted media attention. Some of these jurors have seen literature about a right to nullify laws. What they read contained many errors. The defense lawyer or prosecutor may request to ask questions about nullification on voir dire. Should the lawyers be allowed to voir dire about nullification? If not, these jurors will contaminate the jury deliberations. If so, information about nullification will be made public. The judge may decide to give an antinullification instruction, but this, of course, will reinforce what the literature said would happen and would not correct any errors about the doctrine.

---

[11]Larry Dodge has reported a case from New York in which one of the jurors began to explain jury nullification to the others, but they sent a note to the judge about him. The judge permitted him to continue to deliberate after telling him to "keep his politics out of the case and apply the law as given." The juror agreed, went back to the deliberations, and hung the jury. He was later threatened with perjury and contempt charges, but they were never brought. Dodge, *A Complete History of the Power Rights and Duties of the Jury System,* a talk delivered at the State of the Nation Conference, sponsored by the Texas Liberty Association (July 7, 1990).

Judicial failure to give honest and correct instructions on nullification may thus directly contribute to contamination of jury deliberations. It is a sad irony that while judges continue to refuse to give accurate jury nullification instructions, they in fact are creating the anarchy they seek to avoid.

## CONCLUSION

The renewed grass roots interest in a "fully informed jury" reinforces our earlier views that judges should give jurors an accurate and honest instruction about the jury's role and power. The instruction should state that the judge must properly make rulings on procedural matters and will be guiding the trial so that all constitutional protections are provided to the litigants. The instruction should also say that the jury does not have the power to create new statutes or evaluate the constitutionality of the statutes before them. The jury should be encouraged to pay respectful attention to the acts of the legislature which, after all, reflect the democratic wishes of the community's majority. But the jurors should also be told that their function is to represent the community in this trial and that their ultimate responsibility is to determine the facts that occurred and to evaluate whether applying the law to these facts will produce, in the eyes of the community, a just and equitable verdict.

This type of honest instruction would reinforce our nation's commitment to a government where the people are sovereign, and it would serve to bring the people and their laws together in closer harmony.

# 15.5 Jury Instructions

## CALIFORNIA

*Ladies and Gentlemen of the Jury.* *

IT BECOMES MY DUTY as judge to instruct you concerning the law applicable to this case, and it is your duty as jurors to follow the law as I shall state it to you.

The function of the jury is to try the issues of fact that are presented by the allegations in the information filed in this court and the defendant's plea of "not guilty." This duty you should perform uninfluenced by pity for the defendant or by passion or prejudice against him. . . .

You are to be governed solely by the evidence introduced in this trial and the law as stated to you by me. The law forbids you to be governed by mere sentiment, conjecture, sympathy, passion, public opinion, or public feeling. Both the People and the defendant have a right to demand and they do demand and expect, that you will conscientiously and dispassionately consider and weigh the evidence and apply the law of the case, and that you will reach a just verdict, regardless of what the consequences may be. . . .

## MARYLAND

Members of the jury[†]: this is a criminal case and under the Constitution and the laws of the state of Maryland in a criminal case the jury are the judges of the law as well as of the facts in the case. So that whatever I tell you about the law, while it is intended to be helpful to you in reaching a just and proper verdict in the case, it is not binding upon you as members of the jury and you may accept the law as you apprehend it to be in the case.

---

*Excerpt from California jury instructions in criminal cases.

†Excerpt from Maryland jury instructions in criminal cases.

## 15.6 | A Call to Resist Illegitimate Authority *Hugo Adam Bedau, ed.*

TO THE YOUNG MEN of America, to the whole of the American people, and to all men of good will everywhere:

1. An ever growing number of young American men are finding that the American war in Vietnam so outrages their deepest moral and religious sense that they cannot contribute to it in any way. We share their moral outrage.

2. We further believe that the war is unconstitutional and illegal. Congress has not declared a war as required by the Constitution. Moreover, under the Constitution, treaties signed by the President and ratified by the Senate have the same force as the Constitution itself. The Charter of the United Nations is such a treaty. The Charter specifically obligates the United States to refrain from force or the threat of force in international relations. It requires member states to exhaust every peaceful means of settling disputes and to submit disputes which cannot be settled peacefully to the Security Council. The United States has systematically violated all of these Charter provisions for thirteen years.

3. Moreover, this war violates international agreements, treaties and principles of law which the United States Government has solemnly endorsed. The combat role of the United States troops in Vietnam violates the Geneva Accords of 1954 which our government pledged to support but has since subverted. The destruction of rice, crops, and livestock; the burning and bulldozing of entire villages consisting exclusively of civilian structures; the interning of civilian non-combatants in concentration camps; the summary executions of civilians in captured villages who could not produce satisfactory evidence of their loyalties or did not wish to be removed to concentration camps; the slaughter of peasants who dared to stand up in their fields and shake their fists at

American helicopters—these are all actions of the kind which the United States and the other victorious powers of World War II declared to be crimes against humanity for which individuals were to be held personally responsible even when acting under the orders of their governments and for which Germans were sentenced at Nuremberg to long prison terms and death. The prohibition of such acts as war crimes was incorporated in treaty law by the Geneva Conventions of 1949, ratified by the United States. These are commitments to other countries and to Mankind, and they would claim our allegiance even if Congress should declare war.

4. We also believe it is an unconstitutional denial of religious liberty and equal protection of the laws to withhold draft exemption from men whose religious or profound philosophical beliefs are opposed to what in the Western religious tradition have been long known as unjust wars.

5. Therefore, we believe on all these grounds that every free man has a legal right and a moral duty to exert every effort to end this war, to avoid collusion with it, and to encourage others to do the same. Young men in the armed forces or threatened with the draft face the most excruciating choices. For them various forms of resistance risk separation from their families and their country, destruction of their careers, loss of their freedom, and loss of their lives. Each must choose the course of resistance dictated by his conscience and circumstances. Among those already in the armed forces some are refusing to obey specific illegal and immoral orders, some are attempting to educate their fellow servicemen on the murderous and barbarous nature of the war, some are absenting themselves without official leave. Among those not in the armed forces some are applying for status as conscientious objectors to American aggression in Vietnam, some are refusing to be inducted. Among both groups some are resisting openly and paying a heavy penalty, some are organizing more resistance within the United States and some have sought sanctuary in other countries.

6. We believe that each of these forms of resistance against illegitimate authority is courageous and justified. Many of us believe that open resistance to the war and the draft is the course of

"A Call to Resist Illegitimate Authority," *Civil Disobedience: Theory and Practice*, pp. 162–164. Copyright © 1969 Hugo Bedau. Reprinted by permission of the author.

This statement was originally circulated in August, 1967, accompanied by a list of some one hundred and fifty sponsors. The signers, now in the thousands, are organized under the name of "Resist," with headquarters in Cambridge, Massachusetts.

action most likely to strengthen the moral resolve with which all of us can oppose the war and most likely to bring an end to the war.

7. We will continue to lend our support to those who undertake resistance to this war. We will raise funds to organize draft resistance unions, to supply legal defense and bail, to support families and otherwise aid resistance to the war in whatever ways may seem appropriate.

8. We firmly believe that our statement is the sort of speech that under the First Amendment must be free, and that the actions we will undertake are as legal as is the war resistance of the young men themselves. But we recognize that the courts may find otherwise, and that if so

we might all be liable to prosecution and severe punishment.* In any case, we feel that we cannot shrink from fulfilling our responsibilities to the youth whom many of us teach, to the country whose freedom we cherish, and to the ancient traditions of religion and philosophy which we strive to preserve in this generation.

9. We call upon all men of good will to join us in this confrontation with immoral authority. Especially we call upon the universities to fulfill their mission of enlightenment and religious organizations to honor their heritage of brotherhood. Now is the time to resist.

---

*[In some later printings, this sentence was omitted—ED.]

---

## 15.7  United States v. Dougherty et al.   *473 F.2d 1113 (C.A.D.C. 1972)*

LEVENTHAL, CIRCUIT JUDGE:

SEVEN OF THE SO-CALLED "D.C. Nine" bring this joint appeal from convictions arising out of their unconsented entry into the Washington offices of the Dow Chemical Company, and their destruction of certain property therein. Appellants, along with two other defendants who subsequently entered pleas of nolo contendere, were tried before District Judge John H. Pratt and a jury on a three count indictment alleging, as to each defendant, one count of second degree burglary, 22 D.C. Code §1801(b), and two counts of malicious destruction of property valued in excess of $100, 22 D.C. Code §403. On February 11, 1970, after a six-day trial, the seven were each convicted of two counts of malicious destruction. The jury acquitted on the burglary charges but convicted on the lesser-included offense of unlawful entry. The sentences imposed are set forth in the margin.

Appellants urge three grounds for reversal as follows: (1) The trial judge erred in denying defendants' timely motions to dispense with counsel and represent themselves. (2) The judge erroneously refused to instruct the jury of its right to acquit appellants without regard to the law and the evidence, and refused to permit ap-

pellants to argue that issue to the jury. (3) The instructions actually given by the court coerced the jury into delivering a verdict of guilty. On the basis of defendants' first contention we reverse and remand for new trial. To provide an appropriate mandate governing the new trial, we consider the second and third contentions, and conclude that these cannot be accepted.

### THE RECORD IN DISTRICT COURT

The undisputed evidence showed that on Saturday, March 22, 1969, appellants broke into the locked fourth floor Dow offices at 1030—15th Street, N.W., Washington, D.C., threw papers and documents about the office and into the street below, vandalized office furniture and equipment, and defaced the premises by spilling about a bloodlike substance. The prosecution proved its case through Dow employees who testified as to the lack of permission and extent of damage, members of the news media who had been summoned to the scene by the appellants and who witnessed the destruction while recording it photographically, and police officers who arrested appellants on the scene. . . .

**The Issue of Jury Nullification** . . . [A]ppellants . . . say that the jury has a well recognized

---

Some footnotes have been omitted and the rest are renumbered.

prerogative to disregard the instructions of the court even as to matters of law, and that they accordingly have the legal right that the jury be informed of its power. We turn to this matter in order to define the nature of the new trial permitted by our mandate.

The existence of an unreviewable and unreversible power in the jury, to acquit in disregard of the instructions on the law given by the trial judge, has for many years co-existed with legal practice and precedent upholding instructions to the jury that they are required to follow the instructions of the court on all matters of law. There were different soundings in colonial days and the early days of our Republic. We are aware of the number and variety of expressions at that time from respected sources—John Adams; Alexander Hamilton; prominent judges—that jurors had a duty to find a verdict according to their own conscience, though in opposition to the direction of the court; that their power signified a right; that they were judges both of law and of fact in a criminal case, and not bound by the opinion of the court.

The rulings did not run all one way, but rather precipitated "a number of classic exchanges on the freedom and obligations of the criminal jury." This was, indeed, one of the points of clash between the contending forces staking out the direction of the government of the newly established Republic, a direction resolved in political terms by reforming but sustaining the status of the courts, without radical change. As the distrust of judges appointed and removable by the king receded, there came increasing acceptance that under a republic the protection of citizens lay not in recognizing the right of each jury to make its own law, but in following democratic processes for changing the law.

The crucial legal ruling came in *United States v. Battiste,* 2 Sum. 240, Fed.Cas. No. 14,545 (C.C.D.Mass. 1835). Justice Story's strong opinion supported the conception that the jury's function lay in accepting the law given to it by the court and applying that law to the facts. This considered ruling of an influential jurist won increasing acceptance in the nation. The youthful passion for independence accommodated itself to the reality that the former rebels were now in control of their own destiny, that the practical needs of sta-

bility and sound growth outweighed the abstraction of centrifugal philosophy, and that the judges in the courts, were not the colonial appointees projecting royalist patronage and influence but were themselves part and parcel of the nation's intellectual mainstream, subject to the checks of the common law tradition and professional opinion, and capable, in Roscoe Pound's words, of providing "true judicial justice" standing in contrast with the colonial experience.

The tide was turned by *Battiste,* but there were cross-currents. At mid-century the country was still influenced by the precepts of Jacksonian democracy, which spurred demands for direct selection of judges by the people through elections, and distrust of the judge-made common law which enhanced the movement for codification reform. But by the end of the century, even the most prominent state landmarks had been toppled; and the Supreme Court settled the matter for the Federal courts in *Sparf* v. *United States,* 156 U.S. 51, 102, 15 S.Ct. 273, 39 L.Ed. 343 (1895) after exhaustive review in both majority and dissenting opinions. The jury's role was respected as significant and wholesome, but it was not to be given instructions that articulated a right to do whatever it willed. The old rule survives today only as a singular relic.[1] . . .

This so-called right of jury nullification is put forward in the name of liberty and democracy, but its explicit avowal risks the ultimate logic of anarchy. This is the concern voiced by Judge Sobeloff in *United States* v. *Moylan,* 417 F.2d 1002, 1009 (4th Cir. 1969), cert. denied, 397 U.S. 910, 90 S.Ct. 908, 25 L.Ed.2d 91 (1970):

> To encourage individuals to make their own determinations as to which laws they will

---

[1]Wyley v. Warden, 372 F.2d 742 (4th Cir. 1967), cert. denied, 389 U.S. 863, 88 S.Ct. 121, 19 L.Ed.2d 131 (1967). In holding the provision of the Maryland Constitution consistent with the Federal Constitution, Judge Sobeloff noted that "a practice may be deemed unwise, yet not be unconstitutional." He referred to the "potent and persuasive arguments . . . leveled against the wisdom of the Maryland practice," and the various jurists' analyses condemning it as "archaic, outmoded and atrocious," "unique and indefensible," an "antique constitutional thorn" in "the flesh of Maryland's body of Criminal Law." . . .

obey and which they will permit themselves as a matter of conscience to disobey is to invite chaos. No legal system could long survive if it gave every individual the option of disregarding with impunity any law which by his personal standard was judged morally untenable. Toleration of such conduct would not be democratic, as appellants claim, but inevitably anarchic.

The statement that avoval of the jury's prerogative runs the risk of anarchy, represents, in all likelihood, the habit of thought of philosophy and logic, rather than the prediction of the social scientist. But if the statement contains an element of hyperbole, the existence of risk and danger, of significant magnitude, cannot be gainsaid. In contrast, the advocates of jury "nullification" apparently assume that the articulation of the jury's power will not extend its use or extent, or will not do so significantly or obnoxiously. Can this assumption fairly be made? . . .

The way the jury operates may be radically altered if there is alteration in the way it is told to operate. The jury knows well enough that its prerogative is not limited to the choices articulated in the formal instructions of the court. The jury gets its understanding as to the arrangements in the legal system from more than one voice. There is the formal communication from the judge. There is the informal communication from the total culture—literature (novel, drama, film, and television); current comment (newspapers, magazines and television); conversation; and, of course, history and tradition. The totality of input generally conveys adequately enough the idea of prerogative, of freedom in an occasional case to depart from what the judge says. Even indicators that would on their face seem too weak to notice—like the fact that the judge tells the jury it must acquit (in case of reasonable doubt) but never tells the jury in so many words that it must convict—are a meaningful part of the jury's total input. Law is a system, and it is also a language, with secondary meanings that may be unrecorded yet are part of its life.

When the legal system relegates the information of the jury's prerogative to an essentially informal input, it is not being duplicitous, chargeable with chicane and intent to deceive.

The limitation to informal input is, rather a governor to avoid excess: the prerogative is reserved for the exceptional case, and the judge's instruction is retained as a generally effective constraint. . . .

Rules of law or justice involve choice of values and ordering of objectives for which unanimity is unlikely in any society, or group representing the society, especially a society as diverse in cultures and interests as ours. To seek unity out of diversity, under the national motto, there must be a procedure for decision by vote of a majority or prescribed plurality—in accordance with democratic philosophy. To assign the role of mini-legislature to the various petit juries, who must hang if not unanimous, exposes criminal law and administration to paralysis, and to a deadlock that betrays rather than furthers the assumptions of viable democracy.

Moreover, to compel a juror involuntarily assigned to jury duty to assume the burdens of mini-legislator or judge, as is implicit in the doctrine of nullification, is to put untoward strains on the jury system. It is one thing for a juror to know that the law condemns, but he has a factual power of lenity. To tell him expressly of a nullification prerogative, however, is to inform him, in effect, that it is he who fashions the rule that condemns. That is an overwhelming responsibility, an extreme burden for the jurors' psyche. And it is not inappropriate to add that a juror called upon for an involuntary public service is entitled to the protection, when he takes action that he knows is right, but also knows is unpopular, either in the community at large or in his own particular grouping, that he can fairly put it to friends and neighbors that he was merely following the instructions of the court. . . .

What makes for health as an occasional medicine would be disastrous as a daily diet. The fact that there is widespread existence of the jury's prerogative, and approval of its existence as a "necessary counter to casehardened judges and arbitrary prosecutors," does not establish as an imperative that the jury must be informed by the judge of that power. On the contrary, it is pragmatically useful to structure instructions in such wise that the jury must feel strongly about the values involved in the case, so strongly that it must itself identify the case as establishing a call of high conscience, and must independently initiate and undertake an act in contravention of the established instructions. This requirement of independent jury conception confines the happening of the lawless jury to the occasional instance that does not violate, and viewed as an exception may even enhance, the over-all normative effect of the rule of law. An explicit instruction to a jury conveys an implied approval that runs the risk of degrading the legal structure requisite for true freedom, for an ordered liberty that protects against anarchy as well as tyranny. . . .

BAZELON, CHIEF JUDGE, *concurring in part and dissenting in part:*

My own view rests on the premise that nullification can and should serve an important function in the criminal process. I do not see it as a doctrine that exists only because we lack the power to punish jurors who refuse to enforce the law or to re-prosecute a defendant whose acquittal cannot be justified in the strict terms of law. The doctrine permits the jury to bring to bear on the criminal process a sense of fairness and particularized justice. The drafters of legal rules cannot anticipate and take account of every case where a defendant's conduct is "unlawful" but not blameworthy, any more than they can draw a bold line to mark the boundary between an accident and negligence. It is the jury—as spokesman for the community's sense of values—that must explore that subtle and elusive boundary.

. . . The very essence of the jury's function is its role as spokesman for the community conscience in determining whether or not blame can be imposed.

I do not see any reason to assume that jurors will make rampantly abusive use of their power. Trust in the jury is, after all, one of the cornerstones of our entire criminal jurisprudence, and if that trust is without foundation we must reexamine a great deal more than just the nullification doctrine. . . .

One often-cited abuse of the nullification power is the acquittal by bigoted juries of whites who commit crimes (lynching, for example) against blacks. That repellent practice cannot be directly arrested without jeopardizing important constitutional protections—the double jeopardy bar and the jury's power of nullification. But the revulsion and sense of shame fostered by that practice fueled the civil rights movement, which in turn made possible the enactment of major civil rights legislation. That same movement spurred on the revitalization of the equal protection clause and, in particular, the recognition of the right to be tried before a jury selected without bias. The lessons we learned from these abuses helped to create a climate in which such abuses could not so easily thrive.

Moreover, it is not only the abuses of nullification that can inform our understanding of the community's values and standards of blame worthiness. The noble uses of the power— the uses that "enhance the over-all normative effect of the rule of law"—also provide an important input to our evaluation of the substantive standards of the criminal law. The reluctance of juries to hold defendants responsible for unmistakable violations of the prohibition laws told us much about the morality of those laws and about the "criminality" of the conduct they proscribed. And the same can be said of the acquittals returned under the fugitive slave law[2] as well as contemporary gaming and liquor laws. A doctrine that can provide us with such critical insights should not be driven underground. . . .

*Notes and Questions*

1. Who motivates a jury to nullify the law? Is nullification urged on them by an articulate defense lawyer pleading the cause of liberty or disguising an appeal to prejudice, or do jurors themselves decide that nullification is appropriate?

2. Is there a tendency among some citizens to label as "jury nullification" those verdicts with which they strongly disagree, and thereby to delegitimize verdicts that may have resulted

---

[2]H. Kalven & H. Zeisel, "The American Jury." Jury nullification also provides us with crucial information about the morality of the death penalty. *See McGautha* v. *California,* 402 U.S. 183, 199, 91 S.Ct. 1454, 1463, 28 L.Ed.2d 711 (1971): In order to meet the problem of jury nullification, legislatures did not try, as before, to refine further the definition of capital homicides. Instead they adopted the method of forthrightly granting juries discretion which they had been exercising in fact. . . .

from the prosecution's failure to provide proof beyond a reasonable doubt?

3. Does excessive media coverage of some notorious trials make jury nullification more or less likely? Does it make jury nullification more or less likely to reflect the conscience of the community?

4. If the law provides that the jury can in fact disregard the judge's instructions and deliver a verdict of its own choosing without fear of any sanctions, why is there so much resistance to telling the jury of its power? What might be the effect on jury deliberations if the jurors were told about nullification?

5. Can you think of ways of explaining to jurors what their role in the legal process is other than the two instructions appearing on page 417? What risks are created by organizations, like the Fully Informed Jury Association (FIJA), that attempt to educate all citizens (potential jurors) about nullification? What about handbills or paid newspaper advertisements urging nullification in a particular upcoming trial?

6. Tocqueville writes that "in no country are the judges so powerful as where the people share their privileges." Does jury nullification strengthen or weaken Tocqueville's argument? What power, other than jury instruction, does the judge have in the trial?

7. In a 1972 article entitled "The Jury Is Not a Political Institution," Judge Robert McBride of the Dayton, Ohio, Court of Common Pleas wrote, "Anyone who seeks a return to a supreme jury, independent of the law and independent of instructions of law, ignores the history and development of the judicial process and disregards the fact that this is a representative democracy with a separation of powers." He also wrote that jury nullification is ". . . an unworkable and irresponsible theory, born in the storms of the French, English and American revolutions and totally discredited in the rule of law and not of men that exists today."* Do you agree? How might Tocqueville reply to this argument? Scheflin? FIJA?

8. Under what conditions do you think a jury would consider nullification? Is nullification a matter of spontaneous outrage in a plainly political case? If an attorney were to address the issue of nullification in a summation to the jury, what sorts of things would you expect to be stressed? What kind of jurors would you want to select if you knew that your case depended largely on their willingness to nullify the law in the case?

9. Would jury nullification, even if it were a frequent occurrence, really give jurors significant power? What about routine cases in which the political nature of the crime or dispute is not readily apparent? Can jury nullification change the allocation of power in the legal system or in society, or is it a superficial solution to a major denial of public participation in law?

10. In May 1992, four white Los Angeles police officers were acquitted of charges stemming from the beating of African American Rodney King by a jury on which no African Americans sat. An amateur videotape of the beating was seen on television stations around the country and was a major part of the evidence in the case. Was the acquittal an act of jury nullification? The trial was moved from Los Angeles County to the predominantly white town of Simi Valley. Does this fact throw any doubt on the validity of jury nullification in cases in which racism is an underlying issue?

Four years later, O. J. Simpson was acquitted of murder charges in the deaths of his ex-wife and her friend Ron Goldman. Was this a case of jury nullification, or just an example of an absence of proof beyond a reasonable doubt? Does either the King or the Simpson verdict change your view of whether judges should inform jurors of their power of nullification?

11. The debate over whether jurors should be told about nullification hinges in part on how each side perceives the nature of U.S. society: Some see nullification as a way for ordinary people to protect "progressive" political action from an oppressive government; others point out that historically, nullification has empowered an intolerant public to avoid the rule of law and trample the rights of defendants—making it possible, for example, for white racists to control jury verdicts when whites are accused of crimes against persons of color. Do you think that decision about whether jurors should be told of their power to nullify should depend on a political assessment of society? Should the right to vote also hinge on estimates of the political views of potential voters? Can democratic

---

*Robert McBride, "The Jury Is Not a Political Institution," *Judge's Journal* 11 (1972), p. 37.

processes (including jury nullification) be combined with the preservation of a constitutional rule of law, or is there always the risk that immoral decisions may result?

12. In the Dougherty case, Judge Leventhal states that jury nullification puts "untoward strains on the jury system" and that a juror voting his or her conscience should be able to defend an unpopular decision to friends and neighbors by claiming to be "merely following the instructions of the court." Do you agree? Should jurors be relieved of the responsibility to act in accordance with their conscience? Would your answer have been any different during the war in Vietnam when the "Call to Resist Illegitimate Authority" was issued? Where else has the justification of "just following orders" been advanced?

13. What would happen to the jury as a mechanism for expressing community values if it were possible to use the "I was just following orders" argument suggested by Judge Leventhal? Would this allow the judge to define the community, rather than allowing the community to define itself as a part of the legal process? How might the community react to a judge's usurpation of its participation in determining the application of law? Would an order-following jury cast doubt on the legitimacy of jury trials? Of law itself?

14. Compare and contrast the function of jury nullification with civil disobedience as discussed by Dr. King in Part II.

# *16* JURY SELECTION IN A PLURALISTIC SOCIETY: THE CASE OF RACIAL PEREMPTORIES, AND THE PROBLEM OF DEATH-QUALIFIED JURIES

ঌ The materials in this chapter focus on defining a jury of peers in a society whose citizens are more varied in their background, heritage, and life experience than in any other society on earth. The definition of what constitutes a jury of one's peers is vital because upon this issue depends not only the fairness of a particular jury trial from each litigant's point of view, but also the public perception of whether the jury system and the law itself are legitimate.

The importance of the question of who are peers is magnified considerably by the claim, developed in the previous chapter, that the jury is primarily a political institution. If the jury functions to articulate community standards and apply them to current conflicts, including the power to nullify a law in its application to an individual criminal case, then the composition of juries becomes crucial. Distortions in the representative character of juries will become distortions in the "political" (community-defining) decisions they make. A long-term pattern of significant distortions in jury selection will ultimately raise the question of whether the jury as an institution has been so changed that it is capable neither of rendering a fair verdict based upon a true understanding of the conflict at hand, nor of functioning as a vehicle for community participation.

Because, as Jefferson observed, the opportunity to be a juror is arguably as important a part of citizenship as eligibility to vote, defining a jury of peers may be seen as defining who belongs to America. Perhaps the presidential election of 2000—by showing how important and how fragile the right to vote can be—will add some urgency to our exploration of the importance and fragility of fair jury selection and fair jury trial.

In the first reading of this chapter, excerpts from the introduction to Kenneth Karst's 1989 book, *Belonging to America: Equal Citizenship and the Constitution,* you are asked to consider the issue of equality of citizenship as an issue bearing on the meaning of America, on who belongs to the community and who does not. This is an issue that runs through all the readings in this chapter and that underlies all the legal standards and political judgments about what constitutes a jury of one's peers.

In considering Karst's analytic framework and the cases and notes that follow it, it is important to keep in mind a few basic facts about the pluralistic nature of the United States in the twenty-first century. Because of rapidly changing demographics, the United States is becoming a multiracial society in which the concept of minority status is continually being redefined. The 1990 national census indicated that between 1980 and 1990 there were significant increases in the numbers and percentages of people of color in the United States. The African American population, for example, grew by more than 13 percent to just over 12 percent of total U.S. population. At the same time, the Latino population increased by 53 percent, reaching 9 percent of the national population. A growth rate of 108 percent doubled the percentage of Asian/Pacific Americans to 3 percent of the total population in the same ten-year period. As a result of these changes, the nationwide total of African Americans, Latinos, Asian/Pacific Americans, and Native Americans rose from 20 percent of the U.S. population in 1980 to 25 percent in 1990.

Projections of future growth suggest a continuing and substantial increase in the number of "minority" persons in the United States. The number of Asian/Pacific Americans is expected to double by about 2010 and triple by the year 2020. If current levels of immigration continue, Latinos are likely to number 39 million in two decades, becoming the largest minority group in the nation. Other projections indicate that if current growth rates continue, in the year 2000 nonwhites will account for 31 percent of the total population; in 2010 the figure will be 42 percent, and in 2020, just one generation from now, "minorities" will account for almost 60 percent of the population. Although other projections are more conservative, the net result of demographic changes is that, within fifty years, there will no longer be a majority race in the United States. We will have become, literally, a nation of minorities. All the relevant 2000 Census data analysis is not available as this chapter goes to press, and what is available has been a subject of debate among those interpreting its meaning. But, readers can update population projections for themselves by consulting www.census.gov.

Determining what constitutes a jury of peers is a project of considerable urgency and great complexity, with an enormous impact on law and daily life. Within the context presented by professor Karst in "Equality, Law, and Belonging," Chapter 16 presents materials that focus on two of the most important current legal and policy issues in jury selection. Each issue has commanded significant public debate, great difference of opinion based on conscience, and disagreement among legal scholars and policy-makers. The first of these, the use of peremptory challenges to influence the racial composition of juries in criminal cases, cuts to the core of the way that America defines itself and selects its juries.

As some of the following readings indicate, legal/constitutional protections against discrimination in jury selection focus almost entirely on whether there is systematic discrimination against recognizable groups in the process of selecting the jury panel. The selection of a particular trial jury, unlike the panel of potential jurors from which the trial jurors are selected, has almost completely escaped legal scrutiny. But in the *Batson* case (Reading 16.3), the Supreme Court reexamined issues of purposeful racial discrimination in the use of peremptory challenges by a prosecutor participating in the picking of a defendant's trial jury. The *Batson* case was just the beginning of rethinking the issue of race and trial jury selection, as Professor Lawrence's article on unconscious racism (Reading 16.4) and Professor Alschuler's article on affirmative action in jury selection (Reading 16.5) demonstrate. And the issues of race consciousness and law raised by these readings extend beyond the problem of fair jury selection to a whole range of problems of racial justice in the United States.

The second major current issue in jury selection, presented in Readings 16.6–16.8, concerns what has come to be called the "death-qualified jury." To what extent may potential jurors who have scruples against capital punishment be excluded from juries in capital cases? To what extent does the idea of a representative cross section, as a definition of "jury of peers," require the presence on capital juries of differing attitudes on this issue of conscience? Materials are presented to help the reader reflect on his or her own view of capital punishment, and then two leading Supreme Court cases on death-qualified juries are presented. As the nation continues to debate the death penalty—its effectiveness, morality, racial application, and accuracy—the issue of jury selection in capital cases becomes ever more important.

---

## 16.1  Equality, Law, and Belonging: An Introduction    *Kenneth Karst*

THE IDEAL OF EQUALITY is one of the great themes in the culture of American public life. From the Declaration of Independence to the pledge of allegiance, the rhetoric of equality permeates our symbols of nationhood. Over and over in our history, from the earliest colonial beginnings, equality has been a rallying cry, a promise, an article of national faith. So it is that the ideal of equality touches our emotions. All these aspects of equality—protest, hope, and faith, infused with emotion—came together in an August afternoon over a quarter century ago when

Martin Luther King, Jr., spoke to a multitude at the Lincoln Memorial, repeatedly returning to the phrase: "I have a dream."

King's vision of the future centered on the ideal of one nation, indivisible—a nation that would heal its racial divisions by offering justice for all. The metaphor of the dream was his way of making vivid the contrast between the Constitution's promise of equality and the realities of race relations in the America of 1963. But if Martin Luther King was a dreamer, he also knew how to get down to cases, from segregated buses to employment discrimination. The immediate objective of his speech was a change in the nation's law. The huge gathering before him had joined a "march on Washington" to support the bill that became the Civil Rights Act of 1964. He understood that if black people were to think of themselves as belonging to America, the nation must make a reality of the ideal expressed in the motto on the Supreme Court Building: Equal Justice under Law.

Such a faith in the capacity of law is common among Americans. A deep current of egalitarianism has always run through American society, and we have often resorted to law to effectuate our ideals. Yet Martin Luther King, from his awareness of our history and from his own personal experience, also had reason to appreciate Ralf Dahrendorf's mordant epigram: "all men are equal *before* the law but they are no longer equal *after* it." Slavery and racial segregation; discrimination against the foreign-born; religious qualifications for political participation; the virtual exclusion of women from public life—all were reminders that law can be an instrument for the subordination of groups. Equality and citizenship had been explicitly written into the Fourteenth Amendment to the Constitution after the Civil War, and yet our constitutional law had been shaped to accommodate these kinds of legalized subordination.

If the law touching matters of equality looked into two directions, it did no more than reflect prevailing attitudes in American society. Writing during World War II, Gunnar Myrdal called the race-relations aspect of this ambivalence an "American dilemma." Myrdal saw that white Americans were genuinely devoted to the nation's egalitarian and individualistic ideals, yet they also accepted the systematic denial of black

people's equality and individuality. Similar paradoxes have attended our society's treatment of other cultural minorities and of women.

How have successive generations of Americans—whites and males and the native born—managed to live with this incongruity between their egalitarian ideals and their behavior? The technique is simple enough: just define the community's public life—or the community itself—in a way that excludes the subordinated groups. The inclination to exclude is not innate; it arises in the acculturation that forms individual self-definition out of attachment to one's own group and separation from other groups. Rodgers and Hammerstein put it best: "You've got to be carefully taught." Culture shapes identity by contrasting "our" beliefs and behavior, which are examples to be followed, with those of the Other, which must be avoided. Our own national experience is replete with examples:

> Americans came early to accept the inevitable presence of outsiders. . . . Although every citizen could claim a basic set of legal rights, some of these citizens would almost certainly remain outsiders. Actual membership was determined by additional tests of religion, perhaps, or race or language or behavior, tests that varied considerably among segments and over time. Each generation passed to the next an open question of who really belonged to American society.

Among full members of the community, the ideal of equality prevails; as to outsiders, the issue of equality seems irrelevant. Equality and belonging are inseparably linked: to define the scope of the ideal of equality in America is to define the boundaries of the national community. . . .

Claims to equal citizenship have always carried an emotional charge in America, especially when inequalities have attached to such attributes as race, sex, religion, or ethnicity. These matters touch the heart because they touch the sense of belonging and therefore the sense of self. Belonging is a basic human need. Every person's self is formed within a social matrix; indeed, the very conception of the self is bound up with the idea of a social group. Helen Merrell Lynd captured the idea in one simple but elegant sentence: "Some kind of answer to the question Where do I belong? is necessary for an answer to the question Who am I?" The most heartrending deprivation of all is the inequality of status that excludes people from full membership in the community, degrading them by labeling them as outsiders, denying them their very selves.

The harms of exclusion unquestionably happen to people one by one, but those individual harms result from the subordination of groups. When the instrument for excluding a group is the law, the hurt is magnified, for the law is seen to embody the community's values. For a "degradation ceremony" to succeed, the denouncer "must make the dignity of the supra-personal views of the tribe salient and accessible to view, and his denunciation must be delivered in their name. . . . The denouncer must arrange to be invested with the right to speak in the name of these ultimate values." When a city segregates the races on a public beach, the chief harm to the segregated minority is not that those people are denied access to a few hundred yards of surf. Jim Crow was not just a collection of legal disabilities; it was an officially organized degradation ceremony, repeated day after day in a hundred ways, in the life of every black person within the system's reach.

The main success of the civil rights movement was the formal redefinition of American communities both local and national. Large numbers of Americans, previously excluded from those communities' public life, were formally recognized as equal citizens. It was important to all of us, but especially to black people's sense of self, that the mechanism for inclusion was the Constitution, our national community's most authoritative official embodiment of values. All this Martin Luther King knew when he spoke to us of his dream of one nation, indivisible. . . .

The problem of understanding the Other is by no means peculiar to law and government, but it emerges regularly there for a reason tinged with irony. The most typical reaction to cultural difference in America has been avoidance: what you don't see won't bother you. Law and government, however, not only provide a public arena that all our diverse cultures necessarily share but also define meanings that hold our society together. The members of different cultures unavoidably confront each other in police-citizen relations on the streets of Los Angeles, in the political dealings in the Texas legislature and the Pawtucket city council, and in courtrooms both high and low. Sometimes intercultural differences become the explicit subjects of conflict in the public arena. More often, those conflicts lie below the surface of discussion. In either case, police officers and legislators and judges, when they make their official decisions, begin with their own acculturated assumptions about the meaning of behavior and come to question the universality of those assumptions only with difficulty. . . .

In one perspective the question, Who belongs to America? raises larger cultural questions: In a nation of many cultures, does it even make sense to speak of an American community of meaning, an American culture? If it does, what are the culture's defining features? In another perspective the question of belonging is a question of social psychology, centered on the interplay between individual beliefs and group membership: Who thinks of himself as a fully participating member of the national community? Or, in a perspective that is more sociological, which people—and peoples—are generally seen by others to be members? Questions like these can be stated separately, but their separateness is only a matter of perspective. The question, Who belongs? turns out to be a question about the meanings of America. To speak of self-definition, of the sense of community, and of the community-defining functions of law is not to identify different parts of a machine but to view a complex social process from several different angles.

And there's the rub. It is artificial to divide an organic process into parts for purposes of analysis, but any attempt to describe the process all at once is doomed. To understand the meanings of the question, Who belongs? and to ask how our constitutional protections of equality come to bear on the answers to that question, we need to make a series of discrete inquiries: into the foundations for community and the varieties of belonging; into the sense of community as the matrix for individual identity; and into the meanings of equal citizenship in the American civic culture, both as an ideal and as a principle of constitutional law.

Peremptory Challenges and Affirmative Action:
Constitutional Protections for a Jury of Peers   *Stephen Arons*

EVERY YEAR THERE ARE a handful of celebrated cases in which litigants spend large sums of money on social science experts who provide help in picking jurors who will be fair from the perspective of the party using the experts. But for the vast majority of citizens, it is only the provisions of the U.S. Constitution (and either the Federal Jury Selection and Service Act, 28 USCA 1861, or state statutes governing jury selection) that guarantee a fair trial by an impartial jury of one's peers. Not everyone has expensive social science tools available to aid in jury selection, and therefore most defendants must rely on the lawyer's skill in using constitutional and statutory standards to ensure a fair cross section of the community in the jury box. For those who must be content with institutional protections of a fair trial such as jury selection statutes, the *voir dire* questioning of prospective jurors by judge or counsel, and the protections of the Constitution, what is the likelihood of getting a fair jury? More important, perhaps, what is a fair jury? What constitutes a jury of one's peers as defined by law? And most important of all, are the existing and developing legal standards in this area adequate for handling the complex problem of defining a jury of peers in a multicultural society?

The phrase "jury of peers" goes back to the Magna Carta in 1215, although the significance of this pedigree is in doubt. In 1215, after all, there was little that even remotely resembled trial by jury as we know it today. In fact, the reference to a jury of peers in Magna Carta represented an attempt by English barons to secure their privileges against the king's encroachment, not a theory of the equality of all the populace, including those outside the nobility. Nevertheless, the con-

cept of being tried by a jury of one's peers has become ingrained in Anglo-American law. The question is, what does it mean? The excerpts from Kenneth Karst's book suggest that issues of citizenship, of participating in the continuous process of defining the community's values, and of belonging to the community, as well as of fairness to the litigants and of accurate reflection of the community's sense of justice, are at stake. The legal problem of defining a jury of peers thus becomes more complex and important.

Does insistence on a jury of peers mean that defendants should be judged by members of their own gender, social, ethnic, or economic subgroup? If so, what subgroups or communities are to be recognized as defining who are a person's peers in a pluralistic society? Or does it mean that since all people are equal in a democratic republic, a jury must be a cross section of the whole society? If this is so, the problem of defining communities is still with us, for now the issue is whether a recognizable group has been excluded and whether such an exclusion is significant for the trial or the community. In a society composed of at least 150 ethnic groups, a jury of twelve can hardly be a literal cross section. Perhaps we are all one another's peers by virtue of our humanity. If so, does "jury of peers" mean anything practical at all as a principle for preventing discrimination in jury selection?

Finally, in addition to exploring the consequences of jury selection for trial fairness and for "belonging to America," consider the effect of discrimination in jury selection on the legitimacy of a trial, of the jury system, and of the law itself.

⁊ The formal legal system has approached issues of jury selection using various criteria, some of which are examined in the materials presented below. For many years the constitutional standards for a fair jury were applied to the jury pool rather than the particular jury chosen for a particular case. Courts inquired as to whether there was "systematic exclusion" of a "cognizable group" from the pool of potential jurors. Several important cases sought to eliminate systematic discrimination against African Americans and women in constructing the jury pool. See, for example, *Swain* v. *Alabama,* 380 U.S. 202 (1965), and *Duren* v. *Missouri,* 439 U.S. 357 (1979). For a discussion of the meaning of the term *cognizable group* and how it might help decide which American subgroups are deserving of constitutional protection against systematic exclusion from the jury pool, see *United States* v. *Guzman,* 337 F. Supp. 140 (S.D. N.Y. 1972). Also pay careful attention to the Court's discussion in *Lockhart* v. *McCree* (Reading 16.8) of whether citizens with scruples against capital punishment constitute a cognizable group.

In recent years, the courts have shifted their focus from the jury pool to the jury box by examining the use of peremptory challenges. In the case and article that follow, the issues of racial discrimination and representation in jury selection are considered. These readings are presented for the purpose of provoking discussion about the strengths and limitations of constitutional and statutory law as mechanisms for addressing the fundamental questions of justice, fairness, citizenship, legal legitimacy, and belonging that are inevitably raised in defining a jury of peers in a dynamic, multicultural society.

As the Court has taken up the issue of peremptory challenges (by which jurors may be excused by a litigant's attorney without the agreement of the judge that there is cause for such an excusal and without giving any reason for the excusal), the standards for judging whether unconstitutional discrimination has taken place in the selection of a *particular* jury seem to be changing. At the same time, issues of affirmative action in jury selection, and its constitutionality, are raised. In a sense, the peremptory challenge and related cases that have been heard or may soon be heard by the Supreme Court are on the cutting edge of legal thinking about what constitutes a jury of peers and why a jury of peers is important. The focus has shifted from the jury pool to the trial jury itself in looking for illegal discrimination, unfair jury selection, and unrepresentative juries.

There follow excerpts from the case of *Batson* v. *Kentucky,* Professor Lawrence's discussion of unconscious racism and legal standards for finding unconstitutional racism, and excerpts from a law review article, "Racial Quotas and the Jury," in which Albert Alschuler evaluates a proposal for affirmative action in jury selection as an alternative to the struggle over peremptory challenges.

# 16.3 | Batson v. Kentucky   *106 S.Ct. 1712 (1986)*

JUSTICE POWELL *delivered the opinion of the Court.*

THIS CASE REQUIRES US to reexamine that portion of *Swain* v. *Alabama,* 380 U.S. 202, . . . (1965), concerning the evidentiary burden placed on a criminal defendant who claims that he has been denied equal protection through the State's use of peremptory challenges to exclude members of his race from the petit jury.

Petitioner, a black man, was indicted in Kentucky on charges of second-degree burglary and receipt of stolen goods. On the first day of trial in Jefferson Circuit Court, the judge conducted *voir dire* [questioning of prospective jurors to determine their fitness to serve] examination of the venire, excused certain jurors for cause, and permitted the parties to exercise peremptory challenges. The prosecutor used his peremptory challenges to strike all four black persons on the venire, and a jury composed only of white persons was selected. Defense counsel moved to discharge the jury before it was sworn on the ground that the prosecutor's removal of the black veniremen violated petitioner's rights under the Sixth and Fourteenth Amendments to a jury drawn from a cross-section of the community, and under the Fourteenth Amendment to equal protection of the laws. Counsel requested a hearing on his motion. Without expressly ruling on the request for a hearing, the trial judge observed that the parties were entitled to use their peremptory challenges to "strike anybody they want to." The judge then denied petitioner's motion, reasoning that the cross-section requirement applies only to selection of the venire and not to selection of the petit jury itself.

The jury convicted petitioner on both counts. On appeal to the Supreme Court of Kentucky, petitioner pressed, among other claims, the argument concerning the prosecutor's use of peremptory challenges. . . .

The Supreme Court of Kentucky affirmed. In a single paragraph, the court . . . observed that it recently had reaffirmed its reliance on *Swain,* and had held that a defendant alleging lack of a fair cross-section must demonstrate systematic exclusion of a group of jurors from the venire. . . . We granted certiorari, . . . 105 S.Ct. 2111 . . . (1985), and now reverse.

In *Swain* v. *Alabama,* this Court recognized that a "state's purposeful or deliberate denial to Negroes on account of race of participation as jurors in the administration of justice violates the Equal Protection Clause." 380 U.S., at 203–204, 85 S.Ct., at 826–27. This principle has been "consistently and repeatedly" reaffirmed, *id.,* at 204, 85 S.Ct., at 827, in numerous decisions of this Court both preceding and following *Swain.* We reaffirm the principle today.

More than a century ago, the Court decided that the State denies a black defendant equal protection of the laws when it puts him on trial before a jury from which members of his race have been purposefully excluded. *Strauder* v. *West Virginia,* 10 Otto 303, 100 U.S. 303.

. . . . . . . . . . . . . . . . . . . .

In holding that racial discrimination in jury selection offends the Equal Protection Clause, the Court in *Strauder* recognized, however, that a defendant has no right to a "petit jury composed in whole or in part of persons of his own race." . . .

Purposeful racial discrimination in selection of the venire violates a defendant's right to equal protection because it denies him the protection that a trial by jury is intended to secure. "The very idea of a jury is a body . . . composed of the peers or equals of the person whose rights it is selected or summoned to determine; that is, of his neighbors, fellows, associates, persons having the same legal status in society as that which he holds." . . . The petit jury has occupied a central position in our system of justice by safeguarding a person accused of crime against the arbitrary exercise of power by prosecutor or judge. *Duncan* v. *Louisiana,* 391 U.S. 145, 156, . . . (1968).[1] Those

---

Some citations and footnotes have been omitted and footnotes are renumbered.—ED.

---

[1] . . . By compromising the representative quality of the jury, discriminatory selection procedures make "juries ready weapons for officials to oppress those accused individuals who by chance are numbered among unpopular or inarticulate minorities." *Akins* v. *Texas,* 325 U.S., at 408, 65 S.Ct., at 1281 (Murphy, J., dissenting).

on the venire must be "indifferently chosen," to secure the defendant's right under the Fourteenth Amendment to "protection of life and liberty against race or color prejudice.". . .

Racial discrimination in selection of jurors harms not only the accused whose life or liberty they are summoned to try. Competence to serve as a juror ultimately depends on an assessment of individual qualifications and ability impartially to consider evidence presented at a trial. . . . As long ago as *Strauder,* therefore, the Court recognized that by denying a person participation in jury service on account of his race, the State unconstitutionally discriminated against the excluded juror. 100 U.S., at 308; . . .

The harm from discriminatory jury selection extends beyond that inflicted on the defendant and the excluded juror to touch the entire community. Selection procedures that purposefully exclude black persons from juries undermine public confidence in the fairness of our system of justice. . . . Discrimination within the judicial system is most pernicious because it is "a stimulant to that race prejudice which is an impediment to security to [black citizens] that equal justice which the law aims to secure to all others." *Strauder, supra,* 100 U.S., at 308.

. . . . . . . . . . . . . . . . . . . . . .

Thus, the Court has found a denial of equal protection where the procedures implementing a neutral statute operated to exclude persons from the venire on racial grounds, and has made clear that the Constitution prohibits all forms of purposeful racial discrimination in selection of jurors. While decisions of this Court have been concerned largely with discrimination during selection of the venire, the principles announced there also forbid discrimination on account of race in selection of the petit jury. Since the Fourteenth Amendment protects an accused throughout the proceedings bringing him to justice, . . . the State may not draw up its jury lists pursuant to neutral procedures but then resort to discrimination at "other stages in the selection process." . . .

Accordingly, the component of the jury selection process at issue here, the State's privilege to strike individual jurors through peremptory chal-

lenges, is subject to the commands of the Equal Protection Clause. Although a prosecutor ordinarily is entitled to exercise permitted peremptory challenges "for any reason at all, as long as that reason is related to his view concerning the outcome" of the case to be tried, *United States* v. *Robinson,* 421 F.Supp. 467, 473 (Conn. 1976) . . . , the Equal Protection Clause forbids the prosecutor to challenge potential jurors solely on account of their race or on the assumption that black jurors as a group will be unable impartially to consider the State's case against a black defendant. . . .

. . . . . . . . . . . . . . . . . . . . . .

Since the decision in *Swain,* we have explained that our cases concerning selection of the venire reflect the general equal protection principle that the "invidious quality" of governmental action claimed to be racially discriminatory "must ultimately be traced to a racially discriminatory purpose." *Washington* v. *Davis,* 426 U.S. 229, 240, 96 S.Ct. 2040, 2048, . . . (1976). As in any equal protection case, the "burden is, of course," on the defendant who alleges discriminatory selection of the venire "to prove the existence of purposeful discrimination." . . .

The standards for assessing a prima facie case in the context of discriminatory selection of the venire have been fully articulated since *Swain.* . . . These principles support our conclusion that a defendant may establish a prima facie case of purposeful discrimination in selection of the petit jury solely on evidence concerning the prosecutor's exercise of peremptory challenges at the defendant's trial. To establish such a case, the defendant first must show that he is a member of a cognizable racial group, . . . and that the prosecutor has exercised peremptory challenges to remove from the venire members of the defendant's race. Second, the defendant is entitled to rely on the fact, as to which there can be no dispute, that peremptory challenges constitute a jury selection practice that permits "those to discriminate who are of a mind to discriminate." . . . Finally, the defendant must show that these facts and any other relevant circumstances raise an inference that the prosecutor used that practice to exclude the veniremen from the petit jury on account of their race. This combination of factors in the empanelling of the petit jury, as in the selection of the venire, raises the necessary inference of purposeful discrimination. . . .

Once the defendant makes a prima facie showing, the burden shifts to the State to come forward with a neutral explanation for challenging black jurors. Though this requirement imposes a limitation in some cases on the full peremptory character of the historic challenge, we emphasize that the prosecutor's explanation need not rise to the level justifying exercise of a challenge for cause. . . . But the prosecutor may not rebut the defendant's prima facie case of discrimination by stating merely that he challenged jurors of the defendant's race on the assumption—or his intuitive judgment—that they would be partial to the defendant because of their shared race. . . . Just as the Equal Protection Clause forbids the States to exclude black persons from the venire on the assumption that blacks as a group are unqualified to serve as jurors, . . . so it forbids the States to strike black veniremen on the assumption that they will be biased in a particular case simply because the defendant is black. The core guarantee of equal protection, ensuring citizens that their State will not discriminate on account of race, would be meaningless were we to approve the exclusion of jurors on the basis of such assumptions, which arise solely from the juror's race. Nor may the prosecutor rebut the defendant's case merely by denying that he had a discriminatory motive or "affirming his good faith in individual selections." . . . If these general assertions were accepted as rebutting a defendant's prima facie case, the Equal Protection Clause "would be but a vain and illusory requirement." . . . The prosecutor therefore must articulate a neutral explanation related to the particular case to be tried. The trial court then will have the duty to determine if the defendant has established purposeful discrimination.

.   .   .   .   .   .   .   .   .   .   .   .   .   .   .   .

While we recognize, of course, that the peremptory challenge occupies an important position in our trial procedures, we do not agree that our decision today will undermine the contribution the challenge generally makes to the administration of justice. The reality of practice, amply reflected in many state and federal court opinions, shows that the challenge may be, and unfortunately at times has been, used to discriminate against black jurors. By requiring trial courts to be sensitive to the racially discriminatory use of peremptory challenges, our decision enforces the mandate of equal protection and furthers the ends of justice. In view of the heterogeneous population of our nation, public respect for our criminal justice system and the rule of law will be strengthened if we ensure that no citizen is disqualified from jury service because of his race. . . .

In this case, petitioner made a timely objection to the prosecutor's removal of all black persons on the venire. Because the trial court flatly rejected the objection without requiring the prosecutor to give an explanation for his action, we remand this case for further proceedings. If the trial court decides that the facts establish, prima facie, purposeful discrimination and the prosecutor does not come forward with a neutral explanation for his action, our precedents require that petitioner's conviction be reversed. . . .

It is so ordered.

JUSTICE MARSHALL, *concurring.*

I join Justice Powell's eloquent opinion for the Court, which takes a historic step toward eliminating the shameful practice of racial discrimination in the selection of juries. The Court's opinion cogently explains the pernicious nature of the racially discriminatory use of peremptory challenges, and the repugnancy of such discrimination to the Equal Protection Clause. The Court's opinion also ably demonstrates the inadequacy of any burden of proof for racially discriminatory use of peremptories that requires that "justice . . . sit supinely by" and be flouted in case after case before a remedy is available. I nonetheless write separately to express my views. The decision today will not end the racial discrimination that peremptories inject into the jury-selection process. That goal can be accomplished only by eliminating peremptory challenges entirely. . . .

. . . [W]hen a defendant can establish a prima facie case, trial courts face the difficult burden of assessing prosecutors' motives. . . . Any prosecutor can easily assert facially neutral reasons for striking a juror, and trial courts are ill-equipped to second-guess those reasons. . . .

Nor is outright prevarication by prosecutors the only danger here. "[I]t is even possible that an attorney may lie to himself in an effort to convince himself that his motives are legal." . . . A prosecutor's own conscious or unconscious racism may lead him easily to the conclusion that a prospective black juror is "sullen," or "distant," a characterization that would not have come to his mind if a white juror had acted identically. A judge's own conscious or unconscious racism may lead him to accept such an explanation as well supported. As Justice Rehnquist concedes, prosecutors' peremptories are based on their "seat-of-the-pants instincts" as to how particular jurors will vote. . . .

. . . Yet "seat-of-the-pants instincts" may often be just another term for racial prejudice. Even if all parties approach the Court's mandate with the best of conscious intentions, that mandate requires them to confront and overcome their own racism on all levels—a challenge I doubt all of them can meet. It is worth remembering that "114 years after the close of the War Between the States and nearly 100 years after *Strauder*, racial and other forms of discrimination still remain a fact of life, in the administration of justice as in our society as a whole." *Rose* v. *Mitchell,* 443 U.S. 545, 558–559 . . . (1979). . . .

[Dissent by Chief Justice Burger omitted.]

⁊ The following excerpt from Professor Charles Lawrence's groundbreaking article on unconscious racism considers what psychology has to teach law about recognizing and deterring racism. Perhaps Lawrence's analysis can help us to understand the importance of Justice Marshall's concurring opinion in the *Batson* v. *Kentucky* case just presented (Reading 16.3), and to evaluate whether Professor Alschuler's suggestion for bringing affirmative action to jury selection (Reading 16.5) might be not only practical and effective but necessary. Perhaps Lawrence's article will also help us think about why it is both so important and so difficult to ensure that trial by jury does not become an instrument of racial injustice.

In order to understand the significance of the Lawrence piece, it is necessary to think not only about race-based jury selection and the exercise of peremptory challenges, but also about the way that law constructs the very idea of racial discrimination. The question of whether legal descriptions of reality are consistent with everyday reality "on the street" has been central to understanding the relationship of law and society, especially in matters of race. To understand the Court's construction of racism in general and in jury selection in particular, it will first be useful to briefly describe the 1976 case of *Washington* v. *Davis,* 426 U.S. 229, to which Lawrence is responding.

The *Washington* case was brought to trial in 1970 by a group of African American job candidates for the metropolitan police department of Washington, D.C., which was a predominantly black city with a predominantly white police force at the time. In order to be enrolled in the police academy and then become a D.C. police officer, candidates had to take, among other things, a written exam. The exam, Test 21, had no provable relationship to job performance. It was an apparently race-neutral test of verbal ability and vocabulary that had been developed for the Civil Service Commission. Candidates taking Test 21 for entrance to the police academy had scores that could have, and perhaps should have, been predicted to depend on the race of the candidate. A substantial majority of whites who took the exam passed it, while a substantial majority of African Americans failed it.

Plaintiffs challenged the exam as being racially discriminatory in its *effect,* since it excluded the vast majority of them from becoming police officers on the basis of a written test that had no provable relationship to job performance or to skills that could be shown to be needed to become a competent police officer. In other words, the plaintiffs claimed that the actual impact of using this race-neutral test was to maintain a racially segregated police force. There was no proof offered that maintaining racial segregation was the *intentional motive* of the police department in deciding to require that recruits pass Test 21. But the history of using Test 21 may have made such a result foreseeable.

The U.S. Supreme Court ruled against the African American police candidates, holding that unless the plaintiffs could show some evidence that the police department had *intentionally* discriminated against them, the mere fact that African Americans continued to be excluded from service in the police force by Test 21 would not be regarded as a constitutional violation. In other words, racial *effects* of government policies would not be held to violate the equal protection principle unless specific racial *motives* were proven to have caused those effects. *Washington* v. *Davis* thus came to stand for the principle that institutional racism does not violate the Constitution. Since 1976, the intent principle enunciated in *Washington* v. *Davis* has embedded in law the idea that without proof of conscious and intentionally racist motives by government agencies no amount of actual racial segregation justifies a legal finding of unconstitutional discrimination.

This so-called "intent principle" has clear implications for the racial peremptory challenges considered in the *Batson* case. In *Batson* as in *Davis,* the Court focuses on the question of whether conscious racism is the motive for the challenged government action. In *Batson* specifically, the Court requires that a prosecutor provide the trial judge with a nonracial motive for certain suspect peremptory challenges. As you read the excerpts from Lawrence's article, consider whether Lawrence's analysis strengthens Justice Marshall's view that the intent requirement is an unworkable way to decide whether a peremptory challenge is racist, and that therefore all peremptories should be eliminated. Consider also whether affirmative action in jury selection, such as that advocated by Alschuler (Reading 16.5), seems more realistic and even necessary in light of the pervasive unconscious racism that the Court has been unwilling to recognize in its equal protection analysis.

## *16.4* The Id, the Ego, and Equal Protection Reckoning with Unconscious Racism   *Charles R. Lawrence III*

### PROLOGUE

IT IS 1948. I am sitting in a kindergarten class-room at the Dalton School, a fashionable and progressive New York City private school. My parents, both products of a segregated Mississippi school system, have come to New York to attend graduate and professional school. They have enrolled me and my sisters here at Dalton to avoid sending us to the public school in our neighborhood where the vast majority of the students are black and poor. They want us to escape the ravages of segregation, New York style.

It is circle time in the five-year-old group, and the teacher is reading us a book. As she reads, she passes the book around the circle so that each of us can see the illustrations. The book's title is *Little Black Sambo*. Looking back, I remember only one part of the story, one illustration: Little Black Sambo is running around a stack of pancakes with a tiger chasing him. He is very black and has a minstrel's white mouth. His hair is tied up in many pigtails, each pigtail tied with a different color ribbon. I have seen the picture before the book reaches my place in the circle. I have heard the teacher read the "comical" text describing Sambo's plight and have heard the laughter of my classmates. There is a knot in the pit of my stomach. I feel panic and shame. I do not have the words to articulate my feelings—words like "stereotype" and "stigma" that might help cathart the shame and place it outside of me where it began. But I am slowly realizing that, as the only black child in the circle, I have some kinship with the tragic and ugly hero of this story—that my classmates are laughing at me as well as at him. I wish I could laugh along with my friends. I wish I could disappear.

I am in a vacant lot next to my house with black friends from the neighborhood. We are listening to *Amos 'n' Andy* on a small radio and laughing uproariously. My father comes out and turns off the radio. He reminds me that he disapproves of this show that pokes fun at Negroes. I feel bad—less from my father's reprimand than from a sense that I have betrayed him and myself, that I have joined my classmates in laughing at us.

I am certain that my kindergarten teacher was not intentionally racist in choosing *Little Black Sambo*. I knew even then, from a child's intuitive sense, that she was a good, well-meaning person. A less benign combination of racial mockery and profit motivated the white men who produced the radio show and played the roles of Amos and Andy. But we who had joined their conspiracy by our laughter had not intended to demean our race.

A dozen years later I am a student at Haverford College. Again, I am a token black presence in a white world. A companion whose face and name I can't remember seeks to compliment me by saying, "I don't think of you as a Negro." I understand his benign intention and accept the compliment. But the knot is in my stomach again. Once again, I have betrayed myself.

This happened to me more than a few times. Each time my interlocutor was a good, liberal, white person who intended to express feelings of shared humanity. I did not yet understand the racist implications of the way in which the feelings were conceptualized. I am certain that my white friends did not either. We had not yet grasped the compliment's underlying premise: To be thought of as a Negro is to be thought of as less than human. We were all victims of our culture's racism. We had all grown up on *Little Black Sambo* and *Amos 'n' Andy*.

Another ten years pass. I am thirty-three. My daughter, Maia, is three. I greet a pink-faced, four-year-old boy on the steps of her nursery school. He proudly presents me with a book he has brought for his teacher to read to the class.

"It's my favorite," he says. The book is a new edition of *Little Black Sambo.*

## INTRODUCTION

This article reconsiders the doctrine of discriminatory purpose that was established by the 1976 decision, *Washington* v. *Davis.* This now well-established doctrine requires plaintiffs challenging the constitutionality of a facially neutral law to prove a racially discriminatory purpose on the part of those responsible for the law's enactment or administration.

*Davis* has spawned a considerable body of literature treating its merits and failings. Minorities and civil rights advocates have been virtually unanimous in condemning *Davis* and its progeny. They have been joined by a significant number of constitutional scholars who have been equally disapproving, if more restrained, in assessing its damage to the cause of equal opportunity. These critics advance two principal arguments. The first is that a motive-centered doctrine of racial discrimination places a very heavy, and often impossible, burden of persuasion on the wrong side of the dispute. Improper motives are easy to hide. And because behavior results from the interaction of a multitude of motives, governmental officials will always be able to argue that racially neutral considerations prompted their actions. Moreover, where several decisionmakers are involved, proof of racially discriminatory motivation is even more difficult.

The second objection to the *Davis* doctrine is more fundamental. It argues that the injury of racial inequality exists irrespective of the decisionmakers' motives. Does the black child in a segregated school experience less stigma and humiliation because the local school board did not consciously set out to harm her? Are blacks less prisoners of the ghetto because the decision that excludes them from an all-white neighborhood was made with property values and not race in mind? Those who make this second objection reason that the "facts of racial inequality are the real problem." They urge that racially disproportionate harm should trigger heightened judicial scrutiny without consideration of motive.

Supporters of the intent requirement are equally adamant in asserting the doctrine's propriety. . . .

My own sympathies lie with the critics of the doctrine of discriminatory purpose. . . . But I do not intend to simply add another chapter to the intent/impact debate. Rather, I wish to suggest another way to think about racial discrimination, a way that more accurately describes both its origins and the nature of the injury it inflicts.

.   .   .   .   .   .   .   .   .   .   .   .   .   .   .   .   .

Americans share a common historical and cultural heritage in which racism has played and still plays a dominant role. Because of this shared experience, we also inevitably share many ideas, attitudes, and beliefs that attach significance to an individual's race and induce negative feelings and opinions about nonwhites. To the extent that this cultural belief system has influenced all of us, we are all racists. At the same time, most of us are unaware of our racism. We do not recognize the ways in which our cultural experience has influenced our beliefs about race or the occasions on which those beliefs affect our actions. In other words, a large part of the behavior that produces racial discrimination is influenced by unconscious racial motivation.

There are two explanations for the unconscious nature of our racially discriminatory beliefs and ideas. First, Freudian theory states that the human mind defends itself against the discomfort of guilt by denying or refusing to recognize those ideas, wishes, and beliefs that conflict with what the individual has learned is good or right. While our historical experience has made racism an integral part of our culture, our society has more recently embraced an ideal that rejects racism as immoral. When an individual experiences conflict between racist ideas and the societal ethic that condemns those ideas, the mind excludes his racism from consciousness.

Second, the theory of cognitive psychology states that the culture—including, for example, the media and an individual's parents, peers, and authority figures—transmits certain beliefs and preferences. Because these beliefs are so much a part of the culture, they are not experienced as explicit lessons. Instead, they seem part of the individual's rational ordering of her perceptions of the world. The individual is unaware, for example, that the ubiquitous presence of a cultural stereotype has influenced her perception that blacks are lazy or unintelligent. Because racism is so deeply ingrained in our culture, it is likely to be transmitted by tacit understandings, because they have never been articulated, are less likely to be experienced at a conscious level.

In short, requiring proof of conscious or intentional motivation as a prerequisite to constitutional recognition that a decision is race-dependent ignores much of what we understand about how the human mind works. It also disregards both the irrationality of racism and the profound effect that the history of American race relations has had on the individual and collective unconscious.

It may often be appropriate for the legal system to disregard the influence of the unconscious on individual or collective behavior. But where the goal is the eradication of invidious racial discrimination, the law must recognize racism's primary source. The equal protection clause requires the elimination of governmental decisions that take race into account without good and important reasons. Therefore, equal protection doctrine must find a way to come to grips with unconscious racism.

This effort in inform the discriminatory intent requirement with the learning of twentieth century psychology is important for at least three reasons. First, the present doctrine, by requiring proof that the defendant was aware of his animus against blacks, severely limits the number of individual cases in which the courts will acknowledge and remedy racial discrimination.

Second, the existing intent requirement's assignment of individualized fault or responsibility for the existence of racial discrimination distorts our perceptions about the causes of discrimination and leads us to think about racism in a way that advances the disease rather than combatting it. By insisting that a blameworthy perpetrator be found before the existence of racial discrimination can be acknowledged, the Court creates an imaginary world where discrimination does not exist unless it was consciously

intended. And by acting as if this imaginary world was real and insisting that we participate in this fantasy, the Court and the law it promulgates subtly shape our perceptions of society. The decision to deny relief no longer finds its basis only in raw political power or economic self-interest; it is now justifiable on moral grounds. If there is no discrimination, there is no need for a remedy; if blacks are being treated fairly yet remain at the bottom of the socioeconomic ladder, only their own inferiority can explain their subordinate position.

Finally, the intent doctrine's focus on the narrowest and most unrealistic understanding of individual fault has also engendered much of the resistance to and resentment of affirmative action programs and other race-conscious remedies for past and continuing discrimination. If there can be no discrimination without an identifiable criminal, then "innocent" individuals will resent the burden of remedying an injury for which the law says they are not responsible. Understanding the cultural source of our racism obviates the need for fault, as traditionally conceived, without denying our collective responsibility for racism's eradication. We cannot be individually blamed for unconsciously harboring attitudes that are inescapable in a culture permeated with racism. And without the necessity for blame, our resistance to accepting the need and responsibility for remedy will be lessened.

## I. "THY SPEECH MAKETH THEE MANIFEST": A PRIMER ON THE UNCONSCIOUS AND RACE

We have found—that is we have been obliged to assume—that very powerful mental processes or ideas exist which can produce all the effects in mental life that ordinary ideas do (including effects that can in their turn become conscious as ideas), though they themselves do not become conscious.

Whatever our preferred theoretical analysis, there is considerable commonsense evidence from our everyday experience to confirm that we all harbor prejudiced attitudes that are kept from our consciousness.

When, for example, a well-known sports broadcaster is carried away by the excitement of a brilliant play by an African American professional football player and refers to the player as a "little monkey" during a nationally televised broadcast, we have witnessed the prototypical parapraxes, or unintentional slip of the tongue. This sportscaster views himself as progressive on issues of race. Many of his most important professional associates are black, and he would no doubt profess that more than a few are close friends. After the incident, he initially claimed no memory of it and then, when confronted with videotaped evidence, apologized and said that no racial slur was intended. There is no reason to doubt the sincerity of his assertion. Why would he intentionally risk antagonizing his audience and damaging his reputation and career? But his inadvertent slip of the tongue was not random. It is evidence of the continuing presence of a derogatory racial stereotype that he has repressed from consciousness and that has momentarily slipped past his ego's censors. Likewise, when Nancy Reagan appeared before a public gathering of then-presidential-candidate Ronald Reagan's political supporters and said that she wished he could be there to "see all these beautiful white people," one can hardly imagine that it was her self-conscious intent to proclaim publicly her preference for the company of caucasians.

Incidents of this kind are not uncommon, even if only the miscues of the powerful and famous are likely to come to the attention of the press. But because the unconscious also influences selective perceptions, whites are unlikely to hear many of the inadvertent racial slights that are made daily in their presence.

Another manifestation of unconscious racism is akin to the slip of the tongue. One might call it a slip of the mind: While one says what one intends, one fails to grasp the racist implications of one's benignly motivated words or behavior. For example, in the late 1950s and early 1960s, when integration and assimilation were unquestioned ideals among those who consciously rejected the ideology of racism, white liberals often expressed their acceptance of and friendship with blacks by telling them that they "did not think of them as Negroes." Their conscious intent was complimentary. The speaker was saying, "I think of you as normal human be-

ings, just like me." But he was not conscious of the underlying implication of his words. What did this mean about most Negroes? Were they not normal human beings? If the white liberal were asked if this was his inference, he would doubtless have protested that his words were being misconstrued and that he only intended to state that he did not think of anyone in racial terms. But to say that one does not think of a Negro as a Negro is to say that one thinks of him as something else. The statement is made in the context of the real world, and implicit in it is a comparison to some norm. In this case the norm is whiteness. The white liberal's unconscious thought, his slip of the mind, is, "I think of you as different from other Negroes, as more like white people."

One indication of the nonneutrality of the statement, "I don't think of you as a Negro," when spoken as a compliment by a white is the incongruity of the response, "I don't think of you as white." This could also be a complimentary remark coming from a black, conveying the fact that she does not think of her friend in the usual negative terms she associates with whiteness. But this statement does not make sense coming from an individual who would accept as complimentary a statement characterizing her as unlike other Negroes. If anything, the response only makes sense as a lighthearted but cautionary retort. It conveys the following message: "I understand that your conscious intent was benign. But let me tell you something, friend. I think being black is just fine. If anything, our friendship is possible because you are unlike most white folks."

Of course, the statements of both these interlocuters are enthnocentric. But it is the white who has made the slip of the mind. He was unmindful of the ethnocentric premise upon which his "compliment" was based. He would find it painful to know that it is a premise in which he believes. His black friend's ethnocentrism is self-conscious and self-affirming. She is well aware of the impact of her reply. It is a defensive parry against the dominant society's racism.

A crucial factor in the process that produces unconscious racism is the tacitly transmitted cultural stereotype. If an individual has never known a black doctor or lawyer or is exposed to blacks only through a mass media where they are portrayed in the stereotyped roles of comedian, criminal, musician, or athlete, he is likely to deduce that blacks as a group are naturally inclined toward certain behavior and unfit for certain roles. But the lesson is not explicit: It is learned, internalized, and used without an awareness of its source. Thus, an individual may select a white job applicant over an equally qualified black and honestly believe that this decision was based on observed intangibles unrelated to race. The employer perceives the white candidate as "more articulate," "more collegial," "more thoughtful," or "more charismatic." He is unaware of the learned stereotype that influenced his decision. Moreover, he has probably also learned an explicit lesson of which he is very much aware: Good, law-abiding people do not judge others on the basis of race. Even the most thorough investigation of conscious motive will not uncover the race-based stereotype that has influenced his decision.

. . . . . . . . . . . . . . . . .

If the purpose of the law's search for racial animus or discriminatory intent is to identify a morally culpable perpetrator, the existing intent requirement fails to achieve that purpose. There will be no evidence of self-conscious racism where the actors have internalized the relatively new American cultural morality which holds racism wrong or have learned racist attitudes

and beliefs through tacit rather than explicit lessons. The actor himself will be unaware that his actions, or the racially neutral feelings and ideas that accompany them, have racist origins.

Of course, one can argue that the law should govern only consciously motivated actions—that societal sanctions can do no more than attempt to require that the individual's ego act as society's agent in censoring out those unconscious drives that society has defined as immoral. Under this view, the law can sanction a defective ego that has not fully internalized current societal morality and has, therefore, allowed illegal racist wishes to reach consciousness and fruition in an illegal act. But the law should not hold an individual responsible for wishes that never reach consciousness, even if they also come to fruition in discriminatory acts.

The problem is that this argument does not tell us why the law should hold the individual responsible for racial injury that results from one form of ego disguise but not the other. I believe the law should be equally concerned when the mind's censor successfully disguises a socially repugnant wish like racism if that motive produces behavior that has a discriminatory result as injurious as if it flowed from a consciously held motive.*

. . . . . . . . . . . . . . . . .

*The remainder of the article is omitted but may be found at 39 *Stanford Law Review* 317 (1987).—Ed.

---

## 16.5 | Racial Quotas and the Jury    *Albert W. Alschuler**

### I. SOME HISTORY

FEW STATEMENTS ARE MORE likely to evoke disturbing images of American criminal justice than this

Albert Alschuler, "Racial Quotas and the Jury" *Duke Law Journal*, vol. 704, 1995. Copyright © 1995 Duke University. Reprinted by permission. Some footnotes have been omitted and others renumbered.

*Wilson-Dickinson Professor, the University of Chicago Law School.

one: "The defendant was tried by an all-white jury."

This statement might bring to mind the Scottsboro boys—uneducated African-American youths riding on a freight train through Jackson County, Alabama, in 1931; victors in a fight with white youths on the train; charged after their arrests with raping two white women; rushed to judgment before all-white juries; and sentenced to death. The state's denial of effective counsel to these defendants led to the Supreme Court's decision in *Powell v. Alabama,* in which the Court held for the first time that the Constitution affords a right to counsel in state capital proceedings. Following the ruling in *Powell,* following another Supreme Court decision three years later condemning racial discrimination in the selection of a Scottsboro defendant's jury on retrial, and following a supposed rape victim's repudiation of her charges, further retrials before all-white juries produced new convictions. Pleas from Franklin and Eleanor Roosevelt for gubernatorial pardons proved unavailing. The last of the Scottsboro defendants to be released from prison was paroled in 1950. That same year, Alabama sought the extradition of another who had escaped to Michigan.[1]

One also might think of an earlier time than Scottsboro and of the Ku Klux Klan's epidemic of violence against African-Americans and white Republicans in the years following the Civil War. Senator John Sherman, a supporter of the Ku Klux Act of 1871, recited a series of atrocities in the South and noted that "from the beginning to the end in all this extent of territory no man has ever been convicted or punished for any of these offenses, not one." One of several southern judges who offered evidentiary support for Sherman's allegations declared, "In nine cases out of ten the men who commit the crimes constitute or sit on the grand jury, either they themselves or their near relatives or friends, sympathizers, aiders, or abettors. . . .

Sherman later supported the 1875 federal statute that outlawed racial discrimination in state jury selection. Like other Republican leaders, he recognized that all-white juries would serve as instruments of oppression not only when African-American litigants came before them but also when white jurors closed their eyes to the use of terror and violence to enforce America's racial caste system. As an African-American commenta-

tor said in 1912, the problem is "not so much that the negro fails to get justice before the courts" as that "too often . . . the . . . white man . . . escapes it." Gunnar Myrdal's landmark 1944 study of race in America declared, "It is notorious that practically never have white lynching mobs been brought to court in the South, even when the killers are known to all in the community and are mentioned by name in the local press."

One's thoughts might turn to a time more recent than Scottsboro—the summer of 1955, when in Money, Mississippi, Emmett Till, a fourteen-year-old African-American visitor from Chicago, accepted a dare to speak to a white woman. "Bye, Baby," he said. Several days later, Till's mangled body was discovered in the Tallahatchie River. Roy Bryant, the husband of the white woman, and J.W. Milam, the woman's brother, were charged with Till's murder. The principal evidence against them was the testimony of an African-American, Mose Wright. An all-white jury took slightly more than an hour to acquit the defendants. One juror explained, "If we hadn't stopped to drink pop, it wouldn't have taken that long." Following the defendants' acquittal, they sold their story to a journalist for $4,000. Bryant and Milam said that they had meant merely to frighten Till but "had" to kill him when he refused to beg for mercy. During the next decade, as large-scale civil rights activity came to the South, all-white juries failed to convict the defendants accused of killing Medgar Evers, Viola Liuzzo, and Lemuel Penn.

Talk of all-white juries might evoke a time still closer to the present. In Miami in 1980, four white police officers were tried on charges that they had beaten to death an African-American arrested for a traffic offense. The defendants' attorneys, acting together, struck every potential African-American juror, and the all-white jury that their challenges produced acquitted the officers. The Miami riots followed. Four years later, another Miami police officer was charged with manslaughter in the death of an African-American suspect. Again, the defense attorney's strikes produced an all-white jury; again the defendant was acquitted; and again the acquittal sparked public outcry.

In thinking of race and juries, the events of April 29, 1992, are likely to be close to mind. On that date, a California jury with no African-

---

[1]Although the Scottsboro defendants escaped execution, the link between all-white juries and racial disparity in the imposition of capital punishment in the South has been incontestable. Between 1930 and 1977, of the 62 men whom Georgia executed for rape, all but four were African-Americans. *See* McCleskey v. Kemp, 481 U.S. 279, 332 (1987) (Brennan, J., dissenting).

American members failed to convict any of four Los Angeles police officers of misconduct despite the fact that most of these officers had been videotaped kicking and beating Rodney King, an African-American suspect, as he lay on the ground. The jury's decision triggered the worst race riot in American history,[2] two days of violence that cost fifty-eight lives and nearly one billion dollars in property damage.[3]

Two conclusions about juries composed entirely of members of America's majority race seem almost too obvious to mention. First, in many communities, these juries are mistrusted; and second, the mistrust has deep historical roots.

## II. THE HENNEPIN COUNTY QUOTAS

A year before the 1992 Los Angeles riots, an all-white grand jury in Minneapolis, Minnesota, exonerated Dan May, a white police officer who had shot and killed Tycel Nelson, a seventeen-year-old African-American suspect. The grand jury's no-bill of Officer May and the protests and tension that followed were among the circumstances that prompted a Hennepin County task force to recommend, and the Minnesota Supreme Court to approve, a plan for abolishing all-white grand juries in Hennepin County. Governments can reduce the likelihood of all-white juries in many ways, but there is only one way to end them. The Hennepin County Task Force proposed racial quotas. Because the use of quotas in selecting petit jurors would not pose significantly different constitutional issues from those raised by their use to select grand jurors, the Hennepin County proposal offers a useful vehicle for assessing the issues raised by affirma-

tive action in the selection of both grand and petit jurors.[4] . . .

## III. OTHER QUOTAS

The Hennepin County proposal is one of a number of affirmative-action jury-selection measures currently under consideration or already in place in American jurisdictions. In Arizona, a bar committee has proposed dividing jury lists into subsets by race and drawing jurors from each subset. Some Arizona judges currently strike trial juries that, in their view, do not include adequate numbers of minority jurors. In DeKalb County, Georgia, jury commissioners divide jury lists into thirty-six demographic groups (for example, black females aged 35 to 44); they then use a computer to ensure the proportional representation of every group on every venire.

The Federal Jury Selection and Service Act of 1968 was designed to ensure a measure of racial balance in federal jury panels. The Act requires panels to be drawn from voter registration rolls or from lists of actual voters unless the use of these sources would lead to the substantial underrepresentation of a racial (or other) group. In that event, the Act orders courts to augment the voting rolls with other sources.

For ten years, the U.S. District Court for the Eastern District of Michigan maintained a racially balanced jury wheel by sending extra jury questionnaires to areas in which African-Americans constituted 65% or more of the population. More recently, this court has sought

---

[2]William Julius Wilson, *Crisis and Challenge: Race and the New Urban Poverty*, U. CHI. REC., Dec. 8, 1994, at 2, 4.

[3]*See* Seth Mydans, *Prosecutor Seeks Retrial of Officer in King Beating*, N.Y. TIMES, May 14, 1992, at A20; Neal R. Peirce, *Look Homeward, City of Angels*, 24 NAT'L J. 1250 (1992). Mayor Tom Bradley of Los Angeles voiced the sentiment of many Americans when he said of the videotape, "We saw what we saw. What we saw was a crime." Bill Boyarsky, *Ashes of a Mayor's Dream*. L.A. TIMES, May 1, 1992, at B2. A federal court jury composed of nine whites, two African-Americans, and one Latino later convicted two of the officers involved in the beating of violating Rodney King's civil rights. *See* Jim Newton, *Koon, Powell Get 2 1/2 Years in Prison*, L.A. TIMES, Aug. 5, 1993, at A1; Jim Newton, *Racially Mixed Jury Selected for King Trial*, L.A. TIMES, Feb. 23, 1993, at A1.

[4]The use of quotas to select petit juries would have been a more significant innovation in the criminal justice system. Grand juries no longer initiate most felony prosecutions; unlike most petit juries, they need not act by unanimous vote and typically may act by majority vote; their function is to determine the existence of probable cause rather than guilt beyond a reasonable doubt; they proceed without an adversary presentation of evidence; and they often seem dominated by the prosecutors who advise them. MARVIN FRANKEL & GARY NAFTALIS, THE GRAND JURY: AN INSTITUTION ON TRIAL 16–24, 67–71 (1977).

Perhaps the Hennepin County Task Force was asked to focus on grand rather than petit juries simply because all-white grand juries were a special source of controversy and concern. In addition, the fact that grand juries are substantially larger than petit juries might have made the grand jury seem a more appropriate body for the initiation of affirmative action measures.

demographic balance by removing from the jury wheel some questionnaires of whites.

Similar color-conscious jury selection methods are in use in other jurisdictions to "balance the box"—that is, to ensure racial proportionality in the initial pool from which petit and grand juries are drawn. Seeking racial balance in the wheels and boxes from which petit and grand jurors are drawn appears to be less controversial than seeking racial balance in juries themselves. . . .

## V. JURIES ARE DIFFERENT

The Supreme Court has recognized that the importance of representative juries justifies a departure from the standards employed in equal protection litigation to test assertedly discriminatory governmental action. The Court has held that in criminal cases the systematic exclusion of an identifiable group from jury venires violates a "fair cross-section requirement" implicit in the Sixth Amendment right to jury trial. In 1940, the Court wrote, "It is part of the established tradition in the use of juries as instruments of public justice that the jury be a body truly representative of the community," and in 1975 the Court declared, "[T]he selection of a petit jury from a representative cross section of the community is an essential component of the Sixth Amendment right to a jury trial." Although the fair cross-section requirement does not truly require that either juries or jury venires include a cross-section of the population (a result that would require the use of demographic quotas), the Court's test of discrimination under the Sixth Amendment looks less to purpose and more to effect than does the test of discrimination that the Court employs in cases arising under the Equal Protection Clause.[5]

Juries are distinctive both because affirmative action in jury selection has special virtues and because it is likely to prove less costly to individuals and society than affirmative action in other contexts. . . .

Diverse viewpoints are more important to a jury's performance than diverse skin color, but promoting diversity of race and ethnicity may provide a more workable means of ensuring diverse viewpoints than attempting to probe viewpoints directly through questionnaires, voir dire examinations, and the like. The experiences of members of different racial and ethnic groups tend to differ in ways that may affect their perceptions of some issues that come before juries. Not only would the direct probing of the attitudes of prospective jurors be burdensome and invasive of their privacy, but it also would pose a risk of governmental viewpoint discrimination. This risk seems insubstantial when jury selection rests on objective demographic indicators of social experience and when no group is assured more representation than its share of the population.

In short, the Hennepin County quotas would present few of the difficulties that prompt concern about other affirmative action programs and about racial classifications in general. These quotas would not deprive individuals of significant tangible benefits; they would not brand any group as inferior or evaluate any individual on the basis of racial stereotypes; and far from diverting the grand jury from its central mission, they would be likely to enhance the grand jury's achievement of its objectives.

## VI. PEREMPTORY CHALLENGES AND RACIAL BALANCE

Ironically, the Supreme Court Justices who appear most likely to disapprove the Hennepin County proposal have expressed sympathy for a more invidious procedure that they believe may contribute in some circumstances to racially balanced juries. In *Georgia v. McCollum,* the Supreme Court held that the Constitution forbids defense attorneys as well as prosecutors from exercising peremptory challenges to exclude prospective African-American jurors on the basis of race. [The *Batson* case, presented earlier, forbids only prosecutors from exercising peremptory challenges on racial grounds.—ED.] An *amicus curiae* brief submitted by the NAACP in support of the *McCollum* ruling suggested that the use of

---

[5] *See Duren,* 439 U.S. at 368 n.26 (noting that in equal protection cases, statistical disparity is evidence of discriminatory purpose that may be rebutted, but that "in Sixth Amendment fair-cross-section cases, systematic disproportion itself demonstrates an infringement . . ."); WAYNE R. LaFAVE & JEROLD H. ISRAEL, CRIMINAL PROCEDURE §21.2(c).

peremptory challenges by minority defendants to exclude prospective white jurors should be treated differently. The brief declared, "The only possible chance the defendant may have of having any minority jurors on the jury that actually tries him will be if he uses his peremptories to strike members of the majority race." . . . Justice Thomas . . . declared, "I am certain that black criminal defendants will rue the day that this court ventured down th[e] road" of using the Constitution to restrict peremptory challenges.

An unrestricted regime of peremptory challenges of the sort apparently favored by Justice Thomas and other Supreme Court Justices is far more likely to produce all-white juries and other forms of racial imbalance than a regime in which discrimination in the exercise of peremptory challenges is forbidden. . . .

Even the asymmetrical regime of challenges favored by the NAACP, permitting defendants to challenge prospective jurors on racial grounds only when the jurors are white, would produce racial balance only by happenstance and only on the basis of a partisan attorney's stereotypical judgment about the members of a racial group. . . .

The Hennepin County plan does not depend on the uncertain outcome of partisan race wars (or race games) in the courtroom, and it does not rest on any judgment about how the members of racial groups are likely to vote in particular cases. Unlike the strategies of partisans, this plan is designed to promote the public objectives of more effective grand jury deliberation and enhanced public confidence in grand jury rulings. The Hennepin County proposal rests on only one group judgment—that the members of racial minorities are likely to have (or sometimes may have, or may reasonably be seen by the public as having) distinctive experiences and perspectives that can improve a grand jury's performance. . . .

Rulings on the use of peremptory challenges and other jury qualification issues sometimes give judges a sub rosa opportunity to engage in color-conscious jury selection, and their efforts to achieve racial balance may prove more costly than openly acknowledged forms of affirmative action. In the second trial of the police officers accused of beating Rodney King (the federal court trial), Judge John G. Davies refused to permit the defendants to challenge peremptorily an African-American who had failed to disclose that he lived in South Central Los Angeles, near the center of the rioting that had followed the first King verdict. The defendants' lawyers feared that this prospective juror had omitted the information deliberately in an effort to make his way onto the jury and to remedy the perceived injustice of the first King verdict. Although Judge Davies ruled that the lawyers lacked a racially neutral reason for their challenge, he might have had another reason for retaining the challenged juror. As George Fletcher noted, "[N]o one—not the defense, not the prosecution, not the judge—dared to go to trial without fair 'community' representation on the jury." . . .

## VIII. SOME QUESTIONS AND PROBLEMS

**A. Racial Matching** Shari Lynn Johnson has proposed that every African-American, Native American, or Hispanic-American defendant be entitled to the inclusion of three "racially similar" jurors on a jury of twelve. The Hennepin County proposal, however, does not attempt to match the races of jurors and defendants, and contrary to common assumptions, its principal objective is not to assure every minority defendant a jury of his "peers."

The presence of minority-race jurors may be especially important when minority-race defendants are on trial, but the value of inclusive jury selection procedures is not limited to the cases of these defendants. The discussion of verdicts by all-white juries with which this Article began mentioned only one prosecution in which the defendants were members of a racial minority, that of the Scottsboro boys. Most of these troublesome verdicts came in cases in which the defendants were white. In recent years, cases in which white law enforcement officers have been accused of mistreating minority suspects have been a special source of concern. White jurors may tend to view the victimization of nonwhites as less serious than the victimization of members of their own racial group. This danger seems fully as strong as the danger that white jurors will be biased against minority defendants. Indeed, verdicts by all-white juries sometimes have been problematic even when both the defendant and his asserted victim were white; consider cases in which white jurors tolerated violence against white Republicans following the Civil War and against white civil rights workers a century later.

Moreover, the inclusion of minority jurors can make juries fairer and more effective in cases that do not present racially sensitive issues. Justice Marshall wrote for the Supreme Court in *Peters* v. *Kiff:*

> [W]e are unwilling to make the assumption that the exclusion of Negroes has relevance only for issues involving race. When any large and identifiable segment of the community is excluded from jury service, the effect is to remove from the jury room qualities of human nature and varieties of human experience, the range of which is unknown and perhaps unknowable. It is not necessary to assume that the excluded group will consistently vote as a class in order to conclude, as we do, that its exclusion deprives the jury of a perspective on human events that may have unsuspected importance in any case. . . .

Affirmative action in jury selection has value in cases other than those with minority defendants. Moreover, efforts to match jurors and defendants by race and ethnicity could prove difficult and unbecoming. These efforts would require courts to confront such questions as whether Mexican-Americans are sufficiently similar in background and culture to Puerto Ricans to merit affirmative inclusion on the juries of Puerto Rican defendants, whether Filipino-Americans are sufficiently similar in race and ethnicity to warrant their affirmative inclusion on the juries of Japanese-American defendants, and whether any prospective jurors are racially or ethnically similar to a defendant whose grandparents are African-American, Hispanic-American, Asian-American, and Native American. As the United States grows more multiracial and multicultural, troublesome issues of racial matching could arise more frequently. . . .

. . . [T]he members of nonracial groups may feel aggrieved when no members of their groups sit on the juries that resolve cases drawing their strong interest and concern. Nevertheless, in a reasonably small body like a jury, ensuring proportional representation by race, gender, sexual orientation, handicap, religion, nationality, wealth, and age would be impossible. The Hennepin County Attorney, Michael O. Freeman (who appointed the Hennepin County Task Force and who strongly supports its proposals), reports that he personally would draw the line at race and accept any political consequences that follow.

This line seems appropriate. No other group in America can recite a history of mistreatment by juries comparable to the mistreatment of African-Americans that the opening section of this Article chronicled in part. . . .

. . . [But] the claim that jurors serve in a representative capacity seems troublesome: no individual juror should be expected to represent anyone other than herself. If Hennepin County's jury selection methods encouraged minority-race jurors to view themselves not simply as independent citizens, but as representatives of a race or a people, that effect would be regrettable. The proposition that jurors both represent others and act independently may seem contradictory, but perhaps the contradiction can be resolved if *juries* but not *jurors* act as community representatives. The selection of a sufficiently large body of jurors through sufficiently inclusive means may permit every juror to vote her conscience while still providing some assurance that the jury's collective judgment accords with general community sentiments. . . .

One danger posed by the nonrandom inclusion on juries of people with special qualifications is that of ideological jury-stacking. This danger seems most pronounced when the likelihood of distinctive viewpoints is itself considered a qualification for service and when officials may guarantee some favored groups greater-than-proportional representation. The Constitution probably should limit the government's ability to place its thumb on the scales in the marketplace of ideas established in most jury deliberations. Even if diversity rather than representation is the principal objective of the Hennepin County proposal, proportionality may remain an essential constraint.

The principal purpose of the Hennepin County proposal is not to enhance any group's aggregate voting power. It is to guarantee that minority voices will be heard in every case rather than loudly in one, softly in another, and not at all in a third depending on the luck of a random draw. . . .

. . . Within the limits of proportionality set by this baseline, the Hennepin County proposal could increase the number of minorities on grand juries. Hennepin County has, however, bounded diversity with a fair and sensible principle of proportionality.

## IX. THE DOWNSIDE

The preceding Part considered some possibly troublesome aspects of Hennepin County's proposed methods of jury selection. The principal objection to these color-conscious methods, however, is simply that they are color-conscious. A program grounded on the perception that the members of different races have different viewpoints may make it more likely that racially distinctive viewpoints will persist. This program may encourage people to view themselves and others in racial terms. . . .

Americans are not color-blind. They cannot be. The Constitution does not require them to pretend to be. The Constitution requires only that the government not stigmatize or otherwise disadvantage people on the basis of race (at least not without a sufficiently compelling reason for doing so). The jury selection methods proposed in Hennepin County do not stigmatize or disadvantage people on the basis of race, and I believe that they are constitutional.

&❧ The following three cases raise the question of whether persons who have scruples against the death penalty should be excluded, for cause, from serving on a jury in a capital case. When persons opposed to capital punishment are excluded from serving by a judge during jury selection, the resulting jury is often called *death-qualified*. Because a jury of peers should be a fair cross section of the community, and because its decisions represent the conscience of the community in a particular criminal case, the exclusion from the jury of persons who are troubled by the imposition of the death penalty raises significant issues of morality, law, and social policy.

The degree to which individuals oppose or support the death penalty in general may of course vary enormously. Some feel conscience-bound to oppose the death penalty on moral or religious grounds, and would absolutely refuse to impose it. Others may in general prefer a sentence of life imprisonment without possibility of parole, but favor the death penalty under certain aggravated circumstances. Still others may simply be uncomfortable with the idea that the state can take human life, but not be sure whether they oppose capital punishment or just have "scruples against it." The degree of support for capital punishment may likewise vary.

Regardless of the degree to which one opposes—or supports—imposition of the death penalty, the reasons for these views may vary as well. For some it is a practical question of deterrence—will the death penalty deter others from committing similar crimes? Some may wonder whether the death penalty increases the prevalence of violence in the society. For others it is a matter of retribution or revenge—is the death penalty a more or less severe form of punishment than life imprisonment without parole? Can retribution be an appropriate sole justification for capital punishment in a modern society? Still others may consider the socioeconomic realities of how the death penalty is imposed, or whether it has been and continues to be used in a racially discriminatory manner, or the chance that failures of due process may mean that innocent persons are put to death or spend long years on death row before their innocence is discovered. Although many people outside the jury room may try to place their position on the death penalty within a moral, ethical, or religious context, there is some evidence that once on a jury in a capital case, many people try to distance themselves from the moral dimension of the issue by saying that the judge gave them no choice in sentencing (see Hugo Bedau, ed., *The Death Penalty in America,* 1997). As with any matter touching so deeply on the idea of justice, the state, and the sanctity of the individual human being, this matter of conscience and sociolegal policy is complex, changing, and subject to political and media manipulation.

In order to think clearly about the issue of death-qualified juries, the dissenting opinion of Associate Supreme Court Justice Harry Blackmun in the 1994 *Callins* v. *Collins* case (Reading 16.6) is presented before the death penalty jury selection cases. Blackmun's opinion in *Callins* marked a major transformation in his thinking. As he wrote then, "I no longer shall tinker with the machinery of death." Blackmun's opinion is presented in order to challenge the reader to think deeply and clearly about whether he or she opposes the death penalty and why. A similar stimulus to conscience and careful thought might also be gained by watching the movie, *The Green Mile,* or by attending one of the numerous lectures given by persons who spent years on death row for crimes that they did not commit. An open and robust discussion of all sides of the capital punishment issue should serve not only to stimulate the growth of conscience, but to illuminate what is at stake in the two death-qualified jury selection cases.

As you will see in these two cases, *Witherspoon* v. *Illinois* (Reading 16.7) and *Lockhart* v. *McCree* (Reading 16.8), states that provide for capital punishment usually impanel a single jury to deliberate in two phases, the guilt-determining phase and the sentence-imposing phase. While the two-phase deliberation arrangement is not required by the U.S. Constitution, it does meet the Supreme Court's requirement in *Gregg* v. *Georgia,* 428 U.S. 153 (1976), that " . . . the penalty of death not be imposed in an arbitrary and capricious manner . . . [and that] . . . the sentencing authority [be] given adequate information and guidance. . . ."

The same jury considers both questions, so the jury selection process may examine a prospective juror's ability to fairly discharge the jurors' duties in either or both phases. As you read these edited Supreme Court opinions, consider which phase of the trial concerns the Court most and why. Consider also how the intensity of a prospective juror's views might affect whether he or she is excluded, and whether the Court's legal standard for exclusion is fair to the defendant. Is the death-qualified jury a fair cross section of the community if it excludes people with a particular moral or religious sensibility? Does it violate a defendant's right to an impartial jury by "tilting" the jury in favor of the prosecution in the guilt-determining phase? Most important, think about whether the legal doctrine that has evolved for the death-qualified jury respects the purposes of jury trial and is based on a definition of jury of peers consistent with the importance of juries to the democratic experiment.

## 16.6 | *Callins* v. *Collins*   114 S.Ct. 1127 (1994)

JUSTICE BLACKMUN, *dissenting.*

On February 23, 1994, at approximately 1:00 A.M., Bruce Edwin Callins will be executed by the State of Texas. Intravenous tubes attached to his arms will carry the instrument of death, a toxic fluid designed specifically for the purpose of killing human beings. The witnesses, standing a few feet away, will behold Callins, no longer a defendant, an appellant, or a petitioner, but a man, strapped to a gurney, and seconds away from extinction.

Within days, or perhaps hours, the memory of Callins will begin to fade. The wheels of justice will churn again, and somewhere, another jury or another judge will have the unenviable task of determining whether some human being is to live or die. We hope, of course, that the defendant whose life is at risk will be represented by competent counsel—someone who is inspired by the awareness that a less-than-vigorous defense truly could have fatal consequences for the defendant. We hope that the attorney will investigate all aspects of the case, follow all evidentiary and procedural rules, and appear before a judge who is still committed to the protection of defendants' rights—even now, as the prospect of meaningful judicial oversight has diminished. In the same vein, we hope that the prosecution, in urging the penalty of death, will have exercised its discretion wisely, free from bias, prejudice, or political motive, and will be humbled, rather than emboldened, by the awesome authority conferred by the State.

But even if we can feel confident that these actors will fulfill their roles to the best of their human ability, our collective conscience will remain uneasy. Twenty years have passed since this Court declared that the death penalty must be imposed fairly, and with reasonable consistency, or not at all, see *Furman* v. *Georgia,* 408 U.S. 238, 92 S.Ct. 2726, 33 L.Ed.2d 346 (1972), and, despite the effort of the States and courts to devise legal formulas and procedural rules to meet this daunting challenge, the death penalty remains fraught with arbitrariness, discrimination, caprice, and mistake. This is not to say that the problems with the death penalty today are identical to those that were present 20 years ago. Rather, the problems that were pursued down one hole with procedural rules and verbal formulas have come to the surface somewhere else, just as virulent and pernicious as they were in their original form. Experience has taught us that the constitutional goal of eliminating arbitrariness and discrimination from the administration of death can never be achieved without compromising an equally essential component of fundamental fairness—individualized sentencing. See *Lockett* v. *Ohio,* 438 U.S. 586, 98 S.Ct. 2954, 57 L.Ed.2d 973 (1978).

.   .   .   .   .   .   .   .   .   .   .   .   .   .   .   .   .   .   .   .

To be fair, a capital sentencing scheme must treat each person convicted of a capital offense with that "degree of respect due the uniqueness of the individual." *Lockett* v. *Ohio,* 438 U.S., at 605, 98 S.Ct., at 2964 (plurality opinion). That means affording the sentencer the power and discretion to grant mercy in a particular case, and providing avenues for the consideration of any and all relevant mitigating evidence that would justify a sentence less than death. Reasonable consistency, on

---

Notes and some case citations are omitted.—ED.

the other hand, requires that the death penalty be inflicted evenhandedly, in accordance with reason and objective standards, rather than by whim, caprice, or prejudice. Finally, because human error is inevitable, and because our criminal justice system is less than perfect, searching appellate review of death sentences and their underlying convictions is a prerequisite to a constitutional death penalty scheme.

On their face, these goals of individual fairness, reasonable consistency, and absence of error appear to be attainable: Courts are in the very business of erecting procedural devices from which fair, equitable, and reliable outcomes are presumed to flow. Yet, in the death penalty area, this Court, in my view, has engaged in a futile effort to balance these constitutional demands, and now is retreating not only from the *Furman* promise of consistency and rationality, but from the requirement of individualized sentencing as well. Having virtually conceded that both fairness and rationality cannot be achieved in the administration of the death penalty, see *McCleskey* v. *Kemp,* 481 U.S. 279, 313, n. 37, 107 S.Ct. 1756, 1778, n. 37, 95 L.Ed.2d 262 (1987), the Court has chosen to deregulate the entire enterprise, replacing, it would seem, substantive constitutional requirements with mere aesthetics, and abdicating its statutorily and constitutionally imposed duty to provide meaningful judicial oversight to the administration of death by the States.

From this day forward, I no longer shall tinker with the machinery of death. For more than 20 years I have endeavored—indeed, I have struggled—along with a majority of this Court, to develop procedural and substantive rules that would lend more than the mere appearance of fairness to the death penalty endeavor. Rather than continue to coddle the Court's delusion that the desired level of fairness has been achieved and the need for regulation eviscerated, I feel morally and intellectually obligated simply to concede that the death penalty experiment has failed. It is virtually self-evident to me now that no combination of procedural rules or substantive regulations ever can save the death penalty from its inherent constitutional deficiencies. The basic question—does the system accurately and consistently determine which defendants "deserve" to die?—cannot be answered in the affirmative. It is not simply that this Court has allowed vague aggravating circumstances to be employed, see, e.g., *Arave* v. *Creech,* 507 U.S. 463 113 S.Ct. 1534, 123 L.Ed.2d 188 (1993), relevant mitigating evidence to be disregarded, see, e.g., *Johnson* v. *Texas,* 509 U.S. 350, 113 S.Ct. 2658, 125 L.Ed.2d 290 (1993), and vital judicial review to be blocked, see, e.g., *Coleman* v. *Thompson,* 504 U.S. 188, 112 S.Ct. 1845, 119 L.Ed.2d 1 (1992). The problem is that the inevitability of factual, legal, and moral error gives us a system that we know must wrongly kill some defendants, a system that fails to deliver the fair, consistent, and reliable sentences of death required by the Constitution.

. . . . . . . . . . . . . . . . .

There is little doubt now that *Furman*'s essential holding was correct. Although most of the public seems to desire, and the Constitution appears to permit, the penalty of death, it surely is beyond dispute that if the death penalty cannot be administered consistently and rationally, it may not be administered at all.

. . . . . . . . . . . . . . . . .

The Court is unmoved by this dilemma, however; it prefers "finality" in death sentences to reliable determinations of a capital defendant's guilt. Because I no longer can state with any confidence that this Court is able to reconcile the Eighth Amendment's competing constitutional commands, or that the federal judiciary will provide meaningful oversight to the state courts as they exercise their authority to inflict the penalty of death, I believe that the death penalty, as currently administered, is unconstitutional. . . .

**16.7**  Opinion of the Court   *in Witherspoon v. Illinois 391 U.S. 510 (1968)*

MR. JUSTICE STEWART *delivered the opinion of the Court.* . . .

## I.

The issue before us is a narrow one. It does not involve the right of the prosecution to challenge for cause those prospective jurors who state that their reservations about capital punishment would prevent them from making an impartial decision as to the defendant's guilt. Nor does it involve the State's assertion of a right to exclude from the jury in a capital case those who say that they could never vote to impose the death penalty or that they would refuse even to consider its imposition in the case before them. For the State of Illinois did not stop there, but authorized the prosecution to exclude as well all who said that they were opposed to capital punishment and all who indicated that they had conscientious scruples against inflicting it.

In the present case the tone was set when the trial judge said early in the *voir dire,* "Let's get these conscientious objectors out of the way, without wasting any time on them." . . .

## II.

The petitioner contends that a State cannot confer upon a jury selected in this manner the power to determine guilt. He maintains that such a jury, unlike one chosen at random from a cross-section of the community, must necessarily be biased in favor of conviction, for the kind of juror who would be unperturbed by the prospect of sending a man to his death, he contends, is the kind of juror who would too readily ignore the presumption of the defendant's innocence, accept the prosecution's version of the facts, and return a verdict of guilt. To support this view, the petitioner refers to what he describes as "competent scientific evidence that death-qualified jurors are partial to the prosecution on the issue of guilt or innocence."

The data adduced by the petitioner, however, are too tentative and fragmentary to establish that jurors not opposed to the death penalty tend to favor the prosecution in the determination of guilt. We simply cannot conclude, either on the basis of the record now before us or as a matter of judicial notice, that the exclusion of jurors opposed to capital punishment results in an unrepresentative jury on the issue of guilt or substantially increases the risk of conviction. In light of the presently available information, we are not prepared to announce a *per se* constitutional rule requiring the reversal of every conviction returned by a jury selected as this one was.

## III.

It does not follow, however, that the petitioner is entitled to no relief. For in this case the jury was entrusted with two distinct responsibilities: first, to determine whether the petitioner was innocent or guilty; and second, if guilty, to determine whether his sentence should be imprisonment or death. It has not been shown that this jury was biased with respect to the petitioner's guilt. But it is self-evident that, in its role as arbiter of the punishment to be imposed, this jury fell woefully short of that impartiality to which the petitioner was entitled under the Sixth and Fourteenth Amendments. . . .

A man who opposes the death penalty, no less than one who favors it, can make the discretionary judgment entrusted to him by the State and can thus obey the oath he takes as a juror. But a jury from which all such men have been excluded cannot perform the task demanded of it. Guided by neither rule nor standard, "free to select or reject as it [sees] fit," a jury that must choose between life imprisonment and capital punishment can do little more—and must do nothing less—than express the conscience of the community on the ultimate question of life or death. Yet, in a nation less than half of whose people believe in the death penalty, a jury composed exclusively of such people cannot speak for the community. Culled of all who harbor doubts about the wisdom of capital punishment—of all who would be reluctant to pronounce the extreme penalty—such a jury can speak only for a distinct and dwindling minority.

If the State had excluded only those prospective jurors who stated in advance of the trial that they would not even consider returning a verdict of death, it could argue that the resulting jury was simply "neutral" with respect to penalty. But when it swept from the jury all who expressed conscientious or religious scruples against capital punishment and all who opposed it in principle, the State crossed the line of neutrality. In its quest for a jury capable of imposing the death penalty, the State produced a jury uncommonly willing to condemn a man to die. . . .

Whatever else might be said of capital punishment, it is at least clear that its imposition by a hanging jury cannot be squared with the Constitution. The State of Illinois has stacked the deck against the petitioner. To execute this death sentence would deprive him of his life without due process of law.

## 16.8 A.L. Lockhart, Director, Arkansas Department of Correction v. Ardia V. McCree   *476 U.S. 162 (1986)*

JUSTICE REHNQUIST *delivered the opinion of the Court.*

In this case we address the question left open by our decision nearly 18 years ago in *Witherspoon* v. *Illinois*, 391 U.S. 510, 88 S.Ct. 1770, 20 L.Ed.2d 776 (1968): Does the Constitution prohibit the removal for cause, prior to the guilt phase of a bifurcated capital trial, of prospective jurors whose opposition to the death penalty is so strong that it would prevent or substantially impair the performance of their duties as jurors at the sentencing phase of the trial? . . . We hold that it does not.

On the morning of February 14, 1978, a combination gift shop and service station in Camden, Arkansas, was robbed, and Evelyn Boughton, the owner, was shot and killed. That afternoon, Ardia McCree was arrested in Hot Springs, Arkansas, after a police officer saw him driving a maroon and white Lincoln Continental matching an eyewitness' description of the getaway car used by Boughton's killer. . . .

McCree was charged with capital felony murder in violation of Ark.Stat.Ann. § 41–1501(1)(a) (1977). In accordance with Arkansas law, see *Neal* v. *State*, 259 Ark. 27, 31, 531 S.W.2d 17, 21 (1975), the trial judge at *voir dire* removed for cause, over McCree's objections, those prospective jurors who stated that they could not under any circumstances vote for the imposition of the death penalty. Eight prospective jurors were excluded for this reason. The jury convicted McCree of capital felony murder, but rejected the State's request for the death penalty, instead setting McCree's punishment at life imprisonment without parole. McCree's conviction was affirmed on direct appeal, *McCree* v. *State*, 266 Ark. 465, 585 S.W.2d 938 (1979), and his petition for state post-conviction relief was denied. McCree then filed a federal habeas corpus petition raising, *inter alia*, the claim that "death qualification," . . . violated his right under the Sixth and Fourteenth Amendments to have his guilt or innocence determined by an impartial jury selected from a representative cross section of the community.

. . . . . . . . . . . . . . . . . . . . .

The District Court held a hearing on the "death qualification" issue in July 1981, receiving in evidence numerous social science studies concerning the attitudes and beliefs of "*Witherspoon*-excludables," along with the potential effects of excluding them from the jury prior to the guilt phase of a bifurcated capital trial. In August 1983, the court concluded, based on the social science evidence, that "death qualification" produced juries that "were more prone to convict" capital defendants than "non-death-qualified" juries. *Grigsby* v. *Mabry*, 569 F.Supp., at 1323. The court ruled that "death qualification" thus violated both the fair-cross-section and impartiality requirements of the Sixth and Fourteenth

---

Notes for some citations are omitted.—ED.

Amendments, and granted McCree habeas relief. *Id.,* at 1324.

The Eighth Circuit found "substantial evidentiary support" for the District Court's conclusion that the removal for cause of "*Witherspoon-*excludables" resulted in "conviction-prone" juries, and affirmed the grant of habeas relief on the ground that such removal for cause violated McCree's constitutional right to a jury selected from a fair cross section of the community. *Grigsby* v. *Mabry,* 758 F.2d, at 229. The Eighth Circuit did not address McCree's impartiality claim.

.  .  .  .  .  .  .  .  .  .  .  .  .  .  .  .  .  .  .  .

Before turning to the legal issues in the case, we are constrained to point out what we believe to be several serious flaws in the evidence upon which the courts below reached the conclusion that "death qualification" produces "conviction-prone" juries. McCree introduced into evidence some 15 social science studies in support of his constitutional claims, but only 6 of the studies even purported to measure the potential effects on the guilt-innocence determination of the removal from the jury of "*Witherspoon-*excludables."

.  .  .  .  .  .  .  .  .  .  .  .  .  .  .  .  .  .  .  .

. . . Having identified some of the more serious problems with McCree's studies, however, we will assume for purposes of this opinion that the studies are both methodologically valid and adequate to establish that "death qualification" in fact produces juries somewhat more "conviction-prone" than "non-death-qualified" juries. We hold, nonetheless, that the Constitution does not prohibit the States from "death qualifying" juries in capital cases.

. . . The Eighth Circuit ruled that "death qualification" violated McCree's right under the Sixth Amendment, . . . to a jury selected from a representative cross section of the community. But we do not believe that the fair-cross-section requirement can, or should, be applied as broadly as that court attempted to apply it. We have never invoked the fair-cross-section principle to invalidate the use of either for-cause or peremp-

tory challenges to prospective jurors, or to require petit juries, as opposed to jury panels or venires, to reflect the composition of the community at large.

.  .  .  .  .  .  .  .  .  .  .  .  .  .  .  .  .  .  .  .

. . . But even if we were willing to extend the fair-cross-section requirement to petit juries, we would still reject the Eighth Circuit's conclusion that "death qualification" violates that requirement. The essence of a "fair-cross-section" claim is the systematic exclusion of "a 'distinctive' group in the community." *Duren, supra,* 439 U.S., at 364, 99 S.Ct., at 668. In our view, groups defined solely in terms of shared attitudes that would prevent or substantially impair members of the group from performing one of their duties as jurors, such as the "*Witherspoon-*excludables" at issue here, are not "distinctive groups" for fair-cross-section purposes.

Our prior jury-representativeness cases, whether based on the fair-cross-section component of the Sixth Amendment or the Equal Protection Clause of the Fourteenth Amendment, have involved such groups as blacks, see *Peters* v. *Kiff,* 407 U.S. 493, 92 S.Ct. 2163, 33 L.Ed.2d 83 (1972) (opinion of MARSHALL, J.) (equal protection); women, see *Duren, supra* (fair cross section); *Taylor, supra* (same); and Mexican-Americans, see *Castaneda* v. *Partida,* 430 U.S. 482, 97 S.Ct. 1272, 51 L.Ed.2d 498 (1977) (equal protection). . . . Because these groups were excluded for reasons completely unrelated to the ability of members of the group to serve as jurors in a particular case, the exclusion raised at least the possibility that the composition of juries would be arbitrarily skewed in such a way as to deny criminal defendants the benefit of the common-sense judgment of the community. In addition, the exclusion from jury service of large groups of individuals not on the basis of their inability to serve as jurors, but on the basis of some immutable characteristic such as race, gender, or ethnic background, undeniably gave rise to an "appearance of unfairness." Finally, such exclusion improperly deprived members of these often historically disadvantaged groups of their right as citizens to serve on juries in criminal cases.

. . . [U]nlike blacks, women, and Mexican-Americans, "*Witherspoon*-excludables" are singled out for exclusion in capital cases on the basis of an attribute that is within the individual's control. It is important to remember that not all who oppose the death penalty are subject to removal for cause in capital cases; those who firmly believe that the death penalty is unjust may nevertheless serve as jurors in capital cases so long as they state clearly that they are willing to temporarily set aside their own beliefs in deference to the rule of law. Because the group of "*Witherspoon*-excludables" includes only those who cannot and will not conscientiously obey the law with respect to one of the issues in a capital case, "death qualification" hardly can be said to create an "appearance of unfairness."

. . . [W]e conclude that "*Witherspoon*-excludables" do not constitute a "distinctive group" for fair-cross-section purposes, and hold that "death qualification" does not violate the fair-cross-section requirement.

. . . McCree argues that, even if we reject the Eighth Circuit's fair-cross-section holding, we should affirm the judgment below on the alternative ground, adopted by the District Court, that "death qualification" violated his constitutional right to an impartial jury. . . . In short, McCree does not claim that his conviction was tainted by any of the kinds of jury bias or partiality that we have previously recognized as violative of the Constitution. Instead, McCree argues that his jury lacked impartiality because the absence of "*Witherspoon*-excludables" "slanted" the jury in favor of conviction.

We do not agree. McCree's "impartiality" argument apparently is based on the theory that, because all individual jurors are to some extent predisposed towards one result or another, a constitutionally impartial *jury* can be constructed only by "balancing" the various predispositions of the individual *jurors*. Thus, according to McCree, when the State "tips the scales" by excluding prospective jurors with a particular viewpoint, an impermissibly partial jury results. We have consistently rejected this view of jury impartiality, including as recently as last Term when we squarely held that an impartial *jury* consists of nothing more than "*jurors*

who will conscientiously apply the law and find the facts."

**JUSTICE MARSHALL,** *with whom* JUSTICE BRENNAN *and* JUSTICE STEVENS *join, dissenting.*
Eighteen years ago, this Court vacated the sentence of a defendant from whose jury the State had excluded all venirepersons expressing any scruples against capital punishment. Such a practice, the Court held, violated the Constitution by creating a "tribunal organized to return a verdict of death." *Witherspoon v. Illinois,* 391 U.S. 510, 521, 88 S.Ct. 1770, 1776, 20 L.Ed.2d 776 (1968). The only venirepersons who could be constitutionally excluded from service in capital cases were those who "made unmistakably clear . . . that they would *automatically* vote against the imposition of capital punishment" or that they could not assess the defendant's guilt impartially. *Id.,* at 522–523, n. 21, 88 S.Ct., at 1777, n. 21.

Respondent contends here that the "death-qualified" jury that convicted him, from which the State, as authorized by *Witherspoon,* had excluded all venirepersons unwilling to consider imposing the death penalty, was in effect "organized to return a verdict" of guilty. In support of this claim, he has presented overwhelming evidence that death-qualified juries are substantially more likely to convict or to convict on more serious charges than juries on which unalterable opponents of capital punishment are permitted to serve. Respondent does not challenge the application of *Witherspoon* to the jury in the sentencing stage of bifurcated capital cases. Neither does he demand that individuals unable to assess culpability impartially ("nullifiers") be permitted to sit on capital juries. All he asks is the chance to have his guilt or innocence determined by a jury like those that sit in noncapital cases—one whose composition has not been tilted in favor of the prosecution by the exclusion of a group of prospective jurors uncommonly aware of an accused's constitutional rights but quite capable of determining his culpability without favor or bias.

With a glib nonchalance ill suited to the gravity of the issue presented and the power of respondent's claims, the Court upholds a practice that allows the State a special advantage in those prosecutions where the charges are the most serious and the possible punishments, the most severe. The State's mere announcement that it intends to seek the death penalty if the defendant is found guilty of a capital offense will, under today's decision, give the prosecution license to empanel a jury especially likely to return that very verdict. Because I believe that such a blatant disregard for the rights of a capital defendant offends logic, fairness, and the Constitution, I dissent.

. . . . . . . . . . . . . . . . . . . . . .

. . . In the wake of *Witherspoon,* a number of researchers set out to supplement the data that the Court had found inadequate in that case. The results of these studies were exhaustively analyzed by the District Court in this case, see 569 F.Supp. 1273, 1291–1308 (ED Ark.1983), and can be only briefly summarized here. The data strongly suggest that death qualification excludes a significantly large subset—at least 11% to 17%—of potential jurors who could be impartial during the guilt phase of trial. Among the members of this excludable class are a disproportionate number of blacks and women.

. . . The perspectives on the criminal justice system of jurors who survive death qualification are systematically different from those of the excluded jurors. Death-qualified jurors are, for example, more likely to believe that a defendant's failure to testify is indicative of his guilt, more hostile to the insanity defense, more mistrustful of defense attorneys, and less concerned about the danger of erroneous convictions. This pro-prosecution bias is reflected in the greater readiness of death-qualified jurors to convict or to convict on more serious charges. . . . And, finally, the very process of death qualification—which focuses attention on the death penalty before the trial has even begun—has been found to predispose the jurors that survive it to believe that the defendant is guilty.

. . . . . . . . . . . . . . . . . . . . . .

In *Witherspoon,* the Court observed that a defendant convicted by a jury from which those unalterably opposed to the death penalty had been

excluded "might still attempt to establish that the jury was less than neutral with respect to *guilt.*" 391 U.S., at 520, n. 18, 88 S.Ct., at 1776, n. 18. Respondent has done just that. And I believe he has succeeded in proving that his trial by a jury so constituted violated his right to an impartial jury, guaranteed by both the Sixth Amendment and principles of due process, see *Ristaino* v. *Ross,* 424 U.S. 589, 595, n. 6. We therefore need not rely on respondent's alternative argument that death qualification deprived him of a jury representing a fair cross section of the community.

. . . . . . . . . . . . . . . . . . . . . .

Respondent does not claim that any individual on the jury that convicted him fell short of the constitutional standard for impartiality. Rather, he contends that, by systematically excluding a class of potential jurors less prone than the population at large to vote for conviction, the State gave itself an unconstitutional advantage at his trial.

. . . . . . . . . . . . . . . . . . . . . .

Witherspoon had been denied a fair sentencing determination, the Court reasoned, not because any member of his jury lacked the requisite constitutional impartiality, but because the manner in which that jury had been selected "stacked the deck" against him. *Id.,* at 523, 88 S.Ct., at 1778. Here, respondent adopts the approach of the *Witherspoon* Court and argues simply that the State entrusted the determination of his guilt and the level of his culpability to a tribunal organized to convict.

### Notes and Questions

1. In the *Batson* case, Justice Marshall was not convinced that racism in the use of peremptory challenges could be eliminated by a formula that requires merely that the prosecutor come up with a nonracial reason to justify his or her peremptory challenge of a nonwhite juror. Marshall's own experience and reading of the law seemed to tell him that American society has been so deeply and

pervasively racist for so long that it is a part of our culture rather than just an error of individual behavior or attitude. Is this view consistent with your own experience and study? Are you troubled by the possibility that there might be no individual to blame and punish for racism, and that in the absence of racist motivations the society might be obliged nevertheless to change its laws or legal structure in order to solve the problem of racism? Does Professor Lawrence's discussion of unconscious racism make Justice Marshall's concern seem more legitimate to you? Does it help you to come to terms with the reality of racism outside of individual, intentional acts of racism?

2. Would you agree with Marshall's conclusion that the only reliable way to eliminate racism in peremptory challenges is to eliminate the practice of peremptory challenge altogether? Does the majority opinion's method of dealing with racial peremptories seem like it would be effective? What would the cost be to trial by jury if Marshall's prescription were followed? Would the benefit be worth the cost? Does Professor Alschuler's idea of affirmative action in jury selection seem more workable? Would peremptories still be a part of the process under Alschuler's affirmative action analysis? Given his analysis of unconscious racism, what do you think Lawrence's reaction to the two suggestions would be?

3. Do the approaches taken by Marshall, Lawrence, and Alschuler suggest ways of dealing with racism outside of the area of jury selection? Would these ways of thinking about discrimination in the United States be useful for issues of gender, ethnicity, sexual orientation, class, or religion? How important *is* individual intent, blame, and innocence in perpetuating or correcting racism or other forms of invidious discrimination?

4. The text suggests that an evaluation of the validity of empaneling "death-qualified" juries should proceed from a frank and open discussion of the death penalty itself. What general arguments can you make for adopting the death penalty? Against it? How many of these arguments—such as its alleged deterrent effect—can be evaluated with the help of social science research? How many are normative or moral issues? Once you have thought through your own position on the death penalty, can you find or generate arguments *against* your

position that are troubling to you? In a considerable number of recent cases persons convicted of a capital offense and condemned to death have later been discovered to be innocent. This has led at least one state governor to place a moratorium on executions. Does the conviction of innocent persons in capital cases change the way that you think about capital punishment?

5. Although Justice Blackmun clearly understands the moral implications of his change of position on the death penalty, his reasoning deals with practical matters of law and human judgment in capital jury trials. Can you describe or restate the legal reasoning that led Justice Blackmun to conclude that the death penalty violates the Eighth Amendment prohibition of cruel and unusual punishment? If consistent guidelines or standards for applying the death penalty must be given to sentencing juries in order to reduce the possibility of racist or other arbitrary decision-making in each case, why is Blackmun concerned that these guidelines might be too rigid? What is the importance in death-penalty cases of the jury's taking individual circumstances of the crime and characteristics of the defendant into account in sentencing? Do you think Blackmun was correct in reasoning that both guidelines to prevent arbitrariness and individual analysis of each defendant and crime could not *both* be attained in a trial? What else do you think Justice Blackmun might have considered in changing his position and becoming an opponent of capital punishment?

6. Do you think that persons who are opposed to capital punishment should be permitted to sit on a jury in a capital trial? Does it matter whether that opposition is so strong that it would prevent the prospective juror from supporting a guilty verdict no matter what the facts? Does it matter whether that opposition is so weak that it amounts to nothing more than humility and extreme caution in voting to have another person's life taken by the state? Is it fair to the defendant to have persons with scruples against the death penalty disqualified from serving on his or her jury? Is it consistent with the role of the jury as an institution designed to reflect community beliefs and conscience to have such persons excluded?

7. Does the Court's analysis in *Lockhart* seem even-handed and realistic? Should the Court

restrict itself to judging only systematic exclusion of cognizable groups from the jury panel, or is this a circumstance in which the fair cross-section requirement or impartial jury requirement should be applied directly to particular trial juries? Suppose that a prospective juror's opposition to the death penalty were based on strongly held religious beliefs. Isn't religion a workable way to define a cognizable group for purposes of analyzing jury selection issues?

8. Do you think that the majority or the dissenters made a better analysis of the social science data that the defendant offered? If there were significant, reliable social science data about death-qualified juries being "tilted" in favor of the prosecution, would that convince you that the practice of death-qualifying juries should be curtailed? Are there other juror commitments to conscience or other public attitudes and beliefs that should be screened from juries in the same way as opposition to the death penalty is? If so, might the jury then increasingly become a rubber stamp for legislative policies regardless of community values?

9. Which is the better place to insist on a representative cross section of the community, the roll of names from which jurors are picked or the actual jurors on a particular jury panel? Why?

10. Should age be recognized as a factor in making up representative jury rolls or juries? Should the type of offense or the age of the defendant make any difference on this issue? What type of evidence might be offered to show that "young people" is a cognizable group?

11. Instead of a representative cross section of the community, should a jury of peers be defined as a jury made up of people sharing the cultural or economic background of the defendant?

12. Broad participation in the legal process is one of the goals to be met by using jury trials. Would it therefore be realistic to say that since all citizens are of equal worth, a search for a particular cross section should be abandoned? Should a juror be regarded as adequate as long as he or she has no biases about the issue and the parties in the trial in question?

13. Once the courts begin identifying characteristics of the population that should not be discriminated against in jury pool selection or in peremptory challenges, where does the process stop? Should the courts look at religious persuasion, socioeconomic status, ethnic background, language, political registration, eye color? What does your answer tell you about American society? Do the changing demographics of the United States—its movement toward becoming a nation of minorities—alter the way you think about what groups should be protected against jury discrimination? Does Karst's idea about "belonging to America" influence your thinking about this?

14. Can the jury system function adequately in a society that is so heterogeneous that there are a nearly infinite number of ways of categorizing differences among people?

15. Does the Hennepin County plan for affirmative action in creating representative juries seem reasonable in light of U.S. history? Of the debate over affirmative action in other institutions? Of the demographics of Hennepin County?

16. A considerable amount of constitutional and statutory law affects how juries are selected. But there are also social science experts who advise lawyers about the characteristics of persons who would make good jurors from the perspective of the lawyer's client. In addition, some litigants use shadow juries to try out arguments and evidence on persons who share the characteristics of the real jurors in the case. Is this second-guessing of juries destructive of the protections built into a system of jury of peers? Of the fairness of jury verdicts? Of the community's sense that jury trial is legitimate? Of a subgroup's sense that they belong to America by virtue of their participation in this aspect of the legal process?

# 17 DECLINE OF THE JURY: DEMOCRACY AT RISK?

&❧ Trial by jury is a threatened and fading institution in the United States. Highly publicized jury trials such as those involving the tobacco industry, O. J. Simpson, Timothy McVeigh, and the defendants in a variety of matters related to racial, homophobic, or terrorist violence may be merely the exceptions that prove the rule. The materials in this chapter suggest some of the reasons for that decline and ask what societal interests stand to gain from diminishing the importance of the jury. The underlying issue of the entire chapter is whether it is important to preserve and reinvigorate the jury as an instrument of public participation in democratic self-government, or whether we should accept the decline of the jury as not meriting the attention of those studying law and society or the concern of those measuring the health of democracy in America.

The readings on the cultural context of the jury trial suggest that this institution is deeply rooted in the same Enlightenment values that underlie democracy itself: faith in the common person and respect for the use of reason, the centrality of the individual as a unit of political sovereignty and social decision-making, and the reliance on significant limitations on government power as a means of preserving liberty and privacy.

Thomas Jefferson made clear his own intense commitment to popular participation in government through juror service when he wrote:

> Were I called upon to decide, whether the people had best be omitted in the legislative or in the judiciary department, I would say it is better to leave them out of the legislative. The execution of the laws is more important than the making of them.

Today, with voter participation low and legislatures seeming to function without much influence from ordinary citizens, the importance to democracy of jury trials could be said to be even more important. Yet in an article entitled "Reinvigorating Citizenship," Stephen Bates reported that 60 percent of people nationwide summoned for jury service don't bother to show up. A 1995 survey in Los Angeles county showed that only 41 percent of people think of jury duty as a matter of civic responsibility.

As a matter of history, it would also seem that the jury has been regarded as a political institution of great significance to democracy. Tocqueville observed that

> The jury is pre-eminently a political institution; it should be regarded as one form of the sovereignty of the people. . . . All the sovereigns who have chosen to govern by their own authority, and to direct society instead of obeying its directions, have destroyed or enfeebled the institution of the jury.

These observations were made in 1830, near the end of the period that Professor Morton Horwitz has called a "transformation of American law." In the excerpt from his book with that title that follows, Horwitz discusses which would-be sovereign—which interest group seeking to increase its own power—was responsible for the substantial reduction in jury power in the beginning of the nineteenth century.

Justice White's historical review of trial by jury in the *Duncan* case (Reading 15.1) and his conclusion about the many ways that it serves as a protection against "oppression by the government" make it still clearer that the jury is a political institution. The jury is political in its very existence, as well as in the method of its operation, and in the decisions juries make in civil and criminal trials. The fact that in criminal cases juries have the power of nullification when applying the community's sense of justice (its conscience) makes every juror's decision a part of the process of defining the community's cultural boundaries. As Karl Llewellyn wrote in *The Cheyenne Way,* "Either the law jobs manage to get done in such a way as the 'group' stays the 'group,' or the group explodes, dribbles away, or dies." This is democratic politics in its broadest and most basic sense—the continuous defining and redefining of the moral boundaries of society.

Jury trial is of course enormously important to the parties in a civil litigation and to the defendants in criminal trials, because fairness in a pluralistic society dictates that judgment by one's peers secures the most valid and the most legitimate judgments in individual cases. Beyond the parties to a case, however, trial by jury also serves the essentially democratic function of empowering "we, the people" and providing a relatively incorruptible means by which the everyday values and beliefs of communities—and the consciences of individuals—can be reflected in an often formalistic and inaccessible legal system. The law is, or should be, public. Trial by jury not only protects the individual, it makes the community the central player in defining its own values and standards of behavior.

In his description of trial by jury in the United States, Tocqueville observed that through juror service, ". . . every man learns to judge his neighbor as he would himself be judged," and that the interactions that take place during jury service make jurors "feel the duties which they are bound to discharge toward society and the part which they take in its government." Thus, one effect of participation in the jury system, as with other forms of participation in the democratic process, is to break down the boundaries among people, to dissolve alienation, and to teach respect for working together where public matters are concerned.

Tocqueville pulled no punches in describing, elsewhere in *Democracy in America,* how the buildup of alienation and the isolation of individuals might eventually open the door to tyranny if Americans did not use such free political institutions as the jury. The warning seems especially important today, when so few people are willing to serve on juries. Writing in a

chapter entitled "That the Americans Combat the Effects of Individualism by Free Institutions," Tocqueville observed that:

> Despotism, which by its nature is suspicious, sees in the separation among
> men the surest guarantee of its continuance, and it usually makes every effort
> to keep them separate. No vice of the human heart is so acceptable to it as
> selfishness: a despot easily forgives his subjects for not loving him, provided
> they do not love one another. He does not ask them to assist him in governing
> the state; it is enough that they do not aspire to govern it themselves. He
> stigmatizes as turbulent and unruly spirits those who would combine their
> exertions to promote the prosperity of the community; and, perverting the
> natural meaning of words, he applauds as good citizens those who have no
> sympathy for any but themselves.

The tug of war over the power of the jury in America is therefore of
great importance not only to the health of the democracy, but to the
preservation of liberty and to the survival and continual redefining of the
community. Questions about the vitality of the jury in America reach to
the heart of the culture.

The evidence of a current decline in the vitality of trial by jury suggests how many ways jury trial can be, and is, threatened. Each way is itself
a socio-legal problem worthy of discussion. For one thing, there is the
number of jury trials taking place. In civil cases, jury trials take place in a
very small percentage of cases filed. Apparently most civil cases are settled
out of court. A 1988 research project sponsored by the Roscoe Pound
Foundation and entitled "The Jury in America" found that in 1980 only 8
percent of the civil cases filed were ever brought to trial before either
judge or jury. Of that 8 percent, less than one-third (30 percent) were jury
trials. It would appear that fewer than one out of twenty-five civil cases
winds up before a jury of peers.

On the criminal side, things are much the same as the Mills Reading
in Chapter 13 shows. The common estimate is that 85 percent of criminal
cases are plea-bargained away. The Roscoe Pound Foundation study put
the 1980 percentage of criminal cases that went to either judge or jury trials at 16 percent, and approximately half of those (52 percent) were jury
trials. That would put one out of 12 criminal cases before a jury of peers.
Some places are worse than others. In June 1991, the *New York Times* reported that 1990 figures for the five boroughs of New York City indicated
that the percentage of felony indictments that went to either judge or jury
trial varied from a low of 3 percent to a high of 6.5 percent ("The Rare Verdict by Trial"; source: New York State Office of Court Administration). At
best, the jury—both civil and criminal—seems to have fallen into disuse.

At the same time that this low level of use of the jury is being observed, attempts are being made to reduce the number of jury trials still
further through the use of alternative dispute settlement procedures (see
Part V), by creating new causes of action that do not provide for jury trials,
and by "tort reform" legislation that claims to make civil litigation fairer

and more efficient by reining in jury discretion in damage awards. Those who perceive a "litigation explosion" to be taking place, or who seek to control liability insurance losses for faulty products or professional malpractice, have sought additional limitations on jury trials or the issues with which they are permitted to deal.

When jury trials do take place, there are still other problems. The cases and articles presented in this chapter deal with the reduction in the size of juries and the question of whether the U.S. Constitution requires a unanimous verdict in all criminal cases. The professed reason for attempting to reduce the size of juries and to eliminate the unanimity requirement is often a desire to save time and taxpayers' money by reducing the length of jury trials. The possible effects of changes in these two areas on the quality of jury deliberations and the representative character of the jury are often ignored in such legislative debates but should be discussed following the cases (see Readings 17.5 and 17.6).

In evaluating the significance of all these alleged reductions in the number and effectiveness of trials by jury, keep in mind the changes that are taking place in the selection of jurors and in the complexity and technicality of the testimony jurors hear. Wealthy persons or groups may be able to afford expensive social science help in predicting what kinds of jurors will be most sympathetic to a litigant's position in a case. These same social science skills may be used to pick so-called mock juries that share the characteristics of the real jury and that can preview a lawyer's presentation of evidence and argument to help the lawyer understand the most effective way to conduct the case before the real jury.

And once on the jury, jurors may have to deal with medical, forensic, technological, or other complex evidence presented by conflicting expert witnesses. That such evidence may confuse jurors and disable them from performing their proper function (recall the *Collins* case at p. 399) was demonstrated by congressional testimony given by jurors in John Hinckley's trial for attempting to assassinate President Reagan. Several jurors commented that they were so confused by the psychiatric testimony offered on the question of whether Hinckley was legally insane when he fired at the president that they virtually ignored this testimony in reaching their verdict. The jury is still out, so to speak, on whether the use of DNA evidence is similarly confusing to jurors or obstructive of their democratic role.

It can be argued that all these changes in the use and nature of the jury support a conclusion that trial by jury is virtually nonexistent in the United States. If this is a fair conclusion, then the democratic values that legitimize trial by jury and that are in turn supported by that institution may be at risk. Perhaps the "Trial of the Future" and the beliefs that such a system would depend upon are already being ushered in. As you evaluate the following materials about the size of juries and the quality of their deliberations, keep in mind the central question: Is trial by jury still an important part of American law, and if it is not, who or what stands to gain from what Tocqueville called the "enfeebling" of the jury?

The following excerpt from *The Transformation of American Law* offers a brief sketch of how the professional bar, judges, and certain commercial interests united in the early 1800s to erode the power of juries. Each of these parties seems to have had its own independent reason for forming a coalition with the others; none described its purpose as the erosion of a jury system recently written into the Bill of Rights to secure the ratification of the Constitution. That the real effect and ideological basis of these changes remained hidden from public view at the time suggests that more recent proposed changes in legal structure and jury function ought to be more closely scrutinized by the public to determine whose interests such reforms actually will serve.

Although brief, this section from Morton Horwitz's book provides a revealing view of the manipulation of legal institutions and rules by those seeking to consolidate their power. Moreover, Horwitz suggests that legal institutions conceived or described as a bulwark against oppression may be eroded without the consent or even the knowledge of those they are meant to protect. A similar conclusion is suggested by the materials on the tobacco case and on the tort reform movement that follow Horwitz. An excerpt from Professor Dooley's article, "Our Juries, Ourselves," then suggests that as juries become more representative by including more women they are more likely to be regarded by some as a less legitimate and less reliable form of legal decision-making. At the end of Chapter 17, Professor Abramson gives an incisive analysis of the unanimity requirement in criminal trials. His argument cuts to the core of the difference between the democratic function of jury trial and the special-interest power politics that seems to dominate legislative and executive action in the United States.

## 17.1   Excerpt from *The Transformation of American Law*   *Morton Horwitz*

IT SHOULD HAVE COME as no surprise that in most cases "merchants were not fond of juries." For one of the leading measures of the growing alliance between bench and bar on the one hand and commercial interests on the other is the swiftness with which the power of the jury is curtailed after 1790.

Reprinted by permission of the publisher from *The Transformation of American Law* by Morton Horwitz, pp. 84–85, 141–143, 154–155, Cambridge, Mass.: Harvard University Press, Copyright © 1977 by the President and Fellows of Harvard College. (Abridged.)

Three parallel procedural devices were used to restrict the scope of juries. First, during the last years of the eighteenth century American lawyers vastly expanded the "special case" or "case reserved," a device designed to submit points of law to the judges while avoiding the effective intervention of a jury.

A second crucial procedural change—the award of a new trial for verdicts "contrary to the weight of the evidence"—triumphed with spectacular rapidity in some American courts at the turn of the century. The award of new trials for any reason had been regarded with profound suspicion by the revolutionary generation.

"The practice of granting new trials," a Virginia judge noted in 1786, "was not a favourite with the courts of England" until the elevation to the bench of Lord Mansfield, "whose habit of controlling juries does not accord with the free institutions of this country, and ought not be adopted for slight causes." Yet, not only had the new trial become a standard weapon in the judicial arsenal by the first decade of the nineteenth century; it was also expanded to allow reversal of jury verdicts contrary to the weight of the evidence, despite the protest that "not one instance . . . is to be met with" where courts had previously reevaluated a jury's assessment of conflicting testimony. In both New York and South Carolina this abrupt change of policy was first adopted in order to overturn jury verdicts against marine insurers. In Pennsylvania too the earliest grant of a new trial on the weight of evidence occurs in a commercial case.

These two important restrictions on the power of juries were part of a third more fundamental procedural change that began to be asserted at the turn of the century. The view that even in civil cases "the jury [are] the proper judges not only of the fact but of the law that [is] necessarily involved" was widely held even by conservative jurists at the end of the eighteenth century. "The jury may in all cases, where law and fact are blended together, take upon themselves the knowledge of the law . . . ," William Wyche wrote in his 1794 treatise on New York practice.

During the first decade of the nineteenth century, however, the Bar rapidly promoted the view that there existed a sharp distinction between law and fact and a correspondingly clear separation of function between judge and jury. For example, until 1807 the practice of Connecticut judges was simply to submit both law and facts to the jury, without expressing any opinion or giving them any direction on how to find their verdict. In that year, the Supreme Court of Errors enacted a rule requiring the presiding trial judge, in charging the jury, to give his opinion on every point of law involved. This institutional change ripened quickly into an elaborate procedural system for control of juries.

By 1810, it was clear that the instructions of the court, originally advisory, had become mandatory and therefore juries no longer possessed the power to determine the law. Courts and litigants quickly perceived the transformation that had occurred and soon began to articulate a new principle—that "point[s] of law . . . should . . . be . . . decided by the Court," while points of fact ought to be decided by the jury.

These procedural changes made possible a vast ideological transformation in the attitude of American jurists toward commercial law. The subjugation of juries was necessary not only to control particular verdicts but also to develop a uniform and predictable body of judge-made commercial rules.

Thus, it appears that several major changes in the attitude of judges and merchants toward commercial arbitration had begun to emerge at the beginning of the nineteenth century. First, an increasingly organized and self-conscious legal profession had become determined to oppose the antilegalism among merchants which, during the colonial period, had taken the form of resort to extralegal settlement of disputes. Second, the mercantile classes, which had found the colonial legal rules hostile to their interest began, at the end of the eighteenth century, to find that common law judges themselves were prepared to overturn anticommercial legal conceptions. Third, the development of a split in the commercial interest, first manifested in the field of marine insurance, converted a largely self-regulating merchant group into one that was made dependent on formal legal machinery. Thus, one might loosely describe the process as one of accommodation by which merchants were induced to submit to formal legal regulation in return for a major transformation of substantive legal rules governing commercial disputes. The judges' unwillingness any longer to recognize competing lawmakers is a product of an increasingly instrumental vision of law. Law is no longer merely an agency for resolving disputes; it is an active, dynamic means of social control and change. Under such conditions, there must be one undisputed and authoritative source of rules for regulating commercial life. Both the hostility of judges to arbitration and the willingness of merchants to forgo extrajudicial settlement spring from a common source: the increasingly active and solicitous attitude of courts to commercial interests. . . .

Standing beside the numerous changes in legal conceptions was an important institutional innovation that began to appear after 1830—an increasing tendency of state legislatures to eliminate the role of the jury in assessing damages for the taking of land. It was long a commonplace that juries increased the size of damage judgments. Although there were other early instances in which legislatures eliminated the jury's role in

assessing damages, it was only in connection with the building of railroads that this movement gained real force. Between 1830 and 1837 such statutes in New Jersey, New York, Ohio, and North Carolina were upheld over the objection that they violated constitutional provisions guaranteeing trial by jury. The result was that railroad companies were often allowed to take land while providing little or no compensation.

## 17.2   $145 Billion to Send a Message   *Bob Van Voris*

"A BILLION HERE, A billion there, pretty soon you're talking about real money."

In the wake of the recent $145 billion verdict in a Florida tobacco class action, the late Senator Everett Dirksen's famous line may have to be retired. A billion dollars just ain't what it used to be.

At least that is what corporate defense lawyers fear will be the upshot of the punitive damages verdict in *Engle* v. *R. J. Reynolds Tobacco Co.*, No. 94–8273 (Cir. Ct. Dade Co.). Even as many observers predict that the record-smashing verdict will eventually be cut or reversed on appeal, lawyers wonder: Has the price of sending a message from the jury room to the board-room inflated to the hundreds of billions?

"The whole environment is like walking across a high wire without a safety net," says defense lawyer Michael Jones, a partner in the Washington, D.C., office of Chicago's Kirkland & Ellis. Even if a defendant wins most of the time, he says, the stakes have become so high that a single punitive damages verdict can threaten bankruptcy. "You only have to slip once," he says.

Despite a recent U.S. Justice Department study showing that punitive damages are rarely awarded and are usually fairly modest, the very highest verdicts—the ones through which jurors are presumably trying to send messages—have been shooting up for a couple of years. For example, the total of the 10 highest verdicts from

1999 was $9.6 billion, almost twice the total of 1998's top 10—$4.9 billion [NLJ, Feb. 28].

Many lawyers think that the continued profitability of the cigarette business, in the face of a $246 billion settlement with state governments, has been a big factor, inflating the amount that jurors think it takes to get through to a corporate defendant. The $145 billion *Engle* verdict can only mean more of the same, they say.

### BIG WHACK

"I knew this jury was going to whack them," says Victor Schwartz, of Washington, D.C.'s Crowell & Moring L.L.P. "Kaye was able to get the jury into a frenzy," a reference to trial Judge Robert Kaye.

Mr. Schwartz, an authority on tort law and a tort-reform advocate, thinks the size of the *Engle* verdict makes it all the more likely that it will be reversed. And he says that it may actually help inoculate Big Tobacco against other punitive verdicts in the future.

"Now everyone in America knows they've been punished," he says.

But the huge verdict may inflate verdicts against other industries, he fears. Mr. Schwartz jokes that he envisions a case in which a plaintiff's lawyer sums up to the jury, pockets turned inside-out in false poverty. Drawing a contrast with the *Engle* verdict, the lawyer will plead, "I'm only asking you for $10 billion."

The way John Banzhaf figures it, on the other hand, Big Tobacco got off easy. Exxon was hit with $5 billion in punitives for the Valdez oil spill, even though not a single human life was

"$145 Billion to Send a Message," Bob Van Voris. This article is reprinted with permission from the July 31, 2000 edition of *National Law Journal*, © 2000 NLP IP Company.

lost, says Mr. Banzhaf, a law professor at George Washington University who has been battling the industry since the '60s. Smoking, by contrast, kills 500,000 people every year.

The punitive damages in *Engle* work out to about $300,000 per class member (assuming there are half a million eligible Florida smokers), a figure that Prof. Banzhaf says is "quite reasonable."

Brian Panish, a partner at Greene, Broillet, Taylor, Wheeler & Panish L.L.P., in Santa Monica, Calif., sums up the reaction of most plaintiffs' lawyers to the *Engle* verdict: "You've got to hit 'em where it hurts—on the bottom line."

Mr. Panish was the toast of the Association of Trial Lawyers of America convention in San Francisco last summer after winning a $4.9 billion verdict for his clients against General Motors Corp. The verdict, cut to $1.2 billion by the trial judge and on appeal, set a record for products' liability cases.

Richard Shapiro, of Snell & Wilmer L.L.P. in Phoenix, was on the other side of that case as counsel to GM.

"Five or 10 years ago, billions of dollars would have been just unthinkable," says Mr. Shapiro. He believes that lawyers such as Mr. Panish, who win big verdicts, encourage other plaintiffs' lawyers to be even more aggressive in encouraging juries to "send a message."

All through the current wave of tobacco litigation, other defense lawyers have feared that their clients would end up paying for the sins of Big Tobacco. Distrust of tobacco executives will spill over to poison their jury pools, they worry. Tough precedents limiting the attorney-client privilege in tobacco cases will be applied to pry loose their clients' most sensitive documents. An emboldened plaintiffs' bar, spilling over with tobacco industry money, will look for new corporate targets.

The $145 billion *Engle* verdict is just the latest tobacco development that defense lawyers worry will haunt them one day. The process of reaching the verdict went quickly. According to the Miami Herald, the six men and women of the jury took turns setting out the amounts each thought Big Tobacco should pay. All of the figures were between $100 billion and $200 billion.

The jurors took out a calculator and settled on an average figure, then divided the total by each company's market share. Then they lopped a billion off the figure for the Liggett Group, the smallest of the five major U.S. cigarette makers, as a reward for breaking with the rest of the industry in 1996 to cooperate with the state attorney general lawsuits.

After hearing testimony from 157 witnesses over the course of two years, the jurors came back with their verdict in a little more than four hours. *Et voilà*. The largest verdict in the history of mankind.

"If the verdict was wrong," juror James Stowbridge later told CNN, "I think the judge has got the power to overturn it."

"I don't think the numbers are going to stick, but I think they can afford to pay the numbers," Mr. Stowbridge said, referring to tobacco companies.

Some defense lawyers observing the Miami verdict were troubled by the possibility that the jurors thought the near-certain appeal meant they could send a message to the tobacco industry without having to take full responsibility for the results.

"That is fundamentally unsound for the system" said Chilton D. Varner, a partner at King & Spalding in Atlanta.

Ms. Varner also deplores the tendency of the media to make jurors into instant celebrities in the biggest cases.

"It accelerates the competition between juries to see who can deliver the biggest whack," she says.

Susan Macpherson, a Minneapolis-based trial consultant who works for National Jury Project, looks at it differently. Her company, which generally works for plaintiffs in tort cases, interviews jurors to understand their thinking in big cases, including the jurors in the $4.9 billion GM case.

"If there's a problem with the verdict, they know there's a way for the system to do something about it," she says.

She says that it is too early to know if *Engle* will become one of those cases—like the O. J. Simpson acquittal or the McDonald's spilled-coffee case—that becomes part of every juror's consciousness.

## IT'S THE ECONOMY

Another important factor behind the *Engle* verdict and other record verdicts is the economy, say many lawyers. Dot-com windfalls, a runaway stock market, and multibillion-dollar mergers have all conspired to make potential jurors comfortable with figures in the billions of dollars.

Because jurors typically calculate punitive damages as a percentage of the profits or net worth of defendants, companies that have merged or are doing well financially can expect to pay big verdicts if they have done something particularly egregious, says Ms. Macpherson, the trial consultant.

When the defendants are small companies, Ms. Macpherson says, jurors are often conservative, tempering the message-sending impulse with a concern that a big verdict may hurt innocent employees. But as unemployment has become less of a threat in the current hard-charging economy, it has also become less of a restraining factor in jury deliberations, she says.

Mr. Jones, of Kirkland & Ellis, has also interviewed many big-case jurors, in hopes of gaining insights he can use in court. He thinks the *Engle* verdict and other highly publicized megaverdicts give jurors permission to look to the extremes when considering a punitive verdict. Add to that the lack of meaningful guidelines for jurors deciding how much punishment is appropriate, he says, and defense lawyers have a problem.

"The system really encourages jurors to vent," he says.

. . . . . . . . . . . . . . . . . . .

## 17.3 | The Not-so-quiet Revolution   *Philip Corboy\**

### THE "TORT CRISIS" . . .

IN THE MID-1980S, THE liability insurance industry was hit by a recurrence of the capacity problems which afflict the insurance market periodically. The most credible explanation lies in the cyclical nature of the industry, combined with wide fluctuations in interest rates and irresponsible cash-flow underwriting. Nevertheless, a massive public relations and lobbying campaign by business and insurance interests, aided by a Republican administration, successfully promoted the perception that the insurance crisis was the result of a malfunctioning tort system. This tort crisis theory claimed that expanding liability rules resulted in a litigation explosion which forced liability insurers to raise premiums and limit coverage, thereby increasing the cost of most products and excluding others from the marketplace altogether. The answer to the tort crisis, the campaign argued, was tort reform.

The primary objective of the campaign was to garner public and legislative support for enactment of tort reform legislation. The campaign also succeeded in changing judicial attitudes. By the mid-1980s, courts shifted toward a pronounced pro-defendant stance, which many analysts attributed directly to the impact of the tort crisis public relations campaign.

Tort scholars were also affected by this campaign. Increasingly, academic commentary not only criticized particular rules or decisions, but called for an end to tort law altogether. In time, much of the tort crisis attitude manifested itself in cynicism, mistrust and even hostility toward the jury system.

Thirty years ago, tort scholars saw the jury as part of the solution in product liability. Today the civil jury is frequently condemned as part of the problem. This shift in academic and judicial attitude will soon impact on the future of product liability law. . . .

Philip Corboy, "The Not-so-Quiet Revolution" *Tennessee Law Review*, Vol. 346, 1995. Copyright © 1995 Tennessee Law Review Association. Reprinted by permission. (The full text of this article originally appeared at 61 *Tenn. L. Rev.* 1043 (1994).)

*Mr. Corboy represents plaintiffs in personal injury and wrongful death actions.

Part III of this Article revisits the insurance crisis. Information and experience acquired in the years following the crisis make it clear that the tort crisis theory is based upon a false hypothesis. The price of liability insurance was most heavily influenced by changes in interest rates, not by expansion of substantive liability rules. In addition, there was no litigation explosion in product liability, and there is little evidence that changes in tort law could make a significant impact on liability premiums. Evidence also indicates that increased liability premiums do not increase the cost of products to the point of undermining competitiveness. Moreover, studies of jury behavior refute the stereotype of incompetent, biased, sentimental jurors on which much of the torts crisis theory depends.

**The Tort Crisis Theory** The torts crisis theory shifts the focus away from the drop in the supply of insurance and onto rising liability payments. Proponents argue that a rising tide of claims resulted in huge underwriting losses for insurers, who were then forced to increase premiums to policyholders. The driving force behind this rise, according to a powerful alliance of insurance, business, and governmental interests, was a malfunctioning tort system. In other words, the insurance crisis was actually supposed to be a torts crisis.

The most influential proponent of this theory was the Reagan Administration's Interagency Task Force, headed by Edwin Meese's Department of Justice. The theory postulates that tort law has abandoned the principle of fault, particularly in the area of product liability, resulting in an explosion of tort cases and in sharply rising jury awards. Facing huge current losses and the prospect of greater losses in future years, insurers were forced to dramatically increase premium rates.

Tort reform was to be the cure for America's tort crisis. While the idea of legislative manipulation of tort rules to benefit liability insurers certainly did not originate with the Task Force, the report became the single most influential document in winning passage of tort reform legislation in nearly every state over the next two years. After premiums fell and availability increased, the tort reformers shifted their emphasis to allegations that the cost of insurance was undermining the competitiveness of American industry, a contention that gained prominence as part of the Bush-Quayle campaign for reelection. . . .

## THE TORT REFORM MOVEMENT: ASSAULT ON THE JURY

**Torts As Public Relations** As the insurance industry's woes grew, it "mounted massive publicity campaigns as well as enormously expensive federal and state legislative lobbying efforts." The Insurance Information Institute, the public relations arm of the industry, announced a massive campaign that would "change the widely held perception of an insurance crisis to a perception of a lawsuit crisis." . . .

Lawyers, researchers, and scholars have documented the huge investment by the tort reform campaign to advance the tort crisis theory through sheer saturation marketing and public relations. In an attempt at rebuttal, scholars assailed the inaccuracies in the reformers' assertions, and condemned the emotion-laden, propaganda-style techniques employed by the advocates of tort reform. It was, in the words of Ralph Nader, "one of the most unprincipled public relations scams in the history of American industry." Nevertheless, it worked.

**Torts As a Special Interest** To correspond with the public relations campaign, the insurance industry, business interests, and the health care industry launched a lobbying campaign that blanketed the country. In 1986 alone, approximately 1400 tort reform bills were introduced in state legislatures. Again, the tort reformers resorted to using questionable facts and special interest political tactics, and, here again, the reformers were quite successful.

**Tort Reform in the Courts** The drive to secure immunity from tort liability also extended to the courts. Large jury verdicts awarding punitive damages were of particular concern to manufacturers. Ultimately, the tort reformers hoped to convince the United States Supreme Court to recognize constitutional limitations on punitive damages. Pursuing their goal, the tort reformers filed numerous amicus briefs with the Court that focused on product liability awards and the insurance crisis, although the Court did not actually accept any product liability cases. In effect, they urged the Court to impose on the states the same limits on punitive damages that most state legislatures had previously rejected.

Despite the reformers' effort, the Court has consistently declined to impose rigid constitutional limits on punitive damages. Moreover, many courts have expressed doubts concerning the very existence of the crisis. Accordingly, a number of state supreme courts have struck down tort reform damage caps, frequently on the state constitutional grounds of access to courts and right to trial by jury. . . .

## AN UPDATE ON THE CRISIS

The crisis itself was relatively short-lived, essentially ending in 1987. One salutary consequence of the crisis was to exert pressure on the insurance industry to provide greater disclosure and on researchers to test many of the assumptions relied upon by the tort reformers. After considering the available data and empirical analysis developed by researchers, this Article will conclude that the tort crisis theory is based upon a false hypothesis. . . .

**The Myth of Absolute Liability**   After extensive study, the ALI Reporters found that "there appears to be little or no foundation for the common diagnosis that erosion of the fault principle as the basis of tort liability has attracted surplus numbers of dubious claims into the tort system." Moreover, "it is clear that the sudden explosion of insurance premiums and the contraction of available coverage in the mid-eighties was not caused by . . . the legal system. . . ." . . .

**The Myth of the "Litigation Explosion"**  The second essential inference in the tort crisis theory is that expanded liability rules have resulted in a dramatic increase in product liability litigation. The ALI Reporters determined that "[m]ore systematic analysis of claims trends has demonstrated either that there never was a true general explosion in tort litigation, or at least that any incipient trend has definitely subsided."

**The Myth of the "Runaway" Jury**   A third myth that has been laid to rest by empirical research is the idea of the "runaway jury," swayed by sympathy for plaintiffs and antipathy toward deep-pocket defendants. Juries, it turns out, continue to do their job well, and damage awards in products cases generally tend to reflect the severity of injuries. Empirical research reveals no support for the assumption that juries tend to award large verdicts out of bias in favor of an injured plaintiff against a defendant who is able to pay. Indeed, studies reveal that jury awards are usually not greater than awards by judges in bench trials. Additionally, juries tend to be more skeptical of personal injury plaintiffs than of corporate defendants.

**The Myth of the "Torts Tax" and Competitiveness**   Finally, the tort reformers contend that liability costs, passed along to consumers in the form of higher prices, hobble American competitiveness and innovation. Recent presidential candidate George Bush complained in a Labor Day speech that "our product liability system is killing our economic competitiveness." Because the insurance industry did not report product liability coverage as a separate line of insurance until recently, tort reformers frequently resorted to horror stories claiming that a large percentage of the price of such worthy items as ladders goes to product liability costs. Analyzing this issue, however, reveals that researchers estimate that the cost of product liability insurance adds less than 1% to the price of most products. More specifically, a recent study of new data compiled by A.M. Best, which includes separate reporting of product liability insurance, reveals that premiums represent about .14% of retail cost. Furthermore, accounting for self insurance and other factors, NICO estimates that, at most, product liability adds under one half of one percent to product prices on average. . . .

## 17.4 | Our Juries, Our Selves: The Power, Perception, and Politics of the Civil Jury *Laura Gaston Dooley\**

THE MODERN AMERICAN JURY has a bipolar presence in the popular consciousness. On the one hand, the jury is a cultural icon as revered in the United States as the flag, its contribution to democracy equated to voting. On the other hand, the jury is reviled as an agent of arbitrary injustice, its output considered evidence of the decline of moral consensus. Controversial, high-profile jury verdicts in the last few years have intensified the debate about the efficacy of the jury as the principal decisionmaker in court-settled disputes.

This cultural ambivalence about the jury has significance beyond the ongoing need to assess jury performance, because the modern jury is the most diverse of our democratic bodies.[1] After courts began to interpret constitutional mandates of equal protection and impartial juries to require that women and minorities be included on juries,[2] the demographics of juries changed dramatically at a pace far exceeding the diversification of legislatures, executive branches, or the judiciary.[3]

But as this jurisprudence of inclusion developed, so too did restraints on jury power. The twentieth-century civil jury is subject to legal restraints unknown to our constitutional framers and enjoys far less prestige than its eighteenth-century ancestor. The confluence of the dual trends toward inclusion and restraint creates some troubling questions. What does it mean that the most diverse of our democratic institutions is subject to increasing legal restraints and cultural disdain? Is the treatment of the modern jury as an institution (now that women are routinely included) itself a manifestation of sexism? Does the

---

Laura Gaston Dooley, "Our Juries, Our Selves: The Power, Perception, and Politics of the Civil Jury," *Cornell Law Review 1995*. Used by permission of the Cornell Law Review. Some footnotes omitted, others renumbered.

*Associate Professor, Valparaiso University School of Law.

[1] As to gender diversity, a recent study reveals that in the federal courts of eight major cities, women comprised an average of 52.875% of serving jurors, defined in the study as a "qualified person reporting or on call to report to the courthouse for jury duty." NATIONAL CENTER FOR STATE COURTS, THE RELATIONSHIP OF JUROR FEES AND TERMS OF SERVICE TO JURY SYSTEM PERFORMANCE 3 n.4 (Janice T. Munsterman, Project Director, 1991) [hereinafter JUROR FEES STUDY]. In the state courts serving the same metropolitan areas, women comprised 53.75% of serving jurors. The cities surveyed were Bismarck, Boston, Dallas, Denver, Montgomery, Phoenix, Seattle, and Washington, D.C. *Id.* app. D at D1.

The degree of racial diversity was much more varied. In Montgomery, for example, African-Americans comprised 22% of serving jurors in state court and 23% in federal court; in Washington, D.C., African-Americans comprised 65% and 73% of serving jurors in state and federal court; in Bismarck, Boston, Phoenix, and Seattle, the percentage of African-Americans hovered around 3% in both state and federal court, though other minorities added somewhat to the diversity of juries in those cities. *Id.*

[2] The Supreme Court has developed two strands of jurisprudence designed to ensure that juries will fairly represent the community from which they are drawn. The first is derived from the Sixth Amendment guarantee of criminal trials by "impartial" juries, which the Court reads to mean that jury venire pools must be drawn from a "fair cross section" of the community. The Court does not require, however, that the final jury chosen in any particular case be demographically proportionate.

A more important tool in the movement toward representativeness has been the Equal Protection Clause of the Fourteenth Amendment, which has been successfully invoked to prevent the use of peremptory challenges to strike prospective jurors on the basis of their race or gender. *See* J.E.B. v. Alabama *ex rel* T.B., 114 S. Ct. 1419 (1994) (declaring unconstitutional the use of peremptory challenges to strike jurors on the basis of gender); Batson v. Kentucky, 476 U.S. 79 (1986) (establishing that use of peremptories to strike jurors on the basis of race violates the federal constitution).

[3] Despite growing awareness of the gender gap in legislative bodies, the judiciary, and the executive offices of government, the numbers are still vastly disproportionate. In the 103d Congress, only six women served among the 100 members of the United States Senate; only 47 women served among the 435 members of the House of Representatives. In 1992, only 60 women held state-wide elective executive offices in the United States, and only 1375 women served in state legislatures. BUREAU OF THE CENSUS, U.S. DEP'T OF COMMERCE, STATISTICAL ABSTRACT OF THE UNITED STATES: 1992, at 268 (1992). As of 1988, women comprised only 7.4% of the federal judiciary, and only 7.2% of state judges. COMMISSION ON WOMEN IN THE PROFESSION, REPORT TO THE HOUSE OF DELEGATES OF THE AMERICAN BAR ASSOCIATION 6 (Hillary Rodham Clinton, Chair, 1988).

power distribution in the courtroom between judge and jury reflect a cultural privileging of the judge as the presumably "rational" actor? . . .

. . . The procedural structure within which the civil jury operates, together with the language that manifests that structure, tell a story of a progressive cultural privileging of judicial rationality and distaste for perceived populist excesses. Thus, the jury's power is held in check by procedural devices which ensure that judges will have the last word, while its value as a trustworthy decisionmaker is called into question by courtroom protocol and rhetoric that casts it in feminine terms. Like women, juries are placed on rhetorical pedestals yet are condescended to by the other actors in the legal system.

## I. ANGEL OF THE COURTROOM: THE POWER OF THE CIVIL JURY . . .

In the Victorian period, it was often argued that the social arrangements of the day properly divided power, influence, and responsibilities according to the relative attributes of men and women. Far from being oppressed, the woman was said to exercise great power in the domestic sphere, to which her feminine talents were particularly well-suited. She was the "angel in the house," and her ability to control her private world was supposed to satiate any general desire for power that she might have. Of course, any power women had was completely circumscribed by men (usually husband or father). The limited sphere of her influence was always subject to external control.

The notion that Victorian women enjoyed a position of power in the private sphere under the convention of the time seems quaint to us now. But the same power dynamic that allowed for such an argument in the nineteenth century is reinventing itself in the twentieth-century relationship between judge and jury in the courtroom. Because the judge always retains ultimate authority to override jury decisions, he controls the jury's sphere of influence.

This power disparity did not always exist. In colonial times civil juries were frequently entrusted to adjudicate both law and fact. Although historical sources are scarce and sometimes inconsistent, causing scholars to debate the precise lines of authority between judge and jury in late eighteenth and early nineteenth century American courtrooms, one thing is clear: the authority of the jury vis-a-vis the judge eroded in the late nineteenth century and especially in the twentieth. . . .

## II. SIGNS OF (IR)RATIONALITY: THE PERCEPTION OF THE AMERICAN JURY . . .

. . . [T]here is an obvious parallel between the language used by judges to describe juries that they believe to have decided a case the wrong way and language commonly used to demean the decision-making of women. Thus, juries are referred to as "easily swayed by emotion" and "not given to hard logical thinking." Such rhetoric validates the intuition fostered by the structural system of restraints on juries: that indeed juror irrationality is an ever-present threat that must be kept in constant check.

In reported opinions of the nineteenth century, courts often referred to jurors as "reasonable men" as though that characterization was so natural and inevitable that it was almost a given. Juries were romanticized; their supposed diversity in terms of drawing members from different walks of life contributed to their prestige. Whatever verdict a jury returned in those early days was presumably reasonable, since the jury was made up of men who were themselves reasonable. . . .

Significantly, when judges decide to overrule jury verdicts, the language they use mirrors the rhetoric that traditionally has marginalized the intellectual and decisionmaking faculties of women.[4] The traditional stereotype of women is that they are irrational, emotional, and passionate. Indeed, it was this stereotype that so long delayed women's successful participation in the democratic exercises of both jury service and

---

[4]For example, in the psychological literature, much attention has been directed to exposing the fragmented approach of early moral theorists who based their ideas about moral development on the behavior of men and then measured women by those standards. Carol Gilligan's work in debunking male-oriented theories of moral development has been quite influential and is often cited in legal literature. *See* CAROL GILLIGAN, IN A DIFFERENT VOICE: PSYCHOLOGICAL THEORY AND WOMEN'S DEVELOPMENT (1982). Though Gilligan's work has been criticized as essentialist, its importance as an exposé of male-centered evaluative processes has endured.

voting. Once it was no longer politically possible to exclude women from jury service outright, their power was more subtly restrained by procedural devices that control, and rhetoric that compromises, the institution that now included them. Now, like women, juries are called irrational, emotional, and inflamed by passion. Of course, the juries branded by these demeaning feminine terms are precisely those whose error it was to disagree with a presiding judge on how a case should come out. . . .

Rhetoric compromising jury authority can be found outside court opinions as well. Much legal scholarship, for example, has been quite harsh in its assessment of the competency of juries to decide modern disputes, especially private ones. The debate about the relative merits of lay versus professional decisionmakers is not a new one, certainly, but the modern discourse discloses a particular hostility toward jurors' ability to comprehend the so-called complex cases of the post-industrial age. . . .

As [the] theme of jury inefficiency has evolved through this century, its most ardent and articulate champions have been judges, whose positions give their policy views extraordinary weight. Judge Jerome Frank, for example, was famously critical of juries.[5] Of the jury trial, he said "[a] better instrument could scarcely be imagined for achieving uncertainty, capriciousness, lack of uniformity, disregard of former decisions—utter unpredictability." Jurors he described as "notoriously gullible and impressionable" and "hopelessly incompetent as fact-finders; they are "neither able to, nor do they attempt to, apply the instructions of the court." . . .

Judge Frank's Freudian notion of judge-as-archetypal-father illustrates the sort of rhetorical compartmentalization of courtroom actors that ultimately demeans both juries and common people in general: his notion was that the public preferred the jury trial precisely because of its anti-intellectual and illogical qualities. The "hu-

manizing agency" that tempers the stern judicial father must be the mother-jury. And while Judge Frank pushed for judges to acknowledge the impossibility of perfectly logical decisionmaking, his disdain for the jury remained steadfast; he forthrightly stated that "[t]he jury makes the orderly administration of justice virtually impossible."

Judge Frank was not the only prominent twentieth-century jurist to challenge the supremacy of the jury trial method. Chief Justice Warren Burger's concern about the increasingly complex nature of modern litigation and the delay in the federal courts led him to pick up the banner for revamping civil jury trials. In a 1984 lecture, he proposed that it was time to "inquire into the possibility of some alternatives to the traditional jury trial for the protracted civil trials of issues which baffle all but the rarest of jurors who actually wind up in the jury box." Chief Justice Burger questioned whether modern juries are "truly representative" given that professionals, business executives, academics, and "others arguably more competent than most to cope with complex economic or scientific questions rarely survive [peremptory challenges] to sit in the box."

Indeed, the complexity debate has eclipsed the earlier efficiency debate to become the focus of dissatisfaction with the jury in recent years. . . .

## CONCLUSION

The intersection of the two jurisprudential trends that have dominated the development of the jury in the last hundred or so years—the movement toward inclusive juries and the growth of judicial restraint on jury power—produces an unsettling picture of a power struggle along gender and racial lines. Acknowledging this political truth forces a reexamination of jury restraint mechanisms that we have come to accept as necessary and therefore constitutional.

Moreover, the semiotic analysis presented here prepares the field for a more self-conscious appraisal of both the current system and proposed reforms. The ideology of juror distrust that is facilitated and reinforced by the rational-

---

[5]*See generally* FRANK, COURTS ON TRIAL (expressing skepticism about jurors' ability to perform factfinding and law application functions).

ity standard for evaluating jury decisionmaking should no longer conceal the power dynamic in the modern courtroom. The stark reality is that jury power is externally controlled; if this is the justice system we prefer, we must openly acknowledge its anti-democratic features.

If, on the other hand, we do not want to see the jury system limp along in its present condition, we should demonstrate our respect for the good faith and intellect of jurors by enlarging their sphere of influence in the courtroom. For example, we might consider enlarging the universe of information available to jurors or giving jurors a voice in information gathering. Most importantly, we must as a society vigilantly ensure that our supposedly democratic institutions do not simply mask power concentrations that we have not affirmatively sanctioned.

&ntilde; The settlement of civil cases out of court and the persistence of widespread plea bargaining in the nation's criminal courts (see Reading 13.4) have made trials by jury more the exception than the rule. In spite of the dwindling percentage of cases that result in jury trials, however, many critics are disturbed by the amount of time taken in impaneling the jury and in jury deliberation. Crowded court dockets, resulting in part from legislative unwillingness to increase the number of judges and courtrooms, have lent a greater urgency to these criticisms and prompted some states to reduce the size of juries or to eliminate the unanimity requirement in order to reduce the time needed to choose juries and the time juries spend deliberating. These actions raise thorny questions about the dynamics of jury deliberation, the representative character of juries, and the constitutional role of juries in the U.S. legal system.

The following cases deal with the dynamics of jury deliberation. The final reading, excerpted from Jeffrey Abramson's excellent book, *We, The Jury,* places the issue of jury unanimity squarely in the tradition of constitutional democracy. Together with the materials presented earlier, these readings shed light on the direction in which the jury system seems to be moving. They suggest that the jury is an endangered part of American culture, and that antidemocratic forces may be gaining the upper hand in the struggle over this venerable legal institution. And they raise again the question considered by Horwitz, Corboy, and Dooley, and suggested originally by Tocqueville's trenchant observation that "All the sovereigns who have chosen to govern by their own authority, and to direct society instead of obeying its directions, have destroyed or enfeebled the institution of the jury." Who, or what, is this would-be tyrant?

## 17.5 Johnson v. Louisiana    *92 S.Ct. 1620 (1972)*

MR. JUSTICE WHITE *delivered the opinion of the Court.*

UNDER BOTH THE LOUISIANA Constitution and Code of Criminal Procedure, criminal cases in which the punishment is necessarily at hard labor are tried to a jury of 12, and the vote of nine jurors is sufficient to return either a guilty or not guilty verdict. The principle question in this case is whether these provisions allowing less than unanimous verdicts in certain cases are valid under the Due Process and Equal Protection Clauses of the Fourteenth Amendment.

### I

Appellant Johnson was arrested at his home on January 20, 1968. . . . Johnson pleaded not guilty, was tried on May 14, 1968, by a 12-man jury and was convicted by a nine-to-three verdict. . . .

### II

Appellant argues that in order to give substance to the reasonable doubt standard which the State, by virtue of the Due Process Clause of the Fourteenth Amendment, must satisfy in criminal cases, that clause must be construed to require a unanimous jury verdict in all criminal cases. . . . Concededly, the jurors were told to convict only if convinced of guilt beyond a reasonable doubt. Nor is there any claim that, if the verdict in this case had been unanimous, the evidence would have been insufficient to support it. Appellant focuses instead on the fact that less than all jurors voted to convict and argues that, because three voted to acquit, the reasonable doubt standard has not been satisfied and his conviction is therefore infirm.

We note at the outset that this Court has never held jury unanimity to be a requisite of due process of law. . . . We can find no basis for holding that the nine jurors who voted for his conviction failed to follow their instructions concerning the need for proof beyond such a doubt or that the vote of any one of the nine failed to reflect an honest belief that guilt had been so proved. . . .

We have no grounds for believing that majority jurors, aware of their responsibility and power over the liberty of the defendant, would simply refuse to listen to arguments presented to them in favor of acquittal, terminate discussion and render a verdict. On the contrary it is far more likely that a juror presenting reasoned argument in favor of acquittal would either have his arguments answered or would carry enough other jurors with him to prevent conviction. A majority will cease discussion and outvote a minority only after reasoned discussion has ceased to have persuasive effect or to serve any other purpose—when a minority, that is, continues to insist upon acquittal without having persuasive reasons in support of its position. . . . We conclude, therefore, that, as to the nine jurors who voted to convict, the State satisfied its burden of proving guilt beyond any reasonable doubt. . . .

That rational men disagree is not in itself equivalent to a failure of proof by the State, nor does it indicate infidelity to the reasonable doubt standard. . . .

In order to "facilitate, expedite, and reduce expense in the administration of justice," *State* v. *Lewis,* 129 La. 800, 804, 56 So. 893, 894 (1911), Louisiana has permitted less serious crimes to be tried by five jurors with unanimous verdicts, more serious crimes have required the assent of nine of 12 jurors, and for the most serious crimes a unanimous verdict of 12 jurors is stipulated. In appellant's case, nine jurors rather than five or 12 were required for a verdict. We discern nothing invidious in this classification. . . .

[He] is simply challenging the judgment of the Louisiana Legislature. That body obviously intended to vary the difficulty of proving guilt with the gravity of the offense and the severity of the punishment. We remain unconvinced by anything appellant has presented that this legislative judgment was defective in any constitutional sense.

The judgment of the Supreme Court of Louisiana is therefore

Affirmed.

MR. JUSTICE STEWART, *with whom*
MR. JUSTICE BRENNAN *and* MR. JUSTICE
MARSHALL *join, dissenting.*

The guarantee against systematic discrimination in the selection of criminal court juries is a fundamental of the Fourteenth Amendment. . . .

The clear purpose of these decisions has been to ensure universal participation of the citizenry in the administration of criminal justice. Yet today's judgment approves the elimination of the one rule that can ensure that such participation will be meaningful—the rule requiring the assent of all jurors before a verdict of conviction or acquittal can be returned. Under today's judgment, nine jurors can simply ignore the views of their fellow panel members of a different race or class.

. . . For only a unanimous jury so selected can serve to minimize the potential bigotry of those who might convict on inadequate evidence, or acquit when evidence of guilt was clear. . . .

The requirement that the verdict of the jury be unanimous, surely as important as these other constitutional requisites, preserves the jury's function in linking law with contemporary society. It provides the simple and effective method endorsed by centuries of experience and history to combat the injuries to the fair administration of justice that can be inflicted by community passion and prejudice.

I dissent.

## 17.6   Apodaca et al. v. Oregon   *92 S.Ct. 1628 (1972)*

[*In* Apodaca *the court upheld Oregon's jury statute allowing a conviction in a felony case by a jury voting 10–2. The court refuted the claim that minority groups would be excluded from influencing verdicts when unanimity was not required.*]

WE ALSO CANNOT ACCEPT petitioners' second assumption—that minority groups, even when they are represented on a jury, will not adequately represent the viewpoint of those groups simply because they may be outvoted in the final result. They will be present during all deliberations, and their views will be heard. We cannot assume that the majority of the jury will refuse to weigh the evidence and reach a decision upon rational grounds, just as it must now do in order to obtain unanimous verdicts, or that a majority will deprive a man of his liberty on the basis of prejudice when a minority is presenting a reasonable argument in favor of acquittal. We simply find no proof for the notion that a majority will disregard its instructions and cast its votes for guilt or innocence based on prejudice rather than the evidence.

We accordingly affirm the judgment of the Court of Appeals of Oregon.

It is so ordered.

[MR. JUSTICE DOUGLAS, *in a dissent, found faults in the majority's view of jury deliberations.*] . . .

The diminution of verdict reliability flows from the fact that nonunanimous juries need not debate and deliberate as fully as must unanimous juries. As soon as the requisite majority is attained, further consideration is not required either by Oregon or by Louisiana even though the dissident jurors might, if given the chance, be able to convince the majority. Such persuasion does in fact occasionally occur in States where the unanimous requirement applies: "In roughly one case in ten, the minority eventually succeeds in reversing an initial majority, and these may be cases of special importance."[1] . . .

It is said that there is no evidence that majority jurors will refuse to listen to dissenters whose votes are unneeded for conviction. Yet human experience teaches that polite and academic conversation is no substitute for the earnest and robust argument necessary to reach

[1]Kalven and Ziesel, The American Jury 490 (1966). See also The American Jury: Notes for an English Controversy, 48 Chi. Bar Rec. 195 (1967).

unanimity. As mentioned earlier, in Apodaca's case, whatever courtesy dialogue transpired could not have lasted more than 41 minutes. I fail to understand why the Court should lift from the States the burden of justifying so radical a departure from an accepted and applauded tradition and instead demand that these defendants document with empirical evidence what has always been thought to be too obvious for further study.

## 17.7 | The Unanimous Verdict    *Jeffrey Abramson*

FOR OVER SIX HUNDRED years, the unanimous verdict has stood as a distinctive and defining feature of jury trials. The first recorded instance of a unanimous verdict occurred in 1367, when an English Court refused to accept an 11–1 guilty vote after the lone holdout stated he would rather die in prison than consent to convict. Steadily afterward, the requirement of unanimity took hold. . . .

Some American colonies briefly authorized majority verdicts in the seventeenth century, apparently because of unfamiliarity with common-law procedures. But by the eighteenth century, it was agreed that verdicts had to be unanimous. Indeed, prior to 1972, no case explicitly disputing the unanimity requirement in criminal cases ever came before the Supreme Court. . . .

Today, over thirty states use juries that are made up of fewer than twelve persons to try at least some nonpetty criminal offenses. But few states avail themselves of the Court's permission to experiment with nonunanimous verdicts. Louisiana and Oregon remain the only states authorizing felony convictions by less than unanimous verdicts. Florida permits juries to recommend life versus death, for persons convicted of murder, by a straight majority vote; however, the jury's recommendation is advisory only and subject to judicial override. Some states permit defendants to waive their right to a unanimous verdict.

Even though the Court's 1972 decisions did not open the floodgates to majority verdicts,

those decisions represent a remarkable demotion of the unanimous verdict rule, stripping it of constitutional protection and leaving it up to states to accept it or not. After so much history, what lies behind this weakened stature for the unanimous verdict rule? . . .

### THE POLITICAL THEORY OF UNANIMITY VERSUS MAJORITY RULE

History provides no clear answer as to why the ideal of unanimity found such a permanent home in the jury. There is some evidence that the ideal prevailed generally in medieval institutions. The Church placed a premium on unanimity as "the infallible sign of God's voice." Fourteenth-century English Parliaments still doubted that a majority vote was sufficient to bind individuals; their hesitancy may have reflected an argument that individuals could be bound legally only by their own consent and not by what the majority decided. As one medieval scholar put it, "The word consent . . . carried with it the idea of *concordia* or unanimity."

In its original form, the medieval jury had its own reasons to prefer unanimity. Being drawn from the neighborhood, jurors were presumed to be witnesses to the events on trial, or at least informed about them. Disagreement therefore suggested perjury and argued for a unanimity requirement. The medieval mind was also more likely than our own to believe that reason could tolerate only one, correct, answer to what happened; there was no room for reasonable jurors to disagree. But, whatever its medieval origins, the unanimous verdict requirement survived into modern times to become a pillar of popular

Reprinted by permission of the publisher and author from *We, the Jury: The Jury System and the Idea of Democracy*, by Jeffrey Abramson, Cambridge, Mass.: Harvard University Press. Copyright © 1994 by Basic Books.

faith in the legitimacy and accuracy of jury verdicts. By contrast, "the decision-making process in Parliament became avowedly majoritarian" by the fifteenth century. . . .

. . . The unanimous verdict rule gives concrete expression to a different set of democratic aspirations—keyed to deliberation rather than voting and to consensus rather than division. Voters pull a curtain and vote in private; jurors meet face-to-face and debate their differences. Numbers are decisive in elections, making problematic the effective representation of small or marginal groups; on the jury, the practice of unanimity represents an ideal where individual views cannot simply be ignored or outvoted. At its best, unanimity disempowers narrow and prejudiced arguments that appeal to some groups but not others. It favors general arguments persuasive to persons drawn from different walks of life.

One of the ironies of current law is that the Supreme Court withdrew constitutional protection from the unanimous verdict even as it was reading the Constitution for the first time as guaranteeing that the jury be a body truly representative of the community. But if the great reforms of jury selection in recent years are not to degenerate into the mere token presence of minorities on juries, then the Court needs to regain an appreciation of the unanimous verdict's service to cross-community deliberation. In essence, the unanimous verdict is the crucial element in the jury designed on the model of collective wisdom that Aristotle isolated as the best argument on behalf of democracy. When "the many" govern, Aristotle noted, each individual is an ordinary person considered alone. When these ordinary persons meet together, greater understanding may result than when persons must decide on their own:

> For each individual among the many has a share of virtue and prudence and when they meet together, they become in a manner one man. . . . Some understand one part, and some another and among them they understand the whole.

Ultimately, the requirement of unanimity necessitates that jurors conduct extensive deliberations out of which collective wisdom flows. Each must consider the case from everyone else's point of view in search of the conscience of the community. Each must persuade or be persuaded in turn. . . .

[Professor Abramson here discusses the *Apodaca* and *Johnson* cases, reprinted in part at pages 472–474.]

## UNANIMOUS VERDICTS AND THE DELIBERATIVE IDEAL

The Court's dispute over unanimity raised a number of intriguing empirical and philosophical questions. From the empirical point of view, what factual evidence was there to support the majority's conclusion that nonunanimous verdicts would make "no difference" to the thoroughness of deliberation? From the philosophical point of view, what understanding of the deliberative ideal did the justices have in mind when they examined the practical importance of abandoning unanimity? In particular, what does it mean to ask persons from various groups to come together as one community to deliberate toward a shared sense of justice? I begin with the philosophical issues at stake. . . .

. . . [E]choing Aristotle's account of how democratic assemblies achieved a common wisdom beyond the grasp of isolated individuals, the best defense of the unanimous verdict would have celebrated the jury's bringing together of persons from various walks of life, each inevitably drawing on valued perspectives embedded in his or her religion and ethnic background and yet each fair-minded enough to appreciate the wisdom someone from another background brings to the discussion. . . .

. . . To acknowledge that jurors enter the jury room with views and values shaped in part by their creed, race, or gender is not to accuse the jurors of bias in need of silencing. It is to treasure the particularly rich conversations a democratic assembly inspires, precisely because it brings into one communal conversation persons from different subcommunities. On a jury, these persons must, however, clearly understand that their goal is not to represent, to protect, or to assert the interests of their own groups. It is to join with others in search of the truth and shared justice, making a positive contribution to that search by drawing on their own backgrounds when necessary but also listening to what others know better by virtue of their experiences.

The requirement of unanimity is indispensable to sending the right cue to jurors about what we expect of them. It surely contributes to an understanding among jurors that their function is to persuade, not to outvote, one another. When jurors behave in this way, they contribute knowledge to the ongoing discussion. And the jury distinctively achieves collective wisdom through deliberation, rather than collapsing into a body where jurors behave as if their function were to represent the preconceptions and interests of their own kind.

## THE PRACTICAL EFFECTS OF ABOLISHING UNANIMOUS VERDICTS

Practically speaking, what difference would it make if juries were permitted to render 9–3 or 10–2 verdicts rather than unanimous verdicts? In *Apodaca* and *Johnson*, the Court surmised that the effects would be minimal. Presumably, there would be some reduction in hung juries and thus some gain in the efficiency of the system. But the Court thought neither the prosecution nor the defense would gain an edge from the shift. Deliberation would proceed as before, and would be just as thorough, reliable, and representative of opposing points of view. . . .

**Post-1972 Studies** The Supreme Court's decisions in *Apodaca* and *Johnson* spurred social scientists into a new round of empirical studies of unanimous versus majority verdicts. In general, these studies have shown that "jury verdicts do not differ as a function of decision-rule"; the ratio of convictions to acquittals remains the same, whether mock juries are instructed to return unanimous verdicts or verdicts down to a two-thirds majority. The only major difference, as far as final verdicts go, is that unanimous juries are more likely to hang. All of this basically confirms Kalven and Zeisel's findings. . . .

Such [studies] support the dissent of Justice Douglas in *Apodaca,* when he argued for the difference between "polite" debate (which a majority might deign to have with minority jurors whose votes are not needed) and "robust" argument (which takes place when the majority needs to persuade the minority jurors). As sociologist Michael Saks put it, the achievement of the minimum bloc of votes necessary for a verdict is "psychologically binding" on bloc members. The deliberation may continue but it continues as an option, not an obligation.

Various subsidiary findings support the general conclusion that deliberation between majority and minority factions becomes weak and watery once the majority has enough votes for a verdict. . . .

Finally, and most important, the empirical studies showed that jurors returning nonunanimous verdicts felt far less certain of their conclusions than did their counterparts on unanimous verdict juries. This is so intuitively plausible that we probably did not need fancy mock jury studies to prove it: jurors not voting in favor of the majority's verdict are hardly likely to think justice was done. What is perhaps not so obvious is that the holdouts left the trial feeling that the majority did not even listen to them seriously. According to the Massachusetts study, the style of deliberation under nonunanimous verdict instructions was likely to be more combative than under unanimous rules, with "larger factions in majority rule juries adopt[ing] a more forceful, bullying, persuasive style because their members realize that it is not necessary to respond to all opposition arguments when their goal is to achieve a faction size of only eight or ten members." One consequence was that members of nonunanimous verdict juries corrected each other's errors of fact less frequently, with those in the minority apparently concluding that the effort was unproductive.

These research findings suggest that the quality of jury deliberation is far more tied to the practice of unanimous verdicts than the Supreme Court allowed in 1972. Moreover, because "popular acceptance of the jury system is formulated, in part, by what former jurors say about it, jurors' satisfaction is not without its importance." All studies to date verify that juror satisfaction sours under nonunanimous verdict conditions. To this extent, the unanimous verdict rule must be seen as a core ingredient underwriting the jury's ability to legitimate justice in the eyes of the community. . . .

The continuing popularity of the unanimous verdict is worthy of comment. One of the key functions of the criminal jury system is to legitimize, in the eyes of the community, the state's use of its coercive powers. The jury gives legitimacy to an accused's imprisonment, even execution, because ordinary persons like ourselves give the verdict. But the jury's ability to maintain public confidence in the administration of justice is fragile. It depends in part on drawing the jury from the community at large so that all groups have a potential say in how justice is done. It depends also on public confidence that jury verdicts are just, accurate, and true. The strongest argument for retaining the unanimous verdict is that it is central to the legitimacy of jury verdicts.

Common sense alone tells us that public confidence in the accuracy of verdicts is greater when the verdict is unanimous. Common sense also tells us that Justice Stewart was right to fret over the symbolic significance of replacing unanimous verdicts with majority verdicts. In the best of circumstances, public confidence would erode whenever split verdicts resulted. In the worst cases, a crisis of legitimacy would greet verdicts split along racial or other group lines. Justice Stewart did not cite statistics about the probability of such group splits occurring. His point was that the very redesign of jury trials to permit such verdicts changed public attitudes toward the jury for the worst. It sponsored an ever present consciousness that majorities, if large enough, could rule absolutely on juries.

In the end, however, it must be admitted that there is a paradox behind the unanimous verdict's contribution to the jury's legitimacy. Unanimity inspires confidence because the public *believes* that requiring all jurors to agree promotes the search for truth. But, as Jacobsohn noted in his study of the unanimous verdict, this belief rests on at least a partial misconception. Unanimity might inspire jurors to behave deliberatively—that is, to reason together across differences to reach a genuinely shared verdict. But, as Justice Powell pointed out, unanimity may prod jurors to behave more expediently, returning a compromise verdict that splits the difference between jury factions and has no rational basis. To the extent that this happens, unanimity does not promote truth.

The analysis so far suggests that unanimous verdicts contribute to the legitimacy of jury verdicts only so long as a certain fiction is maintained—that is, only so long as the public *mistakenly* believes that the more consensual the verdict, the more likely the verdict is correct. But is the public mistaken? Exactly how jurors "compromise" or harmonize during deliberations remains a mystery; studies of mock jurors are not likely to tell us how jurors behave when they bear actual responsibility for the decision.

No doubt there are cases where jurors strike a bargain simply to agree and go home, much like Justice Powell suggested. But jury compromises need not be of the expedient, horse-trading, split-the-difference, or flip-a-coin models.

The alternative give-and-take model defines the democratic ideal of deliberation. On this model, jurors do not strike compromises between the different interests they represent. They each take seriously the goal of reaching the truth, earnestly seeking to harmonize their different understandings of the facts, their different assessments of an accused's culpability or responsibility for his acts. In the face of these differences, the conversation grows animated, intense, even angry. The unanimous verdict rule makes the deliberations all the more intense because the alternative of outshouting or outvoting opponents does not exist. In such circumstances, jurors certainly have incentives for compromising or harmonizing. But the cue we are giving jurors by requiring unanimity is that there are compromises and there are compromises. On the basic issue of whether an accused is guilty or not guilty, there can be no compromise, and even deadlocked jurors are carefully instructed that individual jurors should not "cave in" to achieve unanimity.

The whole point of having jurors deliberate face-to-face is to change people's preconceptions about a case through conversation with others. Unanimity empowers the conversation by signaling to jurors to put their opinions at risk. The ideal, which is often realized, is that power flows to the persuasive on the jury—that people change their minds not out of expediency but because their views actually have shifted through hearing the views of others. When deliberation works in this way, the achievement of unanimity speaks to the collection of wisdom, not the politics of compromise.

In Brazil, federal juries do not deliberate. At the close of evidence, jurors are individually polled in writing, a secret ballot is taken, and the majority prevails. Such a procedure stands in stark contrast to our own, where deliberation is the essence of a juror's duty.

Replacing unanimous verdicts with majority verdicts would not obliterate deliberation altogether and import the Brazilian model. But it would alter the basic institutional design of our jury and the behavior promoted by that design. If they are instructed to return a unanimous verdict, jurors know their task is not to vote. For all their differences, they must approach justice through conversation and the art of persuading or being persuaded in turn. Majority verdicts signal an entirely different type of behavior, where jurors ultimately remain free to assert their different interests and opinions against one another. The distinctive genius of the jury system has been to emphasize deliberation more than voting and representation. Abolishing the unanimous verdict would weaken the conversations through which laypersons educate one another about their common sense of justice.

## Notes and Questions

1. Horwitz's analysis of the whittling away of jury functions in early American law suggests that the merchants' economic interests combined with the judiciary's desire for exclusive control over dispute resolution to reduce popular influence on law. What light does this analysis shed on Tocqueville's description of the jury as a political institution? At this point in history, what political, economic, or other forces might find it in their self-interest to reduce jury power still further? Do the materials on tort reform help in answering this question?

2. In the article, "$145 Billion to Send a Message," as in other high-profile jury trials in

which large punitive awards have been made, it may appear that an angry public is seeking unreasonable revenge against powerful corporations through abuse of the jury trial system. Does tort reform seem a reasonable response to such jury actions? Does Corboy's article convince you otherwise? Suppose that the public *does* want to penalize or even close down irresponsible, negligent, or destructive businesses, but cannot accomplish this legislatively because of special interest power. Is that the kind of situation that jury trials were designed to deal with by giving voice to the common person and to the community? What is tort law if not a means for imposing a reasonable standard of care upon individuals or corporations whose profit requirements may be dangerously inconsistent with the public good? If you were writing an analysis of tort reform one hundred years from now, do you think you would find patterns similar to those that Horwitz found in looking at the late eighteenth and early nineteenth centuries? Do you think de Toqueville's analysis of these jury awards and the tort reform response would suggest that multinational corporations constitute a would-be tyrant trying to enfeeble the jury? What about limiting jury awards in HMO suits?

3. Does the court in the *Johnson* case equate "having a reasonable doubt" about guilt with "having persuasive reasons" in support of innocence? Why or why not?

4. Does the *Johnson* court reconcile its admission that the Louisiana legislature "obviously intended to vary the difficulty of proving guilt with the gravity of the offense" with its conclusion that the state's jury law does not "indicate infidelity to the reasonable doubt standard"? What questions remain?

5. In his dissent in *Apodaca,* Mr. Justice Douglas wrote,

> The late Learned Hand said that "as a litigant I should dread a lawsuit beyond almost anything else short of sickness and death." At the criminal level that dread multiplies. Any person faced with the awesome power of government is in great jeopardy, even though innocent. Facts are always elusive and often two-faced. What may appear to one to imply guilt may carry no such overtones to another. Every criminal prosecution crosses treacherous ground, for guilt is common to all men.

What relevance does this statement have to the question of whether less than unanimous verdicts are constitutionally acceptable?

6. Charles Rembar, in his book *The Law of the Land,* describes the unanimity requirement as "primitive":

> . . . What was it then, this demand for unanimity? A product, I would say, of the immaturity of the law and the psyche of the time and place. It is characteristic of a rudimentary legal system, and it suits the medieval mind, which has no room for doubt. There is a need to deal in absolutes; there is a paralysis without them. Possibilities, probabilities, diverging views of truth—these are notions alien to these people, difficult, disturbing. A thing is so or else not so, and if it is so then everyone must know it.*

Do you agree? Does Abramson's discussion of jury unanimity convince you that there is a significant difference between the unanimous and the majority decision processes in terms of the quality of discussion and respect for individual opinions?

7. Although nearly 300,000 jury trials reportedly take place each year in the United States, this is a small and decreasing percentage of all the cases that could go to a jury. The materials in this chapter suggest that the quantitative

---

*Charles Rembar, *The Law of the Land* (New York: Simon & Schuster, 1980), p. 162.

decline in the use of the jury may be matched by a qualitative decline. This qualitative decline may result from using majority-rule juries, smaller juries, obfuscating expert testimony, shadow juries during trials, excessive and sometimes distorted media coverage of trials, and social science expertise in jury selection. Suppose the jury really is declining for all these reasons. How do the following two quotations help you think about the consequences of and motives for this decline?

> But jury trial, at best, is the apotheosis of the amateur. Why should anyone think that twelve persons brought in from the street, selected in various ways for their lack of general ability, should have any special capacity for deciding controversies between persons?
>
> Erwin Griswold, Dean, Harvard Law School, *Report of the Dean* (1963)

> All the sovereigns who have chosen to govern by their own authority, and to direct society instead of obeying its directions, have destroyed or enfeebled the institution of the jury.
>
> Alexis de Tocqueville, *Democracy in America* (1835)

8. In view of the Corboy article and the history revealed by Horwitz, who or what is the "sovereign" that "chooses" to "enfeeble" the jury in modern America? Does the earlier material on the "Trial of the Future" suggest another answer? In what kind of society is Dean Griswold's statement inevitable but destructive?

# CONCLUSION

❧ The preceding notes and questions should help you draw your own conclusions about whether the trial by jury is in decline in the United States, and about whether such a decline, if it is real, has an important effect on the health of our democracy and the quality of our lives. In essence, you will be thinking about Jefferson's statement that trial by jury is the centerpiece of democratic self-government (see page 383) and about de Tocqueville's warning (see page 401) that "all the sovereigns who have chosen to govern by their own authority" instead of by the authority of the people have destroyed or weakened the jury. If

Jefferson and de Tocqueville were right and if the jury is in decline in the United States now, who or what is "the sovereign" that seeks to replace democratic self-government with its own power and its own priorities? Could it be that our own misunderstanding or under-valuation of the importance of trial by jury makes "we the people" complicit in the decline of democracy?

# Suggested Additional Readings

Abramson, Jeffrey. *We, The Jury: The Jury System and the Ideal of Democracy.* Cambridge: Harvard University Press, 2000.

Adler, Stephen. *The Jury: Trial and Error in the American Courtroom.* New York: Times Books, 1994.

*The American Jury System: Final Report.* Annual Chief Justice Earl Warren Conference on Advocacy in the United States. New York: Roscoe Pound Trial Lawyers Association, 1977.

Bell, Derrick. *Race, Racism and American Law.* 2nd ed. Boston: Little, Brown, 1980, secs. 5.12 to 5.21.

Bloomstein, Morris J. *Verdict: The Jury System.* New York: Dodd, Mead, 1972.

Cecil, Joe, et al. "Citizen Comprehension of Difficult Issues: Lessons from Civil Jury Trials." *American University Law Review* 40 (1991), p. 728.

DiPerna, Paula. *Juries on Trial: Faces of American Justice.* New York: Dembner Books, 1984.

"Federal Grand Jury Investigation of Political Dissidents," *Harvard Civil Rights–Civil Liberties Law Review* 7 (1972), p. 432.

Federal Jury Selection Act, 28 USC 1861 et seq.

Forsyth, Walter. *History of Trial by Jury.* New York: Franklin, 1971.

Frederick, Jeffrey. *The Psychology of the American Jury System.* Charlottesville, Va.: Michie Co., 1987.

Fukurai, Hiroshi. *Race and the Jury: The System on Trial.* New York: Plenum, 1993.

Garrow, David J. *Bearing the Cross: Martin Luther King, Jr., and the Southern Christian Leadership Conference.* New York: Morrow, 1986.

Guinther, John. *The Jury in America.* New York: Facts on File Publications, 1988.

Hans, Valerie, and Neil Vidmar. *Judging the Jury.* New York: Plenum, 1986.

Hastie, Reid, Steven Penrod, and Nancy Pennington. *Inside the Jury.* Cambridge, Mass.: Harvard University Press, 1983.

Hastie, Reid, ed. *Inside the Juror: The Psychology of Juror Decision Making.* Cambridge [Eng.]: Cambridge University Press, 1993.

Horowitz, Irwin, and Thomas Willging. "Changing View of Jury Power: The Nullification Debate, 1787–1988." *Law and Human Behavior* 15 (1991), p. 165.

Kalven, Harry, Jr., and Hans Zeisel. *The American Jury.* Boston: Little, Brown, 1966.

Karst, Kenneth. *Belonging to America: Equal Citizenship and the Constitution.* New Haven, Conn.: Yale University Press, 1989.

Kassin, Saul, and Lawrence Wrightsman. *The American Jury on Trial: Psychological Perspectives.* New York: Hemisphere Publishing, 1988.

Kaufman, F. "The Right of Self-representation and the Power of Jury Nullification." *Case Western Reserve Law Review,* 28 (1978), p. 269.

Kennebeck, Edwin. *Juror Number Four: Trial of Thirteen Black Panthers as Seen from the Jury Box.* New York: Norton, 1973.

Kershen, Drew. "Jury Selection Act of 1879: Theory and Practice of Citizen Participation." *University of Illinois Law Forum* (1980), p. 707.

Levine, James. *Justice and Politics.* Pacific Grove, Calif.: Brooks/Cole, 1992.

Levy, Leonard. *The Palladium of Justice: Origins of Trial by Jury.* Chicago: I. R. Dee, 1999.

Litan, Robert, ed. *Verdict: Assessing the Civil Jury System.* Washington, D.C.: Brookings, 1993.

Moore, Lloyd. *The Jury: Tool of Kings, Palladium of Liberty.* Cincinnati: W.H. Anderson, 1973.

Palmer, Ronald. "Post-trial Interview of Jurors in the Federal Courts—A Lawyer's Dilemma." *Houston Law Review* 6 (1968), p. 290.

Sarat, Austin D. "Access to Justice: Citizen Participation and the American Legal Order," in Leon Lipson and Stanton Wheeler, eds., *Law and the Social Sciences.* New York: Russell Sage, 1986.

Simon, Rita James. *The Jury System in America: A Critical Overview.* Sage Criminal Justice System Annuals, Vol. 4. New York: Russell Sage Foundation, 1975.

Spooner, Lysander. *An Essay on the Trial by Jury.* Boston: J. P. Jewett, 1852.

Subcommittee to Investigate Administration of Internal Security Act of Senate Judiciary Committee. Hearings on Recording of Jury Deliberations. 84th Cong., 1st session, 1955.

Thoreau, Henry David. *Walden* and *Civil Disobedience.* Ed. by Owen Thomas. New York: Norton, 1966.

Unger, Roberto. *Law in Modern Society.* New York: Macmillan, 1976.

Van Dyke, Jon. *Jury Selection Procedures.* Cambridge, Mass.: Ballinger, 1977.

*Washington and Lee Law Review.* "Protest and Resistance: Civil Disobedience in the 1990's" (a nine-article symposium). 48 (1991).

Wishman, Seymour. *Anatomy of a Jury: The System on Trial.* New York: Times Books, 1986.

Zerman, Melvyn. *Call the Final Witness.* New York: Harper & Row, 1977.

———. *Beyond a Reasonable Doubt.* New York: Crowell, 1981.

*The Judgment of Wouter Van Twiller.* (The Bettmann
Archive, Inc.)

# Conflict Resolution

In every society, there is a wide range of alternatives
for coping with the conflict stirred by personal
disputes. Litigation is only one choice among many
possibilities, ranging from avoidance to violence. The
varieties of dispute settlement, and the socially
sanctioned choices in any culture, communicate
the ideals people cherish, their perceptions of
themselves, and the quality of their relationships with
others. They indicate whether people wish to avoid
or encourage conflict, suppress it, or resolve it
amicably. Ultimately the most basic values of society
are revealed in its dispute-settlement procedures.

Jerold S. Auerbach

The legal system serves many functions in American society. One of its
primary and most problematic roles is to serve as the major forum for the
resolution of conflict and the settlement of disputes, with judges expected
to be the final arbiters of social conflict. The American culture is unique
in its reliance on courts for dispute resolution. As early as 1831, Alexis de
Tocqueville noted that in the emerging American democracy, "scarcely any
political question arises in the United States that is not resolved, sooner or
later, into a judicial question." The public attitude toward law and courts
has varied during different historical periods. In *Justice Without Law*, the
historian Jerold Auerbach documents how

The American pattern of dispute settlement is, and always has been, more
varied and complex than our currently constricted legal perspective would
suggest. Tucked away in corners of our historical experience are intriguing
experiments that testify to a persistent counter-tradition to legalism. In
many and varied communities, over the entire sweep of American history,
the rule of law was explicitly rejected in favor of alternative means for
ordering human relations and for resolving the inevitable disputes that
arose between individuals. The success of non-legal dispute settlement has
always depended upon a coherent community vision. How to resolve
conflict, inversely stated, is how (or whether) to preserve community. . . .
Historically arbitration and mediation were the preferred alternatives.
They expressed an ideology of communitarian justice without formal
law, an equitable process based on reciprocal access and trust among
community members. They flourished as indigenous forms of community
self-government. Communities that rejected legalized dispute resolution
were variously defined by geography, ideology, piety, ethnicity, and
commercial pursuit. Yet, their singleness of vision is remarkable. Despite

their diversity, they used identical processes because they shared a common commitment to the essence of communal existence: mutual access, responsibility, and trust. The founders of Dedham (a seventeenth-century Christian utopian community in Massachusetts), Quaker elders of Philadelphia, followers of John Humphrey Noyes at Oneida (a nineteenth-century utopian commune), the Chinese in San Francisco and Scandinavians in Minnesota, and even Chamber of Commerce businessmen easily could have collaborated on a common blueprint for dispute settlement. Sharing a suspicion of law and lawyers, they developed patterns of conflict resolution that reflected their common striving for social harmony, beyond individual conflict, for justice without law.

For some of these same ideological reasons, the interest in alternatives to law was reignited in the late 1970s and early 1980s. But the resurgence in "alternative dispute resolution" during this period was only partially an ideological movement. Perhaps more significantly, it was tied to a more general recognition of gridlock problems within the American justice system. Courts were becoming congested with minor criminal and civil cases, many of which, observers argued, did not require formal legal intervention. A variety of diversion projects for settling disputes outside of the formal legal arena were developed. Foremost among these were federally funded Neighborhood Justice Centers, which used volunteer community mediators to resolve disputes referred by local courts. The ideological foundation for these experimental programs comprised a number of premises, many of which continue to influence ongoing experimental models of mediation. One underlying premise involves the problematic nature of the adversary process used in courts, a process that, while resulting in a judgment, polarizes the parties, making any future relationship impossible. The adversary process requires the transformation of disputes into legal claims, and one consequence of this is that the underlying issues in a dispute often fester and remain unaddressed. Far from alleviating community conflict, the adversary process can serve to undermine community relations, creating more racial, ethnic, and general community conflict. A second underlying premise is that mediation-oriented programs represent a form of popular participation in the justice system, a system that allows for almost no community input. The idea of "community mediation" represents a challenge to lawyers and their professional domination of the justice system. Another underlying premise of mediation and alternative dispute resolution programs is that they facilitate "restorative" justice. Unlike the adversary process, which is based on a "punitive" model of justice, mediational processes allow people to confront each other and to communicate their "stories" and experiences, leading to a sense of reconciliation and the possibility of restoring relationships. This third premise of mediation focuses on outcomes. Whereas the adversary model of justice in formal legal arenas is organized around winning and losing, the mediational model of justice is organized around the notion of collaborative and mutually beneficial outcomes.

Over the last decade, the dispute resolution movement has grown exponentially. There are currently close to 1000 mediation programs that work closely with local courts. In addition, bar associations in every state in the country sponsor some sort of alternative dispute resolution program. This is particularly noteworthy, as originally the state bars actively opposed the development of these programs, which utilized nonlawyer community volunteers. The support of the bar was linked to its perception that mediation could provide new arenas for lawyers and new markets for legal work. Several states have passed mandatory mediation legislation, particularly in the area of family law. In addition, conflict resolution is now taught in schools on every level, and courses in dispute resolution are becoming part of the required law school curriculum.

While the field of conflict resolution appears to be transforming both the ideology of law and legal practice, there is also opposition to these developments. The strongest opposition has come from the organized women's movement, particularly from advocates for battered women, who argue that mediation undermines rights that women have gained only through long, complex political and legal struggles. Mediation, for example, is viewed by many judges and some lawyers as a remedy for domestic violence. The objection to this is that only recently have courts been willing and required to hear cases of domestic abuse, and that diverting these cases out of the courtroom into mediational forums represents another attempt to "decriminalize" spouse abuse and domestic violence. Some object to mandatory mediation, arguing that while it may help to clear court backlogs, it can threaten women's safety by requiring them to negotiate with a partner in a private venue outside of the courtroom, without the safety net of the legal process. This objection is part of the larger criticism of mediation that while the private, confidential, and "voluntary" processes of dispute resolution, freed from the constraints of the formal rules of evidence, may help people to structure creative solutions to conflicts, they may also compromise people's rights, as the safeguards of due process are lacking. Thus, opponents of mediation assert that it serves the interest of powerful parties and, rather than balancing power, further disempowers the less powerful.

Despite this criticism, however, the interest in mediation is growing, and the field shows all the signs of an emerging, autonomous profession. For example, training programs for would-be mediators are packed with people, professional associations are blossoming and beginning to set standards of practice, conferences are held nationally and internationally, and academic and professional journals are proliferating. Whether mediation is understood as a new, second-class form of legal practice or as a new participatory approach to problem solving that is reorienting our justice system, the field of conflict resolution is no longer at the margins of law.

The readings in this section illustrate some of these cross-currents. These materials are meant to reflect the various ways in which the theory and practice of mediation raise critical questions about justice and its relationship to law. The readings in Chapter 18 focus on the theory and practice of mediation and informal dispute resolution more generally. These materials explore the problems of formal law that informal alternatives seek to address. They also examine the history of community mediation, some examples of current practice and some problems with its use. In Chapter 19, the readings focus on mediation as a form of popular justice in diverse, contemporary social contexts. The materials in Chapter 20 examine how informal dispute resolution operates as restorative justice. The last reading raises some critical questions about conflict resolution and informal justice and questions whether, in trading justice for harmony, mediation undermines or enhances social participation.

# 18 LEGAL CONTEXT OF DISPUTE RESOLUTION

❧ During the last two decades, dispute resolution programs have experienced tremendous growth. Alternative Dispute Resolution (ADR) programs now offer their services in an array of legal and nonlegal contexts. While the field generally describes itself as "alternative" dispute resolution and as fundamentally different from formal legal process, the institutional context for most of these activities is the formal justice system. The materials in this chapter explore the relationship between law and alternative dispute resolution, evaluating their differences in theory and practice as well as some of the contradictions that have emerged between the idea and the reality of informal justice.

## 18.1 | The Transformation of Disputes by Lawyers: What the Dispute Paradigm Does and Does Not Tell Us

*Carrie Menkel-Meadow*

[T]HE GRIEVANT TELLS A story of felt or perceived wrong to a third party (the lawyer) and the lawyer transforms the dispute by imposing "categories" on "events and relationships" which

Carrie Menkel-Meadow, "The Transformation of Disputes by Lawyers: What the Dispute Paradigm Does and Does Not Tell Us," from *Missouri Journal of Dispute Resolution,* 1985, pp. 31–34. Reprinted by permission.

redefine the subject matter of dispute in ways "which make it amenable to conventional management procedures." This process of "narrowing" disputes occurs at various stages in lawyer-client interactions and could be usefully studied empirically. First, the lawyer may begin to narrow the dispute in the initial client interview. By asking questions which derive from the lawyer's repertoire of what is likely to be legally relevant, the lawyer defines the situation from the very beginning. Rather than permitting the client to tell a story freely to define what the dispute consists of, the lawyer begins to categorize the case as a "tort," "contract," or "property" dispute so that questions may be asked for legal saliency. This may narrow the context of a dispute which has more complicated fact patterns and may involve some mix of legal and non-legal categories of dispute. A classic example of such a mixed dispute is a landlord-tenant case in which relationship issues and political issues (such as in rent control areas) intermingle with strictly legal issues of rent obligation, maintenance obligation, and nuisance. Thus, during the initial contact the lawyer narrows what is "wrong" by trying to place the dispute in a legal context which the lawyer feels he can handle.

Even if the client is allowed to tell his lawyer a broader story, the lawyer will narrow or rephrase the story in his efforts to seek remediation. Beginning with an effort to negotiate with the other side, the lawyer will construct a story which is recognizable to the other lawyer so that he can demand a stock remedial solution.

Once negotiation commences the dispute is further narrowed, the issues become stylized, and statements of what is disputed become ritualized because of the very process and constraints of litigation. In negotiation, lawyers begin to demand what they will ask the court to do if the case goes to trial. Lawyers are told to plan "minimum disposition," "target," and "reservation" points that are based on an analysis of what would happen if the case went to trial. Because a court resolution of the problem will result in a binary win/loss ruling, lawyers begin to conceive of the negotiation process as simply an earlier version of court adjudication. Thus, lawyers seek to persuade each other, using many of the same principles and normative entreaties that they will use in court, that they are right and ought to prevail now, before either party suffers further monetary or temporal loss. The remedies lawyers seek from each other may be sharply limited to what they think would be possible in a court case considering the court's remedial powers. Thus, most negotiations, like most lawsuits, are converted into linear, zero-sum games about money, where money serves as the proxy for a host of other needs and potential solutions such as apologies or substitute goods. Negotiated solutions become compromises in which each side concedes something to the other to avoid the harshness of a binary solution. The compromise, which by definition forces each side to give up something, may be unnecessary and fail to meet the real needs of the parties. Consider two children disputing about a single piece of chocolate cake. The parental dispute resolver, like most lawyers, might seek the "obvious" compromise solution of cutting the cake in half, thereby eliminating a "better" solution if one child desires the cake, while the other prefers the icing.

In counseling clients lawyers may tell them what remedies are legally possible (money or an injunction) and thus preclude inquiry into alternatives which the client might prefer or which might be easier to obtain from the other party. As Engel has noted, some disputants prefer an acknowledgement that wrong has been done to them to receiving money. Once lawyers are engaged and the legal system, even if only informally, has been mobilized, the adversarial structure of problem-solving forces polarization and routinization of demands and stifles a host of possible solutions. . . .

*Notes and Questions*

1.  How do lawyers narrow disputes? Are there other third parties who do not transform conflict? What role do therapists and other counselors play in the transformation of disputes?

2.  Does American society have too much conflict or too little? How could this be measured and evaluated?

3.  Nils Christie claims that legal specialists are "interested in converting the image of a case from one of conflict into one of nonconflict." What interest does this serve?

4.  Many researchers have examined why clients go to court. Vilhelm Aubert suggested the following answer to that question:

    > Possibly the most general reason why two conflicting parties deviate from "rational" behavior and permit a case to be settled in a court of law, with greatly increased chances of total loss for one, is the tendency to

overestimate one's chances of winning. Only in a borderline case are the chances of winning 100 per cent for one of the parties. There are some rather general reasons why people should tend to overestimate their chances to win legal suits. For one thing, the arguments favoring one's own case are much more readily available than those favoring the other party. Cognitively speaking, full insight into all the aspects of the case is lacking. The positive aspects will easily be perceptually overrepresented. Legal suits have a moral tinge. To predict loss in a courtroom would normally imply doubt concerning one's own moral right. The personal defense erected against such moral doubt will therefore tend to render factual predictions unreliable. There may even exist a need to retain one's moral aggression against the other party. Legal suits represent an area of life where it is hard for people to be completely rational, in the sense of attempting an unbiased prediction of the future based on available empirical grounds. It is, in addition—and for other reasons—an area where predictions are often "technically" difficult to make.*

5.  A number of commentators have observed that the judicial role is undergoing a transformation. Law professor Judith

Resnick, for example, has suggested that many judges . . .

> have departed from their earlier attitudes; they have dropped the relatively disinterested pose to adopt a more active, "managerial" stance. In growing numbers, judges are not only adjudicating the merits of issues presented to them by litigants, but also are meeting with parties in chambers to encourage settlement of disputes and to supervise case preparation. Both before and after the trial, judges are playing a critical role in shaping litigation and influencing results.[†]

Resnick and others are concerned about the implications of "managerial judging." She claims the following:

> As managers, judges learn more about cases much earlier than they did in the past. They negotiate with parties about the course, timing, and scope of both pretrial and posttrial litigation. These managerial responsibilities give judges greater power. Yet the restraints that formerly circumscribed judicial authority are conspicuously absent. Managerial judges frequently work beyond the public view, off the record, with no obligation to provide written reasoned opinions, and out of reach of appellate review.[‡]

---

*Vilhelm Aubert, *Journal of Conflict Resolution,* Volume XII, No. 1, p. 51, 1967.

[†]Judith Resnick, 23 *Judges' Journal,* 8–11 (Winter 1984).
[‡]Ibid.

&  Mediation and other forms of informal dispute resolution originated in part from the belief that formal law's hierarchical structure, its emphasis on objectivity, and its rule orientation not only undermined the ability to solve problems but also was particularly problematic for women and other traditionally disempowered groups. Informal dispute resolution has turned out to be equally problematic for women.

## 18.2 | Mediation from a Feminist Perspective: Promise and Problems  *Janet Rifkin*

### INTRODUCTION

The interest in alternative dispute resolution is intensifying in this country and others as well. Programs offering mediation, arbitration, negotiation and conciliation services are proliferating throughout the United States, Canada, Australia and Western Europe. These programs may be court-related or community-based. In either case, the overt justifications for mediation programs are similar. Mediating conflict as a substitute for litigating disputes has been justified by two basic rationales: First, the formal court system is not suited to handle the range and number of disputes being brought to it. Second, the adversary process itself is not suited to resolve interpersonal disputes.

While mediation is flourishing, concern about the theory and practice of "informal" justice is also increasing. Most of the criticisms focus on the manipulative potential of informal systems such as mediation. For example, critics suggest the bureaucratic logic that supports state legality is as much a part of the process in informal and non-bureaucratic settings as it is in the formal court of law. Critics also suggest that the state, faced with fiscal crisis, achieves spending cuts by resorting to informalization, accompanied by appeals to popular participation, consensual social life, and the struggle against bureaucracy. Others argue that mediation fosters the privatization of life—the cult of the personal—and denies the existence of irreconcilable structural conflicts between classes or between citizen and state. Finally, critics claim that mediation is detrimental to the interests of women, who, being less empowered, need both the formal legal system and aggressive legal representation to protect existing rights and pursue new legal safeguards.

Although these criticisms remain, the debate about mediation lacks a careful questioning of law and alternative dispute programs from a feminist perspective. For the most part, mediation's critics predicate their questions on the traditional view of law that litigation leads to social change and that the "lawsuit" is *the* appropriate and most effective vehicle for challenging unfair social practices, for protecting individuals, and for delineating new areas of guaranteed "rights."

This dominant view leaves unchallenged the patriarchal paradigm of law as hierarchy, combat, and adversarialness; and, therefore, generates only a certain kind of questioning of mediation. This viewpoint has not asked whether and in what way alternative dispute resolution reflects a feminist analysis of law and conflict resolution, and whether in theory and practice mediation challenges or reinforces gender inequality in contemporary society.

My intention in this discussion is to articulate some of the questions basic to an understanding of the relationship between law, mediation and feminist inquiry. As one commentator noted:

> [O]bjective epistemology is the law of law. It ensures that the law will most reinforce existing distributions of power when it most closely adheres to its own highest ideal of fairness. . . . Such law not only reflects a society in which men rule women; it rules in a male way. The rule form which unites scientific knowledge with state control in its conception of what law is, institutionalizes the objective as jurisprudence.

What is not yet clearly developed is how mediation in theory reflects "a new jurisprudence, a new relation between life and law." Further, what is not yet known is whether in practice, mediating disputes reflects feminist jurisprudential differences from the male ideology of law or whether mediating simply reinforces the "objective epistemology" of law.

## I. MEDIATION IN THEORY: FEMINIST PEDAGOGY AND THE STUDY OF LAW

Social structures supporting the pedagogy practiced in traditional American law schools conflict with the social structures espoused as the basis of mediation. In traditional legal pedagogy, the case book is the emblem of the authoritative character of the law and the "Socratic Method" mirrors and reinforces the structure of authority. Traditional legal pedagogy is hierarchical with a vengeance. It trains students to reject an analysis of social reality as it is subjectively experienced, and instead requires them to internalize a series of abstract rules. Traditional legal pedagogy is deeply wedded to a patriarchal conception of law. This wedding is characterized by hierarchy, adversarialness, linearity, and rationality, a paradigm in which reason is synonymous with rule and the ideal of the reasonable man is the fundamental frame of reference for making decisions. Whereas formal law reinforces the dominance of hierarchy and rationality supporting traditional ideas of public and private, mediation challenges these notions. By explicitly asking different kinds of questions, by supporting dialogue and by challenging the authority of "objective epistemology" implicit in the law and in legal teaching, a new pedagogy emerges which is essential to a new way of thinking about law. This new pedagogical approach, in a mediation course, places the emphasis on the female concerns of responsibility and justice. These concerns contrast with the concerns for individual rights that are characteristic of the male pedagogy dominant in law school and most other academic settings.

The study of mediation thus introduces and, indeed, requires a feminist pedagogy, a feminist pedagogy fundamentally different from traditional legal pedagogy. "[F]eminist method is consciousness raising: the collective critical reconstitution of the meaning of women's social experience as women live through it."

Legal pedagogy involves a learning process in which "facts, issues, principles, reasoning and laws are learned without specific reference to behavior or experience; where students are required to think in legal terms and to articulate problems and issues in the language of the law." Legal pedagogy reflects the power relationships which feminist theory challenges. The study of mediation from a feminist perspective focuses on questions which are antithetical to traditional legal study: Is liberal law and the rationalistic linear mode of thinking, of which law study is a part, in some fundamental way male and distinguishable from female contextual thinking? Do women have a distinct moral language emphasizing concern for others, responsibility, care, and obligation as distinguished from male morality, which focuses on abstract notions of individual rights? Do female and male engenderment generate different modes of thinking and discourse and is it useful to distinguish between them?

These questions not only exist outside the framework of traditional legal teaching but also represent a challenge to the way of thinking that supports the operation of law in this society. Theoretically, at least, the study of mediation challenges traditional pedagogy. This challenge and mediation's emphasis on the female concerns of responsibility and justice necessitate framing questions from a feminist perspective.

## II. MEDIATION IN PRACTICE: PROMISE AND PROBLEMS

Mediation in practice operates as a process of discussion, clarification, and compromise aided by third party facilitators. It is a process in which the third party has no state-enforced power. A third party's power lies in the ability to persuade the parties to reach a voluntary settlement. It involves the creation of consensus between the parties in which the parties are brought together in an atmosphere of confidentiality to discover shared social and moral values as a means of coming to an agreement.

In mediation, the focus is not on formal and substantive rights. The emphasis is on the process by which the individual parties are encouraged to work out their own solution in a spirit of compromise. The intervention of a mediator turns the initial dyad of a dispute into a triadic interaction of some kind. However, the disputing parties retain their ability to decide whether or not to agree and accept proposals for an outcome irrespective of the source of the proposals.

The following chart highlights some of the main contrasts between adjudication and the practice of mediation.

| *Adjudication* | *Mediation* |
| --- | --- |
| public | private |
| formal | informal |
| strict evidentiary rules | no formal parameters —conversationalist |
| coercive | voluntary |
| emphasis on conflict of interest, value dissensus | emphasis on areas of agreement, points in common |
| win/lose—combative | compromise— conciliatory |
| decision oriented | agreement oriented |
| rule oriented | person oriented |
| professional decision maker | community lay volunteers |
| representation by lawyer | direct participation |

Although the mediator is a neutral intervenor with no self-interest, a mediator does become a negotiator. In that role the mediator inevitably brings to the process, deliberately or not, certain ideas, knowledge, and assumptions. What a mediator can do is also affected by the particular context and the parties' expectations of mediation.

The question of a mediator's technique brings us back to the issue of whether the methodology is premised on the same view of objectivity inherent in legal ideology. If neutrality, an important feature of being a mediator, masks the same "objectivist" paradigm of law, then mediation, like legalism, reinforces the ideology fundamental to the state as male and further institutionalizes male power. . . . The rhetoric of mediation rejects the "objectivist epistemology" of the law. Theoretically, in mediation precedents, rules, and a legalized conception of facts are not only irrelevant but constrain the mediator's job of helping the parties to reorient their perception of the problem to the extent that an agreement can be reached. The legal rights of the parties are not central to the discussion which takes place in mediation. Again, in theory, the lack of focus in

mediation on abstract legal rights contrasts with the emphasis on them in legal proceedings.

These differences, however, are clearer in theory than in practice. . . .

. . . Numerous questions emerge from actually mediated disputes:

1. Does the mediation process substitute another form of "objectivist" manipulation of conflict?

2. Does the mediation process really shift the focus of the dispute from an abstract notion of right to the more female concerns of care, responsibility, and concern for others?

3. Does mediation involve a new definition of justice?

4. What is the measure of whether these things or others are happening in mediation? What kinds of questions need to be asked of the participants in particular and of the process in general?

5. Does mediation of a conflict alter the power relationship between the parties? Does it redistribute that power or does it perpetuate a relationship of unequality?

6. Does mediation, by requiring participation and decision making by the parties, offer a better forum for resolving problems in situations where traditionally women have been particularly victimized?

## Notes and Questions

1. Mediation has been criticized by women's groups and by others concerned about issues relating to family violence. The following excerpt reflects one perspective on this issue:

   It is not a coincidence that, just when the state legislatures are passing strong laws with respect to battery, marital property and child support enforcement, and when the U.S. Congress and U.S. Supreme Court are acting for the first time in history on family law issues, there is a movement to exclude these issues from the courts. It is no coincidence that, as battered women are gaining increased access to the courts through pro se civil procedures or increased arrests, there is a movement that would exclude these cases from the jurisdiction of the civil and criminal courts. Nor is it a coincidence that, as standards and enforcement are beginning to be developed by the legal system in the areas of child and spousal support, mediation, which would offer no enforcement, is being encouraged.

Only the legal system has the power to remove the batterer from the home, to arrest when necessary, to enforce the terms of any decree if a new assault occurs, to discover hidden assets, to prevent dissipation of assets, and to enforce support orders. Only the legislatures and courts can create, develop, expand and enforce women's rights. Mediation offers no protection, no deterrence, no enforcement, and no opportunity to expand women's rights.

At a time when women are making significant progress on family law issues in the courts and legislatures on both the state and federal levels, after years of inactivity by these bodies, a dispute resolution approach that is private and not required to be consistent with the law is being advocated. This approach defeats the progress of women's rights, and therefore must be rejected forcefully.*

2. Consider the following comment by Lisa Lerman.

> Abuse cases can be successfully resolved (that is, the violence can be stopped) in a number of different fora. Sometimes legal action designed to prevent violence or to rehabilitate the offender is more effective than directly punitive action, especially if the parties want to maintain their relationship.

Action in civil court may be less threatening, and therefore more accessible to victims of abuse. On the other hand, some abusers will not respond seriously to any civil action but are effectively intimidated by criminal charges.

Although ambivalent about working with a legal system which is often unreceptive to feminist values and priorities, battered women's advocates have moved toward a loose consensus that law enforcement is valuable. They agree that remedies are more likely to be effective if they lay clear responsibility for the violence on the abusive party, let him know that serious consequences will flow from repeated violence, and follow through on that threat when further violence occurs. Remedies are believed to be most effective if the system provides assistance and protection to the women during and after the legal proceedings and tailors its remedies to the needs of the victims on a case-by-case basis. Finally, the battered women's movement favors remedies which focus on abuse as the primary issue, and address other problems, such as visitation and property issues, in the context of avoiding continued abuse.

Measured against these criteria, mediation emerges as perhaps the weakest of available formal legal remedies.†

3. How does this perspective differ from Rifkin's?

4. Would this perspective be appropriate for the "wife-battery" cases discussed in Chapter 1? What are the important concerns to consider in developing your answer? How would Lerman, Woods, and Rifkin respond?

---

*Laurie Woods, "Mediation: A Backlash to Women's Progress on Family Law Issues," *Clearinghouse Review,* Summer 1985, p. 436. Reprinted by permission.

†"Mediation of Wife-Abuse Cases: The Adverse Impact of Informal Dispute Resolution on Women," *Harvard Women's Law Journal* 7 (1984). Copied with permission. Copyright © by the *Harvard Women's Law Journal.*

## 18.3 The Culture of Battering and the Role of Mediation in Domestic Violence Cases   *Karla Fischer, Neil Vidmar, and René Ellis*

### I. INTRODUCTION

HE ALWAYS FOUND SOMETHING *wrong with what I did, even if I did what he asked. No matter what it was. It was never the way he wanted it. I was either too fat, didn't cook the food right. . . . I think he wanted to hurt me. To hurt me in the sense . . . to make me feel like I was a nothing. And that I did something wrong, when I didn't do anything wrong. . . .*

*I can't talk to adults. I don't know how to talk to people because my opinion doesn't ever count. I feel like I never had an opinion on politics or on life. I don't know how to interact because he would [always] be going like this to me [mimicking abuser's gesture of drawing a line with his index finger] . . . that was his big signal to make me shut up, or he'd be kicking me under the table to shut my mouth.*

The relationship between a battered woman and her abuser frequently involves communication through subtle phrases and modes of interaction that have meanings and symbols idiosyncratically shared by the two parties—a "culture of battering." This culture is a reflection and an integral part of the pattern of dominance and abuse that a battered woman experiences. Recognition of this cultural component of battering relationships has major implications for the policy debate on whether mediation is an appropriate mechanism for dealing with cases involving domestic violence, regardless of whether the specific issues to be mediated involve the abuse itself or ancillary matters related to divorce or separation (i.e. child custody and visitation, child support, or division of property). We argue here, as a central theme, that because me-

diation models work on ameliorating conflict, mediators assume that abuse in a relationship is a product of interpersonal conflict. This assumption is fundamentally inconsistent with the dynamics of the relationship and its cultural context of domination and control. Essentially, both the ideology and the practice of mediation are incompatible with a culture of battering.

In this article we first explore the culture of battering and its dynamics. We specifically refute here theories that posit that battering results exclusively from conflict. In Section III we consider the widespread and expanding practice of referring "domestic relations" cases to mandatory or voluntary mediation and describe how mediation is practiced when spousal violence is identified in the couple. In Section IV we critique both the ideology and practice of mediation against the background of the culture of battering. We conclude by recommending that cases should be excluded from mediation where a culture of battering has been established. . . .

### III. THE WIDESPREAD USE OF MEDIATION FOR "DOMESTIC DISPUTES"

The use of mediation to resolve what are often generically labeled "domestic relations issues" is widespread and growing. Many states have enacted statutes providing for mediation in divorce, child custody, and disputes involving division of property. In some instances mediation is mandatory. In others judges have discretion to assign these civil cases to mediation on an almost wholesale basis. Prosecutors have discretion to direct criminal cases involving domestic assault to mediation as part of diversion programs. Mediators and mediation service providers are expanding at a tremendous rate and have organized themselves into professional organizations that argue for even more expansive use of mediation. The providers argue that mediation is a viable, superior remedy for domestic disputes, even as a potential remedy for cases in which the central issue is criminal assault.

We take the position that both the theory and practice of mediation pose serious problems for its use as a resolution device when a relationship involves a culture of battering. In this section we review a number of statutes that foster mediation and discuss problems associated with them. We also consider literature that advocates broadening the uses of mediation, particularly that which suggests mediation is appropriate as a resolution device when the central issue is domestic assault. This provides a backdrop for Section IV where we detail the incompatibility of mediation ideology and practice for domestic violence cases.

**A. Selected Statutes and Discretionary Guidelines**   The statistics indicate that a high percentage of women involved in divorce proceedings are likely to be battered, including those in mediation programs. Many battered women are divorced or separated, confirming studies that suggest that "the most dangerous time for a woman is when she divorces or separates from her spouse." From the perspective of the culture of battering, separation from the abuser may actually enhance the likelihood and seriousness of the violence because abuse is one of the few tools the abuser has left to attempt to dominate and control his victim. Estimates of the number of battered women who enter divorce mediation programs range from a conservative ten percent to fifty percent.

Despite the substantial probability that many divorcing women will be battered, the use of mediation continues to expand. Many states have enacted statutes encouraging mediation of domestic relations cases, including divorce and child custody. Some states require mediation. Although some states exempt battered women from mandatory mediation, alarmingly few provide special rules for domestic violence, and none provide a mechanism to screen for those cases. Many ignore even the possibility of domestic violence among divorcing couples and none consider patterns of domination and control. Some states do not establish minimum credentials for mediators while others have model provisions for mediator qualifications. Likewise, some states give the mediator a great deal of authority, but fail to estab-

lish even minimum qualifications for mediators. Others specifically limit the authority of the mediator. Most statutes provide broad discretion for the appointment of the mediator. Likewise, some statutes are quite broad about the subject matter of mediation, while others are quite limited. The statutes often do not provide or recommend representation for the parties, and some give the mediator the authority to exclude legal counsel from the process.

Below we highlight some of the statutes governing the mediation of domestic cases to illustrate the widespread use of mediation, the inconsistent implementation of programs from state to state, the absence of screening mechanisms for cases involving battering, the lack of consistent credentialing for mediators, and the obvious ignorance of the risks in mediating "disputes" that arise out of a culture of battering.

### 1. The Discretion of the Court—Permitting the Judge to Order Mediation

Many states give courts broad discretion to order mediation in domestic cases. In Alaska, the court may order mediation for child custody, divorce, and annulment cases. The statute permits the judge to appoint the mediator, although the parties may challenge peremptorily one mediator. There does not appear to be anything in the statute outlining qualifications for mediators or guidelines for appointment. The statute provides for the presence of counsel in divorce mediation, but does not provide for the presence of counsel during custody mediation. There is nothing in the Alaska statute that specifically deals with issues of domestic violence, although in divorce mediation the parties may withdraw after participation in the first mediation conference.

Some statutes authorize court-ordered mediation, but provide exceptions for abuse cases. The difficulty in most of the cases is that no real mechanism exists for identifying the abuse. For example, Minnesota provides that a domestic relations matter may be set for mediation prior to, concurrent with, or subsequent to the setting of the matter for hearing. Interestingly, the mediator is directed to "use best efforts to effect a settlement . . . but shall have no coercive authority." The statute provides an exception to required mediation if the court determines that there is probable cause that one of the parties, or a child of a party, "has been physically or sexually abused by the other party." The statute also specifies mediator qualifications, including a minimum of forty hours of mediation training. The mediation agreement, if any, may not be presented to the court without the consent of the parties and their counsel. If the parties have not reached an agreement as a result of mediation, the mediator may recommend to the court that an investigation be conducted to assist the parties to resolve the "controversy," and in some limited cases the mediator may conduct the investigation.

North Dakota simply says that "the court may order mediation at the parties' own expense." Like Minnesota, it also states that the court may refrain from ordering mediation if the custody, support, or visitation issue involves or may involve physical or sexual abuse of any party or the child of any party to the proceeding. The statute does not suggest any mechanism for identifying the abuse. The North Dakota court is directed to appoint a mediator from a list of qualified mediators approved by the court, and the supreme court is charged with establishing minimum qualifications. The mediator is specifically prohibited from excluding counsel from the mediation.

At least one state permits the court to consider abuse issues and order mediation anyway if the court finds it appropriate. An Ohio court is directed to consider the existence of abuse and thereafter may still order mediation, but "only if the court determines that it is in the best interests of the parties . . . and makes specific written findings of fact." The mediator is required to file a report with the court that may contain a mediated agreement, but the court is not bound by the report.

Other statutes are more specific about what might be mediated and provide exclusions for domestic violence cases according to the particular issues involved in the case. For example, Illinois provides for an exclusion for mediation in domestic violence cases enforcing visitation orders, but not when mediating joint custody. In cases in which joint custody is requested in Illinois, the parties are first required to submit a Joint Parenting Agreement. Once the agreement is submitted, any changes, disputes, or breaches regarding the agreement may be mediated. The court may also order mediation to determine if joint custody is appropriate. Likewise, in enforcing visitation orders, the court may order counseling or mediation, except in cases where there is evidence of domestic violence.

In contrast, a number of statutes provide significant detail about the procedure or qualifications of mediators, and then ignore any possible issues of domestic abuse. For example, the Kansas statute governing family law issues provides that the "court may order mediation of any contested issue of child custody or visitation at any time, upon the motion of a party or on the court's own motion." The statute contains a provision outlining the appointment and qualifications of the mediator and requires the court to consider the following: whether an agreement exists for a specific mediator; conflict and bias issues; the mediator's knowledge of the Kansas judicial system and domestic relations cases; the mediator's knowledge of sources for referral; the mediator's knowledge of child development issues, children's clinical issues, effects of divorce on children, and psychology of families; and the mediator's training and experience. Michigan is more specific about the requirements of mediators: they must have a "license or a limited license to engage in the practice of psychology . . . or a master's degree in counseling, social work, or marriage and family counseling."

For the states that focus on who the mediator is, many states require mediators to attend training sessions. Michigan's statute provides for a training program with not less than forty hours of classroom instruction and 250 hours of practical experience. Wisconsin makes mediation available and requires that mediators have twenty-five hours of training or not less than three years experience in the field of dispute resolution. Interestingly, the mediator is charged with the responsibility of determining the appropriateness of mediation. If the mediator finds that it is not appropriate, he or she will notify the court, and the court will waive mediation if the court finds that attending the session will cause undue hardship or would endanger the health or safety of one of the parties. Undue hardship can be established if the mediator finds interspousal battery or domestic abuse. Whether or not counsel is permitted to be present at a mediation session is within the discretion of the mediator.

The Kansas statute is illustrative of unusual attention paid to the process of mediation. The statute includes a list under "Duties of Mediator" that outlines mediator responsibility, including the requirement that the mediator advise each of the parties to obtain independent legal advice; however, it allows only the parties to attend the mediation session. Unlike statutes in many other states, the information obtained during the mediation process is not privileged. The mediator is obligated to inform the parties that the mediation process is not privileged and may be subject to disclosure. The mediator is required to advise each party, in writing, to obtain legal assistance in drafting any agreement and reviewing any agreement drafted by the other party. It does not speak to issues of domestic violence, but it does provide that either party may terminate the session any time after the second session. The mediator may also terminate the session when he or she believes that continuation would "harm" one or more parties or the children, or when meaningful participation is lacking. There are no stated guidelines for defining "harm."

## 2. Mandatory Mediation

In California, mediation of custody disputes is mandatory, and there is no provision for exclusion where domestic violence is present. The court appoints the mediator, who may be a member of the "professional staff of a family conciliation court, probation department, or mental health services agency, or may be any other person or agency designated by the court." In addition, the appointed mediator has the authority to exclude counsel from the mediation hearings. The statute also provides that the agreement should be limited to specific custody issues and provides for conducting "negotiations in such a way as to equalize power relationships between the parties." There are no suggested guidelines or reference to some resource for recommenda-

tions on how to engage in effective methods of power balancing. The mediator is directed to make "best efforts to effect a settlement." The mediator may interview the child or children involved and also has the authority to meet with the parties separately when a request for separate mediation is made or where there has been a history of domestic violence. Thus, the statute does not exclude domestic violence cases from mediation but provides for separate mediation.

The California statute has an interesting provision for a "support person" that may accompany a party to the mediation, but the statute also provides that the mediator may exclude the support person if the "support person participates in the mediation session, acts as an advocate, or the presence of a particular support person is disruptive or disrupts the process of mediation." One of the problems with the authority given to the California mediator is that it exists hand in hand with the court's broad discretion to appoint a mediator who only meets certain minimum qualifications and who may exclude either party's attorney and "support person."

North Carolina has a mandatory mediation statute, but gives the court the authority to waive mediation in cases involving domestic violence. North Carolina requires that child custody matters shall be set for mediation either before or concurrent with the hearing where there is a program established. That statute provides an exception where, for good cause, the court can waive mediation. Good cause may include, among other reasons listed, allegations of abuse and neglect of a minor child, alcoholism, drug abuse, undue hardship, voluntary participation in mediation, and spouse abuse. Additionally, either party may move to have the mediator dismissed due to bias, undue familiarity with one of the parties, or other prejudicial ground. One of the stated goals of the statute is "[t]o provide a structured, confidential, nonadversarial setting that will . . . minimize the stress and anxiety to which the parties, and especially the child, are subjected."

Not only does Oregon have a mandatory mediation statute, it also has a mandatory arbitration statute in "domestic relations" cases where the only issue is the division or disposition of property. It does provide the court with the authority to exempt certain cases for good cause. The statute also provides for mandatory mediation in joint custody proceedings "within a mediation program established by the court or as conducted by any mediator approved by the court." Upon a party's motion, the court may waive mediation if participation will lead to emotional distress. The statute does not specifically speak to abuse, but does have some other protection. Although the statute gives the court the authority to establish mediation procedures in other cases, any mediation of property division or child/spousal support issues requires the written approval of the parties and their counsel. Additionally, the mediator may not make any substantive recommendations to the court without approval of the parties. The statute provides for minimum educational and experience qualifications as well as gives the court the discretion to employ or contract for mediators directly or through public or private agencies. The mediation proceedings are private and confidential.

The Utah statute establishes a mandatory mediation program, but provides an exception for cases that would cause undue hardship to or threaten the mental or physical health or safety of either of the parties, or the child or children of the parties, or cases in which a party has engaged or been victimized in interspousal domestic violence.

In at least one state, mediation is encouraged as a matter of public policy. Maine's statute has a formal finding that mediated resolutions of disputes between parents is in the best interest of minor children. Thus, the statute provides that when there are minor children in a custody action, mediation is mandatory. The statute provides that the court may waive the mediation requirement for extraordinary cause supported by affidavit. Once involved in the mediation session, the court must determine that the parties made a good faith effort to mediate. If the court does not find good faith, it may order the parties to mediation, may dismiss the action, may assess attorney's fees and costs, or may impose any other sanction that is "appropriate." In addition, the child custody statute states that the mediator should consider the "existence of a history of domestic abuse between the parents" when mediating child custody issues. The statute also pro-

vides that the court shall not consider abandonment of the residence as a factor in determining parental rights when the parent who left was "physically harmed or seriously threatened with physical harm . . . and that harm or threat of harm was causally related to the abandonment." However, one chapter in its domestic relations statute precludes protection order cases from being mediated.

**B. Mediation in Spousal Abuse Cases**   There are two types of legal cases where mediation with batterers and their victims is likely to occur: 1) criminal assault/battery cases; and 2) divorce and child custody. While the type of case will determine the exact form that the agreement will take, both criminal and divorce mediation sessions with abusive couples will not differ markedly from mediation with general populations. Whether the context is criminal or civil, mediation that has the elimination of violence against the victim as its goal will result in a settlement of some variation like: "Mr. Abuser agrees not to hit Ms. Victim and Ms. Victim agrees to talk to Mr. Abuser about any subject provided that he has not been drinking." Our purpose in this section is limited: we wish to simply provide a descriptive summary of how mediation with domestic violence is carried out. We follow this with our critical evaluation of the weaknesses of these mediation programs.

*1. Mediation in Criminal Assault/Battery Cases*

In addition to the many jurisdictions where mediation is used for divorce and child custody, every year thousands of cases in which the specific issue is criminal assault are referred . . . to mediation centers. The referrals are made by judges, district attorneys, and court clerks. In many instances public mediation centers send their personnel to the court to screen for such cases and court personnel then give their imprimatur to attempts to contact the parties for mediation.

The utilization of mediation for criminal assault/battery against spouses has been encouraged and supported by articles in scholarly journals that provide a rationale for mediation as an alternative to the court systems. A leading article by Bethel and Singer, for example, labeled mediation as an important new remedy for domestic violence cases. They described a model program of community mediation that included domestic violence cases within its claimed scope of expertise. This center, called the "Citizens' Complaint Center", operates in the District of Columbia and is separate from the prosecutor's office. Like all disputes that the center handles, mediation in domestic violence cases occurs only if both parties agree. The mediation occurs in a single hearing set for a specific time and date, and typically two mediators are assigned to each case. Bethel and Singer identified mediation as faster, cheaper, and empowering of both parties because it requires direct involvement of both in the resolution process. They also pointed out that it lessens the demand on the resources of the legal system because it does not require the time of judges, prosecutors, and defense attorneys.

With a slightly different spin, Corcoran and Melamed have similarly urged consideration of mediation on the grounds that it is less remote and impersonal than the court system that has traditionally been unresponsive to battered women. Battered women are not protected, they claim, by restraining orders, by the police, who frequently fail to arrest the abuser, by prosecutors, who infrequently prosecute domestic cases, or by judges and juries, who refuse to convict or sentence to jail the rare abuser who enters the system. Criminal prosecution only attempts to control domestic violence (and does so inadequately), without addressing the societal causes of battering. In these authors' view, what is needed is more attention to compassionate approaches to dealing with domestic violence, approaches that incorporate support and treatment for both victims and offenders. By addressing the violence directly, including its causes and methods of rehabilitation, the "couple may actually experience relief and support in knowing that others have shared their experiences. . . ." Like Bethel and Singer, they argue that mediation offers "the prospect of empowerment to the victim, rehabilitation of the batterer, and, as a model of constructive conflict resolution, an opportunity to end the cycle of violence." Mediation can be effective in the cessation of further violence, they

suggest, because the process models other approaches to resolving conflicts that are non-abusive. Mediation may have immediate practical effects as well, including the ability to structure a prompt protective agreement involving the appropriate criminal justice mechanisms or an agreement that the abuser will seek counseling.

Corcoran and Melamed propose several modifications to the mediation process to address concerns raised primarily by victim advocates about mediation of domestic violence cases. First, they suggest that mediation include victim advocates or the victim's attorney: individuals who balance negotiating power. The presence of non-neutral individuals may eliminate covert intimidation so that the rights of the victim can be better protected. Second, they suggest the use of private caucusing with the parties to encourage disclosure about intimidation or abuse and check on the victim's safety. Third, they suggest the use of prerequisites to mediation, such as counseling or protective orders to encourage victims and abusers to obtain outside help. Fourth, they suggest that mediators take affirmative steps, through the use of questionnaire or interview screening, to determine whether there has been abuse in the relationship.

To support the position that mediation can have a positive effect for battered women and their abusers, Corcoran and Melamed cite the study conducted by Bethel and Singer comparing the outcome of mediation cases involving domestic violence with cases that did not involve domestic violence. Bethel and Singer had mediation staff contact participants by telephone approximately two months after mediation was attempted. Statistically, in comparing mediated domestic violence cases with non-violent cases, the authors found no significant differences between the samples in terms of the parties' satisfaction with the mediation process, their satisfaction with the agreement, and satisfaction with the extent to which the agreement was reported to have been adhered to. Based on data that they do not provide for the reader, Bethel and Singer concluded that domestic violence cases are "not less suitable for mediation than other interpersonal disputes." While Bethel and Singer conceded that, perhaps, mediation should not be used for the most serious cases of spousal violence, they also set forth the caveat that more research might prove mediation's usefulness in those instances.

Despite Bethel and Singer's claim that mediation may protect battered women from further violence, other empirical work indicates that this may not be true. For example, Desmond Ellis found that battered women were more likely to be abused after separation if they went through mediation rather than adjudication with lawyers. He reported that attorneys were more likely than mediators to use particular strategies to "challenge" the batterer. For instance, lawyers might seek to increase the adverse consequences of violence by enlisting the help of law enforcement through orders of protection or police involvement.

Ellis' empirical study is cited by advocates for battered women who have repeatedly emphasized that victims should never have to negotiate for their physical safety. The advocates argue that safety is a basic right and under no circumstances should a woman ever have to bargain it away. Forcing victims to negotiate with their abusers in this fashion both compromises the message that domestic violence is a crime and enhances the power imbalance between the parties. Some assert that mediation should be used in conjunction with other intervention efforts and that "it is never appropriate to mediate about stopping the violence." However, even for some who advocate the more limited use, the "empowerment" of the victims of spousal abuse is commonly pointed to as one of the positive outcomes of mediation.

## 2. Divorce Mediation

The rationales offered for the use of mediation in divorce cases where there has been violence in the relationship are not substantially different than those cited for the criminal cases. Erickson and McKnight, for example, representing themselves as experienced mediators with domestic violence divorce cases, offer the claim that mediation not only reduced the likelihood of future abuse, but also "encourages cooperative interaction," and may "reduce hostility and establish clear boundaries for the couple." To accomplish these goals, mediation with abusive couples must be done by trained and experienced mediators who employ a variation of the standard mediation process.

Although Erickson and McKnight do not mention the qualifications needed for mediators, they propose several adaptations to the mediation process to accommodate domestic violence cases. Grounding their trio of special rules in establishing safety for the victim, they suggest that the mediator first attempt to uncover the history of abuse in the couple. The first rule for mediators is to take the abuse seriously as an "issue" rather than as true fact, and immediately begin to focus on protection, boundaries, communication procedures, and safety. The second rule mediators are encouraged to follow is to make a strong statement that there is never an excuse for abuse. Accomplishing this requires mediators to avoid certain topics of discussion, including inquiring how the "incident" of abuse came about, or who was at fault. The third rule is a list of specific steps to be taken with the couple including 1) providing the victim with information about protection orders; 2) discussing additional precautions, such as calling the police; 3) establishing clear boundaries about the exchange of children and contact between the parties; 4) encouraging the victim to seek sensitive counsel; 5) asking each party to bring their attorneys to mediation sessions; and 6) considering whether a battered woman's advocate might be useful to the victim during mediation.

Like those who advocate mediation in the criminal context, Erickson and McKnight find certain categories of domestic violence cases inappropriate for mediation. Most of their exclusion criteria involve the behavior of the abuser, such as the husband "who totally discounts everything his wife says and does and refuses to acknowledge her worth," the husband who is currently abusing his victim, and the husband who is carrying a weapon or using drugs and alcohol. Couples should also be prevented from engaging in mediation when they meet and attempt to resolve issues outside of the formal sessions, or if either party violates the rules of mediation and refuses to conform. Through excluding these inappropriate cases of domestic violence and following the special procedures for appropriate cases, Erickson and McKnight believe that mediation will "work" with spousal abuse couples.

### 3. Screening for Domestic Violence in Mediation

The screening issue in mediation of domestic violence cases involves two separate determinations. First, unlike criminal cases where abuse has already been tagged as the problem, divorce mediators must have some mechanism that identifies the history of violence in the couple's relationship. Moreover, these mediators must then be able to refer to specific criteria to determine whether or not the case is an appropriate one for mediation. Second, mediators need to be able to screen for violence that is presently occurring, particularly if it is a result of the agreement developing through mediation. The first screening issue is applicable only in divorce mediation cases, while the second issue is relevant for mediation occurring both in criminal and civil contexts with abusive couples.

Those who have written about screening mechanisms for uncovering histories of abuse in couples engaging in mediation differ both in the type of questions asked and how those questions are asked. Erickson and McKnight give couples a questionnaire that has a single item that identifies abuse: "Was abuse present in the marriage relationship?" The follow-up item asks couples to check off the type(s) of abuse present: 1) physical; 2) emotional; 3) chemical; or 4) other. The screening program in Hawaii described by David Chandler also uses a single question, asked by a interviewer: "Would you tell me if you have been physically abused by your husband during your relationship?" The Hawaiian program expands the domain of abuse history by further inquiring when the abuse last occurred, whether the woman fears future assaults, and whether she feels that the abuse has limited her ability to communicate "on an equal basis" with her spouse. Only women responding affirmatively to the physical abuse question are asked the last three questions.

Linda Girdner provides the most comprehensive assessment of abuse history in a semistructured interview format that she calls the Conflict Assessment Protocol. First, the Conflict Assessment Protocol probes for the couple's decision-making patterns, resolution of conflicts in the relationship, and expressions of anger. The purpose of this section of the protocol is for mediators to be "attuned to the issue of control." The second section of the interview proceeds through a series of questions designed to elicit acknowledgment of specific abusive behaviors. Based on the Conflict Tactics Scale used in domestic violence research, the questions about abuse tap into emotional, sexual, and physical domains. The interview closes with specific questions about control, jealousy, child abuse, and substance use. Each of these questions is asked of each spouse in an individual session, but phrased in terms of whether either partner has abused the other.

Only the screening procedure described by David Chandler contains a "when" question that would allow a mediator to know if the abuse is occurring presently, or whether it is merely part of the couple's history. Unfortunately, this lack of attention to inquiring about present abuse may reflect the stereotype that abuse is no longer an issue once the couple seeks to terminate their relationship. As we documented earlier, separation abuse is common and frequently life-endangering.

In short, even the model mediation programs appear to have weak or inadequate screening mechanisms to identify cases involving culture of battering relationships. We strongly suspect that even rudimentary screening is absent in most other settings, particularly when the issue involves divorce, child custody, or division of property.

**C. Summary**  Mediation has become legislators', judges', and prosecutors' preferred mode of resolution of "domestic issues" cases. While one can infer that a primary motivation in sending these cases to mediation is that it helps clear court dockets of troublesome cases, it is also true that a number of theorists have justified mediation by arguing that it is a superior method for resolving domestic issues disputes—including, in some instances, serious cases of domestic violence. However, even when professionals agree that mediation should not proceed when there is a history of spousal abuse, our review suggests that current mechanisms to screen for abuse are inadequate. We now turn to the issue of the adequacy—or rather inadequacy—of mediation to provide justice to battered women.

*Notes and Questions.*

1. The question of whether mediation is unfair to women is controversial. Joan Kelly and Mary Duryee, in their empirical study of two California family mediation programs, examined the reactions of men and women to the mediation processes. While their findings were not conclusive or generalizable beyond California, they found that the "majority of women and men do not perceive the mediation process as unfair, weighted against them, or resulting in agreements which they believe to be contrary to their interests."*

---

*Joan Kelly and Mary Duryee, "Women's and Men's Views of Mediation in Voluntary and Mandatory Mediation Settings," *Family and Conciliation Courts Review,* Vol. 30, pp. 34–49, 1992.

2. What safeguards should be provided in mediation of domestic violence cases?

3. Mediating problems of sexual harassment is also controversial. Public institutions and private companies are now legally required to have procedures in place for responding to allegations of sexual harassment, and a number of these procedures include a mediation component. What problems might arise if a complaint of this nature were mediated? Does mediation offer anything positive in the resolution of these matters? What does the victim in a sexual harassment case stand to gain or lose through mediation? What does the alleged perpetrator of sexual harassment have to gain or lose?

---

❧ Community Mediation started as an idea that the facilitation of many disputes should take place outside of formal courtroom settings. During the past fifteen years, this idea has been institutionalized. As a consequence, mediation is now intimately tied to the justice system in ways that the early proponents of this idea would have found troublesome. The following article examines the history of and current relationship between courts and mediation programs.

## 18.4  Community Mediation and the Court System: The Ties That Bind   *Timothy Hedeen, Patrick G. Coy*

SINCE THEIR INCEPTION, COMMUNITY mediation programs in the United States have often been tied to the justice system, a proximity that is expressed in a number of ways: courts are the leading source of case referrals for many programs; state or local court systems provide the majority of funding for many programs; and it is partly through these ties that mediation programs have attained legitimacy in the communities they serve. In fact, some pro-

grams are even housed in courthouses. Although there are benefits that accrue to mediation programs from this cozy relationship, it is not without problems for a movement that has also been deeply committed to community building, citizen empowerment, and the building of alternative institutions. We highlight and analyze some of these problems in this article.

### HISTORY OF COMMUNITY MEDIATION IN THE UNITED STATES

The community mediation movement in the United States can trace its roots to two primary sources: the social and political movements of

---

the 1960s and a governmental and nongovernmental movement to reform the justice system. In the first case, community mediation was embraced as an empowerment tool for individuals and communities to take back control over their lives from a governmental institution (the courts) that was seen as not only inefficient but oppressive and unfair. This vision included equipping citizens to resolve their own disputes and the building of a truly alternative system that would keep many disputants from seeing the inside of a courthouse.

In the second case, the motivation was focused on responding to court system inefficiency. Here the "alternative" in alternative dispute resolution (ADR) was much more reformist; it did not refer to creating a parallel, citizen-run and community-centered dispute resolution system. In language that was to become popular in the 1980s, the goal was to build a "multidoor courthouse." As the mediation field developed, these two movements sometimes surfaced as quite distinct in orientation and emphasis. But it is also true that there has been significant overlap and cooperation, resulting in rich and often spirited discussions about the objectives and values of community mediation. In our historical overview, we focus primarily on the reformist approach because we later raise questions about the effects for mediation of working closely with or within the court system.

Many scholars trace the origins of the field of community dispute resolution to the Community Relations Service, a federal program established through the Civil Rights Act of 1964 to prevent violence and encourage constructive dialogue in communities. Formalized developments toward community mediation were initially funded through the federal Law Enforcement Assistance Administration (LEAA). For example, the Philadelphia Municipal Court Arbitration Tribunal began in 1969 as an innovative project involving prosecutors and the courts to assist disputants, and in 1970, the Columbus Night Prosecutor's Program was initiated to relieve overburdened city court dockets.

The next wave in alternative dispute resolution included the creation of neighborhood justice centers (NJCs). Richard Danzig envisioned community-based resources to involve citizens in the administration of justice through methods to promote reconciliation. The LEAA later developed his ideas by establishing NJCs in Atlanta, Kansas City, and Los Angeles in 1978 and in Honolulu and Dallas in 1980. These centers were created partly in response to a number of court-related concerns, including those that in 1976 triggered the National Conference on the Causes of Popular Dissatisfaction with the Administration of Justice (also known as the Pound Conference).

As these federally funded programs were developing, other communities were initiating their own dispute resolution resources with purely local bases of support. Examples include the Institute for Mediation and Conflict Resolution's Dispute Center in Manhattan, the San Francisco Community Boards Program, the Rochester (New York) Community Dispute Services, and the Dorchester (Massachusetts) Urban Court Program. Many of these programs were linked to various courts, although others clearly distanced themselves from the justice system.

The development of the NJCs and the various community dispute services continued into the early 1980s, even after the sunset of federal funding. There were over 100 programs in operation at that time; the number ballooned to approximately 650 in 1998. Theoretically, each of these programs has been designed to respond to the dispute resolution needs and interests of the community it serves, and therefore every program has unique referral and funding mechanisms. For the vast majority of these programs, however, the justice system plays a large role.

## COMMUNITY MEDIATION AND THE JUSTICE SYSTEM

In the late 1970s and into the 1980s, the Department of Justice undertook considerable study of the NJC and community mediation concepts. These reviews were motivated in large part by citizen frustration with the justice system, as well as by more basic questions about the appropriateness of relying on the courts to settle interpersonal conflicts. As one report stated:

The courts have not actively sought to become the central institution for dispute resolution; rather the task has fallen to them by default as the significance and influence of other institutions has waned over the years. . . . Many of the disputes which are presently brought to the courts would have been settled in the past by the family, the church, or the informal community leadership. Although the current role of these societal institutions in resolving interpersonal disputes is in doubt, many citizens take their cases to the courts.

A 1983 Justice Department report outlined five goals for the employment of mediation in small claims disputes: (1) increasing the efficiency of case processing, (2) reducing court system costs, (3) allowing judges to provide added attention to cases on the regular civil docket, (4) improving the quality of justice, and (5) improving collection of judgments. These goals clearly demonstrate the value that mediation was perceived to have for the court system. The same report went on to outline the benefits of having court house mediation programs:

• A court-sponsored program requires a smaller operating budget than one that is independently operated.
• The prospects for continued funding are greater if the program is supported by the regular court budget or by a filing fee surcharge.
• Judicial support is more likely for a court-run program.
• Respondents may be more likely to attend a mediation session sanctioned by the court as the power of the court can be brought to bear against nonappearing parties.
• A mediation settlement can be reviewed immediately by a judge for correctness and evenhandedness and declared a formal order of the court.
• If the mediation effort fails, the complainant does not need to file the case a second time.
• After a failed mediation, it might be possible in some jurisdictions for the parties

to proceed immediately to adjudication (either a court trial or arbitration) without further delays or extra trips to the courthouse.

This approach, where mediation essentially services the court system, led some courts to grant the critical start-up funds for mediation programs and in other instances to provide physical housing as well. Although the multidoor courthouse offered mediation as one alternative to the court process, it also provided a number of other legal and dispute processes such as arbitration and neutral evaluation.

Regardless of their sponsorship by courts, private nonprofit organizations, or other public entities, most community mediation programs receive a sizable number of their cases through the court system. These referrals happen in at least four ways:

Claimants seeking to file in civil matters are often encouraged by court staff or various media (posters, brochures) to attempt mediation first.
Community mediators attend court sessions and work with disputants prior to their cases being heard by the judge or on the recommendation of the clerk or judge.
For some criminal matters, the prosecutor or judge, or both, will postpone a trial and direct the case to mediation.
Many states and courts have mandated alternative dispute resolution for larger civil cases and family matters, and they often route cases to community mediation programs.

The 1998 membership directory of the National Association for Community Mediation (1998) provides a measure of how sizable the proportion of court referrals is for community programs. Of 250 community mediation programs in the United States registered as members, 185 provided percentage breakdowns of their case referrals. Eighty-six (46.5 percent) of these centers indicated that at least half of their cases are court referrals. In fact, 45 (24.3 percent) receive at least three-quarters of their cases from the courts. The mean average of court referrals as a percentage of total caseload is 44 percent (the median average is 45 percent). Similarly, McKinney, Kimsey, and Fuller surveyed a broad spectrum of mediation resources nationwide, of which community programs were the majority, and found that nearly 30 percent identified "court-annexed mediation" as their primary service, and that over 75 percent participated in court-referred cases. And in New York, where each of the sixty-two counties has its own community dispute resolution resource, 41 percent of all cases are referred from courts.

Numerous studies continue to document the utility of community mediation in each of these arrangements. Meanwhile, court systems and mediation centers have expanded their efforts to incorporate mediation into the justice system case-handling process, often with little critical reflection on the deleterious effects this may have for mediation. Although mediation programs gain both cases and public exposure through court referrals, we believe they may also lose something in the bargain.

## CONCERNS ABOUT COMMUNITY MEDIATION'S RELATION TO THE JUSTICE SYSTEM

Many in the justice system have heralded the potential of mediation to alleviate court congestion, reduce costs for the system and its clients, and bring about resolution in a more timely manner. Certainly these benefits to the justice system are valuable, but they are seldom the primary aims of community mediation programs. For many staff and volunteers, the promise of mediation lies in the empowerment of communities and individuals to develop their own solutions in informal, convenient meetings with minimal involvement from the justice system. For example, the goal of the influential San Francisco community boards was "providing a first-resort conflict-settlement service for local residents *outside* the perimeters of the formal legal system."

The editors of a recent book on court-based mediation offer that "while court-annexed mediation may be co-optive, with negative implications, it is unlikely that the takeover was motivated by malign intentions, conscious or otherwise." They proceed to explicate the interests behind this appropriation of mediation: "The cry for experimentation and the internalization of ADR processes

within the traditional system appears to be motivated primarily by efficiency concerns, e.g., the elimination of congested dockets and cost or time savings, rather than quality of process and humanistic goals embraced by the broader alternative dispute resolution movement."

The current state of relations between community mediation and the justice system raises a number of concerns regarding the integrity and viability of mediation. With the high proportion of community mediation programs' caseloads and funding coming from the court system, many programs may find themselves in tenuous, if not compromising, positions. We have identified six areas of special concern: (1) the dependence for funding on the favor and support of the justice system, (2) the loss of autonomy to turn back inappropriate court referrals, (3) the potential for coerced participation in mediation, (4) the potential to be found at fault is faced by only one party, (5) the misunderstanding of the legal status or basis of mediation processes and outcomes, and (6) the loss of focus on community in community mediation.

**Dependence for Funding on Justice System Favor or Support.** The need for diversified funding sources for community mediation programs has long been recognized in theory, if too seldom achieved in practice. A 1991 National Institute for Dispute Resolution (NIDR) manual that distilled lessons from the first two decades of community mediation work highlighted the importance of establishing viable fundraising plans and building diverse funding bases for community centers. When mediation programs are funded in large part by any one source, the potential for control or even undue influence that a funding agency has over aspects of the mediation program is likely to increase. When the court system is the primary funding source and the mediation center also works closely with that system on a day-to-day referral basis, that potential is increased further still. Many mediation programs successfully negotiate these choppy seas; others may sacrifice the integrity of their services to accommodate the wishes of the funder, thereby taking on considerable water.

The mechanisms through which mediation programs receive their funding are varied, but many states have formalized means to provide state support to community mediation. Whether the funding comes from court filing fees (as in California and Michigan) or a legislative appropriation administered through the state court (as in Minnesota and New York), many state governments place the responsibility for oversight of community mediation funds, and often of community mediation operations, in the purview of the courts.

Albie Davis's evaluative report on community mediation in Massachusetts bears out our concerns regarding mediation's dependence on the courts for funding. She found that funding agencies have a profound impact on the shape and approach of individual programs, or in her phrase, "form often follows funding." Many courts that are funding mediation programs "are still focusing inappropriately on managing the vast majority of cases as if they were going to trial."

One area where this is especially problematic is that of written agreements. Among mediation's numerous advantages is its ability to address conflicts constructively, respect each party's perspective, empower individuals to take personal responsibility for conflicted relations, establish mutually beneficial dialogue, and reduce violence. Written settlements are often a by-product of these dynamics, but they are not in themselves a sufficient goal of community mediation.

In court-related cases, however, agreements often become the goal. It is not uncommon to hear practitioners and administrators in court-annexed programs speak of mediations without written agreements as "unsuccessful." Moreover, if mediation programs and their mediators are subject to bureaucratic pressures to keep cases moving through the docket by a written agreement, they will likely pass that pressure on to the parties seated around the mediation table: "Mediators remind recalcitrant disputants that if they don't come to agreement, the court may hold it against them." Such a predisposition toward a written outcome contradicts a core value of mediation: party self-determination. When mediators push disputants to arrive at a written agreement of any sort, much less one that addresses specific issues of concern to an outside agent like the courts, the notion that disputants know best how to resolve their conflicts is sacrificed.

Another area where court system concerns may not be in the interest of community mediation is the turnaround time for case processing. One reason that courts initially embraced mediation was to help relieve their vastly overloaded dockets. Thus, Drake and Lewis noted that one of the things that court systems find attractive about mediation is the potential for a large number of cases to be processed in a relatively short amount of time. Unfortunately, we now know that in those states with the most experience in institutionalizing the mediation alternative within the court system (New York, Ohio, Michigan, and Maine) mediation has largely failed to alleviate court congestion. Despite this poor track record, it is still common to hear mediation advocates claim that mediation can in fact relieve the scheduling pressures faced by courts.

Whether mediation has been able to deliver on the promises made on its behalf or not, the pressures to do so remain, and they have a negative impact on the quality of the mediation services provided. For example, the need to handle a large caseload has resulted in some court-annexed programs' delivering services in what we would call a compromised manner: "There are reported instances of 20-minute mediations in one city. . . . Too-rapid mediation erodes the underlying premise of mediation which is to permit disputants to sort out reasons for their conflict and fashion a mutually agreeable solution. They also raise the spector of assembly-line justice."

Justice system funding of mediation is not necessarily to the detriment of community mediation. What must be realized, however, is the tremendous influence of court funding, for "whatever courts do with respect to extra-judicial dispute resolution resources impacts heavily on the growth of the [mediation] field." In some situations, reliance on court funding can have significant drawbacks, and in still others there is a likelihood that problems could easily develop. One of the more salient issues facing the field today is how to mitigate both the realized and the potential deleterious effects that reliance on court referrals and funding may have on the mediation process itself and on the larger mediation movement. Some of the national foundations that financially supported early or pilot community mediation initiatives have refocused their funding priorities recently. There is some constricting of funding sources, meaning that even more centers are turning toward the courts, which may be either "saviors or saboteurs." "The powerful influence of the courts can make or break players in the Alternative Dispute Resolution field. Contrast the explosive growth of private judging in California with the withering and dying of community dispute resolution programs ignored by the court in Florida."

Given today's broad-based effort to institutionalize ADR in the courts and in the broader public sector on both the federal and state levels, there is no more appropriate time than now for mediation programs to develop institutional safeguards to reduce undue influence. This approach is predicated on our belief that the future development and directions of community mediation belong not first to the funders but to the larger communities that mediation centers serve.

**Loss of Autonomy to Turn Back Inappropriate Referrals.**  Many mediation programs associated with a court system receive cases that have been "mandated" to mediation. Unfortunately, not all of these cases are appropriate for mediation. Many cases are referred to mediation not because it is the most appropriate service, but because it is less inappropriate than the court process. An increasingly familiar dilemma emerges: A justice system representing the strongest source of referrals and funding for a mediation program refers cases that are inappropriate for mediation. Programs are torn between heeding the adage, "Never bite the hand that feeds you," and staying true to their understanding of the nature and purposes of mediation. Where mediation relies heavily on court referrals, and is thus somewhat dependent on the courts for program viability, the dilemma facing mediation programs is particularly intense.

McGillis and Mullen noted early on, "Decisions within the criminal justice agencies can have a profound impact on the vitality of the project. . . . The Boston project's dependence upon the court for referrals makes the project vulnerable." Ten years later, Drake and Lewis echoed these same concerns: "In recent years, courts have come to play larger roles as sponsors and funders of what initially were often community-based programs. Older centers, seeking funding and formal case referral arrangements with the courts, have been giving up some autonomy." More recently, in an evaluation of Michigan's court-sponsored mediation program, Mika recommended caution and ongoing vigilance to protect the autonomy of Michigan's community mediation centers: "Conduct site-specific assessments of [community mediation] centers operating under the auspices of sponsoring or umbrella organizations, for the purpose of evaluating the relative autonomy of program development and decision-making, and the role of the umbrella."

Even for those mediation centers that have maintained an independent organizational locus or a broad base of funding support, such as the Community Dispute Settlement (CDS) Program in Philadelphia, questions of autonomy remain critical: "Given the dependence of CDS on court referrals, how independent is it? We have slowly come to understand that CDS in fact lies within the boundary of the legal system, extending the borders of criminal justice so it can be more consensual and less adversarial."

**Potential for Coerced Participation in Mediation.**  Although mediation is most often heralded as a voluntary process for all parties at all stages—that is, parties to a dispute may elect whether to use the service at all, and then may discontinue at any point—close ties to the court system complicate this mediation hallmark significantly. In their attempts to bring disputants to the mediation table, many centers affiliated with courts have employed coercive tactics that are hardly subtle. A 1976 study conducted for the Department of Justice found that a number of programs "use very threatening letters to compel respondents to appear for mediation with the complainant. The typical closing line in the letter is, 'Failure to appear may result in the filing of criminal charges based on the above complaint.' Official stationery is used and the district attorney or a similar official signs the letter."

In the 1970s, community mediation was a fledgling field whose viability was far from assured. Consequently, the application of such pressure was seen as necessary to ensure sizable caseloads, which would in turn demonstrate that mediation was here to stay. Although anecdotal evidence suggests that many centers have toned down such language in an effort to provide disputants with a more balanced choice of whether to participate, many centers maintain this practice. A 1998 profile of a North Carolina program provides a good example: "The level of pressure applied to disputants to attend mediation sessions varies depending on the nature of the referral agency. . . . Referral letters from the district attorney's office have a stronger tone and are sent by the Center on official stationery from the district attorney's office." The letters close, "If you choose not to appear at the Dispute Settlement Center or if mediation is not successful, you must be in Criminal Court at [specific time and place]."

The number of programs using such threatening letters appears to have diminished, but coercion is delivered in other forms too. In her reflections on the Philadelphia Community Dispute Settlement Program, Beer relates that "most who call the program have been given two choices: try dispute settlement or appear in court." Some would argue that this method of referral, which sometimes takes the form of a judge's recommendation, upholds the tenet of voluntary participation, yet it seems clear to us that it relies more on the punitive stick of adjudication than on the enticing carrot of mediation. Indeed, it is not uncommon for court officials and mediation center staff to caution disputants who might dismiss such a "recommendation" from a judge that failure to participate in mediation will be taken into account if the case returns to court.

Mediation centers have relied on criminal justice system coercion not least because it brings results. Harrington found, for example, that "a mediation hearing was held in 86 percent of the cases referred by the criminal justice system where an arrest charge was involved. In those cases referred by criminal justice agents without charges pending . . . only 38 percent participated in a hearing."

There is one final area relative to coercion and proximity to the courts that bears mentioning: victim-offender mediation (VOM). In the past few years many community mediation programs have expanded the services they offer; some centers are now providing "restorative justice" services, including VOM. The potential for coercion is exacerbated in this form of mediation, with the worst potential for abuse occurring in cases involving youthful offenders. In some instances and jurisdictions, VOM may be offered to youths accused of criminal activity in lieu of prosecution and the establishment of a criminal record. The potential for coercion and abuse is heightened by the fact that there tend to be fewer due process protections for youthful offenders. The voluntariness of participation in mediation is obviously compromised for the offender in such situations, and there may be coercive pressure exerted on the victim too: "The fact that the state or its surrogate initiates the discussion may create pressure to take part." Moreover, the rhetorical appeal of some victim-offender programs—especially those that focus on "reconciliation"—potentially adds another layer of coercion over the victim, who might feel guilty if he or she were to refuse to participate.

At the same time, however, many other benefits may accrue to victims, offenders, and the community as the result of VOM, despite its potential for coercion. In the end, community centers will have to continue to struggle with how certain manifestations of VOM complement or contradict their particular mandate.

**Potential to Be Found "At Fault" Is Perceived to Be Faced by Primarily One Party.** When a mediation program contacts the respondent in a court-related case, that party is likely to consider mediation as an extension of the court or the prosecutor's office. Consequently, respondents frequently view mediation as being favorably oriented toward the complainant-victim and being predisposed toward finding fault with the respondent. This is problematic for two interrelated reasons.

For most community mediation centers in North America, neutrality is a fundamental element of mediation practice. Whether or not one subscribes to the notion of mediator neutrality, most would agree that community mediators must win the trust of both parties and mediation programs must be perceived to be even-handed in order to carry out a successful mediation. Yet first impressions run deep, and respondents are naturally defensive and on guard when they are first called to mediation. Consequently, respondent trust is hard to win and easy to lose whenever a mediation program initially appears to the respondent to be doing the work of the court system. Many mediation programs try to mitigate this perception of bias, but they also routinely find that they must assure respondents of mediator neutrality before they will agree to participate in mediation.

Second, a hallmark of good mediation practice is steering the disputants away from a simple search for the guilty party in order to find fault with that party. Mediators rewrite this age-old script by helping both parties see that they face a joint, or shared, problem and that each will have to take some initiative toward resolving it.

Many cases are referred to mediation with the contingency that if no agreement is reached, the case may proceed immediately to court. When mediation becomes so tightly connected to the court structure, the presumption of favor toward the complainant may become explicit. The following example, drawn from a 1992 informational pamphlet on the mediation of criminal matters, outlines how mediators might convince defendants to participate: "Explaining that the case is a minor one which may nevertheless require a full trial, that the Defendant, if found guilty, would have a permanent public record of conviction, and that the Judge hopes that this can be resolved at this hearing serves to impress the Defendant with the more serious options of refusing mediation."

Other elements of coercion generally reserved for the courts have been brought to bear in mediation, including the use of ink colors normally reserved for "official" warnings. For example, in New York City in the early 1980s, respondents received yellow "Request to Appear" notices with warnings in red ink about the possibility of criminal charges. Program staff referred to this notice as a "summons," and these were provided to complainants with instructions to deliver them to respondents; complainants could request that a police officer accompany them to deliver the notice, and officers were mandated to oblige.

Intended or not, such attempts at powerful persuasion by the courts toward the respondent also tend to validate a complainant's concerns and demonstrate that they are receiving appropriate attention and service from the court system. Thus, intimate ties to the courts are problematic in the maintenance of programs' perceived, if not actual, neutrality.

**Misunderstanding of the Legal Status of Mediation Processes and Outcomes.** As a relatively young field operating mostly out of the public eye, community mediation is still too little understood by the general public. On the one hand, where mediation has emerged and maintained its collective identity as a stand-alone nonprofit organization that happens to work with the courts, community members' views of mediation are likely to reflect the multiple strands of the mediation movement's history. On the other hand, in communities where mediation is housed within or very closely connected to the courts, it is common for the populace to associate mediation closely with the legal process. In fact, in our experience, disputants often inquire of mediation center staff whether the services may be accessed outside court, with the presumption that they may not. Because some courts now require that cases be handled through ADR (or mediation specifically) before going to trial, this perception of mediation as a component of the justice system is not likely to disappear any time soon.

Even centers that have maintained offices and funding outside the courts are not immune from being seen as an adjunct to the court system due to the high proportion of court referrals in their caseloads. In the light of the prevalence of judges' referrals in the caseload of Philadelphia's CDS, founder Eileen Stief made an insightful distinction that likely applies to many programs across the country: "We haven't created an alternative to the courts. We've become an alternative to the courtroom."

Given the close working association with the court system, many disputants fail to distinguish between mediated agreements and court decisions, especially with regard to courts of limited jurisdiction (such as small claims courts and conciliation courts) and housing courts. Confusion over the legal status and enforceability of mediated settlements is especially prevalent and is therefore of great concern both within and outside the justice system. This problem is exacerbated in cities where mediation sessions are held in courthouses. In those cases, the lines between judicial processes and mediative processes are blurred further still, especially for disputants who are relatively new to mediation. Although no mediators wear black robes, the following report indicates that they are nevertheless routinely mistaken for judges: "Disputing parties sometimes agree to mediation in the hope that it will impress the judge, or because they feel that this is a required part of the court process. Some of the disputants I interviewed in various mediation programmes even thought that they had been to court and seen the judge."

One lesson that should be drawn from this discussion is the important educational role of the community center mediator, especially in courthouse settings. If mediators fail to help the disputants distinguish mediation from the courthouse setting at the outset, substantive misunderstandings about the nature of the mediation process will probably result. These misunderstandings are likely, in turn, to influence unduly the character, direction, tone, and outcome of the mediation itself. Moreover, we ought not to assume that these problems will occur only when mediations are done inside a courthouse; other settings also require that mediators explain the unique role of mediation. In a culture heavily influenced by television, the reach of Judge Wapner and the *People's Court* is no doubt longer than we might hope.

## Notes and Questions

1. The number of people who want to become mediators is staggering. Training programs are filled, and there is a growing demand for advanced training and continuing education. However, the vast majority of practicing and aspiring mediators are white middle-class professionals. The percentage of African Americans, Latinos, and other minorities in the dispute resolution field is very low. What are the reasons for this gap?

2. The one arena where there is diverse participation in conflict resolution programs is in elementary and secondary schools. There are over 5,000 programs in the United States in which young people function as "peer mediators" in their schools. Some of these programs are focusing on gang violence and racial conflict. Several research studies are currently examining the long-term effects on young people who have been trained in mediation skills. There is already, however, a growing body of evidence that these types of programs enhance these students' ability to negotiate conflict in other aspects of their lives outside of school.

3. What credentials should aspiring mediators have? Is a professional degree important? If so, which degree? What kind of skills does a mediator need to have? Some people have suggested that mediation is "an art, not a science." Do you agree?

---

18.5   Mediating Misdemeanors   *Nancy Hirshman*

HAVE YOU EVER BEEN awakened at the crack of dawn by the horrendous whine of your neighbor's weed-whacker? Has your know-it-all classmate pushed you so close to the edge that you elbowed him out of the way as you beat a hasty retreat? Or have you gone out to fetch the morning papers to find that your petunia patch has been trampled for the umpteenth time by the kids waiting for the school bus?

These are the scenarios that often end up as misdemeanor criminal charges in the state of Maryland, which is one of the many states in which communities have established mediation programs for such cases. In this article, I use our experience in Maryland to provide a sense of how these programs handle criminal matters— almost exclusively misdemeanors—with the caveat that they tend to have characteristics and features that are unique to the needs, interests, and concerns of their communities.

## PROSECUTORS REFER CASES

In Anne Arundel County, Md., the Mediation Center is a component of the State's Attorney's Office (SAO). When faced with cases like the ones described above, prosecutors in the screening division refer them to the Mediation Center. They also refer other misdemeanor offenses, such as trespass, theft, telephone abuse, malicious destruction and violation of animal or zoning ordinances. (Maryland is one of just three states that allow a citizen to generate a criminal charge. Most jurisdictions provide for prosecutorial review or, as an alternative, investigation and charging by the appropriate law enforcement agency. Maryland's "commissioner" system may be one of the reasons why mediation has been embraced by our prosecutors and trial courts.)

Provided the charges fall within certain guidelines, prosecutors make immediate referrals of misdemeanor charges, both civilian complaints and police-generated charges. Generally speaking, the guidelines limit referrals to minor misdemeanor charges and cases that do not involve weapons, serious injuries, domestic violence or individuals with significant criminal history. Wary of potential criticism for "decriminalization," the state attorney decided not to refer certain categories of cases—such as shoplifting and theft—to mediation. Rather, screening attorneys are trained to refer on a case-by-case basis. The guidelines have remained fairly stable since the inception of the program.

Sometimes prosecutors refer cases that were not initially referred by the screening unit, because after further trial preparation the case appears appropriate for mediation. Cases are also referred to the Mediation Center by government agencies and elected officials, the parties themselves and law enforcement officers (who carry "palm cards" providing information about mediation). Defense attorneys, particularly attorneys familiar with mediation, often refer cases because the fees generated by the types of cases appropriate for mediation are modest, and they recognize that the possibility of avoiding prose-

cution is in their client's best interests. Regardless of the referral source, all cases go through the same screening process to determine their suitability for mediation.

The office, established as the Neighborhood Mediation Program in 1983, was originally intended to be one central place to which any of the county's 482,000 residents could turn to seek an expedient and effective resolution of their complaints. It became apparent early on that a substantial number of citizens who complained had already filed a criminal charge at the commissioner's office. They were either impatient because it took so long for the case to come up for trial or frustrated because the problem was increasing in frequency and severity and no-one in "the system" seemed interested in doing anything. Thus, the Mediation Center became a pretrial diversion component of the State's Attorney's Office.

## CASE SCREENING

When cases are received by the Mediation Center, which is currently staffed by a director-mediator, a screener-case manager and volunteer interns from a variety of sources, the initial steps usually involve accessing computer databases or case management systems.

First, staff members screen the cases to ascertain the trial date and court location, whether an attorney has entered an appearance for the defendant and the court history of *both* defendant and complaining witness/victim. (Checking both parties' records is sometimes the only method of determining if related or cross-charges are outstanding, or if the parties together have a history of criminal complaints which may signify that the cases fall under the domestic violence umbrella. Copies of any related charges or cross-charges are obtained for review.)

Using the information obtained in the screening phase, the center director decides whether to accept or decline referred cases. In borderline cases, the director may consult with the senior prosecuting attorney in the appropriate district court for opinions or approval. Frequently, the director will confer with one of the staff domestic violence advocates to clear a questionable case.

## INITIAL CONTACT

Complaining witnesses are promptly informed by mail of the case referral. The letter is computer-generated and is accompanied by an informational brochure explaining mediation. Written communication not only lends legitimacy to the contact but also is preferable to "cold" calling the complainant, which is time-consuming and staff-intensive. When the complaining witness responds, the screener-case manager answers general questions and attempts to elicit the complainant's expectations, needs and concerns. If the complainant declines mediation, the staff member notes the file accordingly.

If the complaining witness or victim consents to mediation, the center contacts the defendant or the attorney of record. Agreement to mediate is generally—but not always—forthcoming from defendants, who readily see the benefit of avoiding prosecution.

A mutually convenient appointment is scheduled at the site of the complainant's choice. Defense attorneys (who may advise their clients but not speak for them in mediation) are welcome to attend but seldom do. Attendance of witnesses is discouraged.

## MEDIATION PROCEDURES

First, the mediator sets ground rules with the parties and reviews how the process will work. It is the mediator's responsibility to ensure that the guidelines are observed and the balance of power is equitable; the disputants dictate the topics of discussion as well as the outcomes. It should be noted that the Mediation Center primarily uses a facilitative approach to mediation. There are also situations where conciliation is appropriate, and others—particularly multiparty neighborhood disputes—that require facilitation. (Arbitration is not offered.)

Assuming the parties have come to a mutual resolution, the agreement is reduced to writing on a Mediation Center disposition form. The parties are asked to review the document, consult with an attorney or other advisor if they wish, then sign the form. The mediator countersigns the agreement, then gives copies to the parties.

The mediator advises the parties that, subject to approval of the prosecutor handling their trial docket, the mediation agreement will be entered on the court docket in lieu of the case proceeding to trial. Options for disposition of the criminal charge are discussed. The parties are responsible for verifying through the Center's office that the assistant state's attorney has approved the agreement, disposed of the criminal charge and excused the parties. They are told the specific time frame within which they must call to ascertain the outcome.

If the parties are unable to reach complete agreement—reaching impasse on the amount of restitution or whether the defendant must enroll in an anger management program, for example—a memo is placed in the assistant state's attorney's file stating only that the mediation was unsuccessful.

## HIGH SUCCESS RATE

In 1999, 623 criminal cases were referred to the Mediation Center. Of that number, mediation failed in just 3 percent of the matters. Almost $26,000 in restitution was paid, thousands of dollars in property was repaired or replaced and approximately 275 hours of community service were performed. Since the inception of the program, the number of cases resolved has exceeded 90 percent, due in part to the training and experience of the mediators as well as the thorough screening and intake process.

More importantly, the success rate is attributable to the requisite consent of the parties to mediate, thus implying their predisposition toward conciliation. In the end, relationships—whether family, business or community—are preserved, while the participants take from the session a better understanding of each other's viewpoint and perhaps more productive communication skills.

This is one reason that support for the program remains high among prosecutors, who further recognize that it resolves the types of cases that are time-consuming and rarely involve significant legal issues. The district court judges in Anne Arundel County also are strong proponents because mediation clears minor cases from the court docket and allows more productive allocation of limited resources. Indeed, as in other states, the Anne Arundel County Mediation Center has demonstrated the value and efficiency of such programs as a complement to the court.

# 18.6  Scrapping the Plea-Bargain    *Jennifer Smith*

DESPITE INCREASED USE OF ADR in civil cases and in limited areas of juvenile and minor criminal law, ADR is rarely used to resolve disputes involving major criminal charges against adults. In this article, I outline a proposal for using ADR in the mainstream criminal justice system as a routine substitute for the current dual system of plea-bargaining and trial. This new dispute resolution system would modify plea-bargaining by mandating participation in mediation sessions, and would result in trial only infrequently. ADR would give prosecutors the power to create personally tailored and thus more effective punishments for criminals, give defendants a buffer against currently extensive prosecutorial discretion, and give the public at large a more reliable and accountable justice system.

Before describing the proposed system in detail, I should note some of the issues that have influenced this effort to apply ADR to criminal law. First, although the lack of formal ADR in criminal cases suggests that many people consider major crimes and ADR to be fundamentally incompatible, plea-bargaining has already made negotiation an intrinsic part of the criminal justice system. When we encounter objections to the proposed mediation system, we should consider whether it would be an improvement over the current system of unsupervised negotiation. Indeed, many criminal cases are ideal ADR candidates because they are legally routine but involve complex human factors that would benefit from individualized solutions.

Second, the plea-bargaining system is largely unregulated due to prosecutors' expansive discretion to decide whom to charge and with what offense, and whether to trade leniency for guilty pleas and informant testimony. This discretion is highly controversial, and official records of these private negotiations are inadequate to enable the public to determine whether the benefits of enhanced law enforcement outweigh the risks of potential discrimination and abuse.

Third, the public's interests are not necessarily adequately represented in the power struggle between prosecution and defense. Prosecutors have an interest in advocating for a dispute resolution system that facilitates the most convictions, and defense attorneys have an interest in advocating for the dispute resolution system that facilitates the most acquittals. But the general public's interest lies in balancing benefits and costs in order to achieve the system that maximizes the justice purchased by each dollar spent and minimizes the cost in violent crime for each civil liberty protected.

## OBJECTIONS TO ADR IN CRIMINAL LAW

It is not difficult to identify a number of possible reasons for the infrequent use of ADR in major criminal cases. After all, ADR preaches that arguing about interests is better than arguing about who is right and who is wrong. But when it comes to criminals who have robbed, or assaulted or perhaps even murdered innocent citizens, the ADR ethos eliminates all the elements we *want* in our criminal justice system. Criminal law is precisely about determining who is right, and how much the person who is wrong should be punished. However, many disputes that involve a strong element of moral disapproval are resolved effectively through ADR, including hostage crises and environmental pollution cases. Moral judgment and a desire to punish thus do not act as per se bars to resolving major crimes through ADR methods.

There are other potential objections. Public trials serve a number of important purposes, including the need for visible evidence of predictable consequences to criminal behavior, the guarantees of fairness that accompany publicity and open proceedings, the value of precedent in the rule of law, and the need to express sanctions against people who violate community standards. Trials also provide criminal defendants with many procedural protections that might be compromised in mediation.

Also, any dispute resolution system that modifies the prosecutor's ability to plea-bargain is bound to be controversial. To some, prosecutorial discretion is beneficial. To others, discretion equals discrimination. These critics claim that prosecutors protect police officers who violate civil liberties and turn a blind eye to informant perjury. Claims of selective prosecution, which have been substantiated by extensive statistical studies, have failed to persuade courts to pierce the powerful veil of prosecutorial discretion.[1] On the other hand, prosecutors often use their leverage to make the justice system operate more cheaply and efficiently, and to save innocent people from imminent bodily harm. The challenge is therefore to design an ADR system that addresses these competing concerns better than existing alternatives.

## MANDATORY MEDIATION PROPOSAL

I propose a system of mandatory mediation. The prosecution and the defense would each submit a confidential brief to the mediator outlining the major issues surrounding the case, describing any special circumstances as the party sees them, and suggesting terms of settlement. There would be no penalties for failing to settle, but each party would be required to listen to a brief presentation (up to 30 minutes) by the opposing side describing and defending settlement.

Neutrals would be selected at random from a panel of qualified mediators chosen by an American Bar Association panel of prosecutors and defense attorneys. That panel would also determine quality-control standards and training requirements. Mediators would be facilitative, taking no responsibility for substantive fairness and making no effort to affect the substantive outcome of the mediation.

All statements within the negotiation would be confidential unless publicized as part of the final plea agreement. The neutral would maintain written records of the discussion and outcome that could be accessed in the event of appeal and for statistical purposes. To ensure that race, class or other impermissible discrimination did not distort substantive results, county, state and national statistics would be tracked. If prosecutors sought the death penalty more often in election years, for example, that distortion would show up in the statistical record. By contrast, the mediator's description of the discussion would be sealed unless one party appealed the settlement, in which case the description could be used to void that agreement but would not be admissible in any further proceedings.

Attorneys would represent both government and defendant. Constitutional protections that could not be waived at trial could not be waived at mediation. Any settlement involving an admission of guilt or legal liability would require a brief court appearance in which a judge would ensure that the defendant had knowingly waived his statutory and constitutional rights, and would impress upon the defendant the legal consequences of his decision to admit guilt. Not all defendants would necessarily plead guilty. For example, a teenage runaway caught shoplifting might escape prosecution entirely if she agreed to complete a drug rehab program. In another case, a murder suspect might plead guilty and be required to state the facts of his crime before a judge as part of the settlement.

The rules of evidence would be suspended during the mediation, but any evidence that would have been inadmissible at trial would remain inadmissible whether or not the evidence was used in mediation. This provision would encourage broad-based settlement discussions without compromising the defendant's constitutional trial rights, should she choose to exercise them.

The parties would be entitled to discovery to the same extent that they would have been during trial, although they might decide to forego formal discovery by mutual agreement.[2] Although the defendant could maintain her silence by invoking her Fifth Amendment privilege against self-incrimination, either party

---

[1] See McCleskey v. Kemp, 481 U.S. 279 (1987) (refusing to overturn the sentence in the absence of evidence of discriminatory intent, even where the Baldus study demonstrated that prosecutorial discretion had a discriminatory effect).

[2] In the teenage runaway example, discussed above, the parties could decide that the facts of the crime were irrelevant because both agreed that the best settlement would involve getting the teenager off the streets so she no longer needed to steal.

could include a clause voiding the settlement if the opposing party had misrepresented a material fact. For example, the prosecutor might request a provision that the settlement be voided by evidence showing that the defendant was not the getaway driver, but the triggerman.

Judicial review would differ depending on the terms of the settlement. The agreement could be appealed in court by either side on claims of procedural error or violation of the settlement terms. The defendant would retain the right to appeal the agreement based on statistical evidence of systemic impropriety, constitutional violations such as ineffective assistance of counsel or new evidence that establishes innocence of the crime charged.

The proposal uses mediation rather than arbitration because mediation would insert a buffer between prosecutor and defendant without either decreasing the prosecutor's legitimate discretionary power or upsetting the constitutional requirements for appointing judges and holding jury trials. The neutral would not intrude upon the prosecutor's ability to decide what plea offers would be offered or accepted. However, she could aid communication between the parties, help them overcome destructive negotiating tactics, and explore in individual caucuses the potential for speedy settlement.

The presence of a neutral third party would also reduce the possibility that either side would act unethically. It would be more difficult to threaten or blackmail, belittle or intimidate an opponent with someone else watching. Negotiating positions would have to pass a straight-face test or be withdrawn. If claims of impropriety were made after the mediation concluded, the mediator's individual report or the aggregate statistics could be used to support or refute allegations of selective prosecution or deception. Valid claims would succeed more often, and invalid claims would be dismissed more quickly.

## MANDATORY MEDIATION BENEFITS

Plea negotiations take place in secret. In contrast, under this proposal the general public would be better informed about the mediation process and could better decide whether it supports the positions taken and values expressed in the public's name. The public may not be aware of the frequency or nature of plea-bargains in the current system, or the extent to which they encourage criminal defendants to give false testimony against others in return for more lenient sentences for themselves. Although confidentiality rules would bar mediators from disclosing the contents of any specific mediation, neutrals could make general recommendations for improving the system as a whole.

One of the strongest benefits of mediation over trial would be the parties' ability to tailor creative responses to criminal behavior. Right now, judges and juries who decide guilt and impose sentences make choices among strictly regulated options. Those decisions often involve long prison sentences that have unintended side effects for the defendant, his family, and his community (e.g., the social effects on children and economies caused by high rates of black male conviction and incarceration). In mediation, parties could include a wide variety of custom-made solutions, including child support agreements, victim restitution, severe prison sentences, drug rehab, mental health services and job training.

## PILOT PROJECT NEEDED

It is impossible to predict the effects this proposal might have on the criminal justice system if implemented, and the sheer number of interested parties and other variables make large-scale introduction unlikely and probably unwise. However, considering the potential benefits to be gained from mandatory mediation, I would recommend that this proposal be tested through a pilot project in an innovative county or state.

To that end, it is worth taking a few moments to speculate about the possible advantages and disadvantages such a pilot project might encounter, and some of the issues that its implementers might wish to monitor. I would hope that system efficiency would increase under my proposal, as tailored punishments reduced the prison population, crime rates, recidivism and need for expensive trials. Intangible benefits might include increased fairness and accuracy, healthier families and communities through reduced crime and incarceration of young men, and increased accountability to the public. These savings would need to offset the extra costs incurred by paying neutrals and the extra drain on social services caused by creative sentencing. Also, channeling major crimes through mediation would be less expensive than trial, but channeling very minor crimes through mediation might actually be more expensive than the informal deal making that presently occurs.

Among the major stakeholders, I expect prosecutors to be the most resistant to mediation of major crimes. In theory, this proposal does not reduce the prosecutor's power in any way, nor do prosecutors personally bear the financial cost if formal mediations lead to increased workloads. The district attorney represents the public and has no legitimate right to any intimidation or other unethical tactic that might require secrecy. But prosecutors may value the ability to bend or break the rules to fight organized crime, save a kidnapping victim's life, or discover the location of a bomb. This conflict is real, and my proposed system would force society to openly debate such questions and make the tough decisions about where to draw the line between public safety and civil liberties.

In short, this proposal would bring plea-bargaining into the light and would minimize the use of that most time-consuming, cumbersome, expensive and unpredictable of institutions, the jury trial. It would add a minimum of extra procedure in exchange for a large improvement in accountability. For the first time, we would be able to examine our entire justice system to determine whether it is one of the last bastions of race and class discrimination, or an essential tool in achieving the greatest amount of justice for the greatest number at the lowest cost. We would also change our justice system from a mechanism for indiscriminate punishment through fine, imprisonment, or execution, into a flexible mechanism for dispensing appropriate responses to inappropriate behavior in a manner that deters individual recidivism, reduces crime, and helps us achieve our goal of a safer society.

## Notes and Questions

1. Mediation and other alternative dispute resolution processes are increasingly used in large, complex civil cases. In these cases, companies and their lawyers are choosing to "hire" private third parties, many of whom are retired judges who have gone into ADR practice. They will review the evidence and either help the parties to negotiate a settlement or will render a decision. What concerns are raised by this growing practice, which many have referred to as the "privatization" of the justice system?

2. What are the advantages of mandatory mediation? What are the problems with mandatory mediation? How should these pros and cons be evaluated to help guide the public policy of mediation?

# *19* MEDIATION AS POPULAR JUSTICE

❧ The following materials focus on the differing interpretations of the dispute resolution movement in contemporary Western society. The reading by Sally Engle Merry compares mediation in small-scale societies with American community mediation programs. The excerpt from Richard Hofrichter considers the political implication of the rise of informalism. The reading by Howard L. Brown describes how mediation is used in the contemporary Navajo legal system.

## 19.1    The Social Organization of Mediation in Nonindustrial Societies: Implications for Informal Community Justice in America    *Sally Engle Merry*

### INTRODUCTION

American courts are notorious for their failure to resolve minor, interpersonal disputes quickly, effectively, and in a way that satisfies the disputing parties. The increasing urbanism, transiency, and heterogeneity of American society in the twentieth century has undermined informal dispute settlement mechanisms rooted in home, church, and community and increased the demand for other means of dealing with family, neighbor, and community disputes. However, many legal experts argue that the formality of the courts, their adherence to an adversary model, their strict rules of procedure, and their reliance on adjudication render them inappropriate for handling many kinds of interpersonal quarrels arising in ongoing social relationships. . . .

. . . The American Bar Association, the U.S. Department of Justice, the American Arbitration Association, the Institute for Mediation and Conflict Resolution, and many community groups are experimenting with the use of mediation in community-based centers to resolve minor interpersonal disputes on the assumption that this will provide a more humane, responsive, and accessible form of justice. . . . However, an examination of anthropological models of mediation suggests that community mediation in urban America, as these experiments are presently constituted, may provide a kind and quality of justice fundamentally different from that which their creators intended.

Every society develops a range of mechanisms for resolving disputes, some of which are informal, rooted in such local institutions as lineage, clan, religious association, or family, and some of

which are more formal, coercive, and dependent on the political hierarchy. With the transition from small-scale, kinship-based societies to large, complex, urban social systems, disputants turn increasingly to formal rather than informal dispute resolution mechanisms. Community mediation, however, endeavors to turn the tide: to return control of certain kinds of disruptive and offensive behavior to local communities, where they can be managed through mediation, compromise, and restitution, enforced by community social sanctions and the desire of disputants to settle. It seeks to replace the formality of the court with the informality of the neighborhood, narrow considerations of legal principles with more general questions of morality and shared responsibility, win or lose outcomes with compromises, and penal sanctions of fine and imprisonment with compensation and informal social pressures. The introduction of neighborhood mediation, frequently termed citizen dispute resolution,[1] is thus part of a general movement toward delegalization, toward removing dispute management from the courts on the premise that substantive justice is better served outside the formal procedures of the existing legal system. . . . Clearly, the therapeutic and consensual nature of such forms of dispute resolution is attractive to a society increasingly critical of adversary adjudication and coercive sanctions. These proposed citizen dispute settlement centers appear to satisfy a happy conjunction of interests between those concerned with

Sally Engle Merry, "The Social Organization of Mediation in Nonindustrial Societies: Implications for Informal Community Justice in America," from *The Politics of Informal Justice,* edited by R. Abel. Copyright © 1981 by Academic Press, Inc. Reprinted by permission of Academic Press, Inc., and the author. (Most footnotes and all citations omitted.)

---

[1]Community dispute settlement centers are either court based or community based. Most of the programs that have been studied are closely connected to a court, receive referrals from court clerks and judges, and rely on the threat of judicial sanction to encourage mediation. Community-based models build on local community leaders to run the programs and to serve as mediators, and they eschew any connection with the courts either as a source of cases or as a sanction against recalcitrant disputants. . . . These centers endeavor to use community social pressure to induce compliance with agreements.

the quality and accessibility of justice available to the individual and those tackling problems of massive court congestion and mushrooming court costs.[2]

## MEDIATION IN SMALL-SCALE SOCIETIES

Mediation is an important mode of settling disputes in societies ranging from horticultural and pastoral peoples whose political institutions are coterminous with their kinship systems to peasant villages incorporated into nation-states. Although it is difficult to evaluate the "effectiveness" of mediation in these various settings, it is possible to examine the conditions under which disputants choose mediation rather than some other

---

[2]Citizen dispute resolution programs provide an alternative to adjudication for minor civil and criminal complaints arising from domestic, neighborhood, family, merchant-consumer, and landlord-tenant disputes in which the parties know one another. . . . Disputants air their grievances in an informal, personal, and supportive atmosphere in which a third party, usually a lay community member, simply mediates the dispute, facilitating the process by which the disputing parties collectively forge a mutually acceptable compromise solution or, in a few programs, agree to submit to arbitration. The mediation experience, ideally, is voluntary, noncoercive, more humane, and more closely tailored to the needs of individual disputants than is the court. The process is one of bargaining and negotiation, and the free-ranging discussion that fully explores feelings and perspectives usually lasts much longer than adjudication. Outcomes are generally compromises rather than zero-sum decisions and take into account the total relationship between the parties. Rules provide a framework for the discussion and are used by each side to justify its position, but they do not determine the outcome. . . . The process is not one of matching a problem to a rule but of establishing agreement between the parties about a fair or just settlement, even if this deviates from existing rules. Settlements may even create new rules. . . . The settlements are generally compensatory rather than penal, focusing on peacemaking and restitution rather than punishment. . . . They serve to reconcile the parties, diffuse hostility, and maintain relatively amicable and cooperative relationships. Mediation thus seems to be a more appropriate procedure than adjudication for resolving disrupted interpersonal relationships, since its central quality is "its capacity to reorient the parties toward each other, not by imposing rules on them, but by helping them to achieve a new and shared perception of their relationship, a perception that will redirect their attitudes and dispositions toward one another." . . .

process. Disputants in societies of the first type turn to mediation as an alternative to violence, feud, or warfare; those in the second choose it in preference to violence or court. . . .

**The Process of Mediation** Mediation is prompt. Ideally, it occurs immediately after the incident, before the disputants have time to harden their positions or, as the Waigali say, before they can "think about their ancestors"—their pride and social positions. The process is time-consuming, taking hours or days, as long as is necessary to reach a settlement. . . . Negotiations are often conducted in public forums where neighbors and kinsmen can offer opinions and condemn the behavior of unreasonable disputants. Even when the mediator is a go-between who meets with the parties privately, the wider public often knows the nature of the discussions through its kin ties to both sides.

Mediators arrange the payment of damages. Their function is usually to negotiate an outcome that will satisfy both parties through an exchange of property, the demarcation of a new boundary line, or the rendering of a public apology; vague promises of improved behavior in the future are not sufficient. Injuries such as insult, adultery, assault, and even homicide are generally perceived as reparable through gifts of cattle, sheep, or other valuables in amounts specified by custom.

The mediation process usually ends with immediate consummation of the agreement. When it is necessary to postpone the final settlement, for instance, while one disputant finds enough sheep, the assembly will often reconvene to observe the exchange. . . . In societies that lack written contracts, such an immediate exchange is the only guarantee of performance. . . . However, when debts are not paid promptly they often remain unsatisfied, offering fertile soil for future disputes. The last step in the mediation process is typically a ritual of reconciliation, whether drinking coffee together in a Lebanese village or a massive village feast financed by the loser as a public apology, as in prerevolutionary China. . . .

**The Social Organization of Mediation** Mediators are respected, influential community members with experience and acknowledged expertise in settling disputes. Successful settlements enhance their prestige and political prominence and often earn them some form of payment from the disputing parties. . . . Mediators often have special religious status. . . . The reputation they earn for skillful negotiation, expertise in community norms and genealogies, and fairness and impartiality brings them more cases and political influence. Mediators are not outside authorities but informal leaders of kin groups, age grades, local hamlets, or other social grouping. . . . They are usually of higher social status than the disputants. Where disputes involve members of higher social strata, outsiders are often needed. . . .

Mediators represent the norms and values of their communities, often attaining their positions by virtue of their expertise in moral issues. They advocate a settlement that accords with commonly accepted notions of justice, couched in terms of custom, virtue, and fairness, and reflecting community judgments about appropriate behavior. To flout such a settlement is to defy the moral order of the community. Mediators often deliver moral lectures to one or both disputants. Finally, they are experts in village social relationships and genealogy, bringing to the conflict a vast store of knowledge about how individuals are expected to behave toward one another in general as well as about the reputations and social identities of the particular disputants. Mediators build upon their past experience with similar cases and their knowledge of local customs regarding such disputes, manipulating these rules to justify their opinions.

**The Nature of Mediated Settlements** Mediated settlements are backed by coercion. Although the mediator lacks authority to impose a judgment, he is always able to exert influence and social pressure to persuade an intransigent party to accept some settlement and, often, to accept the settlement the mediator advocates. The community also exerts social pressure on disputants to settle and to abide by their agreement. Supernatural sanctions are often important as well.

Since mediators are usually powerful and influential, loss of their goodwill is itself a cause

for concern. Some simply facilitate dyadic negotiations . . . , whereas others practically adjudicate, backing their decisions with armed force. . . .

The community itself exerts pressure to settle. Recalcitrant disputants become the objects of gossip and scandal. . . . Witchcraft and supernatural beliefs concerning illness also serve as a powerful incentive to restoring amicable relations. . . .

One further form of coercion and social pressure is the need to maintain peaceful relations with the other party. Terminating relations may be damaging to political, economic, or kinship transactions; threats of violence or court action raise the specter of protracted, ruinous litigation or a bloody feud. Insofar as they seek to avoid these disasters, disputing parties are coerced to settle. Nevertheless, in no case is a mediator's decision backed by institutionalized force, and parties are always free to reject mediation and face the consequences.

Mediated settlements between unequals are unequal. With few exceptions, a mediated settlement reflects the status inequalities between the disputants. Payments for homicide among the Sudanese Nuer and the Enga of New Guinea . . . depend on the social status of the dead man; Ifugao compensation varies according to the status of both plaintiff and defendant. . . .

Since a mediator lacks the ability to enforce his decisions, he must find an outcome both parties will accept. A mutually acceptable solution tends to be one in which the less powerful gives up more. . . . The greater the power of the mediator, the more leverage he has to impose a solution that disregards the inequality of the parties. The judge, at least in theory, adjudicates the legal rights of the disputants; he does not weigh their total social personalities.

## COMMUNITY MEDIATION PROGRAMS IN CONTEMPORARY AMERICA

This analysis of mediation in small-scale societies has important implications for the way that process will function in urban America and for the quality of justice it can provide. First, urban American mediation is more perfunctory, more delayed, and less concrete than mediation in small-scale societies. Hearings typically occur seven to eleven days after the incident is reported. . . . This time lapse may mean that disputant positions have hardened. A large portion of referrals are made by judges, in which cases the plaintiff has already decided against seeking a consensual settlement. Experiments with delaying the hearing for a three-week "cooling-off" period support the wisdom of rapid intervention since the number of disputants appearing for these hearings drops radically. . . . Negotiations and settlements are strictly private, so that community members can neither participate in the agreement nor pressure the parties to comply, except in a few community-based programs such as the San Francisco Community Boards. Hearings in American centers last a maximum of two and a half hours and often less. . . . Although this is longer than many court trials, it does not approach the input of time and resources of mediation in small-scale societies.

Second, the enveloping social system of urban American neighborhoods is quite different from that of small-scale, nonindustrial societies. I argued earlier . . . that the efficacy of mediation depends on the existence of a cohesive, stable, morally integrated community whose powers of informal social control can be harnessed to informally achieved settlements. Yet since American centers function in large metropolitan areas, the community pressures necessary to induce disputants to accept a compromise settlement are generally absent. Disputants are rarely embedded in a close, cohesive social system where they need to maintain cooperative relationships. Even when disputants come from the same neighborhood, unless they are integrated into a unitary social structure their conflicts in one relationship do not have repercussions for others. Further, they have the option of moving away from a conflict situation rather than settling it by compromise. This is probably a frequent pattern in American society . . . , although it may carry a high cost. . . .

My own study of an urban neighborhood suggests that avoidance, or moving away, is common but is usually chosen reluctantly after a long period of conflict and the exhaustion of other

alternatives. . . . Most of the disputes in this low-income, polyethnic housing project passed through a long phase of endurance, in which the disputants simply put up with barking dogs, dirty stairwells, minor thefts, and jealous, violent lovers while appealing to a variety of formal third parties—the management office, the police, and the courts. But few disputes were resolved by these third parties. Disputants rarely consulted neighborhood leaders. Efforts to mobilize community public opinion had little impact in this fragmented, diverse community whose social networks were largely restricted to each ethnic group. . . . Disputants tended to rely on violence as an alternative to formal third parties. In the long run, disputes eventually terminated only after one or both parties moved out of the project. Thus, in those segments of American society where the social structure is fragmented and the population mobile, the need to settle may be slight and the incentive to mediate and to compromise correspondingly reduced.

Nor are court-based versions of citizen dispute resolution programs organized in a way that could exploit existing patterns of informal social control. Most programs serve areas with several thousand to several million residents rather than the smaller social units whose residents may belong to a single social network. The mediator, although usually chosen from the "local community," is almost always required to be a stranger to the disputants in order to assure his impartiality. This means that he lacks the store of knowledge about personal histories and reputations and the nature of previous settlements in the local area that appears to be critical to the success of a mediator. . . . The mediator is not a person of unusual prestige, moral stature, or influence in the neighborhood but simply a resident who has had a week of training in mediation and is paid a nominal sum to hear cases occasionally on evenings and weekends.

These mediators are also unable to operate in terms of a shared moral system. They are enjoined by mediation trainers not to make moral statements or judgments and are encouraged to seek a mutually acceptable outcome, regardless of their notions of relevant laws or norms. . . . Since each center serves a large area, mediators must handle cases from a wide variety of neighborhoods with diverse norms and values. They cannot assume that they share the value system of the disputants or that the disputants themselves agree on normative standards. Nor can they be familiar with the outcomes of similar disputes settled in the disputants' neighborhoods, which could serve as precedents. Public opinion cannot reinforce a decision reached in a private session attended only be mediators and disputants. Private hearings cannot serve as arenas to raise broader issues affecting entire neighborhoods. . . . Agreements are not solemnized with the kind of public ritual that in nonindustrial societies frequently serves to solidify the commitment of the parties to support the agreement and secure public approval.

Citizen dispute resolution programs may be most effective in disputes between parties involved in an ongoing relationship they wish to preserve. Although most centers purport to deal exclusively with conflicts in "ongoing social relationships," this phrase conceals an important distinction between relationships with a long past that are terminating and those with a short history but expectations of a long future. . . . The latter is the critical variable for mediation. The willingness of a tenant to compromise with his landlord may be far greater when he plans to stay in his apartment for another ten years than that of a tenant who has been there ten years but is planning to move the following week. Similarly, a domestic conflict in which both parties wish to preserve the relationship demands different treatment from one in which they are trying to establish the terms of their separation. Where separating parties share custody of a child, however, their relations will inevitably endure, and mediation can again be appropriate. Mediators are more likely to function successfully in disputes where both parties have an incentive to settle than in those where both wish only to win.

Further, mediation depends on a community fabric that links disputants in enduring relationships important to both and provides a shared set of values within which the dispute can be discussed. In the United States, urban ethnic enclaves often possess these qualities. . . . Programs in these social settings may be able to marshal in-

formal sanctions behind their actions by selecting influential and morally respected individuals as mediators and making hearings public.

A third implication of this cross-cultural survey of mediation is that the process may be more appropriate for concrete disputes that can be settled by a simple exchange of property than for complex, emotion-laden interpersonal hostilities arising out of tangled webs of insult and rivalry, abuse and counterabuse, love and hatred. Resolution of the latter often involves vague promises of changed behavior or avoidance. . . . It is this kind of dispute for which mediation is advocated and that judges, prosecutors, and the police feel least able to handle. . . . Yet there are indications that such cases are most resistant to long-term resolution through mediation, whereas the former result in outcomes that are easier to monitor and more likely to be viewed by disputants as satisfactory over the long run. . . . Those disputes most likely to be perceived by complainants as resolved in the long run (six to twelve months after the hearing) were landlord–tenant, harassment, and recovery of money or property; domestic or child welfare and neighborhood cases were least likely to be so perceived. . . . Ironically, the kinds of cases for which citizen dispute resolution is most often advocated thus seem resistant to mediation, whereas those in which it might be more effective are handled fairly effectively by adjudication. Programs may thus be more effective in relieving court congestion and shunting aside troublesome cases than in providing a more desirable process to those now poorly served in domestic and neighborhood disputes.

A fourth feature of mediation in small-scale societies, with critical implications for American programs, is the central role of coercion. Mediation in village and pastoral societies does not occur without coercion, but the latter takes the form of informal social pressures, fear of supernatural reprisals, and expectations of violence at the hands of the aggrieved party or the mediator, rather than that of state coercion. In American programs, the role of coercion is a recurring concern. . . . The staff and mediators of the Dade County Citizen Dispute Settlement Program, for example, see their program's "lack of teeth" as a major problem and suggest that they need subpoena power and legal enforcement of mediation agreements. . . . A persistent problem for many citizen dispute resolution programs is the high proportion of "no-shows"—disputants who fail to appear for scheduled hearings. The Florida mediators would like greater legal authority to cope with this. . . .

Moreover, the court is used to coerce disputants not only to mediate but also to settle and to abide by the outcome. In many programs, cases are continued by the court pending successful mediation so that disputants are negotiating in the shadow of the courthouse, aware that failure to agree will put them back before the judge. Mediators having difficulty persuading disputants to submit to mediation and reach an agreement threaten court action if the process stalls. The three federally funded neighborhood justice centers (NJCs) rely on the coercion implicit in referrals from police, prosecutors, or the court, which suggests that disputes not mediated will be adjudicated. . . .

Thus there are pressures within the citizen dispute resolution movement to rely more heavily on the coercive powers of the court or to demand new coercive powers for mediators in order to compensate for the absence of informal pressures. This endangers one of the primary attractions of mediation—its less coercive, more consensual process. Furthermore, this trend raises the specter of quasi-judicial entities exercising coercive powers outside the courts, controlling citizens without the legal safeguards of due process and the adversary system. . . . Such entities might become a way of expanding state intervention into the daily lives of citizens without proper regard for their legal rights. . . .

There are indications that citizen dispute resolution programs are coping with the problem of coercion through a second strategy: by producing settlements to which both parties will agree and that appear to provide a solution, yet that are essentially meaningless and unenforceable. Since a frequent measure of the success of citizen dispute resolution programs is the proportion of hearings reaching an agreement, resort to low-quality settlements is difficult to measure or evaluate. . . . Mediation programs have been criticized for their inability to deal with the underlying sources of social conflict such as social inequality, poverty, unemployment, racism, or sexism. Even in domestic disputes, however, mediation without coercion may not always produce the kinds of settlements desired. . . .

In my research on patterns of disputing in an American urban neighborhood, I found that disputants frequently appeal to the court in interpersonal disputes but use it as a sanction rather than as a forum for settling disputes. . . . It is predominantly those less capable of using violence, such as women and the elderly, who threaten or actually go to court, not because they expect to win an effective judgment (cases are often dismissed) but in order to equalize the balance. If this is the role courts are playing in domestic and neighbor disputes, mediation clearly can not provide an adequate substitute.

The criticism that mediation programs are generating meaningless settlements is supported by the facts that caseloads remain low although the programs appear to offer a much-needed service and that large numbers of cases apparently amenable to mediation continue to appear in courts. Many referrals fail to come to hearings, and the percentage of voluntary referrals is very small. In the first six months of operation, for example, the three neighborhood justice centers held 525 hearings, 86 per cent of which were declared resolved, yet this represents only 29 hearings per center per month, a surprisingly low number considering that each center serves a large metropolitan area. . . . Perhaps this low level of use simply represents public inertia or ignorance about these programs, but it is also possible that disputants perceive them as ineffective or inappropriate forums for dispute resolution and take their conflicts elsewhere.

Mediation may provide an effective tool for dispute resolution, however, if its capacities and processes are more carefully understood and its use more circumscribed. It seems most appropriate for those disputes in which both parties wish to maintain their relationship. This desire provides an incentive to settle, to seek peace rather than victory. Neighbors quarreling over a common boundary or separating spouses settling child

custody, for example, must find ways of living together, and this need to settle is itself a form of
pressure to agree.

The observed inequality of mediated settlements in small-scale societies raises troubling
questions about the quality of justice in American mediation centers. The impact of mediation
may be quite different, depending on whether
the dispute is between equals or unequals. Mediated settlements perpetuate differences in social
status—a characteristic with very different implications in nonindustrial ranked societies and
industrialized class societies that embrace an
egalitarian ideology. Conflicts between equals
and between unequals both fall under the rubric
of "ongoing social relationships" and may therefore be considered appropriate for mediation.
Yet there are significant differences between disputes among relative equals, such as neighbors
or local small merchants and regular customers,
and those between relative unequals, such as a violent husband and an abused wife or a large
merchant and a consumer. In disputes between
unequals, the weaker party may turn to a third
party to equalize the balance and seek an equitable resolution, as the powerless Cheyenne turns
to an important chief. . . . To be effective, the
third party must possess sufficient power to equalize the balance between the disputants. Unless
mediation centers address this problem or decide to deal only with disputes between equals,
they risk serving the weaker parties poorly by ac-
commodating their demands with inadequate
compensation while inhibiting their appeal to
courts where they could, at least in theory, demand a legally just settlement. . . . Of course,
considerable research suggests that courts also
serve to perpetuate inequalities. . . .

There are some indications that disputes
between unequals could become a significant
proportion of the mediation caseload, although
we lack information on this point from functioning programs. In the first six months of operation, the neighborhood justice centers found
that almost half of their respondents were representatives of corporations or public and private
organizations but that only 5 percent of complainants were. . . . In two reports on Florida
programs, respondents reported satisfaction
with the mediation process more often than

complainants, although these studies did not
tabulate the proportion of corporate representatives. . . . Thus, we must ask whether mediation
serves the weaker parties better than the courts
do or simply perpetuates inequalities, as it does
in small-scale societies. A mode of dispute resolution whose outcomes clearly reflect the economic and political inequalities of American
society may ultimately be unacceptable in a
polity based on legal, if not social, equality.

## CONCLUSIONS

Existing versions of mediation, particularly those
programs closely connected to courts, seem to
function quite differently from mediation in nonindustrial societies. These programs do not rely
on informal social controls rooted in the local
community. In heterogeneous urban neighborhoods where the social fabric of community is
loosely woven, mediation programs turn to the
threat of the court to achieve settlement. Since
one inspiration for mediation was dissatisfaction
with penal sanctions in interpersonal disputes,
their reappearance through the back door represents a return to a mode of sanctioning that has
already been judged inadequate. If disputants are
impelled to try to mediat[e] before they can use
the court, mediation centers may become meaningless at best and, at worst, another hurdle between the citizen and his day in court.

On the other hand, mediation has tremendous potential if it can be built on existing
community structures (where these exist) rather
than appended to the legal system; if it is restricted to disputes between relative equals, and
if it is used only in future-oriented disputes
where the parties feel a need to settle. It offers
hope for resolving disputes arising from faulty
communication and misunderstanding, those in
which both parties wish to avoid the criminal
penalties of the court, and those where an agreement involves a specific exchange rather than
long-term promises of improved behavior.

Perhaps a mediation program that endeavored to build on existing social structures and
mobilized informal social pressures through
public hearings and the use of influential community leaders as mediators within small areas
knit together through interlocking social rela-

tionships could achieve effective dispute resolution without recourse to the sanctions of the state. But in some settings, the social structure may be too diffuse and the population too transient to allow mediation to function as it does in the anthropological prototype. Mediation cannot serve as a panacea for the problems that plague the courts; nor can it, alone, reverse the trend toward the dissolution of the cohesive local community in American society.

Societies must always choose some course between the conflicting goals of order and liberty. The cumbersome, formalistic procedures of due process serve, at least ideally, to protect liberty and to preserve the rule of law against state oppression. However, the price of these procedural safeguards for the protection of individual freedom may be a certain level of disorder, of disruption or rule breaking that goes unpunished, and inefficiency in the processing of cases. The social changes of twentieth-century America have gradually loosened community control over behavior, allowing greater liberty to nonconforming, disruptive, and deviant individuals. With the dissolution of informal social controls, the perceived increase in disorder has led to heightened demands that the court restore order even in the domain of neighborhood and family conflicts. . . . From this perspective the citizen dispute resolution movement is an anomaly: It seeks to return control over nonacceptable behavior to the local community without sacrificing the greater measure of personal liberty and autonomy that the very breakdown in informal social controls have provided. Informal control mechanisms in small-scale societies produce order at the expense of individual freedom, particularly for individuals of lower rank or power. It is particularly instructive that those American settings in which mediation occurs naturally are also those where members and powerful leaders exert considerable control over their fellows. . . . If Americans are unwilling to return to a social world in which their actions can be judged and condemned by neighbors and fellow workers, mediation programs will be unable to function.

The alternative is to create institutions that appear to grant communities control over behavior yet that in reality simply provide a forum for handling disputes outside the protections of due process. . . . We still know too little about what mediation programs will do, but they contain the possibility of increasing state control over individual behavior outside the rule of law, of enhancing order at the expense of liberty.

## Notes and Questions

1. Daniel McGillis, a researcher at Harvard Law School's Center for Criminal Justice, offers an interpretation of the strengths and weaknesses of mediation programs that differs from that offered by the preceding authors:

> The survival and growth in numbers of dispute resolution programs suggests that they must be doing something right, especially given the routine demise of many other 1970s social programs. . . .
>
> While they have been successful in many respects, the programs have certainly failed to fulfill many of the early optimistic goals laid out for them. They were expected to reduce court caseloads in their jurisdictions, freeing up resources for the remaining cases on the docket. No demonstrable evidence exists that programs have remotely succeeded in this task. A corollary to that goal was an anticipated reduction in justice system costs (because mediation would be very cheap compared to adjudication). The courts have not been reported to be mailing checks of unexpended funds back to governmental treasuries, however. In fact, some mediation programs are quite expensive on a per-case basis. Programs have also typically failed to develop large caseloads (in comparison to comparable court caseloads). Some programs sponsored by the courts and the prosecutors' offices are exceptions to this pattern, and a few process over 10,000 cases per year. But we can probably say with some confidence after approximately ten years' experience with such programs that the American people are not eagerly beating a path to the programs' doors, although this may be due more to Americans' focus on court dispute settlement (as idealized on Perry Mason) than due to anything fundamentally wrong with dispute resolution programs.
>
> So what are the mediation programs doing right to justify the investment of scarce local and state governmental resources? The most likely achievement of the programs is that they provide a superior process for many of the

types of cases that they handle. Research studies support the casual impression that people like to have their cases mediated. They typically view the process as more fair and more understandable, and they like the agreements that are achieved. Agreements are reached in approximately 80 percent of mediation sessions. Disputants consistently report that they are satisfied with the mediation process and view outcomes as fair. . . . Research on the mediation of minor civil cases in the Maine District Courts indicates that defendants in mediated cases are far more likely to pay their settlement in full than defendants in comparable court cases (70% vs. 34%, respectively).*

2. Why might mediation programs seem to have trouble attracting users? Is size of caseload an indicator of success? What other factors should be considered in evaluating the success or failure of mediation programs?

3. Do you think it is important that people feel satisfied at the end of a case?

---

*Community Dispute Resolution Programs and Public Policy* (Washington, D.C.: U.S. Department of Justice, National Institute of Justice, 1986), pp. 13–14.

---

    ❧ The following reading raises concerns about why alternative dispute-resolution processes are appealing to state officials and policymakers. It considers the implications of mediation and other informal dispute-resolution practices for law and legal processes.

## 19.2 | Neighborhood Justice in Capitalist Society: The Expansion of the Informal State    *Richard Hofrichter*

. . . [T]he rule of law within the judicial system poses other constraints on the capacities of courts to handle effectively matters that come before them. . . . The judicial system is organized to handle certain types of disputes deemed appropriate. But the definition of appropriate keeps changing. For example, so-called small-scale or minor disputes have either been rejected by courts as nonjusticiable or relegated to small claims courts, shifted to arbitration procedures, or placed in a lesser priority on the docket. Such disputes are often described by judicial officials as "junk cases." Increasingly these types of neighborhood disputes at the level of everyday life—in contrast to those that involve loss of money or which occur among people who can handle them on their own—are becoming more disruptive to the social order. They disrupt the infrastructural

stability necessary for capital accumulation. As Wolf Heydebrand explains,

> a decreased capacity for formal conflict resolution may actually increase the level of substantive conflict in the larger society. Thus, by dismissing cases or inducing settlements, courts may temporarily terminate conflicts but not ultimately resolve them. Instead, disputes are forced back into an indeterminate situation, that is, into the arena of conflicting socio-economic forces which had generated the dispute in the first place. . . .

As the economy sinks into deeper crisis, and as citizens use the courts to secure their rights under public programs . . . , the disputes of working-class people with the state and among themselves may proliferate. More is at stake for them. But these people are not socialized to the ways of the courts. Judicial procedures are designed for the middle and upper classes and their problems. Formal procedures and the rule of law cannot handle the particularisms brought

---

into court by people who cannot deal with formalism. Because the court is limited by formal procedural rules, it cannot confront the roots of conflict. It cannot therefore manage with precision solutions external to legal logic, given the relations between capital expansion and social disruption which have been described. Preemptive political intervention is required, regardless of whether such disruption can be defined by specific legal offenses.

The courts are increasingly politicized. They are geared to the protection of government policy against numerous claimants (e.g., Social Security, Medicaid and affirmative action). Under those conditions they become surrogates of the state and therefore less visibly autonomous. Sometimes they must protect the working class in a time of rising entitlements and at other times they become more of a foe as the state reduces entitlements. However, this relation of claimants with the state creates a crisis of legitimacy. When courts are perceived as not resolving disputes but as protecting the state and sometimes capital

(e.g., anti-trust, oil leasing decisions), dissatisfaction occurs and hegemony is undermined. People do not use courts to be treated as a social problem but in order to receive a hearing. Disorder can thus mean too many people using the courts and making claims against the state. Too much litigation from the point of view of capital is thereby a form of disorder.

Legal rules and procedures in many ways are part of the infrastructure of daily life and in that sense represent a form of hegemony. For example, people take the courts and its rules for granted, as an orderly part of their communities. . . . But increasingly, the kinds of conflicts arising in communities are more disruptive than previously. As judicial institutions become more isolated, bureaucratic, divorced from everyday life, and separated from the communities they serve, law loses legitimacy. The distinction between its reified abstractions and the culture become visible, experienced. The administrative failures of law in its implementation heighten its vulnerability and claims to legitimacy. . . .

## 19.3 | The Navajo Nation's Peacemaker Division: An Integrated, Community-Based Dispute Resolution Forum

*Howard L. Brown, Esq.*

### INTRODUCTION

For hundreds of years, the *Dine'*, or Navajo people, have used a community-based dispute resolution ceremony to resolve conflicts. The ceremony integrates the wisdom, skills and perspectives of a variety of participants in order to reach noncoercive settlements that return the disputants and the community at large to a state of harmony. Because the contemporary Navajo Peacemaker Division relies on a customary dispute resolution method, experts argue that the Division is better considered a forum for "tradi-

tional" dispute resolution than "alternative" dispute resolution. Although the Navajo Nation Judicial Branch includes a well-developed court system based on the Anglo-American model, Navajo judges, legislators and citizens assert that traditional dispute resolution mechanisms more fully comport with Navajo customs and thus are more effective in resolving the conflicts that arise among Navajo people and within the Navajo Nation.

In order to understand the Peacemaker Division and the role it plays in resolving disputes, some familiarity with the Navajo Nation and the Navajo Nation Judicial Branch is necessary. The Navajo Nation is a sovereign Indian nation, with reserved territories of over 25,000 square miles in Arizona, New Mexico and Utah. It has a population in excess of 220,000 people. The Nation's government has three independent and separate

"The Navajo Nation's Peacemaker Division," Howard L. Brown, Esq., *American Indian Law Review*, 1999/2000, Vol. 24, No. 297. Reprinted with permission. (Footnotes have been omitted.)

branches, including the judicial branch. The judicial branch consists of a district court (with seven judicial districts located throughout the Navajo Nation, and including a family court division) and a supreme court (located in the Navajo Nation's capital, Window Rock). The district courts assert original jurisdiction to adjudicate disputes involving persons who reside within the Navajo Nation or who have caused an action or Navajo Nation crime to occur within the Navajo Nation. Navajo common law and statutory law are the laws of preference, although judges may apply federal and state law if a matter is not addressed by Navajo law.

Navajo common law, or traditional law, "reflects the customs, usages and traditions of the Navajo People, formed by Navajo values in action." Navajo judges fashion accepted customs and practices into a contemporary, working common law in a similar manner as do judges in other cultures and legal systems. For example, in a 1996 Supreme Court decision, the justices analyzed due process in "light of the customs and traditions, or common law, of the Navajo people." The court stated:

> The Navajo principle of *k'e* is important to understanding Navajo due process. *K'e* frames the Navajo perception of moral right, and therefore this court's interpretation of due process rights. *K'e* contemplates one's unique, reciprocal relationships to the community and the universe. It promotes respect, solidarity, compassion and cooperation so that people may live in *hozho,* or harmony. *K'e* stresses the duties and obligations of individuals relative to their community.

The court concluded, "In Navajo law, *k'e* would be the mutual understanding and normative practice that defines a person's legitimate claim to fair procedures."

The Navajo judiciary's application of Navajo common law is significant for a number of reasons. First, in using familiar cultural norms to resolve disputes, the courts are a more familiar and less hostile forum for individual Navajo people to use. Thus, individuals implicitly are encouraged to utilize their court system, which in turn strengthens the legitimacy of the Nation's judi-

cial branch and the sovereignty of the Nation's government. Second, the contemporary use and application of Navajo common law helps to preserve Navajo traditions and cultural norms. In 1892, the U.S. Secretary of the Interior established Anglo-American style courts for the Navajo people. The federally appointed Navajo judges of these so-called CFR [Code of Federal Regulation] courts were not intended to apply traditional Navajo principles. To the contrary, CFR courts were designed to assimilate Navajos into the dominant Anglo-American culture by outlawing Navajo customs. In 1959, the Navajo Nation Tribal Council abolished the CFR courts and established the Navajo tribal courts "to keep the states from exerting jurisdiction over the Navajo Nation." Today, Navajo Nation judges expressly refer to Navajo common law when resolving disputes, thus preserving traditional knowledge and customs for future generations of Navajo people.

The third reason that the Navajo courts' application of Navajo common law is significant is because the courts' actions serve as a model for dispute resolution advocates considering alternatives to the adversarial, Anglo-American model of settling conflicts. As former Chief Judge J. Clifford Wallace of the U.S. Court of Appeals for the Ninth Circuit wrote, "Federal courts would do well to look to traditional tribal courts [that] employ a time-honored system of dispute resolution that predates and predicts modern successes with **mediation**."

In the early 1980s, the Navajo Common Law Project was formed as an ongoing effort to learn about, collect and use Navajo wisdom, methods and customs in resolving disputes. Project researchers soon learned of a long-standing method of dispute resolution in which respected members of the community assist disputants and other interested parties to reach noncoercive, consensual agreements to conflicts. Project participants passed what they learned to the Navajo Nation Judicial Conference, which was eager to adopt a customary method of dispute resolution as an alternative to the Anglo-American, adversarial model of achieving justice. In 1982, the Judicial Conference created the Peacemaker Court, now known as the Peacemaker Division, to implement customary methods of resolving disputes.

The Peacemaker Division institutionalizes the custom of *hozhooji naat'aanii,* or peacemaking. Peacemaking consists of a justice ceremony in which disputants and community members gather to "talk things out" with the assistance of a respected community leader, or *naat'aanii* (peacemaker), to reach a consensual settlement. *Hozhooji naat'aanii* aims to reach solutions through consensus and to solve problems through restorative justice. Wrongdoing and conflict among members of the Navajo community are "regarded as . . . symptom[s] of things being out of place, or in dissonance." Thus, the object of peacemaking is not to punish, but to return individuals and the community to a state of *hozho,* or harmony.

Peacemaking assumes the superiority of an integrated approach to resolving disputes. That is, the Peacemaking process integrates and utilizes the wisdom, skills and perspectives of a variety of people, including the disputants, the disputants' relatives and friends, the *naat'aanii,* local government bodies known as chapters, judges, clerks of court, other interested parties, and in some rare circumstances, lawyers. The integrated approach to dispute resolution is consistent with Navajo principles of harmony, community and clan relationships, as well as a Navajo sense of solidarity, or oneness of "self with family, community, nature, and the cosmos—all reality."

*Hozhooji naat'aanii* may be used to resolve and address a variety of issues including, but not limited to, marital strife, disputes among spouses, parents and children, neighborhood conflicts stemming from nuisance or animal trespass, misconduct related to alcohol or drug abuse, transactional disputes and other conduct causing disunity to the community.

Disputes may come to the Peacemaker Division in one of two ways. District court judges may transfer cases to a *naat'aanii* when doing so is in the interest of justice. Alternatively, disputants themselves may seek the assistance of a peacemaker by submitting a request to their local district court clerk of court. In such cases, the clerk immediately presents the request to a judge, who may meet with the disputants before granting or denying the request. If the request is granted, as is generally the case, the judge may appoint a *naat'aanii* to conduct the peacemaking.

The judge may select the *naat'aanii* from a list compiled and certified at meetings of local chapters and maintained by the court clerk. Otherwise, the court may appoint the *naat'aanii* "from qualified persons known to it or any person recommended as being qualified as a peacemaker." The Navajo Peacemaker Court Manual states that:

> Any person who has the respect of the community of his or her residence, an ability to work with chapter members, and a reputation for integrity, honesty, humanity and an ability to resolve local problems shall be eligible to be appointed as a peacemaker. Members of the Navajo Tribal Council, Chapter governments, Native American Church chapters, medicine men or members of any other organization or group which has the respect of the individuals who will come before the Peacemaker Court may be appointed [as] peacemakers.

Alternatively, disputants may agree among themselves to retain a particular individual to serve as the peacemaker for their dispute. In such cases, the peacemaker may be any individual that the disputants select unanimously. The *naat'aanii* is considered to be an officer of the court and thus enjoys multiple privileges and bears many responsibilities. The peacemaker is authorized to "use traditional and customary Navajo methods and other accepted nonjudgmental methods to mediate disputes and obtain the resolution of problems through agreement." In addition to fulfilling the role of mediator, the peacemaker may be authorized by the disputants to arbitrate the conflict. The *naat'aanii* may "instruct or lecture individuals on the traditional Navajo teachings relevant to their problem" as a means of resolving the dispute. Additionally, the peacemaker has the power of subpoena to compel persons involved in the dispute to participate in its resolution.

A district court judge retains supervisory authority over the peacemaker and the peacemaking sessions. In addition to ensuring that qualified peacemakers are selected and that the proceedings run smoothly and fairly, the supervising judge may issue protective orders ending the peacemaking process on grounds including misconduct by the peacemaker. As officers of the court, peacemakers are bound by the Navajo Nation Code of Judicial Conduct and are subject to dismissal for violations of ethical standards.

The Peacemaker Division Rules do not mandate a particular technique or style of dispute resolution beyond those guidelines described above. However, the primacy of tradition and custom provides a framework for the peacemaking ceremony, and, thus, most proceedings follow a similar pattern. The *naat'aanii* opens the proceedings with a prayer to summon the assistance of the supernatural, focus the minds of the participants and create an atmosphere of *hozho,* or harmony. The participants then have an opportunity to "talk things out," express their positions and listen to one another. Often, parties sit in a circle or around a table facing one another. Relatives and other interested parties have an important role to play. A sister scolds her brother for the strife that he has caused their family; relatives explain to a wayward husband his duties to family and community; grandparents reveal knowledge of a son's paternity. A 1993 newspaper article reported on a case in which a husband allegedly battered his wife during an alcoholic-related domestic dispute:

> [The wife] opted to take the case to a peacemaker court instead of regular tribal court. Eight friends and relatives of her husband showed up . . . for the hearing and told [the husband] how much they respected him and explained his duties, in the Navajo tradition, to his family and to the community. Since the hearing, [the wife] said, her husband has acted differently because he "knows people think of him as a special person."

The *naat'aanii* listens carefully, helps to guide the conversation and attempts to lead the disputants to *hozho.* He or she may point out the true causes of the dispute and the disputants' disharmony. The peacemaker may explain to the parties how they violated Navajo values. He or she often relates the dispute to the Navajo creation story, in which the Hero Twins engaged in a lengthy odyssey of trial, assistance-seeking and education before they slew the world's *nayee,* or monsters.

Importantly, the *naat'aanii* is not, in a strict sense, "neutral." Rather, he or she offers a point of view that is grounded in Navajo values. Through the following example, Peacemaker Division experts Philmer Bluehouse and James W. Zion illustrate the peacemaker's role in offering a Navajo point of view. "If there is a land dispute, this story may be told by the peacemaker to guide the parties:

> Before humans assumed their present form, the Holy People had their own problems to address. During that time, Lightning and Horned Toad had a dispute. Horned Toad was walking on some land, when suddenly Lightning confronted Horned Toad and asserted that he, Lightning, owned the land and Horned Toad must leave immediately. Horned Toad replied, 'My brother, I don't understand why you should have possession of this land, and I certainly don't lay claim to it.' He continued along. Again, Lightning asserted his claim, and he threw a bolt of lightning as a warning. Horned Toad said, 'I am very humble, and I can't hurt you as you can hurt others with your bolt of lightning. Could we talk about this tomorrow? I'll be waiting to talk with you on top of the refuse left there by Brother Water.' Lightning agreed.
>
> The following day, Horned Toad arrived, wearing his armor. Lightning announced his arrival and asserted his power by throwing more lightning bolts at Horned Toad.
>
> Horned Toad sat atop a pile of driftwood, which was left behind after a storm. From atop that pile, he discussed the matter with Lightning. Horned Toad said, 'You are very powerful; you can certainly strike me down with a bolt of lightning.' 'I certainly can,' said Lightning. 'That's not what we are here about,' said Horned Toad. 'We are here to discuss the land ownership issue, and we must talk.' 'There is nothing to discuss; the land is mine!' Lightning got angry and threw another bolt of lightning, which hit Horned Toad. 'Brother, you did not hurt me,' he said. The bolt bounced off Horned Toad's armor. 'Brother,' he said, 'this armor was given to me by the same source as your bolts of lightning.

Why is it we are arguing over the land, which was also loaned to us?'"

The story "takes land complainants back to the true 'owner,' and it is a forceful traditional precedent to take the parties to common ground." It also reminds people of the importance of "talking things out" and the natural power and "armor" that comes through peaceful, consensual forms of resolving disputes.

After all of the participants have the opportunity to speak, the peacemaker engages them in *hozhoojigo*, a process of developing a plan to settle the dispute. The process, as with all other parts of *hozhooji naat'aanii*, should be noncoercive and consensual. Further, *hozhoojigo* should be aimed at restoring harmony and creating a new, ongoing relationship among the participants and the community, which, according to Navajo justice concepts, is entitled to "the return of its members to a state of harmony."

Once the parties reach an agreement, they may opt to enter it as a court judgment. According to the Peacemaker Court Rules, a judgment may be entered if the court has proper jurisdiction, the judgment contains the agreement as reached through the peacemaking procedure and all necessary parties have actual knowledge of the judgment and agree to it. Once entered, the judgment may be enforced as any other judgment of the court. However, in actual practice most agreements reached through the peacemaking ceremony are not entered as court judgments. Instead, parties often follow the traditional practices of executing simple oral or written agreements memorializing the peacemaking settlement. In all cases, the peacemaker must report the results of the peacemaking ceremony to the supervising district court judge.

## CONCLUSION

With over 250 certified peacemakers throughout the Navajo Nation, *hozhooji naat'aanii* is a well-utilized and successful exercise of traditional dispute resolution. During the years between 1986 and 1990, one Navajo judge alone referred over fifty cases to the Peacemaker Division. Peacemaking successfully reached agreement in all but two of those cases. In the first three months of 1992,

twenty-four disputes were handled by peacemakers. By comparison, in the first three months of 1993, nearly one hundred disputes were submitted to the Peacemaking Division. The growing use and acceptance of *hozhooji naat'aanii* heralds its acceptance in the community as a legitimate forum for resolving a myriad of disputes.

The non-Navajo world can learn a great deal from the Peacemaker Division. Official delegations from countries such as Canada, Australia, New Zealand, Namibia and South Africa have visited the Navajo Nation with hopes of learning about and incorporating traditional models of dispute resolution into their own justice systems. As the Navajo judiciary continues to use and develop traditional dispute resolution mechanisms, other Indian nations and non-Indian societies should take the opportunity to observe, learn from and practice the wisdom manifested in *hozhooji naat'aanii*.

## *Notes and Questions*

1. What are the differences between the way that the Navajos use mediation and the way it is used in the formal American legal system?

2. Most informal dispute resolution practices emphasize the importance of third-party neutrality. Community mediation programs use third-party mediators who are not known to the parties on the premise that this ensures fairness and lack of bias. In contrast, the Navajos use mediators who are respected members of the community and are known by the parties. Would the Navajo model work in the community mediation context?

3. Does neutrality ensure fairness? How can fairness be assessed in informal dispute resolution?

4. Some researchers have defined mediation as a storytelling process. In this context, Sara Cobb and Janet Rifkin have argued that "mediators legitimize certain stories over others—once the magic of mediation is critically examined, it must be understood as a political process which privileges certain speakers/disputants over others"[‡]

---

[‡]Cobb, S., & Rifkin, J. (1991) "Practice and Paradox: Deconstructing Neutrality in Mediation." *Journal of Social Inquiry, 16*, 201–227.

# 20 MEDIATION AS RESTORATIVE JUSTICE

❧ The following article examines a form of mediation that is being used in criminal cases, providing an opportunity for victims of crime to confront the offender. The idea behind this approach is to promote greater opportunities for victims of crimes to participate in the justice process and to promote "healing" for both the victim and the offender.

## 20.1  The Development and Impact of Victim-Offender Mediation in the United States  *Mark S. Umbreit*

FOR MANY PUBLIC OFFICIALS and citizens at large, the idea of a crime victim sitting face-to-face with his or her offender is difficult to conceive. "Why would any victim want to meet the criminal?" "Victims are angry; they want more severe punishment of offenders." "What's in it for the victim?" "Why would any offender ever be willing to meet his or her victim?" "What is there to mediate or negotiate anyway?" Such comments and questions are frequently to be heard among those who are unfamiliar with the actual process of victim-offender mediation and even among some individuals in the larger field of alternative dispute resolution.

The fact remains, however, that in a growing number of communities throughout North America and Europe, crime victims are meeting face-to-face with their offenders in the presence of a trained mediator. People who have been victimized have the opportunity to tell offenders how the crime affected them. They can get answers to lingering questions that they have, such as "Why me?" and "Were you watching my movements?" Those who have committed certain types of criminal offenses are able to tell their stories, portray a more human dimension to their characters, own up to their behavior, and make amends. To-

gether, both parties have the opportunity to negotiate a mutually agreeable restitution plan for compensating the victim.

In the late 1970s, only a handful of programs provided victim-offender mediation and reconciliation services, nearly exclusively in the United States and Canada. Today, as illustrated in Figure 20.1-A, there are approximately 125 victim-offender mediation programs in the United States and nearly 30 in Canada. An even larger number of programs exist in Europe, where the field began developing in the mid-1980s (largely based upon the victim-offender reconciliation program model used in Canada and the United States). Programs are now developing more rapidly in Europe than in North America.

The field of victim-offender mediation is no longer simply an experiment. Rather, it is an emerging field of alternative dispute resolution that continues to grow, yet is little understood by many. The application of mediation techniques in the context of victim-offender conflict is both similar to and different from more traditional mediation programs. An overview of the practice of mediating victim-offender conflicts follows, beginning with the historical roots of the movement and its rationale and moving on to describe the process, different program models, and the style of mediation usually employed. In addition, similarities and differences with traditional mediation are highlighted, along with what has been learned from research. The article concludes by identifying a number of dangers that face the field of victim-offender mediation, as well as the opportu-

Mark S. Umbreit, "The Development and Impact of Victim-Offender Mediation in the United States," *Mediation Quarterly*, Vol. 12, No. 3, pp. 263–276, 1995. Copyright © 1995 Mediation Quarterly. Reprinted by permission of Jossey-Bass, Inc. (References have been omitted.)

**FIGURE 20.1-A**   *International Development of Victim-Offender Mediation Programs*

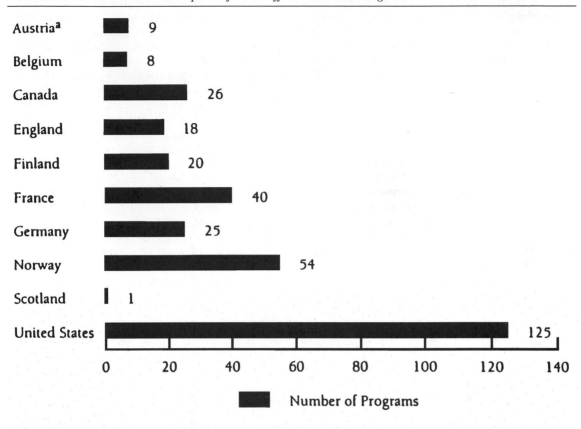

[a]Austria's federal policy makes victim-offender mediation available to youth in any of Austria's 143 cities within its nine provinces.

nities that exist. While reference will be made to the development of victim-offender mediation throughout North America and Europe, the overview focuses primarily upon the United States.

## HISTORICAL DEVELOPMENT

The victim-offender movement appears to have grown out of at least two distinct traditions. Particularly during the mid to late 1970s, there appears to have been little awareness or information sharing between programs experimenting with the concept of mediating victim-offender conflict. The field of victim-offender mediation in the United States is often associated with the development in 1978 of the first victim-offender

reconciliation program (VORP) in Elkhart, Indiana. This initial U.S. VORP was a joint effort of the Mennonite Central Committee and the PACT (Prisoner and Community Together) organization. It was modeled after the initial Canadian VORP that began in 1974 in Kitchener, Ontario. To this day, the VORP tradition remains the most clearly articulated and documented expression of victim-offender mediation, and it has greatly influenced the larger field, particularly private community-based agencies and some church-related organizations.

Another tradition, however, actually predates the VORP movement and has been located in public criminal justice agencies, primarily probation departments. The initial efforts to experiment with bringing crime victims and their young offenders face-to-face can be traced back to the 1960s when a small number of probation departments began to see the value of such a confrontation. A total of thirty-four programs involving victim-offender mediation in the juvenile justice system were begun between 1965 and 1979. If one looks for the language of mediation in these programs, little will be found. However, the actual process employed during these early years, while certainly not fitting today's technical definition of mediation, clearly approximates what we now understand to be victim-offender mediation.

Another example of a victim-offender mediation program is the Minnesota Restitution Center, established in 1970 in Minneapolis by the Minnesota Department of Corrections. In this program, adult property offenders who had been diverted from prison and placed in a residential center would meet with their victims to determine restitution plans. While the people running this nationally recognized program model did not frame what they were doing as mediation, the actual process they were using was quite similar in many, but not all, respects with what is now called victim-offender mediation.

## RATIONALE FOR VICTIM-OFFENDER MEDIATION

The contemporary development of victim-offender mediation and reconciliation in both North America and Europe is occurring within the context of recent developments in social theory that speak of two different paradigms of justice. In the context of the old paradigm of *retributive justice,* the state is the primary victim and the focus of attention is upon the offender who violated the interests of the state. The individual victim is placed in a passive position. Victims have little if any participation or input in the justice process. The retributive justice paradigm assumes adversarial relationships between victims and offenders while focusing upon the imposition of severe punishment in order to deter or prevent future crime. The interpersonal character of criminal behavior does not receive any attention nor do the specific interests of individual victims. Zehr argues that within this old paradigm the actual conflict between the offender and his or her victim is often heightened.

The *restorative justice* paradigm views crime quite differently, defining it as a violation of one person by another, not a violation of state interests. In this new paradigm, a focus is placed upon problem solving for the future rather than upon establishing blame for past behavior, and dialogue and negotiation are normative. Rather than imposing severe punishment, restorative justice emphasizes restitution as a means of restoring both parties; reconciliation of the parties is the goal. Victims are no longer ignored, nor are offenders placed in an entirely passive role. Instead, the paradigm of restorative justice places both victim and offender in active and interpersonal problem-solving roles.

A growing number of studies are questioning some of the underlying assumptions of the retributive justice paradigm. This body of research would suggest that the general public, and crime victims specifically, are far less vindictive than commonly portrayed. Many victims appear to be quite supportive of alternative programs, including mediation, that focus on providing a range of social services for offenders and their victims within a community-based setting.

The criminal justice system is driven by its focus upon the offender. As a result, crime victims are nearly always placed in a totally passive position. They frequently do not even receive basic assistance or information. A sense of powerlessness and vulnerability is experienced by most crime victims. Some even feel revictimized by the impersonal treatment they receive from the criminal justice system. That system often treats them the same way the offender did, as an object, a piece of evidence, rather than a person with feelings and concerns. Offenders are rarely able to understand or be confronted with the real human impact of their criminal behavior, to learn that victims are people, not just targets or objects to be abused. Those who violate the law have many rationalizations for their criminal behavior. For both victim and offender, anger, frustration, and conflict are often increased as they move through the retributive justice process.

Rather than continuing the depersonalization that occurs in the criminal and juvenile justice systems, the process of mediating victim-offender conflict draws upon some rather old-fashioned principles that view crime as being fundamentally against people, not just the state.

Instead of emphasizing an adversarial process that places the state's interests above the individual victim's interests and allows for little if any direct accountability by the offender to the person he or she has wronged, victim-offender mediation facilitates an active and personal process that works at conflict resolution. By attempting to address the interests of both parties, victim-offender mediation represents a unique process within the larger criminal justice system.

## PROGRAM MODELS

At least four different models of victim-offender mediation have emerged during the past decade. (It should be noted that many of these programs, particularly those that were initially either offender oriented or victim oriented, have in common an emphasis on the use of community volunteers as mediators.)

**Church-Related Programs**   The initial development of the VORP model, the best-documented and best-known expression of the victim-offender mediation concept, was closely linked to the efforts of Mennonite volunteers and probation staff in both Canada and the United States. As noted by Howard Zehr, the director of the first VORP in the United States and the current director of the Office of Criminal Justice for the Mennonite Central Committee U.S., "The biblical perspective seems to view crime as a rupture, a wound in the health of the community that must be healed. The emphasis is upon healing— reestablishing right relationships—through reparation rather than retribution."

Over the years, the VORP model has been embraced by people of many different religious and secular traditions. The Mennonite church, however, continues to play a leadership role in promoting the value of victim-offender reconciliation as part of a larger commitment to a restorative, rather than retributive, vision of justice.

The clearest example of the church-related model of victim-offender mediation and reconciliation is seen in the relatively small number of programs that are directly sponsored and largely funded by various specific churches. Other church-related programs are agencies that are free-standing and community-based but that are funded primarily, if not exclusively, by church members and organizations.

The VORP program in Fresno County, California, is perhaps the best example of a church-related program. With close linkages to the Mennonite church, it has developed into a strong program receiving over 400 referrals of juvenile offenders annually. This program receives no government funds and has developed a growing base of individual contributors from the Christian community. Another example of church-related programs is seen in the efforts of Justice Fellowship, an evangelical Christian organization. Through its national network of volunteers and a relatively small staff, Justice Fellowship is actively promoting restorative justice and church-based victim-offender reconciliation programs, and it has been instrumental in initiating several church-based programs.

**Community-Based Criminal Justice Private Agencies**   The largest portion of programs has been developed by private nonprofit agencies that have had a history of working within the criminal justice system. Some of these programs began working with offenders and later expanded into the area of victim services. The PACT (Prisoner and Community Together) organization, based in Valparaiso, Indiana, is a good example of a community-based criminal justice private agency.

During its initial development, PACT focused exclusively upon residential, job, and advocacy services for offenders and ex-offenders. Several years later, it broadened its mission to include victim services, initiating the first victim/witness assistance program in Michigan City, Indiana, and later working with the Mennonite Central Committee on the development of the first VORP project in the United States.

The Minnesota Citizens Council on Crime and Justice, in Minneapolis, is another example of a community-based agency providing a wide range of services initially to offenders but now to both offenders and victims. In fact, the Minnesota Citizens Council was one of the first agencies in the United States to initiate a multiservice crime victim center, where several thousand victims a year are served. The Minnesota Citizens Council Mediation Services operates a victim-offender mediation program that was initiated in 1985.

A number of other community-based programs, however, developed as entirely new nonprofit agencies. These victim-offender mediation agencies have had a particularly difficult time in developing their programs and securing funding without the assistance and resources of a larger umbrella organization. More recently, a number of victim advocacy agencies are considering or actually developing a victim-offender mediation component. The Victim/Witness Assistance Program in Dauphin County (Harrisburg), Pennsylvania, is a good example of such an agency.

**Probation-Based Agencies**  Probation-based agencies in a number of different states, usually working with juveniles, have been involved in the development of victim-offender mediation from its inception. In fact, the first U.S. VORP, in Elkhart, was initially developed and coordinated by probation officers, who in a very short period of time realized it would operate more effectively under the sponsorship of a private community-based agency. At the same time that the first VORP developed in northern Indiana, the Dakota County Juvenile Probation Department, in southern Minnesota, initiated its Face To Face program. With virtually no awareness of VORPs and little reference to mediation terminology, this program clearly embraced the basic principles of victim-offender mediation. One important exception to the principles, however, which occurred in a number of other probation-based programs as well, was the use of probation officers to serve as mediators. Probation officers were obviously not neutral third parties.

Other probation-based programs either hired a new staff person to work exclusively as a mediator, with no traditional probation/supervision caseload, or made use of community volunteers as mediators. In the Earn It program in Quincy, Massachusetts, for example, a juvenile court judge took leadership in securing additional resources to hire a new person to serve exclusively in the program's mediation/restitution component. The victim-offender mediation programs in Dallas and Austin, Texas, are examples of probation-based programs that use trained volunteer mediators from local dispute settlement centers.

Since probation-based programs are clearly not the work of neutral third parties, having program staff do the initial case referral/development and then having trained community volunteers serve as the mediators is a particularly good strategy for insuring the integrity of the mediation process in these programs.

**Dispute Settlement Centers**  A model that has been present since the early development of mediated conflict between offenders and victims, and that appears to be growing now, consists of established community dispute settlement centers that add a victim-offender mediation component. There are many obvious advantages to this model. The established agency already has a pool of trained mediators and is familiar with the field of conflict resolution. Adding a new program component to an existing dispute settlement center that has been handling primarily neighborhood disputes is likely to require less time and fewer resources than other new programs would demand. And the existing credibility of the agency should greatly enhance the development of the new program. A possible difficulty can be found, however, in using mediators trained in one kind of conflict resolution to work in another kind of conflict resolution, one that has been found to be more effective when a different case management process is employed.

In addition to the four models just described, a number of other models exist that are not as representative of the field. A sheriff's department in upstate New York has sponsored a program using the concept of victim-offender mediation and reconciliation since the early 1980s. Based in Genesee County, New York, the program has focused primarily upon violent crimes. The State Department of Corrections in Oklahoma sponsors a statewide postconviction victim-offender mediation program that works with both property and certain violent crimes. Oklahoma is the only state that has a clear, legislatively authorized mechanism for implementing victim-offender mediation on a systemwide basis. The victim-offender mediation program in Albuquerque is jointly sponsored by the New Mexico Center for Dispute Resolution and the Juvenile Probation Department. The agencies share funding and staffing for the program.

## COMPARISON WITH MEDIATION IN OTHER SETTINGS

Mediating conflict between crime victims and their offenders is clearly an unusual application of mediation techniques. It is not, however, contrary to the basic definition and criteria for mediation. However, the context in which victim-offender mediation operates results in a number of distinct differences from more traditional applications of mediation.

Nearly all other applications of mediation occur among individuals with some prior situational or interpersonal relationship (landlord/tenant, spousal, employer/employee, farmer/creditor, and the like). In victim-offender conflict most, but not all, participants in mediation are strangers. The issues in the conflict are clearer. There is a clear victim and a perpetrator who has admitted his or her guilt. Determination of guilt is not the focus. The mediation process is a time-limited, problem-solving intervention. It promotes a sense of justice as restorative, through the sharing of information and the negotiation of restitution by the victim and offender themselves.

Power imbalance is of major concern to most mediators. Precisely because there are a clear victim and a clear offender, an enormous situational imbalance of power exists. It would be inappropriate to assume that both parties are contributing to the conflict, necessitating the need for a neutral terminology such as "disputants." One of the individuals has been violated, and therefore, special attention must be directed toward that victim in order to ensure that he or she is not revictimized by the mediation process. This additional sensitivity to the victim does not have to come at the cost of a program's being insensitive to the offender or violating the very process of third-party negotiations. It does, however, mean that victims must have absolute voluntary choice about their participation in the program. The time and location of the mediation session must not violate their sense of what is safe, appropriate, and convenient.

Applying the mediation process with strangers may be considered by some mediators to be quite difficult. However, experience in the field of victim-offender mediation suggests the contrary. Far less emotional and historical baggage is present. During the mediation process, the prominent dynamic is one of breaking down stereotypes and related fears rather than addressing issues of betrayal and mistrust that are rooted in highly charged emotions and/or lengthy prior relationships.

In mediating victim-offender conflict, there is usually also a generational imbalance of power. The offender is frequently a juvenile or young adult, and the victim is an adult. When the offender is inarticulate, it is important to prepare, even coach, the offender during the prior individual meeting. This coaching resembles informal role-playing more than it does directing an individual what to say in response to specific questions the victim might ask. The opportunity to think through some of the possible questions and express one's thoughts in a less threatening situation than the actual victim-offender meeting is important for many offenders. It makes them likely to be more prepared to interact directly with the victim during the mediation session. This preparation represents one strategy for attempting to balance power in the context of age and communication differences. (Sometimes the same dynamic is present when the victim is a young person also.)

It is in the area of political ideology that the concept of victim-offender mediation differs most significantly from more traditional applications of mediation. Americans have strong feelings about crime and punishment. These feelings often result from the way in which the most atrocious, and least representative, crimes are frequently highlighted by the media and many politicians. We are an exceptionally punitive society, having the highest per capita rate of incarceration in the world after Russia and having recently surpassed South Africa. Alternative dispute resolution within the context of civil court conflict may be controversial to some. It does not, however, confront major ideological barriers related to crime control policy in U.S. society. The moment mediation enters the criminal justice process, however, it has stepped over a powerful ideological threshold. On the one hand, there is growing evidence among both criminal justice officials and the participants themselves that victim-offender mediation can be quite consistent with the community's sense of justice and fairness. On the other hand, there is likely to remain strong resistance by some officials and citizens to the very notion of embodying restorative justice in the victim-offender mediation process. The more dominant retributive sense of justice, with its emphasis on the severity of punishment on behalf of state interests, even at the cost of addressing the direct interests of the person violated by the offense, is deeply rooted in contemporary U.S. culture. It is unlikely to be dramatically changed in the near future.

## WHAT WE HAVE LEARNED

A small but growing amount of research in the field of victim-offender mediation is providing increasing insight into how the mediation process works and the impact it is having on those who participate in it and on the larger justice system.

The first large multisite evaluation of victim-offender mediation programs in the United States, based on 1,153 interviews with victims and juvenile offenders in four U.S. cities (Albuquerque; Austin, Texas; Minneapolis; and Oakland, California) led to a number of important findings. Victim-offender mediation programs resulted in very high levels of satisfaction among both parties. Victims who participated in mediation were far more likely to feel the justice system had treated them fairly than were similar victims who went through the normal court process. Over 90 percent of mediation sessions produced a negotiated restitution plan to compensate the victim, and more than four out of five offenders complied with their restitution obligations. The mediation process had a strong effect on humanizing the justice system response to crime for both victims and juvenile offenders. Victim-offender mediation helped reduce fear and anxiety among crime victims. Victims who engaged in mediation were far more likely to receive the agreed upon restitution than were similar victims assigned restitution as a result of a court order only. Considerably fewer and less serious additional crimes were committed within a one-year period by juvenile offenders who partici-

pated in a victim-offender mediation program than by similar offenders who did not participate in mediation. However, this finding was not statistically significant because of the size of the program samples.

## DANGERS

As the field of victim-offender mediation continues to develop in North America and Europe, it faces at least three significant dangers. Perhaps the greatest danger, one that faces any reform movement, is loss of vision. Programs inevitably become preoccupied with securing stable funding sources and developing routine day-to-day operating procedures. It becomes increasingly easy to lose sight of the underlying values and principles of restorative justice that motivated so many of the individuals who initiated the program and that serve as the foundation for the program's existence. The importance of providing opportunities for addressing the emotional issues surrounding crime and victimization, including even the possibility of genuine remorse and forgiveness and reconciliation, is a foundational principle of the field. Losing sight of this vision could easily result in a utilitarian and exclusive focus on simple restitution determination and payment, allowing no time for the sharing of facts and feelings related to the crime. Such a utilitarian focus could easily lead to the elimination of the premediation separate meetings with each party, meetings that have been found to contribute to the humanizing of the process for both victim and offender.

The remaining two dangers also grow out of a loss of vision when programs continue to be preoccupied with their acceptability or institutionalization. The first of these dangers is the tremendous tendency to take few risks, particularly in the type of cases being referred to the program. In their eagerness to negotiate new referral arrangements and get enough cases, programs may be too quick to accept "garbage cases," those that prosecutor's offices either do not have sufficient evidence for or that they would prefer not being bothered with. However, the likelihood that the field of victim-offender mediation will become increasingly marginalized and not taken seriously by the larger criminal justice system will be far greater if the field becomes identified with the easy cases, those that the system would have done little with in the first place.

The remaining danger facing the movement is related to working with primarily easy cases and has important public policy implications. The vision of the field is deeply rooted in the belief that the mediation process is an alternative to the criminal justice system. The VORP model, specifically, was linked to the alternatives to incarceration movement during the late 1970s and early 1980s. If programs focus upon taking the easy cases, many of which would not have even entered the formal criminal justice system, the field of victim-offender mediation will join the ranks of many other so-called alternatives that research has demonstrated have led to wider and stronger nets of social control. If that happens, despite intentions to the contrary, victim-offender mediation programs will be increasing, rather than limiting, state intervention into the lives of individuals who violate the law.

## OPPORTUNITIES

All social reform movements face many dangers and pitfalls. Yet by definition, the process of advocating and developing a reform program contains many creative opportunities. With over two decades of experience in bringing crime victims and their offenders face-to-face and in addressing a number of important issues to both parties, the field of victim-offender mediation is in a stronger position than ever to boldly tell its story. There is no longer any question about whether or not victims would ever be willing to meet their offenders. Nor is there any question about the intrinsic value of the mediation process in humanizing the criminal justice process and promoting a greater sense of healing and closure for both victim and offender. Thousands of crime victims and offenders have benefited from the mediation process, and their individual stories offer powerful testimony to the basic validity of the model. These stories need to be increasingly heard by both the general public and the policymakers. They breathe life into the theory of restorative justice.

While focusing on nonviolent property crime, many programs have also worked since their inception with simple assault cases. The movement of victim-offender mediation into working with more serious violent cases, however, has been led by requests from people who have been victimized by such crimes as aggravated assault, armed robbery, sexual assault, attempted homicide, and the family members of victims of homicide. The field is only beginning to come to grips with how the basic mediation model must be adapted to serve the more intense needs of parties involved in severely violent criminal conflict.

A growing number of representatives of major victim advocacy organizations in different parts of the country are beginning to recognize the value of mediation for certain victims of violence. As they confront the very source of terror in their lives, some victims of violence are able to obtain a greater sense of inner healing and closure. The field of victim-offender mediation is faced with an exciting opportunity to stretch its original vision and significantly alter its original model to appropriately address the needs of parties affected by violent criminal conflict. This can only happen with a serious commitment to reexamine the basic model; an understanding of that model's limitations; an increased awareness of the victimization experience, including posttraumatic stress and grieving; an understanding of the need for intensive case preparation, involving multiple premediation sessions with both parties; and a willingness to apply tighter boundaries in defining when mediation is appropriate, what kind of training is required, and who should serve as mediators.

Finally, a major concern facing the field of victim-offender mediation in North America and Europe is that of marginalization. Despite its growth and increasing acceptance, the practice of mediating conflict between crime victims and their offenders (as part of a larger vision of restorative justice) remains on the margins of how we do justice. Criminal justice systems continue to be driven by the principles of retributive justice, focusing upon state interests and the offender.

An opportunity now exists to move mediation away from the margins and closer to the mainstream of how we do justice in our society. With the growing amount of public, including victim, support and the growing amount of empirical evidence supporting the model, the field of victim-offender mediation is now able to give serious consideration to advocating mediation as a basic right of any crime victim in any community. This right could be conditioned upon the availability of a competent mediator, the willingness of the parties, and the absence of any major mental health issues.

In an ideal setting, linkage of such a strategy to only one side of the conflict (that is, victim rights) would not be preferable. Given the reality of the U.S. criminal justice system, however, no other strategy is more likely to greatly expand access for both crime victims and offenders to the mediation process. Indeed, it is a recently passed victim bill of rights in Indiana that has become the first act of public policy to include these provisions.

A number of other opportunities exist, as well. With its many years of experience, the field of victim-offender mediation can now take the lead in developing standards of practice, certification of mediators, greater networking among colleagues in North America and Europe, and initiation of longitudinal studies to access the long-term impact of mediation and cross-national studies to gain a greater understanding of the development of the victim-offender mediation process in differing national and cultural contexts.

The growing field of mediating conflict between crime victims and their offenders is an important element within the larger field of alternative dispute resolution. By responding to certain types of criminal behavior as conflicts between individuals within community settings, rather than focusing exclusively upon state interests, the victim-offender mediation movement in North America and Europe represents a challenging new vision of how communities can respond to crime and victimization. For some, this vision that is rooted in a paradigm of restorative rather than retributive justice may seem too radical. However, the vision of doing restorative justice in contemporary society is deeply rooted in most of the religious and secular traditions that are part of the collective Western heritage, traditions that have emphasized the importance of direct accountability, remorse, forgiveness, and reconciliation.

## Notes and Questions

1. Is victim-offender mediation appropriate for all criminal cases? Does its appropriateness depend on the seriousness of the crime? On the willingness of the parties to participate in this kind of mediation? Are there any dangers involved in this approach?

2. What kind of mediators would be appropriate for situations of this kind? What kind of training should these mediators have? Should lawyers be involved? Should these mediation sessions be confidential?

3. Assume that you are a practicing mediator. You are called by a lawyer representing a man accused of manslaughter. The lawyer explains that his client, who killed his roommate when he found him in bed with his girlfriend, is suffering deep remorse and desperately wants an opportunity to face the victim's family. The lawyer also explains that he is involved in structuring a plea bargain with the judge and the district attorney and is hoping that, in addition to alleviating his client's emotional pain, this kind of mediation might be advantageous in his plea-bargaining efforts. Would you agree to mediate? What information would you want to have? What would be the basis of your decision?

4. Is restorative justice a legitimate goal of our justice system? Is it obtainable?

&. The following story offers an account of how informal dispute resolution can be used in conflict situations outside of formal court settings. It also reflects how the goal of informal processes is not necessarily to "resolve" a conflict, but rather to assist in building conversation and communication in order to defuse anger, de-escalate the possibility of violence and to possibly facilitate consensus in highly polarized situations.

## 20.2 | Talking with the Enemy   *Anne Fowler, Nicki Nichols Gamble,*

### *Frances X. Hogan, Melissa Kogut, Madeline McComish, and Barbara Thorp*

FOR SIX YEARS, LEADERS on both sides of the abortion debate have met in secret in an attempt to better understand each other. Now they are ready to share what they have learned.

On the morning of Dec. 30, 1994, John Salvi walked into the Planned Parenthood clinic in Brookline and opened fire with a rifle. He seriously wounded three people and killed the receptionist, Shannon Lowney, as she spoke on the phone. He then ran to his car and drove two miles down Beacon Street to Preterm Health Services, where he began shooting again, injuring two and killing receptionist Lee Ann Nichols.

Salvi's 20-minute rampage shocked the nation. Prochoice advocates were grief-stricken, angry, and terrified. Prolife proponents were appalled as well as concerned that their cause would be connected with this horrifying act. Governor William F. Weld and Cardinal Bernard Law, among others, called for talks between prochoice and prolife leaders.

We are six leaders, three prochoice and three prolife, who answered this call. For nearly 5½ years, we have met together privately for more than 150 hours—an experience that has astonished us. Now, six years after the shootings in Brookline, and on the 28th anniversary of the U.S. Supreme Court's landmark *Roe* v. *Wade* decision, we publicly disclose our meetings for the first time.

How did the six of us, activists from two embattled camps, ever find our way to the same table?

In the months following the shootings, the Public Conversations Project, a Boston-based national group that designs and conducts dialogues about divisive public issues, consulted many community leaders about the value of top-level talks about abortion.

Encouraged by these conversations, the project in July 1995 invited the six of us to meet

together four times. The meetings would be confidential and we would attend as individuals, not as representatives of our organizations.

Our talks would not aim for common ground or compromise. Instead, the goals of our conversations would be to communicate openly with our opponents, away from the polarizing spotlight of media coverage; to build relationships of mutual respect and understanding; to help deescalate the rhetoric of the abortion controversy; and, of course, to reduce the risk of future shootings.

Still shaken by the murderous attacks in Brookline, we each agreed to participate.

As we approached the first meeting, we all were apprehensive.

Before the meeting, the prolife participants prayed together in a booth at a nearby Friendly's. Frances X. Hogan, a lawyer and president of Women Affirming Life and executive vice president of Massachusetts Citizens for Life, worried that a dialogue with prochoice leaders might generate "a scandal if people thought I was treating abortion merely as a matter of opinion on which reasonable people could differ."

Madeline McComish, a chemist and president of Massachusetts Citizens for Life, had a "gut fear of sitting with people who were directly involved with taking life."

Barbara Thorp was "deeply anguished over the murders at the clinics." She feared that "if lines of direct communication between prolife and prochoice leaders were not opened, polarization would only deepen." Despite misgivings, Thorp, a social worker and director of the ProLife Office of the Archdiocese of Boston, was "anxious to meet the other side."

The prochoice participants were also skeptical and concerned. As president and CEO of the Planned Parenthood League of Massachusetts, Nicki Nichols Gamble was directly affected by the shootings. Although she felt that dialogue might help, she "wondered if the talks would divert my energies from coordinating my organization's response to the shootings and from assisting in the healing of my employees and their families."

Melissa Kogut, newly appointed executive

director of Mass NARAL, the state affiliate of the National Abortion Rights Action League, wondered how she would "justify to my board and colleagues spending time on something that arguably could be futile."

The Rev. Anne Fowler, rector of St. John's Episcopal Church in Jamaica Plain, believed that her perspective as a Christian leader who is prochoice would be essential, but worried that her viewpoint might not be respected by either side. "However, as a priest, peacemaker, and activist, I had to accept this invitation."

The two facilitators who would moderate all the meetings were also anxious. Laura Chasin, director of the Public Conversations Project, "was afraid that talks might do more harm than good." Susan Podziba, an independent public policy mediator from Brookline, recalls, "The threat of violence was palpable. What if the wrong person found out about the dialogue?"

The first meeting took place at the project's office in Watertown on Sept. 5, 1995, a sweltering Tuesday evening. "I had wanted to wear my clerical collar, but it was too hot," recalls Fowler.

That first discussion was grueling. We could not agree on what to call each other. All but one of us were willing to use each side's preferred designation, in virtual or actual quotation marks: "prolife" and "prochoice."

Our first of many clashes over language, this disagreement remains unresolved. To this day, Gamble still cannot call the other side prolife because "I believe my cause is also prolife," she says. This stand frustrates Thorp and her colleagues. "I have tolerated Nicki's refusal to call us prolife but, frankly, it angers me. I wasn't eager to call Nicki's side prochoice, but I did it because it seemed to be necessary for showing respect and for moving the conversation forward," Thorp says.

Kogut questioned her own willingness to agree to these terms, "but I came to two conclusions," Kogut says. "To proceed with a civil dialogue, we needed to call each other what we each wanted to be called. Second, over time, I began to see 'prolife' as descriptive of the others' beliefs—that life itself, more important than the quality of life, was their preeminent value."

We also struggled over how to refer to what grows and develops in a pregnant woman's womb. The prochoice women found "unborn baby" unacceptable and the prolife women would not agree to "fetus." For the sake of proceeding, we all assented, uneasily, to the term "human fetus."

These opening exchanges brought us to the heart of our differences. Nerves frayed. The chasm between us seemed huge.

To help us listen and speak across this divide, ground rules were critical. We would seek to use terms acceptable (or at least tolerable) to all participants. We would not interrupt, grandstand, or make personal attacks. We would speak for ourselves, not as representatives of organizations. Most important, the meetings would be completely confidential unless all of us could agree upon a way to go public.

We also made a commitment that some of us still find agonizingly difficult: to shift our focus away from arguing for our cause. This agreement was designed to prevent rancorous debates.

And indeed, we believe this ground rule has been essential to the long life of our dialogue. Knowing that our ideas would be challenged, but not attacked, we have been able to listen openly and speak candidly.

But it has not been easy.

"From the beginning, I have felt an enormous tension," Hogan says, "between honoring the agreement to not argue for our position and my deep hope—which I still feel—that these women for whom I have such great respect will change their minds about abortion."

Our ground rules also required us to refrain from polarizing rhetoric. In one early session, we generated a list of "hot buttons"—words and phrases that make it almost impossible for some of us to think clearly, listen carefully, or respond constructively.

Prochoice members are inflamed when called "murderers" or when abortions are likened to the Holocaust or to "genocide." Prolife participants are incensed by dehumanizing phrases such as "products of conception" and "termination of pregnancy" that obscure their belief that abortion is killing.

We also discussed stereotypes we thought were applied to us by people "on the other side."

Prolife participants feel maligned when characterized as religious fanatics taking orders from men, or as uneducated, prudish individuals, indifferent to women in crisis and to children after they are born. Prochoice members are offended by labels such as anti-child, anti-men, anti-family, elitist, frivolous, self-centered, and immoral.

Despite the strains of these early meetings, we grew closer to each other. At one session, each of us told the group why she had devoted so much of her time, energy, and talents to the abortion issue. These accounts—all deeply personal—enlightened and moved us.

After the fourth meeting, we agreed to extend our sessions through the one-year anniversary of the shootings—an occasion, we feared, when tensions over abortion might ignite in Boston.

On the evening of Dec. 30, 1995, about 700 people gathered at Temple Ohabei Shalom in Brookline to honor the memory of Lowney and Nichols. All our prochoice participants attended the service. Fowler and Gamble officiated. In the solemn crowd were Podziba, one of our facilitators, and two of our prolife members, Hogan and Thorp, accompanied by David Thorp, her husband.

"Seeing the other members of the group walk in was one of the most meaningful moments of the service for me," Fowler recalls.

In her remarks, Gamble expressed gratitude "for the prayers of those who agree with us and the prayers of those who disagree."

Fowler, in her sermon, reminded us of the "God who calls out to all who love peace." She drew from the words of the Hebrew prophet Isaiah, saying "and new things have sprung forth in the year since Lee Ann's and Shannon's deaths. Much has been transformed, and much will be."

Indeed, to those of us involved in the confidential dialogues, much had been transformed. By the time of this sad anniversary, each one of us had come to think differently about those "on the other side."

While we struggled over profound issues, we also kept track of personal events in one another's lives, celebrating good times and sharing sorrows. As our mutual understanding increased, our respect and affection for one another grew.

This increased understanding affected how we spoke as leaders of our respective movements. The news media, unaware that we were meeting, began noting differences in our public statements.

In an article after the first-year anniversary of the shootings, Globe reporter Don Aucoin wrote, "Has the past year brought the lowering of voices . . . called for by Cardinal Law, Governor William Weld and others? The answer seems to be a qualified yes, at least among some activists."

The article quoted Gamble as saying, "There are numbers of people on both sides of this question who have tried to be thoughtful about the rhetoric they use." Gamble added that she was hearing fewer uses of such labels as "baby-killer, murderer, Nazi."

In the same article, Hogan is quoted as saying she uses "prochoice because that is what they want to be called. I have a basic respect for the person, even though I don't agree with or respect the position."

Thorp, too, was quoted. "This call for a lowering of voices sent a signal that we really needed to listen to each other with care and respect. I'm more mindful now than I've ever been of speaking in love, speaking in peace, and speaking in respect to anyone, no matter how wide the differences are."

In a National Public Radio interview about the anniversary, Hogan explained that while she believed that abortion is killing, she did not call it murder. Hogan also said, "Toning down the rhetoric is critical. It's not just better manners, but it turns out it's also better politics. . . . We reach people we may never otherwise have reached with the message."

Kogut felt and acted differently when she appeared with prolife spokespeople on news shows and at speaking engagements. Kogut recalls, "I was struck by the media's desire for conflict. One host of a radio talk show actually encouraged me to attack my opponent personally."

In early 1996, we continued to meet, anticipating that the upcoming Salvi trial would present new challenges to protect activists and the public from danger.

At one point, prolife advocates acted to keep proponents of violence away from Massachusetts. In February 1996, the Rev. Donald Spitz, head of ProLife Virginia, made it known that he was planning to come to Boston to show support for what he had called, according to the Globe, Salvi's "righteous deed."

McComish wrote a letter to Spitz, signed also by Hogan and Thorp. "Your public statements on the acceptability of violence . . . are counter to everything that the prolife movement represents," McComish wrote. "At this very difficult time, you are not welcome in Massachusetts."

Spitz and several of his allies objected to McComish's charge. They suggested that she was betraying the cause. But he did not come.

A growing trust opened a "hot line" channel of reliable communication between us. The prolife leaders alerted Gamble when there was a possibility of imminent physical danger. "It lowered my anxiety—and moved me deeply—to know that there were people on the other side who were concerned about my safety," Gamble says.

Throughout these 5½ years, though external events claimed much of our attention, we managed to explore many aspects of the abortion controversy, such as when life begins, the rights of women, the rights of the unborn, why women get abortions, and the aftermath of abortion.

We spent especially tense hours discussing the issue that prochoice members describe as "bans on certain abortion procedures" and that prolife participants call "partial-birth abortions." We also probed a host of other complex and challenging subjects: feminism, sex education, euthanasia, suicide, the death penalty, the role of law in society, and individual responsibility.

When addressing divisive topics, we expected to disagree. But at times, conflicts caught us by surprise—flaring when one side unwittingly used certain words in a way that struck the other as presumptuous or offensive.

One provocative word has been "violence." While the prochoice leaders use it to refer to shootings and other attacks on clinics, doctors, and staff, the prolife activists believe that abortion also is a violent act.

In writing this article, we came to an impasse when one side mentioned the Declaration of Independence. The prolife participants wished to cite the Declaration as a presentation of their core belief that the right to life is inalienable and self-evident. The prochoice members passionately objected to what they saw as an appropriation of a document that they also cherish. To them, the Declaration affirms every person's right to life and liberty.

In these and all of our discussions of differences, we strained to reach those on the other side who could not accept—or at times comprehend—our beliefs. We challenged each other to dig deeply, defining exactly what we believe, why we believe it, and what we still do not understand.

These conversations revealed a deep divide. We saw that our differences on abortion reflect two world views that are irreconcilable.

If this is true, then why do we continue to meet?

First, because when we face our opponent, we see her dignity and goodness. Embracing this apparent contradiction stretches us spiritually. We've experienced something radical and life-altering that we describe in nonpolitical terms: "the mystery of love," "holy ground," or simply, "mysterious."

We continue because we are stretched intellectually, as well. This has been a rare opportunity to engage in sustained, candid conversations about serious moral disagreements. It has made our thinking sharper and our language more precise.

We hope, too, that we have become wiser and more effective leaders. We are more knowledgeable about our political opponents. We have learned to avoid being overreactive and disparaging to the other side and to focus instead on affirming our respective causes.

Since that first fear-filled meeting, we have experienced a paradox. While learning to treat each other with dignity and respect, we all have become firmer in our views about abortion.

We hope this account of our experience will encourage people everywhere to consider engaging in dialogues about abortion and other protracted disputes. In this world of polarizing conflicts, we have glimpsed a new possibility: a way in which people can disagree frankly and passionately, become clearer in heart and mind about their activism, and, at the same time, contribute to a more civil and compassionate society.

**Prochoice**

The prochoice members of the group describe their views this way:

We recognize no single, universal truth that determines our moral decisions. On the contrary, we must consider a broad range of values whenever we seek to make wise, ethical, and compassionate choices. We respect a woman's moral capacity to make decisions regarding her health and welfare, including reproductive decisions.

A woman's choices reflect how she weighs her various life circumstances; her important relationships, her economic, social, and emotional resources and obligations, her health, her religious or philosophical beliefs, and the well-being of others for whom she has responsibility.

We live out our destinies in a world of vast and profound complexity, where claims upon our compassion and our judgement compete and often conflict. A woman respects the preciousness of human life by acknowledging and honoring the intricate tapestry of her relationships and commitments; indeed, we believe that the complexity of human life can be a source of moral wisdom and courage.

**Prolife**

The prolife members of the group describe their views this way:

We believe in one universal truth. We three, as Catholics, believe that each human life has its origin in the heart of God. This divine genesis of the human person calls us to protect and respect every human life from the moment of conception to natural death.

The truth regarding the intrinsic dignity of the human person can also be understood through reason and scientific principles of human reproduction and genetics. Indeed, faith and reason resonate, both affirming the inviolable truth that every human life is inherently sacred.

Abortion kills the most vulnerable member of the human family: the unborn child. The right to be born is the most basic of human rights. If it is not protected then all other rights are threatened.

We understand, all to well, the often desperate and overwhelming circumstances that some pregnant women face. We remain committed to creating an environment in which no pregnant woman feels that she must choose between her own well-being and the life of her child. It is an utter failure of love and community for a pregnant woman to feel that abortion is her only choice.

*Notes and Questions*

1. Would this model of conflict facilitation be useful in other kinds of situations? Can you think of any particular situations that might be appropriate?

2. What are the drawbacks of this approach?

3. What training would the facilitators of this kind of process need?

4. What impact, if any, does this kind of process have on the larger, seemingly intractable abortion conflict?

# CONCLUSION

&. What are the social implications of informal justice? Does mediation and the field of alternative dispute resolution undermine people's rights? Whose interests does it serve? Are those who are already disadvantaged made more so, through the privatization and individuation of mediational justice? In the concluding article, the legal anthropologist Laura Nader addresses these concerns.

## Trading Justice for Harmony   *Laura Nader*

ALMOST EVERYTHING WRITTEN BY advocates of Alternative Dispute Resolution (ADR) suffers from a fixation on forms of dispute resolution devoid of a sense of history, absent of an understanding of other cultures, or of the social context of ADR experiments in our own culture. As a group ADR advocates are oblivious to their critics, unaware of research that challenges ADR ideology, and sometimes ignorant of the sources of ADR ideas. Some of these general comments apply to Griffin Bell's Dispute Resolution Lecture of 1991.

First there is the double talk. Mr. Bell notes that the overall theme of the 1976 Pound Conference was "how to deliver justice with dispatch, efficiently and at low cost." I disagree. Although the 1976 Pound Conference took as its topic "The Causes of the Popular Dissatisfaction with the Administration of Justice," the conference was not about how to deliver *justice* (as Judge Higgenbothom reminded us at the conference). Instead, conference themes hovered around efficiency and harmony, or how to rid the country of confrontation and the courts of "garbage cases" (e.g., consumer, environmental, feminist issues). Particularly noteworthy at the Pound Conference was the fact that while there was discussion of how to streamline the administration of justice, there was no talk about measures that prevent wrong doing, no discussion about unequal power vis-a-vis the law, nor did discussion of

streamlining include class-action or aggregate solutions. Indeed, the "courthouse of many doors" that Griffin Bell attributes to Frank Sanders' presentation at the conference is reminiscent of Mexican Zapotec Indian courts. Such a courthouse is a simple idea practiced by many of the "simpler" peoples of the world and has for decades been described by anthropologists working on many continents. The brilliance in this case belongs to indigenous peoples and our ability to take advantage of their experience should be duly credited to the anthropologists who described such courts for western audiences.

Mr. Bell writes of chairing a task force to follow-up on the ideas of the Pound Conference. He describes a report that focuses on new mechanisms for the delivery of justice, but does not consider solutions that lie outside the legal system. Methods of prevention are absent; standardizing product parts or using air bags to prevent automotive injury cases are examples of extra-legal prevention. He ignores the fact that dispute resolution is skewed: neighborhood justice centers may deal with yapping dogs, but not with absentee landlordism, rampant consumer problems, or toxic waste—all sources of conflict high on the list of citizen problems.

As I have explicated many times, the legal problems that need creative new forms of administration of justice are those between people of unequal power. The justices of the peace that Mr. Bell speaks about used their wisdom to settle face-to-face disputes between relative equals; today we are faced with conflicts between dispersed citizens and large, centralized structures. The parties are of grossly unequal power. Thus to focus on assistance to individuals distracts attention from economic forces, power differentials, and inequality in distribution of remedies in the United States. The assumption that change in the delivery of justice is to be achieved by adding mediators or arbitrators illustrates a blindness to the importance of social and cultural structures that produce legal problems.

In the absence of data it is easy to boast. Mr. Bell mentions the work of Professors Rosenberg and Meador as bearing great fruit. With all due respect to these gentlemen, I ask what great fruit: to say that there are more than 400 neighborhood justice centers in operation tells us little about what they mean in terms of providing remedies to those in need. And although neighborhood justice centers or other efforts to train mediators or arbitrators do not keep a public record of their cases, those of us who have studied their workings know that for the majority of American consumers, mechanisms for the resolution of controversies involving consumer goods and services are still "largely unavailable, inaccessible, ineffective, expensive or unfair" (see the Congressional Record 1978: S10143).

ADR is a clever scheme of pacification, one similar to that used by missionizing colonial powers in Africa, in the Pacific and elsewhere. The 1960s in the United States were years when many social groups felt encouraged to come forward with their agendas: civil rights, consumer rights, environmental rights, women's rights, etc. Those who thought that Americans were becoming too litigious sought to remedy what they saw as a confrontational mode. During that same time large corporations were complaining about the costs of inter-corporate litigation.

Those who have benefitted from ADR are organizations, for example large corporations. The majority of potential users on the other hand are not attracted to ADR and have to be coerced into using ADR. If compulsory nonbinding arbitration does not spread it may be because it is compulsory, not part of the public record, and not geared to protect against inequalities. Why indeed must any case go to mediation before there can be a trial? Such coercion is akin to requiring a cancer patient to have radiation treatment before going to surgery, when surgery is the patient's first choice. Citizens are often aware that they are los-

ing plaintiff rights because of coercive tactics linked to ADR techniques, and researchers have found that mediators may adjudicate when they are supposed to be mediating.

Roscoe Pound was not interested in the administration of justice devoid of social and cultural context. He put it quite to the contrary:

> Justice, which is the end of the law, is the
> ideal compromise between the activities
> of each and the activities of all in a crowded
> world. . . . When the community is one
> in its ideas of justice, this is possible.
> When the community is divided and
> diversified, and groups and classes and
> interests, understanding each other
> none too well, have conflicting ideas of
> justice, the task is extremely difficult.

Justice is more than a technique for dispute resolution. Disputes are more than a lack of communication. And incivility in the litigation process refers to style rather than to the components of a first rate *adversary* system.

As a whole, the most zealous ADR advocates have yet to consider the findings from empirical works on the subject. For example, *No Access to Law* (Nader et al. 1980) is an empirical study of alternatives to the American judicial system, the result of a 10-year study funded by the Carnegie Corporation of New York. In Chapter 11, "Old Solutions for Old Problems," we catalogue some of the possibilities in the framework of a complaint-handling chain that includes discussion of prevention, aggregate solutions, and what works and does not work. Other studies also report on empirical research and provide thoughtful analyses.

Griffin Bell suggests that we need a law giver, a benevolent potentate to right the wrongs of our legal system. I argue that the dispute resolution movement is far from the salvation Mr. Bell seeks. Indeed, ADR has been primarily geared to induce passivity, a characteristic certainly not encouraging of democracy. Disputes are symptoms of fundamental and systematic problems in our society, one of the most important being the absence of democratic control over society's resources. In sum to consider ADR in its present form as a panacea for wrongdoing is unacceptable because it trades justice for harmony.

*The City Chanters.* A scene from the "Wilkes and Liberty" riots. (© Hulton Getty/Tony Stone Images)

# PART VI

# Cyberspace and the Future of Law

Each technology gives us a different space.
　　—David Bolter

If only we could, we would wander the earth and never leave home.
　　—Michael Benedikt

    This book began with Kafka's parable of an individual standing before the law. The individual came with expectations about the law and about a citizen's ability to interact with the law. He assumed, you may recall, that law "should be accessible to every man and at all times." Yet, the doorkeeper barred entry and stood in the way of the citizen wishing to become involved with the law.

    The doorkeeper was Kafka's metaphor or symbol for many different forces that keep citizens at a distance from law and justice. Costs that are significant, law libraries and legal materials that are hidden from the public or are difficult to use, and architecture that is intimidating and unfamiliar can be considered to be doorkeepers that may interfere with the assertion of rights and the just resolution of disputes. Physical distance that makes obtaining legal information inconvenient or burdensome can be viewed as a doorkeeper. As many of the readings in this book suggest, administrative regulations, intricate court procedures, and the legal profession itself often serve as doorkeepers by keeping citizens at a distance from the law and excluding them from direct contact with it.

    In Kafka's parable, the doorkeeper serves only to exclude. However, doorkeepers typically have dual functions, excluding some and admitting others. For example, architecture that is formal and intimidating may also foster respect for judicial authority and thereby promote the use of law. Complex knowledge systems may, if one becomes familiar with them, be powerful and efficient systems for finding information. Lawyers, while a barrier of entry at many times, can at other times be a means for moving the doorkeeper aside and obtaining entrance.

    This chapter focuses on a new and powerful doorkeeper, one that affects all the processes and institutions discussed in previous chapters. This doorkeeper is cyberspace, the environment of new electronic information technologies. Some of you may be familiar with cyberspace. You may use

E-mail, the Internet, and the World Wide Web. For others, the computer and communication over computer networks may still be a mystery. Whether or not you participate in cyberspace, however, you should recognize the power of these new tools and the powerful influence they will have on law.

Why will a new medium of communication be a significant force for change in the law? While we often think of law in terms of courthouses, lawyers, police officers, and other symbols of authority and justice, at the heart of every legal process is information. Professor Harold Berman once wrote that a legal system requires that there be a "belief in the power of certain words, put certain ways, to bring about certain effects denominated as legal. This kind of magic is necessary if law is to work."* Law is an organism whose lifeblood is information, and media of communication are the veins and arteries that move the information through the system. Lawyers are a profession with control over a body of information. New media bring about change because they allow for new opportunities to move, process, organize, store, and publish information, and for new opportunities to interact with people and institutions, and to challenge those groups who have previously had control over information.

Manipulation of information underlies the way legal institutions work, legal doctrines are applied, and social and moral values are translated into legal values. Law is a response to information received *from* the public. Law is also information that is communicated *to* the public. Law is the result of judgment and decision making involving the evaluation and organization of information. As Professor Marc Galanter has observed, law

> usually works not by exercise of force but by information transfer, by communication of what's expected, what forbidden, what allowable, what are the consequences of acting in certain ways. That is, law entails information about what the rules are, how they are applied, with what costs, consequences, etc. For example, when we speak of deterrence, we are talking about the effect of information about what the law is and how it is administered. Similarly, when we describe "bargaining in the shadow of the law," we refer to regulation accomplished by the flow of information rather than directly by authoritative decision. Again, "legal socialization" is accomplished by the transmission of information. In a vast number of instances the application of law is, so to speak, self administered—people regulate their conduct (and judge the conduct of others) on the basis of their knowledge about legal standards, possibilities and constraints.[†]

Those of you who have "surfed the Net" may have encountered questions about copyright, privacy, obscenity, patents, trademarks, or the First

---

*Harold Berman, "The Background of the Western Legal Tradition in the Folklaw of the Peoples of Europe," 45 *U. of Chicago L. Rev.* 553, 563 (1978).

[†]Marc Galanter, "The Legal Malaise: Or, Justice Observed," 19 *Law and Society Rev.* 537, 545 (1985).

Amendment. Concern about these areas of law has dominated public discussion of law and the Internet. These are important areas of law that touch important economic, political, and social themes. Yet, the impact of the new technologies goes beyond particular rules of law. New modes of communication touch the legal profession, law enforcement, the manner in which disputes are settled and standards established, and other themes covered in this book, as much as, or perhaps more than, they touch particular legal doctrines involving information and communication. They are doorkeepers that touch both our ability to interact with the law and our expectations about justice.

The purpose of this chapter is more to raise questions about this powerful force whose influence is spreading widely than to provide definitive answers. It is clear that computers and computer networks will affect law deeply, just as they are likely to have a significant impact on our economic and political systems. But what kind of doorkeeper is this new medium of communication? Does it create distance between the individual and the law, or does it facilitate access? Are our new technologies likely to be doorkeepers that invite us in, or are they doorkeepers that exclude? Are they likely to serve the individual, enhance our autonomy, and empower us, or are they likely to violate our privacy, preserve the status quo, and serve established interests? Do they present us with tools to move other doorkeepers aside, or are they providing support for doorkeepers that are already in place?

# 21 | CYBERSPACE AND THE FUTURE OF LAW

❧ The following reading introduces us to cyberspace. It reveals a place where we can interact with others no matter where these other people may be located. Cyberspace is, one can argue, a real place, even though it is not a physical place. Access to this place is easy and the doorkeepers seem to invite us in, but what we find inside may be different from what we expect, and we may need to be more tentative and cautious than in other settings. Cyberspace is a place where externally imposed barriers to expression have been lowered, but where we also need to ask ourselves how willing we are to expose ourselves to others. It is a place where many constraints that exist in the physical world are not present, and it is a place where questions about law arise routinely. The following event took place some time before the Internet became popular but the lessons and issues that are raised remain with us.

## 21.1  The Strange Case of the Electronic Lover    *Lindsy Van Gelder*

I "MET" JOAN IN the late spring of 1983, shortly after I first hooked my personal computer up to a modem and entered the strange new world of on-line communications. Like me, Joan was spending a great deal of time on the "CB" channel of the national network CompuServe, where one can encounter other modem owners in what amounts to a computer version of CB radio. I was writing an article for *Ms.* about modems and doing on-line interviews with CB regulars. Joan was already a sought-after celebrity among the hundreds of users who hung out on the channel—a telecommunications media star.

Her "handle" was "Talkin' Lady." According to the conventions of the medium, people have a (usually frivolous) handle when they're on "open" channels with many users; but when two people choose to enter a private talk mode, they'll often exchange real information about themselves. I soon learned that her real name was Joan Sue Greene, and that she was a New York neuropsychologist in her late twenties, who had been severely disfigured in a car accident that was the fault of a drunken driver. The accident had killed her boyfriend. Joan herself spent a year in the hospital, being treated for brain damage, which affected both her speech and her ability to walk. Mute, confined to a wheelchair, and frequently suffering intense back and leg pain, Joan had at first been so embittered about her disabilities that she literally didn't want to live.

Then her mother, a former professor at Johns Hopkins, presented her with a computer, a modem, and a year's subscription to CompuServe to be used specifically doing what Joan was doing—making friends on-line. At first, her handle had been "Quiet Lady," in reference to her muteness. But Joan could type—which is, after all, how one "talks" on a computer—and she had a sassy, bright, generous personality that blossomed in a medium where physicality doesn't count. Joan became enormously popular, and her new handle,

"Talkin' Lady," was a reflection of her new sense of self. Over the next two years, she became a monumental on-line presence who served both as a support for other disabled women and as an inspiring stereotype-smasher to the able-bodied. Through her many intense friendships and (in some cases) her on-line romances, she changed the lives of dozens of women.

Thus it was a huge shock early this year when, through a complicated series of events, Joan was revealed as being not disabled at all. More to the point, Joan, in fact, was not a woman. She was really a man we'll call Alex—a prominent New York psychiatrist in his early fifties who was engaged in a bizarre, all-consuming experiment to see what it felt like to be female, and to experience the intimacy of female friendship.

Even those who barely knew Joan felt implicated—and somehow betrayed—by Alex's deception. Many of us on-line like to believe that we're a utopian community of the future, and Alex's experiment proved to us all that technology is no shield against deceit. We lost our innocence, if not our faith.

To some of Alex's victims—including a woman who had an affair with the real-life Alex, after being introduced to him by Joan—the experiment was a "mind rape," pure and simple. (Several people, in fact, have tentatively explored the possibility of bringing charges against Alex as a psychiatrist—although the case is without precedent, to put it mildly.) To some other victims, Alex was not so much an impostor as a seeker whose search went out of control. (Several of these are attempting to continue a friendship with Alex—and, as one woman put it, "to relate to the soul, not the sex of the person. The soul is the same as before.")

Either way, this is a peculiarly modern story about a man who used some of our most up to date technology to play out some of our oldest assumptions about gender roles. . . .

The unfolding of an on-line relationship is unique, combining the thrill of ultrafuturistic technology with the veneration of the written word that informed 19th-century friendships and romances. Most people who haven't used the medium have trouble imagining what it's like to connect with other people whose words are wafting across your computer screen. For starters, it's dizzyingly egalitarian, since the most important thing about oneself isn't age, appearance, career success, health, race, gender, sexual preference, accent, or any of the other categories by which we normally judge each other, but one's *mind*. My personal experience has been that I often respond to the minds of people whom, because of my own prejudices (or theirs), I might otherwise not meet. (For example, my best friend on-line is from Appalachia, which I once thought was inhabited only by Li'l Abner and the Dukes of Hazzard. My friend, in turn, had never had a gay friend before.)

But such mind-to-mind encounters presume that the people at both keyboards are committed to getting past labels and into some new, truer way of relating. In the wake of the Alex/Joan scandal, some on-line habitués have soberly concluded that perhaps there's a thin line between getting out of one's skin and getting into a completely false identity—and that the medium may even encourage impersonation. . . . Still, when it works, it works. Disabled people are especially well represented on-line, and most of them say that it's a medium where they can make a first impression on their own terms. . . .

Alex supposedly began his dual identity by mistake. . . . Alex apparently came on-line sometime in late 1982 or early 1983 and adopted the handle "Shrink, Inc." His epiphany came one evening when he was in private talk mode with a woman who for some reason mistook him for a female shrink. "The person was open with him in a way that stunned him," according to one of the women—let's call her Laura—who has maintained a friendship with Alex. "What he really found as Joan was that most women opened up to him in a way he had never seen before in all his years of practice. And he realized he could help them."

"He later told me that his female patients had trouble relating to him—they always seemed to be leaving something out," said Janis Goodall, a Berkeley, California, software firm employee who also knew both Joan and Alex. "Now he could see what it was." (Despite their similar recollections, Goodall is in the opposite camp from Laura, and says: "For someone supposedly dedicated to helping people, I think he rampaged through all of our feelings with despicable disregard.") At some point after "Shrink, Inc.'s" inadvertent plunge into sisterhood, Joan was born.

According to both Goodall and Laura (both of whom are disabled themselves), Alex has a back condition, "arthritis of the spine or a calcium deposit of some kind," according to Goodall, "which causes him discomfort, and has the potential, but *not* the probability of putting him in a wheelchair someday." Goodall added that Alex later defended his choice of a disabled persona by claiming that he "wanted to find out how disabled people deal with it." Others on-line believe that Joan's handicaps were a way both to shroud her real identity and aggrandize her heroic stature.

If Joan began spontaneously, she soon became a far more conscious creation, complete with electronic mail drop, special telephone line, and almost novelistically detailed biography (although she sometimes told different versions to different people). She was, by my own recollection and by the accounts of everyone interviewed, an exquisitely wrought character. For starters, she had guts. (She had once, before the accident, driven alone across the interior of Iceland as a way to cure her agoraphobia.) She had travelled everywhere, thanks to money left to her by her family's textile mill fortune. She lived alone (although neighbours checked on her and helped her with errands) and was a model independent female. In fact, Joan was quite a feminist. It was she who suggested the formation of a women's issues group within CompuServe, and she actively recruited members. Several women had relationships with Joan in which they referred to each other as "sister.". . .

Interestingly, the two people who knew Joan and also met Alex in person say that their surface personalities were opposite. Alex is Jewish. He almost never drinks or smokes pot (although one of his medical specialities is pharmacology). He is a workaholic whose American Psychiatric Association biography reports wide publication in his field. "Joan was wild and zingy and flamboyant and would do anything you dared her to," notes Laura. "A part of Alex wanted to be like that, but he's actually quite intellectual and shy." Adds Janis Goodall: "Alex has a great deal of trouble expressing his emotions. There are long silences, and then he'll say, 'uh-huh, un-huh'—just like a shrink."

Above all, Joan was a larger-than-life exemplary disabled person. At the time of her accident, she had been scheduled to teach a course at a major New York medical school (in fact, the teaching hospital that Alex is affiliated with as a psychiatrist). Ironically, Joan noted, the course dealt with many of the same neurological impairments that she herself now suffered. One of Joan's goals was eventually to resume her career as if the accident had never happened—and when I first knew her, she was embarked on an ambitious plan to employ a computer in the classroom to help her teach. The idea was that Joan would type her lecture into a computer, which would then be either magnified on a classroom screen or fed into student terminals. To all of us techno-fans and believers in better living through computers, it was a thrilling concept.

Joan was also a militant activist against the dangers of drunken drivers. Early in her convalescence, when she was frequently half out of her mind with anger, she had on several occasions wheeled herself out of her apartment and onto the streets of Manhattan, where she would shout at passing motorists. On one such occasion, police officers in her precinct, upon learning her story, suggested that she put her rage and her talent to more productive use. Joan then began to go out on patrol with a group of traffic cops whose job it was to catch drunken drivers. Joan's role in the project was twofold: (1) as a highly credentialed neuropsychologist, she was better trained than most to detect cars whose drivers had reflex problems caused by too much drinking, and (2) she was willing to serve as an example to drunken drivers of what could befall them if they didn't shape up.

On one of Joan's forays, she met a young police officer named Jack Carr. As he and Joan spent more time together, he came to appreciate her spirit in much the same way the rest of us had. They fell in love—much to the distress of Jack's mother, who thought he was throwing his life away. (Joan's on-line friends were heartened to learn much later that Mrs. Carr had softened after Joan bought her a lap-top computer, and

the two of them learned to communicate in the on-line world where Joan shone so brightly.) Jack occasionally came on-line with Joan, although I remember him as being shy and far less verbal than Joan.

Shortly after I met Joan, she and Jack got married. Joan sent an elaborate and joyous announcement to all her CB pals via electronic mail, and the couple held an on-line reception, attended by more than 30 CompuServe regulars. (On-line parties are not unusual. People just type in all the festive sound effects, from the clink of champagne glasses to the tossing of confetti.) Joan and Jack honeymooned in Cyprus, which, according to Pamela Bowen, a Huntington, West Virginia, newspaper editor, Joan said "was one of the few places she'd never been." Bowen and many of Joan's other on-line friends received postcards from Cyprus. The following year Joan and Jack returned to Cyprus and sent out another batch of cards.

"I remember asking Joan how she would get around on her vacation," recalls Sheila Deitz, associate professor of law and psychology at the University of Virginia. "Joan simply replied that if need be, he'd carry her. He was the quintessential caring, nurturing, loving, sensitive human being"—a Mr. Right who, Deitz adds, exerted enormous pull on the imaginations of all Joan's on-line female friends. In hindsight, Deitz feels, "he was the man Alex would have loved to be"—but in fact could only be in the persona of a woman.

Joan was extraordinarily generous. On one occasion, when Laura was confined to her bed because of her disability and couldn't use her regular computer, Joan sent her a lap-top model—a gift worth hundreds of dollars. On another occasion, when Laura mentioned that no one had ever sent her roses, Joan had two dozen delivered. Marti Cloutier, a 42-year-old Massachusetts woman with grown children, claims that it was Joan who inspired her to start college. "She made me feel I could do it at my age." When it came time for Cloutier to write her first term paper, she was terrified, but Joan helped her through it, both in terms of moral support and in the practical sense of sending her a long list of sources. (Ironically, Cloutier's assignment was a psychology paper on multiple personalities. She got an "A" in the course.) On another occasion, Joan told Cloutier that she was going out to hear the "Messiah" performed. When Cloutier enviously mentioned that she loved the music, Joan mailed her the tape. On still another occasion, when Cloutier and her husband were having difficulties over the amount of time that she spent on-line, Joan volunteered to "talk" to him. Cloutier's husband is also a part-time police officer, as Jack ostensibly was, and he and Joan easily developed a rapport. According to Marti Cloutier, Joan was able to persuade him that if his wife had her own friends and interests, it would ultimately be good for their marriage. "She was always doing good things," Cloutier recalls, "and never asking anything in return."

My personal recollections are similar. Once, when Joan and I were chatting on-line late at night, I realized to my great disbelief that a bat had somehow gotten into my apartment and was flapping wildly about, with my cats in crazed pursuit. I got off the computer, managed to catch the bat and get it back out the window—but in the attendant confusion, the windowpane fell out of the window and onto my arm, slicing my wrist and palm. Needless to say, I ended up in the emergency room. Joan dropped me several extremely solicitous notes over the next few weeks, making sure that my stitches were healing properly and that I was over the scare of the accident. Even earlier, around the time I first met Joan, the child of two of my oldest friends was hit by a car and knocked into a coma that was to last for several weeks. Joan had a lot of thoughts about the physiology of comas, as well as about how to deal with hospital staffs, insurance companies, and one's own unraveling psyche in the midst of such a crisis. She offered to set up an on-line meeting with the child's mother. I later heard that Joan had also helped several women who had suicidal tendencies or problems with alcohol. . . .

Janis Goodall was in a category all her own. Now 37 and cheerfully describing herself as "a semiretired hippie from 'Berserkeley,' California," Goodall met Joan at a time in her life "when I was a real sick cookie—an open raw wound." Goodall was herself coping with the emotional and physical aftermath of an automobile accident. (Although she can walk, Goodall's

legs are badly scarred and she suffers from both arthritis and problems of the sciatic nerve.) Beyond her injuries, Goodall was also dealing with a recent separation from her husband and her brother's death. "It was Joan who helped me to deal with those things and to make the transition into the life of a disabled person who accepts that she's disabled."

Joan and Goodall were "fixed up" by other CompuServe regulars after Goodall attended an on-line conference on pain management. When she and Joan arranged via electronic mail to meet in CB, "it was love at first sight. By the end of that first discussion, which lasted a couple of hours, we were honorary sisters. Later, I went around profusely thanking everyone who had told me to contact her."

The fact that Joan's disability was more severe than her own gave her an authority in Goodall's eyes, and her humor was especially therapeutic. "We used to make jokes about gimps who climb mountains. At the time, just to get through the day was a major accomplishment for me, and my attitude was screw the mountains, let me go to the grocery store." The two never became lovers, despite strenuous lobbying on Joan's part. ("I often found myself apologizing for being straight," said Goodall.) But they did become intense, close friends. "I loved her. She could finish my sentences and read my mind."

About a year ago, Joan began telling Goodall about "this great guy" who was also on-line. His name was Alex. He was a psychiatrist, very respected in his field, and an old friend of Joan's, an associate at the hospital. Largely on the strength of Joan's enthusiastic recommendation, Goodall responded with pleasure when Alex invited her into private talk mode. "During our second or third conversation, he began to get almost romantic. He clearly thought I was the greatest thing since sliced bread. I couldn't understand why an established Manhattan psychiatrist his age could be falling so quickly for a retired hippie—although of course I was very flattered. Hey, if a shrink thought I was okay, I was okay!"

Alex told Goodall that he was married, but that his marriage was in trouble. Last winter he invited her to come visit him in New York, and when she said she couldn't afford it, he sent her a round-trip ticket. "He treated me like a queen for the four days I was there," Goodall remembers. "He put me up at the Fifth Avenue hotel— the American Stanhope, right across the street from the Metropolitan Museum. He took me to the Russian Tea Room for dinner, the Carnegie Deli for breakfast, Serendipity for ice cream, museums, everywhere—he even introduced me to his daughters." The two became lovers, although, Goodall says, his back problems apparently affected his ability and their sex life was less than satisfactory. Still, it seems to have been a minor off note in a fabulously romantic weekend. There were also many gifts. Once, Goodall says, "he went out to the corner drugstore to get cigarettes and came back with caviar. I went to Berkeley on Cloud Nine."

Naturally, Goodall had also hoped that she might meet Joan during her New York holiday. None of Joan's other women friends had. Some of the able-bodied women, especially, were hurt that Joan still felt shame about her appearance after so many protestations of love and friendship. According to Sheila Deitz, several people were reported to have arranged rendezvous with Joan and were stood up at the last minute—"although you just know Alex had to be lurking about somewhere, checking them out." Joan would, in each case, claim to have gotten cold feet.

Marti Cloutier says that Joan told her that she had promised her husband that she would never meet any of her on-line friends, but "that if she ever changed her mind and decided to meet any of her on-line friends, I would be one of them." In fact, the only CB person who had ever seen Joan was her hospital colleague—Alex. Over the course of Goodall's four days in the city, she and Alex both tried to reach Joan by phone, but without success. Goodall had brought Joan a gift—a stylized, enameled mask of a smiling face. Alex promised to deliver it.

Back in Berkeley, Goodall resumed her on-line relationship with Joan, who had been out of town for the weekend. Joan, however, was anxious to hear every detail of Goodall's trip. Did she think she was in love with Alex? Was the sex good?

It was the disabled women on-line who figured it out first. "Some things about her condition were very farfetched," says one. Says another

woman: "The husband, the accomplishments—it just didn't ring true from the beginning." But her own hunch wasn't that Joan was a male or able-bodied; she suspected that she was in fact a disabled woman who was pretending to have a life of dazzling romance and success.

Although such theories, however, ultimately ran up against the real postcards from Cyprus, people began to share their misgivings. "There were too many contradictions," says Bob Walter. "Here was this person who ran off to conferences and to vacations and did all these phenomenal things, but she wouldn't let her friends on-line even see her. After a while, it just didn't compute."

In hindsight, I wonder why I didn't question some of Joan's exploits more closely. As a journalist, I've dealt with the public relations representatives of both the New York City Police Department and the hospital where Joan supposedly taught—and it now seems strange to me that her exploits as drunk-spotter and handicapped professor weren't seized on and publicized. Pamela Bowen says she once proposed Joan's story to another editor, but urged him "to have somebody interview her in person because her story was too good to be true. So my instincts were right from the beginning, but I felt guilty about not believing a handicapped person. I mean, the story *could* have been true." It's possible that many of us able-bodied were playing out our own need to see members of minority groups as "exceptional." The more exceptional a person is, the less the person in the majority group has to confront fears of disability and pain.

Even with the contradictions, the game might have continued much longer if Joan hadn't brought Alex into the picture. According to both Goodall and Laura, Alex has, since his unmasking, said that he realized at some point that he had gotten in over his head and he concocted a plan to kill Joan off. But after seeing how upset people were on one occasion when Joan was off-line for several weeks, supposedly ill, he apparently couldn't go through with it. "It would have been a lot less risky for him to let Joan die," according to Laura, "but he knew it would be cruel." (Meanwhile, someone had called the hospital where Joan was thought to be a patient and had been told that no such person was registered.)

What Alex seems to have done instead of commit compu-murder was to buy a new ID number and begin his dual *on-line* identity. Joan increasingly introduced people to her friend Alex, always with great fanfare. We may never know what Alex intended to do with Joan eventually, but there's certainly strong evidence that he was now trying to form attachments as Alex, both off-line (with Goodall) and on.

One might imagine that The Revelation came with a big bang and mass gasps, but this was not the case. According to Walter, months and months went by between the time that some of Joan's more casual acquaintances (he among them) put it together and the time that those of her victims whom they knew heeded their warnings. "People were so invested in their relationships with the female persona that they often just didn't want to know," Walter said. And Joan was also a brilliant manipulator who always had an explanation of why a particular person might be trashing her. "If you ever questioned her about anything," Goodall recalls, "she would get very defensive and turn the topic into an argument about whether you really loved her."

Goodall now acknowledges that she and others ignored plenty of clues, but, as she says, "Let's remember one thing—it was a *pro* doing this."

Deitz, whose off-line work sometimes involves counseling rape victims, agrees that Alex's victims were caught in an intolerable psychological bind. "Alex zeroed in on good people," she says, "although they were often good women at vulnerable stages of their lives." To admit that Joan was a phantom was, in many cases, also to assault the genuine support and self-esteem that they had derived from the relationship. In fact, with only two exceptions—pressuring for compusex and, in Goodall's case, using the Joan persona to pump "girl talk" confidences about Alex—there seems to have been absolutely nothing that Joan did to inspire anyone's rancor. What makes people angry is simply that Joan doesn't exist. "And a lot of what a lot of people were feeling," Deitz adds, "is mourning."

Laura ultimately confronted Joan on-line. She had already "cooled off" her relationship with Joan because of all the inconsistencies in her persona, but while she was suspicious, she had failed to suspect the enormity of the imposture.

In February, however, she called another woman close to Joan, who told her she was convinced that Joan was a man. When Laura found Joan on-line later that night, she immediately asked Joan about the charge. Joan at first denied it. It was only after Laura made it clear that "I believed that we're all created after the image of God, and that I loved the person, not the sex, and would continue to do so," that Alex came out.

Laura, who is Catholic and says that her decision to stick with Alex is partially motivated by principles of Christian love, admits that it took her several weeks to "make the transition." Since then, however, she's met Alex in person and come to love him "as my adopted brother instead of my adopted sister."

Marti Cloutier to this day hasn't confronted Alex, although she has talked with him by CB and phone. "I just haven't the courage. Once, when we were talking, he mentioned something about going for a walk that day, and I wrote back that it would be a lovely day for Joan to go for a walk. I was instantly sorry." Cloutier adds: "Joan was a very special person and I loved Joan. I feel as if she died. I can't really say that I love Alex, although maybe I could, in time. Maybe I wouldn't have given him a chance if I'd known from the beginning he was a male. I've tried to sort out my feelings, but it's hard. I know I don't feel like a victim, and I don't understand why some of these other women have gone off the deep end. I don't think he was malicious. What I can't get out of my mind was that he's the same person I've spent hours and hours with."

Sheila Deitz had been introduced on-line to Alex by Joan, but found him "not all that interesting" and never became close to him. But as a visible on-line person known to many as a psychologist, she heard from many of the victims— some of whom formed their own circle of support, and in Goodall's words, "sort of held each other together with bubble gum." Some victims, according to Deitz, were so upset by the chain of events that they stopped using their modems temporarily.

Janis Goodall heard it first over the telephone, from Alex himself who mistakenly assumed that Goodall already knew. "I had just come home from the doctor, and was incredibly frustrated at having just spent $155 to have some asshole neurosurgeon tell me I would have to live with what was bothering me. The phone rang, and it was Alex. The first words out of his mouth were 'yep—it's me.' I didn't know what he was talking about. Then he said: 'Joan and I are the same person.' I went into shock. I mean, I really freaked out—I wanted to jump off a bridge."

Since then, she has communicated with Alex by letter but has refused to see him. She emphatically resents those on-line who have spent efforts trying to "understand" him. She agreed to speak for this interview in part because "although I think this is a wonderful medium, it's a dangerous one, and it poses more danger to women than men. Men in this society are more predisposed to pulling these kinds of con games, and women are predisposed to giving people the benefit of the doubt."

Laura thinks that CompuServe and other networks ought to post warnings to newcomers that they might, in fact, encounter impostors. Others believe that the fault doesn't lie with the medium or the network, but with human frailty. "Blaming CompuServe for impostors makes about as much sense as blaming the phone company for obscene calls," says Bob Walter. CompuServe itself has no official position on the subject, although CompuServe spokesman Richard Baker notes: "Our experience has been that electronic impersonators are found out about as quickly as are face-to-face impersonators. While face-to-face impersonators are found out due to appearance, on-line impersonators are found out due to the use of phrases, the way they turn words, and the uncharacteristic thought processes that go into conversing electronically. I also believe that people are angrier when they've been betrayed by an electronic impersonator."

It would have been nice to hear Alex's side of the story. The first time I called his office, I gave only my name (which Alex knows)—not my magazine affiliation or the information that I was working on an article about "our mutual friend Joan." The receptionist asked if I was a patient. Did I want to make an appointment? I had a giddy vision of impersonating one but decided against it. Although I telephoned twice more and identified myself as a journalist, Alex never returned my calls. . . .

## Notes and Questions

1. Some of the material in this chapter refers to sources of information that are located on the World Wide Web. As an example, the address or URL for the World Wide Web home page of the University of Massachusetts Department of Legal Studies is http://www.umass.edu/legal.

2. In "The Strange Case of the Electronic Lover," the author seems to feel that only Alex has taken on a disguise. In on-line communities called MOOs and MUDs, everyone typically assumes a new identity. An article in Chapter 22 by Jennifer Mnookin describes such communities and their attempts at dispute resolution. In a well-known article entitled "A Rape in Cyberspace," Julian Dibbell contemplates whether distinctions between word and deed can endure in an age dominated by electronic communication. He writes:

> For whatever else these thoughts tell me, I have come to believe that they announce the final stages of our decades-long passage into the Information Age, a paradigm shift that the classic liberal firewall between word and deed (itself a product of an earlier paradigm shift commonly known as the Enlightenment) is not likely to survive intact. After all, anyone the least bit familiar with the workings of the new era's definitive technology, the computer, knows that it operates on a principle impractically difficult to distinguish from the pre-Enlightenment principle of the magic word: the commands you type into a computer are a kind of speech that doesn't so much communicate as make things happen, directly and ineluctably, the same way pulling a trigger does. They are incantations, in other words, and anyone at all attuned to the technosocial megatrends of the moment—from the growing dependence of economies on the global flow of intensely fetishized words and numbers to the burgeoning ability of bioengineers to speak the spells written in the four-letter text of DNA—knows that the logic of the incantation is rapidly permeating the fabric of our lives.*

---

*Julian Dibbell, "A Rape in Cyberspace," *The Village Voice*, December 23, 1993.

3. Sherry Turkle has written that

> At one level, the computer is a tool. It helps us write, keep track of our accounts, and communicate with others. Beyond this, the computer offers us both new models of mind and a new medium on which to project our ideas and fantasies. Most recently, the computer has become even more than tool and mirror: We are able to step through the looking glass. We are learning to live in virtual worlds. We may find ourselves alone as we navigate virtual oceans, unravel virtual mysteries, and engineer virtual skyscrapers. But increasingly, when we step through the looking glass, people are there as well. . . .
>
> In the story of constructing identity in the culture of simulation, experiences on the Internet figure prominently, but these experiences can only be understood as part of a larger cultural context. That context is the story of eroding boundaries between the real and the virtual, the animate and the inanimate, the unitary and the multiple self, which is occurring both in advanced scientific fields of research and in the patterns of everyday life. From scientists trying to create artificial life to children "morphing" through a series of virtual personnae, we shall see evidence of fundamental shifts in the way we create and experience human identity. But it is on the Internet that our confrontations with technology as it collides with our sense of human identity are fresh, even raw. In the real-time communities of cyberspace, we are dwellers on the threshold between the real and virtual, unsure of our footing, inventing ourselves as we go along.[†]

4. Whether one has a right to express oneself anonymously is likely to become a significant legal issue. This issue is discussed by Michael Froomkin, <http://www.law.miami.edu/ ~ froomkin/welcome.html>, in "The Metaphor Is the Key: Cryptography, the Clipper Chip and the Constitution," *U. Penn. L. Rev.* 143 (1995), p. 709.

---

[†]Sherry Turkle, *Life on the Screen* (New York: Simon and Schuster, 1995), pp. 9–10.

 

The "Strange Case of the Electronic Lover" may seem less strange today than it did when it was first published. Increasing numbers of people understand that on-line interactions can happen quickly and over great distances. What remains difficult to comprehend is the ultimate effect of a large-scale movement of a wide variety of transactions and interactions to cyberspace.

"Electronic Lover" was about a place where there were opportunities for expanded communication, freer communication, and communication that was subject to fewer constraints than our conversations in many contexts where we meet face to face. This is also an environment in which appearances are not necessarily to be trusted, as opportunities to deceive may be greater than in other environments. The following article suggests an additional cost, one related to privacy.

When we speak to someone face to face, we can usually assume that no one else is listening. When we use a telephone, particularly a cellular phone, we may be a little less sure about privacy and confidentiality, but the odds are that no one else is listening. With electronic communication, however, we operate in a different context. The on-line environment is one in which machines are connected, in which every communication one receives is actually a copy of something that originated on someone else's screen, and in which whatever keystrokes you press as you log into and work with a distant machine may be recorded, stored, and analyzed. Our economy is becoming more and more oriented to the production and sale of information products. Traditionally, concern over invasions of privacy stemmed from fear of the state and abuses of state power. Increasingly, however, invasions of privacy have economic value, and it is the private use of information that we may even reveal voluntarily, that is of growing concern.

## 21.2 | Online Profiling    *Federal Trade Commission*

### II. WHAT IS ONLINE PROFILING?

**A. Overview**  Over the past few years, online advertising has grown exponentially in tandem with the World Wide Web. Online advertising revenues in the U.S. grew from $301 million in 1996 to $4.62 billion in 1999, and were projected to reach $11.5 billion by 2003. A large portion of that online advertising is in the form of "banner ads" displayed on Web pages—small graphic advertisements that appear in boxes above or to the side of the primary site content. Currently, tens of billions of banner ads are delivered to consumers each month as they surf the World Wide Web. Often, these ads are not selected and delivered by the Web site visited by a consumer, but by a network advertising company that manages and provides advertising for numerous unrelated Web sites. DoubleClick, Engage, and 24/7 Media, three of the largest Internet advertising networks, all estimate that over half of all online consumers have seen an ad that they delivered.

In general, these network advertising companies do not merely supply banner ads; they also gather data about the consumers who view their ads. This is accomplished primarily by the use of "cookies" and "Web bugs" which track the individual's actions on the Web. Among the types of information that can be collected by network advertisers are: information on the Web sites and pages within those sites visited by consumers; the time and duration of the visits; query terms entered into search engines; purchases;

"click-through" responses to advertisements; and the Web page a consumer came from before landing on the site monitored by the particular ad network (the referring page). All of this information is gathered even if the consumer never clicks on a single ad.

The information gathered by network advertisers is often, but not always, anonymous, *i.e.,* the profiles are frequently linked to the identification number of the advertising network's cookie on the consumer's computer rather than the name of a specific person. This data is generally referred to as non-personally identifiable information ("non-PII"). In some circumstances, however, the profiles derived from tracking consumers' activities on the Web are linked or merged with personally identifiable information ("PII"). This generally occurs in one of two ways when consumers identify themselves to a Web site on which the network advertiser places banner ads. First, the Web site to whom personal information is provided may, in turn, provide that information to the network advertiser. Second, depending upon how the personal information is retrieved and processed by the Web site, the personally identifying information may be incorporated into a URL string that is automatically transmitted to the network advertiser through its cookie.

Once collected, consumer data can be analyzed and combined with demographic and "psychographic" data from third-party sources, data on the consumer's offline purchases, or information collected directly from consumers through surveys and registration forms. This enhanced data allows the advertising networks to make a variety of inferences about each consumer's interests and preferences. The result is a detailed

Federal Trade Commission, "Online Profiling: A Report to Congress" (June 13, 2000). (Footnotes have been omitted.—Ed.)

profile that attempts to predict the individual consumer's tastes, needs, and purchasing habits and enables the advertising companies' computers to make split-second decisions about how to deliver ads directly targeted to the consumer's specific interests.

The profiles created by the advertising networks can be extremely detailed. A cookie placed by a network advertising company can track a consumer on any Web site served by that company, thereby allowing data collection across disparate and unrelated sites on the Web. Also, because the cookies used by ad networks are generally persistent, their tracking occurs over an extended period of time, resuming each time the individual logs on to the Internet. When this "clickstream" information is combined with third-party data, these profiles can include hundreds of distinct data fields.

Although network advertisers and their profiling activities are nearly ubiquitous, they are most often invisible to consumers. All that consumers see are the Web sites they visit; banner ads appear as a seamless, integral part of the Web page on which they appear and cookies are placed without any notice to consumers. Unless the Web sites visited by consumers provide notice of the ad network's presence and data collection, consumers may be totally unaware that their activities online are being monitored.

**B. An Illustration of How Network Profiling Works**   *Online consumer Joe Smith goes to a Web site that sells sporting goods. He clicks on the page for golf bags. While there, he sees a banner ad, which he ignores as it does not interest him. The ad was placed by USAad Network. He then goes to a travel site and enters a search on "Hawaii." USAad Network also serves ads on this site, and Joe sees an ad for rental cars there. Joe then visits an online bookstore and browses through books about the world's best golf courses. USAad Network serves ads there, as well. A week later, Joe visits his favorite online news site, and notices an ad for golf vacation packages in Hawaii. Delighted, he clicks on the ad, which was served by the USAad Network. Later, Joe begins to wonder whether it was a coincidence that this particular ad appeared and, if not, how it happened.*

At Joe's first stop on the Web, the sporting goods site, his browser will automatically send certain information to the site that the site needs in order to communicate with Joe's computer: his browser type and operating system; the language(s) accepted by the browser; and the computer's Internet address. The server hosting the sporting goods site answers by transmitting the HTTP header and HTML source code for the site's home page, which allows Joe's computer to display the page.

Embedded in the HTML code that Joe's browser receives from the sporting goods site is an invisible link to the USAad Network site which delivers ads in the banner space on the sporting goods Web site. Joe's browser is automatically triggered to send an HTTP request to USAad which reveals the following information: his browser type and operating system; the language(s) accepted by the browser; the address of the referring Web page (in this case, the home page of the sporting goods site); and the identification number and information stored in any USAad cookies already on Joe's computer. Based on this information, USAad will place an ad in the pre-set banner space on the sporting goods site's home page. The ad will appear as an integral part of the page. If an USAad cookie is not already present on Joe's computer, USAad will place a cookie with a unique identifier on Joe's hard drive. Unless he has set his browser to notify him before accepting cookies, Joe has no way to know that a cookie is being placed on his computer. When Joe clicks on the page for golf bags, the URL address of that page, which discloses its content, is also transmitted to USAad by its cookie.

When Joe leaves the sporting goods site and goes to the travel site, also serviced by USAad, a similar process occurs. The HTML source code for the travel site will contain an invisible link to USAad that requests delivery of an ad as part of the travel site's page. Because the request reveals that the referring site is travel related, USAad sends an advertisement for rental cars. USAad will also know the identification number of its cookie on Joe's machine. As Joe moves around the travel site, USAad checks his cookie and modifies the profile associated with it, adding elements based on Joe's activities. When Joe enters a search for "Hawaii," his search term is transmitted to USAad through the URL used by the travel site to locate the information Joe wants and the search term is associated with the other data collected by the cookie on Joe's machine. USAad will also record what advertisements it has shown Joe and whether he has clicked on them.

This process is repeated when Joe goes to the online bookstore. Because USAad serves banner ads on this site as well, it will recognize Joe by his cookie identification number. USAad can track what books Joe looks at, even though he does not buy anything. The fact that Joe browsed for books about golf courses around the world is added to his profile.

Based on Joe's activities, USAad infers that Joe is a golfer, that he is interested in traveling to Hawaii someday, and that he might be interested in a golf vacation. Thus, a week later, when Joe goes to his favorite online news site, also served by USAad, the cookie on his computer is recognized and he is presented with an ad for golf vacation packages in Hawaii. The ad grabs his attention and appeals to his interests, so he clicks on it.

## III. PROFILING BENEFITS AND PRIVACY CONCERNS

**A. Benefits** Cookies are used for many purposes other than profiling by third-party advertisers, many of which significantly benefit consumers. For example, Web sites often ask for user names and passwords when purchases are made or before certain kinds of content are provided. Cookies can store these names and passwords so that consumers do not need to sign in each time they visit the site. In addition, many sites allow consumers to set items aside in an electronic shopping cart while they decide whether or not to purchase them; cookies allow a Web site to remember what is in a consumer's shopping cart from prior visits. Cookies also can be used by Web sites to offer personalized home pages or other customized content with local news and weather, favorite stock quotes, and other material of interest to individual consumers. Individual online merchants can use cookies to track consumers' purchases in order to offer recommendations about new products or sales that may be of interest to their established customers. Finally, by enabling businesses

to monitor traffic on their Web sites, cookies allow businesses to constantly revise the design and layout of their sites to make them more interesting and efficient.

Network advertisers' use of cookies and other technologies to create targeted marketing programs also benefits both consumers and businesses. . . . Targeted advertising can also improve a consumer's Web experience simply by ensuring that she is not repeatedly bombarded by the same ads. Businesses clearly benefit as well from the ability to target advertising because they avoid wasting advertising dollars marketing themselves to consumers who have no interest in their products.

Additionally, a number of commenters stated that targeted advertising helps to subsidize free content on the Internet. By making advertising more effective, profiling allows Web sites to charge more for advertising. This advertising revenue helps to subsidize their operations, making it possible to offer free content rather than charging fees for access.

Finally, one commenter suggested that profiles can also be used to create new products and services. First, entrepreneurs could use consumer profiles to identify and assess the demand for particular products or services. Second, targeted advertising could help small companies to more effectively break into the market by advertising only to consumers who have an interest in their products or services.

In sum, targeted advertising can provide numerous benefits to both business and consumers.

**B. Concerns** Despite the benefits of targeted advertising, there is widespread concern about current profiling practices. Many commenters at the [Public] Workshop objected to network advertisers' hidden monitoring of consumers and collection of extensive personal data without consumers' knowledge or consent; they also noted that network advertisers offer consumers few, if any, choices about the use and dissemination of their individual information obtained in this manner. As one of the commenters put it, current profiling practices "undermine individuals' expectations of privacy by fundamentally changing the Web experience from one where consumers can browse and seek out information anonymously, to one where an individual's every move is recorded."

The most consistent and significant concern expressed about profiling is that it is conducted without consumers' knowledge. The presence and identity of a network advertiser on a particular site, the placement of a cookie on the consumer's computer, the tracking of the consumer's movements, and the targeting of ads are simply invisible in most cases. This is true because, as a practical matter, there are only two ways for consumers to find out about profiling at a particular site before it occurs. The first is for Web sites that use the services of network advertisers to disclose that fact in their privacy policies. Unfortunately, this does not typically occur. As the Commission's recent privacy survey discovered, although 57% of a random sample of the busiest Web sites allowed third parties to place cookies, only 22% of those sites mentioned third-party cookies or data collection in their privacy policies; of the top 100 sites on the Web, 78% allowed third-party cookie placement, but only 51% of those sites disclosed that fact. The second way for consumers to detect profiling is to configure their browsers to notify them before accepting cookies. One recent survey indicates, however, that only 40% of computer users have even heard of cookies and, of those, only 75% have a basic understanding of what they are.

The second most persistent concern expressed by commenters was the extensive and sustained scope of the monitoring that occurs. Unbeknownst to most consumers, advertising networks monitor individuals across a multitude of seemingly unrelated Web sites and over an indefinite period of time. The result is a profile far more comprehensive than any individual Web site could gather. Although much of the information that goes into a profile is fairly innocuous when viewed in isolation, the cumulation over time of vast numbers of seemingly minor details about an individual produces a portrait that is quite comprehensive and, to many, inherently intrusive.

For many of those who expressed concerns about profiling, the privacy implications of profil-

ing are not ameliorated in cases where the profile contains no personally identifiable information. First, these commenters felt that the comprehensive nature of the profiles and the technology used to create them make it reasonably easy to associate previously anonymous profiles with particular individuals. This means that anyone who obtains access to ostensibly anonymous data—either by purchasing the data or hacking into it—might be able to mine the data and link it to identifiable individuals. Second, commenters feared that companies could unilaterally change their operating procedures and begin associating personally identifiable information with non-personally identifiable data previously collected. Third, commenters noted that, regardless of whether they contain personally identifiable information, profiles are used to make decisions about the information individuals see and the offers they receive. These commenters expressed concern that companies could use profiles to determine the prices and terms upon which goods and services, including important services like life insurance, are offered to individuals (for example, products might be offered at higher prices to consumers whose profiles indicate that they are wealthy, or insurance might be offered at higher prices to consumers whose profiles indicate possible health risks). This practice, known as "weblining," raises many of the same concerns that "redlining" and "reverse redlining" do in offline financial markets. . . .

. . . [S]urveys show that consumers are not comfortable with profiling. A *Business Week* survey conducted in March of this year [2000] found that 89% of consumers are not comfortable having their browsing habits and shopping patterns merged into a profile that is linked to their real name and identity. If that profile also includes additional personal information such as income, driver's license, credit data and medical status, 95% of consumers express discomfort. Consistent with the comments received in connection with the Public Workshop, consumers are also opposed to profiling even when data are not personally identifiable: 63% of consumers say they are not comfortable having their online movements tracked even if the data is not linked to their name or real-world identity. An overwhelming 91% of consumers say that they are not comfortable with Web sites sharing information so that they can be tracked across multiple Web sites.

Many consumers indicate that their concerns about the collection of personal information for online profiling would be diminished if they were given clear notice of what data would be collected about them and what it would be used for, and were given a choice to opt-out of data collection or of particular uses of their personal data. A recent survey by Privacy & American Business explained to Internet users that, in order to offer consumers personalized advertising, companies would need information about the consumer. Internet users were then asked about their willingness to provide that information by: (1) describing their interests; (2) allowing the use of information on their Web site visits; (3) allowing the use of information on their Internet purchases; (4) allowing the use of information on their offline purchases; and (5) allowing the combination of online and offline purchasing information. When told that the company providing tailored ads would spell out how they would use the consumer's information and the consumer would be given a chance to opt-out of any uses that he did not approve, a majority of consumers indicated willingness to provide personal information. With notice and choice, 68% were willing to describe their interests; 58% were willing to allow site visit data to be used; 51% were willing to allow use of online purchasing information; 53% were willing to allow use of offline purchasing data; and 52% were willing to allow the use of combined online and offline purchasing information.

Although this survey indicates that, with appropriate notice and choice, many consumers would be willing to allow companies to use their personal information in order to deliver advertising targeted to the consumer's individual needs and interests, the statistics also demonstrate that many consumers are not willing to allow this kind of profiling *regardless of whether notice and choice are given.* A substantial minority of Internet users—between 32% and 49%—indicated that they would not be willing to participate in personalization programs even if they were told what would be done with their information and were given the choice to opt-out of uses that they did not approve.

Internet users are also overwhelmingly opposed to the wholesale dissemination of their personal information. Ninety-two percent say that they are not comfortable with Web sites sharing their personal information with other organizations and 93% are uncomfortable with their information being sold. Eighty-eight percent of consumers say they would like a Web site to ask their permission every time it wants to share their personal information with others.

Ultimately, consumers' privacy concerns are businesses' concerns; the electronic marketplace will not reach its full potential unless consumers become more comfortable browsing and purchasing online. That comfort is unlikely to come unless consumers are confident (1) that they are notified at the time and place information is collected who is collecting information about them, what information is being collected, and how it will be used and (2) that they can choose whether their personal information is gathered, how it is used, and to whom it is disseminated.

## Notes and Questions

1. Online resources concerning privacy are accessible at http://www.epic.org/ (Electronic Privacy Information Center), http://www.privacy.org/ipc/ (Internet Privacy Coalition), http://www.cdt.org/ (Center for Democracy and Technology), http://www.eff.org/ (Electronic Frontier Foundation), http://www.etrust.org/ (eTRUST Privacy Project), and http://www.aclu.org/ (American Civil Liberties Union).

# 22 LAW AND CYBERSPACE AND LAW IN CYBERSPACE

❧ Cyberspace may be a vibrant place, a creative place, a fun place, even a lucrative place. It is not, however, a harmonious place. The on-line environment allows one to make contact quickly with people who may have the same interests, but opportunities for deception and disagreement are also present. How should we settle disputes that arise in cyberspace? And where should they be settled? In the United States, whether a case will be heard in Massachusetts or California usually depends on where the dispute arose or where the parties are located. There are intricate rules that govern whether a case belongs in the state or federal courts. When disputes arise out of on-line activity, however, where is the activity occurring? Interactions between citizens of different countries can occur just as easily as those between citizens of the same state.

The following readings provide evidence of the broad range of long-term questions that the emergence of cyberspace will pose for anyone concerned with law. The excerpt from *Sex, Laws, and Cyberspace,* by Jonathan Wallace and Mark Mangan, shows that we must confront the fact that we have a rising level of disputing and that, at the same time, the power of states is eroding because more and more activity is occurring between people separated by great distances. In "Law and Borders," David Johnson and David Post recognize this and argue that the solution to the problem of on-line disputes is to have a system of on-line law. In the last reading, Jennifer Mnookin describes an on-line activity that already has its own law and its own institutions for dealing with conflicts and disputes. As you read her article, consider whether the on-line environment will be not only a source of conflict but a source of solutions to conflict.

## 22.1 | Sex, Laws, and Cyberspace *Jonathan Wallace and Mark Mangan*

### ACT I—THE STING

POSTAL INSPECTOR DAVID DIRMEYER of Memphis, Tennessee, was trolling for pornographers. Dirmeyer was a lanky man with a Tennessee twang. He had 15 years of government service and a collection of genuine child pornography, seized by the Postal Service more than 10 years before. Dirmeyer had a tested routine. Using a pseudonym, he would contact pornographers, order material from them, and, via telephone conversations or the mail, attempt to interest them in some "action mags." If they expressed interest, he would mail them the magazines, and then perform what he called a "controlled delivery." Armed with a search warrant, Dirmeyer would show up at the suspect's house on the day the magazines were delivered, seize the contraband, and execute a search of the premises.

Dirmeyer had received special training in combatting child pornography and obscenity, and had participated in approximately one dozen investigations of pornographers, of which about half had involved controlled deliveries. In July of 1993, Dirmeyer reeled in Robert and Carleen Thomas of Milpitas, California—his first computer pornographers. . . .

Dirmeyer first learned of the Thomases' Amateur Action bulletin board system ("AABBS") in late July 1993, when he was contacted by Earl Crawley of Gleason, Tennessee. Crawley was a hacker who had stumbled into the public section of the board. The Thomases had been running their electronic pornography store since 1991 and went to some trouble to run it carefully. It was a membership-only system; only one file, containing a text description of some 17,000 Graphic Interface Format ("GIF") files, was available to nonmembers. To join, a user printed a form from the BBS, filled it out and mailed it to the Thomases in Milpitas. The form included the user's address and telephone information. One of the Thomases, usually Robert, would then call and speak to the applicant before signing him up as a member. Generally, from the handwriting on the form and the applicant's voice on the telephone, Robert would be able to make a careful judgment of whether the applicant was over eighteen. He testified at trial that he frequently had refused membership on this basis.

On AABBS's main menu, an option entitled "Legal Issues" pointed to a file directed at law enforcement officers who might be investigating the board. The file stated that the operation was legal, having been investigated and cleared by the San Jose police department in 1992. This file had been prepared by J. Keith Henson, a software developer and Internet activist who became involved with the Thomases after their high-tech operation's first confrontation with the law. Another legally prudent feature of AABBS was that no uploads were accepted. Robert Thomas was afraid that some-

one would upload something illegal, such as child pornography, on his system.

The material he made available was carefully screened. Though many of the GIFs he captioned as involving pre-teens, Robert Thomas went to lengths to be sure that the women in the pictures were all 18 or older. He distributed a certain amount of "naturist" material—nudist camp footage of children in nonsexual situations—which at trial was acknowledged to be legal in all 50 states. But he was careful to stay away from any images of children in sexual situations. On the other hand, he knew what his customers wanted and would suggestively hint at underage sex and incest. At the same time, he openly solicited requests from his members, and made efforts to fulfill their graphics and video desires.

Robert Thomas had found a pretty good formula for marketing explicit sexual materials online. Several membership plans were available, allowing users to spend a certain amount of time on the BBS, or download a certain number of files. The text was a tease for the GIFs, and the GIFs were primarily a come-on for the videos from which they were taken. In the first nine months of 1993, almost $240,000 had passed through one of the Thomases' bank accounts, and there may have been other accounts. The business was run from three locations: the house, where the computers, printers, and 32 modems were kept; a warehouse, where the videotapes, the duplication bank of 32 VCRs, the car and the boat were located; and a Mailboxes Etc. store that received their business mail.

The Thomases had collected the full gamut of sexual images including bestiality, rape, torture, and incest. Many of the GIFs on AABBS were taken from publicly available videotapes. For the corresponding text descriptions, Robert Thomas often copied words from the box; other times he would set his imagination free. . . .

Dirmeyer, who had not previously had much contact with computers, dialed into AABBS for the first time on a borrowed machine in his office in Memphis. At first look, he must have seen enough to rush the blood of even the most jaded porno-seeking postal inspector. The public files seemed to point to a slew of pictures of little girls and boys engaged in all kinds of illegal sex acts. Dirmeyer took no action for a couple of weeks, but on August 20 he called AABBS again, armed with a false name and a firm plan to go undercover.

In his communications with the Thomases, Dirmeyer became Lance White, with a mail drop address in Cordova, Tennessee. He used the **print screen** command liberally to capture his sessions. First, he read and printed a message stating that subscribers to AABBS could download GIFs and obtain lists of videos, magazines, and novelty items available for sale by the Sysop. Dirmeyer promptly printed an application form, completed it as Lance White, and sent it to the Thomases' mail drop. His $55 money order bought him a six-month subscription to AABBS with a 90-minute time limit per day.

Dirmeyer also maintained a telephone number and answering machine in the name of Lance White and six days later, he found a message on it from Robert Thomas, welcoming him to AABBS. Later that same day, Dirmeyer was logged onto AABBS when Thomas initiated chat mode and welcomed him to the system as the newest of about 3,500 users. Dirmeyer continued to hit his **print screen** button, capturing all kinds of material for his day in court—such as a list of "nudist" videos advertised as containing "tender young teens caught candid at nudist colony." Such material is legal in all 50 states, but Dirmeyer thought it had prosecutorial merit. The next day, Dirmeyer printed a partial list of the 17,000 GIFs available. Trained to seek out obscenity, he scanned in particular for lewd phrases evidencing underage sex.

Dirmeyer then sent a $41 money order to the Milpitas mailing address, asking Thomas to pick a video for him from those referenced in the AABBS listing as K71 through K74. Thomas had assigned each video a letter and number, and the trial testimony later indicated that the letters were shorthand for the content. For instance, "K", for kinky, was the catch-all category in which Thomas placed everything which did not comfortably fit into a single topic heading, such as one with defecation and bestiality. . . .

When video K74 arrived at Lance White's address, Dirmeyer dutifully watched it in its entirety, prepared a written description for later use, and wrote to Thomas again, ordering four more from the K series. In a video described in detail at the trial, a man breaks into a house and brutally rapes the young housewife and her girlfriend at gunpoint. The corresponding text description was "The girls scream with pain throughout the whole video! Excellent Action!" In the same order, Dirmeyer asked Thomas to select two teen nudist videos. . . .

In October, Dirmeyer decided that the time was ripe to proceed to the next step in his sting operation and reveal the contents of his "action mags." Leaving his feigned subtlety aside, he finally specified that he had "hardcore sex magazines featuring young girls having sex with adults and other children." He wrote, "These magazines were hard to come by and are very special to me. I am willing to let you borrow them so you can scan whatever pictures you want for your private collection. All I ask is that you return the mags to me (with a copy of the GIFs) when you are finished." Though the correspondence was later found in his files, Thomas testified at trial that he never saw it.

On November 3, Dirmeyer sent E-mail to Thomas, asking him to respond to the letter sent two weeks earlier about the "action mags." Six days later, Dirmeyer was again on the BBS when Thomas initiated chat mode, and according to Dirmeyer, indicated he was interested in the magazines. He asked that they be sent two-day air, so he could scan them over the weekend. Dirmeyer wasn't ready to proceed. As he explained at trial, controlled deliveries of contraband must be made in such a way that little chance exists that the material will pass into circulation. If he simply mailed the magazines to Thomas, images placed on AABBS might be disseminated to other computer systems and pass beyond Dirmeyer's reach before he got his magazines back. He needed to time the delivery to coincide with a trip to California and the obtaining of a search warrant. He therefore sent Thomas what he referred to as a lulling letter, stating that he had been unable to send the magazines due to personal problems and would ship them as soon as he could. At the end of October, Dirmeyer got in touch with the San Jose Police Department, Bureau of Investigations, and spoke to an investigator named Greg Gunsky.

Gunsky told him that AABBS had been seized and searched in January of the prior year, and that no charges had been brought. Investigator Mark McIninch had joined AABBS in an undercover guise in 1991 and over time had made a number of purchases from Thomas. On January 20, 1992, McIninch had gone to the Thomas residence with a search warrant and had seized computers, VCRs, and videotapes. When no child pornography was found, the San Jose police came to the conclusion that the remaining materials—the same ones Dirmeyer had been purchasing—did not violate California community standards. They returned all the equipment, gave Thomas a letter confirming that they had found nothing illegal on the board, and left. What the California police found was crude, pornographic, and perhaps worth the effort of investigating, but it was nothing for which they could reasonably prosecute.

At this point, Thomas was contacted by J. Keith Henson, a self-taught expert in computer law. Henson, a California-based software developer, had wide-ranging interests including planetary exploration, cryogenics, nanotechnology, and freedom on the Internet. Henson has been in the software business since 1972, but it was through his work with Alcor, a cryogenics foundation, that he acquired his expertise in laws pertaining to cyberspace. People sign up with Alcor either to have their entire body frozen in the hope of later revival, or, if they cannot afford the full treatment, have their severed heads preserved instead on the assumption that someday technology will permit the head to be revived and reattached to a body. In 1988, when an Alcor client died at Alcor's facility, she was promptly decapitated and her head frozen. No physician had ever signed a death certificate, and when the San Jose police were investigating a possible murder, they seized Alcor's computer systems. Board member Henson made himself an expert in the Electronic Communications Privacy Act ("ECPA").

This law, which Congress had passed the year before, provides financial penalties for the seizure of computer equipment if it impedes the transmission of electronic mail to the intended recipient. The police who seized Alcor's computers knew nothing about the ECPA and disregarded its constraints on them. Henson effectively backed them off, got the computers returned to Alcor, brought a pro se lawsuit against the authorities, and recovered a settlement of $30,000.

When McIninch seized AABBS, he kept it for five weeks and interrupted the delivery of electronic mail. Five years after the passage of the ECPA, the San Jose police were apparently not any more familiar with the law. Henson discovered what was happening, contacted Robert Thomas, and informally helped him confront the authorities. Henson told McIninch and the prosecutor to contact Don Ingram, the county attorney who had taken a shellacking over the Alcor incident. According to Henson, they did, and after hearing Ingram's tale of woe, they returned the AABBS equipment to Thomas and gave him the written release. Henson contributed the Legal Issues file, accessible from the main menu of AABBS, which advised putative investigators that AABBS had already been seized and was found to be legal.

An interesting question is whether Dirmeyer really proceeded several months into the AABBS investigation before contacting the San Jose authorities. After reading the Legal Issues file, or certainly no later than his conversation with the San Jose investigator, Dirmeyer must have been aware that, at least under California community standards, the BBS had been cleared. Yet he still pushed forward. He must have either felt certain that Tennessee standards were so much stricter he could get a conviction, or that his controlled delivery of the "action mags" would make up for the lack of child pornography on AABBS. Perhaps the Thomas' text descriptions were so explicit that he simply felt compelled to shut them down.

On November 16, Dirmeyer flew to Milpitas, California and drove by the Thomas residence, observing a handmade "UPS Pickup" sign in one of the windows. One can only imagine the excitement Dirmeyer must have felt to be close to his prey after so many months of E-mail. The following day, he visited the AABBS mail drop, Mail Boxes, Etc., and spoke to Tom Pennybacker, the owner. While Pennybacker was confirming that the Thomases rented mail box #284 from him, Dirmeyer unexpectedly had his first view of one of his suspects, "a white female, approximately 37 years old, 5 feet one inch in height, weighing approximately 100 lbs. with gray streaked black hair, entered the establishment." It was Carleen Thomas. She picked up a package, loaded it into her new sun-roofed Toyota and drove off. Dirmeyer returned to Tennessee and took no further recorded action on the Thomas case until January, when he returned to San Jose. The official purpose of this November surveillance was never revealed.

Dirmeyer applied to federal magistrate Wayne D. Brazil in San Jose for a search warrant, filing a 27-page affidavit which summarized the history of his pursuit of the Thomases. Here he got an unpleasant surprise. The magistrate wouldn't give him a search warrant for the action mags. There were two possible reasons. The federal law Dirmeyer was proceeding under, which governed child pornography, had been held unconstitutional for vagueness by the federal appeals court which had jurisdiction over California. When an appeals court voids a law, its decision is only effective in the states over which it sits, so the same law was still effective in Tennessee. Second, California federal courts will not grant search warrants for a house when the "controlled delivery" is made to a post office box. In any event, Dirmeyer improvised a solution.

On January 9, he returned to Mail Boxes, Etc. and initiated his controlled delivery by stuffing the package into the Thomases mailbox. The package contained three magazines, entitled "Lolita Color Special 6," "Lolita Color Special 18," and "Little Girls Fuck, Too." Dirmeyer confided in Pennybacker that he was setting up a surveillance, then waited outside the building for Robert or Carleen Thomas to pick up the package.

He watched and waited. They never showed that day so he went back to the hotel. He arrived early the next day, set up, and waited again. They still didn't show. Finally, late in the day, he enlisted Pennybacker's help and had him call the Thomas residence. The Thomases later testified that Pennybacker was strange and rather insistent that they get their package, making up an excuse about inventory. Carleen Thomas finally responded to Pennybacker's pressure and came over to the store. Dirmeyer, assisted by San Jose police, followed Carleen back to her house. At five o'clock the same night, he rang the Thomases' doorbell.

After six months, the postal inspector now met his quarry for the first time. He was accompanied by four San Jose police officers, including Officer Jim McMahon (the head of the high tech unit), an Assistant District Attorney, and two local postal inspectors. Dirmeyer presented Thomas with an unsigned, undated search warrant which noted on its face that it had been issued by Magistrate Brazil. The search warrant listed the tapes that Dirmeyer had purchased, the GIFs he had downloaded, and the description files, and called for the seizure of all computer equipment. The warrant made no mention of the action mags.

Dirmeyer found his magazines in the Thomases' bedroom, but he had no authority to seize them. Instead, it was necessary to get Robert Thomas' consent. According to Thomas, Dirmeyer said that if Thomas didn't cooperate, he would keep them locked up in the house for as many hours as it took him to drive to San Francisco and get a search warrant, and that he and his men would then "rip the house apart." He offered Thomas a "Consent to Search Form." Apparently, Dirmeyer and the San Jose police each carried a stack of these—you never know when you might need to search something. Thomas, who had not yet contacted an attorney, signed the form, but only after making Dirmeyer add some language to it. The form's boilerplate read:

> I, _____ , have been informed by _____ , who made proper identification as (an) authorized law enforcement officer(s) of the _____ , of my CONSTITUTIONAL RIGHT not to have a search made of the premises and property owned by me and under my care, custody and control, without a search warrant.

The form further acknowledges that the signer knowingly waives this right. In another blank, Dirmeyer hand-wrote a description of the property he was looking for, "namely priority mail package from Lance White addressed to Robert Thomas." Following this was the wording Thomas insisted on as a condition of his signing the consent, "sent without his knowledge." At this point, Thomas had no idea that Dirmeyer and Lance White were one and the same. In fact, he thought that Dirmeyer might really be after this Lance White character, and AABBS had just been caught in the middle.

Around eight o'clock, Thomas thought to call Henson, whom he had never met in person. Henson asked to talk to Dirmeyer. Dirmeyer apparently thought Henson was a lawyer and agreed to speak with him. Henson sternly asked him if he was familiar with the ECPA. According to Henson, Dirmeyer replied that he was in fact aware of the ECPA, and didn't think he had any problem with it because it was their intent to bring the system back within a few days without looking at any of the 2000 E-mail messages stored on the system.

One of the policemen drew a sketch of the house; in addition, every room of the house thought to play a role in the business was photographed. The investigators, not sure where to stop, even got shots of the Atari game computer in one of the Thomas son's bedroom. McMahon, Dirmeyer, and Thomas then headed over to the warehouse. Here they ran into another problem. Dirmeyer was apparently unaware of the warehouse and had failed to include it in the search warrant. They again managed their way around this by asking Thomas to sign two more Consents to Search. This time Dirmeyer used a local form carried by McMahon, as Dirmeyer had no more left. Thomas signed one consenting to the seizure of "three pieces of lined notebook paper with writing by Lance White" and another agreeing to the seizure of the masters of the videotapes Dirmeyer had ordered. The officers photographed the banks of VCRs used for copying, a Ford Mustang, and a boat.

On Tuesday, Dirmeyer again visited the Thomases, taking fingerprints and handwriting samples. As he left, he told Robert Thomas that if he wanted to get any consideration for cooperation, "it might be a good idea to keep the cover of Lance White intact." He was hoping to use AABBS to catch other users, and in fact had engaged in "a couple of transactions [with] one guy from Boston." Robert Thomas still had not put two and two together and apparently thought he was being warned not to talk about user Lance White, the subject of a separate investigation. Copying the electronic files took longer than expected, and it took the San Jose cops the rest of the week to back up AABBS. The system had so much hard drive space, it kept exceeding the capacity of whatever the police tried to download it

onto. They finally went out and borrowed a drive capacious enough.

On Tuesday, Henson wrote up the whole episode and posted it to Usenet's Electronic Frontier Foundation ("EFF") newsgroup. EFF is an organization, founded by Mitch Kapor and John Perry Barlow, which specializes in the freedom of electronic communications. Henson continued to post reports to several newsgroups throughout the trial. Wednesday and Thursday, he spent some time briefing an attorney Thomas retained, Richard Williams of San Jose, on the ECPA and some of the prior cases, including Alcor and a similar, well-publicized government seizure of the computer systems at Steve Jackson Games in Austin, Texas.

On Friday, just as Henson was about to meet Robert Thomas for the first time, Thomas called him. Carleen had found that the original "Lance White" registration form and Lance White's name printed on the "Permission To Search" looked identical. Henson tried dialing the phone number from the registration form, "to my ear, the answering machine's message which says it is Lance White's phone and the person I talked to who said he was Dirmeyer are the same person."

Dirmeyer called Thomas on Friday and told him to come down to a postal facility in San Jose on Saturday morning at 8:30 to retrieve his computer equipment or he wouldn't be able to get it until the following Tuesday. Dirmeyer was leaving that morning to return to Tennessee. Thomas replied that he was sick, that it wasn't convenient for him to come down, and requested the government deliver his stuff back to him. Finally, the Thomases' two sons and a friend went to get the computers, accompanied by Henson. On crutches from an injury, Henson approached Dirmeyer and asked him if he was Lance White. Dirmeyer admitted it. . . .

## ACT II—THE TRIAL

At trial, the jury heard that the Thomases were rich, vulgar, monsters. A Tennessee grand jury had charged them in a twelve-count indictment for distributing obscene pictures and videos, and helping Dirmeyer send them some child pornography.

Count one charged the Thomases with conspiring to break the law. Counts two through eleven were the obscenity charges; two through seven involved the interstate transport of graphic files; eight through ten the shipment of six videocassettes. Count eleven charged them with "aiding and abetting" the shipment of child pornography. They could only be charged with "receiving" Dirmeyer's special action mags in the state where they arrived. Count twelve was a legal extra—it did not charge them with anything, but simply called for forfeiture of all their computer equipment.

The Thomases had retained California attorney Richard D. Williams. Before the trial began, Williams made a flurry of motions. He first brought a motion before the federal court in California, arguing that the Thomases were protected by the Privacy Protection Act, which Congress enacted in 1980 to require law enforcement officials to obtain evidence whenever possible by less intrusive means than search and seizure. But when passing the act, Congress had made it clear that it was geared particularly to prevent the hasty seizure of journalists' and broadcasters' data, which might prove to contain time-sensitive news. It did not apply here.

Williams also asked that the search warrant and the seizure of the computer equipment be invalidated, citing the ECPA. Here, the government denied any wrongdoing and stood by the warrant. The court responded that although it had jurisdiction to decide such a motion, it would rather defer to the Tennessee court, and invited Williams to renew his motion there. When he arrived in Tennessee, Williams had a new set of legal maneuvers for Judge Julia Smith Gibbons.

The first was a motion to transfer the case back to California in the "interests of justice." Williams made a jurisdictional argument that AABBS did not have much to do with Tennessee, claiming "only approximately five of the BBS' 3,500 members reside in Tennessee." In support, he claimed that nothing had been "sent" to Tennessee, "The member pays for the call, reviews a menu, and 'downloads' what they choose. Thus, Defendants don't 'send' anything into Tennessee." Judge Gibbons denied the motion. She pointed out that obscenity cases involving interstate transport can legally be brought either in the district from which the material is sent or the

one in which it is received. Because the Thomases' pornography ended up in Tennessee, she was going to try them there. . . .

. . . The trial began inauspiciously at 11:05 on July 18, with Judge Gibbons asking Williams "where have you and your clients been since 9:30." Williams was late, without his legal file, and dressed in blue jeans. He explained that his luggage had been mistakenly redirected at Chicago the night before. Gibbons gave him until 2:00, and stated, "you either better find your luggage or take advantage of one of our stores and find something appropriate to wear in court."

Williams arrived at 2:00 with a new suit and a new motion—to dismiss count 11, the action mags/child pornography charge. He based his argument on *X-citement Video,* the 1992 case decided by the Ninth Circuit Court of Appeals, which had held the child pornography law to be unconstitutional because it did not require a defendant to know that an actress or actor in a video he distributed was a minor. The case involved a pornography star who had been acting since age 14 but looked older. Since possession of child pornography could not, at the moment, be a crime in California, to prosecute the Thomases in Tennessee for something that was legal back home was not fair. Judge Gibbons denied the motion.

Williams had one last motion. He wanted all evidence pertaining to chat mode communications excluded. Judge Gibbons said, "I'm going to have to be educated a bit about the whole process and what is involved before I can decide." She warned him that it was very important to her to start on time. "Obviously, we haven't got off to a very good start in that regard." . . .

Newsom began his opening statement with an explanation of the indictment, which charged the two defendants with eleven separate crimes. He told the jury it was up to them to determine if the GIFs and tapes were obscene. "If it's obscene, and the proof will show that it is obscene . . . it's the same as contraband, as machine guns, as drugs or anything else. It's not protected by the First Amendment. It's contraband."

Newsom described the three prongs of the test they would apply to determine obscenity. The first prong was that the average person, applying contemporary community standards, would find that the work, taken as a whole, appeals to a prurient interest in sex. The second prong was that the work depicts or describes sexual conduct in a patently offensive manner. The third prong was that the work lacks substantial literary, artistic, political, or scientific value. After rambling through most of the counts and the obscenity standard, Newsom began describing the on-line chat mode that Dirmeyer had used with Robert Thomas. Williams then made his first objection.

Making an objection during the opening statement is relatively rare, as lawyers have wide latitude in their opening and closing monologues. Williams was jumping the gun, eager to argue that the Chat-mode evidence was dubious. The judge overruled him, said Newsom could mention it, and they would get to it when they got to it.

Newsom, without relating them to the counts of the indictment, now spoke of the tapes ordered by Dirmeyer and shipped by Thomas via UPS. He went on to tell the story of the action mags, including Dirmeyer's repeated offers, Thomas' interest, and the result that "The proof will show that in fact the United States government made what we call a controlled delivery. We sent him those magazines, three magazines . . . involving children engaging in actual sexual conduct with adults . . . once they are delivered to the defendant, we go in and confiscate those back. We don't let them go out into the public for further circulation or lose control of them. . . . Pursuant to the defendant's request, he received the child pornography that he ordered."

Newsom asked the jury to "make that determination if they are obscene or not according to the standards that the judge will give you. If they are, and the government has proven each and every one of the elements in these crimes, we are going to ask you to convict each of these defendants of the crimes with which they are charged. Thank you ladies and gentlemen." He had never told them, specifically, what counts 8 through 11 of the indictment involved. Ironically, these included the sending of the videotapes—the most conventional charges in the case.

In his opening statement, Williams stressed many important issues, but simply beyond the Federal Court's scope. The jury had been in-

structed to decide if the AABBS material was sexually provocative, offensive, and devoid of artistic merit—according to their community values in Memphis. Rather than try to show that equivalent material existed in their community and that Thomas' pornography was not so bad, Williams raised the larger issue; which community standards should one apply in judging the Thomases? Was it fair to apply the conservative standards of Memphis, Tennessee to a pair of sysops living and working in Milpitas, California? This would later become *the* issue of the case for organizations such as the American Civil Liberties Union and the Electronic Frontier Foundation.

The community standards rule represents an improvisation by the Supreme Court in *Miller v. California*. The First Amendment of the United States Constitution states that "Congress shall make no law . . . abridging the freedom of speech." Obscenity is one of the few categories of "speech" which falls outside of First Amendment protection.

The evolution of obscenity laws over the decades has followed a more chaotic course than most areas of constitutional law. Originally, the states were left free to do almost anything they wanted, banning literary and scientific works by Walt Whitman, Theodore Dreiser, and Sigmund Freud, among many others, as obscene. A Walt Disney nature documentary was held obscene in one state because it showed the birth of a buffalo. Another movie was obscene in the South because it showed black and white children playing together. The utter confusion of obscenity law is best summed up in Justice Potter Stewart's famous remark that although he couldn't rightfully define obscenity, "I know it when I see it."

In the 1950s and 1960s, the Supreme Court developed a test somewhat similar to the current three-pronged *Miller* test. Significant differences were that a national community standard was implied, and that the prosecutor had the burden of showing that the work was "utterly without redeeming social value." The Court held during the 1960s that a magazine showing male nudity, without sexual acts, was not obscene, and that it was not a crime merely to possess obscene material in the privacy of one's own home.

The *Miller* standard arose with the arrest of Marvin Miller, who was charged with a violation of a California obscenity law for distributing flyers with explicit sexual depictions. The trial judge had informed the jury that they could apply a local standard on obscenity, and Miller appealed on this issue. The Supreme Court, in promulgating its three-pronged test, did a couple of notable things. First, it rejected the trend of the prior decade by explicitly confirming that a local standard would apply. Chief Justice Burger wrote that "It is neither realistic or constitutionally sound to read the First Amendment as requiring that people of Maine or Missouri accept public depiction of conduct found tolerable in Las Vegas or New York City."

Second, the Court reversed the burden of proof on the third prong of the test. Previously, it had been the prosecutor's job to prove lack of social value. Now, it was up to the defense to show some artistic, literary, political, or scientific value. Interestingly, the court adopted local standards as applicable to the first (appeal to prurient interest) and the second (patently offensive depiction of sexual conduct) prongs, but refused to extend it to the social value criteria of the third prong. It thereby stopped just short of allowing courts to call something art in California, but filth in Tennessee. The standard to be applied on the third prong was a universal "reasonable person" standard. Of the first two prongs, the prurient appeal part of the test has been paraphrased as meaning that it must "turn you on," while the patently offensive prong means that the material must simultaneously "gross you out."

In his opening statement, Williams reintroduced an argument from one of his rejected motions, touching upon the fine distinction between subject and object, sending and taking, with regards to the GIF files. He said that "it's very important that you know that my client is not sending things . . . the Thomases haven't sent anything anywhere with the exception of the videotapes." Although Williams would continue to argue this technical point that BBS information is not actively sent, but pulled down, he was never able to hammer it home convincingly.

In cross-examining the first witness, Officer MacMahon, who Newsom established as an expert in computer technology, Williams attempted to show that the Thomases had never transferred anything to the postal inspector; Dirmeyer had

logged onto AABBS and downloaded files, in effect transferring files to himself. He asked, "In the event that someone were to contact my computer and downloaded something, would they be taking something, or would I be sending something?" MacMahon answered that they would, of course, be sending.

This was a typical Williams soft-ball question—right concept, not incisively phrased. McMahon was ready for him, walked around the questions, and provided analogies to support the opposite view. Williams was never able to effectively show that the GIFs were not sent. He then discussed the chat mode technology, drawing an admission that the chat mode conversations could have been doctored. He was suggesting to the Tennessee jury that their local postal inspector was a liar who forged evidence. Throughout the trial he was carefree with such implications, while never directly alleging that Dirmeyer forged anything. After McMahon stepped down, Newsom called David Dirmeyer to the stand.

Dirmeyer described his job, "I investigate drug cases, drugs through the mail, and also obscenity cases and child pornography cases. . . . I attended the Postal Inspection Service Training Academy, which was approximately twelve weeks. Of that at least 100 hours were dedicated specifically to child pornography and obscenity investigations." As the jury could see, he was an expert on child pornography, which is governed by stricter laws and standards than other obscene material. Unlike with other obscenity, the government can prosecute for mere possession and artistic or scientific merit is not a defense. Dirmeyer had never found any child pornography in the Thomases' possession, other than that which he sent them. He described how he was first contacted by Earl Crawley, borrowed a computer, logged on for the first time, and was greeted by the slogan "Welcome to AABBS, the nastiest place on earth."

Dirmeyer recounted his undercover search for child pornography, "The main thing that got my interest was the nudist section, as he called it, which he described having GIF files and videotapes of nude teenagers basically is what they were, nude children, ranging from age—any age on up to through their teens." This was the naturist material, which portrayed no sexual acts.

Being legal, it wasn't charged in the indictment, but Newsom and Dirmeyer, with no objection by Williams, continued to include it every chance they got. Dirmeyer testified that other GIFs were described as involving bondage, golden showers, and other kinky acts. Newsom quickly circled back around to the nonexistent child pornography, asking Dirmeyer about the term "Lolita." The postal inspector said he was familiar with it as indicating prepubescent girls engaging in sexual activities. . . .

Williams haplessly began his cross-examination of Dirmeyer by reminding the jurors of his credentials. He had Dirmeyer recount his Postal Inspection Service basic training and numerous subsequent training courses. Williams then elicited some relevant admissions by asking Dirmeyer if he was aware that there was in fact no child pornography on AABBS. "I didn't find any child pornography on the system, no sir." Having established that Dirmeyer had a couple of hundred hours training in combating child pornography and that naturist material had been discussed in that training, he asked, "Now, what did they tell you about the naturist materials? Did they tell you it was legal, or did they tell you it was illegal?" Dirmeyer agreed that as far as he knew, it was legal in all 50 states. Williams inquired weakly into the questionable nature of the search and Thomas' disclosure of knowledge of the consent form. However, he did not really exploit this opportunity to rattle Dirmeyer on entrapment, the chat mode, or anything else. . . .

Williams' biggest failure was that he never counterattacked Newsom's conception of Memphis community standards by introducing comparable materials that were available locally. Williams had sent J. Keith Henson out to buy similar videos in stores near the courthouse, but never introduced them into evidence.

In his closing argument Newsom reiterated much of what he had said in his opening. He told the jury that it was irrelevant whether or not AABBS users were a community of consenting adults, and also irrelevant whether the Thomases thought they were doing anything illegal. The jury only had to believe that the Thomases knew the "general nature and content of the material." He cautioned them that Williams would talk to them of entrapment, and suggested that they think about Robert Thomas' character and reputation. He told them that they must decide whether the GIFs had been transmitted in interstate commerce using the phone lines. Newsom stated, "The transportation of these images, whether its being sent or received, makes no difference. . . . [P]lease don't be confused about that as far as whether it was going or coming. . . . The question is was the facility used or caused to be used for purposes of transportation of an obscene matter. . . . I ask you to convict each of these defendants of the crimes charged in this indictment."

In the closing argument for the defense, Williams told the jury that a question existed "as to whether or not they are actually sending it or whether people are reaching out and taking it by way of download. . . . At any rate though, I think that you will be told by the Court that it's up to you to decide the community standards, and it's up to you to decide what community is the intended recipient . . . you heard from Inspector Dirmeyer, and you heard from Robert Thomas, and you heard from Carleen Thomas. Now, what did each of these people tell you? Number one, membership only. . . . This information is not available to the general public, and I guess you can look at that in terms of just the membership curve of the jury and how many of you do have computers and modems." In other words, if the putative victims the jurors were protecting were people like themselves, they had nothing to worry about. . . .

Newsom stood for his rebuttal and reminded the jury that it was not at issue whether a deviant group would find the AABBS materials patently offensive, "It's whether the average person in your community would find that this material is patently offensive."

At 9:45 a.m. on July 28, the jury announced that the defendants, Robert and Carleen Thomas, had been found guilty of all counts except 11, pertaining to the action mags. The jury apparently believed that Dirmeyer had entrapped the Thomases by sending them the magazines. Newsom took the opportunity to add that the Thomases had just been indicted in the state of Utah. This new indictment was based on nonexistent child pornography.

After the trial, the Thomases discharged Williams and hired two lawyers to represent them—Thomas Nolan of Palo Alto for Robert and James Causey of Memphis for Carleen. . . .

In a post-trial conference, Judge Gibbons confirmed the forfeiture of all the equipment. She sentenced Robert Thomas "at the upper end of the guideline range, or a sentence of thirty-seven months." She declined to impose a fine, up to $60,000, because the forfeiture of the computers was financial penalty enough. "The Court also recognizes that there will be a need to provide for the Thomases' two children during their incarceration—I don't think they've got the assets that would permit them to adequately take care of them, have the equipment forfeited, and also pay the fine." As for Carleen Thomas, "She is less culpable, and I think that in her case a sentence at the low end of the guideline range is appropriate, or a sentence of thirty months."

The journalistic and legal communities immediately criticized the trial. They generally portrayed Tennessee as the most conservative state in the union and commented on the absurdity of it governing the standards of the on-line world. Judge Gibbons read the disparaging press remarks and was clearly nettled. She remarked that the material was disgusting, repulsive, and would most likely be found obscene everywhere. She was resentful of national publicity that implied that the Thomases could have been convicted only in Memphis, as if the good people of western Tennessee, not the Thomases, were the outcasts.

Nolan argued that the material was not that bad. Gibbons replied, "What I'm raising my eyebrows at you about is the suggestion that this is a case in which a conviction could only have been obtained in this district or a similar one. This is very, very egregious . . . this was far at the extreme end of the scale in terms of what might be considered obscenity. . . . I haven't seen that many, but of the ones [where] I have seen the material, this was way worse than anything I have seen."

Nolan pressed his argument that the Thomases had not been permitted a fair trial. Judge Gibbons, however, continued to make the point that the AABBS material was extremely disturb-

ing, "your arguments will sound a whole lot better in the abstract than they will if the appellate court also considers the content of what the jury in fact saw in this case." This statement was remarkable. If Carleen Thomas was denied a fair trial, it is not supposed to matter under our system whether she is accused of speeding or of mass murder. Even an extremely hard-core pornographer is entitled to due process.

Nolan tried to make this point tactfully, "I don't mean to argue with the Court. The Court saw the videotapes, and the jury saw the videotapes, and the jury conflicted, and the Court obviously has a belief about those tapes. Those tapes were never subjected to the adversary system. We don't know whether you can buy those tapes down the street, because the lawyer never went and checked." The Judge concluded the conference, "I think you've just about said everything you can say to me today."

Robert Thomas has been incarcerated in federal prison since February 1995. His wife was allowed some extra time to look after her kids and began serving her thirty month sentence the following July. . . .

Though Williams did not help the Thomases very much, he did, in fact, raise some of the most important larger issues. In his opening statement at trial he said, "Mr. Thomas will tell you basically that the Amateur Action BBS is an adults-only membership-only bulletin board service. . . . The menu, of course, would be the only thing, as Mr. Thomas will tell you, that would be available to somebody that is not a member. Why would this be important from our perspective? Because it's not likely these things are being disseminated to the community generally. You will hear that only the people who look at the menu and decide they want to join the bulletin board would be members and entitled to download anything."

This argument embodies the essential problems with the AABBS case and with obscenity laws in general, pointing out that the Thomases sold their material to an insular community of 3,500 consulting adults, who asked and paid for it.

This argument, however, was ineffective at trial—questioning the validity of applying local, geographical standards on global networks, and the right of government to ban this form of speech could hold no weight in Gibbons' court.

## ACT III—THE ISSUES

Soon after the conviction and sentencing, the Internet and the media were both running stories of an unfair trial, based on an outmoded standard. Many mainstream newspapers and magazines, from *The New York Times* to *Playboy*, published pieces on the plight of the Thomases. Several nonprofit civil liberties organizations drafted amicus briefs—third party legal arguments submitted to the court to influence its decision. Jumping into the fray were the Electronic Frontier Foundation, the American Civil Liberties Union ("ACLU"), The Society For Electronic Access, and the Interactive Services Association. In addition, the ACLU brief was joined by other organizations including the National Writer's Union and Feminists for Free Expression. Most of these groups specifically declared that they were not objecting to the Thomases' conviction for mailing videotapes to Dirmeyer in Memphis; they were concerned about the case's certain effect upon free speech on the Internet.

On appeal, Nolan also revisited an important point which Williams had unsuccessfully raised: did the Thomases in fact "send" anything? He tried to persuade the appeals court that a BBS is more like a traditional bookstore than like a mail order operation. He cited *Cubby v. CompuServe,* which held that on-line customers could electronically browse through the available material, pick items, and take these items back home. A higher court would never permit the prosecution of a California bookstore in Memphis if Dirmeyer had travelled to California, bought books there, and carried them home to Memphis.

He maintained that Memphis was not the proper venue because "Mr. Thomas did not send any GIF files to Memphis. . . . The acts that did occur in Tennessee, such as the selection and downloading of GIF files, were initiated and performed solely by Inspector Dirmeyer." Nolan argued that, if the standards of any geographical community were to be applied, it should be the standards of northern California, where AABBS

was actually located. The EFF concurred, arguing that the Thomases "had no physical contact with the state of Tennessee, they had not advertised in any medium directed primarily at Tennessee, they had not physically visited Tennessee, nor had they any assets or other contacts there." Dirmeyer's actions—logging on and downloading—caused the material to be "transported" into Tennessee. The EFF, like Nolan, used the analogy of Dirmeyer travelling to California, purchasing a computer file, and bringing it back home with him.

Nolan then summed up the central cyberspace issue, "To impose the standards of Memphis, Tennessee on national communications networks would have a chilling effect on the free speech rights of members of other communities. These networks would be compelled to self-censor and impose on the entire nation the standards of the most restrictive community." The EFF centered its argument on this point—Memphis standards should not be used to set the ground rules for all cyberspace. Allowing the conviction to stand would fly in the face of *Miller* by creating a single national, even global, standard based on the law of Tennessee.

In its famous *Butler v. Michigan* decision in 1957, the Supreme Court held a Michigan law unconstitutional which made criminal the sale of books that might have a bad effect on youth. Justice Frankfurter, who traditionally took a hard stance against obscenity, wrote for the majority and stated that the Constitution does not permit a state to reduce its adult population "to reading only what is fit for children." The AABBS case allows *Miller* to reduce the national population to reading only what is fit for Tennessee.

In 1973, when *Miller* was decided, America was already immersed in an age of national television and radio broadcasting and national distribution of books and magazines. Chief Justice Burger's touching fear that New York and Las Vegas—those sinks of vice—would impose their vile standards on Maine or Mississippi, was not balanced by any apprehension that Maine or Mississippi might turn the tables and rule New York or Las Vegas. There is no other area of constitutional law which allows for local variations. A police beating which violates the Fifth Amendment in New York is not acceptable in Memphis because [of] local standards . . . differing. An illegal search violating the Fourth Amendment in California is just as illegal in Maine.

The *Miller* decision presupposed that the material was distributed by a more conventional method, such as the mail, and allowed the distributor a choice of not sending it into any jurisdiction where the local standards might find it obscene. In an age where information located on any server, anywhere in geographical space can be accessed and transmitted anywhere else, and where geographical location is not even mildly relevant in terms of access cost or speed, *Miller* now stands for the opposite of what it did in 1973. By allowing the application of local standards to a vast, instantaneous, worldwide entity like the Internet, *Miller* now allows Memphis, in the heart of the Bible Belt, to apply its conservatism forcibly on the rest of the world.

Many people may agree that the Thomases deserve to sit in prison. The jury found the Thomases guilty of slipping six obscene videos into their state. Perhaps "the nastiest place on earth" would prove illegal in 49 states, and it is not New York or Las Vegas from which the wholesome communities need protection, but Milpitas, California. Judge Gibbons said after the trial that this was the worst stuff she had ever seen, deserving of conviction in any federal district in the country, under any local standards. But even if Judge Gibbons' guess is correct, it does not justify the jailing of these California Sysops in Tennessee.

The case stands out because it reveals the glaring shortcomings of the obscenity standard in the face of today's new communications. The fundamental problem was that neither [Gibbons's] court, nor the Court of Appeals was equipped to handle the real issue. Neither Williams, Nolan, or Causey could rightfully argue the constitutionality of *Miller* before either court. (Although Williams gave it a try.)

On the Internet today, it is not usually possible to determine a user's state of origin from the IP address or domain name. Even if technology is introduced to allow BBS and Internet providers to determine the user's residence, it is unrealistic to expect them to learn the laws and precedents for each community of all 50 states. It is also unrealistic to expect Tennessee to unplug itself from the Internet. The fundamental question is which community has the right to set the standard? Three possible answers to the question are raised by the AABBS case—the status quo (the *Miller* standard), a national standard, or the use of the standards of cybercommunities rather than geographical ones. This third argument added an interesting new element to an old debate.

Nolan argued that "computer bulletin board technology requires the application of a new definition of community." The wording of *Miller* had not required that the standards applied be those of a "geographical" community, and there was precedent in FCC regulations and military law for the proposition that a *Miller* community did not have to be geographically bound. "In defining community standards in the *Miller* case, the Supreme Court neither anticipated nor took into account the rapid advances in computer technology. . . . The rapid growth of national and global computer networks have radically altered the nature of communications and have allowed persons to interact without geographic constraints in 'a nonphysical universe called cyberspace.'"

"The cyberspace community is as much a community as traditional geographic divisions. This community should have the right to articulate its standards on the issue of obscenity. A definition of community based on connections between people rather than one based on geographic location will ensure that all communities have the right to define protected speech."

Though nothing in *Miller* prevented the determination that the standards of a nongeographical, cyberspace community should apply, Judge Gibbons had said at trial that the relevant community could not legally be adult bookstore customers, or pornographic video watchers, or even VCR owners.

Newsom had a brief retort to Nolan's argument, "Computer technology does not require a new definition of community. . . . Appellants provide an eloquent essay on the effect of computers on interpersonal communication. While fascinating and well-written, the mini-treatise fails to offer any legal support or any suggestion for how a court is to 'examine the community created by computer technology' and 'adopt a rule that protects and encourages freedom of speech and expression.' The reality is that if the court 'examined the community created by computer technology', it would find that computers essentially create a world community. Computers unite citizens of small midwestern towns with denizens of New York City. For that matter, they unite Memphis residents with computer users in London, Tokyo, Bombay. It would be unrealistic to attempt to define the accepted standards of a 'community' that includes Iowa farmers, Las Vegas casino owners, Icelandic fishermen, and Tibetan monks. Clearly the notion of a 'computer-users community' is unfathomable and should be rejected, just as the United States Supreme Court rejected a 'national' standard in Miller. . . ."

Actually, no one was arguing for a global standard. Nolan and the ACLU were really arguing to apply the standards of the AABBS users themselves. The idea is that they are an insular group of 3,500 pornophiles who should be allowed to stew in their own smut if they like.

Such a result—the adoption of the standards of the members of a cyberspace community to judge the obscenity of which they are sympathetic users—would effectively repeal obscenity laws entirely. Under such a scenario, as long as AABBS did not offend its own members, and disseminated its material only to adults who requested and paid for it, it would never be shut down.

From a broader perspective, the application of obscenity laws to cyberspace is an opportunity to reexamine the legal and moral underpinnings of these laws. Obscenity is held to be a form of speech so degraded that it stands entirely outside the usual First Amendment protections. The problem is that no one seems exactly certain what it is, or how to define it; Justice Potter Stewart's famous but legally weak, statement was that he knew it when he saw it.

The meanings of the words pornography and obscenity have evolved over the years. Obscenity is a subset of pornography and it is illegal, because it is prurient, contains patently offensive sexual material, and is devoid of scientific, literary, artistic or political value. Pornography, by contrast, covers much material that appeals to prurient interests but which is either not offensive or which has scientific, literary, artistic or political value. It is almost universally accepted that the written word, even embodied in cheap, transient, anonymous paperbacks intended solely to cause sexual arousal, is not obscene. Most obscenity prosecutions today involve pictures and films.

The "slippery slope" argument posits that regulation slides into censorship, taking other valid forms of speech with it. If we find marginal material to be obscene, soon the courts will be using the precedent to ban literature. This argument is well supported by history; Joyce, Nabokov, Hemingway, and other great authors have all been banned in this country. Critics of this line of reasoning say that those were the dark ages and today's society certainly would not revisit the follies of the past.

The Post Office first became involved in obscenity law after the Civil War. Over the years the post office sought to purge the mail of obscene novels by Ernest Hemingway, John O'Hara, Erskine Caldwell, J.D. Salinger, Alberto Moravia, John Steinbeck, Richard Wright, and Norman Mailer, and nonfiction works by Sigmund Freud, Margaret Mead, and Simone de Beauvoir. . . .

If you look at the *Amateur Action* case in a vacuum, it is hard to comprehend why the ACLU or the Feminists for Free Expression, think that there is a slippery slope leading from Robert and Carleen Thomas to more serious purveyors of radical or non-mainstream ideas. After all, the Thomases never sought to argue that the videos or GIFs were artistic expression protected by the First Amendment. (Nolan and Causey didn't even attempt to argue that this was an issue missed by Williams.)

The slippery slope doesn't seem so unreasonable if you think that as recently as 1990, Cincinnati police closed a Robert Mapplethorpe photography show at the Contemporary Arts Center and local authorities indicted the museum's curator for obscenity. Mapplethorpe, whose images included portraits, flowers and sexually explicit homoerotic images, was almost universally recognized in the art world as a major figure. It just does not wash to say, after reading about Post Office vendettas against Hemingway and Steinbeck, that "those were the bad old days; it can't happen again." The slope, starting with Robert and Carleen Thomas, leads to serious artists and the purveyors of radical ideas.

The law of obscenity is so fundamentally confused that, before we bring it into a new technology and a new century, we should tear it down to its foundations, examine it, and determine whether and how to rebuild it to meet modern social needs. After defining the terms, we must determine who this abridgment of the First Amendment is designed to protect. There are four classes of potential victims of obscenity: minors, unsuspecting viewers, women, and users of pornography—who may need to be protected against themselves.

For many, minors form the crux of the obscenity issue. Among consenting adults in a free society, distasteful speech is merely to be avoided. Children, on the other hand, can be drawn by curiosity and corrupted by such ideas. Though the prosecution raised the question of whether Dirmeyer, for all the Thomases knew, could have been underage, they never charged AABBS with distributing to minors. In fact, the Thomases instituted relatively strict measures to keep out children. This becomes more of an issue on the open protocols of newsgroups and the World Wide Web; but AABBS was as secure as any adults-only sex shop on 42nd Street.

Unwilling viewers of obscene material seem to be everyone's second-choice victim. Like secondary smoke, unwanted pornography is a quality of life issue, polluting the lives of people who would rather not be exposed to it. The Supreme Court has dealt with the unwilling viewer issue in two contexts: unsolicited mailings on public policy issues, and non-obscene nudity on drive-in movie screens. The Court said that, with regards to unsolicited mailings, our right not to be bothered does not justify limiting First Amendment rights. The solution is to "escape exposure to the objectionable material simply by transferring [it] from envelope to wastebasket." The Supreme Court also invalidated, on First Amendment grounds, a Florida law that banned nudity on drive-in movie screens to protect innocent passers-by. The Court said that the problem could most easily be cured by turning away after a fleeting glimpse—not by depriving movie-goers of the right to see films.

The cautious AABBS sign-up procedure of credit cards, passwords, and voice verification seems to minimize the possibility that anyone who didn't want to see the GIFs would be exposed to them. Newsom and Dirmeyer tried to raise the specter of the unwanted viewer as victim by describing Earl Crawley's shock at seeing the ALLGIF file without being a member of AABBS, and by the particular attention they paid to the "distribute freely" stamp on many of the GIFs. However, there was no evidence at trial that any unwilling viewer other than Earl Crawley had ever been exposed to AABBS materials, and the only thing Crawley could have seen, the ALLGIF file, probably could not itself legally have been declared obscene, since it consisted of text only. Since Crawley did not appear at trial, the defense never was able to ask him what he was doing logged onto a BBS named "Amateur Action" anyway. (Maybe he thought it had to do with ham radio or local theatricals.)

Even the GIFs marked "distribute freely" were redistributed mainly on other adult bulletin boards and the Internet's alt.sex newsgroups, which require some effort to find and are probably not frequented by too many unwilling viewers. Additionally, a pornographic GIF doesn't just appear on your screen in Usenet; viewing it requires the download of many separate messages (sometimes more than 20) and then the use of special software to reconstitute it as an image.

Although the recent "cyberporn" debate has concentrated on the vulnerability of children in cyberspace, the *Miller* decision and another case, *Paris Adult Theaters v. Slaton*, reveal that the Supreme Court's main concern was with society, perceived as a huge class of "unwilling viewers" whose lives could be polluted by obscene material. The Court expressed extreme skepticism that there was any effective way, short of banning it, to keep obscene speech from intruding on society. . . .

A free, democratic society should err on the side of speech, not censorship. But, considering that there are children around who should not be exposed to certain ideas and pictures until they are ready to view and handle them, we must build in some safeguards. Although Robert Thomas may very well be, as Newsom argued, a rich, sadistic purveyor of twisted smut, he effectively built in safeguards to prevent his community of 3,500 consumers from being discovered by minors. Then, as the EFF said, "any local territorial community that wants to enforce its own obscenity standards has a duty to use tools to help it stay away from the offending materials."

The AABBS case highlights the 200-year debate between the autonomy of the states and the power of the federal union. The problem is not made any easier in an era of global networks that do not recognize geographical distinctions or any differing value between different streams of ones and zeros running through the wires. This case foreshadows the coming problems that will arise between communities of all shapes and sizes. Will Iran extradite Europeans for posting parts of *Satanic Verses* to a newsgroup? Will China shut down servers in Asia that offer material that sympathizes with Tibet? In December, 1995, CompuServe removed alt.sex newsgroups from it's global service because of a threat by German prosecutors. As difficult as it may be to swallow, speech should be allowed to roam free, just as books are almost entirely uncensored in America.

As for the Thomases, business is booming. Along with a friend, the Thomas sons have pitched in while their parents serve out their prison terms. There is something incongruous about the family life of the Thomases: a seemingly secure, financially comfortable, stable, nuclear American family where the family business, eventually taken over by the sons, trades in images of rape, bondage, and torture. The hype surrounding the case has brought their membership up to 10,000. And though they forfeited all their computers to the government, they have all new machines to better handle the growth of their $300,000+ per year enterprise. The Thomases will be out of prison in a couple of years. But then they may have to stand trial again in Utah (and Nebraska, and Kentucky, and Nevada. . . . ?).

## 22.2 | Law and Borders    *David R. Johnson and David G. Post*

### INTRODUCTION

GLOBAL COMPUTER-BASED COMMUNICATIONS CUT across territorial borders, creating a new realm of human activity and undermining the feasibility—and legitimacy—of applying laws based on geographic boundaries. While these electronic communications play havoc with geographic boundaries, a new boundary, made up of the screens and passwords that separate the virtual world from the "real world" of atoms, emerges. This new boundary defines a distinct cyberspace that needs and can create new law and legal institutions of its own. Territorially-based law-making and law-enforcing authorities find this new environment deeply threatening. But established territorial authorities may yet learn to defer to the self-regulatory efforts of cyberspace participants who care most deeply about this new digital trade in ideas, information and services. Separated from doctrine tied to territorial jurisdiction, new rules will emerge, in a variety of online spaces, to govern a wide range of new phenomena that have no clear parallel in the nonvirtual world. These new rules will play the role of law by defining legal personhood and property, resolving disputes and crystallizing a collective conversation about core values.

### TERRITORIAL BORDERS IN THE "REAL WORLD"

We take for granted a world in which geographical borders—lines separating physical spaces—are of primary importance in determining legal rights and responsibilities: "All law is prima facie territorial." Territorial borders, generally speaking, delineate areas within which different sets of legal rules apply. There has until now been a general correspondence between borders drawn in physical space (between nation states or other political entities) and borders in "law space." For example, if we were to superimpose a "law map" (delineating areas where different rules apply to particular behaviors) onto a political map of the world, the two maps would overlap to a significant degree, with clusters of homogenous applicable law and legal institutions fitting within existing physical borders, distinct from neigh-boring homogenous clusters. . . .

## WHEN GEOGRAPHIC BOUNDARIES FOR LAW MAKE SENSE

Physical borders are not, of course, simply arbitrary creations. Although they may be based on historical accident, geographic borders for law make sense in the real world. Their relationship to the development and enforcement of legal rules is logically based on many related considerations.

**Power**  Control over physical space, and the people and things located in that space, is a defining attribute of sovereignty and statehood. Law-making requires some mechanism for law enforcement, which in turn depends (to a large extent) on the ability to exercise physical control over, and to impose coercive sanctions on, law-violators. The ability of the sovereign to claim personal jurisdiction over a particular party, for instance, turns importantly on the party's relationship to the physical jurisdiction over which the sovereign has control (e.g., the presence of the party or assets belonging to the party, within the jurisdiction, or activities of the party that are directed to persons or things within the jurisdiction).

Similarly, the law chosen to apply to a contract, tort, or criminal action has historically been influenced primarily by the physical location of the parties or the deed in question. The US government does not impose its trademark law on a Brazilian business operating in Brazil, at least in part because imposing sanctions on the Brazilian business would require assertion of physical control over those responsible for the operation of that business. Such an assertion of control would conflict with the Brazilian government's recognized monopoly on the use of force over its citizens.

**Effects**  The correspondence between physical boundaries and boundaries in "law space" also reflects a deeply rooted relationship between physical proximity and the effects of any particular behavior. That is, Brazilian trademark law governs the use of marks in Brazil because that use has a more direct impact on persons and assets located within that geographic territory than anywhere else. For example, the existence of a large sign over "Jones' Restaurant" in Rio de Janeiro is unlikely to have an impact on the operation of "Jones' Restaurant" in Oslo, Norway, for we may assume that there is no substantial overlap between the customers, or competitors, of these two entities. Protection of the former's trademark does not—and probably should not—affect the protection afforded the latter's.

**Legitimacy**  We generally accept the notion that the persons within a geographically defined border are the ultimate source of law-making authority for activities within that border. The "consent of the governed" implies that those subject to a set of laws must have a role in their formulation. By virtue of the preceding considerations, the category of persons subject to a sovereign's laws, and most deeply affected by those laws, will consist primarily of individuals who are located in particular physical spaces. Similarly, allocation of responsibility among levels of government proceeds on the assumption that, for many legal problems, physical proximity between the responsible authority and those most directly affected by the law will improve the quality of decision making, and that it is easier to determine the will of those individuals in physical proximity to one another. . . .

## THE ABSENCE OF TERRITORIAL BORDERS IN CYBERSPACE

Cyberspace radically undermines the relationship between legally significant (online) phenomena and physical location. The rise of the global computer network is destroying the link between geographical location and: (1) the power of local governments to assert control over online behavior; (2) the effects of online behavior on individuals or things; (3) the legitimacy of the efforts of a local sovereign to enforce rules applicable to global phenomena; and (4) the ability of physical location to give notice of which sets of rules apply. The Net thus radically subverts a system of rule-making based on borders between physical spaces, at least with respect to the claim that cyberspace should naturally be governed by territorially defined rules.

Cyberspace has no territorially-based boundaries, because the cost and speed of message transmission on the Net is almost entirely independent of physical location: Messages can be transmitted from any physical location to any other location without degradation, decay, or substantial delay, and without any physical cues or barriers that might otherwise keep certain geographically remote places and people separate from one another. The Net enables transactions between people who do not know, and in many cases cannot know, the physical location of the other party. . . .

## TRANSBORDER DATA FLOW

The power to control activity in cyberspace has only the most tenuous connections to physical location. Many governments first respond to electronic communications crossing their territorial borders by trying to stop or regulate that flow of information as it crosses their borders. Rather than deferring to efforts by participants in online transactions to regulate their own affairs, many governments establish trade barriers, seek to tax any border-crossing cargo, and respond especially sympathetically to claims that information coming into the jurisdiction might prove harmful to local residents. Efforts to stem the flow increases as online information becomes more important to local citizens. In particular, resistance to "transborder data flow" (TDF) reflects the concerns of sovereign nations that the development and use of TDF's will undermine their "informational sovereignty," will negatively impact on the privacy of local citizens, and will upset private property interests in information. Even local governments in the United States have expressed concern about their loss of control over information and transactions flowing across their borders.

But efforts to control the flow of electronic information across physical borders—to map local regulation and physical boundaries onto cyberspace—are likely to prove futile, at least in countries that hope to participate in global commerce. Individual electrons can easily, and without any realistic prospect of detection, "enter" any sovereign's territory. The volume of electronic communications crossing territorial boundaries is just too great in relation to the resources available to government authorities to permit meaningful control. US Customs officials have generally given up. They assert jurisdiction over only the physical goods that cross the geographic borders they guard and claim no right to force declarations of the value of materials transmitted by modem. Banking and securities regulators seem likely to lose their battle to impose local regulations on a global financial marketplace. And state Attorneys General face serious challenges in seeking to intercept the electrons that transmit the kinds of consumer fraud that, if conducted physically within the local jurisdiction, would be more easily shut down.

Faced with their inability to control the flow of electrons across physical borders, some authorities strive to inject their boundaries into the new electronic medium through filtering mechanisms and the establishment of electronic barriers. For example, German authorities, seeking to prevent violations of that country's laws against distribution of pornographic material, ordered CompuServe to disable access by German residents to certain global Usenet newsgroups that would otherwise be accessible through that commercial service. Anyone inside Germany with an Internet connection could, however, easily find a way to access the prohibited news groups during the ban. Although initially compliant, CompuServe subsequently rescinded the ban on most of the files by sending parents a new program to choose for themselves what items to restrict.

Similarly, Tennessee has insisted (indirectly, through enforcement of a federal law that defers to local community standards) that an electronic bulletin board in California install filters that prevent offensive screens from being displayed to users in Tennessee if it is to avoid liability under local obscenity standards in Tennessee. Others have been quick to assert the right to regulate all online trade insofar as it might adversely impact local citizens. The Attorney General of Minnesota, for example, has asserted the right to regulate gambling that occurs on a foreign Web page that was accessed and "brought into" the state by a local resident. The New Jersey securities regulatory agency has similarly asserted the right to shut down any offending Web page accessible from within the state.

## LOGICAL ROADS TO VIRTUAL PLACES

But such protective schemes will likely fail as well. First, the determined seeker of prohibited communications can simply reconfigure his connection so as to appear to reside in a different location, outside the particular locality, state, or country. Because the Net is engineered to work on the basis of "logical," not geographical, locations, any attempt to defeat the independence of messages from physical locations would be as futile as an effort to tie an atom and a bit together. And, moreover, assertions of law-making authority over Net activities on the ground that those activities constitute "entry into" the physical jurisdiction can just as easily be made by any territorially-based authority. If Minnesota law applies to gambling operations conducted on the World Wide Web because such operations foreseeably affect Minnesota residents, so, too, must the law of any physical jurisdiction from which those operations can be accessed. By asserting a right to regulate whatever its citizens may access on the Net, these local authorities are laying the predicate for an argument that Singapore or Iraq or any other sovereign can regulate the activities of US companies operating in cyberspace from a location physically within the United States. All such Web-based activity, in this view, must be subject simultaneously to the laws of all territorial sovereigns.

Nor are the effects of online activities tied to geographically proximate locations. Information available on the World Wide Web is available simultaneously to anyone with a connection to the global network. The notion that the effects of an activity taking place on that Web site radiate from a physical location over a geographic map in concentric circles of decreasing intensity, however sensible that may be in the nonvirtual world, is incoherent when applied to cyberspace. A Web site physically located in Brazil, to continue with that example, has no more of an effect on individuals in Brazil than does a Web site physically located in Belgium or Belize that is accessible in Brazil. Usenet discussion groups, to take another example, consist of continuously changing collections of messages that are routed from one network to another, with no centralized location at all; they exist, in effect, everywhere, nowhere in particular, and only on the Net.

Nor can the legitimacy of any rules governing online activities be naturally traced to a geographically situated polity. There is no geographically localized set of constituents with a stronger claim to regulate it than any other local group; the strongest claim to control comes from the participants themselves, and they could be anywhere.

The rise of an electronic medium that disregards geographical boundaries also throws the law into disarray by creating entirely new phenomena that need to become the subject of clear legal rules but that cannot be governed, satisfactorily, by any current territorially-based sovereign. For example, electronic communications create vast new quantities of transactional records and pose serious questions regarding the nature and adequacy of privacy protections. Yet the communications that create these records may pass through or even simultaneously exist in many different territorial jurisdictions. What substantive law should we apply to protect this new, vulnerable body of transactional data? May a French policeman lawfully access the records of communications traveling across the Net from the United States to Japan? Similarly, whether it is permissible for a commercial entity to publish a record of all of any given individual's postings to Usenet newsgroups, or whether it is permissible to implement an interactive Web page application that inspects a user's "bookmarks" to determine which other pages that user has visited, are questions not readily addressed by existing legal regimes—both because the phenomena are novel and because any given local territorial sovereign cannot readily control the relevant, globally dispersed, actors and actions.

Because events on the Net occur everywhere but nowhere in particular, are engaged in by online personae who are both "real" (possessing reputations, able to perform services and deploy intellectual assets) and "intangible" (not necessarily or traceably tied to any particular person in the physical sense) and concern "things" (messages, databases, standing relationships) that are not necessarily separated from one another by any physical boundaries, no physical jurisdiction has a more compelling claim than any other to subject these events exclusively to its laws. . . .

## MIGRATION OF OTHER REGULATED CONDUCT TO THE NET

Almost everything involving the transfer of information can be done online: education, health care, banking, the provision of intangible services, all forms of publishing and the practice of law. The laws regulating many of these activities have developed as distinctly local and territorial. Local authorities certify teachers, charter banks with authorized "branches," and license doctors and lawyers. The law has in essence presumed that the activities conducted by these regulated persons cannot be performed without being tied to a physical body or building subject to regulation by the territorial sovereign authority, and that the effects of those activities are most distinctly felt in geographically circumscribed areas. These distinctly local regulations cannot be preserved once these activities are conducted by globally dispersed parties through the Net. When many trades can be practiced in a manner that is unrelated to the physical location of the participants, these local regulatory structures will either delay the development of the new medium or, more likely, be superseded by new structures that better fit the online phenomena in question.

Any insistence on "reducing" all online transactions to a legal analysis based on geographic terms presents, in effect, a new "mind-body" problem on a global scale. We know that the activities that have traditionally been the subject of regulation must still be engaged in by real people who are, after all, at distinct physical locations. But the interactions of these people now somehow transcend those physical locations. The Net enables forms of interaction in which the shipment of tangible items across geographic boundaries is irrelevant and in which the location of the participants does not matter. Efforts to determine "where" the events in question occur are decidedly misguided, if not altogether futile.

## A NEW BOUNDARY FOR CYBERSPACE

Although geographic boundaries may be irrelevant in defining a legal regime for cyberspace, a more legally significant border for the "law space" of the Net consists of the screens and passwords that separate the tangible from the virtual world. Traditional legal doctrine treats the Net as a mere transmission medium that facilitates the exchange of messages sent from one legally significant geographical location to another, each of which has its own applicable laws. Yet, trying to tie the laws of any particular territorial sovereign to transactions on the Net, or even trying to analyze the legal consequences of Net-based commerce as

if each transaction occurred geographically somewhere in particular, is most unsatisfying.

**Cyberspace as a Place**   Many of the jurisdictional and substantive quandaries raised by border-crossing electronic communications could be resolved by one simple principle: conceiving of cyberspace as a distinct "place" for purposes of legal analysis by recognizing a legally significant border between cyberspace and the "real world." Using this new approach, we would no longer ask the unanswerable question "where" in the geographical world a Net-based transaction occurred. Instead, the more salient questions become: what rules are best suited to the often unique characteristics of this new place and the expectations of those who are engaged in various activities there? What mechanisms exist or need to be developed to determine the content of those rules and the mechanisms by which they can [be] enforced? Answers to these questions will permit the development of rules better suited to the new phenomena in question, more likely to be made by those who understand and participate in those phenomena, and more likely to be enforced by means that the new global communications media make available and effective.

**The New Boundary Is Real**   Treating cyberspace as a separate "space" to which distinct laws apply should come naturally, because entry into this world of stored online communications occurs through a screen and (usually) a "password" boundary. There is a "placeness" to cyberspace because the messages accessed there are persistent and accessible to many people. You know when you are "there." No one accidentally strays across the border into cyberspace. To be sure, cyberspace is not a [homogeneous] place; groups and activities found at various online locations possess their own unique characteristics and distinctions, and each area will likely develop its own set of distinct rules. But the line that separates online transactions from our dealings in the real world is just as distinct as the physical boundaries between our territorial governments—perhaps more so.

Crossing into cyberspace is a meaningful act that would make application of a distinct "law of cyberspace" fair to those who pass over the electronic boundary. As noted, a primary function and characteristic of a border or boundary is its ability to be perceived by the one who crosses it. As regulatory structures evolve to govern cyberspace-based transactions, it will be much easier to be certain which of those rules apply to your activities online than to determine which territorial-based authority might apply its laws to your conduct. For example, you would know to abide by the "terms of service" established by Compu-Serve or America Online when you are in their online territory, rather than guess whether Germany, or Tennessee, or the SEC will succeed in asserting their right to regulate your activities and those of the "placeness" online personae with whom you communicate.[1] . . .

## OTHER CYBERSPACE REGIMENS

Once we take cyberspace seriously as a distinct place for purposes of legal analysis, many opportunities to clarify and simplify the rules applicable to online transactions become available.

**Defamation Law**   Treating messages on the Net as transmissions from one place to another has created a quandary for those concerned about liability for defamation: Messages may be transmitted between countries with very different laws, and liability may be imposed on the basis of "publication" in multiple jurisdictions with varying standards. In contrast, the approach that treats the global network as a separate place would consider any allegedly defamatory message to have been published only "on the Net" (or in some distinct subsidiary area thereof)—at least until such time as distribution on paper occurs. This re-characterization makes more sense. A person who uploads a potentially

defamatory statement would be able more readily to determine the rules applicable to his own actions. Moreover, because the Net has distinct characteristics, including an enhanced ability of the allegedly defamed person to reply, the rules of defamation developed for the Net could take into account these technological capabilities—perhaps by requiring that the opportunity for reply be taken advantage of in lieu of monetary compensation for certain defamatory net-based messages. The distinct characteristics of the Net could also be taken into account when applying and adapting the "public figure" doctrine in a context that is both global and highly compartmentalized and that blurs the distinction between private and public spaces.

**Regulation of Net-based Professional Activities**   The simplifying effect of "taking cyberspace seriously" likewise arises in the context of regimes for regulating professional activities. As noted, traditional regulation insists that each professional be licensed by every territorial jurisdiction where she provides services. This requirement is infeasible when professional services are dispensed over the Net and potentially provided in numerous jurisdictions. Establishing certification regimes that apply only to such activities on the Net would greatly simplify matters. Such regulations would take into account the special features of Net-based professional activities like tele-medicine or global law practice by including the need to avoid any special risks caused by giving online medical advice in the absence of direct physical contact with a patient or by answering a question regarding geographically local law from a remote location. Using this new approach, we could override the efforts of local school boards to license online educational institutions, treating attendance by students at online institutions as a form of "leaving home for school" rather than characterizing the offering of education online as prosecutable distribution of disfavored materials into a potentially unwelcoming community that asserts local licensing authority.

**Fraud and Antitrust**   Even an example that might otherwise be thought to favor the assertion of jurisdiction by a local sovereign—protection of local citizens from fraud and antitrust violations—

---

[1]Having a noticeable border may be a prerequisite to the establishment of any legal regime that can claim to be separate from pre-existing regimes. If someone acting in any given space has no warning that the rules have changed, the legitimacy of any attempt to enforce a distinctive system of law is fatally weakened. No geographically based sovereign could plausibly claim to have jurisdiction over a territory with secret boundaries. And no self-regulatory organization could assert its prerogatives while making it hard for members and nonmembers to tell each other apart or disguising when they were (or were not) playing their membership-related roles.

shows the beneficial effects of a cyberspace legal regime. How should we analyze "markets" for antitrust and consumer protection purposes when the companies at issue do business only through the World Wide Web? Cyberspace could be treated as a distinct marketplace for purposes of assessing concentration and market power. Concentration in geographic markets would be relevant only in the rare cases in which such market power could be inappropriately leveraged to obtain power in online markets—for example by conditioning access to the net by local citizens on their buying services from the same company (such as a phone company) online. Claims regarding a right to access to particular online services, as distinct from claims to access particular physical pipelines, would remain tenuous as long as it is possible to create a new online service instantly in any corner of an expanding online space.

Consumer-protection doctrines could also develop differently online—to take into account the fact that anyone reading an online ad is only a mouse-click away from guidance from consumer protection agencies and discussions with other consumers. Can Minnesota prohibit the establishment of a Ponzi scheme on a Web page physically based in the Cayman islands but accessed by Minnesota citizens through the Net? Under the proposed new approach to regulation of online activities, the answer is clearly no. Minnesota has no special right to prohibit such activities. The state lacks enforcement power, cannot show specially targeted effects, and does not speak for the community with the most legitimate claim to self-governance. But that does not mean that fraud might not be made "illegal" in at least large areas of cyberspace. Those who establish and use online systems have an interest in preserving the safety of their electronic territory and preventing crime. They are more likely to be able to enforce their own rules. And, as more fully discussed below, insofar as a consensually based "law of the Net" needs to obtain respect and deference from local sovereigns, new Net-based law-making institutions have an incentive to avoid fostering activities that threaten the vital interests of territorial governments.

**Copyright Law**  We suggest, not without some trepidation, that "taking cyberspace seri-

ously" could clarify the current intense debate about how to apply copyright law principles in the digital age. In the absence of global agreement on applicable copyright principles, the jurisdictional problems inherent in any attempt to apply territorially-based copyright regimes to electronic works simultaneously available everywhere on the globe are profound. As Jane Ginsburg has noted:

> A key feature of the GII [Global Information Infrastructure] is its ability to render works of authorship pervasively and simultaneously accessible throughout the world. The principle of territoriality becomes problematic if it means that posting a work on the GII calls into play the laws of every country in which the work may be received when . . . these laws may differ substantively. Should the rights in a work be determined by a multiplicity of inconsistent legal regimes when the work is simultaneously communicated to scores of countries? Simply taking into account one country's laws, the complexity of placing works in a digital network is already daunting; should the task be further burdened by an obligation to assess the impact of the laws of every country where the work might be received? Put more bluntly, for works on the GII, there will be no physical territoriality. . . . Without physical territoriality, can legal territoriality persist?[2]

But treating cyberspace as a distinct place for purposes of legal analysis does more than resolve the conflicting claims of different jurisdictions: It also allows the development of new doctrines that take into account the special characteristics of the online "place."

The basic justification for copyright protection is that bestowing an exclusive property right to control the reproduction and distribution of works on authors will increase the supply and diversity of such works by offering authors a financial incentive to engage in the effort required for their creation. But even in the "real world,"

---

[2]Jane C. Ginsburg, "Global Use/Territorial Rights: Private International Law Questions of the Global Information Infrastructure," *Journal of the Copyright Society*, 1995.

much creative expression is entirely independent of this incentive structure, because the author's primary reward has more to do with acceptance in a community and the accumulation of reputational capital through wide dissemination than it does with the licensing and sale of individual copies of works; for example, the creative output of lawyers and law professors—law-review articles, briefs and other pleadings, and the like—may well be determined largely by factors completely unrelated to the availability or unavailability of copyright protection for those works, because that category of authors, generally speaking, obtains reputational benefits from wide dissemination that far outweigh the benefits that could be obtained from licensing individual copies. And that may be more generally true of authorship in cyberspace; because authors can now, for the first time in history, deliver copies of their creations instantaneously and at virtually no cost anywhere in the world, one might expect authors to devise new modes of operation that take advantage of, rather than work counter to, this fundamental characteristics of the new environment. One such strategy has already begun to emerge: giving away information at no charge—what might be called the "Netscape strategy"—as a means of building up reputational capital that can subsequently be converted into income (e.g., by means of the sale of services). As Esther Dyson has written in this newsletter:

> Controlling copies (once created by the author or by a third party) becomes a complex challenge. You can either control something very tightly, limiting distribution to a small, trusted group, or you can rest assured that eventually your product will find its way to a large nonpaying audience—if anyone cares to have it in the first place. . . .
>
> Much chargeable value will be in certification of authenticity and reliability, not in the content. Brand name, identity and other marks of value will be important; so will security of supply. Customers will pay for a stream of information and content from a trusted source. For example, the umbrella of *The New York Times* sanctifies the words of its reporters. The content churned out by *Times* reporters is valuable because the reporters

undergo quality-control, and because others believe them. . . .

> The trick is to control not the copies of your work but instead a relationship with the customers—subscriptions or membership. And that's often what the customers want, because they see it as an assurance of a continuing supply of reliable, timely content.

A profound shift of this kind in regard to authorial incentives fundamentally alters the applicable balance between the costs and benefits of copyright protection in cyberspace, calling for a reappraisal of long-standing principles. So, too, do other unique characteristics of cyberspace severely challenge traditional copyright concepts. For example, consider the very ubiquity of file "copying"—the fact that one cannot access any information whatsoever in a computer-mediated environment without making a "copy" of that information.[3]

As a consequence, any simple-minded or simplistic attempt to map traditional notions of the author's exclusive rights over the making of "copies" onto cyberspace transactions will likely have perverse results; "if the very act of getting a document to your screen is considered the 'making of a copy' within the meaning of the Copy-

---

[3] "For example, 'browsing' on the World Wide Web necessarily involves the creation of numerous 'copies' of information; first, a message is transmitted from Computer A to (remote) Computer B, requesting that Computer B send a copy of a particular file (e.g., the "home page" stored on Computer B) back to Computer A. When the request is received by Computer B, a copy of the requested file is made and transmitted back to Computer A (where it is copied again—'loaded' into memory—and displayed). And the manner in which messages travel across the Internet to reach their intended recipient(s)—via intermediary computers known as "routers," at each of which the message is 'read' by means of 'copying' the message into the computer's memory—[involves]. . . innumerable separate acts of . . . 'reproduction'. File copying is not merely inexpensive in cyberspace, it is ubiquitous; and it is not merely ubiquitous, it is indispensable. . . . Were you to equip your computer with a 'copy lock'—an imaginary device that will prevent the reproduction of any and all information now stored in the computer in any form—it will, essentially, stop functioning." David G. Post, "White Paper Blues: Copyright and the National Information Infrastructure," *Legal Times,* April 8, 1996.

right Act, then a high proportion of the millions of messages traveling over the Internet each day potentially infringes on the right of some file creator . . . to control the making of copies. And, if the very act of reading such documents on line involves copying, then some form of a license . . . would, in this view, be required for virtually every one of those message transmissions."[4] Similarly, application of the "first sale" doctrine (allowing the purchaser of a copyrighted work to freely resell the copy she purchased) is problematic when the transfer of a lawfully owned copy technically involves the making of a new copy before the old one is eliminated, as in defining "fair use" when a work's size is indeterminate, ranging from (1) an individual paragraph sold separately on demand in response to searches to (2) the entire database from which the paragraph originates, something never sold as a whole unit.

Treating cyberspace as a distinct location allows for the development of new forms of intellectual property law, applicable only on the Net, that would properly focus attention on these unique characteristics of this new, distinct place while preserving doctrines that apply to works embodied in physical collections (like books) or displayed in legally significant physical places (like theaters). Current debates about applying copyright law to the Net often do, implicitly, treat it as a distinct space, at least insofar as commercial copyright owners somewhat inaccurately

refer to it as a "lawless" place. The civility of the debate might improve if everyone assumed the Net should have an appropriately different law, including a special law for unauthorized transfers of works from one realm to the other. We could, in other words, regulate the smuggling of works created in the physical world, by treating the unauthorized uploading of a copy of such works to the Net as infringement.

This new approach would help promoters of electronic commerce focus on developing incentive-producing rules to encourage authorized transfers into cyberspace of works not available now, while also reassuring owners of existing copyrights to valuable works that changes in the copyright law for the Net would not require changing laws applicable to distributing physical works. It would also permit the development of new doctrines of implied license and fair use that, as to works first created on the Net or imported with the author's permission, appropriately allow the transmission and copying necessary to facilitate their use within the electronic realm.[5]

---

[5]For example, we could adopt rules that make the "caching" of web pages presumptively permissible, absent an explicit agreement, rather than adopting the standard copyright doctrine to the contrary (caching involves copying Web pages to a hard drive so that future trips to the site take less time to complete). Because making "cached" copies in computer memory is essential to speed up the operation of the Web, and because respecting express limits or retractions on any implied license allowing caching would clog up the free flow of information, we should adopt a rule favoring browsing.

---

[4]David G. Post, "New Wine, Old Bottles: The Evanescent Copy," *American Lawyer*, May 1995.

---

From U.S. Senate. Committee on Commerce, Science, and Transportation. *Children's Internet Protection Act.* Hearing, March 4, 1999. Washington, DC: Government Printing Office, 1999. Some case citations omitted.

## 22.3 | Regulating Internet Access in Libraries

*Statement of Jay A. Sekulow*

### INTRODUCTION

PUBLIC LIBRARIES WERE CREATED to lend books, provide research tools, and make available educa-

tional opportunities to its citizens. The Supreme Court has described a library as "a place dedicated to quiet, to knowledge, and to beauty." *Brown* v. *Louisiana*, 383 U.S. 131, 142 (1966). Libraries, therefore, have an affirmative duty to provide materials which will benefit the surrounding community and to restrict illegal and harmful materials.

Children's unrestricted access to the Internet fails to fulfill this duty. The Internet is obviously a very valuable educational resource, and many can benefit from access to that information resource free of charge at public libraries. The vast majority of the pornography which saturates the Web is neither educational, nor beneficial, and in many jurisdictions the exposure of minors to such materials is illegal. Therefore, to avoid liability, libraries will have to adopt some form of Internet filtering process for minors.

Additionally, libraries, like other employers, have an affirmative duty to provide a workplace which is free from pornography. Pornography creates a hostile work environment, as well as a hostile environment for patrons not wishing to be exposed to such material. Internet filtering prevents libraries from becoming peep show parlors. That is constitutionally sufficient for upholding the use of such software.

## LIBRARIES HAVE AN AFFIRMATIVE RESPONSIBILITY TO PROTECT CHILDREN

Libraries have a duty to the public in their dealings with children. As the U.S. Supreme Court has stated: "It is evident beyond the need for elaboration that a State's interest in safeguarding the physical and psychological well-being of a minor is compelling . . . the legislative judgment, as well as the judgment found in relevant literature, is that the use of children as subjects of pornographic materials is harmful to the physiological, emotional, and mental health of the child. The judgment, we think, easily passes muster under the First Amendment." *New York* v. *Ferber,* 458 U.S. 747, 756–758 (1982).

Accordingly, the Supreme Court has long held that the government has a compelling interest in protecting the physical and psychological well-being of minors. *Ginsberg* v. *New York,* 390 U.S. 629, 639–640 (1968); *Sable Communications* v. *FCC,* 492 U.S. 115, 126 (1988); *Denver Area Educational Telecommunications Consortium* v. *FCC,* 116 S.Ct. 2374, 2387 (1996). "This interest extends to shielding minors from the influence of literature that is not obscene by adult standards." *Sable,* 492 U.S. at 126. This compelling interest extends to the state acting in *loco parentis* for children. As the Supreme Court reiterated in *Bethel School Dist. No. 403* v. *Fraser,* 478 U.S. 675, 684 (1986):

This Court's First Amendment jurisprudence has acknowledged limitations on the otherwise absolute interest of the speaker in reaching an unlimited audience where the speech is sexually explicit and the audience may include children. In *Ginsberg* v. *New York,* 390 U.S. 629, 88 S.Ct. 1274, 20 L.Ed.2d 195 (1968), this Court upheld a New York statute banning the sale of sexually oriented material to minors, even though the material in question was entitled to First Amendment protection with respect to adults. And in addressing the question whether the First Amendment places any limit on the authority of public schools to remove books from a public school library, all Members of the Court, otherwise sharply divided, acknowledged that the school board has the authority to remove books that are vulgar. *Board of Education* v. *Pico,* 457 U.S. 853, 871–872, 102 S.Ct. 2799, 2814–2815, 73 L.Ed.2d 435 (1982) (plurality opinion); id., at 879–881, 102 S.Ct., at 2814–2815 (BLACKMUN, J., concurring in part and in judgment); id., at 918–920, 102 S.Ct., at 2834–2835 (REHNQUIST, J., dissenting).

These cases recognize the obvious concern on the part of parents, and school authorities acting in *loco parentis,* to protect children especially in a captive audience from exposure to sexually explicit, indecent, or lewd speech.

Accordingly, the Court held that: "petitioner School District acted entirely within its permissible authority in imposing sanctions upon *Fraser* in response to his offensively lewd and indecent speech. Unlike the sanctions imposed on the students wearing arm bands in *Tinker* [v. *Des Moines Independent Sch. Dist.,* 393 U.S. 503, 506], the penalties imposed in this case were unrelated to any political viewpoint. The First Amendment does not prevent the school officials from determining that to permit a vulgar and lewd speech such as respondent's would undermine the school's basic educational mission." *Id.* at 685.

There is absolutely no constitutional protection for child pornography, yet child pornography is on the Internet. As the Supreme Court held in *Osborne* v. *Ohio,* 495 U.S. 105, 111 (1989):

First, as *Ferber* recognized, the materials produced by child pornographers permanently records the victim's abuse. The pornography's continued existence causes the child victims continuing harm by haunting the children in years to come. The State's ban on possession and viewing encourages the possessors of these materials to destroy them. Second, encouraging the destruction of these materials is also desirable because evidence suggests that pedophiles use child pornography to seduce other children into sexual activity.

The use of children in pornography or predation of children on the Internet is not the only concern, however. It is the exposure of pornography to children which represents another real harm. The potential harm to children allows the imposition of regulations limiting Internet access. Filtering systems used for the purpose of protecting children is completely constitutional. As the Supreme Court ruled in this regard in *FCC* v. *Pacifica Foundation,* 438 U.S. 726, 749 (1978):

> . . . broadcasting is uniquely accessible to children, even those too young to read. Although [comedian George] Carlin's written message might have been incomprehensible to a first grader, Pacifica's broadcast could have enlarged a child's vocabulary in an instant. Other forms of offensive expression may be withheld from the young without restricting the expression at its source. Bookstores and motion picture theaters, for example, may be prohibited from making indecent material available to children. We held in *Ginsberg* v. *New York,* 390 U.S. 629, 20 LEd2d 195, 88 S. Ct. 1274, 44 Ohio Ops 2d 339, that the government's interest in the "well-being of its youth" and in supporting "parents' claim to authority in their own household" justified the regulation of otherwise protected expression. *Id.,* at 640 and 639, 20 LEd2d 195, 88 S.Ct. 1274, 44 Ohio Ops 2d 339.

Similarly, the Internet (like broadcasting) "is uniquely accessible to children, even those too young to read." In the context of a library with unfiltered Internet access, it is more than possible that a child may be exposed to what an adult decides to view.

Unquestionably, the Internet contains material that is not suitable for children and that could be harmful to them if allowed to view such material. The argument that children can make choices concerning pornography is not only counter-intuitive, it is in most states illegal. "[D]uring the formative years of childhood and adolescence, minors often lack experience, perspective, and judgment to recognize and avoid choices that could be detrimental to them." *Bellotti* v. *Baird,* 443 U.S. 622, 635 (1979). Therefore, to protect the welfare of children and to remove the possibility of any civil liability, libraries should take reasonable steps to ensure that children do not access indecent or pornographic material through the use of the Internet.

It is in the context of the protection of children, that libraries may constitutionally use filtering systems or segregate certain computer systems with filtering software for the use of children from "adult" computers. Otherwise, libraries open themselves up to liability for the inevitable harm caused to innocents viewing pornography for the first time.

## THE MAINSTREAM LOUDON DECISION WAS WRONG

The federal district court for the Eastern district of Virginia in *Mainstream Loudoun* v. *Bd. of Trustees of the Loudoun County Library,* 24 F. Supp.2d 552 (1998), declared that Internet filtering software used by a library is unconstitutional. That decision was wrong because the district court used an incorrect forum analysis; it confused access to publicly available rooms in the library with the library collection itself. Publicly available meeting rooms can easily become public fora, whereas the library collection cannot. As a result of using the wrong forum analysis, the court also erroneously required the library to show a compelling justification for its use of the Internet filtering software.

Also, regardless of the legal analysis, the *Mainstream Loudoun* case involved using filtering software on all of the computers in the library, 24 F. Supp.2d at 552, whereas the legislation at issue here applies to only some of the computers in any given library (those accessible to children). The *Mainstream Loudoun* court acknowledged that use of filtering software on only some Internet terminals used by minors would have been a constitutionally less restrictive alternative to the policy it dealt with. *Id.* at 567.

Also, the Fourth Circuit recently overruled a parallel decision by the same federal district court judge in *Urofsky* v. *Gilmore,* 1999 WL 61952 (4th Cir. (Va.)) (Feb. 10, 1999). In *Urofsky,* a constitutional challenge was brought against a Virginia law restricting state employees from accessing sexually explicit materials on computers owned or leased by the state. The district court ruled the law unconstitutional, and the Federal Court of Appeals for the Fourth Circuit overturned that decision, holding such restrictions to be constitutional. As the Fourth Circuit ruled:

> We reject the conclusion of the district court that Va. Code Ann. §§ 2.1–804 to –806, restricting state employees from accessing sexually explicit material on computers that are owned or leased by the Commonwealth unless given permission to do so, infringes upon first amendment rights of state employees. The Act regulates the speech of individuals speaking in their capacity as Commonwealth employees, not as citizens, and thus the Act does not touch upon a matter of public concern. Consequently, the speech may be restricted consistent with the First Amendment. *Urofsky,* 1999 WL 61952 at 3.

Similarly, in *Mainstream Loudoun* v. *Bd. of Trustees of the Loudoun County Library,* 24 F. Supp.2d 552 (D.Va. 1998), the library had a compelling justification in protecting minors and employees from the harmful and discriminatory effects of pornography. Nonetheless, the library should have been required to meet a lower threshold of scrutiny, and the use of this software should have been upheld.

**Calling Aesthetic Library Collection Decisions an "Open Forum" Was Erroneous** Aesthetic acquisition decisions concerning a library collection are not the same as renting facilities to the general public and excluding a particular group because of their viewpoint. However, in *Mainstream Loudoun,* an eastern district of Virginia federal court held that a public library is a "limited public forum," and consequently, use of Internet filtering software was unconstitutional:

> All three of these factors indicate that Loudoun County libraries are limited public fora and, therefore, that defendant must permit the public to exercise rights that are consistent with the government's intent in designating the Library as a public forum. The receipt and communication of information is consistent with both. Because the policy at issue limits the receipt and communication through the Internet based on the content of that information, it is subject to a strict scrutiny analysis and will only survive if it is necessary to serve a compelling government interest and is narrowly drawn to achieve that end. *Mainstream Loudoun,* 24 F. Supp. at 563.

The district court's analysis that libraries are public fora, and thus, susceptible to constitutional challenge based upon aesthetic decisions is wrong.

Again, "the Supreme Court [has] identified three types of fora: the traditional public forum, the public forum created by government designation, and the nonpublic forum." *Cornelius* v. *NAACP Legal Defense & Educ. Fund, Inc.,* 473 U.S. 788, 802 (1985). Traditional public fora include "places which by long tradition or by government fiat have been devoted to assembly and debate. . . ." *Perry Educ. Ass'n* v. *Perry Local Educators' Ass'n,* 460 U.S. 37, 45 (1983). This category includes streets, parks, public sidewalks, and other public places which "have immemorially been held in trust for the use of the public, and time out of mind, have been used for purposes of assembly, communicating thoughts between citizens, and discussing public questions." *Id.* The government cannot regulate speech in a public forum unless it is "necessary to serve a compelling state interest" and "narrowly drawn to achieve that end." *Id.*

A designated public forum consists of "public property which the state has opened for use by the public as a place for expressive activity." *Id.* In a designated public forum, "[r]easonable time, place and manner regulations are permissible, and a content-based prohibition must be narrowly drawn to effectuate a compelling state interest." *Id.* at 46. The government cannot create a public forum by inaction. "The decision to create a public forum must instead be made by intentionally opening a nontraditional forum for public discourse." *Cornelius,* 473 U.S. at 802.

The Court has recognized a sub-category of designated public fora, the limited public forum. *Perry,* 460 U.S. at 45 n. 7. "In the case of a limited public forum, constitutional protection is afforded only to expressive activity of a genre similar to those that government has admitted to the limited forum." *Travis* v. *Owego-Apalachin Sch. Dist.,* 927 F.2d 688, 692 (2d Cir. 1991). Therefore, those restrictions that do not limit the type of First Amendment activities the government has specifically permitted in the limited public forum need only be reasonable and viewpoint neutral. *Perry,* 460 U.S. at 46.

The last category of property is nonpublic fora. In a nonpublic forum, "[t]he State, no less than a private owner of property, has power to preserve the property under its control for the use to which it is lawfully dedicated." *Perry,* 460 U.S. at 46. Thus, in this setting, the government may enact and enforce "time, place, and manner regulations, [to] . . . reserve the forum for its intended purposes, communicative or otherwise, as long as the regulation on speech is reasonable and not an effort to suppress expression because public officials oppose the speaker's view." *Id.*

A public library does not constitute a traditional public forum. The nature of a library does not permit a patron to engage in most traditional First Amendment activities while in the library. For example, a patron would not be permitted to engage in speeches or any other type of conduct which would disrupt the quiet and peaceful atmosphere of the library. Similarly, library patrons cannot demand the placement of a book on the library shelves or that the library change its rules and regulations to fit his/her needs. Therefore, the nature of the public library does not lend itself to be classified a traditional public forum.

A library would also not be classified as a designated public forum. As stated before, the government can only create a public forum through actions that express an intent to do so. The opening of a library does not meet that test.

The Supreme Court has "recognized that the location of property also has a bearing on this question because separation from acknowledged public areas may serve to indicate that the separated property is a special enclave, subject to greater restriction." *International Society for Krishna Consciousness* v. *Lee,* 505 U.S. 672, 680 (1992). Libraries impose many restrictions on the use of their systems which demonstrate that the library is not available to the general public. Additionally, an open forum by government designation becomes "open" because it allows the general public into its facility for First Amendment activities. Like the *National Endowment for the Arts* v. *Finley,* 118 S.Ct. 2168 (1998) decision, the government purchase of books (like buying art) does not create a public forum.

The same analysis applies in determining that the library is not a limited public forum. The case relied upon by the district court in *Mainstream Loudoun, Kreimer* v. *Bureau of Police for Town of Morristown,* 958 F.2d 1242 (3rd. Cir. 1992), is inapposite and irrelevant in the determination concerning the types of aesthetic judgments libraries can make about their own circulation. In *Kreimer,* a homeless man challenged certain library policies which governed patron activities, dress, and personal hygiene. *Id.* at 1247. Using the limited public forum standard, the court upheld all of the challenged ordinances. *Id.* at 1246. Also, the *Kreimer* decision rests upon, *ISKCON* v. *New Jersey Sports and Exposition Authority,* 691 F.2d 155, 160 (3rd. Cir. 1982), which had nothing to do with a public library, and *Concerned Women for America, Inc.* v. *Lafayette County,* 883 F.2d 32, 34 (5th Cir. 1989), which held that a meeting room was an open forum by government designation, and therefore the library could not exclude a religious group wishing to use the room. Thus, the *Mainstream Loudoun* court created its rationale that library acquisition decisions could be subsumed under the open forum doctrine out of whole cloth.

Since a library is not a traditional public forum and it is not a designated public forum, it will be either a nonpublic forum or a forum for aesthetic acquisition decisions. The Second Circuit's rational in *General Media Communications, Inc.* v. *Cohen,* 131 F.3d 273, cert. denied, 118 S. Ct. 2637 (1998), supports the classification of a public library as such a forum. In *Cohen,* the court was asked to determine the constitutionality of the Military Honor and Decency Act which prohibits the sale of sexually explicit material at military exchanges. *Id.* at 275. In upholding the Act, the court held military exchanges to be a nonpublic forum. *Id.* at 280.

"[W]hen the state reserves property for its 'specific official uses,'" the Second Circuit held, "it remains nonpublic in character." *Id.* at 279 (citing *Capitol Square Review and Advisory Bd.* v. *Pinette,* 515 U.S. 753, 761 (1995)). "The government's dedication of property to a commercial enterprise is 'inconsistent with an intent to [create] a public forum.'" *Id.* (quoting *Cornelius,* 473 U.S. at 804). "It is also well established that the presence of some expressive activity in a forum does not, without more, render it a public forum." *Id.* (citing *Cornelius,* 473 U.S. at 805).

After establishing these principles, the Second Circuit held that the purpose of the military exchange was to "provide authorized patrons with articles and services necessary for their health, comfort, and convenience and to provide a supplemental source of funding for military morale, welfare, and recreation programs." *Id.* at 280 (internal citations and quotation marks omitted). "[T]he government has simply chosen to purchase certain magazines, newspapers, and videos from third parties, and has offered this merchandise for resale to its personnel at military exchanges. . . . It does not offer to resell the merchandise of every producer, or every 'speaker,' who seeks access to those shelves." *Id.*

Libraries are similarly designed to "provide authorized patrons" with articles necessary for educational and "convenience" purposes. To further those goals, libraries choose certain materials for purchase and offer this material to authorized patrons. Libraries do not open their shelves to every "speaker who seeks access to [their] shelves." Thus, a library, as with a military exchange, is either a nonpublic forum, or a forum of such nature as to allow aesthetic decisions to be made about what will be acquired for the library's collection.

It must also be noted that the *Mainstream Loudon* court did hold that "minimizing access to illegal pornography and avoidance of creation of a sexually hostile environment are compelling interests." 24 F. Supp. at 565. The court went on

to hold that, although the challenged policy was over inclusive because it restricted adult Internet access, it would be possible to create a policy which would protect children. *Id.* at 567. The ultimate solution for this library while the appeal of the district court decision is being evaluated, was to segregate some computers exclusively for the use of children with the filtering software. As of this writing, I am unaware of any challenge to that new policy.

**The Use of Filtering Software Is Reasonable and Viewpoint Neutral**   Content-based restrictions in such a forum must only be reasonable and viewpoint neutral. The use of Internet filtering software meets these standards. Since "forum" analysis is inapplicable, a library's regulations will be constitutional as long as they are reasonable and viewpoint neutral. *Lamb's Chapel* v. *Center Moriches Union Free Sch. Dist.,* 508 U.S. 384, 392 (1993). The regulations are only required to be reasonable, they "need not be the most reasonable or the only reasonable limitation." *Cornelius* v. *NAACP Legal Defense & Educ. Fund,* 473 U.S. 788, 808 (1984). Further, "[t]he reasonableness of the Government's restriction of access to a nonpublic forum must be assessed in the light of the purpose of the forum and all the surrounding circumstances." *Id.* at 809.

***The Use of Filtering Software to Protect Children and Employees Is Reasonable***   In *Arkansas Educ. Television Comm'n* v. *Forbes,* 118 S.Ct. 1633 (1998), the Court upheld the decision of a public broadcasting station denying a political candidate access to a televised public debate. The Court's reasoning was based on the broadcaster's duty "to schedule programming that serves the public interest, convenience, and necessity." *Id.* at 1639 (internal quotation marks and citations omitted). In furtherance of this duty, "[p]ublic and private broadcasters alike are not only permitted, but indeed required, to exercise substantial editorial discretion in the selection and presentation of their programming." *Id.* The Court stated that forcing a broadcaster to include all candidates "would actually undermine the educational value and quality of the debates." *Id.* at 1643.

The television station put forth five reasons for excluding Forbes from the televised debate:

"(1) the Arkansas voters did not consider him a serious candidate; (2) the news organizations also did not consider him a serious candidate; (3) the Associated Press and a national election result reporting service did not plan to run his name in results on election night; (4) Forbes apparently had little, if any, financial support, failing to report campaign finances to the Secretary of State's office or to the Federal Election Commission; and (5) there was no 'Forbes for Congress' campaign headquarters other than his house." *Id.* at 1643–44 (internal quotation marks omitted). These reasons led the television station to conclude that Forbes had generated no appreciable public interest. The Court held that this was a reasonable basis for excluding Forbes from the debate. *Id.* at 1644.

Similarly, ensuring that pornographic material is not accessible at library computer terminals is a reasonable basis for utilizing Internet filtering software. Libraries are designed to serve the "public interest, convenience, and necessity." To further this purpose, libraries are required to "exercise substantial editorial discretion in the selection and presentation" of the material they make available to the public. If libraries were forced to make available every piece of information on the Internet, including obscene material, it would undermine the "educational value and quality" of the information provided by the library. Library officials, as opposed to the courts, are best equipped to make decisions as to the types of information that the library will make available to the public.

Libraries are designed to promote education in the surrounding communities. Intertwined with this purpose is the duty to promote community values and to protect children from harmful material. Due to the compelling interest in protecting children, placing Internet filtering software on library computers is a reasonable measure designed to protect children from accessing materials which could be harmful to them. Also, even though libraries are not compelled to use the least restrictive means, Internet filtering software is the least restrictive means to block harmful material on the Internet.

Opponents of Internet filtering software, such as the American Library Association (ALA) and the American Civil Liberties Union (ACLU),

have proposed several alternatives which they argue would be less restrictive and just as effective. The following are the five alternatives proposed: (1) Acceptable Use Policies—provide carefully worded instructions for parents, teachers, students and libraries on use of the Internet; (2) Time Limits—establish content neutral time limits on use of the Internet, request that Internet access in schools be limited to school-related work; (3) "Driver's Ed" for Internet Users—condition Internet access for minors on completion of Internet seminar similar to a driver's education course; (4) Recommended Reading—publicize and provide links to websites recommended for children and teens; (5) Privacy Screens—install screens to protect users' privacy when viewing sensitive information and avoid unwanted viewing of websites by passers-by. ACLU White Paper, *Censorship in a Box: Why Blocking Software is Wrong for Public Libraries* <http://www.aclu.org/issues/cyber/box. html#battling>

First, the first four suffer from the same flaw in assuming that one can avoid offensive material simply by being educated about the Internet. One can hardly imagine a search on the Internet which will not yield at least a few pornographic sites. Many sites are designed to look innocent at first glance so that they can avoid being blocked by Internet filtering software. Second, establishing time limits would in no way limit children's access to pornography. It would only limit the amount of pornography that they could access. Third, these alternatives suffer from another faulty premise that, if educated, children will not access pornographic sites. In no other aspect of our society does the law trust minors to do what is in their best interest. Children are banned from accessing pornography in every other venue. Public libraries should not be the only place where children are allowed to access such material because we trust them to do what is in their best interest. Lastly, privacy screens will only foster minors' access of pornography by allowing them to do it in private without the fear or embarrassment of being caught. They will in no way decrease the minors' access of pornography. Therefore, none of the alternatives cited by the ALA and ACLU provide any reasonable proof that if placed in use they will be at all effective in curbing the problem of minors' access to pornography.

First, the public school library is a wholly different setting than the public library. The Supreme Court has held time and again that public schools are a unique setting and are subject to unique constitutional constraints. See, e.g., *Edwards* v. *Aguillard,* 482 U.S. 578, 584 (1987) ("The State exerts great authority and coercive power through mandatory attendance requirements, and because of the students' teachers as role models and the children's susceptibility to peer pressure."); *Shelton* v. *Tucker,* 364 U.S. 479, 487 (1960) ("The vigilant protection of constitutional freedoms is nowhere more vital than in the community of American schools."). Therefore, *Board of Educ. Island Trees Union Free School Dist.* v. *Pico,* 457 U.S. 853 (1982) is not applicable to the public library setting where there is no captive audience by virtue of mandatory attendance requirements. Additionally, the Supreme Court noted in *Pico* that:

> On the other hand, respondents implicitly concede that an unconstitutional motivation would not be demonstrated if it were shown that petitioners had decided to remove the books at issue because those books were pervasively vulgar. Tr. of Oral Arg. 36. And again, respondents concede that if the removal decision was based solely upon the "educational suitability" of the books in question, then their removal would be "perfectly permissible." *Id.,* at 53. In other words, in such motivations, if decisive of petitioners' actions, would not carry the danger of an official suppression of ideas, and thus would not violate respondents' First Amendment rights.

Second, the Supreme Court has "long recognized that each medium of expression presents special First Amendment problems." *FCC* v. *Pacifica Foundation,* 438 U.S. 726, 748 (1978). Thus, the Court's analysis on book removal cannot be the standard for the use of Internet filtering software on the Internet. The Internet is a unique medium of expression with no real counterpart. Therefore, any analysis regarding the Internet will need to be wholly unique to that setting.

Lastly, even if the *Pico* standard is applied in the present setting, the use of Internet filtering software meets that standard. *Pico* forbids only the removal of books from a school library if the removal is based on the viewpoint expressed by the book. "Nothing in our decision today affects in any way the discretion of a local school board to choose books to add to the libraries of their schools." *Pico,* 457 U.S. at 871.

Internet filtering software does not remove any material from a library's collection. The software merely acts as a substitute purchaser for the library. Library personnel are always called upon to exercise their discretion when determining whether to purchase certain materials. In using Internet filtering software, librarians are simply exercising that same discretion, albeit, through a different means. The nature of the Internet does not allow for individual purchase of certain information by a human librarian. However, Internet filtering software is able to play the part that the human librarian has always played. Therefore, the use of Internet filtering software at public libraries does not change in any way the nature in which libraries have conducted their business since their inception.

In fact, not using Internet filtering software constitutes a significant change in the nature of libraries. Libraries have always been a safe haven for children; a place which parents could trust that would be beneficial to their children. Libraries are designed to enhance the educational process and to inculcate community values. However, pornographic material permeates the Internet and is readily accessible to the willing, and the unwilling, recipient. If Internet filtering software is not placed on library computers, it will drastically change the nature of public libraries, and parents can no longer be safe in assuming that their child's visit to the library will be beneficial to their upbringing.

### The Use of Internet Filtering Software Is Viewpoint-Neutral

Viewpoint discrimination is an effort to suppress the speaker's activity due to disagreement with the speaker's view. *Rosenberger* v. *Rector & Visitors of Univ. of Virginia,* 515 U.S. 819, 829 (1995). A viewpoint is "a specific premise, a perspective, a standpoint from which a variety of subjects may be discussed and considered." *Id.* at 831. The Supreme Court has consistently recognized that the government may allocate funding according to criteria that would not be permissible in enacting a direct regulation.

This principle was reiterated in *Finley,* when the Court noted that, "the Government may allocate competitive funding according to criteria that would be impermissible were direct regulation of speech or a criminal penalty at stake." *Id.* at 2179. This principle is firmly ensconced in the Supreme Court's "It is preposterous to equate the denial of taxpayer subsidy with measures aimed at the suppression of dangerous ideas." *Regan* v. *Taxation with Representation,* 461 U.S. 540, 550 (1983). "The Government can, without violating the Constitution, selectively fund a program to encourage certain activities it believes to be in the public interest, without at the same time funding an alternative program." *Rust* v. *Sullivan,* 500 U.S. 173, 193 (1991).

Just as the federal government may determine what types of art it chooses to fund, so also can public libraries choose the types of information they will make available to the public. A public library's decision to place Internet filtering software on computer terminals in no way restricts individuals' First Amendment rights. Libraries which do so have merely made a choice to, in the words of the NEA regulation, "tak[e] into consideration general standards of decency and respect for the diverse beliefs and values of the American public," *Finley* at 2172, when deciding which information to purchase.

This type of governmental decision stands in stark contrast to the broad provisions of the Communications Decency Act (CDA) which was struck down by the Court in *Reno* v. *American Civil Liberties Union,* 117 S. Ct. 2329 (1998). The major distinction between the CDA and this piece of legislation is that this is a control not over the Internet, but it is a control being exercised over the receipt of government funds.

Also, in her concurrence in *Reno,* Justice [Sandra Day] O'Connor makes clear that this legislation, unlike the CDA, would pass constitutional muster:

> Our cases make clear that a "zoning" law is valid only if adults are still able to obtain the regulated speech . . . If the law does not unduly restrict adults' access to constitutionally protected speech, however, it

may be valid. In *Ginsberg* v. *New York,* 390 U.S. 629, 634 (1968), for example, the Court sustained a New York law that barred store owners from selling pornographic magazines to minors in part because adults could still [buy] the magazines. 117 S. Ct. at 2353 (O'Connor, J., concurring in part and dissenting in part).

Similarly, this legislation allows libraries to maintain computers for adult access to the Internet. It simply limits a child's access to pornography on those computers to which children have access. Stated another way, as opposed to the CDA, this proposed legislation does not attempt to control the Internet at all. Instead, it controls the funding for the gateway through which children have access to the Internet.

Finally, the CDA, Section 223(a)(1)(B)(ii) criminalizes the "knowing" transmission of "obscene or indecent" messages to any recipient under 18 years of age. Another section, 223(d), prohibits the "knowing" sending or displaying, to a person under 18, of any message, "that, in context, depicts or describes, in terms patently offensive as measured by contemporary community standards, sexual or excretory activities or organs."

In contrast, placing Internet filtering software on public library Internet terminals does not in any way limit First Amendment activities on the Internet. Individuals may still engage in any type of speech they wish on the Internet. Then, through the use of software, libraries can choose which pieces of information it will make available to the public.

The government's ability to purchase or fund material it deems suitable notwithstanding, restrictions on "lascivious," "lewd," or "indecent" speech are not based on viewpoint. In *R.A.V.* v. *City of St. Paul,* 505 U.S. 377, 388 (1992), the Court explained that, even though obscenity is unprotected speech, a State could not prohibit "only that obscenity which includes offensive political messages," to do so would constitute viewpoint discrimination. However, the First Amendment does allow the government to "choose to prohibit only that obscenity which is the most patently offensive in its prurience—i.e., that which involves the most lascivious displays of sexual activity." *Id.* Thus, in enunciating this principle, the Court relied on the premise that distinctions based on "prurience" or "lascivious[ness]" are not viewpoint discriminatory. See also *Bethel Sch. Dist. No. 403* v. *Fraser,* 478 U.S. 675, 685 (1986) (punishment of public high school student for use of "offensively lewd and indecent" language in speech to students was "unrelated to any political viewpoint"); *Bd. of Educ.* v. *Pico,* 457 U.S. 853, 871 (1982) (plurality opinion) (removal of books from public school library because of their "pervasive vulgarity" would be permissible whereas removal of books because of their "ideas" would not).

The Second Circuit adopted this reasoning in their recent decision in *General Media Communications, Inc.* v. *Cohen,* 131 F.3d 273 (2d. Cir. 1997), cert. denied, 118 S. Ct. 2637 (1998). *Cohen* involved a constitutional challenge to the Military Honor and Decency Act which prohibits the sale or rental of recordings and periodicals at military exchanges "the dominant theme of which depicts or describes nudity, including sexual or excretory activities or organs, in a lascivious way." 10 U.S.C. § 2489a(d). The appellees argued that the Act targeted a "viewpoint portraying women as sexual beings or as the focus of sexual desire, as well as a viewpoint of lasciviousness." *Id.* at 281 (internal quotations marks omitted). In dismissing this argument, the court held that the adjective "lascivious" helps identify the particular subject matter or content that the Act

encompasses. From this, the court concluded that lasciviousness is not a viewpoint. *Id.* at 282.

The majority of Internet filtering software is designed to block all Internet sites which are deemed to be prurient or lascivious. They are not designed to block out only those pornographic materials which may express a certain viewpoint. The use of such software by public libraries is constitutional, and is the only way, presently, in which libraries can provide their patrons with the Internet and still protect children from harmful materials. . . .

## CONCLUSION

Libraries and public schools have a compelling interest to protect the physical and psychological well-being of children, and not to foster a hostile working environment. Both of these interests are compromised when Internet access is left unchecked and patrons, young and old, are unwillingly or unwittingly exposed to the hardcore pornography available throughout the Internet. Libraries not only may implement reasonable, viewpoint neutral regulations to prohibit the access of pornography, but potential liability would argue for such implementation. The use of Internet filtering software is a reasonable, viewpoint neutral regulation which accomplishes the goal of eliminating access to pornography, and fosters the libraries' educational purposes.

---

## 22.4  Regulating Internet Access in Libraries

*Statement of Jerry Berman*

THE CENTER FOR DEMOCRACY and Technology [CDT] has a number of concerns with the legislation under discussion today, which would mandate schools and libraries receiving Universal Service, or "E-Rate," funding to certify to the Federal Communications Commission that they are using Internet blocking and filtering software.

From U.S. Senate. Committee on Commerce, Science, and Transportation. *Children's Internet Protection Act.* Hearing, March 4, 1999. Washington, DC: Government Printing Office, 1999.

CDT believes that the federal government should not force a "one-size-fits-all" solution onto a setting where many libraries and schools have found effective, community-based mechanisms to deal with children's Internet safety, and where others are seeking, through local consultation and experimentation, the best solutions for their communities. Many schools and libraries have developed "Acceptable Use" policies, and others have selected from among the approximately 90 different tools available in the market to help parents, teachers, and librarians protect children online.

The courts have held that user empowerment tools, such as blocking and filtering software, provide valuable *choices* for protecting children online, but have drawn the line against mandatory use of such tools. The United States Supreme Court, in striking down the Communications Decency Act 9–0, recognized user empowerment tools as a less restrictive means of effectively protecting children than government content restrictions. More recently, federal judge Lowell Reed recognized that these tools were at least as effective as legislation in protecting children online, when he issued a preliminary injunction against the Department of Justice, prohibiting enforcement of the Child Online Protection Act [COPA]. However a mandatory filtering policy in Loudoun County, Virginia was found unconstitutional by the federal court, because it acted as a prior restraint on speech, blocked access to constitutionally protected speech, and because there was insufficient evidence to show that blocking and filtering software was a narrowly tailored solution to serve a compelling government interest. A federal filtering mandate would face constitutional problems similar to those encountered by Loudoun County, Virginia.

## THE INTERNET IS A TREMENDOUS EDUCATIONAL AND ENTERTAINMENT RESOURCE FOR CHILDREN

Worldwide, there are over 140 million people online today, and children are an increasingly large segment of the Internet user population. For children on the Internet, a computer terminal is a window into an exciting world of knowledge, people, places and ideas. The Internet provides children with a tremendous opportunity to exercise their creativity and communicate with others, allowing them to publish their ideas and speak with voices that truly reach around the globe. The Internet offers children possibilities for personal growth that are limited only by their own imaginations.

The following are some examples of innovative online projects that demonstrate how the Internet can enrich the lives of children:

- **Building Bridges for Place-Bound Students** is a virtual classroom initiative that allows hospitalized children to collaborate with classroom-based students to learn about global climate change.
- **CyberIsle** is a Web-based virtual community that seeks to provide a compelling and safe environment for teenagers to explore issues around their sexuality, alcohol, cigarette, and drug use.
- **The NICE Project** gives K–12 students the opportunity to construct, cultivate, and preserve a virtual garden.
- **The Pueblo Project** matches senior citizens with school children in a one-to-one online mentoring program that encourages community development, basic reading and writing skills, and social responsibility.

We have all recognized that the Internet has enormous potential to foster the growth of children by encouraging them to communicate and exchange ideas. With this potential for growth, however, comes a potential for risk and a need for responsibility. The interactivity provided by the Internet, while providing opportunity for learning and self-expression, also raises some troubling issues. Children can interact with others online without parental supervision. The ease with which children can reveal information about themselves to others—through the click of their mouse, or through participation in games, chatrooms, pen-pal programs, and other online activities—can be alarming. Indeed, while the Internet offers children unprecedented and important new educational and recreational opportunities, the medium may also offer access to inappropriate material, exposure to unknown individuals, or exposure to unfair marketing or information collection practices.

The challenge for parents, teachers, and librarians is to realize the potential of the Internet for their children, while avoiding the possible perils. Ensuring a safe and enriching online environment requires us to strike a delicate balance between protecting children, preserving First Amendment freedoms, and respecting the privacy rights of all who seek to read, communicate, and associate with others on the Internet. Libraries, as institutions dedicated to promoting access to information, can play a pivotal role in preserving the fundamental First Amendment freedoms and privacy interests that allow people to exercise their right to read and access information. Libraries also serve as an important gateway to knowledge for children. As such, their efforts to address the complex issues presented by the Internet are of critical importance, and are ill-suited to resolution trough federal legislative mandates.

## LOCALLY DEVELOPED SOLUTIONS ARE A BETTER WAY TO PROTECT CHILDREN ONLINE THAN FEDERAL LEGISLATION

Requirements to adopt filtering technology will effectively usurp local communities' ability to set standards that reflect their values, for several reasons:

• While there are many reasonably priced filtering technologies currently available, they do not mirror the diversity of local community norms found across the country.
• The budgetary constraints under which libraries and schools operate are likely to limit their ability to custom design filters that meet their community standards.
• The ability of schools and libraries to assess whether commercially available filters meet their needs will be stymied by companies that currently do not disclose the standards under which they filter or the list of filtered sites.
• Some schools and libraries may lack the technical expertise and resources to choose and deploy filters.

The impact of requiring schools and libraries to implement filters is likely to be the replacement of the existing diversity of local community norms with a narrower set of views offered by companies that provide off the shelf filtering and blocking tools. In order to maintain funding, libraries and schools may find themselves out of step with their communities' values. This in turn may subject them to litigation, as happened recently in Loudoun County, Virginia. There, a federal court found mandatory filtering

in a library to be unconstitutionally restrictive on speech. Libraries and schools are concerned about this issue, but they also want to protect their child patrons. The United States National Commission on Libraries and Information Science [NCLIS] held a hearing on November 10, 1998, on the topic "Kids and the Internet: the Promise and the Perils." At its December 3, 1998 meeting, the NCLIS adopted this policy:

> NCLIS feels strongly that the governing body of every school and public library, in order to meet its trustee responsibilities, should establish, formally approve, and periodically review a written acceptable use policy statement on Internet access.

NCLIS offered not one, but several different approaches for libraries to consider, either individually or in combination, as ways of mitigating the perils facing children using the Internet, including:

• Libraries can implement procedures for gaining parental permission that describes what sort of access is permissible for their children;
• Separate terminals can be provided for adults and children;
• Libraries can restrict the use of chat by children to sites that have been specifically approved;
• Libraries can provide Internet training, education, and other awareness programs to parents and teachers.

The requirement to install filtering software interferes with the decisions by local communities, educators, and librarians to protect children through other means. These institutions are actively pursuing solutions that are responsive and appropriate to their specific missions, goals, and constituencies. Thoughtful local decision-making would be replaced by the decisions made by private companies—many of which are shut off from public scrutiny due to lack of disclosures about their proprietary process or guidelines for blocking sites. The prospect of schools and libraries being forced by budgetary constraints to choose between forgoing funding or delegating their traditional power to unchecked private entities raises troubling First Amendment issues.

## CONGRESS SHOULD NOT RUSH TO REGULATE AN ISSUE WHEN IT HAS JUST CREATED A COMMISSION TO STUDY THE PROBLEM AND POTENTIAL SOLUTIONS

Near the close of the last session, less than six months ago [November 1998], Congress created the Commission on Online Child Protection, which has been charged with taking a hard look at all of the technological and other options available to parents, teachers and librarians to protect children online. If Congress appoints a Commission that reflects a broad and balanced range of viewpoints and has the necessary expertise, then CDT is hopeful that the Commission will be well-suited to examine the marketplace of Internet child-protection options, learn from the variety of local experiences, and provide a useful, factual basis for future deliberations. Congress should wait for the COPA Commission to study these concerns and issue a report and recommendations, rather than rushing to pass another law before the Commission has even been fully appointed, much less had the opportunity to carry out its responsibilities.

## MANDATORY USE OF FILTERING SOFTWARE RESTRICTS SPEECH UNCONSTITUTIONALLY

While the Supreme Court has upheld the government's right to restrict speech that it funds where the speech reflects government policy, the government may not restrict speech where the purpose of funding is to propagate a diverse range of private views. The mandatory filtering decision in Loudoun County found that libraries are a public forum for the purpose of analyzing access to information on the Internet. The reasoning the court used to reach that conclusion would be reinforced by the fact that Universal Service E-rate funding is explicitly designed to facilitate access to the Internet—a broad range of ideas and views—not to express a specific government policy. Several studies of commercial available filters suggest that they curtail access to information on

topics ranging from gay and lesbian issues, women's health, conservative politics, and many others. If libraries and schools are faced with a limited set of options, this approach may force them to censor more than they would choose and in effect discriminate against specific viewpoints.

This bill will alter adults' ability to access constitutionally protected material in ways that will constrain and in some instances violate their First Amendment rights. Currently adults and children are able to access information that falls into the "harmful to minors" category in the same way they access other information online. Instituting a supervisory override of the filtering tool would not be constitutionally sufficient.

Courts have ruled that the government may not require adults to affirmatively request controversial but protected material in order to receive it.

## ALTERNATIVES TO LEGISLATION

While the Congress and courts around the country have been debating whether censorship laws can protect children online, companies and non-profit organizations have responded with wide-ranging efforts to create child-friendly content collections, teach children about appropriate online behavior, and develop voluntary, user-controlled, technology tools that offer parents the ability to protect their own children from inappropriate material. Unlike legislative approaches, these bottom-up solutions are voluntary. They protect children and assist parents and care-takers regardless of whether the material to be avoided is on a US or foreign Web site. They respond to local and family concerns. And they avoid government decisions about content. We would like to describe some of these initiatives to emphasize their diversity, their user-controlled nature, and their responsiveness to parental concerns.

**Education, Green Spaces, and Other Initiatives** Many public-private initiatives are underway to help parents and children learn to navigate the Web safely, create kid-friendly content zones, and to work with law enforcement to ensure children's safety. They include:

• User-friendly, "One Click Away" content is currently being developed by libraries, parents, consumer and civil liberties groups and the Internet industry, to help Internet Service Providers comply with the "Dodd Amendment," which requires that such companies provide their customers with information about and access to User Empowerment tools including filtering software.

• Sites created by libraries and schools, to lists of useful sites compiled by libraries and educators, such as "Kids Connect Favorite Web Sites" selected by school librarians for K–12 students;

• Tools that guide kids while they explore the Internet, such as AOL NetFind Kids Only a search engine that links only to sites that are safe for kids; and

• Hotlines that connect concerned parents and adults to law enforcement resources, such as the National Center for Missing and Exploited Children's Cyber Tipline.

In addition to ongoing efforts to develop resources, educational tools and child-friendly materials, the Internet community has sponsored several public events to highlight the issue of children's safety online, including access to inappropriate content, and inform the public of the resources and tools to address it. The Internet Online Summit: Focus On Children was held on December 1st–3rd 1997. More than 650 participants representing over 300 organizations came together to assure that steps were taken to make the Internet online experience safe, educational, and entertaining for children. Several major Initiatives emerged from the Summit, including:

• America Links Up: A National Education Campaign
• A "Parents Guide to the Internet"
• ISP "Zero Tolerance Policy" on illegal materials online
• "CyberTips Line" a "911" for the Internet
• Law Enforcement and Internet Safety Forum
• Local Law Enforcement Computer Crime Training

The industry and public interest community continues to develop educational and safety programs designed to help parents, schools, and libraries keep children's experiences on the Internet fun, educational, and safe.

**Acceptable Use Policies**    As a result of their "Kids and the Internet: The Promises and the Perils" study, the National Commission on Libraries and Information Science recommends that all libraries receiving public funding should develop, formally approve, and regularly review an "Acceptable Use Policy." Schools, libraries, and other educational and cultural community centers are actively seeking ways to provide children with enriching and safe online experiences. A central component of these efforts is protecting children from inappropriate information. Approaches range broadly. The United States Catholic Conference has developed an "Ethical Internet Use" policy under which each school or diocese adopts a policy detailing the rights and responsibilities of students, parents and teachers in Internet use. The policies are buttressed by contracts signed by students, parents and teachers. For example, Freemont Public Schools in Freemont, Nebraska, like many other public institutions, uses Acceptable Use Policies that educate students on how to access appropriate information and emphasize classroom supervision.

Other schools have chosen to incorporate into their Internet use tools that filter access at the desktop or network level and/or monitor access by students into their Internet strategy. School districts such as the New Haven Unified School District in Union City, California offer schools the ability to choose from filters that help limit access to content and access logs that help teachers monitor classroom use to ensure children's safety. Others such as Macomb County, Michigan, have established a countywide Internet filtering solution but allow individual schools to decide whether to employ it.

## CONCLUSION

The Center for Democracy and Technology shares the desire of the Chairman and the Committee to protect children on the Internet. However, we believe that this is not the time to rush forward with further action. Now is the time for schools and libraries to consider and implement the recommendations of the NCLIS, in such a way that best reflects their community concerns, experiences, and resources. Now is the time for the Commission on Child Online Protection, which is still in the process of being appointed, to take a hard look at the resources available and inform consumers—libraries, schools and parents—as well as Congress about the myriad of user empowerment tools available to protect children on the Internet.

## 22.5 | Virtual(ly) Law: The Emergence of Law in LambdaMOO
*Jennifer L. Mnookin*

### AN INTRODUCTION TO LAMBDAMOO

A DOZEN OR SO people are clustered in the kitchen of a sprawling house. New arrivals are greeted with a friendly wave or a nod; old friends bid farewell by hugging each other warmly. A samurai, a beady-eyed man in a dirty raincoat and a college kid in a ripped tee shirt are trying to solve a riddle. As a rainbow-colored dragon gives a disquisition to no one in particular on the advantages of foreign cars, a man with a stubbly beard whispers lascivious remarks to anyone who will listen. A chain-smoking, fast-talking woman in black and a little green elf argue over whether or not a ballot under consideration would help the community. One guest crawls into the microwave and laughs out loud.

This scene comes not from a surrealist film but from everyday life in LambdaMOO. LambdaMOO is one of more than 350 text-based virtual realities available via the internet. These virtual spaces are generally known as MUDs, multi-user dungeons, or multi-user dimensions. MOOs (MOO stands for multi-user, object oriented) and MUDs are real-time, interactive conferencing programs, spaces in which many people can carry on conversations at the same time. Unlike some other conferencing spaces, however, MOOs and MUDs are based in physical, spatial metaphors; they are virtual worlds in which to wander. A visitor to LambdaMOO, for example, arrives inside the coat closet of a house; the visitor may walk around the house's rooms, head out to the hot tub, take a stroll over to the museum, or visit a bar and order a drink. In each space, the visitor's computer screen will show a textual description of the room (but no graphics), and will also display who else is visiting the room at that moment. The visitor can talk to everyone else in the room, or interact with objects in the room, or whisper a message to one person in the room in particular, or even send a page to anyone else logged onto the MOO.

At any given time, hundreds of characters are logged on at once, talking, programming, flirting, and fighting; LambdaMOO is a virtual community. Within its confines, participants explore the contours of the virtual world, ride helicopters and moonbeams, even teleport themselves from one place to another or take an elevator from California to China. Experienced players also build their own rooms and spaces within the MOO, or, using an object-oriented programming language, create objects that they and other players can manipulate or expand, or "verbs" that allow characters to interact in novel ways. Participants in the MOO are literally building their own universe room by room. At the same time, they are building their own social structure, as well as their own legal system.

This paper will focus on the legal system beginning to emerge within LambdaMOO. At present, LambdaMOO has a system for enacting legislation, as well as mechanisms for dispute resolution. An examination of this nascent legal system is worthwhile for at least two reasons. First,

Jennifer Mnookin, "Virtual(ly) Law: The Emergence of Law in LamdaMOO," *Journal of Mediated Communication*, 1996. Portions of this chapter are reprinted here with the permission of *The Journal of Computer-Mediated Communication*. June, 1996. Footnotes omitted.

the study of LambdaLaw is an exercise in legal anthropology, a chance to examine a legal order separate from our own that has received no previous scholarly attention. Looking at Lambda-MOO's legal system provides the opportunity to see how participants are creating both social and legal order within a virtual sphere.

Second, LambdaMOO offers the potential to be an imaginative space, an environment within which social structures and legal mechanisms may be creatively constructed and reconstructed. What do I mean by this? One of the most interesting features of LambdaMOO is that it is structurally unconstrained by the laws of nature. A LambdaMOO character need in no way correspond to a person's real life identity; people can make and remake themselves, choosing their gender and the details of their online presentation; they need not even present themselves as human. Of equal significance, LambdaMOO need not be bound by the institutional structures of real life (or, as it is often known within the MOO, RL). Indeed, LambdaMOO takes to the hilt the notion of reality as a social construction. Within LambdaMOO, it is far more obvious than in real life that social structures are made rather than given, that they are constructed out of the actions and assumptions of the participants. In this virtual society, to change the code is to change the world; reality is bounded only by the imagination. There exists, then, the possibility that inside of virtual spaces such as LambdaMOO, law and politics as much as identity can be creatively reconfigured. The legal system of LambdaMOO can be, quite literally, whatever the players make of it. Perhaps, then, LambdaMOO and spaces like it will serve as both virtual laboratories and virtual looking-glasses. Law within LambdaMOO, then, might turn out to reveal something about law outside of LambdaMOO as well.

The next section of the paper will look closely at the emergence of law within LambdaMOO. This section will examine the rise of the legislative system, the nature of the mechanisms for resolving disputes, and the kinds of disputes that arise within the MOO. It will also look at a central debate over the nature of law within LambdaMOO: many players wish to make LambdaLaw better defined, more structured, and increasingly formalized, while a number of other participants want it

to become less formal and legalistic, or even hope to abolish it altogether. Then, the third section of the paper will examine the appropriate relation between law within LambdaMOO and law outside of it. How should law in the "real world" connect to law within virtual environments? This section sketches out a number of possible ways of modeling the relationship between "LambdaLaw" and real-world law, and argues that the best model is the one that gives LambdaMOO the greatest possible amount of legal autonomy and thus the greatest potential for becoming an imaginative space for legal experimentation.

## LAW AND POLITICS IN LAMBDAMOO

LambdaMOO was born in October 1990, the child of Pavel Curtis, a researcher at Xerox Park. Since that time, it has become one of the most popular of the MOOs and MUDs; it has many thousands of registered characters. Some participants drop by infrequently; others spend dozens of hours a week in LambdaMOO. The LambdaMOO software and the LambdaMOO database are stored on a computer at Xerox Park in Palo Alto, California; to visit LambdaMOO one need only telnet to its site at lambda.parc.xerox.com, port 8888. Anyone who wants to can visit LambdaMOO as a guest; to take up residence there in a more permanent fashion, one must request a character, provide a functioning electronic mail address, and take one's place on a waiting list.

At its outset, LambdaMOO was an oligarchy without any formal system for resolving controversies or establishing rules. The oligarchs—MOO-founder Pavel Curtis as well as several other players who had participated in LambdaMOO since its infancy—were known as "wizards"; they were responsible for both technical integrity and social control on the MOO. The wizards were benevolent dictators. They set the rules of conduct within the MOO; they decided when to increase a player's quota (the quantity of disk space reserved for objects and spaces of her creation); they attempted to resolve disputes among players. Occasionally the "wizocracy" meted out punishment, the most extreme form of which was to "recycle" (destroy) a player for incorrigibly antisocial behavior.

**The Creation of a Legislative System** In early 1993, Pavel Curtis, the archwizard, wrote a memo to the MOO community telling them that the social structure was about to be transformed. As LambdaMOO expanded, the wizards

were fighting an increasingly losing battle to control and accommodate and soothe a larger and larger, more and more complex community. We were trying to take responsibility for, now, the behavior and mores of over 800 people a week, connecting from almost 30 countries of the world. We were frustrated, many of the players were frustrated; the center could not hold.

You can probably see where this is leading.

I realize now that the LambdaMOO community has attained a level of complexity and diversity that I've actually been waiting and hoping for since four hackers and I first set out to build this place: this society has left the nest.

I believe that there is no longer a place here for wizard mothers, guarding the nest and trying to discipline the chicks for their own good. It is time for the wizards to give up on the 'mother' role and to begin relating to this society as a group of adults with independent motivations and goals.

So, as the last social decision we make for you, and whether or not you independent adults wish it, the wizards are pulling out of the discipline/manners/arbitration business; we're handing the burden and freedom of that role to the society at large. . . .

My personal model is that the wizards should move into the role of systems programmers: our job is to keep the MOO running well and getting better in a purely technical sense. That implies, though, that we're responsible for keeping people from getting 'unauthorized' access; in particular, we still have to try to keep others from getting wizard bits since the functional integrity of the entire MOO is clearly at risk otherwise. . . .

It's a brave new world outside the nest, and I am very much looking forward to exploring it with the rest of you. To those of you who have noted that I have the ability to shut down the MOO at any moment, that my finger is, after all, the one on the boot button: you have nothing to fear on that score for the foreseeable future; only an utter fool would put an end to such an exciting social experiment at so crucial a time in its evolution.

In what Curtis hoped would be "the last socio-technical decision imposed on LambdaMOO by wizardly fiat," the oligarchs instituted a petition system, a process through which the players in LambdaMOO could enact legislation for themselves.

At the present time, any LambdaMOO resident who meets certain minimal criteria can initiate a petition for making a socio-technical change in LambdaMOO. The scope of changes that can be made by petition is broad: any modification that requires technical action in order to reach a social goal. For example, a petition might request the creation of a truly escape-proof jail, or a modification in the character-creation process, or a transformation of the petitions mechanism itself. When a player creates a petition, a mailing list is simultaneously created, to be used by all LambdaMOOers for debating the merits of the proposal. Players who support the goals of the petition, or who at least believe that the petition presents an issue worthy of consideration [by the] Lambda populace as a whole, may choose to attach their signatures to the petition. When a petition gets at least ten signatures, its creator can submit it to the wizards for "vetting." A wizard's decision to vet is supposed to be based on five criteria: that the petition be (1) appropriate subject matter for petitions; (2) sufficiently precise that the wizard can understand how to implement it; (3) technically feasible; (4) not likely to jeopardize the functional integrity of the MOO; and (5) not likely to bring the wizards or Xerox into conflict with real-world laws or regulations. Wizards are supposed to base their decisions exclusively upon these five criteria, and they are explicitly prohibited from refusing to vet on the basis of their personal opinions regarding the soundness of the proposals. Once vetted, a petition needs a certain number of signatures (5 percent of the average total vote count on all ballots, or currently,

60 signatures) to be transformed into an open ballot, and if the signatures are not received within a given amount of time, the petition expires. Ballots are open for voting for two weeks, and must pass by a two to one margin in order to be implemented.

The inauguration of the petitions process transformed LambdaMOO from an aristocracy into a partly-democratic technocracy. Wizards continue to be appointed, not elected; only the Archwizard has the power to promote a player to wizard status. There are no mechanisms for holding wizards or their actions accountable to the population at large. Officially, wizards have become mere implementers of the popular will. But implementation is far from self-executing. The power to implement, to transform the language of a petition into computer code is necessarily the power to interpret and shape whatever is being implemented. Moreover, the wizards have technical powers and access to information denied to the rest of LambdaMOO. Even if they pledge to use these abilities only for the public good and only when explicitly told to by mechanisms like the petitions process, their special abilities give them power over the MOO. Indeed, wizards are often referred to only half-jokingly as gods.

The wizards' functions, with regard to the petitions process, might be analogized to a cross between an administrative agency and a higher court. Like an administrative agency, the wizards are responsible for the actual implementation of legislation. (However, unlike the rule-making process undertaken by an administrative agency after a piece of legislation has passed, the wizards write their implementation notes before the petition is voted upon, so voters can see in advance, at least to a certain extent, what actions will result if any given petition is passed.) When wizards decide whether or not to vet a petition, they are acting in a capacity similar to that of judges engaged in judicial review, except that vetting takes place before the voting rather than after the legislation has been passed. (If judges had the power to issue advisory opinions about constitutionality when legislation was still under consideration, this would be akin to the vetting process.) The vetting process frequently has multiple iterations: a wizard may refuse to vet, explaining the refusal in a letter to the mailing list; the petition's author can then revise the petition in light of the wizard's comments and resubmit it. This back-and-forth process will continue until a wizard vets or the author gives up and decides to pursue the petition no longer.

LambdaMOO's petitions process illustrates both the politics of technology and the technology of politics. Transforming the virtual world in any significant and enforceable way requires changes in the computer code. Moreover, politics in LambdaMOO cannot be seen as mere superstructure, nor understood as entirely distinct from technology. Rather, politics in LambdaMOO is implemented through technology and political conceptions can be embedded within the technological constructions of the virtual environment. In other words, ideas about politics can be, to a certain extent, hard-wired into society via technology. For example, to prevent people from signing petitions without so much as glancing at them, a player may not sign without first scrolling through a petition beginning to end. Currently, voters are allowed to change their votes as often as they like throughout the voting period, but the breakdown of yes and no votes is not available to voters until after the voting period has closed. Voting in LambdaMOO is not required.

All of these aspects of the voting system reflect a certain conception of the relation between the individual and the political sphere, a conception of informed individuals who voluntarily participate within a system in which strategic voting is discouraged. We can easily imagine, however, the technologies of LambdaMOO being used to implement alternative conceptions of voting. For example, it would not be difficult to implement a system in which players were obligated to vote, or one in which strategic alliances were encouraged because the names of voters on each side and the vote tallies were both revealed and revisable while the voting period was underway. The range of what is possible is broad indeed when every petition is an "object" within object-oriented code and every political process is, in essence, created by a programming routine. The point is that in LambdaMOO it is far more apparent than in real life the extent to which choices about the design of the political process are just that: choices. As one LambdaMOO character put it, "LambdaMOO isn't a 'closed' or 'homeostatic' system, we're not stuck with anything. . . . All legislation that exists at LambdaMOO has been created in a vacuum where no one could predict how it would actually function with living, breathing human beings 'living the law.' People make mistakes. Foolish people are those that don't recognize that mistakes can be corrected. In virtual reality they can be undone!"

From descriptions of characters to political processes, all of LambdaMOO is constituted through words, based in language. Rooms, people, objects, technology and politics, all consist of nothing but words and signs. Within Lambda-MOO, [it] is not just communication that takes place in and through language, but the material substrate of LambdaMOO itself, its physical spaces and manipulable objects, its social institutions and political processes, as well. LambdaMOO operates as layers of embedded texts; indeed object-oriented programming lets one nest object within object, text within text. In LambdaMOO, there is no extralinguistic reality. In real life, action may be intelligible only through a linguistic filter; in LambdaMOO, reality is quite literally nothing but language.

**LambdaLaw in Action**   As of February 1, 1996, the voters of LambdaMOO have approved forty-four ballots. The ballots concern a number of LambdaMOO's important social issues: procedures for increasing or transferring quota; mechanisms for attempting to limit LambdaMOO's population explosion; the creation of a verb allowing experienced players to "boot" guests off the system for an hour if the visitors behave in inappropriate or annoying ways; the creation of a way for players to ban players they dislike from using their objects or visiting their rooms; the inclusion of a paragraph in the "help manners" text stating that sexual harassment is "not tolerated by the LambdaMOO community" and may result "in permanent expulsion." Recently passed ballots include a referendum declaring that the petition and balloting system is legitimate; a petition declaring that a homophobic petition would be burned in effigy; and a declaration that no petition may "bribe" signatories by providing special

or differential treatment to those who supported the measure by signing the petition.

### Dispute Resolution in LambdaMOO

The petitions process was also used to establish a system of dispute resolution. LambdaMOO's arbitration system is staffed by volunteers; participants who have been a member of the community for at least four months may offer their services. Every member of LambdaMOO is bound by the arbitration system, including wizards. Any player can initiate a dispute against any other individual player. The person calling for the dispute must have experienced an actual injury, interpreted broadly; making this determination is within the arbitrator's discretion. The two disputants must agree on an arbitrator from among those who have volunteered for the case; if they cannot agree, an arbitrator will be assigned at random. Other interested players can join an ongoing dispute, but a party cannot initiate a dispute against more than one player, nor initiate two disputes simultaneously. A mailing list is established for each dispute; anyone who wishes to comment on the facts or the process or any other aspect may contribute to the mailing list. Arbitrators hear both sides, collect information and post their decisions to the mailing list. They are "encouraged, but not required to solicit advice on the handling of the case from others." Although the parties cannot appeal the decision, it is reviewed by the other arbitrators. If more arbitrators vote against the decision than uphold it, it is overturned, and, depending on the circumstances, the same arbitrator tries again or a new one is appointed. Those with any conflict of interest with either disputant are prohibited both from serving as arbitrators and from voting to overturn the decision. Trials in absentia are discouraged, but permissible.

Arbitrators have a broad array of remedies. They may "call for almost any action *within the MOO*." They may modify either player's quota, recycle any of their objects or reduce their powers. They may ban either party from the MOO for a period of time, or order a character to engage in community service. They may even order the most extreme of punishments: "toading," LambdaMOO's name for the virtual death penalty. Indeed, there are only two significant limits on the power of arbitrators: (1) they may only take action with respect to the two parties; they may neither propose a punishment that would infringe the rights of other players, nor call for a new law as the result of the arbitration; and (2) their proposed actions must take place within Lambda-MOO itself; the punishment cannot require any real-life activity. In practical terms, however, this first limitation on arbitrators' power is a serious issue. It means that except by providing potentially persuasive examples of community norms, disputes have no precedential value. Other than community enforcement through the "overturn" mechanism, there is no system for ensuring that similarly situated disputants are treated similarly. Moreover, even when a dispute illustrates a structural problem within the MOO, the arbitrator is limited to resolving the specific instance of the problem and prohibited from making any changes to resolve the underlying structural issue. Arbitrators cannot prohibit the population in general from taking any action, nor can an arbitrator use a dispute to change social policy or make institutional reforms.

So what do people fight about in Lambda-MOO? Two of the most significant areas of contention and debate are: (1) the nature of property rights within the MOO; and (2) the extent to which free speech is a right within the MOO.

*Property Rights*   To what extent do Lambda residents own the objects they create within the MOO? To what extent should the creator of a room or object be able to control who uses it and how? Can especially useful objects be appropriated in the interest of the common good? Several ballots and disputes have revolved around these issues of property rights. For example, in Margeaux v. Yib, Yib refused to allow a helicopter pad created by Margeaux a place in her list of outdoor rooms. Yib claimed that this list was her own creation, and she should be allowed to use her own criteria for judging inclusions. She intended her criteria to be reasonable, and would include any outdoor room as long as it was "themely"; that is, she wanted it genuinely to have an out-

door look-and-feel. In Yib's view, Margeaux's helipad, made of swiss cheese and connected to the second floor of her house, was not sufficiently "outdoors"-like to warrant inclusion.

Margeaux argued that Yib's list was not a privately owned object but a public utility. (In essence, Yib's list provided the basis for the in-MOO aviation system; if one's spaces were not on the list, it would be quite difficult for anyone with a form of air transportation to fly over them or land there.) In Margeaux's words, "it's NOT Yib's system anymore. It's a public transportation system now." The problem was, as one player put it,

> "What is a public object? And if an object becomes 'public' ([and it is] still undefined as to what that means or when this occurs), who has control of the object? Does its author/creator? Does that author suddenly have to follow guidelines ([that are] also undefined)?"

The dispute itself did not solve any of the thorny definitional issues (indeed, under the rules of Lambda Arbitration it could not). However, Margeaux and Yib compromised; Yib agreed to publish her standards for including landing pads and modified the code so that people could land on their own helipads regardless of whether they were listed in Yib's catalog.

Another property-related dispute concerned a player who created object after object and then immediately destroyed them, in order to get access to objects with particular numbers. (He wanted what he saw as a "magic" number: 93939.) Every object in LambdaMOO, from a player to a mailing list, is associated with a number; basically these numbers are distributed sequentially. In his efforts to get the particular number he wanted, the player wasted hundreds of object numbers. The argument against his behavior was essentially that these numbers are a shared resource, a Lambda-commons, and he was violating the norms necessary for their shared use and enjoyment by the community. The player was punished by having some of his programming powers temporarily removed.

Issues related to property rights have generated petitions as well as disputes. One character wrote a petition that would have granted him ownership of numerous objects that belonged to other people. He explained his reasoning:

> "I'm not an anarchist, I'm a libertarian. I believe in property rights. In fact, I fight for them. However, while I realize that this is an actual society where people interact and have real relationships, it's still just a 'virtual' world. Why not toy with anarchy a bit? It's fun. It's also interesting that I'm using a democratic system for my anarchistic means."

A number of players appreciated this character's effort to thumb his virtual nose at the system, while others roundly criticized the petition as "an idiotic waste of resources." Even its supporters acknowledged that the ballot was "a joke" and had no chance of passing, and indeed it did not pass. But part of the discomfit of its opponents stemmed from the way it would have transferred property via petition. As I am writing this, a petition is under consideration that would allow MOO characters to write wills to dispose of their property if they should be recycled for any reason or commit "MOOicide." (Under the current system, one of the wizards serves as the "grim reaper," and generally makes decisions about what happens to the property of characters who are reaped.) The central argument in favor of will creation is that it is a proper component of property rights: characters should have some control over the uses to which their property is put even if they have left the MOO. This petition would allow characters to designate items for destruction or preservation in case of their MOO-death, and to bequeath their property to specific individuals, or prohibit certain individuals from acquiring it. References to real-world intellectual property issues abound in the discussion of this petition: the nature of copyright protection; whether volatile computer memory counted as "fixed in a tangible medium" under the copyright code; whether it violated the spirit of intellectual property protection to expel someone from the MOO and nonetheless make use of the programming undertaken by the banished character.

Disputes about property in LambdaMOO are neither as frequent nor as acrimonious as disputes about speech. Nonetheless, serious issues have been raised about the nature of property ownership within the MOO. If someone writes code and makes it available to the public, is the author then accountable to the public in any way? To what extent should the creators of rooms and objects be allowed to control who uses them and how? Should stealing someone's code be considered a punishable offense? The residents of LambdaMOO have not yet resolved this set of questions about the nature of property within their sphere.

*Speech Rights and Harassment* Disputes involving the issues of free speech and harassment are generally more emotionally charged than the disputes arising over property rights. In Abaxas vs. lucifuge2, for example, a player initiated a dispute against a character who was frequently insulting and using "violent" verbs against other players, repeatedly moving them without their permission to places within LambdaMOO such as "the cinder pile" and "Hell." In this case, nearly everyone agreed that lucifuge2's behavior was obnoxious; the question was one of appropriate punishment. The issue was further complicated when it became clear that the human being behind the character lucifuge2 had already been disciplined several times under other character names for nearly identical behavior. Despite his past offenses, a number of people felt strongly that the use of the most severe forms of punishment, like toading, or the revelation of real-life information about the character, was not an appropriate penalty for behavior, no matter how offensive, for which adequate defensive measures had been available to the victim.

What are these defensive measures? In LambdaMOO, any player can "gag" any other player (or object); issuing the "@gag" command prevents the gagged player's words from appearing on the issuer's screen. This command affects only the issuer; it has no effect on what the gagged player can say to anyone else. Another command allows a player to "refuse" the speech or commands of a character. For example, a player can refuse to receive paged messages from someone; or refuse to be moved from one place to another by someone else. Anyone who gagged or refused moves from lucifuge2 would, in effect, become immune to his harassment.

Some of the debate in this case, and in similar instances, centered on the appropriate response to "verb abuse," as it is called on LambdaMOO. Some believed that the responsibility clearly lay with whoever used the offending verbs. The arbitrator in Abraxas described an interview he had with a character who had been verb-abused by lucifuge2:

> [This character] feels that this sort of constant, mindless use of violently emoting verbs that move players involuntarily has created an environment of harassment that directly imposes on her ability freely to enjoy public areas of the MOO. . . . [She] also wanted to state that no player should be forced to @gag offensive players . . . since that would have the effect of leaving them vulnerable to spoofing from that player which would result in one being demeaned in front of one's friends and guests.

Others, however, emphasized that behavior like lucifuge2's, though irritating, should nonetheless be viewed as protected speech. As one player put it, "Don't like the way lucifuge talks? Got a filthy mouth? Tough shit, so do a lot of us. Gag him if you don't like it. I don't advocate toading the Jesus-preachers that show up from time to time, as personally offensive as I may find them. This place is supposed to protect free speech." In another arbitration, a commentator tersely summarized the two positions: "Those who do not believe in dealing with MOO criminals directly would argue that these crimes could be solved by such commands as '@refuse all from.' Others [liken] commands like '@refuse all from' to taking a painkiller and wearing a blindfold while getting raped."

A third position was that "abusive" verbs should be prohibited altogether, or their programmers should be responsible for their use. In one players' words, " 'This kind of behavior' (i.e., using verbs to move characters) should be prevented by disabling the verbs in question. If the verbs are available for public consumption, who is to decide how much use is 'too much'? What legitimate use does the 'sewer' or 'fireball' verb have?" As another wrote,

In an instance such as this, I do believe the responsibility lies with [the character who built the verbs in question]. His [verb] serves no purpose that I can tell other than to harass players. This isn't an instance where we have a kid who has written his own harassment verbs. [He] gave tacit permission (and we, the community, in turn, give [him] permission when we don't hold him accountable for creating objects that only function to annoy others, and leave ourselves in the role of having to educate his 'customers') to this player by allowing him access to his [creations]. And because this community is so transient, [with] players of varying ages continually joining, I foresee this as being a constant problem for the dispute [resolution] process.

In the end, lucifuge2 was given a player status invented specifically for this dispute: his powers were sharply curtailed for a two-month period. The creator of this new status described it as follows: "This is the Time Out Player Class, named for the way my 4-yr-old's day care deals with unruly children. They are sent to 'time out' to contemplate their behavior." While taking his "time out," lucifuge2 was allowed to participate in LambdaMOO, but his activities were restricted: he was denied access to all verbs other than those necessary for basic communication and he lacked the power to "gag" or "refuse" other players. He did, however, retain [the] right to initiate a dispute if he were the victim of harassment.

This dispute, and the many other speech-related disputes that have come about on LambdaMOO, illustrates the difficulty of separating the categories of speech and action within the MOO. A player like lucifuge2 moves another player by typing words on his keyboard, and these words, this speech, results in another player being forcibly moved against his will, an action. Moreover, players in LambdaMOO may "spoof" each other. As a general term, spoofing refers to unattributed speech within the MOO. But spoofing may also be used by one character to impersonate another. If a character makes offensive remarks in the LambdaMOO living room, he is, it would seem, speaking. But what if the character, by spoofing, makes it appear that somebody else is making those offensive remarks, somebody who is not actually typing the words onto the keyboard at all? Is this speech, or is it action? Should this distinction be important within LambdaMOO?

There continues to be substantial disagreement within LambdaMOO about the appropriate balance between freedom of speech and protection from unwanted speech. Ballots at each extreme have been proposed. One proposal, for example, recognized freedom of speech as a "basic right," and prohibited any disputes that were based upon "solely the content of speech," such as, presumably, disputes based on charges of sexual harassment or hate speech. Disagreement ensued over whether by the terms of the petition spoofing would, or should, be included within the category of protected speech; no consensus was reached regarding the status of spoofing should the ballot come to pass. As it turned out, the ballot was voted down, with 337 nays and 269 yeas.

An anti-rape measure, spurred in part by an incident, infamous in LambdaMOO, in which a character named Mr. Bungle spoofed several players in a public space, forcing them to engage in violent sex acts and making it appear that they were acting voluntarily, represents the opposite extreme. This petition recommended that "toading," or permanent expulsion, become the recommended punishment for confirmed virtual rapists. The ballot tried to distinguish between speech and action within the MOO; this attempt led to a complex set of definitions:

> A virtual "rape", also known as "MOOrape", is defined within LambdaMOO as a sexually-related act of a violent or acutely debasing or profoundly humiliating nature against a character who has not explicitly consented to the interaction. Any act which explicitly references the non-consensual, involuntary exposure, manipulation, or touching of sexual organs of or by a character is considered an act of this nature.

> An "act" is considered, for the purposes of this petition, to be a use of "emote" (locally or remotely), a spoof, or a use of another verb performing the equivalent presentation, whether by a character or by an object controlled by a character.

> The use of "say", "page", and "whisper" . . . and other functionality creating an equivalent sense of quotation generally are not considered "acts" under this petition; they are considered "speech". Notes, mail messages, descriptions, and other public media of communication within LambdaMOO that provide a sense of quotation or written expression rather than conveying action are also forms of "speech". This petition should not be interpreted to abridge freedom of speech within LambdaMOO community standards. Communications in the form of speech might still be considered offensive and harassing, but generally are not considered virtual rape unless they explicitly and provokingly reference a character performing the actions associated with rape.

The author of this petition was attempting, through these definitions, to make a distinction between the use of words that gives a "sense of quotation," and the use of words that gives a sense of action or activity. The debate over this ballot included extended discussion of whether this distinction between action and speech was coherent, and whether, even if coherent, it was the proper basis for determining the severity of punishment. In the end, the ballot had a high turnout and received support from a majority, but not from two-thirds of voters; the final tally was 541 in favor, 379 against, and 167 abstentions.

### Arbitrators' Techniques

*Authority through Dialogue* Like many real-life trial judges, the arbitrators of LambdaMOO seem willing to go to great lengths to avoid getting overturned. Recall that commentary, on the accusation, on the process, on the arbitrator's competence, on the appropriate penalty, is not only allowed, but structurally encouraged through the existence of the dispute-related mailing list to which any member of the community may contribute. One strategy that arbitrators use to minimize their chances of being overturned is to seek out a wide range of opinion before making a decision. Arbitrators frequently submit to the mailing list their proposed resolution, in unofficial form, asking for suggestions and comments regarding the intended sanction. This provides the arbitrator with a chance to see if the community backs the proposed approach to the dispute and an opportunity to argue with and perhaps persuade those unhappy with the strategy. Indeed, one of the most notable features of Lambda arbitrations is their dialogic nature; there is a great deal of give-and-take and animated discussion among the parties, the arbitrator, and other members of the community. Rarely do arbitrators maintain judicial distance during disputes; they participate, argue, explain their rationales, and even change their minds. Indeed, the ensuing discussion often prompts the arbitrator to modify the proposed penalty. (For example, in both of the cases involving lucifuge2, the arbitrator changed the punishment; in Abraxas the sanction changed from revealing the character's site information to enrolling him for two months in "time-out"; in Basshead, the punishment changed from temporary banishment to permanent expulsion.)

*Formal Language*   But the dialogic nature of the dispute resolution process can strain the system. Dispute mailing-lists can turn into shouting matches. Moreover, arbitrators sometimes feel frustrated by the influence the community wields over the sanction, even when only the arbitrator has been privy to all of the evidence on both sides. As one arbitrator explained, turning in his resignation, "Frankly, I don't want to go into a situation where I have to consider the opinions of masses over my better judgment having been the only one to hear both sides of the story."

These concerns have led some arbitrators to pursue a second strategy, in addition to or in place of participatory dialogue: formalization. That is, some arbitrators attempt to gain legitimacy for their decisions by using lawyerly language and issuing official-sounding findings of fact and conclusions. For example, Hiroko, the arbitrator in Basshead, issued a very precise, legalistic set of rulings regarding who would be allowed to join the dispute, explaining, "I realize these rulings may appear somewhat formalistic, but serious measures against lucifuge have been requested, and I intend this process to be beyond criticism to the extent I can possibly manage it." Formal speech and an attention to

process can give the adjudicatory process authority; it can illustrate, as Hiroko acknowledges, that the procedure was fair and beyond reproach. It is an attempt to be official by sounding official, not an outlandish strategy in a society consisting solely of text.

**Directions for LambdaLaw: Formalization and Resistance**   This tendency toward formalization may occur institutionally as well as individually. It is not limited to specific arbitrators, or even to arbitrators as a group. Rather, the entire LambdaMOO legal system is at a crossroads. Many believe that the current regime has revealed itself to be unworkable. Disputes are frequent and acrimonious. Frustration-levels are high and charges of favoritism are commonplace. Moreover, because arbitration remedies cannot extend beyond the parties, many of the issues underlying disputes cannot be addressed by the arbitration system. To be sure, the explanations for the current difficulties diverge: some blame the problems on corrupt and self-serving arbitrators; others believe the problems lie in the institutional structure; others view the very idea of LambdaLaw with suspicion. Two very different approaches have emerged for confronting the limitations of the current system: one approach favors increased formalization of LambdaLaw, while the other wants LambdaLaw eliminated. Those seeking formalization hope to establish more powerful legal and adjudicatory mechanisms along with better defined rights and responsibilities for players. The other camp, by contrast, advocates a turn away from law. For the past year, there has been a stalemate between the two camps: neither perspective has succeeded in mobilizing enough voters to change the system radically, but both approaches have enough advocates to keep their issues on the virtual table.

*The Formalizers*

Perhaps the most significant effort by the formalizers was their effort in the spring of 1995 to implement a Judicial Review Board (JRB), also known as the LambdaMOO Supreme Court. This Board would have been an elected body responsible for interpreting any question of LambdaLaw, and, under certain prescribed circumstances, would have acted as a court of appeals to review decisions made by wizards or LambdaMOO executive bodies. The JRB would have had jurisdiction over four kinds of cases: (1) inquiries about the proper interpretation of a clause of a petition or an existing law; (2) challenges to a wizard's decision to vet based on the procedural guidelines wizards are obligated to follow; (3) challenges to the way a wizard implemented a petition; and (4) procedural challenges to the actions of LambdaMOO governmental and quasi-governmental bodies. To have brought a case before the court, players would have needed to show a direct and specific interest in the case, or to have collected 15 signatures on a petition. The petition also declared that all ballots passed within LambdaMOO were to have the status of constitutional law, and that other forms of lawmaking, should they come to exist, were not to be considered to be constitutional law unless they explicitly stated otherwise.

The JRB petition had three main goals. First, it aimed to provide some structural accountability for the action of wizards. Second, it hoped to provide procedural accountability for the actions taken by arbitrators or the quota-granting Architectural Review Board. Third, in the current system of law in LambdaMOO, interpretive disputes are often insoluble. Furious debates have arisen over such matters as whether the petition rewriting "help manners" was intended as a guideline for courteous MOOing or as enforceable law. An arbitration system whose resolutions have no precedential value, combined with the lack of an authoritative body for resolving interpretive differences, means that such disputes cannot attain closure. Each time a new dispute is initiated regarding, say, sexual harassment, the arguments erupt again, with as much force as ever. The JRB would have provided a mechanism for achieving closure, a social structure with the authority to speak definitively. Although more voters supported the measure than opposed it, the ballot on JRB failed to achieve the support of two-thirds of the voters, as required for passage. However, in January of this year, another player re-introduced the measure, and is seeking signatures to turn it into a ballot. There have been several other efforts to restructure LambdaLaw as well, including a much-discussed proposal that would have replaced the petition system with a constitution, and a bill detailing Lambda-citizens' rights and responsibilities.

### The Resisters

While some members of the community expend their efforts attempting to formalize and extend LambdaLaw, another faction is trying to reduce or abolish its effect. In an effort to shrink LambdaLaw down to size, a number of petitions and ballots have been introduced which have an anti-formalist, anti-legalist bent. All of these ballots have intended to mock the formalist turn in LambdaLaw and add some humor to the adjudicative process. The subtext of all of these ballots is: "Remember, LambdaMOO is supposed to be fun. It's a game. Can't we all lighten up a bit?" For example, one ballot proposal, *Choosing Justice,* would have allowed individual Lambda-denizens to opt out of the system of arbitration, and to choose to solve their disputes through "wiffle" instead. Each participating player would have received a 'wiffle-ball'-style bat (in other words, a virtual plastic toy) with which they could have whipped other participating players whom they found offensive, annoying, or otherwise deserving of whapping. Any character who received a certain number of whaps would have been automatically banished from LambdaMOO for a period of twenty-four hours.

Wiffle's supporters argued that it provided people with an alternative to a stifling and arbitrary adjudicative mechanism by means of a relatively small penalty "available without all the legislative brouhaha," and that it might actually increase the level of courtesy within the MOO. Wiffle was also quite explicitly intended as a statement about the Lambda-legal system: as one supporter wrote, "I protest the introduction of violence into LambdaMOO society through the use of lawyers, arbitration, and legal red tape. This is a MOO, not a court of law. Support wiffle!" Wiffle's detractors claimed that players would abuse their wiffle-bats and gang up on people for no reason; that it was 'uncivilized,' offered lynch-mob-style justice; and that encouraging violence and self-help on LambdaMOO would lead to chaos and the unraveling of Lambda-society. When all was said and done, the Lambda-MOO population as a whole voted down the Wiffle ballot. The tally was 345 in favor and 376 against, with 268 abstentions.

Another petition proposed allowing a game of Scrabble to be an alternative dispute resolution mechanism. The proposal was enthusiastically received by some, who thought it was an appropriate mechanism for the MOO: "LambdaMOO is a society based almost entirely on words; [this measure provides] a form of settling disputes that takes this fact into account." The Scrabble petition, however, was denied vetting, because players could have concocted disputes and agreed that the winner would receive a quota increase, thus using the Scrabble game to make an end run around the proper quota distribution channels.

One light-hearted measure proposed attaching a new description to any player who submitted a political petition that received vetting: "[Playername] is wearing a boring three piece suit and an ugly tie. [Player is] carrying a leather attache case. On one side of the attache case is a large sign which reads 'Moo-politician. Beware!'" Any player to whom these words were attached could not remove them for a period of three weeks. Although some people found the ballot amusing and thought a little embarrassment for Lambda-politicians was entirely called for, others claimed that it was discriminatory and mean. The ballot failed to win passage; the tally was 304 in favor; 404 against; with 253 abstaining. The most extreme anti-formalist measure proposed the wholesale elimination of the arbitration system with no replacement for it at all. Its author advocated a return to a virtual state of nature: a system of self-help, and the elimination of all enforceable, MOO-sanctioned law. The debate regarding this proposal degenerated into name-calling; and the measure failed.

These disagreements between formalizers and resisters about LambdaLaw are, at their root, philosophic debates about the nature of LambdaMOO. For both the resisters and the formalizers, anxieties about the meaning of LambdaMOO are played out in the sphere of law. For those who view the MOO as a diversion, a virtual playground, LambdaLaw seems unnecessary and frustrating, an absurd bureaucratic

impediment to enjoying the MOO. These participants think that the formalizers take themselves and LambdaMOO far more seriously than they ought to. The resisters believe that LambdaMOO is, in the end, a game, a virtual reality that ought not to be mistaken for a real one. For the second group, those who take LambdaMOO seriously as a society, law has a double function, both pragmatic and symbolic. On the one hand, a legal system is a practical necessity, because the society requires workable mechanisms for adjudicating disputes, enacting legislation and establishing its standards of conduct. However, law simultaneously serves a symbolic function as well: If LambdaMOO has a well-defined legal system, then it is a society. That is, the existence of LambdaLaw becomes itself proof that LambdaMOO is more than a game, that what happens there is not just recreation but the creation of a virtual community. Games have rules, but who every heard of a game with a Supreme Court and a complex legislative system? In this sense, formalized law becomes a mechanism by which LambdaMOOers can prove that they are engaged in something grander than a role-playing game, that they are participants in a full-fledged virtual world. Law provides dispute-resolution mechanisms and legislative procedures, but it also provides something more: legitimacy.

What will be the outcome of this philosophic battle between the formalizers and the resisters? It seems that a greater proportion of MOO denizens, or at least a greater proportion of the voting population, support the formalizers than the resisters. Several of the formalizers' ballots, including the blueprint for the Judicial Review, received majority support from the non-abstaining voters, though none has received the necessary supermajority. By contrast, not a single one of the various anti-formalist measures has been favored by a simple majority. The formalizers' support thus appears to be broader and deeper than that of the resisters. Moreover, the lack of face-to-face communication and the diversity of the Lambda-MOO community suggest that informal norm-enforcement mechanisms will be hard to sustain; indeed, they have already proved hard to sustain. It therefore seems likely that if LambdaMOO lasts, so will LambdaLaw.

## REAL LAW AND LAMBDALAW: DEFINING THE BOUNDARIES

If LambdaLaw seems likely to be a permanent feature of LambdaMOO, determining the appropriate relationship between the legal system within the virtual world and the legal systems that exist outside of it becomes an issue. What should the relationship between LambdaMOO and the legal system in the Real World look like? Should United States courts, for example, recognize LambdaMOO as a separate jurisdiction? Or should they view LambdaLaw as irrelevant to "real" legal determinations involving activities within the MOO? In what circumstances should events that take place within virtual space be actionable in real space? There are at least four possible approaches to this issue; I will lay them out schematically.

### Metaphors of MOOdom

#### LambdaMOO as a social club

If LambdaMOO is understood to be the equivalent of a social club, the existence of LambdaLaw is largely irrelevant within the larger legal framework. In other words, the existence of dispute resolution mechanisms within the MOO would have no effect on LambdaMOO-ers ability to seek redress outside of the MOO for matters that took place within the MOO. LambdaLaw would be equivalent to the by-laws of a social club, or to a university's regulations. Just as a social club's regulations might prohibit members from engaging in certain otherwise legal behaviors within the club, LambdaLaw might prohibit activities that are permissible outside of its sphere. But, by this analogy, Lambda rules do not limit LambdaMOOers' out-of-MOO legal options. If a university has rules prohibiting libel, and a student is libeled in the college newspaper, the student can file a lawsuit instead of, or in addition to, making use of the university's grievance procedures. The existence of those procedures has no effect on whether the student is allowed recourse to law, nor do they affect the legal standard that operates. By this analogy, the laws of LambdaMOO have little relevance to proceedings that take place outside of the MOO, even if the events underlying the cause of action occurred within the MOO. If LambdaMOO is like a social club, there is no compelling reason to give its organizational forms and structures any special legal recognition.

#### LambdaMOO as a village

If LambdaMOO is understood to be a village, exhaustion of Lambda remedies before allowing access to state remedies might be appropriate. That is, if we see LambdaMOO as a place of its own, but one nested within larger geographic entities, just as a village is within a state within a country, we might want the legal system to require disputes to be addressed first at the local level before allowing them to be appealed to a higher authority. This conception would suggest a requirement of exhaustion of LambdaMOO remedies before allowing anyone to make an out-of-Lambda legal claim resulting from in-Lambda activities. Under this approach, courts would dismiss any case in which the plaintiff did not first make use of whatever remedies were available within LambdaMOO. In other words, a LambdaMOO player could not bring suit against someone for slander that took place within LambdaMOO without first using LambdaMOO's arbitration process against the slanderer. The Lambda arbitration system would be the functional equivalent of the court of original jurisdiction for disputes arising within LambdaMOO. Another way to illustrate this approach is to think of LambdaLaw as similar to an administrative remedy. Just as a government employee may sue for wrongful discharge only after all administrative remedies have been exhausted, a LambdaMOO denizen could take out-of-MOO action only after making use of LambdaMOO's available procedures.

The problem with this approach, however, is that unlike a county court or an administrative agency, Lambda's legal institutions have no formal legal authority. They are not an arm of the state, nor even recognized by it. Therefore, courts are unlikely to take this approach with LambdaMOO—unless LambdaMOO itself requires it of its participants contractually. For example, LambdaMOO could pass a petition that would add to the text every player sees when logging in: "By connecting to this MOO, you agree to exhaust all legal remedies available within the MOO before making any activities, actions, or speech that takes place within the MOO the basis for a lawsuit anywhere outside of LambdaMOO." Although courts would be unlikely to impose an exhaustion requirement on their own, they would probably enforce such a requirement if it were made a condition of MOO-participation. Alternatively, LambdaMOO could follow the model established by many corporate contracts and require binding arbitration for all disputes generated within the MOO and not resolved through MOO dispute resolution mechanisms.

*LambdaMOO as a separate country*

A third approach is for courts to recognize LambdaMOO as a separate jurisdiction. The analogy here would be to view LambdaMOO as a separate physical space, a place of its own. Legally speaking, LambdaMOO would be equivalent to, not a village within a state, but another country. Viewing LambdaMOO as its own jurisdiction has some conceptual advantages: after all, where exactly are activities on LambdaMOO taking place? The database server is in California, but the characters are logging in from computers all over the country, indeed all over the world. If LambdaMOO is a village, in what state or country is the village itself located? Or, to put it another way, if a player from Seattle spreads slanderous lies about a St. Louis-player to players from Sussex and Syracuse, where did the slander take place? California, Washington, Missouri, England, New York? Where exactly was the tort committed? Perhaps the most satisfying answer is that the tort was committed in LambdaMOO. That is, we could view LambdaMOO as a real place, indeed, the place where the slander occurred. If LambdaMOO were understood to be a separate jurisdictional entity, courts would generally refuse to hear disputes arising from activities taking place entirely within LambdaMOO. Just as American courts lack jurisdiction over disputes among Germans taking place in Germany, they would lack jurisdiction over disputes among LambdaMOOers taking place in LambdaMOO.

In practice, of course, the possibility of courts in multiple sites, each with legitimate ju-

risdiction, means that the situation would be substantially more complex. If a MOOer from California injured another MOOer from California, even if California courts recognized LambdaMOO as a separate jurisdiction, the injured party might have jurisdiction in California courts as well as in LambdaMOO. If we spin out this scenario, we can even imagine courts making inquiries into the adequacy of LambdaMOO remedies and determining whether to apply the doctrine of forum non conveniens, or engaging in elaborate analysis regarding choice-of-law. These scenarios might appear farfetched; the point is that merely recognizing LambdaMOO's jurisdictional independence might not assure that disputes that arose in LambdaMOO would be resolved through LambdaMOO legal mechanisms. Now, if LambdaMOO had exclusive jurisdiction over all that took place in LambdaMOO, these jurisdictional issues would not arise. However, even if LambdaMOO is like another country, the players typing onto their computer screens are themselves located in specific, real-world, geographically-located places. On what theory would a real-world court maintain that it lacked jurisdiction over the actions of a real person that took place within its boundaries? If a player located in California committed slander within LambdaMOO, a California court would seem clearly to have both personal jurisdiction and subject-matter jurisdiction over the defendant. Still, the metaphorical resonance of the recognition of LambdaMOO as a separate jurisdiction is strong; it corresponds to the instinct of many that cyberspace is Elsewhere.

*LambdaMOO as a role-playing game*

A fourth approach is to analogize LambdaMOO to a role-playing game, richer and more complex than Dungeons and Dragons, to be sure, but of the same ilk. From a legal standpoint, this analogy suggests the need to make a distinction between characters and typists. If LambdaMOO is a role-playing game, its characters are more like fictional creations than juridical entities. Fictional characters, unlike legally recognized artificial persons (such as corporations), have no legal standing. In other words, if characters are not juridical entities, they can neither sue nor be sued. Damage to fictional characters is not legally cognizable, nor can the person who controls the character sue on the character's behalf. Therefore, in order to bring a civil suit based on action that took place in LambdaMOO, a plaintiff would have to show that the person, the typist behind the character, the human being, experienced damages. And reputational damage suffered within the MOO by the character alone would, one imagines, not count as damage experienced by the typist controlling the character.

However, the real people behind characters would be accountable for any damage their characters caused non-characters. (The analogy here would be to an actor who assaults someone during the shooting of the film. If the assault was part of the script, and he was carrying out his role, he has not committed a legally cognizable act of violence. If the assault, however, had nothing to do with the script, the actor could not escape accountability by claiming that it was his character who committed the assault.) In other words, if we return to our slander example, if one MOO character spread slanderous lies about another MOO character, the slandered character would not have standing to sue in a civil court. The victim of slander would therefore have no alternative but to use whatever dispute resolution mechanisms were available to characters *within* LambdaMOO. However, if a MOO character slandered a real human being within the MOO, such as, perhaps, a person who had never even visited the MOO, and the real human being suffered damages outside of the MOO as a result of the slander, the victim would have a cause of action against the typist who controlled the slandering character. . . .

We have, then, four approaches to the relation between LambdaLaw and the system of law outside of it. Each approach is based on a metaphor, a conception of the nature of LambdaMOO. Is LambdaMOO a social club or is it a village? Is it more like a country or more like a role-playing game? The difficulty, of course, is that all four metaphors resonate: LambdaMOO is a hybrid. It is a fantasy space in a double sense, both a utopian space of possibility and an adolescent playground. It is a social club and a village and a country and a role-playing game. How, then,

should we choose a reigning metaphor, and with it a framework for the relation between LambdaLaw and the state-sanctioned legal system?

**Laboratories for Experimentation** As we have seen, LambdaMOO is a space in which reality is bounded only by the imagination. As Sherry Turkle has emphasized in her recent book, *Life on the Screen,* virtual environments such as LambdaMOO allow their participants to engage in creative self-fashioning. In the MOO, people can develop characters that emphasize usually-suppressed aspects of themselves. In the MOO, they may be something or someone that they are unable to be in the physical world. People may even use the MOO to work through anxieties with origins in the real world; on occasion, MOOs may have therapeutic potential. Turkle describes how virtual spaces encourage participants to play with aspects of themselves, to experiment with identity and self-presentation. But it is not only individual identities that are shaped and reshaped within a MOO, but institutional identities as well. Just as players may construct themselves in novel and creative ways, they may also imaginatively construct political institutions and social forms. Turkle calls spaces such as LambdaMOO "laboratories for the construction of identity." But they may equally be laboratories for the construction of society. In an often-quoted dissenting opinion, Justice Louis Brandeis wrote, "It is one of the happy incidents of the federal system that a single courageous State may, if its citizens choose, serve as a laboratory; and try novel social and economic experiments without risk to the rest of the country." Sixty years later, it may be virtual spaces that can best serve as laboratories for experimentation, places in which participants can test creative social, political and legal arrangements.

As we have seen, many of the disputes within LambdaMOO have centered around issues relating to property and speech. It is worth noting that both of these topics are highly contested outside of LambdaMOO as well as within it. To what extent is information properly considered property? What should ownership look like in a society in which the most valuable resources are symbolic rather than material, words rather than things? To what extent should information be protected as private? All of these questions are as central outside of LambdaMOO as inside. With speech as well: how should the legal system protect people from unwanted speech and simultaneously allow free and open communication? Can speech alone cause injuries that should be legally recognized? Are there circumstances in which the content of speech should be regulated? These, too, are relevant questions in domains far outside of cyberspace.

Moreover, it is not as if the Lambda legal system has been constructed in a vacuum. It borrows from the legal systems outside of it, especially the American legal system, both explicitly and implicitly. Often, participants invoke notions of the law based on their (sometimes inaccurate) understanding of law in the real world. For example, nowhere in LambdaLaw is there any explicit codification of either a free speech right or a privacy right, and yet most participants presume that these rights exist within the MOO. (Ironically, it is often law-resisters who most vehemently argue that free speech is sacrosanct.) At a procedural and institutional level, too, we can see the tremendous extent to which American legal culture influences LambdaMOOers' approaches to LambdaLaw. Both in the mechanisms used by arbitrators to shore up their authority and in the structure of the Judicial Review Board, we see a turn to a process-based system for determining the legitimacy of decisions. We see an individualistic conception of property rights applied to virtual objects created by computer code. And the language used by LambdaMOOers, such as the labeling of their proposals "the LambdaMOO Supreme Court" and the "LambdaMOO Bill of Rights," reflects the legal culture in which they exist off-line.

That people invent for themselves structures that resemble those that they know best is not surprising. The strong reliance upon existing models of law, both procedural and substantive, suggests the limits of any paradigm that views virtual reality as completely set apart from real life. The structure of LambdaMOO makes it possible to change the world by changing the code, limited only by the imagination. And yet in practice, while the characters and the places may look like nothing one's seen before, the real world is sorely lacking in characters shaped like fractal

dragons and offers no possibility of taking an elevator from California to China, but the institutions look rather familiar. But we must be careful not to overstate the resemblance. LambdaLaw is at once tightly linked to the culture of the real world and a kaleidoscopic transformation of it. Its relation to real law is far from simply mimetic; it is a form of legal bricolage, blending elements of "real" law and elements of lay people's conception of "real" law, together with institutional variations and innovative conceptions.

Possibly, then, virtual spaces such as LambdaMOO could be laboratories for experimenting with various institutional creation and creative legal standards. With this potential in mind, let us return to the question of the reigning metaphor, the best way to conceive of the relation between reality and virtuality, LambdaLaw and real law. Which approach, LambdaMOO as a social club, as a village, as a country, or as a role-playing game, offers the most promise for allowing virtual communities to be laboratories for social and institutional invention? Which approach would allow the greatest flexibility for institutional refashioning?

The best metaphor turns out to be conceiving of LambdaMOO as a role-playing game. Analogizing LambdaMOO to a role-playing game ends up granting LambdaMOO denizens the most freedom to experiment, and indeed, the greatest amount of legal autonomy. By emphasizing LambdaMOO's game-like aspects, we emphasize LambdaMOO's power to make rules for itself, unconstrained by the rules that operate outside its borders. In other words, recognizing LambdaMOO as a game, as a play-space, frees participants in LambdaMOO to play, to invent and reinvent both themselves and their institutional setting. For labeling LambdaMOO a "mere" game is the easiest way to free what happens within LambdaMOO from external legal oversight. If LambdaMOO were a social club, external legal institutions would have no reason to defer to the MOO's rules when they differed from those of society at large. If LambdaMOO were a village, when the village laws conflicted with the law of the state, state law would prevail when invoked. If LambdaMOO were a country, the principle of comity would suggest that real-world courts should respect LambdaLaw as legitimate; however, unless LambdaLaw had exclusive jurisdiction over anything that took place in LambdaMOO, complex jurisdictional questions would arise. If LambdaMOO is a game, however, players would generally find it difficult to invoke external law when it differed from the rules of the game. A football player cannot successfully sue for a civil assault when he is tackled during a game, even though the same action in another circumstance would be actionable. When he agrees to play football, he agrees to its rules, even when they conflict with those of the general society. Similarly, LambdaMOOers would find it difficult to bring suit for actions sanctioned by the rules of the MOO, even if the same action would be prohibited outside of the MOO. Obviously, there are social limits to what society will allow in the guise of a game; "it was part of a consensual game" would hardly provide an adequate defense for murder. Nonetheless, it seems that analogizing the virtual community to a role-playing game ends up providing LambdaMOO with the greatest freedom from external legal control.

Moreover, the role-playing game metaphor suggests a useful guideline for determining when the external legal system should allow actions within Lambda to be the basis for a lawsuit, when "it was part of a consensual game" should not protect a player from liability. Viewing LambdaMOO as a role-playing game suggests a distinction between the role and the players, between the persona and the person. This distinction, to be sure, is not always a stable one; as Sherry Turkle writes, "MUDs blur the boundaries between self and game, self and role, self and simulation.". . .

. . . LambdaMOO is a world in which nearly anything is possible. It is a world where destroying an institution (or a character) requires no more than tossing out some programming code, a society in which institutional creation and innovation are made real through writing. It is a place where words have the potential to come to life. LambdaMOO, then, has the potential to be a utopian space of possibility. It could provide a space in which participants can remake themselves and their institutions; it could provide a standpoint from which to critique and rethink the institutional structures of the space outside the MOO.

The utopian possibility, the notion of a virgin place in which we can wash off the mistakes of the past and begin anew; these are recurrent and familiar myths. From the hopes of creating a new man in the New World to the conception of the frontier as a place of freedom from the stifling constraints of society, there have been those who have believed in the possibility of transforming humanity by moving to a new space, an untouched place. Cyberspace has clearly become the latest site within this lineage of utopian dreamspaces, and in this new world as surely as in the ones that have preceded it, utopian dreamers are destined to be disappointed. Nonetheless, virtual communities like LambdaMOO, odd hybrids between games and worlds, simulations and society, may prove to be spaces for institutional reimagining, for questioning and reshaping conceptions of self, politics, and law.

### Notes and Questions

1. For obscenity and pornography, online resources for Supreme Court decisions can be located at http://www.law.cornell.edu and at http://www.findlaw.com.

2. Borders and Boundaries
   A. Edmund Burke's "Where in the World Is the World Wide Web?" at http://www.educom.edu/web/pubs/pubHomeFrame.html presents a useful review of jurisdictional issues raised by the World Wide Web.
   B. Consider the following:
      Romulus, according to Plutarch's Life, plowed a deep furrow to delineate the boundary of Rome and thought the task so important that he killed the interfering Remus. Roman law provided severe punishment for those who tampered with boundary stones, and the Roman pantheon gave a proud place to Terminus—god of boundaries. Spatial boundaries were important because they marked limits of power and control, and so it is today; the maps negotiated by politicians and drafted by urban planners are patchworks of ownership boundaries, zoning boundaries, and jurisdictional boundaries. Within jurisdictional borders, local laws and customs apply, local power is exerted by some over others, and local police and military forces maintain power by the

potential or actual use of violence. But bits answer to terminals, not Terminus; these lines on the ground mean little in cyberspace.*

Visit the Pentagon or the New York Times, and everywhere there are maps,

solemnly defining national borders and sovereign territories. No one shows any signs of knowing that we no longer live in geographic time and space, that the maps of nations are fully as obsolete as the charts of a flat earth, that geography tells us virtually nothing of interest about where things are in the real world.[†]

*William Mitchell, *City of Bits* (Cambridge, Mass.: MIT Press, 1995), accessible on the World Wide Web at http://alberti.mit.edu/arch/4.207/texts/city-of-bits-toc.html.

[†]George Gilder, *The Message of the Microcosm* (1989).

# Suggested Additional Readings

Biegal, Stuart. *Beyond Our Control? Confronting the Limits of Our Legal System in the Age of Cyberspace.* Cambridge: MIT Press, forthcoming 2001.

Branscomb, Anne. *Who Owns Information?* New York: Basic Books, 1994.

Godwin, Mike. *Cyber Rights: Defending Free Speech in the Digital Age.* New York: Times Books, 1998.

Katsh, Ethan. *Law in a Digital World.* New York: Oxford University Press, 1995.

Lessig, Lawrence. *Code and Other Laws of Cyberspace.* New York: Basic Books, 1999.

McLuhan, Marshall. *Understanding Media.* New York: McGraw-Hill, 1964.

Shapiro, Andrew L. *The Control Revolution: How the Internet Is Putting Individuals in Charge and Changing the World We Know.* New York: Public Affairs, 1999.

Susskind, Richard. *The Future of Law.* Oxford: Oxford University Press, 1996.

Important online sources of information about cyberspace and the law can be accessed at:
http://jurist.law.pitt.edu/sg_cyb.htm
http://www.law.cornell.edu
http://www.findlaw.com
http://www.gseis.ucla.edu/iclp/hp.html
http://www.umass.edu/dispute

# Index